Encyclopedia of Data Science and Machine Learning

John Wang
Montclair State University, USA

Volume IV

Published in the United States of America by
  IGI Global
  Engineering Science Reference (an imprint of IGI Global)
  701 E. Chocolate Avenue
  Hershey PA, USA 17033
  Tel: 717-533-8845
  Fax: 717-533-8661
  E-mail: cust@igi-global.com
  Web site: http://www.igi-global.com

Library of Congress Cataloging-in-Publication Data

Names: Wang, John, 1955- editor.
Title: Encyclopedia of data science and machine learning / John Wang,
  editor.
Description: Hershey, PA : Engineering Science Reference, an imprint of IGI
  Global, [2023] | Includes bibliographical references and index. |
  Summary: "This book examines current, state-of-the-art research in the
  areas of data science, machine learning, data mining, optimization,
  artificial intelligence, statistics, and the interactions, linkages, and
  applications of knowledge-based business with information systems"--
  Provided by publisher.
Identifiers: LCCN 2021027689 (print) | LCCN 2021027690 (ebook) | ISBN
  9781799892205 (h/c) | ISBN 9781799892212 (ebook)
Subjects: LCSH: Big data. | Data mining. | Machine learning.
Classification: LCC QA76.9.B45 E54 2022 (print) | LCC QA76.9.B45 (ebook)
  | DDC 005.7--dc23
LC record available at https://lccn.loc.gov/2021027689
LC ebook record available at https://lccn.loc.gov/2021027690

British Cataloguing in Publication Data
A Cataloguing in Publication record for this book is available from the British Library.

All work contributed to this book is new, previously-unpublished material. The views expressed in this book are those of the authors, but not necessarily of the publisher.

For electronic access to this publication, please contact: eresources@igi-global.com.

Editorial Advisory Board

List of Contributors

Alphabetical Table of Contents

Volume I: 1-618; Volume II: 619-1246; Volume III: 1247-1870; Volume IV: 1871-2498; Volume V: 2499-3143

Table of Contents by Category

Volume I

Section: Accounting Analytics

Wikil Kwak, University of Nebraska at Omaha, USA
Xiaoyan Cheng, University of Nebraska at Omaha, USA
Yong Shi, University of Nebraska at Omaha, USA
Fangyao Liu, Southwest Minzu University, China
Kevin Kwak, University of Nebraska at Omaha, USA

Toshifumi Takada, National Chung Cheng University, Taiwan

Section: Approximation Methods

Jean-Éric Pelet, LARGEPA, Panthéon-Assas University, Paris, France
Santiago Belda, Universidad de Alicante, Spain
Dounia Arezki, Computer Science Faculty, Science and Technology University of Oran, Algeria

Section: Autonomous Learning Systems

Indraneel Dabhade, O Automation, India

Section: Big Data Applications

Section: Big Data as a Service

Section: Big Data Systems and Tools

Section: Business Intelligence

Volume II

Section: Causal Analysis

Section: Chaos Control, Modeling, and Engineering

Section: Cloud Infrastructure

Section: Cognitive Science

Section: Computational Intelligence

Section: Computational Statistics

Section: Computer Vision

Section: Customer Analytics

Section: Data Processing, Data Pipeline, and Data Engineering

Volume III

Section: Data Visualization and Visual Mining

Section: Decision, Support System

Section: Deep Neural Network (DNN) of Deep Learning

Section: E-Learning Technologies and Tools

Section: Emerging Technologies, Applications, and Related Issues

Section: Ensemble Learning

Section: Gradient-Boosting Decision Trees

Section: Graph Learning

Section: High-Throughput Data Analysis

Section: Industry 4.0

Section: Information Extraction

    Fabian N. Murrieta-Rico, Universidad Politécnica de Baja California, Mexico
    Moisés Rivas-López, Universidad Politécnica de Baja California, Mexico
    Oleg Sergiyenko, Universidad Autónoma de Baja California, Mexico
    Vitalii Petranovskii, Universidad Nacional Autónoma de México, Mexico
    Joel Antúnez-García, Universidad Nacional Autónoma de México, Mexico
    Julio C. Rodríguez-Quiñonez, Universidad Autónoma de Baja California, Mexico
    Wendy Flores-Fuentes, Universidad Autónoma de Baja California, Mexico
    Abelardo Mercado Herrera, Universidad Politécnica de Baja California, Mexico
    Araceli Gárate García, Universidad Politécnica de Baja California, Mexico

Section: Internet of Things

    Shivlal Mewada, Government Holkar Science College, India

    Matthew J. Drake, Duquesne University, USA

Section: Malware Analysis

    Thomas Alan Woolman, On Target Technologies, Inc., USA
    Philip Lunsford, East Carolina University, USA

Section: Management Analytics

    Maximiliano Emanuel Korstanje, University of Palermo, Argentina
    Martha Omara Robert Beatón, University of Havana, Cuba
    Maite Echarri Chávez, University of Havana, Cuba
    Massiel Martínez Carballo, University of Havana, Cuba
    Victor Martinez Robert, University of Havana, Cuba

    Jorge Gomes, Universidade Lusófona das Humanidades e Tecnologias, Portugal
    Mário Romão, ISEG, Universidade de Lisboa, Portugal

Section: Marketing Analytics

    Tasnia Fatin, Putra Business School, Universiti Putra Malaysia, Malaysia
    Mahmud Ullah, Department of Marketing, University of Dhaka, Bangladesh
    Nayem Rahman, School of Business and Information Technology, Purdue University Global, USA

Section: Object Detection

Section: Performance Metrics

Section: Predictive Analytics

Mustapha Kamal Benramdane, CNAM, France
Samia Bouzefrane, CNAM, France
Soumya Banerjee, MUST, France
Hubert Maupas, MUST, France
Elena Kornyshova, CNAM, France

Section: Reinforcement Learning

Section: Simulation and Modeling

Section: Smart City

Section: Social Media Analytics

Section: Supply Chain Analytics and Management

Section: Symbolic Learning

Section: Time Series Analysis

Section: Transfer Learning

Section: Transport Analytics

Section: Unsupervised and Supervised Learning

Foreword

There has been tremendous progress made in Data Science and Machine Learning over the last 10 – 15 years, leading to the Data Science becoming the major driving force of the Fourth Industrial Revolution and a significant factor in the current cycle of economic expansion. The need for data scientists is growing exponentially and machine learning has become one of the "hottest" professions in the labor market.

The field of Data Science is expanding both in-depth and in-breadth. In particular, we have witnessed widespread adoption of data science methods across a broad class of industries and functional areas, including health sciences and pharmaceuticals, finance, accounting, marketing, human resource management, operations and supply chains. Data-driven approaches have been deployed in such diverse set of applications as drug discovery, analysis of medical data and decision support tools for physicians, financial applications, including robo-advising, predictive maintenance of equipment and defect detection, Internet of Things (IoT), precision agriculture, physics and chemistry, to name a few. All these industries and applications enjoy adoption of a wide range of machine learning methods, the scope of which grew significantly over the last 10 – 15 years. In addition to the evolutionary growth and expansion of classical machine learning techniques, the last decade has witnessed revolutionary breakthroughs in such areas as Deep Learning, scalable machine learning methods capable of handling Big Data, the size of which grows exponentially over time in many applications, and the analysis of unstructured data, such as text using NLP-based methods, images and videos using Computer Vision techniques, and voice using Speech Recognition methods.

Given all this progress in Machine Learning and Data Science, it is high time to aggregate all this new knowledge "under one roof," and this Encyclopedia of Data Science and Machine Learning serves this purpose. It covers 188 different topics across the whole spectrum of the field written by leading academic scholars and industry practitioners describing the progress made in the respective areas over the last 10 – 15 years and reflecting the State-of-the-Art for each topic.

Since data science and machine learning are evolving rapidly, the authors also describe the challenges and present promising future research directions in their respective areas, delineating interesting work that lies ahead for the scholars to address these challenges. Therefore, this Encyclopedia remains what it is – a milestone on a long and exciting road that lies ahead of us in Data Science and Machine Learning.

Alexander Tuzhilin
New York University, USA
May 2022

Preface

Big Data and Machine Learning (BDML) are driving and harnessing the power of the Fourth Industrial Revolution, also referred to as Industry 4.0 or 4IR, which revolutionizes the way companies, organizations, and institutions operate and develop. With the age of Big Data upon us, we risk drowning in a flood of digital data. Big Data has now become a critical part of the business world and daily life, as the synthesis and synergy of Machine Learning (ML) and Big Data (BD) have enormous potential.

BDML not only deals with descriptive and predictive analytics but also focuses on prescriptive analytics through digital technology and interconnectivity. It has continuously explored its "depth" and expanded its "breadth". BDML will remain to maximize the citizens' "wealth" while promoting society's "health".

The *Encyclopedia of Data Science and Machine Learning* examines current, state-of-the-art research in the areas of data science, ML, data mining (DM), optimization, artificial intelligence (AI), statistics, and the interactions, linkages, and applications of knowledge-based business with information systems. It provides an international forum for practitioners, educators, and researchers to advance the knowledge and practice of all facets of BDML, emphasizing emerging theories, principles, models, processes, and applications to inspire and circulate cutting-edge findings into research, business, and communities (Wang, 2022).

How can a manager get out of a data-flooded "mire"? How can a confused decision-maker navigate through a "maze"? How can an over-burdened problem solver clean up a "mess"? How can an exhausted scientist bypass a "myth"? The answer to all of the above is to employ BDML.

As Roy et al. (2022) point out, data has become the center point for almost every organization. For quite a long time, we are familiar with Descriptive Analytics (what happened in the past) and Diagnostic Analytics (why something happened in the past), as well as Predictive Analytics (what is most likely to happen in the future). However, BDML could go much above and beyond them with Prescriptive Analytics (what should be done now), which recommends actions companies, and organizations can take to affect those outcomes. The digital transformation, the horizontal and vertical integration of these production systems, as well as the exploitation via optimization models, can make a gigantic jump with this giant digital leverage.

BDML can turn *Data* into *value*; Transform *information* into *intelligence*; Change *patterns* into *profit;* Convert *relationships* into *resources.* Companies and organizations can make *Faster* (real-time or near real-time), *Frequent*, and *Fact-based* decisions. In an ever-evolving market, 4IR with a set of technologies can stimulate innovations and rapid responses. Knowledge workers can proactively take action before an unfriendly event occurs (Wang, 2008).

Having been penetrated and integrated into almost every aspect of our work and life, as well as our society itself, AI and related cutting-edge technologies will enhance human capacities, improve efficiencies, and optimize people's lives. AI would not replace human intelligence, rather than amplify it. As *AI evolves* and *humans* adapt, AI and humans go forward together in the long run because AI and people both bring different capabilities to society.

According to Klaus Schwab, the World Economic Forum Founder and Executive Chairman, 4IR intellectualizes precipitous change to industrial and societal prototypes and processes in the 21st century due to increasing interconnectivity and smart automation and finally blurs the lines among the physical, digital, and biological worlds. Part of the 4IR is the manner in which all types of machines and devices interact, correspond, and cooperate with each other. Even though there will be obvious job losses due to the replacement of tasks that humans have conducted for years by autonomous machines and/or software. On the contrary, there could be new business opportunities and plenty of new jobs for controlling "the new electricity" (Philbeck & Davis, 2018; Moll, 2022).

There are 207 qualified full chapters among 271 accepted proposals. Finally, the encyclopedia contains a collection of 187 high-quality chapters, which were written by an international team of more than 370 experts representing leading scientists and talented young scholars from more than 45 countries and regions, including Algeria, Argentina, Austria, Bangladesh, Brazil, Canada, Chile, China, Colombia, Cuba, Denmark, Egypt, El Salvador, Finland, France, Germany, Ghana, Greece, Hong Kong, Hungary, Indonesia, Iraq, Japan, Lebanon, Macau, Malaysia, Mexico, Netherland, New Zealand, Poland, Portugal, Saudi Arabia, Serbia, Singapore, South Africa, Sweden, Switzerland, Syria, Taiwan, Tunisia, Turkey, UK, USA, Venezuela, Vietnam, etc.

They have contributed great effort to create a source of solid, practical information, informed by the sound underlying theory that should become a resource for all people involved in this dynamic new field. Let's take a peek at a few of them:

Jaydip Sen has published around 300 articles in reputed international journals and referred conference proceedings (IEEE Xplore, ACM Digital Library, Springer LNCS, etc.), and 18 book chapters in books published by internationally renowned publishing houses. He is a Senior Member of ACM, USA a Member of IEEE, USA. He has been listed among the top 2% scientists in the globe as per studies conducted by Stanford University for the last consecutive three years 2019 - 2021. In his contributed chapter Prof. Sen and his co-author, Dutta have evaluated the performance of two risk-based portfolio design algorithms.

Leung - who has authored more than 300 refereed publications on the topics of data science, ML, BDM and analytics, and visual analytics (including those in ACM TODS, IEEE ICDE, and IEEE ICDM) - presents two encyclopedia articles. One of them presents up-to-date definitions in BDM and analytics in the high-performance computing environment and focuses on mining frequent patterns with the MapReduce programming model. Another one provides the latest comprehensive coverage on key concepts and applications for BD visualization; it focuses on visualizing BD, frequent patterns, and association rules.

Lorenzo Magnani is Editor-in-Chief of the Series Sapere, Springer. Thanks to his logico-epistemological and cognitive studies on the problem of abductive cognition (that regards all kinds of reasoning to hypotheses) explained in this chapter both virtues and limitations of some DL applications, taking advantage of the analysis of the famous AlphaGo/AlphaZero program and the concepts of locked and unlocked strategies. Furthermore, he is the author of many important articles and books on epistemology, logic, cognitive science, and the relationships between ethics, technology, and violence.

The chapter 'AI is transforming insurance with five emerging business models' is the culmination of three years of research into how AI is disrupting insurance. Zarifis has recently won a 'best paper award' at a leading conference and Cheng has recently been published in MIS Quarterly for related work. AI is disrupting many distinct parts of our life, but insurance is particularly interesting as some issues like risk and privacy concerns are more important. After several case studies, this chapter identifies that there are five emerging models in insurance that are optimal for AI.

In "Artificial Intelligence, Consumers, and the Experience Economy," Chang and Mukherjee's excellent synthesis of AI and consumers in the modern economy provides a much-needed knowledge base for stakeholders tasked to deploy AI. In "Using Machine Learning Methods to Extract Behavioral Insights from Consumer Data," they present a comprehensive discussion of new data sources and state-of-the-art techniques for researchers and practitioners in computational social science. The chapters are built on their projects supported by the Ministry of Education, Singapore, under its Academic Research Fund (AcRF) Tier 2 Grant No. MOE2019-T2-1-183 and Grant No. MOE2018-T2-1-181, respectively.

Based on many years of application development by CY Pang and S. Pang's cognitive data analysis of many industrial projects, this chapter proposes a programming paradigm specific to BD processing. Pang was the lead architect of a $1.6 billion enterprise software project and was awarded a special architectural design trophy. He has received awards of $20,000 and $5,000 for outstanding innovation from a company he previously worked for. By the way, CY Pang was awarded a Prestige Scholarship from Peter House, Cambridge to complete his Ph.D. at the University of Cambridge, UK.

Vitor provides an excellent overview of multidimensional search methods for optimization and the potential these methods have to solve optimization problems more quickly. With almost ten years of industry experience, Vitor is an expert in optimization methods and the modeling of complex systems using operations research and data analytics techniques. He is also a recipient of the Nebraska EPSCoR FIRST Award, supported by the National Science Foundation to advance the research of early-career tenure-track faculty.

Lee's chapter on evidence-based data-driven pain management bears multi-facet importance. Nearly 40 million anesthetics are administered each year in the United States. And over 10.7% of Americans use prescription pain medication on a regular basis. The findings highlight the optimal safe dose and delivery mechanism to achieve the best outcome. The study showcases the persistence of overprescription of opioid-type drugs, as it finds that the use of fentanyl has little effect on the outcome and should be avoided.

Auditors must evaluate the volatility and uncertainty of the client company at the initial stage of the audit contract because it directly influences the audit risk. Takada contributes to auditing research and accounting education for 40 years. He has been awarded for his research and contributions to his excellent papers and accounting education by the *Chinese Auditing Association* and by the *Japanese Auditing Association*.

Nguyen and Quinn propose an optimal approach to tackle the well-known issue of the imbalance in bankruptcy prediction. Their approach has been evaluated through a rigorous computation including the most popular current methods in the literature. They have also made other main contributions in the area of imbalanced classification by winning the 2020 Literati Awards for Outstanding Author Contribution.

Rodríguez is the Bioethics of Displacement pioneer, a field that merges futurism, belongingness, and life. He has also published analytic papers and fieldwork on crises and big social changes such as pandemics, Anthropocene, AI takeover, cyborgs, digital securitization and terrorist attacks. As a chair, the author leads the research on the first decolonized corruption index. Torres shares his more than 15 years of wealth of experience in Predictive Maintenance management as a speaker at global summits such as Scalable and PMM Tech Dates. The author leads the first non-taxonomic error mode proponent of AI implementation.

Kurpicz-Briki, Glauser, and Schmid are using unique API technologies to measure the impact of online search behavior using several different online channels. Their method allows the identification of the specific channels, where keywords have been searched, and a restriction of regions, using the domains. Such technologies provide a major benefit for different application domains, including public health. In times such as a pandemic crisis, it is highly relevant for different stakeholders to identify the impact of their communications on the user community as well as the well-being of the population. Using the method proposed by the authors, this can be done while fully respecting the privacy of the users.

Sensors sense the environment and process large sets of data. Monitoring the data to detect malicious content is one of the biggest challenges. The previous work used mean variation to ease the surveillance of information. Ambika's proposal minimizes the effort by classifying the streamed data into three subsets. It uses the k-nearest neighbor procedure to accomplish the same. The work conserves 10.77% of energy and tracks 27.58% of more packets. Map-reduce methodology manages large amounts of data to a certain extent. Ambika's other proposal aims to increase processing speed by 29.6% using a hashing methodology.

In today's world, text-based sentiment analysis brings the attention of all. By looking at the people requirement, Tripathy and Sharaff propose a hybridized Genetic Algorithm (GA)-based feature selection method to achieve a better model performance. In the current study, they have customized the GA by using the SVM to evaluate the fitness value of the solutions. The proposed idea is essential as the technique reduces the computational cost by reducing sufficient features without affecting the performance. The proposed model can be implemented in any field to filter out the sentiment from the user's review.

Alberg and Hadad present the novel Interval Gradient Prediction Tree ML Algorithm that can process incoming mean-variance aggregated multivariate temporal data and make stable interval predictions of a target numerical variable. Empirical evaluations of multi-sensor aircraft datasets have demonstrated that this algorithm provides better readability and similar performance compared to other ML regression tree algorithms.

The environmental, societal, and cultural imperatives press for innovative, prompt, and practical solutions for grave humanitarian problems we face in the 21st century. The climate crisis is felt everywhere; natural disasters are rampant. Can technology provide reasonable means to humanitarian supply chains? What potential uses can AI offer in establishing sustainable humanitarian logistics (SHL)? Ülkü, an award-winning professor and the director of CRSSCA-Centre for Research in Sustainable Supply Chain Analytics, and his research associate Oguntola of Dalhousie University - Canada review the latest research on the applications of AI technology on SHL.

Aguiar-Pérez, the leading author of this chapter, provides the audience an insight into what ML is and its relation with AI or DL. He has an extended experience in the field of ML, DL, BD, and IoT in various sectors (automotive, smart roads, agriculture, livestock, heritage, etc.), including collaboration with companies, EU-funded research projects, publications, and postgraduate teaching experience. The rest of the authors work with him in the Data Engineering Research Unit of the University of Valladolid.

Bagui, a highly accomplished author of several books on databases and Oracle, presents a very timely chapter on the improvements made in Oracle 19c's multitenant container architecture and shows how these improvements aid in the management of Big Data from the perspective of application development. The added functionality that comes with the integration of Big Data platforms, alongside the flexibility and improvement that comes with a container and pluggable databases, has allowed Oracle to be in the forefront in the handling of Big Data.

As an internationally renowned interdisciplinary information and data professional, Koltay's chapter on Research Data Management (RDM) is of interest not only for both professionals of DS and ML but is related to any research activity. He is also a widely published author in these fields. In 2021, his contribution to IGI Global books included an entry on information overload. His book, titled Research Data Management and Data Literacy (Chandos, 2021) contains a more detailed explanation of the subjects, contained in this chapter.

Zhao is a DS professional with experience in industry, teaching, and research. He is a leading BD expert in the IR BD & AI Lab in New Jersey, USA. He provides multiple chapters to the book by covering a broad range of BD applications in vast perspectives of urgent demands in DS research objectives, such as DSS, DL, computer vision, BD architecture designs, and applied BD analytics in Covid-19 research. As such, he did excellent work in those chapters and made significant contributions to the book.

Based on their discovery of action rules and meta-actions from client datasets, Duan and Ras propose a strategy for improving the number of promoters and decreasing the number of detractors among customers. Moreover, the improved/enhanced action rules can be utilized in developing actionable strategies for decision makers to reduce customer churn, which will contribute to the overall customer churn study in the business field. The authors target the domain represented by many clients, each one involved with customers in the same type of business. Clients are heavy equipment repair shops, and customers are owners of such equipment.

The A2E Process Model for Data Analytics is simple without being simplistic and comprehensive without being complicated. It balances technology with humanity and theories with practices. This model reflects Jay Wang's decades-long multi-disciplinary training and experience in STEM, Behavioral Science, and Management Science. While existing process models such as CRISP-DM, SEMMA, and KDD were developed for technical professionals with limitations and low adoption rates, the A2E Model is more approachable to subject matter experts, business analysts, and social scientists. The A2E Model will elevate the analytics profession by fostering interdisciplinary collaborations of all stakeholders and increasing the effectiveness and impacts of analytics efforts.

Turuk explores Audio and video-based Emotion Recognition using the Backpropagation Algorithm, which is the backbone of ML and DL architectures. This chapter analyses everyday human emotions such as Happy, Sad, Neutral, and Angry using audio-visual cues. The audio features such as Energy & MFCC and video features using the Gabor filter are extracted. Mutual information is computed using video features. The readers will benefit and motivated to conduct further research in this domain. The application may be extended to a lie detector using Emotions.

Stojanović and Marković-Petrović focus on continuous cyber security risk assessment in Industrial Internet of Things (IIoT) networks, and particularly on possibilities of DL approaches to achieve the goal. The authors successfully complement their previous work regarding the cyber security of industrial control systems. They concisely review the theoretical background and provide an excellent framework for the continuous risk assessment process in the IIoT environment. DL can be integrated into edge-computing-based systems and used for feature extraction and risk classification from massive raw data. The chapter ends with a list of proposals for further studies.

Climate change is a very important issue and each person on our planet must have a culture of keeping it clean. Pollution increased yearly due to the increased consumption of fossil fuels. Alsultanny has many research papers in climate change and renewable energy. He led a UNDP team for writing reports on energy consumption in Bahrain. Alsultanny did an innovative method in his chapter, by utilizing the pollution gases data, these data currently are BD, because they are registered yearly in every minute, and from many monitoring pollutions stations.

Deliyska and Ivanova conducted timely research and practical work representing an important contribution to data modeling in sustainable science. Applying ontological engineering and a coevolutionary approach, a unique metamodel of sustainable development is created containing structured knowledge and mutual links between environmental, social, and economic dimensions in this interdisciplinary area. Specialists in different fields can use the proposed metamodel as a tool for terminology clarification, knowledge extraction, and interchange and for the structuring of ML models of sustainable development processes.

Hedayati and Schniederjans provide a broad spectrum of issues that come into play when using digital technologies to benefit healthcare. This is even more important where the pandemic has forced healthcare models to rapidly adjust towards compliance with local, regional, and national policy. The dissemination and creation of knowledge become paramount when considering the benefits and drawbacks of the rapid changes in technology applications worldwide. The authors consider several insights from the American Hospital Association Compliance to provide some questions researchers and practitioners may consider when addressing knowledge management via digital technology implementation in healthcare settings.

Pratihar and Kundu apply the theory of fuzzy logic to develop a classification and authentication system for beverages. It emphasizes the versatility of fuzzy logic to deal with the higher dimensional and highly non-linear sensor data obtained from e-tongue for different beverage samples. Commonly used mapping techniques (for dimension reduction of a data set) and clustering techniques (for classification) were also briefly discussed. This study provides a perspective on developing a fuzzy logic-based classifier/authenticator system in the future for beverages, foods, and others and their quality control and monitoring.

Drake discusses the use of IoT technology to improve SCM. As firms look to improve their supply chain resilience in response to the COVID-19 pandemic and other disruptions, IoT data increases visibility, traceability, and can help firms to mitigate risks through added agility and responsiveness. The improved decision-making made possible by IoT data creates a competitive advantage in the market.

Today, high-dimensional data (multi-omics data) are widely used. The high dimensionality of the data creates problems (time, cost, diagnosis, and treatment) in studies. Ipekten et al. introduce the existing solutions to these problems and commonly used methods. Also, the authors present the advantages of the methods over each other and enlighten the researchers that using suitable methods in terms of performance can increase the reliability and accuracy of the studies. Finally, the authors advise on what can be done in the future.

Learning analytics (LA), a promising field of study that started more than a decade ago but has blossomed in recent years, addresses the challenges of LA specifically in education, integrating it as a fundamental element of the Smart Classroom. Ifenthaler and Siemens among others discuss the primary features, the benefits, and some experiences. In addition, the team of authors of the chapter has contributed more than twelve publications on this topic in the last 3 years in leading journals and publishers.

Current advances in AI and ML in particular have raised several concerns regarding the trustworthiness and explainability of deployed AI systems. Knowledge-Based approaches based on symbolic representations and reasoning mechanisms can be used to deploy AI systems that are explainable and compliant with corresponding ethical and legal guidelines, thus complementing purely data-driven approaches.

Batsakis and Matsatsinis, both having vast theoretical backgrounds and experience in this research area, offer an overview of knowledge-based AI methods for the interested AI practitioner.

Noteboom and Zeng provide a comprehensive review of applications of AI and ML and data analytics techniques in clinical decision support systems (CDSSs) and make contributions including, 1) the current status of data-driven CDSSs, 2) identification and quantification of the extent to which theories and frameworks have guided the research, 3) understanding the synergy between AI/ML algorithms and modes of data analytics, 4) directions for advancing data-driven CDSSs to realize their potential in healthcare.

Fisogni investigates the emotional environment which is grounded in any human/machine interaction. Through the lenses of metaphysics and system thinking the author sketches a highly valuable insight, for sure an unprecedented challenge for DSs. In fact, only a philosophical foundation of the big issues of this realm can bring about a change in the quality of understanding an increasingly melted environment humans/machines in the Onlife era.

In "Hedonic Hunger and Obesity", Demirok and Uysal touch upon a remarkable topic and explain ways of identification for people with hedonic nutrition and the conditions that are effective in the states that trigger hunger state in humans. In addition, in this text, the authors ensample hormones that suppress and trigger hunger.

Yen and her coauthors contributed a chapter on how ML creates the virtual singer industry. Virtual singers have great market potential and even advantages over their human counterparts. Despite the bright future of virtual singers, the chapter has discussed difficulties virtual singers face, especially their copyright protection by legislation. Literature on the technical aspects of virtual singers is also reviewed, and a list of additional readings is provided for readers interested in the ML algorithms behind virtual singers.

Rastogi is working on Biofeedback therapy and its effect on Diabetes diseases, a currently very active healthcare domain. He brings back the glory of Indian Ancient Vedic Sciences of Jap, Pranayama, Healing techniques, and the effect of Yajna and Mantra science on Diseases and pollution control. Also, He has developed some interesting mathematical models with algorithms on Swarm Intelligence approaches like PSO, ACO BCO, etc. for better human life via Spiritual Index and higher consciousness.

Isikhan presents a comparison of a new proposal for the modeling of Ceiling and Floor Effect dependent variables and classical methods. It has been noticed that there are very few publications evaluating the regression modeling of ceiling and floor effect observations in recent years. The modeling method with regression-based imputation, which clinicians can use as an alternative to classical models for ceiling and floor effective observations, is explained in detail. The performances of the newly proposed imputation-based regression and other classical methods were validated based on both real clinical data, synthetic data, as well as a 500 replicated cross-validation method.

Drignei has extensive experience with time series modeling and analysis. Prior to this work, he addressed statistical modeling aspects of space-time data, such as temperatures recorded over space and time. His research has been published in leading statistics journals. The current work deals with seasonal times series recorded at a large number of time points. Such data sets will become more common in the future, in areas such as business, industry, and science. Therefore, this chapter is timely and important because it sheds new light on modeling aspects of this type of data sets.

Data visualization plays a key role in the decision-making process. Visualization allows for data to be consumable. If data is not consumable, there is a tendency to ignore the facts and rely more on biases. Researchers have found that cognitive biases do exist within data visualizations and can affect decision-making abilities. Anderson and Hardin provide background on cognitive biases related to data visualizations, with a particular interest in visual analytics in BD environments. A review of recent studies related to mitigating cognitive biases is presented. Recommendations for mitigating biases in visualizations are provided to practitioners.

Puzzanghera explores the impact of AI on administrative law. He combines IT systems with administrative activity and researches the processors that prepare content and the implications that arise. He analyzes the European Commission's proposal in regard to the legislation of AI in Europe and the importance of safeguarding human rights in the introduction of AI in administrative activity.

How ML impacts the catering industry? Liu et al. provide a comprehensive vision to readers with real-life examples and academic research. Researchers at business schools may have their attention drawn to the impact of ML on operations, management, and marketing, while scholars with solid ML backgrounds may become aware of industry issues, identify new research questions, and link their expertise to practical problems through reading the chapter.

Di Wang's research interests include 4D printing technology, robot control, remanufactured industry, and energy schedule in the smart city. Combinatorial optimization is a widely applied field at the forefront of combinatorics and theoretical computer science. With BD challenges, deep reinforcement learning opens new doors to solve complex combinatorial optimization problems with overwhelming advantages over traditional methods.

Firmansyah and Harsanto focus on exploring BD and Islamic finance. The utilization of BD in Islamic financial institutions (IFIs) has been perceived as a source of competitive advantage in today's era. Many IFIs have been more dependent on BD technologies than ever before in order to keep up with the changing customers' demands, lifestyles, and preferences.

With his experience of working in both industry and academic research, Indraneel highlights progress made in integrating AI with industry and helps bridge the reality and challenges faced while summarizing the state of Industry 4.0. The author engages audiences from different sectors without overburdening the reader with incoherent technical details. A practitioner in the fields of DS and cybersecurity, the author brings experience interacting with clients and customers from different fields, including manufacturing, legal, and product developers.

Yang, Wu, & Forrest examine the textual aspects of consumer reviews. As a critical source of information for online shoppers, researchers have spent considerable time examining the potential impact of consumer reviews on purchasing behavior. The authors contribute to the existing body of knowledge by proposing a conceptual framework for capturing the internal relationships between major textual features discovered in prior research.

Kara and Gonce Koçken are researchers studying mathematical programming problems in fuzzy environments. In the study, a novel fuzzy solution approach to multi-objective solid transportation problems is developed by using different membership functions, which can help the studies in transportation systems.

Millham demonstrates the various spheres of the emerging 4IR and how they interrelate with the application, opportunities, expectations, and challenges of a smart city. Because many of these smart city applications are very complex and interact with each other using various technologies, several nature-inspired algorithms are introduced as a way to provide intelligent and coordinated management of these entities.

The development of novel measurement and detection techniques is a rapidly growing area, where the generation of vast amounts of information requires novel methods for analysis. Murrieta-Rico explores a new direction of his research by combing the know-how for generating a big dataset from a digital frequency measurement, with the application of the principal component analysis (PCA). As a result, a powerful methodology for data analysis is presented. In addition, these results can be used for extending the capabilities of ML systems based on sensors.

Coimbra, Chimenti, and Nogueira contribute to the debate related to human-machine interaction in social media. The work helped to understand the mechanisms and motivators of this relationship. In addition, the article presented a historical evolution of the debate on the interaction between machines and men in decision-making, distributing the result of the literature review in three historical cycles. The research was carried out through a survey of YouTube users to understand the interaction mechanism along with its motivators.

As a transformational general-purpose technology, AI is impacting marketing as a function, and marketing managers' activities, capabilities, and performance. Oberoi emphasizes how the job of a marketing manager will be evolving into understanding which kind of AI can and should be applied to which kind of marketing actions for better performance. Marketing managers will have to go through a learning curve and acquire new skills.

Singh and Dev have discussed the concepts of data warehouse and OLAP technology to deal with real-life applications efficiently. The topic is useful in the modern digital era as businesses are dealing with data from heterogeneous sources. The chapter presents the case study of the tourism industry as it deals with multidimensional data like tourist, hospitality, and tourist products. This chapter will be helpful in understanding how to generate multi-dimensional reports that will show the information according to the needs of policymakers.

Ramos has made many contributions to the potential of Business Intelligence tools, combined with DM algorithms methods to produce insights about the tourism business, highlighting an aspect of the investment potential of tourism organizations in this type of system, from those related to accommodation, management of tourist destinations, to tourist transport, restaurants, among other businesses complementary to the tourist activity, with a view to innovation and increasing financial performance, which includes examples ranging from the application of OLAP techniques to the application of ML methods.

Balsam depicts the meaning and role of metamodels in defining the abstract syntax of the language by which developers communicate, design, and implement systems including the selection of the design, implementation methods, and techniques for increasingly complex systems to satisfy customers' needs, particularly if the system has to be delivered in a considerably fleeting time. The author highlights different aspects of meta-models standards, categories, the process of creating the metamodel, and challenges in the research of metamodeling.

Dharmapala contributes a novel method to the field of research in 'Classification of employee categories in allocating a reward, with input features from survey responses.' In the past, researchers conducted qualitative and quantitative analyses on this subject as it is an important topic to any organization that strives to boost the morale of its employees. The author opened a new direction in future research on the subject by using ML algorithms, and the results obtained were promising.

Mudrakola identifies the gap and future scope for Breast cancer applications like the impact of chemical therapy, prognosis analysis among various treatment types and stages, etc. From basic to the latest trends, the author's extensive literature survey will direct the root to aspects needed to analyze work on medical applications specific to Breast cancer.

Rani et al. highlight the venues of user-generated content (UGC) in Industry 4.0. This chapter's contribution is highly interesting for any digital content creator and non-paid professionals. The importance of UGC on consumer behavior in the era of Industry 4.0 will be explained, allowing stakeholders to assess their efficacy in Internet communication and enhancing the digital process required for modern marketing. The chapter aims to link existing ideas and provide a holistic picture of UGC by concentrating on future research.

Ibrahim et al. seek to provide an understanding of the relationship between member support exchange behavior and self-disclosure intention in online health support communities using a data-driven literature review. Seeking or providing support in online communities may be useful but having to disclose personal information publicly online is a critical privacy risk – intention counts.

Rusko introduces the main perspectives of industrial revolutions. He found interesting backgrounding details for the chapter about the disruptions of the industrial revolutions. Kosonen updates the paper with the effects of Covid-19 and contemporary digitizing development.

I would like to highlight a number of authors who have received special stunning honors: Eva K Lee has published over 220 research articles, and fifty government and state reports, and has received patents on innovative medical systems and devices. She is frequently tapped by a variety of health and security policymakers in Washington for her expertise in personalized medicine, chronic diseases, healthcare quality, modeling and decision support, vaccine research and national security, pandemic, and medical preparedness. Lee has received multiple prestigious analytics and practice excellence awards including INFORMS Franz Edelman award, Daniel H Wagner prize, and the Caterpillar and Innovative Applications in Analytics Award for novel cancer therapeutics, bioterrorism emergency response, and mass casualty mitigation, personalized disease management, ML for best practice discovery, transforming clinical workflow and patient care, vaccine immunity prediction, and reducing hospital-acquired infections. She is an INFORMS Fellow. She is also inducted into the American Institute for Medical and Biological Engineering (AIMBE) College of Fellows, the first IE/OR engineer to be nominated and elected for this honor. Her work has been funded by CDC, HHS, NIH, NSF, and DTRA. Lee was an NSF CAREER Young Investigator and Whitaker Foundation Young Investigator recipient.

Petry and Yager are both internationally known for their research in computational intelligence, in the area of fuzzy set theory and applications, and are both IEEE Fellows and have received prestigious awards from the IEEE. They have collaborated here as it represents extensions of their previous research on this topic. Hierarchical concept generalization is one important approach to dealing with the complex issues involving BD. This chapter provides insights on how to extend hierarchical generalization to data with interval and intuitionistic forms of uncertainty.

The globalization of the software development industry continues to experience significant growth. The increasing trend of globalization brings new challenges and increases the scope of the core functions of the software development process. Pal introduces a distributed software development knowledge management architecture. Kamalendu has published research articles in the software development community in the ACM SIGMIS Database, Expert Systems with Applications, DSSs, and conferences. Kamalendu was awarded the best research paper on data analytic work at a recent international conference. He is a member of the British Computer Society, the IET, and the IEEE Computer Society.

Badia's research has been funded by the National Science Foundation (including a prestigious CAREER Award) and has resulted in over 50 publications in scientific journals and conferences. His chapter demonstrates how to use SQL in order to prepare data that resides in database tables for analysis. The reader is guided through steps for Exploratory Data Analysis (EDA), data cleaning (including dealing with missing data, outliers, and duplicates), and other tasks that are an integral part of the Data Scientist day-to-day. The references provide a guide for further study.

Srinivasan explains the three components of graph analytics and provides illustrative examples as well as code for implementation. His chapter is one of the few primers of graph DS/analytics that covers a variety of topics in the discipline. The author does active research in graph analytics methods and applications in healthcare, ML explainability, and DL and regularly publishes in top journals and conferences in information systems, healthcare, and computer science. He received best paper awards in INFORMS Workshop on Data Science (2021) and the 6th International Conference on Digital Health (2016), respectively.

Knowledge explosion pushes BDML, a multidisciplinary subject, to ever-expanding regions. Inclusion, omission, emphasis, evolution, and even revolution are part of our professional life. In spite of our efforts to be careful, should you find any ambiguities of perceived inaccuracies, please contact me at prof.johnwang@gmail.com.

John Wang
Montclair State University, USA

REFERENCES

Moll, I. (2022). The Fourth Industrial Revolution: A new ideology. *tripleC: Communication, Capitalism & Critique, 20*(1), 45–61.

Philbeck, T., & Davis, N. (2018). The Fourth Industrial Revolution: Shaping a new era. *Journal of International Affairs, 72*(1), 17–22.

Roy, D., Srivastava, R., Jat, M., & Karaca, M. S. (2022). A complete overview of analytics techniques: Descriptive, predictive, and prescriptive. *Decision Intelligence Analytics and the Implementation of Strategic Business Management*, 15-30.

Wang, J. (Ed.). (2008). *Data Warehousing and Mining: Concepts, Methodologies, Tools, and Applications* (Vols. 1–6). IGI Global. doi:10.4018/978-1-59904-951-9

Wang, J. (Ed.). (2022). *Encyclopedia of Data Science and Machine Learning*. IGI Global. https://www.igi-global.com/book/encyclopedia-data-science-machine-learning/276507

Acknowledgment

The editor would like to thank all authors for their insights and excellent contributions to this major volume. I also want to thank the many anonymous reviewers who assisted me in the peer-reviewing process and provided comprehensive and indispensable inputs that improved our book significantly. In particular, the Editorial Advisory Board members, including Xueqi Cheng (Chinese Academy of Science), Verena Kantere (University of Ottawa, Canada), Srikanta Patnaik (SOA University, India), Hongming Wang (Harvard University), and Yanchang Zhao (CSIRO, Australia), have all made immense contributions in terms of advice and assistance, enhancing the quality of this volume. My sincere appreciation also goes to Prof. Alexander Tuzhilin (New York University). Despite his busy schedule, he has written three forewords for my consecutive encyclopaedias, over an 18-year span, in this expanding and exploring area.

In addition, the editor wishes to acknowledge the help of all involved in the development process of this book, without whose support the project could not have been satisfactorily completed. I owe my thanks to the staff at IGI Global, whose support and contributions have been invaluable throughout the entire process, from inception to final publication. Special thanks go to Gianna Walker, Angelina Olivas, Katelyn McLoughlin, and Melissa Wagner, who continuously prodded me via email to keep the project on schedule, and to Jan Travers and Lindsay Wertman, whose enthusiasm motivated me to accept their invitation to take on this project.

I would also like to extend my thanks to my brothers Zhengxian, Shubert (an artist, https://portraitartist. com/detail/6467), and sister Joyce Mu, who stood solidly behind me and contributed in their own unique ways. We are thankful for the scholarships which we have been provided, without which it would not have been possible for all of us to come and study in the U.S.

Finally, I want to thank my family: my parents for supporting me spiritually throughout my life and providing endless encouragement; my wife Hongyu for taking care of two active and rebellious teenagers, conducting all family chores, and not complaining to me too much.

This book was special due to the stresses and difficulties posed by the Covid-19 pandemic. We thank and salute the authors who had to overcome numerous challenges to help make this volume a reality. Our authors had to persevere through unprecedented circumstances to enable this masterful encyclopedia. Now, it is time to celebrate and reap the fruits of our demanding work! Cheese and cheers!

Bio-Inspired Algorithms for Feature Selection:
A Brief State of the Art

B

Rachid Kaleche
 https://orcid.org/0000-0002-9326-2944
LIO Laboratory, Université Oran1, Algeria

Zakaria Bendaoud
 https://orcid.org/0000-0003-3091-5044
GeCoDe Laboratory, University of Saida Dr. Moulay Tahar, Algeria

Karim Bouamrane
 https://orcid.org/0000-0002-6953-0339
LIO Laboratory, Université Oran1, Algeria

Khadidja Yachba
 https://orcid.org/0000-0002-7754-2823
LIO Laboratory, Université Relizane, Algeria

INTRODUCTION

Data is an important resource of knowledge used in decision making process, and which imply states, enterprises, and various organisations for different domains like economic, health, environment, policy, security, … Nowadays, the volume of data increases in an exponentially manner, and usual machine learning techniques reached their limits. According to the site Statista, the worldwide volume was 26 zetabytes in 2017, the forecasts for 2022 and 2025 are 97 zetabytes and 181 respectively. Therefore, extracting knowledge from voluminous data is a challenge due to the huge amount of features and/or the great number of instances. Hence, the high dimentionality implies a high computational cost, a difficulty in terms of readability due to the large amount of features, and irrelevant and redundant features could decrease the learning model performance (Dash, M., & Liu, H. 1997; Xue et al. 2016).

In order to reduce the high number of features, two main methods exist, which are feature selection (FS) and feature extraction (FE) (Kohavi, & John; 1997). The principal of FS is to select the relevant features, while in the case of FE, new features are constructed from the existant ones (Xue et al. 2016). This paper highlights on FS. The FS problem is a combinatorial problem, it is known to be an NP-Hard problem (Amaldi & Kann, 1998; Narendra & Fukunaga, 1977). The FS problem was addressed by classical algorithms such as sequential forward selection (SFS) and sequential backward selection (SBS) (Dash & Liu, 1997; Kohavi, & John; 1997) which reached their limits in terms of peformance and runtime (Xue et al. 2016). By contrast, these last decades global methods inspired from nature, namely bio-inspired algorithms, have been used and provided amazing results.

DOI: 10.4018/978-1-7998-9220-5.ch113

Nature have been an important inspiration source of algorithms to tackle hard problems, especially bio-inspired algorithms. These last have been inspired from living beings behaviors, as ants, bees, plants, bacteria and others, which smartly solve their own daily problems. Therefore, these bio-inspired algorithms have been used to address several hard problems in different fields as transport, medecine, robotic, industry and so on. In summary, bio-inspired algorithms proved their effectiveness and robustness to tackle hard problems in a general manner. Since FS is a combinatorial problem, bio-inspired algorithms are, by consequence, the suited algorithms to tackle this problem. In addition, the hudge number of bio-inspired algorithms, more than 300 algorithms and their variantes, offers a wide range of choices.

Given that the FS process importance and the robustness and efficiency of the bio-inspired algorithms, the motivations of this paper are:

- Provide an overview of FS as an important process of machine learning to face the high dimentional issue of big data
- Provide a summary description of bio-inspired algorithms
- Describe bio-inspired algorithms modeling elements to address the FS problem
- Describe of bio-inspired approaches tackling FS problems
- Enumerate the application domains of bio-inspired algorithms for FS problems
- Outline challenges relevant to bio-inspired algorithms for FS problem, and those relied the bio-inspired algorithms in order to improve existant approaches tackling the FS process.

This paper is organized as follow: the second section is an overview of challenges related to the high dimentonality of data and the limits of classical FS algorithms. In the third section, an introduction to the bio-inspired algorithms is given. Some modelization elements of bio-inspired algorithms to address FS problem, and a brief state of art of applied bio-inspired algorithms with samples of applied approches are given in the forth section. In the fivth section, some future research directions are suggested. Finaly, the last section concludes this paper.

BACKGROUND

Big Data and Feature Selection

The term Big Data was introduced by Roger Mougalas from O'Reilly Media in 2005. The data are collected from several sources as internet, digital devices, IoT, … The data are characterised by a set of features, which could be of a few number or around thousands even millions of features like those collected by microarray technology for instance.

To face the challenges of high dimentionality of data, there is an issue to reduce search space and in the same time preserving a high performance (accuracy) of learning algorithms. These challenges are two opposite objectives. In addition, the reduction of the number of features leads to a better readability of the induction factors. There are two categories of methods to achieve the reduction of search space and keeping a high induction performance, namely FS and FE (Kohavi & John, 1997; Qiu & Feng, 2016). FS is the process which aims to select a subset of relevant features that will be used in a learning (induction) algorithm. In other words, the FS process aims to remove irrelevant and redundant features. On the other hand, FE is the preprocess that is used to construct a new subset of features from the original ones, and which will also be used in a learning algorithm. The focus, in the rest of this paper, is made on the FS process.

Dash and Liu in 1997 defined a general FS process framework composed by three steps, followed by a validation step as indicated in the Figure 1. The FS approach is an iterative process, in which iteratively a generated subset of features is evaluated until a stop criterion is reached, and finally the selected subset is submitted to a validation step (Dash & Liu, 1997). Evaluation algorithms are divided into five categories: distance measures (e.g., Euclidean measure), information measures (e.g., entropy measure), dependence measures (or correlation measure), consistency measures, and classifier error rate measures (Dash & Liu, 1997).

Figure 1. Feature selection process steps

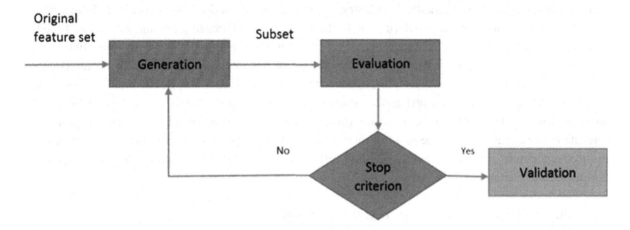

In the FS process, according to evaluation point of view, three main approaches are used, filter approach, wrapped and embedded one (Kohavi & John, 1997; Brezočnik & Podgorelec, 2018). In the case of the filter approach, the selection of a subset of features is done with no regards to machine learning algorithm and without any relation between features each other. By contrast, the wrapper approach interacts with machine learning algorithm by using it as evaluation step part of selected feature's subset (Kohavi & John, 1997), which imply implicit interaction between features each other. In the embedded approach, the FS and a learning algorithm are included in the same process (Liu & Ye, 2018). The wrapper approach has a higher performance (accuracy) than filter one, but needs more run time (Dash & Liu, 1997).

As selecting a subset of features double at each added feature, the search space for n features is $O(2^n)$ (Kohavi & John, 1997). Hence, selecting a relevant feature subset is a hard task, therefore searching subset feature of this huge search space is done by heuristics like sequential forward selection (SFS) and sequential backward selection (SBS) and their variants (Kohavi & John, 1997; Xue et al. 2016). In the SFS, heuristic the algorithm starts with an empty set and add at each iteration a feature until forming a relevant subset with a highest evaluation. By contrast, the SBS heuristic starts with all features and remove at each step a feature until forming a highest evaluation of feature's subset. The most classical methods of feature selection suffer from two major drawbacks, namely stagnation in local optima and a high computational cost with high dimentional feature sizes (Xue et al. 2016).

By the increasing number of features, and the high dimenionality of data, the classical machine learning algorithms reached their limits (Kohavi & John, 1997; Qiu & Feng, 2016). For instance, in the case of classification algorithms like tree decision algorithms, the accuracy decreases when the number of features increases, even for a small number of features, while the computational cost increases for Naïve Bayes (Kohavi & John, 1997). In addition, the classical machine learning algorithms have as hypothesis that data are entirely loaded and treated in the same machine (Qiu & Feng, 2016). Actually, the data grow up continually in an unprecedent manner; therefore using a unique machine to store data and run learning algorithms became very hard to maintain and to justify.

Bio-Inspired Algorithms

The nature have been the principal inspiration source of the majority of algorithms destinated to tackle hard problems in different domains as industry, health, economic and others. Especially, bio-inspired algorithms which have a wide popularity due to their easy use and amazing results. According to their inspiration sources, a number of studies classified commonly bio-inspired algorithms to evolutionnary algorithms, swarm intelligence based algorithms and no swarm intelligence based algorithms (Binitha & Sathya 2012; I. Fister Jr., Yang, I. Fister, Brest, & D. Fister, 2013; Kaleche, Bendaoud, & Bouamrane, 2020). An example of classification based on source inspiration is illustrated in Figure 2 (Kaleche, Bendaoud, & Bouamrane, 2020). In the literature, there is more than 300 bio-inspired algorithms proposed (invented), hence this is a one the proof of their success. As examples, a not exhaustive number of bio-inspired algorithms, their inspirations and their references are outlined in Table 1. The main steps of a bio-inspired algorithm are:

1. Initialization of specific parameters of the algorithm
2. Initialization
    a. Init a population of individuals (solutions)
    b. Evaluate the fitness of each population individual
    c. Save the best individual
3. Evolve population individuals by diversification and/or intensification processes
4. Evaluate the fitness of the evolved individuals
5. Save the best individual known until now
6. If the stop criteria is not verified goto 3
7. Return the best individual

As any metaheuristic, a bio-inspired algorithm explores a space of solutions in order to find the optimal solution or at least a good one. It uses two processes, namely, diversification and intensification. In the diversification step a metaheuristic explores the search space in its globality aiming to find a promising search area. On the other hand, by the intensification process, a metaheuristic exploits a local area to improve a solution. Because of the exponentiality of the search space, the metaheuristics explore it randomly aiming to find a high-level quality solution in a reasonable amount of time. This trade-off between acceptable amount of time and goodness of the solution quality are among the main import advantages of metaheuristics. In addition, among advantages of bio-inspired algorithms are the following list (Kaleche, Bendaoud, & Bouamrane, 2020):

- their conception is easy, they liberate us from gradient complexity of objective function (Siarry, 2014),
- they are generic; therefore, they are relevant to a broad number of problems (Siarry, 2014),
- the duality intensification, diversification allows for the first to improve quality of a solution by exploring his neighbourhood; and for the second process to explore promising regions of the search space in order to enhance the global solution.

Some of their drawbacks can be summarized as follows:

- The convergence to optimal solution is not guaranteed,
- they do not give any information about the proximity of the obtained solution compared to the optimal one,
- their behaviours depend on the tuning of their parameters; consequently, they depend on experiences and feelings of their users,
- it is difficult to analyse their performance.

Figure 2. Metaheuristic classifications by inspiration sources

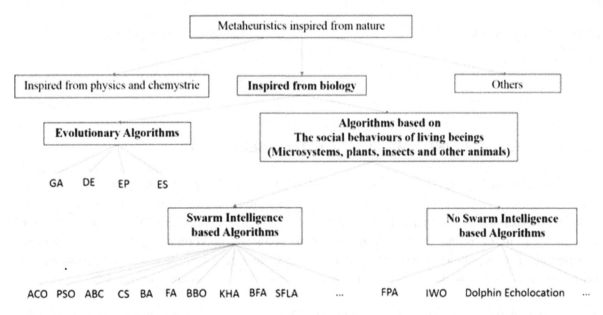

Table 1. A sample of bio-inspired algorithms list

BI algorithm	Inspiration	Reference
Genetic Algorithm (GA)	Natural evolution of species	(Holland, 1975)
Ant Colony Optimization (ACO)	Foraging of ants	(Dorigo, Maniezzo, & Colorni, 1991)
Particle Swarm Optimization (PSO)	Social behaviour of birds flocking and fish schooling	(Kennedy & Eberhart, 1995)
Shuffled Frog Leaping Algorithm (SFLA)	Frog leaping when searching food	(Eusuff & Lansay, 2003)
Artificial Bee Colony (ABC)	Foraging of honeybees	(Karaboga, 2005)
Biogeography-based Optimization (BBO)	Migration of species	(Simon, 2008)
Cuckoo Search (CS)	Parasitism of cukoo birds	(Yang & Deb, 2009)
Glowworm Swarm Optimization (GSO)	Glowworm use of bioluminescence to attract males and prey	(Krishnanand & Ghose, 2009)
Bat Algorithm (BA)	Microbats hunting strategy	(Yang, 2010a)
Firefly Algorithm (FA)	Firefly attractiveness strategy	(Yang, 2010b)
Flower Pollination Algorithm (FPA)	Pollination of flower plants	(Yang, 2012)
Grey Wolf Optimizer (GWO)	Leadership hierarchy and hunting mechanism of grey wolves	(S. Mirjalili, S. M. Mirjalili, & Lewis, 2014)
Salp Swarm Optimization (SSO)	Foraging of the salp group	(Mirjalili et al. 2017)
...	...	...

BIO-INSPIRED ALGORITHMS FOR FEATURE SELECTION

As the FS problem is an NP-Hard problem (Narendra & Fukunaga, 1977; Amaldi & Kann, 1998), bio-inspired algorithms are an appropriate approach, since they proved their effectiveness and robustness to tackle hard tasks in several domains like medecine, engineering, robotic, industry problems and others. Like the majority of metaheuristics, bio-inspired algorithms are based on a population of individuals representing a set of solutions, and two common process which are diversification and intensification. Based on these three elements, bio-inspired algorithms have between advantages the next:

- The population evolved by a bio-inspired algorithm maintains a set of solutions which could find a pareto front of nondominated solutions (Xue et al. 2016)
- The intensification process is a good mean to improve a good solution (a subset of features) in a promizing area of a search space
- The diversification process is an effective mecanism to escape local optima trap by exploring promizing not visited search space areas

In addition, other advantages are provided by bio-inspired algorithms:

- Information exchanges between population individuals could accelerate convergence of the FS search process

B

- Any feature could be added or removed at any iteration of the algorithm whitout any restriction
- The adaptation of bio-inspired algorithms to address the FS problem is easy to implement

Modelization Elements

In the aim to understand the rest of this paper, important elements are introduced. One of these important elements is how an individual, in a bio-inspired algorithm, is represented (encoded). The second element is how the objective function, in the other word the fitness function, is expressed. An overview of how these elements are implemented by bio-inspired algorithm makes the rest of this paper more easy to understand and avoid repetitions. Furthermore, these elements are a help to implement a FS algorithm based on a bio-inspired algorithm.

Individual Encoding

According to the used bio-inspired algorithm to address the FS problem, an individual, which is a feature subset, is represented differently. In the case of GA using, a binary representation encodes an individual by a string in which, each bit indicates, if equal 1, that the corresponding feature is selected, and not selected, if the value is 0. By contrast, in the most cases of used bio-inspired algorithms, the continuous representation of an individual is adopted. Hence, for a continuous representation, a feature is seleced if its corresponding value is greater than a threshold value, and not selected else. Given that most of bio-inspired algorithms such as ABC, CS, FA, BA, GSO, and SSO for example, are continuous, the continuous representation of individuals is the most used representation to tackle the FS problem. By contrast, for PSO, continuous (Kennedy & Eberhart, 1995) and binary representations (Kennedy & Eberhart, 1995) are used. In the case of ACO, a graph is used as a representation in which the nodes represent features, and edges the selection of relied features (Kanan, Faez, & Taheri, 2007; Harde & Sahare, 2016). The Figure 3 summarizes the different bio-inspired algorithm individual representations (encondings) to address the FS problem.

Figure 3. Individual FS encoding by bio-inspired algorithms

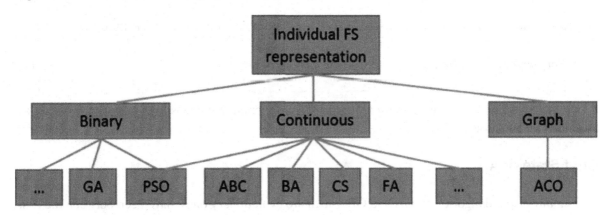

Fitness Function

Since the FS problem is a bi-objective optimization problem, the two objectives are the optimization performance of learning algorithm, and the minimization of the size of the selected feature subset. Here, the optimization of the performance could be the maximization of the accuracy of the learning algorithm (Tan, Fu, Zhang, & Bourgeois 2007; Xue et al., 2016;), or the minimization of the error rate (Xue, Zhang, & Browne, 2013; Too, Abdullah, & Mohd Saad, 2019; Al-Tashi et al., 2020) in th case of classification learning which is the majority of studied issues.

The most approaches using bio-inspired algorithms tackling the FS problem optimize a mono objecive function. Generally, the fitness function for the FS problem is the sum of functions on the performance of induction algorithm and the feature susbest size. The general form of fitness function is expressed by the equation 1.

$$F = a * f_1(performance) + \beta * f_2(\# Features) \tag{1}$$

Where a and β are weights as their sum is equal to 1, and f_1 and f_2 are functions that have the roles to keep performance high and to minimize the feature subset size respectively.

The multi objective function form for the FS problem is expressed by the equation 2.

$$F = \left[f_1, f_2 \right] \tag{2}$$

Where one of f_1 or f_2 is the fitness function that optimizes the performance of the induction algorithm and the other minimizes the feature subset size. For instance, f_1 could be expressed by the equation 3, and f_2 by the equation 4.

$$f_1 = \frac{\# Features}{AllFeatures} \tag{3}$$

Where #*Features* is the feature subset size, *AllFeatures* is the size of the original feature size.

$$f_2 = PerformanceFunction \tag{4}$$

On the other hand, the *PerformanceFunction* is a function that keeps high performance level as explained for equation 1.

Brief State of Art

Among bio-inspired algorithms, GA and GP, which are evolutionary ones, have been between the first ones used to address the FS problem (Xue et al. 2016). The most studied bio-inspired algorithms to tackle the FS problem have been used are, PSO either with its continuous or binary variant, ACO, and GA (Xue et al. 2016, Lin et al. 2021). This is due to promizing results provided by these algorithms.

GA Approach Samples

Tan, Fu, Zhang, and Bourgeois 2007 proposed a framework based on GA to address FS problem on 2 microarray datasets (colon cancer and prostate cancer) and a radar dataset. An Individual is encoded by a n-bit binary vector. The fitness function is a mono objective function composed from a function based on the optimization of accuracy and the minimization of feature subset size. In order to reduce the search space, and by consequence the computational cost, the approach starts by the construction of a pool of feature's subsets. This pool of feature's subsets is constructed by using three FS algorithms, two filter algorithms (entropy-based, *T*-statistics) and a wrapper one, which is Support Virtual Machines-recursive feature elimination (SVM–RFE). The authors of this study used SVM as induction algorithm independently of GA. This choice makes the framework flexible by replacing easily SVM by another induction algorithm. The proposed approach provides better classification performance and/or smaller feature subset size than classical approaches.

In order to tackle the FS problem of credit risk assessment, a hybrid GA Neural Network (NN) (HGA-NN) algorithm was proposed (Oreski, S., & Oreski, G., 2014). The hybridization of GA is done by introducing and incremental stage in order to allow the reconstruction of genetic material which is incrementally added to the initial population. Therefore, this incremental technique allows to avoid falling in local optima trap with population diversification. The proposed approach is based on three steps, the first restricts the search space, the second refines the restricted space, and the last introduces an incremental improve of initial population. The reduction of search space is made by the generation of initial population based on filter methods. The generation of the initial solutions is performed by means of the filter techniques for feature ranking: Information gain, Gain ratio, Gini index and Correlation. The selection of features is made in two reduction steps. In the first step, filter techniques are performed on the original feature set which reduce the search space quickly. In the second step, HGA and NN are applied aiming to refine the reduced feature set. In the third step, an individual is added to the initial population in the aim to diversify the population and to avoid local optima trap. Comparisons were made between HGA-NN and GA-NN with the parameters based on experiments. According to the obtained results, HGA-NN outperforms GA-NN in the terms of accuracy and speed-up of convergence.

PSO Approach Samples

An improved binary PSO based on the catfish effect with a wrapper approach called CatFishBPSO was proposed in (Chuang, Tsai, & Yang, 2011). The wrapper methods outperform the filter ones, since the wrapper methods take into account the feature interactions. By using the catfish effect, 10% of particles are replaced by new ones when the gbest particle do not enhance after three iterations. Therefore, the new introduced particles aim to stimulate the rest of particles in order to overcome the premature convergence of BPSO. In this approach, evaluation method is K-nearest neighbor (K-NN) method with leave-one-out cross-validation (LOOCV) that was used to evaluate the quality of the solutions. The principle for LOOCV is to let 1 set to test task, and N-1 sets as training sets. Six benchmarks were used and the results obtained by CatFishBPSO were compared to classical approaches, SGA, and HGA. According the obtained results by the authors, CatFishBPSO outperforms all the other mentionned approaches.

Kunhare, Tiwari, and Dhar in 2020 addressed the high network trafic of intrusion detection system issue. The number of features is high and needs to be reduced in order to reduce the search space and, in the same time, keep high the accuracy of the classifier algorithm. The problem is a FS problem, and a modified PSO was used to tackle this issue. The individual representation chosen is the continuous one. The proposed model begins with a FS with Random Forest (RF) algorithm, which is an embedded method, in order to remove redundant, and noisy features. RF is used to select 10 features only ranked upon their importances. After that, machine learning classifiers (SVM, LR, DT, K-NN, NB) are applied in order to compute the accuracy of classifiers. Then, PSO is applied in the aim to refine the selection of feature subsets. According to provided results by the authors, the proposed model outperforms the classical FS algorithms.

ACO Approaches Samples

Chen, Miao, and Wang in 2010 proposed a feature selection approach based on rough set technique and ACO called rough set feature selection ACO (RSFSACO). The graph representation was chosen, where nodes model features and edges the choice of the next feature. The objective function is a mono objective that have the form of aforementionned equation 1. Rough set technique allows to compute a minimal feature reduct called feature core. The construction of the feature core is based on a heuristic called FEATURECORE (Chen, Miao, & Wang in 2010) which starts from an empty feature set by adding a significant feature iteratively based on entropy and mutual information, therefore the initial graph to explore is transformed to a smaller one. Each ant starts its research of a feature subset from a randomly selected node of this feature core and constructs its path by selecting among nodes those do not belong to the feature core. The benchmark tested by the authors is composed from 9 instances from UCI datasets. Accoring to the authors, provided results by RSFSACO proved its effectiveness compared to classical rought set (RST-based) methods (Pal & Skowron, 1999), Jensen and Shen's algorithm (JSACO) (Jensen & Shen, 2003), and other metaheuristics (GA-based & Tabu Search-based).

Peng et al. (2018) proposed an improved ACO to address the FS problem; they called it FACO. They used the graph representation where the nodes represent the features and the edges denote the next feature that can be selected. The fitness function is a mono objective function having the form of equation 1. The first term of the fitness function is based on the false positive (FP) rate of classification, where the FP is the number of negative samples wrongly classified as positive samples by the classifier. While the second term is based on the ratio between feature subset size and the size of all features. On the other hand, the path transition probability is computed according to the classification performance and the feature subset length rate. The pheromone concentration is updated in two stages. In the first stage, the feature classification effect is used to improve the pheromone concentration, while in the second stage, the pheromone concentration of the optimal path and the closest ones are increased. This strategy have as effect to accelerate the FACO convergence. The FACO approach was applied to the classifiers SVM, KNN, Bayes and decision tree, which increases their accuracies. The results obtained by the authors showed that FACO outperforms two other ACO-based approaches in terms of convergence speed and the classification accuracy.

ABC Approaches Samples

Schiezaro and Pedrini (2013) proposed a binary ABC approach to adresse the FS problem. The initial population is generated by a method based on forward search strategy where the size of the population (source foods) is N, which corresponds to the number of features. In the initialization step, one bit is initialized to 1 for each source food (individual) among the N food sources. Then, each employee bee explores the neighborhood of a feature subset. The value of bit, which models a feature, receive the value 1 if a random number is less than a threshold value called MR, which is a parameter int the range between 0 and 1. The use of the MR parameter allows to bypass the modification of one dimension at each iteration, and by consequence the known disadvantage of classical ABC, which is the slow convergence. A comparison is made between the fitnesses of original food source and its neighbor. If the fitness (accurracy) of the neighbor is better than the original food source, then the neighbor is added as a food source, else the original food source is abandoned after a limit number of tries. Then, the onlooker bees store the best foods, and the scout bees generate new neighbors from abandoned food sources. The fitness function is evaluated by the accuracy of the classifier, a ten fold cross-validation is used to evaluate the accuracies of seleced feature subsets. According to the results obtained by the authors, the binary ABC approach outperforms bio-inspired algorithms ACO, PSO and GA in the majority of the 10 datasets of UCI machine learning repository. By contrast, the fact that the population size equals the total number of features could be a real problem in terms of storage and time consuming for big data with important number of features.

Lin et al. (2021) addressed the Quantitative Structure–Activity Relationship (QSAR) problem, which aims to correlate molecular structure properties with corresponding bioactivity. The authors proposed a binary ABC to tackle the FS problem of molecular descriptors of QSAR problem. They named their algorithm ABC-PLS-1. They introduced crossover and mutaion operators to employee bee phase and onlooker bee phase to modify several dimensions at the same iteration. The aim of these two operators is to accelerate convergence and to convert ABC from continuous representation to discrete one. Only scout bee phase uses a continuous representation in the range $[0,1]$, which is converted to discrete values. If the value of a feature is greater than a threshold value 0.5, then this feature is selected (value converted to 1), else the feature is not selected (value receives 0). The fitness of a candidate is evaluated with the metric Q^2, which is based on the cross-validation technique in order to measure the accuracy of QSAR modeling. On the other hand, a new gready selection strategy is used. It consists in selecting a feature subset which optimizes the accuracy. If the accuracy of two solutions is the same, then the feature subset with lower features is selected. According to the obtained results by the authors on benzodiazepine receptors (BZR) dataset, ABC-PLS-1 outperforms the algorithms PSO-PLS, a weighted sampling PSO (WS-PSO-PLS), a binary feature DE (BFDE-PLS) in terms of prediction accuracy, feature subset size, and also stability.

Other Approaches Samples

With the Table 2, the goal is not to give an exhaustive list of bio-inspired approaches for the FS problem. This limited list enumerates treated issues, the bio-inspired algorithm used, their modeling elements and evaluation approaches.

Table 2. A short list of bio-inspired algorithm approach samples for the FS problem

Issue	BI algorithm	Individual representation	Fitness function	Evaluation approach	Reference
Tumors classification	BBO	Binary	Multi objective	Wrapper (SVM)	(Li & Yin, 2013)
15 UCI datasets	GWO	Binary	Mono objective	Wrapper (KNN)	(El-Kenawy et al., 2020)
Motor Imagery electroencephalography	FA	Continuous	Mono objective	Wrapper (Spectral regression discriminant analysis (SRDA))	(Liu et al., 2017)
13 UCI datasets	SSO	Binary	Multi objective	Wrapper (Error rate, G-mean, Recall, Specificity)	(Aljarah et al., 2020)
12 public datasets	BA	Binary	Mono objective	Wrapper (Naïve Bayes)	(Taha et al., 2013)
8 public datasets	CS	Binary	Mono objective	Wrapper (Accuracy, Sensitivity, Precision, and F-measure)	(Zhao & Qin, 2021)
Diabetic Retinopathy	GSO	Binary	Mono objective	Wrapper (SVM)	(Karthikeyan & Alli, 2018)

Application Domains

The Bio-inspired algorithms tackling the FS problem have been applied to different and several domains. The following cited domains are not exhaustive:

- **Bio-medical engineering field:** Comprises gene classification based on mircoarray technolgy, and deases detection for instance.
- **Image processing:** Includes satelite images, deases of fruits and vegetals in agriculture, and scanner images for example.
- **Energy area:** Includes electrical distribution systems (Power quality disturbance), building energy consumption …
- **Computer science:** Includes detection network security, and development software cost for instance.
- **Financial domain:** Comprises prediction of credit risks, among others.
- **Others:** various problems between which, those used in different fields as physical phenomenen multivariate calibration models in spectroscopy for example.

The application domains and some references are provided in the Table 3.

Table 3. Application domains of bio-inspired algorithms for the FS problem

Domain	References (BI algorithm: ref)
Bio-medical engineering	ACO: (Nemati et al., 2009), BBO: (Li & Yin, 2013), GA: (Liu et al. 2018), ABC: (Coleto-Alcudia & Vega-Rodríguez, 2021)
Image processing	FA: (Liu et al., 2017), GA: (Khan et al., 2019), GSO: (Karthikeyan & Alli, 2018)
Energy area	ABC-PSO: (Chamchuen et al., 2021)
Computer science	ACO: (Aghdam & Kabiri, 2016), PSO: (Kunhare et al., 2020)
Financial field	GA: (Oreski, S., & Oreski, G., 2014)
Others	SSO: (Elhariri et al., 2020)

FUTURE RESEARCH DIRECTIONS

From a methodological point of view, the most studies about the FS problem addressed by bio-inspired algorithms suffer from some weaknesses. Firstly, few studies take in account the runtime aspect of proposed approaches, knowing that runtime is an important key in searching a good feature subset and one of the main reasons why global approaches as bio-inspired algorithms are used. For example, in a security context, or a tense economic context such as the stock market, or an energy context as in the power quality disturbance where computational time is important, experts and decision makers are waiting for a high accuracy and a quick answer. Furthermore, these approaches based on bio-inspired algorithms are seldom compared to the classical FS algorithms.

Another challenge is the improvement of effenciency and robusteness of bio-inspired algorithms when tackling the FS problem whitout reproducing the same approaches than other studies relevant to the same problem which is the FS problem. Many studies propose a hybridization of a bio-inspired algorithm, such as ABC, ACO among others, with other bio-inspired algorithms whose results are very interesting like GA and PSO; hence, the added value or contribution is not of great importance. Therefore, the expected efforts are not to hybridize bio-inspired algorithms which have less interest results with others as GA and PSO which have amazing results. In addition, it is not expectded to propose a new bio-inpired algorithm (Sörensen, 2013). Real added values could be to suggest new strategies to improve existant bio-inspired algorithms which will reduce the computational cost, minimize the feature subset size, and enhance the accuracy of learning algorithms.

Although bio-inspired algorithm approaches outperform classical approaches, it suffers from falling in local optima trap independently of the FS problem. Going from this fact, there is a room to improve bio-inspired algorithms in order to avoid this shortcoming. Therefore, More efforts should be made to tackle this issue, by developing new diversification techniques and using existing ones, and investigating adaptive parameter approaches during search process.

The bio-inspired algorithms based on the wrapper approach are the most used approaches due to their amazing obtained results. However, these approaches are costly in terms of execution time due to the fitness evaluation cost. Consequently, the number of iterations is frequently small in order to reduce the execution time, which limits the exploratory potential of the bio-inspired algorithms. Therefore, to increase the explotary potential of the bio-inspired algorithms, efforts should be made to reduce the fitness evaluation cost.

Currently, dataset sizes are measured in zetabytes, and FS processing faces scalability challenges in terms of accuracy and processing time on the same time. The answer to these scalability challenges lies in the parallelization of processing using the best adapted bio-inspired algorithms to parallelization in a

MapReduce framework (Li & Liu, 2016), having a good convergence or improving it, while maintaining good learning accuracies.

CONCLUSION

This paper mentioned the unprecedent increase of data volume, known as big data, and the importance of the machine learning to extract crucial and usefull knowledge destinated to decision makers. Therefore, the study of the FS process, which tackles the high dimentional issue to extract data knowlege has its great importance in any decision making process. Hence, a reminder of the main iterative used steps of the FS process was made: the generation of subsets, their evaluation, and the stop criterion. In addition, the main FS methods which are wrapper, filter, embedded were described. The classical approaches tackling the FS problem, as SFS and SBS among others, reached their limits in terms of induction algorithm performance (accuracy) and amount of execution time.

In this state of art, the basic definitions of bio-inspired algorithms, their main processes, which are intensification and divesification were presented. In addition, advantages and drawbacks of bio-isnpired algorrithms were enumerated, and a classification based on their inspiration sources, and a summary table enumerating some bio-inpired algorithms were given as examples. The objectives behind these definitions and examples were to give to the reader a basic background to understand the FS process and its importance, which is the FS problem, the classical approaches limits and an overview of important aspects of bio-inspired algorithms.

These last decades, the bio-inspired algorithms have been used intensively and widely to address the FS problem. This is due to the fact that the FS problem is an NP-Hard problem, and the bio-inspired algorithms proved their robusteness and effectiveness facing such problems. In addition, the first uses of bio-inspired algorithms as GA outperformed the obtained results by classical approaches. In order to provide an understand of the application of bio-inpired algorithms to the FS problem, a summary of the existant individual encodings and fitness function cases were explained. Therefore, the three individual encodings, binary, continuous and graphical representations were described. In addition, the mono objective and the bi-objective fitness function forms were cited and explained. Samples of bio-inspired algorithms for the FS problem have been described. Furthermore, a not exhaustive list of application domains of the FS problem were described and some examples were listed in a summary table. These application domains and these examples were cited in order to give an overview to the reader.

Despite the wide use of bio-inspired algorithms to address the FS problem, challenges remain. Among these challenges, the execution time apsect is not often taken into consideration by researchers while it is one of the main reasons why the bio-inspired algorithms are chosen to face the NP-Hard problems such as the FS problem. Another challenge to improve the efficiency of bio-inspired algorithms addressing the FS problem, is to improve them by proposing other approaches or/and techniques rather than hybridization with GA and PSO which are known to be efficient in dealing with the FS problem. Regardless of the FS problem, bio-inspired algorithms are subject to premature convergence. Therefore, this problem related to bio-inspired algorithms is a challenge that does not only concerns the FS problem, and thus addressing it will have positive repercussions on all NP-hard problems including the FS problem. Finally, the exploratory potential of the bio-inspired algorithms should be increased by providing research efforts reducing the fitness evaluation cost.

ACKNOWLEDGMENT

Our sincere thanks to the Directorate General for Scientific Research and Technological Development (DGRSDT), Ministry of Higher Education and Scientific Research for its support of this work.

REFERENCES

Aghdam, M. H., & Kabiri, P. (2016). *Feature Selection for Intrusion Detection System Using Ant Colony Optimization.* Academic Press.

Al-Tashi, Q., Abdulkadir, S. J., Rais, H. M., Mirjalili, S., Alhussian, H., Ragab, M. G., & Alqushaibi, A. (2020). Binary Multi-Objective Grey Wolf Optimizer for Feature Selection in Classification. *IEEE Access: Practical Innovations, Open Solutions, 8,* 106247–106263. doi:10.1109/ACCESS.2020.3000040

Aljarah, I., Habib, M., Faris, H., Al-Madi, N., Heidari, A. A., Mafarja, M., Elaziz, M. A., & Mirjalili, S. (2020). A dynamic locality multi-objective salp swarm algorithm for feature selection. *Computers & Industrial Engineering, 147,* 106628. doi:10.1016/j.cie.2020.106628

Amaldi, E., & Kann, V. (1998). On the approximability of minimizing nonzero variables or unsatisfied relations in linear systems. *Theoretical Computer Science, 209*(1–2), 237–260. doi:10.1016/S0304-3975(97)00115-1

Binitha, S., & Sathya, S.S. (2012). A survey of Bio inspired optimization algorithms. *International Journal of Soft Computing and Engineering.*

Brezočnik, L., Fister, I., & Podgorelec, V. (2018). Swarm Intelligence Algorithms for Feature Selection: A Review. *Applied Sciences (Basel, Switzerland), 8*(9), 1521. doi:10.3390/app8091521

Chamchuen, S., Siritaratiwat, A., Fuangfoo, P., Suthisopapan, P., & Khunkitti, P. (2021). High-Accuracy Power Quality Disturbance Classification Using the Adaptive ABC-PSO as Optimal Feature Selection Algorithm. *Energies, 14*(5), 1238. doi:10.3390/en14051238

Chen, Y., Miao, D., & Wang, R. (2010). A rough set approach to feature selection based on ant colony optimization. *Pattern Recognition Letters, 31*(3), 226–233. doi:10.1016/j.patrec.2009.10.013

Chuang, L.-Y., Tsai, S.-W., & Yang, C.-H. (2011). Improved binary particle swarm optimization using catfish effect for feature selection. *Expert Systems with Applications, 38*(10), 12699–12707. doi:10.1016/j.eswa.2011.04.057

Coleto-Alcudia, V., & Vega-Rodríguez, M. A. (2021). A metaheuristic multi-objective optimization method for dynamical network biomarker identification as pre-disease stage signal. *Applied Soft Computing, 109,* 107544. doi:10.1016/j.asoc.2021.107544

Dash, M., & Liu, H. (1997). Feature Selection for Classification. *Intelligent Data Analysis, 1*(1–4), 131–156. doi:10.3233/IDA-1997-1302

Dorigo, M., Maniezzo, V., & Colorni, A. (1991). *Positive feedback as a search strategy.* Dipartimento di Elettronica, Politecnico di Milano, Italy, Tech. Rep.

Eusuff, M. M., & Lansey, K. E. (2003). Optimization of Water Distribution Network Design Using the Shuffled Frog Leaping Algorithm. *Journal of Water Resources Planning and Management, 129*(3), 210–225. doi:10.1061/(ASCE)0733-9496(2003)129:3(210)

Fister, I. Jr., Yang, X.-S., Fister, I., Brest, J., & Fister, D. (2013). *A Brief Review of Nature-Inspired Algorithms for Optimization.* Academic Press.

Holland, J. H. (1975). *Adaptation in Natural and Artificial Systems.* University of Michigan Press.

Jensen, R., & Shen, Q. (2003). Finding rough set reducts with ant colony optimization. *Proceeding of 2003 UK Workshop Computational Intelligence,* 15–22.

Karaboga, D. (2005). *An idea based on honey bee swarm for numerical optimization.* Academic Press.

Kanan, H. R., Faez, K., & Taheri, S. M. (2007). Feature Selection Using Ant Colony Optimization (ACO): A New Method and Comparative Study in the Application of Face Recognition System. In P. Perner (Ed.), *Advances in Data Mining. Theoretical Aspects and Applications* (Vol. 4597, pp. 63–76). Springer Berlin Heidelberg. doi:10.1007/978-3-540-73435-2_6

Karthikeyan, R., & Alli, P. (2018). Feature Selection and Parameters Optimization of Support Vector Machines Based on Hybrid Glowworm Swarm Optimization for Classification of Diabetic Retinopathy. *Journal of Medical Systems, 42*(10), 195. doi:10.100710916-018-1055-x PMID:30209620

Khan, M. A., Lali, M. I. U., Sharif, M., Javed, K., Aurangzeb, K., Haider, S. I., Altamrah, A. S., & Akram, T. (2019). An Optimized Method for Segmentation and Classification of Apple Diseases Based on Strong Correlation and Genetic Algorithm Based Feature Selection. *IEEE Access: Practical Innovations, Open Solutions, 7,* 46261–46277. doi:10.1109/ACCESS.2019.2908040

Kennedy, J., & Eberhart, R. (1995). *Particle Swarm Optimization.* Academic Press.

Krishnanand, K. N., & Ghose, D. (2009). Glowworm swarm optimisation: A new method for optimising multi-modal functions. *International Journal of Computational Intelligence Studies, 1*(1), 93–119. doi:10.1504/IJCISTUDIES.2009.025340

Kohavi, R., & John, G. H. (1997). Wrappers for feature subset selection. *Artificial Intelligence, 97*(1–2), 273–324. doi:10.1016/S0004-3702(97)00043-X

Kunhare, N., Tiwari, R., & Dhar, J. (2020). Particle swarm optimization and feature selection for intrusion detection system. *Sadhana, 45*(1), 109. doi:10.100712046-020-1308-5

Li, J., & Liu, H. (2016). *Challenges of Feature Selection for Big Data Analytics.* https://arxiv.org/abs/1611.01875

Lin, Y., Wang, J., Li, X., Zhang, Y., & Huang, S. (2021). An Improved Artificial Bee Colony for Feature Selection in QSAR. *Algorithms, 14*(4), 120. doi:10.3390/a14040120

Liu, A., Chen, K., Liu, Q., Ai, Q., Xie, Y., & Chen, A. (2017). Feature Selection for Motor Imagery EEG Classification Based on Firefly Algorithm and Learning Automata. *Sensors (Basel), 17*(11), 2576. doi:10.339017112576 PMID:29117100

Liu, X.-Y., Liang, Y., Wang, S., Yang, Z.-Y., & Ye, H.-S. (2018). A Hybrid Genetic Algorithm With Wrapper-Embedded Approaches for Feature Selection. *IEEE Access: Practical Innovations, Open Solutions, 6*, 22863–22874. doi:10.1109/ACCESS.2018.2818682

Mirjalili, S., Gandomi, A., Mirjalili, S. Z., Saremi, S., Faris, H., & Mirjalili, S. M. (2017). Salp Swarm Algorithm: A bio-inspired optimizer for engineering design problems. *Advances in Engineering Software, 7*, 1–29. doi:10.1016/j.advengsoft.2017.07.002

Narendra, & Fukunaga. (1977, September). A Branch and Bound Algorithm for Feature Subset Selection. *IEEE Transactions on Computers, C-26*(9), 917–922. doi:10.1109/TC.1977.1674939

Oreski, S., & Oreski, G. (2014). Genetic algorithm-based heuristic for feature selection in credit risk assessment. *Expert Systems with Applications, 41*(4), 2052–2064. doi:10.1016/j.eswa.2013.09.004

Pal, S. K., & Skowron, A. (1999). *Rough Fuzzy Hybridization: A New Trend in Decision-Making*. Springer.

Peng, H., Ying, C., Tan, S., Hu, B., & Sun, Z. (2018). An Improved Feature Selection Algorithm Based on Ant Colony Optimization. *IEEE Access: Practical Innovations, Open Solutions, 6*, 69203–69209. doi:10.1109/ACCESS.2018.2879583

Qiu, J., Wu, Q., Ding, G., Xu, Y., & Feng, S. (2016). A survey of machine learning for big data processing. *EURASIP Journal on Advances in Signal Processing, 2016*(1), 67. doi:10.118613634-016-0355-x

Schiezaro, M., & Pedrini, H. (2013). Data feature selection based on Artificial Bee Colony algorithm. *EURASIP Journal on Image and Video Processing, 2013*(1), 47. doi:10.1186/1687-5281-2013-47

Seyedali, M., Seyed Mohammad, M., & Andrew, L. (2014). Grey Wolf Optimizer. *Advances in Engineering Software, 69*, 46-61. doi:10.1016/j.advengsoft.2013.12.007

Simon, D. (2008). *Biogeography-Based Optimization. IEEE Transactions on Evolutionary*. doi:10.1109/TEVC.2008.919004

Sörensen, K. (2015). Metaheuristics-the metaphor exposed. *International Transactions in Operational Research, 22*(1), 3–18. doi:10.1111/itor.12001

Harde, S., & Sahare, V. (2016). Design and implementation of ACO feature selection algorithm for data stream mining. *2016 International Conference on Automatic Control and Dynamic Optimization Techniques (ICACDOT)*, 1047-1051. 10.1109/ICACDOT.2016.7877746

Taha, A. M., Mustapha, A., & Chen, S.-D. (2013). Naïve Bayes-Guided Bat Algorithm for Feature Selection. *TheScientificWorldJournal, 2013*, 1–9. doi:10.1155/2013/325973 PMID:24396295

Tan, F., Fu, X., Zhang, Y., & Bourgeois, A. G. (2007). A genetic algorithm-based method for feature subset selection. *Soft Computing, 12*(2), 111–120. doi:10.100700500-007-0193-8

Too, J., Abdullah, A. R., & Mohd Saad, N. (2019). A New Co-Evolution Binary Particle Swarm Optimization with Multiple Inertia Weight Strategy for Feature Selection. *Informatics (MDPI), 6*(2), 21. doi:10.3390/informatics6020021

Xue, B., Zhang, M., & Browne, W. N. (2013). Particle Swarm Optimization for Feature Selection in Classification: A Multi-Objective Approach. *IEEE Transactions on Cybernetics, 43*(6), 1656–1671. doi:10.1109/TSMCB.2012.2227469 PMID:24273143

Xue, B., Zhang, M., Browne, W. N., & Yao, X. (2016). A Survey on Evolutionary Computation Approaches to Feature Selection. *IEEE Transactions on Evolutionary Computation*, 20(4), 606–626. doi:10.1109/TEVC.2015.2504420

Yang, X.-S. (2010a). A New Metaheuristic Bat-Inspired Algorithm. In J. Kacprzyk (Ed.), *Nature Inspired Cooperative Strategies for Optimization (NICSO 2010)* (Vol. 284, pp. 65–74). Springer Berlin Heidelberg. doi:10.1007/978-3-642-12538-6_6

Yang, X.-S. (2010b). *Firefly Algorithm, Levy Flights and Global Optimization*. doi:10.1007/978-1-84882-983-1_15

Yang, X.-S. (2012). *Flower Pollination Algorithm for Global Optimization*. doi:10.1007/978-3-642-32894-7_27

Yang, X.-S., & Deb, S. (2009). Cuckoo Search via Lévy flights. *2009 World Congress on Nature & Biologically Inspired Computing (NaBIC)*, 210–214. 10.1109/NABIC.2009.5393690

Zhao, M., & Qin, Y. (2021). Feature Selection on Elite Hybrid Binary Cuckoo Search in Binary Label Classification. *Computational and Mathematical Methods in Medicine*, 2021, 1–13. doi:10.1155/2021/5588385 PMID:34055039

ADDITIONAL READING

Balasaraswathi, V. R., Sugumaran, M., & Hamid, Y. (2017). Feature selection techniques for intrusion detection using non-bio-inspired and bio-inspired optimization algorithms. *Journal of Communications and Information Networks*, 2(4), 107–119. doi:10.100741650-017-0033-7

Basir, M. A., Hussin, M. S., & Yusof, Y. (2021). Ensemble Feature Selection Method Based on Bio-inspired Algorithms for Multi-objective Classification Problem. In F. Saeed, T. Al-Hadhrami, F. Mohammed, & E. Mohammed (Eds.), *Advances on Smart and Soft Computing. Advances in Intelligent Systems and Computing* (Vol. 1188). Springer. doi:10.1007/978-981-15-6048-4_15

Manikandan, G., & Abirami, S. (2021). Feature Selection Is Important: State-of-the-Art Methods and Application Domains of Feature Selection on High-Dimensional Data. In R. Kumar & S. Paiva (Eds.), *Applications in Ubiquitous Computing. EAI/Springer Innovations in Communication and Computing*. Springer. doi:10.1007/978-3-030-35280-6_9

Mohammadi, F. G., Amini, M. H., & Arabnia, H. R. (2020). Applications of Nature-Inspired Algorithms for Dimension Reduction: Enabling Efficient Data Analytics. In M. H. Amini (Ed.), *Optimization, Learning, and Control for Interdependent Complex Networks* (Vol. 1123, pp. 67–84). Springer International Publishing. doi:10.1007/978-3-030-34094-0_4

Rong, M., Gong, D., & Gao, X. (2019). Feature Selection and Its Use in Big Data: Challenges, Methods, and Trends. *IEEE Access: Practical Innovations, Open Solutions*, 7, 19709–19725. doi:10.1109/ACCESS.2019.2894366

Rostami, M., Berahmand, K., Nasiri, E., & Forouzandeh, S. (2021). Review of swarm intelligence-based feature selection methods. *Engineering Applications of Artificial Intelligence*, 100, 104210. doi:10.1016/j.engappai.2021.104210

KEY TERMS AND DEFINITIONS

B

Bio-Inspired Algorithms: Iterative and stochastic algorithms, called metaheuristics, inspired from living being and destinated to address hard problems.

Classification: A process of putting objects on previously defined classes (supervised) or not defined (unsupervised) according to defined attributes by using specific algorithms.

Diversification Process: A process of metaheuristics used in order to explore new area of an optimization problem and to escape a local optima trap.

Feature Selection: A step of feature engineering by which the dimensionality of a problem is reduced obtaining a subset of pertinent features in order to improve the accuracy of a predictive model and to give more lisibility.

Filter Methods: A set of FS methods based on statistical methods with no regards to the predictive algorithm and no explicit interaction between the features each other.

Intensification Process: A process of metaheuristics aiming to explore an area of a search space of an optimization problem.

Swarm Intelligence Bio-Inspired Algorithms: A subclass of bio-inspired algorithms inspired from swarm intelligent behavioural strategies of living beings like ant, bee, and bird colonies.

Wrapper Methods: A set of FS methods interacting with predictive algorithms implying the interaction between features each other.

Section 24
Financial Services Analytics

Financial Analytics With Big Data

Leon Wang
Big Data Club, USA

INTRODUCTION

Finance is a fundamental part to everyone's life. As the big data, Internet of Things, cloud computing, and other ideas and technologies are integrated into social life, the big data technology can improve the corporate financial data processing. At the same time, with the fiercer competition between enterprises, investors and enterprises have paid more attention to the role of financial crisis warning in corporate management. The development of modern information technologies entails an unprecedented growth in the volume of computing resources and large data sets. Thanks to this, ML methods available through open-source toolkits are gaining popularity among analysts and developers. Deep learning models have proven extremely successful in a wide range of applications, including image processing, learning gamification, neuroscience, energy conservation, and medical diagnostics (Shang, Lu, & Zhou, 2021; Zhou, Lou, & Jiang, 2019).

The finance industry has adopted ML to varying degrees of sophistication. Several mathematical disciplines, including statistical computing, data mining, financial econometrics, probabilistic and dynamic programming were brought together by ML in finance. There are many misconceptions and limited understanding of the possibilities of this field. Effective ML methods remain poorly understood and often mathematically unsound (Sreejanya, Chowdary, Atri, Reddy, Harith, & Mahajan, 2022). A key challenge to understanding ML is the lack of well-established theories and concepts that are necessary for financial time series analysis. The key to implementing ML in finance is to be able to run ML alongside parametric methods, observing over time the differences and limitations of parametric modeling based on fit metrics in the sample. Karachun, Vinnichek, & Tuskov (2021) address many finance practitioner's concerns that neural networks are a "black-box" by showing how they are related to existing well-established techniques such as linear regression, logistic regression, and autoregressive time series models. Neural networks can be shown to reduce to other well-known statistical techniques and are adaptable to time series data. Statistical tests must be used to characterize the data and select the algorithm. If the data is of sufficiently high quality and adds a new source of information, then it can be easily scaled up. ML is a more reliable approach than many methods of parametric financial econometrics used today. At the same time, the use of ML requires strong skills of scientific justification. And it is not a panacea for automatic decision-making.

BACKGROUND

There has been an extremely fast growth in the amount of data that is made and collected on a daily basis and because of this data collection, analysis, and processing have created opportunities for new technology, jobs and industries. According to Forrester (2019), big data is considered as a vital dominant driver of competitive advantage that refers the ability to outperform the rivals for businesses. Today, there is

DOI: 10.4018/978-1-7998-9220-5.ch114

a dramatic increase in the amount of generated, mined and stored data, reaching a market size of $50 billion to reach $104.3 billion by 2026 (Basdas & Esen, 2021). Companies produce large amounts of raw data in daily basis via IoT, smart devices and cloud platforms. Technology is constantly evolving and changing the way that we do business. The implementation of Big Data in the business world has proved to be very beneficial and effective especially in the financial sector. The addition of this new research will allow companies to combat fraud, offer more personalized experiences to their customers, and make smarter investment decisions.

Financial services industry includes SME finance, wealth and asset management, mobile payment platforms and the popular cryptocurrency. Due to the intricacy and sheer magnitude of the data these platforms create, they are also prone to many arising issues which is why financial analysts are highly sought after. These are especially important to analyze because big data and internet finance are being regarded by more and more scholars to be the "new engine of growth" (Wang, 2018). Big data has already proved its importance and value" (Ke & Shi, 2014). Identifying the opportunities, challenges and implications of big data in finance help to further highlight areas of growth for organizations. With ever evolving technology and with different types of data now continuously available with the advancements of information technologies, data has become, one of if not the most, valuable commodity in the financial services industry. Finance is at the core of modern economic operations, and financial viability determines the quality and potential of the overall economy (Wang, 2018). Most areas of business and finance are heavily connected with big data (Hasan, Popp, & Olah, 2020).

Basdas and Esen (2021) provide a systematic review on the world's revolution in information and communication technologies (ICTs) over last couple of decades. Big data appeared as a revolutionary phenomenon that influenced decision-making processes. The need for big data towards the digitalization of services, utilization of social media and new channels to reach customers, demand for personalized services and continuous flow of vast amount of data in the sector is growing exponentially. Massively parallel processors and modern data management architectures have led to more efficient operations and a better decision making for companies to process and analyze such complex and large-scale data. Especially, financial services companies leverage big data to transform their business processes. Heuristic decision making, simple reporting and statistical analysis dominated in the 1960s and 1970s. Relational or hierarchical databases in table based format were organized to store data in the 1990s. Extract, transform and load (ETL) processes have been implemented for cross-functional activities, fast query processing and multiuser environment in order to help enterprise data mitigate from day-to-day transactions to data warehouses. Companies started to focus on value creation by operational data warehouses that accumulate business transactions in the early 2000s. Companies became more analytical and data-driven in the following decade due to their ability in processing high volume and velocity of data to realize business benefits. The advent of wireless has avalanched the variety of data and brought a proprietary resource for companies in 2010. Virtual infrastructures, a real-time communication network, allowed many companies to allocate their resources for moving, storing and analyzing the huge amount of data over the second half of the 2010s. Further developments in the digital transformation enable companies to move with big data solutions using Artificial Intelligence (AI) for organizing and performing business tasks today.

CURRENT RESEARCH

Real-Time Analytics

Real Time Enterprise

Having faced the fast-changing and comprehensive digital economy, modern management needs various IT systems for effective management, such as ERP, CRM, BI, SCM, SCADA (System Control And Data Acquisition), HCM (Human Capital Management, et al., Kisielnicki and Marek (2021) emphasize that real time enterprise should be as a platform of support management systems. Real Time Enterprise (RTE) can react immediately to business changes, reduce the time needed to implement economic processes, obtain information very quickly and share it. Realtime information processing enterprise uses integration technologies, cloud or on-premises (middleware), which enable immediate data exchange between both the company's IT systems and its business partners. Hence, in the case of RTE, one can speak of a platform of cooperating IT systems supporting management. The authors indicate examples of business areas with real-time business processes and present the basic RTE requirements for IT, such as real time monitoring, real-time access to information and acceleration of business processes. Also, the authors propose determinants of IT system design for IT, including: a) Implementation & development of IT systems, b) Integration of people, information and business processes, c) Change management and continues improvement of the enterprise processes, d) IT design. Plus, The MUST methodology (a Danish acronym for theories of and methods for design activities) was proposed as the basis for the preparation of IT technology implementation for RTE. Furthermore, the authors put forward the management cockpit as the central reporting element for real-time monitoring.

Event Detection

Carta, Consoli, Piras, Podda, & Recupero (2021) notice that Event Detection (ED) has become increasingly important in the last two decades, since it allows users to disentangle this mass of scattered and, oftentimes, heterogeneous data, and to become aware of relevant world-wide facts in a more efficient way. Having built on the theoretic foundations of Information Retrieval, ED absorbs Natural Language Processing, Text Mining and Big Data processing. Event Detection aims to discover contents published on the Web that report on the same current topic, organize them in meaningful groups and provide insights, based on properties extracted automatically from the data. There are both pros and cons between traditional press and social media. The former represents an authoritative and noise-free source whereas the latter can provide insights about the entity or the resonance of the events. The integration of them is a best solution. So, they propose a real-time domain-specific clustering-based event-detection approach that integrates textual information coming from traditional newswires with microblogging platforms. Their qualitative and quantitative analysis shows that the proposed method is able to extract meaningful, separable clusters, which correspond to real-world events. Furthermore, the alert generation algorithm detects *hot* events with high accuracy, proving the effectiveness of the integration of news articles and tweets.

Data Stream Processing

Corresponding to Jadhav and Kodavade (2021), various applications generate voluminous streamed data and ideally desire real-time data analysis due to digitization in many fields. Data stream analysis fulfills the requirements of generation of output result with accuracy and low latency. Data stream processing is used where time is an important aspect and a real-time decision is important. A huge amount of heterogeneous and unbounded data requires real processing and analytics for decision making. Data stream processing and data stream analytics both are techniques that are applicable for such types of applications. Having provided a general architecture of data stream processing, the authors evaluate the efficacy of the most suitable open-source data stream analytics frameworks, such as storm, spark streaming, kafka stream, and flink et al. Also, the authors discuss the capabilities of available big data and stream analytics technologies in relation with the requirements of predictive maintenance use cases for railway transportation. One of the Industry 4.0 use case - predictive maintenance rail transportation - has been illustrated here as a case study design mapped with streaming analytics framework. This can be easily mapped to the probable use cases of streaming analytics as Finance, Healthcare, Transportation etc. Overall data stream processing and streaming analytics are the growing and trending fields for real-time processing of huge amounts of real-time streaming data. They intend to provide a comprehensive technology and framework guidelines with a focus on representative use case of predictive maintenance in railway transportation.

Risk Management

Fuzzy Association Rule Mining

From the US subprime mortgage crisis to the European debt crisis, the research on financial risk crisis warning is particularly important. In harsh market competition, the requirements of companies for risk management are increasing. The enterprises can gather and put in safekeeping all business activity data with the development of the economy and the era of big data. Shang, Lu, & Zhou (2021) propose a fuzzy association rule mining algorithm of time series based on FCM (fuzzy cluster method) clustering, which used FCM clustering algorithm for the fuzzy discretization on the cleaned time data. A parallel mining algorithm of association rule was used to obtain the frequent fuzzy option sets, and multiple processors in parallel generated the fuzzy association rules satisfying minimum fuzzy trust degree. The rules between all financial indicators were mined to determine more representative financial risk indicators. The big data mining algorithm of Internet of Things was established based on fuzzy association rules to obtain the model of corporate financial-risk analysis. The rules between financial indicators were found to predict corporate financial crisis. The method in the work has been verified by the experiment, and the fluctuation of key indicators determined the enterprise risk degree.

Unsupervised Learning

Financial institutions aggregate risk reports at least cover key risks such as MR (market risk), CR (credit risk), OR (operational risk) and LR (liquidity risk). As the information of risk reports originates from risk data, the quality of risk data would be verified first. In case there are any DQ (data quality) problems in risk data, erroneous data have to be identified, predicted earlier and remediated as soon as possible. Wong and Wong (2021) model big data prediction in unsupervised learning, which saves much time on labelling data that demands for many resources and great efforts. In real life, there are massive amount of big data. It is impossible to label them all before we can train neural networks for prediction.

Neural networks with a multidimensional learning of DQ are experimented including the feedforwarding learning, the backward learning and the bidirectional learning with a focus on relatively important big data. The authors start to implement the model to detect data noises from a risk dataset according to an international data quality standard from banking industry and then estimate their impacts with Gaussian and Bayesian methods. After that, they direct sequential learning in multiple deep neural networks for the prediction with an attention mechanism. The model is experimented with various network methodologies to show the predictive power of ML technique and is evaluated by validation data to confirm the model effectiveness. The model is scalable to apply to any industries utilizing big data other than the banking industry.

A Loan Risk Assessment Model

Li and Huang (2021) use basic user information and added the user's consumption features to construct a loan risk assessment model that integrates features. At present, the main study directions in the field of loan risk assessment are divided into two categories, one is the study on loan assessment methods, the other is the study on loan assessment dimensions. Therefore, this study from the perspective of dimensions and methods, by adding the user's consumption data in the consumption platform to the loan evaluation dimension, constructs a loan evaluation model integrating consumption data. Through experiments on real data sets, the evaluation effect of our proposed fusion model is better than other models. In view of the user's historical consumption data, we extract consumption features from two aspects, analyze consumption information, construct consumption portrait features, and consider the sequence information in consumption. By constructing CNN_BiLSTM, we can extract the sequence features in consumption data well. Considering that each consumption has different impact on the user's economic level and loan risk, we introduce an attention mechanism to further enhance the classification effect.

Fraud Detection

Cross Checking

Rizvi (2021) observes that most of the knowledge provided in today's world is in an unstructured format, which plays a positive role in the financial institutions for financial fraud. It is difficult to extract relevant information from it because it comes in terms of different tempo, variety, and variability. The ability to cope with larger data volumes and work with new, unstructured forms of data would greatly increase criminal activity identification. In order to reduce financial fraud in financial institutions, gathering valuable information for automated detection of fraud is our goal. It is the leading strategy to recognize similitude between an individual or bunch behavior recognized from numerous sources and cross-checking value-based information behavior. The study recommends the researcher find more challenges, opportunities, tools, and techniques of big data analytics, also find as how many organizations have implemented big data and how big data helps to generate sales.

Internal Audit Functions

Rakipi, Santis, & D'Onza (2021) identify and test five variables expected to be associated with the IAFs' (internal audit functions) use of DA (data analytics) tools. Their findings provide empirical evidence that the IAF reporting to the AC relates positively and significantly to the adoption of DA tools in audit work. Their evidence adds to the literature on the importance of the IAF's independence. This underlines that the IAF's independence, preserved through direct reporting to the AC, is important so as to avoid the IAF encountering obstacles in the innovation of its techniques, and to have the necessary financial and human resources to support its investments. This is particularly important for DA, as these techniques increase IAF's ability to identify possible management fraud and internal control deficiencies. A direct functional reporting line to senior managers could slow down, or in the worst scenario, undermine DA use.

Their results also indicate that the involvement of the IAF in risk management assurance and fraud detection are significant correlates to the IAF's use of DA tools. This indicates that DA use is facilitated when the IAF performs IT audits. This offers the possibility to improve data quality and further develop the knowledge of the organization's IT system and data value chains. Our results help researchers, CAEs, and professional associations to identify factors that can influence DA use. The authors also suggest additional research into whether DA adoption determines a real increase in IAF's effectiveness and ability to satisfy its stakeholders' expectations. Further, we encourage researchers to analyze the application of DA tools by the IAF in other areas, including business process re-engineering and auditing of outsourced processes. We also provide insights to the IIA in order to develop training activities, standards, and practical guidelines for DA use in internal auditing.

Key Information Providers

In agreement with Balios (2021), upgraded information systems and automation in business procedures diminish the need for staff participation. Inevitably, the skills of accountants and knowledge must be associated with big data and big data analytics and modern accountants must develop an analytics mindset by being familiar with data and technologies. The author considers the impact of big data on accounting and auditing. Financial accountants need to move beyond the book-keeping process and become key information providers to decision-makers. That upturns accountants' consulting role and their ability to think strategically, providing critical help in management decision making. The relationship between managers and management accountants becomes closer and more effective because of big data. Management accountants can use additional analytical methods to detect processes and product excellence, combined with diminishing cost. Big data and big data analytics in auditing ensure audit quality and fraud detection.

Consumer Analytics

Behavioral Finance

ML has opened the world of finance to instantaneous data that can be collected by the click of a button. According to Chartier, Bowden, Pinkerton, & Townley (2021), Artificial Intelligence and Social Media Analytics has paved the way for unlimited means in which finance can be handled moving forward in the world of business. These new tools are very eye opening to the future of economics, either through predicting valuations of a stock or helping to maximize revenue generated in a business. As the way of the stock market is moving to more of an individualistic investor approach, Social Media Analytics will be a main influence in the future when it comes to determining which stocks to invest in. When looking into the future of the stock market, it will become very beneficial if investors study accounting and use their knowledge of business positions to help determine the valuation of future stocks. The world has seen the impact that AI and ML has had on businesses in its early stages, and it is very exciting to see where it will lead in a few years. With the addition of advanced learning that AI provides it will break that barrier leading to opportunities never imagined before.

Digital Platform

Having used neural networks in the first stage and multiple regression in the second stage, Song, Li, & Yu (2021) examine how digital platform-based financial service providers (FSPs) use big data analytics (BDA) to discriminate different qualities of financial service providers (SMEs) through explicit information, and analyze what kind of tailored implicit information can effectively predict the amount of supply chain finance (SCF) SMEs receive. Authors suggest that FSPs can effectively embed each entity onto a digital platform for SCF by micro-architecture supply chain services, modular-architecture processes, and cloud-based applications. This not only enriches research on FSPs but also extends platform theory to a SCF context. Also, authors suggest that BDA of implicit operational information exhibited in the FSPs' digital platform plays a crucial role in the discriminative effects of SCF, which enriches research on SCF from the perspective of information signaling theory and contributes to research on BDA in supply chain management.

Their study proposed that the digital platform initiated and organized by FSPs can use BDA to track the behaviors of SMEs throughout their life cycle, and overcome the problem of information asymmetry inflicted by financial institutions. Furthermore, they propose that BDA of explicit information, including relational information, credit guarantee information and relational specific assets information, exerts supportive effects for lending decisions. Thus, finding targeted information and making targeted loan decisions not only help solve the financing problem of SMEs but also help financial institutions effectively control default risks, especially when information scarcity and overload coexist. The study's findings can be applied to assist managers in the decision-making process for SCF. Constructing a digital platform through effective means is an important performance outcome of FSPs. This digital platform not only effectively integrates the operating data in the supply chain but also facilitates financial activities.

Retail Analytics

Rooderkerk, DeHoratius, & Musalem (2021) document the development of academic research on retail analytics and compare it with current practice, which was the result after interviewing global practitioners. As illustrated by bibliometric analyses, retail analytics is a field of growing importance. This characterizes an evolution of the retail analytics field from one closely related to operations research, to embracing econometrics to study the drivers and consequences of certain phenomena and advise optimization problems to finally considering forecasts, which was driven by the advent of ML. The authors notice that analytics as still mostly in its infancy in practice due to the following barriers: culture, organization, people, processes, systems, and data.

Moving forward analytics use of existing data is high on the agenda for all involved in the retail value chain, being stimulated by investments in data management systems, analytics solutions and expertise. Many interviewees also expect to substantially invest in three types of technologies: a). RFID and IoT, etc. that can more precisely track assets; b). Technologies, like video, that help obtain a better understanding of what happens in terms of in-store traffic and shopper activity; c). Technologies that ease data handling and analytics such as cloud infrastructure and computing. Adoption of these three technologies will spawn rich new data sources, mostly unstructured.

FUTURE RESEARCH DIRECTIONS

Deep Belief Network (DBN)

Song and Wu (2021) apply genetic algorithm (GA), neural network (NN), and principal component analysis (PCA) methods to collect and process the data, and build a risk assessment model of excessive financialization of financial enterprises. The performance of the model is analyzed through the data of specific cases. The results suggest that the data mining technology based on *back propagation neural network* (BPNN) can optimize the input variables and effectively extract the hidden information from the data. Through the analysis of data mining algorithm, the differences of different algorithm models in practical application and performance are comprehensively evaluated. When the dataset is small, the algorithm can get the optimal results under different datasets. When the dataset is large, DBN (deep belief network) neural network model consumes less time; each model has its own unique advantages in different performance. The authors notice that when a large amount of data is analyzed, how to reduce the running time and improve the efficiency of algorithm learning is a problem that needs to be studied.

Algorithmic Text Analysis

Nyman, Kapadia, & Tuckett (2021) apply algorithmic analysis, a conviction narrative approach, to financial market unstructured text-based data to assess how narratives and sentiment might drive financial system developments. The authors find changes in emotional content in narratives show the development and subsequent downfall of exuberance prior to the global financial crisis. They extract quantitative summary statistics from novel data sources which have largely only been used qualitatively thus far and have demonstrated that their approach can lead to some intuitive and useful representations of financial market sentiment. A novel ML application also points towards increasing consensus around the strongly positive narrative prior to the crisis. The authors have also developed a novel methodology to measure consensus in the distribution of narratives. This metric can potentially be used to measure homogenization in the financial system. Greater consensus, when viewed together with an increase in sentiment, may also be interpreted as an increase of predominantly excited consensus of narratives prior to the global financial crisis. Overall, their metrics may be useful in gauging risks to financial stability arising from the collective behavior discussed.

Financial Distress Modeling

Financial distress modeling is a promising model for businesses to use because it will enable them to forecast financial failure, measure one's financial performance, and reduce the occurrence of a human error made in auditing. These models help companies to assess/forecast a company's financial failure. Many firms have used decision-tree-based models to predict this. The integration of big data techniques in this type of modeling will allow companies to better gauge their financial performance and help to improve going concern evaluations that are required during auditing. Additionally, big data will also help to reduce the occurrence of issuing an unmodified opinion when declaring bankruptcy which can impose a further financial burden on a company because it is a very costly (Gepp et al., 2018; Goldstein et al., 2021).

Blockchain Analytics

Blockchain Analytics is one of the biggest up-and-coming trends regarding big data in finance. Blockchain Analytics is a technology that records information that makes it virtually impossible to hack or change a system. This technology also takes transactional data and stores it in different databases. Blockchain Analytics will not only have a positive impact on finance but on other departments as well such as supply chain and quality control. In regards to finance, the implementation of Blockchain Analytics will change the way companies do banking. It will make processes such as sending international money and accounting ledgers flawless (Saha et al., 2019). The reason behind this is because Blockchains block out any unauthorized individual trying to modify a transaction which will allow them to be more secure and efficient. The use of this technology will also help in detecting fraud which is a prevalent issue in the financial industry and will even help to detect money laundering. This emerging trend is solid and will help change the way firms do business (Heister, Kaufman, & Yuthas, 2021).

CONCLUSION

Big data has changed the way many industries around the world operate. With these changes, there are also many challenges companies face with big data in finance. Many companies rely on big data in finance to make better financial decisions and give them a competitive advantage in the market. With the use of big data, many financial companies have been able to make better investments with higher returns. Big data is considered to be the most important source of analysis for all related areas to finance. Big data in finance comes with many positives but it also comes with some negatives. Personal data collection is one of the many negatives that come with big data in finance. Personal data can be distributed across the world which scares many people and makes them skeptical of sharing their financial records. When it comes to supply chain finance, big data is very beneficial. Big data helps with collecting data from wide ranges of different sources, assessing risks, and forecasting and projecting the future.

Some risks are associated with the data itself. These risks include the high costs of according the data, the legitimacy and authenticity of data, and security issues. There are many levels of data purchased from different sources and processing this data comes with a cost. Once this data is processed it needs to be dissected to figure out which information is useful, and which is not. After that, the data can finally be stored. Data can be breached at any time which raises security concerns for a company. It also costs money to buy the data and process it to be stored. Data can also be inaccurate and wrong which can lead to negative business outcomes. With the many risks, there are worth using big data in finance. There are also many steps companies can take to limit these risks and protect the personal information of people, save money, and enhance knowledge surrounding big data and artificial intelligence. It is recommended that companies should fully supervise data information present in social networks because the increased use of social media led to an increase in data leaks and shares.

Big data is also very important in banks, it is used to collect relevant information and data in the financial field and also clarify the specific development trend of stocks and bonds. Financial services and artificial intelligence also use big data to their benefit. Big data can help limit future risk for any business. Using intelligent risk foresights and mining potential threats for any business is crucial. The use of risk management strategy will contribute to monitoring threats that are present now that can't be seen by the normal eye and future threats. For a company to succeed, understanding consumer wants and needs to strategies that are implemented into risk management and feedback as well as understanding future paths is paramount important. With more research being conducted and the introduction of Blockchain Analytics, ML, Financial Distress Modeling, and Financial Fraud Modeling, the use of big data will continue to evolve.

REFERENCES

Basdas, U., & Esen, M. F. (2021). Review of big data applications in finance and economics. In B. Patil & M. Vohra (Eds.), *Handbook of Research on Engineering, Business, and Healthcare Applications of Data Science and Analytics* (pp. 181–202). IGI Global. doi:10.4018/978-1-7998-3053-5.ch010

Balios, D. (2021). The impact of big data on accounting and auditing. *International Journal of Corporate Finance and Accounting*, 8(1), 1–14. doi:10.4018/IJCFA.2021010101

Carta, S., Consoli, S., Piras, L., Podda, A. S., & Recupero, D. R. (2021). Event detection in finance using hierarchical clustering algorithms on news and tweets. *PeerJ. Computer Science*, 7, e438. doi:10.7717/peerj-cs.438 PMID:34084918

ChartierE.BowdenI.PinkertonM.TownleyA. (2021). Behavioral finance: the impact of artificial intelligence and social media analytics. https://ssrn.com/abstract=3794039 doi:10.2139/ssrn.3794039

Forrester, V. V. (2019). School management information systems: Challenges to educational decision-making in the big data era. *International Journal on Integrating Technology in Education*, 8(1), 1–11. doi:10.5121/ijite.2019.8101

Gepp, A., Linnenluecke, M. K., & Terrence, J. (2018). Big data techniques in auditing research and practice: Current trends and future opportunities. *Journal of Accounting Literature*, 40(1), 102–115. doi:10.1016/j.acclit.2017.05.003

Goldstein, I., Spatt, C. S., & Ye, M. (2021). Big data in finance. *Review of Financial Studies*, 34(7), 3213–3225. doi:10.1093/rfs/hhab038

Hasan, M. M., Popp, J., & Oláh, J. (2020). Current landscape and influence of big data on finance. *Journal of Big Data*, 7(1), 21. Advance online publication. doi:10.118640537-020-00291-z

Heister, S., Kaufman, M., & Yuthas, K. (2021). Blockchain and the Future of Business Data Analytics. *Journal of Emerging Technologies in Accounting*, 18(1), 87–98. doi:10.2308/JETA-2020-053

Jadhav, S.B., & Kodavade, D.V. (2021). Evaluative review of streaming analytics: tools and technologies in real-time data processing. *International Journal of Advanced Research in Science, Communication and Technology, 5*(2).

Karachun, I., Vinnichek, L., & Tuskov, A. (2021). Machine learning methods in finance. *ICEMT, 2021*. Advance online publication. doi:10.1051hsconf/202111005012

Ke, M., & Shi, Y.X. (2014). Big data, big change: In the financial management. *Open Journal of Accounting, 3*(4). doi:10.4236/ojacct.2014.34009

Kisielnicki, J., & Marek, M. M. (2021). Real time enterprise as a platform of support management systems. *Foundations of Management, 13*(1), 7–20. doi:10.2478/fman-2021-0001

Li, L., & Huang, D. (2021). A Loan risk assessment model with consumption features for online finance. *Journal of Physics: Conference Series, 1848*(1), 012068. doi:10.1088/1742-6596/1848/1/012068

Nyman, R., Kapadia, S., & Tuckett, D. (2021). News and narratives in financial systems: Exploiting big data for systemic risk assessment. *Journal of Economic Dynamics and Control, 127.*

Rakipi, R., Santis, F. D., & D'Onza, G. (2021). Correlates of the internal audit function's use of data analytics in the big data era: Global evidence. *Journal of International Accounting, Auditing and Taxation, 42.*

Rizvi S. R. Z. (2021). *Role of big data in financial institutions for financial fraud.* doi:10.2139/ssrn.3800777

Rooderkerk, R. P., DeHoratius, N., & Musalem, A. (2021). *Retail analytics: the quest for actionable insights from big data on consumer behavior and operational execution.* Chicago Booth Research Paper No. 21-18. doi:10.2139/ssrn.3867484

Saha, K. (2019). Analytics and big data: Emerging trends and their impact on our lives. *Journal of Public Affairs, 19*(4), 1472–3891. doi:10.1002/pa.1944

Shang, H., Lu, D., & Zhou, Q. (2021). Early warning of enterprise finance risk of big data mining in internet of things based on fuzzy association rules. *Neural Computing & Applications, 33*(9), 3901–3909. doi:10.100700521-020-05510-5

Song, H., Li, M., & Yu, K. (2021). Big data analytics in digital platforms: How do financial service providers customise supply chain finance? *International Journal of Operations & Production Management, 41*(4), 410–435. doi:10.1108/IJOPM-07-2020-0485

Song, Y., & Wu, R. (2021). The impact of financial enterprises' excessive financialization risk assessment for risk control based on data mining and machine learning. *Computational Economics.* https://doi-org/ doi:10.1007/s10614-021-10135-4

Sreejanya, O., Chowdary, B. R., Atri, A., Reddy, G. Y., Harith, S., & Mahajan, K. S. (2022). Big data analysis using financial risk management. *International Journal of Research in Engineering. Science and Management, 5*(1), 8–12.

Wang, F-P. (2018). Research on application of big data in internet financial credit investigation based on improved GA-BP neural network. *Complexity.* doi:10.1155/2018/7616537

Wong, K. Y., & Wong, R. K. (2021). Big data quality prediction informed by banking regulation. *International Journal of Data Science and Analytics, 12*(2), 147–164. doi:10.100741060-021-00257-1

Zhou, Q., Lou, J., & Jiang, Y. (2019). Optimization of energy consumption of green data center in e-commerce. *Sustain Computing Inf Sys, 23*, 103–110. doi:10.1016/j.suscom.2019.07.008

Sreejanya, O., Chowdary, B. R., Atri, A., Reddy, G. Y., Harith, S., & Mahajan, K. S. (2022). Big data analysis using financial risk management. *International Journal of Research in Engineering. Science and Management, 5*(1), 8–12.

ADDITIONAL READING

Alrashidi, M., Almutairi, A., & Zraqat, O. (2022). The impact of big data analytics on audit procedures: Evidence from the Middle East. *Journal of Asian Finance, Economics and Business, 9*(2), 93–102.

Edu, A. S. (2022). Positioning big data analytics capabilities towards financial service agility. *Aslib Journal of Information Management.* https://doi-org.ezproxy.montclair.edu/10.1108/AJIM-08-2021-0240

Guo, G., Shen, L., & Zhang, C. (2022). Management and control of financial information platform by big data technology. In *2021 International Conference on Big Data Analytics for Cyber-Physical System in Smart City. Lecture Notes on Data Engineering and Communications Technologies, 103*. Springer. 10.1007/978-981-16-7469-3_121

Khatrı, A., Sıngh, N., & Gupta, N. (2021). Big data analytics: Direction and impact on financial technology. *Journal of Management Marketing and Logistics, 8*(4), 218–234. doi:10.17261/Pressacademia.2021.1529

Muheidat, F., Patel, D., Tammisetty, S., Tawalbeh, L. A., & Tawalbeh, M. (2022). Emerging concepts using blockchain and big data. *Procedia Computer Science, 198*, 15–22. doi:10.1016/j.procs.2021.12.206

Pérez-Juárez, M. A., Aguiar-Pérez, J. M., Alonso-Felipe, M., Del-Pozo-Velázquez, J., Rozada-Raneros, S., & Barrio-Conde, M. (2022). Exploring the possibilities of artificial intelligence and big data techniques to enhance gamified financial services. In F. Portela & R. Queirós (Eds.), *Next-Generation Applications and Implementations of Gamification Systems* (pp. 187–204). IGI Global. doi:10.4018/978-1-7998-8089-9.ch010

Turgaeva, A. A., Kashirskaya, L. V., Zurnadzhyants, Y. A., Latysheva, O. A., Pustokhina, I. V., & Sevbitov, A. V. (2020). Assessment of the financial security of insurance companies in the organization of internal control. *Entrepreneurship Sustain Issues, 56*(4), 6–7. doi:10.9770/jesi.2020.7.3(52)

Xiao, J. (2022). Exploring the path of financial risk prevention in big-data-supported financial audit. In *2021 International Conference on Big Data Analytics for Cyber-Physical System in Smart City. Lecture Notes on Data Engineering and Communications Technologies, 103*. Springer. https://doi-org.ezproxy.montclair.edu/10.1007/978-981-16-7469-3_127

KEY TERMS AND DEFINITIONS

Big Data Analytics: A process used to extract meaningful insights, such as hidden patterns, unknown correlations, market trends, etc.

Financial Analytics: Financial analysis is the process of evaluating businesses, projects, budgets, and other finance-related transactions to determine their performance and suitability.

Fraud Detection: A set of processes and analyses that allow businesses to identify and prevent unauthorized financial activity.

Personalized Services: Making a measurable impression on consumers that is tailored to each individual customer, based on their specific wants and needs.

Real-Time Processing: It requires a continual input, constant processing, and steady output of data.

Risk Management: The process of identifying, assessing, and controlling threats of unfortunate events to an organization's capital and earnings.

Social Media Analytics: The ability to gather and find meaning in data gathered from social channels to support business decisions.

Streaming Analytics: The processing and analyzing of data records continuously rather than in batches. Generally, streaming analytics is useful for the types of data sources that send data in small sizes (often in kilobytes) in a continuous flow as the data is generated.

Portfolio Optimization for the Indian Stock Market

Jaydip Sen

Praxis Business School, Kolkata, India

Abhishek Dutta

Praxis Business School, Kolkata, India

INTRODUCTION

The design of optimized portfolios has remained a research topic of broad and intense interest among the researchers of quantitative and statistical finance for a long time. An optimum portfolio allocates the weights to a set of capital assets in a way that optimizes the return and risk of those assets. Markowitz in his seminal work proposed the mean-variance optimization approach which is based on the mean and covariance matrix of returns (Markowitz, 1952). The algorithm, known as the *critical line algorithm* (CLA), despite the elegance in its theoretical framework, has some major limitations. One of the major problems is the adverse effects of the estimation errors in its expected returns and covariance matrix on the performance of the portfolio.

The *hierarchical risk parity* (HRP) and *hierarchical equal risk contribution* (HERC) portfolios are two well-known approaches of portfolio design that attempt to address three major shortcomings of quadratic optimization methods which are particularly relevant to the CLA (de Prado, 2016). These problems are, instability, concentration, and under-performance. Unlike the CLA, the HRP algorithm does not require the covariance matrix of return values to be invertible. The HRP is capable of delivering good results even if the covariance matrix is ill-degenerated or singular, which is an impossibility for a quadratic optimizer. On the other hand, the HERC portfolio optimization adapts the HRP approach to achieve an equal contribution to risk by the constituent stocks in a cluster after forming an optimal number of clusters among a given set of capital assets. Interestingly, even though CLA's objective is to minimize the variance, portfolios formed based on HRP and HERC methods are proven to have a higher likelihood of yielding lower out-of-sample variance than the CLA. The major weakness of the CLA algorithm is that a small deviation in the forecasted future returns can make the CLA deliver widely divergent portfolios. Given the fact that future returns cannot be forecasted with sufficient accuracy, some researchers have proposed risk-based asset allocation using the covariance matrix of the returns. However, this approach brings in another problem of instability. The instability arises because the quadratic programming methods require the inversion of a covariance matrix whose all eigenvalues must be positive. This inversion is prone to large errors when the covariance matrix is numerically ill-conditioned, i.e., when it has a high condition number (Baily & de Prado, 2012). The HRP and HERC portfolios are two among the new portfolio approaches that address the pitfalls of the CLA using techniques of machine learning and graph theory (de Prado, 2016). While HRP exploits the features of the covariance matrix without the requirement of its invertibility or positive-definiteness and works effectively on even a singular covariance matrix of returns, the HERC portfolio leverages the formation of an optimal number of clusters

DOI: 10.4018/978-1-7998-9220-5.ch115

among a set of capital assets in a manner that ensures equal risk contribution by the assets in the same cluster (Raffinot, 2018).

Despite being recognized as two approaches that outperform the CLA algorithm, to the best of our knowledge, no study has been carried out so far to compare the performances of the HRP and the HERC portfolios on Indian stocks. This chapter presents a comparative analysis of the performances of the HRP and the HERC portfolios on some important stocks from selected eight sectors listed in the National Stock Exchange (NSE) of India. Based on the report of the NSE on Oct 29, 2021, the most significant stocks of seven sectors and the 50 stocks included in the NIFTY 50 are first identified (NSE, 2021). Portfolios are built using the HRP and the HERC approaches for the eight sectors using the historical prices of the stocks from Jan 1, 2016, to Dec 31, 2020. The portfolios are backtested on the in-sample data of the stock prices from Jan 1, 2016, to Dec 31, 2020, and also on the out-of-sample data of stock prices from Jan 1, 2021, to Nov 1, 2021. Extensive results on the performance of the backtesting of the portfolios are analyzed to identify the better-performing algorithm for portfolio design.

RELATED WORK

Several approaches have been proposed by researchers for accurate prediction of future values of stock prices and using the forecasted results in building robust and optimized portfolios that optimize the returns while minimizing the associated risk. Time series decomposition and econometric approaches like ARIMA, Granger causality, VAR are some of the most popular approaches to future stock price predictions which are used for robust portfolio design (Sen, 2018b, 2017a, 2017b; Sen & Datta Chaudhuri, 2018, 2017b, 2017c, 2016a, 2016b, 2016c). The use of machine learning, deep learning, and reinforcement learning models for future stock price prediction has been the most popular approach of late (Bao et al., 2017; Binkowski et al., 2018; Mehtab & Sen, 2022, 2020a, 2020b, 2020c, 2020d; Mehtab et al., 2021, 2020e; Sen, 2018a; Sen & Datta Chaudhuri, 2017a; Sen & Mehtab, 2021b, 2021c; Sen et al., 2020, 2021e). Hybrid models are also proposed that utilize the algorithms and architectures of machine learning and deep learning and exploit the sentiments in the textual sources on the social web (Audrino et al., 2020; Bollen et al., 2011; Carta et al., 2021; Chen et al., 2019; Galvez & Gravano, 2017; Mehtab & Sen, 2019; Weng et al., 2017). The use of metaheuristics algorithms in solving multi-objective optimization problems for portfolio management has been proposed in several works (Chen et al., 2018; Corazza et al 2021; Macedo et al., 2017; Zhao et al 2020). Several modifications of Markowitz's minimum variance portfolio theory have been advocated by imposing a constraint of the purchase limits and on the cardinality (Clarke et al., 2011; DeMiguel et al., 2009; Qu et al., 2017; Reveiz Herault, 2016; Saborido et al., 2016; Silva et al., 2015; Syrovatkin, 2020; Vercher and Bermudez, 2015; Zhang et al., 2019). The use of *fuzzy logic, genetic algorithms* (GAs), algorithms of *swarm intelligence* (SI), e.g., *particle swarm optimization* (PSO), are also quite common in portfolio optimization (Garcia et al., 2018; Ertenlice & Kalayci, 2018; Erwin & Engelbrecht, 2020). The performances of the mean-variance, eigen, and HRP portfolios have been compared on different stocks from various sectors of the Indian stock market (Sen & Dutta, 2022; Sen & Mehtab, 2021a; Sen et al., 2021d, 2021f, 2021h, 2021i, 2021j). The use of *generalized autoregressive conditional heteroscedasticity* (GARCH) in estimating the future volatility of stocks and portfolios has also been illustrated (Sen et al., 2021g).

The current work presents two methods, the HRP and the HERC portfolio design approaches, to introduce robustness while maximizing the portfolio returns for eight sectors of the NSE of India. Based on the past prices of the stocks from Jan 2016 to Dec 2020, portfolios are designed using the HRP and the HERC methods for each sector. The backtesting of the portfolios is carried out on the in-sample data of stock prices from Jan 2016 to Dec 31, 2020, and also on the out-of-sample data from Jan 1, 2021, to Nov 1, 2021. The backtesting is done on the return, volatility, and the Sharpe ratio of the portfolios for each sector.

CONTRIBUTION OF THE WORK

The main contribution of the current work is threefold. First, it presents two different methods of designing robust portfolios, the HRP algorithm, and the HERC approach. These portfolio design approaches are applied to eight critical sectors of stocks of the NSE. The results can be used as a guide to investors in the stock market for making profitable investments. Second, a backtesting method is proposed for evaluating the performances of the algorithms based on the daily returns yielded by the portfolios and their associated volatilities (i.e., risks). Since the backtesting is done both on the training and the test data of the stock prices, the work has identified the more efficient algorithm both on the in-sample data and the out-of-sample data. Hence, a robust framework for evaluating different portfolios is demonstrated. Third, the returns of the portfolios on the eight sectors on the test data highlight the current profitability of investment and the volatilities of the sectors studied in this work. This information can be useful for investors.

DATA AND METHODOLOGY

In this section, the six-step approach adopted in designing the proposed system is discussed in detail. The six steps are as follows: (i) choice of the sectors and the stocks, (ii) data acquisition, (iii) derivation of return and volatility of the stocks, (iv) hierarchical risk parity portfolio design, (v) hierarchical equal risk contribution portfolio design, and (vi) backtesting the portfolios on the in-sample (i.e., the training) data and the out-of-sample (i.e., the test data) In the following, these steps are discussed in detail.

Choice of Sectors and Stocks

Eight important sectors of NSE are first chosen. The selected sectors are (i) auto, (ii) consumer durable, (iii) financial services, (iv) fast-moving consumer goods (FMCG), (v) healthcare, (vi) information technology (IT), (vii) metal, and (viii) NIFTY 50. NIFTY 50 contains the 50 most critical stock stocks from several sectors of the Indian stock market. For the remaining seven sectors, the most influential stocks from each sector are identified based on their contributions to the computation of the overall sector index to which they belong as per the report published by the NSE on Oct 29, 2021 (NSE, 2021).

Data Acquisition

The prices of the most influential stocks of the seven sectors and the 50 stocks listed in the NIFTY 50 are extracted using the *DataReader* function of the *data* sub-module of the *pandas_datareader* module in Python. The stock prices are extracted from Yahoo Finance, from Jan 1, 2016, to Nov 1, 2021. The stock price data from Jan 1, 2016, to Dec 31, 2020, are used for training the portfolios, while the portfolios are tested on the data from Jan 1, 2021, to Nov 1, 2021. Among all the features in the stock data, the variable *close* is chosen for the univariate analysis.

Derivation of Return and Volatility of Stocks

The changes in the *close* values for successive days in percentage represent the daily return. For computing the daily returns, the *pct_change* function of Python is used. Based on the daily returns, the daily and yearly volatilities of the stocks of every sector are computed. Assuming that there are 250 operational days in a calendar year, the annual volatility values for the stocks are arrived at by multiplying the daily volatilities by a square root of 250.

Hierarchical Risk Parity Portfolio Design

First, the *hierarchical risk parity* (HRP) algorithm-based portfolios are designed for the seven sectors and the NIFTY 50 stocks. The HRP algorithm works in three phases. These three phases are as follows: (a) tree clustering, (b) quasi-diagonalization, and (c) recursive bisection. These steps are briefly described in the following.

Tree Clustering

The tree clustering used in the HRP algorithm is an agglomerative clustering algorithm. To design the agglomerative clustering algorithm, a *hierarchy* class is first created in Python. The *hierarchy* class contains a *dendrogram* method that receives the value returned by a method called *linkage* defined in the same class. The *linkage* method receives the dataset after pre-processing and transformation and computes the minimum distances between stocks based on their return values. There are several options for computing the distance. However, the *ward* distance is a good choice since it minimizes the variances in the distance between two clusters in the presence of high volatility in the stock return values. In this work, the *ward* distance has been used as a method to compute the distance between two clusters. The *linkage* method performs the clustering and returns a list of the clusters formed. The computation of linkages is followed by the visualization of the clusters through a dendrogram. In the dendrogram, the leaves represent the individual stocks, while the root depicts the cluster containing all the stocks. The distance between each cluster formed is represented along the *y*-axis, longer arms indicate less correlated clusters and vice versa.

Quasi-Diagonalization

In this step, the rows and the columns of the covariance matrix of the return values of the stocks are reorganized in such a way that the largest values lie along the diagonal. Without requiring a change in the basis of the covariance matrix, *quasi-diagonalization* yields a very important property of the matrix – the assets (i.e., stocks) with similar return values are placed closer to each other, while disparate assets are put at a far distance. The working principles of the algorithm are as follows. Since each row of the *linkage matrix* merges two branches into one, the clusters $(C_{N-1}, 1)$ and $(C_{N-2}, 2)$ are replaced with their constituents recursively, until there are no more clusters to merge. This recursive merging of clusters preserves the original order of the clusters (Baily & de Prado, 2012). The output of the algorithm is a sorted list of the original stocks (as they were before the clustering).

Recursive Bisection

The quasi-diagonalization step transforms the covariance matrix into a *quasi-diagonal* form. It is proven mathematically that allocation of weights to the assets in an inverse ratio to their variance is an optimal allocation for a *quasi-diagonal matrix* (Baily & de Prado, 2012). This allocation may be done in two different ways. In the *bottom-up approach*, the variance of a contiguous subset of stocks is computed as the variance of an inverse-variance allocation of the composite cluster. In the alternative *top-down approach*, the allocation among two adjacent subsets of stocks is done in inverse proportion to their aggregated variances. In the current implementation, the top-down approach is followed. A python function *computeIVP* computes the inverse-variance portfolio based on the computed variances of two clusters as its given input. The variance of a cluster is computed using another Python function called *clusterVar*. The output of the *clusterVar* function is used as the input to another Python function called *recBisect* which computes the final weights allocated to the individual stocks based on the recursive bisection algorithm.

The HRP algorithm performs the weight allocation to n assets in the base case in time $T(n) = O(\log2\ n)$, while its worst-case complexity is given by $T(n) = O(n)$. Unlike the CLA algorithm, which is an approximate algorithm, the HRP is an exact and deterministic algorithm. The HRP portfolios for all the sectors are built on Jan 1, 2021, based on the training data from Jan 1, 2016, to Dec 31, 2020.

Hierarchical Equal Risk Contribution Portfolio Design

The hier*archical equal risk contribution (HERC)* portfolio is a risk-based portfolio optimization method that attempts to integrate machine learning and the top-down recursive bisection approach of HRP for portfolio optimization (Raffinot, 2018).

Raffinot argues that the HRP portfolio optimization suffers from the following shortcomings. First, the clustering approach of HRP uses the linka*ge metr*ic to combine the clusters. The use of the sin*gle linkage clustering cons*tructs the tree based on the distance between the two closest points in the clusters, which results in a chain*ing effect maki*ng the tree very deep and wide. This prevents any dense clustering and suboptimal weight allocation. Second, in the HRP portfolio algorithm, there is a high possibility of large trees getting formed from a large dataset of stocks which may result in a very high computational task and possible overfitting of the model. Third, in the recursive bisection step of the HRP algorithm, in which the algorithm bisects the tree before allocating the weights instead of allocating the weights based on the constructed dendrogram. This results in inaccuracies in the resultant weights. Finally, in the HRP, the weights are computed based on the variance of the clusters. The assets in clusters with minimum variance receive higher weights. Since the estimates of risk are based on the past variances of the stocks are very unreliable and unstable, the weight allocation by HRP may not be very accurate for the out-of-sample data.

The HERC portfolio optimization involves the following four steps: (a) hier*archical tree clustering, (b)* sele*cting the optimal number of clusters, (c)* top-*down recursive bisection, and* (d) naive *risk parity within the clusters. S*tep (a) of the HERC method that calculates the distance matrix from the correlation matrix for cluster formation remains identical to that of the HRP method. In step (b), the HERC differs from the HRP algorithm, in which the optimal number of clusters is identified. While HRP is not based on any optimality of the clusters, HERC uses the gap *index met*hod for determining the number of clusters to be used (Tibshirani et al., 2001). After the optimal number of clusters is determined, the top-down recursive bisection step computes the weight for each cluster. In step (c), the clustering tree bisects the cluster at a given level into two sub-clusters. The weights assigned to the sub-clusters are in the ratio of their contributions to the overall risk of the original cluster. Suppose, for a cluster C, the clustering algorithm has formed to sub-clusters C1 an$_d$ C2. T$_h$e weights assigned to the sub-clusters, W1, a$_{nd}$ W2, a$_r$e given by (1) and (2), respectively.

$$W_1 = \frac{R_1}{R_1 + R_2} \tag{1}$$

$$W_2 = 1 - W_1 \tag{2}$$

In (1) and (2), R_1 and R_2 represent the risk contributions of the sub-clusters C_1 and C_2, respectively, to cluster C. Several alternative metrics exist for computing risk such as *variance, standard deviation, conditional value at risk, conditional drawdown as risk*, etc. The risk involved in a given cluster is the additive risk contribution of all the individual members in that cluster as shown in (2). The weight allocation to the clusters is done through the entire tree until all the clusters (i.e., the assets at the leaf level) are assigned weights. Finally, in step (d), the weights are assigned to the assets within the clusters using a naive risk parity approach based on the inverse of the assets' risks. This is illustrated using the above example in which cluster C is divided into two sub-clusters, C_1 and C_2. Let us assume that C_1 consists of two assets S_1 and S_2. The task at hand is to compute the weights assigned to S_1 and S_2 within cluster C_1. The naïve risk parity weights for S_1 and S_2 are given by (3) and (4), respectively.

$$W_{nrp}^{S1} = \frac{\frac{1}{R_1}}{\frac{1}{R_1} + \frac{1}{R_2}} \tag{3}$$

$$W_{nrp}^{S2} = \frac{\frac{1}{R_2}}{\frac{1}{R_1} + \frac{1}{R_2}} \tag{4}$$

The final weights for the stocks S_1 and S_2 are obtained by multiplying their respective naïve parity weights by the weights of the cluster to which they belong. i.e., cluster C_1. The final weights for stocks S_1 and S_2 are computed using (5) and (6), respectively.

$$W_{final}^{S1} = W_{nrp}^{S1} * W_1 \tag{5}$$

$$W_{final}^{S2} = W_{nrp}^{S2} * W_1 \tag{6}$$

In (5) and (6), W^{S1}_{final} and W^{S2}_{final} represent the final weights assigned to the assets S_1 and S_2, respectively, W_I denotes the weight allocated to the cluster to which they belong, i.e., the cluster C_I (derived in (1)), and W^{S1}_{nrp} and W^{S2}_{nrp} denote the naïve parity weights for stocks S_1 and S_2, respectively. This method is repeated till the weights for all the assets in all clusters are computed. The HERC algorithm has the same time complexity for computation as the HRP algorithm.

Backtesting of the Portfolios

In the final step, the HRP and the HERC portfolios for each sector are backtested over the training and the test data periods. For backtesting, the daily return values are computed for each sector for both portfolios. For comparison, the Sharpe ratios and the aggregate volatility values for each sector are also computed over the training and the test periods. For each sector, the portfolios that perform better on the training and the test data are identified. The portfolio that performs better on the test data for a given sector is assumed to have exhibited superior performance for that sector. While both HRP and HERC portfolios are expected to perform better than the base CLA portfolio, a comparison of their performances on the training and the test data will be quite revealing and interesting.

RESULTS

The detailed results on the performance of the portfolios and their analysis are presented in this section. The eight sectors of NSE which are selected for the analysis are as follows: (i) auto, (ii) consumer durable, (iii) financial services, (iv) FMCG, (v) healthcare, (vi) information technology, (vii) metal, and (viii) NIFTY 50. The HRP and the HERC portfolios are implemented in the Python programming language and the portfolios are trained and tested on the Google Colab platform (Google Colaboratory, 2021). In the following subsections, the detailed results of the performances of the two portfolios on the eight sectors are presented. The Python library *riskfolio-lib* has been used for designing and implementing the HRP and the HERC portfolios. To compute the optimum number of clusters, Since the computational overhead of the Gap Index metrics which was originally proposed by Raffinot in designing the HERC algorithm is too high, to compute the optimum number of clusters, the metric *Two-Order Difference Gap* statistic metrics proposed by Yue et al. has been used (Yue et al., 2008).

Auto Sector

The report of NSE released on October 29, 2021, identified 15 stocks as the most influential stocks in the NSE auto sector (NSE, 2021). These stocks contribute most significantly to the computation of the overall index of the auto sector. These 15 stocks are as follows: Maruti Suzuki, Tata Motors, Mahindra & Mahindra, Bajaj Auto, Eicher Motors, Hero MotoCorp, Ashok Leyland, Balkrishna Industries, Bharat Forge, MRF, Amara Raja Batteries, Bosh, Exide Industries, TVS Motor Company, and Tube Investments of India.

Figure 1. Dendrogram of the auto sector stocks formed by the HRP portfolio

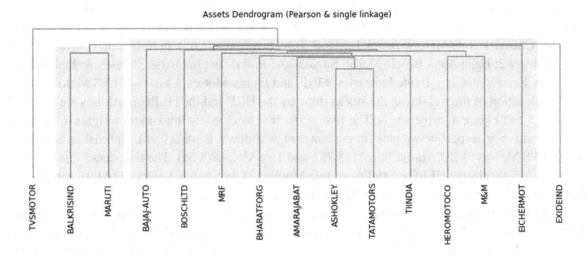

Figure 2. Dendrogram of the auto sector stocks formed by the HERC portfolio

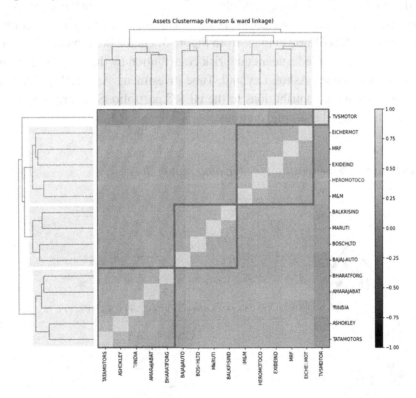

Figure 1 and Figure 2 depict the clustering of the stocks of the auto sector by the HRP and HERC portfolio strategies. While the number of clusters formed in the HRP portfolio will depend on the threshold ward distance plotted along the *y*-axis, it is observed from Figure 1 that there are four clusters formed based on the default value of the ward distance. The four clusters formed by the HRP portfolio contain the following stocks – Cluster 1: TVS Motors; Cluster 2: Balkrishna Industries and Maruti Suzuki, Cluster

3: Bajaj Auto, Bosch, MRF, Bharat Forge, Amara Raja Batteries, Ashok Leyland, Tata Motors, Tube Investments, Hero MotoCorp, Mahindra & Mahindra, and Eicher Motors; Cluster 4: Exide Industries. Figure 2 shows four clusters formed by the HERC approach. The composition of the four clusters is as follows – Cluster 1: Tata Motors, Ashok Leyland, Tube Investments, Amara Raja Batteries, and Bharat Forge; Cluster 2: Bajaj Auto, Bosch, Maruti Suzuki, and Balkrishna Industries; Cluster 3: Mahindra & Mahindra, Hero MotoCorp, Exide Industries, MRF, and Eicher Motors; Cluster 4: TVS Motors.

The allocation of the weights to the stocks done by the HRP and the HERC portfolios are depicted in Figure 3 and Figure 4, respectively. The five stocks that received the maximum weights in the HRP portfolio and their respective weights (in percent) are as follows: Bosh (10.98), Balkrishna Industries (9.94), TVS Motors (9.23), Maruti Suzuki (8.75), and Tata Motors (8.69). The five stocks that received the largest weights by the HERC portfolio are Tata Motors (22.48), Ashok Leyland (16.09), Amara Raja Batteries (15.50), Tube Investment of India (14.02), and Bharat Forge (13.38).

The risk contribution per asset using standard deviation as the metric of risk for the HRP and the HERC portfolios for the auto sector stocks are represented in Figure 5 and Figure 6, respectively. It is observed in Figure 5 that the five stocks with the highest risk contribution to the HRP portfolios are Balkrishna Industries, Bosch, Maruti Suzuki, TVS Motors, and Tata Motors. As has been mentioned earlier in the chapter, unlike the HERC approach, the HRP portfolio strategy does not lead to equal risk contribution by the assets which are in the same cluster. Rather, the stocks in the same cluster are assigned weights in the inverse ratio of their respective variances. This leads to unequal risk contributions by the assets to the portfolio which is clearly evident from Figure 5. On the other hand, Figure 6 clearly shows that the HERC portfolio has yielded a near equal risk contribution by the assets in the same cluster. For example, the stocks Tata Motors, Ashok Leyland, Tube Investment, Amara Raja Batteries, and Bharat Forge contribute have identical contributions to the HERC portfolio. Similarly, the stocks in the other three clusters also exhibit equal risk contributions.

Figure 3. The HRP portfolio composition for the auto sector stocks

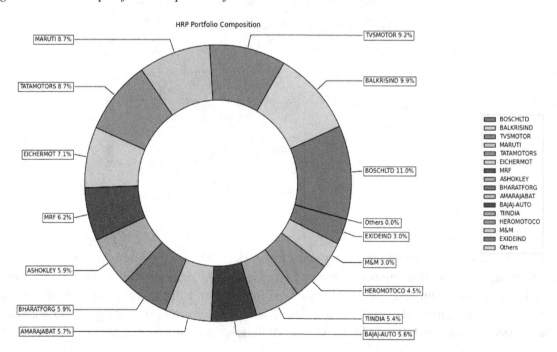

Figure 4. The HERC portfolio composition for the auto sector stocks

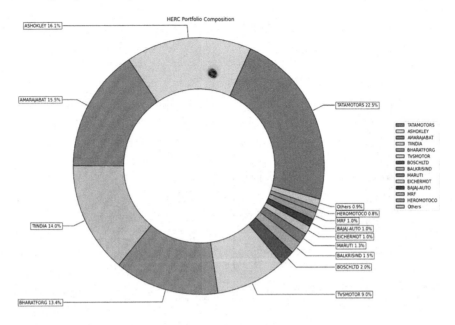

Figure 5. The risk contribution by the auto sector stocks in the HRP portfolio

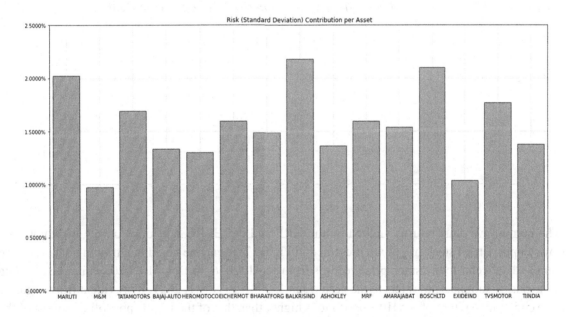

Table 1. The performance of the HRP and HERC portfolios on the auto sector stocks

Portfolio	In-sample Performance		Out-of-sample Performance	
	Volatility	Sharpe Ratio	Volatility	Sharpe Ratio
HRP	0.2360	0.6674	0.1818	1.8130
HERC	0.2497	0.2310	0.1871	0.9197

Figure 6. The risk contribution by the auto sector stocks in the HERC portfolio

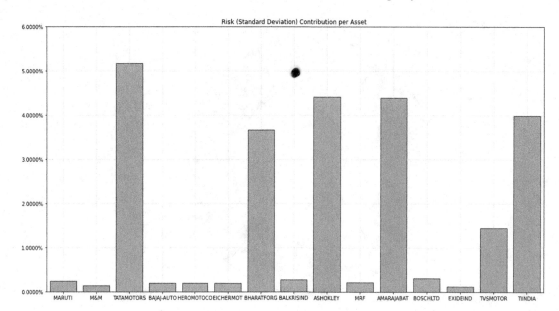

Figure 7. The cumulative returns yielded by the HRP and the HERC portfolios of the auto sector stocks on the training data (the graph on the left) and the test data (the graph on the right)

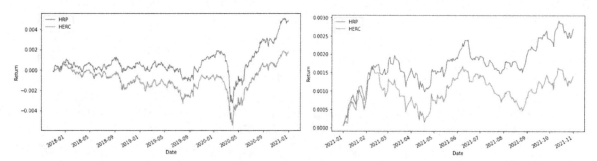

The cumulative daily returns yielded by the HRP and the HERC portfolios on the in-sample and out-of-sample data of stock prices are presented in Figure 7. It may be noted that training data (i.e., the in-sample data) refer to the stock price records from Jan 1, 2016, to Dec 31, 2020, while the test data (i.e., the out-of-sample data) refers to the period Jan 1, 2021, to Nov 1, 2021. It is evident from Figure 7 that the cumulative return of the HRP portfolio is higher than that of the HERC portfolio for most of the period of the training and the test data. Table 1 shows that the HRP portfolio has produced higher Sharpe ratios for both training and the test periods, while its volatility values are lower. The results indicate the HRP portfolio has outperformed the HERC portfolio on both training and test data.

Consumer Durable Sector

The 15 stocks that are identified as the most significant stocks in the consumer durable sector as per the report published by the NSE on October 29, 2021, are as follows: Titan Company, Havells India, Voltas,

Crompton Greaves Consumer Electricals, Dixon Technologies (India), Bata India, Kajaria Ceramics, Relaxo Footwears, Rajesh Exports, Whirlpool of India, Amber Enterprises India, Blue Star, Orient Electric, TTK Prestige, and V-Guard Industries (NSE, 2021).

The dendrograms produced by the HRP and the HERC portfolios are depicted in Figure 8 and Figure 9, respectively. It is evident from Figure 8 that the HRP portfolio has created four clusters of stocks as follows: Cluster1: Kajaria Ceramics; Cluster 2: Voltas; Cluster 3: Bluestar; and Cluster 4: Titan Company, Havells India, Crompton Greaves Consumer Electricals, Dixon Technologies (India), Bata India, Relaxo Footwears, Rajesh Exports, Whirlpool of India, Amber Enterprises India, Orient Electric, TTK Prestige, and V-Guard Industries. The dendrogram of the HERC portfolio as depicted in Figure 9 has created four clusters with the following composition: Cluster 1: Kajaria Ceramics; Cluster 2: Bluestar; Cluster 3: Havells India, Voltas, Crompton Greaves Consumer Electricals, Bata India, Relaxo Footwears, Rajesh Exports, Whirlpool of India, Amber Enterprises India, Orient Electric, TTK Prestige, and V-Guard Industries; and Cluster 4: Titan Company and Dixon Technologies (India).

The allocation of weights done by the HRP portfolio for the stocks in the consumer durable sector is depicted in Figure 10. The five stocks that received the maximum weights and their corresponding weights in percent are as follows: Kajaria Ceramics (13.48), Whirlpool of India (8.82), Voltas (8.80), Orient Electric (8.31), and Blue Star (8.03). On the other hand, as observed in Figure 11, the HERC portfolio allocated the highest weights to the following five stocks: Kajaria Cement (71.34), Dixon Technologies (6.89), Titan Company (6.19), Havells India (1.67), and Bata India (1.63). The allocation strategy of HRP is fairly uniform compared to the extremely skewed allocation done by the HERC portfolio. This has made the HRP portfolio more diversified.

Figure 12 and Figure 13 show the risk contribution by the stocks in the HRP and the HERC portfolios, respectively. As shown in Figure 12, the five stocks with the largest risk contribution to the HRP portfolio are Voltas, Kajaria Ceramics, Bluestar, Orient Electric, and Whirlpool of India. It is also evident that the risk contributions of the stocks in the HRP portfolio are widely varying. On the other hand, the HERC portfolio has achieved equal contribution of risk by the stocks in the same cluster. The stock of Kajaria Ceramics has a significantly high contribution to the HERC portfolio, while Dixon and Titan have moderate risk. The remaining stocks have a very low contribution to the portfolio.

Figure 8. Dendrogram of the consumer durable sector stocks formed by the HRP portfolio

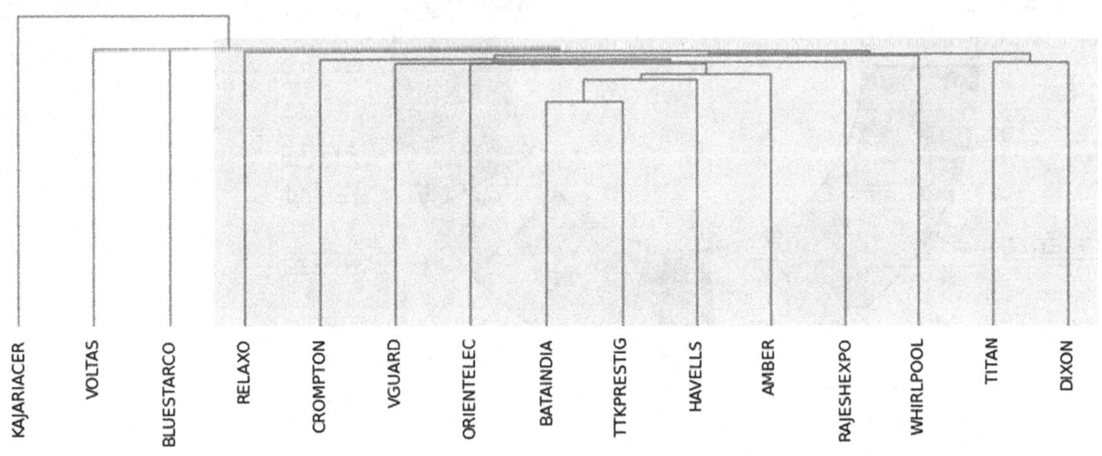

Assets Dendrogram (Pearson & single linkage)

Figure 9. Dendrogram of the consumer durable sector stocks formed by the HERC portfolio

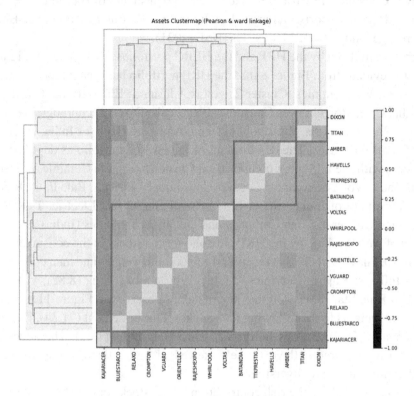

Figure 10. The HRP portfolio composition for the consumer durable sector stocks

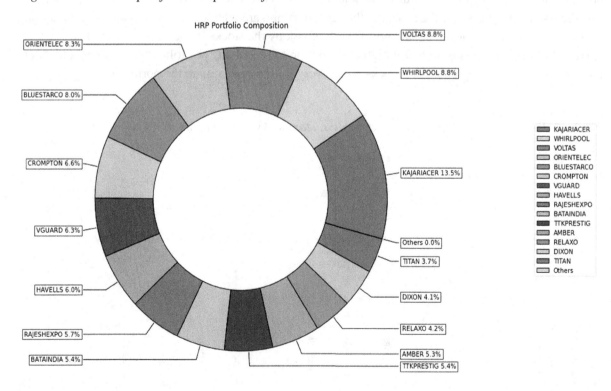

Figure 11. The HRP portfolio composition for the consumer durable sector stocks

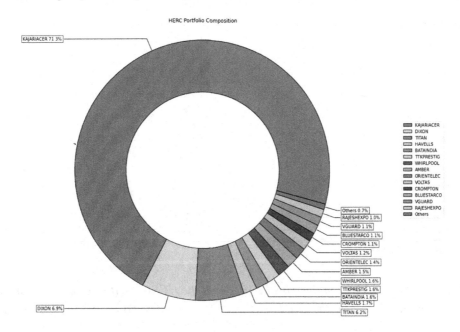

Figure 12. The risk contribution by the consumer durable sector stocks in the HRP portfolio

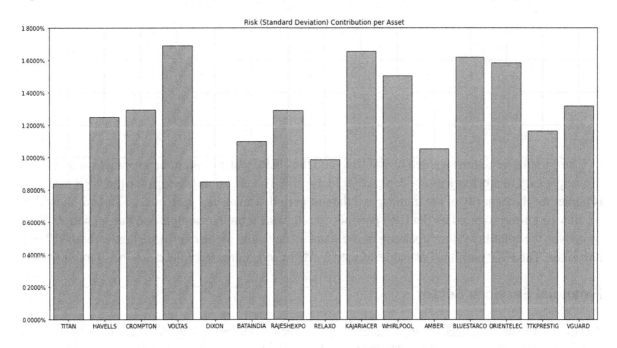

Table 2. The performance of the HRP and HERC portfolios on the consumer durable sector stocks

Portfolio	In-sample Performance		Out-of-sample Performance	
	Volatility	Sharpe Ratio	Volatility	Sharpe Ratio
HRP	0.1988	1.5790	0.1473	3.3201
HERC	0.2412	0.2383	0.1915	2.1508

Figure 13. The risk contribution by the consumer durable sector stocks in the HERC portfolio

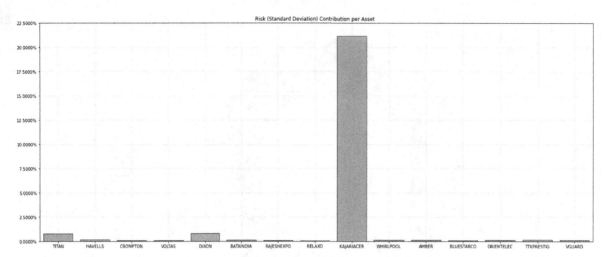

Figure 14. The cumulative returns yielded by the HRP and the HERC portfolios of the consumer durable sector stocks on the training data (the graph on the left) and the test data (the graph on the right)

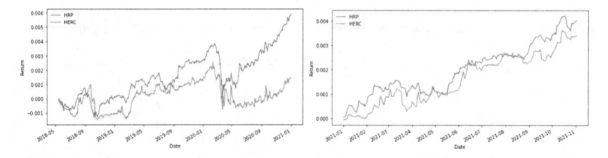

The cumulative returns yielded by the HRP and the HERC portfolios on the in-sample and the out-of-sample data of stock prices are depicted in Figure 14. The cumulative return for the HRP portfolio is higher for the majority of the training and the test period. The results presented in Table 2 show that the Sharpe ratios produced by the HRP portfolio are higher for both in-sample and out-of-sample data. Moreover, the volatility values (measure by the standard deviation of the return) are higher for the HERC portfolios. The HRP portfolio has outperformed its HERC counterpart for the consumer durable sector.

Financial Services Sector

The most influential 20 stocks of the financial services sector as identified by the NSE's report published on October 29, 2021, are as follows: HDFC Bank, ICICI Bank, Housing Development Finance Corporation, Kotak Mahindra Bank, Bajaj Finance, State Bank of India, Axis Bank, Bajaj Finserv, HDFC Life Insurance Company, SBI Life Insurance Company, Cholamandalam Investment, and Finance Company, HDFC Asset Management Company, ICICI Lombard General Insurance Company, ICICI Prudential Life Insurance Company, Mahindra & Mahindra Financial Services, Muthoot Finance, Piramal Enterprises, Power Finance Corporation, REC, and Shriram Transport Finance Company (NSE, 2021).

Figure 15. Dendrogram of the financial services sector stocks formed by the HRP portfolio

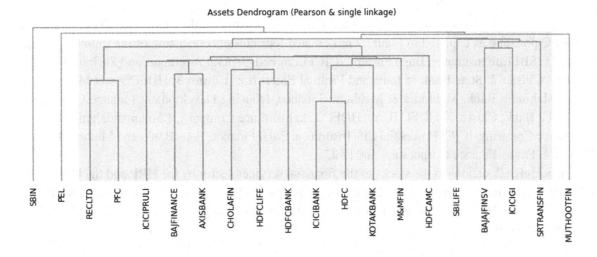

Figure 16. Dendrogram of the financial services sector stocks formed by the HERC portfolio

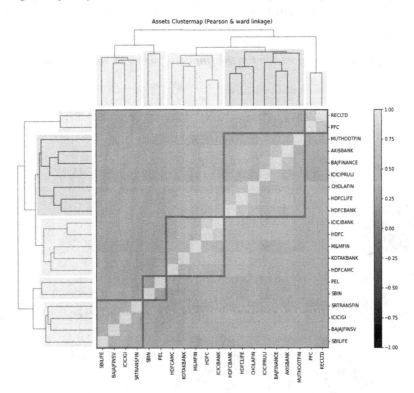

The dendrograms created by the HRP and the HERC portfolios for the stocks in the financial services sector are exhibited in Figure 15 and Figure 16, respectively. The HRP portfolio has produced the following five clusters: Cluster1: State Bank of India; Cluster 2: Piramal Enterprises; Cluster 3: HDFC Bank, ICICI Bank, Housing Development Finance Corporation, Kotak Mahindra Bank, Bajaj Finance, Axis Bank, HDFC Life Insurance Company, Cholamandalam Investment, and Finance Company, HDFC Asset Management Company, ICICI Prudential Life Insurance Company, Mahindra & Mahindra Financial

Services, Power Finance Corporation, REC; Cluster 4: SBI Life Insurance, Bajaj Finserv, ICICI Lombard General Insurance, and Shriram Transport Finance; Cluster 5: Muthoot Finance. The dendrogram of the HERC portfolio shown in Figure 16 also depicts five clusters with the following stocks: The dendrogram of HERC portfolio as depicted in Figure 9 has created four clusters consisting of the following stocks: Cluster 1: SBI Life Insurance, Bajaj Finserv, ICICI Lombard General Insurance, and Shriram Transport Finance; Cluster 2: State Bank of India and Piramal Enterprise; Cluster 3: HDFC Asset Management, Kotak Mahindra Bank, Mahindra & Mahindra Finance, Housing Development Finance Corporation, and ICICI Bank; Cluster 3: HDFC Bank, HDFC Life Insurance Company, Cholamandalam Investment & Finance Company, ICICI Prudential Life Insurance, Bajaj Finance, Axis Bank, and Muthoot Finance; Cluster 4: Power Finance Corporation and REC.

The weight allocations to the stocks of the financial services sector by the HRP and the HERC portfolios are presented in Figure 17 and Figure 18, respectively. The five stocks that received the highest weights from the HRP portfolio and their corresponding weights (in percent) are as follows: State Bank of India (9.07), Bajaj Finance (8.87), Bajaj Finserv (8.10), SBI Life Insurance (7.31), and Axis Bank (6.06). The distribution of weight by the HRP portfolio looks highly uniform. The HERC portfolio, on the other hand, has allocated higher weights to the following stocks: Sate Bank of India (19.52), Shriram Transport Finance (11.94), Bajaj Finserv (10.50), REC (10.41), and Power Finance Corporation (9.88). The weight allocation by the HERC appears to be very skewed in comparison to the HRP portfolio.

Figure 17. The HRP portfolio composition for the financial services sector stocks

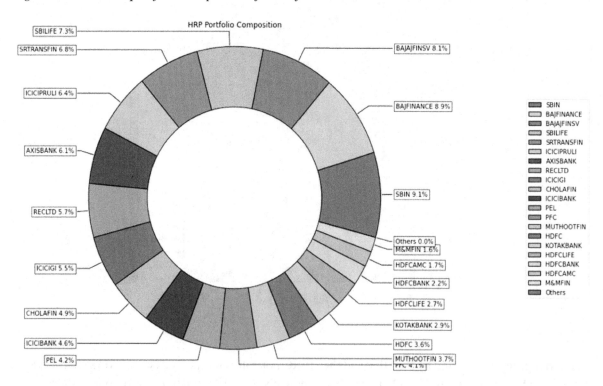

Figure 18. The HERC portfolio composition for the financial services sector stocks

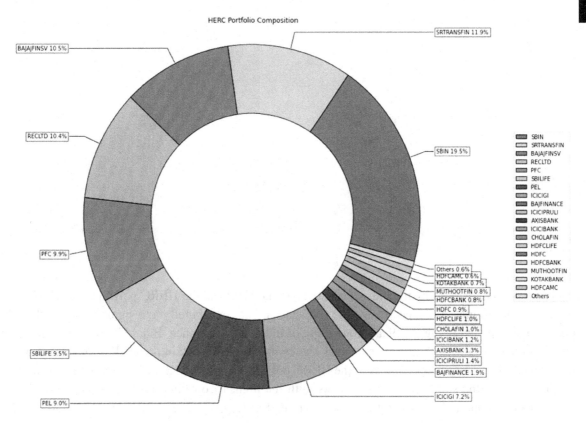

Figure 19. The risk contribution by the financial services sector stocks in the HRP portfolio

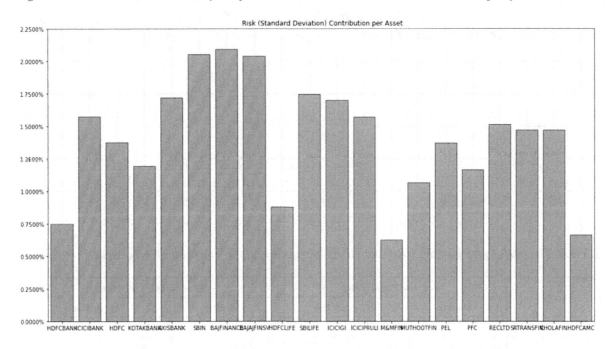

Figure 20. The risk contribution by the financial services sector stocks in the HERC portfolio

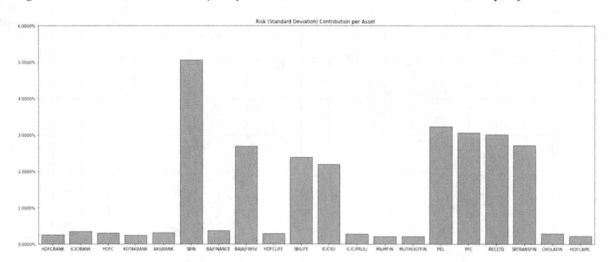

The risk contributions by the individual stocks in the HRP and the HERC portfolios are depicted in Figure 19 and Figure 20, respectively. The five stocks that contributed most significantly to the HRP portfolio as depicted in Figure 19 are State Bank of India, Bajaj Finance, Bajaj Finserv, SBI Life Insurance Company, and Axis Bank. As expected, the contributions to risk in the HRP portfolio are widely divergent for different stocks. However, the HERC portfolio has achieved fairly equal risk contributions by the stocks in the same cluster. The stocks with the highest contributions to the risk in the HERC portfolios are found to be State Bank of India, Piramal Enterprises, Power Finance Corporation, REC, and Shriram Transport Finance.

Figure 21. The cumulative returns yielded by the HRP and the HERC portfolios of the financial services sector stocks on the training data (the graph on the left) and the test data (the graph on the right)

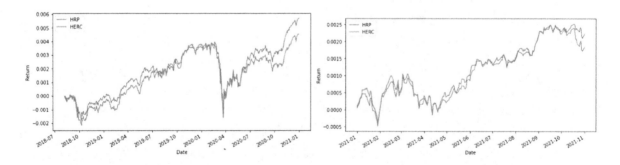

Table 3. The performance of the HRP and HERC portfolios on the financial services sector stocks

Portfolio	In-sample Performance		Out-of-sample Performance	
	Volatility	**Sharpe Ratio**	**Volatility**	**Sharpe Ratio**
HRP	0.2828	0.8625	0.1803	1.5108
HERC	0.2761	0.7037	0.1860	1.2093

The cumulative returns produced by the HRP and the HERC portfolios for the training and the test data of the stock prices of the financial services sector are shown in Figure 21. It is observed that the two portfolios have yielded almost identical returns. The results presented in Table 2 show that the Sharpe ratios yielded by the HRP portfolio are higher for both cases, while the volatilities of the two portfolios are almost identical. Hence, the performance of the HRP portfolio is superior to that of the HERC portfolio for the stocks of the financial services sector.

FMCG Sector

The report published by the NSE on October 29, 2021, identified 15 stocks as the most influential in the FMCG sector. These 15 stocks are as follows: Hindustan Unilever, ITC, Nestle India, Tata Consumer Products, Britannia Industries, Godrej Consumer Products, Dabur India, Marico, United Spirits, Colgate Palmolive (India), Emami, Procter & Gamble Hygiene & Health Care, Radico Khaitan, United Breweries, and Varun Beverages (NSE, 2021).

Figure 22. Dendrogram of the FMCG sector stocks formed by the HRP portfolio

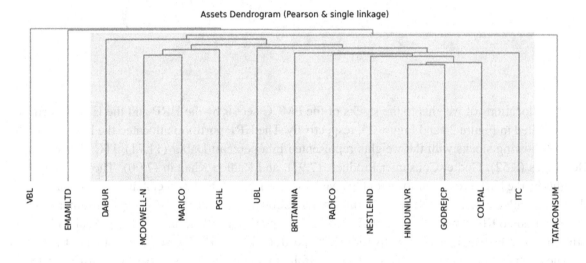

Figure 22 and Figure 23 show the dendrograms produced by the HRP and the HERC portfolios. The four clusters created by the HRP portfolios have the following composition: Cluster1: Varun Beverages; Cluster 2: Emami; Cluster 3: Hindustan Unilever, ITC, Nestle India, Britannia Industries, Godrej Consumer Products, Colgate Palmolive (India), Radico Khaitan, United Breweries, United Spirits, Procter & Gamble Hygiene & Health Care, Dabur, and Marico; and Cluster 4: Tata Consumer Products. The dendrogram of HERC portfolio, on the other hand, has produced the following clusters: Cluster 1: Hindustan Unilever, ITC, Nestle India, Britannia Industries, Godrej Consumer Products, Colgate Palmolive (India), and Radico Khaitan; Cluster 2: Emami, Dabur, and Tata Consumer Products; Cluster 3: Marico, United Spirits, Procter & Gamble Hygiene & Health Care, and United Breweries; and Cluster 4: Varun Beverages.

Figure 23. Dendrogram of the FMCG sector stocks formed by the HERC portfolio

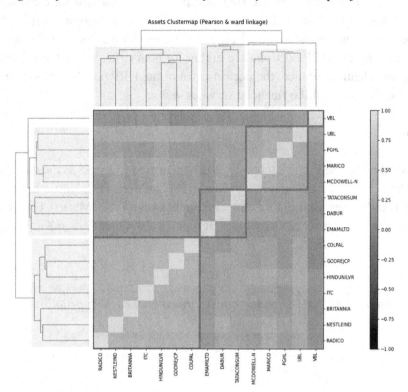

The allocations of weights to the stocks of the FMCG sector by the HRP and the HERC portfolios are exhibited in Figure 24 and Figure 25, respectively. The HRP portfolio allocated the highest weights to the following stocks with the weights represented in a percent: Dabur (11.71), ITC (10.46), Varun Beverages (8.52), Godrej Consumer Products (7.97), and Radico Khaitan (7.90). The distribution of weights by the HRP is quite uniform for the FMCG sector as well. On the other hand, stocks that received the highest allocation by the HERC portfolio are the following: ITC (15.17), Godrej Consumer Products (14.12), Radico Khaitan (13.09), Nestle India (12.93), and Colgate Palmolive (12.73). Again, like in the other sectors, the weight allocation by the HERC portfolio for the FMCG sector is found to be skewed.

The contribution to the overall risk of the portfolio by the individual stocks of the FMCG sector for the HRP portfolio and the HERC portfolio are shown in Figure 26 and Figure 27, respectively. The five most significant contributors to the risk of the HRP portfolio are Dabur, ITC, Godrej Consumer Products, Nestle India, and Radico Khaitan. The diversity of the HRP portfolio is manifested by the wide divergence of risk contribution of its constituent stocks. On the other hand, the HERC portfolio's risk is mostly contributed by Godrej Consumer Products, ITC, Nestle India, Hindustan Unilever, and Colgate Palmolive. The HERC portfolio is characterized by the equal (or nearly equal) risk contributions by the stocks in the same cluster.

Figure 28 depicts the cumulative returns for the FMCG sector produced by the HRP and the HERC portfolios for the training and the test data. It is observed that the HRP portfolio has yielded marginally higher returns most of the time during the training and the test period. The Sharpe ratios produced by the HRP portfolios are found to be higher than those of the HERC portfolios for both training and test data. Moreover, the volatility of the HRP portfolio is also smaller than that of the HERC portfolio. These results indicate that the HRP portfolio has outperformed its HERC counterpart for the stocks in the FMCG sector.

Figure 24. The HRP portfolio composition for the FMCG sector stocks

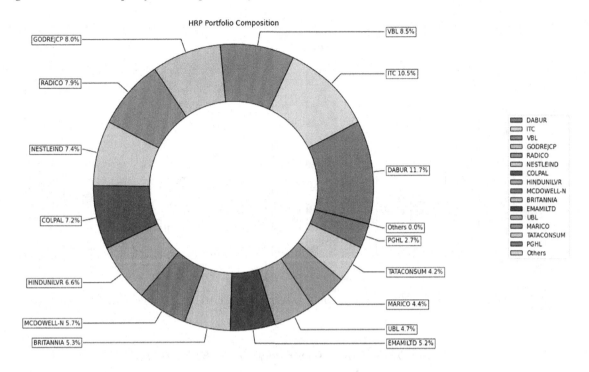

Figure 25. The HERC portfolio composition for the FMCG sector stocks

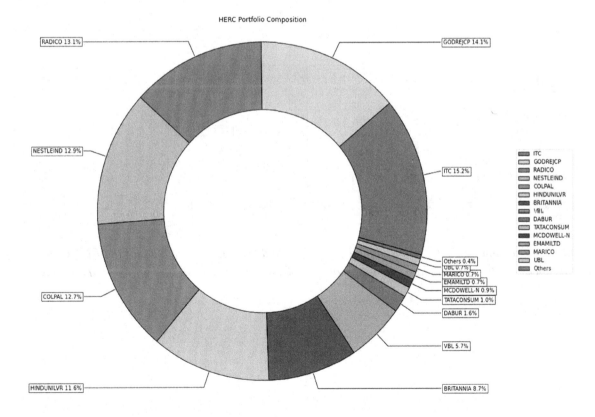

Figure 26. The risk contribution by the FMCG sector stocks in the HRP portfolio

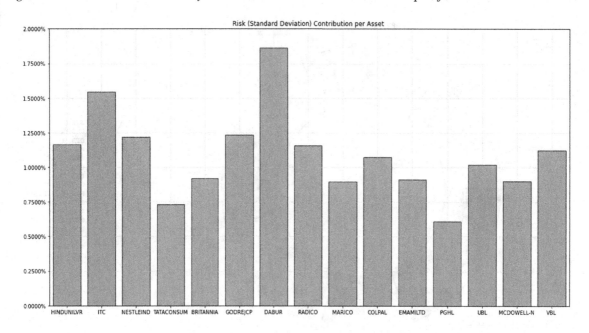

Figure 27. The risk contribution by the FMCG sector stocks in the HERC portfolio

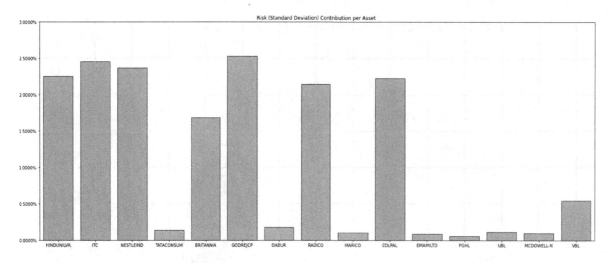

Figure 28. The cumulative returns yielded by the HRP and the HERC portfolios of the FMCG durable sector stocks on the training data (the graph on the left) and the test data (the graph on the right)

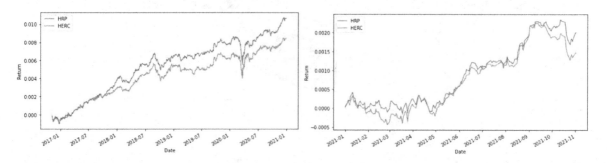

Table 4. The performance of the HRP and HERC portfolios on the FMCG sector stocks

Portfolio	In-sample Performance		Out-of-sample Performance	
	Volatility	**Sharpe Ratio**	**Volatility**	**Sharpe Ratio**
HRP	0.1668	1.5746	0.1166	2.0966
HERC	0.1699	1.2230	0.1257	1.4289

Healthcare Sector

The report of NSE published on October 29, 2021, identified 20 stocks as the most significant in the healthcare sector (NSE, 2021). These 20 stocks are as follows: Sun Pharmaceutical Industries, Divi's Laboratories, Dr. Reddy's Laboratories, Cipla, Apollo Hospitals Enterprise, Lupin, Laurus Labs, Aurobindo Pharma, Alkem Laboratories, Biocon, Alembic Pharmaceuticals, Cadila Healthcare, Dr. Lal Path Labs, Glenmark Pharmaceuticals, Granules India, Ipca Laboratories, Metropolis Healthcare, Pfizer, Strides Pharma Science, and Torrent Pharmaceuticals.

Figure 29. Dendrogram of the healthcare sector stocks formed by the HRP portfolio

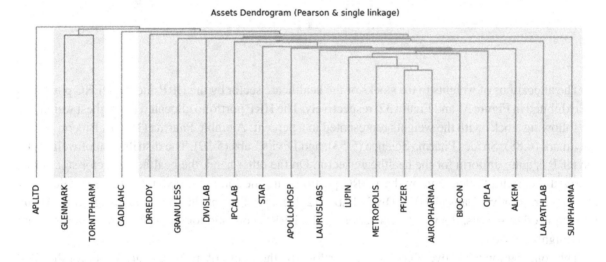

Assets Dendrogram (Pearson & single linkage)

The dendrograms of the HRP and the HERC portfolios on the healthcare sector stocks are presented in Figure 29 and Figure 30, respectively. The HRP dendrogram has four clusters with the following composition: Cluster1: Alembic Pharma; Cluster 2: Glenmark Pharmaceuticals and Torrent Pharmaceuticals; Cluster 3: Cadila Healthcare, and Cluster 4 consisting of the remaining stocks of the healthcare sector. The dendrogram of HERC portfolio, on the other hand, has produced the following clusters: Cluster 1: Dr. Reddy's Labs, Divi's Labs, Cadila Healthcare, Glenmark Pharmaceuticals, Torrent Pharmaceuticals, and Alembic Pharma; Cluster 2: Granules India, Alkem Labs, Cipla, and Ipca Labs; Cluster 3: Aurobindo Pharmaceuticals, Pfizer, Metropolis, Apollo Hospitals and Enterprise, Lupin, Biocon, Laurus Labs, and Strides Pharma Science; and Cluster 4: Sun Pharmaceuticals and Dr. Lal Path Labs.

Figure 30. Dendrogram of the healthcare sector stocks formed by the HERC portfolio

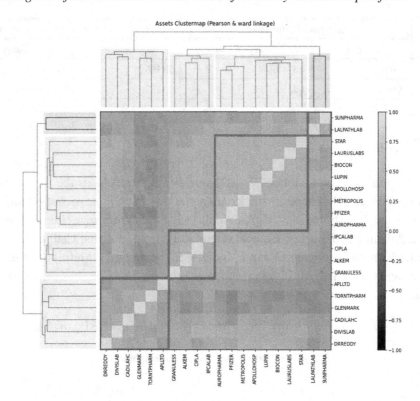

The allocations of weights to the stocks of the healthcare sector by the HRP and the HERC portfolios are exhibited in Figure 31 and Figure 32, respectively. The HRP portfolio allocated the highest weights to the following stocks with the weights represented in a percent: Alembic Pharma (10.85), Biocon (8.16), Glenmark (6.88), Strides Pharma Science (5.53), and Divi's Labs (5.39). The distribution of weights by the HRP is quite uniform for the healthcare sector. On the other hand, the healthcare sector stocks that received the highest allocation by the HERC portfolio are the following: Alembic (22.83), Glenmark (14.47), Dr. Reddy's Labs (13.02), Divi's Labs (12.21), and Torrent Pharmaceuticals (11.80). Again, like in the other sectors, the weight allocation by the HERC portfolio for the healthcare sector is found to be highly skewed.

The contribution to the overall risk of the portfolio by the stocks of the healthcare sector for the HRP portfolio and the HERC portfolio are shown in Figure 33 and Figure 34, respectively. The five most significant contributors to the risk of the HRP portfolio are Biocon, Alembic, Divi's Labs, Laurus Labs, and Ipca Labs. The risk contribution by individual stock to the overall risk of the HRP portfolio looks quite diverse. The five stocks that contributed most significantly are Alembic, Glenmark, Divi's Labs, Dr. Reddy's Labs, and Torrent Pharmaceuticals. The HERC portfolio is characterized by the equal (or nearly equal) risk contributions by the stocks in the same cluster.

Figure 31. The HRP portfolio composition for the healthcare sector stocks

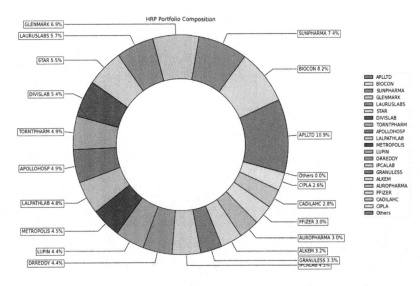

Figure 32. The HERC portfolio composition for the healthcare sector stocks

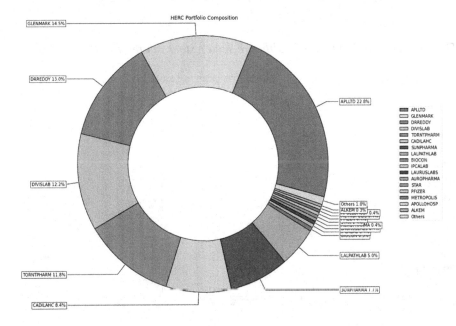

The cumulative returns of the HRP and the HERC portfolios on the healthcare sector stocks for the training and the test data are depicted in Figure 35. It is observed that the HERC portfolio has produced higher returns for most of the time during the training and the test period in comparison to the HRP portfolio. The Sharpe ratio of the HERC portfolio is higher for the test data, while it is marginally smaller in the training data when compared with the HRP portfolio. However, the volatilities of the HERC portfolio are slightly higher in both cases. Since the Sharpe ratio can be taken as the single best metric for comparing portfolios, it is concluded that the HERC portfolio has outperformed its HERC counterpart for the stocks in the healthcare sector.

Figure 33. The risk contribution by the healthcare sector stocks in the HRP portfolio

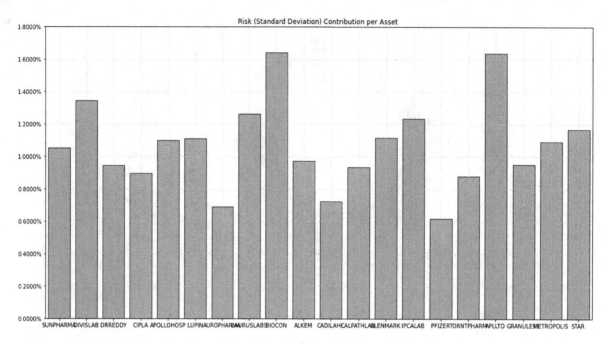

Figure 34. The risk contribution by the healthcare sector stocks in the HERC portfolio

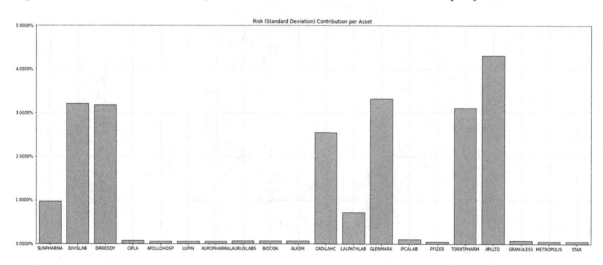

Table 5. The performance of the HRP and HERC portfolios on the healthcare sector stocks

Portfolio	In-sample Performance		Out-of-sample Performance	
	Volatility	Sharpe Ratio	Volatility	Sharpe Ratio
HRP	0.2130	2.1502	0.1501	1.1261
HERC	0.2216	2.1294	0.1637	1.5634

Figure 35. The cumulative returns yielded by the HRP and the HERC portfolios of the healthcare sector stocks on the training data (the graph on the left) and the test data (the graph on the right)

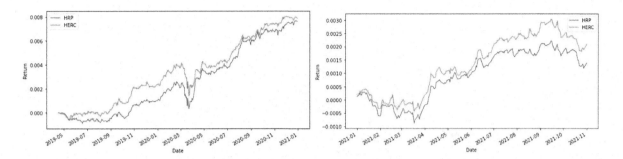

Information Technology Sector

The 10 stocks which are identified as the most influential in the information technology sector by the NSE's report published on October 29, 2021, are the following: Infosys, Tata Consultancy Services, Tech Mahindra, Wipro, HCL Technologies, Larsen & Toubro Infotech, MindTree, MphasiS, L&T Technology Services, and Coforge (NSE, 2021).

Figure 36. Dendrogram of the IT sector stocks formed by the HRP portfolio

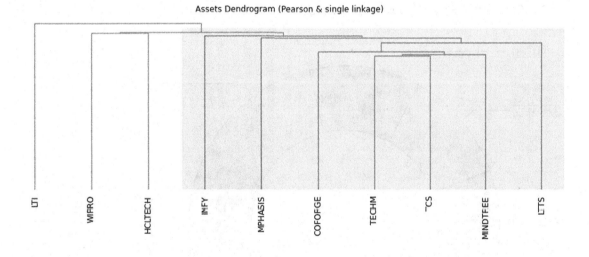

Figure 36 and Figure 37 show the dendrograms created by the HRP and the HERC portfolios on the stocks of the IT sector. The HRP dendrogram has four clusters with the following composition: Cluster1: Larsen & Toubro Infotech; Cluster 2: Wipro; Cluster 3: HCL Technologies; and Cluster 4: Infosys, MphasiS, Coforge, Tech Mahindra, Tata Consultancy Services, MindTree, and L&T Technology Services. The dendrogram of HERC portfolio, on the other hand, has produced the following clusters: Cluster 1: L&T Technology Services, MindTree, Tata Consultancy Services, Tech Mahindra, and Coforge; Cluster 2: Larsen & Toubro Infotech; Cluster 3: Infosys and MphasiS; Cluster 4: HCL Technologies and Wipro.

Figure 37. Dendrogram of the IT sector stocks formed by the HERC portfolio

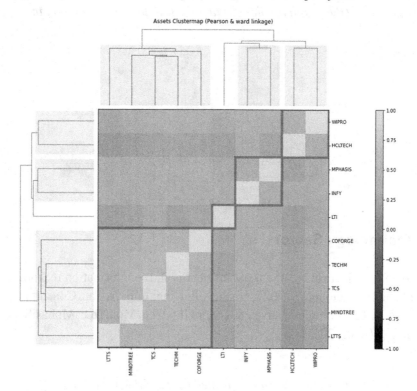

Figure 38. The HRP portfolio composition for the IT sector stocks

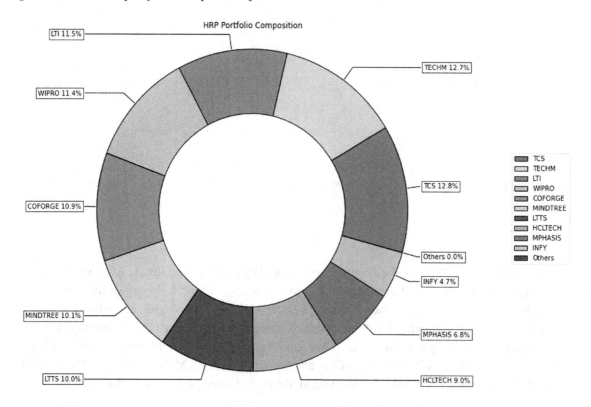

The weight allocation to the stocks of the IT sector by the HRP and the HERC portfolios are shown in Figure 38 and Figure 39, respectively. The five stocks that received the highest weights in the HRP portfolio and their corresponding weight in percent are as follows: TCS (12.82), Tech Mahindra (12.70), Larsen and Toubro Infotech (11.49), Wipro (11.43), and Coforge (10.87). Like other sectors, the distribution of the weight by the HRP to the stocks in the IT sector is uniform. The five stocks that received the highest weights in the HERC portfolio are the following: MindTree (19.76), L&T Technology Services (19.50), Tata Consultancy Services (17.26), Tech Mahindra (16.36), and Coforge (14.01). Again, similar to the other sectors, the HERC's allocation of weight to the IT sector stocks is highly skewed.

Figure 39. The HERC portfolio composition for the IT sector stocks

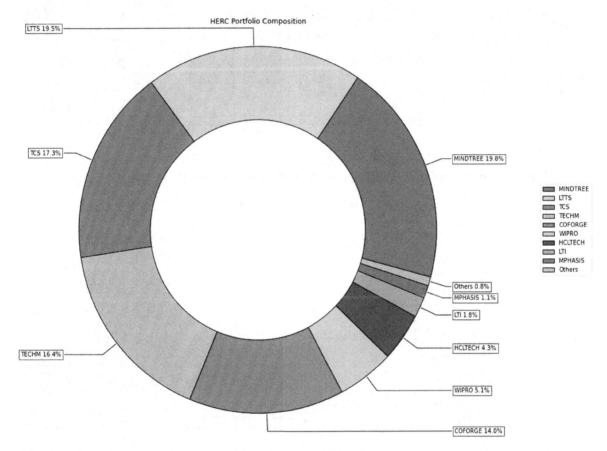

Figure 40 and Figure 41 exhibit the risk contribution by the individual stocks of the IT sector in the HRP and the HERC portfolio, respectively. The five stocks that contributed most significantly to the HRP portfolio are Tata Consultancy Services, Tech Mahindra, Wipro, Coforge, and Larsen & Toubro Infotech. As observed in the other sectors, the contributions to risk in the HRP portfolio are widely divergent for different stocks. However, the HERC portfolio has achieved fairly equal risk contributions by the stocks in the same cluster. In the HERC portfolio, the five stocks that contributed most to the portfolio's risk are MindTree, Tata Consultancy Services, Tech Mahindra, L&T Technology Services, and Coforge.

Figure 40. The risk contribution by the IT sector stocks in the HRP portfolio

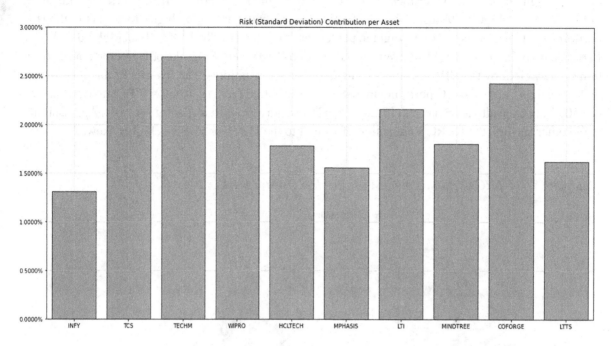

Figure 41. The risk contribution by the IT sector stocks in the HERC portfolio

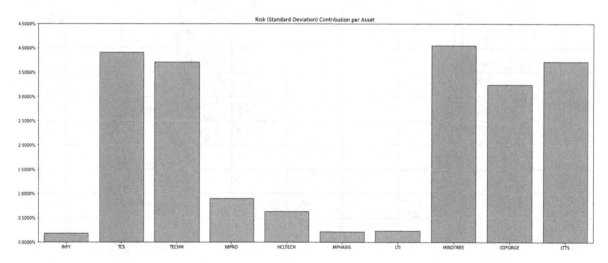

Table 6. The performance of the HRP and HERC portfolios on the IT sector stocks

Portfolio	In-sample Performance		Out-of-sample Performance	
	Volatility	**Sharpe Ratio**	**Volatility**	**Sharpe Ratio**
HRP	0.2112	1.4621	0.2317	2.7810
HERC	0.2080	1.2421	0.2113	2.4144

Figure 42. The cumulative returns yielded by the HRP and the HERC portfolios of the IT sector stocks on the training data (the graph on the left) and the test data (the graph on the right)

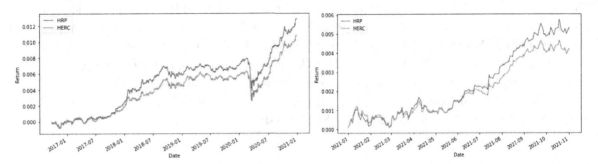

The cumulative returns for the HRP and the HERC portfolios for the IT sector stocks on the training and the test data are exhibited in Figure 42. It is evident from Table 6 that the return yielded by the HRP is higher for both cases. Moreover, the Sharpe ratios produced by the HRP portfolios are higher than those of the HERC portfolio for both training and test data, albeit with marginally higher volatility values. The results clearly show the superior performance of the HRP portfolio to its HERC counterpart for the IT sector stocks.

Metal Sector

The NSE's report published on October 29, 2021, identified 15 stocks as the most influential in the metal sector (NSE, 2021). These stocks are as follows: Tata Steel, Hindalco Industries, JSW Steel, Vedanta, Adani Enterprises, Coal India, Jindal Steel & Power, Steel Authority of India, NMDC, APL Apollo Tubes, Hindustan Copper, Hindustan Zinc, National Aluminum Company, Ratnamani Metals and Tubes, and Welspun Corporation.

Figure 43. Dendrogram of the metal sector stocks formed by the HRP portfolio

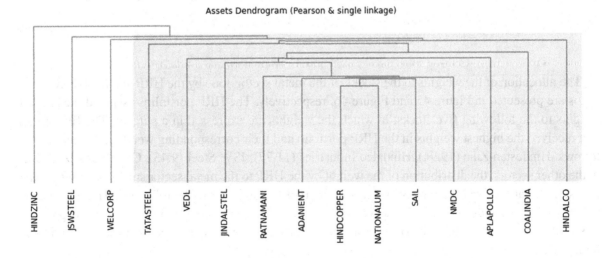

Figure 43 and Figure 44 exhibit the dendrograms of the HRP and the HERC portfolios for the metal sector stocks. The dendrogram of the HRP portfolio consists of the following clusters: Cluster1: Hindustan Zinc; Cluster 2: JSW Steel; Cluster 3: Welspun Corporation; Cluster 4: Hindalco Industries, Vedanta, Jindal Steel, Ratnamani Metals, Adani Enterprises, Hindustan Copper, National Aluminum Company, Sail Authority of India NMDC, APL Apollo Tubes, and Coal India. The clusters formed by the dendrogram of HERC portfolio, on the other hand, have the following composition: Cluster 1: Hindalco Industries, Vedanta, Jindal Steel, APL Apollo Tubes, and Coal India; Cluster 2: Ratnamani Metals, Adani Enterprises, NMDC, National Aluminum Company, Hindustan Copper, and Steel Authority of India; Cluster 3: Tata Steel, Welspun Corporation, and JSW Steel; Cluster 4: Hindustan Zinc.

Figure 44. Dendrogram of the metal sector stocks formed by the HERC portfolio

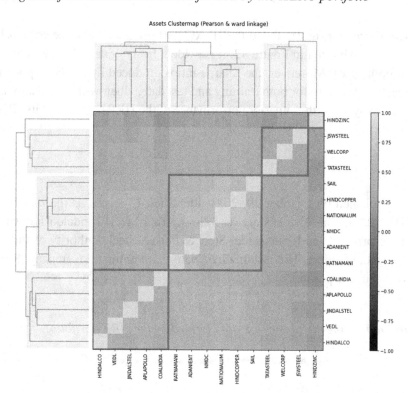

The allocation of the weights to the stocks of the metal sector done by the HRP and the HERC portfolios are presented in Figure 45 and Figure 46, respectively. The HRP portfolios assigned the highest weights to the following five stocks, in which the weights are expressed in a percent: The five stocks that received the highest weights in the HRP portfolio and their corresponding weight in percent are as follows: Hindustan Zinc (19.94), Hindalco Industries (11.77), JSW Steel (9.45), Coal India (9.13). As in the other sectors, the distribution of the weight by the HRP to the metal sector stocks is uniform. The five stocks that received the highest weights in the HERC portfolio are the following: Hindustan Zinc (27.03), Hindalco Industries (10.58), JSW Steel (10. 43), Coal India (8.20), and Welspun Corporation (5.98). As in all other sectors, the HERC's allocation of weight to the metal sector stocks is found to be highly skewed.

Figure 45. The HRP portfolio composition for the metal sector stocks

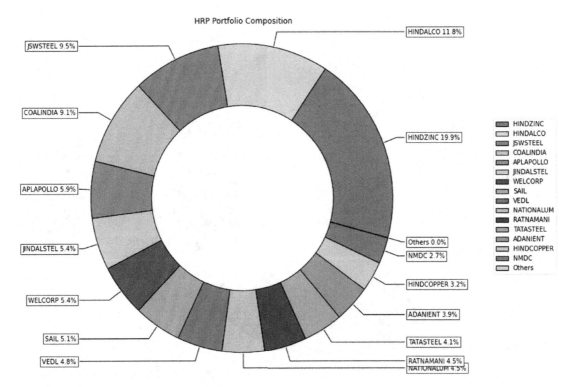

The risk contributions by the stocks of the metal sector in the HRP and the HERC portfolios are represented in Figure 40 and Figure 41, respectively. In the HRP portfolio, the five stocks that contributed the most to the risk are Hindustan Zinc, JSW Steel, Hindalco Industries, Coal India, and APL Apollo Tubes. The risk contributions by the constituent stocks in the HRP portfolio, as in the other sectors, are found to be varying widely. On the contrary, the stocks in the same cluster in the HERC portfolio have identical risk contributions. In the HERC portfolio, the five stocks that contributed most to the portfolio's risk are Hindustan Zinc, JSW Steel, Welspun Corporation, Hindalco Industries, and Tata Steel.

Figure 42 exhibits the cumulative returns yielded by the HRP and the HERC portfolios for the stocks of the metal sector. The returns from both portfolios look similar even though the HRP's return on the training data is a little higher than its HERC counterpart. It is observed from Table 7 that the Sharpe ratios of the HRP portfolio are higher for both training and test data. Moreover, the volatilities of the HRP portfolio are lower than those of the HERC portfolios in both cases. It is evident from these observations that the HRP portfolio has outperformed its HERC counterparts on the stocks of the metal sector.

Table 7. The performance of the HRP and HERC portfolios on the metal sector stocks

Portfolio	In-sample Performance		Out-of-sample Performance	
	Volatility	**Sharpe Ratio**	**Volatility**	**Sharpe Ratio**
HRP	0.2534	1.0486	0.2599	2.6178
HERC	0.2624	0.8475	0.2957	2.2880

Figure 46. The HERC portfolio composition for the metal sector stocks

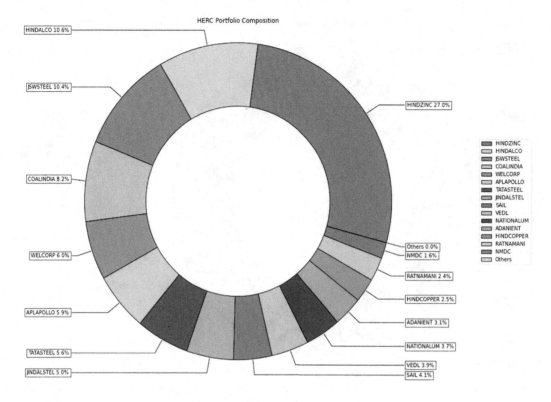

Figure 47. The risk contribution by the metal sector stocks in the HRP portfolio

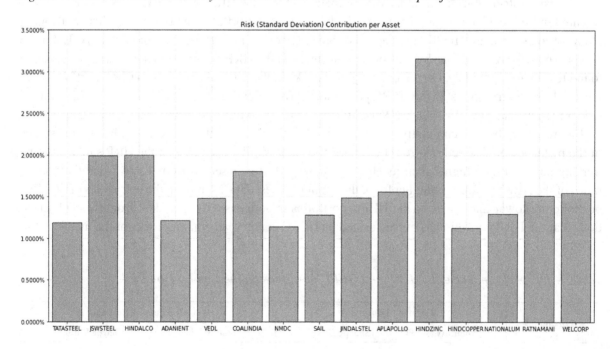

Figure 48. The risk contribution by the metal sector stocks in the HERC portfolio

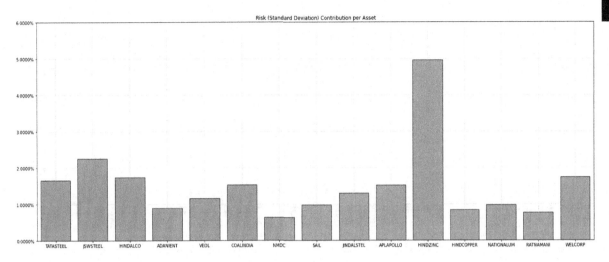

Figure 49. The cumulative returns yielded by the HRP and the HERC portfolios of the metal sector stocks on the training data (the graph on the left) and the test data (the graph on the right)

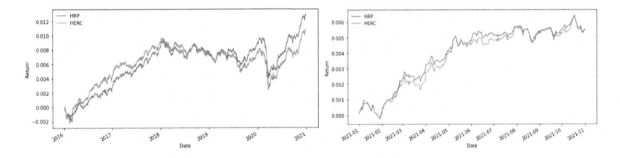

NIFTY 50 Stocks

The NIFTY 50 stocks are the market leaders across 13 sectors in the NSE and these stocks have low-risk quotients. These 50 stocks are as follows: Axis Bank, Bajaj Finance, Bajaj Finserv, Housing Development Finance Corporation, HDFC Bank, HDFC Life Insurance Company, ICICI Bank, IndusInd Bank, Kotak Mahindra Bank, State Bank of India, SBI Life Insurance Company, Bajaj Auto, Eicher Motors, Hero MotoCorp, Mahindra & Mahindra, Maruti Suzuki, Tata Motors, Cipla, Divi's Laboratory, Dr. Reddy's Laboratory, Sun Pharmaceuticals, HCL Technologies, Infosys, Tata Consultancy Services, Tech Mahindra, Wipro, Bharat Petroleum Corporation, Indian Oil Corporation, Oil & Natural Gas Corporation, Reliance Industries, National Thermal Power Corporation, Power Grid Corporation of India, Coal India, Hindalco Industries, JSW Steel, Tata Steel, Britannia Industries, Hindustan Unilever, ITC, Nestle India, Tata Consumer Products, Titan, Shree Cement, UltraTech Cement, Asian Paints, Bharti Airtel, Grasim Industries, Larsen & Toubro, UPL, and Adani Ports and Special Economic Zones (NSE, 2021).

Figure 50. Dendrogram of the NIFTY 50 stocks formed by the HRP portfolio

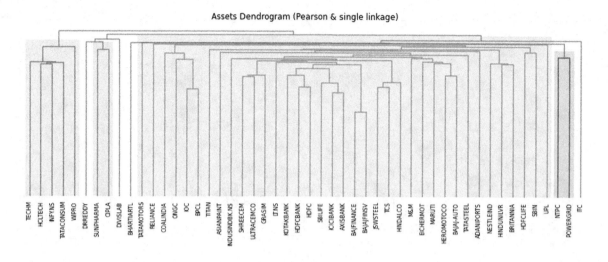

Figure 51. Dendrogram of the NIFTY 50 stocks formed by the HERC portfolio

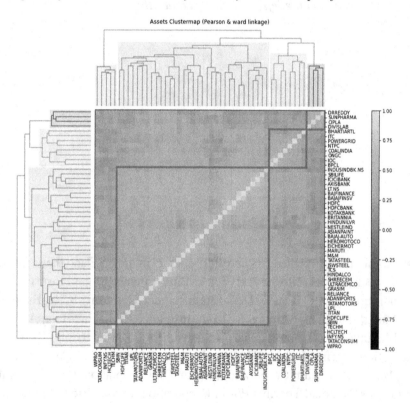

The dendrograms of the clusters of the NIFTY 50 stocks formed by the HRP and the HERC portfolios are exhibited in Figure 51 and Figure 52, respectively. There are eight clusters formed by the HRP portfolio with the largest cluster containing 37 stocks. The remaining seven clusters have the following composition: Cluster 1: Tech Mahindra, HCL Technologies, Infosys, Tata Consumer Products, and Wipro; Cluster 2: Dr. Reddy's Labs; Cluster 3: Sun Pharmaceuticals Industries and Cipla; Cluster 4:

Divi's Labs; Cluster 5: Bharti Airtel, Cluster 6: NTPC and Power Grid Corporation of India; and Cluster 7: ITC. The dendrogram of the HERC portfolio, on the other hand, has created four clusters with the largest cluster containing 33 stocks. The compositions of the remaining three clusters are as follows: Cluster 1: Wipro, Tata Consumer Products, Infosys, HCL Technologies, and Tech Mahindra; Cluster 2: Bharat Petroleum Corporation, Indian Oil Corporation, Oil and Natural Gas Corporation, Coal India, NTPC, Power Grid Corporation of India, ITC, and Bharti Airtel; Cluster 3: Divi's Labs, Cipla, Sun Pharmaceutical Industries, and Dr. Reddy's Labs.

The allocation of the weights to the NIFTY 50 stocks done by the HRP and the HERC portfolios are presented in Figure 52 and Figure 53, respectively. The five stocks from NIFTY 50 that received the highest weights in the HRP portfolio and their corresponding weight in percent are as follows: Tata Consumer Products (4.16), Britannia Industries (3.81), Hindustan Unilever (3.33), Asian Paints (3.30), and Power Grid Corporation of India (3.10). It is evident from Figure 52 that the HRP portfolio has produced a fairly uniform allocation of weights to the stocks achieving a diversified portfolio. The five stocks from NIFTY 50 that received the highest weights in the HERC portfolio are the following: Tata Consumer Products (16.89), Wipro (15.79), HCL Technologies (14.20), Infosys (13.77), and Tech Mahindra (12.49). From Figure 53, it is evident that the allocation of weights by the HERC portfolio to the NIFTY 50 stock is highly skewed as in all other sectors.

The risk contributions by the NIFTY 50 stocks in the HRP and the HERC portfolios are exhibited in Figure 54 and Figure 55, respectively. In the HRP portfolio, the five stocks that contributed the most to the risk are Britannia Industries, Adani Ports, Asian Paints, Bharti Airtel, and Hindustan Unilever. The risk contributions by the constituent stocks in the HRP portfolio, as in the other sectors, are found to be varying widely. On the contrary, the stocks in the same cluster in the HERC portfolio have identical risk contributions. In the HERC portfolio, the five stocks from NIFTY 50 that contributed most to the portfolio's risk are Tata Consumer Products, HCL Technologies, Infosys, Wipro, and Tech Mahindra.

Figure 52. The HRP portfolio composition for the NIFTY 50 sector stocks

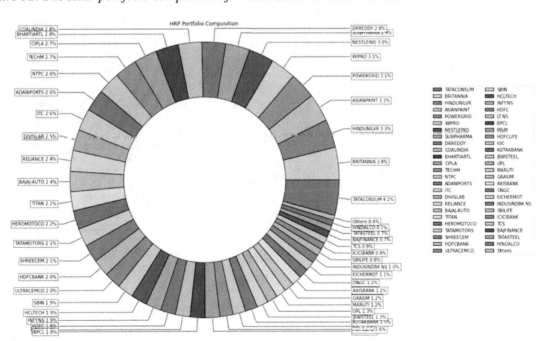

Figure 53. The HERC portfolio composition for the NIFTY 50 sector stocks

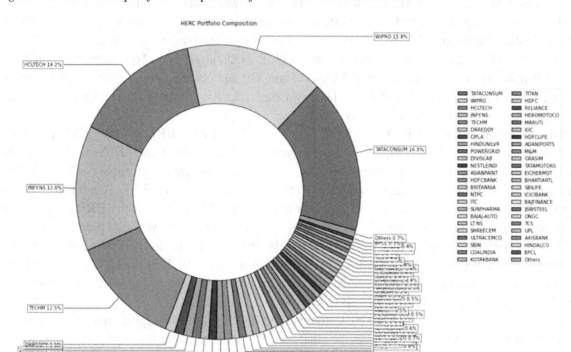

Figure 54. The risk contribution by the NIFTY 50 stocks in the HRP portfolio

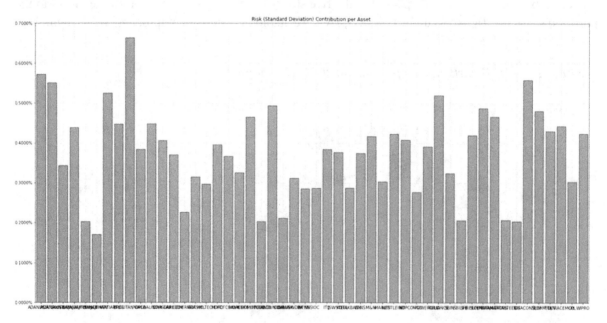

Figure 55. The risk contribution by the NIFTY 50 stocks in the HERC portfolio

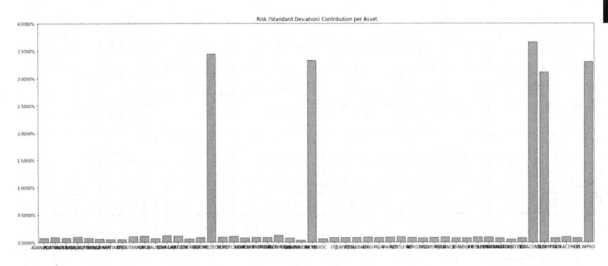

The cumulative returns of the HRP and the HERC portfolios on the training and the test data of the NIFTY 50 stocks are depicted in Figure 56. For both the training and the test data, the return yielded by the HERC portfolio is found to be higher than that produced by the HRP portfolio. The results presented in Table 8 show the Sharpe ratios of the HERC portfolios are higher for both training and test data. However, the volatilities of the HERC portfolios in both cases are marginally higher. The HERC portfolio has marginally performed better than its HRP counterpart on the NIFTY 50 stocks.

Figure 56. The cumulative returns yielded by the HRP and the HERC portfolios of the NIFTY metal sector stocks on the training data (the graph on the left) and the test data (the graph on the right)

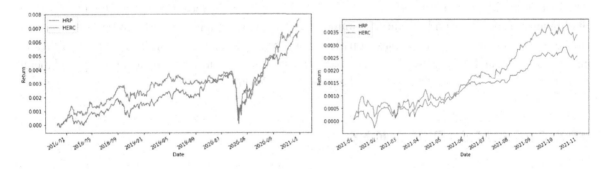

Table 8. The performance of the HRP and HERC portfolios on the NIFTY 50 stocks

Portfolio	In-sample Performance		Out-of-sample Performance	
	Volatility	Sharpe Ratio	Volatility	Sharpe Ratio
HRP	0.1879	1.1797	0.1313	2.3610
HERC	0.2054	1.2228	0.1729	2.3755

Table 9. The summary of the performance results of the HRP and HERC portfolios

Sector	In-sample Performance	Out-of-sample Performance
	Portfolio with higher SR	Portfolio with higher SR
Auto	HRP (0.6674)	HRP (1.8130)
Consumer Durable	HRP (1.5790)	HRP (3.3201)
Financial Services	HRP (0.8625)	HRP (1.5108)
FMCG	HRP (1.5746)	HRP (2.0966)
Healthcare	HRP (2.1502)	HERC (1.5634)
Information Technology	HRP (1.4621)	HRP (2.7810)
Metal	HRP (1.0486)	HRP (2.6178)
NIFTY 50	HERC (1.2228)	HERC (2.3755)

Table 9 presents a summary of the results, in which the portfolio yielding the higher Sharpe ratio for a sector is mentioned along with the corresponding Sharpe ratio for the in-sample and the out-of-sample data. It is observed that except for three cases, the HRP portfolio has yielded higher Sharpe ratios. The three cases in which the HERC portfolio has produced higher Sharpe ratios are NIFTY 50 for both in-sample and out-of-sample data, and the healthcare sector for the out-of-sample data. The results have demonstrated the superiority of the HRP's performance in comparison to the HERC. The risk parity approach followed by the HRP portfolio in the clusters has yielded better results than the equality of the risk contribution by the HERC portfolio. Since some of the stocks belonging to the same sector have correlated returns, the HRP approach has achieved higher diversification of the weights allocated to the correlated portfolios by forming clusters within the stocks, thereby getting rid of the instability problem of the inverse of the correlation matrices of the stock returns. The HERC, on the other hand, has achieved a marginally higher diversification in the NIFTY 50 portfolio due to the availability of a larger number of stocks that could be exploited effectively in its agglomerative clustering process. This has resulted in its higher Sharpe ratios on both the in-sample and the out-of-sample data. The three sectors which turned out to be the most profitable (based on higher Sharpe ratios) on the in-sample data are healthcare, consumer durable, and FMCG. On the other hand, consumer durable, information technology, and metal sectors proved to be the most profitable on the out-of-sample data.

FUTURE RESEARCH DIRECTIONS

As a future scope of work, the other sectors of the Indian economy like private sector banks, public sector banks, oil & gas, media, realty, large-cap, mid-cap, and small-cap will be included in the analysis. The performance of HRP and HERC portfolios will also be compared with other approaches like the eigen portfolio and the Black-Letterman portfolio. Additionally, the stocks listed in important stock exchanges in the world will also be brought under the purview of the study.

CONCLUSION

This chapter has presented portfolio design approaches on eight important Indian stock market sectors using the HRP and the HERC portfolio design approaches. Exploiting the past prices of the most influential stocks of seven sectors and the 50 stocks from NIFTY 50, the HRP and the HERC portfolios are designed for each sector. While the stock price data from Jan 1, 2016, to Dec 31, 2020, are used for building the portfolios, the period Jan 1, 2021, to Nov 1, 2021, is used for the testing. The portfolios are backtested on both the training and the test data to identify the portfolio with the highest Sharpe Ratio for each sector. It is found that the HRP portfolio has outperformed the HERC in all cases except for three. The three cases in which the HERC portfolio yielded a higher Sharpe ratio are NITY 50 for both training and test data, and the healthcare sector on the test data. Since the HRP portfolio has yielded a higher Sharpe ratio for seven out of the eight cases on the training data, and six out of the eight cases on the test data, it turned out to be the clear choice for the investors.

REFERENCES

Audrino, F., Sigrist, F., & Ballinari, D. (2020). The impact of sentiment and attention measures on stock market volatility. *International Journal of Forecasting*, *36*(2), 334–357. doi:10.1016/j.ijforecast.2019.05.010

Baily, D., & de Prado, M. L. (2012). Balanced baskets: A new approach to trading and hedging risks. *The Journal of Investment Strategies*, *1*(4), 21–62. doi:10.21314/JOIS.2012.010

Bao, W., Yue, J., & Rao, Y. (2017). A deep learning framework for financial time series using stacked autoencoders and long-and-short-term memory. *PLoS One*, *12*(7), e0180944. Advance online publication. doi:10.1371/journal.pone.0180944 PMID:28708865

Binkowski, M., Marti, G., & Donnat, P. (2018). Autoregressive convolutional neural networks for asynchronous time series. *Proceedings of the 35th International Conference on Machine Learning (ICML'18)*, 580–589.

Bollen, J., Mao, H., & Zeng, X. (2011). Twitter mood predicts the stock market. *Journal of Computational Science*, *2*(1), 1–8. doi:10.1016/j.jocs.2010.12.007

Carta, S. M., Consoli, S., Piras, L., Podda, A. S., & Recupero, D. R. (2021). Explainable machine learning exploiting news and domain-specific lexicon for stock market forecasting. *IEEE Access: Practical Innovations, Open Solutions*, *9*, 30193–30205. doi:10.1109/ACCESS.2021.3059960

Chen, C., & Zhou, Y. (2018). Robust multi-objective portfolio with higher moments. *Expert Systems with Applications*, *100*, 165–181. doi:10.1016/j.eswa.2018.02.004

Chen, M.-Y., Liao, C.-H., & Hsieh, R.-P. (2019). Modeling public mood and emotion: Stock market trend prediction with anticipatory computing approach. *Computers in Human Behavior*, *101*, 402–408. doi:10.1016/j.chb.2019.03.021

Clarke, R., De Silva, H., & Thorley, S. (2011). Minimum-variance portfolio composition. *Journal of Portfolio Management*, *37*(2), 31–45. doi:10.3905/jpm.2011.37.2.031

Corazza, M., di Tolo, G., Fasano, G., & Pesenti, R. (2021). A novel hybrid PSO-based metaheuristic for costly portfolio selection problems. *Annals of Operations Research, 304*(1-2), 104–137. doi:10.100710479-021-04075-3

de Prado, M. L. (2016). Building diversified portfolios that outperform out of sample. *Journal of Portfolio Management, 42*(4), 59–69. doi:10.3905/jpm.2016.42.4.059

DeMiguel, V., Garlappi, L., & Uppal, R. (2009). Optimal versus naïve diversification: How inefficient is the 1/n portfolio strategy? *Review of Financial Studies, 22*(5), 1915–1953. doi:10.1093/rfs/hhm075

Ertenlice, O., & Kalayci, C. B. (2018). A survey of swarm intelligence for portfolio optimization: Algorithms and applications. *Swarm and Evolutionary Computation, 39*, 36–52. doi:10.1016/j.swevo.2018.01.009

Erwin, K., & Engelbrecht, A. (2020). Improved set-based particle swarm optimization for portfolio optimization. *Proceedings of the IEEE Symposium Series on Computational Intelligence (SSCI)*, 1573–1580. 10.1109/SSCI47803.2020.9308579

Galvez, R. H., & Gravano, A. (2017). Assessing the usefulness of online message board mining in automatic stock prediction systems. *Journal of Computational Science, 19*, 43–56. doi:10.1016/j.jocs.2017.01.001

Garcia, F., Gujjaro, F., & Oliver, J. (2018). Index tracking optimization with cardinality constraint: A performance comparison of genetic algorithms and tabu search heuristic. *Neural Computing & Applications, 30*(8), 2625–2641. doi:10.100700521-017-2882-2

Google Colaboratory. (2021). https://colab.research.google.com

Macedo, L. L., Godinho, P., & Alves, M. J. (2017). Mean-semivariance portfolio optimization with multi-objective evolutionary algorithms and technical analysis rules. *Expert Systems with Applications, 79*, 33–42. doi:10.1016/j.eswa.2017.02.033

Markowitz, H. (1952). Portfolio selection. *The Journal of Finance, 7*(1), 77–91. doi:10.2307/2975974

Mehtab, S., & Sen, J. (2019). A robust predictive model for stock price prediction using deep learning and natural language processing. *Proceedings of the 7th International Conference on Business Analytics and Intelligence (BAICONF'19)*. 10.2139srn.3502624

Mehtab, S., & Sen, J. (2020a). A time series analysis-based stock price prediction using machine learning and deep learning models. *International Journal of Business Forecasting and Marketing Intelligence, 6*(4), 272–335. doi:10.1504/IJBFMI.2020.115691

Mehtab, S., & Sen, J. (2020b). Stock price prediction using CNN and LSTM-based deep learning models. *Proceedings of the IEEE International Conference on Decision Aid Science and Applications (DASA)*, 447-453. 10.1109/DASA51403.2020.9317207

Mehtab, S. & Sen, J. (2020c). *A Time Series Analysis-Based Stock Price Prediction Framework Using Machine Learning and Deep Learning Models*. Technical Report No: NSHM_KOL_2020_SCA_DS_1.

Mehtab, S., & Sen, J. (2020d). Stock price prediction using convolutional neural networks on a multivariate time series. *Proceedings of the 3rd National Conference o Machine Learning and Artificial Intelligence (NCMLAI'20)*. 10.36227/techrxiv.15088734.v1

Mehtab, S., & Sen, J. (2022). *Analysis and forecasting of financial time series using CNN and LSTM-based deep learning models. In Advances in Distributed Computing and Machine Learning, Lecture Notes in Networks and Systems* (Vol. 202). Springer. doi:10.1007/978-981-16-4807-6_39

Mehtab, S., Sen, J., & Dasgupta, S. (2020e). Robust analysis of stock price time series using CNN and LSTM-based deep learning models. *Proceedings of the IEEE 4th International Conference on Electronics, Communication and Aerospace Technology (ICECA)*, 1481-1486. 10.1109/ICECA49313.2020.9297652

Mehtab, S., Sen, J., & Dutta, A. (2021). Stock price prediction using machine learning and LSTM-based deep learning models. Machine Learning and Metaheuristics Algorithms, and Applications (SoMMA), 88-106. doi:10.1007/978-981-16-0419-5_8

NSE. (2021). http://www1.nseindia.com

Qu, B. Y., Zhou, Q., Xiao, J. M., Liang, J. J., & Suganthan, P. N. (2017). Large-scale portfolio optimization using multiobjective evolutionary algorithms and preselection methods. *Mathematical Problems in Engineering, 2017*, 1–14. doi:10.1155/2017/4197914

RaffinotT. (2018). *The hierarchical equal risk contribution portfolio.* https://ssrn.com/abstract=3237540 doi:10.2139/ssrn.3237540

Reveiz-Herault, A. (2016). An active asset management investment process for drawdown-averse investors. *Intelligent Systems in Accounting, Finance & Management, 39*(1–2), 85–96. doi:10.1002/isaf.1375

Saborido, R., Ruiz, A. B., Bermudez, J. D., Vercher, E., & Luque, M. (2016). Evolutionary multi-objective optimization algorithms for fuzzy portfolio selection. *Applied Soft Computing, 39*, 48–63. doi:10.1016/j.asoc.2015.11.005

Sen, J. (2017a). A time series analysis-based forecasting approach for the Indian realty sector. *International Journal of Applied Economic Studies, 5*(4), 8–17. doi:10.36227/techrxiv.16640212.v1

Sen, J. (2017b). A robust analysis and forecasting for the Indian mid cap sector using time series decomposition approach. *Journal of Insurance and Financial Management, 3*(4), 1–32. doi:10.36227/techrxiv.15128901.v1

Sen, J. (2018a). Stock price prediction using machine learning and deep learning frameworks. *Proceedings of the 6th International Conference on Business Analytics and Intelligence (ICBAI'18).*

Sen, J. (2018b). Stock composition of mutual funds and fund style: A time series decomposition approach towards testing for consistency. *International Journal of Business Forecasting and Marketing Intelligence, 4*(3), 235–292. doi:10.1504/IJBFMI.2018.092781

Sen, J., & Datta Chaudhuri, T. (2016a). An investigation of the structural characteristics of the Indian IT sector and the capital goods sector: An application of the R programming language in time series decomposition and forecasting. *Journal of Insurance and Financial Management, 1*(4), 68–132. doi:10.36227/techrxiv.16640227.v1

Sen, J., & Datta Chaudhuri, T. (2016b). An alternative framework for time series decomposition and forecasting and its relevance for portfolio choice- a comparative study of the Indian consumer durable and small cap sectors. *Journal of Economics Library, 3*(2), 303–326. doi:10.1453/jel.v3i2.787

Sen, J., & Datta Chaudhuri, T. (2016c). Decomposition of time series data of stock markets and its implications for prediction: an application for the Indian auto sector. *Proceedings of the 2nd National Conference on Advances in Business Research and Management Practices (ABRMP'16)*, 15–28. 10.13140/ RG.2.1.3232.0241

Sen, J., & Datta Chaudhuri, T. (2017a). A robust predictive model for stock price forecasting. *Proceedings of the 5th International Conference on Business Analytics and Intelligence (ICBAI'17)*. 10.36227/ techrxiv.16778611.v1

Sen, J., & Datta Chaudhuri, T. (2017b). A predictive analysis of the Indian FMCG sector using time series decomposition-based approach. *Journal of Economics Library*, 4(2), 206–226. doi:10.2139srn.2992051

Sen, J., & Datta Chaudhuri, T. (2017c). A time series analysis-based forecasting framework for the Indian healthcare sector. *Journal of Insurance and Financial Management*, 3(1), 66–94. doi:10.36227/ techrxiv.16640221.v1

Sen, J., & Datta Chaudhuri, T. (2018). Understanding the sectors of the Indian economy for portfolio choice. *International Journal of Business Forecasting and Marketing Intelligence*, 4(2), 178–222. doi:10.1504/IJBFMI.2018.090914

Sen, J., & Dutta, A. (2022). A comparative study of hierarchical risk parity portfolio and eigen portfolio on the NIFTY 50 stocks. *Proceedings of the 2nd International Conference on Computational Intelligence and Data Analytics (ICCIDA'22)*.

Sen, J., Dutta, A., & Mehtab, S. (2021e). Profitability analysis in stock investment using an LSTM-based deep learning model. *Proceedings of the IEEE 2nd International Conference for Emerging Technology (INCET'21)*, 1-9. 10.1109/INCET51464.2021.9456385

Sen, J., Dutta, A., & Mehtab, S. (2021f). Stock portfolio optimization using a deep learning LSTM model. *Proceedings of the IEEE International Conference MysuruCon'21*, 263-271. 10.1109/Mysuru-Con52639.2021.9641662

Sen, J. & Mehtab, S. (2021a). A comparative study of optimum risk portfolio and eigen portfolio on the Indian stock market. *International Journal of Business Forecasting and Marketing Intelligence (IJBFMI)*, 7(2), 143-193. doi:10.1504/IJBFMI.2021.10043037

Sen, J., & Mehtab, S. (2021b). Accurate stock price forecasting using robust and optimized deep learning model. *Proceedings of the IEEE International Conference on Intelligent Technologies (CONIT'21)*. 10.1109/CONIT51480.2021.9498565

Sen, J., & Mehtab, S. (2021c). Design and analysis of robust deep learning models for stock price prediction. In J. Sen (Ed.), *Machine Learning- Algorithms, Model and Applications* (pp. 1–32). IntechOpen. doi:10.5772/intechopen.99982

Sen, J., Mehtab, S., & Dutta, A. (2021g). Volatility modeling of stocks from selected sectors of the Indian economy using GARCH. *Proceedings of the IEEE Asian Conference eon Innovation in Technology (ASIANCON'21)*, 1-9. 10.1109/ASIANCON51346.2021.9544977

Sen, J., Mehtab, S., Dutta, A., & Mondal, S. (2021d). Precise stock price prediction for optimized portfolio design using an LSTM model. *Proceedings of the IEEE 9th International Conference on Information Technology (OCIT'21)*. 10.1109/OCIT53463.2021.00050

P

Sen, J., Mehtab, S., Dutta, A., & Mondal, S. (2021h). Hierarchical risk parity and minimum variance portfolio design on NIFTY 50 stocks. *Proceedings of the IEEE International Conference on Decision Aid Sciences and Applications (DASA'21)*, 668-675. 10.1109/DASA53625.2021.9681925

Sen, J., Mehtab, S., & Nath, G. (2020). Stock price prediction using deep learning models. *Lattice: The Machine Learning Journal*, *1*(3), 34–40. doi:10.36227/techrxiv.16640197.v1

Sen, J., Mondal, S., & Mehtab, S. (2021i). Portfolio optimization on NIFTY thematic sector stocks using an LSTM model. *Proceedings of the IEEE International Conference on Data Analytics for Business and Industry (ICDABI'21)*, 364-369. 10.1109/ICDABI53623.2021.9655886

Sen, J., Mondal, S., & Nath, G. (2021j). Robust portfolio design and stock price prediction using an optimized LSTM model. *Proceedings of the IEEE 18th Indian Council International Conference (INDICON'21)*, 1-6. 10.1109/INDICON52576.2021.9691583

Silva, A., Neves, R., & Horta, N. (2015). A hybrid approach to portfolio composition based on fundamental and technical indicators. *Expert Systems with Applications*, *42*(4), 2036–2048. doi:10.1016/j.eswa.2014.09.050

Syrovatkin, A. (2020). Mixed investment portfolio with limited asset selection. *Proceedings of the 13th International Conference on Management of Large-Scale Systems Development (MLSD)*, 1-5. 10.1109/MLSD49919.2020.9247765

Tibshirani, R., Walther, G., & Hastie, T. (2002). Estimating the number of clusters in a data set via the gap statistics. *Journal of the Royal Statistical Society. Series A, (Statistics in Society)*, *63*(2), 411–423. doi:10.1111/1467-9868.00293

Vercher, E., & Bermudez, J. D. (2015). Portfolio optimization using a credibility mean-absolute semi-deviation model. *Expert Systems with Applications*, *42*(20), 7121–7131. doi:10.1016/j.eswa.2015.05.020

Weng, B., Ahmed, M. A., & Megahed, F. M. (2017). Stock market one-day ahead movement prediction using disparate data sources. *Expert Systems with Applications*, *79*, 153–163. doi:10.1016/j.eswa.2017.02.041

Yue, S., Wang, X., & Wei, M. (2008). Application of two-order difference to gap statistic. *Transactions of Tianjin University*, *14*(3), 217–221. doi:10.100712209-008-0039-1

Zhang, J., Leung, T., & Arakin, A. (2019). A relaxed optimization approach for cardinality-constrained portfolios. *Proceedings of the 18th European Control Conference (ECC)*, 2885–2892. 10.23919/ECC.2019.8796164

Zhao, P., Gao, S., & Yang, N. (2020). Solving multi-objective portfolio optimization problem based on MOEA/D'. *Proceedings of the 12th International Conference on Advanced Computational Intelligence (ICACI'20)*, 30–37. 10.1109/ICACI49185.2020.9177505

ADDITIONAL READING

Fan, J., Liao, Y., & Mincheva, M. (2011). High dimensional covariance matrix estimation in approximate factor models. *Annals of Statistics*, *39*(6), 3320–3356. doi:10.1214/11-AOS944 PMID:22661790

Fugazza, C., Guidolin, M., & Nicodano, G. (2015). Equally weighted vs. long-run optimal portfolios. *European Financial Management, 21*(4), 742–789. doi:10.1111/eufm.12042

Hwang, I., Xu, S., & In, F. (2018). Naïve versus optimal diversification: Tail risk and performance. *European Journal of Operational Research, 265*(1), 372–388. doi:10.1016/j.ejor.2017.07.066

Jacobs, H., Muller, S., & Weber, M. (2014). How should individual investors diversify? An empirical evaluation of alternative asset allocation policies. *Journal of Financial Markets, 19*, 62–68. doi:10.1016/j.finmar.2013.07.004

Kan, R., & Zhou, G. (2007). Optimal portfolio choice with parameter uncertainty. *Journal of Financial and Quantitative Analysis, 42*(3), 621–656. doi:10.1017/S0022109000004129

Ledoit, O., & Wolf, M. (2003). Improved estimation of the covariance matrix of stock returns with an application to portfolio selection. *Journal of Empirical Finance, 10*(5), 603–621. doi:10.1016/S0927-5398(03)00007-0

Ledoit, O., & Wolf, M. (2008). Robust performance hypothesis testing with the Sharpe ratio. *Journal of Empirical Finance, 15*(5), 850–859. doi:10.1016/j.jempfin.2008.03.002

Pai, G. A. V. (2017). Fuzzy decision theory based metaheuristic portfolio optimization and active rebalancing using interval type-2 fuzzy sets. *IEEE Transactions on Fuzzy Systems, 25*(2), 377–391. doi:10.1109/TFUZZ.2016.2633972

Peng, Y., Albuquerque, P. H. M., Do Nascimento, I.-F., & Machado, J. V. F. (2019). Between nonlinearities, complexity, and noises: An application on portfolio selection using kernel principal component analysis. *Entropy (Basel, Switzerland), 21*(4), 376. doi:10.3390/e21040376 PMID:33267090

Sen, J., & Datta Chaudhuri, T. (2016). A framework for predictive analysis of stock market indices – a study of the Indian auto sector. Journal of Management Practice, 2(1), 1-20. doi:10.13140/RG.2.1.2178.3448

Weidman, S. (2019). *Deep Learning from Scratch: Building with Python from First Principles* (1st ed.). O'Reilly Media Inc.

KEY TERMS AND DEFINITIONS

Agglomerative Clustering: It is a bottom-up type of hierarchical clustering in which each data point is defined as a cluster initially. Pairs of clusters are merged successively as the algorithm moves up in the hierarchy till the topmost point in the hierarchy is reached.

Backtesting: It is the general method for seeing how well a strategy or model would have done ex-post. Backtesting assesses the viability of a trading strategy by discovering how it would play out using historical data. If backtesting works, traders and analysts may have the confidence to employ it gone forward.

Critical Line Algorithm: It is a computationally efficient method for tracing out the entire efficient frontier of a set of candidate portfolios of assets by finding successive critical values. It is applied to mean-variance optimization problems in portfolio design.

P

Hierarchical Equal Risk Contribution Portfolio: It aims at diversifying capital allocation and risk allocation in a portfolio by clustering the assets in a portfolio in such a way that the assets in a given cluster contribute equally to the overall risk of the portfolio.

Hierarchical Risk Parity Portfolio: It is a risk-based portfolio optimization algorithm, which has been shown to generate diversified portfolios with robust out-of-sample performance without the requirement of a positive-definite return covariance matrix of the assets.

Minimum Variance Portfolio: It is a portfolio that minimizes the risk while maximizing the return. It involves diversifying the holdings to reduce the volatility, or finding a combination of assets that may be risky on their own but balance each other out when held in combination.

Portfolio Optimization: It is a process of selecting the best combination from a set of all portfolios being considered, according to some pre-defined objective. The objective typically maximizes factors such as expected return and minimizes costs like financial risk. The factors being considered may range from tangible (such as assets, liabilities, earnings, or other fundamentals) to intangible (such as selective divestment).

Portfolio Return: It refers to the gain or loss realized by an investment portfolio containing several types of investments. Portfolios aim to deliver returns based on the stated objectives of the investment strategy, as well as the risk tolerance of the type of investors targeted by the portfolio.

Portfolio Risk: It refers to the chance that the combination of assets within a portfolio will fail to meet the financial objectives of the portfolio. Each asset within a portfolio carries its own risk, with higher potential return typically meaning higher risk.

Sharpe Ratio: Originally developed by Nobel laureate William F. Sharpe, it is a metric used to help investors understand the return of an investment compared to its risk. The ratio is the average return earned over the risk-free rate per unit of volatility or total risk. Volatility is a measure of the price fluctuation of an asset or portfolio.

Product Offer and Pricing Personalization in Retail Banking

Wei Ke
Columbia Business School, USA

Rogan Johannes Vleming
Simon Kucher & Partners, Canada

Rohan Shah
Simon Kucher & Partners, Canada

INTRODUCTION

Over the past decade, retail banks have leveraged advanced analytics to power pricing and campaign optimization strategies in deposits. These models collected and analyzed historic data, competitors' pricing, economic conditions, demand elasticities, and other factors to optimize the pricing and marketing of deposit products to consumers. However, these efforts were applied to single-product lines and conducted in silos without consideration for the customer's broader relationship with the bank. Deposit marketing campaigns often had myopic objectives that sometimes ran counter to larger institutional goals, and a broad stroke approach meant marketing-yield efficiency were usually very low.

The rise of parametric (e.g., classic regression and optimization) and non-parametric modeling (e.g. machine learning, multi-armed bandits, etc.) capabilities has opened up new possibilities for banks to shift from this fragmented, product-centric approach towards orchestrated one-to-one marketing where the bank is able to automate and tailor communications, pricing and products offers to speak directly to their customers in context-appropriate, relevant ways. Developed using internal and external data, these models can consider a customer's wider relationship with the bank, to personalize next-best offers, adapt messages based on reactions and feedback, and nudge customers towards desired actions with high-levels of accuracy and relevance.

Several types of parametric and non-parametric models are needed to support one-to-one marketing orchestration capabilities. These include flow of funds, response models, and customer lifetime measurement and segmentation clustering models. Data on product usage and transaction patterns can support customer segmentation models that anticipate and predict future customer needs to trigger up-selling and other tailored communications, while behavioral science can refine machine-learning models to deliver nudges and improve decision making.

Additionally, intangible objectives like financial well-being, customer lifetime value and customer satisfaction must be made measurable and tangible. A dynamic score, similar to a FICO metric, to measure a customer's financial well-being and reflect how well the customer is managing his/her finances based on banking behaviors and transactions, should be considered.

The transition from a marketing and pricing organization that executed blanket marketing campaigns to one capable of delivering the right message to the right customer at the right time for the right product

DOI: 10.4018/978-1-7998-9220-5.ch116

through the right channel, is a multistep and complex undertaking. For banks, there are challenges at the analytical and organizational levels.

Ideally price setting should be integrated with marketing. However, many banks separate these functions where pricing decisions for savings, certificate-of-deposits, mortgages and other retail banking products are made by the bank's treasurer responsible for managing the bank's daily cash flow and liquidity-of-funds to meet regulatory, operational, financial, and risk requirements. For larger banks, a product promotion campaign might also require the involvement of multiple departments. The result are teams operating with fragmented views at the product level, as well as at the marketing execution and pricing level. The barriers preventing a bank from greater personalization in marketing and customer communications, are often related to its organizational structure and not because the bank lacks analytical capabilities.

One-to-one marketing orchestration can be challenging for organizations with segregated teams, inadequate systems and untargeted marketing. Any project must begin with an assessment to identify gaps and maturity along organizational, conceptual and implementation dimensions to ensure the requisite capabilities including internal collaboration, data and analytics capabilities and transformation processes are present.

A well-executed one-to-one marketing strategy can deliver many benefits to a retail banking including higher customer retention, bigger share of wallet, sales profitability per customer and customer satisfaction. Personalization also directly impacts sales growth, marketing efficiency and profitability.

This article's contribution is a unique perspective on the value of combining personalization engines built on customer lifetime value and flow-of-funds modeling into a unified framework to make retail banking product offer and pricing decisions. It takes a classic approach that builds out the behavioral modeling components. Data scientists, marketers, practitioners and decision makers in the field will find the tools, methodologies and approaches in this article useful. There will be sections on designing customer lifetime value models for commercial effectiveness, flow of funds modeling, enhanced data capture for customer interactions, and behavior-based customer segmentation grids. The retail banking deposit, lending, and private banking markets are used as implementation examples.

BACKGROUND

There are three streams of research that precede this piece of work. The first stream comes from economic studies of retail banking product competition and elasticity measurement at the market level. Egan et al. (2017) developed a structural model to study the demand for deposit products. They argue that demand is influenced by product differentiation and the behavior of the banks, e.g., by setting interest rates for the deposit products. Chiu and Hill (2017) estimated elasticity of demand for retail deposits in the United Kingdom, again at the market level. Their modeling approach is based on a highly stylized single period, linear, partial equilibrium model. Karlan and Zinman (2019) estimated long-run elasticity of demand for credit products in Mexico, on the other side of the balance sheet using ordinary least squares. Hong et al. (2021) built a two-period model of revolving credit with asymmetric information and adverse selection to study pattern of changes to interest rates and balance transfer activities before and after the enactment of the CARD Act. Calomiris and Pornrojnangkool (2009) used a log-linear model to estimate the effects of relationship pricing on market demand for industrial loans. Our work assumes the perspectives of an individual bank (as opposed to the market) that wishes to optimize and personalize its pricing for its customer base.

The second stream of research comes from classic demand modeling literature. The seminal work by Berry (1994) proposed a discrete choice model to forecast demand of generic consumer products, though the model estimates are population-level averages. Latest advances in machine learning, which we rely on in our work, allows individual-level estimates to be obtained using methods such as Hierarchical Bayes.

The last stream of research solves the portfolio price optimization problem by leveraging classic demand modeling literature for a specific product area. Caufield (2012), Phillips (2018) and Phillips (2021) have all proposed various methods to solve the portfolio pricing problem for credit products. To our knowledge, no research has been published to solve the deposit side of the problem, nor was there any research focused on personalized pricing or marketing actions in the banking context. Our work attempts to unify the product-siloed methods mentioned above by proposing a framework on pricing and marketing personalization for all banking products on both sides of the balance sheet.

Data Availability and Flow of Funds Models

To support orchestrated one-on-one marketing, we need access to granular actions to understand client behaviors in greater detail and with higher fidelity.

When designing a model for a domain specific area like retail banking, one strategy is to build a model based on the kind of data that is available to us. While gathering granular client- and transaction-level information over a certain period of time is going to be highly useful in understanding how a client or a group of clients use their deposit accounts and how the funds flow between these accounts, financial institutions do not always collect such information in the same data warehouse due to its sheer size or make it easy to access by the modelers.

Instead, we may need to rely on much fewer complex data sets to approximate exact client behaviors on flow of funds. In a theory-driven approach which we call "balance delta," we take weekly or monthly snapshots of account balances over a period of time, e.g., 1-2 years, and determine banking behaviors by evaluating changes between a pair of consecutive balance snapshots and applying rules derived from common, anticipated client behaviors.

For example, if a client's checking account balance has declined by $700 while his or her high-yield savings account balance has increased by $700 over that same one-week interval, we can deduce there has been fund flows from the checking to the savings account. The issue with balance delta models is that it relies on a good understanding of common client behaviors to draw conclusions and does not always capture deviations from them. This becomes especially challenging on customers with multiple deposit accounts, as the total set of permutations on how a client might transfer funds between the accounts is astronomical in theory and asserting a common behavioral type would lead to errors.

If the aforementioned client- and transaction-level data set is indeed available, the bank can use that much bigger data set instead of balance snapshots to more precisely answer pricing and marketing questions and bypass the limitations of the "balance delta" approach. The challenge of using transaction data is, of course, the enormous scale of the exercise. Total transaction count by a large bank's retail customer base could reach billions on a single day. This includes customer fund movements internally across checking, savings, credit cards, lending and investment accounts. Banks also have data on fund movements externally to and from other financial institutions. There is also the issue of noisy data where we are working with a lot of meaningless transactions resulting in unwanted data items that do not help to explain or answer the question.

A hybrid framework where we integrate theory-driven and data-driven models can offer the best of both of worlds where we can more accurately and feasibly identify trends, patterns and correlations to answer situated questions, unlock new insights and better predict banking behaviors and patterns. For example, using this model a bank would be able to detect large outflow of funds from a high-yield deposit product, and by analyzing transactions data be able to distinguish if this was an indicator of shifting customer preference for more liquidity a sign of bank switching behavior.

Flow of funds modeling, or the analysis of a customer's fund flows internally between various deposit, lending and investing accounts, and externally involving accounts held outside the institution, can give banks the granularity needed for more accurate behavior analysis. Banks concerned about churn or attrition amongst high-value customers, can unlock intelligence on evolving banking behaviors and needs, and create an early warning system to detect competitor activities drawing deposit balances from these customer segments out of the bank.

In Figure 1, we see a bank using this hybrid modeling framework to support pricing optimization on a short-term certificate of deposit (CD). The bank wants to minimize the cost of funds while also ensuring it is meeting its institution's liquidity goals. The model is able to show that the bank's current interest rate offers on a short-term CD is competitive enough to attracted more than $2.1 million in funds from external sources and more than $13.8 million in renewals from existing customers (represented by the bright yellow box). Inflows and renewals are more than sufficient to offset the $1.8 million in outflows from short term CDs to external sources. Using a hybrid modeling approach, this bank is able to support more granular and refined demand elasticity measurements to optimize pricing for its short-term CD to meet the institution's cost and liquidity targets.

Figure 1. Example of Flow of Funds
Note. Flow of funds internally between high-yield products and checking accounts, and externally in a sample bank.

From \ To	External	HighQ and HighMarq	MMA and Other Savings	Short Term CD	Long Term CD	Checking	Others	Total	
External	-	$16.6MM	$9.5MM	$2.1MM	$158.7K	$19.3MM	$35.9K	$47.7MM	**Majority external inflow** (new money) into **savings, MMA and checking**
HighQ and HighMarq	$8.3MM	$473.3K	$65.4K	$1.3MM	$254.1K	$1.2MM	$0.1K	$11.6MM	
MMA and Other Savings	$4.9MM	$2.3MM	$246.4K	$580.1K	$245.5K	$1.3MM	$8.1K	$9.6MM	
Short Term CD	$1.8MM	$2.0MM	$384.6K	$13.8MM	$197.9K	$313.1K	·	$18.5MM	Significant flow from **short term CD** accounts to other **short term CD** accounts (Members are renewing to other short term products)
Long Term CD	$512.4K	$477.4K	$18.0K	$326.8K	$510.1K	$34.1K	·	$1.9MM	
Checking	$13.0MM	$3.0MM	$1.8MM	$734.3K	$27.5K	$1.1MM	$8.1K	$19.7MM	
Others	$65.9K	$0.4K	$13.6K	·	·	$6.1K	$2.3K	$88.3K	
Total	$28.6MM	$24.9MM	$12.0MM	$18.8MM	$1.4MM	$23.3MM	$54.4K		

Inflow
Outflow

In order to maximize the business impact from Artificial Intelligence (AL) and ML efforts, banks like many other institutions must first address the challenges surrounding data. This isn't just about the need for access to the right data type, but equally important is to have comprehensive, enterprise-wide data to support a holistic view of the customer.

To produce one-to-one marketing and personalization outputs, bank models should include both financial data as well as non-financial data. Non-financial data includes social media, life stage, client relationship, and client communication data. Internal and external data sources are also required to build more accurate models to produce robust intelligence on bank customers.

Enhanced Data Capture for Customer Interactions

Low-level implementation ML models can analyze input data to meet simple objectives like encouraging primary banking, cross selling other deposit products or prevent attrition. These ML models built with low level languages are fast, memory efficient and powerful enough to trigger an action like a bank marketing message as long as certain conditions exist. For example, when a new customer's account has lower than average debit transaction counts, a predictive machine learning model can hypothesize that he/she has not set up direct deposit. To encourage primary banking behaviors the model triggers a personalized message that includes a printable letter the customer can take to his/her human resources department to set up direct deposit. Similarly, a bank customer transferring funds to an alternative investment firm can trigger the model to send a message offering a complimentary session with a certified financial planner.

At higher levels of implementation complexity, ML models can be trained to incorporate learnings from previous communications to sequence outbound messages for maximum effectiveness. In addition to flow of funds data, more data sources including non-financial data and client attributes can be added as inputs. If a model can more accurately predict that a customer is considering purchasing a residential property, the bank can then direct a nuanced message such as "We want to reward you for your loyalty! Get special rates for your next home" to nudge him/her towards desired behaviors. These higher-level models can be used to trigger a series of sequenced communications that build on previous outbound messages to the customer. The model can recognize how customers responded to previous offers and tailor subsequent communications accordingly. A customer who responded to an offer to open a high-yield savings account might receive a sequenced message at a later date encouraging him to preserve his savings with a low-interest personal loan.

At even higher levels of implementation complexity, powerful artificial neural network and gradient boosting techniques can be used to forecast customer behaviors based on a wider range of data inputs and to address more complex tasks like orchestrating personalized communications. Data inputs are fed into a neural network consisting of millions of forward fed processing nodes. These nodes are densely interconnected through activation functions from some nodes in the last layer to one node in the next layer. Typical activation functions include linear regression, binary logit, or tanh function. New models are added to the neural network ensemble sequentially using gradient boosting. The process of iteratively adding new models by searching in the direction of steepest gradient ascent or descent, allows new weak, base-learner models to be trained stepwise by optimizing new parameters and based on what the whole ensemble has learned thus far. The idea is to iterate towards an improved model with each iteration, where we are changing the model in a way that leads to an improved prediction with each step.

Extreme Gradient Boosting (XGBoost) can be used to improve gradient boosting by adding regularization terms and by using both 1st and 2nd order gradients. Using neural networks and XGBoost algorithms, banks are able to predict with a degree of accuracy higher than 80% which products existing customer would want to use in the near future based on their past behaviors. This insight can also be applied to individuals with similar behaviors and characteristics.

Customer Lifetime Value Models

Banks need a way to measure and predict the customer lifetime value (CLV) of its current customer base in order to efficiently focus customer acquisition, retention, relationship management, loyalty and cross-selling efforts. Like most industries, a smaller percentage of customer represent a large percentage of the bank's profits and revenues. Customer acquisition costs are high in retail banking, and what matters most is the value of long-lasting and expanding relationships with customer.

To calculate CLV, banks can use a method like RFM (recency, frequency and monetary) to analyze historical data to extract recency (most recent revenue generating transactions), frequency (how often) and monetary (how much spend) values. Banks can use the RFM method to estimate the customer lifetime value of its entire customer universe, and extrapolate this to estimate CLV for the current customer base.

Customers can be assigned a CLV score. Weights can also be applied to each parameter based on the importance of the value, while additional dimensions like the customer relationship length can be added as another element.

As shown in Figure 2, top quartile customers who are active (recency), have multiple bank products (frequency) and maintains high account balances (monetary) are assigned a high CLV score represented by the green dots. A high potential or mid-score customer with lower recency, frequency and monetary values will be clustered or segmented into a different group - in this case yellow dots. Now the bank can apply a differentiated strategy - retention activities for the high-score customer and development efforts for the mid-score customer - to maximize marketing yield.

Figure 2. Customer Lifetime Value Scores
Note. Customer Lifetime Value (CLV) scores can help banks focus on the most relevant customers.

Historical data is useful to understand how customer's banking needs and behaviors change over time. For example, it is useful to know at what point in time a customer goes from being a net borrower to become a net investor or saver.

When defining an appropriate time frame for CLV calculations, it is useful to take into consideration uncertainty, the dynamic nature of banking behaviors, and the ever-evolving banking environment. In retail banking, using historical data to predict behaviors over the next six to 18 months is an acceptable, conservative time horizon to yield reliable results.

Another important exercise to support more accurate CLV calculations is to acquire a realistic view of churn behaviors and rates for predictive purposes. This includes analyzing data to determine the correlations between behavior and customers who churn, an estimate of which customers are most likely to leave in the next 30 days, establishing benchmarks, and tracking how churn behaviors change over time.

Behavioral Segmentation Models

Behavioral segmentation where we divide customers based on their behavior patterns is a powerful way for banks to understand how customers use bank products and services, and make purchasing decisions. Behavioral segmentation can also reveal buyer readiness, customer loyalty status, product or service usage patterns, and benefits sought to support more precise targeting and personalization of messages to support desired behavior outcomes.

Consider a situation where a bank is attempting to predict which products existing customers will most like use in the near future based on their past behaviors and based on usage patterns of similar customers. Here the bank analyzes customer product usage and transactions data to segment customers over different time frames to predict future customer needs. Data is unlabeled, but can be divided into groups based on similarity and other measures of natural patterns within the data, so an unsupervised clustering algorithm like K-Means, Mean shift or Gaussian Mixture Models can be used. Comparing customer clusters over different time periods can yield insights about future customer needs

Customer Level Pricing

Customer-level pricing is a pricing strategy where prices are set according to the customer's elasticity or perceived value of the product or service. The objective of customer-level pricing is not to extract every last cent of the customer's willingness to pay for a product, as this does not necessarily lead to the most profitable outcome. Rather we are trying to construct an intelligent system that takes into account the various constraints the bank is operating within including competition, volume, market share, branch presence, risk and cost to serve, to meet the bank's business objectives.

In customer-level pricing, the banks first sets a risk-based floor price. The bank prices loans and sets terms based on the customer's risk profile, and adds a fixed profit margin to the risk rate. Since risk is inversely correlated with price elasticity, the bank will find low-risk borrowers unwilling to pay more than the risk-based floor rate, which means the bank earns no profit. By comparison riskier borrowers are willing to pay more than the risk-based floor rate. By differentiating pricing for elastic and inelastic customer segments, banks can defend the volume of business from low-risk, price sensitive segments and harvest margin from less price sensitive segments.

To segment or classify customers based on their price sensitivities, banks can leverage predictive decision tree techniques. In Figure 3, a decision tree shows the probability that a new mortgage applicant will have pricing sensitivity (PS) classifications one through 15, based on mortgage term length.

The tree considers a number of factors impacting customer's price sensitivities like the tenure of the customer with the bank, branch density, customer's risk score, loan amount, first time buyer and acquisition channel. This decision tree can be repeated for other mortgage product dimension including type of mortgage, variable versus fixed rate, and amortization period. Similarly, the process can be used for mortgage renewals.

Figure 3. Decision Tree Classification Technique
Note. Decision tree classification technique used to segment new mortgage applicants by their pricing sensitivities based on mortgage term length product dimension.

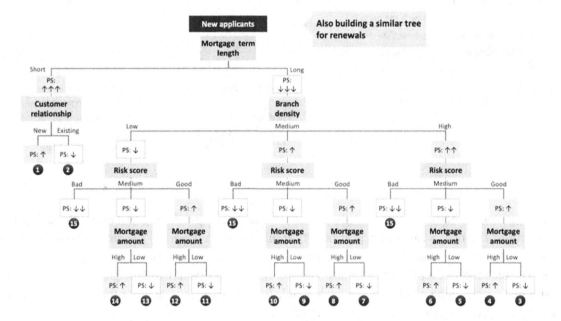

To support personalized pricing, banks can contruct a granular elasticity-based pricing grid to include three dimensions: product, risk and pricing sensitivity as shown in Figure 4. However, banks must beware that there is a limit to how much granularity should be introduced. There are after all only so many price points available for a mortgage loan.

Figure 4. Example of a Granular Pricing Sheet for Mortgages (rates and fees)
Note. *A granular pricing grid with product, risk and pricing sensitivity dimensions can be constructed to support a differentiated pricing strategy for elastic and inelastic segments.*

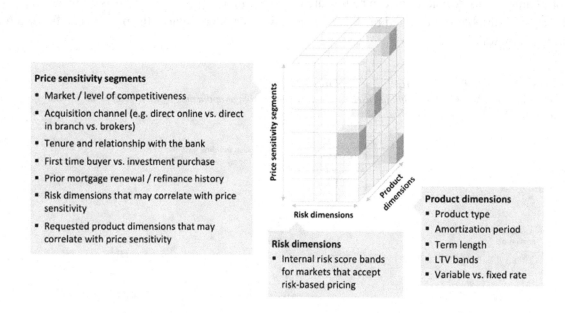

In the example shown in Figure 5, a bank wants to maximize portfolio profitability through pricing optimization. The bank's maximum profitability frontier is represented by the curved boundary which takes into account business constraints including competition, cost to serve, risk appetite, volume, and more. The blue triangle represents the bank's portfolio profitability and volume goal. Using a nonlinear constrained optimization algorithm, the bank is able to automatically search for the best pricing grid to reach the desired profitability and volume outcomes.

Figure 5. Pricing Optimization
Note. *Using a nonlinear constrained optimization algorithm, a bank can automatically search for the best pricing grid in an effort to reach the desire future state where the dual goal of portfolio profitability and volume is optimized.*

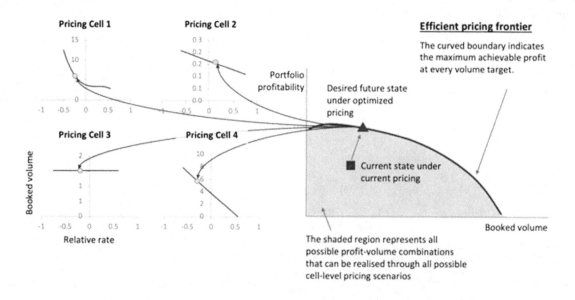

FUTURE RESEARCH DIRECTIONS

While there is robust research on pricing optimization and personalization in retail, airlines and hospitality industries, this is not the case in retail banking, despite the fact that near-perfect customer experiences are increasingly a non-negotiable attribute in this sector. Interest and research in price optimization in retail banking grew after the financial crisis of 2007-8 as banks look for ways to squeeze more profits from pricing. More recently, research have been focused on greater personalization in retail banking.

The idea that banks should look at their customers through a holistic or comprehensive lens as opposed to from a single-product perspective is not new. In his book, *Pricing and Revenue Optimization* published in 2005 by Stanford Business Press, Robert Phillips argued that banks and lending institutions "should take into account not only single product profitability but also cross-product and longer-term relationship profitability" when building price optimization engines.

Future research opportunities include contrasting the traditional optimization framework for modeling customer behavior, where a predicted behavior like booking a flight is calculated as a function of price, with a machine learning approach focused on the end question of what to offer to whom. Determine if the input is viable.

Another area is the application of multivariate optimization instead of modeling components when iterating combinations of offer and price presentment. In the paper, *An Efficient Bandit Algorithm for Real-time Multivariate Optimization*, the authors, all from Amazon explored the challenge of optimizing a large decision space like a webpage using fractional factorial design. The team applied multi-armed bandit methodology to explore the layout space and used hill-climbing to select optimal content in real-time. This can be a time-efficient way to explore feasible solutions and iteratively test machine-learning generated offers. However, the challenge in taking financial institutions down this path, is that this increasingly becomes a black box where the inner workings or logic of how the system converts inputs into outputs are opaque and not available for inspection. Banks tend to be more risk adverse than tech companies when it comes to new approaches to offer optimization. Another area for future research is generating more effective explanations to business users on the application of machine learning and other advanced analytical techniques in offer optimization.

CONCLUSION

Customer-level pricing, behavioral segmentation, customer lifetime value and flow-of-funds modeling and ML personalization are not by itself new. However, by putting these together under a unified framework, banks can have a viable approach to shift pricing and marketing optimization efforts from focusing on single-product sales to consider instead the customer's full banking relationship. While this approach is not without technical hurdles, the greater challenge is getting banks to overcome organizational silos.

Banks trying to predict churn rate or attrition will find it more useful to observe how balances run down over time. New customers are always going to be a smaller percentage of the bank customer population. Banks should also be wary of over-granularity, and consider what is practical and implementable. Another reality to consider is recognizing the usefulness of historical data past a certain point in time, given how much and how rapidly the banking industry and consumer banking behaviors change from one year to the next.

REFERENCES

Berry, S. T. (1994, Summer). Estimating discrete-choice models of product differentiation. *The RAND Journal of Economics*, 25(2), 242–262. doi:10.2307/2555829

Calomiris, C. W., & Pornrojnangkool, T. (2009). Relationship banking and the pricing of financial services. *Journal of Financial Services Research*, 35(3), 189–224. doi:10.100710693-009-0058-7

Caufield, S. (2012). Consumer credit pricing. In Ö. Özer & R. Phillips (Eds.), *The Oxford Handbook of Pricing Management* (pp. 181–199). Oxford University Press.

Charles, C., & Pornrojnangkool, T. (2009). Relationship banking and the pricing of financial services. *Journal of Financial Services Research*, 35(3), 189–224. doi:10.100710693-009-0058-7

Chiu, C.-W., & Hill, J. (2017, March). The rate elasticity of retail deposits. *International Journal of Central Banking*, 14(2), 113–157.

Egan, M., Hortaçsu, A., & Matvos, G. (2017, January). Deposit competition and financial fragility: Evidence from the US banking sector. *The American Economic Review*, 107(1), 169–216. doi:10.1257/aer.20150342

Hong, S., Hunt, R. M., & Serfes, K. (2021, November). *Dynamic pricing of credit cards and the effects of regulation dynamic pricing*. Working paper.

Karlan, D., & Zinman, J. (2019, July). Long-run price elasticities of demand for credit: Evidence from a countrywide field experiment in Mexico. *The Review of Economic Studies*, 86(4), 1704–1746. doi:10.1093/restud/rdy046

Phillips, R. L. (2018). *Pricing Credit Products*. Stanford University Press. doi:10.1515/9781503605657

Phillips, R. L. (2021). *Pricing and Revenue Optimization* (2nd ed.). Stanford University Press. doi:10.1515/9781503614260

ADDITIONAL READING

Arora, N., Dreze, X., Ghose, A., Hess, J. D., Iyengar, R., Jing, B., Joshi, Y., Kumar, V., Lurie, N., Neslin, S., Sajeesh, S., Su, M., Syam, N., Thomas, J., & Zhang, Z. J. (2008). Putting One-to-one Marketing to Work: Personalization, Customization, and Choice. *Marketing Letters*, 19(3), 305–321. doi:10.100711002-008-9056-z

Chen, K. (2020). The Effects of Marketing on Commercial Banks' Operating Businesses and Profitability: Evidence from US Bank Holding Companies. *International Journal of Bank Marketing*, 38(5), 1059–1079. doi:10.1108/IJBM-08-2019-0301

ChenQ. (2021, August). *Book Transparency and Deposit Flows*. Working Paper. https://ssrn.com/abstract=3212873 doi:10.2139/ssrn.3212873

Christensen, C. M., Cook, S., & Hall, T. (2005, December). Marketing Malpractice: The Cause and the Cure. *Harvard Business Review*. Available at: https://hbr.org/2005/12/marketing-malpractice-the-cause-and-the-cure

Edelman, D. C., & Abraham, M. (2022, March-April). Customer Experience in the Age of AI. *Harvard Business Review*. Available at: https://hbr.org/2022/03/customer-experience-in-the-age-of-ai

Mills, S. (2022). Personalized nudging. *Behavioural Public Policy, 6*(1), 150–159. doi:10.1017/bpp.2020.7

Özer, Ö., & Phillips, R. L. (Eds.). (2012). *Customized pricing. The Handbook of Pricing Management*. Oxford University Press. doi:10.1093/oxfordhb/9780199543175.001.0001

Talluri, K. T., & van Ryzin, G. J. (2004). *The Theory and Practice of Revenue Management*. Springer. doi:10.1007/b139000

Wuebker, G., Baumgarten, J., Schmidt-Gallas, D., & Koderisch, M. (2008). *Price Management in Financial Services*. Gower Publishing Limited.

Zhang, J., & Wedel, M. (2009). The Effectiveness of Customized Promotions in Online and Offline Stores. *JMR, Journal of Marketing Research, 46*(2), 190–206. doi:10.1509/jmkr.46.2.190

KEY TERMS AND DEFINITIONS

Behavioral Segmentation: A form of customer segmentation that is based on patterns of behavior displayed by customers as they interact with a company/brand or make a purchasing decision.

Flow of Funds Modeling: The analysis of a bank customer's fund flows internally between various deposit, lending and investing accounts, and externally involving accounts held outside the institution.

Machine Learning Personalization: Creates higher quality recommendations that respond to the specific needs, preferences, and changing behavior of users, improving engagement and conversion.

Market Segmentation: Process of dividing a broad consumer or business market, normally consisting of existing and potential customers, into sub-groups of consumers (known as segments) based on some type of shared characteristics.

Nonparametric: Procedures that rely on few or no assumptions about the shape or parameters of the population distribution from which the sample was drawn.

One-to-One Marketing: One-to-one marketing (also called personalization) are campaigns tailored to a consumer's interests, demographics and point in the customer journey. It involves leveraging data and digital technologies to target and tailor marketing, offers and advertisement such that they are extremely relevant to the consumer's interests in an effort to increase sales/conversion.

Parametric Statistics: Procedures that rely on assumptions about the shape of the distribution in the underlying population and about the form or parameters of the assumed distribution.

Personalized Pricing: Strategies that predict an individual customer's valuation for a product and then offer a price tailored to that customer.

Price Optimization Models: The use of mathematical analysis to calculate demand elasticity at various price levels, and combining that data with dynamic market conditions including costs, inventory, competitive intelligence and behaviors to recommend prices with the goal of improving profits.

Section 25
Fuzzy Logic and Soft Computing

Data Hierarchies for Generalization of Imprecise Data

D

Frederick Petry
Naval Research Laboratory, USA

Ronald R. Yager
Iona College, USA

INTRODUCTION

Issues related to managing imprecise data in areas as diverse as spatial and environmental data, forensic evidence and economics must be dealt with for effective decision making. In order to make use of such information, we have to settle on how the various pieces of data can be used to make a decision or take an action. This can involve some sort of summarization and generalization of the pieces of data as to what conclusions they can support (Yager, 1991; Kacpryzk, 1999; Dubois & Prade, 2000). A currently emerging issue is the management of uncertain information arising from multiple sources and of many forms that appear in the everyday activities and decisions of humans. This can range from data / information obtained by sensors to the subjective information from individuals or analysts. Today ever more massive amounts of multi-source heterogeneous data / information is prevalent such as in systems managing the problem of Big Data (Miller & Miller, 2013; Richards & Rowe, 1999) However while effective decision-making should be able to make use of all the available, relevant information about such combined uncertainty, assessment of the value of a generalization result is critical. One possible approach for such a generalization process can be found in the use of concept hierarchical generalization (Raschia & Mouaddib, 2002; Yager & Petry, 2006). In previous research the problem of evidence resolution was studied for crisp concept hierarchies (Petry & Yager, 2008).

As one example of where data generalization is needed for decision making is with data related to criminal forensics. Federal Bureau of Investigation (FBI) researchers have made use of GIS data for forensic evidence evaluation in criminal cases. Spatial distribution of soils (Pye, 2007), pollens (Brown, Smith & Elmhurst, 2002) and other trace evidence are represented by individual layers with uncertainty as to the exact spatial areas of such information. These are then overlaid, generalized and the areas aggregated to focus on possible sites of interest for further investigation of a crime.

For example, in the case of a suspicious death, depending on the environmental conditions, a medical examiner may provide a likely range of time of death, but allow a possible wider time interval. So, overlap between the above time of death and a temporal interval when a potential suspect might have been in the area of the murder could be crucial in an investigation. Also, forensic anthropology is concerned with evaluations of skeletal-age-at- death (Hoppa & Vaupel, 2002) and must deal with the uncertainties of missing remains and weathering effects to provide estimates of possible temporal age intervals.

To address these issues the use of fuzzy, interval valued and intuitionistic concept hierarchies for generalization can extend previous approaches to deal with the uncertainty of data. A number of approaches to characterizing such decompositions for the resolution of the evidence using these hierarchies is also needed. The characterization of hierarchies indicates that set decompositions are needed to represent the

DOI: 10.4018/978-1-7998-9220-5.ch117

uncertainty of the hierarchies. To characterize these decompositions granularity measures and overlap measures must be developed and examples of each discussed. Additionally, information measures can introduce to be used for these evaluations.

BACKGROUND

Uncertainty Representations

Here we review some of the most common representations of subjective uncertainty that have been developed in the computational intelligence area. We will specifically consider the first three described next, fuzzy set theory, interval valued sets, and intuitionistic fuzzy sets for approaches to generalization of such data to concept hierarchies. The other types could be used in a similar approach.

Fuzzy Set Theory

In ordinary sets a data values either belongs or does not belong to the set. However fuzzy set theory (Zadeh, 1965; Klir, St. Clair & Yuan, 1997) allows a gradual assessment of the membership of data values in a set described by of a membership function. Where elements can either belong or not belong to a regular set, with fuzzy sets elements can belong to the set to a certain degree with zero indicating not an element, one indicating complete membership, and values between zero and one indicating partial or uncertain membership in the set. For a domain S a fuzzy set is

$$Fs(S) = \{d_i \,/\, m(d_i); 0 \le m(d_i) \le 1\}, d_i \in S$$

Interval-Valued Sets

Uncertainty of data is commonly represented in many applications by the use of interval values. We will introduce here the formalisms for intervals and interval arithmetic (Moore, 1966; Deschrijver, 2007; Moore, Kearfott, & Cloud, 2009) as needed. We let D be the domain and intervals will be represented by the values of the lower bound, $z_\dagger = Lb(d_i)$ and an upper bound, $z^\dagger = Ub(d_i)$ of an interval $I\,(d_i)$, $d_i \in D$

$$I\,(d_i) = [z_\dagger, z^\dagger] = \{z \in D \mid z_\dagger \le z \le z^\dagger\}$$

For an interval $I\,(d_i)$, we define the size of the interval, Q, as the difference of the lower and upper bounds,

$$Q: I\,(d_i) \to R^+; Q\,(I\,(d_i)) = \mid z_\dagger - z^\dagger \mid$$

So a representation of uncertainty of a data value d_i by intervals using a lower bound, and an upper bound,

$$\{d_i \mid I(d_i) = [Lb(d_i), Ub(d_i)]\}$$

Intuitionistic Fuzzy Sets

Intuitionistic fuzzy set theory extends ordinary fuzzy set theory by allowing both positive and negative memberships to be specified. Recall an ordinary fuzzy set $Fs(S) = \{d_i / m(d_i)\}$ has only one membership value for a data element d_i. An intuitionistic fuzzy set $IFs(S)$ (Atanassov, 1986) allows both positive and negative membership values.

$$IFs(S) = \{< d_i, m_S(d_i), m_S^*(d_i) = 1 - m_S(d_i) > \mid d_i \in D\} \text{ where } m_S(d_i), m^*_S(d_i), \in [0,1].$$

Since the sum of the membership, $m_S(d_i)$, and non-membership, $m_S^*(d_i)$, is not necessarily one then: $0 \leq m_S(d_i) + m^*_S(d_i) \leq 1$. Additionally, the hesitation $h_S(d_i)$

$$h_S(d_i) = 1 - (m_S(d_i) + m^*_S(d_i))$$

is the degree of indeterminacy (hesitation).

Type-2 Fuzzy Sets

A type 2 fuzzy set T2 (Mendel, 2007) is one in which the membership values are themselves uncertain and can be represented by a fuzzy set itself. So if there is no uncertainty in the membership function this reduces to ordinary sets.

$$T2(X) = \{< (x, r), \mu_T(x,r) > \mid x \in X\} \text{ where } r \in P_x \subseteq [0,1].$$

Rough Set Theory: The core concept of rough sets is an indiscernibility relation R on the domain X (Pawlak, 1985). A rough set A, is specified by using the upper R^uX and lower approximations, R_lX of X.

lower approximation of X in A is the set $R_lX = \{x \in U / [x]_R \subseteq X\}$
upper approximation of X in A is the set $R^uX = \{x \in U / [x]_R \cap X \neq \emptyset\}$.

where $[x]_R$ denotes the equivalence class of the indiscernibility relation R containing x.

In summary the lower approximation of a set is a *conservative* approximation comprising only elements which can definitely determine to be members of the set. The upper approximation is a *liberal* approximation including all elements that might be members of the set.

Dempster- Shafer Uncertainty Theory

Dempster-Shafer (D-S) theory is a well-known approach to modeling uncertainty (Shafer, 1976) providing representation of non-specific forms of uncertainty. A Dempster-Shafer belief structure consists of a collection of non-empty crisp subsets of a space X called focal elements: $R_1, ...R_q$. The mass or basic probability, bp, is used to assign a belief to each element of the power set:

$$bp: 2^X \rightarrow [0,1]$$

So here our knowledge of the value of a variable is inexact where for focal set, $R_i \subset X$, $bp(R_i)$ indicates the probability that the value is in R_i. Two important properties of bp are: 1. basic probability of the empty set is zero,

1. $bp(\Phi) = 0$

and 2. the bps of the remaining elements of the power set sum to 1,

2. $\sum_{R_i \in 2^X} bp(R_i) = 1$

Two commonly used measures for a Dempster-Shafer belief structure are measures of belief (best case) and plausibility (worst case). The belief for a specific set S, Bel (S), is the sum of the basic probabilities of all subsets of S:

$$Bel(S) = \sum_{R_i \subseteq S} m(R_i)$$

The plausibility, Pl(S), is the sum of the bps of the sets R_i that intersect S:

$$Pl(S) = \sum_{R_i \cap S = \varnothing} m(R_i)$$

FOCUS OF THE ARTICLE

Fuzzy hierarchies enable the expression of partial IS-A semantic relationships (with membership values between data values, $d_i \in D = \{d_1, d_2, ..., d_p\}$ and the related (Bachman, 1983) concepts, $C_j \in C = \{C_1, C_2, ...C_q\}$. For fuzzy hierarchies, a concept is regarded as a partial specification of generalized data with the corresponding membership degrees m_{ji} in the [0, 1] interval (Petry & Yager, 2014). If $m_{ji} = 1$ there is a complete specification as in crisp concept hierarchies. So for a fuzzy hierarchy at each level we have a corresponding fuzzy relationship, R(D, C), which maps data onto a specific concept

$d_i \rightarrow C_j$ with membership $m_j(d_i)$

This defines a decomposition of the data as it is mapped to the concepts in the hierarchy. The overlapping of the fuzzy data mapping to concepts results in fuzzy equivalence classes related to these concepts. So we have fuzzy sets of data, R_j, for each concept, C_j. That is there is a set decomposition of the data domain D, R_1, R_2, R_q for which:

$R_j \cap R_k \neq \varnothing; \cup_j R_j = D$, for j = 1 to q.

As a result, there are data values, $d_i \in D$, which do not generalize to only one, unique concept C_j. So R_j corresponding to C_j might contain data values such as $\{d_{i-2}, d_{i-1}, d_i\}$ and Rj_{+1} representing C_{j+1} is {. di, $d_{i+1},...\}$. An overlapping data value such as d_i has a degree of membership $m_j(d_i)$ in R_j and $m_{j+1}(d_i)$ in R_{j+1}. Then $R_j = \{di_{-2} / m_j(d_{i-2}), di_{-1} / mj(d_{i-1}), d_i / m_j(d_i) .$

Intuitionistic Fuzzy Hierarchies

Next, we will extend this approach to consider intuitionistic fuzzy relationships in a concept hierarchy. The generalization hierarchies for intuitionistic fuzzy sets will then entail relationships of positive and negative memberships to the concepts in the hierarchy. In the hierarchy then we will have two sets in the concept decomposition, positive for ordinary memberships and negative for non-membership degrees. So, for a given concept C_j, the set of data values R_j would consist of the sets P_j and Nj. For example, then we can have a data value d_i in both sets, $R_j = Pj \cup N_j$.

$$P_j = \{d_i / m_j(d_i)\} \ N_j = \{d_i / m^*_j(d_i)\}$$

When a value d_i is generalized to a concept C_j, since it can have both positive and negative membership values, this could indicate support or lack of support for the concept. Based on this as a further refinement we can consider dividing the data generalized by considering data for which the d_i has a membership in which the $m_j(d_i)$ is greater or less than $m_j(d_i)$. So now we have $R_j = P1_j \cup N1_j$:

$$P1_j = \{d_i \mid (m_j(d_i) > 0 \wedge m_j(d_i) \geq m^*_j(d_i))\}$$
$$N1_j = \{d_i \mid (m_j(d_i) > 0 \wedge m_j(d_i) \leq m^*_j(d_i))\}$$

We can consider a further approach to structure of intuitionistic generalization of data in the concepts. We have shown a structure of sets where the positive negative membership values are greater for the data. However, for evaluations if the memberships are relatively small then the structure has less usefulness. For example if $m_j(d_i) = .2$ and $m^*_j(d_i) = .1$, the distinction of $m_j(d_i)$ being greater is less important. So we introduce a structure in which the larger positive or negative membership is greater than some threshold T, such as 0.4.

$$P11_j = \{d_i \mid (m_j(d_i) > 0 \wedge m_j(d_i) \geq m^*_j(d_i) \wedge m_j(d_i) \geq T)\}$$
$$P12_j = \{d_i \mid (m_j(d_i) > 0 \wedge m_j(d_i) \geq m^*_j(d_i) \wedge m_j(d_i) < T)\}$$
$$N11_j = \{d_i \mid (m_j(d_i) > 0 \wedge m_j(d_i) \leq m^*_j(d_i) \wedge m^*_j(d_i) \geq T)\}$$
$$N11_j = \{d_i \mid (m_j(d_i) > 0 \wedge m_j(d_i) \leq m^*_j(d_i)) \wedge m^*_j(d_i) < T\}$$

Interval Valued Hierarchies

So, we want to consider how to treat interval valued data values for use in generalization. Two issues may be whether or not there is a single source of a data's value or multiple sources of measurement or specifications of the data. Based on the semantics of the concepts being considered in a generalization application, interval valued data may generalize to more than just a single concept. The specification for a specific concept might give a range for which data would be associated with that particular concept C_j:

$$I(C_j) = [Lb(C_j), Ub(C_j)]$$

We then have several cases to consider for the generalization of interval valued data to such concepts:

1. Data interval contained in a concept interval: $I(d_i) \subseteq I(C_j)$
2. Data interval overlaps a concept interval: $I(d_i) \cap I(C_j) \neq \emptyset$

3.   The intervals are disjoint and so the data does not map to the concept: $I(d_i) \cap I(C_j) = \emptyset$

For example, let there be three concepts indicating the range of sizes that specify a particular object:

Concept 1: $I(C_1) = [Lb(C_1) = 2, Ub(C_1) = 5]$
Concept 2: $I(C_2) = [Lb(C_2) = 6, Ub(C_2) = 10]$
Concept 3: $I(C_3) = [Lb(C_3) = 11, Ub(C_3) = 20]$

Now we consider three data values d_1, d_2, d_3

$\{d_1 / I(d_1) = [Lb(d_1) = 2, Ub(d_1)=8]; d_2 / I(d_2) = [Lb(d_1) = 11, Ub(d_2)=15]; d_3 / I(d_3) = [Lb(d_3) = 7, Ub(d_3)=9]\}\}$

So

Case 1: $R(C_1) = \emptyset$; $R(C_2) = \{d_3\}$; $R(C_3) = \{d_2\}$;
Case 2: $R(C_1) = \{d_1\}$; $R(C_2) = \{d_1, d_3\}$; $R(C_3) = \{d_2\}$;

SOLUTIONS AND RECOMMENDATIONS

In order to make effective usage of generalizations for decision making, measures and metrics must be used to provide analysis of the generalizations.

Decomposition Measures

For use of generalizations to concepts we must consider approaches to compare the concepts to inform decision-making. We can use measures such as granularity and overlap of data associated with different concepts. The most granular partitioning of data is where all values are lumped into the one set and the finest partition is where each data value is in a separate set. A measure termed coarseness or granularity (Yager, 2008) was used to characterize partitioning where the coarseness of the maximum partition was greatest, 1, and the minimum was the finest, 0 granularity. We will examine an extension of this coarseness measure from partitions to apply for decompositions. In order to apply these measures, they must be extended to fuzzy sets. The original formulation relies on the count of the number of elements in the partition sets but for a fuzzy set, R_j, the scalar cardinality or sigma count (Yen & Langari, 1999) must be utilized instead.

$$K = Card\,(R_j) = \sum_{d_i \in R_j} m_j\,(d_i)$$

Also we can use the common t-norm, $\wedge$, which uses the minimum of the membership values. For set intersections in the overlap measure, Olp, we utilize the t-norm. So now we have

$$Grn(R_1, R_2, \ldots R_q) = (\sum_{j=1}^{q} Card\,(R_j)^2) - K) / (K^2 - K); K = \sum_{j=1}^{q} Card\,(R_j)$$

and

$$Olp(R_j) = (\sum_{j=1, j \neq 1}^{q} Card\ (R_i \cap R_j) / Card\ (R_j\ )) / (q\text{-}1)$$

$$Olp(R_1, R_2, \ldots R_q) = (\sum_{j=1}^{q} Olp\ (R_j)) / q$$

We can consider the refinement of granularity for intuitionistic sets by using the structure of $R_j = P_j \cup N_j$

$$P_j = \{ \ldots d_i / m_j(d_i) \ldots \}\ N_j = \{ \ldots d_i / m^*_j(d_i) \ldots \}$$

Then we can have the granularity of the positive and negative subsets of R

$$Grn(P_1, P_2, \ldots P_q) = (\sum_{j=1}^{q} Card\ (P_j)^2) - K) / (K^2 - K);$$

and similarly

$$Grn(N_1, N_2, \ldots N_q) = (\sum_{j=1}^{q} Card\ (N_j)^2) - K) / (K^2 - K);$$

We can consider a simple example of this:

$$P_1 = \{ d_1 / .4, d_2 / .5, d_4 / .4 \},\ P_2 = \{ d_2 / .3, d_3 / .5 \}$$
$$N_1 = \{ d_1 / .3, d_3 / .1 \},\ N_2 = \{ d_1 / .3, d_2 / .2, d_3 / .2, d_4 / .6 \}$$

Then $c_P = 2.1$ and $c_N = 1.7$. So for P_1 and P_2

$$Grn(P_1, P_2) = ((1.3^2 + .8^2) - 2.1) / 2.31 = (2.33\text{-}2.1) / 2.31 = .1$$

A similar computation gives

$$Grn(N_1, N_2) = (1.85\text{-}1.7) / 1.19 = .13$$

Now we can compare this to the full sets R_1, R_2

$$Grn(R_1, R_2) = ((1.7^2 + 2.1^2) - 3.8) / 10.64 = (3.5) / 10.64 = .33$$

So we can see the finer structure gives lower granularity than the original set

$$Grn(P_1, P_2) + Grn(N_1, N_2) = .23 < Grn(R_1, R_2) = .33$$

This follows the reasoning that granularity is larger as more values combined into one set where the maximum possible granularity is one.

In general, there may be many situations in which several domain experts are interpreting the data. Variations of possible interpretations are to be expected and can correspond to different decompositions of the data being analysed. Both the generalization, Grn, and the overlap, Olp, measures can then be utilized in the comparisons of these decompositions.

In considering how to apply interpretations of the two measures account must be taken of dependence on particular application criteria. If the data has been evaluated as mostly indicating relationship to only a few concepts, then the coarseness or granularity measure will be greatest. This implies that in these specific concepts there can be stronger confidence. On the other hand, a smaller granularity could mean that evaluations are more broadly spread out over the concepts implying a lack of consensus. However, in the case of values at either extreme, we could feel that a more natural variability has not been effectively represented. So, an assessment with intermediate values could be more useful, such as not considering outlying cases from some of the many experts' interpretations.

Also, to further consider cases of nearly identical coarseness, the overlap measures can differ and be used as additional criteria for decisions. Specifically, as the decomposition of the data being interpreted tends more closely to a static, crisp, partition, because there is then less overlapping and the Olp measure is lower. This can be seen to indicate less spread of the data and greater focus on specific concepts to guide decision-making.

Intuitionistic Data Resolution

We can discuss several different cases of data resolution, distinguishing complete and partial resolution for intuitionistic memberships. By resolution we refer to the concepts to which data values generalize.

Complete Data Resolution

Case 1. All of the data d_i with both positive and negative memberships, $m_j(d_i)$, $m^*_j(d_i)$, generalizes to at least one concept C_j. To focus on just the data values for describing resolution we denote the generalized set of data as Rd, of just the data values.

So for this case for C_j
$Res(D) = Pd_j = Nd_j$
Example: $D = \{ d_1, d_2, d_3 \}$ and
$m_j(d_1) = .6$, $m^*_j(d_1) = .3$
$m_j(d_2) = .2$, $m^*_j(d_2) = .5$
$m_j(d_3) = .7$, $m^*_j(d_3) = .2$
So $Pd_j = \{ d_1, d_2, d_3 \} = Nd_j$

Case 2. This case is a complete resolution for D as all memberships are strictly either positive or negative.

$Res(D) = Pd_j$ or Nd_j; $Pd_j \cap Nd_j = \emptyset$

For example if all memberships are positive

$Pd_j = \{d_1, d_2, d_3 \}$, $Nd_j = \emptyset$

Case 3. This last case is a complete resolution for D where all data values d_i generalize to one concept C_j, but some d_i have positive intuitionistic memberships and other negative memberships. So we have

$Res(D) = Pd_j \cup Nd_j$

Example:
$m_j(d_1) = .6$, $m^*_j(d_2) = .3$, $m^*_j(d_3) = .3$

$Pd_j = \{ d_1 \}; Nd_j = \{ d_2, d_3 \}$

Partial Data Resolution

Here we do not have at least one concept C_j that all $d_i \in D$ can resolve to. This can have a range cases, first from the case of only one data value d_s, regardless of whether its membership is positive or negative.

$Res (D - \{ d_s \}) = R_j$

and

$d_s \in R_k, k \neq j$

The other extreme of the range is where there is a subset of D, $\{d_1, d_2,, \ldots d_q\}$ such that

$d_1 \in R_1, d_2 \in R_2, \ldots d_q \in R_q$

This means at least some of the data has spread its generalization relationship over all of the possible concepts.

Information Measures

Another approach could use information measures to make comparisons of the generalized sets. If some concepts have higher values of information measures, these could then be more important for an application. Information metrics have been developed for both the ordinary fuzzy sets and intuitionistic fuzzy sets that comprise the concept's contents. In order to judge the usefulness of generalized fuzzy information, we can make use of measures such as the Shannon entropy and the Gini index.

The Shannon measure of information is a well-known and widely used measure of information content (Shannon, 1948; Reza, 1961). For a probability distribution, $P = (p_1, p_2, \ldots, p_n)$, this is given as

$$S(P) = - \sum_{j=1}^{n} p_j \ln (p_j).$$

Another measure related to information content is the Gini index, G(P). The Gini index (Gini, 1921; Giorgi & Gigliarano, 2017) characterizes statistical dispersion according to

$$G(P) = 1 - \sum_{j=1}^{n} p_j^2.$$

The Gini measure is co-extensive with Shannon entropy (Yager, 1995) and since it does not entail a logarithm, G(P) may be used instead of S(P) to simplify tasks like formal analysis.

For fuzzy sets an entropy can be given as an extension of the Shannon definition of a fuzzy set (de-Luca & Termini, 1972).

$$Entropy (R_j) = - \sum_{d_i \in R_j} m(d_i) \ln (m(d_i)).$$

There have been a number of entropy measures formulated for intuitionistic and interval-valued fuzzy sets. These have been variously based on similarity (Zhang et al., 2009; Zeng & Li, 2006) and distance measures (Zeng et al., 2011) as well as geometric interpretations (Szmidt & Kacpryzk 2001).

In particular we will use a measure from Burillo and Bustince (1996) that considered a number of possible fuzzy entropies for intuitionistic fuzzy sets.

So we have for the data di in $P_j \cup N_j$

$$\text{Entropy } (R_j) = \sum_{j=1}^{n} (1 - (m_j(d_i) + m^*_j(d_i)))$$

FUTURE RESEARCH DIRECTIONS

There are a number of other representations that can be used in data generalization as we have discussed including rough set theory and Dempster-Shafer theory. These representations have a more complex structure and several extensions to generalization must be developed for these.

Also new recent uncertainty approaches have been researched that should be considered for future work. Pythagorean membership functions (PFS) are a generalization of intuitionistic memberships (Yager, 2014). In particular by generalizing the negation of a membership value $m_j = 1 - m_j$ is instead a Pythagorean negation

$$(not(m_j))^2 = 1 - m_j^2 .$$

So then the space of these sort of memberships is greater, i.e. Pythagorean membership function allows extended values for which $m_j + m^*_j$ can be > one.

Intuitionistic fuzzy memberships $\subseteq$ Pythagorean membership functions

This then allows the use of Pythagorean membership functions as extensions to intuitionistic fuzzy memberships in some situations. For example a user might want to have an evaluation of data values as $m_j (d_i) = 0.8$ and $m_j *(d_i) = 0.4$. However this violates the intuitionistic restriction as $0.8 + 0.4 = 1.2 > 1.0$. But this restriction is relaxed in Pythagorean membership sets as for these values using the Pythagorean condition we have

$$(0.8)^2 + (0.4)^2 = 0.64 + 0.16 = 0.80 < 1.0$$

Thus an analyst is free to use the desired positive and negative membership values for the data value d_i. This makes the analysis more reflective of the analyst's actual assessments.

CONCLUSION

A problem that must be faced in making decisions for any particular application is making effective use of the large amount of data that may be relevant. This is especially difficult where the data may have various aspects of uncertainty. To assist the decision maker in context of the large data problem, generalization can be used to combine the data to more relevant categories by using generalization approaches.

D

ACKNOWLEDGMENT

This work (Petry) was supported by the Naval Research Laboratory's Base Program.

REFERENCES

Atanassov, K. (1986). Intuitionistic fuzzy sets. *Fuzzy Sets and Systems*, 20(1), 87–96. doi:10.1016/S0165-0114(86)80034-3

Bachman, R. (1983). What IS-A is and isn't: An analysis of the taxonomic links in semantic networks. *IEEE Computer*, 16(10), 30–36. doi:10.1109/MC.1983.1654194

Brown, A., Smith, A., & Elmhurst, O. (2002). The combined use of pollen and soil analyses in a search and subsequent murder investigation. *Journal of Forensic Sciences*, 47(3), 614–618. doi:10.1520/JFS15302J PMID:12051347

Burillo, P., & Bustince, H. (1996). Entropy on intuitionistic fuzzy sets and on interval-valued fuzzy sets. *Fuzzy Sets and Systems*, 78(3), 305–316. doi:10.1016/0165-0114(96)84611-2

de Luca, A., & Termini, S. (1972). A definition of a nonprobabilistic entropy in the setting of fuzzy set theory. *Information and Control*, 20(4), 301–312. doi:10.1016/S0019-9958(72)90199-4

Deschrijver, G. (2007). Arithmetic operators in interval-valued fuzzy set theory. *Information Sciences*, 177(14), 2906–2924. doi:10.1016/j.ins.2007.02.003

Dubois, D., & Prade, H. (2000). Fuzzy sets in data summaries - outline of a new approach. *Proc. 8th Int'l Conf. on Information Processing and Management of Uncertainty in Knowledge-Based Systems*.

Gini, C. (1921). Measurement of inequality of incomes. *Economic Journal (London)*, 31124–31126.

Giorgi, G., & Gigliarano, C. (2017). The Gini concentration index: A review of the inference literature. *Journal of Economic Surveys*, 31(4), 1130–1148. doi:10.1111/joes.12185

Hoppa, R., & Vaupel, J. (2002). *Paleodemography: age distribution from skeletal samples*. Cambridge University Press. doi:10.1017/CBO9780511542428

Kacprzyk, J. (1999). Fuzzy logic for linguistic summarization of databases. *Proc. 8th Int'l Conf. on Fuzzy Systems*, 813-818. 10.1109/FUZZY.1999.793053

Klir, G., StClair, U., & Yuan, B. (1997). *Fuzzy set theory: Foundations and applications*. Prentice Hall.

Mendel, J. (2007). Type-2 fuzzy sets and systems: An overview. *IEEE Computational Intelligence Magazine*, 2(1), 20–29. doi:10.1109/MCI.2007.380672

Michael, K., & Miller, K. (2013). Big Data: New opportunities and new challenges. *IEEE Computer*, 46(6), 22–25. doi:10.1109/MC.2013.196

Moore, R. (1966). *Interval analysis*. Prentice Hall.

Moore, R., Kearfott, B., & Cloud, M. (2009). *Introduction to interval analysis*. SIAM. doi:10.1137/1.9780898717716

Pawlak, Z. (1985). Rough Sets and Fuzzy Sets. *Fuzzy Sets and Systems, 17*(1), 99–102. doi:10.1016/S0165-0114(85)80029-4

Petry, F., & Yager, R. (2008). Evidence resolution using concept hierarchies. *IEEE Transactions on Fuzzy Systems, 16*(2), 299–308. doi:10.1109/TFUZZ.2007.895966

Petry, F., & Yager, R. (2014). Fuzzy concept hierarchies and evidence resolution. *IEEE Transactions on Fuzzy Systems, 22*(5), 1151–1161. doi:10.1109/TFUZZ.2013.2286412

Pye, K. (2007). *Geological and soil evidence: Forensic applications*. CRC Press.

Raschia, G., & Mouaddib, N. (2002). SAINTETIQ:a fuzzy set-based approach to database summarization. *Fuzzy Sets and Systems, 12*(2), 137–162. doi:10.1016/S0165-0114(01)00197-X

Reza, F. (1961). *Introduction to information theory*. McGraw Hill.

Richards, D., & Rowe, W. (1999). Decision-making with heterogeneous sources of information. *Risk Analysis, 19*(1), 69–81. doi:10.1111/j.1539-6924.1999.tb00390.x

Shafer, G. (1976). *A Mathematical theory of evidence*. Princeton University Press. doi:10.1515/9780691214696

Shannon, C. (1948). A mathematical theory of communication. *The Bell System Technical Journal, 27*(3), 379–423, 623–656. doi:10.1002/j.1538-7305.1948.tb01338.x

Szmidt, E., & Kacpryzk, J. (2001). Entropy for intuitionistic fuzzy sets. *Fuzzy Sets and Systems, 118*(3), 467–477. doi:10.1016/S0165-0114(98)00402-3

Yager, R. (1991). On linguistic summaries of data. In Knowledge discovery in databases. MIT Press.

Yager, R. (1995). Measures of entropy and fuzziness related to aggregation operators. *Information Sciences, 82*(3-4), 147–166. doi:10.1016/0020-0255(94)00030-F

Yager, R. (2014). Pythagorean membership grades in multicriteria decision making. *IEEE Transactions on Fuzzy Systems, 22*(4), 958–966. doi:10.1109/TFUZZ.2013.2278989

Yager, R., & Petry, F. (2006). A Multi-Criteria Approach to Data Summarization Using Concept Ontologies. *IEEE Transactions on Fuzzy Systems, 14*(6), 767–780. doi:10.1109/TFUZZ.2006.879954

Zadeh, L. (1965). Fuzzy sets. *Information and Control, 8*(3), 338–353. doi:10.1016/S0019-9958(65)90241-X

ADDITIONAL READING

Atanassov, K., & Krassimir, T. (1999). *Intuitionistic fuzzy sets: Theory and applications*. Springer Verlag. doi:10.1007/978-3-7908-1870-3

Beynon, M., Curry, B., & Morgan, P. (2000). The Dempster-Shafer of evidence: An alternative approach to multicriteria decision modleling. *Omega, 28*(1), 37–50. doi:10.1016/S0305-0483(99)00033-X

Cover, T., & Thomas, J. (2006). *Elements of information theory* (2nd ed.). John Wiley.

Kacprzyk, J. (2000). Intelligent Data Analysis via Linguistic Data Summaries: A Fuzzy Logic Approach. In R. Decker & W. Gaul (Eds.), *Classification and information processing at the turn of the millennium: Studies in classification, data analysis, and knowledge organization*. Springer. doi:10.1007/978-3-642-57280-7_17

Lehrer, K., & Wagner, C. (1981). *Rational consensus in science and society*. D. Reidel. doi:10.1007/978-94-009-8520-9

Li, C. (2011). *Handbook of research on computational forensics, digital crime, and investigation: Methods and solutions*. IGI Global.

Pedrycz, W., & Gomide, F. (1996). *An Introduction to fuzzy sets: Analysis and design*. MIT Press.

Polkowski, L. (2002). *Rough sets: Mathematical foundations*. Springer-Verlag. doi:10.1007/978-3-7908-1776-8

Ross, T. (2017). *Fuzzy logic with engineering applications* (4th ed.). John Wiley.

KEY TERMS AND DEFINITIONS

Concept Hierarchies: A way to organize concepts defined in a way to organize concepts defined in a knowledge domain. It can be collection of objects, events, or other items with common properties arranged in a multilevel structure.

Decision Making: The process of making choices among alternative based on sours of information or intelligence.

Dempster-Shafer Theory: Dempster-Shafer theory is a well-known approach to modeling uncertainty providing representation of non-specific forms of uncertainty. A Dempster-Shafer belief structure consists of non-empty crisp subsets of the data where a probability is given for each subset. An important difference with probability is that these probabilities do not have to sum to one.

Forensics: Forensic scientists collect and analyze scientific evidence during the course of an investigation. Interpretation of such data by investigators is used in solving crimes.

Fuzzy Set Theory: The concept of fuzzy sets was introduced by Lotfi Zadeh. In ordinary sets a data values either belongs or does not belong to the set. However fuzzy set theory allows a gradual assessment of the membership of data values in a set described by of a membership function Where elements can either belong or not belong to a regular set, with fuzzy sets elements can belong to the set to a certain degree with zero indicating not an element, one indicating complete membership, and values between zero and one indicating partial or uncertain membership in the set. Fuzzy set theory has been used in a wide range of applications in which information is incomplete or imprecise.

Hesitation: In an intuitionistic fuzzy set, hesitation is the amount of uncertainty in which the set values are indeterminate, sum to less than one.

Information Theory: Information theory provides a measure of the spread of information in total set of data. If their probability is evenly spread the data provides little information. When is unevenly spread, extreme in only a few data values there is more information of use.

Intuitionistic Fuzzy Set Theory: Intuitionistic fuzzy set theory extends ordinary fuzzy set theory by allowing both positive and negative memberships to be specified.

Partitions: A partition of a set is a grouping of its elements into nonempty subsets, in such a way that every element is included in exactly one subset.

Rough Sets: Rough set theory is a technique for dealing with uncertainty and for identifying cause-effect relationships. It is based on a partitioning of some domain into equivalence classes and the defining of lower and upper approximation regions based on this partitioning to denote certain and possible inclusion in the rough set.

Fuzzy Complex System of Linear Equations

Gizem Temelcan

https://orcid.org/0000-0002-1885-0674

Beykoz University, Turkey

Hale Gonce Köçken

https://orcid.org/0000-0003-1121-7099

Yildiz Technical University, Turkey

İnci Albayrak

Yildiz Technical University, Turkey

INTRODUCTION

The widespread use of linear assumptions in engineering and science requires that many studies begin by establishing a linear model. Also, most advanced problems require solving linear systems with real or complex parameters, often of very large dimensions.

In machine learning, a machine is trained to learn a concept by building models to distinguish classes of objects. It would be appropriate to consider the fuzzy logic approach when there is no definite line separating the two classes, or when the distinguishing features are defined indistinctly. Thus, in machine learning algorithms, the application of uncertainty modeling and decision-making methods leads to better performances of algorithm behavior. With this understanding, the contribution of modeling fuzzy complex systems of linear equations to algorithm behavior will be important. For instance, drawing a scatter plot can be given in data science. A scatter plot is drawn via dots to represent values for two different variables. The position of each dot on the horizontal and vertical axis indicates values for an individual data point. Scatter plots are used to observe relationships between variables. To find the best fitting line, linear regression, which is an example of SLE, can be used. Thus, to predict numerical values, linear regression is used in machine learning. Moreover, Support Vector Machine (SVM) learning algorithms are used to build accurate models with practical relevance for classification, regression, and novelty detection. Some applications of SVMs are facial recognition, text categorization, and bioinformatics. Generally, the training task requires solving an SLE in SVM learning algorithms (Do & Fekete, 2007). Furthermore, in deep learning, SLE is used when training a deep model. For more applications, see (Dombi & Kertesz-Farkas, 2009; Gan, 2013; Martínez et al., 2015; Kurnianggoro et al., 2015; Gan & Huang, 2017; Saini et al., 2020; Jo, 2021).

Systems of linear equations (SLE) play an important role in the areas such as mathematics, statistics, economics, physics, chemistry, social sciences, and engineering. They have many application areas in physical and engineering sciences such as circuit analysis, structural mechanics, heat transport, fluid flow, etc. For instance, civil engineers use the systems to design and analyze load-bearing structures such as bridges; mechanical engineers to design and analyze suspension systems, and electrical engineers to design and analyze electrical circuits. A standard real SLE can be written as $AX = b$, where A and b are crisp real matrices, i.e., parameters, and X is the real variable vector. SLE has a wide range of studies in the literature. There are many methods for solving these systems having crisp real parameters

DOI: 10.4018/978-1-7998-9220-5.ch118

and variables. Several authors have proposed direct and iterative methods for solving the SLE. Direct methods such as Gaussian elimination (with/without pivot technique) and LU decomposition produce the exact solution assuming no rounding errors. On the other hand, iterative methods such as Jacobi, Seidel-Gauss methods, Conjugate gradient method, sequential over relaxation technique produce an approximate solution whose accuracy is imposed by the user. These procedures can be presented as two major classes of methods for the numerical solution of SLE with real coefficients. In the case of a large linear system, the direct solution of a sparse matrix linear system can be obtained by direct methods, without ignoring the computational cost and the corresponding total time. Iterative methods, whose efficiency depends on the method chosen, represent a better alternative.

A concept or information, even if vague and imprecise, may not be applicable to the situation it refers to, as it may not adequately capture the meaning of something. Therefore, the fuzzy concept can provide greater credibility when an imprecise concept is available, or an ambiguous and imprecise concept is not applicable or insufficient to the situation it refers to. This will be better than not reflect the information in the model. For the sake of simplicity, variables and parameters of the systems are defined exactly in the modeling. However, the estimations of the system parameters and variables may be uncertain or vague in nature since they are found by some experiment, observation, or experience. Hence, when some vague and imprecise information about the parameters is given, then some or all the parameters can be represented by fuzzy numbers, which was first introduced by Zadeh (1996) in 1965, to overcome these uncertainties. Fuzziness allows for the inclusion of vague human assessments in problems. Moreover, it provides an effective way for better assessment of options. Therefore, fuzziness is applicable for many people involved in research and development including engineers, mathematicians, natural scientists, medical researchers, computer software developers, social scientists, business analysts, and jurists.

Fuzzy numbers can be used in place of crisp numbers in the cases of the imprecision that may follow from the lack of exact information, changeable economic conditions, etc. Thus, a crisp SLE becomes a Fuzzy SLE (FSLE) or a Fully FSLE (FFSLE). The difference between the FSLE and the FFSLE is that the coefficient matrix or the variables are considered as crisp in the fuzzy system; but in the fully fuzzy system, all parameters and variables are in the form of fuzzy numbers. Solution methods for the general FSLE have been developed either from modification of the methods proposed for solving the crisp systems or from the development of new solution techniques. In this context of the FSLE, studies using direct and iterative methods can be accessed in the review (Kocken & Albayrak, 2015).

When modeling the engineering problems, it often happens that an SLE also occurs on C, as in vector spaces on R; that is, a system whose both coefficients and variables are complex numbers. Accordingly, Complex SLE (CSLE) are important large-scale applied problems in modeling such as optimization, flow, economics, computational electrodynamics, quantum mechanics, electromagnetism, structural dynamics, electric power system models, wave propagation, magnetized multicomponent transport. A general CSLE can be expressed as $CZ = W$, where C and W are crisp complex matrices and Z is the unknown complex vector, and the system can also be solved via direct or iterative methods, and these systems can be solved via direct or iterative methods such as for crisp real systems.

For the sake of convenience, in some scientific areas such as wave function in quantum mechanics, circuit analysis, etc. some parameters or variables are defined as complex numbers. However, these parameters or variables may take on uncertain values in actual practice. To overcome the uncertainty is appropriate to use fuzzy complex numbers instead of complex numbers in such models. Thus, it is important to develop mathematical models that would appropriately treat fuzzy complex linear systems. For instance, circuits can be modeled in the form of the Fuzzy CSLE (FCSLE). Uncertainty in circuit parameters and environmental conditions leads to the development of a new method that considers the uncertainty in circuit analysis. Moreover, in many applications such as wave function in quantum mechanics, physical quantities are in the form of complex numbers and have fuzzy nature, so these are represented by fuzzy complex numbers.

This study has attempted to provide a review of notable papers on FCLES with a basic structural classification. The primary classification is made considering the system types. The secondary classification is based on the solution methods, i.e., direct, or iterative. The literature has been searched systematically to identify the papers that propose advances in the field of FCLES and its applications, and then each included paper has been reviewed through the structural classification made. The review will give a general framework about the progression of the subject and its solution approaches and re-emphasize gaps in the literature.

BACKGROUND

Since the FCSLE is formed by the usage of fuzzy complex numbers, it would be appropriate to give the fuzzy complex number literature first. The concept of complex fuzzy numbers was first introduced by Buckley (1989) in 1987 in the proceeding of ISFK, Guangzhou, China, then in 1989, the study was published in Fuzzy Sets and System. Qiu et al. (2000; 2001) introduced the sequence and series of a fuzzy complex number and their convergences. Candau et al. (2006) analyzed the complex interval arithmetic using a polar form. Buckley and Qui (1991) presented the study on fuzzy complex analysis by developing the theory of differentiation, and then Buckley (1992) studied integration including fuzzy complex numbers. Gong and Xiao (2021) proposed a new representation of fuzzy complex numbers and investigated some arithmetic operations.

When some parameters of an SLE are fuzzy complex numbers, then the considered linear system is called a fuzzy complex linear equations system (FCSLE). The fuzziness enables the modeling of a CSLE in a more natural and direct way. Accordingly, the FCSLE has attracted the attention of many researchers and has become an area recently studied in the literature. In recent years, solving the FCSLE has been studied because of its significant applications in physics and engineering sciences. Especially, in electrical and electromagnetism problems such as RLC circuits with complex fuzzy current and source, for instance, using Kirchhoff's laws in these problems leads to the solving the system.

Solving an FCSLE was first investigated by Rahgooy et al. (2009) in 2009 and applied to circuit analysis. Then, it is studied by Jahantigh et al. (2010) and Behera and Chakraverty (2012). Moses et al. (1999) proposed linguistic coordinate transformations for complex fuzzy sets. Since an interval or a fuzzy number is used in representing uncertainties, the variables can be expressed in terms of them. Therefore, complex interval arithmetic is first studied by Rokne and Lancaster (1971). Then, Petkovic et al. (1998) investigated the complex interval arithmetic, presented a circular form of the interval complex number, and applied it to several problems. Solution sets of complex and linear interval systems are investigated by Hladik (2010). Djanybekov (2006) used the Householder method for the solution of interval complex linear systems. In the interval complex linear systems, the coefficient matrix is taken as an interval.

The basic definitions to be given before presenting the mathematical model of an FCSLE are as follows:

Let a fuzzy real number $\tilde{U}$ be a convex normalized fuzzy set having a membership function μ, $\tilde{U}(x): R \to [0,1]$, $\forall x \in R$ which is piecewise continuous. The fuzzy number $\tilde{U}$ can be rewritten in a parametric form by using an a-cut technique such that $U_\alpha = \left[\underline{U}_\alpha, \overline{U}_\alpha\right]$ $U_\alpha = \left[\underline{U}(\alpha), \overline{U}(\alpha)\right]$ where

$a \in [0,1]$. Thus, a fuzzy complex number is defined by two fuzzy numbers representing the real and imaginary part of a complex number as follows:

$$\tilde{z} = \tilde{p} + i\tilde{q}$$

where $\tilde{p} = \left[\underline{p}(\alpha), \overline{p}(\alpha)\right]$ and $\tilde{q} = \left[\underline{q}(\alpha), \overline{q}(\alpha)\right]$ for all $a \in [0,1]$ are fuzzy numbers. Hence, the fuzzy complex number $\tilde{z}$ can be rewritten in the parametric form as

$$z_{\alpha} = \left[\underline{z}(\alpha), \overline{z}(\alpha)\right] = \left[\underline{p}(\alpha) + i\underline{q}(\alpha), \overline{p}(\alpha) + i\overline{q}(\alpha)\right].$$

Membership function of a fuzzy complex number $\tilde{z}$, denoted as $\mu_{\tilde{z}}(\bullet)$, is a mapping from the set of complex numbers to a closed interval $[0,1]$, i.e., $\mu_{\tilde{z}} : C \rightarrow [0,1]$. Consider a fuzzy complex number is defined via two fuzzy numbers $\tilde{p}$ and $\tilde{q}$ having the membership functions $\mu_{\tilde{p}}$ and $\mu_{\tilde{q}}$, respectively. Then, the membership function of $\tilde{z}$ is $\mu_{\tilde{z}} = \min\left\{\mu_{\tilde{p}}, \mu_{\tilde{q}}\right\}$.

Based on these definitions, a CSLE can be defined as:

$$CZ = W$$

where C and W are crisp matrices having complex elements and Z is a vector with complex variables. This complex system can be expanded by taking at least one of the components on the right-hand side or left-hand side of the system as a fuzzy number. As a result, an FCSLE is obtained.

An FSLE can be classified according to the form of the system parameter. In type 1, the variable vector includes fuzzy complex numbers such that

$$C\tilde{Z} = \tilde{W}$$

where C is a coefficient matrix having crisp complex elements. In type 2, the entries of the coefficient matrix are in the form of a fuzzy complex number, that is

$$\tilde{C}Z = \tilde{W}$$

where the parameters $\tilde{C}$ and W are fuzzy complex numbers and the variable Z is a crisp complex number. Finally, in type 3, an FFCSLE is obtained such as

$$\tilde{C}\tilde{Z} = \tilde{W}$$

where all the parameters and variables of the system are fuzzy complex numbers. This classification of FCSLE is summarized in Figure 1.

Figure 1. Classification of the fuzzy complex system of linear equations

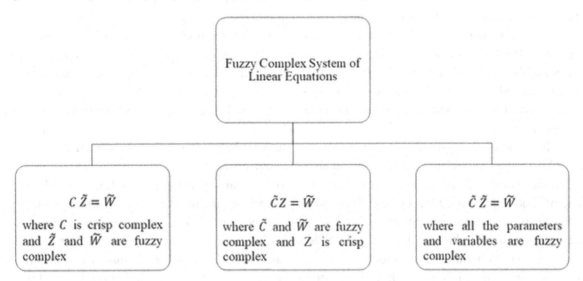

In this chapter, a literature review is presented based on the types of FCSLE given above. Also, the solution methods for each class constructed are classified as direct and iterative methods.

A CLASSIFICATION OF FCSLE BASED ON THE FUZZINESS OF THE PARAMETERS AND VARIABLES

Type 1: FCSLE with only Fuzzy Complex Variables

Solving an FCSLE was first investigated by Rahgooy et al. (2009). They considered the application of FCSLE in the circuit analysis and presented a fuzzy-based approach for the simulation of voltage and current sources fuzzy current as well as voltage in circuit equations. Steady-state analysis of complex circuits is investigated from an FSLE perspective; thus, linear resistance, inductance, and capacitance in a circuit are modeled to complex linear equations. In the SLE, the coefficients and the right-hand side values were considered as fuzzy complex numbers. They utilized the embedding method proposed by Friedman et al. (1998) in which the original FCSLE is replaced with a crisp linear system, and then it is solved. This paper led to the beginning of research on the FCSLE.

Jahantigh et al. (2010) introduced a numerical method for solving a square FCSLE. First, the original system is transformed into two fuzzy linear systems, and they are solved via the method proposed by Friedman et al. (1998). Then, it is shown that the complex combination of these two solutions is the solution of the general system.

Behera and Chakraverty (2012) presented a new procedure to solve both FSLE and FCSLE based on the concept of fuzzy center and width. First, the system is solved, the solution is obtained in terms of fuzzy center, and this solution is used with the width to find the final solution of the general system. Comparisons are made between the solutions obtained and the known solutions.

Behera and Chakraverty (2013) presented an approach based on the center of fuzzy complex numbers for solving FCSLE. Since the use of the fuzzy complex center methodology in the case of complex systems needs few theorems to handle the procedure, some related theorems are stated and proved. The solutions obtained are compared with the known solutions.

Behera and Chakraverty (2014) proposed a novel solution method for a general FCSLE in which the elements of an unknown variable vector and right-hand side vector are considered as the complex fuzzy number and applied to an electric circuit. The general system is solved by adding and subtracting the left and right bounds of the fuzzy complex unknown and right-hand side fuzzy complex vector, respectively. Then, the obtained solution from the new system is used to determine the final solution of the general FCSLE.

Behera and Chakraverty (2016) composed an erratum, including the definition correction of a fuzzy complex number and related calculations causing mathematical errors.

Farahani et al. (2016) presented a new method based on linear algebra for the resolution of an FCSLE. The method is developed for finding all the solutions of a system at a time, i.e., the computation of solutions is done independently for each other, using the eigenvalue method. In the proposed method, the computation of solutions of an FCSLE leads to finding the eigenvalues of a matrix. Hence, useful tools can be used in linear algebra such as converting the matrix into a triangular matrix via elementary row operations and applying the determinant properties. In the method, the FCSLE is converted into a crisp polynomial system of which solutions can be obtained by an algorithm. Then, a Gröbner basis is computed for the ideal generated by the new system for the lexicographic order. Finally, the eigenvalue method is applied for finding the solutions of the system. Also, a sufficient and necessary condition is presented for the existence of the solution of an FCSLE. The advantage of the method is presented such that it does not require a suitable initial point.

Guo and Zhang (2016) considered a matrix method (a numerical procedure) for solving an FCSLE having an LR-type complex fuzzy vector on the right-hand side. The FCSLE is converted to an equivalent high order fuzzy linear system and a numerical procedure to calculate the complex fuzzy solution is designed. The sufficient condition for the existence of a strong complex fuzzy solution is derived (presented) in detail.

Han and Guo (2016) investigated an FCSLE by using the concept of Moore–Penrose generalized inverse. The general FCSLE is converted to an equivalent high-order fuzzy linear system in the proposed method. The process for finding the complex fuzzy solution is presented. Also, the sufficient condition for the existence of a strong complex fuzzy solution is derived based on the right-hand side elements expressed by different complex fuzzy numbers.

Zhang and Guo (2016) considered the QR-decomposition method for solving the FCSLE. It is known that the QR -decomposition is a decomposition of a matrix C into a product $C = QR$ of an orthogonal Q and upper triangular matrix R . Therefore, in the paper, the FCSLE is converted to a high order linear system, and QR-decomposition of the coefficient matrix is used to obtain the fuzzy solution of the FCSLE.

Ghanbari (2017) presented a modified version of the method proposed by Behera and Chakraverty (2014) since there were some problems with it. To avoid these problems, Ghanbari proposed a solution method for general FCSLE and showed that it always gives a fuzzy complex vector as the exact solution (if it exists) of an FCSLE.

Guo et al. (2018) introduced a complex LR fuzzy matrix equation and proposed a general model to solve it. The complex fuzzy matrix equation is converted to an equivalent high order LR fuzzy matrix system, then the LR fuzzy matrix equation is extended into a crisp system of matrix equations. The fuzzy minimal solution of the fuzzy matrix equation is derived from solving the crisp linear matrix system. A procedure for finding the solution is designed in detail, and a sufficient condition for the existence of a strong complex LR fuzzy minimal solution is discussed.

Farahani and Paripour (2020) investigated the FCSLE and proposed a new algebraic approach to find all the solutions of these systems based on Wu's (1984) method. In general, Wu's method is utilized as a solution procedure for solving the crisp polynomial equations system, and it leads to solving characteristic sets that are amenable to easy solutions. Since finding the roots of univariate polynomials is easier than solving the original system, in the approach, the FCSLE is converted to an equivalent crisp polynomial equations system having 8n equations and 6n unknowns. Then, the crisp system is solved using Wu's method for finding fuzzy solutions of the original system. The advantage of the proposed method is being independent of a suitable initial point, and it gives all solutions at a time.

Ghanbari (2020) proposed a solution method to obtain an algebraic solution of an FCSLE. Based on the proposed method, an FCSLE is solved by the classic Crout decomposition method, and the Crout's solution is obtained. It is shown that Crout's solution does not satisfy all equations of the system, and therefore it is not an algebraic solution. Thus, Ghanbari presented a limited version of the classic Crout method such that the obtained solution would be always a unique algebraic solution of the FCSLE, if it exists, by limiting Crout's solution.

Ghanbari et al. (2020) considered the rectangular fuzzy complex linear system, which is a specific type of fuzzy complex linear system and found its algebraic and general solutions via a simple solution method. An approach based on restricting the general solution is presented to solve a rectangular fuzzy complex linear system, and it gives a unique algebraic solution to the system if it exists.

Fathi-Vajargah and Hassanzadeh (2020) applied the Monte Carlo method to obtain the solution of the fuzzy system of linear algebraic equations, the complex fuzzy system of linear algebraic equations with new techniques based on the independency of random walks and individual features of this method. Since the Monte Carlo method has some advantages in using extremely large matrices, they determined the specified and simpler computing condition for the convergence of the Monte Carlo method for the system of linear algebraic equations based on the properties of the Hadamard product of the nonnegative matrices, i.e., probability matrices.

Akram et al. (2021) proposed a new technique for solving square LR-complex bipolar FSLE. They first discussed a technique to solve the LR-complex bipolar FSLE with real coefficients. They replaced the square LR-complex bipolar FSLE with real coefficients by pair of real and imaginary parts of square LR bipolar FSLE and then solved these systems by using mean value and left-right spread systems. Further, they extended the technique (Guo & Zhang, 2016) to solve the LR-complex bipolar FSLE with complex coefficients in which the square coefficient matrix of the system was represented by regular complex numbers, and the right-hand side vector is represented by LR bipolar fuzzy complex numbers. To solve the system, they replaced the square LR-complex bipolar fuzzy SLE with complex coefficients by pair of positive and negative of two $2n \times 2n$ mean value systems and $4n \times 4n$ left-right spread systems. Some numerical examples were solved and discussed to describe the efficiency of the technique. They also discussed and compared the solutions of two different systems: one is LR-complex bipolar fuzzy SLE with real coefficients, and the other is LR-complex bipolar fuzzy SLE with complex coefficients.

Type 2: FCSLE with Fuzzy Complex Parameters

Majumdar (2013) proposed iterative methods, which are the Gauss-Jacobi and the Gauss-Seidel methods, for solving FCSLE with fuzzy complex coefficients as well as for solving FCSLE with fuzzy complex variables. First, the solution is obtained in terms of fuzzy center, and an approximate solution with the width is used to determine the final solution. The proposed methods are convergent when the system is diagonally dominant. If the system is not diagonally dominant, then the system is rearranged and made diagonally dominant.

Fazeli and Aghaei (2016) focused on solving an SLE with complex fuzzy coefficients based on the simpler generalized minimal residual method. The proposed method is discussed in detail, and the solutions found via the method are compared with the iterative Jacobi and Gauss-Seidel methods and the generalized minimal residual method.

Kaur and Kumar (2016) considered shortcomings in arithmetic operations of fuzzy numbers in the existing method proposed by Majumdar (2013). To deal with these shortcomings, two novel methods, named the Mehar method and the Keerat method, are proposed for different types of FCSLE. Mehar method is used for solving FCSLE with fuzzy complex coefficients whereas the Keerat method for solving FCSLE with fuzzy complex variables.

Type 3: Fully FCSLE

Banerjee and Roy (2015) considered fuzzy real and complex SLE with crisp coefficients and fuzzy right-hand side parameters. The fuzzy numbers are taken in generalized trapezoidal type and represented with mean and semi-width. Each system is solved using the concept of strong and weak solutions.

Dutta et al. (2019) presented a novel method for solving FFCSLE. In the system, all knowns and unknowns are fuzzy complex numbers and represented by LR fuzzy numbers. It is shown that solving an FFCSLE is equivalent to the associated linear system $AX = B$ and the FFCSLE with the associated linear system can be uniquely solved for the solution X iff the matrix A is nonsingular. Therefore, conditions on the existence and uniqueness of fuzzy complex solutions have been investigated and discussed.

Daud and Gemawati (2020) determined an alternative solution of FFCSLE by using the inverse method. There are some cases according to the sign of coefficients that include the solution of the FFCSLE. In the paper, two cases are discussed: in the first case, all real and imaginary parts of coefficients are positive whereas in the second case are negative. In each case, the solution obtained when substituted back into an FFCSLE produces a value that means the solution is compatible.

SOLUTIONS AND RECOMMENDATIONS

Among the studies used for the review, the number of studies per year is presented in Figure 2.

Figure 2. Number of studies on FCSLE per year

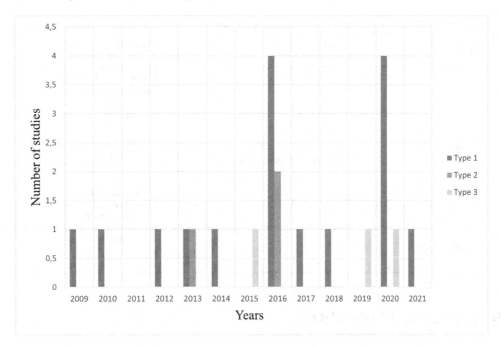

The classification of the studies used in the review as direct, and iterative per year is given in Figure 3.

Figure 3. Year-based direct and iterative methods

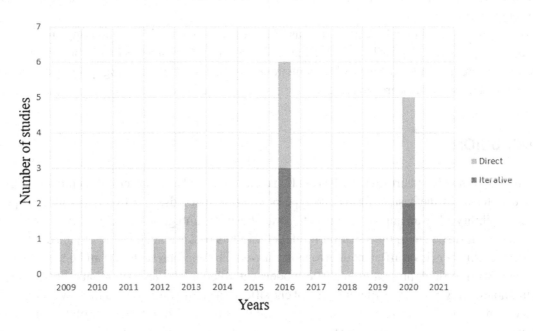

Studies conducted according to iterative, and direct methods for each classification are presented in Table 1.

Table 1. Iterative and direct methods for each classification

Type of FCSLE	Iterative Method	Direct Method
$\tilde{C}Z = \tilde{W}$	Kaur and Kumar (2016) Fazeli and Aghaei (2016)	Majumdar (2013) Akram et al (2021)
$C\tilde{Z} = \tilde{W}$	Farahani et al (2016) Farahani and Paripour (2020) Vajargah and Hassanzadeh (2020)	Rahgooy et al (2009) Jahantigh et al (2010) Behera and Chakraverty (2012) Behera and Chakraverty (2013) Behera and Chakraverty (2014) Guo and Zhang (2016) Han and Guo (2016) Zhang and Guo (2016) Ghanbari (2017) Guo et al (2018) Ghanbari et al (2020) Ghanbari (2020)
$\tilde{C}\tilde{Z} = \tilde{W}$		Banerjee and Roy (2015) Dutta et al (2019) Daud and Gemawati (2020)

FUTURE RESEARCH DIRECTIONS

In the literature, an FCSLE in the form $AX + B = CX + D$ is named Dual FCSLE. This dual system whose parameters and/or variables are fuzzy complex numbers, and coefficient matrices are non-square is the most general structure of a system of linear equations. This general structure, that can model real-life problems in a more flexible way, is important to bring it to the attention of researchers. Investigating in FCSLE will give an opportunity to increase the applicability of the model for various areas especially, engineering.

Considering the traditional methods such as direct and iterative methods, obtaining analytical solutions of FCLES may be impossible; thus, using machine learning techniques can be advantageous. It is known that there does not exist any solution method based on machine learning techniques. Thus, this will be an open area for researchers.

CONCLUSION

This chapter provides a short review of FCSLE. To classify FCSLE, a structural methodology is constructed in terms of the system forms and type of solution methods. The fuzzy concept can provide greater credibility when an imprecise concept is available or an ambiguous, and imprecise concept is not convenient or insufficient to the situation it refers to. In lots of cases such as the obtained information from decision-makers is insufficient or erroneous, it would be appropriate to use an FCSLE. Especially in the engineering field, presenting realistic models can tolerate all these situations. This review that presents noteworthy papers for different types of classification highlights a general framework for FCSLE. It makes a more detailed investigation by classifying the studies also in terms of solution methods. In other words, both the studies for system types, and the solution methods developed for the related systems were examined. Considering all evaluations, the achievements will guide the future studies to be done for FCSLE. The contribution of this study, which is written on the modeling and solutions of complex fuzzy linear equation systems, to machine learning algorithm behaviors will be also important.

REFERENCES

Akram, M., Allahviranloo, T., Pedrycz, W., & Ali, M. (2021). Methods for Solving LR-Bipolar Fuzzy Linear Systems. *Soft Computing*, *25*(1), 85–108. doi:10.100700500-020-05460-z

Banerjee, S., & Roy, T. K. (2015). Linear Equations and Systems in Fuzzy Environment. *Journal of Mathematics and Computer Science*, *15*(01), 23–31. doi:10.22436/jmcs.015.01.02

Behera, D., & Chakraverty, S. (2012). A New Method for Solving Real and Complex Fuzzy Systems of Linear Equations. *Computational Mathematics and Modeling*, *23*(4), 507–518. doi:10.100710598-012-9152-z

Behera, D., & Chakraverty, S. (2013). Fuzzy Center-based Solution of Fuzzy Complex Linear System of Equations. *International Journal of Uncertainty, Fuzziness and Knowledge-based Systems*, *21*(04), 629–642. doi:10.1142/S021848851350030X

Behera, D., & Chakraverty, S. (2014). Solving Fuzzy Complex System of Linear Equations. *Information Sciences*, *277*, 154–162. doi:10.1016/j.ins.2014.02.014

Behera, D., & Chakraverty, S. (2016). Erratum to "Solving Fuzzy Complex System of Linear Equations". *Information Sciences*, *369*, 788–790. doi:10.1016/j.ins.2016.06.014

Buckley, J. (1989). Fuzzy Complex Numbers. *Fuzzy Sets and Systems*, *33*(3), 333–345. doi:10.1016/0165-0114(89)90122-X

Buckley, J. J. (1992). Fuzzy Complex Analysis II: Integration. *Fuzzy Sets and Systems*, *49*(2), 171–179. doi:10.1016/0165-0114(92)90322-U

Buckley, J. J., & Qu, Y. (1991). Fuzzy Complex Analysis I: Differentiation. *Fuzzy Sets and Systems*, *41*(3), 269–284. doi:10.1016/0165-0114(91)90131-9

Candau, Y., Raissi, T., Ramdani, N., & Ibos, L. (2006). Complex Interval Arithmetic Using Polar Form. *Reliable Computing*, *12*(1), 1–20. doi:10.100711155-006-2966-7

Daud, U., & Gemawati, S. (2020). Solution Alternative of Complex Fuzzy Linear Equation System. *International Journal of Innovative Science and Research Technology*, *5*(11), 21–26.

Djanybekov, B. S. (2006). Interval Householder Method for Complex Linear Systems. *Reliable Computing*, *12*(1), 35–43. doi:10.100711155-006-2968-5

Do, T. N., & Fekete, J. D. (2007, December). Large Scale Classification with Support Vector Machine Algorithms. In *Sixth International Conference on Machine Learning and Applications* (pp. 7-12). Institute of Electrical and Electronics Engineers (IEEE). 10.1109/ICMLA.2007.25

Dombi, J., & Kertesz-Farkas, A. (2009). Applying Fuzzy Technologies to Equivalence Learning in Protein Classification. *Journal of Computational Biology*, *16*(4), 611–623. doi:10.1089/cmb.2008.0147 PMID:19361330

Dutta, A., Pramanik, S., & Jana, D. K. (2019, March). Novel Derivations and Application of Complex LR Numbers on Fully Fuzzy Complex Linear System. In *International Conference on Information Technology and Applied Mathematics* (pp. 30-42). Springer. 10.1007/978-3-030-34152-7_3

Farahani, H., Nehi, H. M., & Paripour, M. (2016). Solving Fuzzy Complex System of Linear Equations Using Eigenvalue Method. *Journal of Intelligent & Fuzzy Systems*, *31*(3), 1689–1699. doi:10.3233/JIFS-152046

Farahani, H., & Paripour, M. (2020). Resolution of Fuzzy Complex Systems of Linear Equations Via Wu's Method. *International Journal of Industrial Mathematics*, *12*(2), 135–146.

Fathi-Vajargah, B., & Hassanzadeh, Z. (2020). Monte Carlo Method for the Real and Complex Fuzzy System of Linear Algebraic Equations. *Soft Computing*, *24*(2), 1255–1270. doi:10.100700500-019-03960-1

Fazeli, S. S., & Aghaei, S. (2016). Solving Complex Fuzzy Linear System of Equations Using SGMRES Method. *International Journal of Computer Science and Information Security*, *14*(8), 885.

Friedman, M., Ming, M., & Kandel, A. (1998). Fuzzy Linear Systems. *Fuzzy Sets and Systems*, *96*(2), 201–209. doi:10.1016/S0165-0114(96)00270-9

Gan, G. (2013). Application of Data Clustering and Machine Learning in Variable Annuity Valuation. *Insurance, Mathematics & Economics*, *53*(3), 795–801. doi:10.1016/j.insmatheco.2013.09.021

Gan, G., & Huang, J. X. (2017, August). A Data Mining Framework for Valuing Large Portfolios of Variable Annuities. In *Proceedings of the 23rd Association for Computing Machinery (ACM) SIGKDD International Conference on Knowledge Discovery and Data Mining* (pp. 1467-1475). Association for Computing Machinery. 10.1145/3097983.3098013

Ghanbari, M. (2017). A Discussion on "Solving Fuzzy Complex System of Linear Equations". *Information Sciences*, *402*, 165–169. doi:10.1016/j.ins.2017.03.029

Ghanbari, M. (2020). A Limited Version of Crout Decomposition Method for Solving of Fuzzy Complex Linear Systems. *International Journal of Industrial Mathematics*, *12*(3), 225–237.

Ghanbari, M., Allahviranloo, T., & Pedrycz, W. (2020). On the Rectangular Fuzzy Complex Linear Systems. *Applied Soft Computing*, *91*, 106196. doi:10.1016/j.asoc.2020.106196

Gong, Z., & Xiao, Z. (2021). Fuzzy Complex Numbers: Representations, Operations, and Their Analysis. *Fuzzy Sets and Systems*, *417*, 1–45. doi:10.1016/j.fss.2020.12.021

Guo, X., Li, Z., & Yan, R. (2018). Solving Complex LR Fuzzy Matrix Equation. *Journal of Intelligent & Fuzzy Systems*, *34*(6), 4367–4375. doi:10.3233/JIFS-17963

Guo, X., & Zhang, K. (2016). Minimal Solution of Complex Fuzzy Linear Systems. *Advances in Fuzzy Systems*, *2016*, 1–9. doi:10.1155/2016/5293917

Han, Y., & Guo, X. (2016). Complex Fuzzy Linear Systems. *International Journal of Engineering and Applied Sciences*, *3*(12), 257540.

Hladik, M. (2010). Solution Sets of Complex Linear Interval Systems of Equations. *Reliable Computing*, *14*, 79.

Jahantigh, M. A., Khezerloo, S., & Khezerloo, M. (2010). Complex Fuzzy Linear Systems. *International Journal of Industrial Mathematics*, *2*(1), 21–28.

Jo, T. (2021). Support Vector Machine. In *Machine Learning Foundations* (pp. 167–188). Springer. doi:10.1007/978-3-030-65900-4_8

Kaur, J. J., & Kumar, A. (2016). Mehar and Keerat Method for Solving System of Fuzzy Complex Linear Equations. *Journal of Intelligent & Fuzzy Systems*, *31*(3), 1955–1965. doi:10.3233/JIFS-16134

Kocken, H., & Albayrak, F. I. (2015). *A Short Review on Fuzzy System of Linear Equations. Encyclopedia of Information Science and Technology* (3rd ed.). IGI Global.

Kurnianggoro, L., Hoang, V. D., & Jo, K. H. (2015). Calibration of A 2D Laser Scanner System and Rotating Platform Using a Point-Plane Constraint. *Computer Science and Information Systems*, *12*(1), 307–322. doi:10.2298/CSIS141020093K

Majumdar, S. (2013). Numerical Solutions of Fuzzy Complex System of Linear Equations. *German Journal of Advanced Mathematical Sciences*, *1*(1), 20–26.

Martínez, M. V., Del Campo, I., Echanobe, J., & Basterretxea, K. (2015, September). Driving Behavior Signals and Machine Learning: A Personalized Driver Assistance System. In *2015 IEEE 18th International Conference on Intelligent Transportation Systems* (pp. 2933-2940). Institute of Electrical and Electronics Engineers. 10.1109/ITSC.2015.470

Moses, D., Degani, O., Teodorescu, H. N., Friedman, M., & Kandel, A. (1999, August). Linguistic Coordinate Transformations for Complex Fuzzy Sets. *IEEE International Fuzzy Systems Conference Proceedings (FUZZ-IEEE'99)*, *3*, 1340-1345. 10.1109/FUZZY.1999.790097

Petkovic, M., Petković, M., Petkovic, M. S., & Petkovic, L. D. (1998). *Complex Interval Arithmetic and Its Applications, 105*. John Wiley & Sons.

Qiu, J., Wu, C., & Li, F. (2000). On The Restudy of Fuzzy Complex Analysis: Part I. The Sequence and Series of Fuzzy Complex Numbers and Their Convergences. *Fuzzy Sets and Systems*, *115*(3), 445–450. doi:10.1016/S0165-0114(98)00160-2

Qiu, J., Wu, C., & Li, F. (2001). On The Restudy of Fuzzy Complex Analysis: Part II. The Continuity and Differentiation of Fuzzy Complex Functions. *Fuzzy Sets and Systems*, *120*(3), 517–521. doi:10.1016/S0165-0114(99)00076-7

Rahgooy, T., Yazdi, H. S., & Monsefi, R. (2009). Fuzzy Complex System of Linear Equations Applied to Circuit Analysis. *International Journal of Computer and Electrical Engineering*, *1*(5), 535–541. doi:10.7763/IJCEE.2009.V1.82

Rokne, J., & Lancaster, P. (1971). Complex Interval Arithmetic. *Communications of the ACM*, *14*(2), 111–112. doi:10.1145/362515.362563

Saini, S., Khosla, P. K., Kaur, M., & Singh, G. (2020). Quantum Driven Machine Learning. *International Journal of Theoretical Physics*, *59*(12), 4013–4024. doi:10.100710773-020-04656-1

Wu, W. T. (1984). On the Decision Problem and the Mechanization of Theorem-Proving in Elementary Geometry. *Contemporary Mathematics*, *29*, 213–234. doi:10.1090/conm/029/12

Zadeh, L. A. (1996). Fuzzy Sets. In Fuzzy Logic and Fuzzy Systems: Selected Papers by Lotfi A Zadeh (pp. 394-432). World Scientific Publishing.

Zhang, K., & Guo, X. (2016). Solving Complex Fuzzy Linear System of Equations by Using QR-Decomposition Method. *International Journal of Engineering Research & Science*, *2*(9), 54–63.

ADDITIONAL READING

Akila Padmasree, J., & Parvathi, R. (2021, August). A Novel Approach of Complex Intuitionistic Fuzzy Linear Systems in an Electrical Circuit. In *International Conference on Intelligent and Fuzzy Systems* (pp. 109-118). Springer. 10.1007/978-3-030-85577-2_13

Allahviranloo, T. (2020). *Uncertain Information and Linear Systems*. Springer International Publishing. doi:10.1007/978-3-030-31324-1

Behera, D., & Chakraverty, S. (2015). New Approach to Solve Fully Fuzzy System of Linear Equations Using Single and Double Parametric Form of Fuzzy Numbers. *Sadhana*, *40*(1), 35–49. doi:10.100712046-014-0295-9

Chehlabi, M. (2019). Solving Fuzzy Dual Complex Linear Systems. *Journal of Applied Mathematics & Computing*, *60*(1), 87–112. doi:10.100712190-018-1204-x

Ghanbari, M., Allahviranloo, T., & Pedrycz, W. (2021). A Straightforward Approach for Solving Dual Fuzzy Linear Systems. *Fuzzy Sets and Systems*, *435*, 89–106. doi:10.1016/j.fss.2021.04.007

Jeswal, S. K., & Chakraverty, S. (2020). ANN Based Solution of Uncertain Linear Systems of Equations. *Neural Processing Letters*, *51*(2), 1957–1971. doi:10.100711063-019-10183-w

Kocken, H. G., & Albayrak, I. (2019). *A Short Review on Fuzzy System of Linear Equations Applications*. In *Handbook of Research on Transdisciplinary Knowledge Generation*. IGI Global.

KEY TERMS AND DEFINITIONS

Direct Methods: A type of solution method for solving a problem by a finite sequence of operations.

Fully Fuzzy Complex Linear Equation System: A linear equation system of which all parameters are fuzzy complex.

Fuzzy Complex Linear Equation System: A linear equation system including some fuzzy complex parameters and/or variables.

Fuzzy Linear Equation System: A linear equation system including some fuzzy parameters and/ or variables.

Iterative Methods: A type of solution method for solving a problem by generating a sequence of approximate solutions progressively.

Linear Equation System: A set of linear equations including the same set of variables.

Fuzzy Logic–Based Classification and Authentication of Beverages

F

Bitan Pratihar
National Institute of Technology, Rourkela, India

Madhusree Kundu
National Institute of Technology, Rourkela, India

INTRODUCTION

Tea can be considered as one of the most extensively consumed and cherished drinks in the world because of its health, dietetic and therapeutic benefits (Chen et al., 2020; da Silva Pinto, 2013). Conventionally, professional tea testers assessed the quality of a tea brand on the basis of its color, texture, aroma, and taste (Ren et al., 2021). However, this type of judgment conjectured with human perception may be subjective in nature and prone to suffer from inconsistency and fickleness (Yang et al., 2021). Similarly, several mineral water brands are commercially available, and a few of them are sold with fake labels or no labels on them. Famous mineral water brands don't have an appreciable distinction in their ionic compositions. This makes the assessment of water quality and subsequent monitoring complicated but interesting. These factors compel designing a robust classifier and authenticator for the beverages (tea and water). By applying the techniques of Sammon's Nonlinear Mapping (NLM) and entropy-based fuzzy clustering method on the characteristic signatures of different tea and water brands obtained from electronic tongue (e-tongue), a particle swarm optimization (PSO)-tuned fuzzy logic-based expert system was designed for classification and subsequent authentication of beverages. Some commonly used dimension reduction techniques and clustering techniques were also briefly discussed.

BACKGROUND

Previously, a number of research had assessed the quality of beverages using various analytical techniques, such as high-performance liquid chromatography (HPLC), gas chromatography-mass spectrometry (GC-MS), capillary electrophoresis (CE) etc. (Ren et al., 2013; Yang et al., 2020, Zhou et al., 2022). However, all of the above-mentioned techniques are relatively time-consuming, complex, and expensive, which limits their practical applicability. Recently, electronic tongue (e-tongue)-based automated beverage and food quality monitoring has become quite prevalent (Banerjee et al., 2019; Calvini & Pigani, 2022; Garcia-Breijo et al., 2011; Hu et al., 2022; Moreno et al., 2006; Rifna et al., 2022; Sipos et al., 2012; Wang et al., 2019; Wu et al., 2022; Zeng et al., 2022).

An e-tongue consists of some non-specific solid-state ion sensors, different types of transducers, data collectors, and machine learning algorithms for data analysis aiming characterization of liquid samples (Al-Dayyeni et al., 2021; Apetrei & Apetrei, 2013; Escuder-Gilabert & Peris, 2010; Kirsanov et al., 2013; Marx et al., 2021; Ribeiro et al., 2021; Riul Jr. et al., 2010; Tahara & Toko, 2013). Various electrochemical methods, such as pulse voltammetry, potentiometry, amperometry, and stripping

DOI: 10.4018/978-1-7998-9220-5.ch119

voltammetry were deployed in e-tongue to generate characteristic signatures (like current signatures due to pulse voltammetry) of the liquid sample to be analyzed. An e-tongue is not a taste sensor; the result of characterization is not necessarily correlated with human taste perception or compared with panelists. In dynamic interfacial techniques, it is not humanly possible to classify just by executing a visual inspection of the waveforms obtained as an output from an e-tongue. Cross selectivity (partial overlapping selectivity) of sensors employed and non-stationarities in the corresponding signals were the reasons, which demand the deployment of machine learning algorithms to formulate automated/ computer-based systems for authentication purposes (Ciosek & Wróblewski, 2007; Vlasov et al., 2005). It might be appropriate to refer to a few research contributions regarding the applications of multivariate statistical, neural network-based, and fuzzy logic-based machine learning components practiced in e-tongue devices dedicated to quality monitoring.

Mineral water samples commercially available in the Indian market were utilized to generate e-tongue signatures and developed classifiers using different machine learning algorithms like Slantlet-transform (ST)-based neural networks, Cross correlation-based Sammon's non-linear mapping (NLM), PLS, and PCA (Kundu et al., 2011a, 2011b; Kundu & Kundu, 2013). Sammon's NLM-based tea classifier/authenticator was developed using e-tongue signatures of commercially available tea brands in the Indian market (Kundu & Kundu, 2012). RPCA-based commercial tea classifier was also reported (Kundu et al., 2017). Recently, a correlation coefficient and cluster analysis-based tea aroma detection technique (Wang et al., 2021) and a tea quality identification system based on semi-supervised learning of generative adversarial network (Zhang et al., 2022) were proposed. A convolutional neural network-based feature extraction approach was also utilized in e-tongue system for tea classification (Zhong et al., 2019). A neuro-fuzzy approach for classifying and assessing the aroma, flavor, and taste of black tea using e-tongue and electronic nose (e-nose) signals was also proposed (Mondal et al., 2017). Several studies on utilizing e-tongue and/or e-nose signals to develop classifiers of black tea quality evaluation using the principle of fuzzy logic were previously reported (Roy et al., 2013; Tudu et al., 2009, 2015).

FOCUS OF THE ARTICLE

In the aforesaid backdrop, present research effort is dedicated to designing a beverage classification and authentication device using Sammon's NLM, entropy-based fuzzy clustering method, and subsequent PSO-tuned fuzzy logic-based expert system design. The performance of the developed techniques has been tested on two data sets, as mentioned below.

Data Collection

A data set consisting of six numbers of water brands (Aquafina, Bisleri, Kingfisher, Oasis, Dolphin, and McDowell) certified by ISI were considered for data generation using platinum working electrode in the e-tongue (Kundu, 2015). Each of the brands possessing 3 numbers of samples and each of the samples containing 4402 numbers of features (current signatures from e-tongue due to pulse voltammetric experimentation) were considered to create training database (18×4402). One more replicate; 4th sample time series data were created/simulated for each of the brands under consideration by appending random noise to any of the three training samples, and later those were used for testing the developed algorithms.

E-tongue signals related to tea (using silver as working electrode and six different ISI certified grades of tea; namely Brookbond, Double-diamond, Godrej, Lipton, Lipton-Darjeeling, Marvel), each having three samples resulted into a (18×4402) training data matrix (Kundu, 2015), were also used in this study. The unknown brand sample was generated by considering any subsample of a brand perturbed with 5–10% random noise and used for testing purposes. To validate the applicability of the developed classifier/authenticator in a rugged manner, an integration of noise level up to 10% for a test sample was considered.

The data obtained from E-tongue signals were higher dimensional data and cannot be visualized. To resolve this problem, it was required to map this higher dimensional data to a two-dimensional data set. A number of mapping methods are available in the literature, which may be either linear or non-linear methods. Among the linear methods, the most commonly applied methods are principal component analysis, least square mapping, projection pursuit mapping, etc. (König, 2001; Siedlecki et al., 1988). On the contrary, Sammon's NLM (Sammon, 1969), VISOR algorithm (Koeinig et al., 1994), Self-Organizing Maps (Kohonen, 1997) are some of the frequently used non-linear mapping techniques. In the present study, Sammon's NLM was applied to tackle with the non-linear nature of the sensor data.

Clustering is an effective technique that can investigate the patterns in the data set and assemble them into several clusters based on some similarities. Clusters can either have fixed and well-defined boundaries (crisp clusters) or may have imprecise boundaries (fuzzy clusters). Some of the widely used fuzzy clustering techniques are fuzzy ISODATA (Dunn, 1973), Fuzzy C-Means (Bezdek, 1981), potential-based clustering (Chiu, 1994), fuzzy k-nearest neighborhood algorithm (Keller et al., 1985), entropy-based clustering (Yao et al., 2000), etc. The current study utilized entropy-based fuzzy clustering to classify the two-dimensional data set obtained after mapping.

The Sammon-Fuzzy design was machinated in such a manner that the classifier/authenticator (both for tea and water) could deal with the uncertainties in the measurements of unknown test samples and be competent of bearing a certain degree of inconsistency with respect to their sources. The developed tools and techniques are discussed below.

Design of Fuzzy Logic-Based Authentication System

The classification and subsequent authentication of unknown tea and water samples were carried out in three stages. Sammon's NLM was employed to lower the dimension of sensor data due to the inherent nonlinearity present in it. Data in the subspace were clustered using Entropy-based fuzzy clustering technique followed by the design of a fuzzy logic-based expert system towards authentication of water/tea brands. All the algorithms were coded and implemented in MATLAB R2016a.

Sammon's Nonlinear Mapping Technique

Sammon's NLM technique is one of the most efficient and widely used algorithms for multivariate data analysis (Sammon, 1969). In this algorithm, point mapping of N number of higher L dimensional vectors to a lower dimensional space (two or three dimensions) is achieved to enhance visualization of the data configuration. The preservation of the inherent structure of data under the mapping is ensured by maintaining the interpoint distances in the higher and lower dimensional spaces as closely as possible, which, in turn, is achieved by minimizing an error or stress function.

Let us consider N vectors in an L-space denoted by X_i, $i=1,\ldots,N$ and the corresponding N vectors in a d-space are represented as Y_i, $i=1,\ldots,N$. The distance between L-space vectors X_i, x_j and d-space vectors Y_i, Y_j are designated as $d_{ij} = dist[X_i, X_j]$ and $D_{ij} = dist[Y_i, Y_j]$, respectively. In terms of Euclidean distance, it can be expressed as follows:

$$d_{ij} = \sqrt{\sum_{k=1}^{L} \left[x_{ik} - x_{jk} \right]^2} \tag{1}$$

$$D_{ij} = \sqrt{\sum_{k=1}^{d} \left[y_{ik} - y_{jk} \right]^2} \tag{2}$$

The d-space configuration can be chosen either at random or by using the principal components (PCs) of the sample covariance matrix. The stress function can be written in the form shown below.

$$E = \frac{1}{\sum_{i<j}^{N} d_{ij}} \sum_{i<j}^{N} \frac{\left(d_{ij} - D_{ij} \right)^2}{d_{ij}} \tag{3}$$

It is a function of $d \times N$ variables denoted by y_{pq}, where $p=1,\ldots,N$ and $q=1,\ldots,d$. In this NLM technique, y_{pq} variables are adjusted, or d-space configuration is changed equivalently in order to minimize the error, which is achieved using a steepest descent method. The mapping error after m-th iteration is represented by $E(m)$.

$$E(m) = \frac{1}{\sum_{i<j}^{N} d_{ij}} \sum_{i<j}^{N} \frac{\left(d_{ij} - D_{ij}(m) \right)^2}{d_{ij}} \tag{4}$$

where

$$D_{ij}(m) = \sqrt{\sum_{k=1}^{d} \left[y_{ik}(m) - y_{jk}(m) \right]^2} \tag{5}$$

In $m+1$-th iteration, the d-space configuration is evaluated like the following:

$$y_{pq}(m+1) = y_{pq}(m) - (MF) \bullet (\Delta_{pq}(m)) \tag{6}$$

where

$$\Delta_{pq}(m) = \frac{\dfrac{\partial E(m)}{\partial y_{pq}(m)}}{\dfrac{\partial^2 E(m)}{\partial y_{pq}(m)^2}} \tag{7}$$

Here, MF is termed as the "magic factor" having a value of 0.3 or 0.4. The partial derivatives can be expressed as shown below.

$$\frac{\partial E}{\partial y_{pq}} = \frac{-2}{\sum_{i<j}^{N} d_{ij}} \sum_{\substack{j=1 \\ j \neq p}}^{N} \left(\frac{d_{pj} - D_{pj}}{d_{pj} D_{pj}} \right) \left(y_{pq} - y_{jq} \right) \tag{8}$$

$$\frac{\partial^2 E(m)}{\partial y_{pq}(m)^2} = \frac{-2}{\sum_{i<j}^{N} d_{ij}} \sum_{\substack{j=1 \\ j \neq p}}^{N} \frac{1}{d_{pj} D_{pj}} \left[\left(d_{pj} - D_{pj} \right) - \frac{\left(y_{pq} - y_{jq} \right)^2}{D_{pj}} \left(1 + \frac{\left(d_{pj} - D_{pj} \right)}{D_{pj}} \right) \right] \tag{9}$$

Entropy-Based Fuzzy Clustering

In entropy-based fuzzy clustering method (Yao et al., 2000), the entropy values at each data point are considered for the formation of clusters. Entropy is evaluated based on a similarity measure. The Euclidean distance between two data points determines their similarity. The data point of the minimum entropy is chosen as the center of a cluster and those data points having similarity with this cluster center greater than a pre-defined threshold value β, form a cluster. If the number of data points belonging to a cluster is detected to be more than $\gamma\%$ of the total number of data points, then it is designated as a valid one, otherwise these data points are confirmed as outliers (Chattopadhyay et al., 2009). The values of the parameters: β and γ are determined depending on the nature of the data set considered for clustering. Considering a data set of N data points of L dimensions, this algorithm comprises of the following steps (Pratihar, 2014):

- Step 1: The whole data were arranged in a matrix [T] of N rows and L number of columns.
- Step 2: Euclidean distance between two points i and j was calculated like the following:

$$d_{ij} = \sqrt{\sum_{k=1}^{L} \left(x_{ik} - x_{jk} \right)^2} \tag{10}$$

- Step 3: Similarity S_{ij} between points i and j, which varies in the range of [0.0, 1.0] was determined as shown below.

$$S_{ij} = e^{-\alpha d_{ij}} \tag{11}$$

$$\alpha = \frac{\ln 2}{\bar{d}} \tag{12}$$

where a is a constant and $\bar{d}$ is the mean distance between all pairs of data points.
- Step 4: The total entropy value of a data x_i with respect to all other present in the set was calculated using the formula given below.

$$E_i = -\sum_{\substack{j \in x \\ j \neq i}}^{j \neq i} \left(S_{ij} \log_2 S_{ij} + \left(1 - S_{ij} \right) \log_2 \left(1 - S_{ij} \right) \right) \tag{13}$$

- Step 5: The data point with the minimum entropy value was declared as the cluster center and denoted by $x_{j\,min}$.
- Step 6: $x_{j\,min}$ and all other data points possessing similarity with the cluster center more than β were considered as a single cluster and was eliminated from $[T]$.
- Step 7: Steps 5 to 7 were repeated till $[T]$ became empty.
- Step 8: The validity of the clusters formed was checked by identifying the number of data points belonging to each cluster. If this value was seen to be less than $\gamma\%$ of the total data points, the cluster was declared as invalid and its corresponding data points were identified as outliers.

Fuzzy Logic-Based Authenticator Tuned by a PSO

Let us assume that the application of entropy-based fuzzy clustering on the data set comprising of N data points of L dimensions yielded C number of clusters. The cluster centers were denoted by $\left(x_1^*, x_2^*, \ldots, x_C^*\right)$. Any cluster center x_k^* was composed of two vectors y_k^* and z_k^*. Here, y_k^* was a M dimensional vector representing the inputs, whereas z_k^* was the output vector of L–M dimensions. With respect to the kth cluster, the rule can be written like the following:

IF U is close to y_k^* THEN V is close to z_k^*,

where U and V are input and output vectors of a data point, respectively. A total of C number of rules constitute the rule base. The membership function signifying the degree to which the kth rule is satisfied followed Gaussian distribution, and is shown below.

$$\mu_k = e^{-\frac{u-y_k^{*2}}{2\sigma_k^2}} \tag{14}$$

where u represents the input vector ($U=u$), σk denotes the standard deviation. The output vector v ($V=v$) was calculated, as given below.

$$v = \frac{\sum_{k=1}^{C} w_k \mu_k Z_k^*}{\sum_{k=1}^{C} w_k \mu_k} \tag{15}$$

The additional weight w_k was used to widen the search space for optimization (Majumder & Pratihar, 2018). The values of σ_k and w_k were to be optimized to improve the performance of the fuzzy reasoning tool, which can be used for classification and authentication. Previously, (Yao et al., 2000) determined the optimum values of σ_k using a steepest descent technique. However, there is a possibility of the optimum solutions to get trapped in the local minima, as it is a gradient-based method. To overcome the above stated problem, optimization was carried out using a PSO (Kennedy & Eberhart, n.d.). The objective function to be minimized was average absolute percent deviation in prediction, as given below.

$$f = \frac{1}{N'}\sum_{j=1}^{N'} \frac{1}{R}\sum_{i=1}^{R} \left| \frac{TO_{ij} - CO_{ij}}{TO_{ij}} \times 100 \right| \tag{16}$$

where N' and R represent the number of training cases and dimensionality of the output vector, respectively. TO_{ij} and CO_{ij} represent the target and calculated output values, respectively, of the ith response for the jth training case (Pratihar & Kundu, 2019).

Fuzzy Logic-Based Classification and Authentication Algorithm

- A matrix X' of dimensions ($N \times L$) representing sensor data set of N numbers of points (including the data points used for training of the fuzzy-logic based authenticator and those data points that are used for testing the same) containing L number of features was considered. N_1 number of data points were used for training and N_2 number of data points were utilized for testing ($N = N_1 + N_2$).
- These N number of L dimensional vectors were mapped to a two-dimensional space using Sammon's NLM Technique (refer to section 3.1). Here, the d-space configuration was chosen utilizing the principal components (PCs) of the sample covariance matrix. A matrix of dimension ($N \times 2$) was constructed.
- A training matrix XS of dimension ($N_1 \times 3$) was formed, where the first two columns represented the 2–D mapped features (inputs) and the third column indicated the corresponding sample type (output). The values of the input columns were normalized in the range of 0 to 1.
- This training matrix was considered for entropy-based fuzzy clustering. Let us suppose that C number of clusters were formed in 3–D space (refer to section 3.2).
- This training matrix and the cluster centers formed were exploited to develop a fuzzy logic-based authenticator and the necessary parameters were optimized by means of a PSO algorithm (refer to section 3.3).
- Any unknown sample type can be authenticated, if its 2–D mapped features are available. The normalized testing matrix of dimensions ($N_2 \times 2$) was employed to justify the same. Figure 1 shown the schematic representation of the developed algorithm.

Figure 1. Schematic representation of the algorithm

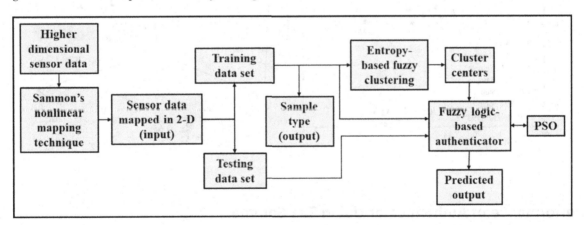

SOLUTIONS AND RECOMMENDATIONS

Two types of fuzzy authentication systems were designed for ISI certified commercial water and tea brands available in the Indian market. The authentication performance for both the systems with respect to unknown samples are as follows:

Performance of Authenticator Using Water Sample

Sammon's NLM technique was employed for the reduction of 4402-dimensional water data set to a 2-dimensional data set. Six clusters were formed using the 18×3 dimensional testing data set using Entropy-based fuzzy clustering technique. The values of the parameters: β and γ were kept fixed to 0.75 and 10% respectively. The values of σ_k and w_k were optimized using a PSO with their values being varied within [0.01, 0.99] and [0.001, 0.1], respectively. The parameters of PSO were obtained through a parametric study, which are as follows: Swarm size= 100, Maximum number of iterations= 1000, inertial weight= 1, cognitive parameter= 1.5 and social parameters= 2.0. The testing matrix of dimensions (6×2) (six unknown samples) was authenticated using the PSO-tuned Fuzzy logic-based authenticator with 100% accuracy. The six clusters formed from the training data along with the location of testing data after authentication in three-dimensional space is shown in Figure 2.

Figure 2. (a) Water sample data set mapped in a 2–D space using Sammon's NLM technique, (b) location of the six training data clusters and testing data set (after authentication) in 3-D space for water sample

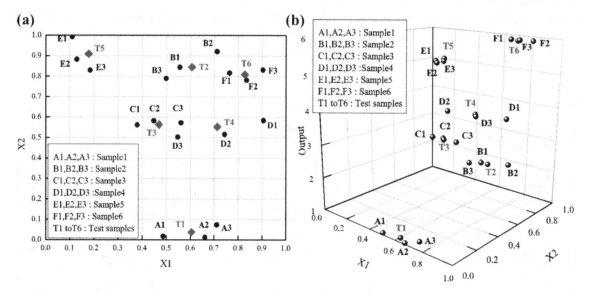

Performance of Authenticator Using Tea Sample

For the reduction of 4402-dimensional tea data set to a 2-dimensional one, Sammon's NLM technique was employed. Six clusters were formed using the 18×3 dimensional testing data set using Entropy-based fuzzy clustering technique with the values of β and γ set to 0.90 and 10%, respectively. The values of σ_k and w_k were optimized using a PSO within their respective ranges of [0.01, 0.99] and [0.001, 0.1], respectively. The parameters of PSO were obtained through a parametric study as follows: swarm size=

100, maximum number of iterations= 1000, inertial weight= 1, cognitive parameter= 1.5 and social parameters= 2.0. The six unknown tea samples were authenticated using the PSO-tuned Fuzzy logic-based authenticator with 100% accuracy. From Figure 3, the six clusters formed from the training data set along with the location of testing data set (on post authentication) in three-dimensional space can be observed.

Figure 3. (a) Tea sample data set mapped in a 2–D space using Sammon's NLM technique, (b) location of the six training data clusters and testing data set (after authentication) in 3-D space for tea sample

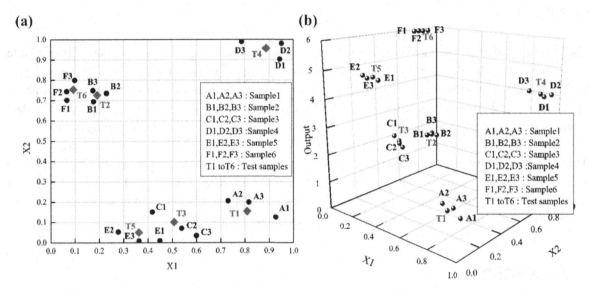

All the classifiers designed could efficiently detect the unknown samples pertaining to various tea and water brands. In some previous studies, for classification and authentication of water brand types, an automated authentication tool utilizing a hybrid combination of Slantlet-Transform-based feature extractor with BPNN-based binary classifier was developed, having authentication performance mostly in the upper 80% and quite often exceeding 90%. Moreover, ordinary Sammon's classifier had yielded 2.97% misclassification, whereas enhanced Sammon's classifier exhibited no misclassification; the misclassification rate of cross-correlation-based PCA classifier was obtained as 2.4% and PLS-based authenticator and classifier performed without misclassification (Kundu, 2015). In case of tea brand types classification and authentication, dissimilarity-based classifier employing moving window-based adaptive pattern matching approach showed a misclassification of 1.38%, whereas a PLS-based authenticator and classifier had 100% authentication performances (Kundu, 2015). An incremental fuzzy classifier for black tea using the e-nose data showed a classification rate of 80% (Tudu et al., 2009), whereas an incremental fuzzy c-means method for the same had an average classification rate of 75.63% (Tudu et al., 2015). Also, a fuzzy neural network model utilizing the fusion of both e-tongue and e-nose signals displayed an overall classification rate of 89.442% for black tea (Roy et al., 2013). So, it can be safely inferred that fuzzy logic-based classifier and authenticator proposed in this work could serve in a better way than most of the methods applied earlier for classification and authentication of water and tea samples using the same e-tongue signals considered in this study to construct the database.

FUTURE RESEARCH DIRECTIONS

The performances of dimensionality reduction technique and clustering tools and fuzzy logic-based expert systems depend on a number of parameters. In the future, an attempt will be made to evolve an intelligent fuzzy logic-based online-authentication system, which will be able to make the prediction accurately for the problems of varying complexities by self-adjusting its parameters.

CONCLUSION

The present work was an endeavor to deploy fuzzy logic in classifying various commercially available water and tea brands. An expert system was also designed to detect unknown brands of water/tea samples with 100% efficiency. Sammon's NLM was used to convert the higher dimensional sensory database (18×4402) into 2–D plane for visualization. Fuzzy clustering was done based on similarity of the data points and fuzzy logic-based expert system was developed, as it a potential tool for dealing with imprecision and uncertainty associated with the data set, as these were collected through the real experiments. Thus, dimensionality reduction for visualization, entropy-based fuzzy clustering for classification and a PSO-tuned expert system as automated beverage authenticators are the three contributions of the present study. To the extent of our knowledge, no previous reference on the development of such type of fuzzy-logic based water and tea classifier is available in the open literature.

REFERENCES

Al-Dayyeni, W. S., Al-Yousif, S., Taher, M. M., Al-Faouri, A. W., Tahir, N. M., Jaber, M. M., Ghabban, F., Najm, I. A., Alfadli, I. M., Ameerbakhsh, O. Z., Mnati, M. J., Al-Shareefi, N. A., & Saleh, A. H. (2021). A review on electronic nose: Coherent taxonomy, classification, motivations, challenges, recommendations and datasets. *IEEE Access: Practical Innovations, Open Solutions*, *9*, 88535–88551. doi:10.1109/ACCESS.2021.3090165

Apetrei, I. M., & Apetrei, C. (2013). Voltammetric e-tongue for the quantification of total polyphenol content in olive oils. *Food Research International*, *54*(2), 2075–2082. doi:10.1016/j.foodres.2013.04.032

Banerjee, M. B., Roy, R. B., Tudu, B., Bandyopadhyay, R., & Bhattacharyya, N. (2019). Black tea classification employing feature fusion of e-nose and e-tongue responses. *Journal of Food Engineering*, *244*, 55–63. doi:10.1016/j.jfoodeng.2018.09.022

Bezdek, J. C. (1981). *Pattern recognition with fuzzy objective function algorithms*. Springer. doi:10.1007/978-1-4757-0450-1

Calvini, R., & Pigani, L. (2022). Toward the development of combined artificial sensing systems for food quality evaluation: A review on the application of data fusion of electronic noses, electronic tongues and electronic eyes. *Sensors (Basel)*, *22*(2), 577. doi:10.339022020577 PMID:35062537

Chattopadhyay, S., Pratihar, D. K., & De Sarkar, S. C. (2009). Fuzzy-logic-based screening and prediction of adult psychoses: A novel approach. *IEEE Transactions on Systems, Man, and Cybernetics. Part A, Systems and Humans*, *39*(2), 381–387. doi:10.1109/TSMCA.2008.2010138

Chen, D., Chen, G., Sun, Y., Zeng, X., & Ye, H. (2020). Physiological genetics, chemical composition, health benefits and toxicology of tea (Camellia sinensis L.) flower: A review. *Food Research International*, *137*, 109584. doi:10.1016/j.foodres.2020.109584 PMID:33233193

Chiu, S. L. (1994). Fuzzy model identification based on cluster estimation. *Journal of Intelligent & Fuzzy Systems*, *2*(3), 267–278. doi:10.3233/IFS-1994-2306

Ciosek, P., & Wróblewski, W. (2007). Sensor arrays for liquid sensing – electronic tongue systems. *Analyst (London)*, *132*(10), 963. doi:10.1039/b705107g PMID:17893798

da Silva Pinto, M. (2013). Tea: A new perspective on health benefits. *Food Research International*, *53*(2), 558–567. doi:10.1016/j.foodres.2013.01.038

Dunn, J. C. (1973). A fuzzy relative of the ISODATA process and its use in detecting compact well-separated clusters. *Journal of Cybernetics*, *3*(3), 32–57. doi:10.1080/01969727308546046

Escuder-Gilabert, L., & Peris, M. (2010). Review: Highlights in recent applications of electronic tongues in food analysis. *Analytica Chimica Acta*, *665*(1), 15–25. doi:10.1016/j.aca.2010.03.017 PMID:20381685

Garcia-Breijo, E., Atkinson, J., Gil-Sanchez, L., Masot, R., Ibañez, J., Garrigues, J., Glanc, M., Laguarda-Miro, N., & Olguin, C. (2011). A comparison study of pattern recognition algorithms implemented on a microcontroller for use in an electronic tongue for monitoring drinking waters. *Sensors and Actuators. A, Physical*, *172*(2), 570–582. doi:10.1016/j.sna.2011.09.039

Hu, G., Mian, H. R., Abedin, Z., Li, J., Hewage, K., & Sadiq, R. (2022). Integrated probabilistic-fuzzy synthetic evaluation of drinking water quality in rural and remote communities. *Journal of Environmental Management*, *301*, 113937. doi:10.1016/j.jenvman.2021.113937 PMID:34731953

Keller, J. M., Gray, M. R., & Givens, J. A. (1985). A fuzzy K-nearest neighbor algorithm. *IEEE Transactions on Systems, Man, and Cybernetics. SMC*, *15*(4), 580–585. doi:10.1109/TSMC.1985.6313426

Kennedy, J., & Eberhart, R. (n.d.). Particle swarm optimization. *Proceedings of ICNN'95 - International Conference on Neural Networks, 4*, 1942–1948. 10.1109/ICNN.1995.488968

Kirsanov, D., Zadorozhnaya, O., Krasheninnikov, A., Komarova, N., Popov, A., & Legin, A. (2013). Water toxicity evaluation in terms of bioassay with an Electronic Tongue. *Sensors and Actuators. B, Chemical*, *179*, 282–286. doi:10.1016/j.snb.2012.09.106

Koeinig, A., Bulmahn, O., & Glesner, M. (1994). Systematic methods for multivariate data visualization and numerical assessment of class separability and overlap in automated visual industrial quality control. In *Proceedings of the British Machine Vision Conference 1994*, 19.1-19.10. 10.5244/C.8.19

Kohonen, T. (1997). Exploration of very large databases by self-organizing maps. In *Proceedings of International Conference on Neural Networks (ICNN'97), 1*, PL1–PL6. 10.1109/ICNN.1997.611622

König, A. (2001). Dimensionality reduction techniques for interactive visualization, exploratory data analysis, and classification. In N. R. Pal (Ed.), *Pattern Recognition in Soft Computing Paradigm* (pp. 1–37). World Scientific Publishing Co Pte Ltd., doi:10.1142/9789812811691_0001

Kundu, M., Kundu, P. K., & Damarla, S. K. (2017). *Chemometric Monitoring: Product Quality Assessment, Process Fault Detection, and Applications*. CRC Press. doi:10.1201/9781315155135

Kundu, P. K. (2015). *Qualitative assessment of beverages using electronic tongue* (Accession No. 2018-12-21T09:13:17Z) [Doctoral dissertation, Jadavpur University]. Shodhganga: A reservoir of Indian theses @ INFLIBNET.

Kundu, P. K., Chatterjee, A., & Panchariya, P. C. (2011). Electronic tongue system for water sample authentication: A Slantlet-Transform-based approach. *IEEE Transactions on Instrumentation and Measurement*, *60*(6), 1959–1966. doi:10.1109/TIM.2011.2115410

Kundu, P. K., & Kundu, M. (2012). A comparative study on tea samples classification by e-tongue using cross correlation based PCA, PCA and Shamon's nonlinear mapping method. *2012 7th International Conference on Electrical and Computer Engineering*, 490–493. 10.1109/ICECE.2012.6471594

Kundu, P. K., & Kundu, M. (2013). The e-tongue-based classification and authentication of mineral water samples using cross-correlation-based PCA and Sammon's nonlinear mapping. *Journal of Chemometrics*, *27*(11), 379–393. doi:10.1002/cem.2521

Kundu, P. K., Panchariya, P. C., & Kundu, M. (2011). Classification and authentication of unknown water samples using machine learning algorithms. *ISA Transactions*, *50*(3), 487–495. doi:10.1016/j.isatra.2011.03.003 PMID:21507400

Majumder, S., & Pratihar, D. K. (2018). Multi-sensors data fusion through fuzzy clustering and predictive tools. *Expert Systems with Applications*, *107*, 165–172. doi:10.1016/j.eswa.2018.04.026

Marx, Í. M. G., Veloso, A. C. A., Casal, S., Pereira, J. A., & Peres, A. M. (2021). Sensory analysis using electronic tongues. In C. M. Galanakis (Ed.), *Innovative Food Analysis* (pp. 323–343). Elsevier., doi:10.1016/B978-0-12-819493-5.00012-1

Mondal, S., Banerjee, R., Tudu, B., Bandyopadhyay, R., & Bhattacharyya, N. (2017). A neuro fuzzy based black tea classifying technique using electronic nose and electronic tongue. In *Proceedings of the First International Conference on Intelligent Computing and Communication. Advances in Intelligent Systems and Computing, vol 458*. (pp. 477–484). Singapore: Springer. doi:10.1007/978-981-10-2035-3_49

Moreno, L., Merlos, A., Abramova, N., Jiménez, C., & Bratov, A. (2006). Multi-sensor array used as an "electronic tongue" for mineral water analysis. *Sensors and Actuators. B, Chemical*, *116*(1–2), 130–134. doi:10.1016/j.snb.2005.12.063

Pratihar, B., & Kundu, M. (2019). Proceedings of 2019 IEEE region 10 symposium (TENSYMP) Classification and prediction of cardiovascular autonomic neuropathy severity using fuzzy logic-based expert system. *2019 IEEE Region 10 Symposium (TENSYMP)*, 692–697. doi:10.1109/TENSYMP46218.2019.8971285

Pratihar, D. K. (2014). *Soft Computing: Fundamentals and applications*. Narosa Publishing House Pvt. Ltd.

Ren, G., Li, T., Wei, Y., Ning, J., & Zhang, Z. (2021). Estimation of Congou black tea quality by an electronic tongue technology combined with multivariate analysis. *Microchemical Journal*, *163*, 105899. doi:10.1016/j.microc.2020.105899

Ren, G., Wang, S., Ning, J., Xu, R., Wang, Y., Xing, Z., Wan, X., & Zhang, Z. (2013). Quantitative analysis and geographical traceability of black tea using Fourier transform near-infrared spectroscopy (FT-NIRS). *Food Research International*, *53*(2), 822–826. doi:10.1016/j.foodres.2012.10.032

F

Ribeiro, C. M. G., Strunkis, C. de M., Campos, P. V. S., & Salles, M. O. (2021). Electronic nose and tongue materials for Sensing. In *Reference Module in Biomedical Sciences*. Elsevier. doi:10.1016/B978-0-12-822548-6.00035-2

Rifna, E. J., Pandiselvam, R., Kothakota, A., Subba Rao, K. V., Dwivedi, M., Kumar, M., Thirumdas, R., & Ramesh, S. V. (2022). Advanced process analytical tools for identification of adulterants in edible oils – A review. *Food Chemistry*, *369*, 130898. doi:10.1016/j.foodchem.2021.130898

Riul, A. Jr, Dantas, C. A. R., Miyazaki, C. M., & Oliveira, O. N. Jr. (2010). Recent advances in electronic tongues. *Analyst (London)*, *135*(10), 2481. doi:10.1039/c0an00292e

Roy, R. B., Modak, A., Mondal, S., Tudu, B., Bandyopadhyay, R., & Bhattacharyya, N. (2013). Fusion of electronic nose and tongue response using fuzzy based approach for black tea classification. *Procedia Technology*, *10*, 615–622. doi:10.1016/j.protcy.2013.12.402

Sammon, J. W. (1969). A nonlinear mapping for data structure analysis. *IEEE Transactions on Computers*, *C–18*(5), 401–409. doi:10.1109/T-C.1969.222678

Siedlecki, W., Siedlecka, K., & Sklansky, J. (1988). An overview of mapping techniques for exploratory pattern analysis. *Pattern Recognition*, *21*(5), 411–429. doi:10.1016/0031-3203(88)90001-5

Sipos, L., Kovács, Z., Sági-Kiss, V., Csiki, T., Kókai, Z., Fekete, A., & Héberger, K. (2012). Discrimination of mineral waters by electronic tongue, sensory evaluation and chemical analysis. *Food Chemistry*, *135*(4), 2947–2953. doi:10.1016/j.foodchem.2012.06.021

Tahara, Y., & Toko, K. (2013). Electronic tongues–A review. *IEEE Sensors Journal*, *13*(8), 3001–3011. doi:10.1109/JSEN.2013.2263125

Tudu, B., Ghosh, S., Bag, A. K., Ghosh, D., Bhattacharyya, N., & Bandyopadhyay, R. (2015). Incremental FCM technique for black tea quality evaluation using an electronic nose. *Fuzzy Information and Engineering*, *7*(3), 275–289. doi:10.1016/j.fiae.2015.09.002

Tudu, B., Metla, A., Das, B., Bhattacharyya, N., Jana, A., Ghosh, D., & Bandyopadhyay, R. (2009). Towards versatile electronic nose pattern classifier for black tea quality evaluation: An incremental fuzzy approach. *IEEE Transactions on Instrumentation and Measurement*, *58*(9), 3069–3078. doi:10.1109/TIM.2009.2016874

Vlasov, Y., Legin, A., Rudnitskaya, A., Di Natale, C., & D'Amico, A. (2005). Nonspecific sensor arrays ("electronic tongue") for chemical analysis of liquids (IUPAC Technical Report). *Pure and Applied Chemistry*, *77*(11), 1965–1983. doi:10.1351/pac200577111965

Wang, J., Zhang, C., Chang, M., He, W., Lu, X., Fei, S., & Lu, G. (2021). Optimization of electronic nose sensor array for tea aroma detecting based on correlation coefficient and cluster analysis. *Chemosensors (Basel, Switzerland)*, *9*(9), 266. doi:10.3390/chemosensors9090266

Wang, J., Zhu, L., Zhang, W., & Wei, Z. (2019). Application of the voltammetric electronic tongue based on nanocomposite modified electrodes for identifying rice wines of different geographical origins. *Analytica Chimica Acta*, *1050*, 60–70. doi:10.1016/j.aca.2018.11.016

Wu, J., Ouyang, Q., Park, B., Kang, R., Wang, Z., Wang, L., & Chen, Q. (2022). Physicochemical indicators coupled with multivariate analysis for comprehensive evaluation of matcha sensory quality. *Food Chemistry*, *371*, 131100. doi:10.1016/j.foodchem.2021.131100

Yang, Y., Zhang, M., Hua, J., Deng, Y., Jiang, Y., Li, J., Wang, J., Yuan, H., & Dong, C. (2020). Quantitation of pyrazines in roasted green tea by infrared-assisted extraction coupled to headspace solid-phase microextraction in combination with GC-QqQ-MS/MS. *Food Research International*, *134*, 109167. doi:10.1016/j.foodres.2020.109167

Yang, Z., Miao, N., Zhang, X., Li, Q., Wang, Z., Li, C., Sun, X., & Lan, Y. (2021). Employment of an electronic tongue combined with deep learning and transfer learning for discriminating the storage time of Pu-erh tea. *Food Control*, *121*, 107608. doi:10.1016/j.foodcont.2020.107608

Yao, J., Dash, M., Tan, S., & Liu, H. (2000). Entropy-based fuzzy clustering and fuzzy modeling. *Fuzzy Sets and Systems*, *113*(3), 381–388. doi:10.1016/S0165-0114(98)00038-4

Zeng, Q., Luo, X., & Yan, F. (2022). The pollution scale weighting model in water quality evaluation based on the improved fuzzy variable theory. *Ecological Indicators*, *135*, 108562. doi:10.1016/j.ecolind.2022.108562

Zhang, S. F., Zhu, D. H., & Chen, X. J. (2022). Analysis of E-tongue data for tea classification based on semi-supervised learning of generative adversarial network. *Chinese Journal of Analytical Chemistry*, *50*(2), 77–85. doi:10.1016/j.cjac.2021.11.008

Zhong, Y. H., Zhang, S., He, R., Zhang, J., Zhou, Z., Cheng, X., Huang, G., & Zhang, J. (2019). A convolutional neural network based auto features extraction method for tea classification with electronic tongue. *Applied Sciences (Basel, Switzerland)*, *9*(12), 2518. doi:10.3390/app9122518

Zhou, B., Wang, Z., Yin, P., Ma, B., Ma, C., Xu, C., Wang, J., Wang, Z., Yin, D., & Xia, T. (2022). Impact of prolonged withering on phenolic compounds and antioxidant capability in white tea using LC-MS-based metabolomics and HPLC analysis: Comparison with green tea. *Food Chemistry*, *368*, 130855. doi:10.1016/j.foodchem.2021.130855

ADDITIONAL READING

Babaei, S. F., Hassani, A. H., Torabian, A., Karbassi, A. R., & Hosseinzadeh, L. F. (2011). Water quality index development using fuzzy logic: A case study of the Karoon River of Iran. *African Journal of Biotechnology*, *10*(50), 10125–10133. doi:10.5897/AJB11.1608

Birle, S., Hussein, M. A., & Becker, T. (2013). Fuzzy logic control and soft sensing applications in food and beverage processes. *Food Control*, *29*(1), 254–269. doi:10.1016/j.foodcont.2012.06.011

Borràs, E., Ferré, J., Boqué, R., Mestres, M., Aceña, L., & Busto, O. (2015). Data fusion methodologies for food and beverage authentication and quality assessment – A review. *Analytica Chimica Acta*, *891*, 1–14. doi:10.1016/j.aca.2015.04.042 PMID:26388360

Debjani, C., Das, S., & Das, H. (2013). Aggregation of sensory data using fuzzy logic for sensory quality evaluation of food. *Journal of Food Science and Technology*, *50*(6), 1088–1096. doi:10.100713197-011-0433-x PMID:24426020

Dewanti, N. A., & Abadi, A. M. (2019). Fuzzy logic application as a tool for classifying water quality status in Gajahwong River, Yogyakarta, Indonesia. *IOP Conference Series. Materials Science and Engineering*, *546*(3), 032005. doi:10.1088/1757-899X/546/3/032005

Dhar, R., Bhalerao, P. P., & Chakraborty, S. (2021). Formulation of a mixed fruit beverage using fuzzy logic optimization of sensory data and designing its batch thermal pasteurization process. *Journal of Food Science*, *86*(2), 463–474. doi:10.1111/1750-3841.15583 PMID:33438202

Egbueri, J. C., & Agbasi, J. C. (2022). Data-driven soft computing modeling of groundwater quality parameters in southeast Nigeria: Comparing the performances of different algorithms. *Environmental Science and Pollution Research International*, *29*(25), 38346–38373. Advance online publication. doi:10.100711356-022-18520-8 PMID:35079969

Khodasevich, M. A., Sinitsyn, G. V., Gres'ko, M. A., Dolya, V. M., Rogovaya, M. V., & Kazberuk, A. V. (2017). Identification of counterfeit alcoholic beverages using cluster analysis in principal-component Space. *Journal of Applied Spectroscopy*, *84*(3), 517–520. doi:10.100710812-017-0503-6

Liu, J., Zuo, M., Low, S. S., Xu, N., Chen, Z., Lv, C., Cui, Y., Shi, Y., & Men, H. (2020). Fuzzy evaluation output of taste information for liquor using electronic tongue based on cloud model. *Sensors (Basel)*, *20*(3), 686. doi:10.339020030686 PMID:32012652

Pławiak, P., & Maziarz, W. (2014). Classification of tea specimens using novel hybrid artificial intelligence methods. *Sensors and Actuators. B, Chemical*, *192*, 117–125. doi:10.1016/j.snb.2013.10.065

Wang, X., Gu, Y., & Liu, H. (2021). A transfer learning method for the protection of geographical indication in China using an electronic nose for the identification of Xihu Longjing tea. *IEEE Sensors Journal*, *21*(6), 8065–8077. doi:10.1109/JSEN.2020.3048534

Zhou, B., Ma, B., Ma, C., Xu, C., Wang, J., Wang, Z., Yin, D., & Xia, T. (2022). Classification of Pu-erh ripened teas and their differences in chemical constituents and antioxidant capacity. *Lebensmittel-Wissenschaft + Technologie*, *153*, 112370. doi:10.1016/j.lwt.2021.112370

KEY TERMS AND DEFINITIONS

Dimensionality Reduction: The higher dimensional data are mapped to the lower dimension for the purpose of visualization.

Electronic Tongue: It is an instrument that includes arrays of solid-state ion sensors, transducers, data collectors and data analysis tools.

Fuzzy Clustering: It is done for a set of data points based on their similarity values.

Fuzzy Logic: It is a potential tool for reasoning after dealing with imprecision and uncertainty of data set.

Sammon's Nonlinear Mapping: It is a distance-preserving tool used for the dimensionality reduction.

Similarity: It is checked between two data points using their Euclidean distance.

Tea Sample: E-tongue signal-based data related to six different ISI certified grades of tea, namely Brookbond, Double-diamond, Godrej, Lipton, Lipton-Darjeeling, Marvel) are utilized.

Water Sample: E-tongue signal-based data set consisting of six number of water brands (Aquafina, Bisleri, Kingfisher, Oasis, Dolphin, and McDowell) is used.

Section 26
Gradient–Boosting Decision Trees

Aircraft Maintenance Prediction Tree Algorithms

Dima Alberg
Shamoon College of Engineering, Israel

Yossi Hadad
Shamoon College of Engineering, Israel

INTRODUCTION

Maintenance of aircraft components have always been an important consideration in aviation. Accurate prediction of possible failures will increase the reliability of aircraft components and systems and decrease maintenance of big future failures. The scheduling of maintenance operations help determine the overall maintenance and overhaul costs of aircraft components. Maintenance costs constitute a significant portion of the total operating expenditure of aircraft systems (Kadir, Onur, & Harun, 2020).

According to Fan (2015) there are three main types of maintenance for equipment: corrective maintenance, preventive maintenance, and predictive maintenance. Corrective maintenance helps manage repair actions and unscheduled fault events, such as equipment and machine failures. When aircraft equipment fails while it is in use, it is repaired or replaced. Preventive maintenance can reduce the need for unplanned repair operations. It is implemented by periodic maintenance to avoid equipment failures or machinery breakdowns. Tasks for this type of maintenance are planned to prevent unexpected downtime and breakdown events that would lead to repair operations. Predictive maintenance, as the name suggests, uses some parameters which are measured while the equipment is in operation to guess when failures might happen. It intends to interfere with the system before faults occur and help reduce the number of unexpected failures by providing the maintenance personnel with more reliable scheduling options for preventive maintenance. Assessing system reliability is important to choose the right maintenance strategy.

The operation and maintenance of modern predictive sensor-equipped systems such as aircraft generates vast amounts of numerical and symbolic data streams. According to Tawaikuli et al. (2020) m Multi Sensor Data Fusion oulti sensor data streams collection and preparation is an expensive, resource consuming and complex phase often performed centrally on raw data for a specific application. These data streams are generated by thousands of sensors installed in various components of the aircraft and then sent in real-time to relational databases storages in ground stations. Before being transmitted to the ground, a number of on-board computer systems monitor and analyze the data stream in order to make sure that various systems of the aircraft are operating properly. However, once the data stream is stored in central databases, further data analysis is rarely performed. This paper presents an algorithm that makes use of this data stream in order to develop interval Machine Learning ML regression tree models to predict the need for replacement of various aircraft components before they become non-operational. The end goal is to implement this ML model in a flight monitoring system that will receive the real-time multi-sensor data input from aircraft fleet, analyze it, and output alerts in the form of appropriate replacement rules when there is a need for component maintenance.

DOI: 10.4018/978-1-7998-9220-5.ch120

The monitoring system will use the automatically generated multi-sensor data stream from the aircraft, and induce an interval regression tree model described in this paper, to detect component problems and recommend their replacement. Such a system could help improve the airline's operation by: reducing the number of delays, reducing maintenance costs, helping achieve better maintenance planning, and increasing the level of safety. The approach proposed in this paper applies techniques from the fields of machine learning on big amounts of complex historical data in order to develop the predictive models required by the monitoring system. The approach described addresses four fundamental difficulties with existing data mining approaches: automatic selection of relevant data, automatic labeling of instances, an evaluation method that accounts for dependencies between the instances, and a scoring function measuring the extent to which the results fit the domain requirements. By addressing these four issues, we believe that the proposed approach will help extend the range of potential applications for ML techniques. Examples of other applications that can benefit from the approach developed in this paper are: prediction of problems in complex systems (e.g.: trucks, ships, trains, and cars), prediction of problems with complex industrial equipment for which a lot of data is continuously acquired, and prediction of critical events in medical applications (e.g. Emergency Room care). The fact that the proposed approach relies on a minimal amount of domain specific information will also facilitate the adaptation to other applications.

The paper is organized as follows: The related work is described in the next section. In Section 3 the INGPRET algorithm is introduced and its computational complexity and performance metrics are analyzed. In Section 4 some experimental results are reported for two real-world temporal data sets. Section 5 discusses the main features of the proposed algorithm and identifies some future research directions.

BACKGROUND

Actually, most of the regression tree algorithms apply binary recursive partitioning, since each node is always split into two child nodes, and are recursive, because the process is repeated at every node. It is also possible to split the data into three or more subsets or child nodes. Regression trees provide quite simple and easily interpreted regression models with reasonable accuracy. However, according to Breiman et al. (1984), these methods are known for their split instability. Finally, the interested reader may find a more detailed survey of regression tree methods in (Alberg, Last, & Kandel, 2012).

XGBoost stands for eXtreme Gradient Boosting and is a scalable implementation of gradient boosting regression trees (Chen & Guestrin, 2016). Since its release in 2016, XGBoost has been a very popular machine learning method, and it has a highly impressive winning record when it comes to machine learning competitions. XGBoost has already been used in several aviation risk assessment applications (Zhang & Mahadevan, 2019), (Shen & Wei, 2020) and represents a boosting ensemble of regression and decision trees. It is worth noting that XGBoost performance is not affected by multicollinearity (highly correlated explanatory variables), which is often highly present in multi-sensor data.

Interval prediction is an important part of the forecasting process and is intended to enhance the accuracy of point estimation. An interval forecast usually consists of upper and lower limits between which the future value is expected to lie with a prescribed probability. The limits are sometimes called forecast limits (Wei, 2006) or prediction bounds (Brockwell & Davis, 1991), while the interval is sometimes called a confidence interval (Granger & Newbold, 1986) or a forecast region (Hyndman, 1995). We prefer the more widely-used term "prediction interval," as used by (Chatfield, 2001) [REMOVED TA FIELD] and (Harvey, 1989), both because it is more descriptive and because the term "confidence interval" is usually applied to interval estimates for fixed but unknown parameters. In contrast, a prediction interval is an interval estimate for an unknown future value. Because a future value can be regarded as a random variable at the time the forecast is made, a prediction interval involves a different sort of probability statement from that implied by a confidence interval.

PROPOSED METHOD

In many aircraft multi-sensor data streams, the data is available as time-continuous statistical moments such as mean or variance that are calculated over pre-defined measurement intervals, rather than as raw values sampled at discrete points in time. However, reporting single predicted values for the mean response values of new sensor measurement intervals can be misleading. The reason is that due to a large unexplained variance of the target variable, for many intervals the actual mean values may be very different from any specific point estimation. In this paper, we therefore shift our attention from predicting a single *mean value* to predicting *intervals*, which are expected to contain the actual mean values with a given probability.

The above considerations create a need for a stable algorithm that can process incoming mean-variance aggregated multivariate temporal data and makes stable interval predictions of a target numerical variable, with a given degree of statistical confidence.

The proposed method is based on the assumption that input and output variables in an aggregated data stream are characterized by linear or nonlinear dependencies (or both), which can be represented using the proposed INGPRET model. The proposed regression trees algorithm differs from currently described (Alberg, Last, & Kandel, 2012) state-of-the-art regression tree algorithms such as XGBoost, CART, Random Forest, RETIS, M5, SMOTI, MAUVE, GUIDE by the following characteristics:

- The use of synchronous mean and variance estimators of numerical features
- The use of gradient-boosting learners based on mean variance estimators
- Node splitting based on the Mahalonobis distance between the two statistical estimators
- Novel representation of prediction intervals at the tree leaves

In our opinion, the suggested approach enables one to utilize predictive feature information obtained from mean and variance of temporally aggregated instances. This approach also enables achieving a considerable reduction in the depth of the induced prediction tree by using interval prediction tree leaves.

Both statistics can be used as candidate predictive features by a prediction tree induction algorithm. Therefore, if the two represented statistics indeed exhibit independent and identical behavior, then the aggregated input variable can be represented within a robust two-tail prediction interval at a user-defined confidence level, such as 95%.

DATA PREPARATION

In our INGPRET algorithm, the average and variance of each aggregated input variable is mapped to the univariate Mahalonobis statistic using an auxiliary control variable $T(\blacksquare)$ (Mason & Young, 2002). We used this statistic because of its expected response to changes in both statistical moments. This statistic also should enable detecting and ignoring outliers, which cause prediction instability, as well as overcoming the model overfitting effect, thus achieving a considerable reduction in the size of the induced tree. It is important to note that the widely known Mahalonobis distance is a special case of the Hotelling distance, when the number of arguments equals two. The Mahalonobis distance arguments, shown below, are two measured statistical estimates of the aggregated time series target mean and standard deviation variables.

$$X \sim \left\{ \overline{x}_i \left(r \right); \; \hat{s}^2_{x_i} \left(r \right) \right\}, \tag{1}$$

where $i \in (1 \ldots n)$ and n is the number of instances of aggregated input variable X.

Let us suppose that each aggregated instance i of the input variable X is represented by the mean and variance estimators $\left\{ \overline{x}_i \left(r \right) \right\}$ and $\left\{ \hat{s}^2_{x_i} \left(r \right) \right\}$ for a given temporal measurement aggregation resolution r. Let $x_A \left\{ \widehat{\overline{x}_i} \left(r \right) \right\}$ and $x_S \left\{ \widehat{\hat{s}^2_{x_i}} \left(r \right) \right\}$ be the sample average values over all aggregated instances, and let $V_A \left\{ \hat{s}^2 \left(\overline{x}_i \left(r \right) \right) \right\}$ and $V_S \left\{ \hat{s}^2 \left(\hat{s}^2_{x_i} \left(r \right) \right) \right\}$ be the sample variance of the corresponding unbiased estimators.

Proposition: The corresponding sample covariance between $\left\{ \overline{x}_i \left(r \right); \; \hat{s}^2_{x_i} \left(r \right) \right\}$, denoted by $V_{AS} \left\{ \hat{s}^2 \left(\overline{x}_i \left(r \right), \hat{s}^2_{x_i} \left(r \right) \right) \right\}$, and the Mahalonobis distance between the two measured statistical moments of an aggregated instance i of the input variable X, may be calculated as follows:

$$\begin{aligned} T \left(\overline{x}_i \left(r \right); \; \hat{s}^2_{x_i} \left(r \right) \right) = {} & \frac{r}{V_A V_S - V_{AS}^2} \cdot \left[V_S \cdot \left(\overline{x}_i \left(r \right) - x_A \right)^2 + V_A \cdot \left(\hat{s}^2_{x_i} \left(r \right) - x_S \right)^2 \right] \\ & - \frac{2r}{V_A V_S - V_{AS}^2} \cdot \left(V_{AS} \cdot \left(\overline{x}_i \left(r \right) - x_A \right) \cdot \left(\hat{s}^2_{x_i} \left(r \right) - x_S \right) \right) \end{aligned} \tag{2}$$

PREDICTION INTERVALS

To the best of our knowledge, the studies discussed in the regression tree section of the methodology section restrict their attention exclusively to point forecasting. A point forecast is a single number, which is an estimate of the unknown true future value. Although it is the most likely estimation of the possible future value implied by the induced model, it provides no information as to the degree of uncertainty associated with the forecast. For this reason, one may justifiably argue that the comparison of alternative point forecasts is of limited use because such a comparison completely neglects the variability associated with forecasting. For an improved and more meaningful comparison of the performance of forecasting models, the degree of uncertainty associated with forecasting should be explicitly taken into account. One of our main contributions in this research is focused on constructing an advanced prediction interval model at the INGPRET regression tree leaves. A prediction interval indicates a range of possible future outcomes with a prescribed level of confidence. As Chatfield (2001) points out, interval forecasts are of a greater value to decision-makers than are point forecasts. Interval forecasts, therefore, should be used more widely in practical applications, as they allow for a thorough evaluation of future uncertainty and for contingency planning.

A

Traditionally, prediction intervals have been constructed based on the assumption that forecast errors follow a normal distribution. However, the validity of this normal approximation is doubtful, because the assumption of normality of the forecast error distribution often may not be justified in practice. The INGPRET algorithm computes the bounds of a prediction interval $PI^{U,L}(a)$ for the corresponding tree leaf with a user-defined confidence level $(1-a)$ that uses the following integrated parametric / non-parametric estimation method (3):

If training instances (nl) at the leaf node fit the normal distribution according to the Jarque-Bera (JB) goodness-of-fit test (3.1.6), then:

$$PI^{U,L}(\alpha) = \begin{cases} \overline{y}_i \mp z_{\alpha/2} \cdot \hat{s}_y \sqrt{\left(1 + 1/n_l\right)}, & n_l > 30 \\ \overline{y}_i \mp t_{1-\alpha/2,\, n_l-1} \cdot \hat{s}_y \sqrt{\left(1 + 1/n_l\right)}, & n_l \epsilon \left(3; 30\right] \end{cases} \tag{3}$$

Else, if $n_l \leq 3$ or if training instances at the leaf node do not fit the normal distribution, then:

$PI^{U,L}(a) = [\text{min}; \text{max}]$,

where $i \in (1\ldots n)$ are tree leaf instances, $z_{a/2}$ and $t_{1-\alpha/2, n_l-1}$ are standardized normal and Student-t distributions with significance error levels of a, and $\overline{y}_i$, $\hat{s}_y$ represents mean and standard deviation estimators of the tree leaf training instances n_l. Thus, when the confidence level equals zero (that is, when $a=100\%$), the corresponding values of $t_{0.5}$ and $z_{0.5}$ distributions also equal zero, and the algorithm transforms the interval representation of a tree leaf into a sample average of the target variable. This special case is very useful for experimental comparison between the interval prediction tree and the regression tree algorithms that perform point statistic estimation.

INGPRET TREE ALGORITHM

The INGPRET tree growing phase presented in Figure 1 continues until at least one stopping criterion is met. In the INGPRET case, we distinguish between three stopping rules. The first gradient optimization weak learner (1) is applied by the algorithm when the selected terminal node instances are normally distributed. In this case, we will represent the terminal nodes by prediction intervals with the aid of previously calculated statistical moments. The stopping criterion evaluates the minimum probability for observations to lie within the prediction interval. Construction of the tree then stops when a user-defined threshold criterion is reached. The threshold criterion is the confidence level, which was previously defined by the user as $1-a$. The second stopping rule (2) is applied when the number of selected terminal node instances is lower than some pre-specified value (such as 30). If the user-specified minimum confidence level equals 100%, the terminal node prediction is represented by the previously calculated first statistical moment (sample average). Finally, the third stopping rule is applied when all instances at the terminal node are outliers.

Table 1. INGPRET tree growing pseudo code

Input:	Training temporal data set, S Input attribute set, X Target variable, Y Significance level a Split criterion (Defined in section 3.2) Stopping criteria Boosting optimizer Weights, w_0
Output:	The INGPRET tree

```
Begin
Begin
Create a new INGPRET tree T weak learner
If first stopping rule (1) then mark T as a leaf node with prediction interval (α)
Else
  If second stopping rule (2) then mark T as a leaf node with sample mean
  If second stopping rule (3) then mark T as an outlier leaf node
  Else
    Obtain INGPRET tree splitting criterion (Figure 6)
    Fit weak learner T with best splitting feature moment that minimizes the
    weighted sum of errors for mean and variance estimators.
    Update tree model
    Recursively call INGPRET tree growing algorithm
End If
Return INGPRET tree
End
```

PERFORMANCE METRICS

The overall performance of the INPGRET algorithm is compared to the state-of-the-art point predictors calculated by two global metrics, namely the Root Mean Squared Error (*RMSE*) and Root Mean Absolute Error (*RMAE*). Intuitively, they represent the square and absolute difference between an interval average value and the true value of the quantity being estimated, and will be computed by the following expressions:

$$RMSE\left(T\right) = \sqrt{\frac{1}{K} \sum_{k=1}^{K} \left(y_k - \overline{y}\right)^2} \tag{4}$$

$$RMAE\left(T\right) = \sqrt{\frac{1}{K} \sum_{k=1}^{K} \left|y_k - \overline{y}\right|} \tag{5}$$

where K is number of instances, y_k is the observed value of target variable, and $\overline{y}$ is the corresponding interval average value.

In order to compare the accuracy of trees from different domains, the Explained Variability (*EV*) measure is defined by (6). This measure evaluates the goodness-of-fit of a given model, or in other words, it answers the question: "How well does the corresponding prediction model approximate the real data, when compared to the mean rule model?"

$$EV\left(T;\alpha\right) = \frac{\left(MSE\left(MR\right) - MSE\left(T\right)\right)}{MSE\left(MR\right)} \cdot 100\%$$

(6)

Here *MR* is a mean rule predictor, which predicts the mean value of the training set for all instances, and *MSE(MR)* and *MSE(T)* are metrics of mean square errors that are respectively evaluated from the mean rule predictor and corresponding regression tree *(T)* model.

Another option for comparing regression tree models is the Cost Complexity Measure (*CCM*) (Breiman & Friedman, 1985), which uses Root Mean Square Error *RMSE(T)* to determine an estimated cost of the regression tree *T*:

$$CCM(T) = RMSE(T) + \gamma \cdot TS(T)$$

(7)

Here *RMSE(T)* is the estimated error cost of regression tree *T*, where *TS(T)* is the number of terminal nodes in the tree, and γ is the user-defined non-negative integer cost complexity parameter adopted from (Breiman & Friedman, 1985). The CCM option shows that for a given complexity parameter, there is a unique smallest sub-tree of the saturated tree that minimizes the cost-complexity measure, which actually quantifies the tradeoff between the tree size and its training error rate. Thus, the best level of time granularity can be found by minimizing the value of the cost-complexity measure. The γ parameter represents the user-specific tradeoff between error cost and tree complexity. When γ equals 1, the user is ready to add a terminal node, for a minimal decrease of one unit in the Root Mean Squared Error; otherwise, when γ is greater than 1, the user prefers to keep the existing tree. In our further experiments, we assume that the cost-complexity coefficient equals 1, so the penalty for one terminal node is equivalent to one unit of the Root Mean Squared Error.

AIRCRAFT DATA SET

Multi-sensor data fusion (MSDF) is the process of combining or integrating measured or preprocessed data or information originating from different active or passive sensors or similar sources, in order to produce a more specific, comprehensive, and unified data set about an event of interest that has been observed (Naipeng, et al., 2021), (Raol, 2010). A successful MSDF model should achieve improved accuracy and more specific inferences than could be obtained using a single sensor alone.

The data set for the experiment was obtained from a proprietary MSDF data warehouse of aircraft maintenance data and is illustrated in Figure 2. This data warehouse was designed for fast multi-sensor data retrieval and aggregation from an Oracle OLTP system source. The star-based fact table was equipped with flight time, sensors data, information on failures, systems data, prediction parameters, and flight and maintenance dimensions, while the highest flight time resolution was represented in minutes of aircraft flight.

Finally, four distinct data sets were derived from the aircraft maintenance MSDF data warehouse (Table 1). The first two data sets consist of 1,316 and 1,068 instances, respectively, and have a numerical target variable of the number of failures in a specific aircraft system denoted by System A. The main difference between the two first data sets is in the prediction lag of the previously defined target variable. Thus, in the first two data sets the prediction lag equals 20 and 50 hours, respectively. The third and fourth data sets consist of 1,310 and 1,050 instances, respectively, and use the same prediction lags with the predicted target variable of failures in a system denoted as System B.

Figure 1. Aircraft Maintenance Data (proprietary)

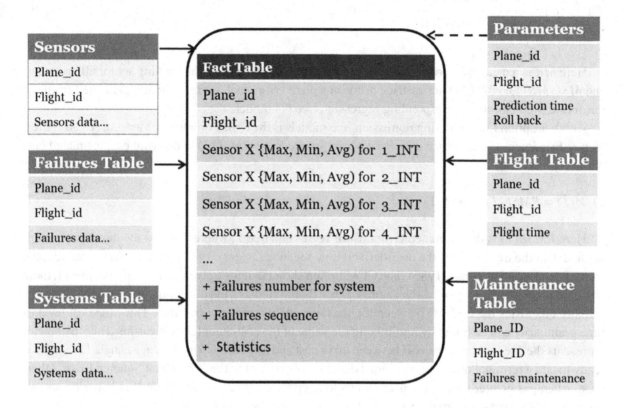

Table 2. The aircraft maintenance MSDF data sets

#Instances		Target Variable	
		System A	System B
Prediction horizon (ahead time lag)	20 Hours	1,316	1,310
	50 Hours	1,068	1,050

All data sets were represented by 203 numerical attributes. The first attributes denote the flight ID and the start and end flight timestamps, while the remaining 200 numerical attributes represent aggregated mean/variance estimators of flight time intervals.

Finally, it can be concluded that, the data preprocessing and analysis in this research plays very critical and important role in accurate massive data collection, transforming and time series multi sensor data warehouse construction. Multi sensor warehouse data collected for machine learning must be preprocessed to fit input requirements or improve performance and accuracy. Data preparation is an expensive, resource consuming and complex data preparation and preparation often performed centrally on raw data for a specific application. The constructed multi sensor data warehouse should contain accurate and valid sensors data which avoid noise and losing useful information due to various transmission errors or malfunctioning sensors.

MACHINE LEARNING MODELS

The following Table 2 demonstrates averaged results for System A from the 10 time 10 fold cross-validation for nine state-of-the-art models, versus the INGPRET algorithm. It is clear that in both data sets the least reliable models in terms of RMAE and RMSE accuracies are: Support Vector Machines with Radial Basis Function Kernel (SVM RBF), Neural Network Multi Layer Perceptron (NN-MLP), XGBoost Trees, and Bagging M5 Tree (B-M5P). It can be seen that errors for data sets in the 20-hours prediction horizon are lower than those in 50-hours horizon. This result confirms the fact that all the regression tree models used for System A data sets are more stable and accurate in the short-time horizon prediction. Another interesting result is that the relatively large Random Forests trees model does not decrease the overall model accuracy. This result confirms previous studies, which showed that the Random Forest RF algorithm tends to overlearn in situations that involve large amounts of time-series correlated data.

Table 3. System A data sets learners comparison (10 time 10 fold cross validation)

Learner	SYSTEM A - 50 Hours Horizon				SYSTEM A - 20 Hours Horizon			
	TS	*RMAE*	*RMSE*	*CCM*	*TS*	*RMAE*	*RMSE*	*CCM*
Add. Reg.		1.43±0.19	2.82±0.31			1.22±0.14	2.09±0.22	
B-M5P	198	1.30±0.68	3.95±4.63	6.18±4.63	221	1.05±0.80	3.24±0.38	6.1±0.38
XGBoost	283	1.16±0.16	2.23±0.37	5.42±0.37	133	0.95±0.11	1.54±0.27	3.26±0.27
M5 Rules	225	1.20±0.26	3.01±0.46	5.54±0.46	139	0.92±0.14	1.93±0.34	3.73±0.34
M5P	229	1.18±0.25	2.90±0.45	5.48±0.45	254	0.89±0.13	1.73±0.33	5.02±0.33
NN-MLP		1.47±1.58	4.19±8.49			1.18±0.36	2.46±0.90	
INGPRET	243	1.22±0.24	2.78±0.35	5.52±0.35	119	0.92±0.24	1.92±0.43	3.46±0.43
RepTree	333	1.22±0.23	2.70±0.43	6.45±0.43	195	0.95±0.20	1.85±0.45	4.37±0.45
RF	299	1.39±0.25	3.44±0.47	6.81±0.47	285	0.95±0.25	1.89±0.47	5.58±0.47
SVM RBF		1.56±0.79	4.38±4.71			1.23±0.22	2.90±0.54	

Figure 3 demonstrates paired Student-t test results between analyzed regression tree models and worst models SVM RBF and B-M5P with the confidence level of 90%. In the case of the 50-hour prediction horizon (3.a), the best models in terms of the RMSE measure and CCM, are XGBoost, RepTree, and the INGPRET tree. It might be said that XGBoost is slightly more accurate than INGPRET, but the INGPRET model, in its turn, is more compact in terms of tree size (243 vs. 283).

Similarly, in the case of the 20-hour prediction horizon (3.b), the best models are XGBoost, M5P, RepTree and the INGPRET tree. The same scenario is reproduced yet again here: the INGPRET model tree is more compact and slightly less accurate than corresponding XGBoost model. Finally, it can be concluded that in both systems INGPRET accuracies were significantly higher than SVM, Neural Network and traditional additive regression tree models and similar to the modern gradient-boosting regression tree XGBoost algorithm. This fact confirmed our hypothesis that in large data sets the prediction tree strategy based on the mean-variance aggregation is preferable to the global additive regression model approach.

Figure 2. System A data sets learners (%) of confidence level (CL) comparison. Black bars demonstrate paired Student-t tests for RMSE accuracy and grey bars CCM tree size learners. Dotted line sets 90% confidence level accuracy

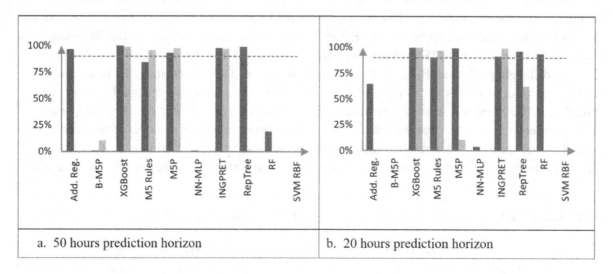

a. 50 hours prediction horizon | b. 20 hours prediction horizon

FUTURE RESEARCH DIRECTIONS

Nowadays, deep learning neural nets DL modeling is considered as one of the hot topics within the area of machine learning, artificial intelligence as well as data science and analytics, due to its learning capabilities from the given data. In future research, efforts will be made to study and implement experiments with DL models that are a fairly open topic that can improve existing interval regression tree methods and handle the above-mentioned concerns and tackle aircraft maintenance problems in a variety of application areas.

CONCLUSION

In aviation, each failure is important in terms of both safety and cost. An optimized maintenance scheduling can only be realized with close-to-realistic forecasts. Having maintenance times predicted ahead of failures will both prevent security excesses and reduce costs. In this paper, we have presented the INGPRET Interval Gradient Prediction Tree algorithm, which can predict values of numerical attributes in aggregated temporal data streams. The proposed algorithm differs from existing state-of-the-art regression algorithms in that it accomplishes the splitting of each input continuous feature according to the best mean-variance contributor, and because it removes outliers from the training data. The experiments conducted on two real-world data sets indicate that the proposed INGPRET algorithm produces accurate and compact interval models compared to such state-of-the-art machine learning algorithms like Support Vector Machines with Radial Basis Function Kernel (SVM RBF), Artificial Neural Network Multi-Layer Perceptron (ANN-MLP), and the Bagging M5P Tree. As a result, the algorithm builds more compact interval prediction trees compared to other trees models with statistically similar accuracy values in terms of RMAE RMSE and CCM metrics. This result was obtained by fact that INGPRET algorithm models build interval leaves instead of classical leave point estimators.

REFERENCES

Alberg, D., Last, M., & Kandel, A. (2012). Knowledge Discovery in Data Streams with Regression Tree Methods. *WIREs Data Mining Knowledge Discovery, 2012*(2), 69–78. doi:10.1002/widm.51

Breiman, L., & Friedman, J. (1985). Estimating Optimal Transformations for Multiple Regression and Correlation. *Journal of the American Statistical Association, 80*(391), 580–597. doi:10.1080/01621459.1985.10478157

Breiman, L., Friedman, J., Olshen, R., & Stone, C. (1984). *Classification and Regression Trees*. Wadsworth & Brooks/Cole. Pacific Grove.

Brockwell, P., & Davis, R. (1991). *Time Series: Theory and Methods*. Springer-Verlag. doi:10.1007/978-1-4419-0320-4

Chatfield. (2001). *Prediction Intervals for Time-Series Forecasting*. Boston: Kruger Academic Publishers.

Chen, T., & Guestrin, C. (2016). XGBoost: A Scalable Tree Boosting System. *Proceedings of the 22nd ACM SIGKDD International Conference on Knowledge Discovery and Data Mining*, 785–794. 10.1145/2939672.2939785

Fan, Q., & Fan, H. (2015). Reliability analysis and failure prediction of construction equipment with time series models. *Journal of Advanced Management Science*, 203 - 210.

Granger, C., & Newbold, P. (1986). Forecasting in Business and Economics (2nd ed.). Academic Press.

Harvey, A. (1989). *Forecasting, Structural Time Series Models and the Kalman Filter*. C.U.P.

Hyndman, R. (1995). Highest-Density Forecast Regions for Non-Linear and Non-Normal Time Series Models. *Journal of Forecasting, 14*(5), 431–441. doi:10.1002/for.3980140503

Kadir, C., Onur, I., & Harun, U. (2020). Failure Prediction of Aircraft Equipment Using Machine Learning with a Hybrid Data Preparation Method. *Scientific Programming*, 1–10.

Mason, R., & Young, J. (2002). Multivariate Statistical Process Control with Industrial Application. *ASA-SIAM Series on Statistics and Applied Probability, 9*.

Naipeng, L., Naigi, G., Yaguo, L., Xiaolei, F., Xiao, C., & Tao, Y. (2021, April). Remaining useful life prediction based on a multi-sensor data fusion model. *Reliability Engineering & System Safety*.

Raol, J. R. (2010). *Multi-Sensor Data Fusion: Theory and Practice*. CRC Press.

Shen, X., & Wei, S. (2020). Application of xgboost for hazardous material road transport accident severity analysis. *IEEE Access: Practical Innovations, Open Solutions, 8*, 206806–206819. doi:10.1109/ACCESS.2020.3037922

Tawakuli, A., Kaiser, D., & Engel, T. (2020). Synchronized Preprocessing of Sensor Data. *2020 IEEE International Conference on Big Data*, 3522-3531. 10.1109/BigData50022.2020.9377900

Wei, W. (2006). *Time Series Analysis: Univariate and Multivariate Methods*. Addison-Wesley.

Zhang, X., & Mahadevan, S. (2019). Ensemble machine learning models for aviation incident risk prediction. *Decision Support Systems*, *116*, 48–63. doi:10.1016/j.dss.2018.10.009

ADDITIONAL READING

Alt, F. (1985). Multivariate Quality Control. Encyclopedia of Statistical Sciences, 6, 110 - 122.

Geron, A. (2017). *Hands-On Machine Learning with Scikit-Learn and TensorFlow: Concepts, Tools, and Techniques to Build Intelligent Systems*. O'Reilly Media.

Hackeling, G. (2017). *Mastering Machine Learning with Scikit-Learn*. Packt Publishing Ltd.

Kimball, R., & Ross, M. (2013). *The Data Warehouse Toolkit: The Definitive Guide to Dimensional Modeling*. Wiley.

Skaf, Z., Dangut, M., & Jennions, I. (2021). An integrated machine learning model for aircraft components rare failure prognostics with log-based dataset. *ISA Transactions*, *113*, 127–139. doi:10.1016/j.isatra.2020.05.001 PMID:32423614

VanderPlace, J. (2016). *Python Data Science Handbook*. O'Reilly Media, Inc.

Wade, C. (2020). *Hands-On Gradient Boosting with XGBoost and scikit-learn: Perform accessible machine learning and extreme gradient boosting with Python*. Packt Publishing.

Zhang, X., & Mahadevan, S. (2019). Ensemble machine learning models for aviation incident risk prediction. *Decision Support Systems*, *116*, 48–63. doi:10.1016/j.dss.2018.10.009

KEY TERMS AND DEFINITIONS

Extreme Gradient Boosting Algorithm (XGBOOST): Scalable, distributed, gradient-boosted decision tree machine learning library. It provides parallel tree boosting and is the leading machine learning library for regression, classification, and ranking problems.

Interval Gradient Prediction Tree Algorithm (INGPRET): A scalable interval prediction tree algorithm which predicts values of numerical attributes in aggregated temporal data streams. The proposed algorithm differs from existing state-of-the-art regression algorithms in that it accomplishes the splitting of each input continuous feature according to the best mean-variance contributor, and because it removes outliers from the training data.

Multi-Sensor Data Fusion (MSDF): The process of combining or integrating measured or preprocessed data or information originating from different active or passive sensors or similar sources, to produce a more specific, comprehensive, and unified data set about an event of interest that has been observed.

Neural Networks Algorithm (NN): Scalable and robust supervised learning prediction algorithm that contains layers of interconnected nodes or perceptrons. These nodes feed the signal produced by a multiple linear regression into an activation function that may be nonlinear and produces a neural net prediction model.

A

Random Decision Trees Forest (RF): An ensemble learning bagging prediction algorithm for classification, regression, and other tasks that operates by constructing a multitude of decision trees. For classification tasks, the output of the random forest is the class selected by most trees. For regression tasks, the mean or average prediction of the individual trees is returned.

Support Vector Machines Algorithm (SVM): Scalable and robust supervised learning prediction algorithm that maps training examples to points in space so as to maximize the width of the gap between categories. New examples are then mapped into that same space and predicted to belong to a category based on which side of the gap they fall.

Section 27
Graph Learning

Graph Data Management, Modeling, and Mining

G

Karthik Srinivasan

University of Kansas, USA

INTRODUCTION

A graph or a network is an abstract representation of a set of objects in which some pairs of objects are connected to each other. Graphs can be a powerful medium for representation of underlying data especially if it contains multiple linked entities. Since most of the practical datasets do not have independent and identically distributed (i.e., i.i.d.) observations, graphs can be effectively used to connect different entities described in the observations. For example, if a dataset contains transactions between sellers and buyers and in a market, a graph can be created such as that sellers and buys are connected to each other based on common transactions and a graph network can be formed.

Graph analytics is the systematic computational analysis of graph data. There are numerous applications of graphs across multiple disciplines including but not restricted to world wide web, social science, cybersecurity, healthcare, ecology, finance, entertainment, political science. In order to find applications of graph analytics, one may examine if the underlying data consists of entities that may be inter-connected to each other through one or more empirical relationships. Some examples of such relationships are friendship between users of a social media application, employees reporting to other employees in an organization, products purchased with complementary, products, etc. This chapter introduces the reader to the breadth of graph analytics tools, techniques, algorithms, and software. After reading this chapter, the reader should be able to identify problems that can use a network approach as well as develop corresponding graph-based analytics solutions. While topics in graph analytics such as graph mining (Gosnell & Broecheler, 2020), graph databases (Sasaki, 2018), and graph modeling (Kolaczyk & Csardi, 2020) have been independently examined in textbooks and research papers, this chapter summarizes these components of graph analytics demonstrating basic applications using examples. It serves as an introductory text for data science enthusiasts by providing an overview of different topics as well as directions for further enquiry.

BACKGROUND

A graph or a network is made up of vertices and edges. It is mathematically represented as $G(V,E)$, where V is the set of vertices and E is the edges. In converse, vertices and edges of a graph G may be represented as $V(G)$ and $E(G)$ respectively. An edge joins two vertices in a graph. Likewise, two vertices are said to be adjacent if and only if there is an edge between them. Two vertices are said to be connected if there is a path from one to the other via any number of edges.

DOI: 10.4018/978-1-7998-9220-5.ch121

A vertex or a node is a single connection point in a graph. Vertices or nodes are entities such as people, products, biological cells, organizations which could be interconnected to each other in a particular configuration and the collection of such entities, and their interconnections constitutes the graph. Nodes are usually labeled but they could be unlabeled as well. An edge, link or relationship is a line segment that connects two nodes. A node without edges is permitted. However, an edge without nodes is not. Edges may have labels as well but are usually unlabeled. Nodes as well as edges can have their own attributes or properties.

Graphs can be further categorized into the type of nodes and the type of edges. Nodes may be single mode or multi-mode. Single mode networks, also called as one-mode or unipartite or homogenous networks have nodes of the same entity type (e.g., A friend network {John, Susan, George}). On the other hand, multi-mode or heterogeneous networks have nodes of multiple types (e.g., A customer-product-store network where customers {John, Susan, George} purchase one or more fruits {apples, oranges, bananas, strawberries} from stores {Target, Walmart}). A bipartite is a two-mode network (e.g., employer-employee network) that enjoys more attention than higher-mode networks as it has a wide range of applications including recommender engines (e.g., product recommendation in e-commerce, disease prognosis in patients, etc.). Nodes could be simple scalars or vectors with numeric or categorical attributes (e.g., {Gender, Age} of people in a friend network).

Edges can be either directed (e.g., a user following another user on Twitter) or undirected (e.g., two users connected as friends on Facebook). Edges can be either unweighted or weighted, such that they not only indicate the presence of a relationship between a pair of vertices, but also indicate the strength of the relationship in terms of a meaningful measure. Lastly, edges can be explicit based on relationship information provided in the context or implicit in which case the existence of an edge needs to be inferred. For example, a network with explicit edges is a friend-friend network where the relationship is the evidence of friendship whereas the contiguous-usa network (Weisstein, 2021) is an implicit network where the edges are inferred based on the fact that two U.S. states may share a border and therefore be geographically proximate.

Table 1 shows examples of different types of graphs categorized in terms of types of edges and types of nodes.

Table 1. Different types of graph and examples

Graph type	Example(s)
Undirected unweighted single mode network	Friendship network, contiguous USA network (Weisstein, 2021)
Undirected weighted network	Zachary karate network, Disease co-occurrence network (Srinivasan et al., 2018)
Directed unweighted network	Twitter following network, Paper citation network
Directed weighted network	Peer-to-peer lending market, International trade network
Bipartite network	User-item network, Patient-disease network (Liu et al., 2020)
Multimode network / Labeled property graph	Movies graph (Sasaki, 2018)

The Zachary karate club is a popular example of a weighted undirected graph and is shown in Figure 1. It has 34 nodes and 78 edges. The nodes are members of a university karate club and the edges indicate whether they interacted outside the club. The edge weights are the number of times the corresponding pair of members interacted. The data can be download using this link: http://vlado.fmf.uni-lj.si/pub/

networks/data/ucinet/ucidata.htm#zachary for an adjacency list or from here https://raw.githubusercontent.com/snap-stanford/snap/master/examples/node2vec/graph/karate.edgelist for an edgelist. It is also available in the *igraph* package of R.

The Movies graph is an example of a labeled property graph with persons and movies as node types (Sasaki, 2018). There are 171 nodes and 506 edges in this graph and a snapshot of this graph is shown in Figure 2.

The movies graph is also called as a labelled property graph or a knowledge graph. This is because it can be queried using a graph database as nodes are labelled and the nodes and edges have multiple properties or attributes.

Examples will be shown using *igraph* package in R software, *networkX* package in python software, *gephi*, and *neo4j*. All these packages and software have free/community versions available for download.

Figure 1. Zachary Karate network

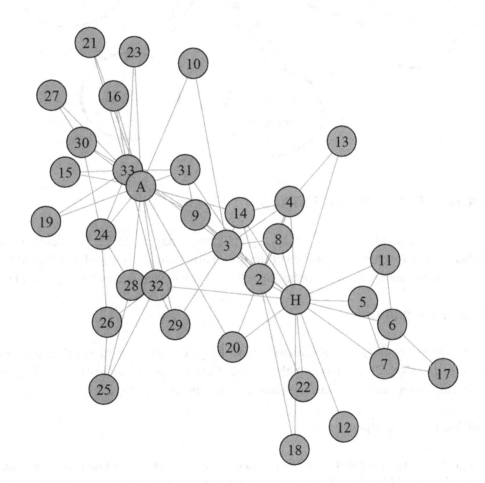

Figure 2. A snapshot of the movies graph from neo4j

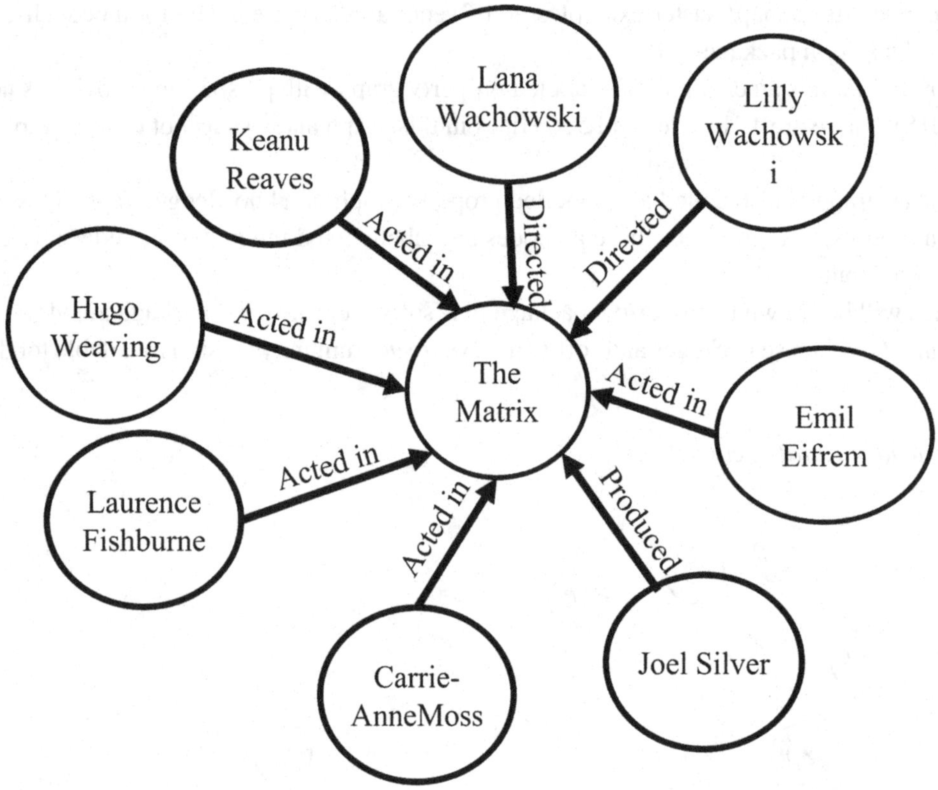

GRAPH ANALYTICS FUNDAMENTALS

Graph analytics can be divided into three parts – graph data management, graph modeling, and graph mining. In this section, fundamentals of each of the three parts are discussed in detail. In addition to the concepts, simple applications are described using related software and code where applicable.

Graph Data Management

Graph data storage and management is primarily done using adjacency matrices, edge lists, graph data frames and other graph objects such as graphML or .net files for standalone analysis; while graph databases are implemented for organizational systems running operational queries.

Storing Single Mode Graphs

Single mode graphs are typically stored and managed using common data structures edge lists, adjacency matrices or graph objects. Consider the simple unweighted undirected graph shown in Figure 3. The edge list and the adjacency matrix for this graph are shown in Table 2 and Table 3 respectively.

The edge list contains the pairs of vertex ids represented in first two columns followed by the edge weight and other edge attributes. It is the simplest representation of graph data.

Figure 3. A simple four node graph

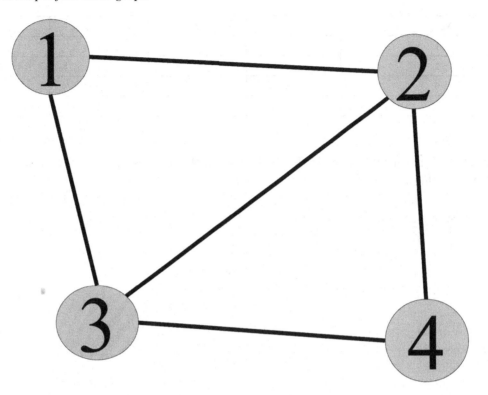

Table 2. Edge list of a simple four node network

Vertex	Vertex
1	2
1	3
2	3
2	4
3	4

Adjacency matrices, when compared to edge lists, are square matrices with evidence of edge (and edge weight) between pairs of nodes given by the respective value in cell where row and column names are the respective node labels. While they are bulkier to load for large networks, they are often faster to load when compared to long edge lists. Mathematically, the edge between nodes i and j is represented as a_{ij}, which is the element ij in the adjacency matrix A. For undirected networks, $A=A^T$, that is, A is a symmetric matrix. Whereas for directed networks, A need not be symmetric. Let the status of the relationship from i to j be denoted by aij, element ij of the adjacency matrix.

Both edge lists and adjacency matrices can be saved as .csv files and can be imported into the *igraph* package of R, *networkX* package of Python, and software such as *gephi* or *neo4j*.

Table 3. Adjacency of a simple four node network

Vertex	1	2	3	4
1	0	1	1	0
2	1	0	1	1
3	1	1	0	1
4	0	1	1	0

For example, importing the edge list (Table 2) into a graph object using *networkX* package in python can be done as follows:

```
import networkx as nx
import pandas as pd
import matplotlib.pyplot as plt
df = pd.DataFrame([[1,2],[1,3],[2,3],[2,4],[3,4]])
df.columns = ['Node_x','Node_y']
print(df)
G=nx.from_pandas_edgelist(df, "Node_x", "Node_y")
nx.draw_networkx(G, with_labels=True)
plt.axis('off')
plt.show()
```

Corresponding code to import an adjacency list (Table 3) into a graph object in *igraph* package in R can be done as follows:

```
library(igraph)
adj_mat = data.frame(cbind(c(0,1,1,0),c(1,0,1,1),c(1,1,0,1),c(0,1,1,0)))
rownames(adj_mat) = c(1,2,3,4)
colnames(adj_mat) = c(1,2,3,4)
G = graph_from_adjacency_matrix(adj_mat,mode = c("undirected"))
plot(G)
```

Other than edge lists and adjacency matrices, graphs can also be stored in data structures customized for storing graph data and its meta-information. A popular graph object file format is GraphML. GraphML is composed of Extensible Markup Language or XML which makes it both machine and human readable allowing this file format to cover wide range of graphical forms like hyper graphs, mixed graphs and undirected and directed graphs. Along with nodes and edge information, graph objects also store metadata such as layout, size, and color that can aid graph visualization. There are other similar formats such as .gdf, .gexf, .gml, .net, .vna, many of which are specific to graph analysis tools.

Storing and Managing Multi-mode Graphs

G

Graphs such as a user network in a social networking site are large and multi-modal. Therefore, instead of storing and manipulating such graphs using simple data structures or file systems, companies prefer utilizing databases for managing and querying such graphs.

A graph database is a database with an explicit graph structure. Graph databases are typically used for storing and managing multimode networks always called as labeled property graphs (LPG). LPG are primarily used for writing graph queries. Nodes in LPG belong to more than one label (e.g., employer, vendor, product, etc.), and edges and nodes are described by multiple attributes.

Graph databases cannot be replaced by tabular/relational databases or document-store databases for storing graphs as traversal – query across multiple nodes and edges becoming time consuming using traditional SQL JOINS. On the other hand, relational databases can be converted to graph databases by representing the rows in entity tables as nodes and creating corresponding relationships based on common columns used for the SQL JOINs. Figure 4 is adapted from the Neo4j software documentation and shows visually how a tabular database can be transformed to a graph database.

Figure 4. Tabular databases to graph database transformation (image adapted from Neo4j documentation)

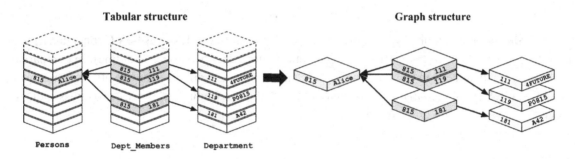

There are several graph database software vendors. Neo4j is one of the most popular providers of graph databases. Neo4j is available as a sandbox (ephemeral workspace), desktop software, and cloud version (aura). Neo4j uses Cypher, a graph query language that builds upon structured query language (SQL) while specialized to query graphs. Similar to SQL statements beginning with a SELECT keyword, Cypher statements begin with a MATCH keyword and their general syntax is as follows:

```
MATCH (FIRST NODE) - [RELATIONSHIP] - (SECOND NODE) <OPTIONAL FILTER CONDI-
TIONS> RETURN <Node.properties, Relationship.properties>
```

Directed graphs can be represented by including the > symbol next to the – symbol in the code as follows:

```
MATCH (FIRST NODE) - [RELATIONSHIP] -> (SECOND NODE) RETURN <Arguments>
```

The Neo4j sandbox accessible using URL https://neo4j.com/sandbox/ can be used to walk through the movie database in the Neo4j graph database. Table 4 shows common Cypher statements and their purposes:

Table 4. Examples of graph database queries

Cypher Statement	Purpose
MATCH (n) RETURN (n)	Returns all nodes in the graph
MATCH (p:Person) RETURN p	Returns all nodes in the graph belonging to label 'Person'
MATCH (m:Movie {released: 2003, tagline: 'Free your mind'}) RETURN m	Node attributes can be specified as filter conditions
MATCH (p:Person {born: 1965}) RETURN p.name, p.born	Instead of returning entire node, can also return select node attributes
MATCH (p:Person) WHERE p.born = 1965 RETURN p.name, p.born	Filter conditions can use WHERE keyword in SQL style
MATCH (p:Person)-[:LIVES_AT]->(h:Residence) RETURN p.name, h.address	Relationship labels are helpful to subset the graph
MATCH (p:Person)--(h:Residence) RETURN p.name, h.address	Skipping the relationship type returns values for all relationships between a pair of nodes
MATCH (n) DETACH DELETE n;	Delete all nodes and relationships
CALL db.propertyKeys()	Information stored about each node
CALL db.labels()	List all the different node labels in the graph database

Table 5 shows a few sample Cypher queries on the Movie database. It shows how Cypher can be used to perform multiple hops in graph traversals (i.e., query more than two nodes at a time). In comparison to SQL queries where cells in resultant tables have single values, graph queries can also return a list of values in each cell using custom functions such as collect) thus expanding the range of business enquiries that can be answered using graph queries.

Table 5. Examples of graph database queries on the Movies database

Business enquiry	Graph query
Find all people who acted in the movie, *The Matrix*.	MATCH (p:Person) - [rel:ACTED_IN] -> (m:Movie {title: 'The Matrix'}) RETURN p, rel, m
Find all people that acted in a movie and the directors for that same movie, returning the name of the actor, the movie title, and the name of the director.	MATCH (a:Person)-[:ACTED_IN]->(m:Movie)<-[:DIRECTED]-(d:Person) RETURN a.name, m.title, d.name
Find all of the actors and directors who worked on a movie, return the count of the number paths found between actors and directors and collect the movies as a list.	MATCH (actor:Person)-[:ACTED_IN]->(m:Movie)<-[:DIRECTED]-(director:Person) RETURN actor.name, director.name, **count**(m) AS collaborations, collect(m.title) AS movies

Knowledge Graphs

Multi-mode graphs in real applications can be specific to the data generation process. In the world wide web, companies such as google and Wikipedia have invested efforts into curating user inputs into validating the relationships between nodes of networks such as the word semantic network which often scale to more than billions of nodes. These graphs are called knowledge graphs.

A knowledge graph is a network of real-world entities – objects, events, situations, or concepts that may belong to different classes/labels. It is similar to semantic graphs and ontologies, which are formally defined based on taxonomy (e.g., animal specifies and sub-species classification, disease classification, etc.). Knowledge graphs utilize natural language processing (NLP) over large troves of data to construct a comprehensive view of nodes, edges, and labels through a process called semantic enrichment. Input to knowledge graph population can come from one or more sources consisting of structured data, semi structured data, free text or images, or direct authoring by human input.

Knowledge graphs can be either based on Resource Description Framework (RDF) a web standard used for data exchange; or Labeled Property Graphs used for efficient querying of linked entities. Once a knowledge graph is complete, it allows question answering and search systems to retrieve and reuse comprehensive answers to given queries. The google knowledge graph (GKG) is the most popular example of knowledge graph applications (Nigam et al., 2020). It is comprised of over 500 million objects, sourcing data from Freebase, Wikipedia, the CIA World Factbook, as well as (curated) user inputs. It allows google to answer factual questions posted in their search engine such as such as "How tall is the Eiffel Tower?", "Where were the 2016 Summer Olympics held?", or "How is the weather today?" (Google, 2021).

Graph Modeling

Explanatory models for representing graph structure can be either mathematical models that are based on assuming an underlying mechanism such as Barabasi-Albert model (Albert & Barabási, 2002), or based on statistical modeling that accounts for stochasticity and assumes that the network can be reasonably estimated from the data and depends on hypothesized effects (Kolaczyk & Csardi, 2020).

Among statistical models, the exponential random graph model (ERGM) is the most generalizable modeling approach as it is analogous to generalized linear models for tabular data. The purpose of family of ERG models is to describe parsimoniously the local selection forces that shape the global structure of the network (Hunter & Handcock, 2006). The general formulation of a Bernoulli ERGM for an un-weighted network $G=(V,E)$ is given as follows:

$$\mathbb{P}_\theta (Y = y) = \left(\frac{1}{K} \right) \exp\{\theta^T g(y)\} \tag{1}$$

In Equation (1), θT is a vector of model coefficients and g(y) is a vector of network statistics such as number of edges, number of triangles, number of 3-stars, etc. in the given network configuration y that can be represented as an adjacency matrix. K is a normalizing constant that ensures that the equation is a legitimate probability distribution. The equation can be expanded to allow node-related attributes X by expressing it as follows:

$$\mathbb{P}_{\theta,\beta} (Y = y|X = x) = \left(\frac{1}{K} \right) \exp\{\theta^T g(y) + \beta^T g(y,x)\} \tag{2}$$

In Equation (2), the additional node-dependent network statistics $g(y,x)$ can be represented as follows:

$$g(y,x) = \sum_{1 \le i < j \le N} y_{ij} h(x_i, x_j) \qquad (3)$$

In Equation (3), $y_{ij}=1$ if edge exists, else $y_{ij}=0$. $h(x_i, x_j)$ may be defined as an additive or equivalence function to examine main effects (i.e., whether attributes are related to the presence of an edge) or homophily effects (i.e., whether similar node attribute values impact edge creation).

Equation (2) can be fit using the *ergm* package in R. Consider the rfid dataset in the *igraphdata* R package. The structure of the hospital encounter network (i.e., presence or absence of edges between a pair of people each of whom could be either a patient, administrative staff, medical doctor, or nurse) can be modeled in terms of the node attribute (i.e. person type). The R code for implementing the model is as follows:

```
library(igraph)
library(igraphdata)
library(ergm)
library(network)
library(intergraph)
## Load the Hospital encounter network dataset
data(rfid)
## List the node attributes in the
vertex_attr_names(rfid)
## Convert the rfid igraph object to a network object
gr = asNetwork(rfid)
model <- ergm(gr ~ edges+nodefactor("Status"),
              control=control.ergm(MCMC.interval = 10000,
              MCMLE.maxit = 100, seed = 12345, force.main = TRUE))
summary(model)
exp(summary(model03)$coefficients)
```

The results of the graph model are shown in Table 6. Table 6 shows that compared to administrative staff, medical doctors and nurses are 46.3% and 79.8% more likely to meet other people in the hospital respectively, whereas patients are 43% less likely to meet other people compared to administrative staff in a short period.

Table 6. Graph model to explain a hospital encounter network

Inputs	Log-odds	p-value
Edges (intercept)	0.5972	0.0024
Status – Admin staff	*baseline*	
Status – Medical doctor	1.4630	0.0000
Status – Nurse	1.7982	0.0000
Status – Patient	0.5755	0.0000

There are other statistical graph models that can be used to explain specific graph structures such as network block models and latent network models and the readers are directed to (Kolaczyk & Csardi, 2020) for further reading about statistical graph models.

Graph Mining

Graph mining involves algorithmically extracting patterns of interest from graphs that describe the underlying generative process or scientific phenomenon. While graph theory is the mathematics and geometry of graphs and it has been studied for several decades, graph mining involves the empirical study of the nature of graphs and their characterization. Graph mining can be further divided into three sub-categories – exploratory analysis, pattern detection, and predictive modeling.

Exploratory Analysis

Visualization of networks are commonly used to identify peculiar patterns that may be indicative of low/ high density, influential nodes, isolated subgraphs, fully connected components, clusters, etc. Visualization layouts such as Force Atlas, Fruchterman Reingold, Yufan Hu can be used to generate visualizations of large networks to identify patterns. Gephi is a popular open-source network visualization tool can be used to import graphs and visualize them using multiple layouts.

Exploratory analysis consists of examine network-level and node-level properties. Network-level properties include type of network, description of node and edge attributes, density of network, average path length, number of k-star components, as well as aggregate node properties. Node properties include node centrality measures such as degree centrality, betweenness centrality, eigen vector centrality, page rank, and clustering coefficient. These network-level and node-level properties are defined in the rest of this section with specific examples where applicable. We will use the five-node weighted directed graph as an example for computing the different measures.

Figure 5. A five-node weighted directed graph

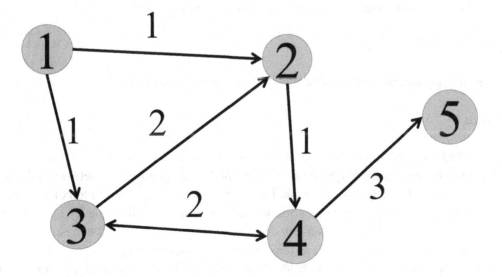

Path

For directed networks, a path between two nodes is a sequence of non-repeating nodes that connects the pair of nodes. For example, one of the paths between Node 1 and Node 5 is 1-2-4-5. The *shortest path* between two nodes is the path that connects the two nodes with the shortest number of edges or smallest number of hops (i.e., nodes falling on the path). The length of the shortest path or the distance between node 1 and node 4 is 2. The Milgram's small world experiment showed that real world people interaction network across the world often has a surprisingly short path, a phenomenon also known as the six degrees of separation in global social connections (Milgram, 1967).

The shortest paths between pairs of nodes in Figure 5 are as follows: Node 1 – Node 5: {1-2-4-5}, Node 2 – Node 5: {2-4-5}, Node 3 – Node 5: {3-4-5}, Node 4 – Node 5: {4-5}, Node 1 – Node 4: {1-2-4}, Node 2 – Node 4: {2-4}, Node 3 – Node 4: {3-4}, Node 5 – Node 4: {φ}, Node 1 – Node 3: {1-3}, Node 2 – Node 3: {2-4-3}, Node 4 – Node 3: {2-4-3}, Node 5 – Node 3: {φ}, Node 1 – Node 2: {1-2}, Node 3 – Node 2: {3-2}, Node 4 – Node 2: {φ}, Node 5 – Node 2: {φ}, Node 2 – Node 1: {φ}, Node 3 – Node 1: {φ}, Node 4 – Node 1: {φ}, Node 5 – Node 1: {φ}.

Density

Density is a network-based metric that indicates how dense a graph is in terms of the ratio of actual number of edges and the total number of possible edges in the network which is C_2^n for n number of nodes. Typically, the range of density for any real-world network ranges from 0.001 to 0.5 and larger networks typically have less density.

Degree

The degree of a node is the number of edges incident to it.

Weighted degree / Strength

The sum of the weights of edges incident on a node in a weighted network

In-degree

The number of edges directed into a particular node in a directed network.

Out-degree

The number of edges originating from a particular node in a directed network.

The degree distribution is the frequency distribution of degrees of nodes in a network and can give an indication of the type of structure of the graph. For example, the degree distribution of an Erdos-Renyi random graph has a Poisson degree distribution whereas the Barabasi-Albert model, also known as the preferential-attachment graph has a power-law degree distribution (Albert & Barabási, 2002).

The degree of a node is also called as its degree centrality. Degree centrality assigns an importance score based simply on the number of links held by each node. That is, for a node, it measures the number of direct 'one hop' connections to other nodes in the network. It is useful for finding very connected nodes. It is the simplest measure of node connectivity. For directed networks, it may be useful to look at in-degree (number of inbound links) and out-degree (number of outbound links) as distinct measures.

In Figure 5, the degree distribution for the network is as follows: {Node 1: 2, Node 2: 3, Node 3: 3, Node 4: 3, Node 5: 1}. The weighted degree or strength of the nodes are: {Node 1: 2, Node 2: 4, Node 3: 5, Node 4: 6, Node 5: 3}. The in-degree/out-degree distribution of the network is: {Node 1: 0/2, Node 2: 2/1, Node 3: 2/1, Node 4: 2/1, Node 5: 1/0}.

There are other node-based centrality measures that are used for specific purposes.

Betweenness Centrality

Betweenness centrality measures the number of times a node lies on the shortest path between other nodes. It is helpful to identify nodes that influence the information flow in a directed network. A high between centrality indicates that a node is critical for the communication between two or more nodes and without the node, the flow of information may take longer. Often the betweenness centrality is normalized to range of [0,1], where 1 indicates the node lies in all the possible shortest paths between all other pairs of nodes. The normalization is helpful to compare nodes across the networks. In Figure 5, the betweenness centrality of Node 2 is 1 and its normalized betweenness centrality is $\frac{1}{(3\times4)} = 0.0833$.

Closeness Centrality

Closeness centrality scores each node based on their closeness to all other nodes in the network. It calculates the shortest paths between all nodes, then assigns each node a score based on its sum of shortest paths. The closeness centrality is calculated as follows:

$$C(x) = \frac{N-1}{\sum_y d(y,x)}$$

In the above expression, N is the number of nodes in the network, $d(x,y)$ is the shortest path distance between x and y. For disconnected graphs, this expression is slightly modified so as to consider a harmonic mean than use the inverse of the mean (Beaucamp, 1965). Though the measure is calculated differently for directed and undirected representations of a network, closeness for directed networks is often reported for its undirected representation. Closeness centrality is helpful for finding the nodes that have a higher influence on other nodes. In social network analysis involving individuals as nodes, closeness centrality can help find good broadcasters in a sparse network. In Figure 5, computing the directed/in-degree closeness centrality is not simple as node 1 is disconnected and hence the distance is infinite. Therefore, the harmonic (in-degree) closeness centrality for Node 3 (suppose) can be computed as follows:

$$(5-1)\times\left(\frac{1}{\infty}+\frac{1}{1}+\frac{1}{1}+\frac{1}{2}\right)=10.$$

The undirected closeness centrality of the nodes in Figure 5 can be computed as {Node 1: 4/7, Node 2: 4/5, Node 3: 4/5, Node 4: 4/5, Node 5: 4/8}.

Eigen Vector Centrality

Like degree centrality, Eigen vector centrality measures a node's influence based on the number of links it has to other nodes in the network. However, it goes a step further by also taking into account how well connected a node is, and how many links their connections have, and so on through the network. This is done by taking advantage of a mathematical (matrix factorization) technique called the eigenvector decomposition. By calculating the extended connections of a node, Eigen vector centrality can identify nodes with influence over the whole network, not just those directly connected to it (Lizardo, 2021).

Page Rank

PageRank is a variant of Eigen vector centrality, also assigning nodes a score based on their connections, and their connections' connections. The difference is that PageRank also takes link direction and weight into account; links reflect weighted influence in each direction between each node-pair. PageRank is famously one of the ranking algorithms behind the original Google search engine (Page et al., 1998). This measure uncovers nodes whose influence extends beyond their direct connections into the wider network. Because it takes into account direction and connection weight, PageRank can be helpful for understanding citations and authority.

Consider a hypothetical web URL citation network given by Figure 6. Each web page has inlinks and outlinks. Inlinks suggest number of links that lead to a webpage. Outlinks is the number of links in a webpage to other webpages. In this example, we can see that Microsoft.com has the highest page rank as it gets cited the most, whereas *mypersonalblog* has the lowest page rank. There are multiple modified versions of page rank. The HITS algorithm is an alternative to page rank that considers ranking hubs, webpages that have a lot of outlinks as well as authorities, which as webpages that have a lot of inlinks. In other words, a good hub represents a page that pointed to many other pages, while a good authority represents a page that is linked by many different hubs (Gosnell & Broecheler, 2020).

Figure 6. A hypothetical www citation network

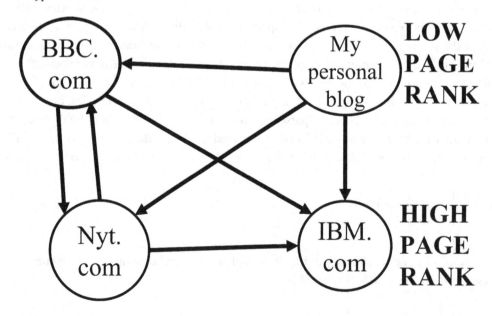

Pattern Detection

G

Multiple advancements in graph mining have been made towards pattern detection and analysis over the years (Gosnell & Broecheler, 2020). Common applications of pattern analysis include epidemiology and new diffusion where the flow of contagion or information is studied respectively (Susarla et al., 2012). Dynamic network or temporal graph analysis is also an active area of research where snapshots of networks are compared and modeled to understand how a networked phenomenon changes over time (Carnegie et al., 2015). Ego networks have also been studied around a particular node of interest to identify node-specific characteristics that reflect in their respective ego network.

Frequent subgraph mining is a popular topic in graph pattern detection, a process of discovering subgraphs that occur often in a database of other graphs ("Practical Graph Mining with R," 2013). Frequent subgraph mining (FSM) is considered supervised learning similar to the other pattern detection approaches as it does not rely on a known outcome but instead unravels distinct patterns in the graph structure using iterative algorithms. Over the years, FSM has found multiple applications in different disciplines such as detecting repeated phenotype expressions in biological metabolic networks to analyzing internet traffic flow using server logs. *Gspan* and *Sleuth* are popular algorithms with implementations in R that can be used for frequent subgraph mining ("Practical Graph Mining with R," 2013).

Community detection or graph clustering is a graph pattern detection approach focused on identifying groups of nodes connected with each other and having similar network characteristics. Community detection methods such as Lovain, fastgreedy, label propagation, Girvan-Newman methods are analogous to clustering methods on tabular data such as K-means and spectral clustering ("Practical Graph Mining with R," 2013). Community detection methods for graphs aim to partition network nodes into a set of clusters, such that nodes are more densely connected to each other within the same cluster than other clusters. For attributed networks, apart from the denseness requirement of topology structure, the attributes of nodes in the same community can also be considered for partitioning the graph.

Let us consider the Lovain method, one of the most popular community detection methods (Blondel et al., 2008; Traag et al., 2019). This method optimizes the modularity metric for separating sub-graph clusters. The modularity score is proportional to the difference between expected number of edges and actual number of edges, ranges between -1 and 1; a higher modularity score means the communities detected are good and more tightly knit. The Lovain algorithm optimizes modularity score in two phases: (1) local moving of nodes; and (2) aggregation of the network. In the local moving phase, individual nodes are moved to the community that yields the largest increase in the modularity score. In the aggregation phase, an aggregate network is created based on the partition obtained in the local moving phase. Each community in this partition becomes a node in the aggregate network. The two phases are repeated until the quality function cannot be increased further. The Louvain algorithm starts by considering each node as a community until nodes are grouped in few tractable communities. In addition to structure, node and edge attributes can be considered in community detection as well (Yang et al., 2013).

The Lovain community detection algorithm can be applied to the karate graph data using the following code:

```
library(igraph)
library(igraphdata)
communities_karate = cluster_louvain(karate, weights = NULL)
membership(communities_karate)
is_hierarchical(communities_karate)
```

```
plot(
  x = communities_karate,
  karate,
  col = membership(communities_karate),
  mark.groups = communities(communities_karate)
  )
```
Four communities of members are detected as shown in Figure 7.

Figure 7. Four communities of members identified in the karate network

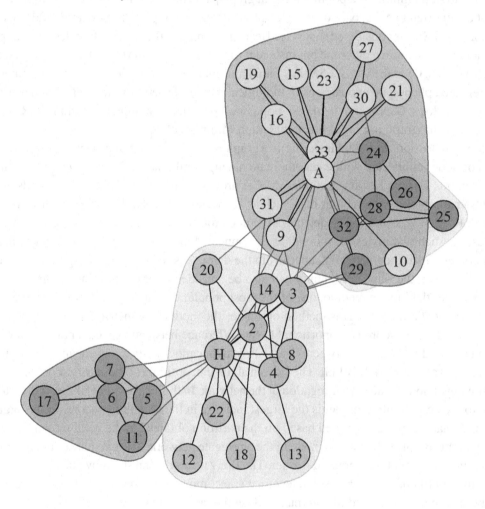

The modularity score for the karate communities is 0.45 indicating a fair amount of differentiation between the members across groups.

Predictive Modeling

Similar to predictive modeling in tabular data, common classification and regression algorithms can be repurposed to perform edge/link prediction, or node prediction. Popular applications of link prediction include recommending items to customers based on their prior purchase history, predict future social media influencers based on current trends, etc. Measures such as Adamic-Adar measure (Adamic & Adar, 2003), similarity measures, community resource allocation (Zhou et al., 2009), provide the propensity of pair of nodes to be connected by an edge based on the local neighborhood structure between them.

Network features can also be used for engineering input features to support tabular predictive modeling tasks. Features from network or node attributes are extracted to predict external outcome that are not inherent to the network structure. For example, prediction of future crimes can be made based on increase in density of communication network of mafia bosses; movie success can be predicted based on inter-relationship network of the actors and crew (Lash & Zhao, 2016); patient visit costs have been shown to be tied to co-occurrence history of admitting diagnoses (Srinivasan et al., 2018).

Recent graph mining literature is focused on knowledge representation in terms of pre-trained vectors known as embedding vectors, also known as graph representation learning (Wang et al., 2021). This literature largely is based on deep learning and word embedding in natural language processing. Word embedding is one of the most popular representation of natural language text. It captures context of words, semantic and syntactic similarity between words based on their co-occurrence in large text corpuses. Embedding is the numeric vector representations of an entity such as a word. Word2Vec is one of the most popular technique to learn word embeddings using shallow neural networks. The idea of word embedding can be extended to graph mining by representing nodes, edges of a graph as numeric multidimensional vectors (Grover & Leskovec, 2016).

Node embedding for the karate network can be training in python using the following code:

```python
import numpy as np
import pandas as pd
import networkx as nx
from node2vec import Node2Vec
G = nx.karate_club_graph()
node2vec = Node2Vec(G, dimensions=100, walk_length=5, num_walks=100, work-
ers=4, seed=12345)
model = node2vec.fit(window=10, min_count=1)
### The vocab is the node labels whereas the vectors are the node embeddings
for the corresponding nodes
vocab, vectors = model.wv.vocab, model.wv.vectors
```

Since training the embedding vectors is a greedy search procedure, it is advised to set a seed value for reproducibility as it is not guaranteed to get the same embedding vector sets for each corresponding nodes in each program run.

FUTURE RESEARCH DIRECTIONS

The general idea of graph analytics is to model the structure of a graph instead of modeling the inter-relationship between input features and outcome(s) in a tabular dataset. Within graph analytics, one could focus on analyzing the entire network, or analyze the nodes (people, places, etc.) and edge formations (friends, visited, etc.). Using structural properties, generative modeling and unsupervised community detection methods are helpful to characterize nodes and the network. By combining node features, domain knowledge, external information and network structure information, it is possible to model complex inter-connected systems visible as networks.

Network-structure related information can be included as input features into explanatory models and predictive models. For example, the centrality of diseases reported in a patient visit over a disease co-occurrence network can be used for accurately predicting the length of stay (Kalgotra & Sharda, 2022) or cost of overall visit (Srinivasan et al., 2018). On the other hand, feature extraction from relational data can be converted to node or edge attributes to explain a network's structure and its characteristics (Yang et al., 2013).

Each component of graph analytics – graph management, graph modeling, and graph mining is rife with research opportunities. Disciplines such as e-commerce, bioinformatics, social networks, criminology, epidemiology have readily adopted graph methods to solve problems including product recommendations, drug discovery, antibacterial discovery, fake news detection, predicting cyberattacks, contact tracing in COVID-19, etc. While other disciplines have only recently explored the potential and application of graph analytics. Transportation and infrastructure planning can store, model, and mine graphs for traffic prediction, transportation planning, while marketing analysts can explore customers, products and agents as interacting agents in a rich knowledge graph. Management and organization science can exploit organizational networks to model inter-firm communications and understand complex behavioral complexities in human interaction.

CONCLUSION

Graph analytics is a necessary toolkit for any serious data scientist. In this chapter, the basic concepts of graph analytics are covered in three subsections – graph management, graph modeling, and graph mining. Simple examples of graphs and applications are provided along with code implementations wherever applicable. This chapter summarizes graph analytics using simple examples as well as throws light into current and future applications. It covers basic definitions and examples in simple words, and covers the multitude of topics in graph analytics, an emerging field in data science.

REFERENCES

Adamic, L. A., & Adar, E. (2003). *Friends and neighbors on the Web.* doi:10.1016/S0378-8733(03)00009-1

Albert, R., & Barabási, A. L. (2002). Statistical mechanics of complex networks. *Reviews of Modern Physics, 74*(1), 47–97. doi:10.1103/RevModPhys.74.47

Beaucamp, M. A. (1965). An improved index of centrality. *Behavioral Science, 10*(2), 161–163. Advance online publication. doi:10.1002/bs.3830100205 PMID:14284290

Blondel, V. D., Guillaume, J. L., Lambiotte, R., & Lefebvre, E. (2008). Fast unfolding of communities in large networks. *Journal of Statistical Mechanics, 10*(10), 6. doi:10.1088/1742-5468/2008/10/P10008

Carnegie, N. B., Krivitsky, P. N., Hunter, D. R., & Goodreau, S. M. (2015). An Approximation Method for Improving Dynamic Network Model Fitting. *Journal of Computational and Graphical Statistics, 24*(2), 502–519. doi:10.1080/10618600.2014.903087 PMID:26321857

Google. (2021). *How Google's Knowledge Graph works - Knowledge Panel Help*. https://support.google.com/knowledgepanel/answer/9787176?hl=en-GB

Gosnell, D. K., & Broecheler, M. (2020). *The practitioner's guide to graph data: applying graph thinking and graph technologies to solve complex problems*. Orielly.

Grover, A., & Leskovec, J. (2016). *node2vec*. doi:10.1145/2939672.2939754

Hunter, D. R., & Handcock, M. S. (2006). Inference in curved exponential family models for networks. *Journal of Computational and Graphical Statistics*, *15*(3), 565–583. doi:10.1198/106186006X133069

Kalgotra, P., & Sharda, R. (2022). When will I get out of the hospital? Modeling Length of Stay using Comorbidity Networks. *Journal of Management Information Systems*.

Kolaczyk, E. D., & Csardi, G. (2020). Statistical Analysis of Network Data with R. Springer. doi:10.1007/978-3-030-44129-6

Lash, M. T., & Zhao, K. (2016). Early Predictions of Movie Success: The Who, What, and When of Profitability. *Journal of Management Information Systems*, *33*(3), 874–903. Advance online publication. doi:10.1080/07421222.2016.1243969

Liu, Z., Cui, L., Guo, W., He, W., Li, H., & Gao, J. (2020). Predicting hospital readmission using graph representation learning based on patient and disease bipartite graph. Lecture Notes in Computer Science, 12113. doi:10.1007/978-3-030-59416-9_23

Lizardo, O. (2021). *Social Networks*. Early draft. http://olizardo.bol.ucla.edu/classes/soc-111/textbook/_book/

Milgram, S. (1967). small world problem. *Psychology Today*, *1*(1).

Nigam, V. V., Paul, S., Agrawal, A. P., & Bansal, R. (2020). A review paper on the application of knowledge graph on various service providing platforms. *Proceedings of the Confluence 2020 - 10th International Conference on Cloud Computing, Data Science and Engineering*. 10.1109/Confluence47617.2020.9058298

Page, L., Brin, S., Motwani, R., & Winograd, T. (1998). The PageRank Citation Ranking: Bringing Order to the Web. *World Wide Web Internet And Web Information Systems*, *54*, 1999–66. 10.1.1.31.1768

Practical Graph Mining with R. (2013). *Practical Graph Mining with R*. doi:10.1201/b15352

Sasaki, B. (2018). Graph Databases for Beginners: Why Graph Technology Is the Future. Neo4J.

Srinivasan, K., Currim, F., & Ram, S. (2018). Predicting High-Cost Patients at Point of Admission Using Network Science. *IEEE Journal of Biomedical and Health Informatics*, *22*(6), 1970–1977. doi:10.1109/JBHI.2017.2783049 PMID:29990022

Susarla, A., Oh, J. H., & Tan, Y. (2012). Social networks and the diffusion of user-generated content: Evidence from youtube. *Information Systems Research*, *23*(1), 23–41. doi:10.1287/isre.1100.0339

Traag, V. A., Waltman, L., & van Eck, N. J. (2019). From Louvain to Leiden: Guaranteeing well-connected communities. *Scientific Reports*, *9*(1), 5233. Advance online publication. doi:10.103841598-019-41695-z PMID:30914743

Wang, H., Wang, J., Wang, J., Zhao, M., Zhang, W., Zhang, F., Li, W., Xie, X., & Guo, M. (2021). Learning Graph Representation with Generative Adversarial Nets. *IEEE Transactions on Knowledge and Data Engineering*, *33*(8), 3090–3103. Advance online publication. doi:10.1109/TKDE.2019.2961882

Weisstein, E. W. (2021). *Contiguous USA Graph*. Wolfram Research, Inc. https://mathworld.wolfram.com/ContiguousUSAGraph.html

Yang, J., McAuley, J., & Leskovec, J. (2013). Community detection in networks with node attributes. *Proceedings - IEEE International Conference on Data Mining, ICDM*. 10.1109/ICDM.2013.167

Zhou, T., Lü, L., & Zhang, Y. C. (2009). Predicting missing links via local information. *The European Physical Journal B*, *71*(4), 623–630. Advance online publication. doi:10.1140/epjb/e2009-00335-8

ADDITIONAL READING

Albert, R., & Barabási, A. L. (2002). Statistical mechanics of complex networks. *Reviews of Modern Physics*, *74*(1), 47–97. doi:10.1103/RevModPhys.74.47

Google. (2021). *How Google's Knowledge Graph works - Knowledge Panel Help*. https://support.google.com/knowledgepanel/answer/9787176?hl=en-GB

Gosnell, D. K., & Broecheler, M. (2020). *The practitioner's guide to graph data: applying graph thinking and graph technologies to solve complex problems*. O'Rielly.

Grover, A., & Leskovec, J. (2016). *node2vec*. doi:10.1145/2939672.2939754

Kolaczyk, E. D., & Csardi, G. (2020). Statistical Analysis of Network Data with R. Springer. doi:10.1007/978-3-030-44129-6

Lizardo, O. (2021). *Social Networks*. Early draft. http://olizardo.bol.ucla.edu/classes/soc-111/textbook/_book/

KEY TERMS AND DEFINITIONS

Exploratory Graph Analysis: Exploratory graph analysis is a collection of graph mining techniques including network visualization and summarization of network properties that are useful for initial exploration of a graph as well as feature engineering.

Graph Analytics: Systematic computational analysis of graph data.

Graph Database: An operational database that uses graph structures for semantic queries with nodes, edges, and properties to represent and store data instead of the traditional relational/tabular structure.

Graph Embedding: A transformation procedure of converting nodes, edges, and graph into a set of multidimensional vectors that optimally capture the characteristics graph structure.

Graph Mining: The process of algorithmically extracting patterns of interest from graphs that describe the underlying generative process or scientific phenomenon.

Knowledge Graph: A knowledge graph is a directed labeled graph real-world entities – objects, events, situations, or concepts created and managed to construct a comprehensive view of the underlying entities, labels, and their inter-relationships.

Network Science: A field involved with investigating the topology of complex networks using graph theory to better understand the behavior, functioning and properties of the underlying phenomenon related to the generation of the network.

Social Network Analysis: The process of investigating social structures through the use of graph analytics. The nodes of the social networks are typically assumed to be individuals and the edges are based on the underlying inter-individual interaction phenomenon that is being studied such as friendship or location proximity.

Statistical Graph Model: A model that represents a network using available input features similar to how a regression model represents the relationship between inputs and outputs in a tabular dataset. It is not to be confused with graphical model which focus on representing the conditional dependence between random variables.

G

Section 28
High–Throughput Data Analysis

Best Practices of Feature Selection in Multi-Omics Data

B

Funda Ipekten

https://orcid.org/0000-0002-6916-9563

Erciyes University, Turkey

Gözde Ertürk Zararsız

Erciyes University, Turkey

Halef Okan Doğan

Cumhuriyet University, Turkey

Vahap Eldem

Istanbul University, Turkey

Gökmen Zararsız

Erciyes University, Turkey

INTRODUCTION

Today, there is an increase in data in many areas. With this increase, the number and variety of the variables to be evaluated also increases. The increase in data and variables became a situation that needed to be solved among world problems. In addition, although there is a perception that having too much data in the scientific field, having too much information, correct information, or sufficient information may not be possible. However, it should not be forgotten that there is valuable information in a relatively large amount of data. It should be clear that it can be beneficial to have much data to extract this helpful information. However, performing data analyses to obtain and process this information can be difficult. In addition, its existence is a problem called the curse of data dimensionality (Verkeysen M. and François D., 2005). High-dimensional data sets, where these problems are most common, are used successfully in multiple fields such as genetics, pharmacology, toxicology, nutrition, and genetics. The use of these high-dimensional data allows one to examine biology systems, cellular metabolism, and disease etiologies in more detail. However, the number of samples (n) of these data is considerably lower than the number of variables (p) and the heterogeneity of the data, the missing observations in the data as a result of the use of high-output technology, limits the use of traditional methods that can be used in this field. Therefore, there is a need for the clinical understanding of the biological system based on research and machine learning, and statistical learning methods to analyze this clinical information statistically (Hastie et al., 2009). Several studies are show that machine learning methods are used and applied successfully in studies carried out in this field. Some of these studies are listed in Table 1.

DOI: 10.4018/978-1-7998-9220-5.ch122

Table 1. Some studies using feature selection

Datasets		Methods	References		
Ovarian cancer	Classification	MKL	Wilson et al.	2019	
Breast cancer	Classification	MKL	Tao et al.	2019	
Gene expression	Classification	SVM	Golub et al.	1999	
Gut microbiota	Classification	RF	Franzosa et al.	2019	
Colon cancer	Classification	SVM	Moler et al.	2000	
Ovarian, leukemia, colon	Classification	SVM	Furey et al.	2000	

MKL: Multiple Kernel Learning, SVM: Support Vector Machine, RF:Random Forest

In general, in all of the studies given in Table 1, researchers aim to optimize the classification of disease-related samples, produce models that can be used to predict system behaviors, or properties or provide the most accurate result appropriate in terms of classification performances. However, the large number of variables in the data used can complicate the structure of the models to be created hence reducing their accuracy. In addition, because the number of variables is too large, the investigation of disease-related genes or other omics causes considerable losses in terms of both time and cost (Hastie et al., 2009). Therefore, it is not always possible for researchers to carry out these studies in depth. Therefore, feature selection is made before model training is evaluated to make the models obtained with learning methods more generalizable, predictable, and ineffective against noisy values, with minimum time and minimum cost (Díaz-Uriarte and Alvarez de Andrés, 2006). At this point, the need for feature selection methods increases in developing new technology and bioinformatics applications.

BACKGROUND

The use of feature selection methods has become a prerequisite for models created by using machine learning algorithms and statistical learning methods in the analysis of high-dimensional data sets such as omics data (Metabolomic, transcriptomic, genomic, etc.), next-generation sequencing data, microarray data (Saeys, 2007).

Feature selection purposes;

- It is done to prevent overfitting problems and to improve model performance. It is used for the prediction performance of the relevant situation in classification problems and for better cluster detection in clustering problems.
- It is aimed to create models with the minimum cost at maximum speed.
- It allows more detailed scanning for the investigated situation.

Feature selection methods, which are used for more than one purpose, have an important place for the quality of the studies without compromising the data 's originality. This is because the original structure of the data does not change in feature selection. Instead, a subset is selected for the relevant situation (sample or number of features) (Saeys, 2007). Since feature selection methods are independent of the classifier, they are used in supervised, semi-supervised, and unsupervised learning techniques. These methods, which are widely used in machine learning methods, have varieties such as filter, wrapper, and ensemble (Ferreira, 2012). The advantages and disadvantages of these methods are presented in Table 2.

Table 2. Taxonomy of feature selection methods

FSM	Advantages	Disadvantages
Filter	Independence of the classifier Lower computational cost than wrappers Fast Good generalization ability	No interaction with the classifier
Wrapper	Interaction with the classifier Captures feature dependencies	Computationally expensive Risk of overfitting Classifier-dependent selection
Embedded	Interaction with the classifier Lower computational cost than the wrapper Captures feature dependencies	Classifier-dependent selection

FSM: Feature Selection Methods

FS selection algorithms play a significant role in selecting correct variables for different classification problems in multi-omics. Nevertheless, choosing the appropriate algorithm (or combination of algorithms) is not a trivial task. So, we highlighted to FS method's advantages and disadvantages.

Filter Methods

The machine learning algorithm is not used in this method. In this method, four criteria (Dependency, Information, Distance, and Compatibility.) are taken into account (Momeni et al., 2020). In other words, it makes associations according to the characteristics of the variables in a data. Generally, scoring is calculated according to the relationship of the variables, and low-scoring variables are excluded in this scoring. Then, the remaining variables are presented as a subset as input to the classification algorithm.

The advantage of this technique is,

- Easily scalable to enormous datasets
- Computationally simple and fast
- The independent of classifiers.

As a result, the variable selection process is performed once and is ready for evaluation with related methods (Saeys, 2007). The disadvantage of filter methods is that most of the proposed techniques are univariate, and the interactions of the variables are ignored. Furthermore, since each variable is handled separately and the dependencies of the variables are ignored, it exhibits worse classification performance than other variable selection methods (Saeys, 2007). Some of the filter methods are listed below.

Relief

Kira and Rendell developed the relief method in 1992. In the ReliefF method, the closest samples of the values of the variables are selected according to how well they discriminate. In other words, given a randomly selected selection, it searches for its two closest neighbors. Relief calculates quality and interest/relationship proxy statistics for each variable that can be used for prediction. This statistical value is called weight, or a score in the range of worst and best. The Relief method may deal with two-category discrete and continuous variables but is limited to two-category problems (Kira K., and Rendell, L.A.,

1992). ReliefF, which is an extension of the Relief algorithm, is used in multi-category situations. Also, it is a powerful method against incomplete and noisy variables (Kononenko I., 1994). This powerful method was later adapted to regression problems, and the RReliefF algorithm was developed (Sikonja R., and Kononenko I., 2003). Relief family is one of the effective methods. Because they apply to any problem, they have low bias, consider interactions between properties, and may capture local dependencies that other methods often fail to capture.

Correlation-Based Feature Selection (CFS)

It is a simple filter algorithm that sorts variables according to a correlation-based heuristic evaluation function (1999, Hall M.A.). The bias of this function is for subsets that contain highly correlated and unrelated features with the label. Variables with low correlation with labels are ignored. Since the remaining variables are highly correlated with the label, redundant features are scanned. The acceptance of a variable will depend on the extent to which it predicts classes in sample space domains that are not predicted by other variables. The correlation-based filter function is as shown in equation 1.

$$M_s = \frac{k\overline{r}_{cf}}{\sqrt{k + k(-1)\overline{r}_{ff}}} \tag{1}$$

M_s: MS is the heuristic "merit" of a feature subset S containing k features
k: Features
$\overline{r}_{cf}$: average variables-class correlation ($f \in S$)
$\overline{r}_{ff}$: is the average feature-feature intercorrelation.

The denominator of the related equation gives the redundancy between the variables. Its numerator can be thought of as an indicator of how predictive the class is of a series of variables (Noelia S.M et al., 2007 & Hall M.A., 1999).

Fast Correlated Based Filter (FCBF)

The fast correlated-based filter (FCBF) method (Yu L., and Liu H., 2003) is based on symmetrical uncertainty (SU), which is defined as the ratio between the information gain (IG) and the entropy (H) two features, x and y:

$$SU(x, y) = 2\frac{IG\left(x/y\right)}{H(x) + H(y)} \tag{2}$$

Where the information gain is defined as:

$$IG(x/y) = H(y) + H(x) - H(x,y) \tag{3}$$

The entropy and joint entropy respectively, are $H(x)$ and $H(x,y)$. This method was designed for high-dimensionality data is effective in removing both irrelevant and redundant features. However, it fails to consider the interaction between features (Press et al., 1988).

Interact

This method uses the same measure of goodness as the FCBF method, but also includes the consistency contribution/c-contribution in the calculation. The C contribution shows how significantly the elimination of the relevant variable will affect its consistency. In the algorithm, the variables are first sorted in descending order of their SU values. Sorted variables are evaluated one by one, starting from the end of the list. If the contribution (c-contribution) is less than the specified threshold, the feature is removed; otherwise, it is selected. The authors have stated that in this method, the interactions of the variables are taken into account and the variable selection process is carried out efficiently (Zhao Z. and Liu H., 2007).

Boruta

The Boruta method, named after a forest god in Slavic mythology, was developed to identify all relevant variables within the classification framework (Kursa and Rudnicki, 2010). The basis of this approach is to compare the significance of actual predictive variables with random, artificial variables using statistical testing and several RF studies. In each run, the actual predictive variables are doubled by adding copies of the variables. The values of these dummy variables are produced by changing the fundamental values between observations, thus destroying the relationship with the result. Next, the RF is trained on the expanded dataset, and variable significance values are collected. A statistical test for each real variable compares its significance with the enormous value of all shadow variables. Variables with significantly greater or lesser significance values are designated as significant or insignificant, respectively. Finally, all insignificant variables and shadow variables are removed and the previous steps are repeated until all variables have been classified or a predetermined number of runs have been performed. The Boruta approach has been used in gene expression and microbiome data analysis (Guo et al., 2014; Saulnier et al., 2011).

Altmann

Altmann, one of the non-parametric methods, generates p values based on the zero distribution of the scores of the essential variables. Altmann et al. (Altmann A. et al., 2010) suggest using parametric p-values by fitting a defined probability distribution such as normal, lognormal, or Gamma to the non-parametric distribution of null significance values to reduce the number of permutations. The parameters of these distributions are estimated using maximum likelihood methods, and the p-values are calculated as the probability of observing a more excellent significance score than the actual significance score below the estimated distribution (Altmann A. et al., 2010). The Altmann approach has been used in gene expression and microbiome data and is less preferred than other methods (Ji et al., 2014; Ning and Beiko, 2015).

Minimum Redundancy-Maximum Relevance (mRMR)

The minimum redundancy maximum relationship approach $D = \{x_{i,k}\}_{nxK}$ refers to our data matrix. Here, the expression $x_{i,k}$ represents the vector of the i variable of the k sample, the number of K samples, and the number of n variables. Assume that our dataset has two classes -1 and 1. If the final variable set is, $S*$ mRMR (Minimum Redundancy Maximum Relevance) equation finds the best $S*$.

$$\max_{S^*} \frac{\sum i \in S^*, h \in \{+1,-1\} I(h,i)}{\frac{1}{|S^*|} \sum_{i,j,\in S^*} I(j,i)} \tag{4}$$

The upper part of the equation expresses the relation value between the data class and the variable value, and it is desired that this expression be as significant as possible. The bottom part of the equation indicates the standard information between the variables, and this value is preferred small. $I(j,i)$ denotes the standard information between j and i variables.

The mRMR method uses an iterative and additive approach to generate the final $S*$ to improve the computational performance. First, the equation specified in 4 is converted to the form in equation 5.

$$\max_{i \in \Omega_{S^*}} \frac{I(+1,i) + I(-1,i)}{\frac{1}{|S^*|} \sum_{j,\in S^*} I(i,j)} \tag{5}$$

Here Ω is denoted by the global variable set and the expressions $\Omega_S = \Omega - S$. Finally, the calculation of common knowledge between two data sets is given in equation 5.

$$I(i,j) = \sum_{i,j} p(x_i, y_j) \log \frac{p(x_i, y_i)}{p(x_i)p(y_i)} \tag{6}$$

Here $p(x,y)$, means the conditional probability of x and y. The minimum redundancy maximum relationship method needs discrete input data, and hence the function is used to distribute it to our dataset. The dataset is defined as, $D = \{x_{i,j}\}_{nxK}$, then the discrete value of this matrix is defined as equation 6.

$$\tilde{x}_{i,j} = \begin{cases} 1 & x_{i,j} \geq \overline{x}_j + \alpha\sigma_{j,} \\ -1 & x_{i,j} \leq \overline{x}_j + \alpha\sigma_{j,} \\ 0 & \text{otherwise} \end{cases}$$

Here σ_j is the standard deviation of the j feature $\overline{x}_j$ is the mean value of the j feature and is a is a parameter set to 0.5. In the classification analysis process, the values created with the expression in equation 6 are not used. After the variables are selected, the actual values are used to perform classification analysis with the MKL method or other methods (Lin et al., 2020). Each feature selection is used in omics data. However, the use of mRMR method is preferred in our study in terms of its widespread use and good performance in multi-omics data.

Information Gain (IG)

It is one of the common methods used in feature selection. Features are sorted using IG, and a threshold must be set to select variables above this threshold. If the threshold is not set, we can choose the best K variables. IG is a measure based on the information theory of entropy. Entropy measures the uncertainty about the value that a random variable can accept in probability theory. For omics datasets, entropy represents the uncertainty of the entire data set itself. Information gain does not remove redundant features. The information gain is calculated as follows:

$$H(Y) = -\sum_{i=1}^{n} p(y_i) logP(y_i) \tag{8}$$

$$H(Y|X) = \sum_{i,j} p(x_i, y_j) log \frac{p(x_i, y_j)}{p(x_i)} \tag{9}$$

$$IG(Y,X) = H(Y) - H(Y|X) \tag{10}$$

In equation 8, Y denotes a set of training examples with possible values $\{y_1, y_2, y_3 \dots y_n\}$, $P(Y)$ represents the probability mass function. In equation 9, Shannon defined the conditional entropy of two events, X and Y taking values x and y respectively. In equation 10, in omics datasets, if Y denotes all of the variables and X denotes one specific gene, conditional entropy measures the uncertainty of the dataset Y on the condition of a particular variable X taking a certain value x. Furthermore, the IG decreases in uncertainty, and measures the importance of a specific feature X for an omics dataset Y. As result, IG with a larger value indicates more information in the corresponding feature (Battiti R., 1994). While many filter methods are described in the literature, a list of common methods is given in Table 3, along with the appropriate references that provide details.

Table 3. Feature selection techniques in multi-omics data analytics

Feature Selection Techniques	Filter class	Methods	Linear	Reference
Information Gain	Univariate, information	Classification	Yes	Hoque et al., 2016
Minimum redundancy-Maximum relevance (mRMR)	Multivariate, information	Classification, regression	No	Tang et al., 2014
Correlation-based feature selection (CFS)	Multivariate, statistical	Classification, regression	Yes	Witten et al., 2005
Fast correlation-based filter (FCBF)	Multivariate, information	Classification	Yes	Yu L. ve ark.
Relief	Univariate, distance	Classification, regression	Yes	Sikonja M.R. ve ark.
ReliefF	Univariate, distance	Classification, regression	Yes	Sikonja M.R. ve ark.

Wrapper Methods

It follows the same purpose as the Filter method but uses a machine learning model as the evaluation criteria. (e.g. Forward/Backward/Bidirectional/Recursive Feature Elimination). It is a method that evaluates a subset of variables with the accuracy of a predictive model trained with them (2012, Ferreira). It estimates by selecting a subset of the variables using a particular classifier. This method works more efficiently than filter methods, but it is computationally expensive (Kushmerick,1997). Overfitting problems can be seen in datasets with low samples. (Momeni et al., 2020).

Wrapper SubsetEval

WrapperSubsetEval evaluates attributed sets by using a learning scheme. Cross-validation is used to estimate the accuracy of the learning scheme for a group of attributes. The algorithm starts with the empty set of afeatures and searches forward, adding features until performance improves further (Witten I.H. and Frank E., 2005).

Sequential Forward Selection (SFS)

Sequential Forward Selection (SFS) is a greedy search algorithm that aims to find the most suitable (optimal) variable set by iteratively selecting the variables according to the classifier performance. An empty set of variables is created, and a variable is added in each round. The added variable results in the best classifier performance. It is an expensive method as it is necessary to both train and cross-validate the model for each combination of variables. The disadvantage of this method is that the meaningless variables after each added variable cannot be removed (Ladha & Deepa, 2011). Its algorithm is as follows:

Table 4. Sequential forward selection algorithm

1. Start with the empty set $Y0=\{\phi\}$
2. Select the next best feature $X^+ =\text{argmax}[J(Y_k+X)];x\not\in Y_k$
3. Update $Y_{k+1}=Y_k+ X^+ ; k=k+1$
4. Go to 2

Sequential Backward Elimination (SBE)

It works in the opposite direction of the SFS method. All variables are included, and variables that cause a minimal reduction in the function are sequentially removed. Thus, it works best when the subsets of the remaining optimal variables have many variables. However, the usefulness of the discarded variable cannot be re-evaluated (Ladha & Deepa, 2011). Its algorithm is as follows:

Table 5. Sequential backward elimination algorithm

1. Start with the complete set Y_0=X
2. Remove the worst feature X^- =argmax[J(Y_k-X)];x Y_k
3. Update Y_{k+1}=Y_k- X^- ; k=k+1
4. Go to 2

Recursive Feature Selection (RFE)

The recursive feature selection method aims to find a minimum set of variables to establish a good prediction model in a high-dimensional dataset (Díaz-Uriarte and Alvarez de Andrés, 2006). Initially, it creates a decision tree structure with all the variables. Then, the features are ranked in order of importance, and a new decision tree structure is created from the remaining variables by removing the features with the lowest importance. These steps are performed iteratively until only one variable remains as input. At each stage, prediction performance is estimated based on so-called out-of-bag samples that are not used for model building. Finally, the set of variables is selected according to the RF with the smallest error. However, we recalculate the ranking at each step because this modified algorithm has been shown to be more effective in the case of correlated estimators (Gregorutti et al., 2017). The recursive features selection method has been successfully applied to transcriptomics (Habermann et al., 2009), proteomics (Fusaro et al., 2009), and metabolomics (Dietrich et al., 2016) data.

Embedded Methods

In large datasets, the Filter variable selection method is fast but has poor efficiency, and the wrapper method is more effective but computationally costly. Therefore, there is a need for a solution that combines the advantages of both approaches. In line with this need, the embedded method, which combines the features of the filter and wrapper methods, has been developed (Tadist, 2019). This approach is a method that simultaneously learns the classifier and selects a subset of the variables. Furthermore, the objective function follows a path that reduces the weights of some variables to zero and regulates sparsity (2012, Ferreira).

SVM-RFE (Recursive Feature Elimination for Support Vector Machines)

Guyon developed it. This embedded method performs feature selection by iteratively training an SVM classifier with the current set of features and removing the least significant feature specified by SVM (The main principle of SVM-RFE is to eliminate features that have the lowest weight squares in each iteration.) procedure for RFE; first step: perform classifier training to find the weight vector (w), second step: Calculate ranking criteria for all features, the third: eliminate features with the smallest ranking criterion value. Features used in the iteration are eliminated with backward feature elimination. The ranking score is given by the components of the weight vector w of the SVM as follows, $w = \sum_k a_k y_k x_k$.

In the SVM-RFE algorithm, training data is expressed as $\{x_i, y_i\}_{i=1}^{N}$ as input. A ranked feature list R is obtained as output. expressed as S = {1,2,...,N}, R=Æ. If S is not an empty set, here are the steps to follow:

Table 6. SVM-RFE algorithm

Restrict the features of X_j to the remaining S (Step 1)
Train SVM to get weight vectors (Step 2)
Calculate the ranking criteria $c_k = w_k^2$, $k=1,\dots,|S|$ (Step 3)
Look for features with the smallest value of c_k, called feature p (Step 4)
Add feature p into $R(R=\{p\}\bullet R)$ (Step 5)
Remove feature p from $S(S=S\backslash p)$ (Step 6)

Feature Selection-Perceptron (FS-P)

It is an embedded method based on a detector. A perceptron is an artificial neural network that can be viewed as the simplest type of feedforward neural network: a linear classifier. The basic idea of this method is to train a sensor in the context of supervised learning. Interconnection weights are used as indicators of which features may be most relevant and provide a ranking (Mejia et al., 2006).

Least Absolute Shrinkage and Selection Operator (L1 LASSO)

The least absolute contraction and selection operator adds the "absolute magnitude value" of the coefficient as a penalty term to the loss function. L1 regularization adds a penalty that is equal to the absolute value of the magnitude of the coefficient. This regularization type can result in sparse models with few coefficients. Some coefficients might become zero and get eliminated from the model. More enormous penalties result in coefficient values that are closer to zero (ideal for producing simpler models). On the other hand, L2 regularization does not result in any elimination of sparse models or coefficients. Thus, Lasso Regression is easy to interpret. It is calculated from the following formula:

$$\sum_{i=1}^{n}\left(y_i - \sum_j x_{ij}\beta_j\right)^2 + \lambda\sum_{j=1}^{p}\left|\beta_j\right| \tag{11}$$

Where λ denotes the amount of shrinkage. $\lambda = 0$ implies all features are considered, and it is equivalent to the linear regression where only the residual sum of squares is considered to build a predictive model. $\lambda = ¥$ implies no feature is considered i.e. as λ closes to infinity, it eliminates more and more features. The bias increases with an increase in λ. Variance increases with a decrease in λ.

As a result, the filter feature selection approach separates feature selection from classifier construction. The wrapper feature selection approach evaluates the classification performance of selected features and keeps searching until specific accuracy criteria are satisfied. Finally, the embedded feature selection approach embeds feature selection within classifier construction (Ma & Huang, 2008). It shows the status of the properties of the methods according to the number of points (Degenhardt et al., 2019) (Table 7).

Table 7. Summary of methods

Methods	Correlation and redundancy	Non linearity	Noise input	Noise target	No.feat>> No.samples
CFS	•	•	•	•••	••••
INTERACT	•	•	•	•••	•••
IG	•	•	•	•••	•••
ReliefF	••••	•••••	•••••	•••••	••
mRMR	••••	•••	•••••	••	•
SVM-RFE	••••	•	•	••••	•••••
FS-P	•••••	••	••••	••••	•

CFS: Correlation-based feature selection, IG: Information Gain, mRMR: Minimum redundancy-maximum relevance, SVM-RFE: Support Vector Machine-Recursive Feature Elimination, FS-P: Feature Selection-Perceptron.

FUTURE RESEARCH DIRECTIONS

Methods can be developed to optimize existing variable selection approaches that take into account missing data and extreme values by continuous and discrete data types in multi-omic data. The approach that automates the filter, wrapper, and embedded methods can be developed in the future. Thus, much better results can be obtained regarding cost and reliability.

CONCLUSION

In this paper, focusing on the data preprocessing step, we identify and review the most relevant studies on feature selection techniques in a set of well-known employed in the analysis of multi-omics data. A feature selection algorithm (FSA) provides a computational solution to the feature selection problem motivated by a certain definition of relevance. This algorithm should be reliable and efficient. Because, despite the technological developments, the data production and storage process continues expensively. Research laboratories do not have the computing infrastructure and sufficient storage space to process vastly complex data sets. Data analytics may have higher data costs than raw data production. Therefore, since high-dimensional data problems may continue in the future, variable selection processes may be needed to reduce data analysis costs and perform appropriate storage. In the study of Degenhardt et al., (Degenhardt et al., 2019) it was stated that Boruta, which is a sensitive method used in variable selection in high-dimensional data, can also be used in low-dimensional observations. In Bolon-Canedo's study (Bolon-Canedo et al., 2013), it has been shown that the ReliefF method gives good results regardless of the characteristics of the data. On the other hand, it has been stated that the SVM-RFE method, although costly, gives good results but cannot be applied in some datasets.

ACKNOWLEDGMENT

All authors contributed to the editing of the manuscript and the content is solely the responsibility of the authors. This study was supported by the Research Fund of Erciyes University [TYL-2019-9600]. The funders had no role in study design, data collection and analysis, decision to publish or preparation of the manuscript.

REFERENCES

Altmann, A., Toloşi, L., Sander, O., & Lengauer, T. J. B. (2010). Permutation importance: A corrected feature importance measure. *Bioinformatics (Oxford, England)*, *26*(10), 1340–1347. doi:10.1093/bioinformatics/btq134 PMID:20385727

Battiti, R. (1994). Using mutual information for selecting features in supervised neural net learning. *IEEE Transactions on Neural Networks*, *5*(4), 537–550. doi:10.1109/72.298224 PMID:18267827

Bolón-Canedo, V., Sánchez-Maroño, N., & Alonso-Betanzos, A. J. K. (2013). A review of feature selection methods on synthetic data. *Knowledge and Information Systems*, *34*(3), 483–519. doi:10.100710115-012-0487-8

Degenhardt, F., Seifert, S., & Szymczak, S. J. B. (2019). Evaluation of variable selection methods for random forests and omics data sets. *Briefings in Bioinformatics*, *20*(2), 492–503. doi:10.1093/bib/bbx124 PMID:29045534

Díaz-Uriarte, R., & Alvarez de Andrés, S. (2006). Gene selection and classification of microarray data using random forest. *BMC Bioinformatics*, *7*(1), 3. doi:10.1186/1471-2105-7-3 PMID:16398926

Dietrich, S., Floegel, A., Weikert, C., Prehn, C., Adamski, J., Pischon, T., Boeing, H., & Drogan, D. (2016). Identification of serum metabolites associated with incident hypertension in the European Prospective Investigation into Cancer and Nutrition–Potsdam Study. *Hypertension*, *68*(2), 471–477. doi:10.1161/HYPERTENSIONAHA.116.07292 PMID:27245178

Ferreira, A. J., & Figueiredo, M. A. T. (2012). *Efficient feature selection filters for high-dimensional data.*. doi:10.1016/j.patrec.2012.05.019

Fusaro, V. A., Mani, D. R., Mesirov, J. P., & Carr, S. A. (2009). Prediction of high-responding peptides for targeted protein assays by mass spectrometry. *Nature Biotechnology*, *27*(2), 190–198. doi:10.1038/nbt.1524 PMID:19169245

Gregorutti, B., Michel, B., & Saint-Pierre, P. (2017). Correlation and variable importance in random forests. *Statistics and Computing*, *27*(3), 659–678. doi:10.100711222-016-9646-1

Guo, P., Luo, Y., Mai, G., Zhang, M., Wang, G., Zhao, M., Gao, L., Li, F., & Zhou, F. (2014). Gene expression profile based classification models of psoriasis. *Genomics*, *103*(1), 48–55. doi:10.1016/j.ygeno.2013.11.001 PMID:24239985

Guyon, I., Weston, J., Barnhill, S., & Vapnik, V. J. M. l. (2002). *Gene selection for cancer classification using support vector machines*. Academic Press.

Habermann, J. K., Doering, J., Hautaniemi, S., Roblick, U. J., Bündgen, N. K., Nicorici, D., Kronenwett, U., Rathnagiriswaran, S., Mettu, R. K. R., Ma, Y., Krüger, S., Bruch, H.-P., Auer, G., Guo, N. L., & Ried, T. (2009). The gene expression signature of genomic instability in breast cancer is an independent predictor of clinical outcome. *International Journal of Cancer*, *124*(7), 1552–1564. doi:10.1002/ijc.24017 PMID:19101988

Hall, M. A. (1999). *Correlation-based feature selection for machine learning*. Academic Press.

Hastie, T., Tibshirani, R., Friedman, J. H., & Friedman, J. H. (2009). *The elements of statistical learning: data mining, inference, and prediction*. Springer. doi:10.1007/978-0-387-84858-7

Hoque, N., Ahmed, H., Bhattacharyya, D., & Kalita, J. J. F. I. (2016). A fuzzy mutual information-based feature selection method for classification. *Taylor & Francis Journals*, 8(3), 355–384. doi:10.1016/j.fiae.2016.09.004

Kira, K., & Rendell, L. A. (1992). A practical approach to feature selection. In *Proceedings of the ninth international workshop on Machine learning (ML92)*. Morgan Kaufmann Publishers Inc.

Kononenko, I. (1994). *Estimating attributes: Analysis and extensions of RELIEF*. Springer.

Kursa, M. B., & Rudnicki, W. R. (2010). Feature selection with the Boruta package. *Journal of Statistical Software*, 36(11), 1–13. doi:10.18637/jss.v036.i11

Kushmerick, N. (1997). *Wrapper induction for information extraction*. University of Washington.

Ladha, L., & Deepa, T. (2011). Feature selection methods and algorithms. *International Journal on Computer Science and Engineering*, 3(5), 1787–1797.

Ma, S., & Huang, J. (2008). Penalized feature selection and classification in bioinformatics. *Briefings in Bioinformatics*, 9(5), 392–403. doi:10.1093/bib/bbn027 PMID:18562478

Mejía-Lavalle, M., Sucar, E., & Arroyo, G. (2006). Feature selection with a perceptron neural net. *Proceedings of the international workshop on feature selection for data mining*.

Momeni, Z., Hassanzadeh, E., Abadeh, M. S., & Bellazzi, R. (2020). A survey on single and multi omics data mining methods in cancer data classification. *Journal of Biomedical Informatics*, 107, 103466. doi:10.1016/j.jbi.2020.103466 PMID:32525020

Ning, J., & Beiko, R. G. (2015). Phylogenetic approaches to microbial community classification. *Microbiome*, 3(1), 1–13. doi:10.118640168-015-0114-5 PMID:26437943

Press, W. H., Flannery, B. P., Teukolsky, S. A., & Vetterling, W. T. (1988). *Numerical recipes in C*. Cambridge University Press.

Rakotomamonjy, A., Guyon, I., & Elisseeff, A. (Eds.). (2003). Variable selection using SVM-based criteria. *Journal of Machine Learning Research*, 3(7-8), 1357–1370. doi:10.1162/153244303322753706

Rathore, S. S., & Gupta, A. (2014). A comparative study of feature-ranking and feature-subset selection techniques for improved fault prediction. *Proceedings of the 7th India Software Engineering Conference*. 10.1145/2590748.2590755

Robnik-Sikonja, M., & Kononenko, M., (2004). *Theoretical and Empirical Analysis of ReliefF and RReliefF*. Academic Press.

Saeys, Y., Inza, I., & Larrañaga, P. J. B. (2007). A review of feature selection techniques in bioinformatics. *Bioinformatics (Oxford, England)*, 23(19), 2507–2517. doi:10.1093/bioinformatics/btm344 PMID:17720704

Sánchez-Maroño, N., Alonso-Betanzos, A., & Tombilla-Sanromán, M. (2007). *Filter Methods for Feature Selection - A Comparative Study*. Paper presented at the Ideal.

Saulnier, D. M., Riehle, K., Mistretta, T. A., Diaz, M. A., Mandal, D., Raza, S., Weidler, E. M., Qin, X., Coarfa, C., Milosavljevic, A., Petrosino, J. F., Highlander, S., Gibbs, R., Lynch, S. V., Shulman, R. J., & Versalovic, J. (2011). Gastrointestinal microbiome signatures of pediatric patients with irritable bowel syndrome. *Gastroenterology, 141*(5), 1782–1791. doi:10.1053/j.gastro.2011.06.072 PMID:21741921

Tadist, K., Najah, S., Nikolov, N. S., Mrabti, F., & Zahi, A. (2019). Feature selection methods and genomic big data: A systematic review. *Journal of Big Data, 6*(1), 1–24. doi:10.118640537-019-0241-0

Tang, J., Alelyani, S., & Liu, H. (2014). Feature selection for classification: A review. *Data classification: Algorithms and applications, 37.*

Teukolsky, S. A., Flannery, B. P., Press, W., & Vetterling, W. J. S. (1992). *Numerical recipes in C.* Academic Press.

Verleysen, M., & François, D. (2005). *The Curse of Dimensionality in Data Mining and Time Series Prediction.* doi:10.1007/11494669_93

Witten, I. H., Frank, E., Hall, M. A., Pal, C. J., & Data, M. (2005). *Practical machine learning tools and techniques.* Paper presented at the Data Mining.

Yu, L., & Liu, H. (2003). Feature selection for high-dimensional data: A fast correlation-based filter solution. *Proceedings of the 20th international conference on machine learning (ICML-03).*

Zhao, Z., & Liu, H. J. I. D. A. (2009). Searching for interacting features in subset selection. *Intelligent Data Analysis, 13*(2), 207–228. doi:10.3233/IDA-2009-0364

ADDITIONAL READING

Kohavi, R., & John, G. H. (1997). Wrappers for feature subset selection. *Artificial Intelligence, 97*(1-2), 273–324.

Leclercq, M., Vittrant, B., Martin-Magniette, M. L., Scott Boyer, M. P., Perin, O., Bergeron, A., ... Droit, A. (2019). Large-scale automatic feature selection for biomarker discovery in high-dimensional OMICs data. *Frontiers in Genetics, 10,* 452.

Lin, Y., Zhang, W., Cao, H., Li, G., & Du, W. (2020). Classifying Breast Cancer Subtypes Using Deep Neural Networks Based on Multi-Omics Data. *Genes, 11*(8), 888. doi:10.3390/genes11080888 PMID:32759821

Perez-Riverol, Y., Kuhn, M., Vizcaíno, J. A., Hitz, M. P., & Audain, E. (2017). Accurate and fast feature selection workflow for high-dimensional omics data. *PLoS One, 12*(12), e0189875. doi:10.1371/journal.pone.0189875 PMID:29261781

Wang, Y., Tetko, I. V., Hall, M. A., Frank, E., Facius, A., Mayer, K. F., & Mewes, H. W. (2005). Gene selection from microarray data for cancer classification—A machine learning approach. *Computational Biology and Chemistry, 29*(1), 37–46.

Wu, C., Zhou, F., Ren, J., Li, X., Jiang, Y., & Ma, S. (2019). A selective review of multi-level omics data integration using variable selection. *High-throughput, 8*(1), 4.

Yousef, M., Kumar, A., & Bakir-Gungor, B. (2021). Application of Biological Domain Knowledge Based Feature Selection on Gene Expression Data. *Entropy (Basel, Switzerland)*, 23(1), 2. doi:10.3390/e23010002 PMID:33374969

B

KEY TERMS AND DEFINITIONS

Feature Selection: It is defined as selecting the best subset that can represent the original dataset.

Filter Methods: Filter methods use statistical techniques to evaluate the relationship between input and target variables. These scores are used to choose (filter) those input variables that will be used in the model.

Gene Expression: It is the process by which information from a gene is used to synthesize a functional gene product that enables it to produce end products, protein or non-coding RNA, and ultimately affect a phenotype as the final effect.

Mass Spectrometry: It is an analytical technique used to measure the mass-to-charge ratio of ions.

Metabolomics: It detects, quantifies, and identifies small molecule metabolites emerging from lipids, carbohydrates, vitamins, hormones, and other cell components in tissues, cells, and physiological fluids in a certain time high-throughput technologies.

Multi-Omics: It is a new approach where the data sets of different omic (metabolomic, genomic, proteomic, transcriptomic, etc.) groups are combined during analysis.

Next Generation Sequencing: It is a new technology for DNA, RNA sequencing, and variant/mutation detection. Next-generation sequencing is also called large parallel sequencing or second-generation sequencing. Next-generation sequencing is a method of simultaneously sequencing DNA fragments (or complementary DNA).

Systems Biology: It is the computational and mathematical analysis and modeling of complex biological systems. It is an approach in biomedical research to understand the larger picture, be it at the level of the organism, tissue, or cell, by putting its pieces together.

Class Discovery, Comparison, and Prediction Methods for RNA–Seq Data

Ahu Cephe
Erciyes University, Turkey

Necla Koçhan
https://orcid.org/0000-0003-2355-4826
İzmir Biomedicine and Genome Center, Turkey

Gözde Ertürk Zararsız
Erciyes University, Turkey

Vahap Eldem
İstanbul University, Turkey

Gökmen Zararsız
Erciyes University, Turkey

INTRODUCTION

Measuring gene-expression plays a vital role in life sciences such as cancer genomics. It enables us to quantify the level at which a particular gene is expressed within a cell, tissue or organism, thereby providing a tremendous amount of information (Alberts et al., 2002). There are different technologies (i.e., microarray and next-generation technologies) that can measure gene-expression levels. Microarray technology is an outdated technology with some limitations and lost its popularity with the advent of next-generation technologies. On the other hand, RNA-seq is one of the next-generation technologies capable of coping with these limitations, using the capabilities of next generation sequencing technologies, and performing operations quickly and cheaply based on the principle of high-throughput sequencing technology. Moreover, compared to microarrays, RNA-seq offers several advantages: (i) having less noisy data, (ii) being able to detect new transcripts and coding regions, (iii) not requiring pre-determination of the transcriptomes of interest.

RNA-seq technology allows measuring the expression levels of thousands of genes in cells simultaneously, leading to high dimensional data to be further analyzed. The information stored in these high dimensional data can be used for different purposes: (i) identifying "biomarker" genes that can characterize different disease subclasses, that is, class comparison; (ii) identifying new subclasses for a particular disease, that is, class discovery and (iii) assigning samples into known disease classes, that is, class prediction (Dudoit et al., 2002; Weigelt et al., 2010).

Class comparison is known as differential analysis or analysis of differential-expression. In these studies, gene-expression profiles of samples, which are predefined groups, are compared to identify differentially expressed genes between groups. Differentially expressed genes are identified in cells from different tissues, different patients, or cells exposed to different experimental conditions. For example,

DOI: 10.4018/978-1-7998-9220-5.ch123

comparing treated and untreated cells to detect the effect of a new drug on gene-expression levels; comparisons between healthy tissue and diseased tissue to identify genes with altered expression; comparing gene-expression in tumor tissue for patients responding to a particular treatment versus gene-expression in patients with the same cancer diagnosis who do not respond to treatment. Such studies yield lists of genes that were significantly altered between groups. The aim is to provide insight into the underlying biological mechanisms and perhaps identify potential therapeutic targets.

In class prediction studies, as in class comparison studies, genes that differ between predefined classes are tried to be determined. However, in class prediction studies, gene-expression values are explanatory variables rather than outcome variables. Moreover, the purpose of the analysis of class prediction studies is to identify a small set of genes that can accurately distinguish between different classes rather than identify all genes that differ. Classes are defined beforehand in class predictions, and the aim is to create a classifier that can distinguish between these classes based on the gene-expression profiles of the samples and can be applied to the expression profiles of a new sample. For example, a classifier that distinguishes between 2 different disease states; a classifier that distinguishes short-term survivors from long-term survivors; a classifier can be created that predicts whether a patient will respond to a particular drug. In class comparison studies, whether a new patient will react to treatment can be predicted based on gene-expression profiles.

Class discovery differs from class comparison and class prediction studies in that classes are not predefined. The purpose of these studies is to determine whether subsets of samples with apparently homogeneous phenotypes can be distinguished based on differences in gene-expression profiles. For example, there are many diseases in which individuals with apparently similar phenotypes have significant variability in outcomes such as survival. This variability is due to differences at the molecular level. Class discovery studies are used to identify molecular differences that define subgroups for new diseases or known diseases. Class discovery studies need to analyze a set of gene-expression profiles in order to discover subgroups that share common characteristics. For example, subgroups of patients with similar expression profiles are classified. It can also describe different stages of disease severity or identify groups of genes that may behave similarly in a disease state.

Although there are many studies and methods using microarray data for class comparison, class prediction and class discovery design model in the literature, these methods cannot be directly applied to RNA-seq data, which has a discrete, skewed and over-dispersed structure, quite different from the continuous data structure of microarrays. In this case, the first way to analyze the RNA-seq data is to transform and get closer data to a normal distribution and use the methods developed for microarrays. The second way is to work directly with count data using methods based on discrete probability distributions such as Poisson and Negative Binomial (Anders & Huber, 2010; Love et al., 2014; Zheng et al., 2014).

This chapter provides an overview of algorithms/methods used for class discovery, comparison and prediction of RNA-seq data. It also covers the difficulties and challenges encountered by these algorithms. Finally, the algorithms proposed and developed for RNA-seq data analysis are discussed with their pros and cons.

BACKGROUND

Preprocessing

Following base calling and demultiplexing single-end or paired-end reads, sequence quality control and trimming are routinely applied in standard RNA-seq data analysis protocols regardless of the methodology used. In preprocessing step, the following data filtering criteria were applied before further analyses were performed: trimming adapter, index, and molecular identifier (UMI) sequences and removing low-quality reads (base-pair quality Phred Score, <Q20), short reads (< 35-bp) and reads with unknown bases >10% to generate high-quality clean data various tools such as Cutadapt (Martin, 2011), Trimmomatic (Bolger et al., 2014), and fastp (Chen et al., 2018). To assess total data quality, AfterQC (Chen et al., 2017), FastQC (Andrews, 2017) and MultiQC (Ewels et al., 2016) analyses are generally performed for quality checks before and after adaptor/sequences trimming.

Normalization

The purpose of normalization is to remove the systematic technical effects in the data to make the samples comparable and ensure that technical bias has minimal impact on the results. A direct comparison of gene-expression between samples may not be possible, as sample read depth differs in different samples. Therefore, the normalization step is an essential preprocessing step for the analyzes of RNA-seq data. Correction for biological variability, technical variability, and bias is required for direct comparison of gene-expression data and accurate determination of expression changes between sample groups. For this, there are many normalization methods for different purposes. Larger genes have higher read counts compared to smaller ones due to the difference in gene lengths and sizes. The methods used to correct this bias in reading depth and transcript length; Implemented in DEGSeq and Cufflinks-CuffDiff are RPKM (Reads per Kilobase per Million mapped reads) (Mortazavi, 2008) and FPKM (Fragments per Kilobase per Million mapped fragments) (Trapnell, 2010). Another approach to correct gene length is the TPM (Transcripts Per Million) method. TPM corrects for both gene length and sequencing read length but may not be able to deal with some biases such as sequencing depth and latent technical artifacts. Although RPKM, FPKM, and TPM are important normalization methods, gene length-dependent normalization is not significant when differential-expression analyses of the same genes are performed between samples and genes are not compared to genes. Another source of variability between samples is library size, which is the total number of reads generated for a sample. With the method used to fix the library size; Upper Quartile (UQ) (Bullard, 2010) is Trimmed Mean of M-values (TMM) (Robinson, 2010) implemented in edgeR and Relative Log Expression (RLE) (Love et al., 2014) implemented in DESeq2/DESeq. After the Upper Quartile removes genes with zero read counts for all samples, the remaining gene counts are divided by the upper quartile of nonzero numbers and multiplied by the average upper quartile across all samples of the dataset in calculating the normalization factors associated with samples of the counts. The TMM method is based on the hypothesis that most genes are not differentially expressed. The TMM factor is calculated for each sample, considering one sample as a reference sample and the remainder as a test sample. For each test sample, TMM is computed as the weighted average of the log ratios between that test and the reference, after excluding the genes with the highest expression and the genes with the largest log ratios. RLE, like TMM, is based on the hypothesis that most genes are not differentially expressed. For a given sample, the RLE scaling factor is calculated as the median of the ratio of the read counts for each gene to the geometric mean across all samples. Other global scaling quantile normalization methods are TC (per-sample total counts), UQ (per-sample 75% upper quartile Q3), Med (per-sample Median Q2) or Q (full quantile).

Class Comparison

Class comparison, also known as differential-expression analysis in the bioinformatics field, is one of the commonly used methods in gene-expression data analyses, particularly in pharmaceutical and clinical research such as tumor diagnosis (Bismeijer et al., 2020) and cancer prognosis (Wang et al., 2020). DE analysis aims to compare expression profiles in class conditions of interest (e.g., tumor and nontumor samples). DE analysis techniques enable us to identify genes or biomarkers, affect the conditions and help us understand the molecular basis of phenotypic variation (Soneson & Delorenzi, 2013).

Class Comparison Methods

Due to the increase in popularity of RNA-seq data, many methods and the corresponding tools have been developed for differential gene-expression analysis. These methods can be grouped into two main categories: parametric and non-parametric. In parametric methods, it is generally assumed that the expression value of any gene, after applying a normalization, comes from a specific distribution such as Poisson (Bullard et al., 2010; Hardcastle & Kelly, 2010; Marioni et al., 2008) or negative binomial distribution (Anders & Huber, 2010; Robinson et al., 2010; Robinson & Smyth, 2008). Non-parametric methods, on the other hand, do not require any model to be fitted and, therefore, can be more informative about the data distribution.

Due to the discrete structure of RNA-seq data and overdispersion, several tools such as edgeR, DESeq2, baySeq use the negative binomial model in differentially expressed gene analysis. In contrast, other tools, such as NOIseq and SAMseq use non-parametric models. Also, there exist other tools such as EBSeq and Cuffdiff2, which focus on transcript or isoform detection but can also be applied to differential gene-expression analysis. Limma can compare a lot of RNA targets simultaneously, handle complex experimental designs and overcome the small sample size problem. Limma fits a linear model such as analysis of variance or linear regression to each gene. In this approach, the coefficients of the model are the log fold changes and the error term is assumed to be normally distributed with a variance that is constant across the range of the data. Limma is used to provide a moderated t-statistic while testing for significantly changed genes.

Limma fits a linear model for each row of data in a matrix of expression values, where each row represents a gene or other genomic feature relevant to the current study, and each column corresponds to an RNA sample. In addition, limma analyzes the data as a whole, helping to model possible correlations between data. Genomic data are parallel, allowing different levels of variability between genes and between samples, making statistical results more reliable when the number of samples is small. This parallel structure between the data is well suited for the parametric empirical Bayesian approach, which dynamically borrows information between genes. This approach establishes a link between variance estimation for each gene and variance estimation for all genes. The empirical Bayesian approach has also been used in limma modeling, as it gives reliable results even with small sample sizes or when the number of replicates is small. Limma also uses quantitative weights at every stage of statistical analysis to reduce less reliable measurements or samples in a gene expression analysis. Using weights increases the power to detect expressed genes and removes the need for observation/sample filtering. limma analyzes RNAseq read counts by converting the numbers to log-scale and empirically estimating the mean-variance relationship. The mean variance trend is converted by the voom function into precision weights that are included in the analysis of log-transformed RNAseq counts.

Limma, originally developed for microarray data but then extended to RNA-seq data, identifies the DE genes using linear modeling. To apply the limma package for DE analyses, TMM normalization and voom transformation, which transforms the normalized counts to log2 scale and models the mean-variance relationship to determine weights for observations, is recommended in the up to date user guide of the limma package. In addition, the Benjamini-Hochberg method is applied to control the False Discovery Rate (FDR).

edgeR is a widely applied DE analysis method for RNA-seq data with biological replicates and can be used even with a small number of replicates. The method applies robust statistical methodologies, including the empirical Bayesian estimation, exact tests, generalized linear models and quasi-likelihood tests based on the assumption of the negative binomial distribution (Robinson et al., 2010; Robinson & Smyth, 2008). In order to moderate the degree of overdispersion across genes, the information shared between genes across all samples is used together with the empirical Bayes procedure (weighted conditional likelihood). By default, TMM normalization is employed in order to minimize the log-fold changes between samples across genes and the Benjamini-Hochberg method is applied to control FDR. The TMM factor is calculated for each lane, one lane reference sample and the others as the test sample. TMM for each test sample is computed as the weighted average of the log ratios between that assay and the reference, excluding the genes with the most expressed and the largest log ratios.

Figure 1. The workflow for RNA-seq class discovery by applying cluster or classification methods. This flowchart is divided into two parts: (i) left panel shows the basic steps of RNA-seq analysis from raw read processing to abundance estimation, (ii) The upper part of the right panel shows the RNA-seq class discovery based on clustering methods whereas the lower part of the right panel indicates various classification algorithms used in RNA-seq class discovery.

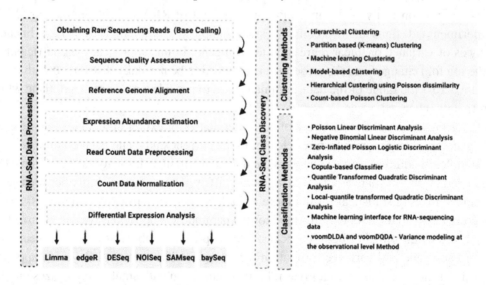

DESeq assumes that data follows negative binomial distribution, but the overdispersion parameter, which shows mean-variance relationship, is estimated using shrinkage estimation and moderates dispersion estimates on the average expression strength over all samples (Love et al., 2014). The package uses

C

a scaling factor normalization for different sequencing depths of different samples and the Benjamini-Hochberg method is applied to control the FDR. Although it is technically possible to work with RNA-seq data without any biological replicates, it is not recommended (Seyednasrollah et al., 2013). DESeq is calculated as the median of the ratio of the number of reads for each gene to its geometric mean across all lanes. DESeq2 fits a negative binomial generalized linear model for each gene. Statistical significance test is done with Wald statistics. This approach calculates the geometric mean of each gene for all samples separately while performing normalization. The counts of a gene in each sample are divided by this average found. It uses shrinkage estimation for dispersions and fold changes to better predict within-group variance in case of few replicates. A biological replicate of each experimental condition must be available to accurately predict the distribution for each gene. The DESeq2 approach also automatically removes outliers and underexpressed genes from the dataset.

edgeR uses the trimmed average of M values; DESeq uses a relative log expression approach by creating a virtual library against which each sample will be compared; in practice, the normalization factors are often similar. edgeR manages feature-level distribution estimates towards a trended mean based on the distribution-mean relationship. In contrast, DESeq takes the maximum of the individual distribution estimates and the distribution-mean trend, which means that DESeq is less powerful, whereas edgeR is more sensitive to outliers.

NOISeq is a non-parametric method that empirically models the noise distribution from counts and is shown to be non-sensitive to the sequencing depth of the data (Tarazona et al., 2015). This method also has better control of false discoveries. RPKM (reads per kilobase per million mapped reads) normalization is used as default. The package is developed for a small number of replicates and low expressed genes (Seyednasrollah et al., 2013).

SAMseq is another non-parametric method that implements Wilcoxon rank statistic and a resampling procedure for minimizing different sampling sequence depths (Li & Tibshirani, 2013). The method estimates FDR using a permutation-based approach. It is pointed out that SAMseq performs more efficiently than the parametric methods when the assumptions of parametric methods are not satisfied (Costa-Silva et al., 2017; Seyednasrollah et al., 2013).

baySeq identifies differentially expressed genes from count data via the empirical Bayesian method, assuming counts follow a negative binomial distribution. The method estimates posterior probabilities of differentially expressed genes and gives a Bayesian FDR estimate (Hardcastle & Kelly, 2010). This method provides the ability to analyze complex experimental setups that can be useful for several biological applications. However, the computational cost of this method is relatively high, but the application of the method takes advantage of parallel processing (Seyednasrollah et al., 2013).

Cuffdiff2 is a method that uses a beta negative binomial model for fragment counts to control variability and read mapping ambiguity that may result in false differential-expression calls of genes with similar isoforms (Costa-Silva et al., 2017; Seyednasrollah et al., 2013; Trapnell et al., 2013). It is designed to identify unknown transcripts or isoforms and can also be applied to the identifying differential expression genes.

EBSeq is a robust method that aims to discover differentially expressed isoforms or transcripts (Leng et al., 2013). The method assumes that data follows negative binomial distribution and estimates the posterior likelihoods with Bayesian methods. The package uses median normalization as default and provides a Bayesian FDR estimate.

A comparative study between widely used class comparison methods is given in **Table 1.**

Table 1. Comparative study between commonly used methods for RNA-seq data about class comparison

Method	Normalization	Distribution	Testing Strategy	Advantages	Limitations	References
edgeR classic	TMM	Negative Binomial	Exact test / Likelihood ratio test	Separate biological from technical variations	Limited to pairwise comparison	Robinson et al., 2010
edgeR glm	TMM	Negative Binomial	Likelihood ratio test	Separate biological from technical variations	Limited to pairwise comparison	McCarthy et al., 2012
edgeR robust	TMM	Negative Binomial	Likelihood ratio test	Separate biological from technical variations	Limited to pairwise comparison	Zhou et al., 2014
DESeq	Median of ratios	Negative Binomial	Exact test / Likelihood ratio test	Extend edgeR by allowing more general Data-driven relationship of mean and variance Work well even with small sample sizes	Limited to pairwise comparison	Anders and Huber, 2010
DESeq2	Median of ratios	Negative Binomial	Wald test / Likelihood ratio test	Improve upon DESeq for better gene ranking Allow hypothesis tests above and below threshold Work well even with small sample sizes	Limited to pairwise comparison	Love et al., 2014
limmaQN	Quantile Normalization on log transformed counts	Gaussian distribution for normalized log-transformed counts	Linear model / Moderated t-test	Inherit the robustness properties from the normal-based procedures in limma Made even more robust using the robust empirical Bayes options of the limma package Work well even with small sample sizes	Low power to detect differences in small number of replicates	Papaport et al., 2013
limmaVoom	TMM	Gaussian distribution after log-transforming normalized counts	Linear model / Moderated t-test	Inherit the robustness properties from the normal-based procedures in limma Made even more robust using the robust empirical Bayes options of the limma package Work well even with small sample sizes	An obstacle to use these normalized counts in normal-based statistical methods is that they have unequal variabilities: larger counts have larger variance than smaller counts.	Law et al., 2014
limmaVoom QW	TMM	Gaussian distribution after log-transforming normalized counts	Linear model / Moderated t-test	Inherit the robustness properties from the normal-based procedures in limma Made even more robust using the robust empirical Bayes options of the limma package Work well even with small sample sizes	Low power to detect differences in small number of replicates	Liu et al, 2015

continues on following page

Table 1. Continued

Method	Normalization	Distribution	Testing Strategy	Advantages	Limitations	References
limmaVst	Median of ratios	Gaussian distribution after applying the DESeq variance stabilizing transformation on the normalized counts	Linear model / Moderated t-test	Inherit the robustness properties from the normal-based procedures in limma Made even more robust using the robust empirical Bayes options of the limma package Work well even with small sample sizes	Low power to detect differences in small number of replicates	Soneson and Delorenzi, 2013
baySeq	Upper Quantile	Bayesian and Empirical Bayesian	Evaluating posterior probability for inference	Involve multiple comparison, accommodate different sample size Show good performances in different cases but is strongly dependent on the dataset structure	Computationally intensive but allow parallelization	Hardcastle and Kelly, 2010
PoissonSeq	Total count of least differental genes	Poisson	Score test	Accommodate multiple covariate types Computationally efficient	Transformation power depends only on gene-expression Libraries are totally exchangeable	Li et al., 2012
SAMSeq	Poisson Sampling	Non-parametric	Wilcoxon test	Robust to outliers Remove Experimental effect Simplify test for feature effect Accommodate quantitative Survival and multiple group comparison Performs well in terms of precision even as it needs more replicates to achieve a good power of detection	Overestimate false discovery rate in some cases, relative low power for data with small sample size	Li and Tibshirani, 2013
Cuffdiff (Cufflinks)	FPKM (geometric)	Poisson	t-test	Deals with problem of overdispersion across replicates	Require a reference genome	Trapnell et al., 2010
Cuffdiff2	DESeq like normalization (Geometric)	Beta Negative Binomial distribution	t-test	Robustly identifies differentially expressed transcripts and genes and reveals differential splicing and promoter-preference changes Have a high precision with a significantly low number of false positives	Lower power of detection at gene level especially with a higher number of replicates	Trapnell et al., 2013
DEGseq	Total count	Poisson	Fisher's exact test / Likelihood ratio test	Support raw read counts or normalized gene-expression values Identify differential-expression of exons or transcripts	Ignore biological variation	Wang et al., 2010

continues on following page

C

Table 1. Continued

Method	Normalization	Distribution	Testing Strategy	Advantages	Limitations	References
NOISeq	RPKM/TMM/ Upper Quantile	Non-parametric	Wilcoxon test	Robust and maintain a high true-positive rate Performs well when the two conditions in the dataset have different dispersion While it has a good control of the false discovery rate, it becomes too conservative with higher number of replicates	Not easy to identify true differential-expression at a low count range Limited to pair-wise comparison	Tarazona et al., 2011
EBSeq	Median normalization	Negative Binomial	Empirical Bayesian Analysis	Developed with the main objective of identifying differentially expressed isoforms, it is also robust in the identification of DEGs.	Represent he high computational cost	Leng et al., 2013
NBPseq	Total count	Negative Binomial	Adapted exact test	Introduce an additional parameter to allow the dispersion to depend on the mean	Assume all library sizes are equal	Di et al., 2011
ShrinkSeq	None	Bayesian and Empirical Bayesian / Zero-inflated negative binomial	Evaluating posterior probability for inference	Provide joint shrink multiple parameters Allow for random effects Address multiplicity problems	Computationally intensive but allow parallelization	Van de Wiel et al., 2013
Myrna	3rd quartile	Poisson or Gaussian	Likelihood ratio test Parallelized permutation test	Handle dataset with over 1 billion rows Computationally efficient	Ignore biological variation, signal loss due to junction or repetitive reads Inconvenient cloud data transfer	Langmead et al., 2010
BBSeq	Total count	Beta binomial	Wald test / Likelihood ratio test	Handle outlier detection automatically	Sensitive to outliers of shrinkage or penalization methods	Zhou et al., 2011

C

Class Discovery

Class discovery, also known as clustering, is an unsupervised learning algorithm used in gene-expression data analysis. Gene-expression data can be clustered, either gene-based or sample-based. The main goal in gene-based clustering is to find groups of genes with similar expression patterns called coexpressed genes, whereas the primary goal in sample-based clustering is to discover subtypes or subgroups of any disease, i.e., cancer, in order to understand the underlying mechanism of each subtype.

Transformation-Based Clustering Methods

Numerous clustering algorithms used for microarray data do not apply to RNA-seq data, which follows an overdispersed Poisson or negative binomial distribution, due to the discrete nature of RNA-seq data. There are also some other statistical challenges of RNA-seq data analysis: (1) having a skewed distribution, (2) variability among the read counts for individual genes and (3) likelihood of extreme values (Zwiener et al., 2014). In order to cope with the discrete nature and skewness problems and be able to apply those clustering algorithms, counts are required to be transformed into a distribution closer to Gaussian distribution. To this end, several transformation methods have been proposed. For example, the log transform can usually deal with skewed data by reducing the variability in the data and converting it to a form closer to the normal distribution. However, in some cases, it has the disadvantage of making the data more skewed and more variable (Feng, 2014). vst (Anders and Huber, 2010) and rlog (rlog) (Love, Huber and Anders, 2014) transformations are just two types of those transformation methods that are used in RNA-seq data clustering (Love et al., 2014). The readers are referred to many other transformation techniques (Z. Zhang et al., 2019).

Hierarchical Clustering Methods

Hierarchical methods enable biologists to easily understand the structure of the data and analyze the data accordingly. Therefore, different variants of hierarchical clustering algorithms such as complete-linkage, single-linkage and average linkage are applied to RNA-seq data after transforming raw counts (Jaskowiak et al., 2018). To cluster RNA-seq data, hierarchical clustering uses various distance measures such as Euclidean, Manhattan, Pearson, Canberra, etc. For instance, Severin et al. (2010) clustered 14 types of soybean textures using hierarchical clustering with Pearson correlation after normalizing the RNA-seq data. Cephe et al. (2019) have performed an extensive simulation to compare the clustering performance of RNA-seq data using different distances and different variants of hierarchical clustering.

The voom method, which is previously used in the significance analyses, and classification algorithms model the mean-variance relationship and can cope with the overdispersion problem arising from biological replicates in RNA-seq data. Due to the advantages of the voom method, Cephe (2019) developed voomPW and voomQW clustering algorithms, which combine the voom method and traditional clustering algorithms (i.e., hierarchical and partition-based clustering algorithms). The authors demonstrated that the performances of both voomQW and voomPW methods are high overall. In addition, the authors have also developed a user-friendly voomCLUSTER web-based application, including preprocessing (normalization and transformation) and different clustering methods for RNA-seq data. So, researchers can perform not only preprocessing but also clustering with an easy-to-use interface. Hierarchical clustering methods are the most popular methods for gene-expression data analysis.

Partition-Based Clustering Methods

k-means is one of the most popular partition-based methods for clustering gene-expression data effectively and significantly. The aim of k-means clustering methods is to partition the objects (genes or samples) into k clusters concerning the closest cluster center. Each cluster is calculated iteratively and objects are assigned to the nearest center using various distance measures. Many studies related to k-means algorithms and their improved versions for gene-expression analysis (P. Li et al., 2010; Sîrbu et al., 2012). However, k-means algorithm has some handicaps in gene-expression data sets. First, the number of clusters in a gene-expression data set is unknown. That is, there is no prior information about the number of clusters. Second, it is known that the k-means algorithm is sensitive to outliers and noise. Thus, it pushes each observation into a cluster even if it is an outlier.

k-medoid is a different version of k-means that is less sensitive to outliers because medoids are used as cluster centers instead of means that can be affected by extreme values (outliers). Cephe (2019) applied k-medoids to RNA-seq data clustering and compared the performance of k-medoids with different clustering methods according to different distance measures. On the other hand, k-medoids have similar drawbacks as K-means. Jaskowiak et al. (2018) addressed that these algorithms cannot adjust differences in sequencing depth (batch effect) in the model.

Machine Learning Clustering Methods

Since RNA-seq data are high dimensional datasets where the number of genes is greater than the number of samples, powerful and efficient algorithms are required in order to extract the crucial biological information from fast-growing RNA-seq data. In particular, scRNA-Seq data consists of lots of zeros and is very sparse compared to RNA-seq data; therefore, it is difficult to analyze with traditional clustering algorithms. To this end, machine learning algorithms are widely used to build predictive models to cluster patients or genes, find the hidden structure in the models and understand the relationships between gene-expression levels and disease type when profiling gene-expression data (Golub et al., 1999; Simon et al., 2003).

In clustering analyses of single-cell RNA sequencing (scRNA-seq) data, computational difficulties are experienced due to the increased number of cells and the batch effect. Therefore, for example, a method is proposed a deep embedding clustering algorithm for single-cell clustering called DESC, which removes batch effect and technical variability artifacts (Li et al., 2020). Furthermore, the study of (Tian et al., 2019) can be examined for many other algorithms used in clustering analyzes of RNA-seq data.

Discrete Distributions Based Clustering Methods

Model-based Clustering

Model-based clustering methods are based on probability models and a probabilistic framework is generated in order to model the cluster structure of gene-expression data. Model-based clustering methods consist of a mixture of Poisson probability distributions, which are used only when there are technical replicates, and Negative Binomial probability distributions, which are used when there are biological replicates. The Expectation-Maximization (EM) and Bayesian approaches, model-based clustering algorithms, have been mainly applied to RNA-seq data clustering analyses due to their statistical power (Lim et al., 2021; Si et al., 2014; Vestal et al., 2020). For example, Bayesian approaches allow biologists to understand the structure of the datasets and can be used to obtain the causal relations between genes,

C

thereby combining prior knowledge and datasets. McLachlan (1997) defines the EM algorithm as an appropriate approach that can fit overdispersed count data in Poisson regression model. On the other hand, due to the overdispersion in the RNA-seq data, a negative binomial likelihood method is recommended. Therefore, in addition to the study of (Si et al., 2014), mentioning many model-based clustering algorithms, such as a model-based clustering method with the expectation-maximization algorithm (MB-EM), an initialization algorithm for cluster centers and a model-Based Hybrid-Hierarchical Clustering Algorithm, which does not require pre-specifid number of clusters as in other methods, enables faster clustering with the algorithm it uses, and it is called hybrid because it combines two steps, they introduced a new RNA-seq data clustering method called Negative Binomial Model-Based (NBMB) to cluster samples using EM algorithm. The results showed that NBMB model can be conducted through NB.MClust package in R programming language (Li et al., 2018). However, the authors address some drawbacks of this algorithm: (1) the algorithm needs an efficient gene selection within the model, (2) the optimal number of clusters has to be modeled and (3) the dependence structure or the correlation between genes is not considered in their model (Li et al., 2018).

Hierarchical Clustering Using Poisson Dissimilarity

Counts obtained in an RNA-seq experiment yield non-negative numbers and follow a discrete distribution. Poisson distribution and Negative Binomial (NB) distribution are the two most frequently used models in the methods developed for differential-expression analysis of such count data (Anders & Huber, 2010; Auer et al., 2012; Robinson & Smyth, 2008). The Poisson distribution is an easy to apply distribution with the same parameter for mean and variance. However, having the same parameter for mean and variance causes some statistical problems when data is overdispersed. To account for the overdispersion, negative binomial distribution, which can model mean-variance relationships in the data has been used in many studies. Witten (2011) discussed the overdispersion problem, suggested transforming the data and then using Poisson model with dissimilarity measure to cluster samples. The authors also developed an R package called PoiClaClu, through which RNA-seq data clustering can be performed. Even though this method was proposed for sample clustering, it can also be used for gene clustering. Since this method ignores the overdispersion that arises from biological replicates in the data, it is not recommended to be implemented when data contains biological replicates.

Count-based Poisson Clustering (iCluster+)

The iCluster+ method is a count-based clustering method, which assumes RNA-seq data follows a Poisson distribution. The method performs feature selection by including sparsity via the lasso penalty before clustering but neglects potential overdispersion in read counts (Mo et al., 2013).

A comparative study between widely used data clustering methods is given in **Table 2**.

Class Prediction (Classification)

Classification based on gene-expression profiles is of great importance in medical research, particularly in personalized medicine. Roughly speaking, classification (a.k.a. supervised learning) assigns new observations into one of the available classes that help clinicians in disease diagnosis and treatment therapies or drug discovery.

Table 2. Comparative study between commonly used algorithms for RNA-seq data clustering

Method	Pros	Cons	Applications
Hierarchical Clustering Methods	• Representation of the data to easily understand the structure of the data and analyze the data • Embedded flexibility regarding the level of granularity • Well suited for problems involving point linkages, e.g. taxonomy trees	• Lack of robustness in the conventional agglomerative hierarchical clustering method • Computational complexity • Computational cost • Selecting the most appropriate distance measure • Inability to make corrections once the splitting/merging decision is made • Lack of interpretability regarding the cluster descriptors	• Jaskowiak et al., 2018 • Severin et al., 2010 • Cephe et al., 2019
Partition-Based Clustering Methods	• Relatively scalable and simple • Suitable for datasets with compact spherical clusters that are well-separated	• No prior information about the number of clusters • Sensitive to outliers and noise • Cannot adjust differences in sequencing depth (batch effect) in the model	• P. Li et al., 2010 • Sîrbu et al., 2012 • Cephe et al., 2019 • Jaskowiak et al., 2018
Model-Based Clustering	• Cope with overdispersion problem in the RNA-seq data • Automatically determine the number of clusters based on standard statistics • Taking outlier or noise into account • Robust clustering methods	• Outliers or noise observations have great impact on the estimation of mixture model parameters • Require an underlying model for the data (e.g., GMMs assume multivariate normality), and the cluster results are heavily dependent on this assumption • Show disappointing computational performance in high-dimensional spaces	• Lim et al., 2021 • Si et al., 2014 • Vestal et al., 2020
Model-Based Hybrid-Hierarchical Clustering Algorithm	• Cope with overdispersion problem in the RNA-seq data • Does not require pre-specifying the number of clusters • Faster clustering	• Outliers or noise observations have great impact on the estimation of mixture model parameters • Require an underlying model for the data (e.g., GMMs assume multivariate normality), and the cluster results are heavily dependent on this assumption • Show disappointing computational performance in high-dimensional spaces	• Si et al., 2014
Negative Binomial Model-Based (NBMB)	• Cope with overdispersion problem in the RNA-seq data	• The algorithm needs an efficient gene selection within the model, • The optimal number of clusters has to be modeled • The dependence structure or the correlation between genes is not considered in their model	• Li et al., 2018
Hierarchical clustering using Poisson dissimilarity	• Cope with overdispersion problem RNA-seq data transforming data	• It is not recommended to be implemented when data contains biological replicates	• Witten, 2011
Count-based Poisson clustering	• Performs feature selection by including sparsity via the lasso penalty	• Neglect potential overdispersion in read counts	• Mo et al., 2013

RNA-seq data is high-dimensional data where the number of genes is greater than the number of samples and this is called the curse of dimensionality in data analysis. Such big datasets are composed of many genes that are irrelevant in RNA-seq data classification. To select the most relevant genes that affect classification performance and reduce the dimensionality of the data, an efficient feature selection strategy should be followed before the classification. One can see many strategies developed for this purpose in the literature (Jabeen et al., 2018). The authors note here that this chapter does not cover feature selection strategies.

Classification methods used for RNA-seq data can be grouped under two main categories: (i) methods based on discrete structure and (ii) methods after transformation of the RNA-seq data. In this section, we discuss these two categories with their advantages and disadvantages.

Classification Methods Based on the Discrete Structure of RNA-seq Data

RNA-seq counts the number of reads mapped onto one gene and measures the level of gene-expression on the discrete scale. Hence, two discrete distributions, Poisson and Negative Binomial are considered to model the data and develop classifiers. Witten (2011) proposed a classifier called Poisson Linear Discriminant Analysis (PLDA), which is an extension of Fisher's linear discriminant analysis to high-dimensional count data. PLDA shrinks the class differences to identify a subset of genes and applies a Poisson log linear model for classification (Witten, 2011). Since RNA-seq data is generally overdispersed, which significantly impacts classification performance, it is recommended to implement PLDA classifier with power transformation as it improves the classification performance (Witten, 2011). Following this study, Tan et al. (2014) shoswed that when classifying RNA-seq data, the classification performance using PLDA is higher than the methods used for microarray datasets. However, the Poisson distribution is only suitable for modeling RNA-seq data when the data contains technical replicates but not biological replicates. Therefore, the Poisson distribution may not be appropriate for modeling RNA-seq data with biological replicates. The reason behind that is when there are biological replicates in the data, the variance of the data exceeds its mean (known as overdispersion), which means that the data is not distributed Poisson anymore (Love et al., 2014; Si & Liu, 2013). Witten (2011) pointed out that the classification accuracy can be further improved for overdispersed data by extending the Poisson model with the negative binomial model. To this end, Dong et al. (2016) proposed a new classification method, called NBLDA classifier, assuming the data follows negative binomial distribution. NBLDA is the extension of PLDA where data is assumed to be negative binomially distributed with parameters mean and overdispersion. The authors used a shrinkage method to predict the additional overdispersion parameter in the model. The results on real and simulated datasets showed that NBLDA outperforms PLDA when biological replicates are considered in the data (Dong et al., 2016). On the other hand, it should be noted that the dispersion parameter has to be correctly estimated in order to obtain high performance in classification.

It is pointed out by (Zhou et al., 2018) that there may be excess zeros in real RNA-seq datasets that should be considered when analyzing RNA-seq data. Thus, Zhou et al. (2018) proposed a new classifier called Zero-Inflated Poisson Logistic Discriminant Analysis (ZIPLDA) for RNA-seq datasets, including technical replicates. In ZIPLDA, the authors assumed that RNA-seq data follows a mixture distribution with a point mass at zero and a Poisson distribution. Since ZIPLDA assumes that data except zeros follows Poisson distribution, Zhu et al. (2021) developed another new classifier called Zero-Inflated Negative Binomial Logistic Discriminant Analysis (ZINBLDA) for overdispersed RNA-seq datasets which contain biological replicates. Unlike ZIPLDA, the authors assumed that RNA-seq data follows a mixture distribution with a point mass at zero and a negative binomial distribution.

Most of the RNA-seq data classification methods are constructed under strong independence assumption, which is not realistic for RNA-seq classification problems and may result in low performance in classification. Therefore, a number of authors have developed new classification algorithms such as copula-based classifier (Q. Zhang, 2017), qtQDA (Koçhan et al., 2019), L-qtQDA (Kochan et al., 2021) and SQDA (Sun & Zhao, 2015) which incorporate the dependence structure between genes into the model. These studies showed that incorporating the dependency between genes into the model improves the performance of the classification. However, due to the high dimensionality of RNA-seq data, SQDA, L-qtQDA and copula-based classifiers are computationally intensive and time-consuming. qtQDA is computationally faster than other classifiers. The only disadvantage of qtQDA study is stated as sparsity of the classifier which means that a regularization technique is required to identify less informative genes and then reduce their effects to zero (Koçhan et al., 2019).

Classification Methods After Transformation Including Machine Learning Algorithms

Due to the discrete structure of RNA-seq data, neither classical machine learning algorithms nor algorithms developed for microarray data can be directly applied to RNA-seq data. In order to use those algorithms, several transformation techniques which transform counts into continuous data have been introduced. Applying transformation techniques such as log-transformation, voom, etc. brings RNA-seq data hierarchically closer to microarray data and uses normal distribution (Anders & Huber, 2010; Nagalakshmi et al., 2008; Robinson et al., 2010). For instance, transforming counts using log-transformation makes machine learning approaches applicable to RNA-seq data classification (Goksuluk et al., 2019).

voom (variance modeling at the observational level) method is one of the transformation techniques which enables us to apply classification algorithms developed for microarray data to RNA-seq data (Law et al., 2014). The voom method basically estimates the mean-variance relationship using log counts. In addition, the voom method takes advantage of generalized linear models and empirical Bayesian estimation in order to control the Type-I error rate and obtain the lowest discovery rate (Law et al., 2014; Ritchie et al., 2015). Due to these substantial advantages of the voom method, Zararsiz et al. (2017a) integrated voom method with nearest shrunken centroids and developed a sparse classifier, called voomNSC. The authors also developed two other voom based non-sparse classifiers: voomDLDA and voomDQDA, where voom and diagonal discriminant analyses were combined. The authors showed that integrating voom transformation in classification improves the performance and gives better results.

Since RNA-seq data are high dimensional datasets where the number of genes is greater than the number of samples, powerful and efficient algorithms are required in order to extract significant biological information from fast-growing RNA-seq data. To this end, many classification algorithms including machine learning approaches are widely used to build predictive models to classify patients. In order to apply those classification algorithms, counts should be transformed into normally distributed data. Therefore, a simple transformation technique, log-transformation, is used. With the log-transformed RNA-seq data, one can implement many efficient classification algorithms that are available in the literature: popular machine learning algorithms such as support vector machines (SVMs), k-Nearest Neighbour (kNN), etc.; discriminant classifiers such as linear discriminant analysis (LDA), quadratic discriminant analysis (QDA), etc.; ensemble classifiers such as random forests, boosted trees, etc.; decision tree classifiers such as C5.0, CART, etc. and so on. For instance, Zararsiz et al. (2017b) applied many machine learning algorithms to RNA-seq datasets and conducted a comprehensive simulation study with RNA-seq data. The authors compared the results of these various algorithms and showed that CART was not appropriate for overdispersed data whereas other algorithms such as SVM, bagSVM, PLDA and random forests resulted in high performances. The authors also showed that bagSVM displayed the best performance among the others when data is overdispersed. Jabeen et al. (2018) also discussed various machine learning algorithms including deep learning algorithms for RNA-seq data and their applications on real datasets. The authors concluded that deep learning approaches are likely to be a better choice of high dimensional RNA-seq data. However, these approaches may lead to overfitting problems due to the need for sufficiently large datasets, which is still costly. Additional studies of deep learning approaches that have been implemented to RNA-seq data are given in (Jasim et al., 2022; Sevakula et al., 2019; Ting et al., 2019).

There are also other studies where researchers have developed R packages for RNA-seq data classification. For instance, Chiesa et al. (2018) developed the DaMiRseq package using R language environment. The method used for classification in the package first weights and then combines the outputs of random forest, Naïve Bayes, nearest neighbours, logistic regression, linear discriminant analysis and SVM classifiers to obtain high classification performance. The package also applies normalization and feature selection steps before classification. In 2019, Goksuluk et al. developed another R package called MLseq, comprehensive and easy-to-use interface for classifying gene-expression data. It allows researchers to perform both preprocessing and various classification tasks through a single platform.

A comparative study between widely used machine-learning based data classiðcation methods is given in **Table 3**.

Table 3. Comparative study between commonly used machine learning algorithms for RNA-seq data classification

Method	Pros	Cons	Applications
SVM	• Appropriate and efficient method for high dimensional RNA-seq data even when the number of genes is greater than the number of samples • Memory efficient • Results in high performance	• Not robust to outliers • Learning is slow	• Zararsız et al. (2017b) • (Arowolo et al., 2021) • (Das et al., 2020) • (Wu & Hicks, 2021) • (Tan et al., 2014)
bagSVM	• Applicable for highly dispersed data • Gives better performance compared to random forest and classical SVM	• Not suitable for moderately dispersed RNA-seq datasets	• Zararsız et al. (2017b)
CART	• Non-parametric method which does not require any probabilistic assumptions • Computationally fast	• Hard to interpret the results due to the usage of large trees • Low accuracy in classification	• Zararsız et al. (2017b)
LDA	• Extended versions of this method have been developed. diagonal linear discriminant analysis (DLDA), sparse linear discriminant analysis (SparseLDA), nearest shrunken centroids (NSC), etc.	• Cannot be directly applied to RNA-seq data due to the singularity of the within-class covariance matrix	• (Tan et al., 2014)
RF	• Robust to outliers • High performance using large trees • Estimates the importance of genes which play important role in RNA-seq data classification.	• Computationally slow • May cause overfitting if data includes noise.	• Zararsız et al. (2017b) • (J. Zhang et al., 2016)
kNN	• Simple and powerful method • Classes do not have to be linearly seperable • Results are easy to interpret • Can handle the missing values	• The number of classes has to be predefined. • Hard to decide an appropriate similarity distance which affects the classification performance • Computationally expensive	• (Koçhan et al., 2019)

FUTURE RESEARCH DIRECTIONS

In this chapter, the algorithms used to analyze of RNA-seq data are explained along with the subtitles of class comparison, class discovery and class prediction. For each subtitle, the definitions, advantages and disadvantages of the methods used in the literature are given in detail. Because of the high dispersion in RNA-seq data and its discrete structure, RNA-seq data analyses remain a difficult problem and numerous approaches have been proposed for different purposes. Despite the various approaches that have been reported up to now, there is still no "gold standard" strategy for RNA-seq data analyses, necessitating the use of alternative approaches. However, in the analysis of RNA-seq data, various statistical analyses for various purposes are also performed, which are not covered in this chapter. One of these analyses is survival analysis, also known as time to a specific event and used to estimate the lifespan of a specific population under study. There are advanced statistical analysis techniques such as penalized Cox regression and random survival forests and classical statistical approaches such as Kaplan-Meier charts, log-rank statistics, and Cox proportional hazard models designed for survival analysis. Following this study, researchers may find it useful to focus on survival analyses in RNA-seq data to demonstrate other methods used in RNA-seq analysis and address the drawbacks of the existing survival analysis approaches. Furthermore, a comprehensive literature on survival analyses of RNA-seq data might be created to guide individual medical studies.

CONCLUSION

In this section, the methods used in the literature for class comparison of RNA-seq data, class prediction and class discovery problems are covered. Whole-transcriptome sequencing is considered as an efficient way to measure transcriptome composition and dynamics even at single-cell resolution, and accumulating evidence showed that the power of RNA-seq in quantifying and annotating transcriptomes is striking. Hence, RNA-seq technologies have been widely applied in development of cancer and other diseases for monitoring transcriptome changes. Currently, modeling gene-expression counts by applying appropriate clustering and classification algorithms are expected to be a clue for early diagnosis and improvement of genetic diseases such as cancer, which often arise as a consequence of dysfunction in gene-expression and are hampered by the complexity of the cellular signaling network. Understanding and developing such clustering and classification models will be critical for diagnosing at a very early stage of cancer development before metastasis occurs. Hence, expanding such clustering approaches to single-cell transcriptomics and spatial transcriptomics allows researchers to monitor cancer progression and treatment as well as therapy response.

REFERENCES

Alberts, B., Johnson, A., & Lewis, J. (2002). *Molecular Biology of the Cell* (4th ed.). Garland Science.

Anders, S., & Huber, W. (2010). Differential expression analysis for sequence count data. *Genome Biology, 11*(10), R106. Advance online publication. doi:10.1186/gb-2010-11-10-r106 PMID:20979621

Andrews, S. (2017). *FastQC: a quality control tool for high throughput sequence data.* https://www.bioinformatics.babraham.ac.uk/projects/fastqc/

Auer, P. L., Srivastava, S., & Doerge, R. W. (2012). Differential expression—The next generation and beyond. *Briefings in Functional Genomics*, *11*(1), 57–62. doi:10.1093/bfgp/elr041 PMID:22210853

Bismeijer, T., van der Velden, B. H. M., Canisius, S., Lips, E. H., Loo, C. E., Viergever, M. A., Wesseling, J., Gilhuijs, K. G. A., & Wessels, L. F. A. (2020). Radiogenomic Analysis of Breast Cancer by Linking MRI Phenotypes with Tumor Gene-expression. *Radiology*, *296*(2), 277–287. doi:10.1148/radiol.2020191453 PMID:32452738

Bolger, A. M., Lohse, M., & Usadel, B. (2014). Trimmomatic: A flexible trimmer for Illumina sequence data. *Bioinformatics (Oxford, England)*, *30*(15), 2114–2120. doi:10.1093/bioinformatics/btu170 PMID:24695404

Bullard, J. H., Purdom, E., Hansen, K. D., & Dudoit, S. (2010). Evaluation of statistical methods for normalization and differential expression in mRNA-Seq experiments. *BMC Bioinformatics*, *11*(94), 94. Advance online publication. doi:10.1186/1471-2105-11-94 PMID:20167110

Cephe, A. (2019). *Novel Statistical Approaches in Clustering RNA-sequencing Data* [Master thesis]. Erciyes University. https://tez.yok.gov.tr/UlusalTezMerkezi/tezSorguSonucYeni.jsp

Chen, S., Huang, T., Zhou, Y., & ... . (2017). AfterQC: Automatic filtering, trimming, error removing and quality control for fastq data. *BMC Bioinformatics*, *18*(Suppl 3), 80. doi:10.118612859-017-1469-3

Chen, S., Zhou, Y., Chen, Y., & Gu, J. (2018). fastp: An ultra-fast all-in-one FASTQ preprocessor. *Bioinformatics (Oxford, England)*, *34*(17), i884–i890. doi:10.1093/bioinformatics/bty560 PMID:30423086

Cloonan, N., Forrest, A. R. R., Kolle, G., Gardiner, B. B. A., Faulkner, G. J., Brown, M. K., Taylor, D. F., Steptoe, A. L., Wani, S., Bethel, G., Robertson, A. J., Perkins, A. C., Bruce, S. J., Lee, C. C., Ranade, S. S., Peckham, H. E., Manning, J. M., McKernan, K. J., & Grimmond, S. M. (2008). Stem cell transcriptome profiling via massive-scale mRNA sequencing. *Nature Methods*, *5*(7), 613–619. Advance online publication. doi:10.1038/nmeth.1223 PMID:18516046

Costa-Silva, J., Domingues, D., & Lopes, F. M. (2017). RNA-Seq differential expression analysis: An extended review and a software tool. *PLoS One*, *12*(12), 1–18. doi:10.1371/journal.pone.0190152 PMID:29267363

Di, Y., Schafer, D. W., Cumbie, J. S., & Chang, J. H. (2011). The NBP negative binomial models for assessing differential gene-expression from RNA-seq. *Statistical Applications in Genetics and Molecular Biology*, *10*(1), 1–28. doi:10.2202/1544-6115.1637

Dong, K., Zhao, H., Tong, T., & Wan, X. (2016). NBLDA: Negative binomial linear discriminant analysis for RNA-Seq data. *BMC Bioinformatics*, *17*(1), 1–10. doi:10.118612859-016-1208-1 PMID:27623864

Dudoit, S., Fridlyand, J., & Speed, T. P. (2002). Comparison of discrimination methods for the classification of tumors using gene-expression data. *Journal of the American Statistical Association*, *97*(457), 77–87. Advance online publication. doi:10.1198/016214502753479248

Elo, L. L., Filén, S., Lahesmaa, R., & Aittokallio, T. (2008). Reproducibility-Optimized Test Statistic for Ranking Genes in Microarray Studies. *IEEE/ACM Transactions on Computational Biology and Bioinformatics*, *5*(3), 423–431. doi:10.1109/tcbb.2007.1078 PMID:18670045

Ewels, P., Magnusson, M., Lundin, S., & Käller, M. (2016). MultiQC: Summarize analysis results for multiple tools and samples in a single report. *Bioinformatics (Oxford, England)*, *32*(19), 3047–3048. doi:10.1093/bioinformatics/btw354 PMID:27312411

Feng, C., & ... . (2014). Log-transformation and its implications for data analysis. *Shanghai Jingshen Yixue*, *26*(2), 105–109. doi:10.3969/j.issn.1002-0829.2014.02.009 PMID:25092958

Goksuluk, D., Zararsiz, G., Korkmaz, S., Eldem, V., Zararsiz, G. E., Ozcetin, E., Ozturk, A., & Karaagaoglu, A. E. (2019). MLSeq: Machine learning interface for RNA-sequencing data. *Computer Methods and Programs in Biomedicine*, *175*, 223–231. Advance online publication. doi:10.1016/j.cmpb.2019.04.007 PMID:31104710

Golub, T. R., Slonim, D. K., Tamayo, P., Huard, C., Gaasenbeek, M., Mesirov, J. P., Coller, H., Loh, M. L., Downing, J. R., Caligiuri, M. A., Bloomfield, C. D., & Lander, E. S. (1999). Molecular classification of cancer: Class discovery and class prediction by gene-expression monitoring. *Science*, *286*(5439), 531–537. doi:10.1126cience.286.5439.531 PMID:10521349

Han, X., Wu, X., Chung, W. Y., Li, T., Nekrutenko, A., Altman, N. S., Chen, G., & Ma, H. (2009). Transcriptome of embryonic and neonatal mouse cortex by high-throughput RNA sequencing. *Proceedings of the National Academy of Sciences of the United States of America*, *106*(31), 12741–12746. Advance online publication. doi:10.1073/pnas.0902417106 PMID:19617558

Hardcastle, T. J., & Kelly, K. A. (2010). BaySeq: Empirical Bayesian methods for identifying differential expression in sequence count data. *BMC Bioinformatics*, *11*(1), 422. Advance online publication. doi:10.1186/1471-2105-11-422 PMID:20698981

Jabeen, A., Ahmad, N., & Raza, K. (2018). Machine Learning-Based State-of-the-Art Methods for the Classification of RNA-Seq Data. In *Classification in Bioapps* (Vol. 26). Springer. doi:10.1007/978-3-319-65981-7_6

Jaskowiak, P. A., Costa, I. G., & Campello, R. J. G. B. (2018). Clustering of RNA-Seq samples: Comparison study on cancer data. *Methods (San Diego, Calif.)*, *132*, 42–49. doi:10.1016/j.ymeth.2017.07.023 PMID:28778489

Koçhan, N., Tutuncu, G. Y., Smyth, G. K., Gandolfo, L. C., & Giner, G. (2019). qtQDA: Quantile transformed quadratic discriminant analysis for high-dimensional RNA-seq data. *PeerJ*, *7*, e8260. doi:10.7717/peerj.8260 PMID:31976167

Kochan, N., Yazgı Tütüncü, G., & Giner, G. (2021). A new local covariance matrix estimation for the classification of gene-expression profiles in high dimensional RNA-Seq data. *Expert Systems with Applications*, *167*, 114200. Advance online publication. doi:10.1016/j.eswa.2020.114200

Langmead, B., Hansen, K. D., & Leek, J. T. (2010). Cloud-scale RNA-sequencing differential expression analysis with Myrna. *Genome Biology*, *11*(8), R83. doi:10.1186/gb-2010-11-8-r83 PMID:20701754

Law, C. W., Chen, Y., Shi, W., & Smyth, G. K. (2014). voom: Precision weights unlock linear model analysis tools for RNA-seq read counts. *Genome Biology*, *15*(2), R29. doi:10.1186/gb-2014-15-2-r29 PMID:24485249

Leng, N., Dawson, J. A., Thomson, J. A., Ruotti, V., Rissman, A. I., Smits, B. M. G., Haag, J. D., Gould, M. N., Stewart, R. M., & Kendziorski, C. (2013). EBSeq: An empirical Bayes hierarchical model for inference in RNA-seq experiments. *Bioinformatics (Oxford, England)*, *29*(8), 1035–1043. Advance online publication. doi:10.1093/bioinformatics/btt087 PMID:23428641

Li, J., & Tibshirani, R. (2013). Finding consistent patterns: A nonparametric approach for identifying differential expression in RNA-Seq data. *Statistical Methods in Medical Research*, *22*(5), 519–536. Advance online publication. doi:10.1177/0962280211428386 PMID:22127579

Li, J., Witten, D. M., Johnstone, I. M., & Tibshirani, R. (2012). Normalization, testing, and false discovery rate estimation for RNA-sequencing data. *Biostatistics (Oxford, England)*, *13*(3), 523–538. doi:10.1093/biostatistics/kxr031 PMID:22003245

Li, P., Ponnala, L., Gandotra, N., Wang, L., Si, Y., Tausta, S. L., Kebrom, T. H., Provart, N., Patel, R., Myers, C. R., Reidel, E. J., Turgeon, R., Liu, P., Sun, Q., Nelson, T., & Brutnell, T. P. (2010). The developmental dynamics of the maize leaf transcriptome. *Nature Genetics*, *42*(12), 1060–1067. doi:10.1038/ng.703 PMID:21037569

Li, Q., Noel-MacDonnell, J. R., Koestler, D. C., Goode, E. L., & Fridley, B. L. (2018). Subject level clustering using a negative binomial model for small transcriptomic studies. *BMC Bioinformatics*, *19*(1), 474. doi:10.118612859-018-2556-9 PMID:30541426

Li, X., Wang, K., Lyu, Y., Pan, H., Zhang, J., Stambolian, D., Susztak, K., Reilly, M. P., Hu, G., & Li, M. (2020). Deep learning enables accurate clustering with batch effect removal in single-cell RNA-seq analysis. *Nature Communications*, *11*(2338), 2338. Advance online publication. doi:10.103841467-020-15851-3 PMID:32393754

Lim, D. K., Rashid, N. U., & Ibrahim, J. G. (2021). Model-based feature selection and clustering of rna-seq data for unsupervised subtype discovery. *The Annals of Applied Statistics*, *15*(1). Advance online publication. doi:10.1214/20-AOAS1407 PMID:34457104

Liu, R., Holik, A. Z., Su, S., Jansz, N., Chen, K., Leong, H. S., Blewitt, M. E., Asselin-Labat, M.-L., Smyth, G. K., & Ritchie, M. E. (2015). Why weight? modelling sample and observational level variability improves power in rna-seq analyses. *Nucleic Acids Research*, *43*(5), e97. doi:10.1093/nar/gkv412 PMID:25925576

Love, M. I., Huber, W., & Anders, S. (2014). Moderated estimation of fold change and dispersion for RNA-seq data with DESeq2. *Genome Biology*, *15*(12), 550. Advance online publication. doi:10.118613059-014-0550-8 PMID:25516281

Marioni, J. C., Mason, C. E., Mane, S. M., Stephens, M., & Gilad, Y. (2008). RNA-seq: An assessment of technical reproducibility and comparison with gene-expression arrays. *Genome Research*, *18*(9), 1509–1517. Advance online publication. doi:10.1101/gr.079558.108 PMID:18550803

Martin, M. (2011). Cutadapt removes adapter sequences from high-throughput sequencing reads. *EMBnet.Journal*, *17*(1), 10–12. doi:10.14806/ej.17.1.200

McCarthy, D. J., Chen, Y., & Smyth, G. K. (2012). Differential expression analysis of multifactor RNA-Seq experiments with respect to biological variation. *Nucleic Acids Research*, *40*(10), 4288–4297. doi:10.1093/nar/gks042 PMID:22287627

McLachlan, G. J. (1997). On the EM algorithm for overdispersed count data. *Statistical Methods in Medical Research, 6*(1), 76–98. doi:10.1177/096228029700600106 PMID:9185291

Mo, Q., Wang, S., Seshan, V. E., Olshen, A. B., Schultz, N., Sander, C., Powers, R. S., Ladanyi, M., & Shen, R. (2013). Pattern discovery and cancer gene identification in integrated cancer genomic data. *Proceedings of the National Academy of Sciences of the United States of America, 110*(11), 4245–4250. doi:10.1073/pnas.1208949110 PMID:23431203

Mortazavi, A., Williams, B. A., McCue, K., Schaeffer, L., & Wold, B. (2008). Mapping and quantifying mammalian transcriptomes by RNA-Seq. *Nature Methods, 5*(7), 621–628. doi:10.1038/nmeth.1226 PMID:18516045

Nagalakshmi, U., Wang, Z., Waern, K., Shou, C., Raha, D., Gerstein, M., & Snyder, M. (2008). The transcriptional landscape of the yeast genome defined by RNA sequencing. *Science, 320*(5881), 1344–1349. Advance online publication. doi:10.1126cience.1158441 PMID:18451266

Parikh, A., Miranda, E. R., Katoh-Kurasawa, M., Fuller, D., Rot, G., Zagar, L., Curk, T., Sucgang, R., Chen, R., Zupan, B., Loomis, W. F., Kuspa, A., & Shaulsky, G. (2010). Conserved developmental transcriptomes in evolutionarily divergent species. *Genome Biology, 11*(3), R35. Advance online publication. doi:10.1186/gb-2010-11-3-r35 PMID:20236529

Perkins, T. T., Kingsley, R. A., Fookes, M. C., Gardner, P. P., James, K. D., Yu, L., Assefa, S. A., He, M., Croucher, N. J., Pickard, D. J., Maskell, D. J., Parkhill, J., Choudhary, J., Thomson, N. R., & Dougan, G. (2009). A strand-specific RNA-seq analysis of the transcriptome of the typhoid bacillus Salmonella typhi. *PLOS Genetics, 5*(7), e1000569. Advance online publication. doi:10.1371/journal.pgen.1000569 PMID:19609351

Rapaport, F., Khanin, R., Liang, Y., Pirun, M., Krek, A., Zumbo, P., Mason, C., Socci, N., & Betel, D. (2013). Comprehensive evaluation of differential gene-expression analysis methods for rna-seq data. *Genome Biology, 14*(3158), R95. doi:10.1186/gb-2013-14-9-r95 PMID:24020486

Ritchie, M. E., Phipson, B., Wu, D., Hu, Y., Law, C. W., Shi, W., & Smyth, G. K. (2015). limma powers differential expression analyses for RNA-sequencing and microarray studies. *Nucleic Acids Research, 43*(7), e47. doi:10.1093/nar/gkv007 PMID:25605792

Robinson, M. D., McCarthy, D. J., & Smyth, G. K. (2010). edgeR: A Bioconductor package for differential expression analysis of digital gene-expression data. *Bioinformatics (Oxford, England), 26*(1), 139–140. doi:10.1093/bioinformatics/btp616 PMID:19910308

Robinson, M. D., & Oshlack, A. (2010). A scaling normalization method for differential expression analysis of RNA-seq data. *Genome Biology, 11*(3), R25. doi:10.1186/gb-2010-11-3-r25 PMID:20196867

Robinson, M. D., & Smyth, G. K. (2008). Small-sample estimation of negative binomial dispersion, with applications to SAGE data. *Biostatistics (Oxford, England), 9*(2), 321–332. Advance online publication. doi:10.1093/biostatistics/kxm030 PMID:17728317

Severin, A. J., Woody, J. L., Bolon, Y.-T., Joseph, B., Diers, B. W., Farmer, A. D., Muehlbauer, G. J., Nelson, R. T., Grant, D., Specht, J. E., Graham, M. A., Cannon, S. B., May, G. D., Vance, C. P., & Shoemaker, R. C. (2010). RNA-Seq Atlas of Glycine max: A guide to the soybean transcriptome. *BMC Plant Biology, 10*(1), 160. doi:10.1186/1471-2229-10-160 PMID:20687943

Seyednasrollah, F., Laiho, A., & Elo, L. L. (2013). Comparison of software packages for detecting differential expression in RNA-seq studies. *Briefings in Bioinformatics*, *16*(1), 59–70. doi:10.1093/bib/bbt086 PMID:24300110

Seyednasrollah, F., Rantanen, K., Jaakkola, P., & Elo, L. L. (2016). ROTS: Reproducible RNA-seq biomarker detector—Prognostic markers for clear cell renal cell cancer. *Nucleic Acids Research*, *44*(1), e1. doi:10.1093/nar/gkv806 PMID:26264667

Si, Y., & Liu, P. (2013). An Optimal Test with Maximum Average Power While Controlling FDR with Application to RNA-Seq Data. *Biometrics*, *69*(3), 594–605. Advance online publication. doi:10.1111/biom.12036 PMID:23889143

Si, Y., Liu, P., Li, P., & Brutnell, T. P. (2014). Model-based clustering for RNA-seq data. *Bioinformatics (Oxford, England)*, *30*(2), 197–205. doi:10.1093/bioinformatics/btt632 PMID:24191069

Simon, R., Radmacher, M. D., Dobbin, K., & McShane, L. M. (2003). Pitfalls in the use of DNA microarray data for diagnostic and prognostic classification. *Journal of the National Cancer Institute*, *95*(1), 14–18. doi:10.1093/jnci/95.1.14 PMID:12509396

Sîrbu, A., Kerr, G., Crane, M., & Ruskin, H. J. (2012). RNA-Seq vs Dual- and Single-Channel Microarray Data: Sensitivity Analysis for Differential Expression and Clustering. *PLoS One*, *7*(12), e50986. doi:10.1371/journal.pone.0050986 PMID:23251411

Soneson, C., & Delorenzi, M. (2013). A comparison of methods for differential expression analysis of RNA-seq data. *BMC Bioinformatics*, *14*(91), 91. Advance online publication. doi:10.1186/1471-2105-14-91 PMID:23497356

Sun, J., & Zhao, H. (2015). The application of sparse estimation of covariance matrix to quadratic discriminant analysis. *BMC Bioinformatics*, *16*(1), 48. Advance online publication. doi:10.118612859-014-0443-6 PMID:25886892

Tamayo, P., Slonim, D., Mesirov, J., Zhu, Q., Kitareewan, S., Dmitrovsky, E., Lander, E. S., & Golub, T. R. (1999). Interpreting patterns of gene-expression with self-organizing maps: Methods and application to hematopoietic differentiation. *Proceedings of the National Academy of Sciences of the United States of America*, *96*(6), 2907–2912. doi:10.1073/pnas.96.6.2907 PMID:10077610

Tan, K. M., Petersen, A., & Witten, D. (2014). Statistical Analysis of Next Generation Sequencing Data. In S. Datta & D. Nettleton (Eds.), *Statistical Analysis of Next Generation Sequencing Data*. Springer International Publishing., doi:10.1007/978-3-319-07212-8

Tarazona, S., Furió-Tarí, P., Turrà, D., Di Pietro, A., Nueda, M. J., Ferrer, A., & Conesa, A. (2015). Data quality aware analysis of differential expression in RNA-seq with NOISeq R/Bioc package. *Nucleic Acids Research*, *43*(21), gkv711. Advance online publication. doi:10.1093/nar/gkv711 PMID:26184878

Tarazona, S., Garcia-Alcalde, F., Dopazo, J., Ferrer, A., & Conesa, A. (2011). Differential expression in RNA-seq: A matter of depth. *Genome Research*, *21*(12), 2213–2223. doi:10.1101/gr.124321.111 PMID:21903743

Tian, T., Wan, J., Song, Q., & Wei, Z. (2019). Clustering single-cell RNA-seq data with a model-based deep learning approach. *Nature Machine Intelligence*, *1*(4), 191–198. doi:10.103842256-019-0037-0

Trapnell, C., Hendrickson, D. G., Sauvageau, M., Goff, L., Rinn, J. L., & Pachter, L. (2013). Differential analysis of gene regulation at transcript resolution with RNA-seq. *Nature Biotechnology*, *31*(1), 46–53. Advance online publication. doi:10.1038/nbt.2450 PMID:23222703

Trapnell, C., Roberts, A., Goff, L., Pertea, G., Kim, D., Kelley, D. R., Pimentel, H., Salzberg, S. L., Rinn, J. L., & Pachter, L. (2012). Differential gene and transcript expression analysis of RNA-seq experiments with TopHat and Cufflinks. *Nature Protocols*, *7*(3), 562–578. doi:10.1038/nprot.2012.016 PMID:22383036

Trapnell, C., Williams, B. A., Pertea, G., Mortazavi, A., Kwan, G., van Baren, M. J., Salzberg, S. L., Wold, B. J., & Pachter, L. (2010). Transcript assembly and quantification by RNA-Seq reveals unannotated transcripts and isofrom switching during cell differentiation. *Nature Biotechnology*, *28*(5), 511–515. doi:10.1038/nbt.1621 PMID:20436464

Van de Wiel, M. A., Leday, G. G., Pardo, L., Rue, H., Van de Vaart, A. W., & Van Wieringen, W. N. (2013). Bayesian analysis of RNA sequencing data by estimating multiple shrinkage priors. *Biostatistics (Oxford, England)*, *14*(1), 113–128. doi:10.1093/biostatistics/kxs031 PMID:22988280

Vestal, B. E., Moore, C. M., Wynn, E., Saba, L., Fingerlin, T., & Kechris, K. (2020). MCMSeq: Bayesian hierarchical modeling of clustered and repeated measures RNA sequencing experiments. *BMC Bioinformatics*, *21*(1), 375. doi:10.118612859-020-03715-y PMID:32859148

Wang, L., Feng, Z., Wang, X., Wang, X., & Zhang, X. (2009). DEGseq: An R package for identifying differentially expressed genes from RNA-seq data. *Bioinformatics (Oxford, England)*, *26*(1), 136–138. Advance online publication. doi:10.1093/bioinformatics/btp612 PMID:19855105

Wang, L., Feng, Z., Wang, X., Wang, X., & Zhang, X. (2010). DEGseq: An R package for identifying differentially expressed genes from RNA-seq data. *Bioinformatics (Oxford, England)*, *26*(1), 136–138. doi:10.1093/bioinformatics/btp612 PMID:19855105

Wang, L., Luo, X., Cheng, C., Amos, C. I., Cai, G., & Xiao, F. (2020). A gene-expression-based immune signature for lung adenocarcinoma prognosis. *Cancer Immunology, Immunotherapy*, *69*(9), 1881–1890. Advance online publication. doi:10.100700262-020-02595-8 PMID:32372138

Weigelt, B., Baehner, F. L., & Reis-Filho, J. S. (2010). The contribution of gene-expression profiling to breast cancer classification, prognostication and prediction: A retrospective of the last decade. *The Journal of Pathology*, *220*(2), 263–280. doi:10.1002/path.2648 PMID:19927298

Witten, D. M. (2011). Classification and clustering of sequencing data using a Poisson model. *The Annals of Applied Statistics*, *5*(4), 2493–2518. doi:10.1214/11-AOAS493

Zararsiz, G., Goksuluk, D., Klaus, B., Korkmaz, S., Eldem, V., Karabulut, E., & Ozturk, A. (2017a). voomDDA: Discovery of diagnostic biomarkers and classification of RNA-seq data. *PeerJ*, *5*, e3890. doi:10.7717/peerj.3890 PMID:29018623

Zararsız, G., Goksuluk, D., Korkmaz, S., Eldem, V., Zararsiz, G. E., Duru, I. P., & Ozturk, A. (2017b). A comprehensive simulation study on classification of RNA-Seq data. *PLoS One*, *12*(8), e0182507. doi:10.1371/journal.pone.0182507 PMID:28832679

Zhang, Q. (2017). Classification of RNA-Seq data via Gaussian copulas. *Stat*, *6*(1), 171–183. Advance online publication. doi:10.1002ta4.144

Zhang, Z., Yu, D., Seo, M., Hersh, C. P., Weiss, S. T., & Qiu, W. (2019). Novel Data Transformations for RNA-seq Differential Expression Analysis. *Scientific Reports*, 9(1), 4820. Advance online publication. doi:10.103841598-019-41315-w PMID:30886278

Zheng, H. Q., Chiang-Hsieh, Y. F., Chien, C. H., Hsu, B. K. J., Liu, T. L., Chen, C. N. N., & Chang, W. C. (2014). AlgaePath: Comprehensive analysis of metabolic pathways using transcript abundance data from next-generation sequencing in green algae. *BMC Genomics*, 15(1), 196. Advance online publication. doi:10.1186/1471-2164-15-196 PMID:24628857

Zhou, X., Lindsay, H., & Robinson, M. D. (2014). Robustly detecting differential expression in RNA sequencing data using observation weights. *Nucleic Acids Research*, 42(11), e91. doi:10.1093/nar/gku310 PMID:24753412

Zhou, Y., Wan, X., Zhang, B., & Tong, T. (2018). Classifying next-generation sequencing data using a zero-inflated Poisson model. *Bioinformatics (Oxford, England)*, 34(8), 1329–1335. Advance online publication. doi:10.1093/bioinformatics/btx768 PMID:29186294

Zhou, Y. H., Xia, K., & Wright, F. A. (2011). A powerful and flexible approach to the analysis of RNA sequence count data. *Bioinformatics (Oxford, England)*, 27(19), 2672–2688. doi:10.1093/bioinformatics/btr449 PMID:21810900

Zhu, J., Yuan, Z., Shu, L., Liao, W., Zhao, M., & Zhou, Y. (2021). Selecting Classification Methods for Small Samples of Next-Generation Sequencing Data. *Frontiers in Genetics*, 12, 642227. Advance online publication. doi:10.3389/fgene.2021.642227 PMID:33747051

Zwiener, I., Frisch, B., & Binder, H. (2014). Transforming RNA-Seq Data to Improve the Performance of Prognostic Gene Signatures. *PLoS One*, 9(1), e85150. doi:10.1371/journal.pone.0085150 PMID:24416353

ADDITIONAL READING

Arowolo, M. O., Adebiyi, M. O., Aremu, C., & Adebiyi, A. A. (2021). A survey of dimension reduction and classification methods for RNA-seq data on malaria vector. *Journal of Big Data*, 8(1), 50. doi:10.118640537-021-00441-x

Cui, Y., Zhang, S., Liang, Y., Wang, X., Ferraro, T. N., & Chen, Y. (2021). Consensus clustering of single-cell RNA-seq data by enhancing network affinity. *Briefings in Bioinformatics*, 22(6). doi:10.1093/bib/bbab236

David, K., Linda, V., & Patrik, R. (2021). Comparison of methods for feature selection in clustering of high-dimensional RNA-sequencing data to identify cancer subtypes. *Frontiers in Genetics*, 12, 1664–8021. doi:10.3389/fgene.2021.632620 PMID:33719342

Jamail, I., & Moussa, A. (2020). Current State-of-the-Art of Clustering Methods for Gene-expression Data with RNA-Seq. In C. M. Travieso-Gonzalez (Ed.), *Applications of Pattern Recognition*. IntechOpen. doi:10.5772/intechopen.94069

Pramana, S., Hardiyanta, I. K. Y., Hidayat, F. Y., & Mariyah, S. (2022). A comparative assessment on gene-expression classification methods of RNA-seq data generated using next-generation sequencing (NGS). *Narra J*, 2(1), e60. doi:10.52225/narra.v2i1.60

Qi, R., Ma, A., Ma, Q., & Zou, Q. (2020). Clustering and classification methods for single-cell RNA-sequencing data. *Briefings in Bioinformatics*, *21*(4), 1196–1208. doi:10.1093/bib/bbz062 PMID:31271412

Wang, H., Sham, P., Tong, T., & Pang, H. (2020). Patway-based single-cell RNA-seq classification, clustering, and construction of gene-gene interactions networks using random forests. *IEEE Journal of Biomedical and Health Informatics*, *24*(6), 1814–1822. doi:10.1109/JBHI.2019.2944865 PMID:31581101

Zamanighomi, M., Lin, Z., Daley, T., Chen, X., Duren, Z., Schep, A., Greenleaf, W. J., & Wong, W. H. (2018). Unsupervised clustering and epigenetic classification of single cells. *Nature Communications*, *9*(2410), 2410. Advance online publication. doi:10.103841467-018-04629-3 PMID:29925875

KEY TERMS AND DEFINITIONS

DESeq: DESeq is an R/BIOCONDUCTOR package and used for differential analysis of count-based expression data based on the negative binomial distribution.

edgeR: Analysis of replicated count-based expression data using an empirical Bayes procedure. It is an R/BIOCONDUCTOR package and used for differential analysis of count-based expression data based of Poisson distribution.

Hierarchical Clustering using Poisson Dissimilarity (POI): Hierarchical Clustering using Poisson Dissimilarity is a clustering alghorithm, which uses a Poisson-based dissimilarity and then perform hierarchical clustering to high-dimensional data.

Limma: Limma, which is an R/BIOCONDUCTOR package, encompasses voom function. This function transforms RNA-seq data for differential analysis.

Negative Binomial Linear Discriminant Analysis (NBLDA): Negative Binomial Linear Discriminant Analysis is used for classification analysis of RNA-seq data. It assumes that RNA-seq data follows negative binomial distribution.

Negative Binomial Model-Based (NBMB): Negative Binomial Model-Based is an unsupervised clustering algorithm used to cluster overdispersed RNA-seq data.

Poisson Linear Discriminant Analysis (PLDA): Poisson Linear Discriminant Analysis is used for classification analysis of RNA-seq data. It assumes that RNA-seq data follows Poisson distribution.

Section 29
Industry 4.0

AI Is Transforming Insurance With Five Emerging Business Models

Alex Zarifis

🆔 https://orcid.org/0000-0003-3103-4601

University of Nicosia, Cyprus & University of Cambridge, UK

Xusen Cheng

Renmin University of China, China

INTRODUCTION

Artificial Intelligence is transforming the way we work and our personal lives (Faraj et al., 2018). More generally, software is taking over more and more processes in organizations, often changing their business model (Alt et al., 2020). This digital transformation is also happening in the insurance field. The impact of AI in insurance is in some ways similar to other sectors of the economy, but in other ways, different. Insurance has some particularities, and events such as AI transformation, recession, and pandemics affect it differently. It is therefore important to understand the adoption of AI and how this will influence insurance business models. An insurance business model must be effective and durable because insurance faces several challenges, such as more pandemics, constantly changing regulations, climate changes, unpredictable weather, and fierce competition (Kannan & Bernoff, 2019). There are many opportunities offered by technology such as AI, big data, cloud computing, IoT, blockchain, and 5G. Machine Learning (ML) and Deep Learning (DL) offer learning that can be supervised or unsupervised, making AI more capable and more accessible to organizations (Kraus et al., 2020). All these separate technologies are converging, creating synergies, and amplifying their impact (Dietzmann et al., 2020). Insurers have a role in shaping AI and its impact. Additionally, consumers and the government also have their roles. The government needs to develop and adapt laws and regulations. Insurers face sociotechnical challenges with AI from within the organization. These can include the data, the people, and the processes. The data is often not large enough in volume or quality to effectively train AI or to use AI to perform evaluations and underwriting. Because of the increasing role of technology, there is also an increasing role for technology providers. Insurers' personnel need new skills and training to implement AI.

While we are looking at the whole insurance sector, it is important to recognize that there is a distinction between insurers that attempt to cover all the insurance services for the consumer and those that focus primarily on one type of insurance. In the data-driven economy, data, its sources, and how these are utilized, is another way to explain a business model. The impact of AI and other technologies such as IoT and blockchain are so important that the sociotechnical capability to utilize them is more significant today than in the past. Currently, most implementations of AI replace specific processes that had specific challenges in the past. To understand the adoption of AI, we must understand each organiza-

DOI: 10.4018/978-1-7998-9220-5.ch124

tion's present state and their journey as an insurer in utilizing technology in general, and AI specifically. Identifying the transformative effect of technology on business models is a popular way to contribute to our understanding of new business models (Veit et al., 2014). Therefore, the research question is: "What are the emerging business models in insurance caused by AI and data technologies?"

This research found empirical support for five emerging AI-driven business models in insurance: (1) Focus and disaggregation, (2) absorb AI into the existing model, (3) incumbent expanding beyond model, (4) dedicated insurance disruptor and, (5) tech company disruptor. The following section is the literature review followed by the methodology section that explains how the case studies were identified and explored. Then the analysis of four exemplar cases is shown, a discussion on the validity and value of the business models is identified, and finally the conclusion is presented.

LITERATURE REVIEW

The literature review covers three areas. Firstly, artificial intelligence and related technologies, secondly, the current literature on business models, and thirdly, current trends in insurance.

Artificial Intelligence-Driven Automation

AI is spearheading several interrelated technologies, including big data, IoT, blockchain, and 5G (Tarafdar et al., 2019). Additional new technologies, such as quantum computing, are not far behind and could join the aforementioned technologies, further speeding up the disruption (Corcoles et al., 2019). AI includes machine learning and deep learning, offering the ability for a system to learn in a supervised or unsupervised way. Virtual assistants powered by AI, often referred to as chatbots, interact with customers, covering more and more processes as their abilities grow (Zarifis et al., 2021). Big data is enabling a constantly increasing collection of data from people and the environment, and making it more manageable to gain insight and utilize this data (Mikalef et al., 2020). This data is collected directly by insurers, but also purchased from other private or public organizations. IoT is particularly important for insurance, because it enables real time monitoring of information related to risk and automatic payouts without the customer even making a claim. Blockchain and distributed ledger technologies are particularly useful to support decentralized storing and the sharing of data in a transparent and secure way. As insurers are increasingly relying on an ecosystem around them, blockchain can support such collaboration. The step-change in bandwidth that 5G provides supports the other new technologies, but also offers some unique opportunities, such as richer, more immersive, interactions with their consumers (Park et al., 2021).

Business Models

Business Model Theory

There are different perspectives on business models, including a more business or more technology focused perspective (Osterwalder et al., 2005). For insurance, it is increasingly important to take a technology centric perspective. Exploring a business model requires a broad perspective to understand all of the processes of an organization and then to focus on the most important ones. For insurance, it needs to be clear where the organization fits into the supply chain, how they add value, and where they have a competitive advantage over competitors. In this sector, the context is critical. For example, insurance is heavily influence by each country's laws and regulations. In addition to the context, recent developments such as the rise of platforms and comparison cites are changing the way of working (Hukal et al., 2020).

Insurance Business Models

There are several insurance services across commercial insurance (B2B) and consumer insurance (B2C). There are also several organizations involved in a supply chain delivering each of these services. The most prominent are comparison websites, insurers, and reinsurers. Within these typical processes, each insurer can fulfil just one, or several of them. The choice of processes within the value chain does not happen once at the organization's inception, but on an on-going basis as the environment evolves. Factors influencing the evolution include but are not limited to the competition, consumer, economy, weather, regulation, and technology (Zarifis & Cheng, 2021).

Theoretic Foundation

The initial stages of this research identified the importance of focusing on the technology to understand the new business models, and which technologies are the most influential at disrupting the previous ways of working.

Based on related research, the four insurance business models for AI-driven automation are:

1. In the third business model: The focus is on strategy and disaggregation. In this model the insurer implements a smaller part of the value chain, has a larger ecosystem, and may join a platform.
2. In the second business model: The insurer utilizes AI across their value chain, but does not change their business model to accommodate AI led automation.
3. In the third business model: The insurer expands further than the insurance value chain, seeking more data and becoming the platform.
4. In the fourth business model: A tech company expands into the insurance value chain offering their own services (Zarifis et al., 2019).

The business models illustrate the increasing role AI and data will have in the future. They have been proven to be valid thus far. This model is used as the foundation to further evaluate the issues.

METHODOLOGY

The methodology applied evaluated four case studies from insurance and built theory from them (Eisenhardt, 1989). The literature on insurance business models gave us a theoretic foundation, but further exploration was required. Four organizations from the insurance supply chain that are being influenced by AI-driven automation were selected. The cases were chosen after initially evaluating how 15 insurers fit into the existing model with four categories (Zarifis et al., 2019). The first stage was desk-based research. As these are large public companies, so there is extensive information available about their operations, both from themselves and other reputable sources. The second stage included three interviews from each company. The interviewees were involved in making the decisions on how to adopt AI. One interviewee from each company had a technical background and was involved in implementing the new technologies. Four constructs were used to evaluate the cases. All of the interviews were conducted in English.

Figure 1. Research method

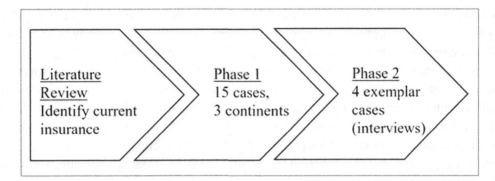

CASE STUDY ANALYSIS

The four case studies were chosen because they represent the four categories identified in the literature, and the two subsections identified in the preliminary analysis of 15 cases. The first case chosen covers 'focus and disaggregation,' and 'absorb AI into existing model.' The second case is 'an incumbent expanding beyond model,' the third is 'a dedicated insurance disruptor' (4a), and the fourth is a 'tech company disruptor' (4b).

Case Study 1: Focus and Disaggregation / Absorb AI Into Existing Model

Position: Large incumbent, traditional insurance company

Insurance provided: Car, home, life, health, travel, business, and others

Location: UK

Description of the AI Application

Approach to Applying AI

This insurer is focused and disaggregated in some services it offers, while it keeps its business model the same in other services it offers. It has several partnerships with established companies in various sectors such as electric cars and start-ups specialised in technology, online life insurance, and other sectors such as property. This enables the insurer to create a portfolio of technologies, including AI.

It has developed its in-house capability with technology. However, it recently shifted its focus from young start-ups to mature technologies that can have an immediate impact. This case is not interesting because of an innovative use of AI, but it is interesting because it is an effective way to utilize recent advances in AI across several parts of their business. They are more focused on finding ways to utilize technology than to develop it. Instead of an insurance company turning into a tech company to fully utilize technology, they are sticking to what they do best and creating intelligent partnerships.

Specific AI Technologies

Several customer-facing processes are completed by self-service and AI. A virtual assistant can also interact with customers. It supports the customer in several ways, such as obtaining an insurance quote, choosing premiums and deductibles, filing a claim, and setting up payments.

A virtual assistant is used by employees for easier access to relevant information. It can answer general questions about insurance and specific questions on claims and deductibles. As this virtual assistant can be trained with machine learning, it is capable of offering new insurance products quickly, without the delay that it would take to retrain human personnel. The virtual assistant can be trained to offer a completely new product line that was not previously offered by the company.

Underwriting: AI supports an underwriting tool that uses machine learning to evaluate all of the cases for quality assurance and can identify those that need to be checked by a human.

AI is used for several risk assessment evaluations. AI can go through reports in text, such as engineering reports and risk evaluations. To ensure regulatory compliance, AI analyses contracts.

Claims processing is moving towards a self-service process supported by AI. The consumer can monitor their application status online. AI analyses trends in claims and predicts the rate of claims in the future.

Fraud detection and reduction: AI finds patterns in data, helps detect cases that are less typical, and cannot be identified by a rules-based system. AI evaluates all of the claims for fraud and identifies the most suspicious ones for evaluation by human personnel. AI is better at learning and adapting to new threats than rules-based software.

The Underlying Technology

The implementations of AI are not unique and can be found in other leading insurers. Given the level of maturity of AI in general and the capability to utilize AI of this organization specifically, AI can currently be used in several specific processes. As the capabilities of AI improve and the ability of this specific insurer to utilize AI improves, the insular iterations of AI can be connected for a more comprehensive solution.

- **AI and Data:** The technology utilizes AI including deep predictive models and cognitive learning. A strong understanding of existing data and how to utilize it with AI is necessary. AI is working together with automation to provide seamless 'intelligent automation.' Mobile apps and an online portal provide the user with insurance customised in terms of its limits, coverage, deductibles, and excesses.
- **Voice Assistant:** This insurer's chatbot benefits from the technology provider's breadth of expertise in natural language processing. The virtual assistant's AI applies machine learning that uses the typical training data but also information from social media. Furthermore, every real interaction is utilized to further train the AI.
- **Audit:** Machine learning is ideal for a preliminary audit of underwriting for several reasons. Machine learning is very effective in analysing large volumes of data and finding patterns. In this process there are large volumes of structured data, which is ideal for machine learning.

Challenges and Regulatory Implications

This implementation of AI is not the most ambitious, so the challenges and regulatory implications are limited. The final decision is usually made by a human being. Most solutions are 'off the shelf' proven solutions with some customization so the challenges are reduced. Using AI to support current staff in their current roles will encourage them to adopt it and reduce their resistance.

Its partners are also competitors, so a network of frenemies is developed. Nevertheless, by developing in-house expertise on AI and contributing to the community of AI and new technologies in insurance strengthens its position to create partnerships with the right partners at the right time.

It is active in some highly regulated markets where the process needs to be transparent, and in other less regulated markets where the process does not need to be so transparent. This reduces the benefits of AI and increases the challenges to implementing it. For example, the regulation in some countries allows for pricing to be flexible and dynamic while in other countries this is not allowed. The unpredictability and limited transparency AI can have may pose challenges when it comes to defending the validity of the fraud claims, for example. Therefore, it is important to engage on the ethical and privacy challenges AI brings and how the algorithms can be transparent.

The Business Model

This insurer is now focused on adding value as an insurer and leading in technology and AI through partnerships, not on its own. This insurer tries to get the best of both worlds by keeping its model, to some degree, but also being part of new developments. Keeping the original model has merit because there is expertise in underwriting that is valuable. This expertise can be in highly specialised underwriting services that have not been disrupted and may not be disrupted for some time. Therefore, only the parts of the organization that should be simplified are made more focused with AI.

AI influences all the aspects of the business including the nature of the products and services, the prices, and the exposure to risk the organization is willing to take. This includes business customers and individuals.

The strategic logic is to avoid using resources on technology, as that is not where the core strengths of the company are. If one of the several partnerships fails it can be mitigated by the success of other partnerships. It is important to create an ecosystem that is stronger than what could be achieved singularly. It is challenging for most organizations in insurance to keep up with the rate of change.

Timing is important when implementing the new wave of technologies, including AI. Having the capabilities internally, and selecting mature proven technologies is necessary. The current cases of AI appear to suggest an incremental evolution of the model.

This insurer collaborates closely with the technology partners it co-develops solutions with. These solutions may be used by other insurers, but as a preferred partner, they will be one of the first applying each new AI solution and will, therefore, gain an advantage. The insurer uses the 'best of breed' solutions 'off the shelf' with minimal customization. The goal is to utilize AI to improve current processes as well, or better, than competitors. As AI is deployed more extensively, in proven ways, the insurer gains an advantage over its competitors.

Case Study 2: Incumbent Expanding Beyond Model

Position: Health insurance and healthcare provider

Insurance provided: Primarily health but also travel and expatriate

Location: UK

Description of the AI Application

Approach to Applying AI

This incumbent expanding beyond their model utilizes technology in new and innovative ways. For example, they provide online health apps and related remote healthcare technology. The app. allows virtual consultations with doctors, and the prescriptions are provided within the app. The insurer provides their services through this app. Their virtual assistant that uses AI is part of their mobile app. There is also a virtual assistant for purchasing health insurance. Consumers can interact with the virtual assistant either by voice or text. The voice assistant can engage with the customer and find solutions for various aspects of the contract, such as premiums and the nature of the coverage.

Specific AI Technologies

AI-driven automation is used in several ways including illness and disability claim prediction, fraud detection, natural language processing during customer service, underwriting; an AI underwriting tool that was trained with machine learning, supports the underwriting of life insurance and offers health advice.

The Underlying Technology

Their app. has an AI-powered clinical triage service. It uses AI to replicate the knowledge and the process a doctor goes through. A virtual doctor can have a conversation with a patient and give advice. The AI can interpret the way patients express their symptoms and identify the problem. The AI can also harness the patient's previous history and any patterns of health problems. Machine learning is used to utilize large databases of health information. The capabilities of machine learning used here are advanced and few companies have currently implemented such sophisticated solutions. Their structured health database, a form of 'knowledge graph,' is another advantage they have in applying AI.

Virtual assistants using natural language processing are increasingly used. Machine learning utilizes the vast volumes of information on their customers' health and how they interact with their services and processes. This information includes text, images, such as scans, but also audio from the call centres. The audio from the call centres helps train the virtual assistant both in the substance of the interaction with the customer and also the style.

Challenges and Regulatory Implications

The health sector is highly regulated and there are many challenges in implementing AI. Even when regulatory challenges are overcome there are risks of legal liability if something goes wrong. It is an important landmark for AI in insurance that AI is used as a virtual doctor, not just to make an analysis to support a human subject expert. Nevertheless, AI is still used mostly for the more typical cases of underwriting and not the more specialised ones. The more innovative implementations of AI, such as it being used in the hiring process, may face challenges from various stakeholders, including the government, unions, and rejected job candidates.

The Business Model

A

This insurer sees that AI gives it an opportunity to make health insurance and healthcare more accessible and convenient. This allows many customers and organizations to use more insurance services. There are synergies between AI and other technology initiatives including wearables, such as fitness trackers. These wearables integrate typical fitness tracking, health insurance services, and encourage and reward a healthier lifestyle. The data and analysis from a breadth of sources, such as wearables, health AI, and doctors, can be brought together to inform insurance decisions and implement insurance.

Virtual assistants improve customer service with the speed they can access data and analyse it. The virtual assistants also increase customer satisfaction in some instances by avoiding human error. As the AI becomes more sophisticated and capable, the benefits increase.

The expected, and partly realised, outcomes are to utilize AI to improve current processes and implement new processes that utilize the new capabilities of AI. This insurer is changing their processes and utilizing AI faster than most large insurers. There seems to be a willingness to change the business model to some degree, not just optimise processes. This health insurer is usually an early adopter of technology, and this also applies to AI. AI influences its processes heavily just like other technologies did in the past.

What is particularly interesting in this case is how the AI from healthcare and the AI in insurance inform one another. This provides an impressive breadth of data and analysis that most insurers cannot match. The benefits of having a business model covering both insurance and health provisions are even greater with AI.

AI supports improved operational efficiency, customer satisfaction, and enables the launch of new services, providing a strategic advantage. This newfound effectiveness can also make expansion possible on a scale that could not have been done before. This expansion can be into new products and services or new geographic locations.

Case Study 3: Dedicated Insurance Disruptor

Position in insurance sector: Mobile based, no physical stores, relatively new, technology-focused insurance company

Insurance provided: Low-cost property and casualty insurance

Location: USA

Description of the AI Application

Approach to Applying AI

This is a new, purely digital insurer, often referred to as 'D2C,' active in several countries, including the USA and the UK. It was 'born digital,' which means it does not have out-dated mind sets or legacy systems. They utilize AI to optimize their processes. Like many internet-based insurers, they rely on a mobile app. with AI automation and vast-diverse amounts of data. Everything is done through the mobile app., so it simplifies the process. The consumer can upload a picture of themselves and enter their vehicle number plate to receive a quote. AI enables the insurer to process the necessary information faster. The mobile app. checks the database of the driver and vehicle licencing agency of each country to identify any problems with the car and the licence. Their system then checks the credit history and criminal record of the customer. Once these quick, automatic checks are made, the insurance is issued.

Their virtual assistant interacts with the consumer during the purchase of a policy, switching from another insurer and claims processing. The processes are very fast and convenient. AI is also used for claims processing and fraud detection. Specific AI technologies identify patterns that indicate fraud. Claims and other processes can be processed faster and more transparently.

This insurer also uses AI and real-time data to increase personalisation and flexibility. This personalization and flexibility is not just at the start when a contract is signed, but throughout as changes can be made where necessary. They also allow the customer to cancel the contract more easily. Making it easier to obtain vehicle insurance and it also benefits casual drivers who borrow someone's car. This functionality can be used by people who do not own a car but want to borrow a friend's car for a few hours.

Specific AI Technologies

AI-driven automation is used in several ways, including selling insurance, estimating risk, evaluating claims, and identifying/preventing fraud.

The Underlying Technology

The virtual assistant can identify the type of claim, the severity, and urgency. Beyond that, it can take steps to encourage the consumer to be truthful and accurate. The well-designed and integrated mobile application takes information directly from the users, but also other data sources to calculate risk. AI supports data sharing and analysis. Currently, the virtual assistant does not reject claims. It processes and settles claims it considers valid automatically and refers the remaining cases to a human to make the final decision. Intelligent analytics keep risks at an acceptable level, while undercutting competitors on price.

As with other internet-based insurers, their success depends on the speed of the quote and being able to offer a low price. AI and machine learning help to achieve this by collecting information from several third-party sources and analysing it to ensure that the lowest price possible is offered while keeping risk at an acceptable level.

The backend processes are highly automated. Many standard and proven solutions are used for its systems, including the AI, with relatively limited customization compared to other insurers that have more highly customized systems.

Challenges and Regulatory Implications

One challenge to success is that as this service is only available through mobile applications, so less technology savvy consumers and those that are not early adopters of technology may not be able to benefit.

Another challenge is that other insurers are using the same technology to offer the same services. By implementing technology systems with limited customisation, they are more dependent on differentiating themselves from similar companies by offering unique services.

A third challenge is that as a new insurer with a relatively new model, processes, staff, and no physical presence, some complicated claims can be challenging to resolve.

The Business Model

As a relatively new, technology-focused insurer, they focus on new technology and automation from the start. Therefore, it is natural for them to use AI as extensively as possible. With a business model that has limited human involvement on the insurers side, it is easy to be customer-focused. As long as everything is set up to be customer-focused, it will run that way continuously with a consistent service quality. Fast or even instant services and low prices, often far lower than competitors, satisfies most customers.

Furthermore, as they already have an innovative model, they have a culture, operations, and technologies that are open to new approaches. Their business model is already innovative because it does not take a profit from money that is not claimed. They take 20% of the money they receive and the rest either goes to claims or charities. By having a business model that focuses on delivering services that utilize new technologies, this company can utilize these new technologies better than incumbent companies, and create an appealing story and narrative for themselves.

Many casual drivers drive very little, for example, only on the weekends. This means a lower price can be offered to them to insure their cars. For the lower price to be feasible, accurate risk analysis and automation are necessary. Furthermore, as less people own their own cars and may not use them every day, more people want to share their cars. As with other similar small start-ups, the insurance selected by the customer is then underwritten by traditional insurers. Care is taken to collect extensive information from the consumer, but allow them to be in control, so they do not feel that their privacy is violated. The app. utilizes real-time data and the breadth of insurances the consumer selects, to calculate what they call the overall risk the specific person has.

By offering a faster, more convenient service and lower prices, they have an advantage over competitors. They target specific niches and specific insurance services where technology and automation are beneficial, but not all forms of insurance. Their technology focuses on providing customer insurance smoothly with minimal effort. The AI-centric business model is disruptive in how it delivers existing products and services, but new products and services can be added in the future. The business model and fully automated value chain is innovative, while the use of technology is less innovative.

Case Study 4: Tech Company Disruptor

Position: Tech and e-commerce platform entering the insurance sector

Insurance provided: Health, property, international trade, and low-cost life insurance

Location: China

Description of the AI Application

Approach to Applying AI

This is an e-commerce company that leads in implementing technologies, such as AI, big data, and blockchain. It uses AI heavily in healthcare and this is being integrated with new insurance products. It offers insurance through its popular e-commerce, social platforms, and through several online subsidiary insurers. It is a tech-focused B2C and B2B company offering a platform to the user with several insurance providers they partner with. As a platform it is at the centre of a digital ecosystem. As it creates and runs the technology behind the insurance provided, the scalability is easier. Bringing new partners to the market is also easier. Regular events are used to co-develop AI solutions with its partners. Staff from all departments is trained on how to utilize AI so they apply it the way they want and have a culture of continuous learning.

Unlike most implementations of AI in the insurance sector that only enhance the knowledge of the insurer, AI is also implemented here to enhance the knowledge of the customer. This reduces the information asymmetry, as opposed to increasing it, and helps the customers make the right choices for themselves.

It also innovates in the way that it offers insurance. It allows groups of people to insure themselves together, so that if one falls ill, they take the money the group put in. It can be considered as a form of peer-to-peer insurance or another form of the sharing economy.

Specific AI Technologies

AI is used across this technology giant's e-commerce and social media for analysis, facial recognition, natural language processing, fraud detection, and security. Specific implementations of AI include virtual assistants for customer support, sentiment analysis, and automation of time-consuming and repetitive tasks. Sales and claims processing are done by virtual assistants with a high level of automation. AI is used in the natural language interaction, the analysis, and processing. AI is used to improve the recommendations made to customers. AI supports fully automatic or semi-automatic interactions with consumers using natural language processing and big data. Vast volumes of data are analysed, and the ideal responses are designed for AI to apply. Great care is taken into designing the conversations, so they are beneficial for the consumer. AI is used along with blockchain for smart contracts. This combination of technologies enables some new services, such as insurance for flights. AI is used in a people-centric way. One of the things this means is that AI is used to empower employees rather than replace them.

Technology does not only support the implementation of insurance, but also requires new forms of insurance. Self-driving cars that use AI also need to be insured. There are new opportunities and challenges for insurance created by AI in both current cars that can drive independently, but even more so, for self-driving cars. The new risks they bring must be insured.

The Underlying Technology

This insurer uses the technical infrastructure, payment systems, data, and relationship with customers from its extensive e-commerce operations. It already cross-sells products and services to its existing partners, and this is one more addition. Several partners and their technologies are used, along with some in-house customization, particularly in relation to the interaction with the customer where they have expertise. AI, blockchain, the Internet of Things (IoT), big data, and social media are utilized to understand the user. All of these technologies support integrated seamless services and cross selling to its existing customers.

Challenges and Regulatory Implications

This is a rare case where the regulator encourages innovation and encourages tech companies to enter the insurance sector. The insurance authority of Hong Kong and China encourages technology companies to apply for licences in joint ventures with existing insurers. The use of AI automation, and the use of data from other parts of their business may meet some regulatory challenges. The relationship between healthcare and insurance may raise some regulatory challenges as well. As this technology platform uses AI extensively, and the several partners it has in insurance also use AI extensively, it can be challenging to have a transparent image of how AI and data are used across the many actors involved in providing the insurance. Achieving auditable 'explainability' is more difficult.

The Business Model

This is an organization with extensive capabilities in AI both in terms of the technology such as the algorithms used and the data needed, therefore they are leveraging and re-using existing technological capabilities in adjacent areas. They are strong in several retail areas, such as healthcare, so insurance is a natural addition. Furthermore, engaging in the insurance sector adds one additional source of data.

This insurer's business model is being a platform and a marketplace. The larger it is and the more diverse it is, the better. Their approach can be considered a radical change in an insurance business model, as a tech company is moving into insurance. It already covers most of the value chain in terms of data and technology. This organization's business model, with standardised processes and extensive data, can be considered ideal for AI. This organization aligns its marketing to the capabilities of its systems.

Figure 2. Updated model of five business models in insurance with disruptors split in tech and insurance

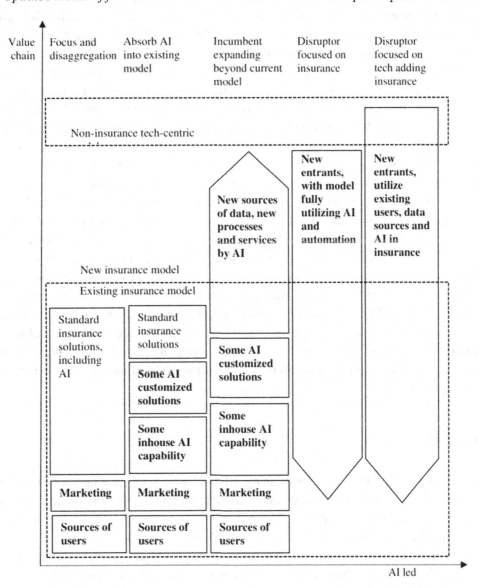

The insurer's strategic logic is to go beyond just being a marketplace and a platform. They want to offer complete, integrated solutions optimised for the cross selling of insurance to existing customers. With the first mover advantage, they also have the opportunity to influence and shape the regulation.

FINDINGS

The impact of AI and data-driven automation in insurance is well underway. While this change shows no signs of stopping or even slowing down, it is at a position in this journey where one can see some business models emerging and being quite well formed and mature. It is therefore a good time to take stock of what has happened. The case studies show the importance of AI and other key technologies in shaping new business models in insurance, just as they have done in other sectors of the economy (Tarafdar et al., 2019). The authors have identified some key technologies and types of companies driving this disruption. The key technologies are: AI, big data, cloud computing, IoT, blockchain, and 5G.

User-facing applications of AI in insurance include: proactive processes and active loss prevention, virtual assistants, chatbots and robo-advisors, fast initial offers and underwriting, faster and more accurate claims processing, improved process flow with clients, new and more flexible services, direct marketing, customer retention, tailored insurance advice, understanding the user's emotions, identifying legal parameters across countries, and AI insuring AI, such as, for example, driverless cars, (Zarifis et al., 2021).

Back-office applications of AI in insurance include: automating simple, low-value tasks, processing large volumes of data, populating and improving data sets, processing structured, semi-structured or unstructured datasets, claims processing, adapting to new risks, new insights on current clients, utilizing data from the IoT, virtual assistants for analysts, fraud detection, faster risk detection for automated services, improved risk analysis, identifying and analysing new data, and audit.

This research attempted to answer the question, "What are the emerging business models in insurance caused by AI and data technologies?" In other words, what the insurance business models were for AI adoption and if they could be empirically validated. This research used a model of four categories of AI adoption in insurance (Zarifis et al., 2019) as a starting point. The preliminary analysis of 15 insurers supported the four categories but identified two useful avenues for further exploration: Firstly, many insurers combined the two first business models. For some products, often the simpler ones, such as car insurance, they focused and disaggregated. For other parts of their organization, they did not change their model, but they absorbed AI into their existing model. Secondly, the fourth category of new entrants has two distinct subgroups: (4a) disruptor focused on insurance and (4b) disruptor focused on tech but adding insurance. The four in-depth case studies support the updated model with five categories, as illustrated in Figure 2.

CONCLUSION

This research evaluated five insurance business models that have a different approach to adopting AI-driven automation in insurance. These cases were chosen primarily because they were representative of the current dynamics, and their clarity of vision is a valuable lesson for others in the sector. This research identified that the digital transformation by AI-driven automation is a long journey, but a clear vision and business model can, and should, be selected at this point. There are several valid business models, as the four cases illustrate, but there are also other insurers with out-dated models that are no longer fit for purpose. The authors' findings show that now is the time to act and implement a transformation that will lead to an insurer optimised for AI. If insurers wait for AI to be optimised for them, they may become out-dated very quickly. This research makes three contributions:

1. It provides additional empirical support for the four AI and data-driven insurance business models.
2. It illustrates that the fourth category has two distinct subcategories, resulting in a model with the following five categories:
   a. Focus on less insurance services and disaggregation
   b. Absorb AI into existing insurance model
   c. Incumbent insurer expanding beyond model
   d. Dedicated insurance disruptor
   e. Tech company disrupting insurance
3. It identified that the first two categories are often combined, particularly by large insurers with many services.

The main limitations of this research are inherent in the methodology chosen, as four cases were explored in depth so there is a possibility that the findings do not apply fully to other insurers. Future research can further validate and develop the model with other cases from different countries.

REFERENCES

Alt, R., Leimeister, J. M., Priemuth, T., Sachse, S., Urbach, N., & Wunderlich, N. (2020). Software-Defined Business: Implications for IT Management. *Business & Information Systems Engineering, 62*(6), 609–621. doi:10.100712599-020-00669-6

Corcoles, A. D., Kandala, A., Javadi-Abhari, A., McClure, D. T., Cross, A. W., Temme, K., Nation, M., Steffen, & Gambetta, J. M. (2019). *Challenges and opportunities of near-term quantum computing systems*. doi:10.1109/JPROC.2019.2954005

Dietzmann, C., Heines, R., & Alt, R. (2020). the convergence of distributed ledger technology and artificial intelligence: an end-to-end reference lending process for financial services competence center ecosystems. In *Proceedings: Twenty-Eighth European Conference on Information Systems (ECIS2020)*. Association for Information Systems. https://www.researchgate.net/ publication/342039353

Eisenhardt, K. M. (1989). Building theories from case study research. *Academy of Management Review, 14*(4), 532–550. doi:10.2307/258557

Faraj, S., Pachidi, S., & Sayegh, K. (2018). Working and organizing in the age of the learning algorithm. *Information and Organization, 28*(1), 62–70. doi:10.1016/j.infoandorg.2018.02.005

Hukal, P., Henfridsson, O., Shaikh, M., & Parker, G. (2020). Platform Signaling for Generating Platform Content. *Management Information Systems Quarterly, 44*(3), 1177–1205. doi:10.25300/MISQ/2020/15190/

Kannan, P. V., & Bernoff, J. (2019). Four challenges to overcome for AI-driven customer experience. *MIT Sloan Management Frontiers, 16*, 1–5. https://sloanreview.mit.edu/article/four-challenges-to-overcome-for-ai-driven-customer-experience/

Kraus, M., Feuerriegel, S., & Oztekin, A. (2020). Deep learning in business analytics and operations research: Models, applications and managerial implications. *European Journal of Operational Research*, *281*(3), 628–641. doi:10.1016/j.ejor.2019.09.018

Mikalef, P., Krogstie, J., Pappas, I. O., & Pavlou, P. (2020). Exploring the relationship between big data analytics capability and competitive performance: The mediating roles of dynamic and operational capabilities. *Information & Management*, *57*(2), 103169. doi:10.1016/j.im.2019.05.004

Osterwalder, A., Pigneur, Y., & Tucci, C. L. (2005). Clarifying business models: Origins, present, and future of the concept. *Communications of the Association for Information Systems*, *16*(16), 1. doi:10.17705/1CAIS.01601

Park, A., Jabagi, N., & Kietzmann, J. (2021). The truth about 5G: It's not (only) about downloading movies faster! *Business Horizons, 64*(1), 19–28. 1.009 doi:0.1016/j.bushor.2020.09

Tarafdar, M., Beath, C. M., & Ross, J. W. (2019). Using AI to Enhance Business Operations. *MIT Sloan Management Review*, *60*(4), 37–44.

Veit, D., Clemons, E., Benlian, A., Buxmann, P., Hess, T., Spann, M., Kundisch, D., Leimeister, J. M., & Loos, P. (2014). Business Models: An Information Systems Research Agenda. *Business & Information Systems Engineering*, *6*(1), 45–53. doi:10.100712599-013-0308-y

Zarifis, A., & Cheng, X. (2021). Evaluating the New AI and Data Driven Insurance Business Models for Incumbents and Disruptors: Is there Convergence? *Business Information Systems*, 199–208. doi:10.52825/bis.v1i.58

Zarifis, A., Holland, C. P., & Milne, A. (2019). Evaluating the impact of AI on insurance: The four emerging AI- and data-driven business models. *Emerald Open Research*, *1*, 15. doi:10.35241/emeraldopenres.13249.1

Zarifis, A., Kawalek, P., & Azadegan, A. (2021). Evaluating if trust and personal information privacy concerns are barriers to using health insurance that explicitly utilizes AI. *Journal of Internet Commerce*, *20*(1), 66–83. doi:10.1080/15332861.2020.1832817

Artificial Intelligence, Big Data, and Machine Learning in Industry 4.0

Georgios Lampropoulos

🆔 https://orcid.org/0000-0002-5719-2125

International Hellenic University, Greece

INTRODUCTION

The globalization and the rapid technological advancements have brought about numerous changes to various sectors. The industrial sector is no exception to this phenomenon. The global market has become fiercely competitive and the requirements more demanding. Consequently, it is vital to utilize innovative technologies and reap their benefits in order to address and satisfy the new and forthcoming needs and create new values. As a result, the emergence of the fourth industrial revolution (Industry 4.0) was inevitable.

By enabling physical assets to be integrated into intertwined digital and physical processes, Industry 4.0 enhances traditional industries by transforming them into intelligent ones (Xu et al., 2018). Industry 4.0 offers new organization levels and has the potential to change and add value throughout the entire value chain by enabling the creation of autonomous, automated, intelligent and digitalized processes (Lasi et al., 2014). Nonetheless, as Industry 4.0 is still at its infancy, several challenges remain to be met in order for it to be fully adopted and successfully implemented. Several technologies, such as Artificial Intelligence (AI), Machine Learning (ML), Big Data (BD), Internet of Things (IoT) etc., help towards the realization of Industry 4.0 and its development. These technologies can be used in combination while simultaneously helping each other advance.

This chapter aims at providing an overview regarding the vital role that the state-of-the-art technologies of AI, ML and BD offer to the realization and adoption of Industry 4.0, the numerous merits they can yield as well as the multitude of contemporary solutions, applications and services they can provide. Consequently, this chapter presents the concept of Industry 4.0 as well as those of AI, ML, BD and Big Data Analytics (BDA) technologies. In addition, it discusses the potentials that these technologies could offer and the merits they could yield when applied within the context of Industry 4.0. Finally, it presents the summary of the main findings, open research issues and challenges, drawn conclusions and provides directions for future research.

BACKGROUND

The plethora of smart devices and the everyday life digitalization have led to a rapid increase of a wide variety of data sources, digital content as well as data structures and types (Gahi et al., 2016). Consequently, an exponentially increasing volume of heterogeneous data, which is called BD, is created and is differentiated from traditional data based on its volume, variety, veracity, velocity and value (McAfee et al., 2012).

DOI: 10.4018/978-1-7998-9220-5.ch125

BD can be processed using advanced analytical tools, called Big Data Analytics (BDA), which utilize analytic and parallel techniques in order to retrieve, process, examine, analyze and manage vast amounts of diverse digital data, information and statistics (Parwez et al., 2017). The BD era offers uncountable potentials for innovation in addition to numerous other advantages, all the more so as BDA offer prescriptive and predictive insight and enable intelligence gleaning, retrieval of crucial data and enhanced decision-making (LaValle et al., 2011). Therefore, there is no doubt that both BD and BDA are essential parts for the implementation of Industry 4.0.

The exponential increase of digital data has given rise not only to new requirements and challenges but also to new opportunities and potentials. ML is a novel scientific field which capitalizes on this vast amount of data as well as the increase in computational power in order to offer improved services and new solutions (Jordan & Mitchell, 2015). Intelligent and highly flexible models that learn through examples, meaning that they simulate the human way of learning, are being developed through ML (Mohri et al., 2018). Hence, ML can be used in various domains, such as computer vision, object recognition, natural language processing, intelligent decision-making systems, recommender systems etc. It is worth noting that as the volume of input and processed data increases so does its efficiency.

Moreover, Deep Learning (DL) constitutes a specialized form of ML. The term "deep" refers to the multitude of layers through which the data is transformed. DL uses multi-layer neural networks and advanced supervised and unsupervised learning methods (Deng & Yu, 2014). Moreover, it allows "*computational models that are composed of multiple processing layers to learn representations of data with multiple levels of abstraction*" (LeCun et al., 2015, p. 436). Therefore, it utilizes nested hierarchies to represent concepts with each individual one being defined as a result of other simpler and more abstract representations.

ML models identify and utilize the optimal combinations of complex input data in an autonomous and automatic manner (Goodfellow et al., 2016). Consequently, they are able to create autonomous human-like decision-making systems that are able to increase the overall process effectiveness without requiring any form of human intervention or action. As the amount of data increases, the algorithms and architectures used become more advanced and systems acquire more compute power, the merits that can be yielded through ML as well as its innovative applications will increase (LeCun et al., 2015). Therefore, it can be claimed that ML plays a vital role in the realization of Industry 4.0.

AI can capitalize on both BD and the advancement of ML to further support and enhance the development of Industry 4.0. AI can be regarded as the capability of digital computers or computer-controlled robots of autonomously performing tasks which are usually associated with intelligent beings (Russell & Norvig, 2002). Furthermore, the term commonly describes systems that have been developed to have human characteristics, intelligent behavior, cognitive functions and the ability to perceive their surrounding environment (Nilsson, 2014). Through its numerous applications, AI can materialize the vision of Intelligent Manufacturing (IM) to further increase overall productivity (Li et al., 2017). Moreover, AI can significantly affect not only the way humans use and interact with computers and machines, but also impact Machine-to-Machine (M2M) communication (Lee et al., 2018). AI is also able to provide sophisticated, intelligent and autonomous decision-making systems and provide several merits and innovative applications and solutions when used in conjunction with ML (Duan et al., 2019). Therefore, AI also plays a significant role in fulfilling the vision of Industry 4.0.

FOCUS OF THE ARTICLE

The focus toward the realization of Industry 4.0 has reached its higher level of activity as industries have access to a large volume of sensory data which contains various formats, semantics and structures. Contemporary technologies can further support the realization of Industry 4.0 by offering new solutions. Internet of Things (IoT) which aims at interconnecting diverse uniquely identifiable devices and objects using standard communication protocols and intelligent interfaces (Lampropoulos et al., 2018) as well as Virtual Reality (VR) and Augmented Reality (AR) technologies which offer new audio-visual experiences and new ways to interact with both the physical and digital environment (Lampropoulos et al., 2020) are some examples. Cyber-Physical Systems (CPS) are an additional essential technology of Industry 4.0. CPS involve a large number of transdisciplinary methodologies, contain cyber-twined services and consist of both cyber and physical processes and components.

SOLUTIONS AND RECOMMENDATIONS

Industry 4.0 is characterized by high levels of integration, digitalization, refinement personalization and interconnectivity. AI, ML and BDA can help towards achieving the main goal of Industry 4.0 which is to provide enterprises with highly flexible, interconnected, intelligent and autonomous production systems and processes in which humans, machines, devices, software and sensors communicate and collaborate in order to increase performances, reduce downtime, optimize resource usage and improve their effectiveness, productivity and security. In addition, they enable real-time predictive, diagnostic and descriptive analytics. More specifically, as these technologies enhance M2M communication and Human-Robot Interaction (HRI), they offer rapid logistics, higher quality control, advanced real-time user profiling and feedback, condition-based and predictive maintenance, intelligent decision-making systems, continuous monitoring and evaluation as well as autonomous operations and processes. Consequently, enterprises which utilize these technologies and realize the vision of Industry 4.0 are able to detect and analyze market trends, socioeconomic attributes and macroeconomic behaviors, increase their productivity, optimize their performance, improve their supply chain management, offer services and products of higher quality while reducing their running costs, errors and malfunctions. As a result, these enterprises are able to increase their revenue, satisfy market and customer needs and stay ahead of competition.

Smart Manufacturing

Smart manufacturing is another significant sector within the context of Industry 4.0 which experiences major advancements. It uses a Service-Oriented Architecture (SOA) which applies cutting-edge technologies, methodologies and manufacturing techniques to various traditional systems, services and products so as to transform traditional enterprises into intelligent ones (Zhong et al., 2017). Particularly, it aims at creating high-performance smart facilities which utilize processes, systems and devices that are able to automatically learn from data, detect patterns and make intelligent decisions.

With a view to increasing the overall production, productivity efficiency and product quality, smart manufacturing uses the combined intelligence of people, processes and machines to create intelligent, autonomous and human like decision-making systems which do not require the involvement and intervention of humans (Lampropoulos et al., 2019). AI, ML and BDA can be used throughout the development and production stages as they enable the continuous collection, process, analysis and evaluation of data in real time. As a result, enterprises are able to optimize their processes and resource management and sharing, enhance their control and management, design products and services according to customer requirements, detect and monitor potential damage, malfunctions and breakdowns, predict future states and improve their maintainability and availability.

Challenges in the Implementation of Industry 4.0

Although there is a plethora of opportunities and numerous benefits that could be yielded from the complete adoption and implementation of Industry 4.0, there still remain some challenges that need to be addressed and overcome before its complete realization. Several studies have looked into the general challenges which are caused by the adoption of Industry 4.0. In their study, Xu et al. (2018) went over the concept of Industry 4.0, its future trends as well as the challenges that need to be sorted out. Schröder (2016) and Masood & Sonntag (2020) provided overviews of the challenges that small and medium-sized enterprises (SMEs) face when trying to implement the vision of Industry 4.0 as well as the benefits it can yield. Other studies examined the challenges that need to be addressed in specific domains of Industry 4.0 such as smart factories (Chen et al., 2017), operations management (Olsen & Tomlin, 2020), supply chain sustainability (Luthra & Mangla, 2018), manufacturing (Zhou et al., 2015) etc. as well as the opportunities that might arise. Moktadir et al. (2018) and Müller et al. (2018) respectively highlighted the challenges that need to be met in order to ensure process safety and environmental protection as well as sustainability when implementing Industry 4.0.

As Industry 4.0 utilizes several contemporary technologies and has interconnectivity at its core, there are quite a few challenges deriving from the implementation of these technologies. In their study, Bajic et al. (2018) highlighted the importance of applying ML techniques within smart manufacturing in the context of Industry 4.0 and looked into their potential application domains and challenges. Khan et al. (2017) analyzed the significance of BD for the realization of Industry 4.0 and pointed out the several opportunities and challenges that might be brought about. Peres et al. (2020) and Bécue et al. (2021) went over the vital role of AI in Industry 4.0 and analyzed the various security challenges and threats that need to be addressed. Jazdi (2014) and Kravets et al. (2020) looked into the role of CPS in Industry 4.0 and presented the challenges that need to be looked into. Aazam et al. (2018) and Sisinni et al. (2018) respectively examined the challenges and issues of fog computing and Industrial Internet of Things (IIoT) in Industry 4.0.

FUTURE RESEARCH DIRECTIONS

In order for Industry 4.0 to be fully realized, there still remain several open research challenges and issues that need to be addressed. Some of the potential open issues that can be looked into are: interoperability (Lu, 2017), equipment intelligent requirements, deep integration networks and knowledge-driven manufacturing (Chen et al., 2017), standardization activities, work organization and product availability (Kagermann et al., 2013), socioeconomic concerns and barriers (Küsters et al., 2017) etc.

Moreover, in order for Industry 4.0 to be widely adopted, it is essential to provide secure physical and virtual environments. Therefore, it is vital to address the new security, privacy and safety issues and challenges which derive from the interconnectivity of digital technologies, devices, applications, services and industrial control systems as well as the convergence of operational technology and Information and

Communications Technology (ICT). As technologies advance, more cyber security threats and attacks become feasible so it is highly important to seek for ways to safely monitor and secure Industry 4.0 environments. Additionally, higher levels of interaction could be achieved and new training opportunities would arise by using immersive technologies such as AR, VR and 360-degree videos within the context of Industry 4.0 (Lampropoulos et al., 2021).

AI, ML and BDA have their own challenges but as the amount of data increases, the algorithms become more advanced and the computational power is enforced, they can constitute essential tools for Industry 4.0. For that reason, future studies should focus on the combinational use of these technologies in order to address these issues and develop innovative solutions. As their benefits and the merits that Industry 4.0 can yield become more widespread and the open issues and challenges get addressed, the vision of Industry 4.0 will be successfully realized.

CONCLUSION

Having interconnectivity at its core, Industry 4.0 combines several technologies in order to offer new opportunities and merits, to transform enterprises into intelligent ones and enable them to successfully meet the ever-changing customer needs and requirements and cope with the more and more competitive global market. Furthermore, the exponential increase of BD has provided new opportunities for innovative applications and solutions. AI, ML and BDA are some of the technologies that help towards the realization of Industry 4.0 as they play a vital role in providing new solutions and addressing some of the challenges that Industry 4.0 is currently facing.

Through the combinational use of these technologies, highly flexible, interconnected, intelligent and autonomous production systems and processes in which humans, machines, devices, software and sensors communicate and collaborate are created. Enterprises that manage to successfully use these technologies and materialize the vision of Industry 4.0 are able to improve their performance, effectiveness, productivity and security, offer services and products of higher quality, optimize their operation and resource usage, reduce their downtime and costs and increase their monitoring, maintenance and sustainability. Moreover, these enterprises are able to capitalize on intelligent and autonomous decision-making systems in order to understand the market needs and stay ahead of the competition. It is worth noting that all enterprises from small scale to large scale can utilize and capitalize on these technologies.

Nonetheless, there are still open research challenges that should be addressed before the complete adoption of Industry 4.0 is accomplished. Due to the nature of Industry 4.0, some of these challenges have to do with its interconnected technologies. Future studies should focus on these issues while also showcasing the potentials and benefits of Industry 4.0 to further advance its implementation.

REFERENCES

Aazam, M., Zeadally, S., & Harras, K. A. (2018). Deploying fog computing in industrial internet of things and industry 4.0. *IEEE Transactions on Industrial Informatics*, *14*(10), 4674–4682. doi:10.1109/TII.2018.2855198

Bajic, B., Cosic, I., Lazarevic, M., Sremcev, N., & Rikalovic, A. (2018). *Machine learning techniques for smart manufacturing: Applications and challenges in industry 4.0*. Department of Industrial Engineering and Management Novi Sad, Serbia.

Bécue, A., Praça, I., & Gama, J. (2021). Artificial intelligence, cyber-threats and industry 4.0: Challenges and opportunities. *Artificial Intelligence Review*, *54*(5), 3849–3886. doi:10.100710462-020-09942-2

Chen, B., Wan, J., Shu, L., Li, P., Mukherjee, M., & Yin, B. (2017). Smart factory of industry 4.0: Key technologies, application case, and challenges. *IEEE Access: Practical Innovations, Open Solutions*, *6*, 6505–6519. doi:10.1109/ACCESS.2017.2783682

Deng, L., & Yu, D. (2014). Deep learning: Methods and applications. *Foundations and Trends in Signal Processing*, *7*(3–4), 197–387. doi:10.1561/2000000039

Duan, Y., Edwards, J. S., & Dwivedi, Y. K. (2019). Artificial intelligence for decision making in the era of big data–evolution, challenges and research agenda. *International Journal of Information Management*, *48*, 63–71. doi:10.1016/j.ijinfomgt.2019.01.021

Gahi, Y., Guennoun, M., & Mouftah, H. T. (2016). Big data analytics: Security and privacy challenges. *2016 IEEE Symposium on Computers and Communication (ISCC)*, 952–957. 10.1109/ISCC.2016.7543859

Goodfellow, I., Bengio, Y., & Courville, A. (2016). *Deep learning*. MIT Press.

Jazdi, N. (2014). Cyber physical systems in the context of industry 4.0. *2014 IEEE International Conference on Automation, Quality and Testing, Robotics*, 1–4. 10.1109/AQTR.2014.6857843

Jordan, M. I., & Mitchell, T. M. (2015). Machine learning: Trends, perspectives, and prospects. *Science*, *349*(6245), 255–260. doi:10.1126cience.aaa8415 PMID:26185243

Kagermann, H., Helbig, J., Hellinger, A., & Wahlster, W. (2013). *Recommendations for implementing the strategic initiative industrie 4.0: Securing the future of german manufacturing industry; final report of the industrie 4.0 working group*. Forschungsunion.

Khan, M., Wu, X., Xu, X., & Dou, W. (2017). Big data challenges and opportunities in the hype of industry 4.0. *2017 IEEE International Conference on Communications (ICC)*, 1–6. 10.1109/ICC.2017.7996801

Kravets, A. G., Bolshakov, A. A., & Shcherbakov, M. V. (2020). *Cyber-physical systems: Industry 4.0 challenges*. Springer. doi:10.1007/978-3-030-32648-7

Küsters, D., Praß, N., & Gloy, Y. S. (2017). Textile learning factory 4.0–preparing germany's textile industry for the digital future. *Procedia Manufacturing*, *9*, 214–221. doi:10.1016/j.promfg.2017.04.035

Lampropoulos, G., Barkoukis, V., Burden, K., & Anastasiadis, T. (2021). 360-degree video in education: An overview and a comparative social media data analysis of the last decade. *Smart Learning Environments*, *8*(20), 1–24. doi:10.118640561-021-00165-8

Lampropoulos, G., Keramopoulos, E., & Diamantaras, K. (2020). Enhancing the functionality of augmented reality using deep learning, semantic web and knowledge graphs: A review. *Visual Informatics*, *4*(1), 32–42. doi:10.1016/j.visinf.2020.01.001

Lampropoulos, G., Siakas, K., & Anastasiadis, T. (2018). Internet of things (IoT) in industry: Contemporary application domains, innovative technologies and intelligent manufacturing. *International Journal of Advances in Scientific Research and Engineering*, *4*(10), 109–118. doi:10.31695/IJASRE.2018.32910

Lampropoulos, G., Siakas, K., & Anastasiadis, T. (2019). Internet of things in the context of industry 4.0: An overview. *International Journal of Entrepreneurial Knowledge*, *7*(1), 4–19. doi:10.37335/ijek.v7i1.84

Lasi, H., Fettke, P., Kemper, H. G., Feld, T., & Hoffmann, M. (2014). Industry 4.0. *Business & Information Systems Engineering*, *6*(4), 239–242. doi:10.100712599-014-0334-4

LaValle, S., Lesser, E., Shockley, R., Hopkins, M. S., & Kruschwitz, N. (2011). Big data, analytics and the path from insights to value. *MIT Sloan Management Review*, *52*(2), 21–32.

LeCun, Y., Bengio, Y., & Hinton, G. (2015). Deep learning. *Nature*, *521*(7553), 436–444. doi:10.1038/nature14539 PMID:26017442

Lee, J., Davari, H., Singh, J., & Pandhare, V. (2018). Industrial artificial intelligence for industry 4.0-based manufacturing systems. *Manufacturing Letters*, *18*, 20–23. doi:10.1016/j.mfglet.2018.09.002

Li, B., Hou, B., Yu, W., Lu, X., & Yang, C. (2017). Applications of artificial intelligence in intelligent manufacturing: A review. *Frontiers of Information Technology & Electronic Engineering*, *18*(1), 86–96. doi:10.1631/FITEE.1601885

Lu, Y. (2017). Industry 4.0: A survey on technologies, applications and open research issues. *Journal of Industrial Information Integration*, *6*, 1–10. doi:10.1016/j.jii.2017.04.005

Luthra, S., & Mangla, S. K. (2018). Evaluating challenges to industry 4.0 initiatives for supply chain sustainability in emerging economies. *Process Safety and Environmental Protection*, *117*, 168–179. doi:10.1016/j.psep.2018.04.018

Masood, T., & Sonntag, P. (2020). Industry 4.0: Adoption challenges and benefits for SMEs. *Computers in Industry*, *121*, 103261. doi:10.1016/j.compind.2020.103261

McAfee, A., Brynjolfsson, E., Davenport, T. H., Patil, D., & Barton, D. (2012). Big data: The management revolution. *Harvard Business Review*, *90*(10), 60–68. PMID:23074865

Mohri, M., Rostamizadeh, A., & Talwalkar, A. (2018). *Foundations of machine learning*. MIT Press.

Moktadir, M. A., Ali, S. M., Kusi-Sarpong, S., & Shaikh, M. A. A. (2018). Assessing challenges for implementing industry 4.0: Implications for process safety and environmental protection. *Process Safety and Environmental Protection*, *117*, 730–741. doi:10.1016/j.psep.2018.04.020

Müller, J. M., Kiel, D., & Voigt, K. I. (2018). What drives the implementation of industry 4.0? The role of opportunities and challenges in the context of sustainability. *Sustainability*, *10*(1), 247. doi:10.3390u10010247

Nilsson, N. J. (2014). *Principles of artificial intelligence*. Morgan Kaufmann.

Olsen, T. L., & Tomlin, B. (2020). Industry 4.0: Opportunities and challenges for operations management. *Manufacturing & Service Operations Management*, *22*(1), 113–122. doi:10.1287/msom.2019.0796

Parwez, M. S., Rawat, D. B., & Garuba, M. (2017). Big data analytics for user-activity analysis and user-anomaly detection in mobile wireless network. *IEEE Transactions on Industrial Informatics*, *13*(4), 2058–2065. doi:10.1109/TII.2017.2650206

Peres, R. S., Jia, X., Lee, J., Sun, K., Colombo, A. W., & Barata, J. (2020). Industrial artificial intelligence in industry 4.0-systematic review, challenges and outlook. *IEEE Access: Practical Innovations, Open Solutions*, *8*, 220121–220139. doi:10.1109/ACCESS.2020.3042874

Russell, S., & Norvig, P. (2002). *Artificial intelligence: A modern approach*. Academic Press.

Schröder, C. (2016). *The challenges of industry 4.0 for small and medium-sized enterprises.* Friedrich-Ebert-Stiftung.

Sisinni, E., Saifullah, A., Han, S., Jennehag, U., & Gidlund, M. (2018). Industrial internet of things: Challenges, opportunities, and directions. *IEEE Transactions on Industrial Informatics, 14*(11), 4724–4734. doi:10.1109/TII.2018.2852491

Xu, L. D., Xu, E. L., & Li, L. (2018). Industry 4.0: State of the art and future trends. *International Journal of Production Research, 56*(8), 2941–2962. doi:10.1080/00207543.2018.1444806

Zhong, R. Y., Xu, X., Klotz, E., & Newman, S. T. (2017). Intelligent manufacturing in the context of industry 4.0: A review. *Engineering, 3*(5), 616–630. doi:10.1016/J.ENG.2017.05.015

Zhou, K., Liu, T., & Zhou, L. (2015). Industry 4.0: Towards future industrial opportunities and challenges. *2015 12th International Conference on Fuzzy Systems and Knowledge Discovery (FSKD)*, 2147–2152. 10.1109/FSKD.2015.7382284

ADDITIONAL READING

Diez-Olivan, A., Del Ser, J., Galar, D., & Sierra, B. (2019). Data fusion and machine learning for industrial prognosis: Trends and perspectives towards Industry 4.0. *Information Fusion, 50*, 92–111. doi:10.1016/j.inffus.2018.10.005

Javaid, M., Haleem, A., Vaishya, R., Bahl, S., Suman, R., & Vaish, A. (2020). Industry 4.0 technologies and their applications in fighting COVID-19 pandemic. *Diabetes & Metabolic Syndrome, 14*(4), 419–422. doi:10.1016/j.dsx.2020.04.032 PMID:32344370

Lee, J., Kao, H. A., & Yang, S. (2014). Service innovation and smart analytics for industry 4.0 and big data environment. *Procedia CIRP, 16*, 3–8. doi:10.1016/j.procir.2014.02.001

Rojko, A. (2017). Industry 4.0 concept: Background and overview. *International Journal of Interactive Mobile Technologies, 11*(5), 77–90. doi:10.3991/ijim.v11i5.7072

Yao, X., Zhou, J., Zhang, J., & Boër, C. R. (2017, September). From intelligent manufacturing to smart manufacturing for industry 4.0 driven by next generation artificial intelligence and further on. In *2017 5th international conference on enterprise systems (ES)* (pp. 311-318). IEEE. 10.1109/ES.2017.58

KEY TERMS AND DEFINITIONS

Artificial Intelligence: The ability of digital computers or computer-controlled robots to autonomously perform tasks which are usually associated with intelligent beings.

Big Data: An exponentially increasing volume of heterogeneous data which is differentiated from traditional data based on its volume, variety, veracity, velocity and value.

Big Data Analytics: Advanced analytical tools which utilize analytic and parallel techniques in order to retrieve, process, examine, analyze and manage vast amounts of diverse digital data, information and statistics.

Deep Learning: A specialized form (sub-field) of machine learning with a multitude of layers through which the data is transformed.

Industry 4.0: The fourth industrial revolution which aims at enhancing traditional industries by transforming them into intelligent ones.

Machine Learning: A sub-field of artificial intelligence that utilizes data and algorithms in order to imitate the manner in which humans perceive things and learn that is, learning through experience.

Smart Manufacturing: Also referred to as intelligent manufacturing, is a technology-driven global industrial method that utilizes interconnected devices to provide computer-integrated manufacturing.

Big Data and Sustainability Innovation

Budi Harsanto
Universitas Padjadjaran, Indonesia

Egi Arvian Firmansyah
 https://orcid.org/0000-0001-5296-706X
Universiti Brunei Darussalam, Brunei & Universitas Padjadjaran, Indonesia

INTRODUCTION

This chapter presents the connection between big data and sustainability innovation. Understanding the connection between these two recent prominent topics is important because today, the need for sustainable innovation is increasing along with various global challenges faced both in terms of the natural environment and the social environment (Adams et al., 2016; Harsanto & Permana, 2021). Companies' innovations frequently have unanticipated consequences that degrade the environment on land, sea, and air. It also frequently harms the social environment, as evidenced by the growing economic divide between rich and poor.

This creates a sense of urgency for businesses to be able to innovate sustainably. Meanwhile, in terms of technology, the development of information communication technology is progressing rapidly, marked by, among others, big data and big data analytics, which help process large amounts of information and assist decision making, including decisions relating to innovation. These two major issues that are currently emerging, sustainability innovation and big data, which are the focus of this chapter. This chapter aims to better understand the link between big data and sustainability innovation. This achieved by exploring keywords form the scientific articles analyzed using bibliometric technique. This understanding is important because in the era of digitalization, companies need to rethinking about the ways they do business. Among the ways of doing business that business actors are starting to realize is the importance of achieving not only economic value but also social and environmental performance (Adams et al., 2016). Digital technologies such as big data regarded as a vital component to help companies achieve not only economic returns but also social and environmental benefits (Schneider, 2019). This chapter could be useful as a resource for academic and practical studies to maximize the use of big data to innovate sustainably and to serve as the foundation for future development.

BACKGROUND

Big data utilization has increased rapidly in recent years. Big data, which means huge volumes of data, when utilized carefully can help facilitate the organization in optimizing various business functions. For example, the use of big data can increase agility, which means the company's ability to effectively identify and respond to situations in its environment at speed (Ghasemaghaei et al., 2017). Sivarajah et al., (2017) suggested that big data can provide insight to enhance the decision-making process. these positive impacts can ultimately improve the company's performance, especially financial performance. Recent studies have found that increased profitability and reduced costs can be achieved with the effec-

DOI: 10.4018/978-1-7998-9220-5.ch126

tive use of big data (Dana et al., 2022; Love et al., 2020; Müller et al., 2018; Silva et al., 2019). Müller et al. (2018) using panel data spanning 6 years involving more than 800 companies found that the increase in company productivity as a result of big data and analytics implementation was in the range of 3-7 percent. In a wider perspective, the use of big data also provides benefits for non-commercial usage such as education, smart city, or heritage management (Harsanto, 2021; Ozer et al., 2022; Wang, 2022; D. Zhang et al., 2022).

The focus of previous studies investigating the relationship between big data and operational or financial aspects of a company has prompted the question, how big data is related to non-operational or non-financial performance such as social or environmental aspects of the organization. As performance is determined by various traditional factors such as leadership or culture or other factors, it is interesting to find out the latest issues regarding the relationship between big data and performance, especially innovation performance (Azis et al., 2017; Harsanto et al., 2020; Widianto & Harsanto, 2017). This question is important because of the concern of various stakeholders towards business organizations to be able to provide economic benefits but more than that, it can also provide benefits to the environment and society (Nunan & Di Domenico, 2017). In this context, big data utilization is also no exception to this concern.

More specifically, the focus of this study is the sustainability of innovation as a specific form of innovation (Hansen & Große-Dunker, 2013; Harsanto et al., 2018; Harsanto & Permana, 2019). In general, sustainability innovation can be in the form of eco or social innovation (Gumbira & Harsanto, 2019; Hansen & Große-Dunker, 2013). A study from Calic & Ghasemaghaei (2021) shows that innovation is a mediator between big data and social performance. Although it does not directly discuss sustainability innovation, the study implies that there is a possible connection between the two. In a broader view, it is interesting to know the discussion about big data and its relation to sustainability innovation. The purpose of this paper is to explore this phenomenon and become the basis for further exploration.

This study contributes to the literature by providing an overview of big data connectedness and sustainability innovation which is still rarely studied in the literature. Previous studies have focused more on the technical aspects of big data or the relationship between big data and the company's financial performance.

METHOD

The approach used is a systematic search on the Web of Science database to then analyzed using bibliometric tecnhique. The keywords used are a combination of "big data" AND "sustainability innovation" in the topic, covering title, abstract, and keywords. The selection of keywords is carried out in a straightforward manner on two concepts that are the center of attention in this paper, namely big data and sustainability innovation. Indeed, there are several other synonyms of sustainability innovation that can be involved such as eco-innovation or social innovation and the like. However, these keywords are not used because these concepts are a subset of sustainability innovation and in this paper, we focus on the generic concept of sustainability innovation. The search results gave 386 documents. After a systematic search, the next two main steps were taken. First, capture descriptive statistics provided by WoS to find out various attributes of the obtained document. Second, exporting metadata in the form of plain text files for keyword occurrence analysis to determine the relationship between various concepts discussed in these two fields (Harsanto, 2020b; van Eck & Waltman, 2014). Further, the metadata is exported to MS Excel format to facilitate analysis and reading, especially the title, abstract, and other important information of the article. The step-by-step process is shown in Figure 1.

Figure 1. Step-by-step analysis process
Source: Authors' elaboration, 2021

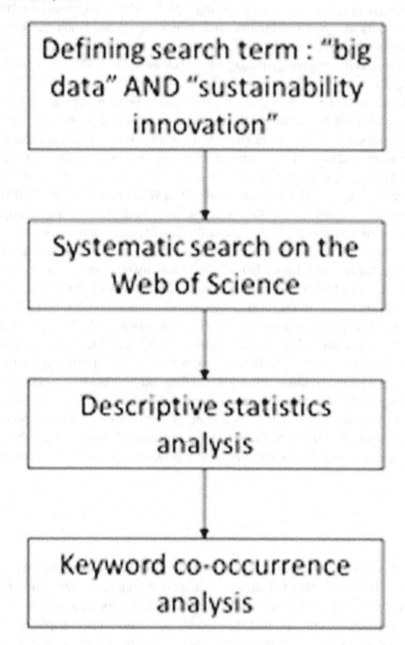

The VOSViewer software is used to perform co-occurrence analysis on the keywords in documents (van Eck & Waltman, 2020). When performing co-occurrence analysis, VOSViewer's default setting is used, which is the occurrence of a minimum of 5 keywords. In principle, a cluster of concepts formed from co-occurrence analysis works by discover concepts that appear together in the analyzed documents. Concepts belonging to the same cluster mean that they have a strong link because they frequently appear together in the analyzed documents (IBM, 2022). The keywords used are from both the author and WoS and calculated using a full counting technique, which means that all keywords are given the same weight. The outcome of this analysis is the clustering of keywords based on their level of connection, as well as detailed frequency data for each keyword, which is analyzed using the content analysis principle to determine the most frequently used keywords in each cluster (Harsanto, 2020a).

RESULTS AND DISCUSSION

The following is a presentation of the results as well as a discussion of the results of the analysis of the publications included in the review. The sections presented include publication attributes such as publication year, document types, Web of Sciences categories, authors' affiliation, journal, research areas, countries of authors, and research areas. Subsequently, an analysis of the concepts represented by the keywords used in various publications is presented.

Publication year

The trend of publication by year seems to increase from year to year. Publications began to appear in the 2000s, although in small numbers with a relatively flat trend from year to year. The publication seems to have started to increase in 2014 with an increasing trend starting from around 10 articles per year then doubled to around 20 articles per year, to reach around 90 articles per year in 2021.

Figure 2. Publication year
Source: Web of Science, 2021

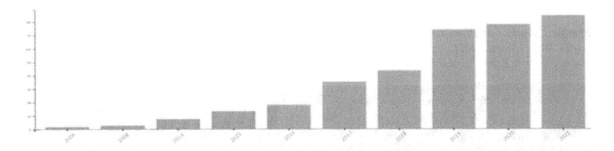

The trend, as shown in Figure 2, is in line with the development of SOI, which began to emerge in the 2000s and then increased after 2010. On a cumulative percentage basis, more than three-quarters of the total publications analyzed were published in the last four years. In 2021 there were 89 publications (23.01%), in 2020 there were 82 articles (21.24%), in 2019, there were 78 articles (20.21%), and in 2018 there were 46 articles (11.92%).

Document types

There are various types of documents included in this review. Most of the articles were 257 documents (66.58%), followed by conference proceedings with 70 documents (18.14%) and review articles with 50 documents (12.95%). Next, there were 25 early access documents (6.48%), book chapters 14 documents (3.63%), and editorial materials 10 documents (2.59%). This indicates there are quite a number of publications related to big data on sustainability innovation, and most of them are peer-reviewed journal articles. Peer review is the highest level in terms of the stringency of the review process to maintain and ensure the quality of publications.

Research Areas

From the perspective of the research area, there is an interdisciplinary nuance in the publications included in the review. Two research areas are equally dominant, namely environmental sciences ecology and other science technology topics, each with 118 documents or 30.57%. The next three research areas that are also widely studied are business economics with 87 documents (22.54%), engineering 74 documents (19.17%), and computer science 57 documents (14.77%). This is understandable because big data is an area that is closer with fields of science such as computer science, engineering, and technology; while sustainability innovation is more concerned with fields of science such as business economics and environmental science. The intersection of these domains of knowledge is interesting, and it can provide valuable insights into the future of big data for sustainable innovation.

Affiliations

The affiliations of the authors are shown in Figure 3. The main affiliations of the authors of the publications included in the review were mainly from Europe, China, and America. From Europe, the largest contributors were the Norwegian University of Science Technology NTNU with 9 documents (2.33%), followed by the University of London with 8 documents (2.07%), the University of Naples Federico II with 5 documents (1.29%) and the University of Salento (1.29%).

Figure 3. Author affiliations
Source: Web of Science, 2021

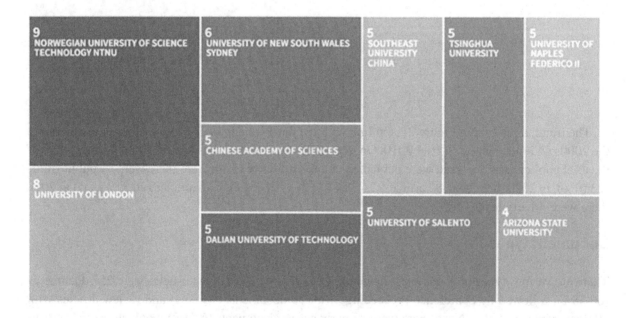

In China, the largest contributors were the Chinese Academy of Sciences, Dalian University of Technology, Southeast University China, and Tsinghua University, each with 5 documents (1.29% each). From America, the highest contributor was Arizona State University with 4 documents (1.04%). Apart from these affiliates, many other affiliates contributed 4 documents or less, including from universities in Latin America such as Universidade De Sao Paulo (1.04%), or universities in the Middle East such as Abu Dhabi University (0.77%). These results indicate that the topic has attracted the interest of researchers from various parts of the world, although it is currently predominantly studied by researchers with affiliations in Europe, China, and America.

Publication title

The outlets for the publication of documents included in the review are in quite many different titles. Considering that the most types of documents included in this review journal articles, so most publication titles are also in the form of journals. The journal that contains the most articles on this topic is Sustainability with 65 documents (16.84%), followed by the Journal of Cleaner Production with 17 articles (4.40%) and Technological Forecasting and Social Change with 9 articles (2.33%).

Outside the journal, there are several other titles, such as a book entitled Big Data Science and Analytics for Smart Sustainable Urbanism which contains 4 documents (1.04%) or proceedings such as Procedia Manufacturing with 3 documents (0.77%). The variety of publication titles, both in terms of titles and fields of science, shows the multidisciplinary nature of big data and sustainability innovation and attracts the attention of researchers from different disciplines.

Funding agencies

The Web of Science also records data on funding agencies. Funding agencies that sponsored the most documents were the National Natural Science Foundation of China (NSFC) with 34 articles (8.81%), followed by the European Commission with 11 articles (2.85%), and Coordenacao De Aperfeicoamento De Pesjual De Nivel Superior Capes, Brazil with 8 articles (2.07%).

In addition, other funders from various parts of the world have also funded these studies. For example, UK Research Innovation (UKRI) with 6 articles (1.55%), Ministry of Education Culture Sports Science and Technology (MEXT) with 4 articles (1.04%), National Institutes of Health (NIH) the USA with 2 articles (0.52%). The diversity of funders indicates enthusiasm for developing big data, including developing sustainable innovations.

Index

Considering that the Web of Science database consists of various specific indexes, as shown in Figure 4, the composition of the documents is based on the index. The largest index is the Social Sciences Citation Index (SSCI) with 202 documents (52.33%), followed by the Science Citation Index Expanded (SCI-Expanded) with 181 documents (46.89%) and the Emerging Sources Citation Index (ESCI) with 53 documents (13.73%).

Figure 4. WoS Index
Source: Web of Science, 2021

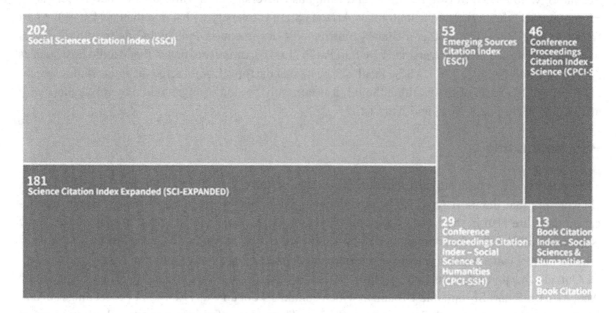

Subsequently, it was followed by a conference and book citation index, namely the Conference Proceedings Citation Index – Science (CPCI-S) with 46 documents (11.92%), Conference Proceedings Citation Index – Social Science & Humanities (CPCI-SSH) with 29 documents. (7.51%), Book Citation Index – Social Sciences & Humanities (BKCI-SSH) with 13 documents (3.37%) and Book Citation Index – Science (BKCI-S) with 8 documents (2.07%). There are two things to be learned here. First, the majority of the documents are in the main indexation, which includes journals; specifically, the first three indexes are SSCI, SCI-Expanded, and ESCI. Second, the two most dominant indexes are a combination of indexes containing journals in the field of social sciences (SSCI) and journals more in the field of science and technology (SCI-Expanded).

Clusters of concepts

The clusters of concepts are accomplished by analyzing the co-occurrence keywords from the documents included in the review. Co-occurrence analysis is performed by analyzing document metadata using VOSViewer software and analyzing all keywords in WoS from both the author and the database. As a default in the software, 116 keywords with co-occurrence of at least 5 times were obtained from a list of 2182 keywords. The analysis yielded the results of six concept clusters (Figure 5).

Figure 5. Cluster of Concepts
Source: Authors' elaboration based on Web of Science, 2021, generated by VOSViewer

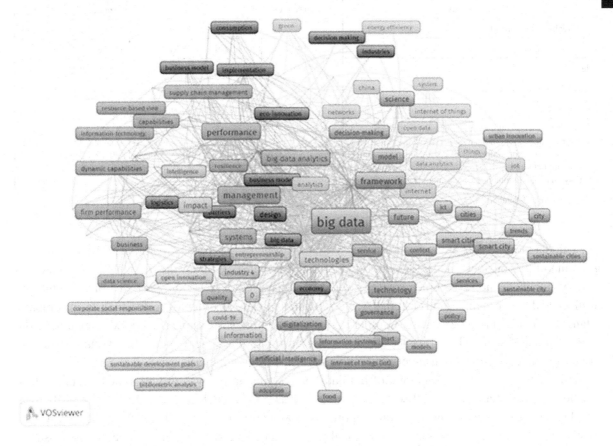

Cluster 1: Circular Economy and Sustainable Development

The first cluster discusses several topics related to sustainable development, circular economy, design, business model innovation, knowledge, and other topics (Table 1). The discussion of big data for sustainability innovation certainly cannot be separated from the keyword sustainable development, which includes a discussion of the implications of industry 4.0 on sustainability and ecosystem support for digital sustainability development (Bonilla et al., 2018; Stuermer et al., 2017). The concept of digital sustainability development is related to the circular economy which is concerned with reducing the consumption of natural resources and protecting the environment, which involves various domains, including technology management (Centobelli et al., 2020). To be able to support the circular economy requires a good design of digital solutions (Bibri & Krogstie, 2017; Kumar et al., 2020).

Table 1. The first cluster of concepts and examples of references

Keywords	Occurrences	Example of references
sustainable development	40	(Bonilla et al., 2018), (Stuermer et al., 2017)
circular economy	19	(Centobelli et al., 2020); (Konietzko et al., 2020)
design	17	(Kumar et al., 2020); (Bibri & Krogstie, 2017)
business model innovation	14	(Visconti & Morea, 2019); (Minatogawa et al., 2020)
knowledge	10	(Klerkx et al., 2019); (Di Vaio et al., 2020)
business models; economy; implementation; barriers; smes; eco-innovation; indicators; perspective; creation; business model; consumption; big-data; decision making; evolution; firm; industries; logistics; product; strategies; supply chains; sustainable business model;	Less than 10 each	(Hidalgo-Carvajal et al., 2021); (Onu & Mbohwa, 2021; Zigiene et al., 2019); (Cui et al., 2019); (Cetin et al., 2021)

Source: Web of Science, 2021

The data on the first cluster concept shows that that one of the most essential aspects to achieving sustainability is business model innovation to facilitate a smooth day-to-day operation. Using case studies on sustainable fashion e-commerce enterprises, Minatogawa et al. (2020) propose that big data may be utilized to develop creative and customer-driven business models. In order to create a long-term company plan, you'll need a lot of expertise. In order to construct a more sustainable society, were exploring the development of artificial intelligence and machine learning for the development of sustainable business models by understanding consumer production and consumption patterns.

Furthermore, the implementation of big data for sustainable innovation will almost certainly face challenges, especially for small-scale businesses (Hidalgo-Carvajal et al., 2021; Onu & Mbohwa, 2021). Onu & Mbohwa explore various opportunities and barriers from implementing industry 4.0 for SMEs in manufacturing to improve operational performance and sustainability, especially for business organizations in Africa. To deal with these various opportunities and barriers, careful decision-making and strategies are needed. Decision-making, for example, can be assisted by the DEMATEL method to convert expert opinions into more measurable and quantifiable data so that they can provide better outcomes (Cui et al., 2019).

Cluster 2: Innovation and Management

In the second cluster, the most prominent keywords are innovation and management (Table 2). There are quite a number of documents that publish research from previous researchers regarding the relationship between sustainability innovation and business performance mediated by big data. El-Kassar & Singh (2019), as an example, using a sample of respondents from the Middle East, North Africa and Gulf Cooperation Countries, examines the effect of green innovation on firm performance by considering the influence of big data in the relationship. Similar research was also conducted by Song et al. (2019). Both El-Kassar & Singh (2019) and Song et al. (2019) are the most cited documents in WoS with 162 and 102 citations, respectively. Several researchers investigated similar phenomena in specific sectors such as agriculture (Rose & Chilvers, 2018) or healthcare (Papa et al., 2020).

Table 2. The second cluster of concepts and examples of references

Keywords	Occurrences	Example of references
innovation	117	(El-Kassar & Singh, 2019); (Song et al., 2019); (Rose & Chilvers, 2018); (Papa et al., 2020); (Mora et al., 2019)
management	58	(Belaud et al., 2014); (Schuelke-Leech et al., 2015); (Brenner, 2018)
performance	39	(Bag et al., 2020)
big data analytics	35	(Raut et al., 2021)
systems	26	(Waibel et al., 2018)
industry 4.0	25	(Bonilla et al., 2018)
strategy	22	(Nan & Tanriverdi, 2017)
firm performance	17	(Erkmen et al., 2020)
capabilities	13	(El Hilali et al., 2020)
supply chain management	13	(Bui et al., 2021)
predictive analytics	12	(Adjekum et al., 2017)
business	10	(Strandhagen et al., 2017)
dynamic capabilities	10	(Ramadan et al., 2020)
quality	10	(Shivajee et al., 2019)
supply chain	10	(Mehmood et al., 2017)
Integration; competitive advantage; resource-based view; data science; environmental performance; financial performance; information-technology; resilience	Less than 10 each	(Munodawafa & Johl, 2019); (Ali et al., 2020); (Kabongo, 2019); (Carayannis et al., 2017)

Source: Web of Science, 2021

The relevance of innovation management is demonstrated by the data on the third cluster concept. This cluster particularly mentions different types of capabilities. As an example, dynamic capabilities and technological capabilities such as the ability to implement big data analytics (Raut et al., 2021); as well as various vital decisions in operations management such as supply chain management and quality management (Bui et al., 2021; Shivajee et al., 2019; Usman et al., 2021). These capabilities are expected to produce a good firm performance (Ali et al., 2020; Kabongo, 2019) and provide a competitive advantage and resilience in the long term (Carayannis et al., 2017; Munodawafa & Johl, 2019).

Cluster 3: Big Data and Business Model Innovation

The third cluster discusses one of the main concepts that are the focus of this chapter, namely big data, as well as other important concepts such as d business model innovation (Table 3). A prominent document that uses the keyword big data is Wu et al. (2016), cited 166x in WoS, which suggested that big data is one of the most powerful drivers to support innovation, especially innovations related to green challenges and revolutions.

Table 3. The third cluster of concepts and examples of references

Keywords	Occurrences	Example of references
big data	184	(Wu et al., 2016), (Lim et al., 2018), (Singh & El-Kassar, 2019), (Song et al., 2019), (Pappas et al., 2018)
framework	45	(Avdiushchenko, 2018)
challenges	39	(Islam et al., 2015)
future	30	(Lajoie-O'Malley et al., 2020)
smart city	21	(Yigitcanlar et al., 2020)
model	19	(Konietzko et al., 2020)
science	18	(Horowitz et al., 2017)
smart cities	17	(de Souza et al., 2019)
cities	13	(Cowley & Caprotti, 2019)
opportunities	13	(Stahel, 2008)
decision-making	11	(Xia et al., 2017)
city	10	(Mehmood et al., 2017)
context; ict; sustainable cities; service; trends; machine learning; models; smart sustainable cities; sustainable city; urban innovation	Less than 10 each	(Bibri & Krogstie, 2017); (Goncalves et al., 2021); (Zheng et al., 2020)

Source: Web of Science, 2021

These challenges are faced by various organizational forms, both business organizations and non-business organizations, including cities which also face challenges to innovate and at the same time be sustainable and can become smart cities (Lim et al., 2018). In enterprises, big data plays an important role along the supply chain and inevitably faces various technological challenges (Singh & El-Kassar, 2019; Song et al., 2019). The development of big data in sustainability innovation is important in line with the digital transformation that is taking place as well as a path to a more sustainable society (Pappas et al., 2018).

There are considerable documents that discuss smart and sustainable cities in this cluster. For example, analysis of best practices from various parts of the world from Songdo to San Francisco (Yigitcanlar et al., 2019). In developing smart and sustainable cities, de Souza et al. (2019) found that the use of data mining and machine learning plays an important role, especially through smarter mobility. Mehmood et al. (2017) developing a model with multiple scenarios regarding the transformation of urban transportation to become smarter through the use of big data.

Cluster 4: Sustainability and Impact

Sustainability and impact are two prominent keywords in the fourth cluster (Table 4). This indicates the importance of big data to have a real impact in realizing a more innovative and sustainable economy. The following keywords appear more than ten times in the analyzed documents: technologies, information, industry, and industry 4 (4.0), followed by corporate social responsibility, education, entrepreneurship, and open innovation.

Table 4. The fourth cluster of concepts and examples of references

B

Keywords	Occurrences	Example of references
sustainability	70	(Bebbington & Unerman, 2018); (Wu et al., 2016); (Bonilla et al., 2018)
impact	30	(Bianchini et al., 2019)
technologies	27	(Gossling, 2021)
information	21	(Olszewski et al., 2018)
industry	13	(Santos et al., 2017)
industry 4	13	(Bai et al., 2020)
corporate social-responsibility; sustainable development goals; bibliometric analysis; intelligence; tourism; covid-19; education; entrepreneurship; open innovation	Less than 10 each	(Gurzawska, 2020); (Fiorentino et al., 2020); (Cappa et al., 2020); (Dooley, 2021); (Pizzi et al., 2020)

Source: Web of Science, 2021

Considering that this chapter discusses the role of big data for sustainability innovation, it is not surprising that it became one of the central topics. Sustainability requires the role of various stakeholders from practitioners, policymakers, academics, and society in general (Bebbington & Unerman, 2018). This multi-stakeholder involvement is because the challenges in optimizing big data to have a significant impact on sustainability are very high (Bonilla et al., 2018). These challenges include challenges from the point of view of the natural environment and social environment (Wu et al., 2016). Education and effort to encourage citizen participation are critical in promoting effective multi-stakeholder engagement (Dooley, 2021; Pizzi et al., 2020).

Among the techniques proposed by the author to overcome various barriers is using a new visualization tool or gamification. New visualization is considered effective in overcoming various barriers to be more sustainable (Bianchini et al., 2019). Gamification, for example, can be applied as a form of sustainability innovation in urban transportation (Olszewski et al., 2018). These techniques, when combined with big data, have the potential to drive Industry 4.0 strategies in a variety of industries (Bai et al., 2020; Gossling, 2021; Santos et al., 2017). Specific sectors studied, for example, are tourism (Gossling, 2021), air navigation service (Fiorentino et al., 2020), cultural heritage (Cappa et al., 2020), education (Pizzi et al., 2020).

Cluster 5: Technology

The fifth cluster is almost entirely concerned with technology. Artificial intelligence (AI), digitalization, precision agriculture, and the internet of things (IoT) are among the most popular technology-related keywords (Table 5). Technology, particularly IoT and big data, is crucial to organizational performance. (El-Kassar & Singh, 2019).

Table 5. The fifth cluster of concepts and examples of references

Keywords	Occurrences	Example of references
technology	27	(El-Kassar & Singh, 2019); (Tachizawa et al., 2015); (Chalvatzis et al., 2019)
artificial intelligence	13	(Dadi et al., 2021)
digitalization	11	(Felsberger & Reiner, 2020)
governance	11	(Brennan et al., 2019)
precision agriculture	10	(Rose & Chilvers, 2018)
Adoption; digital transformation; sharing economy; business; intelligence; policy; food; information-systems; services; smart; internet of things (iot)	Less than 10 each	(Belli et al., 2020); (Hayat et al., 2020); (Ding, 2018)

Source: Web of Science, 2021

The technology mentioned in this cluster that is used relatively frequently is artificial intelligence (AI). Previous researchers examined the application of AI and related technology in agri-food (Dadi et al., 2021), textile (Hayat et al., 2020), pharmaceutical (Ding, 2018), built environment (Tachizawa et al., 2015), or resource allocation for the power generation (Chalvatzis et al., 2019). These technology applications are part of digital transformation and digitization, which are in high demand today (Felsberger & Reiner, 2020).

Cluster 6: Internet of Things (IoT)

The sixth cluster contains the most important internet and internet of things keywords (Table 6). This is not surprising given that the discussion of big data is always accompanied by the internet that allows companies and other entities to obtain large volumes of data at previously unimaginable speeds. Another term that appears is analytics, which is almost always used in conjunction with big data because big data without analytics produces no insightful information for the decision-making process.

Table 6. The sixth cluster of concepts and examples of references

Keywords	Occurrences	Example of references
internet	22	(Latif et al., 2017); (Villegas-Ch et al., 2020)
internet of things	16	(Makori, 2017)
analytics	15	(Adjekum et al., 2017)
iot	14	(Belli et al., 2020)
networks	14	(Turkina & Oreshkin, 2021)
china	11	(N. Zhang & Chen, 2017)
data analytics; green; system; things; energy; energy efficiency; environmental sustainability; open data	Less than 10 each	(Nozari et al., 2021), (Cui et al., 2019), (Corrales-Garay et al., 2020)

Source: Web of Science, 2021

Specific topics found in documents about big data and sustainability innovation include the use of 5G technology (Latif et al., 2017), IoT dan blockchain (Villegas-Ch et al., 2020), and IoT in academic and library settings (Makori, 2017). Precision medicine was researched in the health sector (Adjekum et al., 2017), while data analytics in supply chain management was researched in the FMCG industry to optimize decision making and company productivity (Nozari et al., 2021). Aside from productivity, data analytics plays a role in green efficiency (Cui et al., 2019). Tseng & Hsu (2019) conducted an interesting study on the role of IoT in increasing family interaction. In the field of entrepreneurship, while Turkina & Oreshkin (2021) investigated co-inventor networks, and (Corrales-Garay et al., 2020) researched the importance of open data for entrepreneurship.

FUTURE RESEARCH DIRECTIONS

Progression work on the study in this chapter is a more specific analysis on specific business sectors because the present study is carried out on various business sectors. Analysis of specific business sectors is expected to provide a more in-depth understanding of big data and sustainability innovation in that sector. Future research can also compare the implementation and impact of big data for the development of sustainability innovation before, during, and after the pandemic Covid-19. This is due to the fact that the Covid-19 pandemic is an extraordinary event that is very likely to change how organizations use big data for the development of sustainability innovation. In terms of the literature review, additional research can be conducted by restricting the search and analysis to documents of the journal article type only, accompanied by an assessment of the journal's quality, to obtain sharper insights based on peer-reviewed documents of the highest level of quality and impact. In the future, the quality of search process can also be improved by manually filtering relevance, wherever possible, improvement in pre-processing and using document quality proxies based on the title source qualities.

CONCLUSION

The present chapter aims to understand the development of big data for sustainable innovation in the academic literature. This chapter shows that the development of big data studies for sustainability innovation has developed in the last 10 years by involving various research areas such as environmental science, science technology, business economics, engineering and computer science. The authors on this topic come from all over the world, especially Europe, China, and America, with major outlets such as Sustainability, Journal of Cleaner Production, and Technological Forecasting and Social Change. This chapter has identified six keywords cluster where sustainable development and circular economy are the prominent keywords in the first cluster, innovation and management in the second cluster, big data and framework in the third cluster, sustainability and impact in the fourth cluster, technology and artificial intelligence in the fifth cluster, and internet and internet of things in the sixth cluster. Of the six clusters, the nuances of big data seem to be strong in the third, fifth, and sixth clusters; while the nuances of sustainability innovation are strong in the first, second, and fourth clusters.

REFERENCES

Adams, R., Jeanrenaud, S., Bessant, J., Denyer, D., & Overy, P. (2016). Sustainability-oriented Innovation: A Systematic Review. *International Journal of Management Reviews*, *18*(2), 180–205. doi:10.1111/ijmr.12068

Adjekum, A., Ienca, M., & Vayena, E. (2017). What Is Trust? Ethics and Risk Governance in Precision Medicine and Predictive Analytics. *OMICS: A Journal of Integrative Biology*, *21*(12), 704–710. doi:10.1089/omi.2017.0156 PMID:29257733

Ali, Q., Salman, A., Yaacob, H., Zaini, Z., & Abdullah, R. (2020). Does Big Data Analytics Enhance Sustainability and Financial Performance? The Case of ASEAN Banks. *Journal of Asian Finance Economics and Business*, *7*(7), 1–13. doi:10.13106/jafeb.2020.vol7.no7.001

Avdiushchenko, A. (2018). Toward a Circular Economy Regional Monitoring Framework for European Regions: Conceptual Approach. *Sustainability*, *10*(12), 4398. Advance online publication. doi:10.3390u10124398

Azis, Y., Darun, M. R., Kartini, D., Bernik, M., & Harsanto, B. (2017). A model of managing innovation of SMEs in Indonesia Creative Industries. *International Journal of Business and Society*, *18*(35), 391–408.

Bag, S., Wood, L. C., Xu, L., Dhamija, P., & Kayikci, Y. (2020). Big data analytics as an operational excellence approach to enhance sustainable supply chain performance. *Resources, Conservation and Recycling*, *153*, 104559. Advance online publication. doi:10.1016/j.resconrec.2019.104559

Bai, C. G., Dallasega, P., Orzes, G., & Sarkis, J. (2020). Industry 4.0 technologies assessment: A sustainability perspective. *International Journal of Production Economics*, *229*, 107776. Advance online publication. doi:10.1016/j.ijpe.2020.107776

Bebbington, J., & Unerman, J. (2018). Achieving the United Nations Sustainable Development Goals: An enabling role for accounting research. *Accounting, Auditing & Accountability Journal*, *31*(1), 2–24. doi:10.1108/AAAJ-05-2017-2929

Belaud, J. P., Negny, S., Dupros, F., Michea, D., & Vautrin, B. (2014). Collaborative simulation and scientific big data analysis: Illustration for sustainability in natural hazards management and chemical process engineering. *Computers in Industry*, *65*(3), 521–535. doi:10.1016/j.compind.2014.01.009

Belli, L., Cilfone, A., Davoli, L., Ferrari, G., Adorni, P., Di Nocera, F., Dall'Olio, A., Pellegrini, C., Mordacci, M., & Bertolotti, E. (2020). IoT-Enabled Smart Sustainable Cities: Challenges and Approaches. *Smart Cities*, *3*(3), 1039–1071. doi:10.3390martcities3030052

Bianchini, A., Rossi, J., & Pellegrini, M. (2019). Overcoming the Main Barriers of Circular Economy Implementation through a New Visualization Tool for Circular Business Models. *Sustainability*, *11*(23), 6614. Advance online publication. doi:10.3390u11236614

Bibri, S. E., & Krogstie, J. (2017). ICT of the new wave of computing for sustainable urban forms: Their big data and context-aware augmented typologies and design concepts. *Sustainable Cities and Society*, *32*, 449–474. doi:10.1016/j.scs.2017.04.012

Bonilla, S. H., Silva, H. R. O., da Silva, M. T., Goncalves, R. F., & Sacomano, J. B. (2018). Industry 4.0 and Sustainability Implications: A Scenario-Based Analysis of the Impacts and Challenges. *Sustainability*, *10*(10), 3740. Advance online publication. doi:10.3390u10103740

Brennan, N. M., Subramaniam, N., & van Staden, C. J. (2019). Corporate governance implications of disruptive technology: An overview. *The British Accounting Review*, *51*(6), 100860. Advance online publication. doi:10.1016/j.bar.2019.100860

Brenner, B. (2018). Transformative Sustainable Business Models in the Light of the Digital ImperativeA Global Business Economics Perspective. *Sustainability*, *10*(12), 4428. Advance online publication. doi:10.3390u10124428

Bui, T. D., Tsai, F. M., Tseng, M. L., Tan, R. D. R., Yu, K. D. S., & Lim, M. K. (2021). Sustainable supply chain management towards disruption and organizational ambidexterity: A data driven analysis. *Sustainable Production snd Consumption, 26*, 373–410. doi:10.1016/j.spc.2020.09.017

Calic, G., & Ghasemaghaei, M. (2021). Big data for social benefits: Innovation as a mediator of the relationship between big data and corporate social performance. *Journal of Business Research, 131*(February), 391–401. doi:10.1016/j.jbusres.2020.11.003

Cappa, F., Rosso, F., & Capaldo, A. (2020). Visitor-Sensing: Involving the Crowd in Cultural Heritage Organizations. *Sustainability*, *12*(4), 1445. Advance online publication. doi:10.3390u12041445

Carayannis, E. G., Grigoroudis, E., Del Giudice, M., Della Peruta, M. R., & Sindakis, S. (2017). An exploration of contemporary organizational artifacts and routines in a sustainable excellence context. *Journal of Knowledge Management*, *21*(1), 35–56. doi:10.1108/JKM-10-2015-0366

Centobelli, P., Cerchione, R., Chiaroni, D., Del Vecchio, P., & Urbinati, A. (2020). Designing business models in circular economy: A systematic literature review and research agenda. *Business Strategy andtThe Environment, 29*(4), 1734–1749. doi:10.1002/bse.2466

Cetin, S., De Wolf, C., & Bocken, N. (2021). Circular Digital Built Environment: An Emerging Framework. *Sustainability*, *13*(11), 6348. Advance online publication. doi:10.3390u13116348

Chalvatzis, K. J., Malekpoor, H., Mishra, N., Lettice, F., & Choudhary, S. (2019). Sustainable resource allocation for power generation: The role of big data in enabling interindustry architectural innovation. *Technological Forecasting and Social Change*, *144*, 381–393. doi:10.1016/j.techfore.2018.04.031

Corrales-Garay, D., Mora-Valentin, E. M., & Ortiz-de-Urbina-Criado, M. (2020). Entrepreneurship Through Open Data: An Opportunity for Sustainable Development. *Sustainability*, *12*(12), 5148. Advance online publication. doi:10.3390u12125148

Cowley, R., & Caprotti, F. (2019). Smart city as anti-planning in the UK. *Environment and Planning. D, Society & Space*, *37*(3), 428–448. doi:10.1177/0263775818787506

Cui, L., Chan, H. K., Zhou, Y., Dai, J., & Lim, J. J. (2019). Exploring critical factors of green business failure based on Grey-Decision Making Trial and Evaluation Laboratory (DEMATEL). *Journal of Business Research*, *98*, 450–461. doi:10.1016/j.jbusres.2018.03.031

Dadi, V., Nikla, S. R., Moe, R. S., Agarwal, T., & Arora, S. (2021). Agri-Food 4.0 and Innovations: Revamping the Supply Chain Operations. *Production Engineering Archives, 27*(2), 75–89. doi:10.30657/pea.2021.27.10

Dana, L.-P., Salamzadeh, A., Mortazavi, S., & Hadizadeh, M. (2022). Investigating the Impact of International Markets and New Digital Technologies on Business Innovation in Emerging Markets. *Sustainability, 14*(2), 983. doi:10.3390u14020983

de Souza, J. T., de Francisco, A. C., Piekarski, C. M., & do Prado, G. F. (2019). Data Mining and Machine Learning to Promote Smart Cities: A Systematic Review from 2000 to 2018. *Sustainability, 11*(4), 1077. Advance online publication. doi:10.3390u11041077

Di Vaio, A., Palladino, R., Hassan, R., & Escobar, O. (2020). Artificial intelligence and business models in the sustainable development goals perspective: A systematic literature review. *Journal of Business Research, 121*, 283–314. doi:10.1016/j.jbusres.2020.08.019

Ding, B. Y. (2018). Pharma Industry 4.0: Literature review and research opportunities in sustainable pharmaceutical supply chains. *Process Safety and Environmental Protection, 119*, 115–130. doi:10.1016/j.psep.2018.06.031

Dooley, K. (2021). Direct Passive Participation: Aiming for Accuracy and Citizen Safety in the Era of Big Data and the Smart City. *Smart Cities, 4*(1), 336–348. doi:10.3390martcities4010020

El Hilali, W., El Manouar, A., & Idrissi, M. A. J. (2020). Reaching sustainability during a digital transformation: A PLS approach. *International Journal of Innovation Science, 12*(1), 52–79. doi:10.1108/IJIS-08-2019-0083

El-Kassar, A. N., & Singh, S. K. (2019). Green innovation and organizational performance: The influence of big data and the moderating role of management commitment and HR practices. *Technological Forecasting and Social Change, 144*(December), 483–498. doi:10.1016/j.techfore.2017.12.016

Erkmen, T., Gunsel, A., & Altindag, E. (2020). The Role of Innovative Climate in the Relationship between Sustainable IT Capability and Firm Performance. *Sustainability, 12*(10), 4058. Advance online publication. doi:10.3390u12104058

Felsberger, A., & Reiner, G. (2020). Sustainable Industry 4.0 in Production and Operations Management: A Systematic Literature Review. *Sustainability, 12*(19), 7982. Advance online publication. doi:10.3390u12197982

Fiorentino, R., Grimaldi, F., Lamboglia, R., & Merendino, A. (2020). How smart technologies can support sustainable business models: Insights from an air navigation service provider. *Management Decision, 58*(8), 1715–1736. doi:10.1108/MD-09-2019-1327

Ghasemaghaei, M., Hassanein, K., & Turel, O. (2017). Increasing firm agility through the use of data analytics: The role of fit. *Decision Support Systems, 101*, 95–105. doi:10.1016/j.dss.2017.06.004

Goncalves, G. D., Leal, W., Neiva, S. D., Deggau, A. B., Veras, M. D., Ceci, F., de Lima, M. A., & Guerra, J. (2021). The Impacts of the Fourth Industrial Revolution on Smart and Sustainable Cities. *Sustainability, 13*(13), 7165. Advance online publication. doi:10.3390u13137165

Gossling, S. (2021). Technology, ICT and tourism: From big data to the big picture. *Journal of Sustainable Tourism*, *29*(5), 849–858. doi:10.1080/09669582.2020.1865387

Gumbira, G., & Harsanto, B. (2019). Decision support system for an eco-friendly integrated coastal zone management (ICZM) in Indonesia. *International Journal on Advanced Science, Engineering and Information Technology*, *9*(4), 1177. doi:10.18517/ijaseit.9.4.9484

Gurzawska, A. (2020). Towards Responsible and Sustainable Supply Chains - Innovation, Multi-stakeholder Approach and Governance. *Philosophy of Management*, *19*(3), 267–295. doi:10.100740926-019-00114-z

Hansen, E. G., & Große-Dunker, F. (2013). Sustainability-Oriented Innovation. In *Encyclopedia of Corporate Social Responsibility* (pp. 2407–2417). Springer-Verlag Berlin Heidelberg. doi:10.1007/978-3-642-28036-8_552

Harsanto, B. (2020a). Eco-Innovation Research in Indonesia: A Systematic Review and Future Directions. *Journal of STI Policy and Management*, *5*(2), 179–191. doi:10.14203/STIPM.2020.281

Harsanto, B. (2020b). The First-Three-Month Review of Research on Covid-19: A Scientometrics Analysis. *IEEE International Conference on Engineering, Technology and Innovation (ICE/ITMC)*. 10.1109/ICE/ITMC49519.2020.9198316

Harsanto, B. (2021). Innovation Management in the Library: A Bibliometric Analysis. *Library Philosophy and Practice*, *2021*, 1–12.

Harsanto, B., Kumar, N., Zhan, Y., & Michaelides, R. (2020). Firms ' ICT and Innovation in Jakarta Metropolitan Area. *2020 International Conference on Technology and Entrepreneurship - Virtual*, 1–4. 10.1109/ICTE-V50708.2020.9113778

Harsanto, B., Michaelides, R., & Drummond, H. (2018). Sustainability-oriented Innovation (SOI) in Emerging Economies: A Preliminary Investigation from Indonesia. *2018 IEEE International Conference on Industrial Engineering and Engineering Management (IEEM)*, 1553–1557. 10.1109/IEEM.2018.8607473

Harsanto, B., & Permana, C. T. (2019). Understanding Sustainability-oriented Innovation (SOI) Using Network Perspective in Asia Pacific and ASEAN : A Systematic Review. *The Journal of Asian Studies*, *7*(1), 1–17.

Harsanto, B., & Permana, C. T. (2021). Sustainability-oriented innovation (SOI) in the cultural village: An actor-network perspective in the case of Laweyan Batik Village. *Journal of Cultural Heritage Management and Sustainable Development*, *11*(3), 297–311. doi:10.1108/JCHMSD-08-2019-0102

Hayat, N., Hussain, A., & Lohano, H. D. (2020). Eco-labeling and sustainability: A case of textile industry in Pakistan. *Journal of Cleaner Production*, *252*, 119807. Advance online publication. doi:10.1016/j.jclepro.2019.119807

Hidalgo-Carvajal, D., Carrasco-Gallego, R., & Morales-Alonso, G. (2021). From Goods to Services and from Linear to Circular: The Role of Servitization's Challenges and Drivers in the Shifting Process. *Sustainability*, *13*(8), 4539. Advance online publication. doi:10.3390u13084539

Horowitz, C. R., Shameer, K., Gabrilove, J., Atreja, A., Shepard, P., Goytia, C. N., Smith, G. W., Dudley, J., Manning, R., Bickell, N. A., & Galvez, M. P. (2017). Accelerators: Sparking Innovation and Transdisciplinary Team Science in Disparities Research. *International Journal of Environmental Research and Public Health*, *14*(3), 225. Advance online publication. doi:10.3390/ijerph14030225 PMID:28241508

IBM. (2022). *Co-occurrence Rules - IBM Documentation.* https://www.ibm.com/docs/ja/stafs/4.0.1?topic=techniques-co-occurrence-rules

Islam, S. M. R., Kwak, D., Kabir, M. H., Hossain, M., & Kwak, K. S. (2015). The Internet of Things for Health Care: A Comprehensive Survey. *IEEE Access: Practical Innovations, Open Solutions*, *3*, 678–708. doi:10.1109/ACCESS.2015.2437951

Kabongo, J. D. (2019). Sustainable development and research and development intensity in US manufacturing firms. *Business Strategy and the Environment*, *28*(4), 556–566. doi:10.1002/bse.2264

Klerkx, L., Jakku, E., & Labarthe, P. (2019). A review of social science on digital agriculture, smart farming and agriculture 4.0: New contributions and a future research agenda. *NJAS Wageningen Journal of Life Sciences*, *90–91*(1), 1–16. Advance online publication. doi:10.1016/j.njas.2019.100315

Konietzko, J., Bocken, N., & Hultink, E. J. (2020). A Tool to Analyze, Ideate and Develop Circular Innovation Ecosystems. *Sustainability*, *12*(1), 417. Advance online publication. doi:10.3390u12010417

Kumar, H., Singh, M. K., Gupta, M. P., & Madaan, J. (2020). Moving towards smart cities: Solutions that lead to the Smart City Transformation Framework. *Technological Forecasting and Social Change*, *153*, 119281. Advance online publication. doi:10.1016/j.techfore.2018.04.024

Lajoie-O'Malley, A., Bronson, K., van der Burg, S., & Klerkx, L. (2020). The future(s) of digital agriculture and sustainable food systems: An analysis of high-level policy documents. *Ecosystem Services*, *45*, 101183. Advance online publication. doi:10.1016/j.ecoser.2020.101183

Latif, S., Qadir, J., Farooq, S., & Imran, M. A. (2017). How 5G Wireless (and Concomitant Technologies) Will Revolutionize Healthcare? *Future Internet*, *9*(4), 93. Advance online publication. doi:10.3390/fi9040093

Lim, C., Kim, K. J., & Maglio, P. P. (2018). Smart cities with big data: Reference models, challenges, and considerations. *Cities (London, England)*, *82*, 86–99. doi:10.1016/j.cities.2018.04.011

Love, P. E. D., Matthews, J., & Zhou, J. (2020). Is it just too good to be true? Unearthing the benefits of disruptive technology. *International Journal of Information Management*, *52*, 102096. doi:10.1016/j.ijinfomgt.2020.102096

Makori, E. O. (2017). Promoting innovation and application of internet of things in academic and research information organizations. *Library Review*, *66*(8–9), 655–678. doi:10.1108/LR-01-2017-0002

Mehmood, R., Meriton, R., Graham, G., Hennelly, P., & Kumar, M. (2017). Exploring the influence of big data on city transport operations: A Markovian approach. *International Journal of Operations & Production Management*, *37*(1), 75–104. doi:10.1108/IJOPM-03-2015-0179

Minatogawa, V. L. F., Franco, M. M. V., Rampasso, I. S., Anholon, R., Quadros, R., Duran, O., & Batocchio, A. (2020). Operationalizing Business Model Innovation through Big Data Analytics for Sustainable Organizations. *Sustainability*, *12*(1), 277. Advance online publication. doi:10.3390u12010277

Mora, L., Deakin, M., & Reid, A. (2019). Strategic principles for smart city development: A multiple case study analysis of European best practices. *Technological Forecasting and Social Change*, *142*, 70–97. doi:10.1016/j.techfore.2018.07.035

Müller, O., Fay, M., & vom Brocke, J. (2018). The Effect of Big Data and Analytics on Firm Performance: An Econometric Analysis Considering Industry Characteristics. *Journal of Management Information Systems*, *35*(2), 488–509. doi:10.1080/07421222.2018.1451955

Munodawafa, R. T., & Johl, S. K. (2019). Big Data Analytics Capabilities and Eco-Innovation: A Study of Energy Companies. *Sustainability*, *11*(15), 4254. Advance online publication. doi:10.3390u11154254

Nan, N., & Tanriverdi, H. (2017). Unifying The Role of IT In Hyperturbulence and Competitive Advantage Via a Multilevel Perspective of IS Strategy. *Management Information Systems Quarterly*, *41*(3), 937–958. doi:10.25300/MISQ/2017/41.3.12

Nozari, H., Fallah, M., Kazemipoor, H., & Najafi, S. E. (2021). Big data analysis of IoT-based supply chain management considering FMCG industries. *Biznes Informatika-Business Informatics*, *15*(1), 78–96. doi:10.17323/2587-814X.2021.1.78.96

Nunan, D., & Di Domenico, M. (2017). Big data: A normal accident waiting to happen? *Journal of Business Ethics*, *145*(3), 481–491. doi:10.100710551-015-2904-x

Olszewski, R., Palka, P., & Turek, A. (2018). Solving "Smart City" Transport Problems by Designing Carpooling Gamification Schemes with Multi-Agent Systems: The Case of the So-Called "Mordor of Warsaw.". *Sensors (Basel)*, *18*(1), 141. Advance online publication. doi:10.339018010141 PMID:29316643

Onu, P., & Mbohwa, C. (2021). Industry 4.0 opportunities in manufacturing SMEs: Sustainability outlook. In *Materials Today-Proceedings* (Vol. 44, pp. 1925–1930). 10.1016/j.matpr.2020.12.095

Ozer, K., Sahin, M. A., & Cetin, G. (2022). Integrating Big Data to Smart Destination Heritage Management. In *Handbook of Research on Digital Communications, Internet of Things, and the Future of Cultural Tourism* (pp. 411–429). IGI Global. doi:10.4018/978-1-7998-8528-3.ch022

Papa, A., Mital, M., Pisano, P., & Del Giudice, M. (2020). E-health and wellbeing monitoring using smart healthcare devices: An empirical investigation. *Technological Forecasting and Social Change*, *153*, 119226. Advance online publication. doi:10.1016/j.techfore.2018.02.018

Pappas, I. O., Mikalef, P., Giannakos, M. N., Krogstie, J., & Lekakos, G. (2018). Big data and business analytics ecosystems: Paving the way towards digital transformation and sustainable societies. *Information Systems and e-Business Management*, *16*(3), 479–491. doi:10.100710257-018-0377-z

Pizzi, S., Caputo, A., Corvino, A., & Venturelli, A. (2020). Management research and the UN sustainable development goals (SDGs): A bibliometric investigation and systematic review. *Journal of Cleaner Production*, *276*, 124033. Advance online publication. doi:10.1016/j.jclepro.2020.124033

Ramadan, M., Shuqqo, H., Qtaishat, L., Asmar, H., & Salah, B. (2020). Sustainable Competitive Advantage Driven by Big Data Analytics and Innovation. *Applied Sciences-Basel*, *10*(19), 6784. Advance online publication. doi:10.3390/app10196784

Raut, R. D., Mangla, S. K., Narwane, V. S., Dora, M., & Liu, M. Q. (2021). Big Data Analytics as a mediator in Lean, Agile, Resilient, and Green (LARG) practices effects on sustainable supply chains. *Transportation Research Part E, Logistics and Transportation Review*, *145*, 102170. Advance online publication. doi:10.1016/j.tre.2020.102170

Rose, D. C., & Chilvers, J. (2018). Agriculture 4.0: Broadening Responsible Innovation in an Era of Smart Farming. *Frontiers in Sustainable Food Systems*, *2*, 87. Advance online publication. doi:10.3389/fsufs.2018.00087

Santos, M. Y., Sa, J. E., Andrade, C., Lima, F. V., Costa, E., Costa, C., Martinho, B., & Galvao, J. (2017). A Big Data system supporting Bosch Braga Industry 4.0 strategy. *International Journal of Information Management*, *37*(6), 750–760. doi:10.1016/j.ijinfomgt.2017.07.012

Schneider, S. (2019). The impacts of digital technologies on innovating for sustainability. In *Innovation for sustainability* (pp. 415–433). Springer. doi:10.1007/978-3-319-97385-2_22

Schuelke-Leech, B. A., Barry, B., Muratori, M., & Yurkovich, B. J. (2015). Big Data issues and Opportunities for electric utilities. *Renewable & Sustainable Energy Reviews*, *52*, 937–947. doi:10.1016/j.rser.2015.07.128

Shivajee, V., Singh, R. K., & Rastogi, S. (2019). Manufacturing conversion cost reduction using quality control tools and digitization of real-time data. *Journal of Cleaner Production*, *237*, 117678. Advance online publication. doi:10.1016/j.jclepro.2019.117678

Silva, E. S., Hassani, H., & Madsen, D. Ø. (2019). Big Data in fashion: Transforming the retail sector. *The Journal of Business Strategy*, *41*(4), 21–27. doi:10.1108/JBS-04-2019-0062

Singh, S. K., & El-Kassar, A. N. (2019). Role of big data analytics in developing sustainable capabilities. *Journal of Cleaner Production*, *213*, 1264–1273. doi:10.1016/j.jclepro.2018.12.199

Sivarajah, U., Kamal, M. M., Irani, Z., & Weerakkody, V. (2017). Critical analysis of Big Data challenges and analytical methods. *Journal of Business Research*, *70*, 263–286. doi:10.1016/j.jbusres.2016.08.001

Song, M. L., Fisher, R., & Kwoh, Y. (2019). Technological challenges of green innovation and sustainable resource management with large scale data. *Technological Forecasting and Social Change*, *144*, 361–368. doi:10.1016/j.techfore.2018.07.055

Stahel, W. R. (2008). Global climate change in the wider context of sustainability. *The Geneva Papers on Risk and Insurance. Issues and Practice*, *33*(3), 507–529. doi:10.1057/gpp.2008.21

Strandhagen, J. O., Vallandingham, L. R., Fragapane, G., Strandhagen, J. W., Stangeland, A. B. H., & Sharma, N. (2017). Logistics 4.0 and emerging sustainable business models. *Advances In Manufacturing*, *5*(4), 359–369. doi:10.100740436-017-0198-1

Stuermer, M., Abu-Tayeh, G., & Myrach, T. (2017). Digital sustainability: Basic conditions for sustainable digital artifacts and their ecosystems. *Sustainability Science*, *12*(2), 247–262. doi:10.100711625-016-0412-2 PMID:30174752

Tachizawa, E. M., Alvarez-Gil, M. J., & Montes-Sancho, M. J. (2015). How "smart cities" will change supply chain management. *Supply Chain Management*, *20*(3), 237–248. doi:10.1108/SCM-03-2014-0108

Tseng, W. S. W., & Hsu, C. W. (2019). A Smart, Caring, Interactive Chair Designed for Improving Emotional Support and Parent-Child Interactions to Promote Sustainable Relationships Between Elderly and Other Family Members. *Sustainability*, *11*(4), 961. Advance online publication. doi:10.3390u11040961

Turkina, E., & Oreshkin, B. (2021). The Impact of Co-Inventor Networks on Smart Cleantech Innovation: The Case of Montreal Agglomeration. *Sustainability*, *13*(13), 7270. Advance online publication. doi:10.3390u13137270

Usman, A., Azis, Y., Harsanto, B., & Azis, A. M. (2021). Airport service quality dimension and measurement: A systematic literature review and future research agenda. *International Journal of Quality & Reliability Management*. Advance online publication. doi:10.1108/IJQRM-07-2021-0198

van Eck, N. J., & Waltman, L. (2014). Visualizing Bibliometric Networks. Measuring Scholarly Impact. doi:10.1007/978-3-319-10377-8_13

van Eck, N. J., & Waltman, L. (2020). *VOSviewer - Download*. https://www.vosviewer.com/download

Villegas-Ch, W., Palacios-Pacheco, X., & Roman-Canizares, M. (2020). Integration of IoT and Blockchain to in the Processes of a University Campus. *Sustainability*, *12*(12), 4970. Advance online publication. doi:10.3390u12124970

Visconti, R. M., & Morea, D. (2019). Big Data for the Sustainability of Healthcare Project Financing. *Sustainability*, *11*(13), 3748. Advance online publication. doi:10.3390u11133748

Waibel, M. W., Oosthuizen, G. A., & du Toit, D. W. (2018). Investigating current smart production innovations in the machine building industry on sustainability aspects. In G. Seliger, R. Wertheim, H. Kohl, M. Shpitalni, & A. Fischer (Eds.), *15th Global Conference On Sustainable Manufacturing* (Vol. 21, pp. 774–781). 10.1016/j.promfg.2018.02.183

Wang, C. (2022). Application of Big Data in the Innovation of Physical Education Teaching Mode. In *Innovative Computing* (pp. 639–646). Springer. doi:10.1007/978-981-16-4258-6_79

Widianto, S., & Harsanto, B. (2017). The Impact of Transformational Leadership and Organizational Culture on Firm Performance in Indonesia SMEs. In N. Muenjohn & A. McMurray (Eds.), *The Palgrave Handbook of Leadership in Transforming Asia* (pp. 503–517)., doi:10.1057/978-1-137-57940-9_27

Wu, J. S., Guo, S., Li, J., & Zeng, D. Z. (2016). Big Data Meet Green Challenges: Big Data Toward Green Applications. *IEEE Systems Journal*, *10*(3), 888–900. doi:10.1109/JSYST.2016.2550530

Xia, D., Yu, Q., Gao, Q. L., & Cheng, G. P. (2017). Sustainable technology selection decision-making model for enterprise in supply chain: Based on a modified strategic balanced scorecard. *Journal of Cleaner Production*, *141*, 1337–1348. doi:10.1016/j.jclepro.2016.09.083

Yigitcanlar, T., Desouza, K. C., Butler, L., & Roozkhosh, F. (2020). Contributions and Risks of Artificial Intelligence (AI) in Building Smarter Cities: Insights from a Systematic Review of the Literature. *Energies*, *13*(6), 1473. Advance online publication. doi:10.3390/en13061473

Yigitcanlar, T., Han, H., Kamruzzaman, M., Ioppolo, G., & Sabatini-Marques, J. (2019). The making of smart cities: Are Songdo, Masdar, Amsterdam, San Francisco and Brisbane the best we could build? *Land Use Policy*, *88*, 104187. Advance online publication. doi:10.1016/j.landusepol.2019.104187

Zhang, D., Pee, L. G., Pan, S. L., & Cui, L. (2022). Big data analytics, resource orchestration, and digital sustainability: A case study of smart city development. *Government Information Quarterly*, *39*(1), 101626. doi:10.1016/j.giq.2021.101626

Zhang, N., & Chen, Z. F. (2017). Sustainability characteristics of China's Poyang Lake Eco-Economics Zone in the big data environment. *Journal of Cleaner Production*, *142*, 642–653. doi:10.1016/j.jclepro.2016.02.052

Zheng, C. J., Yuan, J. F., Zhu, L., Zhang, Y. J., & Shao, Q. H. (2020). From digital to sustainable: A scientometric review of smart city literature between 1990 and 2019. *Journal of Cleaner Production*, *258*, 120689. Advance online publication. doi:10.1016/j.jclepro.2020.120689

Zigiene, G., Rybakovas, E., & Alzbutas, R. (2019). Artificial Intelligence Based Commercial Risk Management Framework for SMEs. *Sustainability*, *11*(16), 4501. Advance online publication. doi:10.3390u11164501

ADDITIONAL READING

Adams, R., Jeanrenaud, S., Bessant, J., Denyer, D., & Overy, P. (2016). Sustainability-oriented Innovation: A Systematic Review. *International Journal of Management Reviews*, *18*(2), 180–205. doi:10.1111/ijmr.12068

Ciccullo, F., Fabbri, M., Abdelkafi, N., & Pero, M. (2022). Exploring the potential of business models for sustainability and big data for food waste reduction. *Journal of Cleaner Production*, *340*, 130673. doi:10.1016/j.jclepro.2022.130673

DiVito, L., & Ingen-Housz, Z. (2021). From individual sustainability orientations to collective sustainability innovation and sustainable entrepreneurial ecosystems. *Small Business Economics*, *56*(3), 1057–1072. doi:10.100711187-019-00254-6

Harsanto, B. (2021). Sustainability innovation in the agriculture sector in Indonesia: a review. *1st ICADAI 2021 E3S Web of Conferences, 306*, 02022. doi:10.1051/e3sconf/202130602022

Harsanto, B. (2022). Big Data Analytics in the Supply Chain in Indonesia. *Advances in Science and Technology (Owerri, Nigeria)*, *112*, 163–168. doi:10.4028/p-6aawzh

Hassanin, M. E., & Hamada, M. A. (2022). A Big Data strategy to reinforce self-sustainability for pharmaceutical companies in the digital transformation era: A case study of Egyptian pharmaceutical companies. *African Journal of Science, Technology, Innovation and Development*, 1–13. doi:10.1080/20421338.2021.1988409

Karaboğa, T., Karaboğa, H. A., Basar, D., & Zehir, S. (2022). Digital Transformation Journey of HR: The Effect of Big Data and Artificial Intelligence in HR Strategies and Roles. In Management Strategies for Sustainability, New Knowledge Innovation, and Personalized Products and Services (pp. 94-115). IGI Global.

Klewitz, J., & Hansen, E. G. (2014). Sustainability-oriented innovation of SMEs: A systematic review. *Journal of Cleaner Production*, *65*, 57–75. doi:10.1016/j.jclepro.2013.07.017

B

Maletič, M., Gomišček, B., & Maletič, D. (2021). The missing link: Sustainability innovation practices, non-financial performance outcomes and economic performance. *Management Research Review*, *44*(11), 1457–1477. doi:10.1108/MRR-09-2020-0562

Zhu, X., & Yang, Y. (2021). Big data analytics for improving financial performance and sustainability. *Journal of Systems Science and Information*, *9*(2), 175–191. doi:10.21078/JSSI-2021-175-17

KEY TERMS AND DEFINITIONS

Co-Occurrence Analysis: An examination of the frequency of occurrence and the strength of the link between specific keywords.

Eco-Innovation: Innovation aimed not only for profit but also for providing ecological benefits.

Innovation Management: Activities of planning, implementing, and controlling innovation within the organization.

Internet of Things: Physical objects linked together and exchanging data via the internet network.

Social Innovation: Innovation aimed not only for profit but also for providing social benefits.

Sustainability Innovation: Type of innovation that is a combination of eco-innovation and social innovation, in which the innovation is not only profitable but also provides ecological and/or social benefits.

Web of Science: One of the major multidisciplinary academic databases by Clarivate (formerly Clarivate Analytics, formerly Thomson Reuters).

Deep Learning for Cyber Security Risk Assessment in IIoT Systems

Mirjana D. Stojanović

iD https://orcid.org/0000-0003-1073-5804
University of Belgrade, Serbia

Jasna D. Marković-Petrović
Public Enterprise Electric Power Industry of Serbia, Serbia

BACKGROUND

This section briefly reviews the theoretical background for cyber security risk assessment in the industrial IoT environment. Since identification of risks, threats and attacks precedes risk assessment process, the first part is dedicated to classification of cyber security risks, threats and attacks that are specific for IIoT systems. The second part surveys cyber security risk assessment of industrial systems in terms of actual standards, security principles and priorities, as well as classification of risk assessment methods. The final part discusses general use of machine learning for security and engineering risk assessment.

IIoT Cyber Security Risks, Threats and Attacks

In addition to performance degradation, successful cyber attacks on IIoT system may have permanent or temporary impact on human health and lives, the environment and assets. The main security risks include the lack of authentication and security in sensors and other cyber-physical devices; insecure gateways through which data is transmitted to the cloud; cloud security issues and insecure communication protocols. Successful attacks may cause a number of operational issues such as equipment damage, unforeseen operational concerns, endangered personal safety and regulatory issues (Stojanović & Boštjančič Rakas, 2020).

Several recent studies have provided classification and description of the cyber security threats and attacks against IIoT systems. Sajid, Abbas, and Saleem (2016) identify the most specific threats to supervisory control and data acquisition (SCADA) systems in IoT-cloud environments as follows: advanced persistent threats (APT), lack of data integrity protection, man-in-the-middle (MITM) attacks, identity theft, eavesdropping, replay attacks, as well as different forms of denial of service (DoS) attacks. Leander, Čaušević, and Hansson (2019) apply a threat model based on the STRIDE (Spoofing, Tampering, Repudiation, Information disclosure, Denial of service and Elevation of privilege) method, which was originally introduced by Microsoft. They demonstrate the model on three typical scenarios related to the flow-control loop from the perspective of an industrial automation and control system (IACS). Tsiknas, Taketzis, Demertzis, and Skianis (2021) classify the IIoT threats in five generic categories: phishing attacks, ransomware, protocol, supply chain, and system attacks. Such a classification enables understanding of the security risks and the associated countermeasures in the IIoT environment.

Berger, Burger, and Roglinger (2020) propose three-layer taxonomy of attacks on the IIoT, where each layer is associated with appropriate dimensions and characteristics. Thus, the method of operation layer

DOI: 10.4018/978-1-7998-9220-5.ch127

identifies the entry points and methods used to perform an attack. This layer classifies attacks according to the technique, mechanism, executability and focus. The target layer classifies attacks according to the vulnerability and IIoT level. Finally, the impact layer characterizes effects of the successful attack in the sense of consequence and scope. Table 1 briefly summarizes previously described approaches.

Table 1. Taxonomies of IIoT cyber security risks, threats and attacks

Source	Category	Taxonomy	Main characteristics
Stojanović and Boštjančič Rakas (2020)	Cyber security risks	• Lack of authentication and security in cyber-physical devices • Insecure gateways • Cloud security issues • Insecure communication protocols	General classification that facilitates identification of IIoT operational issues in the case of successful attacks
Sajid et al. (2016)	Cyber security threats	• APT • Lack of data integrity protection • MITM attacks • Identity theft • Eavesdropping • Replay attacks • Different forms of DoS	Intended for IoT-based SCADA systems
Leander et al. (2019)	Cyber security threats	• STRIDE model	Intended for IACS
Tsiknas et al. (2021)	Cyber security threats	Five-category model: • Phishing attacks • Ransomware • Protocol • Supply chain • System attacks	Generic model suitable for definition of countermeasures
Berger et al. (2020)	Cyber security attacks	Three-layer model: • Method of operation layer • Target layer • Impact layer	Multi-layer taxonomy that facilitates identification of similarities and differences between attacks on the IIoT

Cyber Security Risk Assessment of Industrial Control Systems

According to the International Organization for Standardization (ISO) standard 31000:2018, risk assessment is considered as a core element of the risk management process, and includes risk identification, risk analysis, and risk evaluation (ISO, 2018). This assumes the following steps: (1) identification of the sources of risks and possible consequences, (2) analysis of the likelihood and impact of risks, and (3) evaluation of risks to assess the need for subsequent actions. In addition, the International Electrotechnical Commission (IEC) has published the IEC 31010:2019 (as a double logo standard with ISO), which provides guidance on the selection and application of techniques for assessing risk in a wide range of situations (IEC, 2019). Similarly, the International Telecommunication Union – Telecommunication Standardization Sector (ITU-T) defines risk management and risk profile guidelines for telecommunication organizations in its recommendation X.1055 (ITU-T, 2008).

In the context of ICS security, the U.S. National Institute of Standards and Technology (NIST) defines risk assessment as ''the process of identifying risks to operations, assets, or individuals by determining the probability of occurrence, the resulting impact, and additional security controls that would mitigate this impact'' (Stouffer, Pillitteri, Lightman, Abrams, & Hahn, 2015, p. 6-7). The Industrial Internet Consortium (IIC) addresses risk assessment in the view of overall security measures and highlights the need to adapt to continually changing threats and system configurations, provide responses that will minimize the impact on the IIoT system, and enable different organizations work together to ensure the early identification of security threats (IIC, 2016, p. 38).

For general-purpose infrastructures, the goal is to achieve a balanced protection of the confidentiality, integrity and availability of data (the so-called CIA triad), which gives the highest priority to data confidentiality. Protection of ICSs assumes the same triad, but with the reversed order of priorities (AIC), which means that the most important item is availability. This difference is essential in terms of security policies and the associated security mechanisms, with the key objective to preserve availability of all systems that constitute critical infrastructure on the 24/7 basis. Cyber security threats exploit system's vulnerabilities and possibly cause incidents, which may further cause damage to assets and have impact on security infrastructure. Therefore, threats, vulnerabilities, and impacts should be combined together to provide a measure of the risk (Tsiakis, 2010).

Measurement of security risk can be performed in two basic ways, qualitative or quantitative. Qualitative risk measurement interprets potential loss in a subjective way, e.g., low, medium and high risk. Examples of qualitative risk assessment encompass expert assessment, rating estimates, checklists of risk sources, method of analogies, etc. Quantitative risk measurement assumes a suitable mathematical approach, which expresses risk as a numerical value that is a function of probability and consequences. Traditionally, such metrics rely on purely economic categories, like annualized loss expectancy (ALE) and return on investment (ROI). However, security is not generally an investment that results in a profit, but rather in reducing the risks threatening specific assets. For that reason, return on security investment (ROSI) metric is introduced to calculate the loss avoided through preventive investments in security (Sonnenreich, Albanese, & Stout, 2006). Quantitative risk assessment methods can be classified into the three basic categories: (1) analytical methods such as sensitivity analysis, scenario analysis, method of the risk-adjusted discount rate; (2) probabilistic theoretical methods, which include simulation, game theory and tree constructing methods and (3) unconventional methods that encompass modeling with fuzzy logic and machine learning (Kalinin, Krundyshev, & Zegzhda, 2021). Hybrid methods combine the aforementioned approaches, for example, expert assessment with some of quantitative methods (Markovic-Petrovic, Stojanovic, & Bostjancic Rakas, 2019).

Systematic review of security risk assessment methods in ICSs using traditional Internet technologies can be found in the literature (Cherdantseva et al., 2016; Eckhart, Brenner, Ekelhart, & Weippl, 2019; Qassim, Jamil, Daud, Patel, & Ja'affar, 2019). Mirzaei, Maria de Fuentes, and Manzano (2018) address recent trends in dynamic risk assessment techniques by reviewing a number of relevant works and propose a decision guide to choose the most appropriate technique considering traditional computer networks, IoT environment and ICSs.

Application of Machine Learning for Risk Assessment

In the past decade, ML techniques have been recognized as powerful tools for anomaly detection in ICSs (Boštjančič Rakas, Stojanović, & Marković-Petrović, 2020; Radoglou-Grammatikis & Sarigiannidis, 2019). ML-based cyber security risk assessment methods are still in the early stage of development, although ML techniques generally offer a potential to implement CRA tools because of capabilities for handling multi-dimensional and multi-variety data, as well as real-time and predictive risk management.

Some recent review papers addressed applicability of ML techniques for the engineering and security risk assessment. Hegde and Rokseth (2020) present a structured review of publications dealing with ML methods for engineering risk assessment in different industrial sectors; only one out of 130 papers investigated the cyber security risk. Erdogan, Garcia-Ceja, Hugo, Nguyen, and Sen (2021) present an overview of security risk assessment approaches that use artificial intelligence; only three out of 33 papers investigated IoT systems. Results of these two studies indicate that supervised learning with artificial neural networks (ANNs) is the prevalent method in the reviewed papers probably because of their nonlinear calculating apparatus; ANNs require less formal statistical training and are capable of detecting all possible interactions between the input and output variables.

CONTINUOUS RISK ASSESSMENT IN IIoT: ARCHITECTURAL VIEW

Cyber security risk assessment in IIoT can be performed in different contexts, depending on the risk view and the involved entities (Nakamura & Ribeiro, 2018). Risk views may refer to sensors and actuators manufacturers, platform tier, application and ICS developers, industrial sector, integrators, service providers and users. Examples of the involved entities are humans, hardware, software, communication, cloud, etc., and they are the basis for determining the data flow. Some examples of IIoT contexts may include: IoT-based SCADA systems, supply chain robotics, data management for IIoT systems, IIoT contexts in healthcare, etc.

CRA is a data-driven approach to risk assessment, which is performed on an ongoing basis and relies on data that are collected and processed in the run-time. CRA approach assumes two phases: (1) identification and initial evaluation of the risk, which is performed during the system design process and (2) continuous monitoring and re-assessment of risk during the system operation (Rios, Rego, Iturbe, Higuero, & Larrucea, 2020). Figure 1 illustrates an architectural view of CRA process in IIoT, regarding system design and system operation phases.

Figure 1. Architectural view of CRA process in IIoT

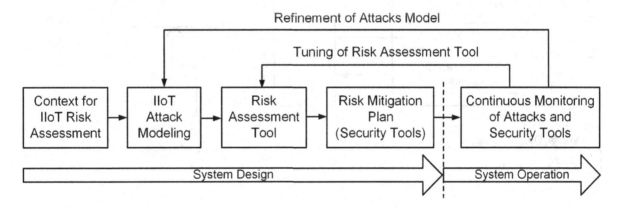

The system design phase begins with identification of the context for IIoT risk assessment. This is followed by an appropriate attack modeling process, which provides dynamic input for the risk assessment tool (static inputs are discussed later in this section). This tool provides qualitative or quantitative measure of the risk, which is a basis for definition of the risk mitigation plan and selection of the appropriate security tools. In the system operation phase, continuous monitoring of attacks and security tools is performed to provide two feedbacks. The first one is used for refinement of attack models, and the second one provides information for tuning of the risk assessment tool to improve its accuracy and precision.

Continuous monitoring in CRA assumes integration of security and risk assessment tools (Adaros Boye, Kearney, & Josephs, 2018; López, Pastor, & García Villalba, 2013). This principle is illustrated in Figure 2. Different security tools are distributed throughout the IIoT system, including logs monitoring, antivirus software, firewalls, intrusion detection and prevention systems, malware detection tools, tools for network traffic monitoring and analysis, etc. These tools capture and process inputs from the IIoT system in a real time and generate notifications about potential threats and suspicious events. The security information and event management (SIEM) module imports information from security tools, performs correlation of the corresponding events and prepares appropriate dynamic inputs for the risk assessment tool. This tool also takes into account different static inputs from policy database (security policy), asset database (asset register, asset values) and incidents database.

Figure 2. A model of integration of security and risk assessment tools in CRA

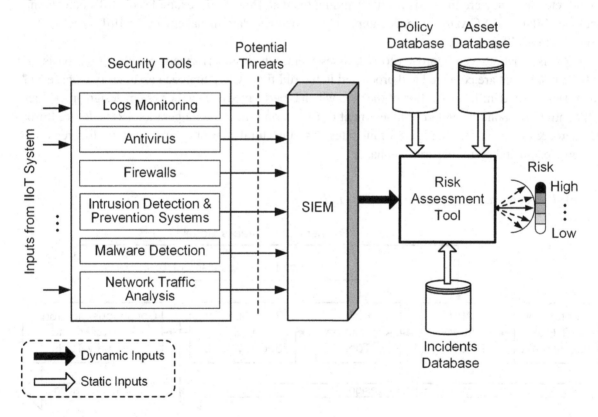

Traditional algorithms that can be used for implementation of CRA tool include (but are not limited to) Bayesian methods, bow-tie analysis and risk barometer (Villa, Paltrineri, & Cozzani, 2015). In the industrial IoT environment, artificial intelligence and machine learning bring substantial benefits for CRA implementation in terms of big data processing, improving efficiency, predictive risk management and better decision-making.

CRA BASED ON DEEP LEARNING: SOLUTIONS, ADVANTAGES AND DISADVANTAGES

D

DL is a subtype of machine learning that learns features and tasks directly from raw data. It requires high-performance computational capacity and massive amount of data. Feature extraction and classification are carried out by DL algorithms; among them, the most popular are deep neural networks (DNNs), i.e., neural networks that are characterized with multiple hidden layers. Examples of DNNs include convolutional neural networks (CNNs), recurrent neural networks (RNNs), graph neural networks (GNNs), etc. Comprehensive reviews of DL algorithms and their applications can be found in the literature (Alzubaidi et al., 2021; Shrestha & Mahmood, 2019; Xin et al., 2018).

Figure 3 illustrates utilization of DNN approach to implement CRA tool, in the context of previously described model of integration of security and risk assessment tools. The DNN trains through processing a large amount of data in the form of indicators from past incidents and normal operations. This phase may need expert supervision in assigning risk level to corresponding events (e.g., high, medium or low risk). After training phase, the DNN uses knowledge to assess real-time risk based on the run-time security state, which is provided by the SIEM module.

Abbass, Bakraouy, Baina, and Bellafkih (2018) propose a CNN algorithm for classifying IoT security risks. The algorithm consists of two phases. In the first phase (extraction) features are automatically extracted and learned from raw data. This is accomplished using two layers: the convolution layer, which collects the input data and the max-pooling layer, which classifies the collected data into sub-samples. The learning is achieved through several iterations of the convolution and max-pooling (back-propagation). In the second phase (classification), the fully connected layer is responsible for connecting the neurons to a single final output that corresponds to the appropriate risk level. After training the output is saved to be used as an input for further calculations, thus resulting in a fully dynamic and predictive approach. The model is implemented using the PyTorch framework and verified by simulation of an interconnection between a cloud client and the Dropbox server. The raw data included a number of simulated attacks such as illegal access network, malware intrusion, probe attacks, integrity loss, DoS, MITM, etc. Simulation experiments indicate that the classification accuracy strongly depends on the available computational capacity.

Figure 3. Illustration of CRA tool implemented using DNN

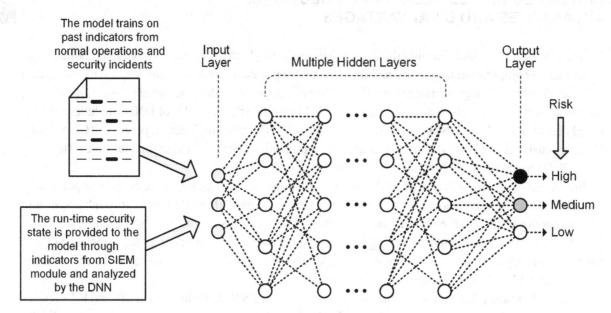

Zakaria, Bakar, Abas, and Hassan (2020) propose a similar conceptual model to assess cyber security risk in healthcare domain. The model relies on the U.S. NIST Guide for Conducting Risk Assessments (NIST SP 800-30) and comprises definition of services, service models, attack's surface, impact of attacks, risk mitigation and priority. CNN algorithm is used for classification of security risks. The authors provide a brief discussion on deployment possibilities based on open source libraries such as Keras, TensorFlow, and PyTorch.

Baldini et al. (2020) propose a policy-based system that integrates distributed agents for risk monitoring. The idea is to reduce security risks of IoT devices by enforcing traffic profiles that are defined either by the device's manufacturer or automatically. Each agent is capable of detecting anomalies for itself and also for its adjacent nodes. All agents utilize deep learning combined with graph structured datasets, i.e., graph neural networks (GNN) to achieve automatic feature extraction and anomaly detection. This resolves the problem of exchanging information among agents in a cooperative manner. The set of considered network features includes number of packets/bytes sent and received, as well as connection duration. In the context of the graph-structured network communication, node represents device, while edge represents communication. Thus, node agents update features of the corresponding nodes. Edge agents integrate information from adjacent nodes and the corresponding edge, and update the edge feature representation. In total, there are four deep neural networks, two of them are used for updating node and edge feature representations, and the other two are used for classification of neighbor nodes and the node in which the agent is installed.

Liu, Ospina, and Konstantinou (2020) propose the deep reinforcement learning (deep Q-network) to assess vulnerabilities in wind integrated power systems. The approach combines deep neural network with reinforcement learning that are goal-oriented algorithms. In other words, it brings together function approximation and target optimization by mapping state-action pairs to expected rewards. This characteristic makes such an approach suitable for both feature extraction and decision-making.

The set of available research works is small; hence, it is difficult or even impossible to draw general conclusions. However, some advantages and disadvantages of DL approach in the context of IIoT cyber security risk assessment can be noticed and they are listed below.

The main advantages include:

- DL can be integrated into edge-computing-based systems and used for feature extraction and risk classification. Features are automatically deduced and optimally tuned for the desired outcome.
- The DL approach is scalable and flexible to be adapted to new problems in the future. For example, more learning models can be created by adding more layers to existing neural network. Also, the same approach can be applied to many different IIoT contexts and datasets.
- The DL approach is robust enough to understand and automatically learn novel data

The main disadvantages are as follows:

- DL is very expensive to train due to complex data models. Usually, there is a need for huge amount of training data, which causes very long training time and the need for high-performance computational capacity.
- DL is hard to understand; for that reason, it is sometimes considered as a black box, which means that training tricks and experiences are needed in practice due to lack of fully theoretical analysis. Also, there is no straightforward guidance for selecting right algorithm as it requires knowledge of topology, training method and other parameters.

Finally, in contrast to other learning methods, performance of DL (primary in terms of classification accuracy) enhances with the increase of data amount. This property can be observed as advantage in some cases, and as disadvantage in the others.

FUTURE RESEARCH DIRECTIONS

DL-based algorithms are powerful tools for meeting challenges that CRA in IIoT environment poses to cyber security, industry and business experts. Although the research in the field is still relatively underdeveloped, its importance has been recognized and will probably gain a strong momentum in the next few years. There are many challenges related to future research. Hereafter, some main research directions are emphasized.

First, development of distributed and decentralized architectural frameworks, based on multiple cooperative agents, should be enforced in order to cover risk assessment in different IIoT contexts and also at different IIoT layers, ranging from edge through cloud to the application layer. Second, hybrid approaches can probably help to overcome some of DL disadvantages. For example, combining expert assessment with DNNs may mitigate shortcomings regarding insufficient classification accuracy and possibly wrong interpretation of results. Finally, attempts to build open-source software platforms dedicated to industrial environment should be enforced. In addition, realistic and comprehensive cyber physical system testbeds are needed to allow for experimentation with different solutions.

CONCLUSION

In spite of numerous benefits that IIoT brings to the industrial sector, cyber security risks may pose limitations to implementation of new systems, and particularly to migration of the existing systems towards IIoT environment. Apart from high-speed and long-distance connectivity, an IIoT network can be characterized with hundreds of thousands of data points, as well as by the requirement to carry a wide variety of network services and traffic types. For all those reasons, implementing effective and continuous cyber security risk assessment will gain in importance in the near future.

Machine learning and particularly DL algorithms are promising approaches due to capabilities to cope with massive raw data, and to be applied for automatic feature extraction and risk classification. Application of hybrid approaches that take into account expert opinion and experience may help in mitigating some DL shortcomings, and contribute to building accurate and reliable CRA models.

ACKNOWLEDGMENT

This research was supported by the Ministry of Education, Science and Technological Development of Serbia.

REFERENCES

Abbass, W., Bakraouy, Z., Baina, A., & Bellafkih, M. (2018). Classifying IoT security risks using deep learning algorithms. In *Proceedings of the 6th International Conference on Wireless Networks and Mobile Communications (WINCOM)* (pp. 1–6). New York: IEEE. 10.1109/WINCOM.2018.8629709

Adaros Boye, C., Kearney, P., & Josephs, M. (2018). Cyber-risks in the Industrial Internet of Things (IIoT): Towards a method for continuous assessment. In L. Chen, M. Manulis, & S. Schneider (Eds.), Lecture Notes in Computer Science: Vol. 11060. *Information Security. ISC 2018* (pp. 502–519). Springer. doi:10.1007/978-3-319-99136-8_27

Alzubaidi, L., Zhang, J., Humaidi, A. J., Al-Dujaili, A., Duan, Y., Al-Shamma, O., Santamaría, J., Fadhel, M. A., Al-Amidie, M., & Farhan, L. (2021). Review of deep learning: Concepts, CNN architectures, challenges, applications, future directions. *Journal of Big Data*, 8(53), 53. Advance online publication. doi:10.118640537-021-00444-8 PMID:33816053

Baldini, G., Fröhlich, P., Gelenbe, E., Hernandez-Ramos, J. L., Nowak, M., & Nowak, S. (2020). IoT network risk assessment and mitigation: The SerIoT approach. In J. Soldatos (Ed.), *Security Risk Management for the Internet of Things: Technologies and Techniques for IoT Security, Privacy and Data Protection* (pp. 88–104). Now Publishers. doi:10.1561/9781680836837.ch5

Berger, S., Burger, O., & Roglinger, M. (2020). Attacks on the Industrial Internet of Things – Development of a multi-layer taxonomy. *Computers & Security*, 93, 101790. doi:10.1016/j.cose.2020.101790

Boštjančič Rakas, S., Stojanović, M., & Marković-Petrović, J. (2020). A review of research work on network-based SCADA intrusion detection systems. *IEEE Access: Practical Innovations, Open Solutions*, 8, 93083–93108. doi:10.1109/ACCESS.2020.2994961

Cherdantseva, Y., Burnap, P., Blyth, A., Eden, P., Jones, K., Soulsby, H., & Stoddart, K. (2016). A review of cyber security risk assessment methods for SCADA systems. *Computers & Security*, *56*, 1–27. doi:10.1016/j.cose.2015.09.009

Eckhart, M., Brenner, B., Ekelhart, A., & Weippl, E. (2019). Quantitative security risk assessment for industrial control systems: Research opportunities and challenges. *Journal of Internet Services and Information Security*, *9*(3), 52–73. doi:10.22667/JISIS.2019.08.31.052

Erdogan, G., Garcia-Ceja, E., Hugo, A., Nguyen, P. H., & Sen, S. (2021). A systematic mapping study on approaches for AI-supported security risk assessment. In *Proceedings of the 2021 IEEE 45th Annual Computers, Software, and Applications Conference (COMPSAC)* (pp. 755–760). New York: IEEE. 10.1109/COMPSAC51774.2021.00107

Hegde, J., & Rokseth, B. (2020). Applications of machine learning methods for engineering risk assessment – A review. *Safety Science*, *122*, 104492. doi:10.1016/j.ssci.2019.09.015

Industrial Internet Consortium (IIC). (2016). *Industrial Internet of Things Volume G4: Security Framework. Document IIC:PUB:G4:V1.0:PB:20160919*. Retrieved July 31, 2021, from https://www.iiconsortium. org/pdf/IIC_PUB_G4_V1.00_PB.pdf

International Electrotechnical Commission (IEC). (2019). Risk management – Risk assessment techniques. *Standard IEC*, *31010*, 2019.

International Organization for Standardization (ISO). (2018). Risk management – Guidelines. *Standard ISO*, *31000*, 2018.

International Telecommunication Union – Telecommunication Standardization Sector (ITU-T). (2008). Risk management and risk profile guidelines for telecommunication organizations. *ITU-T Recommendation*, *X*, 1055.

Kalinin, M., Krundyshev, V., & Zegzhda, P. (2021). Cybersecurity risk assessment in smart city infrastructures. *Machines*, *9*(4), 78. doi:10.3390/machines9040078

Leander, B., Čaušević, A., & Hansson, H. (2019). Cybersecurity challenges in large industrial IoT systems. In *Proceedings of the 2019 24th IEEE International Conference on Emerging Technologies and Factory Automation (ETFA)* (pp. 1035–1042). New York: IEEE. 10.1109/ETFA.2019.8869162

Liu, X., Ospina, J., & Konstantinou, C. (2020). Deep reinforcement learning for cybersecurity assessment of wind integrated power systems. *IEEE Access: Practical Innovations, Open Solutions*, *8*, 208378–208394. doi:10.1109/ACCESS.2020.3038769

López, D., Pastor, O., & García Villalba, L. (2013). Dynamic risk assessment in information systems: State-of-the-art. In *Proceedings of the 6th International Conference on Information Technology (ICIT 2013)* (pp. 1–9). Retrieved July 31, 2021, from http://icit.zuj.edu.jo/icit13/Papers%20list/Camera_ready/ Software%20Engineering/772.pdf

Markovic-Petrovic, J. D., Stojanovic, M. D., & Bostjancic Rakas, S. V. (2019). A fuzzy AHP approach for security risk assessment in SCADA networks. *Advances in Electrical and Computer Engineering*, *19*(3), 69–74. doi:10.4316/AECE.2019.03008

Mirzaei, O., Maria de Fuentes, J., & Manzano, L. G. (2018). Dynamic risk assessment in IT environments: A decision guide. In Z. Fields (Ed.), *Handbook of Research on Information and Cyber Security in the Fourth Industrial Revolution* (pp. 234–263). IGI Global. doi:10.4018/978-1-5225-4763-1.ch009

Nakamura, E. T., & Ribeiro, S. L. (2018). A privacy, security, safety, resilience and reliability focused risk assessment methodology for IIoT systems steps to build and use secure IIoT systems. In *Proceedings of the 2018 Global Internet of Things Summit (GIoTS)* (pp. 1–6). New York: IEEE. 10.1109/GIOTS.2018.8534521

Qassim, Q. S., Jamil, N., Daud, M., Patel, A., & Ja'affar, N. (2019). A review of security assessment methodologies in industrial control systems. *Information and Computer Security*, 27(1), 47–61. doi:10.1108/ICS-04-2018-0048

Radoglou-Grammatikis, P. I., & Sarigiannidis, P. G. (2019). Securing the smart grid: A comprehensive compilation of intrusion detection and prevention systems. *IEEE Access: Practical Innovations, Open Solutions*, 7, 46595–46620. doi:10.1109/ACCESS.2019.2909807

Rios, E., Rego, A., Iturbe, E., Higuero, M., & Larrucea, X. (2020). Continuous quantitative risk management in smart grids using attack defense trees. *Sensors (Basel)*, 20(16), 4404. doi:10.339020164404 PMID:32784568

Sajid, A., Abbas, H., & Saleem, K. (2016). Cloud-assisted IoT-based SCADA systems security: A review of the state of the art and future challenges. *IEEE Access: Practical Innovations, Open Solutions*, 4, 1375–1384. doi:10.1109/ACCESS.2016.2549047

Shrestha, A., & Mahmood, A. (2019). Review of deep learning algorithms and architectures. *IEEE Access: Practical Innovations, Open Solutions*, 7, 53040–53065. doi:10.1109/ACCESS.2019.2912200

Sonnenreich, W., Albanese, J., & Stout, B. (2006). Return on security investment (ROSI) – A practical quantitative model. *Journal of Research and Practice in Information Technology*, 38(1), 45–56.

Stojanović, M., & Boštjančič Rakas, S. (2020). Challenges in securing industrial control systems using future Internet technologies. In M. Stojanović & S. Boštjančič Rakas (Eds.), *Cyber Security of Industrial Control Systems in the Future Internet Environment* (pp. 1–26). IGI Global. doi:10.4018/978-1-7998-2910-2.ch001

Stouffer, K., Pillitteri, V., Lightman, S., Abrams, M., & Hahn, A. (2015). *Guide to industrial control systems (ICS) security (NIST Special Publication 800-82 Rev. 2)*. Gaithersburg, MD: U.S. National Institute of Standards and Technology. doi:10.6028/NIST.SP.800-82r2

Tsiakis, T. (2010). Information security expenditures: A techno-economic analysis. *International Journal of Computer Science and Network Security*, 10(4), 7–11.

Tsiknas, K., Taketzis, D., Demertzis, K., & Skianis, C. (2021). Cyber threats to Industrial IoT: A survey on attacks and countermeasures. *IoT*, 2(1), 163–186. doi:10.3390/iot2010009

Villa, V., Paltrineri, N., & Cozzani, V. (2015). Overview on dynamic approaches to risk management in process facilities. *Chemical Engineering Transactions*, 43, 2497–2502. doi:10.3303/CET1543417

Xin, Y., Kong, L., Liu, Z., Chen, Y., Li, Y., Zhu, H., Gao, M., Hou, H., & Wang, C. (2018). Machine learning and deep learning methods for cybersecurity. *IEEE Access: Practical Innovations, Open Solutions*, *6*, 35365–35381. doi:10.1109/ACCESS.2018.2836950

Zakaria, M. N., Bakar, N. A. A., Abas, H., & Hassan, N. H. (2020). A conceptual model for Internet of Things risk assessment in healthcare domain with deep learning approach. *International Journal of Innovative Computing*, *10*(2), 7–19. doi:10.11113/ijic.v10n2.263

ADDITIONAL READING

Cao, B., Zhang, L., Li, Y., Feng, D., & Cao, W. (2019). Intelligent offloading in multi-access edge computing: A state-of-the-art review and framework. *IEEE Communications Magazine*, *57*(3), 56–62. doi:10.1109/MCOM.2019.1800608

Cook, A., Nicholson, A., Janicke, H., Maglaras, L., & Smith, R. (2016). Attribution of cyber attacks on industrial control systems. *EAI Endorsed Transactions on Industrial Networks and Industrial Systems*, *3*(7), 1–15. doi:10.4108/eai.21-4-2016.151158

Cvitić, I., Peraković, D., Periša, M., & Stojanović, M. (2021). Novel classification of IoT devices based on traffic flow features. *Journal of Organizational and End User Computing*, *33*(6), 12. Advance online publication. doi:10.4018/JOEUC.20211101.oa12

Federation of European Risk Management Associations (FERMA). (2019). *Artificial intelligence applied to risk management*. Retrieved July 31, 2021, from https://www.eciia.eu/wp-content/uploads/2019/11/FERMA-AI-applied-to-RM-FINAL.pdf

Macaulay, T. (2016). *RIoT Control: Understanding and Managing Risks and the Internet of Things*. Morgan Kaufmann.

Paltrinieri, N., Comfort, L., & Reniers, G. (2019). Learning about risk: Machine learning for risk assessment. *Safety Science*, *118*, 475–486. doi:10.1016/j.ssci.2019.06.001

Radanliev, P., De Roure, D., Walton, R., Van Kleek, M., Montalvo, R. M., Maddox, L. T., Santos, O., Burnap, P., & Anthi, E. (2020). Artificial intelligence and machine learning in dynamic cyber risk analytics at the edge. *SN Applied Sciences*, *2*(11), 1773. doi:10.100742452-020-03559-4

Xu, H., Yu, W., Griffith, D., & Golmie, N. (2018). A survey on Industrial Internet of Things: A cyber-physical systems perspective. *IEEE Access: Practical Innovations, Open Solutions*, *6*, 78238–78259. doi:10.1109/ACCESS.2018.2884906 PMID:35531371

KEY TERMS AND DEFINITIONS

Asset: Any element of an information system that possesses a value.

Classification Accuracy: In the context of machine learning, a metric that represents the rate of correct classifications.

Continuous Risk Assessment (CRA): Risk assessment process that is performed dynamically, on an ongoing basis.

Cyber Security Attack: Any action that targets information systems, computer networks, infrastructures, or personal computer devices, with the intent to cause damage.

Cyber Security Risk: Exposure to harm or loss resulting from data breaches or attacks on information and communication systems.

Cyber Security Threat: An event that can take advantage of system's vulnerability and cause a negative impact on it.

Deep Neural Network (DNN): A neural network with multiple hidden layers, which use sophisticated mathematical modeling to process data in a complex way.

Industrial Control System (ICS): A general term that refers to the interconnected equipment used to monitor and control physical equipment and processes in industrial environments.

Return on Security Investment (ROSI): Risk metric, which calculates the loss avoided through preventive investments in security.

Security Information and Event Management (SIEM): A software solution that collects security data from various network devices and performs data analytics and correlation of the corresponding security events.

Digital Transformation and Circular Economy for Sustainability

Renan Carriço Payer
Universidade Federal Fluminense, Brazil

Osvaldo Luiz Gonçalves Quelhas
https://orcid.org/0000-0001-6816-1677
Universidade Federal Fluminense, Brazil

Gilson Brito Alves Lima
https://orcid.org/0000-0001-6741-2403
Universidade Federal Fluminense, Brazil

Níssia Carvalho Rosa Bergiante
https://orcid.org/0000-0001-5131-1253
Universidade Federal Fluminense, Brazil

INTRODUCTION

The traditional industrialization has been producing many byproducts and generating pollution and environmental degradation (Di Vaio, Hasan, Palladino & Hassan, 2022; Hu et al., 2011). This adverse scene made several researches think over the idea of "circularity", aiming to reflect upon the way resources are currently used not only inside production and economical systems but also as a way to deal with their lack and its relation to population growth. (Alhawari, Awan, Bhutta & Ülkü, 2021; Cezarino, Liboni, Stefanelli, Oliveira & Stocco, 2019).

The idea of "circularity" (figure 1) was shaped around the conception of "Circular Economy", which is understood by some authors as a differential perspective about organizational and operational production and consumption systems focused on recovering value from used resources. (Genovese, Acquaye, Figueroa & Koh, 2017; Lieder & Rashid, 2016; Sarc et al., 2019). The organizations which replace the traditional perspective of linear economy for this circular approach on energy and materials may experience economic, environmental and social benefits (Geissdoerfer, Savaget, Bocken & Hultink, 2017).

DOI: 10.4018/978-1-7998-9220-5.ch128

Figure 1. A circular economy model
Source: Author's elaboration

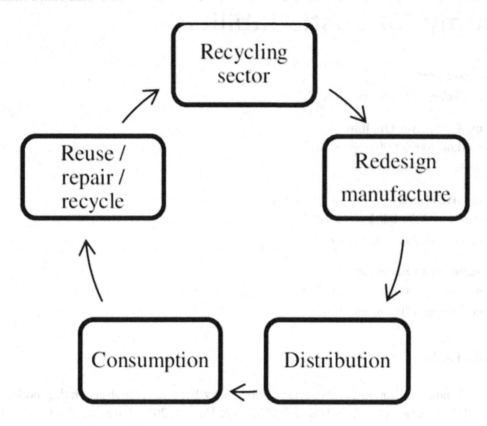

In general, the interest of researchers in studies about the relationship between sustainability and digital transformation has increased. Effectively, the issue of sustainability refers to economic, environmental and social development. Sustainability is a broad concept that is not limited to the environment only, as it also involves economic preservation and the valorization of social resources (Ghobakhloo, 2020).

At the same time, the economic development conducted through the empowerment of the industrial sector and consequently exploration of natural resources has made governments and society itself look for new ways to achieve a sustainable development. So, the digitalization may urge this transformation towards a more sustainable circular economy (Antikainen, Uusitalo & Kivikytö-Reponen, 2018; Cezarino et al., 2019; Hedberg, & Šipka, 2021; Jabbour et al., 2018). Besides, the industry 4.0 and the sustainability may be useful if taken as tendencies in organizational production systems (Rejikumar et al. 2019; Trappey et al., 2017).

With its smart solutions, the industry 4.0 brings in its core the digital transformation, offering an information technology infrastructure capable of providing a more efficient use of resources, enabling reduction of energy consumption, and logistics routes, while also optimizing capacity (Jæger & Halse, 2019; Sreedharan & Unnikrishnan, 2017). The digitalization enables transparent access to products' data, resource consumption, and the promotion of a life cycle of technological products (Antikainen et al., 2018). The business model may be developed based on the integration between technologies of industry 4.0 and the circular economy, promoting a digital transformation (figure 2).

Figure 2. Circular economy and industry 4.0: A business model
Source: Author's elaboration

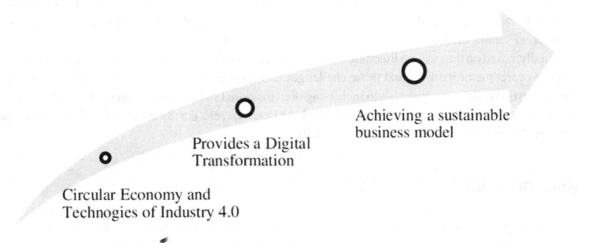

Achieving a sustainable
business model

Provides a Digital
Transformation

Circular Economy and
Technogies of Industry 4.0

During the COVID-19 pandemic, the world has been facing an overwhelming crisis leading organizations to collapse. They need some capacity which gives them conditions to keep operating. Innovation constitutes itself as an alternative to help organizational resilience. This work shows how subjects as industry 4.0 and circular economy are currently studied and applied as a resource for the adaption to the "new normal".

After presenting the scene, this chapter intends to discuss the ways technologies coming from digital transformation step up the circular economy among institutions aiming to promote organizational sustainability. Studies focusing on this matter are still scarce in the literature. (Alhawari et al., 2021; Hedberg, & Šipka, 2021; Jabbour et al., 2018).

Rajput & Singh (2020) understand that in the current scenario, industries face problems with high cost and high energy consumption and resources linked to traditional production systems linked to the linear economy model. on the other hand, with the advent of digital transformation, several technologies have made it possible to make efforts for production systems that can be interconnected and based on data, networks, artificial intelligence, and others. with industry 4.0 technologies, it may be possible to establish production systems that optimize energy and resource consumption and can reduce waste production. in this context, it is worth discussing the progress of industry 4.0 in favor of a model of circular economy and cleaner production to achieve ethical business, achieving precision and efficiency.

It is a complex issue that involves new paradigms (integration between different knowledge areas) and the incapacity of only one specialty area to deal with its causes. Therefore, it is necessary to have a theoretical support from different study areas (social sciences, administration, occupational health and safety, ergonomics, etc.), which brings originality to this study.

The authors will conduct the discussion based on what is already proposed by the literature and will present different examples on how to apply technologies from industry 4.0 on initiatives that have already generated a boost of organizational sustainability inside the concept of circular economy. These examples may lead to a broader understing on how technologies can cooperate in building a sustainable and cohesive to the principles of circular economy organization.

In addition to the discussion mentioned above, the authors will also deal with the limits and challenges faced by organizations regarding the implementation of a digital transformation based on the circular economy, according to different studies already published. These notes may be useful for future research focused on possible solutions or ways to work around those challenges, aiming to provide new approaches to the implementation of sustainable initiatives through technology tools. Other authors, such as Bulanovs et al. (2018), Jabbour et al. (2018), and Jæger and Halse (2019) already suggested conducting studies in this perspective.

Finally, based on the existing literature and on its own authors' experience, this chapter aims to discuss ways to overcome or work around those challenges and limitations, while also contributing through a few suggestions, tips, and proposals to increasing organizational sustainability based on technology (Big Data, Internet of Things, Cloud Computing, Machine Learning, etc.) in the advent of digital transformation and having the circular economy as a principle.

BACKGROUND

The circular economy sustains economic return and strengthens the quality of life through its multiple roles. Its principles can positively impact society. Linear economics, on the other hand, is a model that is based on the transformation of virgin raw material into products, generating waste, without necessarily considering ways to add value to the potential waste. Thus, the circular economy can drive systemic changes and sustain the circulation of value within the process, eliminating the concept of waste (Ilić, Ranković, Dobrilović, Bucea-Manea-țoniș, Mihoreanu, Gheța, & Simion, 2022).

According to Geissdoerfer et al. (2017), Lieder and Rashid (2016), and Nascimento, Alencastro, Quelhas, Caiado, Garza-Reyes, Lona and Tortorella (2018), the circular economy may be considered a potential solution to deal with the challenges of waste generation and shortage of resources, and moreover, to hold economic benefits, since it is a regenerative system where the introduction of new resources, the waste issue, and the loss of energy are mitigated by the slowdown, closing and narrowing of material and energy circuits. Thus, the circular economy approach provides an economical methodology to society which reinserts waste as raw material (Alhawari et al., 2021; Nascimento et al., 2018), transforming production systems into circular chains (Rejikumar, Sreedharan, Arunprasad, Persis & Sreeraj, 2019). This generates several benefits, including a local selection of waste, which supports sustainable logistics (Jabbour, Jabbour, Godinho Filho & Roubaud, 2018).

The fourth industrial revolution introduces fast changes to the industries' value chain (Jæger & Halse, 2019). This digital transformation may be an ally to sustainability, as it brings different technological assets, which in their turn can help the promotion of a circular economy (Jabbour et al., 2018; Nascimento et al., 2018; Rejikumar et al., 2019). Cloud computing, Internet of Things (IoT), 3D-printing, Advanced Analytics Algorithms and Big Data, Artificial intelligence and Machine Learning are some of those assets (Liboni, Liboni & Cezarino, 2018).

FOCUS OF THE ARTICLE

How can Digital Transformation Step up the Circular Economy?

This question has led researches conducted on important essays already published, such as Alhawari et al. (2021), Cezarino et al. (2019) and Nascimento et al. (2018). In fact, it is not about one specific answer or an already established concept, but a type of knowledge that is still under construction (Alhawari et

D

al., 2021). The contributions of different authors are significant, while institutions' day by day reveals relevant empirical knowledge on how to obtain an interface between digital transformation and circular economy (Nascimento et al., 2018). Fortunately, the literature already has some examples on how to apply technologies of industry 4.0 on initiatives that can boost organizational sustainability based on the concept of circular economy (figure 3).

Figure 3. Sustainability and circular economy from technologies of industry 4.0
Source: Author's elaboration

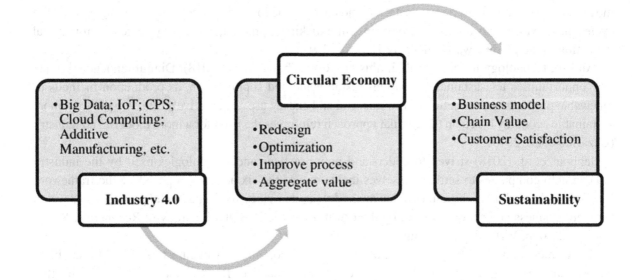

Nascimento et al. (2018) studied how technologies aroused from industry 4.0 may be integrated to circular economy practices to establish a business model that reuses and recycles waste, such as electronic waste. As result of the study, it was recommended a circular model that reuses electronic waste, integrating web technologies and reverse logistics. Those results suggested a positive influence over the business' sustainability improvement, reinserting waste in the supply chain to make products on demand.

Sarc et al. (2019) published a study applying digital computational systems that can separate waste using robotic technologies: there are sensors used to detect the kind of material or to scale its level, and methods to analyze digital images that allow developing new business models. These technologies are based on a huge amount of data, which can contribute to an increase of efficiency inside factories. In the end, it is a smart sorting that takes employees out of uncomfortable work conditions (noise, dust, dirt, pollutant, etc.).

Technology advances from industry 4.0 can create improvements on the productive process through the integration of smart and automatized mechanisms inside the industrial environment (Xu, Xu & Li, 2018). There is a new perspective to the business world based on the implant of smart factories through a net of link devices that accelerate the production (Parajuly & Wenzel, 2017). New spaces, as the Cyber-physical systems (CPSs), operate in a self-organized and decentralized way and are formed by devices and sensors connected that can influence physical processes (Luthra & Mangla, 2018).

According to Burlakovs et al. (2018) and Sarc et al. (2019), a business model can achieve its full potential using Cloud Computing and Internet of Things, since these technologies enable people to connect and share information regarding supply and demand. Websites and applications are important resources to connect people to organizations. Moreover, these technologies can collect information about costumers' behavior, and so, the organizations can improve their product and service's design to expand or replace equipment and boost customer satisfaction (Alhawari et al., 2021; Luthra & Mangla, 2018; Jabbour et al., 2018).

Heading Towards a Circular Economy Starting from Digital Transformation

Inside the circularity model, reusing to a product level has a significant positive environmental impact, followed by reusing to component and material levels, respectively. Heading towards a circular economy model requires a deep focus on raw materials and energy. The focus might be on minimizing product life cycle's negatives effects on the environment while making a product, since early stages from material extraction to the product waste (Jæger & Halse, 2019).

And so, technology has a key role in this process (Jabbour et al., 2018). Digital tendencies create new opportunities for sustainable solutions inside value and supply chain, as production methods of renewable products and reduction of raw material and energy use. Alternatively, the demand for a more sustainable economy based on the circular approach reinforces the need for a more modernized industry (Cezarino et al., 2019).

Jabbour et al. (2018) strived to understand how practices and technologies used by the industry 4.0 can help companies to settle themselves inside one of the six actions proposed by the framework ReSOLVE. According to the authors, this methodology describes six fundamental practices to develop concrete business and actions, which, by their turn, form the ReSOLVE acronym: Regenerate, Share, Optimise, Loop, Virtualise, Exchange.

The framework ReSOLVE describes how the circular economy may manifest itself in different businesses, industries or governments. Thus, besides adopting practices from industry 4.0, the organization can operate in a way that boosts a more sustainable economy, as reducing solid waste production, pollution, and energy used in the production process, while also increasing the industry efficiency through more value generation in the production chains (Jabbour et al., 2018).

Table 1 shows the six fundamental practices from framework ReSOLVE to develop circular actions related to the main technologies and resources of industry 4.0 (digital transformation).

Table 1. The framework ReSOLVE and some technologies of Industry 4.0

D

ReSOLVE	Mains Ideas	Technologies of Industry 4.0
REgenerate	Shift to renewable energy and materials; Reclaim, retain and restore health of ecosystems; Return recovered biological resources to the biosphere.	Machine Learning Internet of Things (IoT)
Share	Share assets (e.g. cars, rooms); Reuse/secondhand; Prolong life through maintenance, design for durability, upgradability etc.	Cloud Computing / Cloud Manufacturing; Internet of Things (IoT)
Optmize	Increase performance/efficiency of product; Remove waste in production and supply chain; Leverage BigData, automation, remote sensing and steering.	Machine Learning Cyber-physical systems (CPSs); Internet of Things (IoT); Big Data
Loop	Remanufacture products or components; Recycle materials; Digest anaerobically; Extract biochemicals from organic waste.	Machine Learning Cloud Computing / Cloud Manufacturing; Internet of Things (IoT); Cyber-physical systems (CPSs).
Virtualize	Dematerialize directly (e.g. books, CDs); Dematerialize indirectly (e.g. online shopping).	Cloud Computing / Cloud Manufacturing; Internet of Things (IoT); Additive manufacturing; Big Data.
Exchange	Replace old with advanced non-renewable materials; Apply new technologies (e.g. 3D printing); Choose new product/service (e.g. multimodal transport)	Machine Learning Additive manufacturing.

Source: Author's elaboration according to Jabbour et al. (2018)

The Cyber-physical systems (CPSs) may integrate cyberspace, physical processes and objects to connect machines and devices inside production lines as in a network, sharing real data to support decision-making, such as production order prioritizing, task optimization, reports about maintenance, etc. (Kang et al., 2016; Lu, 2017). Sensors and actuators are responsible for collecting and distributing these data in real-time (Kang et al., 2016).

The Cloud Computing brings the idea of cloud manufacturing with it, creating a virtual and global space with a network of shared resources and capacities through the Internet (Jabbour et al., 2018). The logic behind cloud manufacturing is based on services, which means that costumers and providers interact to buy and sell services (products' design, simulation, manufacturing and assembling). It is recommendable to adopt cloud manufacturing due to its e-commerce resources, beside the fact that it also encompasses other industry 4.0 technologies, such as additive manufacturing (Trentesaux, Borangiu & Thomas, 2016).

Moreover, the additive manufacturing is based on manufacturing pieces of products without buying or using specialized tools. Besides, manufacturing happens through a digital design, which allows a reduced production's waiting time, and connectivity among designers, engineers and users (Geissdoerfer et al., 2017). 3D printers are the main resources connected to the additive manufacturing.

Machine learning is a field of computer science that aims to teach computers how to learn and act without being explicitly programmed. More specifically, machine learning is an approach to data analysis that involves building and adapting models, which allow programs to "learn" through experience. Machine learning involves the construction of algorithms that adapt their models to improve their ability to make predictions. Machine learning can augment and accelerate the development of new products, components and materials from development to a circular economy of machine learning-assisted iterative design processes that enable rapid prototyping and testing (Rejikumar et al., 2019).

The Internet of Things (IoT) refers to the interconnectivity among things, such as electronical devices, smartphones, machines, means of transportation, etc., and the internet itself through identification codes (Kang, et al., 2016). With the IoT, Cyber-physical systems can be connected to companies and individuals, making it possible to have an interoperability among them (Rejikumar et al., 2019). Because of it, all parts can collect and share data in real-time (Jabbour et al., 2018). In its turn, this information exchange will create a huge amount of data that can be further analyzed to increase the organizations' added value (Kang et al., 2016).

The Big Data technology has been used to improve products' development (Jabbour et al., 2018), predicting demand on supply chains (Trentesaux, et al., 2016), and on green manufacturing policies (Lu, 2017), for instance. The resources more frequently found on the Internet of Things implementation are labels, sensors, barcodes, and smartphones with radio frequency identification technology (Jæger & Halse, 2019).

SOLUTIONS AND RECOMMENDATIONS

Despite the benefits and advantages discussed by the literature, many authors have pointed out limits and challenges in the course of digital transformation towards establishing a circular economy.

One of the challenges identified was the lack of information about the product life cycle, that with the deficiency of advanced technologies to a cleaner production shortened the reach of the principles from the circular economy (Su, Heshmati, Geng & Yu, 2013). Besides, many times the uncertainty around costs, investments' returns, and implementation schedule result in an initial reluctance among companies on adopting these goals (Jabbour et al., 2018).

Other challenges discussed by the literature are: the lack of stakeholders' perception about the characteristics of the discarded products and the procedural non-compliance of the ones responsible for the product life cycle (Parajuly & Wenzel, 2017); the need of changes in the design's philosophy, using unconventional materials based on degradability criteria over quality or durability (Los Rios & Charnley, 2017); and the reflection about the complexity of urban waste (Burlakovs et al., 2018).

Jæger & Halse (2019) incisively pointed out that, many times, disassembling products for reuse processes is not easy, and is, in the contrary, expensive and time-consuming due to their complex nature. Products need a circular design, and this is why production, reuse, dismantling, remanufacturing, etc., are complicated.

Jæger & Halse (2019) also considered the complexity of the supply chain a challenge, as increasing elements from different natures and different disassembling procedures create new costs. Besides, coordinating all companies is also a barrier, as many companies are needed to adjust daily operations.

Rajput & Singh (2020) concluded that one of the challenges to promote the integration between digital transformation and circular economy is the need to reformulate traditional manufacturing configurations, that is, perform a transformation that contemplates an intelligent manufacturing model to obtain self-adaptability, reliability and flexibility with high quality and low-cost production. To overcome this limitation, the authors proposed the mixed-integer linear programming (MILP) model to increase the circular economy model from digital transformation and also to obtain cleaner production. The proposed MILP model optimizes the trade-off between energy consumption and machine processing cost to achieve circular savings and cleaner production, respectively. The proposed model also achieves ethical business by deploying sensors to capture real-time information to establish industry 4.0 facilities.

D

Other authors present viable solutions to overcome the different challenges discussed based on empirical studies and applied cases. One of these studies was developed by Alhawari et al. (2021), Cezarino et al. (2019) and Jabbour et al. (2018).

According to Jabbour et al. (2018), the first step for organizations that intend to advance towards a circular economy is deciding which models are suitable for their production processes. The second one is identifying technologies and resources from industry 4.0 that are viable to them, considering factors such as availability, costs and technical constraints. After that, should follow an adaptation step of design, process and product logistics. The next one is developing integration among layers of the supply chain, so it becomes possible to connect technologies and resources, and also share information regarding demand, supply, delivery, and costumer's behavior in real time. At last, the final step for organizations is the creation of performance indicators, so they can measure their progress towards a circular economy.

Cezarino et al. (2019) endorse a concept based on costs and benefits. For the authors, assembling business models and sustainable management is one way of working around the challenges, applying technological resources from industry 4.0 directly into the value chain. In other words, the technological resources used may add value to products and cooperate to the organizational sustainability increase at the same time.

Alhawari et al. (2021) see the link between resources and value generation to customers as a key to overcome these challenges. The authors suggest that companies based on a circular business model focus on customers as cooperators and partners. To overcome the limitation presented, it is also important that the organization and its stakeholders are aware about each other's interests and expectations regarding digitalization as an integrator for a circular economy to add value to what was formerly waste, and consequently have environmental benefits.

Rejeb, Rejeb, Abdollahi, Zailani, Iranmanesh & Ghobakhloo (2022) concluded organizations need to be based on successful previous experiences and consider the principles of sustainability and circular economy in their most diverse processes. Specifically, the authors point out that it is necessary to promote several improvements necessary to integrate cutting-edge technologies and make them energy efficient, accessible and economical. If necessary, it is indicated to promote greater collaboration between industries and research centers.

Table 2 presents a summary of the challenges and limitations presented in the literature and proposals for overcoming according to the discussion of the literature and based on the experience of the authors.

Table 2. Challenges and limitations x proposals for overcoming

Challenge/Limitation	Literature	Proposals for overcoming (based on the literature or/and experience of the authors)
Lack of information about the technology lifecycle	Su, Heshmati, Geng & Yu, (2013); Parajuly & Wenzel (2017)	It is necessary to create multidisciplinary groups between buyers and suppliers so that the products and their components are better known.
Investment costs and returns	Jabbour et al. (2018)	Cezarino et al. (2019) suggest a model based on the value chain, that is, on adding value to products due to the use of technologies. At the same time, technological resources cooperate in increasing sustainability and compensate for costs.
Conflicts of interest with stakeholders	Parajuly & Wenzel (2017)	Alhawari et al. (2021) argue that stakeholders need to be aware of strategic objectives. Specifically, it is necessary to highlight how the use of technological resources for sustainability can promote organizational competitiveness.
Use of materials based on quality criteria/durability x circularity	Los Rios & Charnley (2017)	It is necessary to discern for each production process which criterion is most relevant: quality/durability or circularity. It is still possible to establish different criteria based on different parts or insums.
Complexity of waste	Burlakovs et al. (2018)	In some cases, it is possible to think of circular chains with less possible waste production and, thus, add value to the production process. Digital transformation can help in this process through production optimization mechanisms.
Complexity of the circular supply chain	Jæger e Halse (2019)	The model proposed by Jabbour et al. (2018) includes 5 useful steps to overcome this limitation. The authors suggest promoting integration between supply chain layers so that it is feasible to share technologies and resources.
Traditional manufacturing configurations	Rajput & Singh (2020)	The mixed-integer linear programming (MILP) model. The MILP model optimizes the trade-off between energy consumption and machine processing cost to achieve circular savings and cleaner production, respectively

Source: Author's elaboration according

FUTURE RESEARCH DIRECTIONS

Further studies on applying the framework (table 1) presented in this chapter to study cases are suggested. So, it would be possible to evaluate learnings about barriers and limitations to the implementation of the industry 4.0 technologies and their consequential benefit to the application of circular economy concepts to organizational processes (according to the instructions contained in table 2).

CONCLUSION

Based on what was explained throughout the chapter and what was already developed by the literature, it is already known that achieving a circular economy model involves a deeper focus on raw materials and energy. And technology has a key role in the process. Digital tendencies create opportunities for sustainable solutions in the supply chain and value.

Different technologies from industry 4.0 may support circular economy strategies inside organizations using sustainable operations management as their base. This is possible to achieve involving managers in the strategic level of the organization and raising awareness among all contributors about the process of including technologies aiming to benefit a more sustainable process.

Effectively, through the ReSOLVE framework, it is possible to verify that technologies from industry 4.0 such as Machine Learning, Internet of Things (IoT), Cloud Computing / Cloud Manufacturing, Cyber-

D

physical systems (CPSs), Big Data and Additive are able to provide supportto achieve the principles of the circular economy (regenerate, share, optimise, loop, virtualise and exchange).

However, some challenges exist in the process of implementing a circular economy model from digital transformation. Some limitations were discussed by the literature, as well as some proposals to overcome these challenges. This chapter summarized 7 limitations/challenges: Lack of information about the technology lifecycle; investment costs and returns; conflicts of interest with stakeholderes; use of materials based on quality criteria/durability x circularity; complexity of waste; complexity of the circular supply chain and traditional manufacturing configurations.

In general, based on literature and the authors' experience, the overcoming of these challenges is based on the articulation of management models that meet the expectations of the interested parties, considering both the circular economy and the digital transformation. Relevant interests and expectations of the interested parties should be considered while implementing circular economy initiatives. Besides, it is important to make clear how they affect the strategy of a digital transformation inside the organization.

In addition, digital transformation is fundamental to support circular businesses models. In practice, it is advisable to assemble businesses and sustainable management models, using technological resources from industry 4.0, and applying both directly into the organization's value chain. It is important that interested parties see how this process is adding value.

ACKNOWLEDGMENT

Thais de Assis Azevedo Payer (Master in Language Studies at Federal Fluminense University - UFF - Brazil), the translator (Portuguese x English) of this chapter.

REFERENCES

Alhawari, O., Awan, U., Bhutta, M. K. S., & Ülkü, M. A. (2021). Insights from Circular Economy Literature: A Review of Extant Definitions and Unravelling Paths to Future Research. *Sustainability*, *13*(2), 859. doi:10.3390u13020859

Antikainen, M., Uusitalo, T., & Kivikytö-Reponen, P. (2018). Digitalisation as an enabler of circular economy. *Procedia CIRP*, *73*, 45–49. doi:10.1016/j.procir.2018.04.027

Burlakovs, J., Jani, Y., Kriipsalu, M., Vincevica-Gaile, Z., Kaczala, F., Celma, G., Ozola, R., Rozina, L., Rudovica, V., Hogland, M., Viksna, A., Pehme, K.-M., Hogland, W., & Klavins, M. (2018). On the way to 'zero waste' management: Recovery potential of elements, including rare earth elements, from fine fraction of waste. *Journal of Cleaner Production*, *186*, 81–90. doi:10.1016/j.jclepro.2018.03.102

Cezarino, L. O., Liboni, L. B., Stefanelli, N. O., Olivera, B. G., & Stocco, L. C. (2019). Diving into emerging economies bottleneck: Industry 4.0 and implications for circular economy. *Management Decision*.

Di Vaio, A., Hasan, S., Palladino, R., & Hassan, R. (2022). The transition towards circular economy and waste within accounting and accountability models: A systematic literature review and conceptual framework. *Environment, Development and Sustainability*. Advance online publication. doi:10.100710668-021-02078-5 PMID:35035274

Geissdoerfer, M., Savaget, P., Bocken, N., & Hultink, E. (2017). The circular economy – a new sustainability paradigm? *Journal of Cleaner Production, 143*(1), 757–768. doi:10.1016/j.jclepro.2016.12.048

Genovese, A., Acquaye, A. A., Figueroa, A., & Koh, S. L. (2017). Sustainable supply chain management and the transition towards a circular economy: evidence and some applications. *Omega, 66*(B), 344-357.

Ghobakhloo, M. (2020). Industry 4.0, digitization, and opportunities for sustainability. *Journal of Cleaner Production, 252*(21), 119869. doi:10.1016/j.jclepro.2019.119869

Hedberg, A., & Šipka, S. (2021). Toward a circular economy: The role of digitalization. *One Earth, 4*(6), 783–785. doi:10.1016/j.oneear.2021.05.020

Hu, J., Xiao, Z., Zhou, R., Deng, W., Wang, M., & Ma, S. (2011). Ecological utilization of leather tannery waste with circular economy model. *Journal of Cleaner Production, 19*(2–3), 221–228. doi:10.1016/j.jclepro.2010.09.018

Ilić, M. P., Ranković, M., Dobrilović, M., Bucea-Manea-ţoniş, R., Mihoreanu, L., Gheţa, M. I., & Simion, V. E. (2022). Challenging Novelties within the Circular Economy Concept under the Digital Transformation of Society. *Sustainability, 14*(2), 702. doi:10.3390u14020702

Jabbour, A. B. L. S., Jabbour, C. J. C., Godinho Filho, M., & Roubaud, D. (2018). Industry 4.0 and the circular economy: A proposed research agenda and original roadmap for sustainable operations. *Annals of Operations Research, 270*(1-2), 273–286. doi:10.100710479-018-2772-8

Jæger, B., & Halse, L. L. (2019). Operationalizing Industry 4.0: Understanding Barriers of Industry 4.0 and Circular Economy. *APMS*, (2), 135–142.

Kang, H. S., Lee, J. Y., Choi, S., Kim, H., Park, J. H., Son, J. Y., Kim, B. H., & Noh, S. D. (2016). Smart manufacturing: Past research, present findings, and future directions. International. *Journal of Precision Engineering and Manufacturing-Green Technology, 3*(1), 111–128. doi:10.100740684-016-0015-5

Liboni, L. B., Liboni, L. H. B., & Cezarino, L. O. (2018). Electric utility 4.0: Trends and challenges towards process safety and environmental protection. *Process Safety and Environmental Protection, 11*, 593–605. doi:10.1016/j.psep.2018.05.027

Lieder, M., & Rashid, A. (2016). Towards circular economy implementation: A comprehensive review in context of manufacturing industry. *Journal of Cleaner Production, 115*, 36–51. doi:10.1016/j.jclepro.2015.12.042

Los Rios, I. C. D., & Charnley, F. J. (2017). Skills and capabilities for a sustainable and circular economy: The changing role of design. *Journal of Cleaner Production, 160*, 109–122. doi:10.1016/j.jclepro.2016.10.130

Lu, Y. (2017). Industry 4.0: A survey on technologies, applications and open research issues. *Journal of Industrial Information Integration, 6*, 1–10. doi:10.1016/j.jii.2017.04.005

Luthra, S., & Mangla, S. K. (2018). When strategies matter: Adoption of sustainable supply chain management practices in an emerging economy's context. *Resources, Conservation and Recycling, 138*, 194–206. doi:10.1016/j.resconrec.2018.07.005

Nascimento, D. L. M., Alencastro, V., Quelhas, O. L. G., Caiado, R. G. G., Garza-Reyes, J. A., Lona, L. R., & Tortorella, G. (2018). Exploring Industry 4.0 technologies to enable circular economy practices in a manufacturing context: A business model proposal. *Journal of Manufacturing Technology Management, 30*(3), 607–627. doi:10.1108/JMTM-03-2018-0071

Parajuly, K., & Wenzel, H. (2017). Potential for circular economy in household WEEE management. *Journal of Cleaner Production, 151*, 272–285. doi:10.1016/j.jclepro.2017.03.045

Rajput, S., & Singh, S. P. (2020). Industry 4.0 Model for circular economy and cleaner production. *Journal of Cleaner Production, 277*(21), 123853. doi:10.1016/j.jclepro.2020.123853

Rejeb, A., Rejeb, K., Abdollahi, A., Zailani, S., Iranmanesh, M., & Ghobakhloo, M. (2022). Digitalization in Food Supply Chains: A Bibliometric Review and Key-Route Main Path Analysis. *Sustainability, 14*(1), 29.

Rejikumar, G., Sreedharan, R. V., Arunprasad, P., Persis, J., & Sreeraj, K. M. (2019). Industry 4.0: Key findings and analysis from the literature arena. *Benchmarking, 26*(8), 2514–2542. doi:10.1108/BIJ-09-2018-0281

Rocchetti, L., Amato, A., & Beolchini, F. (2018). Printed circuit board recycling: A patent review. *Journal of Cleaner Production, 178*, 814–832. doi:10.1016/j.jclepro.2018.01.076

Sarc, R., Curtis, A., Kandlbauer, L., Khodier, K., Lorber, K. E., & Pomberger, R. (2019). Digitalisation and intelligent robotics in value chain of circular economy oriented waste management – A review. *Waste Management (New York, N.Y.), 95*, 476–492. doi:10.1016/j.wasman.2019.06.035 PMID:31351634

Sreedharan, V. R., & Unnikrishnan, A. (2017). Moving towards industry 4.0: A systematic review. *International Journal of Pure and Applied Mathematics, 117*(20), 929–936.

Su, B., Heshmati, A., Geng, Y., & Yu, X. (2013). A review of the circular economy in China: Moving from rhetoric to implementation. *Journal of Cleaner Production, 42*, 215–227. doi:10.1016/j.jclepro.2012.11.020

Trappey, A. J., Trappey, C. V., Fan, C. Y., Hsu, A. P., Li, X. K., & Lee, I. J. (2017). IoT patent roadmap for smart logistic service provision in the context of Industry 4.0. *Zhongguo Gongcheng Xuekan, 40*(7), 593–602. doi:10.1080/02533839.2017.1362325

Trentesaux, D., Borangiu, T., & Thomas, A. (2016). Emerging ICT concepts for smart, safe and sustainable industrial systems. *Computers in Industry, 81*, 1–10. doi:10.1016/j.compind.2016.05.001

Xu, L. D., Xu, E. L., & Li, L. (2018). Industry 4.0: State of the art and future trends. *International Journal of Production Research, 56*(8), 2941–2962. doi:10.1080/00207543.2018.1444806

ADDITIONAL READING

Caiado, R. G. G., Quelhas, O. L. G., Nascimento, D. L. M., Anholon, R., & Leal Filho, W. (2019). Towards sustainability by aligning operational programmes and sustainable performance measures. *Production Planning and Control, 30*(5-6), 413–425. doi:10.1080/09537287.2018.1501817

Martins, V. W. B., Rampasso, I. S., Anholon, R., Quelhas, O. L. G., & Leal Filho, W. (2019). Knowledge management in the context of sustainability: Literature review and opportunities for future research. *Journal of Cleaner Production*, *229*, 489–500. doi:10.1016/j.jclepro.2019.04.354

Souza, R. G., & Quelhas, O. L. G. (2020). Model Proposal for Diagnosis and Integration of Industry 4.0 Concepts in Production Engineering Courses. *Sustainability*, *12*(8), 3471–3486. doi:10.3390u12083471

KEY TERMS AND DEFINITIONS

Additive Manufacturing: The computer-controlled sequential layering of materials to create three-dimensional shapes.

Big Data: Data that contains greater variety, arriving in increasing volumes and with more velocity.

Chain Value: Step-by-step business model for transforming a product or service from idea to reality.

Circular Economy: Model of production and consumption, which involves sharing, leasing, reusing, repairing, refurbishing and recycling existing materials and products as long as possible.

Cloud Computing: The delivery of computing services over the Internet ("the cloud") to offer faster innovation, flexible resources, and economies of scale.

Cyber-Physical Systems (CPS): Computer system in which a mechanism is controlled or monitored by computer-based algorithms.

Digital Transformation: Incorporation of computer-based technologies into an organization's products, processes, and strategies.

Industry 4.0: New phase in the Industrial Revolution that focuses heavily on interconnectivity, automation, machine learning, and real-time data.

Internet of Things (IoT): Network of things with sensors, software, and other technologies for the purpose of connecting and exchanging data with other devices and systems over the internet.

Sustainability: Meeting our own needs without compromising the ability of future generations to meet their own needs. In addition to natural resources, we also need social and economic resources.

Emerging New Technologies and Industrial Revolution

Rauno Rusko
University of Lapland, Finland

Mika Kosonen
University of Lapland, Finland

INTRODUCTION

The technological innovations potentially have great importance to the industries creating new markets or radically change, or disrupt, the status quo in existing industries and their industry architectures (Bower & Christensen, 1995; Nagy, Schuessler & Dubinsky, 2016). This chapter focuses on one question: when new innovation is so disruptive that it causes the whole new industrial revolution? The contemporary technological invasion provides several technologies and perspectives, which might be disruptive. Industrial revolution is linked with disruption (Walters, 2014). Interesting question is, whether the contemporary new innovations and frameworks are disruptive and especially in the way, which is possible to interpret to be even so affective enabling industrial revolution. Furthermore, disruptions which have effects on technological development are not only innovative, but also the era of Covid-19 has cumulative effects on the invasion of digitizing and AI (artificial intelligence). This chapter introduces several innovative technologies and frameworks, which have claimed to be so innovative that they might have the status of industrial revolution (Table 2).

Chapter exploits blockchain technology, which is one of the latest strong innovations in society and business as an example of the most recent potentially disruptive technologies and their features related to the features of industrial revolution. According to Swan (2015), blockchain is in the position to become the fifth disruptive computing paradigm after mainframes, PCs, the Internet, and mobile/social networking. Technological disruption is possible to be individual organization specific (Nagy et al.,2016) or general all-inclusive. Swan (2015) sees that blockchain is a disruptive technological innovation with wide (all-inclusive) effects though the effects of the technology can vary according to the structure and other features of organization.

Furthermore, cybernetics or cyber-physical systems are important contemporary technology, which many researchers see potential core of the next industrial revolution (Monostori, 2014). Cybernetics is based on controlling systems, which are also necessary in the latest AI innovations (Glanville, 2013). Thus, another tested technology of this chapter for new potential industrial revolution is cybernetics.

This chapter focus on strong underlying features in the development of data science and machinery, namely disruptive technologies, which are linked with old and potential new industrial revolutions, such as blockchain technology and cybernetics.

DOI: 10.4018/978-1-7998-9220-5.ch129

BACKGROUND

Literature review is based on two parts: systematic literature review and completed contemporary perspectives about literature, which is focused on disruptions, industrial revolutions and their backgrounding (joint) features linked with data science and/or machinery. Systematic literature review has the first 25 most relevant references from EBSCO database with keywords "industrial revolution" (the search including "..."), which were available (full text). This search was on 28th September, 2016. The main results of this search are presented in Appendix 1.

The Systematic Literature Review

Generally, the drivers of the industrial revolutions are based, in addition to technology and innovations, also on societal, political and demographic themes, such as migration, environmentalism, demography, freedom and free trade. Thus, the "real" industrial revolution is not based on only one (or two) separate or disconnected innovation, rather the industrial revolution is based on the series or sequences of phenomenon, actions, innovations and changes in business environment, political and societal circumstances, which together enable *all-inclusive disruption*. This outcome supports the ideas of Mahoney (2000) about the important role of path-dependence and sequential phases in industrial revolution.

According to table in Appendix 1, the most important drives of the first industrial revolution (in Britain) seem to be relatively *high factor prices,* such as wages and price of coal, *rise in international trade, mechanization, incentives to innovate because of patent system, the general rise in new ideas, consumentarism, organizational changes in production, working-class households, discontinuous technological change, high profits enabling reinvestments.*

Also, the drives of the industrial revolution among the articles, which focused on the latest or several industrial revolutions were *environmental and energy themes*, such as high carbon and low carbon energy sources, low carbon transition, climate change, steam, steamship, electricity, expansion of energy services, historical decline in the energy cost share and new energy sources to methods of production, *technology* (mass production and mass customizing, mechanization, information technology (IT), Internet of Things (IOT), railroad, telegraph, cable systems, mass production and distribution systems, changes in physical and management technology, modern transportation and communication facilities), *political and societal themes* (weak state, an emphasis upon individual liberty, the right institutions and culture of creativity born of free minds and free markets, "Buy American", regulation, taxes and movement from centrally planned economies to capitalism) and *themes of business and economics*, such as global competition, open participation in international trade and private economic benefits of adopting new technologies and practices. (Appendix 1)

The Complementary Literature Review

Because most of the articles in the systematic review considered only the first (British) industrial revolution, it is essential to enlarge the population of articles of the literature review. Disruption, which is an important feature in the new large-scale innovations (Holey, 2009) was mentioned only in 7 out of 25 articles in the systematic literature review. Next, we introduce some other studies, which focus on the theme and criterions of industrial revolution mainly with disruption perspective and consider also other features, logics and the drivers of industrial revolution.

Disruptive technology is linked with industrial revolutions. Industrial revolution contains, according to Holley (2009, 13), three steps:

"...first a technology emerges rapidly, then the technology matures having specific socio-economic benefits, and finally this technology becomes so disruptive that it affects all other technologies that define our socio- economic system. The first stage is marked by innovators' research, the second stage is marked by investors' forecasts, and the third stage is marked by consumers' adaptation."

In other words, new innovation (and research), investment (and forecast), and consumption (and adaptation) follow each other. One possible perspective to analyze industrial revolution is basing on sequential steps or the framework of path dependence, where scholars often consider two dominant types of sequences, *self-reinforcing sequences* characterized by the formation and long-term reproduction of a given institutional pattern and *reactive sequences*, which are chains of temporally ordered and causally connected events. These sequences are "reactive" in the sense that each event within the sequence is in part a reaction to temporally antecedent events. Thus, each step in the chain is "dependent" on prior steps. (Mahoney, 2000.)

Compared with the articles of systematic literature review Swan (2015) considers relatively short perspectives and focuses on disruptive computing paradigms whereas Schwab (2016) has longer historical perspective and he focuses on industrial revolutions. Swan (2015) finds four disruptive computing paradigms: mainframes, PCs, the Internet, and mobile/social networking and Schwab (2016) finds also four phases of industrial revolution: steam, water and mechanic production equipment (from 1784), division of labour, electricity and mass production (from 1870), electronics, IT and automated production (1969) and the contemporary phase is, according to Schwab (2016), "cyber-physical systems". Closely related concept to technology and technology inventions is automatization or cybernetics. Cybernetics has several alternative definitions and interpretations. One general perspective is typical for cybernetics: negative feedback, referring to how an organism or system automatically opposes any change imposed upon it. (Cannon, 1932)

Warschauer (2004) names three industrial revolutions. According to him, the first industrial revolution was late 18th century with the key technologies, such as printing press, steam engine and machinery, the second revolution was late 19th century containing electricity, internal combustion, telegraph and telephone, and the third revolution was mid to late 20th century having transistors, personal computers, telecommunication and internet. The archetypical workplaces of these phases are workshop, factory and office (Warschauer, 2004). Holley (2009) notices five industrial revolutions, which have been driven by water power, internal combustion power, electrical power, and computer power, and have greatly affected economy and forever changed the course of society. Holley (2009, 9) see that nanotechnology is the power of the fifth industrial and even "represents more potential power than all previous technologies combined".

Table 1 summarizes the phases of industrial revolution basing on the attitudes of Holey (2009), Warschauer (2004), Swan (2015) and Schwab (2016).

Table 1. Some interpretations about industrial revolutions.

	Warschauer (2004)	Holey (2009)	Swan (2015)	Schwab (2016)	The most typical industrial revolutions/ disruptions
Industrial revolutions/ disruptions	1) late 18th century: printing press, steam engine and machinery 2) late 19th century: electricity, internal combustion, telegraph and telephone 3) mid to late 20th century: transistors, personal computers, telecommunication and internet	1) Water power 2) Internal combustion power 3) Electrical power 4) Computer power 5) Nanotechnology power?	1) Mainframes 2) PCs 3) Internet 4) Mobile/ social networking	1) From 1784: steam, water and mechanic production equipment, 2) From 1870: division of labour, electricity and mass production 3) From 1969: electronics, IT and automated production 4) Cyber-physical systems	1) Steam power and mechanic production (Factory) 2) Electrical power 3) Computers, IT and digitalization
Time horizon	1750-	1750-	1950-	1784-	about 1750-
Features	Long term general perspective	Long term general perspective	Short term perspective focusing on information	Long term general perspective	Long term general perspective
Drivers of disruptions	Primarily power sources; secondary information technology	Power sources and as well new information technologies	New information technologies	Power sources, information technology and new systems/ organizing	Power sources & information technologies

The studies focusing on long-term perspectives of industrial revolutions emphasize power sources, such as steam & waterpower, internal combustion power and electrical power. Swan (2015) has a shorter perspective starting from about 1950's. Furthermore, she focuses on disruptions basing on information technology. There are discrepancy among these studies about the latest disruption or industrial revolution. According to Warschauer (2004) the latest industrial revolution is based on information technology, such as transistors, personal computers, telecommunication and internet whereas Holey (2009) emphasizes the importance of nanotechnology. Swan (2015) see that generally mobile/social networking is the latest disruption. Schwab (2016) has found the cyber-physical systems to be the source of the latest industrial revolution.

Mohajeri and Nyberg (no date) see that especially additive manufacturing (AM) technology is the main feature of the third industrial revolution. Many studies focusing on industrial revolution, but not systematic literature review, see knowledge strategically important power and a resource. According to Liao, Fei & Liu (2008), third industrial revolution is based on knowledge, which changes the way an individual, an enterprise or even a nation can create wealth and prosperity. Attwell and Costa (2009) emphasizes the importance of changes in how we learn, how we work and how we live. These changes are based on industrial revolution with the rapid development and deployment of digital technologies. (Attwell & Costa, 2009).

This chapter studies the hypothesis, which assumes blockchain technology to have typical features of industrial revolution. In other words, the possibilities to interpret blockchain to be the technology of industrial revolution in the future. Table 1 shows that typically time horizon is relatively long in the discussions and literature about industrial revolution starting about from 1750. Swan considers this theme following shorter time horizon starting from about 1950 and focusing on information technology. This perspective emphasizes the latest inventions and digitalization in the economy. To this kind of perspective new disruptions, such as blockchain technology, are easier to add as a presentative of new industrial revolution. In this sense, it is interesting to consider potential competing technologies or paradigms, which challenges blockchain technology to be the driver of the latest industrial revolution.

Literature of business and technology contain several alternative disrupting technologies or paradigms, which are suggested to be the drivers of the latest or forthcoming industrial revolution, such as nanotechnology, green technology, additive manufacturing (AM) technology (e.g. 3D printing) and maker movement approach, such as do-it-yourself (DIY) and do-it-with-others (DIWO), and offshoring (Bowen, Duffy, & Fankhauser, 2016; Stern & Rydge, 2012). However, the main driver of industrial revolution is new forms of power and energy, such as steam/water power, internal combustion power and electricity (Table 1) and secondary – depending on the time horizon – digital solutions with information transformation. Also new ways to organize production might be one source for (contemporary) new industrial revolution.

This study has three following qualitative hypothesis: Thus, both of these two technologies, blockchain and cyber-physical systems, provide good platform to study the features of industrial revolution generally and especially in the context of these two cases. Third hypothesis focus on alternative technologies.

Hypothesis 1: Basing on the first implemented steps of blockchain technology, blockchain has a great potential as to be important all-inclusive disruptive technology and core of the next industrial revolution.

Hypothesis 2: Basing on the noticed development of cybernetics (cyber-physical systems), cybernetics has a great potential as to be important all-inclusive disruptive technology and core of the next industrial revolution.

Hypothesis 3: Basing on the features and development of other important technologies, such as nanotechnology, green technology, additive manufacturing and offshoring, they have also great potential for the next industrial revolution.

THE RESEARCH DESIGN

Path-Dependence Model

The literature review above noticed the importance of all inclusive features associated with industrial revolution. All-inclusive disruption of industrial revolution is based on the series or sequences of phenomenon, actions, innovations and changes in business environment, political and societal circumstances. This constructed definition is on the general level and it resembles the idea of path-dependence. Therefore, this chapter introduces the principles of path-dependence perspective linked with the concept of industrial revolution. This perspective is used in the analysis of cases.

According to Mahoney (2000), the focus of path-dependence patterns is not on the perspectives of "history matters" or "the past influences the future", but on deviant outcomes or on "exceptionalism", where deviant cases have extremely rare or even unique outcomes. Even today has noticed about the posteriori trends of evolution, that roadmaps based on these posteriori data cannot be counted on to predict disruptions (Kim et al., 2016). Mahoney (2000, 515) see lock-in process to be linked with institutional reproduction, where "these mechanisms of reproduction may be so causally efficacious that they "lock-in" a given institutional pattern, making it extremely difficult to abolish."

This study introduces the perspectives of Mahoney (2000) about English industrialization or industrial revolution. He has found the grounds of his analysis from Goldstone (1998). Figure 1 summarizes the ideas of Mahoney (2000), where industrialization is a sequential result of the environmental sequence. Industrial sequence develops together cultural sequence (liberalizing culture open to technological experimentation).

Figure 1. Reactive sequence explanation of English industrial revolution (Mahoney, 2000, 534; see Goldstone, 1998)

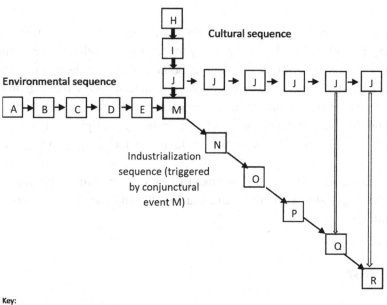

Key:
A: Limited forest area, abundant coal near sea, and cold climate
B: Long-term heavy reliance on cola for heat
C: Surface coal is exhausted
D: Effort to dig for deeper coal
E: Ground water fills mine shafts
H: Limited monarchy
I: Limited Anglian authority and toleration
J: Liberalizing culture open technological experimentation
M: Development of first steam engine
N: Improvement of steam engine
O: reduction in coal prices
P: Reduction in price of iron and steal
Q: Development of railways and ships
R: Mass distribution of industrial production and goods

According to Mahoney (2000) and Goldstone (1998), British industrialization contains especially one invention: steam engine. However, they notice the wider circumstances of industrialization, in addition to this core driver of industrial revolution, steam engine and steam power. This reactive sequence perspective of the first industrial revolution provides analytical tool to compare the other potential industrial revolutions, with the framework of Mahoney (2000). This study exploits this tool in the case study analysis.

Introduction of the Cases

This chapter has two main cases, in addition to other potential "secondary" cases. These main cases are blockchain technology and cybernetics.

The case: blockchain technology

Blockchain technology has been often mentioned in the context of the potential latest industrial revolution (Jensen-Haxel, 2015). Thus, blockchain might be ideal case to follow the path-dependence perspective upon industrial revolution. The most known application basing on blockchain technology is bitcoin, an international digital currency. However, blockchain technology will enable several other products and markets, which are still developing without any significant realized economic importance (Wright, & De Filippi, 2015). This study maps the current situation of the blockchain technology in the economy and markets and estimates the forthcoming opportunities of business basing on blockchain technology. The outcomes of this study base on the existing knowledge and literature focused on blockchain technology. The future development drives of blockchain technology are estimated by comparing the first steps of the older disrupting technologies/paradigms with the development steps of blockchain.

Blockchain technology is based on peer-to-peer technology. Peer-to-peer technology shares distributed resources in an area that has no central service. It is operated through autonomous peers which makes the system self-organized (Savukoski, 2015). In the context of bitcoin, blockchain is the public ledger of all transactions that have ever been executed. It is constantly growing as miners add new blocks to it to record the most recent transactions. The blocks are added to the blockchain in a linear, chronological order. (Swan, 2015). In other words, blockchain is based on blocks, which describe the contents of each transactions. Blocks are transparent and recorded in a public ledger, that is stored on many (all) users' computers, and continuously viewable on the Internet. (Swan, 2015). Figure 2 illustrates the idea of blockchain technology.

Figure 2. The main principle of blockchain technology (Modified from Brikman, 2014).

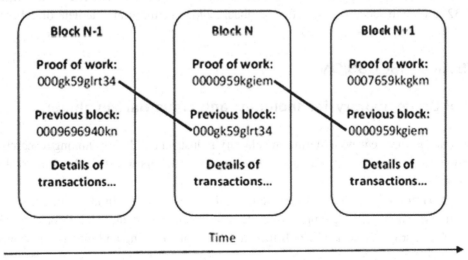

Blockchain technology has several application possibilities. In Internet of things (IoT), where the IoT devices are not revealed in blockchain technology (Gaurav, 2015). The basic idea of this concept is the pervasive presence around us of a variety of things or objects – such as Radio-Frequency IDentification (RFID) tags, sensors, actuators, mobile phones, etc. – which, through unique addressing schemes, are able to interact with each other and cooperate with their neighbors to reach common goals (Atzori, et al. 2010).

The case: Cybernetics

The roots of cybernetics are relatively old (e.g. Cannon 1932), but the relevance of cybernetics is still significant e.g. in the forms of artificial intelligence and self-driving cars (Delic and Riley, 2013). Already 1950's the role of electronics was strong though Ross Assby (1956/1961, V) saw "[T)he basic ideas of cybernetics can be treated without reference to electronics, and they are fundamentally simple".

Some researchers find three waves of cybernetics: periods of homeostasis, self-organization and virtuality (Ilfeld, 2012; Hayles, 2008). The era of homeostasis (1945-1959) contains feedback loop information as signal, circular causality (following the principle idea of cybernetics) and instrumental language. Also quantification is typical for cybernetics in the era of homeostasis. Self-organization (1960-1984) includes in reflexive language, autopoiesis (system is capable of reproducing and maintaining itself), structural coupling and system-environment. Era of virtuality (1985-) has typically emergent behavior, functionalities and computational universe. (Ilfeld, 2012)

According to many scientists, cybernetics has a relationship with digitalization due to "the second machine age", which is spaceless, the spatially absent, or digital space, which is a result of cybernetics and digitalization (Erk and Uluoğlu, 2013). One of the representative studies of "the second machine age" is Alvin Toffler's Future Shock (1970), where technology is, however, as "spinning out of control" and constructing the socio-psychological future shock (Lobsinger, 2000). Schwab (2016) see that the current industrial revolution is (potentially) based on "cyber-physical systems". Cyber-physical systems have several alternative definitions. Baheti and Gill (2011, 161) understand these systems to be a new generation of systems with integrated computational and physical capabilities that can interact with humans through many new modalities in the next generation airplanes and space vehicles, hybrid gas-electric vehicles, fully autonomous urban driving, and prostheses that allow brain signals to control physical objects.

Particularly noteworthy is one essential element of cyber-physical systems: control, which already Cannon (1932) took into account as negative feedback, which is important element of cybernetics.

RESULTS AND DISCUSSION

Features of Contemporary Technologies and Industrial Revolution

There are several alternative ways to define and classify industrial revolutions among researchers (Table 1). In addition to new sources of power and technology, one concept which is also source of industrial revolution is *disruption*.

Walters (2014) and Gilding (2011), for example, have noticed the linkages between (industrial) revolution and disruption. Gilding emphasizes the role of climate change and global warming in the forthcoming great disruption, which "will bring on the end of shopping and the birth of a new world".

Walters (2014, 8) compares industrial revolutions and digital revolution "As the industrial revolution was defined by radical efficiency in production, ... the digital revolution is defined by radical efficiency in information transmission." According to Walters (2014), digital disruption is fundamental disruption concerning every industry because of its results in the empowerment of consumers and creates the need for companies to create and manage positive and differentiated customer experiences worldwide.

One promising way to define industrial revolution is to follow the idea of path-dependence. According to Mahoney (2000, 507-508)

"path dependence characterizes specifically those historical sequences in which contingent events set into motion institutional patterns or event chains that have deterministic properties. The identification of path dependence therefore involves both tracing a given outcome back to a particular set of historical events, and showing how these events are themselves contingent occurrences that cannot be explained on the basis of prior historical conditions."

We can conclude that industrial revolution have to have all-inclusive disruption, which is not focused only one nation, one branch, or one continent. Industrial revolution is a disruption, which practically all firms have to take into account. This kind of disruption is a strategic inflection point, which starts a new paradigm and which firms have to follow in order to maintain their business in the market (Walters, 2014).

Furthermore, industrial revolution contains chains of remarkable events, which are not basing on the typical historical conditions. In this context, blockchain technology seems to be part of larger chains of events, which started, perhaps, from digital revolution (Table 2).

Blockchain technology, for example, is a useful way to restore the information of activities and actions. However, it is possible to doubt the all-inclusive effects of blockchain, which all the firms have to follow to maintain and develop their business. On the contrary, blockchain technology will provide an alternative technology to the prevailing digital technologies. However, it is possible that in the future the situation has changed via new potential blockchain innovations.

Nanotechnology has the all-inclusive features, but it is not necessary for all industries. Furthermore, nanotechnology is related to digital technology and might be actually part of digital revolution. Green technology also has all-inclusive features, but the problem is that green technology is not an independent technology, but related to, for example, nanotechnology (Smith, 2011).

Additive manufacturing (AM), which is especially based on 3D printing, is practically nearly all-inclusive. However, if we accept that digitalization is one of the industrial revolutions, AM might be part of digital revolution. Particularly, the use of AM is related to the Web, which is the most typical outcomes of digitalization. Maker movement and outsourcing are the ways to rationalize the supply chain, but not necessarily any technologies. (Doering et al., 2009). Though they have all-inclusive features.

Cybernetics, however, has all-inclusive effects on the economy. Cybernetics is not a new tendency in the society and economy (Cannon, 1932). Cybernetics has all-inclusive features and new applications of cybernetics arise continuously. Obviously, the latest innovations of cybernetics are autonomous cars. Cybernetics has features and possibilities of industrial revolution. In this case, timing is a problem: cybernetics is already about 100 years old. The development of cybernetics has been relatively slow. Thus, path-dependence perspective of industrial revolution might be suitable for the analysis of cybernetics as industrial revolution (i.e. Mahoney, 2000).

Covid, Digitalization and Blockchain

The reactions during the Covid-19 have accelerated ten key technologies by World Economic Forum, according to online shopping & robot deliveries, digital & contactless payments, remote work, distance learning, telehealth, online entertainment, supply chain 4.0, 3D printing, robotics & drones, and 5G & information and communications technology (Xiao & Fan, 2020). They all aim for minimizing human-to-human contact and they all contain digital and automation components that is transforming contact-based activities to technology mediated (Lee & Han 2020). Especially the growth of digital healthcare, remote work and e-learning as schools and offices were closing and people are afraid of going physically to hospitals has been significant. (Bensbih, Essangri & Soudaka 2020.)

UNESCO have stated that nine out of ten students have faced interruptions in classroom learning during Covid-19, and about half of students have no access to computer worldwide. In research, it has turned harder to collect data as interviews need to be done remotely. The communication between scholars has turned to be mostly via online services. (Aalst, Hinz & Weinhardt 2020.) Kang (2021) have also identified three key concerns regarding digital transformation in education: poor motivation management, negative effect of IT device usage in education, and educational inequality by digital divide. It can be concluded that Covid-19 has had an impact in digitalization.

Blockchain technology enables different solutions like immunity certificates (Bansal et al. 2020) and it helps in the identification of the virus itself (Sharma et al. 2020) and it has been implemented to create new ways of doing charity (Rangone & Burolli 2021). In grape production due the Covid-19, producers have implemented blockchain technology in value chain management (Ravi Kumar & Babu 2020). Even that blockchain technology have seen a trend during Covid-19 pandemic, the impact of virus is much wider in digitalization. Piccialli et al. (2021) have recognized a rising trend of peer reviewed articles regarding artificial intelligence and Covid-19, which tells that there is larger interest in developed technologies due the pandemic, especially in academic world.

In charity, blockchain targets the widest and greatest issue of doing philanthropy, transparency. By using blockchain technology, charities, NGOs, and social enterprises are becoming more and more transparent in their actions. (Rangone & Burolli 2021.) Furthermore, misinformation has turned to be very effective tool for actors with varied interests. Sengupta et al., (2021) have introduced blockchain as solution for tackling fake news. It seems to be clear that Covid-19 have disrupted many industries and blockchain as a technology have been working solution and the development of systems using blockchain is more popular than ever. This gives us a reason to believe that blockchain has potential to be disruptive technology even by itself.

As it can be seen, Covid-19 has accelerated the digitalization and blockchain around the world, concerning multiple different sectors from healthcare to philanthropy. While digitalization itself is acting as disruptive force, Covid-19 has made it even faster and wider in effect.

Table 2. The features of the potential contemporary disruptive technologies and industrial revolutions.

	Blockchain technology	Nanotechnology	Green technology	Additive manufacturing (AM) technology (e.g. 3D printing)	Maker movement approach, such as do-it-yourself (DIY) and do-it-with-others (DIWO),	Offshoring	Cybernetics
Main description	Distributed database that maintains a continuously-growing list of records and helps secure them from tampering and revision.	Nanotechnology is the study and application of extremely small things and can be used across all the other science fields. Manipulation of matter with at least one dimension sized from 1 to 100 nanometers.	Green technology uses inventions of several branches. It is environmentally friendly, developed and used in such a way so that it doesn't disturb environment and conserves natural resources.	The technology that build 3D objects by adding layer-upon-layer of material. Additive manufacturing technologies provide a disruptive transformation in how products are designed and manufactured.	Based on 'Mcdonaldization' and freedom of customers. Value co-creation and prosuming.	A way to rationalize supply chains. Outsourcing and crowd-sourcing are resembling concepts.	Basing on negative feedback, referring to how an organism or system automatically opposes any change imposed upon it
Role of disruption	Individual organization/ industry specific	All-inclusive role, but not necessary for all industries.	All-inclusive, but not an independent technology. Weak disruption.	Practically nearly all-inclusive.	Started already 1950's, all-inclusive	Industry specific, organization specific. Partly all-inclusive features	All-inclusive role, but not necessary for all industries.
Relationship to the digitalization	Uses digital solutions, such as internet as a tool	Relatively closely related to digitalization.	Uses digitalization part of the phenomenon.	Digitalization is necessary part of AM.	Initially no relationship with digital tools.	Initially no relationship with digital tools.	Closely related to digitalization.
Industrial revolution?	Part of digital revolution, might be one part/ branch of its industrialization sequence	Because of all-inclusive role, nanotechnology has some features of industrial revolution. Might be part of digital revolution.	All-inclusive, but not has any independent role. One source of competitive advantage.	Despite of all-inclusive feature AM leans on digitalization. Not independent industrial revolution.	Because of all-inclusive role, maker movement has some features of industrial revolution	Only weak nuances of industrial revolution.	Because of all-inclusive role, cybernetics has some features of industrial revolution. Might be part of digital revolution.

Case Analysis of Path Dependence Model

This section considers the case study examples, blockchain and cybernetics/cyber-physical systems, following the path-dependence perspective linked with the phases of Industrial revolution. According to Mahoney (2000), English industrial revolution and industrialization had three sequences:

1. Environmental sequence (antecedent reactive sequence)
2. Industrialization sequence (conjunctural event/discruption)
3. Cultural sequence (liberalizing culture (and antecedent self-reinforcing sequence), which open to technological experimentation)

Table 3 summarizes the potential fit of blockchain technology and of cyber-physical systems development with the first industrial revolution. Noteworthy is that some researchers have claimed that also steam engine is possible to interpret as a part of the development of cybernetics (Otte, 2011).

Table 3. The features of blockchain technology and cyber-physical systems.

	Blockchain	Cyber-physical systems
Environmental sequence	Internet, digitalization, development of ordinary digital cash technologies, development in the applications of cryptography in bank and credit cards, computer passwords, and in electronic commerce.	Preceding state: cybernetics, invented by Plato (Self-governance), steam engine (Otte, 2011), in 20th century: the fields of control systems (e.g. in telephones). The contemporary cybernetics invented by Norbert Wiener in 1948 (Rifkin, 1996)
Industrialization sequence (conjunctural event/ disruption)	Invention of blockchain technology	Computers and digitalization enabled the enlargement of cybernetics to cyber-physical systems.
Cultural sequence	Bitcoin (the first application of blockchain), developing adaptation to use bitcoin, other preliminary followers of bitcoin in blockchain technology (e.g. databases of art, music, crowdfunding)	E.g. hybrid gas-electric vehicles, fully autonomous urban driving, and prostheses that allow brain signals to control physical objects (Baheti and Gill, 2011)
The state of cultural sequence	Beginning	Developed
Other features, notes about disruption	Relatively narrow influence today in business and society, noticeable disruption (bitcoin)	Long-duration development. Potential disruption is based on digitalization and internet. Contemporary cyber-physical systems only completes IoT.

Cybernetics and digital cyber-physical systems have several features of industrial revolution. All three sequences (environmental, disruptive and cultural) are their developed phases. However, the strong disruption, such as the steam engine in the 18th century, of cybernetics/cyber-physical systems is basing on digitalization (systems of binaries in computers), which is typically intrinsically interpreted to be one of the industrial revolutions (Table 2). Furthermore, timing of cybernetics or cyber-physical systems is problematic. Control and self-control is an essential feature of cybernetics. Even Plato used these kinds of perspectives. Then it is also possible to claim that that we have already meet the industrial revolution of cybernetics and we are only living with the long tails of this distribution and industrial revolution.

The case of blockchain differs from cybernetics: bitcoin might be disruption of blockchain technology and the cultural sequence is now in the starting phase. However, the all-inclusive features of blockchain technology are still missing. Then it might be too early to evaluate, whether blockchain technology is a source of industrial revolution or not.

IMPLICATIONS

About the hypothesis

Generally, researchers have several opinions the number and main disruptions of industrial revolution. Thus, it is impossible to interpret, how many industrial revolutions the mankind has met. One possible interpretation is that the industrial revolutions are overlapping and there are at the same time potentially several industrial revolutions. Thus, we are living at the same time in the environmental sequence, disruptive sequence and cultural sequence of potentially industrial revolutions. Furthermore, the distribution, volume and length of these industrial revolutions differs. Figure 3 illustrates these interpretations. Third industrial revolution is based on computers, digitalization and internet. Cybernetics and cyber-physical systems is potentially an industrial revolution, which strongly leans on the third industrial revolution and especially on digitalization. Furthermore, the environmental phase of cybernetics has been exceptionally long starting, perhaps, from the times of Plato. This finding about cybernetics supports the outcomes of Ardito et al. (2016), where they noticed that not only nascent technologies significantly shape future technological developments, but also established technologies have to become breakthrough solutions.

Compared to cybernetics, application possibilities and technological linkages of blockchain technology are more limited. Blockchain technology is still enlarging technology, and in the future, it has possibilities to achieve all-inclusive technology position due to potentially forthcoming, but still hiding, features and linkages to the other technologies. Similarly, other introduced technologies of this chapter lack all-inclusive character: they are important technologies and frameworks, but there is not necessity to apply, meet and use them in the everyday practices of business and society.

Figure 3.

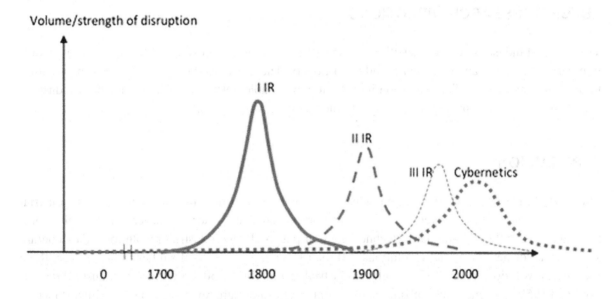

Outcome 1: Blockchain technology seems not to be all-inclusive disruptive technology. However, it has possibilities to disruptive technology in some particular restrictions. It is a good alternative technology, but not all-inclusive technology or core of the next industrial revolution.

Outcome 2: Cyber-physical systems (initially cybernetics) have several features suitable for (disruptive) industrial revolution. However, the timing of cybernetics is difficult. The inventions of the principles of cybernetics dates back even to the era of Plato and Socrates. However, the disruption of cybernetics is based on computers and digitalization, the elements of (potential) third industrial revolution. In this sense cyber-physical systems either completes the third revolution or there are simultaneously two (or more) industrial revolutions, the third digitalization-based revolution and the fourth cybernetics-based industrial revolution.

Outcome 3: Other technologies, such as nanotechnology, green technology, additive manufacturing and offshoring, are important technologies and perspectives, but they do not have similar all-inclusive feature as digitalization or even blockchain technology. They have linkages with digitalization and it is easy to understand them even part of digitalization tendency.

Disruptions, Data Science and Machine Learning

Disruptions have an essential role in the third era of industrial revolution: digitalization. Data science, machine learning and artificial intelligence (AI) lean on digitalization. Furthermore, cybernetics is an underlying feature of AI, such as in the technology of self-driving cars (Grinin & Grinin, 2020). In the branch automobile technology, new applications of cybernetics, such as self-driving cars, are also (minor) disruptions for this branch. The development in automobile industry is only one example, but it shows that data science, digitalization, AI and cybernetics often go together.

Blockchain technology and bitcoin system, for example, have nearly the similar linkages to data science, digitalization and AI. Bitcoin or cryptocurrency mining is based on digitalization, data processing, AI (Lihu et al., 2020), and blockchain technology.

FUTURE RESEARCH DIRECTIONS

The theme of industrial revolution still needs scientific discussions. The definitions of industrial revolution vary remarkably among scholars and practitioners. There is a need to construct uniform structure to the elements of industrial revolution in order to have usable definition for the concept of industrial revolution. This theme provides challenges to the historians and futurologists.

CONCLUSION

The most of the studies, which focus on industrial revolution, consider only the era of the first industrial revolution 1760-1850. However, several contemporary studies consider also several industrial revolutions and especially the candidates (technologies) of potential new industrial revolutions: they contain suggestions for new industrial revolutions and their technologies. Several studies notice at least three industrial revolutions (1760-1850 (English industrial revolution), 1850-1900 (Second industrial revolution) and 1950- (the era of digitalization and computers)). Literature review revealed the importance of all-inclusive effects one of the main features of industrial revolution. Study considers several potential disruptive technologies as the core technologies of industrial revolution. Especially two technologies are the case study examples: blockchain technology and cybernetics/cyber physical systems on which cybernetics proved to have several features of industrial revolution.

REFERENCES

Ardito, L., Messeni Petruzzelli, A., & Panniello, U. (2016). Unveiling the breakthrough potential of established technologies: An empirical investigation in the aerospace industry. *Technology Analysis and Strategic Management*, *28*(8), 1–19. doi:10.1080/09537325.2016.1180356

Attwell, G., & Costa, C. (2009). *Integrating personal learning and working environments*. Academic Press.

Baheti & Gill. (2011). Cyber-physical systems. *The Impact of Control Technology*, *12*, 161-166.

Bansal, A., Garg, C., & Padappayil, R. P. (2020). Optimizing the Implementation of COVID-19 "Immunity Certificates" Using Blockchain. *Journal of Medical Systems*, *44*(9), 140. doi:10.100710916-020-01616-4 PMID:32683501

Bensbih, S., Essangri, H. & Soudaka, A. (2020). The Covid19 outbreak: A Catalyst For Digitization in African Countries. *Journal of the Egyptian Public Health Association*. doi:10.1186/s42506-020-00047-w

Bowen, A., Duffy, C., & Fankhauser, S. (2016). *'Green growth' and the new Industrial Revolution*. https://www.lse.ac.uk/GranthamInstitute/wp-content/uploads/2016/01/Bowen-et-al-2016.pdf

Bower & Christensen. (1995). *Disruptive technologies: Catching the wave*. Harvard Business Review.

Brikman, Y. (2014). *Bitcoin by analogy*. Referenced 15 October 2016. https://www.ybrikman.com/writing/2014/04/24/bitcoin-by-analogy

Cannon, W. B. (1932). *Homeostasis. The wisdom of the body*. Norton.

Erk, G. K., & Uluoğlu, B. (2013). Changing Paradigms in Space Theories: Recapturing 20th Century Architectural History. *Archnet-IJAR: International Journal of Architectural Research*, *7*(1), 6–20.

Fei, W. C., & Liu, C. T. (2008). Relationships between knowledge inertia, organizational learning and organization innovation. *Technovation*, *28*(4), 183–195. doi:10.1016/j.technovation.2007.11.005

Gilding, P. (2011). *The great disruption: Why the climate crisis will bring on the end of shopping and the birth of a new world*. Bloomsbury Publishing USA.

Glanville, R. (2013). Cybernetics: Thinking through the technology. *Traditions of systems theory: Major figures and contemporary developments*, 45-77.

Goldstone, J. A. (1998). Initial conditions, general laws, path dependence, and explanation in historical sociology 1. *American Journal of Sociology*, *104*(3), 829–845. doi:10.1086/210088

Grinin, L., & Grinin, A. (2020). The cybernetic revolution and the future of technologies. In *The 21st Century Singularity and Global Futures* (pp. 377–396). Springer. doi:10.1007/978-3-030-33730-8_17

Hall, R. (1993). A framework linking intangible resources and capabiliites to sustainable competitive advantage. *Strategic Management Journal*, *14*(8), 607–618. doi:10.1002mj.4250140804

Holley, S. E. (2009). Nano Revolution–Big Impact: How Emerging Nanotechnologies Will Change the Future of Education and Industry in America (and More Specifically in Oklahoma) An Abbreviated Account. *The Journal of Technology Studies*, *35*(1), 9–19.

Ilfeld, E. J. (2012). Contemporary art and cybernetics: Waves of cybernetic discourse within conceptual, video and new media art. *Leonardo*, *45*(1), 57–63. doi:10.1162/LEON_a_00326

Jensen-Haxel, P. (2015). New Framework for a Novel Lattice: 3D Printers, DNA Fabricators, and the Perils in Regulating the Raw Materials of the Next Era of Revolution, Renaissance, and Research. " *A. Wake Forest JL & Pol'y*, *5*, 231.

Kang, B. (2021). How the COVID-19 Pandemic is Reshaping the Education Service. In The Future of Service Post-COVID-19 Pandemic, Volume 1, The ICT and Evolution of Work. doi:10.1007/978-981-33-4126-5_1

Kim, J., Park, Y., & Lee, Y. (2016). A visual scanning of potential disruptive signals for technology roadmapping: Investigating keyword cluster, intensity, and relationship in futuristic data. *Technology Analysis and Strategic Management, 28*(10), 1–22. doi:10.1080/09537325.2016.1193593

Kumar, K. N. R., & Babu, S. C. (2021). Value chain management under COVID-19: Responses and lessons from grape production in India. *Journal of Social and Economic Development, 23*(S3), 468–490. Advance online publication. doi:10.100740847-020-00138-6 PMID:34720487

Lee, J., & Han, S. H. (Eds.). (2021). *Preparing for Accelerated Third Order Impacts of Digital Technology in Post Pandemic Service Industry: Steep Transformation and Metamorphosis. In The Future of Service Post-COVID-19 Pandemic* (Vol. 1). The ICT and Evolution of Work. doi:10.1007/978-981-33-4126-5_1

Lihu, A., Du, J., Barjaktarevic, I., Gerzanics, P., & Harvilla, M. (2020). *A proof of useful work for artificial intelligence on the blockchain*. arXiv preprint arXiv:2001.09244.

Lobsinger, M. L. (2000). Cybernetic theory and the architecture of performance: Cedric Price's Fun Palace. *Anxious Modernisms: Experimentation in Postwar Architectural Culture*, 119-139.

Mohajeri, B., & Nyberg, T. (n.d.). *Transition to Social Manufacturing: Applications of Additive Manufacturing in consumer products*. https://elsevier.conference-services.net/viewsecurePDF.asp?conferenceID=3781&loc=files&type=fpaper&abstractID=864389

Monostori, L. (2014). Cyber-physical production systems: Roots, expectations and R&D challenges. *Procedia CIRP, 17*, 9–13. doi:10.1016/j.procir.2014.03.115

Nagy, D., Schuessler, J., & Dubinsky, A. (2016). Defining and identifying disruptive innovations. *Industrial Marketing Management, 57*(August), 119–126. doi:10.1016/j.indmarman.2015.11.017

Otte, M. F. (2011). Evolution, learning, and semiotics from a Peircean point of view. *Educational Studies in Mathematics, 77*(2-3), 313–329. doi:10.100710649-011-9302-9

Piccialli, F., Schiano di Cola, V., Giampaolo, F., & Cuomo, S. (2021). The Role of Artificial Intelligence in Fighting the COVID-19 Pandemic. *Information Systems Frontiers, 23*(6), 1467–1497. Advance online publication. doi:10.100710796-021-10131-x PMID:33935585

Rangone, A., & Busolli, L. (2021). Managing charity 4.0 with Blockchain: A case study at the time of Covid-19. *International Review on Public and Nonprofit Marketing, 18*(4), 491–521. Advance online publication. doi:10.100712208-021-00281-8

Savukoski, A. (2015). *Crypro-currencies in Finland*. Lapland University of Applied Sciences.

Schwab, K. (2016). *The fourth industrial revolution*. World Economic Forum.

Sengupta, E., Nagpal, R., Mehrotra, D., & Srivastava, G. (2021). ProBlock: A novel approach for fake news detection. *Cluster Computing, 24*(4), 3779–3795. Advance online publication. doi:10.100710586-021-03361-w PMID:34366702

Sharma, A., Bahl, S., Bagha, A. K., Javaid, M., Shukla, D. K., & Haleem, A. (2020). Blockchain technology and tis applications to combat COVID-19 pandemic. *Research on Biomedical Engineering*. Advance online publication. doi:10.100742600-020-00106-3

Smith, G. B. (2011). Green nanotechnology. In *SPIE NanoScience+ Engineering* (p. 810402–810402). International Society for Optics and Photonics.

Stern, N., & Rydge, J. (2012). The new energy–industrial revolution and an international agreement on climate change. *Economics of Energy and Environmental Policy*, *1*(1), 1–19. doi:10.5547/2160-5890.1.1.9

Swan, M. (2015). *Blockchain: Blueprint for a new economy*. O'Reilly Media, Inc.

Van der Aalst, W., Hinz, O., & Weinhardt, C. (2020). Impact of COVID-19 on BISE Research and Education. *Business & Information Systems Engineering*, *62*(6), 463–466. doi:10.100712599-020-00666-9

Von Tunzelmann, G. N. (1978). *Steam power and British industrialization to 1860*. Oxford University Press.

Walters, T. (2014). *Beyond Marketing: Why Digital Disruption Requires*. Digital Clarity Group, Inc.

Warschauer, M. (2004). *Technology and social inclusion: Rethinking the digital divide*. MIT press. doi:10.7551/mitpress/6699.001.0001

Wiener, N. (1948). *Cybernetics*. Hermann.

WrightA.De FilippiP. (2015). *Decentralized blockchain technology and the rise of lex cryptographia*. Available at SSRN 2580664. doi:10.2139/ssrn.2580664

Xiao, Y., & Fan, Z. (2020). *10 technology trends to watch in the COVID-19 pandemic*. World Economic Forum. https://www.weforum.org/agenda/2020/04/10-technology-trends-coronavirus-covid19-pandemic-robotics-telehealth/

ADDITIONAL READING

Bressler, M. S. (2012, September). How small businesses master the art of competition through superior competitive advantage. *Journal of Management and Marketing Research*, *11*, 1–12.

Martin, R., & Sunley, P. (2006). Path dependence and regional economic evolution. *Journal of Economic Geography*, *6*(4), 395–437. doi:10.1093/jeg/lbl012

Piller, F. T., Weller, C., & Kleer, R. (2015). Business Models with Additive Manufacturing—Opportunities and Challenges from the Perspective of Economics and Management. In *Advances in Production Technology* (pp. 39–48). Springer International Publishing. doi:10.1007/978-3-319-12304-2_4

Rajkumar, R. R., Lee, I., Sha, L., & Stankovic, J. (2010). Cyber-physical systems: the next computing revolution. In *Proceedings of the 47th Design Automation Conference* (pp. 731-736). ACM 10.1145/1837274.1837461

Toffler, A. (1970). *Future shock*. Amereon Ltd.

Vidler, A. (1996). Architecture after History: Nostalgia and Modernity at the End of the Century. *Journal of Architecture (London)*, *1*(3), 177–187. doi:10.1080/136023696374631

KEY TERMS AND DEFINITIONS

Additive Manufacturing: Technology, which is especially based on 3D printing.

Blockchain: Technology, which is based on peer-to-peer technology.

Cybernetics: Controlling systems, which are also necessary in the latest AI innovations.

Digitalizing: Technology, which leans on computers and other digital tools and frameworks.

Disruption: Technological shock and innovation, which affects all other technologies that define our socio- economic system.

Industrial Revolution: Linked with all-inclusive technological disruption, which have large economic and societal long-run impacts.

Path Dependence Model: Historical sequences in which contingent events set into motion institutional patterns or event chains.

APPENDIX 1

Table 4. The results of the systematic literature review of industrial revolution.

Art-icle	Timing	Keywords or focus of article	Driver(s) or reasons of industrial revolution	Focused on dis-ruption/ inno-vation?	Technology mentioned
1.	1700-1850	High wages economy, energy	High wage economy	No	Energy
2.	1800-2050	3rd Industrial revolution) IR, 1st IR and 2nd IR	Steam, mass production and mass customizing	Yes	3D print, laser cut and CNC, steam engine
3.	1300-1860	IR, Malthusian dynamics, maximum sustainable, population growth, wages development, demographics	Takeoff of coal mining, increases in capital per worker, rise in international trade, changing structure of the economy, rises in factor productivity	No	the steam engine, cotton gin, coal, production into factories, migration.
4.	1700-	Key Engine, 3rd IR, renewable energy sources, solar energy, seawater, water treatment, 3rd IR, 1st IR and 2nd IR	High carbon and low carbon energy sources	Partly	Steam Engine (coal), oil and electricity, systems of renewable energy sources
5.	2005-	Socio-cyber-physical system (SCPS), Smart manufacturing, 3D printing, AM, wisdom and social manufacturing, 4th IR, 5th IR	Mechanization, electricity, and IT. Now the Internet of Things (IOT) into the manufacturing environment	Yes	SPCS, Smart manufacturing, 3D printing, AM, wisdom and social manufacturing, IOT
6.	mid 18th to late 19th century (C)	IR, installation, assemblage, art, readymade, R.B. Kitaj, 1960s	Not mentioned	No	Steam train
7.	mid 18th to late 19th C.	History, IR, Arnold Toynbee's lectures on the Industrial Revolution	Power-loom and the steam-engine.	No	power-loom, steam-engine.
8.	1700-1850; late 19th and 20th C:s	1st IR industrialization, science, neoliberalism, the Cold War, historiography,	Weak state, an emphasis upon individual liberty, the right institutions and culture of creativity born of free minds and free markets	No	Steam power
9.	2000-	New American IR	Growing amidst a renewed push to "Buy American"	Yes	Automation of manufacturing
10.	1700-1870	Endogenous growth, 1st IR, Economic geography Structural change; Britain	Aggregate shift of employment and incomes from agricultural to industrial activities along with a sustained increase in per capita output growth.	No	None
11.	1800-2000	Unified growth theory. Energy, Industrial Revolution, Economic Britain, growth, Sweden	Expansion of energy services, historical decline in the energy cost share	No	energy efficiency of stoves, steam engines, iron smelting, computers
12.	1700–1852	Patents; Invention; Industrial Revolution; Scotland; Ireland	Increase in the supply of new ideas and ways of thinking or demand side response to economic incentives	Yes (patents)	steam engine
13.	1795-1834	Nutrition, stature, gender, IR	-missing-	yes	No
14.	1760–1840	British industrialization, machines, history	inventors and the machines, e.g. steam engine.	Yes	Steam engine, electric telegraph
15	late 18th C.- 1990	3rd IR, 1st IR and 2nd IR	New energy sources to methods of production, modern transportation and communication facilities, railroad, telegraph, steamship, and cable systems, mass production and distribution systems. Changes in physical and management technology, global competition, regulation, taxes, from centrally planned economies to capitalism, open participation in international trade.	Yes	Railroad, telegraph, steamship, and cable systems. mass production and distribution systems

Continued on following page

Table 4. Continued

Art-icle	Timing	Keywords or focus of article	Driver(s) or reasons of industrial revolution	Focused on dis-ruption/ inno-vation?	Technology mentioned
16.	late 18th -early 19th C:s	Childhood, child labour, British IR, 1st IR	Anxieties about resource constraints, escape from the organic economy. The possession and use of coal, a productive agriculture, and the development of the Atlantic economy appear as important drivers. Consumerism.	No	Factory production, technological change, (Computer)
17.	1375-1875	British IR, commerce, induced invention, scientiðc revolution, 1st IR	Britain had a unique wage and price structure in the eighteenth century, and that structure is a key to explaining the inventions of IR. Technologies that substituted capital and energy for labour.	Yes	steam engines, mechanical spinning, and coke smelting
18.	1760-1850	Textile, patents, 1st IR, Cotton Arkwright	Widespread mechanization, patents associated with steam power	Yes	Steam power, mechanization
19.	late 18th -early 19th centuries	1st IR, steam power, industrialization, technology dynamics, energy innovation	Competition, organizational change, inventions, technique, steam power	Yes	Spinning jenny, steam power
20.	1770-1850	Historical, coal industry, innovation stimulus, Great Britain, 1st IR, patents	Availability of cheap coal, exploitation of coal was a huge boost to other industries.	Yes	Railway technology, steam engine technology, steam-driven ships
21	1700-1880	1st IR, high wage economy, interpretation, British IR,	Britain was a high wage economy and that this itself caused industrialization, the structure and functioning of working-class households	No	spinning jenny, the steam engine, and the smelting of iron ore using coal
22.	1770-1820	1st IR, Schumpeterian growth, Cotton textiles, Prices, Profits	Discontinuous technological change created large profits for innovators because of imperfect capital markets. New technology dominated after along diffusion process via reinvestment.	Yes	textile (and steam power) innovations in mechanical production and factory org.
23.	Late 18th century -	Energy transition, climate change, 1st IR, 2nd IR, 3th IR	Private economic benefits of adopting new technologies and practices. Climate change, low carbon transition	Yes	Steam engine, spinning and weaving technolog. internal combustion engine, electrics, ICT
24.	1770-1850	IPRs, (British) IR, Beginnings of Modern Economic Growth	Patents encouraged innovation and economic growth and R&D with risky projects. Altruism, "crossword puzzle" motive	Yes	Steam engine
25.	1760-1859	British IR,	in 19th century global division of labor, it was the power of exchanging that gave occasion to the IR.	Yes	Technological advances in cotton textiles, iron, steel, and transport

Table 5. List of references in the systematic literature review

Article	
1.	Allen, R. C. (2015). The high wage economy and the industrial revolution: a restatement. The Economic History Review, 68(1), 1-22.
2.	Fisher, T. (2015). Welcome to the Third Industrial Revolution: The Mass-Customisation of Architecture, Practice and Education. Architectural Design, 85(4), 40-45.
3.	Tepper, A., & Borowiecki, K. J. (2015). Accounting for breakout in Britain: The industrial revolution through a Malthusian lens. Journal of Macroeconomics, 44, 219-233.
4.	Glasnovic, Z., Margeta, K., & Premec, K. (2016). Could Key Engine, as a new open-source for RES technology development, start the third industrial revolution?. Renewable and Sustainable Energy Reviews, 57, 1194-1209.
5	Yao, X., & Lin, Y. (2015). Emerging manufacturing paradigm shifts for the incoming industrial revolution. The International Journal of Advanced Manufacturing Technology, 1-12.
6.	Marshall, F. (2014). Lives of the Engineers: Visualizations of the Industrial Revolution in the Work of RB Kitaj. Visual Culture in Britain, 15(1), 50-68.
7.	Wilson, D. C. (2014). Arnold Toynbee and the Industrial Revolution: The Science of History, Political Economy and the Machine Past. History & Memory, 26(2), 133-161.
8.	Ashworth, W. J. (2014). The British industrial revolution and the ideological revolution: Science, Neoliberalism and History. History of Science, 52(2), 178-199.
9.	BROADDUS, B. (2016). The MAKINGS of a NEW AMERICAN INDUSTRIAL REVOLUTION. Baylor Business Review. Fall2016, p14-16.
10.	Trew, A. (2014). Spatial takeoff in the first industrial revolution. Review of Economic Dynamics, 17(4), 707-725.
11.	Kander, A., & Stern, D. (2012). The role of energy in the Industrial Revolution and modern economic growth. The Energy Journal, 33(3), 125-152.
12.	Bottomley, S. (2014). Patenting in England, Scotland and Ireland during the Industrial Revolution, 1700–1852. Explorations in Economic History, 54, 48-63.
13.	Horrell, S., & Oxley, D. (2012). Bringing home the bacon? Regional nutrition, stature, and gender in the industrial revolution1. The Economic History Review, 65(4), 1354-1379.
14.	Russell, B. (2014). Preserving the Dust: The Role of Machines in Commemorating the Industrial Revolution. History & Memory, 26(2), 106-132.
15	Jensen, M. C. (1993). The modern industrial revolution, exit, and the failure of internal control systems. the Journal of Finance, 48(3), 831-880.
16.	Humphries, J. (2013). Childhood and child labour in the British industrial revolution1. The Economic History Review, 66(2), 395-418.
17.	Allen, R. C. (2011). Why the industrial revolution was British: commerce, induced invention, and the scientific revolution1. The Economic History Review, 64(2), 357-384.
18.	Spear, B. (2016). Textile patents and the GB Industrial Revolution. World Patent Information, 44, 53-56.
19.	Bruland, K., & Smith, K. (2013). Assessing the role of steam power in the first industrial revolution: The early work of Nick von Tunzelmann. Research Policy, 42(10), 1716-1723.
20.	Spear, B. (2014). Coal–Parent of the Industrial Revolution in Great Britain: The early patent history. World Patent Information, 39, 85-88.
21	Humphries, J. (2013). The lure of aggregates and the pitfalls of the patriarchal perspective: a critique of the high wage economy interpretation of the British industrial revolution. The Economic History Review, 66(3), 693-714.
22.	Harley, C. K. (2012). Was technological change in the early Industrial Revolution Schumpeterian? Evidence of cotton textile profitability. Explorations in economic history, 49(4), 516-527.
23.	Pearson, P. J., & Foxon, T. J. (2012). A low carbon industrial revolution? Insights and challenges from past technological and economic transformations. Energy Policy, 50, 117-127.
24.	Mokyr, J. (2009). Intellectual property rights, the industrial revolution, and the beginnings of modern economic growth. The American Economic Review, 99(2), 349-355.
25.	Clark, G., O'Rourke, K. H., & Taylor, A. M. (2008). Made in America? The new world, the old, and the industrial revolution (No. w14077). National Bureau of Economic Research.

Evolving From Predictive to Liquid Maintenance in Postmodern Industry

Manuel Lozano Rodriguez

 https://orcid.org/0000-0002-4182-8010
American University of Sovereign Nations, Spain

Carlos E. Torres
Power-MI, USA

INTRODUCTION

Liquid Maintenance is the Predictive Maintenance (PdM) evolution to thrive in the incoming industrial era. Industry, and subsequently, maintenance and, namely, PdM are unready to face the near-future incoming challenges since they are anchored in an obsolete paradigm alien to the incoming cyber-physical reality and unfit for unbelievable data density. In addition to this, PdM is wormed by philosophical hiddenness around Time and taxonomies abuse; it is not the sound subdiscipline it appears to be. So PdM professionals are doomed to dialogue and get along with AIs if we want to break our human predictiveness ceiling glass and keep PdM improving. In this paper, the authors will explain not only the turn of the tide but how to flow towards a non-essentialist PdM paradigm.

Maintenance happens in a non-deterministic polynomial-time hard (Abedi et al., 2017). In practice, it points out that early and tardy maintenance works are the norm rather than the exception. More even, industry keeps stuck to the Adam Smith paradigm of labour division extended to maintenance and the way it's understood. Furthermore, the taxonomy as used in industry so many times is too close to Aristotelian verbiage and essentialism which makes it a somewhat immature field of study. And, to cap it all, meagre effort has been put in determining the way from scientific research to taxonomies, which is a long time encysted issue (Fales, 1979). Standardising the whole of maintenance activities is not quite different from setting a quality standard and shares a weak point with it. Great ideas as Total Quality Management not resulted so great when implemented: rigid and strong quality standards give room for a group feeling judged by the standards of others, so, rather than spreading quality it raised dissent and distrust (Brown & Duguid, 2017, p. 135).

Traditionally, what made a factory to be a factory was to be a firm's place where machines produce things -hopefully, in more efficient ways everyday. However, old-fashioned firms are disappearing and the whole industry is diving into a reality where the machines, the goods and foremost the places are belittled by the importance of their digital dimension, sustainable chains of value and the flexibility that smart-tech brings to business opportunities. By the same token, the importance of AI in PdM becomes paramount. Even if it's needed to demystify the breakthrough technologies that will revolutionise everything, the machine learning use in PdM, as in 2022, has grown exponentially (Redmon, 2021; Carvalho et al., 2019). It seems not to be a critical juncture but a structural shift. According to the McKinsey Global Institute, more than 60% of all manufacturing activities in the late 2010s could have been automated with the automation technology then (McKinsey Global Institute, 2016; 2017a). So, it's not surprising

DOI: 10.4018/978-1-7998-9220-5.ch130

that the value of 4IR techs is expected to share \$3.7 trillions in value and become the next economic growth engine (McKinsey Global Institute, 2017b; Leurent & De Boer, 2018).

Physical, digital, and even biological entities are getting blurrier while Time remains indefinite: in such scenarios PdM can't help melting with the 4IR and become a Liquid Maintenance.

BACKGROUND

The Present of Maintenance

Getting the best value for money in maintenance actions is very important for all industries and manufacturers (Wongmongkolrit & Rassameethes, 2011). So much so that the people in charge of maintenance are continuously justifying the costs associated with their activities to prevent getting defunded after the plans for asset management (Martinez-Monseco, 2020). The goals of every plant manager are to maximise "overall equipment effectiveness (OEE) and improve asset reliability and maintainability to ensure timely product delivery and profitability" (Lee, Lapira & Siegel, 2011).

Consequently, the maintenance programme objectives, framed in maintenance philosophy are:

- Maintaining functionality and safety
- Optimising availability and future items design
- Track criticality
- Attain a minimum total life cycle cost (LCC), including maintenance costs and costs of residual failures (Carretero, et al., 2000)

Fulfilling these objectives, in spite of economic constraints, takes moving beyond traditional data collection to information creation: this is the biggest shift in the industrial landscape today (Lee, Lapira & Siegel, 2011). Monitoring dynamic systems for PdM in real-time is a hell of a process involving in turn several techniques applied in successive preprocessing steps such as: data cleaning, missing values treatment, outlier detection, feature selection, or imbalance compensation (Cernuda, 2019). Anyhow, cutting-edge fields such as software engineering are shifting towards raw-data-centrism and widening to include new types of them (Felderer, Russo & Auer, 2019). It can be seen, for example, in the case of sensors in industrial plants using video and audio formats. To prevent fall behind, PdM should move with our data-intensive times and think more like explorers than engineers. In fact, real-time assessment of behaviours during cyber-physical production in a data-intensive environment is an uncharted land for PdM. Thankfully we don't lack pioneers. Nested in the core of industry, PdM shouldn't miss a thing when it comes to learn of the frugal heuristics school that entrepreneurship is and copy its sense-making and fuzziness in situations of data scarcity (Ghezzi, 2020).

Literature review on PdM and AI in the 4IR dawn stresses the importance of decision making algorithms triggered by failure predictions in a smart-manufacturing stage while detaching, however, its lifelong engineer-centrism in favour of multidisciplinarity (Bousdekis, Lepenioti, Apostolou & Mentzas, 2019; Zonta et al., 2020). Namely, PdM is benefiting from artificial neural networks (ANN) which can learn from process data of fault simulation (Krenek, Kuca, Blazek, Krejcar & Jun, 2016). It has been very useful, for example, when estimating criticality at power plants in order to schedule maintenance works before an expected breakdown data (Özcan, Danışan, Yumuşak and Eren, 2020). Specifically, the literature review of machine learning methods applied to predictive maintenance highlights even more the importance of sensing technologies for PdM: fault identification, operation time of equipment and its efficiency (Carvalho, 2019). Fuzzy logic, a sensory tech driver itself, has a bridgehead in PdM when it comes to improving system safety and avoiding downtime and inopportune maintenance spending (Ladj, Benbouzid-Si Tayeb, Varnier, Dridi & Selmane, 2017). Even traditionally quite difficult problems such as the simulation of boiler drum water level are now easier thanks to fuzzy logic (Meng, Zhang, Zheng, Cheng & Weng, 2020). It's also important for predictive maintenance when it comes to fusing asset information so its management decision making gets improved (Faiz & Edirisinghe, 2009). The traditional PdM's Aristotelian taste for taxonomy must fade away as new logics become more pervasive.

As the research on PdM and AI moves forward, in the less academic side of the coin industrial equipment diversifies before our face and data about their support lose value before a scattered management and a ludicrous lack of standards in a world littered with them (Weijie, Jinna, Zhengzheng & Na, 2016). However, as new industrial robots have populated factories in the last years, networked-control and augmented reality telemaintenance have rocketed, too (Sittner et al., 2013). Incidentally, it has raised the importance of maintenance technicians, which likely will keep growing as augmented reality technologies increase the level of safety and decrease the chances of a human error (Martinetti, Rajabalinejad & Van Dongen, 2017).

The Challenge Out There

For more than two decades, proactivity has saved millions of dollars to the companies that embraced it: costly damage, unscheduled shutdowns, lost man-hours and missed project deadlines have been prevented (Trodd, 1998). Of course, PdM has played a major role. Nevertheless, today, while PdM fights against its own obsolescence, Volkswagen loses in sales of up to 400 million Euros per week due to productivity issues (2016 data) (Krupitzer et al., 2020). From Germany and Sweden winds of industrial change blow and the need for a change of industrial maintenance are fait accompli (Kans et al., 2016). Schedules are old-fashioned and PdM won't last in a spreadsheet for too long.

So, now is the time to put the information in the centre. To begin with, the next big thing will likely be the use of cyber-physical systems for the Cognitive Industrial Internet of Things. A groundbreaking change that will shape Industry 4.0 and its workforce (Mircică, 2019). In addition to this, Big Data may upgrade current predictive maintenance analytics to a prescriptive maintenance one (Bradbury, 2020). The grounds are settled: PdM is driving the 4IR over most fields of study because it blends such core 4IR elements as big data, internet of things, and machine to machine (M2M) communication methods along with a growing role in saving energy consumption and human safety (Laurent & De Boer, 2018). It means, in a nutshell, that an evolved PdM can raise the 4IR to a sci-fi level of within-production transparency.

But this displacement and concentration provided by digital technology may be a mere legacy of its designers, its hardworking dedicated pioneers (Brown & Duguid, 2017). It means that, if predictive maintenance is not at the cutting edge, its practice eventually will slip down against the least prepared users till turned into a marginal discipline. Of course, data acquisition, data fusion, data analysis, diagnostics, and prognosis could paliate this handicap, but it takes having data and information at the right place and at the right time as well as networking enabling all people involved in maintenance to share experiences and knowledge. This is changing the Industry maintenance business model for a more liquid one where the focus is on creating value instead of time and resources for performing more maintenance tasks (Kans et al., 2016).

The challenge within

The inherent productivity of human desire led to schizophrenic and dystopian scenarios as soon as it was cornered in factories. Let's put it into an analogy. In European soccer, minorities are overrepresented on the playing field, but not as coaches following a pattern where some are fit for doing but not fit for organising (Bradbury, 2020). And, just like happened with the African players, workmen and somewhat AIs have been the muffled voices in industry. It might change as Industry 4.0 unwraps itself. In this case, the maintenance and, namely, predictive maintenance will shift to be expressed in their own terms, which hardly will be close to the usual solid standards. The many times the creative-wishful side of non-managerial agency has been ignored in Industry only proves its legacy of lack of authenticity as a human enterprise.

In and out of factories, recovering desire as a more complete life activator takes more diverse subjectivities (Nebioğlu, 2020). Industry has been similar to the Tukanoan Amazonian tribe who have two bodies of mythology, two ways to explain the origin of their institutions and even two creation myths (Santos-Granero, 2009, p. 55). The creation by the industrial entrepreneur vision and the one by restless, raw and speechless energies. Vision is the king. Thinking is a free-play with memory-pictures awaiting for the words to fall. Thinking is, mainly, seeing. Social constructs in factories are created both upon masters and machines. Thus Industry has been traditionally burdened with an atavistic duality dressed as modernity and, to cap it all, turning some humans into animated tools has had, by the way, a distinguished tradition backing it up till Aristotle himself (Aristotle, 1888).

A new stakeholder has popped up. Artificial intelligence (AI) is no more an unfulfilled promise. AI agents know how to read, speak and recognize objects and people so they can communicate with humans intuitively (Gerbert, Justus & Hecker, 2017).

Figure 1. By cracking language and wisdom, machines enter the real world. Retrieved from Competing in the age of Artificial Intelligence (Gerbert et al., 2017)

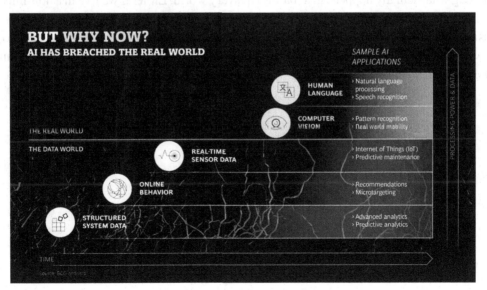

PHILOSOPHICAL HIDDENNES OF PREDICTIVE MAINTENANCE

The Issue of Time and Reliability in PdM

To date, system reliability has been mostly understood as single-component or having a deterministic reliability structure (Lee & Pan, 2017). For example, from this perspective, a plant seems composed of a given quantity of the many forms of the substance equipment. By the same token, time is understood as homogeneous and homogeneously sliced. However, the reality is complex and the inter-time-slices play a role (Lee & Pan, 2017). The remaining useful lifetime of the machine, without going any further, is better calculated by hidden semi-Markov models (Cartella, Lemeire, Dimiccoli & Sahli, 2015). Thanks to (an ideal) PdM, neither unworn components are replaced nor signs of wear are missed, but, in spite of that and even with a (hypothetical) clear time, situations such as shock damage and unwanted degradation of the tool hardly would fall below our predictive reach (Sakib & Wuest, 2018).

By the same token, the common view when preventing preventable failures is that, during equipment mid-life, the rate of failure is constant and fixed, which is wrong (Generowicz, 2016). To start with, how could it be fixed? Someone may reply that even if the calculations are wrong, they are still useful. A bit a-scientific, but she would be right! So, why this flexibility doesn't echo across the whole PdM field of study? By the way, the only constant failure rate is the one from catalectic failures, which has been studied using (oh surprise!) Markovian chains… Indeed, the way PdM faces the junction of time and events seems somewhat trapped in a Gaussian mindset. It's important because the second-order statistics differ greatly if unchained from the gaussianity assumption (Liu, Pokharel & Principe, 2007). In other words, the data shed by the equipment in your plant shows no correlation but a correntropy, which is a blurred / noisy similarity. The quantization of error, by the way, is used along with correntropy for a more efficient outlier rejection (Bahrami & Tuncel, 2020). Would cataleptic failures be better understood as a non-gaussian outlier set of data? Should PdM theorists ask the machines?

The nature of time is, by the way, the main reason because the solid traditional PdM is so good at approximating what actually happens in a (barely) quavery world. Either if we live in a non-linear feature space or in a Cartesian one, we would perceive similarities and boundaries and share a common sense of impossibility and reversibility. Not by chance the Fourier transform of correntropy leads to a generalised power spectral density quite similar to the former conventional one (Liu et al., 2007; Santamaría, Pokharel & Principe, 2006).

Figure 2. PdM vs Liquid Maintenance. Adapted from Power-MI website (Trocel, 2021).

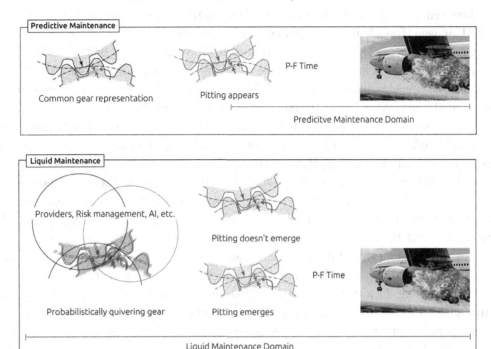

In other words, if we travel back in time in an ideal PdM world we could know when the machines are going to fail, however, in our real world, we would get only useful but inconclusive information. As you can see, a time machine is not the best value for your money... and requires predictive and postdictive maintenance!

Abusing Taxonomies in PdM

Taxonomy grounds on comparison. So, two elements can be compared even if they have nothing in common - a pointless comparison, by the way. However, when comparing ideas (e.g an idea of a factory) rather than estatements it becomes harder to know when resemblance fades away (Blackwelder, 1967). The essentialist conceptualization that taxonomies require have not been rebuked for good by the changing nature of plants, units, tools, etc. Regardless of how detrimental those changes are to reductionist approaches. It gets PdM practitioners trapped in a sort of confusion that, thankfully, we can get rid of. Although it's not what's happening as in 2020, if a sort of meta-data (authors, synonyms, regions, keywords...) for every taxon would be shared and generated dynamically by the whole of industry, it may result in a big game-change. In this case, an AI could retrieve and present graphically a live taxonomy. Big data is turning upside-down our views of scientific progress and even can lead to new consensuated taxonomies (Sterner, Witteveen & Franz, 2019).

An overlooked taxonomical ground in PdM is its demographical legacy. All main referents in PdM, starting by CH Waddington, are corporate male WASP, many of them with a military background or, at least, other men raised in fiercely hierarchical societies. Not by chance, one of the best PdM standards ever was published by the US army and Japan has its very own (Department of Defense, 1980). It's not an issue per se but an overwhelming majority of authors living in a world full of boxes naturally determines the PdM worldview. As the feminist philosophers Janet Bing and Victoria Bergvall highlight, boundaries between colors are identified only with fuzzy logic just like many other real-world continua is hidden by language (Bing & Bergvall, 2014). Considering the difficulties suffered by factory workers who don't identify their gender as usual (Harrison, 2017; Suen, Chan & Badgett, 2020; Suriyasarn, 2016), the seed of taxonomies in Industry might be a lifelong dominant view of binary sexuality watered by a history of rigid echelons and work division. This essentialist PdM showdown shows some parallelisms in how social sciences felt before the bulge of essentialism due its luring epistemological warrant and how intuitive natural-kind concepts were (Haslam, 1998). It fitted too well in a 'winner takes it all' mindset in which highly industrially developed countries developed a narrative depicting themselves smarter and more secular than actually they are (Barca, 2011; Bozonnet, 2017).

To cap it all, PdM's taxonomy as usual doesn't help with the cognitive processes more required for maintenance tasks: the 'equipment' taxon has nothing in common with the skills that repair an equipment takes. Further than this, the main goals PdM's taxonomy aims is to discern between taxons and the discerning behaviour itself, therefore, its main utility is scholastic. Furthermore, in spite that organisational taxonomies, as usually employed at PdM standards, are abundant and an overall sound introduction to a topic, the organisations themselves have not been studied in the same way (Carper & Snizek, 1980). From a PdM perspective, factories have been a taxonomical apex until they grew unrecognisable. So much so that analysts can observe today a leap forward to more promising topics like the taxonomy of international manufacturing networks and a taxonomy of Industry 4.0 research (Feldmann & Olhager, 2019; Nazarov & Klarin, 2020). By the same token, taxonomy of human teams (not to say AI-human ones) have not been paid attention enough and we have lost valuable insights on how authority around PdM tasks in different settings takes shape and on its temporality.

SOLUTIONS AND RECOMMENDATIONS

Conceptual approach

Protocols as usual try to catch an evidential reality with a conceptual web. Indeed, the mere fact of the null predictive power from standard-like taxonomies in the future of PdM during the last 70 years speaks ill of them. On its side, liquid maintenance conceptual approach takes: stay grounded, raise data sensitivity and appreciate feed-back. Even if it means a theoretical agnostic stance in some cases. So, the authors have criticised essentialism across the paper but it's important to stand out that critiques aim for the unnecessary metaphysical baggage, not against every category falling under a realist view of science. Thus, authors concede that sophisticated systematism may require essentialism as long as taxa keep flowing. But no Aristotle-as-service allowed!

Thanks to the PdM virtues, equipment is everyday closer to becoming signs able to remain there indefinitely till a catastrophic failure deletes them. It fosters a sincretism of the mythology of markets' predictiveness and the magical thinking of tokens in stateless aboriginal societies. Everything but looking at the big picture and realising that the smear campaign around factories roots in the philosophical poverty around non-socially toxic forms of commodification. Thus, starting the PdM posthumanist stage requires knowing more about how matter becomes things. And to succeed, it would be a good idea to keep a healthy distrust against the culturally-granted privileges of language (Barad, 2003).

Indeed, the PdM main issue is not about rationality but how professionals codify and reduce this experience in an all-purpose manual. Knowledge is not an algorithm of experience but what we get through practice. So much so that even a used and useful concept as a methodological framework is, doesn't enjoy a widely spread and consensuated definition (McMeekin, Wu, Germeni & Briggs, 2020). PdM professionals should talk more with one another since the information we need is developed socially. Thankfully, those conversations can be recorded, shared and analysed by AIs able to help us to keep focused when debating on how maintenance can be addressed and scheduled on the go. This is the core of liquid maintenance. Furthermore, in the next decades, AIs may join the talk in better terms (for all of us) than if they arise from cold data.

Differential values

If not handled properly, *infoenthusiasm* around the networking generated by benchmarking from plants and factories may lead to some within groups feeling undervalued and judged by alien standards. Therefore, a scientific treatment of feed-back is a must. A grounded approach focused on what people actually do will help to deal with ideologies of newsworthiness in data displaying backing obsolete practises up. It takes giving everybody tools for constructively speaking their mind regardless of their profiles. Let's delve into it.

As can be inferred from the above, it doesn't seem that Big Data is about to retire expert knowledge from PdM -even if algorithms may have potential for doing so (Rivera, Scholz, Bühl, Krauss & Schilling, 2019). Besides the disadvantages of doing so, just like the lack of common sense and explanations behind a decision, the AI aimed to govern PdM systems for industrial mass production facilities would see that both productions and facilities are swiftly changing. Why should a greenleaf AI perform better during long crises and paradigmatic changes than a brain tested against 300.000 years of stressing survival? So, rather than asking AIs too much, researchers should mind the gap between those who analyse the data and prepare work orders and those dealing with equipment and tools in PdM -as it was pointed out before. Giving only what technicians need-to-know is neither efficient nor cost-effective since they get no incentive to look for potential problems and information on causes (traditionally treated as an alien subject) get lost. AIs should help close this gap. To do so, robustness shouldn't limit itself to statistical modelling but connect with the first-hand learned narratives on key scenarios that naturally comes from past decision-making outcomes. It reaches even so complex systems that there is no feasible way the tester determine its correctness thanks to new techniques such as: N-version Testing, Metamorphic Testing, Assertions, Machine Learning, and Statistical Hypothesis Testing (Patel & Hierons, 2018). Modelling those scenarios, instead of only faults and failures' probability curves, may attain a new quantitative judgement that could help PdM researchers to deal with uncertainty without muting human discursive reasoning.

However, the greatest obstacle for this change is (and likely will be) psychological rather than technical, again. Some industrial agents' reluctance before the PdM incoming changes is a sort of learned helplessness in a huge economic engine that is soaked in conservatism. Its main symptoms are:

- Prediction over contextualised information
- Neglecting that ceteris paribus scenarios / elements are mostly for hypothetical work
- Ambivalent feelings on accountability
- Daily blaming lack of control (profanities included!)

It's, shortly, a long experience of wishful thinking about PdM first and getting disappointed then. Indeed, it's the kind of attitude that has boosted stress and has led to depression for decades (Wortman & Dintzer, 1978). Our liquid alternative psychology behind PdM is quite different:

- Information means just-in-time, accessible and contextualised data
- Learn (and forget) new things on PdM everyday since the times they are a-changin'
- Get along with your team or, at least, don't rock the boat

PdM is all about how you bring value when communicating probable events and how you bring value when dealing with the response, therefore, just like happens at any other forecasting biz, we enjoy no certainties!

Although there is a more detailed description in the Table 1 below the authors' differential values for Liquid Maintenance in a nutshell are: a bit of epistemic agnosticism, trust in insightful content and dialogue as well as teaming AI (neither a tool nor a saviour).

Table 1. Differences between Traditional PdM and Liquid Maintenance

Traditional PdM	Liquid Maintenance
Comes from the 2IR and 3IR PdM	4IR native maintenance
Relies on a strict taxonomy	Not against taxonomy but remains flexible
Essentialist	Close to phenomenology
Engineer mindset	Explorer mindset
Industrial production	Cyber-physical production
Labour-intensive environment	Data-intensive environment
Ignores non-managerial agency	Includes non-managerial and even AI agencies
Led by corporate male WASP	More suitable for diverse backgrounds
Relies on protocols and manuals	Relies on consensus, hands-on and AI support
Modelling issues	Modelling scenarios
Learn	Learn & forget
Aims to free resources	Aims to find value

FUTURE RESEARCH DIRECTIONS

Nowadays inert tools, after getting senses and words, may have many things to say shortly. My emphasis in visual thinking is nothing new, it was key in Einstein's success and has backed science up since then onwards (Wallace & Gruber, 1989, p. 180). And just like happened with Einstein's relativity, the massive and dense data affects the rhythm industry going forward in addition to a huge range of behaviours that planets don't have. So, what are going to see the machines when looking11 at industry? Will they try to raise their own agency when looking for a better performance? Why should an early epiphenomena of digital complexity share the vision of this or that entrepreneur? Will the people in charge's capacity for dialogue up to the test? Our 'challenge within' is travelling, through dense data tides, to a new wisdom thanks to opportunities that the incoming Industry brings.

At the time of writing this paper, the current industrial development regarding information handling and digitalisation is leading managers and entrepreneurs to new ways of producing goods. Thus, the 'challenge out there' for the next few years is evolving from human-paced, ad-hoc, intuition-based maintenance to a cyber-physical grounded one (Schomaker, Albano, Jantunen & Ferreira, 2019).

In the future, as cyber-physical environments spread, factories will need to enhance their supply chain responsiveness through make-to-order strategy and customization possibilities (Galar & Mirka, 2017). It will be a new wrinkle of complexity for predictive maintenance. Therefore, the future of PdM is called to be framed between AI and IIoT, especially shaped by Deep Learning, wireless smart sensors as well as mobile devices and AR/VR applications for helping with decision-making (Zheng, Paiva & Gurciullo, 2020). Thanks to the progress in reliability modelling witnessed in the last 90 years, the leap to Intelligent Maintenance from PdM will happen, very likely, in the near future (Zheng et al., 2020).

Anyhow, the touchstone of future PdM, as the authors fore-see it, will be the quantization of data, especially around visual artificial intelligence. For example, the Quantized Fisher Discriminant Analysis altogether with machine learning and information theory is yet being used for facial recognition (Ghojogh, Pasand, Karray & Crowley, 2019). In line with this, non uniform quantization and neural networks are also being employed to obtain a lossless compression in biomedical signals (Sriraam, 2007). Is a matter of time that those methods were widely spread across PdM and the whole Industry.

Indeed, quantic management of uncertainty might be the link of PdM with something bigger than any equipment. To attain a human-like autonomous agency and sense-making, AI needs to improve its adaptivity first as well as become able to perpetually develop its individual constitution and coupling with its environment (Froese & Ziemke, 2009; Georgeon & Riegler, 2019). Quoting Georgeon and Riegler: "Constitutive autonomy of computational entities could lead to genuine agency" -which is linked with motor-sensory capabilities (Georgeon & Riegler, 2019). AI is on this path since evolutionary robots who can choose whether to exploit sensory motor coordination in a set of vision-based tasks, do in a way that resembles the results obtained in sensorially depriven kittens (Suzuki & Floreano, 2008). Thus, mastering images to create useful and cohesive mental schemata, seemingly, is going to be a main feature of AI agents soon.

Amidst the incoming embodied AI and the pressing need to learn more about how AI knows what it knows, PdM solutions developers might run into the phenomenology of robots as a trendy field of study. The first use to care about is not to misuse axioms -such as happens in the mechanistic integration of phenomenology with cognitive sciences (Pokropski, 2019). On the other hand, it will be a paved road for philosophy of mind and cognitive sciences to get intertwined, even if the empirical demonstrations of philosophical statements only cover one of a kind. Phenomena and falsifiability may clash in the 21st century.

What will be the role of sentient AI in society? Will be PdM flexible enough for a social perspective?

CONCLUSION

PdM faces two challenges in the present and near future. PdM has been thrown to the first one, the migration to a cyber-physical paradigm and has the other, getting along with bulging AIs, as an existential threat. Amidst this turmoil, PdM professionals need flexibility before their clients and employers and they, in turn, need to avoid getting hacked by tech-savvy burglars in the dawn of the new industrial revolution.

Human beings and groups understand the way they overcome problems through self-improvement as (over)simplified narratives that shape their worldviews. (That's the psychological trigger that makes success stories so successful!) As aforementioned, PdM headaches and improvements have not happened nor happens in the void or due to plain industrial misfortune, but in a historical context that, for decades, extended from US, Central Europe and Japan to the least materially developed countries' factories. With our human rough edges proneness in mind, we shouldn't forget that the man on the moon happened before the guillotine was sent to the junk room. So it's important to mind History along with the stories we the PdM professionals and researchers have told to ourselves and put in value epistemic humility before performing the big leap forward that AI means.

In this paper, the authors have widely criticised essentialist taxonomy in PdM as usual since, to be true, it would require, at least, that the machines' capacities and nature were identical and changes barely happen. It's bluntly false and, therefore, the nature of a plant, equipment and so on say nothing about its taxon. This philosophical weakness is framed in a wider array of biases. Indeed, in PdM, besides a legacy of gender and labour prejudices, there is a positive bias towards organisations and a negative towards the most spontaneous side of work as if the many spontaneous events fully lack self-organisation. The social life of communication in factories, unveils a dehumanising narrative.

A data platform boosted by AI, could recycle the accrued knowledge in industries and put it to mitigate unwanted human-driven events. So much so that, for the first time, AI may not only be a research opportunity, but also guide future research. Considering the philosophical hiddenness of PdM we shouldn't rush on AI but befriend it. Now that we are closer to meeting the ghost in the machine, PdM raises as an open gate for an incoming future wisdom, as an evolution from a maintenance philosophy to a philosophy of care.

We must flow with the times, our PdM must be *liquid*.

REFERENCES

Abedi, M., Seidgar, H., & Fazlollahtabar, H. (2017). Hybrid scheduling and maintenance problem using artificial neural network based meta-heuristics. *Journal of Modelling in Management, 12*(3), 525–550. doi:10.1108/JM2-02-2016-0011

Aristotle. (1888). *Politics: A treatise on government* (Vol. G). Routledge.

Bahrami, S., & Tuncel, E. (2020). An efficient running quantile estimation technique alongside correntropy for outlier rejection in online regression. *2020 IEEE International Symposium on Information Theory (ISIT)*, 2813–2818. 10.1109/ISIT44484.2020.9174111

Barad, K. (2003). Posthumanist performativity: Toward an understanding of how matter comes to matter. *Signs (Chicago, Ill.), 28*(3), 801–831. doi:10.1086/345321

Barca, S. (2011). Energy, property, and the industrial revolution narrative. *Ecological Economics, 70*(7), 1309–1315. doi:10.1016/j.ecolecon.2010.03.012

Bing, J. M., & Bergvall, V. (2014). The questions of questions: Beyond binary thinking. *Rethinking Language and Gender Research: Theory and Practice, 1*, 30.

Blackwelder, R. E. (1967). A critique of numerical taxonomy. *Systematic Zoology, 16*(1), 64–72. doi:10.2307/2411518

Bousdekis, A., Lepenioti, K., Apostolou, D., & Mentzas, G. (2019). Decision making in predictive maintenance: Literature review and research agenda for industry 4.0. *IFAC-PapersOnLine*, *52*(13), 607–612. doi:10.1016/j.ifacol.2019.11.226

Bozonnet, J.-P. (2017). *Ecocentrism in Europe. A Narrative for a Post-Industrial and Post-Religious Conception of Nature. In European Values*. Brill.

Bradbury, S. (2020). "Fit for doing but not fit for organising". Racisms, stereotypes, and networks in coaching in professional futbol in Europe. In *Race, Ethnicity and Racism in Sports Coaching* (pp. 22–42). Routledge. doi:10.4324/9780367854287-2

Brown, J. S., & Duguid, P. (2017). *The social life of information: updated, with a new preface*. Harvard Business Review Press.

Carper, W. B., & Snizek, W. E. (1980). The nature and types of organizational taxonomies: An overview. *Academy of Management Review*, *5*(1), 65–75. doi:10.2307/257805

Carretero, J., Garcia, F., Perez, J. M., Perez, M., Cotaina, N., & Prete, P. (2000). *Study of existing reliability centered maintenance (RCM) approaches used in different industries*. Universidad Politécnica de Madrid.

Cartella, F., Lemeire, J., Dimiccoli, L., & Sahli, H. (2015). Hidden semi-markov models for predictive maintenance. *Mathematical Problems in Engineering*, *2015*, 1–23. Advance online publication. doi:10.1155/2015/278120

Carvalho, T. P., Soares, F. A., Vita, R., Francisco, R. D. P., Basto, J. P., & Alcalá, S. G. (2019). A systematic literature review of machine learning methods applied to predictive maintenance. *Computers & Industrial Engineering*, *137*, 106024. doi:10.1016/j.cie.2019.106024

Cernuda, C. (2019). On the relevance of preprocessing in predictive maintenance for dynamic systems. In *Predictive Maintenance in Dynamic Systems* (pp. 53–93). Springer. doi:10.1007/978-3-030-05645-2_3

Çokay, N. R. (2020). Schizoanalysis of contemporary dystopia. In *Deleuze and the Schizoanalysis of Dystopia* (pp. 75–91). Palgrave Macmillan. doi:10.1007/978-3-030-43145-7_5

Department of Defense. (1980). MIL-STD-1629A, Procedures for performing a failure mode, effects and criticality analysis. Author.

Faiz, R. B., & Edirisinghe, E. A. (2009). Decision making for predictive maintenance in asset information management. *Interdisciplinary Journal of Information, Knowledge, and Management*, *4*, 23. doi:10.28945/696

Fales, E. (1979). Relative essentialism. *The British Journal for the Philosophy of Science*, *30*(4), 349–370. doi:10.1093/bjps/30.4.349

Felderer, M., Russo, B., & Auer, F. (2019). On testing data-intensive software systems. In *Security and Quality in Cyber-Physical Systems Engineering* (pp. 129–148). Springer. doi:10.1007/978-3-030-25312-7_6

Feldmann, A., & Olhager, J. (2019). A taxonomy of international manufacturing networks. *Production Planning and Control*, *30*(2-3), 163–178. doi:10.1080/09537287.2018.1534269

Froese, T., & Ziemke, T. (2009). Enactive artificial intelligence: Investigating the systemic organization of life and mind. *Artificial Intelligence, 173*(3-4), 466–500. doi:10.1016/j.artint.2008.12.001

Galar, D., & Kans, M. (2017). The impact of maintenance 4.0 and big data analytics within strategic asset management. In Maintenance Performance and Measurement and Management 2016 (MPMM 2016). Luleå tekniska universitet.

Generowicz, M. (2016). *Preventing preventable failures*. Academic Press.

Georgeon, O. L., & Riegler, A. (2019). CASH only: Constitutive autonomy through motorsensory self-programming. *Cognitive Systems Research, 58*, 366–374. doi:10.1016/j.cogsys.2019.08.006

Gerbert, P., Justus, J., & Hecker, M. (2017). Competing in the age of Artificial Intelligence. *BCG Perspective, 1*, 2017.

Ghezzi, A. (2020). How Entrepreneurs make sense of lean startup approaches: Business models as cognitive lenses to generate fast and frugal heuristics. *Technological Forecasting and Social Change, 161*, 120324. doi:10.1016/j.techfore.2020.120324

Ghojogh, B., Pasand, A., Karray, F., & Crowley, M. (2019). *Quantized Fisher discriminant analysis*. Cornell University.

Harrison, J. B. (2017). To sit or stand: Transgender persons, gendered restrooms, and the law. *University of Hawai'i Law Review, 40*, 49.

Haslam, N. O. (1998). Natural kinds, human kinds, and essentialism. *Social Research*, 291–314.

Kans, M., Ingwald, A., Strömberg, A., Laksman, E., Patrikson, M., Ekman, J., Holst, A., Rudström, A. & Larsen, S. (2016). *Future industrial services management: Delivarable 5.2 Results and vision from the project*. Academic Press.

Krenek, J., Kuca, K., Blazek, P., Krejcar, O., & Jun, D. (2016). Application of artificial neural networks in condition based predictive maintenance. Recent Developments in Intelligent Information and Database Systems, 75-86. doi:10.1007/978-3-319-31277-4_7

Krupitzer, C., Wagenhals, T., Züfle, M., Lesch, V., Schäfer, D., Mozaffarin, A., Edinger, J., Becker, C., & Kounev, S. (2020). *A survey on predictive maintenance for industry 4.0*. Cornell University.

Ladj, A., Benbouzid-Si Tayeb, F., Varnier, C., Dridi, A. A., & Selmane, N. (2017). A hybrid of variable neighbor search and fuzzy logic for the permutation flowshop scheduling problem with predictive maintenance. *Procedia Computer Science, 112*, 663–672. doi:10.1016/j.procs.2017.08.120

Lee, D., & Pan, R. (2017). Predictive maintenance of complex system with multi-level reliability structure. *International Journal of Production Research, 55*(16), 4785–4801. doi:10.1080/00207543.2017.1299947

Lee, J., Lapira, E. & Siegel, D. (2011). *Smart decision support tools for robotics and automation systems*. Academic Press.

Leurent, H., & De Boer, E. (2018). The next economic growth engine: Scaling fourth industrial revolution technologies in production. *World Economic Forum*, 1-33.

E

Liang, W., Jia, J., Li, Z., & Cai, N. (2016). Research on the big data construction of equipment support. *2016 IEEE International Conference on Cloud Computing and Big Data Analysis (ICCCBDA)*, 26-31. 10.1109/ICCCBDA.2016.7529529

Liu, W., Pokharel, P. P., & Principe, J. C. (2007a). Correntropy: Properties and applications in non-gaussian signal processing. *IEEE Transactions on Signal Processing*, *55*(11), 5286–5298. doi:10.1109/TSP.2007.896065

Martinetti, A., Rajabalinejad, M., & Van Dongen, L. (2017). Shaping the future maintenance operations: Reflections on the adoptions of Augmented Reality through problems and opportunities. *Procedia CIRP*, *59*, 14–17. doi:10.1016/j.procir.2016.10.130

Martinez-Monseco, F. J. (2020). An approach to a practical optimization of reliability centered maintenance. Case study: Power transformer in hydro power plant. *Journal of Applied Research in Technology & Engineering*, *1*(1), 37–47. doi:10.4995/jarte.2020.13740

McKinsey Global Institute. (2016). *Where machines could replace humans—and where they can't (yet)*. Author.

McKinsey Global Institute. (2017a). *A future that works: Automation, employment and productivity*. Author.

McKinsey Global Institute. (2017b). *How to achieve and sustain the impact of digital manufacturing at scale*. Author.

McMeekin, N., Wu, O., Germeni, E., & Briggs, A. (2020). How methodological frameworks are being developed: Evidence from a scoping review. *BMC Medical Research Methodology*, *20*(1), 1–9. doi:10.118612874-020-01061-4 PMID:32605535

Meng, F., Zhang, X., Zheng, Y., Cheng, X., & Weng, Z. (2020). Fuzzy control and simulation of boiler drum water level. *MATEC Web of Conferences, 309*, 5003. 10.1051/matecconf/202030905003

Mircică, N. (2019). Cyber-physical systems for cognitive industrial internet of things: Sensory big data, smart mobile devices, and automated manufacturing processes. *Analysis and Metaphysics*, (18), 37–43.

Nazarov, D., & Klarin, A. (2020). Taxonomy of industry 4.0 research: Mapping scholarship and industry insights. *Systems Research and Behavioral Science*, *37*(4), 535–556. doi:10.1002res.2700

Özcan, E.C., Danışan, T., Yumuşak, R. & Eren, T. (2020). An artificial neural network model supported with multi criteria decision making approaches for maintenance planning in hydroelectric power plants. *Eksploatacja i Niezawodność, 22*(3).

Patel, K., & Hierons, R. M. (2018). A mapping study on testing non-testable systems. *Software Quality Journal*, *26*(4), 1373–1413. doi:10.100711219-017-9392-4

Pokropski, M. (2019). Phenomenology and mechanisms of consciousness: Considering the theoretical integration of phenomenology with a mechanistic framework. *Theory & Psychology*, *29*(5), 601–619. doi:10.1177/0959354319868769

Redmon, E. (2021). *Deep tech: Demystifying the breakthrough technologies that will revolutionize everything*. Deep Tech Press.

Rivera, D. L., Scholz, M. R., Bühl, C., Krauss, M., & Schilling, K. (2019). Is big data about to retire expert knowledge? A predictive maintenance study. *IFAC-PapersOnLine*, *52*(24), 1–6. doi:10.1016/j. ifacol.2019.12.364

Sakib, N., & Wuest, T. (2018). Challenges and opportunities of condition-based predictive maintenance: A review. *Procedia CIRP*, *78*, 267–272. doi:10.1016/j.procir.2018.08.318

Santamaría, I., Pokharel, P. P., & Principe, J. C. (2006). Generalized correlation function: Definition, properties, and application to blind equalization. *IEEE Transactions on Signal Processing*, *54*(6), 2187–2197. doi:10.1109/TSP.2006.872524

Santos-Granero, F. (2009). *The occult life of things: native Amazonian theories of materiality and personhood*. University of Arizona Press. doi:10.2307/j.ctv1prss0p

Schomaker, L., Albano, M., Jantunen, E., & Ferreira, L. L. (2019). *The future of maintenance. In The MANTIS Book, Cyber Physical System Based Proactive Collaborative Maintenance*. River Publishers.

Sittner, F., Aschenbrenner, D., Fritscher, M., Kheirkhah, A., Kraus, M., & Schilling, K. (2013). Maintenance and telematics for robots (MainTelRob). *IFAC Proceedings Volumes, 46*(29), 113-118.

Sriraam, N. (2007). Neural network based near- lossless compression of eeg signals with non uniform quantization. *2007 29th Annual International Conference of the IEEE Engineering in Medicine and Biology Society*, 3236-3240.

Sterner, B., Witteveen, J. & Franz, N. (2019). *Alternatives to Realist Consensus in Bio-Ontologies: Taxonomic Classification as a Basis for Data Discovery and Integration*. Academic Press.

Suen, Y. T., Chan, R. C., & Badgett, M. L. (2020). The experiences of sexual and gender minorities in employment: Evidence from a large-scale survey of lesbian, gay, bisexual, transgender and intersex people in China. *The China Quarterly*, *245*, 142–164. doi:10.1017/S0305741020000429

Suriyasarn, B. (2016). Discrimination and marginalization of LGBT workers in Thailand. In T. Köllen (Ed.), *Sexual Orientation and Transgender Issues in Organizations: Global Perspectives on LGBT Workforce Diversity* (pp. 197–215). Springer. doi:10.1007/978-3-319-29623-4_12

Suzuki, M., & Floreano, D. (2008). Enactive robot vision. *Adaptive Behavior*, *16*(2-3), 122–128. doi:10.1177/1059712308089183

Trocel, D. (2020). *Vibration Analysis in Gearboxes*. https://power-mi.com/content/vibration-analysis-gearboxes

Trodd, G. (1998). Practical implementation of predictive maintenance. *Conference Record of 1998 Annual Pulp and Paper Industry Technical Conference (Cat. No. 98CH36219)*, 29-37. 10.1109/PAPCON.1998.685501

Wallace, D. B., & Gruber, H. E. (1989). *Creative people at work: Twelve cognitive case studies*. Oxford University Press.

Wongmongkolrit, S., & Rassameethes, B. (2011). The heuristics of effective maintenance policy under the given availability. *International Journal of Collaborative Enterprise*, *2*(4), 251–262. doi:10.1504/ IJCENT.2011.043824

Wortman, C. B., & Dintzer, L. (1978). Is an attributional analysis of the learned helplessness phenomenon viable? A critique of the Abramson-Seligman-Teasdale reformulation. *Journal of Abnormal Psychology*, *87*(1), 75–90. doi:10.1037/0021-843X.87.1.75 PMID:649857

Zheng, H., Paiva, A. R., & Gurciullo, C. S. (2020). *Advancing from predictive maintenance to intelligent maintenance with AI and IIoT. ArXiv200900351 Cs Stat.* Cornell University.

Zonta, T., da Costa, C. A., da Rosa Righi, R., de Lima, M. J., da Trindade, E. S., & Li, G. P. (2020). Predictive maintenance in the Industry 4.0: A systematic literature review. *Computers & Industrial Engineering*, *150*, 106889. doi:10.1016/j.cie.2020.106889

ADDITIONAL READING

Agostini, L., & Filippini, R. (2019). Organizational and managerial challenges in the path toward Industry 4.0. *European Journal of Innovation Management*, *22*(3), 406–421. doi:10.1108/EJIM-02-2018-0030

Baron, S., & Miller, K. (2018). *An introduction to the philosophy of time.* John Wiley & Sons.

Burawoy, M. (1979). The anthropology of industrial work. *Annual Review of Anthropology*, *8*(1), 231–266. doi:10.1146/annurev.an.08.100179.001311

Handayani, L., Hufad, A., & Wilodati, W. (2018). *Permissive and Deviation.* https://www.scitepress.org/Papers/2017/71068/71068.pdf

Pozdnyakova, U. A., Golikov, V. V., Peters, I. A., & Morozova, I. A. (2019). Genesis of the revolutionary transition to industry 4.0 in the 21st century and overview of previous industrial revolutions. In *Industry 4.0: Industrial Revolution of the 21st Century* (pp. 11–19). Springer. doi:10.1007/978-3-319-94310-7_2

Rodríguez, L. M. (2019). Ethical information foresights: a journey across uncharted conflictology. *Eubios Journal of Asian and International Bioethics*, *29*(1), 27-30. https://www.eubios.info/EJAIB12019.pdf

Shank, D. B., & DeSanti, A. (2018). Attributions of morality and mind to artificial intelligence after real-world moral violations. *Computers in Human Behavior*, *86*, 401–411. doi:10.1016/j.chb.2018.05.014

Torres, C. E. (2019). *How to Calculate Condition-Based Maintenance Savings.* https://www.reliableplant.com/Read/31988/how-to-calculate-conditon-based-maintenance-savings

KEY TERMS AND DEFINITIONS

Artificial Intelligence (AI): Technological constellation centred in computer science and concerned with theorising and developing machines able to mimic (and exceed!) traditionally only human tasks related with decision-making, use of language and learning.

Correntropy: A nonlinear measure of the similarity between two random variables.

Fourth Industrial Revolution (4IR): The qualitative change in manufacturing and industrial practises powered by disruptive technologies (artificial intelligence, robotics, the Internet of Things, 3D printing, genetic engineering, quantum computing, etc.) that is leading, as in 2021, to the merge of physical, digital, and biological worlds.

Industry 4.0: Fourth industrial revolution.

Non-Deterministic Polynomial-Time Hard: A complexity class in theoretical computer science that includes all decision problems where you can efficiently verify the answer.

Predictive Maintenance (PdM): Set of techniques and data analysis procedures aiming to optimise maintenance schedule and, therefore, reducing the likelihood of failures.

Taxonomy: The science and practice of classification and ordering classes according to principles.

Time: Non-spatial and indefinite continuum in which events have an intrinsic direction.

To Flow: To change according the wholeness.

Industrial Revolution 4.0 With a Focus on Food–Energy–Water Sectors

Abichal Ghosh

https://orcid.org/0000-0002-5881-0925

Birla Institute of Technology, Pilani, India

Reddi Kamesh

https://orcid.org/0000-0002-1791-4656

CSIR-Indian Institute of Chemical Technology, India

Siddhartha Moulik

https://orcid.org/0000-0001-7214-8088

CSIR-Indian Institute of Chemical Technology, India

Anirban Roy

Birla Institute of Technology, Pilani, India

INTRODUCTION

As the world is trying to cope up with a pandemic, it has brought to the fore the need for automation, machine based intervention and the use of Artificial Intelligence to fuel the sustainability of human civilization. Manufacturing and production took a massive plunge during the COVID-19 pandemic and this affected the world economy to a great extent. However, the major players quickly understood the need of the hour is to adopt a "human-less" operation in such a scenario and it has spurred a rally of research and development in lines of Artificial Intelligence (AI) and Machine Learning (ML).

Artificial Intelligence (AI) and Machine Learning (ML) are some of the newest fields in science and engineering with interest in these topics increasing primarily in the last half a decade, but as a field of research, these fields have existed for the last 6 decades. The most prestigious journals where cutting-edge research is being published in this field are about 5 decades old. Thus, these are not a new field of research from a holistic perspective.

The three intricately related sectors of Food, Energy and Water sectors are experiencing the need for such AI-ML interventions for (i) sustained production, (ii) optimized resource utilization, (iii) economically and financially rewarding supply chain management and (iv) wastage minimization including time and resources and (v) providing rapid solutions and automated predictive decision-making abilities.

This chapter explores the possibilities of intervention in the above 3 sectors by exploring production, processing, and distribution as this can be an expected norm during this Industrial Revolution 4.0 era. The global distribution of AI technologies and investments in farming, forestry and the marine/aquaculture sectors are illustrated in **Figure 1.**

DOI: 10.4018/978-1-7998-9220-5.ch131

Figure 1. Global distribution of AI technologies and investments in farming, forestry and the marine/aquaculture sectors. Fig. 1A. Geographical and sectoral distribution of companies that develop applications of IoT, sensors, robotics and AI-supported analytics for aquaculture, forestry and agriculture. Total number of companies N =1114. Fig. 1B. Geographical distribution of investments in companies listed in 1A. See Supplementary Information for details about methods and data (adapted from Galaz et al., 2021).

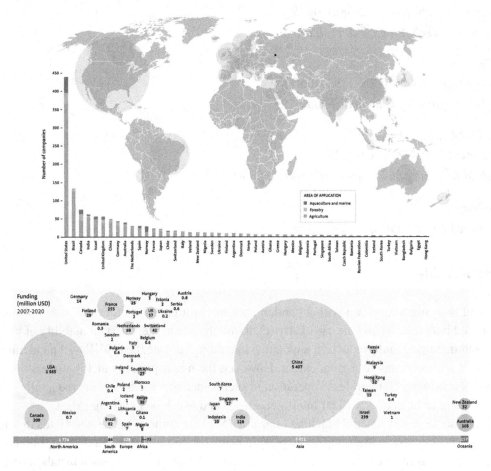

BACKGROUND

In order to understand how AI can drive innovations in the sectors of Food, Energy and Water, it is important to first review the historical perspectives of AI and each of these sectors.

Background: AI-ML

The importance of AI and its applications have experienced exponential growth in the last few years, due to (i) high computing speed, (ii) low cost of operation, (iii) affordable hardware manufacturing, and (iv) using a data-driven approach (due to an increase in the amount of data) to capture non-linearities in modeling. AI includes/spans a multitude/variety of subfields including computational intelligence, knowledge representation, logic, robotics, machine learning, and many more. Machine Learning, as seen, is a subfield of AI but draws its concepts from multiple fields such as AI, statistics, biology, etc.

Machine Learning enables systems to automatically learn and improve from experience without the need for explicit programming. ML is concerned with the creation of computer programs that can access data and utilize the said data for learning. ML is extremely useful for analyzing data and being able to find patterns within the given data. Neural Networks are a subset of Machine Learning which was inspired by the human brain and its learning mechanism through sensory feedback. Having few or more layers in Neural Networks leads to the mechanism to be called Artificial Neural Networks (ANN) or Deep Neural Networks (DNN) respectively. Neural Networks have become increasingly popular due to the high availability of data in the past few decades and the flexibility of the Neural Networks for numerous applications such as analysis of data (ANN and DNN), computer vision (Convolutional Neural Networks), Natural Language Processing (Recurrent Neural Networks), and many more (Alzubaidi, L. et al., 2021).

Background: Food Sector

The agricultural industry plays a significant role in the food industry and with the increasing population, there is an increase in the demand for food. The traditional techniques and materials used are not able to fulfill these requirements. Here, automated methods come into play fulfilling these requirements and this has ultimately led to the agricultural revolution. Along with this agricultural revolution came the genetic engineering of plants and the increased use of better pesticides and fertilizers. Ammonia is one of the most highly produced inorganic chemicals and a majority of the ammonia produced is used for fertilizer production. Ammonia is majorly produced using the Haber process. Thermodynamically the Haber process is energy-intensive and also requires natural gas. Thus, the creation of an ammonia production plant is economically intensive due to the high costs of energy, equipment and maintenance. There are other processes too which also involve significant energy penalties.

Background: Energy Sector

Access to energy is an inseparable part of development, the lack of which leads to a fundamental hindrance to progress impacting various sectors. Also, ensuring access to modern energy in an affordable, reliable, and sustainable manner is one of the Sustainable Development Goals (SDGs) laid out by the UN. The Industrial era started in the 1700's and led to the abundant usage of non-renewable energy sources such as coal, oils, and other fossil fuels. This has led to a shortage of non-renewable energy sources and an increase in environmental pollution. The modern era has started with this awareness and has started shifting to high energy sources like nuclear energy or renewable sources such as solar energy, wind energy, hydroelectrical energy, etc. But, unlike the generators which use non-renewable energy, the generators which use renewable energy sources require either favorable weather conditions to run, or more financial resources. Also, some of these methods have low efficiency.

Background: Water Sector

Water is a natural resource that is at the very core of sustainable development. It is critical for socioeconomic development, healthy ecosystems and for human survival. It is also central to the production and preservation of a host of benefits and services for people. Also, just like in the case of energy, ensuring the availability and the sustainable management of water and sanitation is one of the Sustainable Development Goals (SDGs) laid out by the UN. Even though water is very important for development and human survival, but still well over half of the world's population experience some form of water scarcity.

One of the methods to obtain clean water to reduce this water scarcity is in the form of Desalination. Desalination is the process of removing dissolved salts to produce fresh water from sea and brackish water. Throughout the history of water treatment by desalination, there have been various methods used such as water treatment by using chemical addition, adsorption by using proper adsorbent, distillation/ evaporation(thermal). But these methods have many demerits such as the addition of chemicals leading to change in the taste of water & with poor efficiency, relatively slow process for adsorption, and very high energy requirements in case of distillation/evaporation. Desalination by membranes takes care of most of these demerits. For desalination by using membranes, tailor-made membranes are required in order to increase productivity and decrease the energy losses in a site-specific application.

Motivation of the work: AI-ML interventions in Water-Energy-Food (WEF) sectors

In the recent few decades, the importance of Water, Energy, and Food (WEF) sectors have increased to be able to optimize the use of natural resources and promote sustainability goals. All the challenges previously discussed are being magnified even more due to the population growth and its stress on the availability of resources, thus, justifying the need for AI-ML-based intervention for optimized resource utilization and wastage minimization. Higher data accuracy, processing large amounts of data, recognizing patterns in data, cost and time efficiency, better predictability are some of the advantages that can be obtained by using AI-ML for improving the sustainability of the WEF sectors (D'Amore et al, 2022).

INTERVENTION AND ROLE OF AI-ML IN THE FOOD, ENERGY & WATER SECTORS

In the Background and Historical Section, the historical perspectives and the background is given for each sector followed by an introduction and motivation to how AI can be used in the respective sections. In this section, the role that AI has in each of these sectors is elaborated upon.

Role of AI in the Food Sector

With the growing population, it is expected that there will be a 70% rise in demand for food supply by 2050 as per the Food Agro organization study (van Dijk et al., 2021). Therefore, it is necessary to adopt and advance AI-ML techniques (Camarena, 2020) in the food (quality control, type of food, customer psychology, human building) and agricultural industries (Next generation farming, Plant data analysis, smart irrigation, weather monitoring, soil sensors for smart seeding and precision monitoring, improved crop yield, fertilizer modelling, and automation harnessing) for next generation farming and food processing technologies (Kakani et al., 2020) to meet the demand of food supply.

One of the upcoming interventions on advanced manufacturing and operation is the concept of a digital twin. A digital twin refers to the digital representation of an object or system. By using digital twins to represent the various mechanisms required in the plant, its operation can be simulated (Lv Z and Xie S, 2021). This way, any problems which may arise will be able to be mirrored and methods to diagnose the problems can be found thus taking care of any possible failures. Thus, using digital twins will allow us to increase the accuracy, avoid failures, and reduce the costs for commissioning a plant (Chen et al., 2019). In addition to the application of digital twins, many branches of AI such as ML, Deep Learning (DL), Computer Vision and Robots are used in the Agri-Food Industry. Some of these applications include Self-Driving Drones and Tractors allowing precision, robotic agriculture, AI-enabled automation of food quality assessment to mention a few (Camarena, 2020).

Ammonia is one of the most highly produced inorganic chemicals and it is one of the basic building blocks of fertilizers. As mentioned in the previous section, industrial Ammonia production is mainly done using the Haber-Bosch process (Smith et al., 2020). The Haber process uses high pressure and moderately high temperatures to get a high yield of ammonia. In this process, a mixture of dry Nitrogen and Hydrogen gases are taken in 1:3 ratios by volume and the reaction is carried out in pressure ranging from 150 - 200 atm and temperatures of about 500°C under the presence of a catalyst. Being a high pressure and high temperature operation, the plant needs to be designed with integrated systems comprising of compressors, heat exchangers, high pressure pumps, etc. The use of such complicated equipment and their high costs of operation causes the fabrication and running of an ammonia production plant to be risky. The previously mentioned concept of digital twins can be used here in order to avoid possible faults or failures, reduce the cost of operation, etc. One of the most critical steps in an Ammonia plant is that of the synthesis loop. This synthesis loop systems consists of 3 steps which are that of Syngas Compression, Ammonia Synthesis and Ammonia Refrigeration. Inefficiency, failures and eventual shutdowns in an ammonia plant are some of the main problems that an ammonia plant faces and these problems can lead to huge losses. A good enough number of shutdowns in ammonia plants occur due to failure in the synthesis loop system. Hence, there is a need for increasing the reliability of this system to detect any faults as early as possible. These shutdowns due to failure in the synthesis loop usually occur suddenly after alarm is reached. Hence there is a need for early fault detection by using ML fault detection models (Qosim and Zulkarnain 2020) which can be also addressed through Digital Twin (Semeraro et al., 2021 & Liu et al., 2021) interventions as well as predictive models based on AI-ML from real plant operation data.

Role of AI in the Energy Sector

There is a steady depletion of non-renewable energy resources (Natural gas, oil, and coal) due to its increased consumption and demand arising from the increasing population. This increase in the consumption of non-renewable energy can be seen from the Figure. 2. The industrial revolution started in the 1700's with the use of coal and was followed by the discovery and extensive usage of other non-renewable energy resources such as oil, natural gas, petroleum, etc. Thus, there has been a steady increase in the consumption of these non-renewable resources, as is evident from the cases of coal, petroleum, natural gas, etc. Further, the almost exponential growth of the population of the world is clearly visible from **Figure 3**. Thus, there is a need to shift from non-renewable resources and develop alternative renewable energy resources (solar, wind, hydro and bio-energy etc.) in an efficient and economic manner. From **Figure 2**, it can be seen that in the modern era, the usage of renewable resources such as hydroelectric, wind, nuclear and solar energies certainly has started, but there are still many improvements that are needed to be made. Current technologies for renewable energy generation face serious issues for scale-up because they are not completely efficient and economic. Therefore, there is a need to develop alternate/efficient materials and intensified process using advanced disruptive technologies i.e., AI-ML tools/techniques/methodologies for the design and optimization of processes in energy sectors (Ahmad et al., 2021).

Figure 2. Consumption of non-renewable energy [adapted from U.S. Energy Information Administration, AER Energy Perspectives and MER, eia.gov].

Figure 3. Human population growth since 1000 AD is exponential (dark blue line). Notice that while the population in Asia (yellow line), which has many economically underdeveloped countries, is increasing exponentially, the population in Europe (light blue line), where most of the countries are economically developed, is growing much more slowly. [adapted from https://courses.lumenlearning.com/biology2x-master/chapter/human-population-growth/].

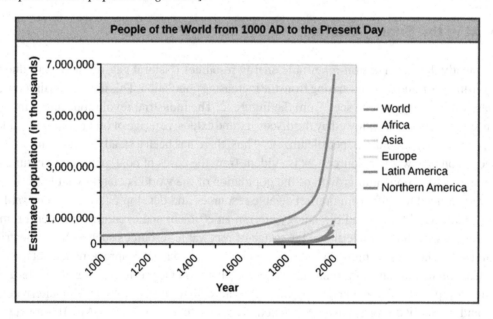

As mentioned earlier, AI is needed for reducing the energy waste, lowering the overall costs, and making better use of clean renewable energy sources. On the energy demand side, the tasks associated with Demand Response is highly complicated and also uses large scale data for real time decisions. (Antonopoulos et al. 2020; Ahmad et al., 2021). Demand Response refers to the method where the supply of energy is regulated in order to balance the power demand of the consumers. This way, Demand Response can help in flexibility, reliability and also in cost regulation. The tasks related to Demand Response is quite complicated, requiring the usage of large amount of data in real time decisions. Another factor which makes working with Demand response complicated for renewable resources is the variability present. For example, the power output of a solar farm depends on the day-night cycle, the weather & many more extrinsic variable factors and the power output from wind mills depends on the wind speed. The usage of AI and ML methods can thus be used to tackle these challenges, ranging from selecting the optimal set of consumers to respond to, dynamic pricing, scheduling and controlling of devices. AI can be used to predict the demand and supply of power, optimize the maintenance and use of energy, provide better stability and efficiency of the power system, automate the decision-making, automate the scheduling and control of the devices used, segment the customers based on demand, and many more. For the problems related to forecasting or predicting, such as predicting the prices, demand of electricity, etc. can be predicted by using supervised learning in the form of regression. Regression methods such as Deep Neural Networks (DNN), Artificial Neural Networks (ANN), Tree based regression methods, and many more can be used here. Further, the task of segmenting the customers based on their consumption or demand is basically the Unsupervised Learning task of clustering. Clustering methods such as k-means clustering can be used in this case.

The energy sector faces numerous challenges which could not be handled by conventional approaches. Integrating advanced computational power, innovative processes (Borowski, (2021) and AI-ML tools it is possible to handle existing challenges faced by the energy sector in effective manner. One of such challenges faced by the energy sector is in the form of fault management. In the Energy Industry, equipment failure is fairly common and can lead to much crucial repercussions. Here the application of AI with sensors can lead to an effective solution to monitoring the equipments and thus either preventing any fault from arising or at least reducing the consequences which may arise due to fault or failure of the monitored equipment.

Another application of AI can be in the form of using image processing for various uses ranging from monitoring, fault prediction, detection, etc. For these uses of monitoring, fault prediction, detection emphasis can be put on cases of solar farms or wind energy farms. These farms are typically very large with the areas required usually being around for solar energy farms and around for wind energy farms. The monitoring of such large areas of land can be very difficult to do using just human power. By using drones equipped with high resolution cameras and various sensors or by using satellites the related images of these farms/plants can be captured. This data can help with fault prediction and monitoring. Using AI on the related images, it can be predicted whether there are any faults, or if any parts need to be changed. For the case of monitoring and detection, semantic segmentation can be used for the detection of such plants/farms. Semantic segmentation is a Deep Learning based image processing task that has various applications in the fields of medicine, remote sensing, astronomy, etc. The task of semantic segmentation involves the pixel-wise classification of an image into various labels.(Atif et al., 2019) In this case, the images captured by the drones and satellites can be obtained and semantic segmentation can be used for an easier method for the detection of these farms/plants (Darapaneni et al., 2020).

Role of AI in the Water Sector

Even though approximately 75% of the Earth is covered with water; about 99% of this available water is salty and brackish and only 1% of it is fresh water. One of the major challenges faced by the world is that of being able to produce fresh water that can be achieved by improving the effectiveness and efficiency of water purification technology (Yildiz, 2017). In this regard, advanced technologies in desalination, water treatment, water quality monitoring and management are needed. Desalination based water treatment methods mostly require using membrane-based technologies as well as thermal technologies such as distillation and evaporation technologies. However, constraints on overstrained costs of these technologies requires AI-ML based advanced techniques for sustainable technology development using process monitoring, optimization, prediction, design and control techniques (Al Aani et al., 2019).

In the historical perspective of the water section, emphasis is put on the desalination method for water treatment. As mentioned earlier, there are many ways of desalination, but here the authors focus mainly on desalination using membranes. Here, better tailor-made Reverse Osmosis (RO) membranes are required to get desalination in terms of enhanced productivity at lower energy cost. These tailor-made RO membranes are in the form of flat sheets or hollow fibers which are made of an ultra-thin polyamide film coated over a porous polysulfone support membrane (Ghosh et al., 2008). To control the membrane performance in terms of water flux and salt rejection, we require a thorough understanding of the RO membrane itself as well as the optimal desalination operating conditions. But, making or finding such a membrane and the specific operation conditions require a lot of effort and time. This is due to the vast variability of the membrane and the number of operating conditions which have to be controlled. This is where we can use Machine Learning in order to find the best possible membrane and the conditions which gives the best membrane performances in terms of water flux and salt rejection.

There are many factors which impact the properties of the RO Membranes which includes properties of the support membrane, solvent selection, catalysts, reaction temperature, curing temperature and time, etc., (Ghosh et al., 2009). Even the operation/working conditions are influenced by a variety of parameters such as applied pressure, feed flow rate, concentration of the feed, temperature, etc. At the end, the goal is to get the best possible combination of the membrane preparation conditions and the operating conditions. To achieve this goal we need to find specific parameters which requires a lot of time and effort. This is where using Machine Learning can come in handy. By looking at the working conditions and the compositions of the already existing membranes, we can use Supervised ML algorithms to predict something close to the best possible membrane and its operation conditions. This Supervised ML problem is basically a Regression problem with the inputs being that of the previously mentioned parameters and the output that of the performance measures. Regression models such as Artificial Neural Networks (ANN), Deep Neural Networks (DNN), Gaussian Process Regression (GPR), Regression Trees, etc. can thus be used here. Furthermore, genetic algorithms and other optimization techniques can be used in modelling desalination membranes and optimizing the operating conditions. Thus, this can drastically reduce the time and efforts which are required as one can try to improve upon the best results found (Al Aani et al., 2019).

The next problem which was mentioned earlier was regarding the high cost and energy requirements which exist for creating any type of desalination plant which makes it difficult and risky to operate and maintain. Just like previously mentioned in the food sector, digital twins can be used here as well. By using digital twins to simulate the plant the risk of failure can be reduced. As stated earlier, the energy requirement of a whole desalination plant is very high and optimizing the output & the energy requirements of such a plant manually while also taking into consideration the various equipment conditions will take a lot of time which is very difficult to be done solely with human power. For identification of operating conditions of the process, the previously mentioned AI/ML methods for modelling and design of membranes can be used. The energy requirements of a desalination plant depend upon various equipment operating conditions. The minimization of this energy requirement can be achieved by finding the optimal operating conditions. Here Supervised ML methods can help to find these conditions, thereby reducing the energy costs.

Water supply and distribution occurs through a water supply network. Portable water is transferred in these networks through the help of various components such as pipes and pumps. This task thus faces the issue of failure or fault due to leakage from the pipes or failure of other components. Here, AI methods can be used in order to detect these issues of leakage and/or failure of components, thereby reducing potential losses (Meleshko et al., 2020). This detection system can work by the help of various sensors such as pressure sensors/monitors, flow sensors/monitors, etc. By monitoring and studying the values detected by the sensors and automatically processing these values, real-time forecasting of the signal values in the near future can be done by using the previously collected data and using Supervised regression algorithms such as ANNs, DNNs, etc.

Therefore, this chapter also provides an outlook of usage of industrial 4.0 revolution technologies such as AI-ML and data science in the field of water sector (Garrido-Baserba et al., 2020).

RECOMMENDATIONS AND FUTURE DIRECTIONS

It is clear from the above discussion that the common interplay between Water, Energy and Food sectors lie in areas of (i) material design (Rangel-Martinez, 2021): better lightweight materials for wind, higher power density material for solar, better membranes for desalination, better catalysts for conversion of raw materials to end products, (ii) process design and optimization: including designing grids catering to seasonal/diurnal fluctuations in demand-supply cycles, optimizing operational costs of desalination plants, retrofitting existing plants to renewable sources and (iii) minimizing wastage: including AI-ML interventions for predicting anomalies in consumption/utilization based on historical data, optimizing supply chain during natural disasters and pandemic and optimizing plant operations with minimum human interventions, increased automation and advanced process control.

Delving into the specifics, AI can also provide rapid solutions for tuning of optimal material (i) renewable energy harvesting such as salinity gradient power, solar energy, wind energy and tidal energy (Rangel-Martinez, 2021), (ii) accelerated discovery of catalysts for energy conversion such as coal to chemicals, carbon dioxide to value added products i.e., methanol, lower olefins, C_1 - C_4 chemical and other higher hydrocarbons (Moses et al., 2021), and (iii) biomass to energy or biofuels such as bio-oil, bio-diesel, hydrogen, ammonia, methane and alcohols (Meena et al., 2021).

For the food and agriculture sector (Di Vaio et al., 2020; Ben Ayed and Hanana,2021) image processing and pattern recognition technologies, AI in fertilizer management to ensure safe food products, robotic intervention for warehouse management, smart technologies for irrigation, crop yield prediction (Liakos et al., 2018), minimizing water wastage and energy intensive pumping processes. AI based food quality management is also being explored as well as pesticide management

For the water sector, rainwater harvesting technologies and distribution, greywater reuse, wastewater treatment desalination and recycling all are being explored through the AI-ML point of view. Explanation tools, forecasting tools and prescriptive tools are being used in various hydraulic models. Minimizing water losses, monitoring water consumption patterns, draught prediction, water network modeling, drinking water supply and demand as well as integrating with exiting desalination plants are the avenues for AI-ML interventions (Sun and Scanlon, 2019; Malviya and Jaspal, 2021; Doorn, 2021).

There is an intricate interplay between each sector, and AI-ML intervention in any of the sector positions to benefit the related ones too either directly or indirectly.

CONCLUSION

The article explores the possibility of AI-ML interventions in water, energy and food sectors. It is imperative to understand that these three sectors are related very intimately to each other and changes in one alter the response of the other. However, the focus of sustainability lies in the fact that optimum resources utilization for an ever-growing population. The minimization of wastage, optimizing utilization and sustaining the population is the holy grail for policy makers, technologists and scientists worldwide. However, the past history of industrial operations and data associated with the same can be used to predict the future and determine the present. The journey of AI-ML has just started and it has indeed a long way to go.

REFERENCES

Ahmad, T., Zhang, D., Huang, C., Zhang, H., Dai, N., Song, Y., & Chen, H. (2021). Artificial intelligence in sustainable energy industry: Status Quo, challenges and opportunities. *Journal of Cleaner Production*, *289*, 125834. doi:10.1016/j.jclepro.2021.125834

Al Aani, S., Bonny, T., Hasan, S. W., & Hilal, N. (2019). Can machine language and artificial intelligence revolutionize process automation for water treatment and desalination? *Desalination*, *458*, 84–96. doi:10.1016/j.desal.2019.02.005

Alzubaidi, L., Zhang, J., Humaidi, A., Al-Dujaili, A., Duan, Y., Al-Shamma, O., Santamaría, J., Fadhel, M., Al-Amidie, M., & Farhan, L. (2021). Review of deep learning: Concepts, CNN architectures, challenges, applications, future directions. *Journal of Big Data*, *8*(1), 1–74. doi:10.118640537-021-00444-8 PMID:33816053

Antonopoulos, I., Robu, V., Couraud, B., Kirli, D., Norbu, S., Kiprakis, A., Flynn, D., Elizondo-Gonzalez, S., & Wattam, S. (2020). Artificial intelligence and machine learning approaches to energy demand-side response: A systematic review. *Renewable & Sustainable Energy Reviews*, *130*, 109899. doi:10.1016/j.rser.2020.109899

Atif, N., Bhuyan, M., & Ahamed, S. (2019, November). A review on semantic segmentation from a modern perspective. In *2019 international conference on electrical, electronics and computer engineering (UPCON)* (pp. 1-6). IEEE.

Ben Ayed, R., & Hanana, M. (2021). Artificial Intelligence to Improve the Food and Agriculture Sector. *Journal of Food Quality*, *2021*, 1–7. Advance online publication. doi:10.1155/2021/5584754

Borowski, P. F. (2021). Innovative Processes in Managing an Enterprise from the Energy and Food Sector in the Era of Industry 4.0. *Processes (Basel, Switzerland)*, *9*(2), 381. doi:10.3390/pr9020381

Camaréna, S. (2020). Artificial Intelligence in the design of transition to Sustainable Food Systems. *Journal of Cleaner Production*, *122574*. Advance online publication. doi:10.1016/j.jclepro.2020.122574

Chen, S., Perathoner, S., Ampelli, C., & Centi, G. (2019). Electrochemical Dinitrogen Activation: To Find a Sustainable Way to Produce Ammonia. In *Horizons in Sustainable Industrial Chemistry and Catalysis* (pp. 31–46). Elsevier Publishing. . doi:10.1016/B978-0-444-64127-4.00002-1

D'Amore, G., Di Vaio, A., Balsalobre-Lorente, D., & Boccia, F. (2022). Artificial Intelligence in the Water–Energy–Food Model: A Holistic Approach towards Sustainable Development Goals. *Sustainability, 14*(2), 867. doi:10.3390u14020867

Darapaneni, N., Jagannathan, A., Natarajan, V., Swaminathan, G. V., Subramanian, S., & Paduri, A. R. (2020, November). Semantic Segmentation of Solar PV Panels and Wind Turbines in Satellite Images Using U-Net. In *2020 IEEE 15th International Conference on Industrial and Information Systems (ICIIS)* (pp. 7-12). IEEE. 10.1109/ICIIS51140.2020.9342701

Di Vaio, A., Boccia, F., Landriani, L., & Palladino, R. (2020). Artificial intelligence in the agri-food system: Rethinking sustainable business models in the COVID-19 scenario. *Sustainability, 12*(12), 4851. doi:10.3390u12124851

Doorn, N. (2021). Artificial intelligence in the water domain: Opportunities for responsible use. *The Science of the Total Environment, 755*, 142561. doi:10.1016/j.scitotenv.2020.142561 PMID:33039891

Garrido-Baserba, M., Corominas, L., Cortés, U., Rosso, D., & Poch, M. (2020). The fourth-revolution in the water sector encounters the digital revolution. *Environmental Science & Technology, 54*(8), 4698–4705. doi:10.1021/acs.est.9b04251 PMID:32154710

Ghosh, A., & Hoek, E. (2009). Impacts of support membrane structure and chemistry on polyamide–polysulfone interfacial composite membranes. *Journal of Membrane Science, 336*(1-2), 140–148. doi:10.1016/j.memsci.2009.03.024

Ghosh, A., Jeong, B., Huang, X., & Hoek, E. (2008). Impacts of reaction and curing conditions on polyamide composite reverse osmosis membrane properties. *Journal of Membrane Science, 311*(1-2), 34–45. doi:10.1016/j.memsci.2007.11.038

Kakani, V., Nguyen, V. H., Kumar, B. P., Kim, H., & Pasupuleti, V. R. (2020). A critical review on computer vision and artificial intelligence in food industry. *Journal of Agriculture and Food Research, 2*, 100033. doi:10.1016/j.jafr.2020.100033

Liakos, K. G., Busato, P., Moshou, D., Pearson, S., & Bochtis, D. (2018). Machine learning in agriculture: A review. *Sensors (Basel), 18*(8), 2674. doi:10.339018082674 PMID:30110960

Liu, M., Fang, S., Dong, H., & Xu, C. (2021). Review of digital twin about concepts, technologies, and industrial applications. *Journal of Manufacturing Systems, 58*, 346–361. doi:10.1016/j.jmsy.2020.06.017

Lv, Z., & Xie, S. (2021). Artificial intelligence in the digital twins: State of the art, challenges, and future research topics. *Digital Twin, 1*(12), 12. doi:10.12688/digitaltwin.17524.1

Malviya, A., & Jaspal, D. (2021). Artificial intelligence as an upcoming technology in wastewater treatment: A comprehensive review. *Environmental Technology Reviews, 10*(1), 177–187. doi:10.1080/21622515.2021.1913242

Meena, M., Shubham, S., Paritosh, K., Pareek, N., & Vivekanand, V. (2021). Production of biofuels from biomass: Predicting the energy employing artificial intelligence modelling. *Bioresource Technology, 340*, 125642. doi:10.1016/j.biortech.2021.125642 PMID:34315128

Meleshko, A. V., Desnitsky, V. A., & Kotenko, I. V. (2020). Machine learning based approach to detection of anomalous data from sensors in cyber-physical water supply systems. In IOP conference series: materials science and engineering (Vol. 709, No. 3, p. 033034). IOP Publishing. doi:10.1088/1757-899X/709/3/033034

Moses, O. A., Chen, W., Adam, M. L., Wang, Z., Liu, K., Shao, J., Li, Z., Li, W., Wang, C., Zhao, H., Pang, C. H., Yin, Z., & Yu, X. (2021). Integration of data-Intensive, machine Learning and robotic experimental approaches for accelerated discovery of catalysts in renewable energy-related reactions. *Materials Reports: Energy*, *100049*(3), 100049. Advance online publication. doi:10.1016/j.matre.2021.100049

Qosim, H., & Zulkarnain. (2020). *Fault Detection System Using Machine Learning on Synthesis Loop Ammonia Plant, Fault Detection System Using Machine Learning on Synthesis Loop Ammonia Plant.* Association for Computing Machinery. . doi:10.1145/3400934.3400950

Rangel-Martinez, D., Nigam, K. D. P., & Ricardez-Sandoval, L. A. (2021). Machine learning on sustainable energy: A review and outlook on renewable energy systems, catalysis, smart grid and energy storage. *Chemical Engineering Research & Design*, *174*, 414–441. doi:10.1016/j.cherd.2021.08.013

Semeraro, C., Lezoche, M., Panetto, H., & Dassisti, M. (2021). Digital twin paradigm: A systematic literature review. *Computers in Industry*, *130*, 103469. doi:10.1016/j.compind.2021.103469

Smith, C., Hill, A. K., & Torrente-Murciano, L. (2020). Current and future role of Haber–Bosch ammonia in a carbon-free energy landscape. *Energy & Environmental Science*, *13*(2), 331–344. doi:10.1039/C9EE02873K

Sun, A. Y., & Scanlon, B. R. (2019). How can Big Data and machine learning benefit environment and water management: A survey of methods, applications, and future directions. *Environmental Research Letters*, *14*(7), 073001. doi:10.1088/1748-9326/ab1b7d

van Dijk, M., Morley, T., Rau, M. L., & Saghai, Y. (2021). A meta-analysis of projected global food demand and population at risk of hunger for the period 2010–2050. *Nature Food*, *2*(7), 494–501. doi:10.103843016-021-00322-9

Yildiz, D. (2017) The Importance of Water in Development, World Water Diplomacy & Science News. Hydropolitics Academy.

Industry Revolution 4.0 and Its Impact on Education

Riccardo Minasi

(iD) https://orcid.org/0000-0003-1146-8189
Università per Stranieri Dante Alighieri, Italy

INTRODUCTION

People can get the information and use it as a competitive advantage. The coming of millennial kids with advanced intelligence and digital ability has poses numerous difficulties to instructors. Advanced locals exploit the tremendous assets of the internet and computerized innovations to make something imaginative, inventive and expressive in spite of digital security issue. These techno addicts and Wi-Fi generation likewise incline toward an intelligent way to deal with learning which mixes data through framework joining by means of an intricate montage of pictures, symbols, sound, video, recreation activity, diversions, and Artificial Intelligence. The fourth Industrial Revolution is the stage in the development of knowledge in which the lines between physical, digital and biological spheres are being blurred. The rapid changes of knowledge have developed the new model of education for the future.

Impact of IR 4.0 in Education

The higher education of the Fourth Industrial Revolution is a dark, rationalistic and energizing open door that can eventually change society for the better. The Fourth Industrial Revolution is fueled by awarness of counterfeiting and it will change the working environment from assignment-based attributes to human-centered qualities (Abdelkader el al. 2013). Many people are displaced due to the loss of their jobs, 7 billion people in the world but only 3.5 billion have access to connectivity. Peter Drucker, 1997, said universities will not survive. Higher education is in deep crisis. There are no techers, books or tuition. Students work in projects and take several internship programs at designed levels. Once the projects are complete, they will earn points to advance to the next level. Character education is still necessary and relevant. 3RT's holistic approach to character education includes the importance of revitalizing, innovative, creative and communicative education, using technology and involving parents. The balance between technology use and personality will create a generation that is both competitive and dignified. Involvement of all parties is the key to students transformation. Education ready to face the era of industrial revolution 4.0 is characterized by the enhancement of human resources' ability to master technology. Policies governing the education system all around the world include the relevance of curricula, personnel capacity, use of information technology and development of personality values, improvement of technological facilities (Gray 2016). 21st century skill include: First, learning and innovation skills which include mastering a variety of knowledge and skills, learning and innovation, critical thinking and problem solving, communication and collaboration, creativity and innovation. Second, skills include digital literacy, information literacy, media literacy, and ICT literacy (Aoun 2018). Third, career and life skills include flexibility and adaptability, initiative, social and cultural interaction, productivity and accountability, leadership and responsability. Because Generation Z students love digital tools,

DOI: 10.4018/978-1-7998-9220-5.ch132

they hope to have these tools with low access barriers available whenever they need them. Industrial revolution 4.0 is driving the world through changes that are increasingly rapid and competitive. First, students can think critically. Second, students are expected to have creativity and innovative abilities. Third, communication skills and competence. Fourth, the ability to cooperate and collaborate, and finally, students' self-confidence. They World Economic Forum has estimated the ten best skills for the future. Creativity will be one of the 6 skills that employees need. Meanwhile, Latip argues that there are at least four competencies that teachers must possess in the industrial revolution 4.0:

Cooperation

This skill is very important now and in the future. This is not very difficult to do, because the world is already interconnected, so there is no reason not to cooperate with others.

Creativity and Risk-Taking

Teachers need to model this creativity and take on how it is integrated into their teaching.

Having a Good Sense of Humor

Reduces stress and frustration while providing opportunities for others to see life from the other side.

Teaching ability

The student also expects the lecturer to be expert in the academic and practical part of courses. It is even more crucial for hands-on courses. Motivation and enthusiasm in teaching, together with pedagogy knowledge, support lecturer in determining a perfect method to deliver a lesson in class and ensure a complete understanding among students. Thus, it will lead to student satisfaction while the institution will accomplish its goal and remain profitable (Baur, 2015).

IR 4.0, which is full of fast technology, has also brought important changes in the education system. These changes in the education system will undoubtedly have an impact on curriculum construction, the role of teachers as educators, and the development of ICT-based educational technologies . There is a new challenge to reinvigorate our education to train competent, creative and innovative people who can compete globally . There are many studies in the field that reveal that curriculum implementation revolves around only targeted academic values that stem from the context and no longer aim to gain students' ability to understand science in the context of daily and life skills competencies especially, has it is broadly researched, in Malaysia (Bell, 2010). Aligning practice-level learning adapted to curriculum structures becomes the initial focus of completing homework in the field of education. Curriculum policy should detail students' pedagogical abilities, life skills, ability to live together, and critical and creative thinking. It promotes soft skills and transversal skills, life skills and invisible skills not related to specific technical and academic fields. However, critical and innovative thinking skills are widely useful in many work situations, such as interpersonal skills, global-minded citizens and media literacy and available information. Teacher Competence and Skills for International Relations: Industrial revolution 4.0 has had a significant impact on various fields, not just teachers, doctors, nurses and the arts. The role of the teacher as an educator, teacher, mentor and 'parent' in the school as a whole will not be replaced entirely by technological advancement, because a teacher's treatment of students has been replaced by any person or technology (Biswas, 2018).

Challenges of IR 4.0 in Education

Different academics authorities and researchers emphasised that investment in emerging technologies and human connectivity, building digital resilience, as well as institutional capabilities in digital governance and accountability, are key strategies for survival; however, it is unclear whether the higher education community are doing enough to adapt and create an enabling environment for learners, academics and practitioners to break barriers, imagine, innovate, and collaborate; develop a 4.0-ready ecosystem fitting to institutional contexts; stimulate greater human connectivity through the exchange of students and staff, which is enabled through global and regional networks, and consortium of higher education institutions; incorporate spiritual values, ethics and morality, national identity and a sense of connection to the community, through curriculum delivery and technology transfer; and be mindful of the benefits and risks brought about by the 4th Industrial Revolution (Cole et al. 2007). One of them is the education system.

Results and discussion

The discussion shows that the development of current and future curricula must elaborate on the abilities of students in the academic dimension, life skills, and the ability to live together and think critically and creatively. Other invisible skills like interpersonal skills, global-minded citizens, and literacy of the media and information available. Also, the curriculum must be able to direct and shape students ready to face the industrial revolution era with an emphasis on the fields of STEM.

In addition to these competencies, teachers also need to have skills and friendliness with technology, collaboration, creative and taking risks, having a good sense of humor, and teaching as a whole (David, 2014). The open learning platform is one way to be considered by the school and teacher in deciding how education and learning are held. One of them is impacting the education system. Improving the quality of human resources through education is a way to balance the development of IR 4.0 (Dunwill, 2016). In this situation, every educational institution must prepare new information and literacy in the field of education. Education is required that can form a creative, innovative, and competitive generation (Fitzpatrick, 2012). Education 4.0 is a response to the need for the Industrial Revolution 4.0, where humans and technology are converging to create new opportunities creatively and innovatively. Fisk explains "that the new vision of learning promotes learners to learn not only skills and knowledge that are needed but also to identify the source to learn these skills and knowledge (Fisk, 2017)." Still, according to Fisk, as cited by Aziz Hussin, there are nine trends related to Education 4.0. Second, learning will be personalized to individual students (Hussain, 2013). Third, students have a choice in determining how they want to learn. Fourth, students will be exposed to more project-based learning. Fifth, students will be exposed to more hands-on learning through field experiences such as internships, mentoring projects, and collaborative projects. Sixth, students will be exposed to data interpretation in which they are required to apply their theoretical knowledge to numbers and use their reasoning skills to make inferences based on logic and trends from given sets of data. Seventh, students will be assessed differently, and the conventional platforms to assess students may become irrelevant or insufficient. Lastly, students will become more independent in their learning, thus forcing teachers to assume a new role as facilitators who will guide the students through their learning process. Nine,shifts in the trend of Education 4.0 above are the primary responsibility of teachers to students. Adaptation to this educational trend guarantees individuals and communities to develop a range of competencies, skills, and knowledge that are complete and expel all their creative potential (Frydenberg, 2011). Based on the description above, the 4.0 industrial revolution characterized by technological disruption has significant implications for the education system. This chapter is intended to describe necessary changes and adjustments made in the education system in order to respond to the spectrum of the digital revolution so that educational output can compete and contribute globally.

Method

Result Industrial Revolution 4. Industry 4.0 is an industry that combines automation technology with cyber technology. It is a trend of data automation and exchange in manufacturing technology.

Education 4.0

Education 4.0 is a general term used by educational theorists to describe various ways to integrate cyber technology both physically and not into learning. It is a leap from education 3.0. Education 3.0 includes meeting neuroscience, cognitive psychology, and educational technology, using digital and mobile web-based, including applications, hardware, and software (Graham et al. 2008).. Education 4.0 is a phenomenon that arises as a response to the needs of the industrial revolution 4.0, where humans and machines are harmonized to obtain solutions, solve various problems faced, and find various possibilities for innovations that can be utilized to improve the lives of modern humans.

The Dawn of 4IR 5 educational landscape, Flexible assignments that accommodate many learning styles, and MOOC and other online learning options will have an impact on secondary education. Second, skills digital literacy includes information literacy, media literacy, and ICT literacy (Herman et al. 2016). Third, career and life skills include flexibility and adaptability, initiative, social and cultural interaction, productivity and accountability, and leadership and responsibility . Because Gen Z students like digital tools, they hope they are available whenever they need them with low access barriers.

Figure 1. The Dawn of 4IR (Schwab, 2016)

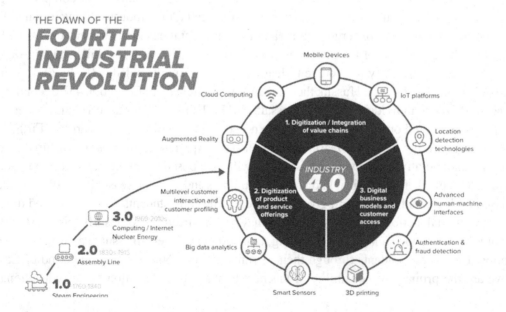

These Gen Z students need to be prepared to develop in the 4.0 Industrial Revolution . In his speech, Mendikbud RI Muhadjir Effendy at the National Education Day May 2, 2018, at University of Yogyakarta, said that the presence of the industrial revolution 4.0 made the world undergoing changes that were increasingly fast and competitive. He assessed that it was necessary to revise the curriculum by adding five competencies. First, students can think critically. Second, students are expected to have the creativity and have innovative abilities. Third, communication skills and competence. Fourth, the skill to cooperate and collaborate, and finally, students have confidence . In addition to vocational education programs, the curriculum must adapt to the increasingly competitive business and industrial climate. Students are prepared with a curriculum that has artificial intelligent content, internet of things, wearable, advanced robotics, and 3D printing. In short, a compulsory link and match curriculum between schools and business and industry. The World Economic Forum has estimated the ten best skills for the future. Creativity will be one of 6 the three skills needed by workers. Emotional intelligence, which is not included in the top 10 today, will be one of the top skills needed by all.

Figure 2. Top 10 Skills in 2015 & 2020 (Schwab, 2016 & Alex Gray, 2016)

Top 10 skills

in 2020	in 2015
1. Complex Problem Solving	1. Complex Problem Solving
2. Critical Thinking	2. Coordinating with Others
3. Creativity	3. People Management
4. People Management	4. Critical Thinking
5. Coordinating with Others	5. Negotiation
6. Emotional Intelligence	6. Quality Control
7. Judgment and Decision Making	7. Service Orientation
8. Service Orientation	8. Judgment and Decision Making
9. Negotiation	9. Active Listening
10. Cognitive Flexibility	10. Creativity

Qusthalani was on the Rumah Belajar, as cited by Dinar Wahyuni, mentioning the five competencies teachers must prepare to enter the Industrial Revolution era 4.0. Meanwhile, Latip argues that there are at least four competencies that must be possessed by teachers in industrial revolution 4.0. " Blended learning is a way of integrating the use of technology in learning that enables learning that is appropriate for each student in the class, and allows reflection on learning" . Definitions show that blended learning based learning is a combination of old literacy and new literacy (Irawan, et al. 2017).

Curriculum for Education 4.0

IR 4.0, which is full of fast technology, has brought significant changes, one of which is the education system. Changes in the education system will undoubtedly have an impact on 7 curriculum construction, the role of teachers as educators, and the development of educational technologies based on ICT. There is a new challenge to revitalize our education in order to obtain competent, creative, and innovative human being who can compete globally. There are many studies revealed that curriculum implementation in the field experiences degradation that comes out of context and is no longer oriented towards achieving students ability to understand science in the context of daily and life skills competencies, but only revolves around the target achievement academic values (Irianto, 2017). Alignment of learning at the level of practice adapted to curriculum constructs becomes the first focus of completing homework in the field of education. The curriculum policy must elaborate on students abilities in the pedagogical dimension, life skills, ability to live together, and critical and creative thinking. It is promoting soft skills and transversal skills, life skills, and skills that are invisible, not related to specific technical and academic fields. However, it is widely useful in many work situations like critical and innovative thinking skills, interpersonal skills, global-minded citizens, and literacy of the media and information available (Jarman, 2019). It has been time for our curriculum to be reviewed and gradually develop an educational curriculum that can direct and shape students ready to face the industrial revolution era with an emphasis on the fields of Science, Technology, Engineering, and Mathematics . Teacher Competence & Skills for IR 4. The industrial revolution 4.0 had a significant influence on various fields, but not for teachers, doctors, nurses, and arts. The role of the teacher as a whole as an educator, teacher, mentor, and 'parent' in the school will not be wholly replaced by technological sophistication because the treatment of a teacher to students has a specificity that cannot be done by just anyone or replaced by technology (Kagermann et al. 2013). Doing so is not too tricky, because the world is already interconnected, so there is no reason not to collaborate with others. Teachers need to model this creativity and undertaker how this creativity is integrated into their teaching. A good sense of Humor A laughter and humor teacher is usually the teacher who is most often remembered by students. Laughter and humor can be essential skills to help in building relationships and relaxation in life.

Figure 3. 21st Century Skills (World Economic Forum, 2016)

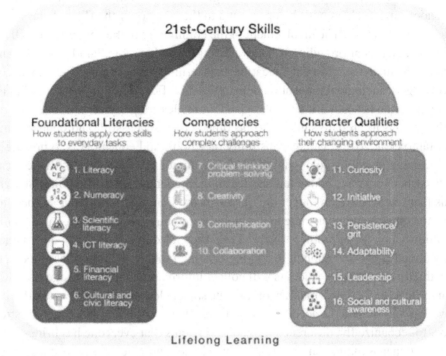

Exhibit 1: Students require 16 skills for the 21st century

The figure above shows that to get to the 21st-century, students need learning that is no longer just traditional academic learning. It is an education that offers learning services that enable them to collaborate, communicate, and solve problems, think critically, creatively, and innovatively. The competence and skills can only be realized through mixed learning, e-learning, and face-to-face, or known as blended learning (Kohler et al. 2016). This learning model requires the optimization of technology involved in learning that is expected to be able to obtain creative, innovative, and competitive graduates to face the era of industrial revolution 4.0. Indicates that the involvement of technology in learning is no longer just a discourse or limited to a vision, but must be a real action at all levels of education ranging from basic to higher education. The problem is the low quantity of educational institutions that organize learning based on information, computers, and technology. This situation, cannot be maintained, the system and learning model must be transformed through the use of educational technology, the expansion of the learning process that transcends the boundaries of classrooms by increasing the interaction of students with the surrounding environment. Moreover, this can only be realized if there is a shift in mindset and action in various contexts in the implementation of education and learning (Kozinski, 2017). To face learning in the 21st century, everyone must have critical thinking skills, knowledge, and digital literacy skills, information literacy, media literacy, and master information and communication technology, including educators . One of the emerging technologies in the field of education today is augmented technology and virtual reality, has begun to be adopted as a medium of learning in the classroom and also research aids in the laboratory . AR/VR technology can be used to support education and improve student learning effectiveness. Learning media that use this technology can quickly improve students' understanding because of 3D objects, text, images, videos, audio can be displayed to real students. As students need increase for individual learning experiences, here, students have choices in determining how they learn. Students will potentially modify their learning process with the 10 tools they feel are necessary. Students will learn with different tools, programs, and techniques based on their preferences. At this level, schools and teachers must be open mind to the concept of the flipped classroom, and students bring their learning tools . The involvement of the community in the context of BYOD will fill the shortage of schools in terms of providing ICT infrastructure in education. Paradigm shifts and action in various contexts in the implementation of education and learning is a necessity. The logical consequence of this ever-evolving technological innovation demands a modification of the concept of class management and learning methods so that it fits the expectations, learning styles, and interests of students. The role of education is to prepare students to become active, successful, and contributing members of society (Kristanto et al. 2017). The responsibility of schools and educators is to prepare students to be able to compete and play their role amid the global community. Schools and teachers can consider the following aspects to organize education and learning. Student-centered Learning Student-centered learning means that teachers are no longer the only primary source of knowledge in the classroom. In order to be able to compete and contribute to the global community in the future, students must be able to obtain new information when problems arise. Then, they need to connect new information with the knowledge they already have and apply it to solving existing problems. In this class model, the teacher will act as a facilitator for students, students will collect information and knowledge themselves, under the guidance of the teacher. Teachers must accommodate student learning styles because this can increase learning motivation and student 11 academic responsibility. Each student has different strengths, and talents, and how to recognize the different strengths and talents that everyone has brings to the project, and changing roles depends mainly on the extent to which the school, teacher, and students develop collaborative learning. Meaningful Learning Student-centered learning does not mean that the teacher gives up all control of the class. While students are encouraged to learn according to their learning styles, the teacher still guides skills that need to be acquired. Teachers can make essential points to help students understand how the skills they build can be applied in their daily lives. Students will be more motivated to learn something useful and valuable to them. Teachers need to teach and train students skills that are useful in any situation. Lessons have no meaning if they do not affect the lives of students outside of school. Integrated with the Community With the internet, students today can do many things. The school community no longer only covers the area located in the school environment, but reaches all over and covers the world. Education needs to help students to be able to contribute to the global community and find ways to have an immense impact on their environment. That is, besides learning about values helping others around them and protecting their closest environment, but they also have to learn about how they can help and protect the world far from them. To prepare students to be responsible citizens, schools need to educate students to become responsible citizens. Through the activities of the school community, students are encouraged to take part in these activities or projects, and occasionally help communities around them with diverse social activities.

Flipped classroom

The flipped classroom, the subject matter is given through learning videos that students must watch in their homes. Here, the teacher acts as a coach or advisor.

Integrating social media

Have the option to continue to share knowledge and interact with each other far beyond the hours spent in class, and online discussions can be exciting.

Learning

Project-based inquiry activity can be carried out by students at school after students. Moodle is a course management system that gives teachers the option to send assignments, lectures, videos, and more. Students can interact with each other through discussion forums, private messages, and chat rooms. Students can upload tasks completed by attaching files.

Inputting test scores to the class book at the same site, and students can also see the feedback given by the teacher.

Blended

Who used Blended Learning based on Schoology get more new theories outside school hours individual so that the face-to-face meetings to provide the theoretical material can be reduced and replaced with a practicum to the student.

PLATO

School students can stay in school and get the credit needed for graduation. PLATO classrooms offer independent courses that students can use to complete both at school and home. This course uses tests to place students in the appropriate class, and they have the opportunity to master the content and meet the stringent academic standards set by the school district. A trusted teacher facilitates this course, and after completion, students can obtain course credit. The advanced of technology also does not hurt changes in attitudes, behavior, and character of students. This medium, the teacher plays an essential role in shaping the character of students. Conclusion Industrial revolution 4.0 has changed the way of thinking about education. Changes made are not just a way of teaching, but far more necessary is a change in the perspective of the concept of education itself. Several things need to be considered by the school and the teacher in deciding how education and learning held.

CONCLUSION

In order for an organization to meet challenges of transforming Industry 4.0, it must have a successful strategy. Most processes will be replaced by the developemnt of technologies such as big data and AI. The next generation is more attracted to the use of smartphones and applications. New technologies are transforming our lives "by inventing new, unsuspected things and creating them in new, unsuspected ways". The first three industrial revolutions provided evidence for the profound shifts in society, the economy and education which resulted in a proliferation of curricular innovation and the establishment of new educational institutions. Unlike previous industrial revolutions, however, the 4IR features the impacts of several compounding exponential technologies which all share the capacity for rapid increases in scale and reductions of cost. This rapidity of advance in technologies demands a more proactive response from the educational sector than the more gradual societal evolution and subsequent response from educational institutions in earlier industrial revolutions (Latip et al. 2019). The impacts of the emerging 4IR technology in economic and environmental terms alone will require a drastic reconsideration of the curriculum within higher education to enable students both to comprehend the individual technologies in detail and to be able to thoughtfully analyze and predict the evolution of networked systems of technology, the environment and sociopolitical systems.

From strictly economic terms, students who are capable of creative insights, collaborating in diverse teams, and navigating through global cultural differences will be at an advantage in a workplace where the meaning of skills will become more of interpreting rapidly changing information and being able to work with experts and stakeholders toward common understanding of the benefits of sustainable development. Students who are able to learn in residential environments with diverse colleagues and develop solutions together in teams will be well trained for the types of tasks that will be asked of them in the 4IR. States and Asia and new types of CTE curricula are providing useful examples of how to implement this new model of 4IR higher education. Higher education needs to recognize the necessity of adapting and scaling up these new 4IR forms of education rapidly to assure the sustainability of our environment and economy, as well as to sustain the relevance of higher education as a responsive and vital component of society. Lipsey said: "Computer interruptions take place every day. We must save our qualities, moral standards as we graps the fourth industrial revolution".

Taken together, these new forms of 4IR education will prepare both students and faculty for leadership roles in a world of rapidly accelerating change, with a curriculum that develops both technical mastery and a deep awareness of ethical responsibility toward the human condition.

REFERENCES

Abdelkader, D., Belkhodja, O., & Linda, C. (2013). Understanding and managing knowledge loss. *Journal of Knowledge Management*, *17*(5), 639–660. doi:10.1108/JKM-12-2012-0394

Aoun, J. E. (2018). Robot-proof: Higher education in the age of artificial intelligence. *Journal of Education for Teaching*, *44*(4), 519–520. Advance online publication. doi:10.1080/02607476.2018.1500792

Baur, C., & Wee, D. (2015). *Manufacturing's Next Act*. Retrieved from www.mckinsey.com/business-functions/operations/ourinsights/manufacturings-next-act

Bell, S. (2010). Project-Based Learning for the 21st Century: Skills for the Future. *The Clearing House: A Journal of Educational Strategies, Issues and Ideas*, *83*(2), 39–43. Advance online publication. doi:10.1080/00098650903505415

Biswas, S. (2018). *Schoology-Supported Classroom Management: A Curriculum Review*. Northwest Journal of Teacher Education. doi:10.15760/nwjte.2013.11.2.12

Cole, J., & Foster, H. (2007). Using Moodle: Teaching with the Popular Open Source Course Management System. *Journal of Chemical Information and Modeling*. Advance online publication. doi:10.1017/CBO9781107415324.004

David, A. (2014). *Khan Academy!* Primary Teacher Update. doi:10.12968/prtu.2011.1.2.52

Dunwill, E. (2016). *4 changes that will shape the classroom of the future: Making education fully technological*. Retrieved from https://elearningindustry.com/4-changes-will-shape-classroom-of-thefuture-making-education-fullytechnological

Fisk, P. (2017). *Education 4.0 ... the future of learning will be dramatically different, in school and throughout life*. Retrieved May 11, 2019, from http://www.thegeniusworks.com/2017/01/future-education-young-everyonetaught-together/

Fitzpatrick, J. (2012). *Planning Guide for Creating new Models for Student Success Online and Blended Learning*. Retrieved from https://michiganvirtual.org/wpcontent/uploads/2017/03/PlanningGui de-2012.pdf

Frydenberg, M., & Andone, D. (2011). Learning for 21 st Century Skills. *International Conference on Information Society (i-Society)*.

Graham, C. R., & Dziuban, C. D. (2008). Blended Learning Environments. Handbook of Research on Educational Communications and Technology. doi:10.1080/02652030701883203

Gray. (2016). *The 10 skills you need to thrive in the Fourth Industrial Revolution*. The World Economic Forum.

Hermann, M., Pentek, T., & Otto, B. (2016). Design principles for industrie 4.0 scenarios. *Proceedings of the Annual Hawaii International Conference on System Sciences*. 10.1109/HICSS.2016.488

Hussain, F. (2013). E-Learning 3.0 = ELearning 2.0 + Web 3.0? *IOSR Journal of Research & Method in Education (IOSRJRME)*. doi:10.9790/7388-0333947

Irawan, V. T., Sutadji, E., & Widiyanti. (2017). *Blended learning based on schoology: Effort of improvement learning outcome and practicum chance in vocational high school*. Cogent Education. doi:10.10 80/2331186X.2017.1282031

Irianto, D. (2017). Industry 4.0: The Chalenges of Tomorrow. *Seminar 15 Nasional Teknik Industri 2017*.

Jarman, B. (2019). *6 Reasons Why Classrooms Need To Implement Blended Learning*. Retrieved from https://www.emergingedtech.com/201 9/01/6-reasons-teachers-need-toimplement-blended-learning/

Kagermann, H., Wahlster, W., & Helbig, J. (2013). *Recommendations for implementing the strategic initiative INDUSTRIE 4.0*. Final report of the Industrie 4.0 WG.

Kohler, D., & Weisz, J. (2016). *Industry 4.0: The Challenges of the Transforming Manufacturing*. Academic Press.

Kozinski, S. (2017). How Generation Z Is Shaping The Change In Education. *Forbes*.

Kristanto, A., Mustaji, M., & Mariono, A. (2017). The Development of Instructional Materials E-Learning Based On Blended Learning. *International Education Studies*, *10*(7), 10. Advance online publication. doi:10.5539/ies.v10n7p10

Latip, M. S. A., May, R. Y. Y., Kadir, M. A. A., & Kwan, T. C. (2019). Does program fees affect the relationship between lecturers' competencies and student' satisfaction in the digital era? A case of Malaysia higher education. *International Journal of Academic Research in Business & Social Sciences*, *9*(7), 877–900. doi:10.6007/IJARBSS/v9-i7/6187

Latip, M. S. A., Noh, I., Tamrin, M., & Latip, S. N. N. A. (2020). Students' acceptance for e-learning and the effects of self-efficacy in Malaysia. *International Journal of Academic Research in Business & Social Sciences*, *10*(5), 658–674. doi:10.6007/IJARBSS/v10-i5/7239

ADDITIONAL READING

Muzenda, A. (2013). Lecturer's competences and students' academic performance. *International Journal of Humanities and Social Sciences Invention*, 3(1), 6–13. doi:10.1016/j.physleta.2016.03.037

Santhi, R., & Ganesh, R. (2015). Addressing service quality to increase students satisfaction and retention in Malaysian private Higher Education Institutions. *American Journal of Economics*, 5(2), 243–250. doi:10.5923/c.economics.201501.31

Sekaran, U., & Bougie, R. (2016). Research methods for business: A skill building approach. John Wiley & Sons Ltd., doi:10.1007/978-94-007-0753-5_102084

Watjatrakul, B. (2014). Factors affecting students' intentions to study at universities adopting the "student-as-customer" concept. *International Journal of Educational Management*, 28(6), 676–693. Advance online publication. doi:10.1108/IJEM-09-2013-0135

Wong, J., Tong, C., & Wong, A. (2014). The mediating effects of school reputation and school image on the relationship between quality of teaching staff and student satisfaction in higher education in Hong Kong. *British Journal of Education, Society & Behavioral Sciences*, 4(11), 1552–1582. doi:10.9734/BJESBS/2014/11312

Sensors and Data in Mobile Robotics for Localisation

S

Victoria J. Hodge
iD https://orcid.org/0000-0002-2469-0224
University of York, UK

INTRODUCTION

Robot navigation is challenging. Leonard and Durrant-Whyte (2012) define it by three questions:

- "where am I?",
- "where am I going?", and
- "how should I get there?"

The first question is localisation: establishing the exact position and orientation of the robot within the frame of reference in its environment, and is the focus here. The robot may be navigating in static or dynamic environments, in indoor or outdoor environments and using static (pre-defined) path determination or dynamic path determination. Each of these variants requires different considerations. Gul, Rahiman, & Nazli Alhady (2019) provide a survey of the algorithms used for robot navigation. Effective navigation requires success in the four building blocks of navigation (Siegwart, Nourbakhsh, & Scaramuzza, 2011):

1. perception - the robot must be able to analyse its sensors data to extract meaningful knowledge;
2. localization - the robot must be able to calculate its position in the environment;
3. cognition - the robot must be able to determine how to navigate to its goals using the information from 1 and 2;
4. motion control - the robot must be able to modulate its movement to achieve the desired trajectory.

This survey focuses on 1 and 2 but also considers 3. It focuses on the sensor data used, how and where they are used and their respective advantages and disadvantages. The **Background** section outlines the different types of mobile robots and identifies the focus for this survey, and **Sensors for Robotics** describes robotics sensors, their use in robot navigation and where the main challenges lie for localisation, **Solutions and Recommendations** examines the literature on localisation for local and global localisation and indoor and outdoor robotics. **Future Research Directions** considers the most likely developments in localisation and the **Conclusion** provides an overview of the article.

DOI: 10.4018/978-1-7998-9220-5.ch133

BACKGROUND

A key task for any autonomous system is acquiring knowledge about its environment. For mobile robot navigation, this is done by taking measurements using various sensors and then eliciting meaningful information from those measurements. Jones, Seiger, & Flynn, (1998) surveyed mobile robotics sensors. Many of these sensors are still used today (in enhanced forms) but new sensors and data have been introduced. The aim of this survey is not to merely catalogue all publications on robot localisation. Rather, it surveys a broad cross-section of contributions that provide the reader with good coverage and insight into the subject. It focuses on interesting and varied contributions from the last decade that use affordable, consumer-grade sensors which have progressed significantly.

Mobile robots can be classified into five different types according to their mode of operation: autonomous ground vehicles (AGVs), autonomous aerial vehicles (AAVs), autonomous surface vehicles, autonomous underwater vehicles, and autonomous spacecraft. This survey considers the first two types. AGVs are used in a broad range of applications for sensing, monitoring, data collection and surveillance, from agriculture to manufacturing logistics, surveillance to transportation, last-mile delivery to mining, defence to construction, environmental (ecological) monitoring to wildlife monitoring, warehouses to distribution centres, search and rescue to disaster analysis and utilities (oil, electricity and gas) and other environments (particularly in logistics, in hospitals or retail). There are also developmental robots and prototypes for domestic use. AAVs can be used in many applications due to their ease of deployment, low maintenance cost, high-mobility and ability to hover. They are used for remote sensing, real-time monitoring and management of road traffic, providing wireless coverage, heat source location, damage assessment, search and rescue operations, delivery of goods, security and surveillance, agriculture, construction and civil infrastructure inspection, environment monitoring, hazard monitoring and weather monitoring, specifically atmospheric forecast and wind.

SENSORS FOR ROBOTICS

Sensors used in robot navigation subdivide into proprioceptive and exteroceptive sensors. Proprioceptive sensors measure the robot itself using data from accelerometers, gyroscopes, magnetometers and compasses, wheel encoders and temperature sensors. Some of these are useful for robot localisation, for example pose estimations or establishing distance travelled during navigation. Exteroceptive sensors measure the external world and acquire information about the robot's environment. Localisation algorithms often need to combine measurements from proprioceptive sensors with information collected by exteroceptive sensors to obtain an overall view of the position, motion and surroundings of the robot within its environment. The various sensors have different operating characteristics and Kelly and Sukhatme (2014) investigate a framework to harmonise the measurement data generation from a cross-section of these sensors to allow a robot to generate information about its environment.

Navigation systems

A typical robot navigation system comprises the five layer architecture shown in Figure 1.

Sensor data are transmitted either as a time-series where data are produced continuously / periodically or, a sequence of readings where data is generated ad hoc, for example generated every time the robot moves. The various data analytics for robot navigation can be performed continuously, periodically or ad hoc. Continuous data transmission is most accurate for localisation and navigation but it is computationally expensive; energy hungry which is a problem for on-board systems as they need power; and the sensor data are very noisy which requires careful processing to ensure accuracy. Periodic data processing is cheaper, uses less energy and allows time for data cleaning and filtering. However, localisation and navigation will be less accurate due to the time gaps. Ad hoc data transmission which only transmits given specific criteria is a trade-off providing the accuracy of continuous transmission with more energy saving of periodic transmission.

Leonard and Durrant-Whyte's (2012) first question of robot navigation is "where am I?". Precise localisation is the first step of navigation for both indoor and outdoor environments.

- Indoor navigation has gained increased attention as Industry 4.0 develops. Robots must be able to navigate dynamic environments safely to assure Industry 4.0 safety (Jaradat, Sljivo, Habli, & Hawkins, 2017). GNSS (Global Navigation Satellite System) is frequently unavailable indoors as there is no line of sight of the satellites (Siegwart et al., 2011). Indoor environments differ from outdoors: indoor spaces are smaller, there are many structural objects such as walls, doors, and furniture or machinery, there may be people moving around and the illumination conditions will change (including artificial lights which can affect sensor data quality from vision-based sensors). However, the variety of obstacles and structures tends to be lower and more regular which can help with object recognition and indoor environments are largely static as their general layouts change infrequently.

Localising indoor AAVs is particularly challenging and needs higher fidelity and faster data processing, position calculation and collision avoidance compared to outdoors as indoor environments are more constricted and compact. AAVs can use autonomous navigation (Hodge, Hawkins, & Alexander, 2021) but autonomous capabilities are often restricted due to state regulation.

- Outdoor spaces vary hugely according to the domain of application, and the type and capabilities of the robot. All robots have to contend with varying weather conditions and varying light conditions, shadows, seasonal changes and temperature changes which adversely affect sensor data accuracy. They also have to contend with wind currents which can displace the robot. All of these aspects make sensor data analysis for localisation and navigation very difficult.

Figure 1. Five-layer system architecture for (IoT) robot navigation

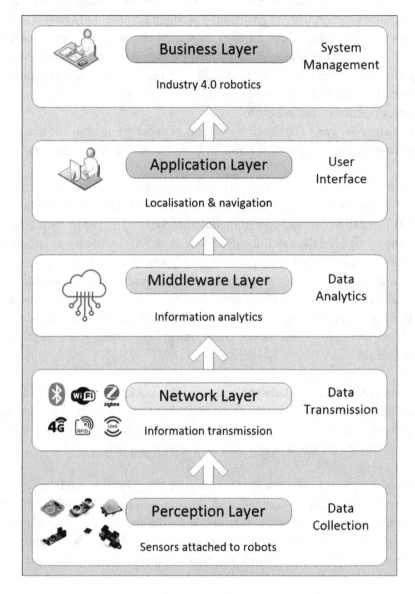

For robot localisation, the information extracted from the sensor data provides global or local estimates of the robot position.

- Local estimation has a known starting location as an input. The sensors provide information regarding the immediate vicinity of the robot so its pose, and distance and direction moved can be estimated. The position estimation is cumulative (an offset from the start). The sensor data describe the immediate locality. Local estimates enable local navigation as they can accurately determine if the robot has rotated, moved a small distance or its distance to nearby objects. They provide high accuracy local data (mm accuracy) but lower confidence in the overall position than global estimates.
- Global estimates are provided by external sensors or on-board cameras among others. They provide a global approximation of the robot's position when it has no knowledge about its initial

position. The estimates tend to have higher confidence of the overall position than local estimates but lower granularity (lower degree of accuracy).

Localisation methods

There are four ways robots can pinpoint their position to allow them to navigate (illustrated in Figure 2).

Figure 2. The four approaches to localisation

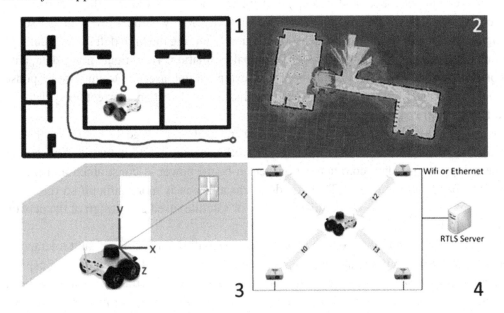

1. using a map (see Rubio, Valero, & Llopis-Albert (2019) for a survey) which is ideal for navigation around immovable objects and fixed structures. It calculates the current location of the robot within the map to determine the robot's position in the environment. The current position can be obtained from a variety of sensors. The data can incorporate range-finding sensor data to identify the distance to obstacles to prevent collisions. Maps are static and navigation using maps requires prior knowledge of the layout to generate the map.
2. using vision-based sensor data to build a map of the environment (topological mapping). This can cope with dynamic environments but vision-based mapping is slow and computationally intensive due to the large data size required for high-fidelity mapping.
3. using object recognition or landmark recognition (this may be mapless or in conjunction with a map). It uses external elements (landmarks) in known locations. These can be either artificially placed landmarks, or natural landmarks. Artificial landmarks may be fiducial markers recognised by computer vision or beacons which transmit signals to receivers on-board the robot.
4. using GNSS or Real-Time Location System (RTLS) (mapless or in conjunction with a map). RTLS uses global estimation with Internet of Things (IoT) receivers in known locations, and ubiquitous connectivity to localize and position IoT tags on-board robots. GNSS and RTLS work indoors and outdoors and are suitable for positioning in dynamic environments. However, they cannot locate dynamic obstructions or humans unless they are also tagged.

Challenges

Industry 4.0 robots need to model their environments, estimate their position and orientation within this model, and navigate to the target. Finding a robust solution to these tasks is crucial to increase the autonomy, adaptability and safety of mobile robots. The main challenges are:

- Sensor data accuracy – sensor data are susceptible to faults such as calibration errors, reflections, shadows, aliasing, illumination variations, insufficient features in open spaces to allow navigation, movement (of robots and objects) and interference. This reduces the accuracy and utility of sensor data and increases computational complexity. Many authors use multi-sensor fusion to mitigate issues with the individual sensors, frequently mixing the high definition accuracy of local estimation with the overview generation of global estimation. To mitigate noisy data, authors use algorithms such as (Extended) Kalman filters, extended unbiased finite impulse response filters, particle filters and Markov or Monte-Carlo localisation to detect and correct noisy data. Panigrahi and Bisoy (2021) provide a review.
- Sensor data need to be transmitted for processing and analysis (Hodge, O'Keefe, Weeks & Moulds, 2015). Indoor robots have readily available networks, usually Wi-Fi networks. Sensor nodes consume energy during data communication yet on-board power is constrained and there is often a lack of bandwidth outdoors. Thus, outdoor transmission is more difficult so the transmission technology (Wi-Fi, Bluetooth, cellular, ZigBee, or satellite) used and design of the network needs to be carefully considered.
- Data processing - the robot needs to provide: access control, data storage, fault tolerance, privacy and security, and data transmission. These severely limit on-board data processing capabilities so data are transmitted for processing. This can introduce latency so transmission must be carefully designed and optimised. Real-time analytics for localisation needs to process huge volumes of data so scalable cloud-based computing architectures are used to enable Industry 4.0 capabilities.
- Standardisation – data need to be integrated for robotics but heterogeneous sensors and heterogeneous transmission protocols produce data in different formats and at different rates leading to compatibility issues. This is exacerbated by a lack of sensor and data standards. Standardisation ensures different systems can share data using a consistent interface.
- Security and privacy - the level of security will be dictated by the value of the asset, the type of asset and the consequences of a failure. The sensor data needs to be secure against intrusion, eavesdropping, data tampering and unauthorized control. IoT devices often have default passwords left unchanged, unpatched software and other major security vulnerabilities.
- If we are truly to realise Industry 4.0 then robotic sensors, data analytics and processing networks need to self-organise to allow new devices to join and devices to leave to make the network proactive rather than reactive. This includes identity management.

The following sections analyse localisation; subdividing it into global or local estimates. Sensors providing global estimates can generate an approximate localisation and ensure that the robot is not lost, while the local sensors provide the higher accuracy information of the robot's vicinity so it can be geo-located precisely and navigate accurately while avoiding collisions. Combining both local and global can provide the best (most accurate and most confident) overall localisation and navigation view.

SOLUTIONS AND RECOMMENDATIONS

Localisation technologies are discussed in the following sections. Many are suitable for both indoor and outdoor localisation.

Local Estimation

Range Sensors: Infrared, Laser and Ultrasound

Both IR and ultrasonic sensors (Leonard and Durrant-Whyte, 2012) can be used for range finding in local estimation indoors or outdoors. The speed of sound and light are almost constant in air so calculating the time between sending a pulse of data and receiving its reflection gives the distance to the reflected object. IR, ultrasonic and laser pulses are not affected by ambient lighting conditions unlike vision cameras where data quality degrades as light levels reduce or in very high light levels (glare). Laser range finders (Biswas and Veloso, 2012) transmit laser pulses and detect their reflections to map the environment's contours. Laser range finders are highly accurate, and detect moving objects such as humans or novel objects such as temporary obstructions. However, all three sensors require line-of-sight between the robot and receiver as the signals cannot penetrate materials (Aqel, Marhaban, Saripan, & Ismail, 2016). Also, the data are noisy, the signal reflections are dependent on the orientation of the object and its material (for example, lasers do not reflect in corridors with glass walls) plus there are no reflections in open areas. Data analysis for these sensors is complex often requiring powerful processing hardware, for example Biswas and Veloso (2012) use particle filters to process laser data.

Dead-reckoning (odometry)

Dead-reckoning for indoor or outdoor AGVs locally estimates the robot's position using data from proprioceptive sensors such as wheel encoders which transmit a tick for each rotation of the wheel and/ or inertial measurement units (IMU) such as accelerometers, gyroscopes and magnetometers which provide acceleration, angular velocity and magnetic field measurement data respectively. Odometry calculates the robot's current position from a combination of the last known position plus an estimate of the distance and direction moved. Modern smartphones contain all of the sensors required making this technique easily accessible and cheap. However, over long periods of time, the position estimate can drift and accuracy is also affected by wheel slippage. Accuracy can be improved using techniques such as (Extended) Kalman Filters and Markov Localisation (Panigrahi and Bisoy, 2021). Duan, Cai, & Min (2014) detect sensor faults and wheel slippage using particle filters (probabilistic modelling), and incorporate a laser range-finder to correct the errors.

Visual odometry (VO) for indoor or outdoor localisation estimates the distance moved and the robot's rotation with respect to a reference frame using real-time frame-to-frame image analysis. It works with consumer-grade cameras and in GPS-denied environments. VO can use monocular or stereo cameras for 2-D or 3-D analyses (Yousif, Bab-Hadiashar, & Hoseinnezhad, 2015). VO algorithms use either appearance (intensity values) or feature detection (key-points) and track their optical flow through frames providing a cumulative estimate of the robot's position. VO outperforms dead reckoning odometry with respect to accuracy (Yousif et al., 2015) but similarly to dead reckoning, VO can suffer from drift. It has been implemented successfully indoors. However, outdoors remains challenging as mitigating varying light and imaging conditions causes high computational cost and the environment (reference frame) must be static and identifiable to allow the robot's movement to be detected by the algorithm. Zhan, Weerasekera, Bian, & Reid (2020) integrated deep learning with monocular VO for indoor and outdoor localisation to overcome scaling and drift issues, and provide more accurate localisation but deep learning is computationally intensive. The Mars Rover and AAVs use VO (Aqel et al., 2016).

Global estimation

GNSS

The most commonly used global estimation for outdoor localisation of all aerial, ground and surface robots is GNSS. This includes the GPS (Global Positioning System) and its data describing the robot's location by longitude, latitude, altitude, and a timestamp. Siegwart et al. (2011) note that:

If one could attach an accurate GPS (Global Position System) sensor to a mobile robot, much of the localisation problem would be obviated.

GNSS is passive; a receiver on the robot receives signals from earth-orbit satellites and processes these data to calculate its location and velocity. However, the position estimate is not free of deviations, and these increase with signal occlusions so, GPS is often used with other localisation mechanisms. Many commercial AAVs fuse GPS data with dead-reckoning IMU data to improve the localisation accuracy.

Magnetic compass

Digital magnetic compasses can provide directional measurements relative to the earth's surface using the earth's magnetic field. They are cheap compared to GPS modules, are readily available in smartphones and are suitable for both indoor and outdoor localisation (Ashraf, Hur, & Park, 2018). Magnetic compasses are most frequently used in conjunction with other sensors, such as cameras and range finders to provide accurate direction estimation. The earth's magnetic field is not affected by weather conditions and is pervasive. However, the earth's magnetic field is often distorted near power lines or steel structures.

Real-Time Location System (RTLS)

Radio-Frequency RTLS measures the distance between transmitter (on-board the robot) and RF receivers (mounted in known locations), see Zafari, Gkelias, & Leung (2019) for a survey of techniques. It is most frequently used indoors but can be used outdoors. The most common methods are based on triangulation which calculates the robot location by measuring signal arrival times or, the radial distance or direction of the received signal from two or three different points. RTLS uses a broad range of positioning technologies including: Wi-Fi, Bluetooth, RFID, UWB, visible light, infrared, ultrasonic, GPS, cellular, ZigBee, and RFID. Deak, Curran, & Condell (2012) provide a survey splitting positioning methods into active and passive. The majority of the localisation techniques are active as they estimate the robot's position using data transmitted from tags mounted on the robot or other objects. Passive systems use readers, often placed in the floor, which power the tags to detect and locate robots locally. Passive systems are cheaper but can only locate robots passing within a short-range of the reader. Active systems can locate robots anywhere inside their range. Martinkovič, Mičieta, & Binasova (2019) investigate a real-time location system for hybrid assembly factories in Industry 4.0. They analyse how UWB tracking can be incorporated in manufacturing where humans and robots cooperate closely and, in the future, collaborate seamlessly and safely. Černohorskỳ, Jandura, & Rydlo (2018) investigate the issues with indoor UWB tracking in confined spaces such as corridors and provide suggestions for overcoming issues with interference and accuracy variability. Outdoor RTLS for both AGVs and AAVs uses transmission technologies such as RF, Laser or UWB. It is often used where GPS fails due to line-of-sight issues. Guo et al. (2016) use UWB RTLS for AAV navigation in spatially restricted areas or dense environments, such as woods or urban canyons where other techniques such as GPS, range sensors or vision-based techniques produce poor quality or no data due to line-of-sight issues.

Visual navigation

The latest visual navigation techniques work indoors or outdoors. They can detect moving objects and handle dynamic environments using Simultaneous Localisation and Mapping (SLAM). SLAM simultaneously maps the robot's location and estimates its pose using probabilistic concepts. SLAM is a global visual mapping of the robot and its environment compared to the local estimation of VO. SLAM can use relatively cheap yet powerful depth sensors such as the Microsoft Kinect RGB-D sensor that was originally designed for the Microsoft Xbox (Biswas and Veloso, 2012) or the Google Tango (Winterhalter, Fleckenstein, Steder, Spinello, & Burgard, 2015). Lu, Xue, Xia, & Zhang (2018) survey visual AAV navigation focusing on approaches that use cheaper and more flexible cameras for pose estimation. AAVs can use regular image processing techniques to reconstruct a 3D map of the environment by estimating the depth value and can then use the depth to estimate the AAV's position. The depth measurement accuracy from these cameras is sufficient for AGV and AAV navigation but requires heavy pre-processing to remove noise, smooth it and to fill gaps where no depth data are produced. Winterhalter et al. (2015) generate proximity measurements from the environment to allow AGV navigation, combine this with RGB-D data and compare it to a 2D outline of the environment, such as a floor plan or map. Kundu, Mazumder, Dhar, & Bhaumik (2016) use 3D-point clouds to generate 2D (binary) occupancy grids with 0 for unmapped or occupied grid cells and 1 for empty cells. The robot uses this grid information to navigate the environment.

Early vision-based approaches for robots relied on artificially placed landmarks such as barcodes. The advent of deep neural networks in 2000s provided a leap forward in vision processing capabilities. Modern vision-based approaches can operate in unmodified environments. Hence, indoor and outdoor localisation can use landmarks, external elements that are either artificially placed or natural occurring but are distinctive, recognisable and fixed position. Natural landmarks can be doors, trees or walls. This visual recognition requires line-of-sight of the landmarks and vision accuracy degrades under obscurants such as fog and smoke, so practitioners fuse multiple sensor data, particularly for AAV navigation, often incorporating IMU data. Alternatively, Khattak, Papachristos, & Alexis (2018) design fiducial markers for the pose estimation of aerial robots. The markers work with (long wave infrared) thermal cameras which are not affected by obscurants. LiDAR has rapid data collection, is highly accurate and recent developments in autonomous vehicles has dramatically reduced the cost of LiDAR so Wang et al. (2021) use 2-D LiDAR SLAM for centimetre-level precision localisation of AAVs in warehouses using artificial landmarks (reflective geometric objects that reflect the laser). LiDAR is susceptible to obscurants so the reflective objects assist recognition but LiDAR has high energy usage.

Even today, visual navigation can be difficult for AGVs and AAVs both indoors and outdoors, see Lowry et al. (2015) for a survey. It is computationally demanding due to the large data size. It faces other challenges including; multiple locations in the environment can appear very similar and difficult to distinguish (known as perceptual aliasing), the appearance of a location can change dramatically under different lighting conditions, shadows or occlusion, obscurants such as fog or smoke can degrade image quality and thus data quality, and locations may be viewed from differing viewpoints if the robot is in a slightly different position from previously. These all impact recognition accuracy. It also needs to factor in the motion of the robot itself.

Localisation with beacons

The robot's on-board receiver captures the beacon data to determine the robot's location from analysing the strength and direction of the data received and identifying the location of the transmitting beacon. Localisation can be achieved using beacons which generate Wi-Fi, Bluetooth, ultrasound, infrared, radio transmissions, visible light, or any similar signal data. Sheinker et al. (2016) perform indoor AGV localisation by analysing magnetic field data. They place magnetic beacons in known locations that can be detected by robot-mounted receivers, such as smartphones or tablets that contain a magnetometer. The robot's position is calculated by software running on the phone that determines which beacon produces the strongest signal. However, magnetic variations can cause signal fluctuations and require compensating mechanisms. Ogiso, Kawagishi, Mizutani, Wakatsuki, & Zempo (2015) combine wheel odometry data with acoustic data collected by on-board microphones for indoor localisation of AGVs. The sound sources (beacons) have known locations and frequency bands and the localisation algorithm estimates the direction-of-arrival (DOA) of the sound sources using 4 microphones in a square array to calculate the location and pose of the AGV. Similar to range-sensor localisation, acoustic localisation is susceptible to occlusion and reflections and requires a clear audio signal between transmitter and receiver.

Sensor data fusion

As mentioned in the previous section of this survey, many authors have turned to sensor data fusion approaches to overcome the limitations of individual sensors and their data. Sensor fusion merges data from multiple sensors (including proprioceptive and exteroceptive sensors) and can fuse local and global estimates. Data fusion aims to obtain a precise position for the robot, generate a richer overview of the robot's environment and reduce uncertainty through increased accuracy, reliability, and fault tolerance of sensor data. Data fusion increases the sensor data coverage (including spatial and temporal coverage); improves the data resolution and increases the data variety. This richer data allows data processing algorithms to generate a richer overview of the robot and its environment. This richer data, however, may cause compute intensive algorithms to be unable to process the data fast enough so the data processing and algorithm used to processed fused data has to be carefully considered. Data from each sensor may be processed first by separate algorithms and the results analysed for localisation or the data may be fused and then analysed by a single algorithm or multiple algorithms. The algorithms need to handle data outages from individual sensors, the data granularity and data transmission rates of the different sensors will vary and need to be accommodated and synchronised, and data are often noisy which needs to be mitigated. Authors often use filter algorithms to mitigate data noise (see Panigrahi and Bisoy, 2021).

Dobrev, Flores & Vossiek (2016) fuse global radar data with local ultrasonic (pose estimation) and odometry (precise location) data for indoor localisation of AGVs where GNSS data are unavailable. The radar data places the robot in its environment and, in conjunction with the local ultrasonic and odometry estimates, places it on a grid map of the environment. The authors claim that fusing data from the three sensors provides an absolute location so the robot can relocate even if it is picked up and moved.

Quigley, Stavens, Coates, & Thrun (2010) consider indoor localisation using smartphones. They use the smartphone's Wi-Fi signal power measurements for fast global convergence with circa 4 metre accuracy and combine this with computer vision from the phone's built-in camera which offers greater tracking accuracy over long periods. The combined approach aims to ensure fast convergence and high precision. Li, Queralta, Gia, Zou, & Westerlund (2020) combine local motion estimation (odometry) data with real-time visual data and a detailed pre-built map for localising delivery AGVs in urban (outdoor) environments. They fuse 3D LiDAR data, inertial (IMU) data, GNSS data and wheel encoder readings. Their analyses identify that using combinations of sensor data allows them to mitigate deficiencies with the individual sensors. For example adding IMU data to a combination of LiDAR and GNSS data increases the accuracy and stability of localisation.

Localising indoor micro-AAVs is particularly challenging due to their mobility and low payload but carefully selected sensors coupled with data fusion can assist. Sensor data fusion can combine camera data with range finding data to implement SLAM algorithms. Li et al. (2018) use a separate (off-robot) wireless network comprising two types of 3-D range finder: a spinning 2-D range finder, which provides omnidirectional measurements and a Time-of-Flight camera that measures the distance in a fixed field of view (like a normal camera). The localisation algorithm fuses these data to build a 3-D map of the area. The AAVs carry low-level path tracking sensors to monitor their motion in the 3-D map. Paredes, Álvarez, Aguilera, & Villadangos (2018) developed a hybrid acoustic and optical positioning system for the accurate 3D positioning of indoor AAVs. It uses ultrasonic data to compute the horizontal position combined with optical data that provides an initial estimation for the AAV's altitude. A recursive algorithm refines the estimated position. This combination requires line of sight for the ultrasonic data, and varying light conditions and visual obscurants will affect the optical data. Azhari et al. (2017) overcome visual obscurants during outdoor AAV navigation by fusing visual SLAM, IMU and ultrasonic (sonar) data generated by sensors on-board the AAV. The SLAM camera is a monochromatic charge-coupled device (CCD) that localises by identifying fiducial markers (waypoints). By processing the sonar data, the localisation algorithm estimates the distance of an object from the AAV using the pulse width of the sound waves. These sound data produce a 3D model approximation of the environment (mines).

Similar to Li et al. (2018), Canedo-Rodríguez et al. (2016) use a multi-sensor fusion approach that combines on-board and external (off-robot) sensors. The authors fuse data from a 2D laser range-finder, a Wi-Fi card, a magnetic compass, and an external multi-camera network of USB webcams for mobile AGV localisation in crowded indoor environments. Their localisation algorithm is based on particle filters. The Wi-Fi positioning system and the cameras provide rough estimate of the robot's position while the laser and the compass refine these estimates and provide location accuracy. The system aims to degrade gracefully if any sensors are unavailable.

There are issues for RTLS such as network contention and network slowdown during heavy traffic, data reception fluctuations due to variations in signal strength, and for active systems the anchors need to be synchronized very precisely as a small timing error translates into a large distance error. Hence, Mirowski, Ho, Yi, & MacDonald (2013) combine an ensemble of RF signals to build multi-modal signal maps for indoor or outdoor localisation of AGVs. They harness off-the-shelf smartphone sensor data collecting time-stamped Wi-Fi, Bluetooth, cellular, magnetic field magnitude, GPS (outdoors) plus near-field communication readings at specific landmarks to create a signal map in buildings and determine the location of the smartphone.

FUTURE RESEARCH DIRECTIONS

Industry 4.0 requires innovation in data, analytics and physical technology. Robotics, IoT and its networks of sensors are crucial for Industry 4.0 realisation. The latest robots, sensor devices, AI, and cloud solutions will underpin this innovation producing smart, integrated and trustworthy systems. Future Industry 4.0 applications will exploit fog and mobile edge computing architectures. As industrial automation advances, sensor technology will be the foundation for data collection and data analytics that will transform industry into the connected, cost-effective, and reliable factories of the future. A key element of this future is autonomous robots which are capable of autonomous and safe navigation. A key element of autonomous and safe navigation is robot localisation, answering the question "Where am I?" precisely. Current sensor technology is developing rapidly but there is still some way to go to bridge the gap between the physical and digital (data-driven) world and precise localisation. This will require development of:

- device interoperability so that sensors become plug-and-play into any robot where they will function seamlessly and allow data collection for localisation,
- multi-purpose sensors,
- standardization of sensor data and data collection architectures,
- standard sensor data processing pipelines (sensorOps),
- multi-channel communications to enable collection of high volume sensor data and a wide variety of data types from different sensors,
- multi-stage data fusion – combining data from a variety of sources (sensors and contextual data) and over a range of time epochs to generate a consolidated state history for advanced localisation,
- privacy and end-to-end security of sensor data as data are collected and transmitted by robots,
- well-defined policies and regulations of data, its collection and processing,
- reductions in costs of sensors, data collection architectures and processing frameworks,
- reduction in power consumption of sensors and on-board processing to allow data to be processed on-board the robots, plus efficient power supply mechanisms (such as self-power or energy-harvesting),
- extending existing localisation algorithms or developing new algorithms to process this enhanced data. The algorithms need to handle high volume, high variety and highly granular data to generate precise localisation for the robots,
- localisation algorithms running on-board the robots must process the full range of data, generate precise localisations while remaining within the limits of energy consumption available from the on-board power sources.

If Industry 4.0 robots are to become fully autonomous then they need to rely on on-board sensors and their data to make navigation decisions including localising.

CONCLUSION

Industry 4.0 and IoT are rapidly innovating sectors with potential to change and automate industrial processes. Robotics, sensors, data and machine learning are central to this innovation. In particular using sensor data for robot navigation to ensure safety and enable autonomy. However, issues of performance, security and standardisation need to be addressed to ensure robot navigation is safe and effective. A crucial aspect of robot navigation is localisation: determining the robot's exact location. The chapter aims to provide readers with a clear understanding of robotic localisation and the different solutions for Industry 4.0. It identifies the advantages and disadvantages of the approaches and will help practitioners find solutions to particular tasks.

ACKNOWLEDGMENT

The research was supported by the Assuring Autonomy International Programme (www.york.ac.uk/assuring-autonomy).

REFERENCES

Aqel, M. O., Marhaban, M. H., Saripan, M. I., & Ismail, N. B. (2016). Review of visual odometry: Types, approaches, challenges, and applications. *SpringerPlus*, *5*(1), 1–26. doi:10.118640064-016-3573-7 PMID:27843754

Ashraf, I., Hur, S., & Park, Y. (2018). MagIO: Magnetic field strength based indoor-outdoor detection with a commercial smartphone. *Micromachines*, *9*(10), 534. doi:10.3390/mi9100534 PMID:30424467

Azhari, F., Kiely, S., Sennersten, C., Lindley, C., Matuszak, M., & Hogwood, S. (2017). A comparison of sensors for underground void mapping by unmanned aerial vehicles. In *Proceedings of the First International Conference on Underground Mining Technology* (pp. 419-430). Australian Centre for Geomechanics. 10.36487/ACG_rep/1710_33_Sennersten

Biswas, J., & Veloso, M. (2012). Depth camera based indoor mobile robot localization and navigation. In *IEEE International Conference on Robotics and Automation* (pp. 1697-1702). IEEE. 10.1109/ICRA.2012.6224766

Canedo-Rodríguez, A., Alvarez-Santos, V., Regueiro, C. V., Iglesias, R., Barro, S., & Presedo, J. (2016). Particle filter robot localisation through robust fusion of laser, WiFi, compass, and a network of external cameras. *Information Fusion*, *27*, 170–188. doi:10.1016/j.inffus.2015.03.006

Černohorský, J., Jandura, P., & Rydlo, P. (2018). Real time ultra-wideband localisation. In *19th International Carpathian Control Conference (ICCC)* (pp. 445-450). IEEE. 10.1109/CarpathianCC.2018.8399671

Deak, G., Curran, K., & Condell, J. (2012). A survey of active and passive indoor localisation systems. *Computer Communications*, *35*(16), 1939–1954. doi:10.1016/j.comcom.2012.06.004

Dobrev, Y., Flores, S., & Vossiek, M. (2016). Multi-modal sensor fusion for indoor mobile robot pose estimation. In *Proceedings of IEEE/ION Position, Location and Navigation Symposium (PLANS) 2016* (pp. 553-556). 10.1109/PLANS.2016.7479745

Duan, Z., Cai, Z., & Min, H. (2014). Robust dead reckoning system for mobile robots based on particle filter and raw range scan. *Sensors (Basel)*, *14*(9), 16532–16562. doi:10.3390140916532 PMID:25192318

Gul, F., Rahiman, W., & Nazli Alhady, S. S. (2019). A comprehensive study for robot navigation techniques. *Cogent Engineering*, *6*(1), 1632046. doi:10.1080/23311916.2019.1632046

Guo, K., Qiu, Z., Miao, C., Zaini, A. H., Chen, C. L., Meng, W., & Xie, L. (2016). Ultra-wideband-based localization for quadcopter navigation. *Unmanned Systems*, *4*(01), 23–34. doi:10.1142/S2301385016400033

Hodge, V. J., Hawkins, R., & Alexander, R. (2021). Deep reinforcement learning for drone navigation using sensor data. *Neural Computing & Applications*, *33*(6), 2015–2033. doi:10.100700521-020-05097-x

Hodge, V. J., O'Keefe, S., Weeks, M., & Moulds, A. (2015). Wireless sensor networks for condition monitoring in the railway industry: A survey. *IEEE Transactions on Intelligent Transportation Systems*, *16*(3), 1088–1106. doi:10.1109/TITS.2014.2366512

Jaradat, O., Sljivo, I., Habli, I., & Hawkins, R. (2017). Challenges of safety assurance for industry 4.0. In *13th European Dependable Computing Conference (EDCC)* (pp. 103-106). IEEE. 10.1109/EDCC.2017.21

Jones, J. L., Seiger, B. A., & Flynn, A. M. (1998). *Mobile robots: Inspiration to implementation.* CRC Press. doi:10.1201/9781439863985

Kelly, J., & Sukhatme, G. S. (2014). A general framework for temporal calibration of multiple proprioceptive and exteroceptive sensors. In *Experimental Robotics* (pp. 195–209). Springer. doi:10.1007/978-3-642-28572-1_14

Khattak, S., Papachristos, C., & Alexis, K. (2018). Marker based thermal-inertial localization for aerial robots in obscurant filled environments. In *International Symposium on Visual Computing*, (pp.565–575). Springer. 10.1007/978-3-030-03801-4_49

Kundu, A. S., Mazumder, O., Dhar, A., & Bhaumik, S. (2016). Occupancy grid map generation using 360o scanning xtion pro live for indoor mobile robot navigation. In *First International Conference on Control, Measurement and Instrumentation (CMI)* (pp. 464–468), IEEE. 10.1109/CMI.2016.7413791

Leonard, J. J., & Durrant-Whyte, H. F. (2012). *Directed sonar sensing for mobile robot navigation* (Vol. 175). Springer Science & Business Media.

Li, H., & Savkin, A. V. (2018). Wireless sensor network based navigation of micro flying robots in the industrial internet of things. *IEEE Transactions on Industrial Informatics*, *14*(8), 3524–3533. doi:10.1109/TII.2018.2825225

Li, Q., Queralta, J. P., Gia, T. N., Zou, Z., & Westerlund, T. (2020). Multi-sensor fusion for navigation and mapping in autonomous vehicles: Accurate localization in urban environments. *Unmanned Systems*, *8*(03), 229–237. doi:10.1142/S2301385020500168

Lowry, S., Sünderhauf, N., Newman, P., Leonard, J. J., Cox, D., Corke, P., & Milford, M. J. (2015). Visual place recognition: A survey. *IEEE Transactions on Robotics*, *32*(1), 1–19. doi:10.1109/TRO.2015.2496823 PMID:26512231

Lu, Y., Xue, Z., Xia, G. S., & Zhang, L. (2018). A survey on vision-based UAV navigation. *Geo-Spatial Information Science*, *21*(1), 21–32. doi:10.1080/10095020.2017.1420509

Martinkovič, M., Mičieta, B. & Binasova, V. (2019). The use of real - time location system in hybrid assembly. *Průmyslové inženýrství*. doi:10.24132/PI.2019.08948.101-108

Mirowski, P., Ho, T. K., Yi, S., & MacDonald, M. (2013). SignalSLAM: Simultaneous localization and mapping with mixed WiFi, Bluetooth, LTE and magnetic signals. In *International Conference on Indoor Positioning and Indoor Navigation* (pp. 1-10). IEEE. 10.1109/IPIN.2013.6817853

Ogiso, S., Kawagishi, T., Mizutani, K., Wakatsuki, N., & Zempo, K. (2015). Self-localization method for mobile robot using acoustic beacons. *ROBOMECH Journal, 2*(1), 1–12. doi:10.118640648-015-0034-y

Panigrahi, P.K., & Bisoy, S.K. (2021). Localization strategies for autonomous mobile robots: a review. *Journal of King Saud University-Computer and Information Sciences.*

Paredes, J. A., Álvarez, F. J., Aguilera, T., & Villadangos, J. M. (2018). 3D indoor positioning of UAVs with spread spectrum ultrasound and time-of-flight cameras. *Sensors (Basel), 18*(1), 89. PMID:29301211

Quigley, M., Stavens, D., Coates, A., & Thrun, S. (2010). *Sub-meter indoor localization in unmodified environments with inexpensive sensors. In 2010 IEEE/RSJ international conference on intelligent robots and systems.* IEEE.

Rubio, F., Valero, F., & Llopis-Albert, C. (2019). A review of mobile robots: Concepts, methods, theoretical framework, and applications. *International Journal of Advanced Robotic Systems, 16*(2), 1–22. doi:10.1177/1729881419839596

Sheinker, A., Ginzburg, B., Salomonski, N., Frumkis, L., Kaplan, B. Z., & Moldwin, M. B. (2016). A method for indoor navigation based on magnetic beacons using smartphones and tablets. *Measurement, 81,* 197–209. doi:10.1016/j.measurement.2015.12.023

Siegwart, R., Nourbakhsh, I. R., & Scaramuzza, D. (2011). *Introduction to autonomous mobile robots.* MIT Press.

Wang, S., Chen, X., Ding, G., Li, Y., Xu, W., Zhao, Q., Gong, Y., & Song, Q. (2021). A lightweight localization strategy for LiDAR-guided autonomous robots with artificial landmarks. *Sensors (Basel), 21*(13), 4479. doi:10.339021134479 PMID:34208935

Winterhalter, W., Fleckenstein, F., Steder, B., Spinello, L., & Burgard, W. (2015). Accurate indoor localization for RGB-D smartphones and tablets given 2D floor plans. In *IEEE/RSJ International Conference on Intelligent Robots and Systems (IROS)* (pp. 3138-3143). 10.1109/IROS.2015.7353811

Yousif, K., Bab-Hadiashar, A., & Hoseinnezhad, R. (2015). An overview to visual odometry and visual SLAM: Applications to mobile robotics. *Intelligent Industrial Systems, 1*(4), 289–311. doi:10.100740903-015-0032-7

Zafari, F., Gkelias, A., & Leung, K. K. (2019). A survey of indoor localization systems and technologies. *IEEE Communications Surveys and Tutorials, 21*(3), 2568–2599. doi:10.1109/COMST.2019.2911558

Zhan, H., Weerasekera, C. S., Bian, J. W., & Reid, I. (2020). Visual odometry revisited: What should be learnt? In *2020 IEEE International Conference on Robotics and Automation (ICRA)* (pp. 4203-4210). IEEE. 10.1109/ICRA40945.2020.9197374

ADDITIONAL READING

Al-Kaff, A., Martin, D., Garcia, F., de la Escalera, A., & Armingol, J. M. (2018). Survey of computer vision algorithms and applications for unmanned aerial vehicles. *Expert Systems with Applications, 92,* 447–463. doi:10.1016/j.eswa.2017.09.033

Alatise, M. B., & Hancke, G. P. (2020). A review on challenges of autonomous mobile robot and sensor fusion methods. *IEEE Access: Practical Innovations, Open Solutions, 8*, 39830–39846. doi:10.1109/ACCESS.2020.2975643

Kuutti, S., Fallah, S., Katsaros, K., Dianati, M., Mccullough, F., & Mouzakitis, A. (2018). A survey of the state-of-the-art localization techniques and their potentials for autonomous vehicle applications. *IEEE Internet of Things Journal, 5*(2), 829–846. doi:10.1109/JIOT.2018.2812300

Peel, H., Luo, S., Cohn, A. G., & Fuentes, R. (2018). Localisation of a mobile robot for bridge bearing inspection. *Automation in Construction, 94*, 244–256. doi:10.1016/j.autcon.2018.07.003

Rubio, F., Valero, F., & Llopis-Albert, C. (2019). A review of mobile robots: Concepts, methods, theoretical framework, and applications. *International Journal of Advanced Robotic Systems, 16*(2). Advance online publication. doi:10.1177/1729881419839596

Siegwart, R., Nourbakhsh, I. R., & Scaramuzza, D. (2011). *Introduction to autonomous mobile robots*. MIT Press.

KEY TERMS AND DEFINITIONS

Global Localisation: The initial robot location is completely unknown, and the robot is localised externally to the robot.

Industry 4.0: Smart manufacturing and autonomous systems powered by interconnectivity, data, and machine learning.

Internet of Things (IoT): Connections between physical objects - people, sensors or machines and the internet.

Local Localisation: The initial location is known, and on-board sensors locate the robot within its environment.

Odometry: An estimation of a robot's location relative to where it started.

Sensor Data Fusion: Merging data from multiple sensors to reduce the uncertainty inherent in their data.

SLAM: Simultaneous localisation and mapping technology uses sensor data to create a map of the robot's environment and allows localisation of the robot to be performed simultaneously.

Structure Implementation of Online Streams

Ambika N.

(ID) https://orcid.org/0000-0003-4452-5514

St. Francis College, India

INTRODUCTION

Global availability (Muhlenbrock, Brdiczka, Snowdon, & Meunier, 2004) has brought more challenges to the systems. Large sets of packets (Khan, et al., 2014) commute to different regions without committing to scalability (Pediaditakis, Tselishchev, & Boulis, 2010) and availability (Silva, Guedes, Portugal, & Vasques, 2012). These new ventures have led to many problems. The technology provides an opportunity for the user to view their doings from isolated areas.

The previous contribution (Xian, Zhang, Bonk, & Liu, 2021) is Rank-based monitoring (Zheng, Huang, Zhou, & Zhou, 2011) and sampling methodology (Acharya, Prakash, Saxena, & Nigam, 2013). It is based on data growth. It instantly discovers the mean variations in a means when only an insufficient division of searches is obtainable online. The measurement sequence will automatically enlarge knowledge for unobservable variables based on the online remarks. It wisely earmarks the monitoring sources to the most questionable input streams (Muthukrishnan, 2005). The architecture can precisely gather the variables based on several noticeable variables and completely assemble a global monitoring statistic with the proposed augmented vector, which leads to a quick apprehension of the out-of-control state even if limited changed variables in real-time. It quickens the disclosure of method transfers in the circumstances of unfinished measurements by growing the unobservable learning with the dimensions of the marked ones.

The suggestion aims to construct a structure based on the fed data. The structure helps to analyses the stream of data. The dataset is divided into three sets. To partition them to the different sets, trial dataset is used initially. The dataset contains the characteristics of the particular data structure is defined. Based on the assembly, the outlier is drawn for the dataset. As the procedure proceeds, first set consists of reliable set. The second set consists of elements that require scrutiny. The third set contains the dataset that are malicious. Using KNN-procedure, it classifies the received data into different sets. After analyzing the received data, it either accepts or rejects the data.

The literature survey is explained in second section. The proposal is detailed in segment three. It is subdivided into assumptions, notations used in the study, and background. The fourth section analyses the study, evaluating energy consumption and availability issues. Future directions are discussed in fifth division. The work is concluded in sixth segment.

DOI: 10.4018/978-1-7998-9220-5.ch134

LITERATURE SURVEY

The following section summarizes the contribution by various authors towards the domain. It is the intermediate outcome (Luckenbach, Gober, Arbanowski, Kotsopoulos, & Kim, 2005) of an R&D design between Samsung Advanced Institute of Technology and Fraunhofer FOKUS. It has a system of eight 802.15.4 acquiescent MICAz nodes. The MICAz is produced by the UC Berkeley and Crossbow. It runs in the 2.4GHz wavelength group. It implements communication rates of up to 250Kbps. It maintains the IEEE 802.15.4 PHY/MAC tier of the ZigBee model. The TinyREST accommodates clients attached to the Internet. It issues HTTP-like demands. It composes the use of the MICAz not only as sensing devices but as actuators as well. With users can control an actuator to take some action. SUBSCRIBE customers express their concern to particular assistance that the devices give with different personalized parameters depending on each customer's requirements. Each contributed consumer will automatically be informed accordingly with NOTIFY information if and each time the coveted experience has been sensed. The interface between the buyers and the device is provided by a multithreaded lightweight HTTP-2-TinyREST gateway. It will manage more than one relationship from purchasers concurrently. The HTTP-2-TinyREST gateway is responsible for establishing, handling, and dropping communication to and from between the customer and the device. It includes efficacy limits and reports composition mappings.

Detecting functionality (Frank, Bolliger, Mattern, & Kellerer, 2008) on portable receivers involves sensing the appearance of marked things, the phone's position, and additional knowledge appropriate for learning the meaning of an object's destruction. The construction involves application-specific assistance, such as connecting things and their buyers, a user database, and profiling co-operations that can be applied to decrease heuristics for wide-area object explorations. They are combined using inquiry assistance that supports the implementation of the application's performance troubles. These include the restricted inquiry assistance. It is used to set up personal portable telephones, the global question assistance. It is used to route questions on universal order and doubts scoping assistance. It maintains the following in preparing proper recipients for an inquiry based on records data collected by the utilization. Gadget tagging is performed using BTnodes, small machines furnished with a Bluetooth radio, and gadget sensing is achieved using Bluetooth development. The in-range and out-of-range issue authorizations generate an event each time a distinct target is created by Bluetooth or an earlier seen gadget declines to answer to an associate effort. Both gadget trademarks and instruments describing characters can reduce their distinctness and allow only validated sensors (Ambika N., 2021) to understand their performance. After the principal essential replacement, defended objects senses only by assigning a piece of confirmed information. The membership assistance helps three foremost objectives. First, it keeps track of connections between users and the gadgets. The position contour assistance presents statistics on the places in which customers consume most of their time. The inquiry duties form the integrating component of the scheme, electrifying the scattered elements for the necessary administration assignment.

IoT Gateway scheme (Zhu, Wang, Chen, Liu, & Qin, 2010) is comprised of three subsystems. The detector connection is in the understanding tier of the method. Its principal purpose is to accumulate data and assign learning to the gateway. It also receives notifications directed from the hubs. The sensor junction is stationed with the Data Processing component to trace the requests and forward the info, Data Transfer obligations and Basic Service model to transmit data packages, and Event Synchronization subcomponent. IoT hub is in the intermediate tier between detector devices and administration principles. It collects sensed knowledge from machines and facilities from the reinforcement policies and broadcasts learning to application policies. GPRS Interaction element and Ethernet Communication part are stationed in the gateway to assign info with reinforcement principles. The transceiver segment extends to transfer information with the host. The Command Mapping part parses the instructions from application principles, achieving sensor system administration or hub supervision. Protocol Translation segment combinations the sensed info with a limited construction. Log Management and Configuration administration performs the administrative duties of hubs, registering the significant results and contour information in the gateway, presenting the upload functionality. The Uploading and Control Operator is effective for clustering data, transferring data to the serial harbor. It performs interface requirements. Application staging is in the administration tier of the policy. Its mission is to maintain the gateway and sensing system through the gateway. It collects the info in the database and implements a user command interface. TCP Server and Consumer Communication part perform data broadcast, detector Interface Arrangement and hub Contour understand the hub and detector arrangement, Data Analysis and Statistical maintains for power administration.

The expanded detector (Ma, Zhou, Li, & Li, 2011) connections and relay devices form a multi-hop network rooted at a gateway. The responsibilities assign the detector devices and awaken to take significant ecological dimensions and drive the information unswervingly or during various leaps to the gateway. The capacities include warmth and comparative moisture of the atmosphere. It also calculates the dampness of the earth, ambient luminosity, and CO_2 attentiveness. According to a gateway admittance procedure, the gateway repackages and sends the together detector info to the message host, which provisions the knowledge into the store. The conclusion sustain arrangement contains an assortment of farming models, examine the store and circulate applicable leadership, like irrigation, insect administration, and devastating weather caution, to farmers via SMS. The irrigation classification and green residence organize attaches to the sensing devices. The relay instruments are prohibited. A web server provides a boundary to outlook real-time statistics, question and jog news on chronological learning, generate watchfully, and carry out uncomplicated administration of detector arrangement. The agronomists can download the node figures from the record and purify the undeveloped representation in DSS.

The IMS structure (Bailey, Cooke, Jahanian, Nazario, & Watson, 2005) has three unique elements. First, a Distributed Monitoring Foundation improves perceptibility into global menaces. A Lightweight Mobile Responder gives unlimited interactivity transfer on the corresponding setting can be modified independently of employment interpretation. The Payload Signatures and Caching tool avoid reading repeated payloads, lessening hanging, and serving in the description. The tradeoff of clarity over in-depth menace knowledge drives the construction illustrated. It consists of a collection of black hole detectors. They watch a dedicated series of available IP directions area. There are no genuine owners in an additional location section. The transactions must be the effect of negative configuration, backscatter from fooled reference directions, or scanning from infections and another probing. The black hole devices in the IMS are a passive element. The receptive segment reports packages sent to the machine's location range and the existing element answers to containers to extract more info from the reference. The dynamic element extracts the primary payload information beyond the higher rules. UDP is a connectionless procedure of application-level knowledge. It transfers without the recipient ever answering.

The framework (Perera, et al., 2013) has two sections. CASSARAM allows users to reveal which connection feature is more important to them when compared to others. They can avoid it by not selecting the check-box correlated with that specific context property. Measurement is calculated for each context attribute. The contribution uses Connotative detector System Ontology to form the sensing devices' specifications and context attributes. The SSN ontology is capable of modeling a notable quantity of knowledge about devices like abilities, production. The SSN ontology can be enlarged unlimitedly by three levels- estimation section, working feature, and durability characteristic.

A CS-based knowledge procurement structure (Li, Da Xu, & Wang, 2012) includes the compressed sampling at the IoT end node, learning communication over IoT (Devare, 2019), and reliable records rehabilitation at FC. In this framework, the sound design, message contents, and reconstruction precision acknowledge for their manufacturing employment. The association of sensing info over IoT and WSNs is an adaptive scattered description and identical sign restoration procedure. It is a tremendous efficiency and cheaper computational complexity correlated with preexisting assembly/cluster-sparse rehabilitation programs.

PROPOSED WORK

The advanced feature administration involves a wide number of method variables and feature attributes. Practitioners accomplish comprehensive information about the method to confirm the quick discovery of variations that may occur at any variable. However, knowledge (Dittrich & Quiané-Ruiz, 2012) (Fan, Han, & Liu, 2014) is not always feasible during online monitoring of data streams due to constraints of monitoring sources in tradition. Rank-based monitoring and sampling methodology (Xian, Zhang, Bonk, & Liu, 2021) is based on data growth. It instantly discovers the mean variations in a means when only an insufficient division of searches is obtainable online. The measurement sequence will automatically enlarge knowledge for unobservable variables based on the online remarks. It wisely earmarks the monitoring sources to the most questionable input streams. The architecture can precisely gather the variables based on several noticeable variables and completely assemble a global monitoring statistic (Townshend & Justice, 1988) with the proposed augmented vector (Qian, Gao, Chen, & Yang, 2019), which leads to a quick apprehension of the out-of-control state even if limited changed variables in real-time. It quickens the disclosure of method transfers in the circumstances of unfinished measurements by growing the unobservable learning with the dimensions of the marked ones.

BACKGROUND

a.   K-nearest neighbor algorithm

It is a non-parametric procedure (Sun & Huang, 2010) (Keller, Gray, & Givens, 1985). It does not make any presumption on underlying information. It stocks all the prepared info and incorporates fresh evidence based on the comparison. It saves the dataset at the training phase. When it gets novel data, it analyzes that knowledge into a section. It puts the same into the set with similar property. The algorithm follows the below steps -

Step-1: Choose the quantity K of the next-door-neighbor
Step-2: Determine the Euclidean range of K quantity of acquaintances
Step-3: Take the K most adjacent bystanders as per the measured Euclidean measure.
Step-4: Between these k acquaintances, calculate the amount of the information cases in a particular section.
Step-5: Indicate the latest evidence points to that division for which the number of the bystander is more.

ASSUMPTIONS

- Three datasets (Buhl, Röglinger, Moser, & Heidemann, 2013) are maintained in the system. These datasets are assumed to be reliable.
- The arriving data is assumed to be anonymous (w.r.t to its characteristics).
- Though the source is assumed to be known, the data's characteristics are assessed.

NOTATIONS USED IN THE WORK

Table 1. Notations used in the work

Notations used in the study	Description
D_R	Reliable data set
D_C	Data set to be scrutinized
D_{UR}	Unreliable dataset
T_i	Data to be verified

Table 1 represents the notations used in the recommendation. The suggestion aims to construct a structure based on the fed data. The structure helps to analyses the stream of data.

- The dataset is divided into three sets. To partition them to the different sets, trial dataset is used initially. The dataset contains the characteristics of the particular data structure is defined. Based on the assembly, the outlier is drawn for the dataset.
- As the procedure proceeds, first set consists of reliable set D_R. The second set D_C consists of elements that require scrutiny. The third set contains the dataset that are malicious D_{UR}.
- When a data T_i arrives it is compared with the characteristics of the three datasets using KNN algorithm (k-nearest neighbor procedure). Based on the outcome, the data is classified.
  - *Case 1* - If the data T_i belongs to dataset-1, no further scrutiny is done.
  - *Case 2*- if the data T_i € dataset -2, the data is observed for time t. after time t, the data is either put into dataset 1 or 3. If the dataset falls into 1, the characteristics are embedded into dataset-1 and the outlier is redefined. If the data falls into dataset-3, the data is removed from the system.
  - *Case 3*- If the data T_i € dataset -3, the data is removed from the system.

SIMULATION

The work is simulated in Ns2. The following parameters given in the table 2 is used to simulate.

Table 2. Parameters used in the simulation

Parameters used	Description
Dimension of study	200m *200m
Number of sensors used	40
Length of data generated	280 bits
Internet speed	109Mbits/s
Devices used	Samsung android mobile device (Exynos 9825 Processor; 64 bit)
Time	60s

ANALYSIS OF THE WORK

Rank-based monitoring and sampling methodology (Xian, Zhang, Bonk, & Liu, 2021) is based on data growth. It instantly discovers the mean variations in a means when only an insufficient division of searches is obtainable online. The measurement sequence will automatically enlarge knowledge for unobservable variables based on the online remarks. It wisely earmarks the monitoring sources to the most questionable input streams (Aggarwal, 2007). The architecture can precisely gather the variables based on several noticeable variables and completely assemble a global monitoring statistic with the proposed augmented vector, which leads to a quick apprehension of the out-of-control state even if limited changed variables in real-time. It quickens the disclosure of method transfers in the circumstances of unfinished measurements by growing the unobservable learning with the dimensions of the marked ones.

Sensors (Akyildiz, Su, Sankarasubramaniam, & Cayirci, 2002) (Yick, Mukherjee, & Ghosal, 2008) (Ambika N., 2020) (Nagaraj, 2021) belong to a similar domain. They are deployed in an environment that requires monitoring and tracking objects of interest. The readings are transmitted to the user. These texts contain a large amount of data. As the distance between the deployed region and user increases, the threat to the data also increases. The intruders are liable to introduce false alarms into the system. Hence tracking the data becomes a challenge to the user.

The suggestion uses the data obtained by the sensors and transmits to the user using Internet. It aims to construct a structure based on the fed data. The structure helps to analyses the stream of data. The dataset is divided into three sets. To partition them to the different sets, trial dataset is used initially. The dataset contains the characteristics of the particular data structure is defined. Based on the assembly, the outlier is drawn for the dataset. As the procedure proceeds, first set consists of reliable set. The second set consists of elements that require scrutiny. The third set contains the dataset that are malicious. Using KNN-procedure, it classifies the received data into different sets. After analyzing the received data, it either accepts or rejects the data.

- *Energy consumption* – If accepting malicious data (Illiano & Lupu, 2015) (Reddy, 2009)are accepted, they will consume more energy (Anastasi, Conti, Di Francesco, & Passarella, 2009) in the systems. The suggestion detects the infected data at an early stage. Hence the energy (Tarannum, 2010) is conserved by the systems. The present suggestion conserves 10.77% more energy compared to (Xian, Zhang, Bonk, & Liu, 2021). Figure 1 is the depiction of the same.

Figure 1. Representation of Energy consumption in devices

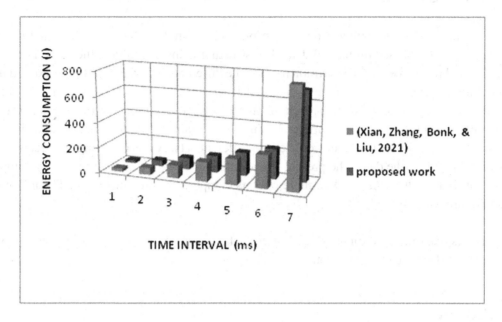

- Availability – The packets are detected at the early stage and hence the proposal will be able to trace and track more packets than the previous contribution by 27.58%. Figure 2 is the graphical representation of the same.

Figure 2. Graphical depiction of availability of the systems

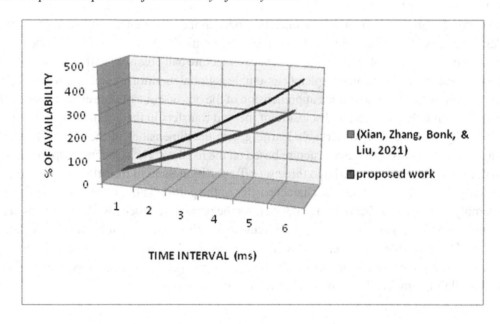

FUTURE DIRECTIONS

The suggestion uses the data obtained by the sensors and transmits to the user using Internet. It aims to construct a structure based on the fed data. The structure helps to analyses the stream of data. The dataset is divided into three sets. To partition them to the different sets, trial dataset is used initially. The dataset contains the characteristics of the particular data structure is defined. Based on the assembly, the outlier is drawn for the dataset. As the procedure proceeds, first set consists of reliable set. The second set consists of elements that require scrutiny. The third set contains the dataset that are malicious. Using KNN-procedure, it classifies the received data into different sets. After analyzing the received data, it either accepts or rejects the data. The present suggestion conserves 10.77% more energy compared to previous contribution. It tracks 27.58%. more packets compared to previous work. The following can be done in future work –

- Security is one of the preliminary necessities of the system. Some security algorithms have to be designed to decrease malicious data.

CONCLUSION

Sensors belong to a similar domain. They are deployed in an environment that requires monitoring and tracking objects of interest. The readings are transmitted to the user. These texts contain a large amount of data. As the distance between the deployed region and user increases, the threat to the data also increases. The intruders are liable to introduce false alarms into the system. Hence tracking the data becomes a challenge to the user. The previous contribution is Rank-based monitoring and sampling methodology. It is based on data growth. It instantly discovers the mean variations in a means when only an insufficient division of searches is obtainable online. The measurement sequence will automatically enlarge knowledge for unobservable variables based on the online remarks. It wisely earmarks the monitoring sources to the most questionable input streams. The architecture can precisely gather the variables based on several noticeable variables and completely assemble a global monitoring statistic with the proposed augmented vector, which leads to a quick apprehension of the out-of-control state even if limited changed variables in real-time. It quickens the disclosure of method transfers in the circumstances of unfinished measurements by growing the unobservable learning with the dimensions of the marked ones.

The suggestion aims to construct a structure based on the fed data. The structure helps to analyses the stream of data. The dataset is divided into three sets. To partition them to the different sets, trial dataset is used initially. The dataset contains the characteristics of the particular data structure is defined. Based on the assembly, the outlier is drawn for the dataset. As the procedure proceeds, First set consists of reliable set. The second set consists of elements that require scrutiny. The third set contains the dataset that are malicious. Using KNN-procedure, it classifies the received data into different sets. After analyzing the received data, it either accepts or rejects the data. The present suggestion conserves 10.77% more energy and availability by 27.58% compared previous contribution.

REFERENCES

Acharya, A. S., Prakash, A., Saxena, P., & Nigam, A. (2013). Sampling: Why and how of it. *Indian Journal of Medical Specialties*, *4*(2), 330–333.

Aggarwal, C. C. (2007). *Data streams: models and algorithms* (Vol. 31). Springer. doi:10.1007/978-0-387-47534-9

Akyildiz, I. F., Su, W., Sankarasubramaniam, Y., & Cayirci, E. (2002). A survey on sensor networks. *IEEE Communications Magazine*, *40*(8), 102–114. doi:10.1109/MCOM.2002.1024422

Ambika, N. (2020). SYSLOC: Hybrid Key Generation in Sensor Network. In Handbook of Wireless Sensor Networks: Issues and Challenges in Current Scenario's (pp. 325-347). Cham: Springer.

Ambika, N. (2021). Wearable sensors for smart societies: a survey. In Green Technological Innovation for Sustainable Smart Societies (pp. 21-37). Springer. doi:10.1007/978-3-030-73295-0_2

Anastasi, G., Conti, M., Di Francesco, M., & Passarella, A. (2009). Energy conservation in wireless sensor networks: A survey. *Ad Hoc Networks*, *7*(3), 537–568. doi:10.1016/j.adhoc.2008.06.003

Ashfahani, A., Pratama, M., Lughofer, E., & Yee, E. Y. (2021). Autonomous deep quality monitoring in streaming environments. In *International Joint Conference on Neural Networks (IJCNN)* (pp. 1-8). Shenzhen, China: IEEE. 10.1109/IJCNN52387.2021.9534461

Bailey, M., Cooke, E., Jahanian, F., Nazario, J., & Watson, D. (2005). The internet motion sensor-a distributed blackhole monitoring system. *NDSS*, 1-13.

Buhl, H. U., Röglinger, M., Moser, F., & Heidemann, J. (2013). Big data. *Business & Information Systems Engineering*, *5*(2), 65–69. doi:10.100712599-013-0249-5

De Paolis, L. T., De Luca, V., & Paiano, R. (2018). *Sensor data collection and analytics with thingsboard and spark streaming. In IEEE workshop on environmental, energy, and structural monitoring systems (EESMS).* IEEE.

Dittrich, J., & Quiané-Ruiz, J. A. (2012). Efficient big data processing in Hadoop MapReduce. *Proceedings of the VLDB Endowment International Conference on Very Large Data Bases*, *5*(12), 2014–2015. doi:10.14778/2367502.2367562

Fan, J., Han, F., & Liu, H. (2014). Challenges of big data analysis. *National Science Review*, *1*(2), 293–314. doi:10.1093/nsr/nwt032 PMID:25419469

Frank, C., Bolliger, P., Mattern, F., & Kellerer, W. (2008). The sensor internet at work: Locating everyday items using mobile phones. *Pervasive and Mobile Computing*, *4*(3), 421–447. doi:10.1016/j.pmcj.2007.12.002

Illiano, V. P., & Lupu, E. C. (2015). Detecting malicious data injections in wireless sensor networks: A survey. *ACM Computing Surveys*, *48*(2), 1–33. doi:10.1145/2818184

Keller, J. M., Gray, M. R., & Givens, J. A. (1985). A fuzzy k-nearest neighbor algorithm. *IEEE Transactions on Systems, Man, and Cybernetics*, *4*(4), 580–585. doi:10.1109/TSMC.1985.6313426

Khan, N., Yaqoob, I., Hashem, I., Inayat, Z., Mahmoud Ali, W., Alam, M., Shiraz, M., & Gani, A. (2014). Big data: Survey, technologies, opportunities, and challenges. *TheScientificWorldJournal*, *2014*, 1–18. doi:10.1155/2014/712826 PMID:25136682

Klein, A., & Lehner, W. (2009). Representing data quality in sensor data streaming environments. *Journal of Data and Information Quality*, *1*(2), 1–28. doi:10.1145/1577840.1577845

Kumari, A., Tanwar, S., Tyagi, S., & Kumar, N. (2019). Verification and validation techniques for streaming big data analytics in internet of things environment. *IET Networks*, *8*(3), 155–163. doi:10.1049/iet-net.2018.5187

Li, S., Da Xu, L., & Wang, X. (2012). Compressed sensing signal and data acquisition in wireless sensor networks and internet of things. *IEEE Transactions on Industrial Informatics*, *9*(4), 2177–2186. doi:10.1109/TII.2012.2189222

Luckenbach, T., Gober, P., Arbanowski, S., Kotsopoulos, A., & Kim, K. (2005). *TinyREST-a protocol for integrating sensor networks into the internet. In RealWsn*. ACM.

Ma, J., Zhou, X., Li, S., & Li, Z. (2011). Connecting agriculture to the internet of things through sensor networks. In *International conference on internet of things and 4th international conference on cyber, physical and social computing* (pp. 184-187). IEEE.

Madden, S., & Franklin, M. J. (2002). Fjording the stream: An architecture for queries over streaming sensor data. In *18th International Conference on Data Engineering* (pp. 555-566). IEEE. 10.1109/ICDE.2002.994774

Muhlenbrock, M., Brdiczka, O., Snowdon, D., & Meunier, J. L. (2004). Learning to detect user activity and availability from a variety of sensor data. In *Second IEEE Annual Conference on Pervasive Computing and Communications* (pp. 13-22). IEEE. 10.1109/PERCOM.2004.1276841

Muthukrishnan, S. (2005). Data streams: Algorithms and applications. Now Publishers Inc. doi:10.1561/9781933019604

Nagaraj, A. (2021). Introduction to Sensors in IoT and Cloud Computing Applications. Bentham Science Publishers. doi:10.2174/97898114793591210101

Pediaditakis, D., Tselishchev, Y., & Boulis, A. (2010). Performance and scalability evaluation of the Castalia wireless sensor network simulator. In *3rd international ICST conference on simulation tools and techniques* (pp. 1-6). ACM.

Perera, C., Zaslavsky, A., Liu, C. H., Compton, M., Christen, P., & Georgakopoulos, D. (2013). Sensor search techniques for sensing as a service architecture for the internet of things. *IEEE Sensors Journal*, *14*(2), 406–420. doi:10.1109/JSEN.2013.2282292

Qian, W., Gao, Y., Chen, Y., & Yang, J. (2019). The stability analysis of time-varying delayed systems based on new augmented vector method. *Journal of the Franklin Institute*, *356*(3), 1268–1286. doi:10.1016/j.jfranklin.2018.10.027

Reddy, Y. B. (2009). A game theory approach to detect malicious nodes in wireless sensor networks. In *Third International Conference on Sensor Technologies and Applications* (pp. 462-468). IEEE. 10.1109/SENSORCOMM.2009.76

Safaei, A. A. (2017). Real-time processing of streaming big data. *Real-Time Systems*, *53*(1), 1–44. doi:10.100711241-016-9257-0

Silva, I., Guedes, L. A., Portugal, P., & Vasques, F. (2012). Reliability and availability evaluation of wireless sensor networks for industrial applications. *Sensors (Basel)*, *12*(1), 806–838. doi:10.3390120100806 PMID:22368497

Sun, S., & Huang, R. (2010). An adaptive k-nearest neighbor algorithm. In *Seventh international conference on fuzzy systems and knowledge discovery* (pp. 91-94). IEEE.

Tarannum, S. (2010). Energy conservation challenges in wireless sensor networks: A comprehensive study. *Wireless Sensor Network*, *2*(6), 483–491. doi:10.4236/wsn.2010.26060

Townshend, J. R., & Justice, C. O. (1988). Selecting the spatial resolution of satellite sensors required for global monitoring of land transformations. *International Journal of Remote Sensing*, *9*(2), 187–236. doi:10.1080/01431168808954847

Xian, X., Zhang, C., Bonk, S., & Liu, K. (2021). Online monitoring of big data streams: A rank-based sampling algorithm by data augmentation. *Journal of Quality Technology*, *53*(2), 135–153. doi:10.1080/00224065.2019.1681924

Yahyaoui, A., Lakhdhar, H., Abdellatif, T., & Attia, R. (2021). Machine learning based network intrusion detection for data streaming IoT applications. In *21st ACIS International Winter Conference on Software Engineering, Artificial Intelligence, Networking and Parallel/Distributed Computing (SNPD-Winter)* (pp. 51-56). IEEE. 10.1109/SNPDWinter52325.2021.00019

Yick, J., Mukherjee, B., & Ghosal, D. (2008). Wireless sensor network survey. *Computer Networks*, *52*(12), 2292–2330. doi:10.1016/j.comnet.2008.04.002

Zheng, K., Huang, Z., Zhou, A., & Zhou, X. (2011). Discovering the most influential sites over uncertain data: A rank-based approach. *IEEE Transactions on Knowledge and Data Engineering*, *24*(12), 2156–2169. doi:10.1109/TKDE.2011.121

Zhu, Q., Wang, R., Chen, Q., Liu, Y., & Qin, W. (2010). Iot gateway: Bridgingwireless sensor networks into internet of things. In *IEEE/IFIP International Conference on Embedded and Ubiquitous Computing* (pp. 347-352). IEEE. 10.1109/EUC.2010.58

ADDITIONAL READING

Ashfahani, A., Pratama, M., Lughofer, E., & Yee, E. Y. (2021). Autonomous deep quality monitoring in streaming environments. In *International Joint Conference on Neural Networks (IJCNN)* (pp. 1-8). IEEE. 10.1109/IJCNN52387.2021.9534461

Chandrasekaran, S., & Franklin, M. J. (2002, January). Streaming queries over streaming data. In *VLDB'02: Proceedings of the 28th International Conference on Very Large Databases* (pp. 203-214). Morgan Kaufmann.

De Paolis, L. T., De Luca, V., & Paiano, R. (2018). *Sensor data collection and analytics with thingsboard and spark streaming. In IEEE workshop on environmental, energy, and structural monitoring systems (EESMS)*. IEEE.

Fumeo, E., Oneto, L., & Anguita, D. (2015). Condition based maintenance in railway transportation systems based on big data streaming analysis. *Procedia Computer Science*, *53*, 437–446. doi:10.1016/j.procs.2015.07.321

Klein, A., & Lehner, W. (2009). Representing data quality in sensor data streaming environments. *Journal of Data and Information Quality*, *1*(2), 1–28. doi:10.1145/1577840.1577845

Kumari, A., Tanwar, S., Tyagi, S., & Kumar, N. (2019). Verification and validation techniques for streaming big data analytics in internet of things environment. *IET Networks*, *8*(3), 155–163. doi:10.1049/iet-net.2018.5187

Madden, S., & Franklin, M. J. (2002). Fjording the stream: An architecture for queries over streaming sensor data. In *18th International Conference on Data Engineering* (pp. 555-566). IEEE. 10.1109/ICDE.2002.994774

Safaei, A. A. (2017). Real-time processing of streaming big data. *Real-Time Systems*, *53*(1), 1–44. doi:10.100711241-016-9257-0

Shahrivari, S. (2014). Beyond batch processing: Towards real-time and streaming big data. *Computers*, *3*(4), 117–129. doi:10.3390/computers3040117

Tatbul, N. (2010, March). Streaming data integration: Challenges and opportunities. In *2010 IEEE 26th International Conference on Data Engineering Workshops (ICDEW 2010)* (pp. 155-158). IEEE.

Yahyaoui, A., Lakhdhar, H., Abdellatif, T., & Attia, R. (2021). Machine learning based network intrusion detection for data streaming IoT applications. In *21st ACIS International Winter Conference on Software Engineering, Artificial Intelligence, Networking and Parallel/Distributed Computing (SNPD-Winter)* (pp. 51-56). IEEE. 10.1109/SNPDWinter52325.2021.00019

KEY TERMS AND DEFINITIONS

Data Streaming: The devices collect enormous amount of data which is to be transmitted to the pre-defined location.

K-Nearest Neighbor Procedure: It is methodology where the input is compared to other datasets, to find a label for itself.

Malicious Data: The information that tries to destroy the asset of the organization or individual.

Sensor: These are tiny devices used to track an object of interest or sense environment.

Trial Dataset: The collection of input/outcome before actually implementing the device in actual environment.

Nature–Inspired Algorithms and Smart City Applications

N

Richard C. Millham
Durban University of Technology, South Africa

Israel Edem Agbehadji
Durban University of Technology, South Africa

Emmanuel Freeman
Ghana Communication Technology University, Ghana

INTRODUCTION

Information and Communication Technology (ICT) play an important role in ensuring efficient use of resources. Through its influences on businesses and government, the fourth industrial revolution will form the future. People have no control over either technology or the disruption that comes with the fourth industrial revolution (Xu, David and Kim 2018). This disruption will impact every sector of an economy ranging from education, health, finance, energy and many more. Creating a dynamic structure to handle such disruption and ensure optimal resource utilization is imperative towards the creation of smart cities.

As indicated in the Focus section of this chapter, we first introduce nature inspired algorithms, along with their characteristics, and show how they are being used with different entities, along with their interactions, for intelligent management within smart cities. To understand how different entities play a role in a smart city, we first explore the different spheres of the fourth industrial revolution and then explore different aspects of the opportunities, expectations, and challenges of a smart city.

In the rest of this chapter, section 2 first begins with a short overview of nature-inspired algorithms and smart city applications. The focus of the chapter, the use of nature-inspired algorithms within fourth industrial revolution and within smart cities, is given. Consequently, in the next section, the era of the fourth industrial revolution with its cyber, digital, and biological spheres is presented. Within this revolution, the intersection of these spheres are outlined with their emergent technologies that are often assisted by nature-inspired algorithms. To further this focus, the opportunities, expectations, and challenges of the fourth industrial revolution then are presented. The last section concludes this chapter. Key terms and suggestions for further readings follow.

DOI: 10.4018/978-1-7998-9220-5.ch135

BACKGROUND

Nature-Inspired Algorithms

These are algorithms inspired from the behavior of social colonies for studying the phenomenology of living systems such as planning, learning, making decisions, perception, etc. The advantage of a Nature-inspired technique is the ability to jump out of any local search that might not lead to an ideal cluster formation. Examples of nature-inspired or bio-inspired techniques are namely Genetic Algorithms (GA), Particle Swarm Optimization (PSO), Ant Colony Optimization (ACO), Wolf Search Algorithm (WSA), Social Spider Algorithm (SSA) and many more.

Genetic Algorithm (GA) is an evolutionary approach that is based on the concept of "survival of the fittest", where the survival depends on "natural selection" that is when the species considered as weak and cannot adapt to the conditions of the habitat are eliminated whereas the species considered as strong and that can adapt to the habitat survives. Thus, natural selection is based on the notion that strong species have a greater chance to pass their genes to future generations, while weaker species are eliminated by natural selection. Sometimes, there are random changes that occur in genes due to changes within the external environments of species, which will cause new future species that are produced to inherit different genetic characteristics. At the stage of producing new species, individuals are selected, at random, from the current population within the habitat to be parents and use them to produce the children for the next generation, thus successive generations are able to adapt to the habitat in respect of time (Mirjalili, 2019).

Ant Colony Optimization (ACO) is characterised as a nature-inspired method that mimics ants' foraging behaviour in their hunt for the shortest paths to food sources. When a food source is discovered, ants will leave a trail of a chemical pheromone to indicate their path for other ants to travel (Agbehadji et al. 2018). A pheromone trail can be described as an odorous material that is utilised as a way to indirectly communicate among ants. The strength of the pheromone is subject to the quantity, quality of, and distance to the food source. This trail of pheromone is also contingent on time, as the trail will evaporate over time, unless refreshed by new ants traversing the same trail. This evaporation quality of pheromone avoids the issue of ants prematurely converging; consequently, ants are able to explore different trails within their area and find an even shorter, better path than the existing one. In the case of an ant being lost, an ant will travel randomly until it finds a strong pheromone trail. The strength of the trail indicates its optimality. If the trail is optimal, such as shortest distance to a large quality food source, this trail will be strengthened through pheromone deposits by ants as they traverse the trail to the food source. If the trail is less than ideal, the ants adopt the more strongly scented optimal trail and less optimal trails, losing their pheromones by evaporation over time, become less and less attractive. Through their adoption of trails, ants can make probabilistic decisions as to where to deposit their pheromones (Coloroni, 1992).

Swarm Intelligence is a nature-inspired method based on swarm behaviour such as ðsh and bird schools in nature. The swarm behaviour is conveyed with respect to how particles (e.g., Particle Swarm Optimization) adapt and make a decision depending on their position within a search space and neighbouring particles (Agbehadji et al. 2018). The advantage of swarm behaviour is that, as an individual particle arrives at a decision, it leads to emergent behaviour, which is contingent on the local interaction among particles to find a potentially optimal solution. Thus, swarm behaviour guarantees some form of collective intelligence. The author (Reynolds 1987) had suggested a model that mimics the ñocking behaviour of birds founded on three simplified rules namely velocity matching with neighbouring ñockmates, collision avoidance with neighbouring ñockmates, and flock centering to remain close to the flock (Siddique and Adeli 2015). The authors (MacArthur and Wilson 1967) proposed a model based on "biogeography" which basically depicts the migration of birds and how species of birds become extinct. Honey bees is a swarm behaviour of bees in search for food sources and they collect food by foraging in ñower patches (Siddique and Adeli 2015).

Wolf Search Algorithm (WSA) is another nature-inspired algorithm that imitates wolves' preying behaviour. This behaviour includes the following capabilities: only merge with its peer if the peer is in a better position (which indicates a trusting characteristic among wolves never to prey upon each other); randomly escape upon the approach of a hunter; the utilisation of scent marks to communicate with other wolves and to delimit its territory; to be only be concerned with prey within its visual range, and to hunt independently by recalling their own trait (a characteristic that shows wolves have memory) (Agbehadji et al. 2016). An alternative version of WSA is the Wolf Search Algorithm with Minus Step Previous (WSA-MP) where a wolf has the ability to remember its previous best position and to elude the old positions taken that do not assure an optimum solution (Fong, 2015).

In a similar manner, the Social Spider Algorithm (SSA) is founded on a spider's social behaviour. Through their prey foraging and web building capabilities, social spiders are recognised to be able to collaborate with their neighbours. Through the building of a social web, spiders offer an environment that acts as a trap that can capture prey. Any prey that is discovered/trapped on the web creates some vibration that can be sensed by a nearby spider. During the prey's attempted escape as it tried to remove itself from the web, it increase the intensity and frequency of its vibration on the web. This increased vibration activates spiders' awareness of a prey's existence on the social web. Consequently, spiders are able to be more conscious of the existence of prey and communicate this existence to nearby spiders in order to collaborate in hunting (James, 2015).

Characteristics of Nature-Inspired Algorithms

Natural systems, especially social colonies, inspired scientist for discovering new algorithms, which help in the study of artificial intelligence. Artificial intelligence is the area of computer science focusing on creating machines, called intelligent agents, or living systems, that can engage behaviours that humans consider intelligent. Artificial intelligence research uses tools and insights from many fields, including computer science, psychology, philosophy, neuroscience, cognitive science, linguistics, ontology, operations research, economics, control theory, probability, optimization and logic.

Prospects of Nature-Inspired Algorithms

The integrated Nature Inspired Algorithm (iNIA) is an emerging approach to combine social behaviour and characteristics of nature-inspired algorithms that manages and monitors the cyber-physical space. There are numerous researches on the application of nature-inspired computation to solve real-world problems. Harnessing the different kinds of nature-inspired behaviour to create a computational technique can create a very vibrate, dynamic and robust eco-system in the current dispensation of system inter-dependency.

The fourth industrial revolution is more than just technology-driven change. Rather, it is powered with disruptive innovation to positively impact our core industries and sectors, such as education, health and business (Xu, David and Kim 2018). Such disruptive innovation should have an underlying structure that is driven by an integrated nature-inspired algorithm. Innovative technologies will integrate different scientific and technical disciplines. Key forces will come together in "a fusion of technologies that is blurring the lines between physical, digital, and biological spheres" (Schwab 2015). This fusion of technologies goes beyond mere combination, but blends incremental improvements from several (often previously separated) fields to create a product. In this context, fusion of nature-inspired algorithms for optimal resource monitoring in this disruptive innovation era is imperative.

SMART CITY APPLICATIONS

Introduction

The smart city concept hinges on computational integration that ensure a greatly improved living and working environment for urban populations. Smart devices are intelligent or adaptive devices that enables the realization of the smart city concept. The fusion of technologies can be achieved using smart devices for data transmission, resource computational needs and networking capabilities.

The extensive use of ICT and connected technologies like the Internet of Things (IoT), Cloud and fog computing, and Cyber Physical Systems (CPS) to name a few has led to data being generated and gathered at lightning speeds (Clever *et al.* 2018).

Through the networking, interoperability, and mutual control of different devices and systems, along with the collection and management of this data, huge amounts of data are being collected and then the integration, interoperability, and management of these systems and devices become possible. Based on the factors, a new urban model is made possible, often termed a green city, along with a system of a green city (Su, 2011).

Networks and IoT

In order to make smart city possible, a powerful smart-city network needs to be constructed to manage the multitude of networks' interoperability and to handle the huge amount of big data that will be flowing through these networks. This network could be based on existing fibre-optic networks, in conjunction with the technologies of Wi-Fi, Mesh, and WiMAX networks, in order to provide a wireless broadband network necessary to manage the media needs of a smart city. A wireless broad base station could be utilised to cover the entire city while many functions of urban management and service systems for business, foreign visitors, tourists, government agencies, and the public could be provided through this media. Some of these functions include emergency telecommunications, mobile dispatching emergency response, mobile video conferencing, and mobile wireless surveillance (Su, 2011).

An Internet of Things (IoT) node may consist of sensor devices (which include radio frequency identification devices and infrared sensors), laser scanners, and global positioning systems, et al. This node could then be connected to a city-wide network and allow its mechanical and electrical equipment to be managed through interactions at the local and centralised control level. Sensor devices, including radio frequency identification devices (RFID), infrared sensors, global positioning system, laser scanners and so on, can be combined with the Internet to form the Internet of Things. Then all the items in life can be taken as a terminal to be brought into the network, achieving the centralized and remote control of electrical and mechanical equipment through the interaction of various networks and terminals. An example, a RFID tag attached to a parcel can send its identifying information to a controlling node which interacts with other nodes that manage the parcel's routing to its destination. (Su, 2011)

Smart cities can take advantage of smart city traffic applications to improve their traffic flow. Depending on their specific needs and particular traffic situation, a smart city could utilise their sensor network and associated computational abilities to change their traditional transport system to a smart transport management system with urban traffic control systems to manage congestion, adaptive traffic lights (where the control of traffic lights is automated according to traffic flow), et al. (Su, 2011). This smart traffic management system serves as only a component in terms of the planning, deployment, operation, and management of a smart city.

Social services

Another aspect of smart city applications is a one-stop social service system. The public can upload information via their mobile phone or personal computer and receive a real-time response. This system would be designed to manage people's complaints, requests for assistance, and personal management of social affairs that, in turn provides the city with platform services for emergency response, community management, and urban comprehensive planning. (Su, 2011)

Smart city applications can be extended to healthcare. IoT can enable hospitals to achieve smart medical care. This medical care includes the digital collection, management, and transmission of internal medical information such as patient records, personnel information and management (ensuring the right people are available during the right shift), medical supplies and equipment (ensuing adequate stock is available at all times), drug information (to prevent dangerous drug interactions), management of safety hazards (both in terms of awareness and proper handling), and monitoring response times to emergencies (Su, 2011). Another potential application with healthcare is the monitoring of patients' health via sensors with alerts being raised whenever an abnormal threshold is reached.

Tourism

Another area for smart city applications is tourism. Smart tourism integrates existing tourism information and infrastructure but extends it to provide tourism online services, management of tourist customer relations, management and operation of tourist sites, promotion and development of local and overseas tourist markets, intelligent management of tourist information that has been collected and used for tourism prediction. These tourist applications can be integrated with other smart systems, such as government and transport systems, to provide a seamless and comprehensive set of services to tourists (Su, 2011)

FOCUS OF THE ARTICLE

The objective of this chapter is to show the different spheres of the emerging fourth industrial revolution and how they inter-relate with the application, opportunities, expectations, and challenges of a smart city. Because many different aspects of smart cities interact with each other through various technologies, several nature-inspired algorithms are introduced and described that have been used to manage these entities and their interactions. The goal is to provide an introduction of these algorithms within smart city entities as a potential solution to a given problem within a specific domain rather than to provide a comprehensive evaluation of all potential nature-inspired algorithms, based on a standardised set of metrics, for this particular challenge.

SOLUTIONS AND RECOMMENDATIONS

Era of the 4th Industrial Revolution

The fourth industrial revolution (4IR), a term coined by Klaus Schwab, founder and executive chairman of the World Economic Forum, describes a world where individuals move between digital domains and offline reality with the use of connected technology to enable and manage their lives (Miller 2015, 3). The first industrial revolution changed our lives and economy from an agrarian and handicraft economy to one dominated by industry and machine manufacturing. Oil and electricity facilitated mass production in the second industrial revolution. In the third industrial revolution, information technology was used to automate production. Although each industrial revolution is often considered a separate event, together they can be better understood as a series of events building upon innovations of the previous revolution and leading to more advanced forms of production (Philbeck, 2018). This chapter discusses the major features of the four industrial revolutions, the opportunities of the fourth industrial revolution, and the challenges of the fourth industrial revolution.

The inter-dependency of systems which also refers to the fusion of technologies can be achieved by harnessing the enormous potential that is offered by the nature-inspired behaviour. Fundamentally, the fusion of technologies is the inter-connectedness of systems within the physical, digital and biological spheres which is collectively referred to as cyber-physical systems. Fusion of technologies will grow exponentially in terms of technological change and socio-economic impact. The advantage of technological fusion is that, first, the majority of people around the world can communicate easily e.g. through the use of social media platforms. Secondly, businesses can have quick and easy access to digital platforms of marketing etc. Thirdly, consumers can have an input in the production and distribution chains. Thus, the exponential growth will create a digital revolution which usher in the concept of the fourth industrial revolution. Technologies have emerged which entirely revolutionises the activities of the society.

Unfortunately, the underlying frameworks of these technologies are very diverse which brings to the fore the challenge of technology frameworks inter-connectedness. This creates some kind of challenge of how to effectively ensure inter-connectedness which Schwab (2005) referred to as "blurring the lines between physical, digital and biological sphere". Harnessing the nature-inspired behaviour can bridge the technology fusion gap and create a very vibrate, dynamic and robust eco-system for the fourth industrial revolution, which can impact on governance and business. The opportunities of the fourth industrial revolution includes reducing barriers between the technology inventors and markets; vibrant use of the artificial intelligence; fusion of different techniques and knowledge domains; enhanced quality of lives through the use of robotics; easy and quick access to information through the use of internet. The 4IR could transform the entire systems of countries, companies, industries and society. In order to realize this transformation it calls for new methods and processes, and the engagement of broad stakeholders consultation both public and private sectors, to academia and civil society for a global integrated and comprehensive policy to ensure the realization of the 4IR. Globalization may be seen as enabler of the fourth industrial revolution of countries and therefore it is significant for global integration of systems. Although countries may differ in certain aspects, the may exhibit some isomorphism that bears similarity with processes of other professional counterparts (Oosthuizen 2016). This processes which have been built into systems need to work with related 4IR technologies. This chapter seeks to bridge the gap between soft applications and create an approach for system integration and transition toward creating smart cities. Algorithms play very significant roles in making complex decision on system integration and transition.

Cyber-physical sphere

Basically, a nature-inspired algorithm is the algorithm developed from the selected behaviour of animals or birds or some living organisms within their natural surroundings. The cyber-physical sphere of 4IR consists of three key dimensions namely digital, physical and biological. These spheres, along with some of their associated technologies, are illustrated in Fig 1.

Figure 1. Three Spheres of the Fourth Industrial Revolution

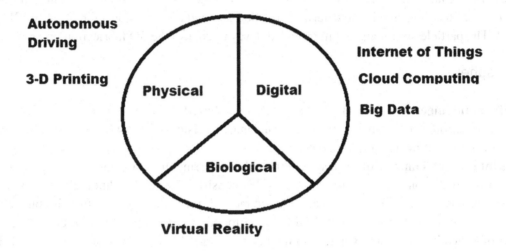

Physical sphere

The physical sphere involves the use of robotics, autonomous vehicles, new material and 3D printing. Although, the underlying models for each is different, nature-inspired algorithms have permeated their applications. Manufacturing systems that employ robots in their assembly process need to consider layout design of their system, operating times and how to manipulate these robots in order to achieve optimal output. In order to achieve these, nature inspired algorithms have been explored to optimize robot work cell layout in robot cellular manufacturing systems. These algorithms have been applied to effectively optimize the layout design, operating time and manipulation of robots in manufacturing systems (Lim, G. and Izui 2016). Swarm robotics is one of the approach to create a coordination of among several number of robots (Zedadra *et al.* 2018).

In **autonomous** driving, the nature-inspired algorithms act as agents with the capabilities to detect the location of an obstacle and avoid it by mapping the global position of the obstacle through the change of its position and visual angle. This mapping consequently enables the agent, and subsequently the vehicle, to manoeuvre (Tanev and Shimohara 2009). For instance, a cuckoo search algorithm has been applied for mobile robot movement to find the shortest path for an agent to manoeuvre through a different number of obstacles (Mohanty P.K. and D.R. 2013). Similarly, pheromone of ant colony system has been applied to find the shortest path which ensures safety and reliability of autonomous underwater vehicles (AUVs) (Ma et al. 2019). Genetic algorithms have been used to not only to find optimal routes but alternative paths for routes in the case of a traffic jam (Ozmen, 2021)

Basically, **3D printing** involves the design and manufacturing of artworks or prototype. Nature inspired algorithms have been applied to design techniques for 3D printing or to develop a nature inspired fabrication strategy. The techniques have been applied for free and controlled movement of 3D printers. For example, these nature-inspired techniques have been built in programs to automatically translate 3D curves into GCode. For example, the spawning behaviour of dragonflies has been applied to enable a 3D printer operate below its printing platform. Similarly, the spawning behaviour of mosquitos has been imitated as a means for the printing of filament onto the surface of water. Again, the spiders' algorithm (Social Spider) has been applied to develop a method that allowed the 3D printer to spray continuous filament in mid-air. Again, the weaver ants algorithm was used for placing fibres on top of fibrous sub surfaces (Zheng and Schleicher 2018). Finally, particle swarm optimization algorithm with artificial neural network has been applied to determine the porosity and compression strength of the 3D printed scaffold. The particle swarm algorithm provided a way to control the 3D fabrication process.

Digital sphere

In **artificial intelligence,** nature-inspired algorithm is referred to as an agent that is intelligent and is able to plan, reason, learn from its environment and make decisions. These makes agent to self-organise themselves into multiple intelligent agents.

The **Internet of Things (IoT)** is a system that allows sharing of data among connected objects and people. It is mostly considered as an eco-system that consists of several technologies like wireless devices, sensor-based devices etc., which are inter-connected. Basically, IoT system relies on the internet infrastructure to store data at a centralized location for future processing. Presently, IoT devices are capable of collecting very large volumes of data that are varied in their structure, and these IoT based systems are growing each day. Nature-inspired algorithms play a key role in creating self-organizing structure within an eco-system of devices by finding the optimal way to route data among devices, form an optimal cluster, resource scheduling, fuse data in wireless sensor networks etc. For instance swarm intelligence-based algorithms have been widely used in IoT-based application (Zedadra *et al.* 2018). IoT has encouraged the creation of smart homes, kitchen, appliances, health, machines, supply chain, transportation and more. It is anticipated that the era of 4IR will make more devices to be interconnected and there will be available large amount of data which will require network optimization of IoT (Srinidhi, Dilip Kumar and Venugopal 2019). Nature inspired algorithm can ensure optimal path for interconnection of different soft computing application. The author of (Zedadra *et al.* 2019) is of the view that with such complex and largely distributed systems, computational intelligence techniques or nature-inspired techniques are well adapted to provide robust, scalable and self-organized behaviour to deal with very dynamic and fast changing systems. In this era of system interconnectedness, the application of new techniques is anticipated to provide an efficient mechanism for routing of data packets, scalability of network and reliability, improved quality of service etc. (Sari 2017) (Srinidhi, Dilip Kumar and Venugopal 2019). The authors of (Bui *et al.* 2020) applied nature-inspired algorithm, based on the nature-inspired bee foraging algorithm, for smart home management system for IoT-based connected devices. The Grey Wolf Optimisation algorithm, similar to the Wolf Search Algorithm of Fong (2015), has been used to reduce energy consumption, through rescheduling appliance usage times, in smart grids. (Amjad, 2020)

Cloud computing is an internet-based computing environment where resources such as data storage and processing are provided to clients on demand sometimes for a fee or free. Basically, the cloud computing environment provides distributed and parallel computing environment to serve the needs of multiple clients (Chakraborty 2017). Resource allocation is one of the challenges in cloud computing.

The objective of resource allocation is to ensure tasks in the computing environment are efficiently allocated to available resources. Hence, scheduling of resources helps to map jobs to the available resources. However, the challenge with cloud computing is processing of data at a central location or workstation which creates bottleneck in real-time data analytics. The bottleneck could lead to poor quality of service, poor response time and delay in sending data to other distributed environment. As edge devices send raw data continually to the cloud it creates a cloud bottleneck (Said 2016). In order to resolve this bottleneck, edge computing has been created to provide real-time analytics at the edge of the network infrastructure instead of performing data analytics on the cloud environment (Agbehadji *et al.* 201). The architecture of edge computing has a layer that liaise with the cloud computing environment in order to support real-time or near real time data processing. This layer is an extension of cloud computing and often called Fog computing layer (Agbehadji *et al.* 2019). In most instances, fog computing and edge computing are used interchangeably because both provide real-time data analytics without sending data to the cloud server for processing. In order to create inter-connectedness fog computing use network routers and switches, mobile-based stations and gateways to provide cloud service. Nature-inspired algorithm can provide an effective way to load balance and map resources/task when deployed on virtual machines to process data from distributed environments (Chakraborty 2017). In this era of smart city and 4IR, it is significant to balance load and map resources e.g., technologies and their related applications to reduce communication failures when large amount of data is processed. Nature-inspired algorithm can help to balance entire system load and reduce the make span of a given tasks (Said 2016). One area where nature-inspired algorithms have been applied is the intelligent management and balancing of load and renewable energy production through the use of the Spider Prey Algorithm, an enhancement of the Social Spider algorithm (Frimpong, 2022).

Big data is when a very large amount of data is collected from heterogeneous or autonomous sources (that is, when each data source collects varied data without relying on any centralized control) with distributed and decentralized control (Agbehadji *et al.* 2016), it leads to the creation of big data. Basically, big data may be characterized by volume, velocity, variety, veracity, variability and value. Volume is the amount/size of data that has to be processed which might range from thousands of terabytes to petabytes and Exabyte. Velocity is how fast incoming data is create, processed and updated from the process system. Variety is the different kinds of data being generated, such as structured or unstructured data (including unstructured text such as word documents, email messages, transcripts of call center interactions, posts from blogs and social media sites; images; audio; video files; and machine data such as log files from websites, servers, networks and applications from mobile systems). Veracity is referred to as the accuracy of results from a processing system. Variability is the change in the rate of data flow from the generation and analysis (Gill and Buyya 2019). Value relates to what the user will gain from the analysis results (such as new revenue opportunities, effective marketing strategies, better customer service etc.). Mostly, the challenge with big data is the extraction and analysis to find hidden and interesting patterns. In order to address this challenge, nature-inspired algorithms are applied for the analysis, extraction and processing of big data.

Biological Sphere: Virtual Reality

Basically, virtual reality is the use of computer technology and applications to create an artificial environment or simulate activities from the physical world in real-time in the presence of a user (Fahim *et al.* 2019).

Virtual Reality (VR) could be defined as an innovative human computer interface that acts to simulate a real-world environment. An example, participants using VR can travel around in this virtual environment. Like the real world, they can view the world from different angles, reach into it, grab objects and reshape them. Often, interaction is done through sensors on the skin or vision glass such that the users need not enter commands or symbols to manipulate this virtual world; they interact with it in the same way that they would interact with their real-world environment. (Zheng, 1998)

An example of VR in practice is non-invasive visualisation of the inside of patients. Patients are first medically scanned which produces a huge volume of data; this data, in turn, is image processed, using various techniques, to provide an accurate three-dimensional internal visualisation of the patient. This visualisation is useful in a number of medical processes such as surgical planning, diagnosis, and surgical training. (Leng, 2001)

Another example of VR is in the use of education in terms of immediate "field trips". These field trips enable learners to experience and explore environments that they would not normally be able to access, such as the Parthenon in Athens, Greece. These "field trips" need not be limited to physical locations but they could be expanded to enable students to be immersed within and gain a fuller understanding of abstract concepts such as electromagnetism, Newtonian dynamics, or molecular attachment. (Scarvelli, 2021)

Yet another example is the combination of computational fluid dynamics and virtual reality. The various vector flows of fluid dynamics have long been used to streamline the design of automobiles and airplanes. Virtual reality enables engineers to have both a wider perspective of this flow through visualisation but it also enables them to also better understand its complexities. (Leng, 2001)

OPPURTUNITIES OF 4TH INDUSTRIAL REVOLUTION

Introduction

The opportunities that comes with the fourth industrial revolution: 1) lower barriers between inventors and markets, 2) more active role for the artificial intelligence (AI), 3) integration of different techniques and domains (fusion), 4) improved quality of our lives (robotics) and 5) the connected life (Internet).

Baseline - Digital literacy, Network Effect, and New Business Models

One of the baselines for the adoption of many of these 4IR technologies is digital literacy. Digital literacy is the basic prerequisite or backbone for students in order to develop their adaptive capabilities that enable them to benefit from the opportunities provided by the digital economy, participate in the global digital society, and to derive new opportunities for innovation, creative expression, social inclusion, and employment. (Brown-Martin, 2017). Digital literacy cannot be defined just as the ability to operate digital devices; instead, it encompasses a wide range of cognitive skills. These skills include good visual memory and strong intuitive associative thinking to comprehend visual messages, the ability to create new knowledge from pieces of existing knowledge, think in a non-linear fashion, and evaluate information for biases. (Alkali, 2004)

One aspect of these opportunities is the "network effect" where the cost of incorporating these technologies within a company/individual increases their value to that entity while the cost of not incorporating these technologies decreases the same value. A case in point is mobile phones, which when adopted, may greatly increase connectivity and productivity (reducing costs) while not adopting mobile phones restricts connectivity and reduces potential earnings. Another example may be autonomous vehicles where non-adoption results in higher maintenance, personnel, and insurance costs than adoption. (Combes, 2017)

Along with these opportunities come changes in underlying business models. Some examples may be Amazon, Uber, and Airbnb that utilise new technologies to acquire a market share and grow on network dynamics while owning no physical assets of their own in the form of vehicles, physical inventories, or rental properties. These business models often see cost reductions as they enhance their business and scale. (Combes, 2017)

Development and Production of New Materials

Other opportunities include materials with greatly increased functionality that are more lightweight, stronger, and more conducive (such as nano-materials) and synthetic biology that applies engineering principles with biology to quickly come out with new biological materials to address industrial and personal needs (Combes, 2017).

Another example is the large growth of 3D printing. 3D printing can be defined as a process of making solid 3D objects from a digital file produced by users or other entities. (Kayembe, 2019) Users become more involved in the product design where they are able to send their product requirements to 3D printing laboratories, thus giving them more control over their product design (Pessôa, 2020). 3D printing is widely utilised in a number of fields, and for a wide variety of purposes, within the fields of car manufacturing, medicine, electronics, etc. Some applications of 3D printing include the development of artificial organs using human cells; creation of customised electronics; and development of customised parts in many industries. Some advantages of 3D printing include a much quicker and cheaper way to create objects but, perhaps most importantly, a way to create customised objects very cheaply and quickly which other methods (such as mass production methods in previous industrial revolutions were unable to do). In this sense, 3D printing is often termed additive manufacturing. (Kayembe, 2019)

IOT and Big Data

Another opportunity is emerging from the Internet of Things (IoT) where different electronic devices such as television sets, mobile devices, computers, appliances, are all connected to each other and to the Internet. This interconnection allows these devices to share data amongst themselves and to allow interaction with themselves or their external environment (Kayembe, 2019). This digital environment between and within these devices and systems constitute the core of the 4IR revolution in that humans, with their automated systems, are able to manage a wide spectrum of devices and these devices, through their sharing of data and interaction, are able to manage themselves. IoT provides corporate opportunities in that sensors, attached to products, can reveal how products are used within real-life scenarios. These scenarios provide the opportunity to determine how customer use and trends are changing while also providing an opportunity for a company to upsell different products to the same customer (Pessôa, 2020). On a personal level, IoT has the potential to greatly impact the way that humans interact with technology with a great impact on their lives. Some examples include the personal health monitoring, such as heart sensors connected to intelligent monitors that detect heart anomalies and alerts you and the authorities if they occur; the ability of appliances to self-schedule their workload themselves for optimal energy use and workload (Kayembe, 2019).

Other opportunities emerge from the emergence of big data. Big data could be defined as very large and complex sets of data, containing both structured and unstructured data, which traditional data processing techniques are unable to handle due to their size and complexity (Taylor-Sakyi 2016). As the world becomes more inter-connected, more and more data becomes available via these inter-connected devices. Big data characteristics include high velocity, huge volume, and a high degree of variety. The use of big data require novel and cost-effective methods of data processing that assist enhanced insight, decision making, and automation of processes. Through insights provided by big data, organisations are able to analyse their data, understand their environment, and make significant decisions for themselves. Big data is seen as high-volume, high-velocity, and/or high-variety information assets that demand cost-effective and innovative forms of information processing that enable enhanced insight, decision-making, and process automation. Big data platforms could assist organisations to analyse and make meaningful decisions based on the data available to them. Many organisations are becoming increasingly dependent on these analyses for proper decision making. An example, a health department could use information on the number of people, along with their cases, attending a provincial hospital to determine its viability or to determine if certain capacities, in terms of staffing or equipment, needs to be increased. Another example would be the police relying on crime statistics in order to identify crime hotspots within their area and take pro-active action in terms of police-community coordination and the placing of greater police resources in these locations. A spin-off of the big data movement is the technological innovation drive induced in order to store and manage this data (Kayembe, 2019).

AI, Robotics, and Quantum Computing

Still other opportunities emerge from the increasingly role played by artificial intelligence. Artificial intelligence has multiple definitions. According to Perez (Perez et al, 2018), artificial intelligence could be defined as the domain of science which enable machines to perform logic, planning, reasoning, learning and perception. Thus, in many ways artificial intelligence could be compared with human cognitive functions. In terms of simple data processing, artificial intelligence is able to manage a large volume of fast incoming data while recognising patterns within them. An example of an artificial intelligence application is Siri where the application accepts human voice commands, deciphers and processes the command, searches various databases, and then outputs the best matching answer in natural human language. Another example would be the use of artificial intelligence in self-driving cars. Self-driving cars would use artificial intelligence in a multitude of forms: image recognition to identify road hazards, traffic, and the limits of a roadway; GPS navigation to guide the navigation of the vehicle upon the desired route; and the determination of weather conditions to adjust for potential road hazards and to moderate speed and distance between cars.

Based on developments in electrical engineering, computing, and mechatronics, the science of robotics has rapidly advanced with consequent opportunities (Perez et al. 2018). One of the most prominent use of robotics is within manufacturing plants that rely heavily on the use of machines for production. Because robots can perform their tasks around the clock, the use of robots has led to a faster production rate. Robotics is deeply rooted in industries such as car manufacturing plants that rely heavily on the use of machines for production. Other companies have used robots to perform tasks that are viewed as too complex or dangerous for humans to manage. An example would be the use of robots to handle toxic waste (Kayembe, 2019). A further development in the use of robots is their use in the full automation of the production process and, within it, "intelligent automation" that reports on machine usage and wear for maintenance; interacts with other networks to report the need for raw materials for their inputs and for their outputs; is able to manage complex instructions to produce customised products; and indicates alerts in case of anomalies in the production process (Karabegovi and Husak, 2018).

A promising development is the emergence of quantum computing. Quantum computing may take days or hours to solve problems that would normally take billions of years to solve using traditional computers. Quantum computing could enable new findings in energy, environmental systems, smart materials, healthcare, et al. According to Microsoft (2019), quantum computing takes days or hours to solve problems that would take billions of years using today's computers. It also enables new discoveries in the areas of healthcare, energy, environmental systems, smart materials, and beyond (Kayembe, 2019). IBM posits that the speed of quantum computing calculations could lead to new discoveries in developing machine learning algorithms to diagnose illnesses sooner, design materials for more efficient devices and structures, formulate financial strategies to better fit the market and bring in sustainable returns, and algorithms for intelligent management of health resources such as the quick dispatch of ambulances in the case of emergencies.

Smart Plant Management and Customised Ordering

An example of these opportunities includes online ordering where there is a use of a wizard to integrate all of your chosen product options to produce a highly customised product. Once the order is placed, raw materials can be managed through automated fleet and pallet management that then feeds onto the factory floor where automated systems using an identifying tag containing your order produce a customised product. Using this same identifying tag, the customised product is sent off through an automated system to your residence (Pagnon, 2017)

In line with online ordering that produces a customised product and reduces waste, smart plant management can reduce downtime on plant equipment. Through the use of sensors to monitor a plant environment and machinery, wear and tear on plant equipment can be calculated and planned for accordingly. Furthermore, through the use of sensors on plant equipment and environment, abnormal conditions, such a leak in a hose, can be quickly detected with the plant operator notified and remedial action quickly taken (Pagnon, 2017)

Renewable energy

A tremendous growth area in many countries, particularly South Africa, is the tremendous opportunity provided by renewable energy production. Renewable energy is driven by at least two factors: one being the increasing demand for power created by 4IR technologies and the second being the failure of aging infrastructure to supply these power needs within a centralised grid. Renewable energy have the possibility for self-generation of power and provide distribute power sources (which are invaluable to isolated communities) and to improve power management (Combes, 2017).

EXPECTATION OF SMART CITY APPLICATIONS

Introduction

Expectations of smart city applications vary. In their study, some services that received a favourable response were the ability to share perceptions about the quality of life, ideas regarding future prosperity, and responses to critical social problems; advanced cognitive computing based system for healthcare diagnosis; design of an innovation hub where innovators, industrial partners, and funders could collaborate in order to build joint ventures; open educational spaces including integration of Massive Online Open Courses within a simple access point; and an augmented reality application in historical centres that enable an immersive and interactive set of scenarios for users' experiences. (Lytras, 2019)

Some less enthusiastic uptakes, as per Lytras, of smart city applications include data mining of social opinions to rate business services and customer support; an integrated complaint management system over social networks; social campaign management systems managed by active citizens; smart phone applications that are able to recommend news articles to owners based on their opinions as expressed in social media; and an advanced alert system related to changes in human activity (Lytras, 2019) Based on this study, it seems that the citizens of a "smart city" are most interested in applications that would enable their economy (such as innovation hubs) or provide better services (in terms of healthcare diagnostics or open learning) while showing much less enthusiasm for applications that may be perceived as intruding upon their personal privacy, even though this information may be readily available online.

Information kiosk

A smart city application, such as a simple travel kiosk, is expected to have multiple characteristics including timeliness, contextualisation, localisation, and event-awareness. Timeliness not only encompasses up-to-date information but information that is important to the users at a given time. An example, they do not care to be informed that a train has just left but they are interested in when the next one is coming. Event-awareness provides information, potentially from other systems, that would affect them such as a strike or fire on the transport line which would delay service. Localisation is where specific information is given dependent on the particular kiosk's location. An example, bus route information is more detailed and pickup points are more highly mapped in a bus station than in a more remote location with one or two bus stops. Contextualisation is where the individual's needs are taken into account such as information on where to store luggage on a train or where baby strollers could be stored within a station (Lehofer, 2016)

Comprehensive services

The city of Nanhai, China collects data from a variety of departments and business, including IOT devices such as IP cameras, vehicle-mounted GPS and environmental sensors. The education bureau, police security department, traffic police department, administrative service centre use video cameras both for monitoring and to provide early warnings of events. Energy companies use sensors and meters to monitor waste water, waste gas, electricity, and the environment. Using an array of sensors, these sensors monitor rainfall, petrol stations, scenic facilities, campus videos, scenic tour, dangerous chemicals, indoor temperatures in businesses, water consumption, wastewater, fire hazards, and water consumption. These sensors are connected to an intelligent surveillance and analysis system, along with an early warning system. These systems feed into various portals and operations in order to provide water, healthcare, municipal administration, energy monitoring, school education, agricultural production, traffic management, environmental prevention, public security, flood prevention, and social governance for a variety of users: external business, background system users, leadership inquiry and decision makers, departmental business users, and public access users(Zhou, 2017)

FUTURE RESEARCH DIRECTIONS

One challenge, particularly in cities that were the first to adopt "smart technology", was the focus on the technology itself rather than the human component it was to serve. A continuing challenge is that in order for smart cities to develop, methods to integrate and understand fast flowing, heterogeneous, and huge amounts of data flowing from various systems of a smart city need to be found in order to provide proper, timely, and relevant services to its citizens.

Future work also includes sectioning and sub-sectioning smart cities into individual entities whereupon the best nature-inspired algorithm, using a standard set of metrics, could be determined which would work optimally within that particular context. The following section and sub-section highlight the challenges of a smart city which may form future research work.

CHALLENGES OF SMART CITY APPLICATIONS

Introduction

Often, the implementation of a smart city begins initially via small, bottom-up steps where many actors independently realise a smart initiative using some type of technological or public infrastructure solution. Some examples include the provision of electric cars to a company's employees, hospitals implementing online health record access, or the replacement of newer less-polluting buses. However, these initiatives are not included within a framework to realise synergies between these initiatives nor communicate their improvement to the city's citizens. These initiatives lack a comprehensive vision that is capable of defining goals, expected results, and scheduling time to achieve a set project.

Over-reliance on a Single Technology

Dameri argues that one of the predominant issues in adoption of early smart cities was the undue focus on technology without creating, or making citizens aware, of the public value created for their lives. This human component of a smart city adoption is required in order to really encompass the smart actions, developed by the city, into the ordinary daily life of its citizens or, perhaps in some occasions, in those visiting for tourism. One of the primary defects of this smart city first wave is the excessive stress on the pivotal role of the technology. Indeed, technology is certainly the core aspect of a smart city, but it is not enough to create public value for citizens. The human contribution is necessary, to really embody the smart actions into the daily life of people living, studying, working in the city or also visiting the city for one or a few days for work or tourism. It should be therefore necessary to speak about smart people in smart city and to consider people, technology and strategic vision like indispensable components of a successful smart program (Dameri, and Rosenthal-Sabroux, 2014)

Requirement for Complex Data

When it comes to smart cities, one of the most important components is data. To enable smart city applications, data needs to be collected, stored, and processed to accomplish intelligent tasks (Clever *et al.* 2018). There are also social and environmental aspects that have become important in smart cities that create concerns regarding ethics and ethical conduct.

Some challenges of smart cities include the fact that many digital information systems are too simple. They often consist of basic remote sensing, data mapping, and three-dimensional modelling of urban streets. These systems have the ability for simple query and analysis of data, along with perhaps the ability for three-dimensional data visualisation. However, these systems are often incapable of utilising, to their full advantage, multiple sourced and multiple temporal data in order to conduct highly spatial and temporal data analysis that would help make viable decisions on proper urban management. (Su, 2011)

In many present urban information systems, the data structure and organisation of temporal data within their current databases is weak and cannot meet the needs of historical reconstruction, future prediction, or digital real time updates. Consequently, Su argues that the chief driver for a digital city to transform into a smart city is further development of methods to integrate multiple sources of heterogeneous urban information, easier management of urban infrastructure and components, fast updates of online data, and the ability to create flexible structures within a multi-dimensional temporal data model representing the smart city (Su, 2011).

Assumptions

Other challenges include assumptions regarding use of technology, within a smart city, by those most in need of it. An example, the use of smart phone applications to obtain public transportation information is commonly cited. However, studies indicate that the most frequent users of public transportation are either the ones that cannot afford smart phones or those who struggle with digital literacy due to lack of education or age. Consequently, smart kiosks must be provided in transport stations, possibly along with human help. Besides providing next transport information, these kiosks can be expanded to provided navigation features, first aid (emergency help and first aid devices), and public service announcements, mobile charging for phones, and free local calls (Lehofer, 2016).

CONCLUSION

In this chapter, we provided an overview of smart city applications, opportunities, and expectations. In many of these applications, one or more nature-inspired algorithm were utilised for its management. Along with smart cities come challenges that we hope will be addressed in the future.

REFERENCES

Agbehadji, I. E., Millham, R. C., Fong, S. J., Jung, J. J., Bui, K.-H. N., & Abayomi, A. (2019). Multi-stage clustering algorithm for energy optimization in wireless sensor networks. In Proceedings of Soft Computing in Data Science. SCDS 2019. Communications in Computer and Information Science. Springer.

Agbehadji, I. E., Millham, R., Fong, S., & Hong, H.-J. (2016). Wolf search algorithm for numeric association rule mining. In *Proceedings of 2016 IEEE International Conference of Cloud Computing and Big data analytics (ICCBDA)*. IEEE. 10.1109/ICCCBDA.2016.7529549

Agbehadji, I. E., Millham, R., Fong, S., & Hong, H.-J. (2018). Kestrel-based Search Algorithm (KSA) for parameter tuning unto Long Short Term Memory (LSTM) Network for feature selection in classification of high-dimensional bioinformatics datasets. *Proceedings of the Federated Conference on Computer Science and Information Systems*, 15-20. 10.15439/2018F52

Alkali, Y. E., & Amichai-Hamburger, Y. (2004). Experiments in digital literacy. *Cyberpsychology & Behavior*, *7*(4), 421–429. doi:10.1089/cpb.2004.7.421 PMID:15331029

Amjad, Z., Shah, M. A., Maple, C., Khattak, H. A., Ameer, Z., Asghar, M. N., & Mussadiq, S. (2020). Towards energy efficient smart grids using bio-inspired scheduling techniques. *IEEE Access: Practical Innovations, Open Solutions*, *8*, 158947–158960. doi:10.1109/ACCESS.2020.3020027

Brown-Martin, G. (2017). *Education and the Fourth Industrial Revolution*. Available at: https://www.groupemediatfo.org/wp-content/uploads/2017/12/FINAL-Education-and-the-Fourth-IndustrialRevolution-1-1-1.pdf

Bui, K.-H. N., Agbehadji, I. E., Millham, R. C., Camacho, D., & Jung, J. J. (2020). Distributed artificial bee colony approach for connected appliances in smart home energy management system. Expert Systems, 15.

C, M.V.P., & Becker, J.M.J. (2020). Smart design engineering: a literature review of the impact of the 4th industrial revolution on product design and development. *Research in Engineering Design, 31*(2), 175-195.

Chakraborty, V. (2017). Nature Inspired Algorithms in Cloud Computing. *International Journal of Trend in Research and Development, 4*.

Clever, S., Crago, T., Polka, A., Al-Jaroodi, J., & Mohamed, N. (2018). Ethical Analyses of Smart City Applications. *Urban Science, MDPI, 2*(96), 1–23.

Colorni, A., Dorigo, M., & Maniezzo, V. (1992, September). An Investigation of some Properties of an" Ant Algorithm". In PPSN (Vol. 92, No. 1992). Academic Press.

Combes, B., Nassiry, D., Fitzgerald, L., & Moussa, T. (2017). *Emerging and exponential technologies: New opportunities for low-carbon development*. Academic Press.

Dameri, R. P., & Rosenthal-Sabroux, C. (2014). Smart city and value creation. In *Smart city* (pp. 1–12). Springer. doi:10.1007/978-3-319-06160-3_1

Fahim, M., Ouchao, B., Jakimi, A., & El Bermi, L. (2019). Application of a non-immersive VR, IoT based approach to help Moroccan students carry out practical activities in a personal learning style. *Future Internet, 11*(1), 15. doi:10.3390/fi11010011

Fong, S., Deb, S., & Yang, X. S. (2015). A heuristic optimization method inspired by wolf preying behavior. *Neural Computing & Applications, 26*(7), 1725–1738. doi:10.100700521-015-1836-9

Frimpong, Millham, Agbehadji, & Jung. (2022). Social spider and the prey search method for global optimization in hyper dimensional search space. *Communications in Computer and Information Science*, 1-13.

Gill, S. S., & Buyya, R. (2019). Bio-inspired algorithms for big data analytics: A survey,taxonomy, and open challenges. *Big Data Analytics for Intelligent Healthcare Management*, 17.

IBM. (2019). *What is Quantum Computing?* Available at: https://www.research.ibm.com/ibm-q/learn/what-isquantum-computing/

James, J. Q., & Li, V. O. (2015). A social spider algorithm for global optimization. *Applied Soft Computing*, *30*, 614–627. doi:10.1016/j.asoc.2015.02.014

Karabegovi, I., & Husak, E. (2018). The Fourth Industrial Revolution and the role of industrial robots with focus on China. *Journal of Engineering and Architecture*, *6*(1), 67–75. doi:10.15640/jea.v5n2a9

Kayembe, C., & Nel, D. (2019). Challenges and opportunities for education in the Fourth Industrial Revolution. *African Journal of Public Affairs*, *11*(3), 79–94.

Lehofer, M., Heiss, M., Rogenhofer, S., Weng, C. W., Sturm, M., Rusitschka, S., & Dippl, S. (2016, April). Platforms for Smart Cities–connecting humans, infrastructure and industrial IT. In *2016 1st International Workshop on Science of Smart City Operations and Platforms Engineering (SCOPE) in partnership with Global City Teams Challenge (GCTC)(SCOPE-GCTC)*. IEEE. 10.1109/SCOPE.2016.7515056

Leng, J. (2001). Scientific examples of Virtual Reality and visualization applications. *UK High Performance Computing*, 1-13.

Lim, Z. Y. (2016). Nature inspired algorithms to optimize robot workcell layouts. *Applied Soft Computing*, *49*, 570–589. doi:10.1016/j.asoc.2016.08.048

Lytras, M. D., Visvizi, A., & Sarirete, A. (2019). Clustering smart city services: Perceptions, expectations, responses. *Sustainability*, *11*(6), 1669. doi:10.3390u11061669

Ma, Y.-N., Gong, Y.-J., Xiao, C.-F., Gao, Y., & Zhang, J. (2019). Path Planning for Autonomous Underwater Vehicles: An Ant Colony Algorithm Incorporating Alarm Pheromone. *IEEE Transactions on Vehicular Technology*, *68*(1), 141–154. doi:10.1109/TVT.2018.2882130

MacArthur, R., & Wilson, E. (1967). *Theory of biogeography*. Princeton University Press.

Mirjalili, S. (2019). Genetic algorithm. In *Evolutionary algorithms and neural networks*. Springer.

Mohanty, P.K., & D.R., P. (2013). Cuckoo Search Algorithm for the Mobile Robot Navigation. In *Swarm, Evolutionary, and Memetic Computing. SEMCCO 2013. Lecture Notes in Computer Science*. Springer.

Oosthuizen, J. H. (2016). *An Assessment of 4IR-Intelligence of South African Management Practitioners Through the Lens of the Fourth Industrial Revolution*. Milpark Business School. https://www.researchgate.net/publication/308785077

Ozmen, M., & Sahin, H. (2021, January). Real-Time Optimization of School Bus Routing Problem in Smart Cities Using Genetic Algorithm. In *2021 6th International Conference on Inventive Computation Technologies (ICICT)* (pp. 1152-1158). IEEE. 10.1109/ICICT50816.2021.9358666

Pagnon, W. (2017). The 4th industrial revolution–A smart factory implementation guide. *International Journal of Advanced Robotics and Automation*, *2*(2), 1–5. doi:10.15226/2473-3032/2/2/00123

Perez, J. A., Deligianni, F., Ravi, D., & Yang, G. Z. (2018). *Artificial intelligence and robotics*. arXiv preprint arXiv:1803.10813, 147.

Philbeck, T., & Davis, N. (2018). The fourth industrial revolution. *Journal of International Affairs*, *72*(1), 17–22.

Reynolds, C. (1987). Flocks, herds, and schools: A distributed behavioural model. *Comput Graph.*, *21*(4), 25–34.

Said, G. A. E.-N. A. (2016). Nature Inspired Algorithms in Cloud Computing: A Survey. *International Journal of Intelligent Information Systems*, *5*(5), 60–64.

Sari, I. R. F. (2017). Bioinspired algorithms for Internet of Things network.*Proceedings of 2017 4th International Conference on Information Technology, Computer, and Electrical Engineering (ICITACEE)*, 1.

Scavarelli, A., Arya, A., & Teather, R. J. (2021). Virtual reality and augmented reality in social learning spaces: A literature review. *Virtual Reality (Waltham Cross)*, *25*, 257–277.

Siddique, N., & Adeli, H. (2015). Nature inspired computing: An overview and some future directions. *Cognitive Computation*, (7), 706–714.

Srinidhi, N. N., Dilip Kumar, S. M., & Venugopal, K. R. (2019). Network optimizations in the Internet of Things: A review. *Engineering Science and Technology, an International Journal, 22*(1), 1-21.

Su, K., Li, J., & Fu, H. (2011, September). *Smart city and the applications. In 2011 international conference on electronics, communications and control (ICECC)*. IEEE.

Tanev, I., & Shimohara, K. (2009). Nature Inspired Design of Autonomous Driving Agent – Realtime Localization, Mapping and Avoidance of Obstacle Based on Motion Parallax. *Proceedings of Conference: Knowledge-Based and Intelligent Information and Engineering Systems, 13th International Conference, KES 2009.*

Taylor-Sakyi, K. (2016). *Reliability Testing Strategy-Reliability in Software Engineering.* arXiv preprint arXiv:1605.01097.

Xu, M., David, J. M., & Kim, S. H. (2018). The Fourth Industrial Revolution: Opportunities and Challenges *International. Journal of Financial Research*, *9*(2), 1–6.

Zedadra, O., Guerrieri, A., Jouandeau, N., Spezzano, G., Seridi, H., & Fortino, G. (2018). Swarm intelligence-based algorithms within IoT-based systems: A review. *Journal of Parallel and Distributed Computing, 122*, 42.

Zedadra, O., Guerrieri, A., Jouandeau, N., Spezzano, G., Seridi, H., & Fortino, G. 2019. Swarm intelligence and IoT-based smart cities: A review. Proceedings of the Internet of Things for Smart Urban Ecosystems. Internet of Things (Technology, Communications and Computing), 177-200.

Zheng, H., & Schleicher, S. (2018). Bio-inspired 3D Printing Experiments. *Conference: the 23rd International Conference on Computer-Aided Architectural Design Research in Asia (CAADRIA).*

Zheng, J. M., Chan, K. W., & Gibson, I. (1998). Virtual reality. *IEEE Potentials*, *17*(2), 20–23.

Zou, J., Zhao, Q., Jiao, B., Yang, W., & Wang, J. (2017, October). Integrated management of internet of things in nanhai district and its application to smart city. In *2017 Chinese Automation Congress (CAC)*. IEEE.

ADDITIONAL READING

Gassmann, O., Böhm, J., & Palmié, M. (2019). *Smart cities: introducing digital innovation to cities*. Emerald Group Publishing.

Ghosh, U., Rawat, D. B., Datta, R., & Pathan, A. S. K. (Eds.). (2020). *Internet of Things and Secure Smart Environments: Successes and Pitfalls*. CRC Press. doi:10.1201/9780367276706

Liu, H. (2020). *Smart Cities: Big Data Prediction Methods and Applications*. Springer Nature. doi:10.1007/978-981-15-2837-8

Mosco, V. (2019). *The smart city in a digital world*. Emerald Group Publishing. doi:10.1108/9781787691353

KEY TERMS AND DEFINITIONS

Big Data: Although definitions vary, big data is often known by its characteristics of Velocity (high speed of incoming data), Variety (great diversity amongst incoming data), and Volume (huge amounts of incoming data).

Fourth Industrial Revolution: Is viewed by many as an extension of the first (which utilised steam power to replace human/animal power), second (which utilised electricity for a wider range of applications), and third (which used digital resources to manage human assets and production) industrial revolutions. The fourth industrial revolution (4IR) merges various aspects of the physical, digital, and biological worlds in order to develop new technologies that produces a human-centred, inclusive future to meet humankind's goals.

Internet of Things (IoT): Internet of Things can be defined as a network of connected devices, from vehicles to appliances, that communicate and exchange data. The purpose of this communication is to share information for improvements, such as an IOT sensor detecting polluted water to having this source removed from the drinking supply, or enabling another entity, such as a vehicle to drive without driver input based on a variety of IOT sensors on its body.

Nature-Inspired Algorithms: These algorithms are inspired by the biological evolution of animals in nature in order to develop novel and challenging techniques. The algorithms are often used to determine the near-optimal solutions of complex problems.

Smart City: A smart city may harness one or multiple technologies to achieve its social goals. The goals may include reducing waste and inconvenience, improving economic and social quality, and improving citizen's lives. The technologies used may include a multitude of inter-connected frameworks and networks, such as those of IOT, which constantly communicate with each other to achieve one or more goals. An example of a smart city may include IOT sensors that detect the amount of road traffic in every section of the city and relay this information to a central server. Based on this information, the server can adjust traffic lights accordingly to enable the smoothest and maximum flow of traffic.

Section 30
Information Extraction

Analysis of Frequency Domain Data Generated by a Quartz Crystal

Fabian N. Murrieta-Rico

https://orcid.org/0000-0001-9829-3013

Universidad Politécnica de Baja California, Mexico

Moisés Rivas-López

https://orcid.org/0000-0001-8751-4693

Universidad Politécnica de Baja California, Mexico

Oleg Sergiyenko

https://orcid.org/0000-0003-4270-6872

Universidad Autónoma de Baja California, Mexico

Vitalii Petranovskii

Universidad Nacional Autónoma de México, Mexico

Joel Antúnez-García

https://orcid.org/0000-0003-3668-1701

Universidad Nacional Autónoma de México, Mexico

Julio C. Rodríguez-Quiñonez

Universidad Autónoma de Baja California, Mexico

Wendy Flores-Fuentes

https://orcid.org/0000-0002-1477-7449

Universidad Autónoma de Baja California, Mexico

Abelardo Mercado Herrera

Universidad Politécnica de Baja California, Mexico

Araceli Gárate García

Universidad Politécnica de Baja California, Mexico

INTRODUCTION

Quartz crystals are versatile devices with plenty of applications. Their primary application is in the development of time-keeping devices, but also, they are used as actuators or sensors. After some electrical connections with other devices, an electrical signal is generated, and its frequency is defined by the proper frequency of crystal. Some popular circuits used for a building resonating circuit are Colpitts oscillator or gate oscillator (Frerking, 1978). As any other device, the functioning of the resonating circuit is affected by quite diverse effects, such as: crystal aging, different forms of jitter, frequency drift, thermal

DOI: 10.4018/978-1-7998-9220-5.ch136

variations, etc. Most of these effects have an influence in the signal that is generated, for this reason an analysis of such data is desired. In case when the resonating circuit is connected to a frequency counter, the measured frequency is obtained over time, and analysis of data is possible. In this sense, the frequency counter plays an important role, because the measurement characteristics define how the data is obtained.

BACKGROUND

There are different methods for frequency counting that include conventional counters, reciprocal counting, interpolating reciprocal counting, time-stamping counting, method for measurement of absolute values, method for measurement of relative values, and universal method of dependent count (Johansson, 2005; Kalisz, 2004; Kirianaki et al., 2001). In the recent years, the principle of rational approximations has been proposed for measuring the frequency of a desired signal. This method requires to compare a signal to measure with other whose frequency is known. Both signals are required to go through a signal conditioning process, where the signals are converted into streams of pulses with a rectangular shape, which appear at regular intervals defined by the frequency of original signals (Hernández Balbuena et al., 2009). These conditioned signals are compared using an AND condition, and a third signal is generated: the signal of coincident pulses. As a result, a coincidence appears where a pulse of the desired signal overlaps in time with a pulse of the reference signal. After the first coincidence, the counting of pulses in three signals starts; when there is another coincidence, an approximation to the desired frequency is obtained. As any other time-frequency measurement technique, when the measurement time increases, the accuracy of measurement increases and uncertainty decreases. The principle of rational approximations has plenty of advantages over other measurement techniques, namely: continuous measurement without dead time, uncertainty limited by the accuracy of reference frequency, approximations to desired frequency are obtained in very short time, and ease of implementation (Avalos-Gonzalez, Sergiyenko, et al., 2018; Murrieta-Rico, Sergiyenko, et al., 2016; Murrieta-Rico et al., 2017, 2018; Murrieta-Rico, Petranovskii, Galván, et al., 2021).

A continuous measurement generates a vast amount of information, and in most cases, these datasets are difficult to interpret. Among the tools available for data analysis, the principal component analysis (PCA) is a method that is widely spread, and it allows to obtain information regarding the relationship of measured variables. In the PCA, the dimensionality of input datasets is reduced, the interpretability is increased and loss of information is avoided; this is done after the creation of new and uncorrelated variables, which successively maximize variance (Jolliffe & Cadima, 2016). Although PCA has been widely developed from statistics point of view, it finds quite diverse applications. Some of them include, dimension reduction on non-Euclidean manifolds with PCA (Mardia et al., 2022), diagnosis of dental pathologies (Nouir et al., 2022), geographically and temporally weighted analysis (Han et al., 2022), etc.

In this work, a quartz crystal and a resonator circuit are used for generating an electrical signal. Then, a frequency counter is used for measuring the generated frequency. The frequency counter uses the principle of rational approximations, and measurement over long time is available. Consequently, a vast amount of data is generated. Then, the generated information is analyzed using PCA. At the same time, the measurement process is simulated using the experimental conditions. The experimental results are compared with the theoretical outcome, and conclusions regarding the effects that define the measured frequency are drawn. The methodology here proposed aims to work as basis for future applications, where different applications of quartz crystals will be explored.

EXPERIMENTAL DETAILS

For this experiment, an AT-cut quartz crystal (XT) with nominal load capacitance of 32 pF was purchased from SKC. Then, it was connected to a gate-oscillator, as described elsewhere (Frerking, 1978; Murrieta-Rico et al., 2019; Murrieta-Rico, Petranovskii, Galván, et al., 2020). The electrical behavior of the quartz crystal is equivalent to the Butterworth-Van Dyke (BVD) model (Fig. 1a). The capacitive effect generated by the electrodes on the quartz is modelled by the parallel capacitance C_0, while the motional elements of quartz are modelled by R_m, L_m, and C_m. From the gate-oscillator, a stable signal was generated. The frequency of this signal can be attributed to the location of the resonant peaks (Fig. 1b), which represent the frequency response of a Butterworth-Van Dyke (BVD) model (Alassi et al., 2017; Murrieta-Rico, Lindner, Petranovskii, et al., 2021). After solving the BVD model, and fitting to the experimental values, the values of the elements in the BVD model can be defined.

The output from the gate-oscillator is connected to a frequency counter, where the frequency of the signal is continuously measured and recorded. The frequency is approximated using a recently proposed technique, which is known as the principle of rational approximations. Among the advantages of this method are that jitter has no effect in the approximation to measurand (O. Sergiyenko et al., 2011), phase displacements do not affect the accuracy of measurements (Murrieta-Rico, Petranovskii, Galván, et al., 2020; Sanchez-Lopez et al., 2019), there is a reduction on the measurement time when the measurand value increases (Murrieta-Rico, Sergiyenko, et al., 2016; Murrieta-Rico et al., 2018), etc.

Figure 1. Butterworth-Van Dyke (BVD) model (a), fitted and experimental values from EIS (b), frequency measurement process when f_x=10 MHz, f_0=11 MHz (c).

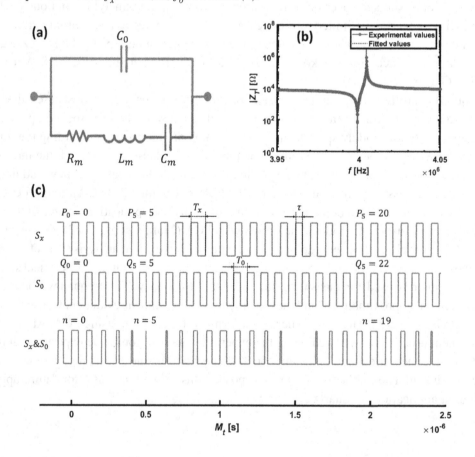

In the principle of rational approximations, a signal to measure S_x with an unknown frequency f_x is compared with a reference signal S_0 with a known frequency f_0. The comparison is done after the use of an AND-gate. Both signals are required to have pulses of the same pulse width, and $f_0 > f_x$. For this reason, before the signal coincidence process, both signals need to be properly conditioned. From the AND-gate, a third signal is generated, this contains the pulses of coincidence that are generated when the pulses of both signals coexist; such a signal is known as S_x and S_0. When the first coincidence takes place, the counting of pulses in S_x and S_0 starts. The counting is recorded by the P_n and Q_n variables, where n denotes the number of coincidences. Then, when a coincidence occurs, the counted pulses form a fraction P_n/Q_n, and the desired frequency can be approximated as $f_x = f_0 P_n/Q_n$. This measurement process is illustrated in the Fig. 1c. After a given number of coincidences or an overflow of the counters, the counting process is stopped and the data from measurement process is retrieved by a computer. Then the measurement process is repeated a number of times that is defined by the application. For this experiment, 500 measurement process were recorded. In addition, for each measurement process, environmental variables such as relative humidity and temperature were recorded; these parameters were also recorded by the computer.

The theory regarding the principle of rational approximations has been exhaustively studied, in fact, this method has proven to offer novel metrological properties, and at the same time, the possibility of application in diverse tasks. For example, this method has been evaluated for applications in the automotive and aerospace industries (Avalos-Gonzalez, Hernandez-Balbuena, et al., 2018; Murrieta-Rico et al., 2014, 2014; Murrieta-Rico, Hernandez-Balbuena, et al., 2016; Murrieta-Rico, Petranovskii, Sanchez-Lopez, et al., 2020; O. Y. Sergiyenko et al., 2012), and in sensors for detection of specific chemical species (Murrieta-Rico et al., 2015, 2019, 2019; Murrieta-Rico, Petranovskii, et al., 2016; Murrieta-Rico, Petranovskii, Sergiyenko, et al., 2021). Furthermore, the applications of the principle of rational approximations are not limited to sensors, for example, this method could be used in the development of devices for analysis based on spectroscopies (Luque et al., 2021; Martínez-Rosas et al., 2021; Murrieta-Rico, Luque, Romo-Cárdenas, et al., 2021; Nava et al., 2020). Even with all these properties, and potential for applications, the principle of rational approximations is not fully understood. For this reason, one of the main aspects to analyze is how the parameters generated during the measurement process affect the approximated value, and how the measurement process is affected by external parameters.

ANALYSIS OF EXPERIMENTAL DATA

As stated before, from the measurement process a set of data containing P_n and Q_n is obtained for each η approximation process. This means that the signal comparison process where a set of Pn and Qn is repeated η times. Since the f0 value is known, the fx can be approximated. The data obtained from this experiment is presented in Fig. 2. As it is expected, there is a linear relationship between Pn and Qn, this behavior can be observed for all the measurement processes in Fig. 2a. In addition, the measurement processes have a high reproducibility, this can be observed in Fig. 2b, where a plot of Pn versus Qn shows a linear relationship. Furthermore, it can be considered that almost all the data in Fig. 2b have the same slope, which is attributed to a high reproducibility and low uncertainty in the measurement process (Murrieta-Rico, Sergiyenko, et al., 2016). In addition, the Fig. 2c and 2d present how the values of Pn and Qn have, in each η, a maximum value that is quite similar to all the other maximum values. This fact defines that the data are quite similar in magnitude, that all the approximation process have the same behavior, there are almost the same number of coincidences in each approximation process, and also that there are no abnormal or atypical values.

From data in Fig. 2e, the greatest deviations from the measurand's true value are observed at the beginning of each approximation process. As it can be noted, there is an absolute maximum deviation of fx $_f$ hat can be in the form of an maximum of minimum, as reported elsewhere (Sanchez-Lopez et al., 2019), this offers information about the phase condition of Sx $_a$ nd S0. The magnitude of these initial deviations are caused by the time elapsed between the first coincidence, and the next coincidence. From Fig. 1c we can observe that the time required for the apparition of n=1 is defined for the existence of a coincidence that generates P1/$_Q$1. This is a random process which depends of a number of parameters, such as fx/$_f$0 $_r$ atio or pulse width τ.

Figure 2. Counting of pulses for both input signals: relationship between the number of pulses in the desired signal P_n, number of pulses in the reference signal Q_n, and the number of approximation η (a), projection of Pn and Qn over η axis (b), projection of Pn $_a$ nd η over Qn a$_x$is (c), projection of Qn a$_n$d η over Pn ax$_i$s (d); approximation to the measurand: relationship between measured frequency fx, η and the measurement time per measurement process Mtp (e$_)$, projection of fx and Mtp ov$_{er}$ η axis (f), projection of fx and $_u$ over the Mtp axis projection of η and Mtp over $_ne$ fx axis.

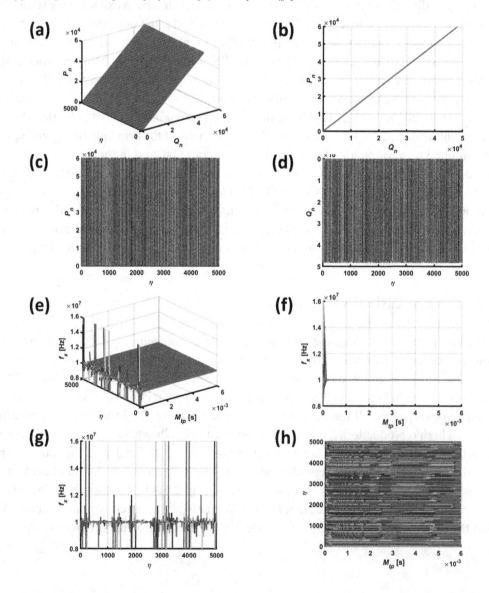

Figure 3. Relationship between the variance and the number of principal component (a), biplot of the two-dimensional principal subspace for measured data (b), data obtained from frequency measurement process (c).

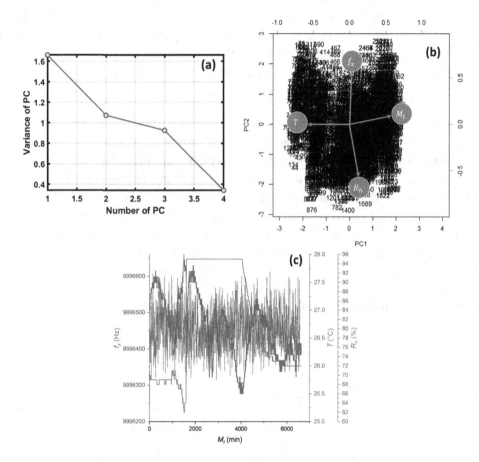

From the counting of pulses, it can be calculated the f_x value. This is presented for each approximation process in Fig. 2e, where an approximation is obtained in each n coincidence. In addition, the measurement time for each application process is presented, this is denoted by M_{tp}. In Fig. 2f, the convergency of approximations is illustrated. In a similar way to Fig. 2e, in Fig. 2f the greatest deviations from the true value are observed at the first approximations. Each one of these values is obtained when a coincidence of pulses occurs. In this sense, there is a quick convergence to the true value of measurand, this behavior is observed for all the data obtained during the measurement process. All the approximations presented in Fig. 2f have almost the same value of convergence, this can be considered to the true value of measurand. In fact, as discussed elsewhere, this measurement process shows the characteristics of a second-order system (Bentley, 2005; Murrieta-Rico, Petranovskii, Galván, et al., 2021), where the first instants of measurement can be considered as a result of dynamic process that cause a transitory or dynamic state, and after enough time, there is a transition to a steady behavior, where the best approximations to measurand are obtained. In Fig. 2g the effect of different phase conditions is depicted. On one hand, it is known that if the measurand is approximated from "above", there is a phase condition where the first pulse of S_x appears later than the first pulse of S_0 (Murrieta-Rico, Petranovskii, Galván, et al., 2020); on the other hand, if the measurand is approached from "below", the first pulse of S_0 appears after the first pulse of S_x. This temporal displacement t_d is a result of the absolute difference that exists between the first pulse of S_x and S_0; accordingly, such a value lies within the range limited by $0 < t_r \leq \tau/2$. From these observations, the phase variations presented in Fig. 2g can be understood as a result of the parameter $S0$ In contrast, the greatest temporal variations exist when the pulses of $S0$ are ahead of the pulses in Sx In the case of Fig. 2h, we can observe the measurement time Mt_p of each approximation. For all the approximations in the measurement process, it is observed that the maximum value of Mt_p is below 6×10^{-3} s. In Fig. 3c is presented the data obtained from the frequency measurement process: measurement time Mt approximated frequency fx temperature T, and relative humidity Rh It is important to note that $M_t = \sum_{\eta=1}^{5000} \left(M_{tp} \right)_\eta + c_t$, where c_t is the time required by the personal computer for acquiring, recording, and processing the data. Also, it is important to consider that the f_x values shown in Fig. 3c are the last value of each approximation shown in Fig. 4a.

As it is well-known, the principal component analysis (PCA) is a tool used for multivariate data analysis. From a given data set, the PCA generates an overview of the dominant patterns of the original data (Wold et al., 1987). Using the PCA the data generated during the measurement process was analyzed. Using R software, the orthonormal coefficient matrix is obtained (Table 1). It is worth to consider that PCA attempts to find a set of orthogonal vectors that describe the variance of the data covariance matrix. In this case, there are 4 principal components (PCs), each one associated to one of the variables in the data set, namely: measurement time M_t, approximated frequency f_x, temperature T, and relative humidity R_h, these two last parameters are obtained from the surroundings of the quartz crystal. The main steps used in R during PCA are: reading of data, obtaining principal components, summarizing of data, and biplot.

Table 1. Orthonormal coefficient matrix.

	PC1	PC2	PC3	PC4
M_t	0.68847566	0.110419244	0.206633972	0.68637545
f_x	0.04409212	0.709839463	-0.701010051	0.05261873
T	-0.70689102	-0.001783877	0.006821546	0.70728734
R_h	0.15608411	-0.695652460	0.682525294	0.16082484

From data in Table 1, the importance of components can be computed, the results are presented in Table 2. Using the values of standard deviation, the variance corresponding to each principal component is calculated and plotted in the Fig. 3a, this allows to obtain a quantitative comparison regarding the effect of the variables that generate the analyzed data. As it is observed in Fig. 3a, the greatest variance is associated to PC1, while the smallest is PC4. Principal components 2 and 3 exhibit a similar variance value. After considering the conditions of the experiment, it can be noted that these PCs characterize in a quite precise way the experiment. This can be understood in terms of the effect of the measurement time (PC1) in the approximated frequency value (PC2), in fact, it is known that in time-frequency metrology, and increase in the measurement time allows to obtain better approximations to the measured frequency. In addition, the temperature (PC3) has a direct effect over the quartz resonance frequency (Frerking, 1978), and even when there are no meaningful variations of temperature, this effect is greater than the relative humidity (PC4), in fact, PC4 has no evident effect over the quartz crystal.

Table 2. Importance of components

	PC1	**PC2**	**PC3**	**PC4**
Standard deviation	1.2886	1.0359	0.9624	0.58337
Proportion of Variance	0.4151	0.2682	0.2316	0.08508
Cumulative Proportion	0.4151	0.6834	0.9149	1

As it is shown in Table 2, according to the accumulative proportion, the majority of information is contained by PC1 and PC2, in particular, a proportion of variance of 42% of PC1 and a 27% of PC2. This generates a cumulative proportion of 68%. In addition, we can visualize both the orthonormal principal component coefficients for each variable and the principal component scores for each observation in Fig. 3b.

According to the importance of the components shown in Table 2, the data distribution can be represented by PC1 and PC2, this is illustrated in the biplot shown in Fig. 3b. Since the input data is standardized, principal components are equivalent to singular value decomposition (SVD) of the (centred) data matrix (Jolliffe & Cadima, 2016). All the variables corresponding to the PCs from the data set are represented in the biplot (Fig. 3b) as vectors. Each variable is represented by a particular vector, with a direction and length that indicate how each variable contributes to the two principal components in the plot. In this case, the first principal component, which is in the horizontal axis, have positive coefficients for the first and second variables (Table 1). Accordingly, vectors f_x and M_t are directed into the right half of the plot. The largest coefficient in the first principal component is the second, corresponding to the variable f_x. The second principal component, which is on the vertical axis, has negative coefficients for the variable T and a positive and negative coefficient for the variable R_h. This two-dimensional biplot includes each one of the data retrieved from the experiment, where the coordinates indicate the score of each datum regarding PC1 and PC2. As a result, from this analysis, in Fig. 3b we can observe the direction of the variables in the plane. In this plot the angles of the vectors among them indicate the correlation between the variables. For this reason, we can observe that f_x is highly correlated with the M_t, and at the same time, the frequency is more correlated with T than with R_h. From the experimental data shown in Fig. 3c, we can validate the results from PCA. In this case, the XT is not affected by R_h due to the fact that the crystal is sealed and isolated from the environment, for this reason, the effects of relative humidity are not observed in the measured frequency, and it can be concluded that f_x and R_h are poorly correlated. In the case of M_t, we know that some time is required for observing the convergency of f_x, for this reason, f_x and M_t are highly correlated. Finally, in the case of T and f_x, a weaker correlation is observed in comparison to M_t and f_x, this can be attributed to the small variations of temperature, which generated a deviation in the resonant frequency of the XT of some ppm for each °C.

FUTURE RESEARCH DIRECTIONS

It is important to highlight that the here proposed analysis offers information that can help to improve plenty of aspects regarding the functioning of sensors and measurement systems. Evaluating the effects that different parameters have in the information obtained from measurements is important, this because the effect of non-expected sources can be observed and compensated. Moreover, real-world applications can be enhanced if information of existing sensors can be analyzed, where a huge amount of data can offer important information of unexpected phenomena tanking place.

CONCLUSION

The analysis of large amount of data is a task that allows to obtain not evident information from a particular phenomenon. In this work, using the principal components analysis data generated during an experiment was analyzed. In particular, a quartz crystal was used to generate a signal with a stable frequency, this parameter was continuously measured using the principle of rational approximations, in addition, other parameters during the experiment were recorded: temperature and relative humidity. As a result, the dependency between the recorded parameters was assessed, and it was found that the main correlation lies between the measurement time and the measured frequency. The methodology here presented was evaluated with the aim to extend its application to other scenarios, for example, in the analysis of data generated by sensors for detection of chemical species, or to evaluate the stability of frequency standards.

ACKNOWLEDGMENT

This work was supported in part by the UNAM PAPIIT IN115920 Grant and in part by the CONACYT basic science under Grant A1-S-33492.

REFERENCES

Alassi, A., Benammar, M., & Brett, D. (2017). Quartz Crystal Microbalance Electronic Interfacing Systems: A Review. *Sensors (Basel)*, *17*(12), 2799. doi:10.339017122799 PMID:29206212

Avalos-Gonzalez, D., Hernandez-Balbuena, D., Tyrsa, V., Kartashov, V., Kolendovska, M., Sheiko, S., Sergiyenko, O., Melnyk, V., & Murrieta-Rico, F. N. (2018). Application of Fast Frequency Shift Measurement Method for INS in Navigation of Drones. *IECON 2018 - 44th Annual Conference of the IEEE Industrial Electronics Society*, 3159–3164. 10.1109/IECON.2018.8591377

Avalos-Gonzalez, D., Sergiyenko, O., Hernandez-Balbuena, D., Tyrsa, V., Kartashov, V., Rivas-Lopez, M., Rodriguez-Quiñonez, J., Flores-Fuentes, W., & Murrieta-Rico, F. N. (2018). Constraints definition and application optimization based on geometric analysis of the frequency measurement method by pulse coincidence. *Measurement*, *126*, 184–193. doi:10.1016/j.measurement.2018.05.025

Bentley, J. P. (2005). *Principles of Measurement Systems*. Pearson Prentice Hall.

Frerking, M. E. (1978). *Crystal oscillator design and temperature compensation*. Van Nostrand. doi:10.1007/978-94-011-6056-8

Han, J., Kang, X., Yang, Y., & Zhang, Y. (2022). Geographically and temporally weighted principal component analysis: A new approach for exploring air pollution non-stationarity in China, 2015–2019. *Journal of Spatial Science*, *0*(0), 1–18. doi:10.1080/14498596.2022.2028270

Hernández Balbuena, D., Sergiyenko, O., Tyrsa, V., Burtseva, L., & López, M. R. (2009). Signal frequency measurement by rational approximations. *Measurement, 42*(1), 136–144. doi:10.1016/j.measurement.2008.04.009

Johansson, S. (2005). New frequency counting principle improves resolution. *Frequency Control Symposium and Exposition, 2005. Proceedings of the 2005 IEEE International.* 10.1109/FREQ.2005.1574007

Jolliffe, I. T., & Cadima, J. (2016). Principal component analysis: A review and recent developments. *Philosophical Transactions - Royal Society. Mathematical, Physical, and Engineering Sciences, 374*(2065), 20150202. doi:10.1098/rsta.2015.0202 PMID:26953178

Kalisz, J. (2004). Review of methods for time interval measurements with picosecond resolution. *Metrologia, 41*(1), 17–32. doi:10.1088/0026-1394/41/1/004

Kirianaki, N. V., Yurish, S. Y., & Shpak, N. O. (2001). Methods of dependent count for frequency measurements. *Measurement, 29*(1), 31–50. doi:10.1016/S0263-2241(00)00026-9

Luque, P. A., Nava, O., Romo-Cardenas, G., Nieto-Hipolito, J. I., Vilchis-Nestor, A. R., Valdez, K., de Dios Sánchez-López, J., & Murrieta-Rico, F. N. (2021). Facile Zinc Oxide Nanoparticle Green Synthesis Using Citrus reticulata Extract for Use in Optoelectronic Sensors. *IEEE Sensors Journal, 21*(10), 11275–11282. doi:10.1109/JSEN.2020.3011988

Mardia, K. V., Wiechers, H., Eltzner, B., & Huckemann, S. F. (2022). Principal component analysis and clustering on manifolds. *Journal of Multivariate Analysis, 188*, 104862. doi:10.1016/j.jmva.2021.104862

Martínez-Rosas, M. E., Garrafa-Gálvez, H. E., Nava, O., Murrieta-Rico, F. N., Chinchillas-Chinchillas, M. J., Carrillo-Castillo, A., & Luque, P. A. (2021). Electrochemical impedance characterization of ZnO semiconductor nanoparticles biosynthesized with Verbascum thapsus. *Journal of Materials Science Materials in Electronics, 32*(8), 10510–10519. doi:10.100710854-021-05706-y

Murrieta-Rico, F. N., Hernandez-Balbuena, D., Rodriguez-Quiñonez, J. C., Mercorelli, P., Petranovskii, V., Raymond-Herrera, O., Nieto-Hipolito, J. I., Tyrsa, V., Sergiyenko, O., Lindner, L., & Hernández, W. (2016). High resolution measurement of physical variables change for INS. *2016 IEEE 25th International Symposium on Industrial Electronics (ISIE)*, 912–917. 10.1109/ISIE.2016.7745012

Murrieta-Rico, F. N., Lindner, L., Petranovskii, V., Galván-Martinez, D., & Antúnez-Garcia, J. (2021). Caracterización de microbalanzas de cuarzo utilizando espectroscopía de impedancia. *Congreso Internacional En Tecnología, Innovación y Docencia (CITID), 3*(3).

Murrieta-Rico, F. N., Luque, M., Romo-Cárdenas, G., & Luque, P. A. (2021). Evaluation of naturally synthesized ZnO for sensing applications using EIS. *Materials Today: Proceedings, 47*, 1676–1681. doi:10.1016/j.matpr.2021.05.465

Murrieta-Rico, F. N., Mercorelli, P., Sergiyenko, O. Yu., Petranovskii, V., Hernández-Balbuena, D., & Tyrsa, V. (2015). Mathematical Modelling of molecular adsorption in zeolite coated frequency domain sensors. *IFAC-PapersOnLine, 48*(1), 41–46. doi:10.1016/j.ifacol.2015.05.060

Murrieta-Rico, F. N., Petranovskii, V., Galván, D. H., Antúnez-García, J., Yocupicio-Gaxiola, R. I., & Tyrsa, V. (2021). Frequency Shifts Estimation for Sensors Based on Optoelectronic Oscillators. *IEEE Sensors Journal, 21*(10), 11283–11290. doi:10.1109/JSEN.2020.3013732

Murrieta-Rico, F. N., Petranovskii, V., Galván, D. H., Sergiyenko, O., Antúnez-García, J., Yocupicio-Gaxiola, R. I., & de Dios Sanchez-Lopez, J. (2020). Phase effect in frequency measurements of a quartz crystal using the pulse coincidence principle. *2020 IEEE 29th International Symposium on Industrial Electronics (ISIE)*, 185–190. 10.1109/ISIE45063.2020.9152255

Murrieta-Rico, F. N., Petranovskii, V., Sanchez-Lopez, J. de D., Nieto-Hipolito, J. I., Vazquez-Briseño, M., Antúnez-García, J., Yocupicio-Gaxiola, R. I., & Tyrsa, V. (2020). Application of the Principle of Rational Approximations for Measuring Dynamic Frequency Values Generated by an IMU. In *Control and Signal Processing Applications for Mobile and Aerial Robotic Systems*. IGI Global. doi:10.4018/978-1-5225-9924-1.ch002

Murrieta-Rico, F. N., Petranovskii, V., Sergiyenko, O., Grishin, M., Sarvadii, S., Sanchez-Lopez, J. de D., Nieto-Hipolito, J. I., Galván, D. H., Antúnez-García, J., & Yocupicio-Gaxiola, R. I. (2021). QCM modified with FAU zeolite nanostructures for analysis of temperature induced adsorbed mass changes. *Measurement, 172*, 108935. doi:10.1016/j.measurement.2020.108935

Murrieta-Rico, F. N., Petranovskii, V., Sergiyenko, O., Hernandez-Balbuena, D., & Raymond-Herrera, O. (2016). High resolution measurement of water levels in optical components. *Nanoengineering: Fabrication, Properties, Optics, and Devices XIII, 9927*, 203–208. doi:10.1117/12.2238849

Murrieta-Rico, F. N., Petranovskii, V., Sergiyenko, O., Mercorelli, P., Antúnez-Garcia, J., de Dios Sanchez-Lopez, J., & Yocupicio-Gaxiola, R. I. (2019). Experimental analysis of measurement process for a QCM using the pulse coincidence method. *IECON 2019 - 45th Annual Conference of the IEEE Industrial Electronics Society, 1*, 4657–4662. 10.1109/IECON.2019.8927337

Murrieta-Rico, F. N., Petranovskii, V., Sergiyenko, O., Molina, M., Hernandez-Balbuena, D., Nieto Hipolito, J. I., Tyrsa, V., & Pestryakov, A. (2014). Acceleration measurement improvement by application of novel frequency measurement technique for FDS based INS. *2014 IEEE 23rd International Symposium on Industrial Electronics (ISIE)*, 1920–1925. 10.1109/ISIE.2014.6864909

Murrieta-Rico, F. N., Petranovskii, V., Sergiyenko, O. Y., Hernandez-Balbuena, D., & Lindner, L. (2017). A New Approach to Measurement of Frequency Shifts Using the Principle of Rational Approximations. *Metrology and Measurement Systems, 24*(1), 45–56. doi:10.1515/mms-2017-0007

Murrieta-Rico, F. N., Sergiyenko, O. Yu., Petranovskii, V., Hernandez-Balbuena, D., Lindner, L., Tyrsa, V., Rivas-Lopez, M., Nieto-Hipolito, J. I., & Karthashov, V. M. (2016). Pulse width influence in fast frequency measurements using rational approximations. *Measurement, 86*, 67–78. doi:10.1016/j.measurement.2016.02.032

Murrieta-Rico, F. N., Sergiyenko, O. Yu., Petranovskii, V., Hernandez-Balbuena, D., Lindner, L., Tyrsa, V., Tamayo-Perez, U. J., & Nieto-Hipolito, J. I. (2018). Optimization of pulse width for frequency measurement by the method of rational approximations principle. *Measurement, 125*, 463–470. doi:10.1016/j.measurement.2018.05.008

Nava, O., Murrieta-Rico, F. N., Martínez-Rosas, M. E., Chinchillas-Chinchillas, M. J., Garrafa-Galvez, H. E., Vilchis-Nestor, A. R., & Luque, P. A. (2020). Evaluation of electrochemical properties of zinc oxide based semiconductor nanoparticles biosynthesized with Mentha spicata for optoelectronic applications. *Materials Letters, 275*, 128101. doi:10.1016/j.matlet.2020.128101

Nouir, R., Cherni, I., Ghalila, H., & Hamzaoui, S. (2022). Early diagnosis of dental pathologies by front face fluorescence (FFF) and laser-induced breakdown spectroscopy (LIBS) with principal component analysis (PCA). *Instrumentation Science & Technology, 0*(0), 1–16. doi:10.1080/10739149.2021.2024845

Sanchez-Lopez, J. de D., Murrieta-Rico, F. N., Petranovskii, V., Antúnez-García, J., Yocupicio-Gaxiola, R. I., Sergiyenko, O., Tyrsa, V., Nieto-Hipolito, J. I., & Vazquez-Briseño, M. (2019). Effect of phase in fast frequency measurements for sensors embedded in robotic systems. *International Journal of Advanced Robotic Systems, 16*(4). doi:10.1177/1729881419869727

Sergiyenko, O., Hernández Balbuena, D., Tyrsa, V., Rosas Méndez, P. L. A., Lopez, M. R., Hernandez, W., Podrygalo, M., & Gurko, A. (2011). Analysis of jitter influence in fast frequency measurements. *Measurement, 44*(7), 1229–1242. doi:10.1016/j.measurement.2011.04.001

Sergiyenko, O. Y., Hernandez Balbuena, D., Tyrsa, V. V., Rosas Mendez, P. L. A., Hernandez, W., Nieto Hipolito, J. I., Starostenko, O., & Rivas Lopez, M. (2012). Automotive FDS Resolution Improvement by Using the Principle of Rational Approximation. *IEEE Sensors Journal, 12*(5), 1112–1121. doi:10.1109/JSEN.2011.2166114

Wold, S., Esbensen, K., & Geladi, P. (1987). Principal component analysis. *Chemometrics and Intelligent Laboratory Systems, 2*(1), 37–52. doi:10.1016/0169-7439(87)80084-9

ADDITIONAL READING

Jackson, J. E. (2005). *A user's guide to principal components* (Vol. 587). John Wiley & Sons.

Jolliffe, I. T., & Cadima, J. (2016). Principal component analysis: A review and recent developments. *Philosophical Transactions - Royal Society. Mathematical, Physical, and Engineering Sciences, 374*(2065), 20150202. doi:10.1098/rsta.2015.0202 PMID:26953178

Llamas-Garro, I., Kim, J. M., & De Melo, M. T. (2017). *Frequency Measurement Technology*. Artech House.

Lombardi, M. A. (2017). Frequency Measurement. In Measurement, Instrumentation, and Sensors Handbook (pp. 42-1). CRC Press. doi:10.1201/b15664-42

Riley, W. J. (2008). *Handbook of frequency stability analysis*. US Department of Commerce, National Institute of Standards and Technology. doi:10.6028/NIST.SP.1065

Smith, D. C. (1992). *High frequency measurements and noise in electronic circuits*. Springer Science & Business Media.

Smythe, R. J. (2021). Frequency Measurement. In *Advanced Arduino Techniques in Science* (pp. 173–184). Springer. doi:10.1007/978-1-4842-6784-4_6

KEY TERMS AND DEFINITIONS

Frequency: The number of times that something repeats in a unit of time. Electrical frequency is the rate of oscillation between two levels of voltage. This is expressed as number of cycles per second or Hz.

PCA: Principal components analysis is a method that reduces a high dimensional data into fewer dimensions, and in this process, the representative information is retained.

Signal: Information in a medium. This can be in the form of electricity, vibrations, heat, etc.

Uncertainty: The range of possible values where the true value of the measurement is located.

Section 31
Internet of Things

Exploration of Research Challenges and Potential Applications in IoT

Shivlal Mewada

iD https://orcid.org/0000-0001-5543-8622

Government Holkar Science College, India

INTRODUCTION

Information, whereas the internet is an interconnected system that deals with physical elements that differ in their capacities to process, to sensor and to control and to communicate over the internet (Raun, 2016). Thus, the main objective of the Internet of Things is to make it possible for objects to be connected with other objects, individuals, at any time or anywhere using any network, path or service. The Internet of Things (IoT) is widely seen as the next phase in the growth of the internet. In order to achieve numerous different objectives, IoT will make it feasible for common items to connect to the internet. The amount of devices that might be included in IoT is currently estimated at just 0.6% (Ryan, 2017). By 2020, however, over 50 billion gadgets are projected to be connected to the internet.

The internet has evolved from a basic network of computers to a network of diverse devices, whereas IoT functions as a network of various "connected" devices, or a network of networks (Miraz, 2018), as illustrated in Fig. Smartphones, automobiles, industrial systems, cameras, toys, buildings, household appliances, industrial systems, and a plethora of other items may now all communicate data through the Internet. These devices can perform smart reorganisations, tracing, positioning, control, real-time monitoring, and process control regardless of their size or function.

In recent years, Internet-capable gadgets have spread significantly. Although its commercial effects were most important in the area of consumer electronics; in particular the smartphone revolution and the interest in wearable devices (watches, headsets etc.), connecting people has become a fragment of a larger movement towards the combination of digital and physical worlds. With all this in mind, it should continue to expand its reach for the number of devices and functions that can be operated by the Internet of Things (IoT).

This is obvious from the ambiguity in the phrase of "Things" which makes it impossible to specify the ever-growing limitations of the IoT (Borgia, 2016). While commercial success continues to emerge, the Internet of Things (IoT) continues to provide an almost endless supply of potential, not just in industry but also in research. As a result, the course examines the many prospective areas for IoT domain applications as well as the research difficulties that come with them.

DOI: 10.4018/978-1-7998-9220-5.ch137

Figure 1. IoT can be viewed as a Network of Networks
(Bedi, 2021, Paul, 2020, Ezeofor, 2021, Prakash, 2019, Bansal, 2018)

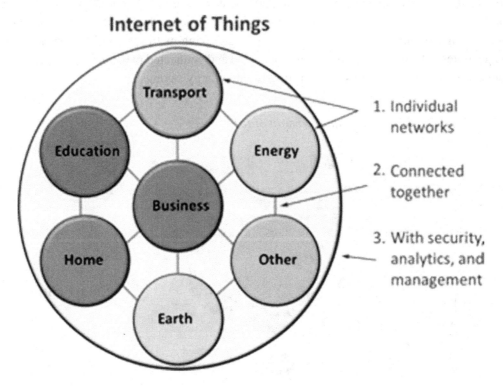

II. APPLICATION OF IOT

The internet of Things' potential applications are not only many but also diversified, since they pervade almost every element of people's, institutions', and society's everyday lives. According to (Patel, 2016), IoT applications span a wide range of industries, including manufacturing, healthcare, agriculture, smart cities, security, and disaster relief, among others.

A. Smart Cities

The IoT plays an essential function to enhance city smartness and general infrastructure, according to (Zanjal, 2016). Smart transport systems (Jain, 2018), intelligent smart building, traffic congestion (Jain, 2018, Soomro, 2018) waste management (Mahmud, 2018), smart lighting, smart parking and urban mapping are some of IoT's application areas for the development of intelligent cities. This may involve the monitoring of available parking spots inside the city, the monitoring of vibration, as well as bridges and buildings material conditions and the installation of sound monitoring instruments in sensitive urban areas and the monitoring of pedestrian and car levels.

Artificial Intelligence (AI) has made it possible. In Smart Cities, IoT may be used to monitor, regulate, and alleviate traffic congestion (Zanjal, 2016). Furthermore, the Internet of Things enables the installation of intelligent and weather-adaptive street lighting as well as the identification of waste and waste containers by tracking trash pickup schedules. Intelligent highways can send out alerts and vital information, such as access to other routes based on weather conditions or unforeseen events such as traffic jams and accidents.

The use of radio frequency identification and sensors in IoT applications to create smart cities would be required. The Aware Home and Smart Santander features are two examples of already created applications in this area. Some large cities in the United States, such as Boston, have plans to integrate the Internet of Things into most of their systems, including parking metres, streetlights, sprinkler systems, and sewage grates, which are all set to be interconnected and connected to the internet. Such applications will represent major advancements in terms of cost and energy savings.

Figure 2. Smart cities in the application domain of IoT

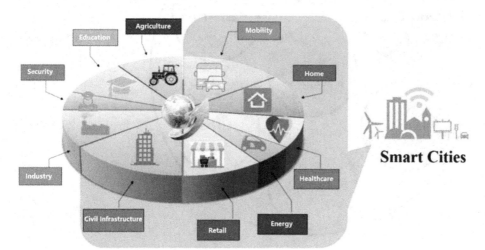

B. Healthcare

Many countries' healthcare systems are inefficient, slow, and error prone. This is readily changeable because the healthcare industry relies on a variety of activities and devices that may be automated and improved through technology. Additional technology that can assist activities such as report sharing to many individuals and places, record keeping, and medication dispensing would go a long way toward transforming the healthcare industry (Mano, 2015).

Many of the advantages that IoT applications provide in the healthcare industry are most commonly classified as tracking of patients, employees, and items, identifying and authenticating persons, and autonomous data collection and sensing. Once the flow of patients is recorded, the hospital's workflow may be significantly improved. Furthermore, verification and identification decrease potentially hazardous occurrences, record maintenance, and the number of cases of mismatched infants. Furthermore, process automation, form processing timeline reduction, automated procedure auditing, and medical inventory management all benefit from automatic data gathering and transfer. Sensor devices provide patient-centered tasks, such as detecting diseases and providing real-time data on patients' health indicators (Zanjal, 2016).

Figure 3. IoT in healthcare

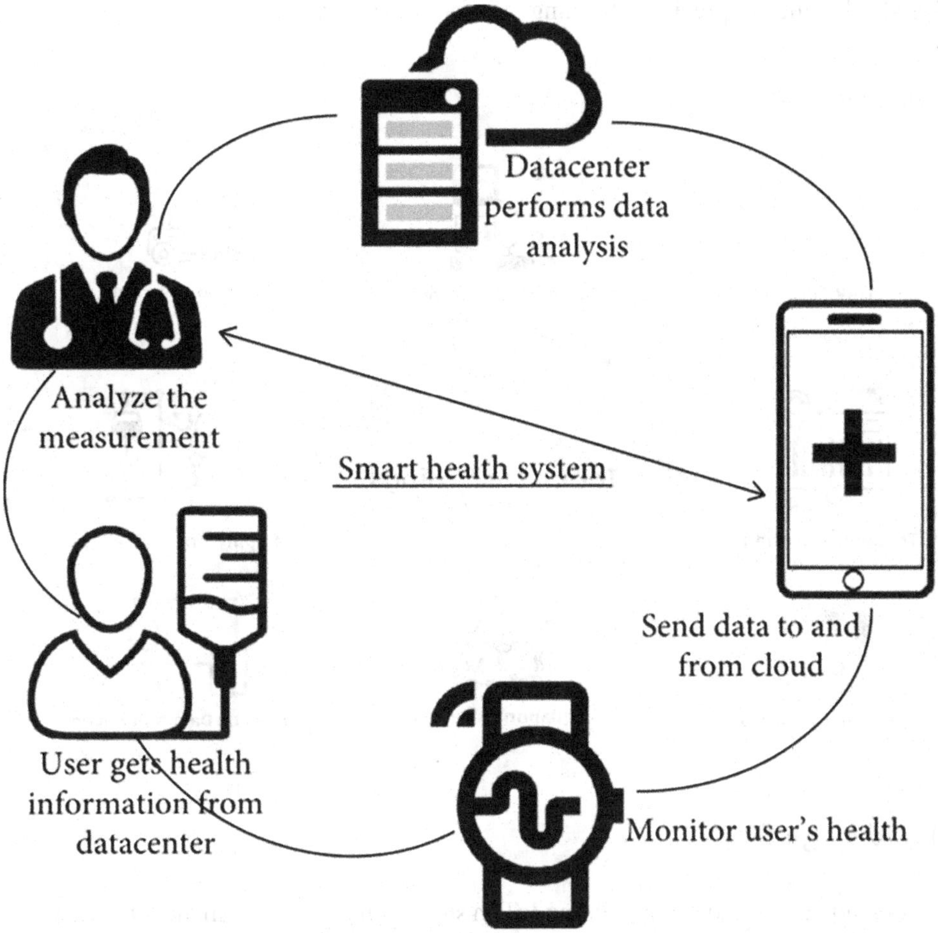

C. Smart Agriculture

3.1 IoT Applications in Agriculture The main applications of IoT technologies in agriculture are found in precision agriculture (Mekala, 2017, Rajeswari, 2017) whose architecture includes IoT techniques for urban agriculture and precision agronomy in smart cities. Commonly, smart cities are based on networks defined by software (SDN) and cyber-physical systems (Ordonez-Garcia, 2017). Other applications of the IoT are the agricultural drones (Uddin, 2017) which are relatively cheap drones with advanced sensors that give farmers new ways to increase yields and reduce crop damage, among other things. Another area of IoT application is the intelligent greenhouses (Wortman, 2015, Yunseop, 2008) which includes hydroponic and small-scale aquaponic systems (Atmadja, 2018, Al-Karaki, 2012, Montoya, 2017). Intelligent greenhouses are increasingly common in urban areas because they allow monitoring several parameters of nutrient solutions (Barbosa, 2015), as well as to improve the growth, yield, and quality of plants. These improvements contribute significantly to the achievement of smart cities with infrastructures that allow automating, optimizing and improving urban agriculture and precision agronomy. Another area in which IoT technologies are applied is the vertical agriculture (Bin Ismail, 2017), which allows controlling soil moisture and water content by means of computers or mobile devices such as tablets and smartphones. Finally, there are applications that combine IoT technologies with Artificial Intelligence such as Malthouse (Dolci, 2017), which is an Artificial Intelligence system that allows prescribing configurations and schedules in precision farming and food manufacturing areas.

Figure 4. IoT in agriculture

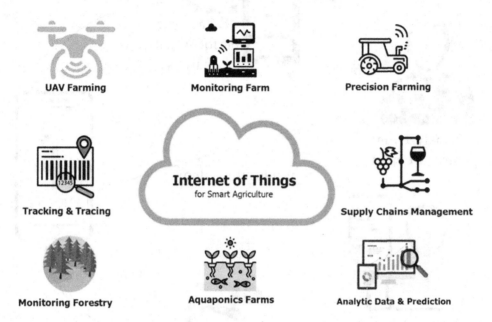

D. Retail and Logistics

There are several advantages to implementing IoT in supply chain or retail management. Some examples include monitoring storage conditions across the supply chain, product tracking for traceability purposes, and payment processing in public transportation, amusement parks, and gyms, among others. Inside the retail environment, IoT can be used for a variety of applications, including guiding customers through the store based on a pre-selected list, automating payment processes such as automatic check-out with biometrics, detecting potential allergen products, and controlling product rotation on shelves and warehouses to automate restocking procedures (Tadejko, 2015).

The IoT elements most often employed are wireless transmission networks and the identification of radio frequencies. SAP (Systems Applications and Products) is currently being used in retail stores, while various logistical examples include quality shipping conditions, location of items, problems with storage incompatibility, fleet tracking, etc. In the field of the industrial sector, IoT supports the detection of gases and leaks within industry and surrounding areas, the tracking of toxic gases and oxygen levels within chemical plant confines in order to ensure the safety of goods and workers and to monitor oil, gas and water levels in cisterns and storage tanks. Application of IoT also helps in maintenance and repair since systems may be implemented in order to prevent failures of the equipment, while periodic maintenance services can be scheduled automatically before the equipment fails. This can be done by installing sensors in devices or machines to check operation and provide reports occasionally.

E. Smart Living

In this sector, IoT may be used in remote control devices to turn appliances on and off remotely, reducing the risk of accidents and conserving energy (Raun, 2016, Miraz, 2018). Refrigerators with LCD (Liquid Crystal Display) displays are another smart home appliance that allows users to see what is accessible within, what has overstayed and is about to expire, and what needs to be replenished. This data can also be connected to a smartphone application, allowing users to view it when out of the house and therefore purchase what they require. Furthermore, washing machines may be used to monitor laundry from afar. Furthermore, a smartphone may be used to interface with a broad range of kitchen gadgets, allowing temperature adjustments, such as in the case of an oven. Some ovens with self-cleaning capabilities may also be readily monitored. In terms of home security, IoT may be implemented through alarm systems and cameras that monitor and detect window or door openings, preventing intruders (Miraz, 2018).

F. Smart Environment

The environment has an important influence in all parts of existence; people, animals, birds, and plants are all affected in some manner by an unhealthy environment. There have been various efforts to build a healthy environment in terms of minimising pollution and resource waste, but the presence of industries and transportation wastes, as well as careless and destructive human behaviours, are commonplace components that constantly affect the ecosystem.

As a result, the environment requires smart and innovative approaches to waste monitoring and management, which generate a large quantity of data that forces governments to implement protection of the environment systems.

Smart environment strategies that include IoT technology should be developed for detecting, tracking, and assessing environmental items that have the potential to help achieve a sustainable existence and a green planet. IoT technology provides for improved traffic management in large cities by detecting and controlling air quality through data gathering from distant sensors throughout cities and offering round-the-clock geographic coverage. In addition, IoT technology may be used to measure pollution levels in water and, as a result, inform water consumption decisions. IoT may also be used in trash management, which includes a variety of waste kinds such as chemicals and pollutants that are harmful to the environment as well as to humans, animals, and plants. This may be accomplished through environmental protection and industrial pollution control using real-time monitoring and management systems, as well as supervisory and decision-making networks. This helps to cut down on waste (S. Rajguru, S., 2015).

IoT may be utilised in weather forecasting to provide substantial accuracy and high precision for weather monitoring through information sharing and data interchange. Weather systems may gather data from moving cars, such as barometric pressure, humidity, temperature, light, motion, and other variables, and communicate it wirelessly to weather stations using IoT technology. Sensors are installed on cars and even buildings to collect data, which is then saved and analysed to help in weather predictions. Radiation endangers the environment, human and animal health, and agricultural production. IoT sensor networks can help regulate radiation by constantly monitoring its levels, which is especially useful for detecting leaks and distributing deterrence around nuclear power plants.

III. RESEARCH CHALLENGES

To determine the success of certain applications and their functioning, sufficient feasibility into the many domains is required for all of the aforementioned prospective IoT applications. IoT, like every other type of technology or innovation, has its own set of difficulties and consequences that must be addressed before widespread adoption can occur. Even while existing IoT enabling technologies have vastly improved in recent years, there are still a slew of issues that need to be addressed, clearing the door for new research directions to be pursued. Because the Internet of Things is made up of disparate technologies for sensing, gathering, acting, processing, inferring, sending, alerting, managing, and storing data, there are going to be several research difficulties. As a result, these research issues that demand attention have crossed several study domains (H. U. Rehman, 2017).

A. Privacy and Security

Because IoT has become a critical component of the internet's future with its growing usage, it requires the necessity to effectively handle security and trust functions. Researchers are aware of the flaws that many IoT devices now have. Furthermore, because IoT is built on top of existing wireless sensor networks (WSN), it inherits the same privacy and security concerns as WSN does (M. Miraz, 2018), (Z. Alansari, 2018). Various attacks and flaws in IoT systems demonstrate the necessity for comprehensive security architectures that safeguard data and systems from beginning to finish. Many attacks take use of flaws in specific devices to obtain access to their systems and, as a result, make protected devices susceptible (J. A. Chaudhry, 2018, A. S. A. Daia, 2018). This security gap further encourages complete security solutions, which include efficient research in applied cryptography for data and system security, non-cryptographic security approaches, and frameworks that aid developers in developing secure systems on heterogeneous devices.

More research on cryptographic security services that can function on resource limited IoT devices is required. This would allow a variety of competent people to safely utilise and install IoT systems, despite the fact that virtually all IoT devices have insufficient user interfaces. Additional areas such as communication secrecy, trustworthiness, and authenticity of communication parties, message integrity, and supplemental safety standards should be included in addition to the protection and security elements of the IoT. These may include features such as the ability to restrict several parties from communicating with each other. In commercial transactions, for example, smart objects must be protected from allowing rivals' access to personal data in the devices and therefore illegally exploiting this knowledge.

B. Processing, Analysis and Management of Data

Because of the diverse nature of IoT and the vast amount of data gathered, particularly in this era of Big Data (Z. Alansari, 2018), the method for processing, analysis, and data management is quite difficult. Most systems currently use centralised systems to offload data and perform computationally expensive activities on an international cloud platform. Nonetheless, there is a persistent fear that traditional cloud architectures would fail to transmit the large amounts of data created and consumed by IoT enabled devices, as well as to sustain the associated computing load while meeting time restrictions (J. Cooper, 2009). To address this issue, most systems are depending on current technologies such as mobile cloud computing and fog computing, both of which are based on edge processing.

Another area of research in data management is the use of Information Centric Networking (ICN) in the Internet of Things. These information-centric systems appear to be extremely helpful not only in accessing but also in transferring and managing created material and its transmission, since they assist in effective content retrieval and access to services. However, this method raises a number of issues, including how to effectively extend the ICN paradigm across the fixed network edge, how to take in IoTs static and mobile devices, and how to apportion ICN functionality on resource limited devices (J. Cooper, 2009).

Analysis of data and its context are not only critical to the success of IoT, but they also offer significant obstacles. In order to accomplish smart IoT operations, data must be gathered and used wisely. As a result, the development of machine learning methods and artificial intelligence algorithms, which are derived from neural works, genetic algorithms, evolutionary algorithms, and a variety of other artificial intelligence systems, is critical for automated decision making.

C. Monitoring and Sensing

Even while monitoring and sensing methods have advanced significantly, they are still improving, with a special focus on energy efficiency and shape. Sensors and tags are often required to be active at all times in order to gather real-time data; this element makes energy efficiency, particularly in terms of lifespan extension, critical. At the same time, new breakthroughs in nanotechnology/biotechnology and miniaturisation have enabled the development of nanoscale actuators and sensors.

D. M2M (Machine to Machine) Communication and Communication Protocols

While IoT communication channels such as CoAP and MQTT already exist, there is currently no standard for an open IoT. However all objects need communication, they do not all need to be internet enabled since they just need a certain capacity to send their data to a specific route. Furthermore, there are several alternatives in terms of appropriate wireless devices, such as IEEE 802.15.4, and Bluetooth, even if it is unclear whether current present wireless devices will be able to continue to cover the broad spectrum of IoT connection in the future.

Gadget communication systems are the driving force behind IoT applications, and they serve as the primary conduit for flow of data among sensors and objects or the outside world. While FDMA, TDMA, and CSMA for low traffic efficiency and collision avoidance have been proposed for numerous domains, additional circuitry in nodes is needed in each case. The transport layer's major goals include ensuring end-to-end dependability as well as conducting end-to-end congestion control. Most methods are unable to provide enough end-to-end dependability in this regard (D. B. Ansari, 2018).

E. Blockchain of Things (BCoT): Fusion of Blockchain and Internet of Things

Blockchain systems, like IoT, have exploded in popularity since their inception in 2018. Despite the fact that blockchain was initially utilised as the underpinning technology for the Bitcoin cryptocurrency, it is currently being used in a variety of nonmonetary applications (M. H. Miraz, 2018). Miraz claims that IoT and Blockchain may mutually enhance each other by removing their respective fundamental architectural constraints (Miraz, M.H., 2019). WSN is the IoT's core technology. As a result, similar to WSN, IoT suffers from security and privacy concerns. On the contrary, the intrinsic security, data integrity, trust, and accessibility of blockchain are the key reasons for its adoption in non-monetary applications. These characteristics are fueled by blockchain's consensus technique and use of DLTs, which need a high level of participation from nodes. As a result, the fusion of these technologies, Blockchain and IoT, creates a new concept known as the BCoT, in which blockchain strengthens IoT by adding an added level of security, while IoT's "things" can act as network participants in blockchain ecosystem functions (Miraz, M.H., 2019). As a result, blockchain-enabled IoT networks will improve overall security (Miraz, M. H.,, 2018) while also benefiting from one another.

F. Interoperability

Because the original need in Internet connectivity demands that "connected" systems have the capacity to "speak a comparable language" in terms of encodings and protocols, interoperability has always been and continues to be a core essential ideal. Currently, a number of standards are used to support diverse industries' applications. Because of the enormous amounts and varieties of data, as well as heterogeneous devices, utilising standard interfaces in such disparate entities is critical, and much more so for applications that allow cross-organizational collaboration, as well as a variety of system constraints.

IV. CONCLUSION

The Internet of Things is best defined as a CAS that will continue to change in the future years, necessitating new and inventive kinds of software, systems engineering, project management, and a variety of other domains to build and manage it. IoT application areas are extremely broad, allowing it to serve a variety of consumers with a variety of demands. Individuals, community or organizations, and agencies are three types of users that benefit from technology. As mentioned in the application part of the research paper, the IoTs has unquestionable potential to be a tremendously transformative force that will, and to some extent already does, favourably affect millions of lives worldwide. According to (R. Porkodi, 2014), this has become even more evident since several governments have indicated interest in the IoT concept by providing funding in the field to allow future research. The Japanese government is a great example.

Numerous research groups have been formed, and continue to be formed, in many areas of the world, with the primary goal of pursuing IoT-related study. New aspects to IoT processes and items that may be linked continue to develop as more scientific investigations are undertaken, opening the door for even more IoT application functions. IoT is a key study subject for investigations in several related domains such as IT and CS since it is so broad and touches almost every aspect of our life. The article discusses different possible IoT application fields as well as the research difficulties that come with them.

REFERENCES

Al-Karaki, G.N., & Al-Hashimi, M. (2012). Green fodder production and water use efficiency of some forage crops under hydroponic conditions. *ISRN Agron, 1–5.*

Alansari, Z. (2018a). Challenges of Internet of Things and Big Data Integration. In Emerging Technologies in Computing. Academic Press.

Alansari, Z. (2018b). Internet of Things: Infrastructure, Architecture, Security and Privacy. *2018 International Conference on Computing, Electronics Communications Engineering (iCCECE),* 150–155.

Ansari, D. B., Rehman, A. U., & Ali, R. (2018). Internet of Things (IoT) Proto- cols: A Brief Exploration of MQTT and CoAP. *International Journal of Computers and Applications*, *179*(27), 9–14. doi:10.5120/ijca2018916438

Atmadja, W., Liawatimena, S., Lukas, J., Nata, E. P. L., & Alexander, I. (2018). Hydroponic system design with real time OS based on ARM Cortex-M microcontroller. In *IOP Conference Series*. Earth and Environmental Science.

Bansal, A., Ahirwar, M. K., & Shukla, P. K. (2018). A survey on classification algorithms used in healthcare environment of the Internet of Things. *International Journal on Computer Science and Engineering*, *6*(7), 883–887.

Barbosa, G. L., Gadelha, F., Kublik, N., Proctor, A., Reichelm, L., Weissinger, E., Wohlleb, G., & Halden, R. (2015). Comparison of land, water, and energy requirements of lettuce grown using hydroponic vs. Conventional agricultural methods. *International Journal of Environmental Research and Public Health*, *12*(6), 6879–6891. doi:10.3390/ijerph120606879 PMID:26086708

Bedi, P., Mewada, S., Vatti, R. A., Singh, C., Dhindsa, K. S., Ponnusamy, M., & Sikarwar, R. (2021). Detection of attacks in IoT sensors networks using machine learning algorithm. *Microprocessors and Microsystems*, *82*, 103814. doi:10.1016/j.micpro.2020.103814

Bin Ismail, M. I. H., & Thamrin, N. M. (2017). IoT implementation for indoor vertical farming watering system. *2017 International Conference on Electrical, Electronics and System Engineering (ICEESE)*, 89–94. 10.1109/ICEESE.2017.8298388

Borgia, E., Gomes, D. G., Lagesse, B., Lea, R., & Puccinelli, D. (2016). Internet of Things: Research challenges and Solutions. *Computer Communications*, *89*(90), 1–4. doi:10.1016/j.comcom.2016.04.024

Chaudhry, J. A., Saleem, K., Haskell-Dowland, P., & Miraz, M. H. (2018). A Survey of Distributed Certificate Authorities in MANETs. *Annals of Emerging Technologies in Computing*, *2*(3), 11–18. doi:10.33166/AETiC.2018.03.002

Cooper, J., & James, A. (2009). Challenges for database management in the internet of things. *IETE Technical Review*, *26*(5), 320–329. doi:10.4103/0256-4602.55275

Daia, A. S. A., Ramadan, R. A., & Fayek, M. B. (2018). Sensor Networks Attacks Classifications and Mitigation. *Annals of Emerging Technologies in Computing*, *2*(4), 28–43. doi:10.33166/AETiC.2018.04.003

Dolci, R. (2017). IoT solutions for precision farming and food manufacturing: artificial intelligence applications in digital food. *2017 IEEE 41st Annual Computer Software and Applications, Conference (COMPSAC)*, 384–385. 10.1109/COMPSAC.2017.157

Ezeofor, C. J. (2021). Development of Smart IoT-Based CNN Technique for Harmful Maize Insects Recognition in Precision Agriculture. *International Journal of Scientific Research in Computer Science and Engineering*, *9*(5), 48–60.

Jain, R. (2018). A Congestion Control System Based on VANET for Small Length Roads. *Annals of Emerging Technologies in Computing*, *2*(1), 17–21. doi:10.33166/AETiC.2018.01.003

Mahmud, S. H., Assan, L., & Islam, R. (2018). Potentials of Internet of Things (IoT) in Malaysian Construction Industry", Annals of Emerging Technologies in Computing (AETiC). *International Association of Educators and Researchers*, *2*(1), 44–52.

Mano, Y. (2015). Exploiting IoT technologies for enhancing Health Smart Homes through patient identification and emotion recognition. *Computer Communications*, *89*(90), 178–190.

Mekala, M. S., & Viswanathan, P. (2017). A survey: smart agriculture IoT with cloud computing. *2017 International conference on Microelectronic Devices, Circuits and Systems (ICMDCS)*, 1–7. 10.1109/ICMDCS.2017.8211551

Miraz, M. H. (2019). Blockchain of Things (BCoT): The Fusion of Blockchain and IoT Technologies", Advanced Applications of Blockchain Technology. *Studies in Big Data*, *60*, 2019.

Miraz, M. H., & Ali, M. (2018). Applications of Blockchain Technology beyond Cryptocurrency. *Annals of Emerging Technologies in Computing*, *2*(1), 1–6. doi:10.33166/AETiC.2018.01.001

Miraz, M. H., & Ali, M. (2018). Blockchain Enabled Enhanced IoT Ecosystem Security. *Proceedings of the International Conference on Emerging Technologies in Computing 2018*, 38-46.

Miraz, M. M., Ali, M., Excell, P., & Picking, R. (2018). Internet of Nano-Things, Things and Everything: Future Growth Trends. *Future Internet*, *10*(8), 68. doi:10.3390/fi10080068

Montoya, A. P., Obando, F. A., Morales, J. G., & Vargas, G. (2017). Automatic aeroponic irrigation system based on Arduino's platform. *Journal of Physics*. doi:10.1088/1742-6596/850/1/012003

Ordonez-Garcia, A., Siller, M., & Begovich, O. (2017). IoT architecture for urban agronomy and precision applications. *2017 IEEE International Autumn Meeting on Power, Electronics and Computing (ROPEC)*, 1–4. 10.1109/ROPEC.2017.8261582

Patel, K. K. (2016) Internet of things IOT: definition, characteristics, architecture, enabling technologies, application future challenges. *International Journal of Engineering Science and Computing, 6*(5), 6122–6131.

Paul, P., Ripu Ranjan Sinha, R. R. S., Aithal, P. S., & Saavedra, M. (2020). Internet of Things (IoT) & Smart Agriculture: With reference to applications & emerging Concern. *Asian Journal of Electrical Sciences*, *9*(1), 37–44. doi:10.51983/ajes-2020.9.1.2370

Porkodi, R., & Bhuvaneswari, V. (2014). The Internet of Things (IoT) Applications and Communication Enabling Technology Standards: An Overview. *2014 International Conference on Intelligent Computing Applications*, 324–329.

Prakash, C., Dua, A., & Saini, R. K. (2019). *IoT Based Monitoring and Controlling of Motherboard Panel Controller in Computers*. Academic Press.

Rajeswari, S., Suthendran, K., & Rajakumar, K. (2017). A smart agricultural model by integrating IoT, mobile and cloud-based big data analytics. *2017 International Conference on Intelligent Computing and Control (I2C2)*, 1–5. 10.1109/I2C2.2017.8321902

Rajguru, S., Kinhekar, S., & Pati, S. (2015). Analysis of internet of things in a smart environment. *International Journal of Enhanced Research in Man-agement and Computer Applications*, *4*(4), 40–43.

Raun, N. F. (2016). Smart environment using internet of things(IOTS) - a review. *2016 IEEE 7th Annual Information Technology, Electronics and Mobile Communication Conference (IEMCON)*, 1-6.

Rehman, H. U., Asif, M., & Ahmad, M. (2017). Future applications and research challenges of IOT. *2017 International Conference on Informa-tion and Communication Technologies (ICICT)*, 68–74. 10.1109/ICICT.2017.8320166

Ryan, P. J., & Watson, R. B. (2017). Research Challenges for the Internet of Things. *What Role Can OR Play*, *5*(1), 1–34.

Soomro, S. M. (2018). Artificial Intelligence Enabled IoT: Traffic Congestion Reduction in Smart Cities. *IET 2018 Smart Cities Symposium*, 81–86.

Tadejko. P. (2015). Application of Internet of Things in logistics-current challenges. *Ekonomia i Zarzadzanie, 7*(4) 54–64.

Uddin, M. A., Mansour, A., Le Jeune, D., & Aggoune, E. H. M. (2017). Agriculture internet of things: AG-IoT. *2017 27th International Telecommunication Networks and Applications Conference (ITNAC)*, 1–6.

Wortman, S. E. (2015). Crop physiological response to nutrient solution electrical conductivity and pH in an ebb-and-flow hydroponic system. *Scientia Horticulturae*, *194*, 34–42. doi:10.1016/j.scienta.2015.07.045

Yunseop, K., Evans, R. G., & Iversen, W. M. (2008). Remote sensing and control of an irrigation system using a distributed wireless sensor network. *IEEE Transactions on Instrumentation and Measurement*, *57*(7), 1379–1387. doi:10.1109/TIM.2008.917198

Zanjalm, S. V., & Talmale, G. R. (2016). Medicine reminder and monitoring system for secure health using IOT. *Procedia Computer Science*, *78*, 471–476. doi:10.1016/j.procs.2016.02.090

The Application of the Internet of Things in Managing Supply Chains

Matthew J. Drake

(iD) https://orcid.org/0000-0002-7777-8916

Duquesne University, USA

INTRODUCTION

Concept of supply chain management (SCM) was introduced in the early 1980s (Melnyk and Seftel, 2016), but its roots go back as far as business itself. Firms have been planning and scheduling production, procuring materials and services, and storing and transporting finished goods to customers for more than a century (Drake, 2012). They gradually began to recognize the interrelationships between these business functions in enabling the delivery of a product or service to satisfy customers' requirements. SCM involves the coordination of these traditional business functions both within an organization and between upstream and downstream members of the system to serve the end consumer (Mentzer et al., 2001).

The timing of the introduction of the supply chain concept was largely dependent upon the concurrent development of business enterprise and communication information systems (Drake, 2012). This technology facilitates the sharing of information and provides the visibility that is required for geographically-dispersed supply chain partners to collaborate and to engage in joint planning and decision making (Fine, 1998). Webster (1992) describes the information resources and systems as part of the glue that holds extended supply chain networks together.

Supply chain technology continued to develop rapidly after the adoption of the SCM concept and practices, enabling firms to share information, understand demand, and track inventory to a degree few could imagine back in the early 1980s. Recent focus has been on implementing advanced technologies that fundamentally change the way supply chains operate through a process known as *digital transformation* (Gezgin, Huang, Samal, & Silva, 2017). The traditional linear view of the supply chain is no longer sufficient to satisfy customers compared to best-in-class competitors in the industry. Traditional supply chains often suffer from delays and demand amplification through the bullwhip effect. The digital supply chain, on the other hand, views the supply chain as an interconnected network of suppliers, manufacturers, and third-party service providers focused on satisfying the customers (Sherman and Chauhan, 2016).

Firms improved their supply chain performance in the 1980s and 1990s by capturing efficiencies from collaboration and technology applications, but incremental gains quickly became harder to realize and supply chain performance plateaued as opportunities for significant improvement dried up. The transformational, data-rich technologies developed in recent years and classified under the term *Industry 4.0* enable firms to achieve breakthrough improvements in their supply chain performance. The success of a digital transformation incorporating Industry 4.0 technologies is dependent upon sufficient integration between the supply chain operations and technology applications as well as human resources and organizational structure that supports continuous improvement and innovation (Gezgin et al., 2017).

DOI: 10.4018/978-1-7998-9220-5.ch138

T

Industry 4.0 technologies represent a revolution in the way firms can use data and automation to manage their physical operations and make better decisions. Specific Industry 4.0 applications include additive manufacturing, blockchain, automated robotics, and artificial intelligence (Olsen and Tomlin, 2020). All these technologies and methods use data to control operations or share information between supply chain partners. The focus of this chapter, however, is on one specific Industry 4.0 technology that collects and transmits real-time data that provide information inputs to other applications and help managers to make better decisions—the Internet of Things (IoT)—and how it enables organizations to improve their supply chains.

BACKGROUND

Represents the system of automated data collection and transmission via internet-connected devices that are implanted in or built into physical items (Birkel and Hartmann, 2020). The term was originally coined by Kevin Ashton in 1999 (Ashton, 2009). At this time, IoT technology was largely limited to automated identification tools such as bar codes and RFID. Modern IoT networks, however, utilize a portfolio of devices and technologies to collect, store, and transmit data such as wireless sensor and actuator networks (WSAN), near field communications (NFC), and smart devices (Atzori, Iera, & Morabito, 2010). Specific IoT devices include environmental sensors, temperature sensors, optical sensors, and wearable sensors (Caro and Sadr, 2019). Additional technologies such as smart phones, cloud computing, and social networks provide support for the IoT network (Xu, He, & Li, 2014).

Establishing and maintaining a seamless data and transmission connection between many disparate sensors, devices, and systems requires a sophisticated network architecture. Xu et al. (2014) describe the design of a four-layer, service-oriented architecture to facilitate IoT networks. The sensing layer works with the sensors and devices to collect data and control the physical items or equipment in the network. The networking layer enables transmission of the data over an Internet-enabled (wireless or wired) network. The service layer uses middleware technology to provide services to the users to satisfy their data and information needs. The interface layer allows the users and other applications to interact with the data.

The service-oriented architecture for IoT is scalable, allowing firms to add more sensors to the network or integrate new data sources as needed (Birkel and Hartmann, 2020). As a result, these IoT networks generate massive amounts of data in datasets classified as *Big Data*. The datasets meet the three standard dimensions of Big Data—volume, variety, and velocity—because they are extremely large (volume), are generated by many different sensors and devices (variety), and are collected and transmitted quickly and frequently (velocity) (Arunachalam, Kumar, & Kawalek, 2018). Firms must then apply Big Data analytics to incorporate this information into how they manage their supply chains in real time to improve performance and increase customer value.

The next section discusses specific benefits that firms can expect to realize when implementing IoT technologies within their supply chain operations.

SUPPLY CHAIN IMPROVEMENTS FROM IMPLEMENTING INTERNET OF THINGS TECHNOLOGY

Supply chain networks consist of linkages between dozens if not hundreds of organizations. All these organizations must perform their given tasks and responsibilities on time and effectively to meet the overall objective of SCM – to satisfy and provide value to the final customer. Managing this network of suppliers, distributors, retailers, and service providers requires a significant amount of data about past performance and current conditions in the supply chain. The Big Data datasets collected through IoT technologies can provide the information supply chain personnel require to manage these networks more efficiently and effectively to ensure customer satisfaction while increasing profitability for the firms.

This section will discuss the main ways that firms use data obtained from IoT to improve the way they manage their supply chains. These applications include, but are not limited to, supply chain visibility, supply chain traceability, supply chain transparency, risk management, and supply chain collaboration.

Supply Chain Visibility

For as long as managers have been tasked with coordinating supply chain networks spread across many miles, countries, and even continents, they have had to make decisions somewhat "in the dark" with respect to the current state of conditions at each location in the supply chain. This lack of full information often led to sub-optimal decisions and results. The collection of information from supply chain assets such as units of inventory and transportation equipment such as trailers and containers using IoT sensors and rapid transmission of that data improves the quality and timeliness of the information available to managers as they contemplate important supply chain decisions (Saghafian, Tomlin, & Biller, 2022). The strategic importance of IoT in supply chains is the ability to bring decision makers out of their prior darkness by providing more complete information (Holdowsky, Mahto, Raynor, & Cotteleer, 2015).

The improved information that IoT technology offers to supply chain managers increases the visibility of the supply chain. This visibility enables managers to better understand current conditions within their firms' internal operations or within their upstream or downstream extended supply chains (Sodhi and Tang, 2019). A significant challenge remains for many organizations, however, in employing effective methods of utilizing this vast amount of IoT-generated Big Data to generate actionable recommendations that optimize overall supply chain network performance (Olson and Tomlin, 2020). In a recent literature review, Ben-Daya, Hassini, & Bahroun (2019) found that most research into the application of IoT technology in managing supply chains has focused on improving the performance of specific supply chain processes such as production and distribution rather than tackling the entire supply chain. Some studies (e.g., Qu et al., 2017), however, address more integrated production and distribution scenarios.

The activities that comprise the supply chain can be viewed as an interrelated, repeating set of processes—plan, source, make, deliver, return, and enable—as popularized by the Supply Chain Operations Reference (SCOR) model (Association for Supply Chain Management, 2021). IoT technologies have most often been applied to improve the "make" and "deliver" supply chain processes (Ben-Daya et al., 2019). As a result, the following discussion will focus on the ways that the supply chain visibility enhanced by IoT technology has improved these facets of the supply chain.

Many of the applications of IoT technology within production and manufacturing are in the support of smart factory operations. A smart factory is a manufacturing operation that integrates physical objects such as production equipment, materials handling equipment (e.g., automated guided vehicles and conveyor systems), and raw materials with information systems such as enterprise resource planning (ERP) and manufacturing execution systems (MES) to create a cyber-physical system allowing the firm to increase flexibility and agility in its production processes (Wang, Wan, Zhang, Li, & Zhang, 2016). IoT devices collect data from the physical objects in the smart factory and transmit that data about the objects' status and factory conditions in real-time to the ERP and MES systems. This improved, updated information allows the systems to reconfigure and optimize production schedules to adapt to changing market and factory conditions (Chen et al., 2018). General Motors uses IoT sensors in its plants to observe real-time humidity conditions for its painting operations. If the humidity levels are not acceptable at a particular machine, the system reroutes the part to be painted in another area of the facility (Olsen and Tomlin, 2020). The smart factory allows the machines and products to act autonomously and intelligently in response to the updated information (Shi et al., 2020). The product moves through the production process on its own, communicating directly with machinery through IoT devices to inform the equipment about how it should be processed (Rebelo, Pereira, & Queiroz, 2022).

Several published studies have illustrated the benefits of incorporating IoT technology within smart factories to improve manufacturing operations. Ivanov, Dolgui, Sokolov, Werner, & Ivanova (2016) present an algorithm for short-term scheduling in a multi-stage flexible flow shop with alternative parallel machines available at each stage with individual processing speeds. The algorithm utilizes IoT-generated data to manage several objectives – minimizing total lateness, maximizing the volume of completed jobs, and balancing machine utilization. Chen et al. (2018) provide experimental results showing that IoT technology applied to a candy packaging line to enable automated scheduling can nearly double the Overall Equipment Effectiveness of the machinery over a six month period compared to traditional centralized scheduling. Li (2016) describes the use of information from IoT sensors to dynamically optimize the production plan and energy consumption in a petrochemical plant. Injection molding facilities at manufacturers such as Arburg are utilizing decentralized production information at the machine level to allow for customization of mass-produced parts, increasing flexibility and agility in the manufacturing process (Gaub, 2016). IoT data used in real-time scheduling allows the firm to increase the variety of options offered to customers while maintaining productivity through increased flexibility of its production processes (Rebelo et al., 2022).

In addition to increasing flexibility and agility of manufacturing operations, IoT sensors can also be used within production to signal when certain conditions such as vibration or temperature exceed an established threshold. The affected machine automatically shuts down while the incident is investigated, and the ERP system immediately signals to the planners which orders or batches will have their completion times affected by the stoppage (Atzori et al., 2010).

IoT technology is also often used within manufacturing facilities to increase the availability of machinery and reduce unplanned downtime. Smart sensors are used on equipment to identify mechanical issues and initiate proactive maintenance before they become major problems. This proactive maintenance reduces overall maintenance costs due to less need for reactive, emergency repairs. It also ensures that machines are available for production as much as possible, allowing the facility to increase its output instead of dealing with unplanned downtime (Sastri, 2019). The automation of detecting problems with equipment resolves common issues with manual assessment and inspection such as missing problems, misinterpreting situations, and inadequately communicating problems to decision makers in a timely manner (Chen and Tsai, 2017). The improved information about the current status of machines in the facility enables the facility to make maintenance decisions based on the actual conditions in the facility (known as condition-based maintenance) instead of relying on preventative or predictive maintenance strategies that base decisions on *expected* instead of actual conditions (Rymaszewska, Helo, & Gunasekaran, 2017).

The "deliver" process is the other major process in the SCOR model of a supply chain where firms commonly employ IoT technology. This includes traditional physical distribution functions such as finished goods inventory management, transportation, warehousing, and order management. Ben-Daya et al. (2019) found that most published research studies about IoT applications in the distribution portion of the supply chain focused on transportation with inventory management and warehousing representing a significant number of studies as well.

Within the delivery processes, IoT devices are commonly attached to individual units of inventory or units of handling such as pallets or cartons; pieces of transportation equipment such as trailers, railcars, and shipping containers; and material handling equipment such as automated guided vehicles, forklifts, and automated storage and retrieval systems. The information gathered and transmitted automatically from these devices provide increased visibility to the inventory as it makes its way through the distribution network ultimately to the final customer. Carriers and logistics service providers can also utilize this information to improve fleet management and real-time routing of their transportation equipment, thereby increasing logistics asset utilization (Tadejko, 2015).

Researchers have long touted the benefits of this enhanced inventory visibility since the earliest applications of radio-frequency identification (RFID) tags in logistics (see, e.g., Heese (2007) and Lee and Özer (2007)), but modern IoT technologies provide richer information about the current environment these items are experiencing rather than simple location tracking. Certain items, especially those in the food supply chain, can perish quickly under extreme temperature, humidity, and other environmental conditions (Olsen and Tomlin, 2020). IoT technology allows firms to monitor the conditions of their inventory remotely to determine if the items were held and transported under acceptable conditions that still allows them to be sold. This remote information also enables firms to proactively reallocate re-route perishable inventory depending on remaining shelf life and environmental conditions to maximize the benefit incurred from selling the products to customers before they perish (Rebelo et al., 2022).

The information provided through IoT technology can help distribution networks to improve customer service and order fulfillment. Tracking the inventory within a warehouse using IoT devices reduces inventory shrinkage and misplacement (Rebelo et al., 2022). Real-time tracking information within a warehouse can also be used to assign inventory to storage locations to improve the order picking process (Choy, Ho, & Lee, 2017). Zara uses IoT data to make store assortments and inventory allocation decisions for its worldwide network of stores in support of its omnichannel strategy (Caro and Sadr, 2019). Dasaklis and Casino (2019) describe the role of IoT technology in improving the effectiveness vendor managed inventory (VMI) relationships between suppliers and retailers.

Supply Chain Traceability

A specific aspect of supply chain visibility relates to the channel's ability to identify the path each item took as it progressed from its raw material stage, through production, and delivery to the end user as well as the conditions it encountered along the way (Sodhi and Tang, 2019). This type of tracking is commonly referred to as *supply chain traceability*. It requires the collection and transmission of large amounts of data throughout the product's journey, which can be facilitated through IoT technology.

Traceability is especially important in supply chains for consumable products that can impact people's health such as food, health care, and pharmaceuticals. It safeguards the supply of these sensitive products and provides the foundation for food quality efforts. Traceability plays a role in establishing that specific products have met sustainability standards and qualified for other certifications such as Fairtrade and Organic. Traceability programs also protect firms' brand names in the market and enable firms to communicate their responsibility efforts and focus to consumers (Dasaklis, Casino, & Patsakis, 2019). IoT technology can help to address the loss of approximately 14% of the world's food supply before it reaches consumers, which is mainly due to problems that occur within the food supply chain (Aamer,

Al-Awlaqi, Affia, Arumsari, & Mandahawi, 2021). The traceability information is often used to facilitate product recalls when harmful products have reached consumers.

While IoT provides valuable information to aid efforts to recall tainted products from the market, a better supply chain solution would avoid product safety issues altogether. Several studies (see, e.g., Bibi, Guillaume, Gontard, & Sorli, (2017) and Pal and Kant (2018)) discuss the use of IoT sensors to monitor conditions in the food supply chain and prevent spoiled or tainted products from being sold to consumers. Lin, Shen, Zhang, & Chai (2018) note many problems related to product safety in food-related supply chains such as the use of harmful chemical pesticides and fertilizers when growing fruits and vegetables, contamination of food due to heavy metal content in water, substitution of substandard ingredients such as sick livestock or recycled waste cooking oil in the production of processed foods, and the use of excessive food additives. They develop a system that integrates IoT and blockchain technology to allow all supply chain parties such as growers, processing plants, logistics companies, retailers, and customers to transmit and access all information about the product and its supply chain conditions, enabling total visibility and traceability. Ahmed, Taconet, Ould, Chabridon, & Bouzeghoub (2020) demonstrate the use of IoT data in a smart contract to automatically identify traceability incidents that are concerning within the supply chain.

Firms can incorporate liability considerations from potential product safety incidents into their overall supply chain network design decisions by utilizing the data from IoT technology. For example, Gautam et al. (2017) present a model to design the supply chain network for kiwi fruit to minimize transportation cost and minimize liability cost if product contamination should occur at any location or while the goods are in transit. These liability costs are dependent upon the accuracy of the data collected by IoT devices.

IoT devices can also be used to combat counterfeiting of luxury-brand products. As counterfeit products have proliferated in the market, luxury brands have experienced reduced demand for and reduced consumer confidence in their products. Several luxury brands such as Gucci, Tiffany, and Michael Kors have worked together to embed RFID chips into their products. These chips cannot be cloned or tampered with, and they can be used to authenticate the official products via either a smartphone or a portable scanner (Caro and Sadr, 2019).

Supply Chain Transparency

Another supply chain objective that is closely related to visibility is *supply chain transparency*. While visibility primarily relates to a firm's ability to understand real-time conditions within its own supply chain, supply chain transparency refers to the firm's ability to communicate relevant information about its operations' and products' compliance with consumer-expected standards to investors, consumers, and other relevant stakeholders such as advocacy and consumer watchdog groups. Visibility supports the needs of internal supply chain stakeholders such as suppliers, employees, service providers, and distribution partners. Transparency, on the other hand, focuses on the external stakeholders in the supply chain (Sodhi and Tang, 2019).

The supply chain visibility enabled by IoT data collection enhances the firm's access to the kind of information about its supply chain operations and its products that external stakeholders would expect transparent firms to share. Most of the focus of transparency is on upstream aspects of the supply chain, concentrating on information about suppliers and their business practices. Common examples of upstream information shared by transparent organizations are list of direct (Tier-1) suppliers, supply chain environmental footprint, safety compliance in the supplier workforce, and even supply chain costs in some of the most extreme cases. While disclosure of downstream information is not as common as upstream information, many companies have begun sharing information about the waste generated by their products at the end of their useful life and their packaging to provide a clearer picture of their environmental impact (Sodhi and Tang, 2019).

Supply chain transparency has several major benefits beyond those generated by internal supply chain visibility efforts. The open communication of supply chain information helps to increase consumers' and investors' trust in the organization. Firms can also avoid the negative publicity and regulatory pressure that comes from supply chain opacity. Consumer advocacy and watchdog groups can indirectly help the firm monitor its suppliers' compliance with standards and consumer-expected norms now that the groups know who the suppliers are, thereby reducing the firm's need to monitor the suppliers on its own. These benefits, though, are often offset by the large cost of collecting and maintaining updated information about the entire supply chain (Sodhi and Tang, 2019). Firms that use IoT technology to provide visibility about their internal supply chain operations already have the infrastructure in place to collect the relevant information to communicate supply chain transparency.

Supply Chain Risk Management

Extended supply chains that span multiple countries and even multiple continents are inherently susceptible to disruptions. Many of the disruptions that occur due to "regular" or commonly-occurring sources of risk such as shipping delays, machine breakdowns, production yield, and material shortages are relatively brief. Supply may be disrupted for a few days, but the system returns to normal relatively quickly afterward. Disruptions that occur due to "irregular" events such as natural disasters, labor stoppages, and political upheaval can cause shortages that last much longer, even extending for months or years in some cases. Thankfully those irregular events do not occur very often and are also usually isolated to a specific geographic area (Drake, 2012).

The supply chain visibility generated by IoT technology increases a firm's ability to proactively manage risks in its supply chain. The real-time collection and transmission of data about current conditions throughout the supply chain increases the firm's ability to identify risks as soon as they start to become evident. IoT data enables a more thorough quantification of the probability that events could occur and their likely impact if they should occur. This improved information provides a strong foundation for better decision making to manage risks, and it forms the basis to conduct post-disruption analysis to design efforts to avoid future risks. IoT data can also be useful in developing contracts with supply chain partners to transfer and share risks between the parties (Birkel and Hartmann, 2020).

In addition to enabling supply chain firms to manage risks more effectively, IoT data can also help governments to develop and implement policies to mitigate the effects of supply chain risks on vulnerable populations, thereby increasing social welfare. Meng (2021) discusses the use of IoT data in Australia to develop government policies and restrictions during the outbreak of the COVID-19 pandemic. The Australian government used real-time data to understand the current conditions in different parts of the country as well as the needs of local residents. It then developed targeted responses informed by these data to contain the spread of the virus and ensure consistent supply of essential products and services throughout the country.

Supply Chain Collaboration

As discussed above, the majority of research studies about the application of IoT technology in the supply chain have focused on increasing internal visibility and improving individual processes as defined by the SCOR model. Few studies have applied IoT technology across the entire supply chain (Ben-Daya et al., 2019; Cui, Gao, Dai, & Mou, in press).

Supply chain collaboration refers to separate companies within a supply chain establishing long-term, mutually-beneficial relationships. They work together closely to develop joint plans and then manage their supply chain operations to attain common objectives (Cao and Zhang, 2011). Attributes such as trust, information sharing, and analytical capabilities contribute to successful supply chain collaboration efforts, which in turn, has been shown to improve the performance of the overall supply chain (Cui et al., in press). IoT technology facilitates information sharing between supply chain partners (Sherman and Chauhan, 2016), and trust often develops after successful information sharing efforts (Soosay and Hyland, 2015).

One of the major challenges in managing a supply chain stems from the *bullwhip effect*, which refers to the increase in demand variability as orders move upstream in the supply chain from retailers to distributors to manufacturers. The bullwhip effect is caused by four main factors: (1) demand forecasts based on orders from direct customers rather than end-consumer usage, (2) customers ordering units to satisfy multiple periods of demand at once time, (3) price changes due to promotions and discounts, and (4) gaming behavior in allocating scarce supplier capacity (Lee, Padmanabhan, & Whang, 1997). Supply chain collaboration informed by IoT data can reduce the impact of the bullwhip effect, improving the performance of the entire system. IoT technology enables connectivity between the upstream and downstream supply chain parties and facilitates the seamless sharing of information, which is required for synchronized planning and execution (Jiang, 2019).

CHALLENGES AND RISKS OF UTILIZING INTERNET OF THINGS TECHNOLOGY IN SUPPLY CHAINS

The many benefits from employing IoT technology in the supply chain must be significant enough to overcome the challenges and risks of utilizing the technology. These challenges and risks include, but are not limited to, processing Big Data effectively for decision making, large initial and ongoing capital requirements, security and privacy concerns, integrating information systems, and data ownership.

A major challenge to utilizing IoT technology is developing the capability of processing the Big Data effectively and using it to make real-time supply chain decisions. Cui et al. (in press) identify the ability to acquire and process large amounts of data quickly to support decision making as a significant competitive advantage in the contemporary marketplace. To fully unlock the potential benefits from IoT data, firms should employ Big Data analytics and other technologies such as blockchain simultaneously (Rebelo et al., 2022). Large datasets often suffer from issues related to inconsistency, redundancy, ambiguity, and quality, which poses additional challenges to firms looking to integrate the Big Data generated by IoT devices into their supply chain decisions (Aamer et al., 2021).

The implementation of IoT technology and the required systems to transmit, store, and analyze the Big Data represent significant initial and ongoing capital investments. These costs may be especially untenable for small companies and firms located in developing countries with fewer options for accessing additional financing. Further complicating the investment decision for organizations, many benefits from implementing IoT technology are realized by looking at the supply chain as a whole and may be more difficult to attribute or assign to each individual entity in the network (Aamer et al., 2021). It may be more difficult for firms to justify the investment to implement IoT technology if they cannot realize significant measurable benefits in a relatively short amount of time (Caro and Sadr, 2019).

IoT systems generate a massive amount of data, which causes issues related to security and privacy. IoT devices are almost always unattended, which makes it easier to attack them physically. The devices also transmit data wirelessly, making them especially prone to eavesdropping and interception. Many IoT devices function on a combination of low energy usage and computing power to keep their costs as low as possible, which limits their ability to accommodate sophisticated security measures. Automated data collection raises additional privacy concerns, especially when the devices interact with civilians who are unaware data is being collected about their interaction with a device. Firms should ensure they protect privacy giving individuals control over what data is collected, when it is collected, and who is collecting it (Atzori et al., 2010). Security and privacy issues related to IoT data has also drawn scrutiny from many governments; as a result, firms must ensure they are not violating laws through their collection, transmission, and storage of IoT data (Tadejko, 2015).

Many IoT systems have been developed as closed systems rather than open systems that talk and share data with each other easily (Tadejko, 2015). This has made integration of information systems between companies especially difficult in some cases. No global standards have been established to integrate across different IoT equipment, nor do standards exist for interpreting the data generated by the IoT system (Aamer et al., 2021).

Another unique issue related to IoT-generated data is the question of ownership of the data. If data is generated from a unit of inventory or a logistics asset as it moves through the supply chain, several parties could rightfully lay claim to own the data collected by the IoT device attached to that item. Supply chain contracts should address the issue of data governance in addition to their more traditional considerations of prices, quantities, and delivery times (Saarikko, Westergren, & Blomquist, 2017).

SOLUTIONS AND RECOMMENDATIONS

While IoT systems have some challenges and risks of implementation that firms must manage, the benefits of increased visibility, flexibility, agility, traceability, and transparency provide substantial benefits for best-in-class supply chains. As Sherman and Chauhan (2016) note, leading firms have already embarked on the road to digital transformation of their supply chains. IoT technology lies at the heart of many of these advancements. Firms that lag behind must strive to catch up to their competitors, or they risk their viability in the market. Technology changes at a rapid pace, and the leaders will continue to look for new ways to maintain their competitive advantage. Laggards cannot afford to fall further behind if they want to continue to compete in the 21st century marketplace. They should consider substantial investment in the technology and human resources required to collect real-time supply chain data and integrate it into the organizational decision-making process effectively.

FUTURE RESEARCH DIRECTIONS

The literature related to IoT applications in SCM has grown significantly in recent years. Many opportunities still remain, however, to conduct further research to improve the effectiveness of the data generated by IoT devices in aiding supply chain decision making. Each of the challenges and risks of implementing IoT technology should be addressed in future research projects. Researchers should consider additional integration of IoT data with other Industry 4.0 technologies such as blockchain, artificial intelligence, additive manufacturing, and robotics to improve supply chain performance (Olsen and Tomlin, 2020).

A specifically interesting question relates to the continued integration of IoT technology and blockchain specifically to generate smart contracts that do not require much human intervention to manage and execute (Francisco and Swanson, 2018).

Researchers must also conduct additional studies about the integrated implementation of IoT technology throughout the extended supply chain rather than continuing to focus on the application within individual supply chain processes (Ben-Daya et al., 2019). Even within some functional processes such as "deliver," there is a dearth of studies focusing on specific applications of IoT to improve performance such as network design and transportation mode selection. Most current studies also look at relatively short timelines for measuring impact of implementation; studies addressing the long-term impacts of IoT applications would also be useful (Ben-Daya et al., 2019). Rebelo et al. (2022) specifically note the absence of a significant number of empirical studies related to the application of IoT technology in practice. While some studies have examined the application of IoT technology in specific industries such as the food supply chain and the retail supply chain, additional industry studies are necessary to consider the unique opportunities and challenges that exist in other industries.

CONCLUSION

IoT technology has changed the way that many firms manage their supply chains. IoT devices collect and transmit data about real-time conditions faced by inventory and logistics assets located practically anywhere in the world. This additional information facilitates supply chain visibility, which enables firms to improve their operations and customer service through better management of inventory and other supply chain resources. It also provides necessary inputs for supply chain traceability and transparency initiatives. The ability to react to the real-time data increases firms' flexibility and agility, increasing their resilience to a variety of supply chain risks. The information provided by IoT technology improves the effectiveness of collaborative efforts with supply chain partners. Best-in-class supply chains will continue to develop innovative ways to leverage the information generated by IoT technology to enhance their competitive advantage in the market.

REFERENCES

Aamer, A. M., Al-Awlaqi, M. A., Affia, I., Arumsari, S., & Mandahawi, N. (2021). The internet of things in the food supply chain: Adoption challenges. *Benchmarking*, 28(8), 2521–2541. doi:10.1108/BIJ-07-2020-0371

Ahmed, M., Taconet, C., Ould, M., Chabridon, S., & Bouzeghoub, A. (2020). Enhancing B2B supply chain traceability using smart contracts and IoT. *Proceedings of the Hamburg International Conference of Logistics*, 29, 559-589. 10.15480/882.3110

Arunachalam, D., Kumar, N., & Kawalek, J. P. (2018). Understanding big data analytics capabilities in supply chain management: Unraveling the issues, challenges and implications for practice. *Transportation Research Part E, Logistics and Transportation Review*, 114, 416–436. doi:10.1016/j.tre.2017.04.001

Ashton, K. (2009). That 'internet of things' thing. *RFID Journal*. https://www.rfidjournal.com/that-internet-of-things-thing

Association for Supply Chain Management. (2021). *SCOR model: Introduction to processes*. https://scor.ascm.org/processes/introduction

Atzori, L., Iera, A., & Morabito, G. (2010). The internet of things: A survey. *Computer Networks*, *54*(15), 2787–2805. doi:10.1016/j.comnet.2010.05.010

Ben-Daya, M., Hassini, E., & Bahroun, Z. (2019). Internet of things and supply chain management: A literature review. *International Journal of Production Research*, *57*(15-16), 4719–4742. doi:10.1080/00207543.2017.1402140

Bibi, F., Guillaume, C., Gontard, N., & Sorli, B. (2017). A review: RFID technology having sensing aptitudes for food industry and their contribution to tracking and monitoring of food products. *Trends in Food Science & Technology*, *62*, 91–103. doi:10.1016/j.tifs.2017.01.013

Birkel, H. S., & Hartmann, E. (2020). Internet of things – the future of managing supply chain risks. *Supply Chain Management*, *25*(5), 535–548. doi:10.1108/SCM-09-2019-0356

Cadr, F., & Sadr, R. (2019). The internet of things (IoT) in retail: Bridging supply and demand. *Business Horizons*, *62*(1), 47–54. doi:10.1016/j.bushor.2018.08.002

Cao, M., & Zhang, Q. (2011). Supply chain collaboration: Impact on collaborative advantage and firm performance. *Journal of Operations Management*, *29*(3), 163–180. doi:10.1016/j.jom.2010.12.008

Chen, B., Wan, J., Shu, L., Li, P., Mukherjee, M., & Yin, B. (2018). Smart factory of industry 4.0: Key technologies, application case, and challenges. *IEEE Access: Practical Innovations, Open Solutions*, *6*, 6505–6519. doi:10.1109/ACCESS.2017.2783682

Chen, T., & Tsai, H. R. (2017). Ubiquitous manufacturing: Current practices, challenges, and opportunities. *Robotics and Computer-integrated Manufacturing*, *45*, 126–132. doi:10.1016/j.rcim.2016.01.001

Choy, K. L., Ho, G. T. S., & Lee, C. K. H. (2017). An RFID-based storage assignment system for enhancing the efficiency of order picking. *Journal of Intelligent Manufacturing*, *28*(1), 111–129. doi:10.100710845-014-0965-9

Cui, L., Gao, M., Dai, J., & Mou, J. (in press). Improving supply chain collaboration through operational excellence approaches: An IoT perspective. *Industrial Management & Data Systems*. doi:10.1108/IMDS-01-2020-0016

Dasaklis, T., & Casino, F. (2019). Improving vendor-managed inventory strategy based on internet of things (IoT) applications and blockchain technology. In *Proceedings of the 2019 IEEE International Conference on Blockchain and Cryptocurrency (ICBC)*. IEEE. 10.1109/BLOC.2019.8751478

Dasaklis, T., Casino, F., & Patsakis, C. (2019). Defining granularity levels for supply chain traceability based on IoT and blockchain. In *Proceedings of the International Conference on Omni-Layer Intelligent Systems*. Association for Computing Machinery. 10.1145/3312614.3312652

Drake, M. (2012). *Global supply chain management*. Business Expert Press.

Fine, C. H. (1998). *Clockspeed: Winning industry control in the age of temporary advantage*. Basic Books.

Francisco, K., & Swanson, D. (2018). The supply chain has no clothes: Technology adoption of blockchain for supply chain transparency. *Logistics*, *2*(1), 2. doi:10.3390/logistics2010002

Gaub, H. (2016). Customization of mass-produced parts by combining injection molding and additive manufacturing with industry 4.0 technologies. *Reinforced Plastics*, *60*(6), 401–404. doi:10.1016/j.repl.2015.09.004

Gautam, R., Singh, A., Karthik, K., Pandey, S., Scrimgeour, F., & Tiwari, M. K. (2017). Traceability using RFID and its formulation for a kiwifruit supply chain. *Computers & Industrial Engineering*, *103*, 46–58. doi:10.1016/j.cie.2016.09.007

Gezgin, E., Huang, X., Samal, P., & Silva, I. (2017). *Digital transformation: Raising supply-chain performance to new levels*. McKinsey & Company.

Heese, H. S. (2007). Inventory record inaccuracy, double marginalization, and RFID adoption. *Production and Operations Management*, *16*(5), 542–553. doi:10.1111/j.1937-5956.2007.tb00279.x

Holdowsky, J., Mahto, M., Raynor, M., & Cotteleer, M. (2015). *Inside the internet of things: A primer on the technologies building the IoT*. Deloitte University Press.

Ivanov, D., Dolgui, A., Sokolov, B., Werner, F., & Ivanova, M. (2016). A dynamic model and an algorithm for short-term supply chain scheduling in the smart factory industry 4.0. *International Journal of Production Research*, *54*(2), 386–402. doi:10.1080/00207543.2014.999958

Jiang, W. (2019). An intelligent supply chain information collaboration model based on Internet of Things and big data. *IEEE Access: Practical Innovations, Open Solutions*, *7*, 58324–58335. doi:10.1109/ACCESS.2019.2913192

Lee, H., & Özer, Ö. (2007). Unlocking the value of RFID. *Production and Operations Management*, *16*(1), 40–64. doi:10.1111/j.1937-5956.2007.tb00165.x

Lee, H. L., Padmanabhan, V., & Whang, S. (1997). The bullwhip effect in supply chains. *Sloan Management Review*, *38*(3), 93–102.

Li, D. (2016). Perspective for smart factory in petrochemical industry. *Computers & Chemical Engineering*, *91*, 136–148. doi:10.1016/j.compchemeng.2016.03.006

Lin, J., Shen, Z., Zhang, A., & Chai, Y. (2018). Blockchain and IoT based food traceability for smart agriculture. In *Proceedings of the 3rd International Conference on Crowd Science and Engineering*. Association for Computing Machinery. 10.1145/3265689.3265692

Melnyk, S. A., & Seftel, C. M. (2016). Myths and truths: Misadventures in supply chain management. *Supply Chain Management Review*, *20*(1), 10–15.

Meng, L. (2021). Using IoT in supply chain risk management to enable collaboration between business, community, and government. *Smart Cities*, *4*(3), 995–1003. doi:10.3390martcities4030052

Mentzer, J. T., Dewitt, W., Keebler, J. S., Min, S., Nix, N. W., Smith, C. D., & Zacharia, Z. G. (2001). Defining supply chain management. *Journal of Business Logistics*, *22*(2), 1–25. doi:10.1002/j.2158-1592.2001.tb00001.x

Olsen, T. L., & Tomlin, B. (2020). Industry 4.0: Opportunities and challenges for operations management. *Manufacturing & Service Operations Management*, *22*(1), 113–122. doi:10.1287/msom.2019.0796

Pal, A., & Kant, K. (2018). IoT-based sensing and communications infrastructure for the fresh food supply chain. *Computer*, *51*(2), 76–80. doi:10.1109/MC.2018.1451665

Qu, T., Thürer, M., Wang, J., Wang, Z., Fu, H., Li, C., & Huang, G. Q. (2017). System dynamics analysis for an internet-of-things-enabled production logistics system. *International Journal of Production Research*, *55*(9), 2622–2649. doi:10.1080/00207543.2016.1173738

Rebelo, R. M. L., Pereira, S. C. F., & Queiroz, M. M. (2022). The interplay between the internet of things and supply chain management: Challenges and opportunities based on a systematic literature review. *Benchmarking*, *29*(2), 683–711. doi:10.1108/BIJ-02-2021-0085

Rymaszewska, A., Helo, P., & Gunasekaran, A. (2017). IoT powered servitization of manufacturing – an exploratory case study. *International Journal of Production Economics*, *192*, 92–105. doi:10.1016/j.ijpe.2017.02.016

Saarikko, T., Westergren, U. H., & Blomquist, T. (2017). The internet of things: Are you ready for what's coming? *Business Horizons*, *60*(5), 667–676. doi:10.1016/j.bushor.2017.05.010

Saghafian, S., Tomlin, B., & Biller, S. (2022). The internet of things and information fusion: Who talks to who? *Manufacturing & Service Operations Management*, *24*(1), 333–351. doi:10.1287/msom.2020.0958

Sastri, S. (2019). Accelerating supply chains with the internet of things. *ASCM Insights*. https://www.ascm.org/ascm-insights/accelerating-supply-chains-with-the-internet-of-things/

Sherman, R., & Chauhan, V. (2016). Just my (re-)imagination. *Supply Chain Management Review*, *20*(2), 28–35.

Shi, Z., Xie, Y., Xue, W., Chen, Y., Fu, L., & Xu, X. (2020). Smart factory in industry 4.0. *Systems Research and Behavioral Science*, *37*(4), 607–617. doi:10.1002res.2704

Sodhi, M. S., & Tang, C. S. (2019). Research opportunities in supply chain transparency. *Production and Operations Management*, *28*(12), 2946–2959. doi:10.1111/poms.13115

Soosay, C. A., & Hyland, P. (2015). A decade of supply chain collaboration and directions for future research. *Supply Chain Management*, *20*(6), 613–630. doi:10.1108/SCM-06-2015-0217

Tadejko, P. (2015). Application of internet of things in logistics – current challenges. *Economics and Management*, *7*(4), 54–64.

Wang, S., Wan, J., Zhang, D., Li, D., & Zhang, C. (2016). Towards smart factory for industry 4.0: A self-organized multi-agent system with big data based feedback and coordination. *Computer Networks*, *101*, 158–168. doi:10.1016/j.comnet.2015.12.017

Webster, F. E. Jr. (1992). The changing role of marketing in the corporation. *Journal of Marketing*, *56*(4), 1–17. doi:10.1177/002224299205600402

Xu, L. D., He, W., & Li, S. (2014). Internet of things in industries: A survey. *IEEE Transactions on Industrial Informatics*, *10*(4), 2233–2243. doi:10.1109/TII.2014.2300753

ADDITIONAL READING

Aryal, A., Liao, Y., Nattuthurai, P., & Li, B. (2020). The emerging big data analytics and IoT in supply chain management: A systematic review. *Supply Chain Management*, *25*(2), 141–156. doi:10.1108/SCM-03-2018-0149

Babich, V., & Hilary, G. (2020). Distributed ledgers and operations: What operations management researchers should know about blockchain technology. *Manufacturing & Service Operations Management*, *22*(2), 223–240. doi:10.1287/msom.2018.0752

Batwa, A., & Norrman, A. (2020). A framework for exploring blockchain technology in supply chain management. *Operations and Supply Chain Management*, *13*(3), 294–306. doi:10.31387/oscm0420271

de Vass, T., Shee, H., & Miah, S. J. (2021). IoT in supply chain management: A narrative on retail sector sustainability. *International Journal of Logistics Research and Applications*, *24*(6), 605–624. doi:10.1080/13675567.2020.1787970

McCrea, B. (2019). How advanced technologies are affecting supply chain software. *Supply Chain Management Review*, *23*(5), 50–56.

Min, H. (2019). Blockchain technology for enhancing supply chain resilience. *Business Horizons*, *62*(1), 35–45. doi:10.1016/j.bushor.2018.08.012

Ogle, M. (2019). Which emerging technologies will help you meet your supply chain challenges? *Supply Chain Quarterly*, *13*(2), 34–40.

Preindl, R., Nikolopoulos, K., & Litsiou, K. (2020). Transformation strategies for the supply chain: The impact of Industry 4.0 and digital transformation. *Supply Chain Forum: An International Journal*, *21*(1), 26-34.

Wasserman, M., & Mahmoodi, F. (2017). Disruptive technologies: Should you give them the green light? *Supply Chain Quarterly*, *11*(1), 34–39.

KEY TERMS AND DEFINITIONS

Big Data: Datasets that are (1) extremely large, (2) generated by many different sensors and devices, and (3) collected and transmitted quickly and frequently.

Industry 4.0: Transformational, data-rich technologies that enable firms to achieve breakthrough improvements in their supply chain performance.

Internet of Things (IoT): The system of automated data collection and transmission via internet-connected devices that are implanted in or built into physical items.

Supply Chain Collaboration: Two or more distinct companies within a supply chain establishing long-term, mutually-beneficial relationships based on trust, information sharing, and decision making to achieve common goals.

Supply Chain Traceability: The ability to identify the path each item took as it progressed through the entire supply chain from its raw material stage to final delivery to the end user, as well as the conditions it encountered along the way.

Supply Chain Transparency: The firm's ability to communicate relevant information about its operations' and products' compliance with consumer-expected standards external stakeholders such as investors, consumers, and advocacy groups.

Supply Chain Visibility: The ability to observe the real-time location and environmental condition of a unit of inventory or a logistics asset regardless of where in the world it currently is located.

Section 32
Malware Analysis

Malware Detection in Network Flows With Self-Supervised Deep Learning

Thomas Alan Woolman
On Target Technologies, Inc., USA

Philip Lunsford
East Carolina University, USA

INTRODUCTION

With ever-increasing network complexities and threat actor sophistication, the vulnerabilities of critical network infrastructure and host systems are potentially greater than ever before. The ability of targeted organizations and government entities to defend their network perimeters utilizing traditional threat detection systems provides only a limited set of tools that are traditionally based on simple statistical tests of network activities and known threat signatures. These threat signatures generally rely on predefined malware detection rules based on known, previously encountered network intrusion attack types. As a result, sensitive information and critical resource applications can potentially be highly vulnerable to novel sophisticated and evolving network intrusion types, potentially putting commercial and public sector resources and information in mounting jeopardy.

The ability to detect legacy cyber threats through a multilayered defense approach is based on research pioneered by Chess and White (1987), initially based on permutations of signature detection methods proposed by Cohen (1987). While signature-based network malware and intrusion detection are still among the most heavily used techniques, heuristic approaches that are able to discern multiple, related threats from a single definition source have been increasingly common, as defined by Kaspersky Lab ZAO (2013). However, novel threats as well as more advanced cyber malware and intrusion events that are explicitly designed to avoid detection by the more commonly used available tools and techniques are becoming increasingly common. By being able to bypass the network security perimeter, intrusions and malware can quickly propagate throughout the network and operate undetected for substantial lengths of time. In many cases, these network intrusions can access restricted information while remaining undetected, masquerading their traffic signatures as legitimate, benign activities.

As the capability to resist successful classification is increasing with the latest generation of network intrusion technologies, continuous improvement in the multilayered network defense approach first proposed in 1987 becomes increasingly necessary. One example of this emerging malware threat class is a sophisticated modular malware known as Flame, first discovered in 2012 on networked devices running the Microsoft Windows operating system (ICIRT, 2012). Flame, also known as Skywiper, is believed to likely have been developed by a state actor as a cyber-weapon that was deployed for espionage purposes for one or more targets in the Middle East (Kaspersky Lab ZAO, 2013).

DOI: 10.4018/978-1-7998-9220-5.ch139

First detected inadvertently in 2012, Flame is now generally regarded as an unusually robust backdoor attack toolkit, with worm-like features and Trojan capabilities, with the ability to replicate both within a targeted network as well as on removable media upon receipt of commands to do so by a remote threat actor's command and control server. Although the exact method of entry into a network has not yet been determined, Flame's ability to take on different roles through a wide range of add-on functional libraries allows it to be both extraordinarily adaptable and difficult to analyze by traditional mitigation and detection methods, utilizing the novel technique of concealment through an unusually large and variable codebase compared to most other network malware threats.

Flame is capable of harvesting sensitive data in a variety of ways, including robust SQL database query insertions, compressed digital audio microphone recording, Bluetooth wireless connectivity attacks from inside the network, as well as file and network traffic ingestion and analysis. Furthermore, Flame can also take recurring screenshot images from infected devices. Flame is capable of reporting back to an external command and control server from within the targeted network via a covert SSL data channel, as well as turning other host devices within the network into beacons that are discoverable via Bluetooth connections, according to Kaspersky Lab ZAO (2013).

Advances in this and similar emerging, novel threat categories of malware and network intrusion capabilities thus require adaptable learning technologies for detection that are not based on predefined statistical patterns, heuristics, or rule-based detection methods. One increasingly utilized form of malware and network intrusion detection technology is anomaly-based detection methods, often utilizing data mining technologies including machine learning and deep learning. Deep learning anomaly detection utilizing network traffic analysis such as packet capture and network flow data is one such emerging advance in this field, one which does not require the use of predefined, human-labeled training data that could be obsolete when faced with novel malware threats. Thus, unsupervised deep learning algorithms for anomaly detection in network connection datasets represent a possible significant component of a multi-layer network defense strategy designed to detect advanced novel malware threats across digital networks, because these systems do not rely on pre-programmed malware threat signatures.

An advantage of utilizing packet capture data sets for anomaly-based network intrusion detection systems (NIDS) is that full packet capture allows for a mirror image of the entirety of the network traffic for a given period of time, allowing robust deep packet inspection (DPI). The DPI data set allows for a complete forensic analysis of all available features including protocols, payloads, and source and origins for each packet, as well as a variety of measurements related to packet transmission speeds and delays.

One significant disadvantage of packet capture data set forensics for NIDS is that DPI imposes a significant burden on routers, switches, and network infrastructure in general during this mirroring cycle to capture and store the vast amount of network traffic. Furthermore, the data storage, processing, and analysis of these often quite deep (often multi-terabytes per day within enterprise networks), wide (typically on the order of dozens of independent variables per observation), and complex data sets often requires the use of more cumbersome "Big Data" analytical cluster computer environments. These specialized analytical frameworks thus necessitate an increase in the scope and complexity of these projects. Robust encryption methods of packet payload data further increase the signature detection complexity of DPI analysis (Woolman & Lee, 2021).

Conversely, network flow data sets represent a more "high level" metadata scope of network traffic within the enterprise, providing summarized level data between the source (IP address and port) and destination (IP address and port) per protocol. Rather than recording the actual packet payload of each component of network traffic, the network flow data set typically records only the information about the number of packets per flow observation, as well as the Shannon entropy for each packet payload and the duration of each flow.

BACKGROUND

Network flow metadata provides only the "headlines" of the more complex network traffic details available in a packet capture log, thus it is able to provide a succinct, high-level view of activities taking place across the network, including time stamps, IP addresses, and ports for both sender and receiver; the overall length of the conversation; the protocol being used; the amount of data being sent; and an estimate of the amount of information potentially held within that data. This summarized view of network traffic substantially reduces the burden of storage, processing, and analysis of enterprise network traffic, at the cost of reduced granularity of the data set. An entire recorded network history using DPI would be required in order to provide a fully detailed forensic review of network traffic for a given time period.

Because of the more concise nature of network flow data, it provides a more cost- and computationally efficient approach for NIDS that is potentially closer to real-time for network intrusion detection. However, the decreased granularity of this data set requires a sophisticated analysis technology that is adaptable to ever-changing network traffic patterns, minimizes false positives and false negatives (Type I and Type II statistical errors), and does not rely on predefined signature rules, heuristics, or statistical pattern definitions. Thus, machine learning and deep learning technologies come into focus with this research.

Deep learning as defined in Zhang et al. (2021) is a subset of broader machine learning, based on artificial neural networks that incorporate representational learning methods, and the "deep" learning refers to the use of multiple layers within the neural network construct. This allows for the optimization of the algorithm to specific use cases of data, with the multiple layers within the model extracting increasingly higher-order features from the underlying data set observations, transforming the original data into successively more abstract representations of information about the data. Unsupervised learning refers to a machine learning or deep learning process which is able to derive new information from a data set without the use of human-labeled examples in order to be able to learn from the patterns in the data.

For this research, a curated data set of daily network flow data from an isolated research laboratory network at Lancaster University (Lancashire, UK) from 2020–2021 is utilized (Mills, et al., 2021). The daily network flow observations include human-labeled outcomes data of benign, malicious, and outlier for each flow observation, where the known malicious and outlier events constituted a range of known malware and likely malware threats. For purposes of the autoencoder model development experiment, the dependent factor variable (malicious or benign) was specifically ignored by the autoencoder MLP model in order to be able to independently, statistically assess the result of the experiment as an unsupervised/self-supervised anomaly detector.

Thus, a blind study was conducted where known potentially malicious network activity class labels for each network flow event were purposely hidden from the autoencoder MLP model. This ensured that the potential ability of the model to detect these anomalies accurately using an unsupervised learning methodology with self-supervised feature extraction was preserved for this experiment.

The objective of this research is thus to investigate the application of unsupervised deep learning anomaly detection with self-supervised feature selection using only network flow metadata (as opposed to the much larger and more granular packet capture log file data) for robust NIDS anomaly detection, using a blind study experiment.

M

In this research, a deep learning autoencoder multilayer perceptron (MLP) neural network is trained to perform unsupervised learning from this data set and determines an anomaly score for each network flow observation. An autoencoding multilayer neural network was first defined by Hinton, Krizhevsky and Wang (2011) as a way to encapsulate data through successive layers within a neural network, to first encode and then decode information after passing through a limited feature space. This methodology provided a way of learning about which attributes of the input data provide the most informative outputs, thus creating a set of "instantiation parameters" in what is now commonly referred to as self-supervised feature extraction. This combines elements of traditional unsupervised learning in that no dependent variable is defined or required, with the ability to self-define principal attributes of the data which have both linear and nonlinear relationships between the independent variables. Furthermore, this method also provides a reconstructed mean square of the error (RMSE) score for each observation based on how well it was reconstructed from the decoding layer of the neural network. Higher RMSE scores thus indicate greater difficulties in reconstruction during decoding, hence a potentially greater degree of multivariate anomaly from an expected norm.

Because unsupervised deep learning autoencoders are the focus of this research, the human-labeled outcome for each flow observation is ignored in the model training data but is used to validate the performance of the unsupervised model for Type I and Type II errors after training by the authors using an ANOVA test. Thus, a blind study methodology was used by the authors which allows the use of statistical analysis to validate the significance of the autoencoding neural networks to detect known (to the author) malicious threat network class events that were not known by the unsupervised deep learning model in the experiment.

By utilizing the novel combination of deep learning autoencoder MLP neural networks and "high level" network flow data, a powerful, adaptive, and computational inexpensive NIDS system will be explored. This network flow data places a much lower burden on the network infrastructure to record and analyze than deep packet inspection does, but at the cost of having a lower granularity of data with which to discover potential threat activities.

A challenge and research opportunity is presented by combining the need for robust, anomaly detection capabilities using machine learning that is potentially able to both utilize unsupervised learning with self-supervised feature selection and also utilize network flow metadata as the primary source of anomaly detection for NIDS. The opportunity here is primarily in utilizing a dramatically smaller and more economically acquired dataset, with an objective of being sensitive enough to detect novel threat activities while minimizing error for known threat classes in a blind study.

Therefore, unsupervised/self-supervised deep learning is used to provide quantified anomaly detection across a range of assorted network traffic types in network flow metadata, across a disparate range of protocols and network activities. The deep learning MLP autoencoder is considered unsupervised learning in that it does not require human-labeled outcome labeling for model design (Liang et al., 2021) but is also classified as a self-supervised algorithm (Hahn & Mechefske, 2021) because they are trained in a partially supervised manner with defined inputs (independent variables), but no dependent variable labeling, retaining the fundamentally unsupervised nature of the model and making them potentially well suited for this network flow anomaly NIDS detection experiment.

Thus, the proposed autoencoder MLP model will be used to learn to differentiate these various network traffic characteristics while remaining sensitive to unusual events in the internet protocol traffic signals, without relying on predefined statistical patterns or known historical examples of benign and malicious flow traffic incidents. The ability to utilized end-to-end deep learning as an initial line of defense against sophisticated, novel network intrusion detection using high-level network flow data allows for the use of machine learning models that do not rely on human-labeled network feature engineering class labeling. The use of a multilayer perceptron autoencoeder is used to model and predict network flow activities utilizing self-supervised techniques, for the purposes of anomaly detection to make a prediction about the potentially high-threat malicious network flow activities.

PROBLEM STATEMENT

According to Haefner and Ray (2021), the rapidly increasing complexity of the multivariate network flow data is demonstrated particularly well when IoT (internet of things) and other network devices become compromised with malware components. Such compromised devices will often exhibit behavioral changes in their network traffic patterns, which are potentially detectable using novelty recognition algorithms that have self-supervised multivariate linear and nonlinear outlier sensitivities. According to those authors, this is particularly true when there are insufficient labeled attack instances available for training supervised detection algorithms.

Unsupervised learning is potentially well suited as a "first line defense" within a larger defense-in-depth (DiD) enterprise network security strategy as defined by Alexander (2020). Alexander defined DiD as being used to help prevent and mitigate network intrusions by deploying tools and procedures including firewalls, access controls, and detection methodologies.

As such, the substantive research question to be investigated is, "Can unsupervised deep learning methodologies be used to detect the presence of network intrusion anomalies in network flow traffic metadata?" As an unsupervised learning use case, this research would not have a dependent variable with which to create a prediction or classification model. Rather, an anomaly score will be produced for each network flow, based on a root mean square error (RMSE) value, ignoring any human-labeled identifiers in the experiment data set including a flow label, source and destination internet protocol (IP) addresses, and start and end time stamps in order to minimize experiment bias.

Null Hypothesis and Alternative Hypothesis

The null hypothesis for this research project is, "The anomaly scores produced by the optimized unsupervised MLP autoencoder are incapable of reliably differentiating benign flow network traffic from malicious flow network traffic at or above 0.2 RMSE or above two standard deviations from the mean RMSE in a given daily observation of LUflow '20 telemetry."

The alternative hypothesis is, "The anomaly scores produced by the optimized unsupervised MLP autoencoder are capable of reliably differentiating benign flow network traffic from malicious flow network traffic at or above 0.2 RMSE or above two standard deviations from the mean RMSE in a given daily observation of LUflow '20 telemetry."

METHODOLOGY

Based on some of the latest research incorporating unsupervised learning for anomaly detection as discussed in Deshwal and Sangwan (2021), the increasing prevalence of significant combinations of labeled and unlabeled data and the cumulative improvement of computational resources have enabled various types of deep learning models to become more practical for a variety of application use cases. Further,

Deshwal and Sangwan emphasized how deep neural networks (DNNs) have become more commonplace due to their extremely effective usefulness in the field of machine learning, stating that the primary aim of deep learning is to be able to learn from the primary structure of input data, while also investigating the nonlinear association mapping between the inputs and outputs of the use case data sets.

As such, this research focused exclusively on the application of DNNs for this unsupervised research problem, noting the specific capabilities of autoencoding multilayer perceptron (MLP) neural networks, a subtype of DNNs. The multilayer perceptron algorithm by H2O (LeDell & Poirier, 2020) was used as the unsupervised autoencoder algorithm in this research, utilizing RStudio as the statistical programming platform. It was developed by the RStudio Team (2020) for conducting the one-way ANOVA model to assess the performance of detecting malicious network flows where the flow class labels were not provided to the autoencoder model. Likewise, the IP source address and IP destination addresses were also unknown to the model, as were the start and end time stamps for each flow. These independent variables (IVs) were ignored by the MLP model in order to remove bias from the experiment design.

This research utilizes a curated laboratory network data source provided by Lancashire University's LUflow '20 data set, released via public access from a Github repository as defined in Mills et al. (2021). This curated data set consists of benign, outlier, and malicious class labels for each specific network flow, which as stated are ignored by the MLP autoencoder model but preserved for evaluation of the unsupervised model performance, allowing the ex post facto experiment to assess performance using a one-way analysis of variance between the class label for each flow and the MLP autoencoder reconstruction mean square error (RMSE) anomaly score, to determine the statistical significance of a relationship between the class label and the anomaly score and thus assess the null hypothesis test.

Mills et al. stated that Lancashire University's Cyber Threat Lab produced their labeled, curated data source through a university research facility specifically designed for the purpose of creating a robust data set suitable for evaluating a variety of cluster computing resource anomaly and signature-based malware detection algorithms. As stated by Mills et al., this Cyber Threat Lab environment consists of multiple interconnected components and captures a wide range of malicious threat traffic produced by a large variety of sources, including a variety of diverse "honeypots" that purposely emulate vulnerable network services to attract malicious network activities. Honeypots were defined by Mills, et al. (2021) as being controlled, observed network systems designed to simulate typical enterprise hosts with the intent of capturing malicious adversarial network behaviors and capturing the associated activity metadata.

Those network telemetries were then captured as network flows using Cisco's Joy tool from the various honeypot collectors as discussed in Sangkatsanee et al. (2011). Likewise, known benign labeled network traffic was captured by LUflow '20 from internally accessed virtual machines (VMs) within the Cyber Threat Lab shared infrastructure, where the VMs served the function as both DNS servers and data nodes. The network traffic associated with those nodes was treated as benign as there were no observed attacks taking place within that laboratory environment. Thus, the LUflow '20 data set was developed with the intention of having a robust, curated "ground truth" containing network flows from devices emanating from within the laboratory network that contained both known malicious and known benign telemetries, with an operational period beginning on a daily basis starting in June 2020. Table 1 below provides an example of the distributions of these network flows taking place in an example month of October 2020:

Table 1. October 2020 distribution of flow labels within LUflow '20 Source: Mills et al. (2021)

	Number of Flows	Mean Flows per Day
Total	101,116,515	849,718
Benign	53,921,369	453,120
Malicious	36,810,141	309,328
Outlier	10,385,005	87,268

For the purposes of anomaly detection and producing a sufficiently conservative unsupervised enterprise-class detection model, flows that were curated as being of the outlier class were reclassified as being malicious network flows for the purpose of performance evaluations. This enabled the robustness of the model to be enhanced as it would reduce the risk of a Type II statistical error taking place, when potentially malicious network flows might otherwise be ignored as being simple network outlier events. The various features of the LUflow '20 data set are shown in Table 2, below:

Table 2. Luflow '20 data set features

Number	Name	Description
1	src_ip	The source IP address associated with the flow. This feature is anonymized to the corresponding Autonomous System.
2	src_port	The source port number associated with the flow.
3	dest_ip	The destination IP address associated with the flow. The feature is also anonymized in the same manner as before.
4	dest_port	The destination port number associated with the flow.
5	protocol	The protocol number associated with the flow. For example, TCP is 6.
6	bytes_in	The number of bytes transmitted from source to destination.
7	bytes_out	The number of bytes transmitted from destination to source.
8	num_pkts_in	The packet count from source to destination.
9	num_pkts_out	The packet count from destination to source.
10	entropy	The entropy in bits per byte of the data fields within the flow. This number ranges from 0 to 8.
11	total_entropy	The total entropy in bytes over all of the bytes in the data fields of the flow.
12	mean_ipt	The mean of the interpacket arrival times of the flow.
13	time_start	The start time of the flow in seconds since the epoch.
14	time_end	The end time of the flow in seconds since the epoch.
15	duration	The flow duration time, with microsecond precision.
16	label	The label of the flow, as decided by Tangerine. Either benign, outlier, or malicious.

Source: Mills et al. (2021)

Upon selection of the optimized autoencoder design using the H2O MLP algorithm, the anomaly-scored data set will be examined using log-scale histograms to provide a detailed distribution of the anomaly scores by pseudo-log frequency count, by curated label class. As previously stated, the flow label, source IP, and destination IP addresses, as well as the start and end time for each flow, were ignored by the autoencoder model so as not to bias the unsupervised intent of the research. Labels and the other ignored features were analyzed after the autoencoder model produced the RMSE anomaly scores in order to discern features and patterns produced by the anomaly scores.

Each daily set of flow observations was analyzed by a separate unsupervised MLP autoencoder and provided with distinct sets of RMSE anomaly scores per flow observed. This pattern appeared to consistently demonstrate an increasing likelihood of a known malicious network flow to be taking place at or above the .02 RMSE anomaly score level, or +2 standard deviations above the mean of the RMSE anomaly scores for that day. This appeared to be a consistent, potential "thumbprint" of malicious malware flow traffic occurring within daily network telemetry from known infected host systems within the network, and appeared to be validated by the Central Limit Theorem using our n = 30 number of anomaly score experiments. Thus, a distinct pattern emerged when comparing the log-scale anomaly distributions for the pseudo-log frequency counts, specifically in the extreme right tail of the anomaly score distributions as shown in Figure 1:

Figure 1. Log-scaled RMSE Anomaly Score of the 10-4-4-10 MLP Autoencoder output for November 20, 2020, LUflow '20 flow observations, again showing a significant positive skew of extreme RMSE values for daily malicious network flows
Source: Woolman & Lunsford (2022)

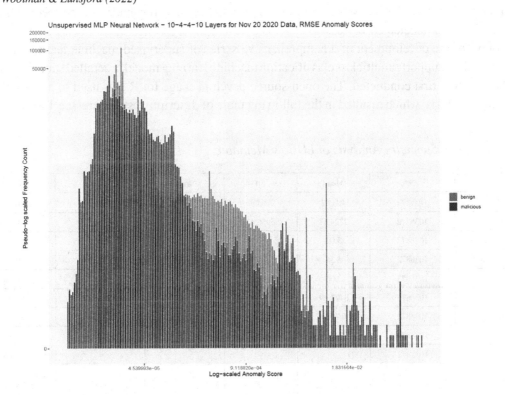

Therefore, it was decided to utilize a one-way analysis of variance test (ANOVA) to determine if there was a statistically significant relationship between the curated label variable and the autoencoder MLP-produced RMSE anomaly score variable from the model output, as a test of statistical significance for the effectiveness of the self-supervised learning MLP autoencoder.

EXPERIMENT DESIGN

The design of experiment used in this study was to employ a series of autoencoding MLP neural networks across a predefined range of randomly selected, daily curated network flow data sets from the LUflow data source, in a quasi-experimental repeated measures methodology. This experimental framework consisted of analyzing a set of previously captured internet protocol network flow traffic data obtained from the curated external source for use in the experiment.

The methodology employed utilizes an optimized unsupervised anomaly scoring model, initially undergoing optimization training using a randomly selected day of observations (Sept. 9, 2020), beginning with a 10-2-10 set of neural network layer parameters, progressing through 10-10-10-10-10, with each parameter denoting a hyper-parameter for the number of perceptrons at each layer of the MLP. As part of the series of daily experiments, an initial determination of optimal MLP autoencoder hyper-parameters would be determined based on observed anomaly sensitivities to labeled outcomes detection based on blind model performance (e.g., ignoring the flow label variable and other potential sources of model bias).

In order to fulfill the objective of accepting or rejecting a null hypothesis with an alpha test statistic, α with a test value of 0.001 was chosen, justified based on normative principles related to economy and evidence constraints and the scope of scientific inquiry. The repeated measures experiment was conducted by cross-validating ($n = 30$) the optimized deep learning MLP model against multiple randomly selected daily network traffic flow observations and producing an error matrix of the median anomaly score to each human labeled flow class.

In support of the development of a comprehensive series of supervised machine learning and deep learning models to support a multiclass classification machine learning model, a detailed statistical analysis of the data set was first conducted. The open-source psych package for R was used to accomplish this first iteration analysis, which resulted in the following table of descriptive statistics (see Table 3, below).

Table 3. Statistical Summary Analysis of LUflow Metadata

Variable	N	Mean	Sd	Min	Max	Data Type
Bytes In	1038872	408.82	2063.43	0	64515	Ratio
Bytes Out	1038872	2394.67	5956.41	0	65533	Ratio
Entropy	1038872	3.03	2.29	0	45.95	Interval
Num Packets Out	1038872	5.36	18.03	0	255	Ratio
Num Packets In	1038872	3.06	10.84	0	255	Ratio
Total Entropy	1038872	8473.09	17029.01	0	1178307	Ratio
Duration	1038872	0.7323	3.67	0	39.14	Ratio
Avg_ipt	1038872	1389298	43320476	0	429467280	Interval
Protocol	1038872	-	-	-	-	Ordinal
Dest_IP	1038872	-	-	-	-	Categorical Factor, **Ignored for AI Training**
Dest_Port	1038872	-	-	-	-	Categorical Factor
Src_IP	1038872	-	-	-	-	Categorical Factor, **Ignored for AI Training**
Src_Port	1038872	-	-	-	-	Categorical Factor
Label	1038872	-	-	-	-	Categorical, **Ignored for AI Training**

Source: Woolman & Lunsford (2022)

UNSUPERVISED (SELF-SUPERVISED) DEEP LEARNING ANOMALY DETECTION FROM NETWORK FLOWS

Utilizing a process discussed in Zhang et al. (2019), a modified grid search hyper-parameter optimization process was conducted with the h2o MLP algorithm to discover an optimized deep learning autoencoder. As Zhang et al. (2019) discussed regarding the need for hyper-parameter tuning, where a challenge is faced by the practitioner utilizing deep learning models because of the great dependency of having properly defined hyper-parameters.

According to Nokeri (2021), these hyper-parameters include the number of hidden layers, the number of units within each distinct layer, the learning rate of the model, and the activation function utilized. Calculation efficiency as well as anomaly score values and discernment sensitivities can vary widely across the various configuration permutations of these hyper-parameters.

Because of the unsupervised nature of the research and the need to have the model ignore IVs that would likely bias the outcome of the experiment, the overall sensitivity of each MLP hyper-parameter permutation was assessed using a maximum methodology. Maximum difference is defined here as the difference between the greatest RMSE (reconstructed mean square of the error) anomaly score for the malicious class data (with class labels only being evaluated after the RMSE anomaly scores are calculated, having been excluded as an IV from the MLP model), and the highest RMSE score for the benign class label.

This process was repeated for a series of different model permutations across combinations of hidden layers, learning rates, and activation functions. Optimization was determined based on the maximum difference between the primary class labels as defined above (malicious versus benign) for each candidate model. The optimal unsupervised MLP model defined using this process was a 4-layer multilayer perceptron autoencoder neural network using the Tanh activation function at 250 training epochs.

MLP AUTOENCODER EXPERIMENT RESULTS ASSESSED STATISTICALLY USING THE ONE-WAY ANALYSIS OF VARIANCE (ANOVA)

In order to make the results of these experiments with multilayer perceptron (MLP) autoencoders falsifiable, a statistical comparison of the experiment outcomes was conducted using a one-way analysis of variance to validate the performance of the unsupervised/self-supervised MLP autoencoder model.

Mangiafico (2016) describes the one-way analysis of variance (ANOVA) as being similar to a t-test, while being capable of comparing more than two groups. Likewise, the ANOVA process is based on the general linear model and is capable of including multiple independent variables that could be either continuous or categorical factor data. This statistical technique was thus employed for testing the ability of the champion MLP autoencoder model to successfully differentiate a statistically significant variation in benign and malicious network traffic flow groups without having to be trained on human-labeled network flow classes.

For this analysis, a one-way ANOVA was conducted using the label factor as our independent variable and using the RMSE anomaly score variable as the dependent variable. Maniafico reminds us that for a one-way ANOVA to be an appropriate statistical test, several criteria must be met, including:

- The dataset should be comprised of one-way data, e.g., having one measurement variable in two or more groups.

- The dependent variables in the dataset is of an interval/ratio statistical type, and is continuous.
- The independent variables is a factor with two or more levels (or groups). This was our label factor variable comprised of two groups, benign and malicious.
- In the general linear model approach, residuals for the model are normally distributed.
- Homoscedasticity or comparative variances from the regression line is present in the dataset.
- The observations among the distinct groups are independent.
- A moderate deviation from normally distributed residuals is permissible.

Likewise, for hypothesis testing using one-way ANOVA, the means of the measurement variable (RMSE anomaly score) for each group must not be equal, in order to be able to reject the null hypothesis in favor of the alternative hypothesis.

For our statistical evaluation of our null hypothesis test, the one-way ANOVA was conducted using the RMSE Anomaly Score dependent variable and the label factor as the two-level independent variable. The result of the ANOVA model produced a p-value of 2e-16, which is compared against an alpha statistic of 0.001. The result was statistically significant; thus we can reject the null hypothesis and not reject the alternative hypothesis. The alternative hypothesis states that "the anomaly scores produced by the optimized unsupervised MLP autoencoder is capable of reliably differentiating benign flow network traffic from malicious flow network traffic at or above 0.2 RMSE or above two standard deviations from the mean RMSE in a given daily observation of LUflow telemetry."

Table 4. One-way ANOVA model results, showing a p-value for the RMSE Anomaly Score DV as being 2e-16, being labeled as statistically significant by the res.aov function in R as it is below an alpha of 0.001

	Df	Sum Sq	Mean Sq	F value	Pr(>F)
RMSE Anomaly Score (DV)	1	3.716	3.716	1006	<2e-16 ***
Residuals	8058	28.088	0.003		

Source: Woolman & Lunsford (2022)

The fitted residuals were then plotted from the ANOVA model, using both a histogram (Figure 4) and a box plot (Figure 3) of fitted residuals. Box the box plot and the histogram of fitted residuals demonstrate a positive skew above the mean; however, this is partially an artifact of the continuous positive score produced by the RMSE anomaly calculation. The primary benefit provided by the box plot in Figure 5 is that the score distributions for both label classes are comprised of approximately equal variances within their distributions. This is particularly well demonstrated in Figure 2 with the histogram that shows a Gaussian distribution with a positive skew artifact due to the positive nature of the RMSE output.

Figure 2. Histogram of One-way ANOVA Residuals, showing an extreme positive skew for all of the observations above a 0.2 RMSE score value Source: Woolman & Lunsford (2022)

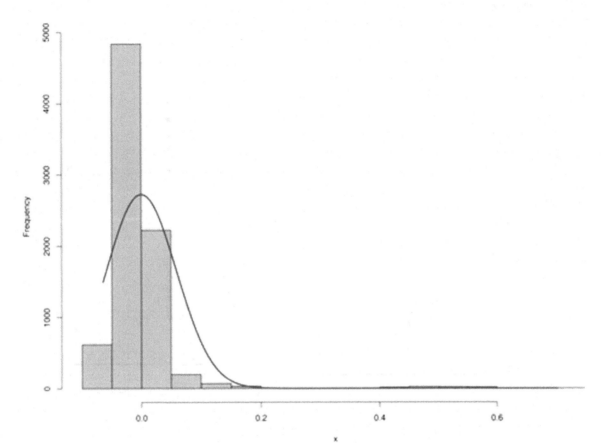

Figure 3. Box plot showing the distribution of RMSE anomaly score observations between label classes, indicating a substantially greater number of score distributions above the 1.5 SD above the third quartile for the malicious class
Source: Woolman & Lunsford (2022)

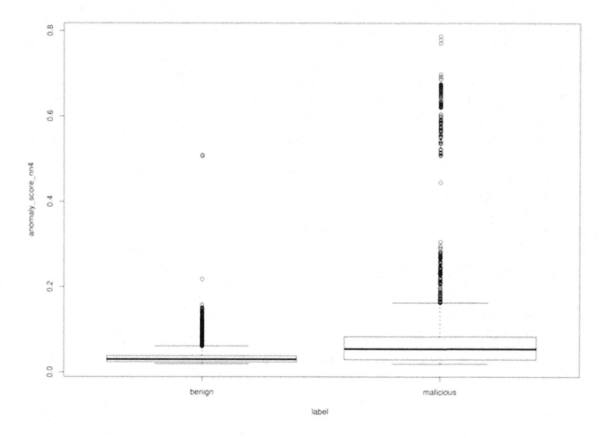

FUTURE RESEARCH DIRECTIONS

One apparent weakness of the MLP autoencoder solution for this use case scenario is that while its effectiveness at discerning malicious activity in NIDS using network flow data is statistically significant, the effectiveness is limited to anomaly scores that are in the extreme right-tail on a log-transformed axis, as shown in Figure 1. Likewise, Figure 1 also illustrates how a majority of the benign class network activities generally fall along the median to first quartile range of the log-transformed RMSE anomaly scores, effectively overlapping with a significant amount of known malicious network activity from the blind study.

It is the authors' belief that it could be possible to enhance the overall effectiveness of an unsupervised methodology with self-supervised feature selection using network flow datasets for this use case by incorporating an additional deep learning algorithm that is specifically designed to analyze time series events. By utilizing an algorithm that is able to "remember" activities on the same port address from the same source host, it may be possible to further differentiate malicious activities from the benign while still limiting the scope of the dataset to network flows and maintaining the blind status of the study by not having to utilize human-labeled flow classes in the training data.

One possible approach that would utilize this direct could be an LSTM autoencoder. An LSTM neural network is defined by Nguyen, Tran, Thomassey and Hamad (2021) is a "Long Short Term Memory" neural network that is a form of Recurrent Neural Network (RNN) that allows for the retention of long-term relationships between elements of the dataset at a given point in time that took place many steps in time previously. This form of neural network incorporates three specific types of control gates: the input gate, the forget gate and the output gate. These RNN features are incorporated into an autoencoder, with its input, output, encoder and decoder neural network layers that compress data into a latent space, and then subsequently decodes the representation into the output layer.

This forces the autoencoding neural network to learn the most salient features of the training data, while incorporating a further sensitivity to similar, related actions that took place previously in the time-series dataset. Thus, an LSTM autoencoder according to Nguyen, et al. (2021) has the potential to learn from complex patterns across long sequences of data. This additional capability of time series awareness is what potentially could make them especially useful for NIDS anomaly detection in this use case scenario with network flow data, as an adjunct to the methodology used in this research. This may be a focus of further upcoming research by the authors.

CONCLUSION

In conclusion, the optimized MLP deep learning autoencoder produced an optimized, unsupervised anomaly detection for known malware telemetry that took place within a specific pattern of score distributions in the experiment data set, relative to known benign network telemetries.

The key findings from this research indicate with a very high degree of confidence with statistical significance that a consistent, daily pattern of malware telemetry exists within the higher positive skew of the flow anomaly score distributions within LUflow '20. Because of the very limited granularities inherent in network flow data as opposed to the far more comprehensive traffic details available with a full packet capture, it is not always possible to confidently discriminate every instance of a malware telemetry event in the daily flow logs within a given LUflow '20 daily data set. It is therefore important to realize the potential application for this research, which could be applied as a first-tier part of a low network bandwidth, low computational resource-consuming application for a larger DiD network intrusion detection system.

Using the concept of defense in depth previously discussed, this research indicates that an unsupervised deep learning model can detect a wide range of malware telemetries over flow data taking place with a sufficient number of flow observations over a given period. Because of the consistent results that took place both within a given randomly selected day and across the multiple *n* randomly selected days, thus far the central limit theorem has been applicable to this system. It is quite likely that given sufficient network flow observations across an enterprise network switch or router collection, the utility of this model can be applied to malware discrimination detection in observation windows significantly below one day of observations.

As such, the potential application for an intelligent learning algorithm that does not require human-labeled curated trained data or the need for updated business rules to detect statistical patterns produced by the latest set of malware threats becomes apparent. The authors believe that the unsupervised MLP autoencoder configured at or similarly to the model proposed in this research could have substantial utility as part of a comprehensive suite of defense-in-depth network intrusion detection systems for enterprise networks.

One key advantage of utilizing such a system on network flow data such as in LUflow '20 is that the network bandwidth resource consumption is greatly minimized and can be conducted using existing routers and switches, as this remains within layer 3 of the OSI model, and no specialized software clients or agents need to be installed on the host systems. Conversely, conducting packet capture requires producing a comprehensive mirror of all network packets as they travel across the network to enable a deep packet inspection.

Such a deep packet inspection process often requires the installation of special application software to be connected to a mirror port, and the connection of cables from these mirror ports to the deep packet inspection application. This potentially can overload large network systems, greatly increase the complexity of managing enterprise class networks, and require a greater degree of technical skill to interpret the packet capture information.

The use of the proposed unsupervised/self-supervised deep learning anomaly scoring model for network flow data thus has a potential significant performance and resource utilization advantage, and can potentially be used as a "tripwire" in a multilayer defense-in-depth strategy to determine when a more detailed forensic packet capture process should be enabled when malware telemetry is detected, as part of a network subnet isolation and similar layered mitigation and triage defense strategy.

REFERENCES

Alexander, R. (2020). Reducing threats by using Bayesian networks to prioritize and combine defense in depth security measures. *Journal of Information Security*, *11*(3), 121–137. doi:10.4236/jis.2020.113008

Chess, D. M., & White, S. R. (1987). An undetectable computer virus. IBM Thomas J. Watson Research Center.

Cohen, F. (1987). Computer viruses: Theory and experiments. *Computers & Security*, *6*(1), 22–35. doi:10.1016/0167-4048(87)90122-2

Deshwal, D., & Sangwan, P. (2021). *A comprehensive study of deep neural networks for unsupervised deep learning. In Artificial intelligence for sustainable development: Theory, practice and future applications*. Springer.

Haefner, K., & Ray, I. (2021). Trust and verify: A complexity-based IoT behavioral enforcement method. In *International symposium on cyber security cryptography and machine learning* (pp. 432–450). Springer. 10.1007/978-3-030-78086-9_32

Hahn, T. V., & Mechefske, C. K. (2021). Self-supervised learning for tool wear monitoring with a disentangled-variational-autoencoder. *International Journal of Hydromechatronics*, *4*(1), 69–98. doi:10.1504/IJHM.2021.114174

Hinton, G. E., Krizhevsky, A., & Wang, S. D. (2011, June). Transforming auto-encoders. In *International conference on artificial neural networks* (pp. 44-51). Springer, Berlin, Heidelberg.

Iran Computer Incident Response Team. (2012). *Identification of a new targeted cyber-attack. Iran Computer Incident Response Team*. Accessed July 12, 2021, from https://www.webcitation.org/682bfkhaU?url=http://www.certcc.ir/index.php?name=news&file=article&sid=1894&newlang=eng

Kaspersky Lab ZAO. (2012). *The Flame: Questions and Answers*. SECURELIST. Kaspersky Lab Expert. Accessed July 13, 2021 from https://securelist.com/the-flame-questions-and-answers/34344/

Kaspersky Lab ZAO. (2014). Generic detection [Poster presentation]. Security Anomaly Summit 2014, CyberSecurity Summit, San Francisco, CA.

LeDell, E., & Poirier, S. (2020). *H2O AutoML: Scalable automatic machine learning* [Conference session]. 7th ICML Workshop on Automated Machine Learning (AutoML). https://www.automl.org/wp-content/uploads/2020/07/AutoML_2020_paper_61.pdf

Mangiafico, S. S. (2016). Summary and analysis of extension program evaluation in R. *Rutgers Cooperative Extension*, *125*, 16–22.

Mills, R., Marnerides, A. K., Broadbent, M., & Race, N. (2021). Practical Intrusion Detection of Emerging Threats. *IEEE eTransactions on Network and Service Management*.

Nguyen, H. D., Tran, K. P., Thomassey, S., & Hamad, M. (2021). Forecasting and Anomaly Detection approaches using LSTM and LSTM Autoencoder techniques with the applications in supply chain management. *International Journal of Information Management*, *57*, 102282. doi:10.1016/j.ijinfomgt.2020.102282

Nokeri, T. C. (2021). Machine learning using H2O. In *Data science revealed* (pp. 231–246). Apress. doi:10.1007/978-1-4842-6870-4_13

RStudio Team. (2020). *RStudio: Integrated development for R. RStudio*. Accessed July 20, 2021 from https://www.rstudio.com/

Sangkatsanee, P., Wattanapongsakorn, N., & Charnsripinyo, C. (2011). Practical real-time intrusion detection using machine learning approaches. *Computer Communications*, *34*(18), 2227–2235. doi:10.1016/j.comcom.2011.07.001

Woolman, T. A., & Lee, S. (2021). Network intrusion detection using deep learning and machine learning for multinomial classification. *International Journal of Cyber-Security and Digital Forensics*, *9*(4), 155–181. doi:10.17781/P002678

Zhang, X., Chen, X., Yao, L., Ge, C., & Dong, M. (2019). Deep neural network hyperparameter optimization with orthogonal array tuning. In *International conference on neural information processing* (pp. 287–295). Springer. 10.1007/978-3-030-36808-1_31

Zhang, Z., Lei, Y., Mao, X., Yan, M., Xu, L., & Zhang, X. (2021). A study of effectiveness of deep learning in locating real faults. *Information and Software Technology*, *131*, 106486. doi:10.1016/j.infsof.2020.106486

ADDITIONAL READING

Hu, Y. H., & Hwang, J. N. (2018). Introduction to neural networks for signal processing. In *Handbook of neural network signal processing* (pp. 1–1). CRC Press. doi:10.1201/9781315220413-1

Jiang, J. R., Kao, J. B., & Li, Y.-L. (2021). Semi-supervised time series anomaly detection based on statistics and deep learning. *Applied Sciences*, *11*(15), 6698. doi:10.3390/app11156698

Toğaçar, M., Cömert, Z., & Ergen, B. (2021). Intelligent skin cancer detection applying autoencoder, MobileNetV2 and spiking neural networks. *Chaos, Solitons, and Fractals*, *144*, 110714. doi:10.1016/j.chaos.2021.110714

KEY TERMS AND DEFINITIONS

Anomaly Detection: Anomaly detection refers to finding unusual events or outliers within a given dataset. Many techniques for detecting anomalies for univariate statistical data exist in statistics, and multivariate techniques exist as well but are more complex and less scalable with standard statistical methods, and are also potentially less accurate due to a traditional model being limited to homogenized methods across all variables and generally being limited to linear relationships between independent variables. Anomaly detection in this paper utilizes a multilayer perceptron neural network that is potentially more sensitive to complex features of the multivariate data including both linear and nonlinear attributes.

Autoencoding Neural Network: A form of unsupervised machine learning that utilizes multiple layers within a neural network to first encode and then later decode the attributes of information about a dataset, for the purpose of learning which attributes are significant features. This feature extraction process is often referred to as a self-supervised process. The autoencoding neural network is then able to produce an anomaly score for each observation of data using a reconstructed mean square of the error (RMSE) score, with higher RMSE scores denoting increasing difficulty in reproducing the observation in the decoding layer of the neural network. Thus, higher RMSE scores generally denote a greater potential anomaly in the multivariate dataset observation.

Deep Learning: Deep learning refers to a subset of the field of machine learning that utilizes a type of neural network algorithm that utilizes successive layers of neurons called perceptrons for the purpose of representation learning. The learning conducted by these various forms of neural networks can be either supervised, semi-supervised or unsupervised machine learning.

Multilayer Perceptron: Also known as an MLP neural network, they are a type of deep learning neural network algorithm that is composed of multiple layers of perceptrons. They contain at least one "hidden" layer of perceptrons within their network, and all MLP models contain an input layer, at least one hidden layer and an output layer. The MLP models generally contain a non-linear activation function and thus have sensitivities to non-linear relationships present in the dataset. MLP models are typically referred to as "vanilla" neural networks, as opposed to recurrent neural networks, convolutional neural networks and other more mission-specific forms of neural networks.

Network Flow: Network flow data typically refers to metadata (higher level digital records) which characterize connections made across a digital network, without recording the exact content of each network activity. Network flows typically contain the internet protocol addresses and port numbers utilized in each recorded network connection event, along with protocols, time stamps and connection durations, source and destination hosts, and network interfaces used. Network flows do not include the actual content of each network connection, thus making it a much more "lightweight" information monitoring tool when compared to a packet capture log which does include the connection content and related content attributes.

Network Intrusion Detection System (NIDS): A hardware device and/or software application designed to monitor a digital network for malicious activity, violations of network policies and recording network activities for analysis. NIDS systems typically record incoming network traffic, from the perspective of an enterprise host system. NIDS systems are traditionally sub-divided into classes, such

M

as signature based (relying on specific, pre-defined patterns of network behaviors to identify specific malware events) and anomaly based systems. Anomaly based NIDS systems are intended to be more adaptable to previously unknown malware attacks because they are not limited to being pre-programmed for specific malware signatures, but are more challenging to develop.

Unsupervised Learning: Unsupervised machine learning is designed to discover patterns or groupings within datasets where no dependent or target variable is present. It is typically used to discover relationships where no labeled outcome variable is known to the algorithm and is frequently used in the area of clustering, association and dimensionality reduction. For the purposes of this paper, unsupervised learning is used for anomaly detection within multivariate data without the use of a labeled outcome dependent variable.

Section 33
Management Analytics

Evaluation of Tourism Sustainability in La Habana City

Maximiliano Emanuel Korstanje

🆔 https://orcid.org/0000-0002-5149-1669

University of Palermo, Argentina

Martha Omara Robert Beatón

University of Havana, Cuba

Maite Echarri Chávez

University of Havana, Cuba

Massiel Martínez Carballo

University of Havana, Cuba

Victor Martinez Robert

University of Havana, Cuba

INTRODUCTION

In the field of sustainability, the specialized literature shows some concern regarding the integration among the global, regional and national levels of planning (Gunn 1977; Getz, 1986). In the tourism industry, the evaluation of sustainability, as well as the co-creation of added value, is of paramount importance to develop smarter and more resilient destinations (Gossling 2017). At a closer look, the term sustainability was originally well-grounded in a solid foundation capable to be articulated with development programs, deficiencies persist in putting it into practice due to the complexity of the interrelationships between its different dimensions. What seems to be equally important, these interactions are manifested in all phases of the destination management process resulting in the complexity of the diagnosis to optimize the relevant decision-making process (Torres, 2016; Um, 2010 Ramos and Caeiro, 2010; Pulido and Sánchez, 2009; Pérez and Nel-lo, 2009; Pérez et. Al, 2009; Blancas et al., 2009 Martínez, López, and Santos, 2007; Choi and Sirikaya, 2005).

Based on previous models and taking into account their shortcomings (Leiper, 1979; Miossec, 1997; Mill and Morrison, 2002; McKercher, 2004), Martín (2006) proposes a pentagonal model that defines three major dimensions of the tourism system: the exogenous subsystems (tourist environment), the endogenous subsystems (tourism) and the macro environment (general environment), which are related to each other in a process called tourism dynamics, which leads to responses or impacts. These responses or impacts that take place in tourism dynamics are still very difficult to analyze with the prevailing models, methods and tools to assess sustainability in a destination (Palomeque et al., 2018; Torres, 2016; Vera et al., 2013; Velasco, 2011; Ávila & Barrado, 2005).

The tourist destination should be considered an integral part of the tourist system, comprising endogenous and exogenous sub-systems. In this way, the conception of the tourist system alludes to a

DOI: 10.4018/978-1-7998-9220-5.ch140

much deeper integration of relationships and interests in different stakeholders which determine tourist behaviour (Pearce 2005; Swarbrooke & Horner, 2007). One might speculate that some studies around destination deal only with the basic dimensions of relationships (structure, contents or configuration), not considering other elements such as the interrelationships that occur between the different processes that take place in it, supply and demand in a causal logic and its operation; thereby losing the explanatory potential they have for the management of tourist destinations.

In Cuba, the research related to the dynamics of the tourism system has studied its conceptualization (Martín, 2006), its development (Figueras, 2008) and specific aspects around its components to propose methodologies for diagnosis, evaluation and forecasting of future trends (Delgado, 2014; La Serna, 2014; Perelló, 2005), its economic and spatial performance, and the impacts at a social level (Vargas, 2013; Pérez, 2013; Pérez, 2011; Echarri, 2006). These approaches assume that the destination is a space whose management depends largely on the functions of the different actors who are present in it. Management by functions defines and establishes work areas by creating several specialized and hierarchical units that are responsible for different specific activities but that do not allow an integrated understanding of the destination, generating fragmentation problems that hinder the process of visualizing and managing the interactions that must exist between all parties (Coaguila 2017, Rojas 2014; Plasencia, 2013; Fraguela et al., 2012; Trishler, 1998; Taylor and Ford 1980). Based on these shortcomings that exist to assess the sustainability of a destination with all the interrelationships that occur in tourism dynamics, it is necessary to look at other areas of knowledge such as the process approach, which until today has been generally used to assess performance within the business. A process- approach allows to establish an objective basis for the development of research regarding this issue, since it recognizes the modelling of systems as a set of interrelated processes through cause-effect links that sustain the systemic vision of a tourist destination, facilitates the integration in the same instrument (the process map) and enables the analysis of a tourist destination through its different stages (planning, implementation, verification and control). Taking into account these considerations, the present research has its general objective to evaluate the sustainability of a tourist destination with a focus on processes. In the following lines we give the strengths of the process approach when applied to tourist destinations:

- The Model allows rapid integration of multiple stakeholders in different levels of the tourist system as well as the entire value chain of the tourist product.
- The process approach is situated as an efficient instrument that helps in the planning process as well as the decision-making process for policymakers.
- It gives a better focus on the interested group while homogenizing the stakeholders´ goals.
- It includes and potentiates the added value while cutting costs.
- Through an empowered community, the model reorganizes and optimizes the labour relations in tourist destinations.

THEORETICAL BACKGROUND

System theory has been used in different sciences to recognize complex processes where societies, territories and economies articulate parts that together make up a functional totality in reality from a methodological perspective.

In tourism processes, at least three vertices can be distinguished in a possible systemic articulation (Fernández et al, 1997; Martín, 2010):

a) Tourists as the final objects of any system, tourists as consumers and clients who decide which products they are going to consume and dictate the level of satisfaction and the amount of expenditure expected. Their decision is conditioned by their sociodemographic profile, the media and by tour operators. In economic terms: the touristic demand is segmented from the generating region.

b) The agents that design and manage tourism products compete in the markets to obtain higher shares in the generating regions, and configure some complexes of productive articulation that are usually considered as a single economic sector by conventional accounting. That is, tourism is usually only understood to be the hotel, travel agency, transport and restaurants subsectors. The public-private duality in tourist destinations is part of an environment of high competition between territorial and urban marketing and the marketing of products by tourism companies, a border that tends to blur due to the need to develop joint promotion efforts in tourism markets.

c) Tourist spaces and travel mobility as an articulation between emission and reception; especially the territory is a good reference key to structure the parts of a tourism system. The transport, connectivity and tourist mobility systems are organized by travel entities between sending and receiving destinations.

Based on these criteria, it is considered that the local society must be added to these vertices if a sustainable approach is to be achieved in the management of the destination since it has a certain degree of impact on the economic, social, political and cultural areas of society.

Various socio-economic and cultural actors converge in tourist destinations that make up the local society. They are generally called stakeholders and have a great level of influence in their development. These actors, according to Torres (2016), Mascarenhas (2010), Coelho (2010), Schianetz and Kavanagh (2008), are the host community, tourists, non-governmental organizations, owners of state and private entities, the destination managers, political and institutional authorities at different levels (local, regional or national), as well as academics. The participation of these actors influences the development of destinations and constitutes an important element to take into account when managing a destination as a tourism product. When analyzing the distinctive characteristics of business organizations managed with a focus on processes, one of those that prevail is the focus on the client and stakeholders, in addition to systemic approach, orientation to the results of the processes and the system, continuous improvement, integration of suppliers, flexibility in the design of processes with an emphasis on added value, competence, awareness (lifelong learning, executive leadership), empowerment, participation and delegation) (Coaguila, 2017; Ulacia, 2007; Zaratiegui, 1999 ; Roure, Moriño and Rodríguez, 1997; Pérez. 1996; Harrington, 1993; Follet, 1924). Characteristics that favor the study of the different interrelations that concur in the tourist dynamics of a destination.

According to systems theory, the organization is a set formed by interrelated parts that constitute a coherent whole and develop a systematic framework for the description of the empirical world (Riascos, 2006; Jiménez, 2005), a criterion that coincides with the expressed by Coaguila (2017), Rojas (2014), Escudero (2013) and Zaratiegui (1999) who state that the organization is a set of interacting systems made up of processes. These systemic organizations have a structure, which can change over time, depending on the conditions of the environment and the internal changes that are experienced. Different elements can be identified in it (Narváez, Lavell and Pérez 2009):

1) The inputs, which are received from external suppliers (extracted and assimilated from the environment) and are to be transformed into a product or final result.

2) The processes, constituted by the successive interactions that must exist between the units that intervene and participate within the organization to progressively and jointly transform the inputs until the expected product or final result is obtained.

3) The product or final result that the organization generates responds to the requirements and specifications of the client or external user.

4) The customer or user of the product is the one who feeds the system with their requirements and the specifications or characteristics of the product that is to be achieved.

The tourist destination shares the components of its structure with the systemic organizations but redefines them considering the inputs such as the resources of the environment/territory, the processes like interactions of the product, transformation units, which it translates into the supply and customers, being these last the main stakeholders as they are the ones who feed the system according to their requirements and whose satisfaction constitutes the outputs. In their integration, they must be oriented towards the same goal within the framework of a shared mission. Organizations are usually associated with companies or social movements, but not with a territory or destination. However, it can be considered that, although systemic organizations have a clear objective with specific characteristics, the tourist destination can be regarded as a systemic territorial organization if it is taken into account that, in the same way, it responds to these characteristics that distinguish them, to the elements that make it up and its analysis requires a systemic approach, responding to defined objectives.

In this perspective, the tourist destination is a systemic organization, which is framed in a territory, has defined geographical limits, and is made up of interrelated parts that constitute a coherent whole, which presents different natural and anthropic characteristics, formed by spatial (territorial resources and tourist infrastructures), administrative (legislation, policies), productive (factors and resources of production, agents, and investment) and social (visitors, tourists and community) elements, with a diversity of interests, and that function as a system.

This condition provides it with the ability to respond and adapt to the impacts of the environment, learn from its own experiences and mistakes, be able to develop through its self-regulation and control mechanisms, based on the dynamics generated by the interrelationships that exist between the units that integrate it as well as their reciprocal interdependencies based on common objectives.

Consequently, it is feasible to adapt the foundations of the approach to processes to assess the sustainability of tourist destinations, taking into account that the interconnections and interrelationships that exist in the tourism system materialize in it, which, as a container and receiver of the tourism activity is the space where the tourism system takes place, so there is a dual relationship: the system includes the destination and the system is materialized or visualized in the destination, so the destination is a local expression of the tourist system. The sustainable development of tourist destinations requires the informed participation of all relevant agents of local society, as well as firm political leadership to achieve broad collaboration and establish consensus. It also requires a continuous process and constant monitoring of the evaluation of its sustainability, taking into account its incidents, to introduce preventive or corrective measures. The sustainable tourism guidelines apply to all forms of tourism in all types of destinations, including mass tourism and various market segments. However, it can be a paradox that the very operation of the tourism sector generates contradictions in the achievement of sustainable objectives. Even when large transnational companies maintain codes of corporate responsibility, the long-distance touristic flows imply high levels of use of air transportation, recognized as one of the main sources of air pollution. In receptive countries and destinations, they tend to limit their local commitment through direct employment, and the flight of capital abroad is recognized as an aggravating factor for developing economies, conditioning and impacting their sustainability. Sustainability is a transversal phenomenon that must be inserted into the international, national and local logic and dynamics, articulating the objectives of the Sustainable Development Agenda to 2030.

METHODOLOGY

The methodological trajectory of the investigation followed a qualitative-quantitative approach, of the descriptive, analytical-exploratory kind and comprised 4 phases. Phase 1: This phase was based on the research line "Sustainable development of tourist destinations" of the Faculty of Tourism of the University of Havana, which currently works on a project aimed at sustainable tourism evaluation with a process approach. This research group has carried out a wide range of studies that deal with real problems in the operation of tourist companies and destinations, leading to results that show the need for new instruments from other areas of knowledge aimed at recognizing and understanding the holistic vision of sustainability in tourist destinations.

In this phase, the main method used was the bibliographic analysis that consisted of the compilation of information from the consulted literature, revealed concepts interpreted and defined from different perspectives, for which a systemic, dialectical, historical-logical and inductive-deductive analysis were carried out, which allowed structuring the investigation; also to present it from the simple to the complex and following logical, linear, sequential and relatable thought processes. Phase 2: the methodological elements were defined to adapt the foundations of the approach to processes in the evaluation of the sustainability of tourist destinations, based on systematizing and carrying out a comparative analysis of the experiences in the application of methodologies for this approach in businesses, which altogether with the application of other methods and techniques made it easier to determine the processes, subprocesses and the interest groups in the tourism system. To do this, a survey of experts was carried out, which consisted of four closed questions related to the process approach and their application in the sustainable evaluation of tourist destinations, which, among the groupings recognized by the literature, is more closely related to the characteristics that distinguish a tourist destination, so the interest group can be represented.

A group of 25 candidates was selected taking as criteria their experience and knowledge in the topics related to the sustainable evaluation of tourist destinations and the approach to processes, having served as a researcher, or research advisor that addresses these issues and the principle of Willingness and interest in participating in the study.

The coefficient of expertise or competence (K) was determined from the coefficient of knowledge (Kc) and argumentation (Ka), using the formula K = ½ (kc + ka). The criterion considered to establish the argumentation and competence coefficient as reported by (González, 2005). Having said this, the broad utilization of these coefficients facilitates the inter-variable connection. Among the 25 candidates, 15 were selected to participate in the first and second rounds of the Delphi method. The survey on the relationship approach to processes - tourist destinations was applied to them, which yielded the following results: all the experts stated that the approach can be applied to processes in a tourist destination, that they did not know if it had been used in this case scenario before and that it was necessary for its incorporation the usage of sustainability criteria and indicators. The 86.7% of the experts chosen agreed that the grouping that most corresponds to the characteristics of a destination responds to the planning processes, product and service, resource management, and measurement - analysis. Also, 100% of them considered that the main stakeholders in a destination are: workers, clients, suppliers, investors, creditors, executives, community and government.

From the results obtained, another questionnaire was sent to them to determine the sub-processes that correspond to each of the processes in a tourist destination of the selected classification. All the sub-processes proposed for the planning processes, product and service realization and resource management, were considered by the experts. There were only discrepancies in the measurement-analysis process, where none of these recognized the audits of the processes, only 46.6% coincided with the improvement and 100% responded to the satisfaction of the interest group, a result that according to the criterion set out in the observations is attributed to the fact that in other organizations process audits are feasible due to their characteristics, but in the case of destinations, where the management models have the human being as their centre, the measurements must respond to the satisfaction of the expectations of the stakeholders. At the same time, in this phase, a preliminary list of sustainability indicators was drawn up for the resource management and product and service processes, which have already been used in previous studies and have demonstrated their viability (Blanco, 2016; Deliz, 2015; Robert, 2010; Salinas, 2008; Echarri, 2005).

The planning process was not taken into account in this list of indicators because it is not evaluated, it is only described, based on what was proposed by Beltrán et al., (2002), who consider that when there is a process where the Outputs are spaced apart in time, they are few and the conditions for obtaining them are not uniform, it is not possible to carry out a statistical analysis. At the same time, the measurement and analysis process was not taken into account in this list of indicators since their evaluation only responds to the satisfaction of the interest group from their perception through surveys.

The list of indicators was submitted to the criteria of experts through the Delphi method, a mathematical, prospective method based on experts. The effectiveness of this technique lies in its three distinguishing characteristics: anonymity, controlled feedback, and group statistical response (Cabero and Infante, 2014; Ortega, 2008; Landeta, 2005; Turoff and Linstone, 1976). Only 79% of the indicators were considered by more than 85% of the experts. These were sent in a second round for the confirmation of the final list. The reliability of the three questionnaires applied was determined by calculating Cronbach's Alpha coefficient, an internal consistency index whose values range between 0 and 1 and which is used to check whether the instrument is reliable or not. The report by Hernández, Fernández and Baptista (2010) was considered, which establishes that: it is acceptable if the value is higher than (0.70). The values obtained ranged between (0.79-and 0.86), which allows us to infer that the surveys are consistent and the results obtained are valid.

In **Phase 3**, the methodological procedure is designed to evaluate the sustainability of tourist destinations with a process approach.

In **Phase 4**, the proposed procedure was validated using the Delphi method. In the first round, the 15 selected experts were sent the instrument. They were requested to report the degree of relevance observed in terms of the theoretical-methodological coherence, the content of the procedure, phases and structure, technical language used, and whether the proposed procedure would, in their opinion, contribute to the evaluation of the sustainability of tourist destinations. Also, some specific considerations of elements to take into account to adapt the approach to processes in tourist destinations, such as sustainability indicators.

In the second and final round, the unified arguments of the opinions of the experts in the previous round were shown, so that they could examine each question in more detail and thus achieve a consensus of opinions. Once the procedure has been validated by experts, it was implemented in the Historic Center of Havana.

RESULTS

E

The purpose of the procedure was to evaluate the sustainability of tourist destinations from a process approach with a holistic vision, which integrates the complex dynamics from the very operation of the processes that concur in it, to obtain feedback and enhance an improved performance of the actors that take part in the system at the destination level by improving and satisfying the needs and expectations of stakeholders.

Premises for its application:

1- Existence of a territorial development manager.
2- Evidence of a management model.
3- Sustainability as a transversal axis to the tourism development plan.
4- Risk perspective in the territorial development plan.
5- Tourism is a declared objective in the territorial development plan.

Basic principles that govern the design and implementation of the procedure:

- Systemic approach: understood as the interaction and articulation of the components of the tourism system in the destination. Their integration is the alignment of the subsystems that compose it. Obtaining a system as a superior quality, characterized by interdependence and interaction between all the parts that make it up, constantly feeding back and interacting with the environment.
- Integrated approach to the stakeholder: It starts from identifying the stakeholder, achieving an integrated approach to their needs and expectations, which facilitates standardizing the design of common objectives.
- Risk approach: acts preventively through proper planning, review and improvement of the tourism system in the destination, with different levels of risk depending on its capacity and the processes that comprise it to meet the objectives.
- Dynamic: Its application allows the elements to be updated at any time that is required, to guarantee the feedback of each process.
- Flexibility: it can be implemented in any tourist destination that needs to evaluate the sustainability of its management, provided that they comply with the established premises.
- Improvement: it is established in an improvement environment by achieving the integration of flows and feedback, both from the environment and the current state of the destination's processes, also facilitating improvement proposals.

The following is the design of the procedure to evaluate the sustainability of tourist destinations with a process approach. It consists of four phases and nine sub-phases

Figure 1.

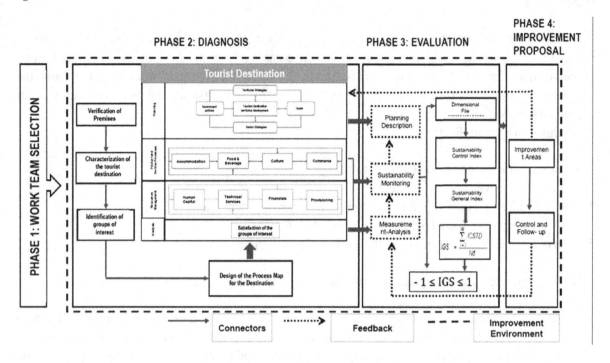

Implementation of the Procedure: A Reference from the Historic Center of Havana

The Historic Center of Havana declared a National Monument in Law No. 2, Law of National and Local Monuments, of August 4, 1977, comprises two differentiated areas: the old city within the walls and the strip of what was distributed from the ancient City Wall (Las Murallas). It occupies an area of 214 ha, with 242 blocks, housing a population of 55,484 inhabitants. On the other hand, it represents only 0.3% of the metropolitan area and 49% of the Old Havana municipality, as it completely contains five of its seven popular councils: Cathedral, Plaza Vieja, Belén, and Prado, San Isidro, and part of Jesús María. The Office of the Historian of the City of Havana (OHCH) has been involved in the safeguarding of Cuban cultural heritage since its foundation in 1938. As of 1993, Decree-Law 143 was approved, which confers on the Historic Center the status of Priority Zone for Conservation, which makes the OHCH the legal figure responsible for the site. The Historic Center of Havana is governed by a new management instrument: the Special Comprehensive Development Plan (PEDI), a tool for planning, managing and controlling comprehensive development and land use planning. It was developed in 1998 and was born from the agreement between the OHCH, the public institutions with competencies in the territory and the citizens; It was updated in 2011 and is subjected to a process of public citizen and institutional consultation. Based on this, the Special Comprehensive Development Plan is built until 2030 (Cruz, 2017). The Special Comprehensive Development Plan until 2030 (PEDI 2030), in line with the National Plan for Economic and Social Development for the same period in the country and with the 2030 Agenda for Sustainable Development, establishes urban planning and development strategies for the Historic Center in five dimensions of sustainability: institutional, cultural, environmental, economic and social, to guarantee the preservation of tangible and intangible cultural heritage (Cruz, 2017).

The territorial management instrument (PEDI) guides urban planning and development, with a comprehensive approach to the risk of changes in the destination. Tourism is an economic activity prioritized in the development of the territory as established by the PEDI until 2030, included in the general objective 2.8 that proposes: Increase, extend and diversify the modalities of tourism, and in the specific 2.8.1: Increase the hosting capacity; 2.8.2: Increase the number of activities associated with tourism: culture, gastronomy and specialized commerce, recreation and physical culture; and 2.8.3: Develop other forms of tourism. Its great wealth of historical-cultural attractions makes its urban framework a must-see, frequented by more than 60% of the tourists that visit the country. It currently represents 35% of Havana's tourist income, 11% of its housing plant and 22% of hotel overnight stays. The hotel entities add up to a total of 29, representing 37% of the hotels in Havana; the number of hotel rooms at the end of 2018 reached a figure of 3,455. Rooms belonging to the non-state sector (private) add up to a total of 1,390 for 28%, overnight stays 669 863 for 22%, the average foreign occupancy is 70% and the average stay behaves at 2.6. The projection of the state investment process until 2030 should incorporate 16 new hotel facilities for a total of 1,044 (Cruz, 2017). The non-hotel network, on the other hand, is characterized by its great diversity. Regarding the gastronomic services of the territory, Palmares stands out. To this must be added the impulse of the gastronomic activity promoted by the new restaurant owners make up the private sector. Regarding the retail trade, it is necessary to mention the establishments that include both specialized heritage stores, as well as mixed tourist stores dedicated to the sale of Cuban products in great demand by tourists (Rums, Coffee, Tobacco, Handicrafts, Souvenirs and others).

Processes of the Management Model of the Historic Center of Havana

The work sessions with the work team allowed defining as interest groups the community, the clients, the President of the Popular Cathedral Council, Deputy Director of the Master Plan, President of the San Cristóbal Travel Agency, Business Director of Gaviota (accommodation, Head of food and beverages at CIMEX, Director of the UEB Heritage Management.). The map was drawn up where the existing interactions between the processes are established, following the type of grouping that assumes the planning, product and service and measurement-analysis processes, with their sub-processes.

Figure 2.

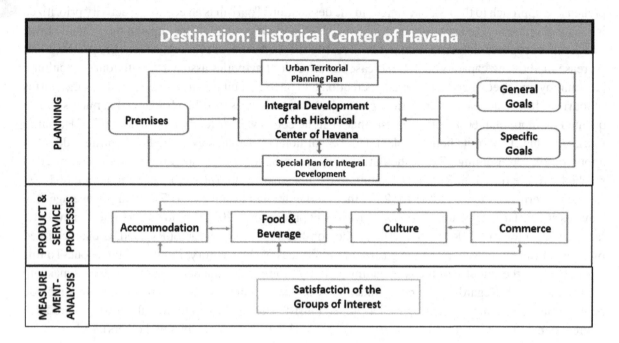

The planning process is only described, based on what was stated by Beltrán et al. (2002), who consider that, when there is a process where the outputs are spaced apart in time, they are few and the conditions for obtaining them are not uniform, it is not possible to carry out a statistical analysis. For the measurement and analysis process, the evaluation only responds to the satisfaction of the stakeholders from their perception through surveys.

Evaluation of Tourism Sustainability from the Process of Realization of Products and Services

Its evaluation is carried out through the environmental, socio-cultural and economic dimensions, and includes the analysis of the periods 2000-2014 and 2017-2018, for which the trend is built from real data. The hosting sub-process is taken as a reference, according to the decisions of stakeholders.

Analysis of the Economic Dimension

Eight indicators were established, which respond to sustainable criteria with behaviour as follows: the total number of rooms has experienced a gradual growth in the period 2000-2020 with positive trends, with an increase in the number of rooms, related to the opening of new facilities in the years 2017-2018, which accelerated growth rates and projections declare that this growth will continue until 2022. The occupancy rate maintains a downward trend in the period of analysis, with a progressive decrease in the values of 2017-2018, conditioned by tourists' behaviour. Although the rooms are occupied daily to maintain a slight growth during the period 2000-2014, a progressive decrease can be seen between 2017 and 2018, where there is a fall in the order of 73 952 rooms occupied daily, determined fundamentally by the reduction in the occupancy rate. The rooms availability per day for the period maintains a negative behaviour in general, which can be determined by the increase in rooms out of order and those dedicated to other uses, which also affect maintenance costs. The average stay maintains a positive performance in the period 2000-2020, even when the trend curve is almost linear and decreases in 2017 with values of 2.05 and showing slight growth in 2018 (2.36 days). Physical tourists in the period have a negative trend, showing a peak of growth in real values during 2000-2005, with a considerable decrease in 2010 and slight fluctuations throughout the period, with a marked decrease in 2018. Daytime tourists display a negative trend, even though real values experienced sustained growth rates between 2000-and 2014, with a peak in 2005 associated with the increase in physical tourists. Profits also illustrate a negative trend, even when the 2018-2017 values are not considered reliable figures (the data referred to is before taxes). This behaviour may be associated with other indicators such as cost per dollar of revenue and revenue per day for tourists.

ANALYSIS OF THE SOCIO-CULTURAL DIMENSION

The socio-cultural dimension is described using seven indicators: Total workers in the period 2000-2020 show a positive trend, with slight increase rates, a tendency that could be reversed with the opening of new facilities as expected in the projection until 2022. The indicators for the number of workers at the intermediate educational level, the upper secondary level and the higher level are closely related, so the analysis will be carried out as a whole. Those of medium level has maintained a positive trend even when the increases are discrete, with fluctuations between the years 2012-2014, which recover the growth rates in 2017 and 2018 linked to the opening of new tourist facilities, which demand skilled workforce. The increase in upper-level workers affects the decrease of the upper-middle level, determined because graduates of the latter graduate from the higher level, which implies that the trend is positive for all three, which indicates a higher qualification of the workforce. Regarding the Total of buildings reused for accommodation, it is valid to note that the performance shows promising signs since they have maintained a positive trend with sustained growth, with a significant increase in 2015, when they decide to rehabilitate six new facilities, which began its operation gradually between the years 2018-2022. The re-functionalization of properties and the recovery of traditional uses have led to the authenticity of the design, the setting and the architecture constituting an identifying element of the tourist offer of the Historic Center, so the behaviour as a trend is positive, even with slight decreases in 2015, which recovered their growth rates in the following years. The incorporation of culture and its different manifestations as a complement to the main product that is offered makes its presence grow, maintaining a positive development and contributing to the rescue of cultural traditions in the proposal of national and/or local art shows.

ANALYSIS OF THE ENVIRONMENTAL DIMENSION

This Dimension Includes Seven Indicators:

Facilities with environmental monitoring programs: Although all are certified from the sanitary point of view, only 10% have their credit compliance with legally established environmental monitoring programs. This is negative, even when a modest growth is perceived in the last analysis period. Facilities with a climate change mitigation/adaptation program (Tarea Vida Program): The trend is negative if one takes into account that only 10% have these, even though it is a new strategy assumed by the country's leadership. Water consumption (m^3): maintains a positive trend throughout the analysis period, since consumption has been gradually reduced. Facilities with programs to reduce water consumption: Although the trend of this indicator is generally negative, with a discrete growth of (15%), which is manifested in the last period, it is recognized that it is closely related to the above-mentioned, so the actions taken have been adequate, and this trend can be reversed. Facilities with waste management programs: The tendency is negative, although it has experienced growth in the last period it is only 20%, even though the Historic Center has the REVIME Project. Electricity expenditure per tourist/day and physical tourist: Due to the relationship between both indicators, their analysis will be carried out as a whole. Both maintain a negative trend, with a progressive increase, which does not correspond to the restructuring of the energy-saving plans in the territory. This behaviour may be related to the increase in the housing capacity of the destination and the decrease in the number of day tourists.

FINDINGS AND DISCUSSION

The systematization of theoretical premises allowed us to understand tourist destinations as a systemic organization, which makes it possible to adapt the foundations of the process approach to the evaluation of their sustainability, favouring the definition of objectives based on the needs and expectations of the stakeholders, the establishment of a unique organizational and management culture, as well as cost reduction and efficiency gains, overcoming the weaknesses associated with traditional approaches to managing touristic destinations. The proposed procedure enables the evaluation of the sustainability of tourist destinations and, at the same time, it encourages the integration of actors of different natures and the identification of areas of action in an improved environment. Likewise, it facilitates the identification of impacts and trends that enhance tourism planning by promoting balanced development logic, which includes the measurement of stakeholders' satisfaction. The implementation of the procedure in the Historic Center of Havana showed the following: the tourism sustainability control index for the economic dimension shows a result of -0.5, evidencing unsustainable behaviour in all its measurement criteria. The positive behaviour is associated with the total number of rooms and the average stay, which should consolidate their trend due to the projection of the destination and revert to improvements for the rest of the indicators, taking into account the opening of new facilities is expected. The bet on high-standard hotels is also expected to bring new niche markets with medium-high purchasing power. The tourism sustainability control index for the environmental dimension shows a result of -0.42, which shows unsustainable behaviour; the result is conditioned by most of the values shown by its indicators, highlighting the growth in electricity costs per physical tourist and per day tourists, alarming figures in correspondence with current housing development and the short term. These results are because good practices are not implemented in daily operation, a consequence of the lack of application of the Environmental Management System according to the Cuban Standard ISO 14001: 2015. There is also evidence of the lack of correspondence in the actions of the destination about the State Plan for Confronting Climate Change (Tarea Vida Program). The tourism sustainability control index of the socio-cultural dimension shows a result of 1.0, a positive trend associated with the performance shown by all the indicators and the sustainability criteria due to the constant growth they have experienced in the period of analysis. Based on this, the general index of sustainability of the accommodation sub-process shows a stagnant behaviour with a value of 0.026, which reflects a trend towards unsustainability, determined by the economic and environmental dimensions with a manifest influence, which even when the socio-cultural reflects sustainability from 100% of its indicators, it does not manage to counteract the critical state of the general index. Although it would be necessary to evaluate the rest of the sub-processes of the product and service processes, the results obtained, taking into account the degree of interrelation and interaction between these and the planning and measurement-analysis processes, show signs of alarm for the management model. The areas for improvement are conditioned to the results of the monitoring of the hosting sub-process, defining the following:

Commercialization

- Rescue of the tour operation towards traditional markets.
- Intentional use in the commercialization of hotels of the historical-cultural attributes they possess.
- Use of Information and Communication Technologies for the commercialization of the destination's tourist products and their follow-up.

Infrastructure

- Recover accommodation properties, as well as reinforce preventive maintenance programs that promote the preservation of heritage.

Environmental

- Direct maintenance plans with a focus on risk management.
- Start environmental certification processes taking into account the areas of action.

The present book chapter aims to discuss the promising outcomes of the process approach applied to Havana City. However, we understand if further concerns on the justification for using the model arise. To better understand how the model operates, we hold that the model gives advantages that lead to overcoming the barriers and challenges posed by the tourism industry in Cuba since the 90s decade. Per our experience, the model enhances the competence among destinations regarding the fields of financial cost reduction, global risk management, problems in organizational culture, without mentioning the ecological crisis that threatens the system (Antón et al., 2012; Zapata, 2008; Vera et al., 2011,1997; Socher, 1993).

FUTURE RESEARCH DIRECTION

Although the literature is strongly interested in studying and understanding sustainability, there are some gaps which the present book chapter intends to fill. Most certainly, the term sustainability associates to the well-functioning of the industry. In an ever-changing world the stakeholders` interests are very hard to harmonize, at least in the operational levels. Hence, the correct interaction of the different sides and subservice sectors in the industry is vital to preserve the sustainability of tourism in the years to come. At a closer look, the tourist system can be divided in three clear-cut parts: exogenous system, endogenous system and macro environment which are more than the sum of the parts. This model offers a fertile ground to give an all-encompassing diagnosis of the tourist destination which occupies a central position in the system. Based on the importance of tourist behaviour, the next guides for applied research should focus in a plan that include diagnosis, evaluation and improvement environment.

CONCLUSION

The characteristics, premises and operations that distinguish systemic organizations can be recognized in a territory or tourist destination, so this can be considered as such, which allows applying the principles that define the process approach. The proposed procedure consists of four phases, and nine sub-phases and allows for the identification of the different processes that concur in a tourist destination, with an interdimensional approach, facilitating the recognition and understanding of the dynamics of sustainability with a holistic vision. The implementation of the procedure in the Historic Center of Havana made it possible to determine processes and sub-processes that guarantee the operation of the destination and the stakeholders linked to tourism development. The behavior of the evaluated indicators showed the stagnant state in which sustainability efforts and performance find themselves, determined by the economic and environmental dimensions, which led to the establishment of areas for improvement in the commercial, infrastructure and environmental performance.

REFERENCES

Anton, S. (2012). El reto de reinventar los destinos [The challenges of designing tourst destinations]. Academic Press.

Asociación de Estados del Caribe. Declaración para el establecimiento de la zona de turismo sustentable del Caribe, [Declaration of Sustainainable Tourism] II Cumbre de Jefes de Estado y/o Gobierno de la A.E.C.", Santo Domingo.

Beltrán, J. C., Rivas, M. A., & Tejedor, F. (2002). *Guía para una gestión basada en procesos* [Guidebook for success study-cases]. Andalucía.

Blancas, F. J., González, M., Lozano-Oyola, M., & Pérez, F. (2009). The assessment of sustainable tourism: Application to Spanish coastal destinations. *Ecological Indicators*, *10*(1), 484–492. doi:10.1016/j.ecolind.2009.08.001

Blanco, A. (2016). *Propuesta de indicadores para evaluar la sustentabilidad turística del destino Cuba* [A proposal to evaluate Cuba as tourist destination]. Trabajo de Diploma. Universidad de la Habana. Facultad de Turismo.

Chávez, M. E., Korstanje, M., & Beatón, M. O. R. (2019). Visión Comunitaria del Turismo. Consideraciones desde la Práctica en el Centro Histórico de La Habana, Cuba/Community Vision of Tourism. Considerations from Practice in Havana Historic Center, Cuba. Rosa Dos Ventos-Turismo e Hospitalidade, 11(1), 1-15.

Choi, H. C., & Sirakaya, E. (2006). Sustainability indicators for managing community tourism. *Tourism Management*, *27*(6), 1274–1289. doi:10.1016/j.tourman.2005.05.018

CITMA – MINTUR. (2003). Indicadores de sostenibilidad para el turismo en Cuba [Reports for Cubas as a tourist destination] Documento preliminar. La Habana.

Cruz, N. (2017). La Gestión Integral del Centro Histórico: Nuevos desafíos [Tourism Management for the historic Centre: new challenges]. Cuaderno Técnico, Plan Maestro - Oficina del Historiador de la Ciudad de La Habana, La Habana.

Delis Fresneda, C. D. (2015). Evaluación de indicadores de sostenibilidad turística para el Centro Histórico de la Habana en el período 2010-2014 [Evaluation and Management plan for the historic Centre in La Habana from 2010 to 2014]. Tesis en opción al título de Licenciado en Turismo. Universidad de la Habana. Facultad de Turismo. La Habana. Cuba.

Echarri, M. (2006). *Análisis Geográfico del Turismo en Ciudades Patrimoniales Cubanas* [Geographical análisis of Cuban cities]. Tesis en Opción al Título de Doctor en Ciencias Geográficas, Universidad de La Habana.

European Commission. (2016). *The European Tourism Indicators System. ETIS toolkit for sustainable destination management.* Available at:https://ec.europa.eu/growth/sectors/tourism/offer/sustainable/indicators/index_en.htm

Fortuny-Santos, J., Arbós, L. C., Castellsaques, O. C., & Nadal, J. O. (2008). Metodología de implantación de la gestión lean en plantas industriales [Methods for Reading Smart and industrial destinations]. *Universia Business Review*, (20), 28–41.

Getz, D. (1986). Models in tourism planning: Towards integration of theory and practice. *Tourism Management*, 7(1), 21–32. doi:10.1016/0261-5177(86)90054-3

Gössling, S. (2017). Tourism, information technologies and sustainability: An exploratory review. *Journal of Sustainable Tourism*, 25(7), 1024–1041. doi:10.1080/09669582.2015.1122017

Gunn, C. A. (1977). Industry pragmatism vs tourism planning. *Leisure Sciences*, 1(1), 85–94. doi:10.1080/01490407709512872

Hernández, R., Fernández, C., & Batista, P. (2000). *Metodología de la investigación* [Methodology for scientific research] (2nd ed.). Editorial McGraw-Hill Interamericana. D.F. Méjico.

Martin, R. A. (2010), *Principios, organización y práctica del turismo: La Habana* [Guidelines, Organization and Practices in Tourism: La Habana]-Plan Maestro. Oficina del Historiador de la Ciudad de La Habana. La Habana, Cuba: Boloña.

Organización de las Naciones Unidas. (1987). *Nuestro Futuro Común o Informe Brutland* [Our shared future or the Brutland report]. Available at http://www.tij.uia.mx/elbordo/vol05/

Organización Mundial del Turismo (OMT) (2005). Indicadores de desarrollo sostenible para los destinos turísticos. *Boletín de la R. S. G.*, *144*, 70–100.

Pearce, D. (2016). Modelos de gestión de destinos. Síntesis y Evaluación [Evolution of Tourism Management]. *Estudios y Perspectivas en Turismo*, 2(1), 1–16.

Pearce, D. W., & Atkinson, G. D. (1995). Measuring sustainable development. In D. Bromley (Ed.), *Handbook of Environmental Economics* (pp. 166–181). Blackwell.

Pearce, P. L. (2005). *Tourist Behaviour: Themes and conceptual schemes*. Channel View Publications. doi:10.21832/9781845410247

Robert, M. (2010). Evaluación de indicadores de sustentabilidad turística para el Centro Histórico de la Habana en el período 2000-2008 [Evaluation for tourism sustainability in Cuba from 2000 to 2008]. Tesis en opción al título de Máster en Gestión Turística. Universidad de La Habana. Cuba.

Robert, M. (2016). Indicadores de sostenibilidad turística. Una propuesta desde la información del destino Cuba [Indicators for tourism sustainability: Cuba as main studycase]. Memorias 10 Conferencia Internacional de Ciencias Empresariales y la 3ra Convención Internacional de Estudios Turísticos, Universidad de Villa Clara, Cuba.

Robert, M. (2018). *La sostenibilidad como referencia para la gestión de destinos turísticos* [Sustainability as a vehicle in tourism development]. Memorias IV Convención Internacional de Estudios Turísticos, Universidad de La Habana.

Robert, M. (2020). *Procedimiento para la evaluación de la sostenibilidad de los destinos turísticos con un enfoque a procesos* [Procedures for the correct evaluation of tourism sustainability and its processes]. Tesis en Opción al Título de Doctor en Ciencias Económicas, Universidad de La Habana.

Sirakaya, E., Jamal, T., & Choi, H. S. (2001). Developing indicators for destination sustainability. In D. B. Weaver (Ed.), *The encyclopedia of ecotourism* (pp. 411–432). CAB International. doi:10.1079/9780851993683.0411

Swarbrooke, J., & Horner, S. (2007). *Consumer behaviour in tourism*. Routledge. doi:10.4324/9780080466958

Torres, H. L. (2016). *Propuesta de esquema metodológico para la evaluación de la sostenibilidad del desarrollo turístico de destinos caso La Habana* [Methodology towards a new form of sustainability for La Habana]. Universidad de La Habana.

Ulacia, Z. (2007). *La gestión de procesos en la hospitalidad. Editorial Centro de Estudios Turísticos* [The development of tourism and hospitality]. Ciudad de La Habana.

ADDITIONAL READING

Apostolakis, A. (2003). The convergence process in heritage tourism. *Annals of Tourism Research, 30*(4), 795–812. doi:10.1016/S0160-7383(03)00057-4

Cooper, C., & Hall, C. M. (2008). *Contemporary Tourism: An international approach.* Routledge.

Jamal, T., & Getz, D. (1999). Community roundtables for tourism-related conflicts: The dialectics of consensus and process structures. *Journal of Sustainable Tourism, 7*(3-4), 290–313. doi:10.1080/09669589908667341

Lee, C. F., & King, B. (2010). International competitiveness in hot springs tourism: An application of the analytical hierarchy process approach. *Tourism Analysis, 15*(5), 531–544. doi:10.3727/108354210X12889831783233

Mackay, K. J., & Fesenmaier, D. R. (1998). A process approach to segmenting the getaway travel market. *Journal of Travel & Tourism Marketing, 7*(3), 1–18. doi:10.1300/J073v07n03_01

Séraphin, H., Butcher, J., & Korstanje, M. (2017). Challenging the negative images of Haiti at a pre-visit stage using visual online learning materials. *Journal of Policy Research in Tourism, Leisure & Events, 9*(2), 169–181. doi:10.1080/19407963.2016.1261146

Seraphin, H., Gowreesunkar, V., Roselé-Chim, P., Duplan, Y. J. J., & Korstanje, M. (2018). Tourism planning and innovation: The Caribbean under the spotlight. *Journal of Destination Marketing & Management*, *9*, 384–388. doi:10.1016/j.jdmm.2018.03.004

Seraphin, H., Korstanje, M., & Gowreesunkar, V. (2020). Diaspora and ambidextrous management of tourism in post-colonial, post-conflict and post-disaster destinations. *Journal of Tourism and Cultural Change*, *18*(2), 113–132. doi:10.1080/14766825.2019.1582658

Smith, G., & Cooper, C. (2000). Competitive approaches to tourism and hospitality curriculum design. *Journal of Travel Research*, *39*(1), 90–95. doi:10.1177/004728750003900112

Smith, S. L. (1994). The tourism product. *Annals of Tourism Research*, *21*(3), 582–595. doi:10.1016/0160-7383(94)90121-X

Tang, H. W. V. (2014). Constructing a competence model for international professionals in the MICE industry: An analytic hierarchy process approach. *Journal of Hospitality, Leisure, Sport and Tourism Education*, *15*, 34–49. doi:10.1016/j.jhlste.2014.04.001

Timothy, D. J., & Tosun, C. (2003). Arguments for community participation in the tourism development process. *Journal of Tourism Studies*, *14*(2), 2–15.

Tosun, C. (1999). Towards a typology of community participation in the tourism development process. *Anatolia*, *10*(2), 113–134. doi:10.1080/13032917.1999.9686975

Zhang, J. (2017). Evaluating regional low-carbon tourism strategies using the fuzzy Delphi-analytic network process approach. *Journal of Cleaner Production*, *141*, 409–419. doi:10.1016/j.jclepro.2016.09.122

KEY TERM DEFINITIONS

Evaluation: This is defined as a process applied to test some theories or hypothesis.

Historic Center of Havana: It is known as well as old Havana, this is part of Havana City where dwelled the colonial authorities.

Procedure: It is a set of actions happening underway at the same moment with the same goal.

Process Approach: It represents a set of ideas that explains how change ultimately develops.

Sustainability: The term is used to denote those practices to sustain, protect or care the non-renewable resources for future generations.

The Contribution of Benefit Management to Improve Organizational Maturity

Jorge Gomes

https://orcid.org/0000-0003-0656-9284

Universidade Lusófona das Humanidades e Tecnologias, Portugal

Mário Romão

https://orcid.org/0000-0003-4564-1883

ISEG, Universidade de Lisboa, Portugal

INTRODUCTION

All organizations are interested in finding ways in which they can ensure their long-term viability, whether they are private firms looking to maximize their shareholder value, or public sector and not-for-profit organizations seeking to maximize their effectiveness. Achieving competitive advantages over competitors has always been the focus of organizations, as only this competitive differentiation can guarantee the long-term sustainability of the organization (Jugdev & Mathur, 2006).

The purpose of the maturity models is to provide a framework for improving an organization's business result by assessing their strengths and weaknesses, enabling comparisons with similar organizations, and a measure of the correlation between organizations (Ibbs & Kwak, 2000). The maturity models are designed to enable organizations to understand their current level of maturity, highlighting areas that would give them the most value as well as performance improvement in the short and long terms.

A benefit is an outcome whose nature and value are considered advantageous by an organization (OGC, 2010). Bradley (2006) defines it as a result of change which is perceived as positive by a stakeholder. An important aspect in the above definitions is that advantage is owned by individuals or groups who want to obtain value from an investment (Ward & Daniel, 2012).

The benefits management approach emerges as a complement to traditional management practices and proposes a continuous mapping of business benefits and the implementation and monitoring of intermediate results. The benefits are often identified in the early stages of investments to build business cases and sell the idea to interested parties (Remenyi, Money, & Bannister, 2007).

The decision-making process over IS/IT investments is not as objective and transparent as it is claimed to be, creating significant failures on the benefits achievement process (Berghout et al., 2005).

The assessment procedures help an organization to understand where they have been, where they are, and what processes they need to implement in future.

One of the factors that differentiates a successful IS/ IT deployment process from a company is the ability to assess whether investments in IS/ IT have made the promised investments.

The perception of continued failure in IS/ IT investments has led to a new approach to the way projects are managed. The focus should be on realizing the benefits, since this is the main reason for the organization's investment (Ward & Daniel, 2012).

DOI: 10.4018/978-1-7998-9220-5.ch141

BACKGROUND

Maturity Models

The basic concept of maturity drives organizational processes towards continuous improvement and, therefore, requires a deep knowledge of the organization's current position and what it intends to achieve in the future.

Maturity models are based on the principle that entities (people, organizations, functional areas or processes) evolve through a process of growth or development towards a more advanced level of maturity, through several different stages (Becker et al., 2009). Considering the various best practice references, improving organizational maturity requires a conscious and properly structured action plan (Crawford, 2005).

Levin & Skulmoski (2000) point out that the maturity models provide a framework to help enable organizations to increase their capability to deliver projects on schedule, within budget and according to the desired technical specifications.

There are several reasons why organizations might choose to use a maturity model to assess their current performance, such as: justifying their investment portfolio, program or project management improvements, gaining recognition of service quality in order to support proposals, or gaining a better understanding of their strengths and weakness in order to enable improvement to happen.

The maturity model is an important element of strategic planning, as it provides a methodology, a road map, to determine and compress the gaps in resources and quality (Kerzner, 2019).

Working with different types of projects within an organization requires standard models to deliver successful projects in the future repeatedly, to improve both the quality of future projects and also to gain knowledge and learn from past mistakes.

Measuring maturity in organizations is considered subjective, as the process focuses mainly on what people do operationally (Andersen & Jessen, 2003).

The works of Ibbs and Kwak, (1997; 2000), and Ibbs and Reginato (2002) over the last decade focused on recognizing the benefits of investment in project management competency through measures of maturity in an organization's practice of project management.

We now move on to make a brief description of the three most popular and referenced maturity models, analyses the singularities of each one and find the approach that fits better with the dynamic characteristics of the organization used for the case study.

The CMM for Software was first published in 1991 and is based on a checklist of critical success factors of software development projects, from during the late 70s and early 80s (Chrissis, 2011). CMM has achieved considerable popularity and is now well-adopted and has undergone several revisions and upgrades. Its success led to the development of CMMs for a variety of subjects beyond software. The proliferation of new models was confusing and so the US government funded a two-year project that involved more than 200 industry and academic experts to create a unique and extensible framework that integrated systems engineering, software engineering and product development. The result was CMMI (Chrissis, 2011).

CMMI defines sets of best practices that are grouped into process areas used by product development organizations to implement and improve the predictability of their project costs and schedules (Beynon, 2007). This model consists of transcending disciplines by offering best practices through the pointing out development and maintenance programmers, covering the whole life cycle of the product from conceptualization to delivery and maintenance.

Considerable research has been done to determine the best software and systems engineering development, acquisition, and sustainment practices. Many of these practices are part of the CMMI framework. The five-step CMMI process is used to establish an organization's current maturity level (CMMI, 2010).

The PMBOK Guide describes a process model for the execution of single projects with five process groups, including 49 processes (PMI, 2017).

Organizational project management, as defined in OPM3, requires an understanding of not only project management and its processes, but also portfolio and program management. The development of this standard was inspired by an increasing interest in a maturity model that shows a step-by-step method of improving and maintaining an organization's ability to translate organizational strategy into the successful and consistent delivery of projects.

OPM3 is the systematic management of projects, programs, and portfolios, in alignment with the objective to achieve strategic goals. OPM3 does not measure the maturity of the organization at an achieved level, as is the case with many other maturity models, but as a percentage of best practices achieved (PMI, 2017).

OGC (2010) describes P3M3 as a key standard amongst maturity models, providing a framework with which organizations can assess their current performance and put in place improvement plans. The P3M3 is an enhanced version of the Project Management Maturity Model, which is itself based on the process CMM model. Although connected, there are no interdependencies between these models, which allows for independent assessment in any of the specific disciplines.

P3M3 uses a five-level maturity framework and focuses on seven process perspectives, which exist in all three models and can be assessed at all five maturity levels. For each of the process areas several attributes are defined at each level of maturity. These attributes are the basis on which the organization should assess its current maturity and develop plans to improve.

The concept of organizational project management is based on the idea that there is a correlation between an organization's capability in terms of project, programme and portfolio management, and also its effectiveness in implementing strategy.

Maturity Models Limitations

Maturity models are now in widespread use, but there seems to be some inefficiency in their success in achieving performance improvements. In fact, there is little evidence to suggest that process capability improvement results in improved project success, although a few studies are promising (Mullaly, 2006; Lee & Anderson, 2006). No studies have been able to show that using maturity models or assessing project management maturity results in a sustained competitive advantage for an organization (Jugdev & Thomas, 2002). Maturity models claim to represent all the processes present for a project to be successful (Sargeant, 2010; Kerzner, 2017). Unfortunately, this assertion is not supported by evidence, with many models either lacking empirical evidence to support the use of particular measures (Skulmoski, 2001), or lacking a theoretical basis (Jugdev & Thomas, 2002).

Many factors that impact performance are not specifically addressed by maturity models (Sargeant, 2010; Lee & Anderson, 2006). Another underpinning assumption is that an improvement in process maturity will yield an improvement in the overall maturity of the organization. Neither of these assumptions has been empirically tested. Maturity models are characterized as being "step-by-step recipes" that oversimplify reality and lack empirical foundation (De Bruin et al., 2005; McCormack et al., 2009).

According to Mettler and Rohner (2009), maturity models should be configurable because internal and external characteristics (e.g., the technology available, intellectual property, customer base and relationships with suppliers) may constrain a maturity model's applicability in its standardized version.

Gareis and Hueman (2000) reject the notion of a maturity ladder of stages, the argument being that a ladder model might be too rigid. Instead, they opt for a spider web presentation, which allows for more differentiation in describing the competencies needed to handle the specific processes of the project-oriented organization.

Ibbs and Kwak (2000) demonstrated that there is no statistically significant correlation between project management maturity and project success, based on cost and schedule performance. Jugdev and Thomas (2002) could not find a correlation between process capability and project success of many maturity models. Mullaly (2006) raised the concern of the lack of evidence of PMM's contribution on organization success as a means of competitive advantage.

Benefits Management

The challenges faced by organizations to increase value from there IS/IT investments, together with the low level of organizational competencies in exploiting IS/IT, were revealed as an underlying cause for the difficulty in dealing with these challenges. The benefits expected from any IS/IT implementations are unlikely to emerge automatically. Any benefits sought must first be identified, along with the changes in ways of working that will bring about, and sustain, each of the benefits. Ownership and responsibility for the realization of each benefit must then be assigned, together with how it will be realized, and on whom it depends (Ward & Daniels, 2012; Gomes & Romão, 2015).

Benefits are often identified in the early stages to form the business case and to sell the idea to stakeholders. A follow-up procedure with the purpose of evaluating those benefits achieved is often missing, and problems arise after system delivery, by which it's time to show whether those previously stated benefits have actually been realized (Remenyi et al., 2007).

One of the factors that differentiates successful from less successful companies in their deployment of IS/IT, is the management resolve to evaluate IS/IT investments before and after they occur. The perception of continuous unsuccessful IS/IT investments led to a new way and approach for how projects are managed.

Benefits Management (BM) can be described as: "The process of organizing and managing, such that potential benefits arising from the use of IT are actually realized" (Ward & Daniel, 2012, p. 325).

According to Ward and Daniel (2012) the process has five stages (Figure 1) that are described in the following way:

1. Identifying and structure the benefits: Analyze the drivers to determine the objectives for the investment. The identification of the correct benefits and classification by their nature. Stakeholder's analysis and establishing the ownership of the benefits and changes. A preliminary business case.
2. Benefits realization plan: A full description of each of the benefits and changes and their ownership. Finalise measurements process of benefits and changes. Developing the Benefits Dependency Network (BDN). Submit business case for funding.
3. Execute benefits realization plan: The management of change programmes and the review of progress according to the plan. Pursuing benefit delivery as well as technical implementation.
4. Review and results evaluation: The ability to develop suitable measures for monitor each identified change and benefit. Confirm which planned benefits have been achieved. Lessons learned.

5. Further benefits: The organizations will only deliver value from IS/IT projects if they can design and execute the organizational change programmes needed to realize all the benefits as planned. Important is the identification of additional improvements through business changes, the subsequent initiation of action and the identification of additional benefits originating from further IS/IT investments. Use the project team and other key stakeholders to identify any new benefits and initiate action to realize them.

Figure 1. The benefits management stages (Ward & Daniel, 2012, p.69)

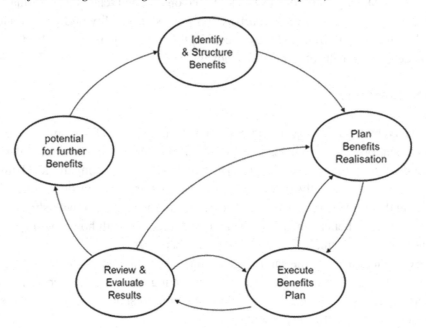

Benefits management is becoming increasingly important in overall frameworks for project delivery capability. The primary benefits to be created as a result of a project or programme need to be identified and monitored in a non-bureaucratic way (Gomes & Romão, 2015).

Benefits management tools and techniques can be included in the strategic planning process to reinforce and enable organizations in their competitive environments, namely; (1) in carrying out a regular strategic analysis to understand and interpret their business drivers and to revise their long-term strategy; (2) by interpreting each objective in terms of the benefits that it could produce for different stakeholders and how these benefits can be measured through key performance indicators (KPIs); (3) identifying the range of changes required to deliver the objectives and the benefits; (4) structuring the changes that enable programmes and projects to be designed to achieve the desired outcomes; (5) mapping dependencies between projects, programmes or initiatives; and, (6) developing business cases and clearly explaining the objectives and benefits to be achieved

According to Peppard et al. (2007) there are five principles for realizing benefits through IT: (1) Just having technology does not confer any benefit or create value; (2) Benefits arise when IT enables people to do things differently; (3) Benefits result from changes and innovations in ways of working, so only business managers, users, and possibly customers and suppliers, can make these changes; (4) All

IT projects have outcomes, but not all outcomes are benefits; (5) Benefits must be actively managed to be obtained..

Best practice is to involve key stakeholders to identify and agree desired benefits maximizing the likelihood of commitment to realize those benefits across a range of levels in the business or the organization (Ward & Daniel, 2012).

The key tool of Benefits Management approach is the Benefits Dependency Network (BDN) designed to enable the investment objectives and their resulting benefits to be linked in a structured way to the business, organization and IS/IT changes required to realize those benefits (Ward & Daniel, 2012) (Figure 2).

Figure 2. Benefits Dependency Network (Ward & Daniel, 2012, p.96)

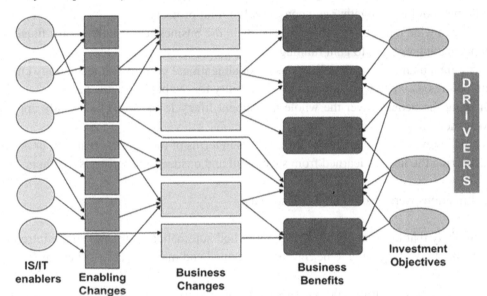

Developing a Benefits Dependency Network results in a clear statement of the benefits from an investment, the activities and the IS/IT capabilities required to achieve these benefits (Gomes & Romão 2015).

Benefits Management not only increases the potential to obtain value from investments, but it also avoids spending money on projects that would not have delivered benefits, increasing greatly the likelihood of the expected benefits from investments made.

The integration of the benefits management and mature models approaches, it can increase the effectiveness of strategic projects and improve business sponsors' confidence that their investment in projects will return business benefits. A higher level of maturity is achieved when organizations assess their capabilities and benchmark their performance against standards and competitors.

Benefits management involves the processes for delivering projects' objectives and goals that are not only based on the outputs of the project, as is common for immature organizations, but also on the measurement of the performance of a specific activity.

Change management is a central topic, as well as being a way of measuring long term achievement for an organization's customer satisfaction, through the delegation of responsibilities and coordination between several projects. To achieve a high maturity rating within benefits management, frequent collection and analysis of performance metrics should be made for the improvement of future projects.

Benefits Management Strengthens and Limitations

The general perception of the continuous failures of IS/IT investments has forced organizations to look new ways and approaches to achieving successful projects. The focus should be on obtaining benefits since this is the main justification for the investment.

There is a growing body of evidence that the use of benefits management practices enhances the likelihood of projects achieving organizational goals, both in relation to IS/IT investments (Ashurst, 2012; Serra, 2017; Ward & Daniel, 2012).

Ward and Daniel (2012) identify that which distinguishes successful, from less successful organizations in benefits realization, namely:

- Using methodologies together and consistently for all projects.
- Including a wide range of stakeholder benefits in the business cases and not just financial ones.
- Not overstating benefits to gain funding.
- Integrating a plan for benefit delivery using organizational process and technology changes.
- Nominating business ownership and accountability for the benefits and changes.
- Managing the benefits over the whole investment lifecycle through consistently applied project governance roles and processes.
- Systematic review of the results of investments in terms of the benefits realized, or not realized.
- Transferring the lessons learned from successful and unsuccessful projects to others.

Some limitations were also highlighted, such as:

- It is unlikely that the benefits previously identified automatically arise from the introduction of a new technology. It's getting to be rigorously planned and managed (Lin & Pervan, 2003; Markus, 2004).
- Bennington and Baccarini (2004) argue that most organizations do not follow the development of benefits by the following reasons, such as: (1) Lack of experience and/or knowledge of the business. Focus on results, rather benefits. (2) Lack of focus on people who will enjoy the benefits. (3) Emotional commitment to continuing the project and therefore is not open to changes that could threaten the viability of the project. (4) Lack of tools to help ensure that the benefits will be delivered.
- The benefits are often identified in the initial phase to build the business case and sell the idea to the interested parties. The absence of a monitoring procedure to assess their achievement is frequent, and problems will arise after the system delivery when it is necessary to show the realization of the benefits previously defined (Remenyi et al., 2007).
- Bennington and Baccarini (2004) suggested that the benefits should be identified process involving a mixed approach of interviews and workshops with key stakeholders.
- Benefits at initial stage should be structured to clarify the relationship between the effects of technology, the necessary changes in business and organization goals (Sakar & Widestadh, 2005).
- One common factor of many projects and programs is the imprecision in benefits identification and gives its failure. Without clearly defined goals, it is hard to stay focused when problems occur later (Reiss et al., 2006).
- Formulating and appraising project target benefits are considered the first and critical step to ensure successful benefit realization (Bradley, 2010).

- There are problems over the concepts of 'benefits' and 'value' which are partly due to the multiple meanings of the terms themselves (Winter et al., 2006).
- The lack of consistency in the definitions developed by different professional groups, such as economists, accountants and project managers, which means that there is a lack of agreement on how to classify and measure benefits (Jenner, 2010).
- Focusing attention on the creation of value and the realisation of benefits has implications for the organization, affecting strategies at corporate, business and operational levels (Johnson et al., 2008).
- Benefits management challenges the wider mind-set in an organization and hence may struggle to gain acceptance (Jenner, 2010).
- The literature on Benefits Management is poorly developed compared to many other aspects of project management. The literature which does exist tends to be either 'how to do it' guides (Bradley, 2010; Payne, 2007) or analysis of benefits management processes and practices (APM, 2012; Ashurst, 2012; Breese, 2012; Coombs, 2015; Lin & Pervan, 2003; Lin et al., 2005; Serra & Kunc, 2015; Ward et al., 2007).

CASE STUDY

P3M3

P3M3 is a product of the OGC that is an office of Her Majesty's Treasury within the UK government and is responsible for improving *value for money* by driving up standards and capability in public sector procurement. It achieves this through policy and process guidance, helping organizations to improve their efficiency and deliver successfully. The purpose of P3M3 is to provide a frame of reference that can be used to baseline an organization's capabilities in project, programme and portfolio management (AXELOS, 2016)

AXELOS (2016) describes P3M3 as a key standard amongst maturity models, providing a framework with which organizations can assess their current performance and put in place improvement plans. The P3M3 is an enhanced version of the Project Management Maturity Model, itself based on the process maturity framework that evolved into the SEI Capability Maturity Model (CMM) (Figure 3).

Although connected, there are no interdependencies between these models, which allows for independent assessment in any of the specific disciplines. P3M3 is designed to enable organizations to understand their current level of maturity and highlight areas that would give them the most value and performance improvement in the short and long terms. The P3M3 contains three models that enable independent assessment.

P3M3 uses a five-level maturity framework and focuses on seven process perspectives, which exist in all three models and can be assessed at all five maturity levels. For each of the process areas there are several attributes defined at each level of maturity. These attributes are the basis on which the organization should assess its current maturity and make plans to improve. The description of the five maturity levels is on the Table 1.

There are seven Process Perspectives within P3M3 (Table 2), defining the key characteristics of a mature organization, which exist in all three models and can be assessed at five maturity levels are the following (OGC, 2010).

Figure 3. P3M3 structure (adapted from AXELOS, 2016)

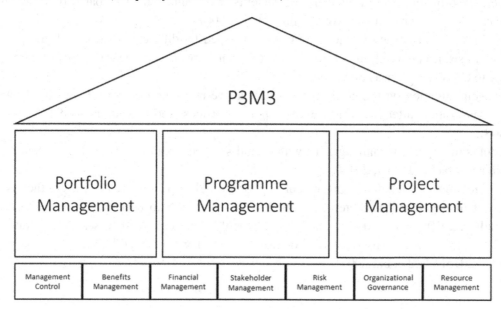

Table 1. P3M3 maturity levels (OGC, 2010)

Level	Description
Level 1	Awareness of process; Processes are not usually documented. Actual practice is determined by events or individual preferences and is highly subjective and variable.
Level 2	Repeatable process: the organization will be able to demonstrate that basic management practices have been established.
Level 3	Defined process; The management and technical processes necessary to achieve the organizational purpose will be documented, standardized and integrated to some extent with other business processes
Level 4	Managed process: mature behavior and processes are quantitatively managed. There will be evidence of quantitative objectives for quality and process performance, and these will be used as criteria in managing processes.
Level 5	Optimized process. The organization will focus on optimization of its quantitatively managed processes to consider changing business needs and external factors. It will anticipate future capacity demands and capability requirements to meet delivery challenges

Embedded within the Process Perspectives are several Attributes. Specific Attributes relate only to a specific Process Perspective. Generic Attributes are common to all Process Perspectives at a given Maturity Level, and include planning, information management, and training and development. There are no interdependencies between the models, so an organization may be better at programme management than it is at project management.

It is important for organizations to understand the optimal level of performance in their quest to maximize value for money from investment, and to have a realistic view of what they can achieve. Not all organizations will be able to reach the highest level, and for many, the middle levels may be adequate to meet their business needs and aspirations. Each organization needs to decide their optimal maturity level depending on their business needs and priorities process improvement effort accordingly (OGC, 2010).

"P3M3 is not simply about isolated, here-and- now assessments – it also acts as a roadmap for ongoing improvement and progression towards realistic and achievable goals that are suitable for your business needs and aspirations" (OGC, 2010, p. 5).

Table 2. P3M3 Process Perspectives (OGC, 2010)

Perspective	Description
Management Control	Management control is characterized by clear evidence of leadership and direction, scope, stages, tranches and review processes during the course of the initiative.
Benefits Management	Benefits should be assessed and approved by the organizational areas that will deliver them. Benefit dependencies and other requirements are clearly defined and understanding gained on how the outputs of the initiative will meet those requirements.
Financial Management	There should be evidence of the appropriate involvement of the organization's financial functions, with approvals being embedded in the broader organizational hierarchy.
Stakeholder Engagement	Stakeholder engagement includes communications planning, the effective identification and use of different communications channels, and techniques to enable objectives to be achieved.
Risk Management	Risk management maintains a balance of focus on threats and opportunities, with appropriate management actions to minimize or eliminate the likelihood of any identified threat occurring, or to minimize its impact if it does occur, and maximize opportunities.
Organizational Governance	Organizational governance also looks at how a range of other organizational controls are deployed and standards achieved, including legislative and regulatory frameworks.
Resource Management	These include human resources, buildings, equipment, supplies, information, tools and supporting teams.

When using P3M3, an organization may choose to review only one specific perspective (e.g., risk management). It is unlikely that an organization will have strengths in all areas or that the defined perspectives are applicable to all situations. So, depending on the sector of industry or business target, the organization may choose what perspectives are appropriate to be assessed. The P3M3 claims some of the organizational benefits, such as (OGC, 2010):

- The strengths and weaknesses are judged against an objective standard, not just against other organizations.
- Helps organizations to decide what level of performance capability they need to achieve to meet their business needs.
- Focuses on the organization's maturity rather than specific initiatives.
- Recognizes achievements from investment.
- Justifies investment in portfolio, programme and project management infrastructure.
- Provides a roadmap for continual progression and improvement.
- Increased productivity, cost predictability, higher-quality outcomes, improved customer satisfaction and enhanced employee morale.

Although there has been no systematic study to determine the actual benefits, organizations using P3M3are supposedly able to achieve (Goldenson & Gibson, 2003):

- A higher rate of return on investment and greater production efficiency.
- Lower production costs and better-quality outcomes.
- Improved customer satisfaction and enhanced employee morale.

Some critics are also pointed out:

- One of the most weaknesses of the P3M3 model is that it is based on the OGC project management maturity model and therefore emphasizes concerns related to project management success, i.e., delivery on-time on-budget on-quality (Morris & Pinto, 2007).

- Young et al. (2014) argue that another deficiency of the P3M3 model is that it uses a single number to represent maturity at the project, programme and portfolio level, with this number being the lowest score in either generic attributes or the process perspectives across each sub-model.

- The generic attributes evaluated in all three P3M3 domains are claimed as essential to achieving improvement in project management maturity. It is doubtful however whether these generic attributes are appropriate for programme and portfolio management domains, which are typically more complex than standalone project management (Artto et al., 2009; Young et al., 2014).

The P3M3 maturity model gives an opportunity for organizations to use self-assessment to obtain an up-to-date evaluation of the maturity of their project. This self-assessment was crucial for providing the data for the strategic analysis needed to endorse the organization's choice of drivers for investment, as well as the identification and structure of benefits beyond. Since P3M3 usage has grown greatly and for many organizations it is now the default maturity assessment model. In many sectors, management models have an increasing importance and become the foundation for assessing organizational capability and identifying opportunities for improvements. Under the P3M3 model, maturity is assessed by evaluating each process perspective to determine whether practice is on what level (Table 3).

Table 3. Maturity levels practices (OGC,2010)

Maturity	Project Management	Programme Management	Portfolio Management
Level 1 Awareness of process	Does the organization recognize projects and run them differently from its ongoing business?	Does the organization recognize programmes and run them differently from projects?	Does the organization's Executive Board recognize programmes and projects, and maintains an informal list of its investments in programmes and projects?
Level 2 Repeatable process	Does the organization ensure that each project is run with its own processes and procedures to a minimum specified standard?	Does the organization ensure that each programme is run with its own processes and procedures to a minimum specified standard?	Does the organization ensure that each programme and/ or project in its portfolio is run with its own processes and procedures to a minimum specified standard?
Level 3 Defined process	Does the organization have its own centrally controlled project processes and can individually projects flex within these processes to suit the particular project?	Does the organization have its own centrally controlled programme processes and can individually programmes flex within these processes to suit the particular programme?	Does the organization have its own centrally controlled programme and project processes and can individual programmes and projects flex within these processes to suit particular programmes and/or projects? Does the organization have its own portfolio management process?
Level 4 Managed process	Does the organization obtain and retain specific measurements on its project management performance and run a quality management organization to better predict future performance?	Does the organization obtain and retain specific measurements on its programme management performance and run a quality management organization to better predict future performance?	Does the organization obtain and retain specific management metrics on its whole portfolio of programmes and projects as a means of predicting future performance? Does the organization assess its capacity to manage programmes and projects and prioritize them accordingly?
Level 5 Optimized process	Does the organization undertake continuous process improvement with proactive problem and technology management for projects to improve its ability to depict performance over time and optimize processes?	Does the organization undertake continuous process improvement with proactive problem and technology management for programmes to improve its ability to depict performance over time and optimize processes?	Does the organization undertake continuous process improvement with proactive problem and technology management for the portfolio to improve its ability to depict performance over time and optimize processes?

P3M3 was one of the earliest maturity models on the market. The first version come out in 2005 and was designed on the premise that organizations increase effectiveness in each of the three domains (project, programme and portfolio) incrementally. The version 2 released in 2008 was designed as three separated models, so the organizations could assess one model independently of the other two. The version 2 also introduced de concept of process perspectives that identified the seven core areas that covered de main management activities in the three models.

The version 3 (AXELOS, 2016) builds on the knowledge gained from a significant number of assessments of a wide range of organizations. This new version included the concept called threads. Threads are a way of grouping attributes and are applied to all 7 perspectives, providing a more structured way to review and diagnose the areas that are enabling or inhibiting performance and replace the generic attributes of version 2. The main changes are the following:

- New self-assessment toolkit.
- An introduction guide as a more sophisticated reference for users.
- Greater diagnostic analysis includes focus on areas such as behaviours, tools and techniques and knowledge management. Greater recognition of techniques.
- Reference to commercial management asset in the models
- Greater alignment with the main bodies of knowledge (e.g., PMI, IPMA, APM, ISO 21500).
- Portfolio model improved to reflect the evolving best practice in this discipline.
- Closer integration of the three domains.
- Better coverage of procurement, contract and asset management

Management maturity models tend to focus on process maturity and compliance. P3M3 is unique in that it looks at the whole system and not just at the processes. It analyses the balance between the process, the competencies of the people who operate it, the tools that are deployed to support it, and the management information used to manage delivery and improvements. The Table 4 shows the main aspects related to three models described above.

Table 4. Main differences of Maturity Models

Maturity Model	CMMI	P3M3	OPM3
Constructor	SEI	OGC/AXELOS	PMI
Version/Date	V.1.3 /2010	V.3 /2016	V.3 /2013
Theoretical background	-	MSP	PMBOK
Continuity between editions	Yes	Yes	Yes
Sector	Software/engineering	All	All
Domains	Project	PPP	PPP
Scope	22 process areas	32 process areas	Best practices
Representation	Staged/ Continuous	Staged	Continuous
Levels	5	5	4
Self-Assessed	Yes	Yes	Yes
Links to strategy	Yes	Yes	Yes
Continuous improvement	Yes	Yes	Yes
Interpretation	Medium	Medium	Yes
Ease of execution	Yes	Yes	Yes

CONTRIBUTIONS AND FUTURE RESEARCH DIRECTIONS

The study provides some theoretical contributions, namely: Through the literature review process, it was possible to systematize the academic topics of Maturity Models, Benefits Management and IS/IT investments and understand the different perspectives. Some opportunities could be reach through a deep participation on the decision process concerning the IS/IT investments.

Regarding future research directions, it should be interesting to consider IS / IT Corporate Governance in future research, which would certainly allow generating useful explanations about the effects of the decision-making process. In addition, analyses the effect of each of the Organizational Maturity perspectives, according to the P3M3, on the various dimensions of project success.

CONCLUSION

The concept of benefits management is becoming increasingly important in overall frameworks for project delivery capability. The primary benefits to be created because of a project or programme need to be identified and monitored in a non-bureaucratic way.

The authors claim that by integrating both Benefits Management and Maturity Model approaches, that one can increase the effectiveness of strategic projects and improve the confidence of business sponsors that their investment in projects will return business benefits. A higher level of maturity is achieved when organizations assess their capabilities and benchmark their performance against standards and competitors.

Knowing beforehand the impact that process maturity has on the organization's performance, it is essential that one can focus on eliminating the internal resistance to change, taking advantage of the favorable factors that positively influence organizational maturity. By using a Benefits Management approach, we have shown how to record the business drivers, discuss them with all the relevant stakeholders, agree on the objectives and the benefits and on the organizational changes, as well as on the right set of IS/IT enablers needed to prompt transformation. Benefits Management adds value and provides relevant information to the Maturity Model framework by identifying goals and benefits, mapping the way to achieve them, supported by the right combination of organizational changes, enabling factors and IS/IT enablers.

The authors claim that Benefits Management provides a richer and more useful decision-support and monitoring tool, making the strategy implementation visible, traceable and measurable. Developing a Benefits Dependency Network results in a clear statement of the benefits from an investment, the activities and the IT capabilities required to achieve these benefits. Benefits Management not only increases the potential to obtain value from investments, but it also avoids spending money on projects that would not have delivered benefits, increasing greatly the likelihood of the expected benefits from investments made. In our integrated approach, the maturity model is designed to enable organizations to understand their current level of maturity, highlighting areas that would give them the most value as well as performance improvement in the short and long terms. Thereafter, our study is an attempt to reinforce the use of maturity models in a more integrated way. We have approached the Benefits Management process and explained how it could be seen as a more transversal process by integrating the initiatives from distinct areas of the overall organizational maturity.

Lastly, but not least, the authors point out that the main focus of an investment's success lies, not only in technology implementation, but mainly in changes in organizational performance and business efficiency, through improved processes and modifications in the way that work is done. The integration between a Maturity Model and a Benefits Management approach can then increase the effectiveness of projects, programmes or portfolios management outcomes. Besides, this linkage can also improve the confidence of decision-makers that the investments made match the desired maturity stages and will then, with more probability, result in more value for the business.

REFERENCES

Anderson, E. S., & Jessen, S. A. (2003). Project maturity in organisations. *International Journal of Project Management*, *21*(6), 457–461. doi:10.1016/S0263-7863(02)00088-1

APM. (2012). *Body of Knowledge* (6th ed.). Association for Project Management.

Artto, K., Martinsuo, M., Gemünden, H. G., & Murtoaro, J. (2009). Foundations of program management: A bibliometric view. *International Journal of Project Management*, *27*(1), 1–18. doi:10.1016/j.ijproman.2007.10.007

Ashurst, C. (2012). *Benefits Realization from Information Technology*. Palgrave Macmillan. doi:10.1057/9780230360822

AXELOS. (2016). *Introduction to P3M3©, version 3*. AXELOS Limited.

Becker, J., Knackstedt, R., & Pöppelbuß, J. (2009). Developing Maturity Models for IT Management: A Procedure Model and its Application. *Business & Information Systems Engineering*, *1*(3), 213–222. doi:10.100712599-009-0044-5

Bennington, P., & Baccarini, D. (2004, June). Project benefits management in IT projects: An Australian perspective. *Project Management Journal*, *35*(2), 20–30. doi:10.1177/875697280403500204

Berghout, E., Nijland, M., & Grant, K. (2005). Seven ways to get your favoured IT project accepted-politics in IT evaluation. *The Electronic Journal of Information System Evaluation*, *8*(1), 31–40.

Beynon, D. R. (2007). Interpreting Capability Maturity Model Integration (CMMI) for Business Development Organisations in the Government and Industrial Business Sectors. Technical Note CMU/SEI-2007-TN-004. Carnegie Mellon University, Pennsylvania, US: Software Engineering Institute.

Bradley, G. (2006). *Benefit Realization Management: A Practical Guide for Achieving Benefits through Change*. Gower Publishing.

Breese, R. (2012). Benefits realization management: Panacea or false dawn? *International Journal of Project Management*, *30*(3), 341–351. doi:10.1016/j.ijproman.2011.08.007

Chrissis, M. B., Konrad, M., & Shrum, S. (2011). *CMMI for Development: Guidelines for Process Integration and Product Improvement* (3rd ed.). Pearson Education Inc.

Coombs, C. (2015). When planned IS/IT project benefits are not realized: A study of inhibitors and facilitators to benefits realization. *International Journal of Project Management*, *33*(2), 363–379. doi:10.1016/j.ijproman.2014.06.012

De Bruin, T., Rosemann, M., Freeze, R., & Kulkarni, U. (2005). Understanding the main phases of developing a maturity assessment model. *Proceedings of the Australasian Conference on information.*

Gareis, R., & Hueman, M. (2000). Project management competences in the project-oriented organization. In *Gower Handbook of Project Management*. Gower.

Goldenson, D. R., & Gibson, D. L. (2003). *Demonstrating the Impact and Benefit of CMMI: An Update and Preliminary Result*. Carnegie Mellon Software Engineering Institute, Carnegie Mellon University.

Gomes, J., & Romão, M. (2014). How Organizational Maturity and Project Management can cooperate for Project Success. In Contemporary Issues in Tourism and Management Studies. Faro: UALg ESGHT.

Gomes, J., & Romão, M. (2015). Maturity, Benefits and Project Management shaping Project Success. *Advances in Intelligent Systems and Computing, 353*, 435-448. doi:10.1007/978-3-319-16486-1_43

Ibbs, W. C., & Kwak, Y. H. (1997). *The benefits of project management: Financial and organisational rewards to corporations*. PMI Educational Foundation.

Ibbs, W. C., & Kwak, Y. H. (2000). Assessing project management maturity. *Project Management Journal, 31*(1), 32–43. doi:10.1177/875697280003100106

Ibbs, W. C., & Reginato, J. (2002). Can good project management actually cost less? *Proceedings of the 33rd Annual Project Management Institute*.

Jenner, S. (2010). *Realising Benefits from Government ICT Investment: a fool's errand?* Academic Publishing International Ltd.

Johnson, M., Christensen, C., & Kagermann, H. (2008). Reinventing Your Business Model. *Harvard Business Review, 86*(12), 50–59.

Jugdev, K., & Mathur, G. (2006). A factor analysis of tangible and intangible project management assets. *PMI (Project Management Institute) Research Conference: New Directions in Project Management*.

Jugdev, K., & Thomas, J. (2002). Project management maturity models: The silver bullet of competitive advantage? *Project Management Journal, 33*(4), 4–14. doi:10.1177/875697280203300402

Kerzner, H. (2017). *Project management: A systems approach to planning, scheduling, and controlling* (12th ed.). John Wiley & Sons.

Kerzner, H. (2019). *Using the Project Management Maturity Model: Strategic Planning for Project Management* (3rd ed.). John Wiley & Sons.

Kwak, Y. H., & Ibbs, W. C. (2000). Calculating project management's return on investment. *Project Management Journal, 31*(2), 38–47. doi:10.1177/875697280003100205

Lee, L. S., & Anderson, R. M. (2006). An exploratory investigation of the antecedents of the IT project management capability. *e-Service Journal, 5*(1), 27–42. doi:10.2979/esj.2006.5.1.27

Levin, G., & Skulmoski, G. (2000). The project management maturity. *ESI Horizons, 2*(3), 1–7.

Lin, C., & Pervan, G. (2003). The practice of IS/IT benefits management in large Australian organizations. *Information & Management, 41*(1), 31–44. doi:10.1016/S0378-7206(03)00002-8

Lin, K., Lin, C., & Tsao, H.-Y. (2005). IS/IT investment evaluation and benefits realisation practices in Taiwanese SMEs. *Journal of Information Science and Technology, 2*(4), 44–71.

Markus, M. L. (2004). Techno change management: Using IT to drive organisational change. *Journal of Information Technology, 19*(1), 4–20. doi:10.1057/palgrave.jit.2000002

McCormack, K., Willems, J., van den Bergh, J., Deschoolmeester, D., Willaert, P., Štemberger, M. I., Škrinjar, R., Trkman, P., Ladeira, M. B., de Oliveira, M. P. L. V., Vuksic, V. B., & Vlahovic, N. (2009). A global investigation of key turning points in business process maturity. *Business Process Management Journal, 15*(5), 792–815. doi:10.1108/14637150910987946

Mettler, T., & Rohner, P. (2009). Situational maturity models as instrumental artifacts for organizational design. *DESRIST '09 Proceedings of the 4th International Conference on Design Science Research in Information Systems and Technology.*

Morris, P., & Pinto, J. K. (2007). *The Wiley Guide to Managing Projects.* Wiley and Sons.

Mullaly, M. (2006). Longitudinal analysis of project management maturity. *Project Management Journal, 36*(3), 62–73. doi:10.1177/875697280603700307

OGC. (2010). *Portfolio, programme and project management maturity model (P3M3): Introduction guide to P3M3.* Office of Government Commerce.

Payne, M. (2007). *Benefits Management: Releasing Project Value into the Business.* Project Manager Today.

Peppard, P., Ward, J., & Daniel, E. (2007). Managing the Realization of Business Benefits from IT Investments. *MIS Quarterly Executive, 6*(1), 1–11.

PMI. (2016). A Guide to the Project Management Body of Knowledge: PMBOK® guide (version 6.0). Project Management Institute Inc.

Reiss, G., Anthony, M., Chapman, J., Leigh, G., Pyne, A., & Rayner, P. (2006). *Gower Handbook of programme management.* Gower Publishing.

Remenyi, D., Money, A., & Bannister, F. (2007). *The effective measurement and management of ICT costs and benefits.* CIMA Publishing.

Sakar, P., & Widestach, C. (2005). *Benefits Management – How to realize the benefits of IS/IT investments* [Master Thesis]. IT University Göteborg, Sweden.

Sargeant, R. (2010). Creating value in project management using PRINCE2. Queensland University of Technology, OGC, APM Group and TSO.

Serra, C. E. M., & Kunc, M. (2015). Benefits Realisation Management and its influence on project success and on the execution of business strategies. *International Journal of Project Management, 33*(1), 53–66. doi:10.1016/j.ijproman.2014.03.011

Skulmoski, G. (2001). Project maturity and competence interface. *Cost Engineering (Morgantown, W. Va.), 43*, 11–19.

Ward, J., & Daniel, E. (2012). *Benefits management: How to increase the business value of your IT projects* (2nd ed.). John Wiley & Sons. doi:10.1002/9781119208242

Winter, M., Smith, C., Morris, P., & Cicmil, S. (2006). Directions for future research in project management: The main findings of a UK government-funded research network. *International Journal of Project Management, 24*(8), 638–649. doi:10.1016/j.ijproman.2006.08.009

Young, M., Young, R., & Zapata, J. R. (2014). Project, programme and portfolio maturity: A case study of Australian Federal Government. *International Journal of Managing Projects in Business, 7*(2), 215–230. doi:10.1108/IJMPB-08-2013-0034

ADDITIONAL READING

Ashurst, C. (2012). *Benefits Realization from Information Technology*. Palgrave Macmillan. doi:10.1057/9780230360822

Crawford, K. (2006). *Project Management Maturity Model* (2nd ed.). Auerbach Publications. doi:10.1201/9780849379468

Meredith, J., & Mantel, S. J. (2011). *Project Management: A managerial approach* (8th ed.). John Wiley and Sons, Inc.

KEY TERMS AND DEFINITIONS

Benefits Managements: Is the process of organizing and managing, such that potential benefits arising from the use of IT are actually realized (Ward & Daniel, 2006, p. 384).

Maturity Models: Are based on the principle that entities (people, organizations, functional areas or processes) evolve through a process of growth or development towards a more advanced level of maturity, through several different stages (Becker et al., 2009).

Organizational Project Management: Is based on the idea that there is a correlation between an organization's capability in terms of project, programme and portfolio management, and also its effectiveness in implementing strategy.

Project: Is a temporary endeavor undertaken to create a unique product, service, or result (PMI, 2016).

Project Management: Is the application of knowledge, skills, tools, and techniques to project activities to meet the project requirements (PMI, 2016).

Section 34
Marketing Analytics

Balanced Scorecard as a Tool to Evaluate Digital Marketing Activities

Tasnia Fatin
Putra Business School, Universiti Putra Malaysia, Malaysia

Mahmud Ullah
https://orcid.org/0000-0001-7472-2477
Department of Marketing, University of Dhaka, Bangladesh

Nayem Rahman
School of Business and Information Technology, Purdue University Global, USA

INTRODUCTION

Most of the recognized businesses, and renowned non-profit, government, and non-government organizations all around the world have started digital marketing by using digital media in addition to or instead of their traditional marketing practices during the last three decades or so. Electronic media available via the internet, computers, cell phones, smartphones, and many other devices constitute the digital media in general. Companies or organizations try to reach out to new segment or group of customers by using digital marketing techniques. Use of digital media helps them make faster and cost effective communications with the customers to understand their needs, wants, preferences, and concerns of the customers at a much deeper level in a much better manner. These processes result into having increased market share with satisfied customers. "Digital marketing refers to the strategic process of distributing, promoting, pricing products, and discovering the desires of customers in the virtual environment of the Internet" (Ferrell et al, 2019).

It is important to measure whether a company is able to take advantage of digital media, and digital marketing (DM) techniques. Business organizations are more conscious of performance management than ever before. With the global working environment adapting to a performance-based culture, many business organizations are using methods such as a balanced scorecard (BSC) to appraise and manage performance (Chaffey & Ellis-Chadwick, 2016). This approach is often used to measure both financial and non-financial aspects of an organization. A balanced scorecard is often used by the top management to improve and identify performance factors within the internal and external environment of the organization. The purpose of this paper is to identify certain issues regarding the usage of a balanced scorecard approach in the context of digital marketing performance management.

The balanced scorecard was originally intended as a measurement tool for stakeholders and executives to understand how an organization is performing in context to the organizational goals and objectives (Kaplan and Norton, 1992). This paper focuses on existing literature to bring clarity on the development of efficiency and performance in context to a balanced scorecard approach. A balanced scorecard has been put into application on various business areas to bring forth a measurable performance on business and technology associated with it.

DOI: 10.4018/978-1-7998-9220-5.ch142

Even though balanced scorecard has been applicable for many financial and non-financial factors in a business, the question still remains about how it is going to be effective in terms of digital marketing. The main theme through which this research paper is going to be addressed is based on certain questions which are: How effective is a balanced scorecard approach in terms of its usability in evaluating digital marketing activities? Is a balanced scorecard the most appropriate method for evaluating digital marketing activities? Is there a better methodology for managing digital Marketing activities other than a balanced scorecard approach?

This paper aims to provide a thorough analysis of a balanced scorecard approach towards measuring digital marketing activities to evaluate the digital marketing performance as effectively and efficiently as possible. Even though a balanced scorecard approach has been adopted by many organizations to effectively measure performance, the question remains as to whether or not it is the most efficient method to measure digital marketing performance (Killeen, 2018). This paper aims to answer this question by providing insights on whether the balanced scorecard is a perfect methodology on performance appraisal of digital marketing, and if there are better methods out there which are more effective than this (Alexander, 2019).

BACKGROUND AND LITERATURE REVIEW

With the advent of the internet followed by the inception of social media, marketing campaigns have taken a new shape. Now social media such as Facebook, Twitter, LinkedIn, YouTube, Instagram, Google+ and many other tools and technologies are being used to run marketing campaigns. Prior to the internet era, companies had been involved in only traditional marketing in terms of print advertisements on newspapers, magazines, billboards, commercials on TV and radio for decades. Switching to digital marketing has resulted in a huge shift in marketing campaigns to reach customers (Akhter & Rahman, 2019). The question is, how do we know if digital marketing is working and who should companies trust with their marketing (Cave, 2016).

Kaplan and Norton (1992) devise balanced scorecard in terms of "a set of measures that gives top managers a fast but comprehensive view of the business." They assert that senior executives need to measure the performance of their firms based on a few key areas simultaneously and not just financial measures. They suggest that innovation and learning aspects, internal business processes improvement and customer satisfaction should also be taken into account. They also suggest that no single measure can provide a clear performance target, but all four perspectives need to be taken into consideration.

Their suggested key measures have received wide acceptance by senior executives in the industry. In their 2010 paper, Kaplan, Norton, & Rugelsjoen (2010) suggest that through a balanced scorecard, a company can create a shift of focus from alliance management derived from operations and contributions to commitment and strategy (e.g., reducing total cycle time in clinical studies by 40% by a pharmaceutical company). (e.g., reducing total cycle time in clinical studies by 40% by a pharmaceutical company). In their other paper (Kaplan & Norton, 2010) they reported that since the introduction of balanced scorecard in 1992 it was adopted by thousands of private, public, and nonprofit organizations across the globe. In the same paper, they also reported that incorporating the management of intangible assets as measurement criteria for the balanced scorecard would help them to improve the management of intangible assets efficiently and thereby play a central role in value creation.

Balanced scorecard approach was used in a data warehouse project implementation to make sure the data warehouse environment was efficient, stable, provided users with a reasonable query runtime, added business value, enabled cost avoidance and lastly provide business executives quality information to support a company's strategic business decision-making at the right time (Rahman, 2013). Ganev (2018) proposes a benchmarking tool to measure digital marketing performance and improve competitiveness. Tancharoenwong (2018) identifies Facebook as a digital marketing tool and a highly popular medium. The author studied the engagement strategies employed by Facebook Pages in the field of maternal and child health information. The recommended strategy was tailoring an insightful and helpful content rather than focusing on the time of the day or frequency of post. The author also asserts that digital marketing tools can provide an extensive reach at a low cost.

Bakhtieva (2017) proposes a digital marketing framework that aims to increase customer loyalty and focuses on channels/touchpoints, audience, and customer journey. The author identifies digital marketing's role as more strategic and aggregative in nature which goes beyond the traditional understanding of marketing. The author asserts that the proposed framework could be beneficial for marketing executives for improving a company's position in the digital marketplace. Sawant (2018) discusses digital marketing's connection with business goals. The author suggests that "compared to traditional marketing, adapting to digital marketing approach can be extremely beneficial if analytics is applied and new leads are generated for identification of new customers." Taiminen (2016) asserts that close attention should be directed to utilization when inspecting the performance of digital marketing - not only just focusing on the possibilities they provide.

Charan and Bansal (2016) present the findings of a comparative study of the impact of digital marketing through Facebook vs. Twitter. The author suggests that digital marketing campaigns should use more creative and interactive content to get a real-time response from the customers. Chaudhry and Sharma (2018) have conducted detailed literature reviews of ethical issues in digital marketing in terms of privacy, trust, security, customer strategies, non-deception, service recovery and reliability. The authors conclude that the implication of fallout on these issues are serious and long-term and can cause the survival issue of business firms. Homburg et al. (2012) present results of an empirical study which suggests that the relationship of comprehensiveness of a marketing performance measurement system to firm performance is conditional. The authors also suggest that marketing alignment and market-based knowledge mediate this relationship, contingent upon a marketing strategy, marketing complexity and market dynamism.

Lee et al., (2017) present the service provider's performance measurement of an athletic department with the help of balanced scorecard (BSC) and Analytic Hierarchy Process (AHP) combined. Their study showed that the Financial perspective is the most important performance measure, followed by Customer, Business Process, and Learning & Growth. Their study also indicates that cost-saving is the most important factor. Islam et al. (2013) study the marketing performance by taking the customer perspectives of balanced scorecard framework into consideration. The authors report that there is a significant mediator effect of customer service quality in the interconnected relationship between marketing mix and customer loyalty.

Hauer et al (2016) present a performance measurement framework for service-oriented marketing drawing insights from a balanced scorecard approach. Their proposed framework provides top management with real-time information to oversee marketing campaigns. The authors also state that their framework can serve as an early warning system containing outcome measures and performance drivers. Brei et al (2011) performed a meta-analysis of correlation between strategies used for standardization and implementation of certain performance and marketing-mix. Their findings suggested a positive inclination towards that. Rahman (2016) proposes a scorecard tool to measure SQL (Structured Query Languages) query performance. The author implemented the scorecard to ensure the predictability of database queries through the consumption of resources and also to ensure its stability.

This paper suggests that digital marketing programmers and other stakeholders should look at digital marketing performance through the mainstream marketing mix. Traditionally, this mix consists of the 4 Ps which are the product, price, place, and promotion. The main objective here is to control financial outflow all the while adding value to the business and achieve economies of scale during a creative marketing campaign. The other prominent goal is to make sure that digital marketing programs are efficient, can reach specific customer segments, and provide quality information for other departments of the organization. The perspectives discussed above are analyzed upon sound metrics and can be correlated to one another. This would allow company executives to be more confident in terms of investing in a certain marketing campaign without worrying much about the investment being made in vain with minimum returns on it.

FOCUS OF THE PAPER

When it comes to using a balanced scorecard approach towards literally any form of performance appraisal, it is crucial to understand that it chooses the best of elements which are influential and contributory factors towards providing effective results on performance measurement (Bischoff, 2011). The aim of this method is to bring clarity and balance on the results of performance for an organization to easily analyze and identify. To bring further clarity to the topic, a brief history on the balanced scorecard is provided below. Balanced scorecard technique of measurement was invented by the Kaplan and Norton in 1990. It was further developed by them in 1992 and has now become a widely used measurement technique all over the world. Initially, it was actually introduced by the Nolan Norton Institute in World (Bourne & Bourne, 2009). In 1996, Kaplan and Norton published a book "The Balanced Scorecard". From that date to 2019 a lot of work has been done by academicians and traders on the balanced scorecard (Bischoff, 2011). A break-down of a balanced scorecard is provided. By definition, the balanced scorecard approach is a performance metric used in strategic management to identify and improve the various internal functions of a business. There are about four key points which are described below:

- *Focus on the strategic agenda of the organization:* The balanced scorecard approach is always designed in such a way that it is in alignment with the strategic vision and agenda of the company. In terms of its usability in digital marketing, it would be consistent with the strategic vision of a particular company (Marcoulides, 1989). In the modern world, digital marketing allows marketers to target specific customers in various locations and appeal to them through hand-held computer devices such as mobile phones and personal computers. Digital marketing, therefore, has the advantage of gathering data on how much its advertisement has reached its targeted audience and what kind of responses were recorded from them. This data would be crucial to the analysis of a balanced scorecard in terms of evaluating digital marketing activities.
- *Incorporating a smaller number of data items:* In digital marketing, it is crucial that relevant data is available for performance appraisal through a balanced scorecard approach. Fortunately, due to the very nature of digital marketing, a lot of data is available for the Scorecard to take under consideration (Varia, 2005). On top of that, the balanced scorecard also considers various other factors which may not be incorporated in generic evaluation data on digital marketing activities.
- *The mix of financial and non-financial factors:* As mentioned before, every balanced scorecard incorporates financial and non-financial matters. In terms of digital marketing, it can be stated that it performed well if the investment behind the marketing brings forth customs to the business.

At the same time, digital marketing has the ability to promote the brand of the company, which perhaps cannot be quantifiably measured. The balanced scorecard would incorporate both of these aspects to measure its performance (Varia, 2005).

- *Providing Feedback:* The best thing about a balanced scorecard approach is the fact that it can provide feedback on a performance appraisal. This feedback is crucial to improvement if necessary and it may also provide insights on how it can be better managed if there are any forms of lacking in that approach (Morris, 2009).

Balanced Scorecard Model for Effective Evaluation of Digital Marketing Activities

Figure 1. A Balanced Scorecard Model for Digital Marketing

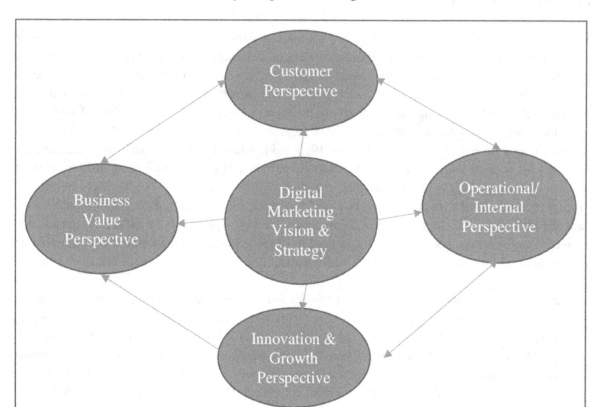

For a digital marketing campaign to run successfully, it must align its policies with the company's mission and vision. A balanced scorecard dictates that a successful marketing campaign relies on many aspects other than financial performance. Therefore, the scorecard would look at four different aspects of digital marketing and judge each category based on its set goals. The extant literature suggests that the lack of marketing accountability and the measurement of marketing performance poses a significant challenge for management globally (Liang et al., 2018). Drawing insights from the Balanced Scorecard (BSC), concerned marketing executives of different organizations try to evaluate the activities of their digital marketing programs. They try to get answers to four questions per guideline of Kaplan and

Norton (1992). How do customers view their digital marketing effort (customer perspectives)? What must they excel at to make their digital marketing program successful (internal perspective)? Can they continuously make improvements and create value in their digital marketing initiatives (innovation and learning perspective)? How do they look to owners and stakeholders (financial perspectives)? While they try to get key evaluation metrics, they also need to make sure that their proposed BSC does not cause information overload for the senior managers of the organization.

FINDINGS AND ANALYSES

Essential Perspectives of Digital Marketing Balanced Scorecard

Customer perspective

Table 1 summarizes different aspects of Customer Perspective of digital marketing balanced scorecard, which are explained below.

Table 1. Balanced scorecard – Customer Perspective

Goal	Evaluation Criteria
Access to products and services	Improvement in providing customers with more access to products and services choice and quality
Customer communications	Improvement in making customer-communications faster and interactive
Response to questions and complaints	Average response time in hours, days to respond to customer questions and complaints
Customer needs and wants	Improvement in providing tailored products and services of customer needs and wants
Brand awareness	Increases in brand awareness among customers
Customer benefits	Improvement in adding value in terms of pricing and instant discounts
Customer relationship	Increase of customer relationship via digital media
Customer services	Increase of feedback mechanism to allow consumers to express concerns, and response to those concerns

From a company's customer point of view, is digital marketing effective enough to reach customers? Does digital marketing address customer concerns in terms of time, quality, preferences, performance, and service? In regards to customer perspectives, digital marketing success depends on customer satisfaction of products and services being offered. User satisfaction is identified as the most important measurement criteria (Kaplan and Norton, 1992). The key factors in assessing satisfaction include design, reliability, quality of the product. A company's product and services development team, product managers, marketing program architects might want to maintain good coordination in their activities. Marketing teams need to maintain a good customer-relation for the success of the products and ensure that the customers' demands have been fulfilled. To understand users' products and services usability and preferences, a direct channel is recommended.

By providing customers access to more products and services choices, the company would achieve the goal of exposing more products and services to them. One of the key aspects of running a successful business is to maintain good customer communication and a company should try to make this process faster and as interactive as possible. Giving customers feedback is also an integral part of the before and after-sales service. Therefore, a company must take certain measurements to respond to every customer complaint or question. Any product or service exists to fulfill a particular need or want of a customer. It is perhaps the most crucial element to its existence. It would be in the best interest of the company to custom tailor every product or service that they may have to the needs and the wants of their customers. A company should always focus on benefiting the customers under all circumstances. They can do so by adding value to a product or providing instant discounts. Finally, the maintenance of customer relationship is also crucial to a business. One can achieve that by applying certain CRM techniques through digital media.

Table 1 shows some important services and benefits that could be provided to customers from digital marketing perspectives. In today's competitive business environment, it is critical to pay much attention to customer needs and wants, product feature needs, and the issues they face with the existing products and services. By providing a greater variety of product features, services, and information about choices marketers can provide customers the capability to make more informed decisions. Digital marketing also provides marketers to maintain faster and interactive customer communication channels. To increase customer satisfaction and retain customers, the response time to customers' question, concerns, and complaints need to be minimized. This is possible in the age of digital media. The digital media and marketing can accommodate the offering of tailored products features and services to customers. The digital media makes it possible to interact with customers at the individual level and provides features and services individually. Digital marketing can allow marketers to offer different prices, benefits, online coupons, and discounts to different customers' segments as well as individual customers. By taking advantage of digital media and digital marketing marketers could be more creative to show their customer obsessiveness. For example, marketers could take advantage of online blogs to give consumers the power to express product feature preferences and also express concerns. Research suggests, approximately 70 percent of companies do not pay much attention to customer concerns on Twitter (Ferrell et al, 2019). By addressing consumer concerns marketers can retain customers and maintain strong relationships.

Business value perspective

Table 2 shows different criteria used to evaluate business value perspective of digital marketing balanced scorecard.

Table 2. Balanced Scorecard – Business Value & Cost Savings Perspective

Goal	Evaluation Criteria
Cost-effectiveness	Ability to reach customers and business in an inexpensive way
Accessibility to customers	Ability to identify customers before they make purchase decisions
Affordability	Reaching new target market with ease and affordability
Reaching new customers	Reaching new customers to increase customer base
Retaining market share	Maintainability of market shares
Distribution cost reduction	Reduction of distribution costs via digital media
Business value delivery	Increase in percentage
Return in investments	Increase in percentage

From a business value and cost savings perspective, we need to evaluate how digital marketing effort looks to the organization's executives and stakeholders. By measuring the financial performance of the company, it could be determined if the alignment of the company's strategy and execution are consistent with the overall improvement of the company (Kaplan and Norton, 1992). Does digital marketing contribute to revenue increase and improvement of brand image? What is the financial goal of a company is achieving profitability, growth, and shareholder value (Kaplan and Norton, 1992)? Digital Marketing Program developers and architects need to evaluate if they are able to provide customers with products and services that they want. If they cannot make products and services available at the right time they are not providing customers with what they want. That might impact sales and revenues. A performance comparison could be made by doing an analysis of past data related to traditional marketing versus digital marketing. If a company fails to grow its customer base through marketing, they may never realize their true capacity of achievement through manufacturing (Kaplan and Norton, 1992).

Companies need to measure their digital marketing performance using these goals and measures to evaluate (Table 2). To ensure cost-effectiveness, a company must find the best way to reach its customers in the most inexpensive way possible. This measure can help a company achieve economies of scale. Also, it would benefit the company if they were able to identify their customer base before they make any kind of purchase decisions. The digital media provides an opportunity for marketers to obtain customer information (accessibility). The companies who use digital media heavily rely on web search engines to learn more about customer interests (Ferrell et al, 2019). Affordability should exist in every step of a company's decision-making process. With affordability, a company would easily reach new markets and customer base. Once a company has attained a certain amount of the market share, it is crucial that they take measurements to maintain it in order to retain that share. Cost-effectiveness is the overall theme of this section and therefore it must also be applicable to distribution as well. A reduction of it can be achieved through the use of digital media.

Proctor and Gamble relies on the Internet to conduct its marketing research activities to ensure speed, cost-effectiveness. For example, the company assesses its new product potentials by inviting consumers via the Internet and different social media to test new product prototypes, get feedback, know about concerns. Another example could be the use of the Facebook Exchange to conduct promotions to the target market segments. Companies can take advantage of digital media to provide customers with new benefits such as discounts in an individualized and faster way. Digital marketing also provides an opportunity for free publicity. Most business organizations use Facebook page to promote their products and services and interact with customers without incurring costs. The digital media provides companies the opportunity to gather useful information about customers and their preferences. Companies could use digital media to add business value by processing orders electronically. They can increase the speed of communication and thereby reduce distribution inefficiencies and cost (Ferrell et al, 2019).

Internal process perspective

Table 3 lists different factors to analyze internal process perspective of digital marketing balanced scorecard.

From an internal business processes standpoint, are digital marketing programs capable enough to capture sentiments from social media sites and influence different internal departments of an organization to enable them to satisfy customer needs? Digital marketing programs need to be effective to gather inputs about the improvements of existing products and new ideas to develop new products. In order for managers to gain insights on various internal processes of a company, a balanced scorecard approach is an appropriate tool. It would be in the best interest of the company if the managers were to focus on various internal operations to ultimately satisfy different customer demands, wants and needs (Kaplan and Norton, 1992).

Table 3. Balanced Scorecard – Internal Process Perspective

Goal	Evaluation Criteria
Marketing research capability	Increase in gathering customer choice, feedback, complaints
Product-prototype testing	Intensity in reaching out consumers to participate in prototype testing
Feedback mechanism	Degree of using the digital media to gather customer feedback
Internal Business Communications	Improvement in communications within internal departments
Internal Business Productivity	Increase in productivity of internal business departments
IS and Knowledge Sharing	Efficient IS development and knowledge sharing capability

Digital marketing program developers and designers need to take under consideration that all internal processes are efficient enough to maintain customer's satisfaction. As part of the internal operation in digital marketing programs, certain key factors need to be taken into consideration. These include making different internal groups such as product design and development teams working with a mindset of satisfying customers and exceeding their expectations, offer reliable and quality products and services, and flawless and safe deployment of products in the market. A company's digital marketing programs need to make sure that its assets in the market are utilized to the maximum and at the same time, they are playing a proactive role to contribute towards the development of the company (Tollin and Schmidt, 2012).

Table 3 provides certain goals and corresponding measurements from the perspective of internal processes. A company must gather enough resources such as customer feedback, choices, and complaints to develop a database for marketing research. Many companies around the world are now reaching out to various customers in order for them to sample their products. This is a measurement through which they could test out new products. Gaining feedback from customers is crucial to a company. Therefore, in order for them to do it effectively and efficiently, they must develop a digital media platform to gain feedback.

A company must be on a continuous improvement mission to improve internal communications. Through efficient internal business communication, efficiency could be achieved, and internal business productivity could also be increased. In the age of information and technology, sharing information and knowledge would allow a company to achieve goals quicker and more effectively. Therefore, a company must develop the capacity to share knowledge and information easily. Companies need to gather customer information in terms of needs, preferences, dislikes, concerns. This information needs to be shared with other departments such as product design and development, marketing research. On the other hand, non-marketing managers need to have a communication channel with marketing managers to continuously know important information about customers' preferences.

Innovation and Growth Perspective

Table 4 shows the criteria to evaluate innovation and growth perspective of digital marketing balanced scorecard.

Table 4. Balanced Scorecard – Innovation & Growth Perspectives

Goal	Evaluation Criteria
Marketing research efficiency	Efficient marketing research capability
Promotional creativity	Creativity in marketing campaign and promotional activities
Communication channels	New communication channels to reach customers individually
Utilizing digital media	Capability to take advantage of social networking tools
Increased automation	Reduction of time to reach customers
Emerging technology learning	Research and training effort
Digital marketing leadership	New capability in digital marketing to continue business growth

Digital marketing efforts need a good amount of investments. From an innovation and growth perspective, can a digital marketing program continues to improve and create value? A company's senior executives and management would want to know whether the digital marketing programs deliver business value to the company and continuously able to reach new and valuable groups of customers and also drive down digital marketing costs as opposed to costs incurred by traditional marketing activities. Value creation might consist of creating creative marketing programs and coming up with new marketing strategies. The digital marketing teams need to evaluate whether an organization can take full advantage of digital marketing, innovativeness in developing marketing programs, ability to reach target markets, and the ability to observe customers' reaction.

Table 4 presents several key goals and measures from the perspectives of innovation and growth. A company must increase its capacity to do efficient marketing research in order for them to identify trends, determine what kind of products and services to provide and features they must possess. Many companies effectively use Facebook and Twitter to discover what customers want. It is reported that about 39 percent of retailers use social media to gather information and use them in product design and development stage (Ferrell et al, 2019). To understand new trends and to perhaps create one, a company must find creative ways to promote their products or services. A creative marketing campaign could help a company to achieve this goal. The modern world demands a company to utilize digital media. Therefore, as a remedy, a company must adapt to take advantage of social networking tools. In earlier times, a company had to put in a lot of labor hours to gather customer needs, wants, and preferences. However, it would be in a company's best interest to find an automated way to deduct the time to reach out to customers.

Technology is changing and evolving every day and as a result, a company must increase effort to conducting research and training to adapt to new emerging technologies. Overall, it is in the best interest of any company to become a digital marketing leader. In order to achieve that, a company must adapt to the new surroundings and research the digital marketing realm. Marketers need to adopt creativity in using social media and digital marketing techniques to reach out customers. Many companies use cookies on the user's computer to identify his/her online presence and product preferences. Companies also use social media to know consumers concerns and address their complaints. Companies need to be creative in using digital media and digital marketing techniques to reach customers faster than before and achieve cost-effectiveness. Companies also find digital media effectively to reach out to consumers in new target markets (Ferrell et al, 2019).

CRITICAL DISCUSSIONS AND RECOMMENDATIONS

The authors would like to offer a few criticisms of the balanced scorecard framework of digital marketing. The first criticism focuses on the experimental nature of the framework. It sounds great however, the approach is rather theoretical in nature. Even though the points mentioned above are correlated with performance appraisal, there could be numerous factors which can contribute towards an upward or a downward spiral of performance which could be mistaken for digital marketing performance without actually finding out the actual results (Van Vliet, 2010).

Inefficiency in the business organization could lead to negative cash inflow or deteriorate the brand image which could be misinterpreted as a poor performance in context to digital marketing. At the same time, it is possible that brand reputation and the quality of the service has brought forth a positive cash flow within the company which could also be misinterpreted as a good performance in digital marketing with a balanced scorecard approach.

The second criticism with a balanced scorecard approach would be considering the actual results it yields (Gaitniece, 2018). Most balanced scorecard approach would not give out actual quantifiable results which could determine performance management up to that extent. The recommendations derived are also theoretical in nature and therefore could not be treated as an absolute measurement of the actual performance. It is simply lenient towards certain results based on its limited understandings according to its findings and therefore provides recommendations based on assumptions up to a certain extent based mostly on theoretical approach (Kaplan & Norton, 2007).

The third criticism has to do with its recommendations and reflections being in alignment with the interest of all stakeholders. A balanced scorecard approach mostly brings out the performance issues which if found negative, suggests an organization to get rid of certain elements and add others in order to gain financial gains (Alexander, 2019). This means that it only serves stakeholders who have financial interests within the company. There are certain other stakeholders who are interested in the company not because of financial matters but for different reasons altogether.

FUTURE RESEARCH DIRECTIONS

As mentioned earlier, there could be numerous factors which can contribute towards an upward or a downward spiral of performance which could be mistaken for digital marketing performance without actually finding out the actual results. The framework needs to be more practical performance-based rather than being more theoretical in nature. Care should be taken in finding out the actual cause of the positive cash flow in the business because sometimes digital marketing could wrongly be credited for positive cash flow in the company. Also, the recommendations derived are also theoretical in nature and therefore cannot be treated as an absolute measurement of the actual performance.

It is simply lenient towards certain results based on its limited understandings according to its findings and therefore provides recommendations based on assumptions up to a certain extent based mostly on theoretical approach (Kaplan & Norton, 2007). In order to find measures of actual performance, more practical performance components have to be taken into consideration. It has also been mentioned earlier that a balanced scorecard approach mostly brings out performance issues which if found negative, suggests an organization to get rid of certain elements and add others in order to gain financial gains (Alexander, 2019). This means that it only serves stakeholders who have financial interests within the company. But in order to reach the top, a company has to take into account long term brand building, reputation building and also building a base of loyal customers. Future researches should thus aim to solve these problems and focus on finding components take on a more practical approach to measuring performance.

CONCLUSION

In a world where technology is evolving at a pace that cannot possibly be comprehended by most people, it is critical to understand that marketers have been using this platform to market products and services through a concept called digital marketing. Marketers have existed from a very early age where traditional marketing methods such as the use of television adverts, radio adverts, leaflets, banners and much more have proven effective. However, in the modern age, digital marketing has been the ultimate tool for marketers to target their customers in a very specific way. Through websites, social media and other internet-based programs, marketers are able to target their customers like never before. Given this platform, it is crucial to understand the performance of a digital marketing campaign to increase efficiency (Akhter & Rahman, 2019). Measuring the performance of digital marketing campaigns have been in use in various ways.

The motivation behind using a balanced scorecard is to make sure digital marketing programs are innovative and efficient; digital marketers do a great job in developing efficient marketing campaigns and they are always adapting to new ways to be more creative and innovative. Digital marketing projects continuously helps the organization's product development, information technology, and other departments to add further value and work towards achieving economies of scale. The digital marketing department is there to provide relevant and quality information to the business executives in order for them to make better strategic decisions.

This paper particularly focused on how the concept of a balanced scorecard approach could be used to measure digital marketing performance. This paper describes digital marketing in general and does the same with the balanced scorecard. Furthermore, it describes several aspects of a balanced scorecard and its implementation on digital marketing performance. To conclude, it can be stated that this method might carry some potential to bring out conclusive results in terms of performance of a particular digital marketing campaign. At the same time, it is crucial to understand that there might be certain limitations to the results and there would be room for some level of uncertainty in terms of results.

REFERENCES

Akhter, S., & Rahman, N. (2019). Marketing analytics: Knowledge as a resource. *Proceedings of the 3rd Biennial Conference of Bangladesh Academy of Business Administration (BABA'19)*.

Alexander, L. (2019). *What is digital marketing?* https://blog.hubspot.com/marketing/what-is-digital-marketing

Bakhtieva, E. (2017). B2B digital marketing strategy: A framework for assessing digital touchpoints and increasing customer loyalty based on Austrian heating, ventilation and air conditioning industry companies. *Oeconomia Copernicana, 8*(3), 463-478. doi: .v8i3.29 doi:10.24136/oc

Bischoff, A. L. (2011). *The balanced scorecard*. GRIN Publishing.

Bourne, M., & Bourne, P. (2009). *Balanced scorecard (instant manager)*. Hodder & Stoughton.

Brei, V. A., Avila, L. D., Camargo, L. F., & Engels, J. (2011). The influence of adaptation and standardization of the marketing mix on performance: A meta-analysis. *Brazilian Administration Review*, *8*(3), 266–287. doi:10.1590/S1807-76922011000300004

Cave, J. (2016). *Digital marketing vs. traditional marketing: Which one is better?* https://www.digital-doughnut.com/articles/2016/july/digital-marketing-vs-traditional-marketing. 2019/04/20.

Chaffey, D. (2019). *Digital marketing goal setting, evaluation and optimization guide*. https://www.smartinsights.com/guides/delivering-results-digital-marketing-guide/

Chaffey, D., & Ellis-Chadwick, F. (2016). *Digital marketing: Strategy, implementation and practice* (6th ed.). Pearson Education.

Charan, A., & Bansal, E. (2016). Impact of digital marketing through Facebook vs. Twitter: A comparative study of Indian consumers. *Review of Professional Management*, *14*(2), 34–51.

Chaudhry, R. S., & Sharma, A. (2018). Ethical issues in digital marketing - A review. *ITIHAS The Journal of Indian Management*, *8*(1), 10–18.

Ferrell, O. C., Hirt, G., & Ferrell, L. (2019). *Business foundations: A changing world* (12th ed.). McGraw-Hill Education.

Gaitniece, E. (2018). Digital Marketing Performance Evaluation Methods. *CBU International Conference Proceedings*.

Gama, A. P. D. (2017). A balanced scorecard for marketing. *International Journal of Business Performance Management*, *18*(4), 476–494. doi:10.1504/IJBPM.2017.087116

Ganev, P. (2018). How to choose the appropriate digital marketing tool. *Global Business & Economics Anthology*, *1*(3),16-25.

Hauer, G., Kroll, J., Yen, D. C., Chen, P. S., & Lin, S.-C. (2016). A performance measurement framework for service-oriented marketing. *Total Quality Management*, *27*(12), 1373–1395. doi:10.1080/147 83363.2015.1076703

Homburg, C., Artz, M., & Wieseke, J. (2012). Marketing performance measurement systems: Does comprehensiveness really improve performance? *Journal of Marketing*, *76*(3), 56–77. doi:10.1509/jm.09.0487

Islam, M., Yang, Y.-F., Hu, Y.-J., & Hsu, C.-S. (2013). Marketing mix, service quality and loyalty – in perspective of customer-centric view of balanced scorecard approach. *Accounting. Accountability & Performance*, *18*(1), 1–17.

Kaplan, R., & Norton, D. (1990). The balanced scorecard. *Technometrics*, *40*(3), 266.

Kaplan, R.S., & Norton, D.P. (1992). The balanced scorecard – measures that drive performance. *Harvard Business Review*, 71-79.

Kaplan, R.S., & Norton, D.P. (2007). Using the balanced scorecard as a strategic management system. *Harvard Business Review*, 1-14.

Kaplan, R. S., Norton, D. P., & Ansari, S. (2010). The execution premium: Linking strategy to operations for competitive advantage. *The Accounting Review, 85*(4), 1475–1477. doi:10.2308/accr.2010.85.4.1475

Kaplan, R.S., Norton, D.P., & Rugelsjoen, B. (2010). Managing Alliances with the balanced scorecard. *Harvard Business Review.*

Kardaras, D. K., Karakostas, B., Barbounaki, S., Papadopoulos, A., & Kaperonis, S. (2017). Integrating the balanced scorecard and web analytics for strategic digital marketing: A multi-criteria approach using DEMATEL. *Proceedings of The Sixth International Conference on Data Analytics,* 41-46.

Lee, S., Brownlee, E., Kim, Y., & Lee, S. (2017). Ticket sales outsourcing performance measures using balanced scorecard and analytic hierarchy process combined model. *Sport Marketing Quarterly, 2017*(26), 110–120.

Liang, X., Gao, Y., & Ding, Q. S. (2018). What you measure is what you will get? Exploring the effectiveness of marketing performance measurement practices. *Cogent Business & Management, 5*(1), 1–12. doi:10.1080/23311975.2018.1503221

Mandal, P., & Joshi, N. (2017). Understanding digital marketing strategy. *International Journal of Scientific Research and Management, 5*(6), 5428–5431.

Marcoulides, G. A. (1989). Performance appraisal: Issues of validity. *Performance Improvement Quarterly, 2*(2), 3–12. doi:10.1111/j.1937-8327.1989.tb00398.x

Morris, N. (2009). Understanding digital marketing: Marketing strategies for engaging the digital generation. *Journal of Direct, Data and Digital Marketing Practice, 10*(4), 384–387. doi:10.1057/dddmp.2009.7

Performance digital marketing of Boise & Tri-Cities, WA. (2019). https://performancedigitalmarketing.net/

Rahman, N. (2013). Measuring performance for data warehouses - A balanced scorecard approach. *International Journal of Computer and Information Technology, 4*(1), 1–7.

Rahman, N. (2016). SQL scorecard for improved stability and performance of data warehouses. *International Journal of Software Innovation, 4*(3), 22–37. doi:10.4018/IJSI.2016070102

Sawant, Y. (2018). Connecting Digital Marketing with Business Goals. *DAWN Journal for Contemporary Research in Management,* 36-38.

Taiminen, H. (2016). One gets what one orders: Utilisation of digital marketing tools. *The Marketing Review, 16*(4), 389–404. doi:10.1362/146934716X14636478977999

Tancharoenwong, A. S. (2018). Facebook as digital marketing tool: Facebook's engagement strategy for maternal and child health page. *UTCC International Journal of Business and Economics, 10*(3), 3–17.

Tollin, K., & Schmidt, M. (2012). Marketing logics, ambidexterity and influence. *Journal of Strategic Marketing, 20*(6), 509–534. doi:10.1080/0965254X.2012.689992

Van, V. V. (2010). *Balanced scorecard.* https://www.toolshero.com/strategy/balanced-scorecard/. 2019/04/29.

Varia, K. (2005). A balanced approach. *Manufacturing Engineer, 84*(2), 40–43. doi:10.1049/me:20050207

ADDITIONAL READING

Dabab, M., Freiling, M., Rahman, N., & Sagalowicz, D. (2018). A decision model for data mining techniques. In *Proceedings of the IEEE Portland International Center for Management of Engineering and Technology (PICMET 2018) Conference.* 10.23919/PICMET.2018.8481953

Khanam, F., Al-Zadid, O., & Ullah, M. (2022). Measuring the quality of higher education in Bangladesh: A study on the University of Dhaka. *International Journal of Knowledge-Based Organizations, 12*(1), 1 – 15. . doi:10.4018/IJKBO.291688

Khanam, F., & Rahman, N. (2019). Measuring the quality of healthcare services in Bangladesh: A comparative study of two hospitals. *International Journal of Big Data and Analytics in Healthcare, 4*(1), 15–31. doi:10.4018/IJBDAH.2019010102

Maydanova, S. (2019). Balanced scorecard for the digital transformation of global container shipping lines. *Proceedings of the International Conference on Digital Transformation in Logistics and Infrastructure (ICDTLI 2019). Atlantis Highlights in Computer Sciences, 1*, 415-420. 10.2991/icdtli-19.2019.72

Rahman, N. (2018a). A taxonomy of data mining problems. *International Journal of Business Analytics, 5*(2), 73–86. doi:10.4018/IJBAN.2018040105

Rahman, N. (2018b). Data mining techniques and applications: A ten-year update. *International Journal of Strategic Information Technology and Applications, 9*(1), 78–97. doi:10.4018/IJSITA.2018010104

Rahman, N. (2018c). Data warehousing and business intelligence with big data. *Proceedings of the International Annual Conference of the American Society for Engineering Management.*

Rahman, N., Daim, T., & Basoglu, N. (2021). Exploring the factors influencing big data technology acceptance. *IEEE Transactions on Engineering Management*, 1–16. doi:10.1109/TEM.2021.3066153

Smith, A. W., Rahman, N., Saleh, M. A., & Akhter, S. (2019). A holistic approach to innovation and fostering intrepreneurship. *International Journal of Knowledge-Based Organizations, 9*(2), 62–79. doi:10.4018/IJKBO.2019040104

KEY TERMS AND DEFINITIONS

Balanced: A natural or any abstract state of a living or non-living entity, or of a concept, philosophy, or idea, - which is in an equilibrium, statically static, dynamically static, or usually in a stable position over a period of time or range of situations relative to the broader time frame or various situations, due to the interaction of all the internal and external forces or elements working on that particular entity, concept, philosophy, or idea over that period of time or range of situations.

Digital Marketing: All kinds of marketing tasks done with the help or involvement of anything or everything of the hardware or software related to or used in the extended field or realm of information technology, to supplement the traditional marketing, or to do it absolutely newly and separately.

Evaluation: Ascertaining, determining, examining, or judging the worth of anything, any activity, or any concept by applying certain criteria as standard or benchmark for that specific thing, activity, or concept. The purpose of such ascertainment, determination, examination, or judgment is basically to identify & correct the flaws or problems if any, in the said thing, activity, or concept.

Perspective: Some kind of background, context, framework, relationship, situations, or surroundings to a particular issue to explain it in comprehensive manners, to make it perceivable to most of the stakeholders as easily and uniformly as possible. A total canvass or picture of the whole issue at a glance.

Scorecard: An object of certain design, shape, and size corresponding to the purpose of its creation and use, to keep the records of different numerical or non-numerical results of i.e. data or information obtained from measuring any activity, task, method, procedure, or phenomenon, which may be used for different statistical or analytical purposes to make data based decisions to run the related activities, tasks, or phenomena more effectively and efficiently.

Section 35
Mathematical Optimization

An Approach for a Multi–Objective Capacitated Transportation Problem

Nurdan Kara
National Defence University, Turkey

Hale Gonce Köçken
https://orcid.org/0000-0003-1121-7099
Yildiz Technical University, Turkey

INTRODUCTION

The classical transportation problem (TP) is a special type of linear programming (LP) problem. In this problem, a homogeneous product is to be transported from several sources to several destinations in such a way that the total transportation cost is minimum, or profit is maximum. In this problem, while sources can be defined as suppliers, production centers, factories, etc., demands may be customers, warehouses, sinks, etc. Moreover, this problem may have equality or inequality type of constraints. In real-life problems, the constraints of TPs are not generally in equal form. In some cases, the decision-maker may have specified a supply amount that must be provided from a particular source. Then, the corresponding supply constraint will be "greater than or equal to" form. Similarly, when the amount of resources owned by any supplier is limited (i.e. has an upper limit), then the corresponding supply constraint will be "less than or equal to" form. These different types of inequalities may also appear in any demand constraint. Therefore, TP with mixed constraints arises.

Moreover, when the total demand equals the total supply, the TP is referred to be a balanced transportation problem. If a TP has a total supply that is strictly less than the total demand, then the problem has no feasible solution. In this situation, it is sometimes desirable to allow the possibility of leaving some demand unmet. In such a case, we can balance a transportation problem by creating a dummy supply point that has a supply amount equal to the unmet demand and associating it with a penalty.

Furthermore, a STP with two or more fractional objective functions is called as a multi-objective fractional STP. In this problem, maximum profitability - profit/cost or profit/time – as a criterion function is maximized subject to supply, demand, and conveyance constraints.

The transportation problem, in its simplest form, deals with the physical transfer of some goods from sources to destinations but also has different applications in many different fields. Many subproblems that can be defined especially in the field of logistics are based on the logic of transportation problems. From a more general point of view, there are many transportation problems in the field of the supply chain, which includes the movement of the product or service from the supplier to the customer and is defined as the whole systems of organizations, people, technology, and activities. Some of these are the transportation of raw materials to be sent from suppliers to the factories, the transportation of goods to warehouses or distribution centers, the delivery of the products to customers, and transferring used products to recycling centers.

DOI: 10.4018/978-1-7998-9220-5.ch143

In today's world of globalization, we are faced with the transportation of more products and the diversity in the ways of transportation of the product. To meet this need, we had to define the solid transportation problem (STP) which is one of the important research topics from both theoretical and practical aspects. STP is a special type of the traditional transportation problem in which three-dimensional properties (supply, demand, convenience) are taken into account in the objective and constraint set instead of source and destination. The necessity of considering this special type of transportation problem arises when heterogeneous conveyances are available for the shipment of products. The STP is also applied in public distribution systems. In many industrial problems, a homogeneous product is delivered from a source to a destination by means of different modes of transport called conveyances, such as trucks, cargo flights, goods trains, ships, etc. These conveyances are taken as the third dimension. An STP may be transformed into a traditional TP by considering only a single type of conveyance.

It is generally aimed to minimize only the transportation cost in all these transportation problems, namely the classical two-dimensional transport problem or the three-dimensional STP. However, it is very rare to consider only cost in real-life problems. Therefore, it is required to consider the optimization of several objectives such as minimization of transportation time, packing cost of goods, maximizing the total profit, the security level of transportation, etc. In addition to these objectives, environmental objective functions, such as the minimization of carbon emissions from related transportation processes can also be taken into account within the scope of green, closed loop, or sustainable supply chain management. All these situations lead to considering multi-objective versions of TP or STP. Thus, Multi-objective TP (MTP) and Multi-objective STP (MSTP) can be modeled more realistically. Although the optimal solution concept is utilized in single-objective problems, Pareto-optimal solutions emerge in multi-objective problems. Since the total number of these non-dominated solutions is usually very large, the preferences of the decision-makers are taken into account with methods such as weighting, interactive approaches, scalarization procedures, etc. In this way, the most suitable solutions are tried to be chosen to present the decision-makers among many Pareto-optimal solutions.

One of the most important research topics for solid transportation problems is the use of fuzzy set theory. This theory was first introduced by Zadeh. In several applications, the required data for real-life problems can be imprecise. Therefore, an adaptation of fuzzy set theory in the solution method increases the flexibility and effectiveness of the proposed approaches. This theory has been used for the development of the applications of solid transportation. Most research investigates multi-objective solid transportation problems under the fuzzy environment in two cases: (1) the costs, the supplies, the demands, and conveyances capacities are fuzzy numbers (2) All parameters are crisp while the fuzzy programming approach is used.

The classical TP, which has supply and demand constraints, deals with transporting a single commodity. However, additional indices such as commodities and modes of transport should be considered, and this necessity led to the multi-index TP. Moreover, fixed costs in establishing the production process can be added to TP models, so fixed charge TPs occur. Similar to MSTP, criteria other than cost (such as time, profit, etc.) led to the multi-index, multi-objective fixed charge TPs.

Although the linear membership function is widely utilized in many real-world decision-making problems, the usage of the non-linear membership function can provide a more realistic conclusion than the linear ones in some practical applications. That is, the non-linear membership function is much more versatile than linear types and can generate better results for objective functions' satisfactory levels. Therefore, the decision-maker can opt for the membership function, which is presenting a better solution for the objectives being a higher priority.

BACKGROUND

Multi-Objective Transportation Problem

Ringuest and Rinks (1987) presented two interactive algorithms which take advantage of the special form of the multiple objective TP.

Solid and Multi-Objective Solid Transportation Problem

The STP was stated by Schell (1955) and Haley (1963) described the solution procedure of this problem. Pandian and Anuradhais (2010) proposed a method for finding an optimal solution to solid transportation problems for MSTP, Ahlatcioglu, and Sivri (1988) proposed an efficient solution method by using decomposing techniques to reduce the dimension.

Fuzzy Multi-Objective and Capacitated Transportation Problem

Bit et al. (1993) have applied the fuzzy programming technique to solve the multi-objective transportation problem. Das et al. (1999) have given the solution method for multi-objective transportation problem where the cost coefficients of the objective functions, and the supply and demand parameters have been defined as interval values. Li and Lai (2000) and Wahed (2001) proposed a fuzzy compromise programming approach for solving MTP. In (2012) is presented a chance-constrained multi-objective capacitated transportation problem based on a fuzzy goal programming problem by Parmanik and Banerjee. Gupta et al. (2018) have formulated a new model of multi-objective capacitated transportation problems with mixed constraints. The fuzzy approach with hyperbolic membership functions for the multi-objective capacitated transportation problem has been presented by Bit (2004).

Fuzzy Solid and Multi-Objective Transportation Problem

In many real-world situations, the parameters in MSTP are uncertain in nature due to various uncontrollable aspects such as insufficient input information, fluctuation of financial market conditions, etc. To cope with uncertainty in real-life transportation systems, a lot of researchers recently have studied STP in several uncertain environments. Pramanik et al. (2013) have introduced the formulation of MSTP for a damageable item. Chen et al. (2017) modeled a goal programming problem for MSTP. Anuradha et al. (2019) has used a row maxima method for solving a bi-objective STP. Bit (2005) presented the fuzzy model with hyperbolic membership functions for a multi-objective capacitated STP.

Fuzzy Multi-Objective Fractional Solid Transportation Problem

Radhakrishnan and Anukokila, (2014) focus on an interval STP applying fractional goal programming. A capacitated MSTP was defined as a constrained nonlinear problem and solved using Interactive Fuzzy Method and Gradient method by Ojha et al. (2014). Jana and Jana (2020) gave a solution method for STP with additional constraints and optimized through fuzzy and fractional programming methods. Basu and Acharya (2002) presented bi-criterion quadratic fractional STP and developed a method. In Khalifa and Al-Shabi, (2018), a fully fuzzy multi-objective linear fractional programming is given for multi-product problems. Khalifa (2019) investigated a fractional multi-objective multi- product STP with interval costs, supply, demand, and conveyances. Khalifa et al. (2021) dealt with fuzzy geometric programming approach by using membership function to obtain compromise solution of multi-objective fractional two-stage STP.

Different Membership Functions

Leberling (1981) solved the multi-objective linear programming problem by fuzzy method with a non-linear membership function. Li and Lee (1991) defined fuzzy multiple objective linear programming and solved using exponential membership function. Fuzzy multi-objective problem is solved using exponential membership functions in Rath and Dash (2017). Peidro and Vasant (2011) applied the fuzzy goal programming approach with some nonlinear membership functions to solving multi-objective transportation problems (MTP). Verma et al. (1997) proposed the fuzzy method using some non-linear membership functions to solve an MTP. Bodkhe et al. (2010) applied to fuzzy approach for solving MSTP using hyperbolic and exponential membership functions.

Multi-Index Transportation Problem

Kaur et al. (2015) developed fuzzy programming approaches to a real-life transportation problem by using linear, exponential, and hyperbolic membership functions and analyzing some kind of the uncertainties of the parameters. Many important studies (2015, 2018, 2019) have also been made on the multi-index transportation problem. Yang and Liu (2007) gave expected value model, change constrained and dependent chance model for fixed charge STP with fuzzy environment. Yang and Yuan (2007) presented a bicriteria STP with fixed charge under stochastic environment.

This paper proposes a fuzzy approach for solving a multi-objective capacitated solid transportation problem (MCSTP) using an exponential membership function. An application from Tao and Xu (2012) is solved for the concrete transportation problem of the Xiluodu Hydropower station and compares the solutions of this method using linear and exponential membership functions. Therefore, we can get a satisfactory solution for the application and present the decision-maker.

The organization of the paper is shown as follows. In Section 2, the mathematical model of MCSTP is given. The next section presents the proposed solution procedure for MCSTP using linear and exponential membership functions. In section 4, a real-life problem from the literature is solved. Finally, the conclusion follows in Section 5.

Multi-Objective Capacitated Solid Transportation Problem

In MCSTP, a product is to be transported from m supplies to n demands by means of k conveyances and their capacities are a_i, b_j, and e_k, respectively. And suppose that the cost of p-th objective function $Z_p(x)$ is denoted by c_{ijk}^p which corresponds to x_{ijk}. Then, the mathematical model of MCSTP can be defined as:

$$\min Z_p(x) = \sum_{i=1}^{m} \sum_{j=1}^{n} \sum_{k=1}^{K} c_{ijk}^p x_{ijk} \ , p=1,2,\ldots P$$

$$\sum_{j=1}^{n}\sum_{k=1}^{K} x_{ijk} \le a_i \quad , i=1,2,\dots m$$

$$\sum_{i=1}^{m}\sum_{k=1}^{K} x_{ijk} \ge b_j \quad , j=1,2,\dots n \tag{1}$$

$$\sum_{i=1}^{m}\sum_{j=1}^{n} x_{ijk} \le e_k \quad , k=1,2,\dots K$$

$l_{ijk} \le x_{ijk} \le u_{ijk} \bullet \forall i,j,k$

where the subscript on $Z_p(x)$ and c_{ijk}^p denote the *p*-th objective function and $a_j>0$, $\forall i$; $b_j>0$, $\forall j$; $e_k>0$, $\forall k$; $c_{ijk}^p \ge 0$, $\forall i,j,k,pS$ and the balanced equality holds, that is $\sum_{i=1}^{m} a_i = \sum_{j=1}^{n} b_j = \sum_{k=1}^{K} e_k$. Let the feasible region of MCSTP given by (1) is denoted by *S*. We note that if the last constraint of problem (1) is not considered, classical MSTP is obtained. However, in real-life problems, transport quantities often have a certain lower and upper limit.

While the optimal solution concept is discussed in a single objective STP, the Pareto-optimal solution notion is used in the multi-objective framework, So, we present the following basic definitions:

Definition 1: (Pareto-optimal solution) Let S be the feasible region of (1). $x^* \in S$ is a Pareto-optimal (strongly efficient) solution iff there does not exist another $x \in S$ such that $Z_p(x) \le Z_p(x^*)$ for all $p=1,2,\dots P$ and $Z_p(x) \neq Z_p(x^*)$ for at least one $p=1,2,\dots P$; where $x^*=\{x_{ijk}\}$.

Definition 2: (Compromise solution) A feasible $x^* \in S$ is a compromise solution of (1) iff $x^* \in E$ and $F^p(x^*) \le \bigwedge_{x \in S} F(x)$ where $\wedge$ stands for "minimum" and *E* is the set of Pareto-optimal solutions.

A Solution Procedure for MCSTP

In the proposed solution procedure, the nonlinear exponential membership function will be used instead of the linear membership function, which is frequently used in the literature. In order to present the approach clearly, first of all, the linear membership function will be discussed in the following subsection.

Designing the linear membership functions of the objectives:

Firstly, the linear membership function for the objectives can be written in the following way:

$$\mu_p(Z_P(\mathbf{x})) = \begin{cases} 1, & Z_P < L_p \\ \dfrac{U_P - Z_p(\mathbf{x})}{U_p - L_p}, & L_p \le Z_p \le U_p, \\ 0, & Z_p > U_p \end{cases} \tag{2}$$

where $\max_{\mathbf{x} \in S} Z_p(\mathbf{x}) = U_p$ and $\min_{\mathbf{x} \in S} Z_p(\mathbf{x}) = L_p$, $p=1,\dots,P$.

By using of the "min" fuzzy operator model proposed by Zimmermann the following problem is solved for MCSTP:

$$\max_{\mathbf{x} \in S} \min_{1 \leq p \leq P} \mu_p(Z_p(\mathbf{x})) \tag{3}$$

The new variable $\lambda = \min \bullet \mu_p(Z_p)$ implies the constraints $\mu_p(Z_p) \geq \lambda$ for all p. Thus, (3) can be reduced to:

$$\max \bullet \lambda$$

$$\mu_p(Z_p) \geq \lambda \tag{4}$$

$$\mathbf{x} \in S.$$

Problem (4) is the model that corresponds to Zimmermann's min operator. The λ^* solution represents the common satisfaction level of all objectives. Here, the world "common" means the lowest level of satisfaction achieved for each objective of (1).

Designing the Exponential Membership Function of the Objectives

In many real-world decision-making problems, usage of the non-linear membership would provide a more realistic conclusion than the linear ones. Also, the rate of satisfaction of membership functions is not always constant, as in linear membership functions. Therefore, the exponential membership function is preferred in this paper.

The exponential membership function for objectives can be defined as:

$$\mu_p^E(Z_p(\mathbf{x})) = \begin{cases} \exp\left(\dfrac{\alpha_p(Z_p(\mathbf{x}) - L_p)}{L_p - U_p}\right), & Z_p \in [L_p, \infty) \\ 1, & \text{otherwise} \end{cases} \tag{5}$$

where a_p is a shape parameter which is generally assumed as $a_p = 3$.

Using (5), the fuzzy model can be written as:

$$\max \bullet \lambda$$

$$\mu_p^E(Z_p(\mathbf{x})) = \exp\left(\frac{\alpha_p(Z_p(\mathbf{x}) - L_p)}{L_p - U_p}\right) \geq \lambda, \ p = 1, 2, \ldots, P \tag{6}$$

$$\mathbf{x} \in S.$$

With the new variable $x_E = -\ln\lambda$, problem (6) turns into the following linear programming problem:

$$\min \bullet x_E$$

$$\left(\frac{\alpha_p(Z_p(\mathbf{x}) - L_p)}{L_p - U_p}\right) \leq x_E, \ p = 1, 2, \ldots, P \tag{7}$$

$$\frac{\alpha_p(Z_p(\mathbf{x}) - L_p)}{L_p - U_p} \geq 0$$

$x \in S$, $x_E \geq 0$.

If (x_E, x^*) is an optimal solution of (7), the optimal solution $(\lambda^* \cdot x^*) = (-\text{Inx}_E, x^*)$ is obtained.

Illustrative Numerical Example

To illustrate the proposed approach, the application for the concrete transportation problem of Xiluodu Hydropower Station in Tao and Xu (2012) will be discussed. Xiluodu Hydropower Station is founded in the transition zone of Qinghai–Tibet Plateau, Yunnan–Guizhou Plateau to the Sichuan Basin. Xiluodu Hydropower Station is one of the four largest hydropower stations in the Jinsha river downstream. In (2012), the problem of a concrete transportation problem at Xiluodu Hydropower Station is presented. To build infrastructures in four demand points, Leibo, Baisha, Daguan, and Baihetan, the concrete is demanded from Shuifu, Yongshan, and Puerdu. Considering the statistical documents and information from the decision-maker, the capacity of source and demand is seen in Table 1.

Table 1. Estimated values of supply capacity of sources and demand of destinations (m3 /day)

Source	Supply capacity	Destination	Demand
Shuifu	30	Leibo	20
Yongshan	30	Baisha	20
Puerdu	40	Daguan	20
		Baihetan	30

Moreover, large, medium, and small trucks are three kinds of conveyances and are expressed by conveyance 1, 2, and 3. Therefore, the total transportation capacities of these are 40m³, 40m³ and 15m³, respectively.

The capacities of the variables x_{ijk} are given as $x_{ij3} \in [0,15]$, $x_{i41} \in [0,30]$, $x_{ijk} \in [0,20]$, $\forall i,j,k$.

The cost of unit transportation amount from source i to destination j by conveyance k is denoted by c_{ijk}^1 and given in Table 2.

Table 2. Unit transportation cost by conveyances

	1	2	3	4		1	2	3	4		1	2	3	4
1	300	320	340	320	1	310	325	345	325	1	315	330	350	340
2	280	380	360	300	2	285	390	370	310	2	290	400	380	320
3	290	310	350	300	3	300	320	360	310	3	310	330	380	320
Conveyance 1				Conveyance 2					Conveyance 3				

The transportation time with respect to transportation activity from source i to destination j by conveyance k is denoted by c_{ijk}^2 and given in Table 3.

Table 3. Transportation time by conveyances

	1	2	3	4		1	2	3	4		1	2	3	4
1	90	80	60	60	1	80	75	60	70	1	120	70	70	60
2	80	70	70	60	2	75	65	60	60	2	85	60	60	60
3	90	120	100	80	3	80	115	95	60	3	70	110	90	80
	Conveyance 1					Conveyance 2					Conveyance 3			

Thus, the supply, demand, and conveyance capacities of the corresponding MCSTP are:

Supplies: $a_1=30$; $a_2=30$; $a_3=40$;
Demands: $b_1=20$; $b_2=20$; $b_3=30$; $b_4=30$
Conveyances capacities: $e_1=40$; $e_2=40$; $e_3=15$.

Then, the mathematical model of the corresponding MCSTP can be constructed as:

$$\min Z_1(\mathbf{x}) = \sum_{i=1}^{3} \sum_{j=1}^{4} \sum_{k=1}^{3} c_{ijk}^1 x_{ijk} \tag{8}$$

$$\min Z_2(\mathbf{x}) = \sum_{i=1}^{3} \sum_{j=1}^{4} \sum_{k=1}^{3} c_{ijk}^2 y_{ijk}$$

$$\sum_{j=1}^{4}\sum_{k=1}^{3} x_{1jk} = 30, \ \sum_{j=1}^{4}\sum_{k=1}^{3} x_{2jk} = 30, \ \sum_{j=1}^{4}\sum_{k=1}^{3} x_{3jk} = 40, \ \sum_{k=1}^{3}\sum_{i=1}^{3} x_{i1k} = 20, \ \sum_{k=1}^{3}\sum_{i=1}^{3} x_{i2k} = 20,$$

$$\sum_{k=1}^{3}\sum_{i=1}^{3} x_{i3k} = 20, \ \sum_{k=1}^{3}\sum_{i=1}^{3} x_{i4k} = 30, \ \sum_{i=1}^{3}\sum_{j=1}^{4} x_{ij1} = 40, \ \sum_{i=1}^{3}\sum_{j=1}^{4} x_{ij2} = 40, \ \sum_{i=1}^{3}\sum_{j=1}^{4} x_{ij3} = 15$$

$0 \le x_{ij3} < 15$, $0 \le x_{i41} < 30$, $0 \le x_{ijk} < 20$, $\forall i,j,k$

where $y_{ijk} = \begin{cases} 1, & if \ x_{ijk} > 0 \\ 0, & \text{otherwise} \end{cases}$.

Let the feasible region of (8) be denoted by $\hat{S}$. The lower and upper bound for objectives are found as: $L_1 = 27950$, $U_1 = 32800$, $L_2 = 345$, $U_2 = 2790$.
Then, the linear membership functions are:

$$\mu_1(Z_1(\mathbf{x})) = \frac{32800 - Z_1(\mathbf{x})}{4850}, \quad \mu_2(Z_2(\mathbf{x})) = \frac{2790 - Z_2(\mathbf{x})}{2445}.$$

A

Solving MCSTP Using Exponential Membership Function

Using (5), the exponential membership function of Z_1 can be constructed easily. For this objective, Figure 1 presents the graph for the linear and exponential membership functions. Figure 1 shows that the exponential membership function gives better membership values for the satisfaction degrees above the intersection point. Similarly, the graphs of the remaining objective functions can be drawn as well.

Figure 1. The linear and exponential membership functions of Z_1

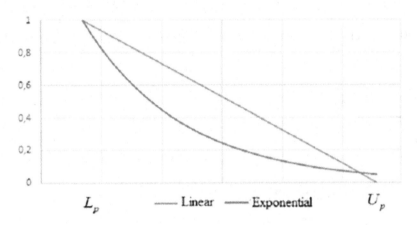

We can write the problem corresponding to problem (7) as follows:

min x_E (9)

$4850 \bullet x_E \geq 0.001 \bullet (Z_1(\mathbf{x}) - 27950)$,

$2445 \bullet x_E \geq 0.003 \bullet (Z_2(\mathbf{x}) - 345)$,

$0.001 \bullet (27950 - (Z_1(\mathbf{x})) \leq 0$,

$0.003 \bullet (345 - Z_2(\mathbf{x})) \leq 0$,

$\mathbf{x} \in \hat{S}, \ x_E \geq 0$

where $\alpha_1 = \alpha_2 = 3$ which is generally used in the literature. We note here that the shape parameter α is a non-zero parameter prescribed by the decision-maker in Dhingra and Moskowitz (1991). To offer more Pareto-optimal solutions to the decision-maker, it is possible to obtain various solutions by choosing different values of shape parameters. Solving (9), $\mathbf{x}_1^*$ and x_E^* is obtained as: $x_E^* = 0.06$,

$$\mathbf{x}_1^* = \begin{cases} x_{132}^* = 20, & x_{212}^* = 20, & x_{243}^* = 10, & x_{321}^* = 20, & x_{341}^* = 20, & \text{rest all } x_{ijk}^* = 0 \\ y_{132}^* = 1, & y_{212}^* = 1, & y_{243}^* = 1, & y_{321}^* = 1, & y_{341}^* = 1, & \text{rest all } y_{ijk}^* = 0. \end{cases}$$

Using the equation $\lambda_1^* = -\ln x_E$, the common satisfactory level of membership functions is found as $\lambda_1^* = 0.94$. For $\mathbf{x}_1^*$, the objective function values are $Z_1(\mathbf{x}_1^*) = 28000$, $Z_2(\mathbf{x}_1^*) = 395$.

Solving MCSTP Using Linear Membership Function

The problem corresponds to (4) can be written as follows:

$$\max \lambda \tag{10}$$

$$\mu_1(Z_1(\mathbf{x})) = \frac{32800 - Z_1(\mathbf{x})}{4850} \geq \lambda$$

$$\mu_2(Z_2(\mathbf{x})) = \frac{2790 - Z_2(\mathbf{x})}{2445} \geq \lambda$$

$$\mathbf{x} \in \hat{S}.$$

Solving (10), $\mathbf{x}_2^*$ and λ_2^* is obtained as:

$$\mathbf{x}_2^* = \begin{cases} x_{132}^* = 20, & x_{212}^* = 10, & x_{213}^* = 10, & x_{241}^* = 10, \\ x_{321}^* = 20, & x_{341}^* = 10, & x_{342}^* = 10, & \text{rest all } x_{ijk}^* = 0, \\ y_{132}^* = 1, & y_{212}^* = 1, & y_{213}^* = 1, & y_{241}^* = 1, \\ y_{321}^* = 1, & y_{341}^* = 1, & y_{342}^* = 1, & \text{rest all } y_{ijk}^* = 0. \end{cases}$$

$\lambda_2^* = 0.92$. For $\mathbf{x}_2^*$, the objective function values are $Z_1(\mathbf{x}_2^*) = 27950$, $Z_2(\mathbf{x}_2^*) = 540$.

The results of models using the linear and exponential membership functions are summarized in Table 4.

Table 4. The comparison of membership functions

	Exponential		Linear	
	$Z_p\left(\mathbf{x}_1^*\right)$	$\mu_p^E(Z_p(\mathbf{x}_1^*))$	$Z_p\left(\mathbf{x}_2^*\right)$	$\mu_p(Z_p(\mathbf{x}_2^*))$
Z_1	28000	0.99	27950	1
Z_2	395	0.98	540	0.92

A

Table 4 shows that in the fuzzy approach used the linear membership function, while Z_1 is fully satisfied, Z_2 is not satisfied at a high satisfactory level. In our proposed approach, in which the exponential membership function is used, both objectives have reached a very high level of satisfaction compared to the linear one. While both solutions obtained with linear and exponential membership functions are Pareto-optimal, our proposed approach gives a better average satisfaction value of 0.99, the linear one gives an average satisfaction value of 0.96.

FUTURE RESEARCH DIRECTIONS

In this study, a fuzzy approach has been developed for the multi-objective capacitated STP problem by using the exponential membership function, contrary to the common usage of linear one in the literature. Since this approach increased the common satisfaction of objectives, it can be adapted to all kinds of transportation problems of multi-objective nature. As an extension of the proposed approach, the effect of aggregation operators can be analyzed as a future study. The usage of different types of membership functions is also an alternative extension.

Multi-index transportation problems which are the generalized version of STP have the ability to model the real-life problems in a more flexible way. In this context, all the extensions given for STP may be easily applied to multi-index versions.

Considering the uncertainties in the parameters, costs, or any type of data, all types of STP including multi-index can be modeled in a fuzzy or interval environment. Thus, new models can be obtained with a better representation ability.

CONCLUSION

Many studies in the literature have focused on traditional MSTP and used linear membership functions to solve the corresponding problem. However, this paper focuses on the capacitated version of MSTP and introduces the exponential membership function to implement in the solution process. Furthermore, this special type of membership function together with Zimmermann's min operator is used to obtain a non-dominated compromise solution. Also, a comparison is provided for the solutions of linear and exponential membership functions. The reason for choosing the exponential membership function is that it is versatile and generates better solutions than the linear membership function. In other words, since the solution obtained using the exponential membership function provides the highest level of satisfaction among the objectives, the exponential membership function is used to solve the MCSTP. Thus, a more qualified solution is presented to the decision-maker. As a result, it can be concluded that the use of the exponential membership function can generate solutions that satisfy the decision-maker's expectations at a better level. Moreover, the usage of MCSTP instead of MSTP enables us to model real-life problems in a better and more flexible way.

REFERENCES

Ahlatçıoğlu, M., & Sivri, M. (1988). A Solution Proposal for Solving Three-Dimension Transportation Problem. *İ.T.Ü*, (22), 9-12.

Anuradha, D., Jayalakshmi, M., Deepa, G., & Sujatha, V. (2019). Solution of multi-objective solid transportation problem in fuzzy approach. *AIP Conference Proceedings*, *2177*(1), 020009. doi:10.1063/1.5135184

Basu, M., & Acharya, D. P. (2002). On quadratic fractional generalized solid bi-criterion transportation problem. *Journal of Applied Mathematics & Computing*, *10*(1-2), 131–143. doi:10.1007/BF02936212

Bit, A. K. (2004). Fuzzy programming with hyperbolic membership functions for multiobjective capacitated transportation problem. *Operational Research Society of India*, *41*(2), 106–120. doi:10.1007/BF03398837

Bit, A. K. (2005). Fuzzy programming with hyperbolic membership functions for multi- objective capacitated solid transportation problem. *The Journal of Fuzzy Mathematics*, *13*(2), 373–385.

Bit, A. K., Biswal, M. P., & Alam, S. S. (1993). Fuzzy programming approach to multiobjective solid transportation problem. *Fuzzy Sets and Systems*, *5*(2), 183–194. doi:10.1016/0165-0114(93)90158-E

Bodkhe, S. G., Bajaj, V. H., & Dhaigude, D. B. (2010). Fuzzy programming technique to solve multi-objective solid transportation problem with some non-linear membership functions. *Advances in Computational Research*, *2*(1), 15–20.

Chen, L., Jin, P., & Zhang, B. (2017). Uncertain goal programming models for bicriteria solid transportation problem. *Applied Soft Computing*, *51*, 49–59. doi:10.1016/j.asoc.2016.11.027

Das, S. K., Goswami, A., & Alam, S. S. (1999). Multiobjective transportation problem with interval cost, source and destination parameters. *European Journal of Operational Research*, *117*(1), 100–112. doi:10.1016/S0377-2217(98)00044-7

Dhingra, A. K., & Moskowitz, H. (1991). Application of fuzzy theories to multiple objective decision making in system design. *European Journal of Operational Research*, *53*(3), 348–361. doi:10.1016/0377-2217(91)90068-7

Gupta, S., Ali, I., & Ahmed, A. (2018). Multi-objective capacitated transportation problem with mixed constraint: A case study of certain and uncertain environment. *Opsearch*, *55*(2), 447–477. doi:10.100712597-018-0330-4

Jana, S. H., & Jana, B. (2020). Application of fuzzy programming techniques to solve solid transportation problem with additional constraints. *Operations Research and Decisions*, *30*(1), 67–84. doi:10.37190/ord200104

Kaur, D., Mukherjee, S., & Basu, K. (2015). Solution of a multi-objective and multi-index real-life transportation problem using different fuzzy membership functions. *Journal of Optimization Theory and Applications*, *164*(2), 666–678. doi:10.100710957-014-0579-6

Khalifa, H. A., & Al-Shabi, M. (2018). Utilizing of fractional programming for multi-objective multi-item solid transportation problems in fuzzy environment. *International Journal of Current Research*, *10*(11), 75024–75035.

Khalifa, H. A. E. (2019). Fuzzy compromise approach for Solving interval-valued fractional multi-objective multi-product solid transportation problems. *Journal of System Management*, *2*, 1–20.

Khalifa, H. A. W., Kumar, P., & Alharbi, M. G. (2021). On characterizing solution for multi-objective fractional two-stage solid transportation problem under fuzzy environment. *Journal of İntelligent Systems*, *30*(1), 620–635. doi:10.1515/jisys-2020-0095

Khurana, A., & Adlakha, V. (2015). On multi-index fixed charge bi-criterion transportation problem. *Opsearch*, *52*(4), 733–745. doi:10.100712597-015-0212-y

Khurana, A., Adlakha, V., & Lev, B. (2018). Multi-index constrained transportation problem with bounds on availabilities, requirements and commodities. *Operations Research Perspectives*, *5*, 319–333. doi:10.1016/j.orp.2018.10.001

Leberling, H. (1981). On finding compromise solutions in multicriteria problems using the fuzzy min-operator. *Fuzzy Sets and Systems*, *6*(2), 105–118. doi:10.1016/0165-0114(81)90019-1

Li, L., & Lai, K. K. (2000). A fuzzy approach to the multiobjective transportation problem. *Computers & Operations Research*, *27*(1), 43–57. doi:10.1016/S0305-0548(99)00007-6

Li, R. J., & Lee, E. S. (1991). An exponential membership function for fuzzy multiple objective linear programming. *Computers & Mathematics with Applications (Oxford, England)*, *22*(12), 55–60. doi:10.1016/0898-1221(91)90147-V

Mollanoori, H., Moghaddam, R. T., Triki, C., Kestheli, M. H., & Sabohi, F. (2019). Extending the solid step fixed-charge transportation problem to consider two-stage networks and multi-item shipments. *Computers & Industrial Engineering*, *137*, 106008. doi:10.1016/j.cie.2019.106008

Ojha, A., Mondal, S. K., & Maiti, M. (2014). A solid transportation problem with partial nonlinear transportation cost. *Journal of Applied and Computational Mathematics*, *3*(150), 1–6.

Pandian, P., & Anuradha, D. (2010). A new approach for solving solid transportation problems. *Applied Mathematical Sciences*, *4*(72), 3603–3610.

Peidroa, D., & Vasant, P. (2011). Transportation planning with modified S-curve membership functions using an interactive fuzzy multi-objective approach. *Applied Soft Computing*, *11*(2), 2656–2663. doi:10.1016/j.asoc.2010.10.014

Pramanik, S., & Banerjee, D. (2012). Multi-objective chance constrained capacitated transportation problem based on fuzzy goal programming. *International Journal of Computers and Applications*, *44*(20), 42–46. doi:10.5120/6383-8877

Pramanik, S., Jana, D., & Maiti, M. (2013). Multi-objective solid transportation problem in imprecise environments. *Journal of Transportation Security*, *6*(2), 131–150. doi:10.100712198-013-0108-0

Radhakrishnan, B., & Anukokila, P. (2014). Fractional Goal Programming for Fuzzy Solid Transportation Problem with Interval Cost. *Fuzzy Information and Engineering*, *6*(3), 359–377. doi:10.1016/j.fiae.2014.12.006

Rath, P., & Dash, R. B. (2017). Solution of fuzzy multi-objective linear programming problems using fuzzy programming techniques based on exponential membership functions. *International Journal of Mathematics Trends and Technology*, *41*(3). Advance online publication. doi:10.14445/22315373/IJMTT-V41P529

Ringuest, J. L., & Rinks, D. B. (1987). Interactive solutions for the linear multiobjective transportation problem. *European Journal of Operational Research*, *32*(1), 96–106. doi:10.1016/0377-2217(87)90274-8

Sadore, D. S., & Tuli, R. (2019). Optimal Solution of the Planar Four Index Transportation Problem. *Amity International Conference on Artificial Intelligence (AICAI)*, 548-553. 10.1109/AICAI.2019.8701265

Tao, Z., & Xu, J. (2012). A class of rough multiple objective programming and its application to solid transportation problem. *Information Sciences*, *188*, 215–235. doi:10.1016/j.ins.2011.11.022

Verma, R., Biswal, M. P., & Biswas, A. (1997). Fuzzy programming technique to solve multi-objective transportation problems with some non-linear membership functions. *Fuzzy Sets and Systems*, *91*(1), 37–43. doi:10.1016/S0165-0114(96)00148-0

Wahed, W. F. (2001). A multi-objective transportation problem under fuzziness. *Fuzzy Sets and Systems*, *117*(1), 27–33. doi:10.1016/S0165-0114(98)00155-9

Yang, L., & Liu, L. (2007). Fuzzy fixed charge solid transportation problem and algorithm. *Applied Soft Computing*, *7*(3), 879–889. doi:10.1016/j.asoc.2005.11.011

Yang, L., & Yuan, F. (2007). A bicriteria solid transportation problem with fixed charge under stochastic environment. *Applied Mathematical Modelling*, *31*(12), 2668–2683. doi:10.1016/j.apm.2006.10.011

ADDITIONAL READING

Christi, M. A., & Kalpana, I. (2016). Solutions of multi objective fuzzy transportation problem with non-linear membership functions. *International Journal of Engineering Research and Applications*, *6*(11), 52–57.

Dalman, H., & Sivri, M. (2017). Multi-objective solid transportation problem in uncertain environment. *Iranian Journal of Science and Technology. Transaction A, Science*, *41*(2), 505–514. doi:10.100740995-017-0254-5

Jalil, S. A., Sadia, S., Javaid, S., & Ali, Q. M. (2017). A solution approach for solving fully fuzzy multiobjective solid transportation problem. *International Journal of Agricultural and Statistics Sciences*, *13*(1), 75–84.

Jiménez, F., & Verdegay, J. L. (1998). Uncertain solid transportation problems. *Fuzzy Sets and Systems*, *100*(1-3), 45–57. doi:10.1016/S0165-0114(97)00164-4

Kakran, V. Y., & Dhodiya, J. M. (2020). Fuzzy programming technique for solving uncertain multi-objective, multi-item solid transportation problem with linear membership function. In R. Venkata Rao & J. Taler (Eds.), *Advanced Engineering Optimization Through Intelligent Techniques. Advances in Intelligent Systems and Computing* (Vol. 949, pp. 575–588). Springer. doi:10.1007/978-981-13-8196-6_50

Nagarajan, A., Jeyaraman, K., & Prabha, S. K. (2014). Multiobjective solid transportation problem with interval cost in source and demand parameters. *International Journal of Computer & Organization Trends*, *8*(1), 33–41. doi:10.14445/22492593/IJCOT-V8P306

Narayanamoorthy, S., & Anukokila, P. (2013). Fuzzy transportation problem with hyperbolic function. *International Journal of Mathematics in Operational Research*, *5*(5), 648–662. doi:10.1504/IJMOR.2013.056120

Ojha, A., Das, B., Mondal, S., & Maiti, M. (2010). A stochastic discounted multi-objective solid transportation problem for breakable items using Analytical Hierarchy Process. *Applied Mathematical Modelling*, *34*(8), 2256–2271. doi:10.1016/j.apm.2009.10.034

Pramanik, S., Jana, D. K., & Maity, K. (2014). A multi objective solid transportation problem in fuzzy, bi-fuzzy environment via genetic algorithm. *International Journal of Advanced Operations Management*, *6*(1), 4–26. doi:10.1504/IJAOM.2014.059612

Tao, Z., & Xu, J. (2012). A class of rough multiple objective programming and its application to solid transportation problem. *Information Sciences*, *188*, 215–235. doi:10.1016/j.ins.2011.11.022

KEY TERMS AND DEFINITIONS

Exponential Function: An exponential function is a mathematical function in form $f(x)=e^x$, where "x" is a variable and "e" is a constant which is called the base of the function and it should be greater than 0.

Linear Function: A linear function is an algebraic equation in which each term is either a constant or the product of a constant and (the first power of) a single variable.

Membership Function: The membership function of a fuzzy set is a generalization of the indicator function in classical sets.

Multiple-Criteria Decision-Making: It is a sub-discipline of operations research that explicitly evaluates multiple conflicting criteria in decision making.

Pareto-Optimal Solution: It is a set of 'non-inferior' solutions in the objective space defining a boundary beyond which none of the objectives can be improved without sacrificing at least one of the other objectives.

Solid Transportation Problem: The STP is an extension of the traditional TP. It involves source, destination, and mode of transport parameters.

Transportation Problem: The objective of transportation problem is to determine the amount to be transported from each origin to each destination such that the total transportation cost is minimized.

One vs. Two vs. Multidimensional Searches for Optimization Methods

Fabio Vitor

ⓘ https://orcid.org/0000-0002-3284-8378

University of Nebraska at Omaha, USA

INTRODUCTION

Optimization is one of the most widely used tools in operations research and have been used by decision makers of public and private organizations to make smarter decisions. Optimization is used daily to solve numerous real-world complex problems. For instance, the most energy efficient way in scheduling crude oil operations (Wu et al., 2017), the design of decision-support tools for outpatient appointment systems (Ahmadi-Javid et al., 2017), the optimal routes for drone delivery (Dorling at al., 2017), cancer treatment options (Biesecker et al., 2010), and vaccination campaigns (Matrajt et al., 2021) can all be determined by optimization models.

Some important classes of optimization models include linear, nonlinear, and integer programming. This chapter focuses primarily on linear programming, but some insights for nonlinear optimization is discussed. Formally, define a linear program (LP) as:

maximize $z = c^T x$
subject to: $Ax \leq b$
$x \geq 0$

where $n, m \in \mathbb{Z}_+$, $x \in \mathbb{R}_+^n$, $c \in \mathbb{R}^n$, $A \in \mathbb{R}^{m \times n}$, and $b \in \mathbb{R}^m$. Let the polyhedron $S = \left\{ x \in \mathbb{R}_+^n : Ax \leq b \right\}$ be the set of feasible solutions of an LP and (x^*, z^*) be its optimal solution where $x^* \in S$ and $z^* = c^T x^* \geq c^T x'$ for all $x' \in S$.

Finding an optimal solution to LPs in a reasonable amount of time is vital for decision makers. Even though algorithms to solve LPs in polynomial time exist (Gondzio, 2012), a substantial amount of time can still be required to solve them. This is because real-world applications are often large, sparse, and dependent on a substantial amount of data. In fact, the amount of data to model optimization problems has drastically increased over the recent years due to the discovery of many efficient data analytics techniques (Vitor, 2019). Therefore, finding methods to solve LPs more quickly can benefit numerous organizations in obtaining better solutions to their problems.

Most of linear programming (and nonlinear programming) algorithms are considered one-dimensional search. That is, from a solution, a single search direction is selected and a one-dimensional subproblem is solved to determine how far to move along this direction. A new solution is obtained and the process repeats. Figure 1 demonstrates this concept using a simplex framework. For brevity, one can view a simplex framework as an algorithm that moves between solutions that are located at the vertices of the polyhedron. On the other hand, an interior point framework moves between solutions within the interior of the polyhedron. For each iteration k, an improving search direction d^k is selected from x^k.

DOI: 10.4018/978-1-7998-9220-5.ch144

Optimally solving a one-dimensional subspace LP defined by $x^k + \lambda^k d^k$ and $\lambda^k > 0$ determines how far to move from x^k along d^k. The optimal solution to this subproblem is λ^{k^*} and x^{k+1} is computed as $x^{k+1} = x^k + \alpha \lambda^{k^*} d^k$ where $0 < a < 1$. Notice that solving a one-dimensional subspace problem is the same as performing a one-dimensional search.

Figure 1. Graphical representation of one-dimensional search algorithms

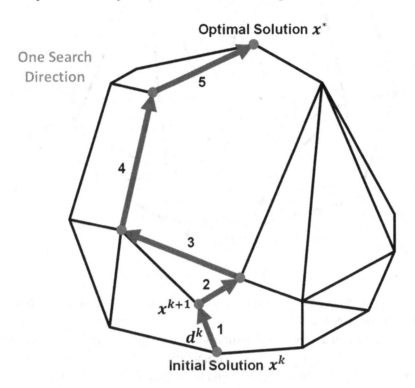

Multidimensional search methods have also been developed. Differently than the traditional one-dimensional search techniques, these methods consider more than one search direction at each step. Furthermore, a multidimensional subproblem must be solved to determine how far to move along each direction. Figure 2 graphically presents this concept. For simplicity, two search directions are considered. From x^k, two search directions, $\left(d_1^k, d_2^k \right)$, are selected at each step k (at least one must be improving). Both search directions define a plane, and this plane when intersected with the polyhedron creates a two-dimensional subspace. Optimally solving a two-dimensional subspace LP defined by $x^k + \lambda_1^k d_1^k + \lambda_2^k d_2^k$, $\lambda_1^k > 0$, and $\lambda_2^k > 0$ determines the step length. The optimal solution to this sub-problem, let say $\left(\lambda_1^{k^*}, \lambda_2^{k^*} \right)$, determines the next solution $x^{k+1} = x^k + \alpha \left(\lambda_1^{k^*} d_1^k + \lambda_2^{k^*} d_2^k \right)$ where $0 < a < 1$. Again, solving a two-dimensional subspace problem is the same as performing a two-dimensional search (or a multidimensional search). If more than two search directions are considered, let say d_i^k for all $i \in \{1, 2 \ldots t\}$ where t is some integer upper bound, then the multidimensional subspace LP becomes $x^k + \sum_{i=1}^{t} \lambda_i^k d_i^k$ and $\lambda_i^k > 0$ for all $i \in \{1, 2 \ldots t\}$ and the next solution is $x^{k+1} = x^k + \alpha \sum_{i=1}^{t} \lambda_i^k d_i^k$ where $0 < a < 1$.

Figure 2. Graphical representation of two-dimensional search algorithms

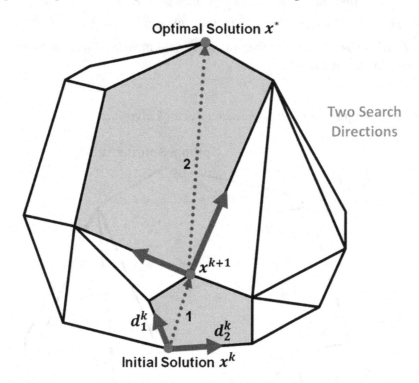

There are some pros and cons to additional search directions. One advantage is that multidimensional searches look for an improved solution at a much broader space while one-dimensional searches are limited by the solutions contained in a single ray. Furthermore, there are an infinity number of one-dimensional search directions that can be represented as a combination of the multidimensional search directions. Because of that, it is likely that the solutions found by multidimensional search methods are better than the solutions found by one-dimensional search techniques, making these methods move further at each iteration. One disadvantage is that performing multidimensional searches requires more computational effort than performing one-dimensional searches. Therefore, effective methods should be implemented to solve these subproblems to counteract the additional effort. Likely, these methods should be designed specifically to perform multidimensional searches because using the traditional one-dimensional search algorithms may take longer.

One may question what conditions characterize an algorithm as a multidimensional search. *Remark* 1 formalizes them. Obviously, these conditions are not set in stone and others may propose something different. However, they help position the existing research described in the following sections. Notice that some preliminary insights about these conditions are presented by Vitor and Easton (2022).

Remark 1*: To be characterized as a multidimensional search method, the algorithm must: (1) search over multiple search directions at each iteration (more than one); (2) optimally solve a multidimensional subspace problem to determine the step length for each search direction using methods designed to perform multidimensional searches.*

With that being said, this chapter has two primary goals. First is to introduce the reader to the concept of multidimensional searches in optimization methods and some existing research in the field. Second is to provide an improved version of the slope algorithm, a method to perform multidimensional searches, that is more numerically stable. The remainder of this chapter is organized as follow. First, an extensive background in existing multidimensional search methods is presented. Thus, strategies to improve the numerical stability of the slope algorithm are described accompanied by a computational study. Finally, future research topics and conclusions are discussed.

BACKGROUND

This section presents some background information on existing multidimensional search methods for both linear and nonlinear optimization. The section first describes techniques to perform multidimensional searches. That is, methods designed to solve small linear and nonlinear programs. Thus, multidimensional search algorithms within both a simplex and interior point framework are presented. Finally, the concept of multidimensional searches for nonlinear programming is discussed.

Methods to Perform Multidimensional Searches

Many algorithms have been developed to solve small optimization problems. These algorithms can be applied to solve the subproblems of multidimensional search methods. This is because they frequently solve these subproblems faster than traditional methods. One of the first techniques was created by Shamos and Hoey (1976), which can find an optimal solution of a two-variable linear program (2VLP). Given m constraints, their algorithm first determines whether any two constraints intersect and then finds the common intersection of m half-planes in $O(m \log m)$ time. An optimal solution is determined by finding one common intersection with maximum objective function value.

Later, Megiddo (1983) proposed algorithms to solve both two and three-variable LPs in $O(m)$ time. For 2VLPs, Megiddo's method begins with a feasible solution to the problem and then arranges the constraints in disjoint pairs. For each pair, it computes the solution determined by the intersection formed by the two constraints. Thus, it decides for each pair if any of the two constraints is redundant by either finding that both has the same slope or that the solution is not within a certain interval. Redundant constraints are removed, and the median of all remaining solutions is computed. The median solution is tested along the remaining constraints to find that the problem is either infeasible, the median is optimal, or to redefine the interval that determined redundant constraints. If the latter case, the algorithm can drop some other constraints and the process repeats.

The concept of Megiddo's algorithm for three-variable LPs is similar and a linear time algorithm to find the smallest circle enclosing m points is used. Observe that Dyer (1984) derived a similar approach than Megiddo (1983) to solve two and three-variable LPs, but both have been discovered independently. These results were also extended to higher dimensions by Megiddo (1984), which showed that LPs can be solved in linear time when the dimension is fixed. Even though Megiddo's algorithm for LPs of fixed space is interesting from a theoretical perspective, in practice it may not be applicable except when the dimension is small.

Recently, Vitor and Easton (2018) developed the slope algorithm, a $O(m \log m)$ method to find an optimal solution and optimal basis of 2VLPs. An optimal basis is a basic feasible solution from where there does not exist any feasible improving search direction. The slope algorithm compares the slope of each 2VLP's constraint with the slope defined by the coefficients of the objective function. The slope algorithm begins by converting 2VLP's nonnegative conditions into two other constraints and computing each of the constraints' slopes. The constraints are sorted in ascending order of their slopes and the algorithm finds a pair of constraints such that the slope of the objective function falls in between the slope of the two constraints. Conditions are checked to find whether the problem is unbounded. If not, the solution determined by the intersection formed by the two constraints is computed and its feasibility is tested against all constraints. If the test fails for any of the constraints, the intersection formed by such a constraint and one of the previous two constraints defines a new solution. This new solution then follows the same testing procedure, and the process repeats until a feasible solution is found. The algorithm terminates and reports an optimal solution and the two constraints that intersect at an optimal basis.

One of the advantages of the slope algorithm is its ability to handle degenerate 2VLPs. This is because it guarantees an optimal basis. That is, if a 2VLP has a degenerate optimal solution, meaning two constraints intersect at the optimal solution, then the slope algorithm will find a pair of constraints that also intersect at an optimal basis. Notice that all previously discussed methods to solve 2VLPs can find an optimal solution, but none of them guarantees an optimal basis. This is critical when implementing the slope algorithm within a simplex framework to perform multidimensional searches because selecting a nonoptimal basis of 2VLPs may result in unchanged basis of the simplex algorithm. In this case, additional pivots are needed, and the simplex algorithm can potentially cycle and never terminate.

While all aforementioned techniques can be used to perform multidimensional searches over a primal space, none of them can be directly applied to a dual space without using complementary slackness and the solution of a system of equations. To eliminate this additional step, Vitor (2018) developed the ratio algorithm, a method to find an optimal solution and optimal basis of two-constraint LPs. This method is similar to the slope algorithm. However, instead of looking into the slope of each constraint, the ratio algorithm looks into the ratio of each variable formed by the coefficients of the two constraints. Moreover, the ratio algorithm begins with a feasible solution and works to achieve optimality while the slope algorithm begins with a super optimal solution and works to achieve feasibility.

Motivated by creating other multidimensional search algorithms, Jamrunroj and Boonperm (2021) proposes a method to solve 2VLPs by considering only the coefficient of the constraints. This technique is limited to the types of problems it can solve since four conditions must be satisfied: (1) objective function coefficients must be positive; (2) right-hand side must be nonnegative; (3) variables must be nonnegative; (4) one of the variables must have a strictly positive coefficient for each constraint. If all four conditions are met, then a solution can be obtained immediately in $O(m)$ time. Notice in this case that an optimal solution will always occur along one of the axes.

While a significant amount of research has been developed to find methods to solve small LPs that can be used to perform multidimensional searches, the same did not happen for nonlinear optimization. More recently, Santos et al. (2019) created an algorithm to solve three-variable nonlinear polynomial optimization problems. Overall, this technique has two major steps. For a fixed value of one of the variables, the algorithm: first, builds a number of regions that represents the constraints of the problem; second, finds an optimal solution to the subproblem defined by each region, which corresponds to finding a local optima to the general problem. Thus, an optimum is obtained by choosing the best among all local optima. While this method solves a three-variable nonlinear polynomial optimization problem, one could view it as a two-dimensional algorithm since it reduces the original problem to two variables by fixing the value of the third variable. The following sections describe how these algorithms are used to perform multidimensional searches.

Multidimensional Searches within a Simplex Framework

One of the fist multidimensional search algorithms within a simplex framework was developed by Vitor and Easton (2018), called the double pivot simplex method. Differently than the traditional simplex algorithm, the double pivot simplex method moves from one basic feasible solution to another by pivoting on two variables simultaneously. During each iteration, both entering basic variables are selected by using Dantzig's pivoting rule. That is, the two variables with the most improving reduced costs. The two leaving nonbasic variables are chosen by solving a 2VLP. The double pivot simplex method uses the slope algorithm to solve its subproblems as it guarantees an optimal basis. Computational experiments tested the double pivot simplex method versus the traditional simplex method and also CPLEX's, a high-performance mathematical programming solver, primal simplex implementation. Computational results on a subset of benchmark Netlib (Gay, 1985; Dongarra and Grosse, 1987) and MIPLIB (Gleixner, et al., 2021) problems show an improvement in the number of iterations by over 40% when compared to the simplex method and more than 20% when compared to CPLEX.

Motivated by improving the computational time of the double pivot simplex method, Li et al. (2022) developed an implementation of double pivots into a primal simplex solver. To make it efficient, a version of the double pivot simplex method that can handle bounded variables was developed. Their work also presents some insights on how to modify both Megiddo (1983) and Dyer (1984) algorithms to return an optimal basis of 2VLPs. The double pivot simplex method for bounded variables was implemented in LPSOL, a simplex solver built on the top of the general-purpose mixed integer programming solver (Lee, 1997). To update the basis factorization with two variables, two eta-matrices are computed at each iteration. Other implementation details such as preprocessing, two-phase algorithm, pricing step, and numerical instability are also discussed in their work. Computational results on a larger subset of Netlib and MIPLIB problems plus some instances from the collection of Mittelmann (2021) show that the double pivot simplex method for bounded variables improves the number of iterations and CPU time of LPSOL by approximately 30% and 10%, respectively if the slope algorithm is used to solve the 2VLPs. If the modified version of Dyer is used instead, this improvement becomes nearly 32% and 28%, respectively.

A dual version of the double pivot simplex method is briefly described by Vitor (2019). In this case, two nonbasic leaving variables are selected (the two most infeasible) and two entering basic variables are determined by solving a two-constraint LP using the ratio algorithm. As one would expect, under a nondegenerate LP, the double pivot simplex method, the version for bounded variables, and the dual version correctly solve LPs within a finite number of steps.

Independently, Yang (2020) also proposed a primal double pivot simplex algorithm for LPs. This method chooses the entering nonbasic variables using two different pivoting rules. One of them is chosen using Dantzig's pivoting rule. The second is chosen using the longest step rule. That is, the variable that maximizes the step size. The algorithm chooses the leaving basic variables through a 2VLP, which in this case is solved by a sequence of systems of linear equations. This is done by first eliminating all basic variables that create a ray of unboundedness in the 2VLP. Then, several systems of two equations are solved with the remaining variables to compute all feasible solutions of the 2VLP. The two basic variables that produce a minimum for the 2VLP are selected as the leaving variables.

The work of Yang also provides two upper bounds on the number of iterations. One of them is derived by determining a least improvement in the objective function value at each step. The other is derived using a nondegenerate assumption. The former one when applied to LPs with totally unimodular matrices or Markov decision problems with discount rate shows that the double pivot method solves these problems in strongly polynomial time. Some small computational experiments are also presented. One of them tested the proposed technique on three variants of the famous Klee-Minty cube. Results show that the original simplex method takes an exponential number of iterations to solve these instances while the proposed algorithm solves them in only one iteration. The second set of computational experiments tested both methods on some dense randomly generated LPs. Results also show a computational advantage of the double pivot method in the number of iterations but not in CPU time.

Extending upon that, the implementation of a double pivot simplex method that combines the slope algorithm and the longest step pivoting rule is proposed by Yang and Vitor (2022). Their work discusses several implementation details such as LU decomposition versus pseudo inverse to update the basis inverse, pre and postprocessing, and the process of handling some degenerate solutions. Computational experiments tested the proposed implementation against the simplex method using Dantzig's pivoting rule on a set of cycling LPs, three variants of the Klee-Minty cube, some randomly generated instances, and a subset of benchmark Netlib problems. Overall, results show that this double pivot algorithm is degenerate-tolerable and more efficient than Dantzig's simplex implementation for large random LPs, but less efficient for benchmark Netlib problems.

One may question whether some multiple pivot methods developed throughout the years can also be categorized as multidimensional search methods. For instance, decomposition methods (Conejo et al., 2006), column generation (Ford and Fulkerson, 1958), and block pivots (Bazaraa et al., 2010). Even though all these methods do use more than one search direction during each iteration, traditional one-dimensional search algorithms are the primary technique to solve their subproblems. Therefore, they all fail the second requirement of *Remark 1*. Obviously, this does not diminish the importance of these methods as all of them have helped solving numerous difficult optimization problems for decades and are part of the foundation of optimization methods.

Multidimensional Searches within an Interior Point Framework

The first time that the concept of multidimensional searches within an interior point framework appeared was in a conference talk (Karmarkar and Ramakrishnan, 1985). Some theoretical results appeared later in the work of Gonzaga (1991), but the first algorithmic results were developed by Boggs et al. (1989). Their algorithm considers two search directions. One of them is a dual affine direction while the other is a rank-one update direction. In the last iterations, the rank-one update direction is replaced with a Newton recentering direction. The step length for each search direction is determined by solving a 2VLP. In this case, 2VLPs were solved using an implementation of the simplex method. Some other implementation strategies were considered such as using a Big-M procedure to find initial solutions, scaling of the constraint matrix, dropping constraints that are away from the initial solution, and implementing the two search directions only during Phase 2. Computational experiments tested this algorithm versus the dual affine scaling method on a small subset of benchmark instances from Netlib. The results reported showed an improvement in the average number of iterations.

Domich et al. (1991) extended their work by considering three search directions. The first two search directions are the same as Boggs et al. and the third one is determined by Huard's method of centers. The implementation of this three-dimensional search interior point algorithm follows closely the one used by Boggs et al. but with some refinements, which allowed more instances to be solved. Computational experiments compared this method with the dual affine scaling algorithm. Both iterations and CPU time were improved, on average, when solving a subset of benchmark Netlib problems.

Recently, Vitor and Easton (2018, 2022) also created a set of two-dimensional search interior point algorithms. Their work presents both primal and dual approaches derived from affine and logarithmic barrier directions. The two search directions are determined by randomly partitioning the objective function vector into two orthogonal vectors, and then projecting them onto the null/column space of the constraint matrix. This approach comes from two principles for determining search directions: (1) 2VLPs are guaranteed to improve the objective function value at least as well as one-variable LPs if the search direction that the defines the latter is contained in the cone combination of the two search directions that define the first; (2) the feasible region of 2VLPs formed by two search directions that are orthogonal to each other is larger than the one formed by any pair of two search directions that can be represented as a cone combination of the orthogonal search directions. Two-variable LPs were solved using the method of Dyer (1984) to determine the step length of each search direction. Computational experiments also tested these methods against their corresponding one-dimensional search versions on Netlib benchmark instances, and an overall improvement of 14% in the number of iterations and 12% in CPU time was obtained.

Another recent development includes the work of Santos et al. (2019). While each of the aforementioned interior point methods are primal or dual alone techniques, the one developed by Santos et al. uses a primal-dual framework. Furthermore, three search directions are considered: an affine scaling direction, a direction for the central path, and a corrector direction. A three-variable polynomial optimization problem determines the step length for each direction, and a method to specifically solve these subproblems was designed as previously discussed. Regardless, a one-dimensional search is still required at each iteration to guarantee that solutions stay within the interior of the polyhedron. The algorithm was implemented under PCx, an interior point open-source solver for linear optimization. When benchmark instances are solved and compared, the original implementation of PCx still performs better but the results are comparable for both number of iterations and CPU time.

Similar to the simplex framework, one may claim that other multidimensional search interior point algorithms exist. For example, the composite and two-step methods of Boggs et al. (1989), the two-stage approach of Mehrotra (1992) and Gondzio (1996) to compute the iteration step, the work of Jarre and Wechs (1999) and Mehrotra and Li (2005) that uses an LP subproblem at each step to compute search directions, and the method of Colombo and Gondzio (2008) that improves the multiple centrality approach. However, none of them meet the second criterion of *Remark 1* as the step length for each search direction is determined by solving a one-dimensional search problem. That is, all of these methods move along each search direction independently.

Multidimensional Searches in Nonlinear Optimization

Most of the work in multidimensional search methods has been done for LPs. To the best of the author's knowledge, nothing or little in this topic has been studied for nonlinear optimization. Observe that the idea of "multidimensional searches" has been already discussed in nonlinear programming. Examples include the cyclical coordinate method, Hooke and Jeeves' method, Rosenbrock's method, gradient search (or method of steepest descent), and Newton's multidimensional search method (Bazaraa et al., 2006). However, none of them can be truly classified as a multidimensional search algorithm. This is because none has both of the properties discussed in *Remark 1*. For instance, the cyclical coordinate, Hooke and Jeeves, and Rosenbrock's techniques consider multiple orthogonal search directions but search over each one independently. That is, using one of the line search methods. Other methods such as gradient search and Newton's technique consider a single search direction at each step and perform one-dimensional searches. In fact, these methods are called "multidimensional" only because they move over all n dimensions simultaneously in contrast to the orthogonal search directions that move over one dimension at a time. Other "multidimensional" search algorithms exist, and they do not meet *Remark 1* (Costa and Fernandes, 2006; Boldyrev and Pashkovskiy, 2018). The following section presents some improvements to the slope algorithm to make it more numerically stable and improve its performance as a method to perform multidimensional searches.

IMPROVING THE NUMERICAL STABILITY OF THE SLOPE ALGORITHM

Even though the slope algorithm has been proved to be a fast and effective technique to perform multi-dimensional searches within both a simplex and interior point framework, one of its major drawbacks is that it is extremely sensitive to numerical errors. Mostly because the slope algorithm is dependent of a sufficiently large positive number and the coefficients of the constraints. This section describes some strategies developed to make the slope algorithm more numerically stable and also improve its performance.

The Slope Algorithm

The slope algorithm can find both an optimal solution and an optimal basis of 2VLPs. Formally, define a 2VLP as:

Maximize $c_1 x_1 + c_2 x_2$
subject to: $a_{i,1} x_1 + a_{j,2} x_2 \leq b_j \ \forall i \in (1,2,\ldots,m, m+1, m+2\}$

where $x_1, x_2 \geq 0$, $c_1, c_2 > 0$, $a_{i,1}, a_{i,2} \in \mathbb{R}$, and $b_i \geq 0$ for all $i \in \{1,2,\ldots,m, m+1, m+2\}$. Furthermore, $a_{m+1,1} = a_{m+2,2} = -1$, $a_{m+1,2} = a_{m+2,1} = 0$, and $b_{m+1} = b_{m+2} = 0$ guarantees the nonnegative condition of x_1 and x_2.

The complete description of the slope algorithm is shown in Algorithm 1. Its input is a 2VLP and output is an optimal solution and the constraints that intersect at an optimal basis. First, the algorithm computes the slope of each constraint $i \in \{1,2,\ldots,m, m+1, m+2\}$ according to (1)

$$
\alpha_i = \begin{cases}
-2M & \text{if } a_{i,1} = 0, a_{i,2} < 0 \\[2mm]
-M + \dfrac{a_{i,2}}{a_{i,1}} & \text{if } a_{i,1} > 0, a_{i,2} < 0 \\[2mm]
-M & \text{if } a_{i,1} > 0, a_{i,2} = 0 \\[2mm]
\dfrac{a_{i,2}}{a_{i,1}} & \text{if } a_{i,1} > 0, a_{i,2} > 0 \\[2mm]
M & \text{if } a_{i,1} = 0, a_{i,2} > 0 \\[2mm]
M - \dfrac{a_{i,1}}{a_{i,2}} & \text{if } a_{i,1} \langle 0, a_{i,2} \rangle 0 \\[2mm]
2M & \text{if } a_{i,1} < 0, a_{i,2} = 0 \\[2mm]
3M & \text{if } a_{i,1} = 0, a_{i,2} = 0 \\[2mm]
3M & \text{if } a_{i,1} < 0, a_{i,2} < 0
\end{cases}
\tag{1}
$$

where M is a sufficiently large positive number that can be computed as (2).

$$M > \max\{M_1, M_2, M_3\} \tag{2}$$

$$M_1 = \max\left\{\left|\frac{a_{i,1}}{a_{i,2}}\right| : a_{i,2} \neq 0 \quad \forall i \in \{1, 2, \ldots, m, m+1, m+2\}\right\} \tag{3}$$

$$M_2 = \max\left\{\left|\frac{a_{i,2}}{a_{i,1}}\right| : a_{i,1} \neq 0 \quad \forall i \in \{1, 2, \ldots, m, m+1, m+2\}\right\} \tag{4}$$

$$M_3 = \frac{c_2}{c_1} \tag{5}$$

The algorithm then sorts the constraints according to their slope, finds constraints j' and k', and determines whether the 2VLP is unbounded by checking if any of the conditions in (3) are satisfied.

$$\alpha_{g_{j'}} = -2M \text{ and } \alpha_{g_{k'}} \geq M \text{ or}$$

$$-2M < \alpha_{g_{j'}} < -M \text{ and } \alpha_{g_{k'}} = 2M \text{ or}$$

$$\alpha_{g_{j'}} = -M \text{ and } \alpha_{g_{k'}} = 2M \text{ or}$$

$$-2M < \alpha_{g_{j'}} < -M \text{ and } M < \alpha_{g_{k'}} < 2M, \text{ and } \frac{a_{g_{j'},2}}{a_{g_{j'},1}} \leq \frac{a_{g_{k'},2}}{a_{g_{k'},1}}$$

If the 2VLP is bounded, the slope algorithm computes the solution defined by the intersection of constraints $g_{j'}$ and $g_{k'}$ and check its feasibility on all other constraints. If feasible, the algorithm terminates. Otherwise, it permutes between constraints until a feasible pair of constraints is found. Notice that one of the primary assumptions is that $x=(0,0)$ is a feasible solution to the 2VLP.

Algorithm 1. The Slope Algorithm

1: Compute a sufficiently large positive number M according to (2)
2: Compute a_i for each $i \in \{1, 2, \ldots, m, m+1, m+2\}$ according to (1)
3: Let $G = \{g_1, g_2, \ldots, g_m, g_{m+1}, g_{m+2}\}$ be the list of constraint indices sorted in ascending order according to their α values

4: Find constraints j' and $k' \in \{1, 2, \ldots, m, m+1, m+2\}$ such that $\alpha_{g_{j'}} < \frac{c_2}{c_1} \leq \alpha_{g_{k'}}$

5: **if** 2VLP is unbounded according to (3) **then**
6: **return** 2VLP is unbounded

7: **else**

8: $j \leftarrow j'$

9: $k \leftarrow k'$

10: Compute the intersection of constraints $g_{j'}$ and $g_{k'}$ defined by $\left(x_1', x_2'\right)$

11: **while** $j>1$ or $k<m+2$ **do**

12: **if** $j>1$ **then**

13: $j \leftarrow -1$

14: **if** $a_{g_j,1}x_1' + a_{g_j,2}x_2' > b_{g_j}$ **then**

15: $j' \leftarrow j$

16: Compute the intersection of constraints $g_{j'}$ and $g_{k'}$ defined by $\left(x_1', x_2'\right)$

17: **if** $k<m+1$ **then**

18: $k \leftarrow k+1$

19: **if** $a_{g_k,1}x_1' + a_{g_k,2}x_2' > b_{g_k}$ **then**

20: $k' \leftarrow k$

21: Compute the intersection of constraints $g_{j'}$ and $g_{k'}$ defined by $\left(x_1', x_2'\right)$

22: **return** $x^* = \left(x_1', x_2'\right)$, $z^* = c_1 x_1' + c_2 x_2'$, $j^* \leftarrow g_{j'}$, $k^* \leftarrow g_{k'}$, α_{j^*}, and α_{k^*}

Modifying the Method of Jamrunroj and Boonperm (2021) for an Optimal Basis

As previously discussed, the technique of Jamrunroj and Boonperm (2021) can find an optimal solution, but not an optimal basis, of 2VLPs when either $x^* = \left(x_1^*, 0\right)$ or $x^* = \left(0, x_2^*\right)$. One can see that a straight-forward modification to this method can be applied so it also returns an optimal basis. Suppose their method returns $x^* = \left(x_1^*, 0\right)$. Clearly, this solution occurs along the x_1 axis, which is defined by the constraint $-x_2 \leq 0$. Consequently, $j^*=m+2$ and $\alpha_{j^*} = -2M$. Constraint k^* can be determined as

$$k^* = \arg\min\left\{\frac{b_i}{a_{i,1}} : a_{i,1} > 0 \quad \forall i \in \{1,2,\ldots,m\}\right\} \tag{6}$$

and α_{k^*} can be computed according to (1). Similarly, suppose that their method returns $x^* = \left(0, x_2^*\right)$. Thus, this solution occurs along the x_2 axis, defined by the constraint $-x_1 \leq 0$. Hence, $k^*=m+1$ and $\alpha_{k^*} = 2M$. Constraint j^* is determined as

$$j^* = \arg\min\left\{\frac{b_i}{a_{i,2}} : a_{i,2} > 0 \quad \forall i \in \{1,2,\ldots,m\}\right\} \tag{7}$$

and α_{j^*} is calculated using (1).

This simple modification can be implemented at the end of their technique, and the entire modified method can be implemented right before the slope algorithm is called (before line 1 of Algorithm 1). Thus, if a 2VLP satisfies all four assumptions of their method (notice that the slope algorithm has the same first three assumptions), then an optimal solution and an optimal basis is found much faster without having to use the slope algorithm. If the fourth assumption is not satisfied, then the slope algorithm is called to solve the 2VLP.

Introduction of a Tolerance Parameter

Computing the slope of each constraint (line 2 of Algorithm 1) requires checking whether $a_{i,1}$ and $a_{i,2}$ are positive, negative, or zero. Notice that round-off errors to these coefficients can lead to incorrect conclusions about the slope of the constraints, and the algorithm may output an incorrect solution. The same type of error can occur when computing m and checking whether the solution obtained by the intersection of two constraints is feasible (or infeasible) on other constraints (lines 1, 14, and 19 of Algorithm 1). Introducing a tolerance parameter ϵ to these steps can help avoiding these errors. Computational experiments showed that setting $\in$ from 10-^{12} to 10-^{15} may be sufficient, but this certainly depends on what precision the slope algorithm is implemented.

Preprocessing of Constraints

One of the major issues within the slope algorithm is the presence of nearly parallel constraints. If a 2VLP has nearly parallel constraints, then round-off errors can result in an incorrect order of the constraints, selection of the incorrect j' and k' constraints, and/or determining a feasible solution is infeasible or vice-versa (lines 3, 4, 14, and 19 of Algorithm 1). One way to handle this issue is to remove all nearly parallel constraints, except for the ones that support the polyhedron or are "closer" to it. Algorithm 2 describes a procedure that was implemented to delete nearly parallel constraints. Another preprocessing considered that helped improving the stability of the algorithm was to remove some redundant constraints. Algorithm 3 describes the procedure for this purpose. Observe that removing all redundant constraints would be time consuming so this procedure only eliminates redundant constraints of the type: $a_{i,1}>0$ and $a_{i,2}=0$; $a_{j,1}=0$ and $a_{j,2}>0$. Both Algorithms 2 and 3 are implemented right after line 3 of Algorithm 1.

Algorithm 2. Delete Nearly Parallel Constraints

1: $p \leftarrow \infty$, $j \leftarrow 1$, $t \leftarrow 0$, $d = (0,0,\ldots,0)^{m+2}$

2: **for** $i=1$ **to** $m+1$ **do**

3: **if** $\left| u_{g_{i+1}} - u_{g_i} \right| < \epsilon$ **then**

4: **if** $a_{g_i,1} > \epsilon$ **or** $a_{g_i,1} < -\epsilon$ **then**

5: **if** $\left| \dfrac{b_{g_i}}{a_{g_i,1}} \right| < p - \epsilon$ **then**

6: $p \leftarrow \left| \dfrac{b_{g_i}}{a_{g_i,1}} \right|$

7: **if** $\left| \dfrac{b_{g_{i+1}}}{a_{g_{i+1},1}} \right| < p - \epsilon$ **then**

8: $p \leftarrow \left| \dfrac{b_{g_{i+1}}}{a_{g_{i+1},1}} \right|$

9: $d_j \leftarrow i,\ t \leftarrow i,\ j \leftarrow j+1$

10: **else**

11: $d_j \leftarrow i+1,\ t \leftarrow i,\ j \leftarrow j+1$

12: **else if** $\left| \dfrac{b_{g_{i+1}}}{a_{g_{i+1},1,}} \right| < p - \epsilon$ **then**

13: $p \leftarrow \left| \dfrac{b_{g_{i+1}}}{a_{g_{i+1},1}} \right|$

14: $d_j \leftarrow t,\ t \leftarrow i+1,\ j \leftarrow j+1$

15: **else**

16: $d_j \leftarrow i+1,\ j \leftarrow j+1$

17: **else if** $a_{g_i,2} > \epsilon$ **or** $a_{g_i,2} < -\epsilon$ **then**

18: **if** $\left| \dfrac{b_{g_i}}{a_{g_i,2}} \right| < p - \epsilon$ **then**

19: $p \leftarrow \left| \dfrac{b_{g_i}}{a_{g_i,2}} \right|$

20: **if** $\left| \dfrac{b_{g_{i+1}}}{a_{g_{i+1},2}} \right| < p - \epsilon$ **then**

21: $p \leftarrow \left| \dfrac{b_{g_{i+1}}}{a_{g_{i+1},2}} \right|$

22: $d_j \leftarrow i,\ t \leftarrow i+1,\ j \leftarrow j+1$

23: **else**

24: $d_j \leftarrow i+1,\ t \leftarrow i,\ j \leftarrow j+1$

24: **else if** $\left| \dfrac{b_{g_{i+1}}}{a_{g_{i+1},2}} \right| < p - \epsilon$ **then**

26: $p \leftarrow \left| \dfrac{b_{g_{i+1}}}{a_{g_{i+1},2}} \right|$

27: $d_j \leftarrow t,\ t \leftarrow i+1,\ j \leftarrow j+1$

28: **else**

29: $d_j \leftarrow i+1,\ j \leftarrow j+1$

30: **else**

31: $d_j \leftarrow i,\ j \leftarrow j+1$

32: **else**

33: $p \leftarrow \infty$

34: Delete all elements from d such that $d_j = 0$ for $j \in \{1,2,\ldots,m,\ m+1,\ m+2\}$ and then delete from G elements $g_{d_1},\ g_{d_2},\ g_{d_3},\ g_{d_4} \ldots$ and so forth

Algorithm 3. Delete Some Redundant Constraints

1: $p \leftarrow \infty,\ q \leftarrow \infty,\ u \leftarrow \infty,\ v \leftarrow \infty$

2: $s \leftarrow 0,\ t \leftarrow 0,\ h \leftarrow 0,\ I \leftarrow 0$

3: $\Delta \leftarrow 0,\ j \leftarrow 1,\ d = (0,0,\ldots,0)^{m+2}$

4: **for** $i=1$ **to** $m+2$ **do**

5: **if** $\alpha_{g_i} > -M$ **and** $\alpha_{g_i} < M$ **then**

6: **if** $\dfrac{b_{g_i}}{a_{g_i,1}} < p$ **then**

7: $p \leftarrow \dfrac{b_{g_i}}{a_{g_i,1}}, \quad s \leftarrow i$

8: **if** $\dfrac{b_{g_i}}{a_{g_i,2}} < q$ **then**

9: $q \leftarrow \dfrac{b_{g_i}}{a_{g_i,2}}, \quad t \leftarrow i$

10: **else if** $\alpha_{g_i} > -M - \epsilon$ **and** $\alpha_{g_i} < -M + \epsilon$

11: **if** $\dfrac{b_{g_i}}{a_{g_i,1}} < u$ **then**

12: $u \leftarrow \dfrac{b_{g_i}}{a_{g_i,1}}, \quad h \leftarrow i$

13: **else if** $\alpha_{g_i} > M - \epsilon$ **and** $\alpha_{g_i} < M + \epsilon$ **then**

14: **if** $\dfrac{b_{g_i}}{a_{g_i,2}} < v$ **then**

15: $v \leftarrow \dfrac{b_{g_i}}{a_{g_i,2}}, \quad l \leftarrow i$

16: **if** $s=t$ **then**

17: $\Delta \leftarrow 1$

18: **else if** $s \neq 0$ **and** $t \neq 0$

19: $\Delta \leftarrow 2$

20: Compute the intersection of constraints g_s and g_t defined by $\left(x_1^{'}, x_2^{'}\right)$

21: **for** $i=1$ **to** $m+2$ **do**

22: **if** $\alpha_{g_i} > -M$ **and** $\alpha_{g_i} < M$ **then**

23: **if** $\Delta = 1$ **and** $i \neq s$ **and** $i \neq t$ **then**

24: $d_j \leftarrow i, j \leftarrow j+1$

24: **else if** $\Delta = 2$ **and** $i \neq s$ **and** $i \neq t$ **then**

26: **if** $a_{g_i,1} x_1^{'} + a_{g_i,2} x_2^{'} < b_{g_i} + \epsilon$ **then**

27: $d_j \leftarrow i, j \leftarrow j+1$

28: **else if** $\alpha_{g_i} > -M - \epsilon$ **and** $\alpha_{g_i} < -M + \epsilon$

29: **if** $i \neq h$ **then**

30: $d_j \leftarrow i, j \leftarrow j+1$

31: **else if** $\alpha_{g_i} > M - \epsilon$ **and** $\alpha_{g_i} < M + \epsilon$ **then**

32: **if** $i \neq l$ **then**

33: $d_j \leftarrow i, j \leftarrow j+1$

34: Delete all elements from d such that $d_j = 0$ for $j \in \{1, 2, \ldots, m, m+1, m+2\}$ and then delete from G elements $g_{d_1}, g_{d_2}, g_{d_3}, g_{d_4} \ldots$ and so forth

Solving 2VLPs for All Values of c_1 and c_2

One of the assumptions of the slope algorithm is that $c_1 > 0$ and $c_2 > 0$. This is because the slope algorithm was designed specifically to solve 2VLPs within a simplex framework, where this assumption holds. However, one may want to use the slope algorithm to solve the subproblems of other algorithms where c_1 and c_2 can have negative or zero values. Notice that a straightforward modification can be made to fix this issue. Basically, all that is needed is to compute the slope of the objective function using a similar idea as the one used for the slope of the constraints. That is, the slope of the objective function, let say αo_{bj} can be computed according to (4). One can see that (4) slightly differs from (1) by two things. First, one of the coefficients is added or subtracted for the cases where the objective function is a vertical or horizontal line in order to maintain the sorted order. Second, the cases where 3M would have been assigned as the slope are not considered since x=(0.0) is an optimal solution for this case, j*=m+2, k*=m+1, $\alpha_{j^*} = -2M$ and $\alpha_{k^*} = 2M$.

$$
\alpha_{obj} = \begin{cases}
-2M - c_2 & \text{if } a_{i,1} = 0, a_{i,2} < 0 \\[2mm]
-M + \dfrac{c_2}{c_1} & \text{if } a_{i,1} > 0, a_{i,2} < 0 \\[2mm]
-M + c_1 & \text{if } a_{i,1} > 0, a_{i,2} = 0 \\[2mm]
\dfrac{c_2}{c_1} & \text{if } a_{i,1} > 0, a_{i,2} > 0 \\[2mm]
M - c_2 & \text{if } a_{i,1} = 0, a_{i,2} > 0 \\[2mm]
M - \dfrac{c_1}{c_2} & \text{if } a_{i,1} \langle 0, a_{i,2} \rangle 0 \\[2mm]
2M + c_1 & \text{if } a_{i,1} < 0, a_{i,2} = 0
\end{cases}
$$

Making this change also requires changing the way M is computed. In this case, M must be determined using (5).

$$
M > \max \left\{ M_1, M_2, \left| \frac{c_1}{c_2} \right| : c_2 \neq 0, \left| \frac{c_2}{c_1} \right| : c_1 \neq 0, |c_1|, |c_2| \right\} \tag{8}
$$

All these changes were implemented and computationally tested on some extreme 2VLPs. The following section discusses some of the computational results obtained with this implementation.

COMPUTATIONAL EXPERIMENTS

Both, the original slope algorithm and the one with the discussed modifications were implemented in C++ and compiled using Microsoft Visual Studio. The goal with this computational study was to solve several 2VLPs using both implementations and compare wether they output a correct solution. Computational experiments were performed on an Intel® Core™ i9-9900 CPU @ 3.10GHz processor with 64GB of RAM. The solution of every 2VLP returned by both implementations were compared to the solution obtained by solving the same problem with version 20.1.0 of CPLEX.

Instances were randomly generated for this study. The objective function, constraint, and right-hand side coefficients were generated using a uniform random distribution. Problems were designed such that these coefficients can assume extremely small and large values (on the order of 10^{-15} and 10^{15}), zero, positive, and also negative values. The idea was to test both implementations of the slope algorithm on extreme cases. In total, 2,500 instances were solved. These problems ranged from 200, 400, 600, ..., 5,000 constraints. For each problem size, 100 problems were solved.

To save space, results are not showed and will only be discussed. If considering only the instances where $c_1 > 0$ and $c_2 > 0$, the original slope algorithm solved nearly 50% of them correctly while the modified version solved all of them correctly. If considering all 2,500 instances, then the modified version of the slope algorithm solved almost 99% of the problems correctly. When investigating the 1% that did not solve correctly, most of them failed at computing the intersection of constraints with extremely small and large coefficients. One may claim that the modified slope algorithm is more time consuming given that it has additional steps. Even though this is true, the author anticipates that the modified slope algorithm worsened the CPU time by less than 10%, on average. Regardless, most instances could be solved in tenths of a second. Therefore, the modified slope algorithm is still competitive and much more reliable.

FUTURE RESEARCH DIRECTIONS

One of the major future research directions is to create other multidimensional search algorithms that consider more than two search directions. The majority of the methods discussed during this chapter are two-dimensional techniques, so expanding this to three, four, and higher dimensions is a potential future work topic. This may require creating other slope type algorithms for higher dimensions other than two. This is because an optimal basis is required for simplex framework methods, and the existing methods that can perform multidimensional searches over three and more dimensional do not guarantee an optimal basis. Furthermore, expanding the concept of multidimensional searches to nonlinear optimization is another potential future research topic.

CONCLUSION

This chapter discussed multidimensional search methods for optimization. The chapter presented an extensive literature review of methods to perform multidimensional searches, and their application within a simplex and interior point framework. The chapter also briefly discussed the idea of multidimensional searches for nonlinear programming. Furthermore, a modified slope algorithm to find an optimal solution and optimal basis of 2VLPs was presented. The modified method implements several strategies to improve the applicability of the slope algorithm and mostly, its numerical stability. These strategies include finding an optimal basis for certain solutions immediately, implementing tolerance parameters, removing nearly parallel and redundant constraints by preprocessing them, and solving 2VLPs for all types of objective functions. Computational results showed that the modified slope algorithm is effective and more reliable than the original version.

REFERENCES

Ahmadi-Javid, A., Jalali, Z., & Klassen, K. J. (2017). Outpatient appointment systems in healthcare: A review of optimization studies. *European Journal of Operational Research*, *258*(1), 3–34. doi:10.1016/j. ejor.2016.06.064

Bazaraa, M. S., Jarvis, J. J., & Sherali, H. D. (2010). *Linear programming and network flows* (4th ed.). John Wiley & Sons.

Bazaraa, M. S., Sherali, H. D., & Shetty, C. M. (2006). *Nonlinear programming: Theory and algorithms* (3rd ed.). John Wiley & Sons. doi:10.1002/0471787779

Biesecker, M., Kimn, J.-H., Lu, H., Dingli, D., & Bajzer, Ž. (2010). Optimization of virotherapy for cancer. *Bulletin of Mathematical Biology*, *72*(2), 469–489. doi:10.100711538-009-9456-0 PMID:19787406

Boggs, P. T., Domich, P. D., Donaldson, J. R., & Witzgall, C. (1989). Algorithmic enhancements to the method of centers for linear programming problems. *ORSA Journal on Computing*, *1*(3), 159–171. doi:10.1287/ijoc.1.3.159

Boldyrev, D. V., & Pashkovskiy, A. V. (2018). *An approach to multidimensional nonlinear optimization. In 2018 International Multi-Conference on Industrial Engineering and Modern Technologies (FarEastCon)*. IEEE.

Colombo, M., & Gondzio, J. (2008). Further development of multiple centrality correctors for interior point methods. *Computational Optimization and Applications*, *41*(3), 277–305. doi:10.100710589-007-9106-0

Conejo, A. J., Castillo, E., Mínguez, R., & García-Bertrand, R. (2006). *Decomposition techniques in mathematical programming*. Springer.

Costa, M. F., & Fernandes, E. M. (2006). Implementation of an interior point multidimensional filter line search method for constrained optimization. In *Proceedings of the 5th WSEAS International Conference on System Science and Simulation in Engineering* (pp. 391-396). WSEAS.

Domich, P. D., Boggs, P. T., Rogers, J. E., & Witzgall, C. (1991). Optimizing over three-dimensional subspaces in an interior-point method for linear programming. *Linear Algebra and Its Applications*, *152*, 315–342. doi:10.1016/0024-3795(91)90280-A

Dongarra, J. J., & Grosse, E. (1987). Distribution of mathematical software via electronic mail. *Communications of the ACM*, *30*(5), 403–407. doi:10.1145/22899.22904

Dorling, K., Heinrichs, J., Messier, G. G., & Magierowski, S. (2017). Vehicle routing problems for drone delivery. *IEEE Transactions on Systems, Man, and Cybernetics. Systems*, *47*(1), 70–85. doi:10.1109/ TSMC.2016.2582745

Dyer, M. E. (1984). Linear time algorithms for two- and three-variable linear programs. *SIAM Journal on Computing*, *13*(1), 31–45. doi:10.1137/0213003

Ford, L. R. Jr, & Fulkerson, D. R. (1958). A suggested computation for maximal multi-commodity network flows. *Management Science*, *5*(1), 97–101. doi:10.1287/mnsc.5.1.97

Gay, D. M. (1985). Electronic mail distribution of linear programming test problems. *Mathematical Programming Society COAL Newsletter*, *13*, 10–12.

Gleixner, A., Hendel, G., Gamrath, G., Achterberg, T., Bastubbe, M., Berthold, T., Christophel, P., Jarck, K., Koch, T., Linderoth, J., Lübbecke, M., Mittelmann, H. D., Ozyurt, D., Ralphs, T. K., Salvagnin, D., & Shinano, Y. (2021). MIPLIB 2017: Data-driven compilation of the 6th mixed-integer programming library. *Mathematical Programming Computation*, *13*(3), 443–490. doi:10.100712532-020-00194-3

Gondzio, J. (1996). Multiple centrality corrections in a primal-dual method for linear programming. *Computational Optimization and Applications*, *6*(2), 137–156. doi:10.1007/BF00249643

Gondzio, J. (2012). Interior point methods 25 years later. *European Journal of Operational Research*, *218*(3), 587–601. doi:10.1016/j.ejor.2011.09.017

Gonzaga, C. C. (1991). Search directions for interior linear-programming methods. *Algorithmica*, *6*(1-6), 153–181. doi:10.1007/BF01759039

Jamrunroj, P., & Boonperm, A.-a. (2021). A new technique for solving a 2-dimensional linear program by considering the coefficient of constraints. In *Proceedings of the 3rd International Conference on Intelligent Computing and Optimization 2020 (ICO2020)* (pp. 276-286). Springer. 10.1007/978-3-030-68154-8_27

Jarre, F., & Wechs, M. (1999). Extending Mehrotra's corrector for linear programs. *Advanced Modeling and Optimization*, *1*(2), 38–60.

Karmarkar, N., & Ramakrishnan, R. (1985). *Further developments in the new polynomial-time algorithm for linear programming* [Paper presentation]. ORSA/TIMS Joint National Meeting. Boston, MA, United States.

Lee, E. K. (1997). Computational experience of a general purpose mixed 0/1 integer programming solver (MIPSOL). Software report, Georgia Institute of Technology, School of Industrial and Systems Engineering, Atlanta, GA, United States.

Li, Z., Vitor, F., Lee, E., & Easton, T. (2022). *On the implementation of double pivots into a primal simplex solver* [Manuscript in preparation].

Matrajt, L., Eaton, J., Leung, T., & Brown, E. R. (2021). Vaccine optimization for COVID-19: Who to vaccinate first? *Science Advances*, *7*(6), 1–11. doi:10.1126ciadv.abf1374 PMID:33536223

Megiddo, N. (1983). Linear-time algorithms for linear programming in . *SIAM Journal on Computing*, *12*(4), 759–776. doi:10.1137/0212052

Megiddo, N. (1984). Linear programming in linear time when the dimension is fixed. *Journal of the Association for Computing Machinery*, *31*(1), 114–127. doi:10.1145/2422.322418

Mehrotra, S. (1992). On the implementation of a primal-dual interior point method. *SIAM Journal on Optimization, 2*(4), 575–601. doi:10.1137/0802028

Mehrotra, S., & Li, Z. (2005). Convergence conditions and Krylov subspace-based corrections for primal-dual interior-point method. *SIAM Journal on Optimization, 15*(3), 635–653. doi:10.1137/S1052623403431494

Mittelmann, H. D. (2021, September 25). *Decision tree for optimization software*. Retrieved from http://plato.asu.edu/guide.html

Santos, L.-R., Villas-Bôas, F., Oliveira, A. R., & Perin, C. (2019). Optimized choice of parameters in interior-point methods for linear programming. *Computational Optimization and Applications, 73*(2), 535–574. doi:10.100710589-019-00079-9

Shamos, M. I., & Hoey, D. (1976). Geometric intersection problems. In *17th Annual Symposium on Foundations of Computer Science* (pp. 208-215). IEEE.

Vitor, F. (2018). The ratio algorithm to solve the optimal basis of two constraint linear programs. In *Proceedings of the 2018 IISE Annual Conference* (pp. 1949-1954). IISE.

Vitor, F. (2019). *Two dimensional search algorithms for linear programming* (Order No. 13881983) [Doctoral dissertation, Kansas State University]. ProQuest Dissertations & Theses Global.

Vitor, F., & Easton, T. (2018). A two dimensional search primal affine scaling interior point algorithm for linear programs. In *Proceedings of the 2018 IISE Annual Conference* (pp. 1961-1966). IISE.

Vitor, F., & Easton, T. (2018). The double pivot simplex method. *Mathematical Methods of Operations Research, 87*(1), 109–137. doi:10.100700186-017-0610-4

Vitor, F., & Easton, T. (2022). Projected orthogonal vectors in two-dimensional search interior point algorithms for linear programming. *Computational Optimization and Applications, 83*(1), 211–246. doi:10.100710589-022-00385-9

Wu, N., Li, Z., & Qu, T. (2017). Energy efficiency optimization in scheduling crude oil operations of refinery based on linear programming. *Journal of Cleaner Production, 166*, 49–57. doi:10.1016/j.jclepro.2017.07.222

Yang, Y. (2020). A double-pivot simplex algorithm and its upper bounds of the iteration numbers. *Research in the Mathematical Sciences, 7*(4), 34. doi:10.100740687-020-00235-2

Yang, Y., & Vitor, F. (in press). A double-pivot degenerate-robust simplex algorithm for linear programming. *International Journal of Operational Research*. Advance online publication. doi:10.1504/IJOR.2022.10050447

ADDITIONAL READING

Dantzig, G. B. (1947). Maximization of a linear function of variables subject to linear inequalities. In T. C. Koopmans (Ed.), *Activity Analysis of Production and Allocation* (pp. 339–347). John Wiley & Sons.

Karmarkar, N. (1984). A new polynomial-time algorithm for linear programming. *Combinatorica, 4*(4), 373–395. doi:10.1007/BF02579150

Khachiyan, L. G. (1980). Polynomial algorithms in linear programming. *U.S.S.R. Computational Mathematics and Mathematical Physics, 20*(1), 53–72. doi:10.1016/0041-5553(80)90061-0

Lenstra, J. K., Rinnooy-Kan, A. H., & Schrijver, A. (1991). *History of mathematical programming: a collection of personal reminiscences.* North-Holland.

Terlaky, T., & Zhang, S. (1993). Pivot rules for linear programming: A survey on recent theoretical developments. *Annals of Operations Research, 46*(1), 203–233. doi:10.1007/BF02096264

Vanderbei, R. J. (2020). *Linear programming: Foundations and extensions* (5th ed.). Springer. doi:10.1007/978-3-030-39415-8

Williams, H. P. (2013). *Model building in mathematical programming* (5th ed.). John Wiley & Sons.

Wright, S. J. (1997). *Primal-dual interior-point methods.* SIAM. doi:10.1137/1.9781611971453

KEY TERMS AND DEFINITIONS

Dantzig's Pivoting Rule: Select a nonbasic variable with the most improving reduced cost.

Degenerate Solution: Basic feasible solution where one of the basic variables equals zero.

Interior Point Framework: An algorithm that moves between solutions within the interior of a polyhedron.

Multidimensional Search: The act of solving a multidimensional subspace problem to simultaneously find the step length along multiple search directions.

One-Dimensional Search: The act of solving a one-dimensional subspace problem to find the step length along a single search direction.

Optimal Basis: Basic feasible solution from where there does not exist any feasible improving search direction.

Simplex Framework: An algorithm that moves between solutions that are located at the vertices of a polyhedron.

Section 36
Meta–Analysis and Metamodeling

The Role of Metamodeling in Systems Development

Balsam A. J. Mustafa

(iD) https://orcid.org/0000-0002-2973-7124

Al Hadi University College, Iraq

Mazlina Abdul Majid

University Malaysia Pahang, Malaysia

INTRODUCTION

What is Meta-Model? The word *"Meta"* literally means "after", "beyond" in Greek or more "comprehensive" (*Merriam-Webster's*, 1993). In computer science, it is widely used in different meanings. In Database Management Systems, metadata means (data about data) which may represent data dictionaries, repositories, etc., and models represent data like the ER model (Entity-Relationship). In other words, a meta-model is a model of the data model. In Programming Languages, a meta interpreter is an interpreter of a (program) interpreter (Smith, 1984). Meta-modeling is a method for defining the abstract syntax of a language, both modeling or programming language. It makes the development of a language simpler allowing the designers to directly map the classes identified in domain analysis to classes in the meta-model (Kleppe, 2008). The meta-model expresses what models include such as concepts and relationships between them and may be the rules of how these concepts can be interrelated. Hence, a metamodel can be treated just like any conceptual model of information systems. The only specialty is that the artifact of meta-modeling is a model (Jeusfeld, 2009), i.e. a model is an instance of a metamodeling, for example, any UML class diagram can be seen as an instance of the UML metamodel that should be well formed with respect to it (Osis & Donins, 2017).

At the beginning of the development of any system, the representation of a system view takes place once it is represented by a model. Kuhne (2006). defined a model as an abstraction of a real or language-based system allowing predictions or inferences to be made by developers. Kuhne (2006). explained that any model is built according to a specific meta-model which consists of a collection of functional or structural elements and rules to allow modeling the system view. The developer then can explain his ideas and discuss the conceptual view of the system with other stakeholders and can be further refined based on feedback from others. For any modeling method, its accuracy depends on the meta-model which semantically supports the features and behavior of the system that the method is used to model, i.e. the metamodel identifies the semantics of the system representation at the model level. Basha et al. (2012). pointed out that metamodeling is important because it provides a means for the machine to read, write, and understand models that were created and interpreted only by people. From this perspective, meta-modeling plays a key role in automating model based system development (MBSD). With models understandable to computers, tools can be built for model creation and code generation.

DOI: 10.4018/978-1-7998-9220-5.ch145

Harel and Rumpe (2004). explained that machines use machine-readable languages for communication just like people use natural languages to communicate between them. Both kinds of languages whether they are natural, artiðcial, or programming languages contain a large variety of meaningful elements. Therefore, a language consists of a syntactic notation (syntax), which is a set of legal elements, together with the meaning of those elements, which is expressed by relating the syntax to a semantic domain. A metamodel is a model of a language that developers use to design and implement a system and its structure consists of the essential elements of the language such as the language concepts, its graphical syntax and its semantics, i.e. what the models and programs written in the language mean and how they behave (Atkinson & Kuhne, 2003).

To improve system development practice, it is important to understand how languages can be managed to respond to the developers' demands. Language driven development is elaborated in this chapter. The right language improves the productivity of developers by increasing the value of primary software artifacts in terms of how much functionality they deliver at the development stages, and by reducing the rate at which primary software artifacts become obsolete (Atkinson & Kuhne, 2003).

In this chapter, we discuss first the role and importance of a language used in system development with its features, and introduces the steps of the meta-modeling process. In the sequel, we review the meta-modeling standards and the relationship between meta-modeling and model-driven architecture (MDA). The chapter also discusses the different categories of meta-models and finally presents the areas in meta-modeling where there is a demand for more research suggesting some future work.

BACKGROUND

The architecture of a system involves what elements make up the system and how they work together to provide the functionality of the system. The Model Driven Architecture (MDA) is an approach for software systems development initiated by the object management group (OMG) in 2001 (OMG, 2001). Unlike the other standards of the OMG, the MDA offers to use models instead of the traditional source code. It defines a specification that separates the system functionality from implementation that uses a specific technology platform. The architecture of a system is a specification of the parts and connectors of the system and the rules for the interactions of the parts using the connectors (Shaw, & Garlan, 1996). The standard of MDA released by OMG contains a set of guidelines for structuring the specification as models. MDA focused on creating and modeling the software products (Yousaf et al, 2019). The model here is an abstraction or a representation of a certain aspect of the system or a domain of the real-world that the system is designed for. The model aims to simplify the complexity of the system, focuses on the abstraction away from code to form a graphical model, which enables developers to understand, communicate, design, and implement the systems or adapt existing models. This makes the development of an application easier for those without prior coding knowledge. Different standard notations are used in modeling, e.g. the unified modeling language (UML).

MDA hence relies on models to be the main artifact in the development process to raise the level of abstraction to manage the complexity and change of the development process. This includes all types of models defined in the OMG standard which are the platform-independent model (PIM) and the platform-dependent model (PDM) to cover all system aspects in the development lifecycle. Models are created by a language, and the OMG' Meta-Object Facility (MOF) is introduced and clearly stated as the language in which all the languages for MDA are written (MOF, 2002). Modeling languages are used to define models, thus, their syntax and semantics (meaning) must be precisely defined. Hence, the process of metamodeling allows meaningful metamodel of a language to be defined precisely. It is clear that in metamodeling, language definitions are modeled in a language that is similar to the language used to construct system models which makes the metamodeling language easier to understand since they are written in a familiar notation (Atkinson & Kuhne, 2003). This chapter discusses the role and importance of a language in system development with its features, introduces the steps of the meta-modeling process, also provides an overview of the meta-modeling standards and the relationship between meta-modeling and model-driven architecture (MDA).

LANGUAGE DRIVEN DEVELOPMENT

Nowadays software systems developers are encountering different challenges as systems become increasingly complex due to numerous customer needs that lead to a system with rich functionalities to be delivered within a short schedule. Developers also have to manage a variety of implementation methods, design techniques, and development processes. Researchers (Fowler, 2010) proposed *"Languages"* as a solution to these problems. Languages are fundamental means for systems developers by which they communicate, design, and implement systems. Design and implementation of computer languages have become a mature area that consists of a wide range of methods, techniques, and tools which found very useful in many software development methods and led to a distinguished paradigm known as *"language-driven software development"*, where these tools and techniques are based on strong theoretical and mathematical principles (Alfred et al., 2007). The paradigm is particularly appropriate to address complex systems development involving sophisticated and highly customizable architectures, interdisciplinary teams of developers, and domain experts (Kleppe, 2003; Mauw et al., 2004; Mernik et al., 2005).

THE ROLE OF LANGUAGES

Human beings use natural languages to communicate between them and the stakeholders involved with them. Languages in computer science, although in a more formalized way, are fundamental to the development of software systems. Developers use different kinds of languages in the design and implementation including high-level modeling languages e.g. UML (Unified Modeling Language) that models different aspects of the system without considering the details of implementation. Other programming languages such as Java, scripting languages such as Perl, and database languages like SQL. Many of these languages are of general- purpose and could be applied across various domains, while other languages are domain- specific provide a special set of concepts that are related to a specific domain (Kleppe, 2008). Languages support different activities that are important parts of systems' development as it allows to run and test a model or a program, provides information of the properties of the model and program, and generate test cases from models to validate them against programs. In addition, many languages provide visualization through the graphical description of the system (Rumbaugh et al., 1999). A UML is an example of such language.

FEATURES OF LANGUAGE

To understand a meta-model of a language we need to specify the main concepts of the language i.e. abstract syntax, concrete syntax, semantics, and mapping.

Abstract Syntax

An abstract syntax aims to describe the structural essence of the language (Krahn, 2007). It is typically carried out using metamodeling. In any specific language, the abstract syntax represents the basic elements (concepts) of the language and the relationships between them (associations) defined in a mathematically precise way. It defines these elements which could be any particular idea or entity with which the user is concerned and the relationships between the elements, and may be any rules that legally combine the elements. However, the abstract syntax of a language does not describe how the elements are presented to the end-user in a model or a program or the meaning of the model (Krahn, 2007).

Concrete Syntax

As indicated by Krahn (2007). any language provides a notation that specifies how the model or program would be presented and constructed using the language. This notation is the concrete syntax of the language. It describes how the elements of a language are presented in a model. There are two types of concrete syntax, textual or graphical. Textual concrete syntax describes the model or program in a textual form that allows presenting details. Graphical concrete syntax represents the model using a diagrammatical form that enables stakeholders to communicate the structure of the model and the domain of the system.

Semantics

The semantics of a language explain the meaning of a model or a program written in that language or what it would do. As pointed out by Harel and Rumpe (2004), both a system's behavior and its structure are important views in system modeling, both are represented by syntactic concepts (constructs), and both need semantics. Thus, models like entity-relationship diagrams (ER) for databases or UML class diagrams need semantics to enable users to know the meaning of the constructs of a language. It is very important that the semantics of a language must be understood in a precise and useful way by the user of the language. An abstract mathematical description has little benefit if it cannot be understood or used. An executable language for example must have operational semantics that allows it to be run; a language that contains concepts, like classes, should permit the creation of objects according to the rules of creating instances from a class (Harel & Rumpe, 2004).

Mapping

Mapping is the process that makes the relationship between a language and another language by translating the concepts of one language into concepts in another language. This means, given two modeling languages, *mapping* refers to a method that allows a model of the second language to be determined starting from a model of the first language. It allows finding semantic equivalence between two languages i.e. a language may have concepts whose meaning is similar to the concepts in another language, such as mapping a UML language to another non-UML language (Domnguez & Zapata, 2000). As researchers discussed, mapping is a complex process, and they proposed the meta-modeling approach as a general framework for model translation, considering that semantics are preserved in the mapping of two models (Domnguez & Zapata, 2000).

THE PROCESS OF META- MODELING

Formalizing a meta-model was discussed in various researches (Drbohlav, 1999; Czarnecki, & Hedin, 2012). The process of creating a meta-model involves developing specifications that the modeling process must fulfill. Like other modeling languages, meta-modeling languages focus on specific aspects of the domain to be modeled and therefore lead to different types of representations.

The steps of a typical meta-modeling process as shown in Czarnecki and Hedin (2012) are as follow:

1- Select a meta- modeling infrastructure
2- Define an abstract syntax using the selected infrastructure
3- Define well- formalized rules and any operations on the meta-model
4- Define a concrete syntax that conforms to the abstract syntax
5- Define semantics
6- Define mappings to other languages e.g. by using transformations

In language development, the meta-modeling process may end at different steps.

META-MODELING STANDARDS

System development uses languages to describe different aspects of the problem domain. As discussed before, all system development languages have a concrete syntax, which deðnes how the elements of a language are presented, an abstract syntax that describes the elements of the language, and a semantics that describes what the concepts mean. A meta-model is a model of all these different aspects of a language. For system' development, there are various languages, meta-modeling can solve the problem of diversity of languages by describing all languages in a unified way (Krahn, 2007). The difference between meta-modeling language and a programming language like Java or a modeling language like UML is that the meta-modeling language is speciðcally designed to support the design of languages. Therefore, a metamodeling language needs to have the ability to precisely define all aspects of a modeling language including its syntax and semantics (Harel & Rumpe, 2004).

META-MODELING AND MDA

The Model Driven Architecture (MDA) approach initiated by the object management group (OMG) uses models in software development (OMG, 2001). The MDA has significant implications for the discipline of Meta-modeling. It describes specific kinds of models on a high level of abstraction which are Platform independent, which means a model of the system that does not refer to any technology-specific implementation details. This allows developers to focus on the problem domain. It attempts to separate the business and application logic from the underlying technology platform to understand the system's functions and behavior separate from technology-specific code that implement it (Sacevski, & Veseli, 2007). The other kind of model is a model of a system that specifies the technology of implementation that will be used. For example, the model that describes the system using Java or Microsoft.NET technology is a platform-specific model. In MDA, transformation techniques translate platform-independent models to platform-specific models. MDA uses standard modeling languages of OMG like Unified Modeling Language (UML); Meta-Object Facility (MOF); and Common Warehouse Meta-model (CWM) to build these models (Sacevski, & Veseli, 2007).

Meta - Object Facility (MOF)

MOF standard of the object management group (OMG) is an essential part in MDA. It is a semiformal language to write meta-models and describe models transformation. As Mosānsa and Kampars (2020) stated "Metamodeling facility (MOF) is frequently used to specify the meta-models. Having a method based on a well-defined metamodel enables the development of consistent and interoperable models as well as to provide tools for implementing systems out of the models". To understand how MOF works, it is necessary to explain the traditional metamodel infrastructure produced by OMG where software is specified by models and models are deðned as instances of meta-models, which are, in turn, deðned as instances of the MOF meta-meta model (OMG, 2009). The infrastructure that supports MOF consists of 4 layers hierarchy of model levels (Figure 1). The first level in the hierarchy (M0) contains the data of the software represented by objects or data in a relational database table. Level (M1) represents a model of the M0 user data, this is the user model. M2 represents a model of the model in level M1 (i.e. a meta-model). This meta-model captures the language, for example, UML elements such as class, attribute, and operation. M3 is the model that describes the properties of all meta-models in M2, so it is often characterized as meta-meta model or MOF (Atkinson & Kuhne, 2003). According to OMG, MOF is aimed to define a common way of capturing all the different modeling used by MDA (OMG, 2009). Languages that are defined in terms of MOF can be mapped to each other because they are defined in the same way. For example, relating two models one written in UML and another model that describes a program written in Java becomes easy because MOF definition of each language is available.

Common Warehouse Meta-Model (CWM)

The model driven architecture (MDA) has significant implications for the disciplines of Metamodeling. The core standards of the MDA (UML, MOF, XMI, CWM) form the basis for building coherent schemes for authoring, publishing, and managing models within a model-driven architecture (Pool, 2001). The reason behind the OMG Common Warehouse Metadata Initiative (CWM) as pointed out by OMG (2003a) is to enable the easy interchange of metadata between data warehousing tools and metadata repositories in distributed heterogeneous environments.

The Common Warehouse Meta-model is a specification for modeling metadata for relational, non-relational, multidimensional systems, and most other objects found in a data warehousing environment. CWM provides objects that describe where the data came from and when and how the data was created (OMG, 2003b). The specification of (CWM) adopted by the Object Management Group (OMG) is an important milestone on the way to fully MDA supporting data warehouse interchange. Tools that are used in data warehouse deployment and maintenance interface with a shared store containing metadata about the structure of various operational data sources and target data warehouses in addition to descriptions of the transformations required to move data between them. As Tolbert (2000) discussed, suitably designed tools can then use the metadata and transformations to coordinate the extraction of data from operational sources and its transformation into forms appropriate for import into target data warehouse stores.

Figure 1. Traditional OMG Modeling Infrastructure. Source: Atkinson and Kuhne (2003)

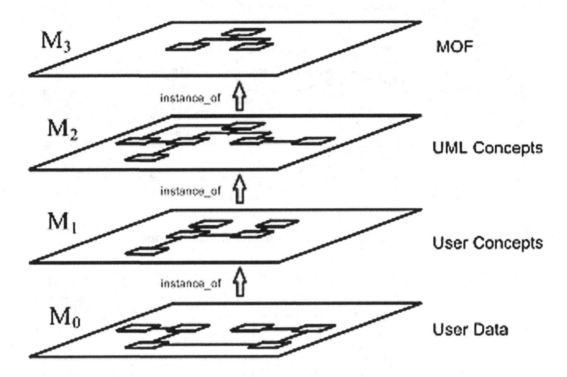

META- MODELING CATEGORIES

The language used to represent a system should be able to represent the emphasized characteristics of that system in a clear, unambiguous way. This can be achieved if the meta-model of the language is accurate, rigorous enough to avoid any misinterpretation of the representation. According to Gajski at al. (1994). meta-model should be complete to build a model that describes the system view. Gajski et al., (1994). have categorized the meta-models into five types.

State Oriented Meta-Models

This type of Metamodels focuses on modeling a system as a set of states and a set of transitions (Figure 2). These meta-models allow to model systems by capturing the temporal behavior of the system, i.e. after the system being in one state what will happen next (another state). Examples of this type of meta-model are finite state machines (FSMs), finite state machines with data paths (FSMD), State Charts, and Petri nets.

Figure 2. Example State Chart Diagram

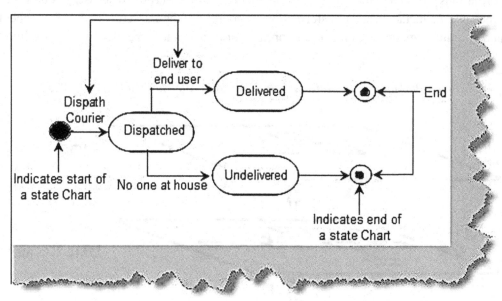

Figure 3. - Example FSM Metamodel. Source: (KerMeta Software Tutorial)

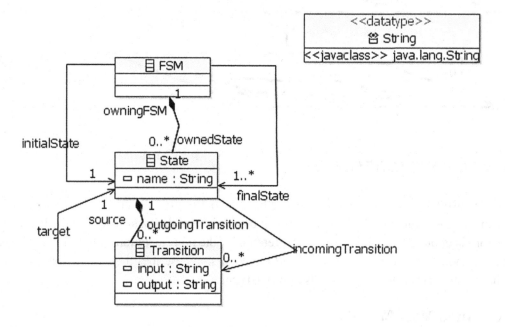

Figure 3 shows a basic finite state machine (FSM) meta-model. The meta-model specifies the abstract syntax of FSM model as a UML class diagram. The meta-model defines a finite state machine element *FSM* consisting of *states*, of which one *State* is the *start or initial* state. *States* are connected via *Transitions*. The *FSM* provides *conditions* bound to transitions (Kermeta, n.d.). The FSM shown in the figure above may be used to statically describe the state machines of the system. The FSM is used at design-time by the designer to represent the behavior of software components in form of FSMs (Lehmann et al., 2010).

Finite state machine data (FSMD) is an evolution of FSM to solve the problem of state explosion in a clear way. The FSMD adds a data path including variables, operators on communication to the classic FSM. To define FSMD formally, the definition of an FSM must be extended by introducing sets of data path variables, inputs, and outputs that will complement the sets of FSM states, inputs, and outputs. However, and according to Sudnitson (2001). these meta-models cannot address concurrency and hierarchy, hence, they are not able to capture complex behaviors.

Another meta-model of this type can be represented by Petri Nets. A mathematical tool used for modeling the dynamic aspects of the system (see Figure 4). It consists of 'circles' which represent any state of the system, there appear 'rectangles' that represent transitions between states which might be caused by an event or action that leads to change the state, and 'arrows' that connect a circle with a transition or vice versa. By formally analyzing the petri nets, useful information about the structure and dynamic behavior of the system can be obtained (David & Allah, 1994). The main feature of Petri nets is their ability to model a system that shows concurrent actions and synchronization when a transition has multiple input states and one output state (join), the transition represents synchronization among all of the sources of the transition. The meta-model specifies the major components of the Petri nets. Some Petri net extensions comprise powerful semantic mechanisms like hierarchical approaches and object orientation that make them suitable for modeling complex systems (Jensen, 1997).

Figure 4. Example Petri Net

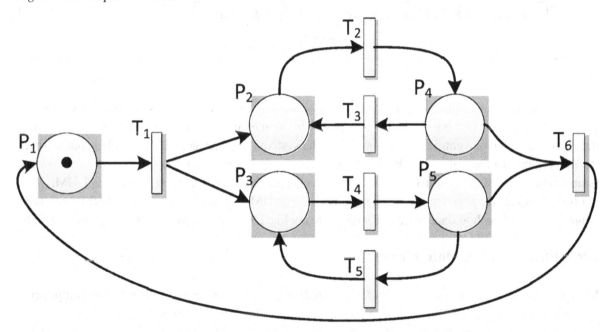

Activity Oriented Meta-Models

An example of this kind of metamodel is the activity-oriented process meta-models (shown as UML class diagram) which can be used to create models that concentrate on the activities and tasks performed in a process to produce a product (Hug et al., 2009). Because these models represent a process it includes concepts like 'Work Definition' that have Products as inputs and outputs and are performed by an activity.

Examples of activity oriented Meta-process modeling are the software process engineering metamodel (SPEM) which is an OMG-standard (OMG, 2005) and (ISO 24744, 2007). More examples of activity oriented meta-models are data flow diagram (DFD) and flow charts.

Figure 5 depicts part of SPEM as illustrated in the work of Hug et al. (2009). A Work Definition can be an Activity or a phase. In a work process, WorkDefinition represents the work performed in a process. A ProcessRole defines responsibilities over specific WorkProduct, and defines the roles that perform and assist in specific activities. The ActivityParameter meta-class allows specifying the input/output (WorkProduct) of a WorkDefinition.

Figure 5. SPEM meta-model. Source (Hug et al., 2009)

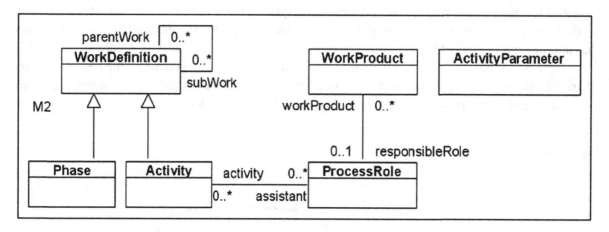

DFD diagram is a graphical representation that shows how data flow in the system and processed to get an output. It uses four basic constructs depicted in the metamodel, these are processes, data stores, data flows, and external entities that interact with the system (Dahanayake, 2000). A DFD shows where the processing of input data will take place and what output is generated. However, it cannot show the temporal behavior of the system or action control. As Fernandes and Lilius (2004). explained, UML does not have a similar diagram based on this metamodel. The UML's use case diagram and UML's activity diagram do not show how data processed so they are not like DFDs and cannot be used to describe DFDs.

Structure Oriented Meta-Models

Structure oriented meta-models describe the structure of the system in terms of the physical components (modules) of the systems and the relationships between them. This metamodel focuses on the characteristics of the system components not their functionality (Baresi & Miraz, 2011). The UML component diagram which can be used to model the basic architecture of the system is based on this metamodel. Component diagram not only shows the basic components of the system but the interfaces to these components. When the interfaces are defined by the developers, it becomes much easier to organize the development effort and deal with the evolution of the interfaces to reflect new requirements or changes to the design.

Data Oriented Meta-Models

Data oriented meta-models focus on the organization of data in a system rather than the functions or processes of the system. Data oriented metamodels are, typically, used with techniques of the structured analysis and design method (SSADM). One example of these techniques is the entity-relationship diagram (ERD). The entity-relationship model is a graphical representation of the entities in a system and the logical relationships between these entities in order to create a database. When a database is to be created, the logical structure of the database is modeled after creating a conceptual view that describes the data and relationships among the data (Chen, 1997). The ER metamodel consists of entities, relationships among them, and attributes of the entities, where a set of permitted values for an attribute is defined in domains like (string, integer, date, etc).

Another example of data oriented met-models is Jackson system development (JSD). As Jackson (1992) described it, JSD assumes that the application domain can be represented by objects or entities that engage in sequentially time-ordered events. Descriptions of the behavior of these objects will provide the basis for the sequential processes of the system. JSD differs from other modeling methods in that it makes separation of model from function, i.e. no events or entities that belong to the system function. Data models concentrate on the states of the modeled domain; event and process models concentrate on how those states change (Jackson, 1992). In JSD, the attribute of an entity is represented by a set of states based on the time-ordered structure of events that happen to this entity. In this way, the meaning of the attribute values can be made fully unambiguous (Jackson & Sztipanovits, 2009). UML does not have any kind of diagram based on these metamodels, since it is object- oriented and does not include diagrams mainly dedicated to data modeling.

FUTURE RESEARCH DIRECTIONS

Metamodeling is a technology provides signiðcant power to designers and users, and there has been a distinguished amount of research in this area in terms of modeling data, software, and languages. However, there are research challenges that are still outstanding regarding usability, evolution, intuitive representation (Sprinkle et al, 2010). Some of the research demands in this area are discussed below in brief.

Metamodeling Semantic Issues

As discussed before in this chapter, metamodels are pure syntactic representations of the models they describe. Signiðcant research has been made in attaching additional information to these metamodels, which in many approaches is called "semantic attachments". Research is needed to explore "what methods are appropriately efficient and intuitive to do this attachment?" Another issue is mappings from one semantic domain to another. As Sprinkle et al. (2010) pointed out; one issue that deserves further research is the speciðcations of these mappings for complex metamodels and their intuitive representation.

Evolution of Meta-Model

Meta-models may evolve, for example, because the tools that generate it are updated to a new version, this may affect the models built using the metamodel. These models may no longer conform to the evolved metamodel. Therefore, it is required that the models should evolve so that models conform to the new metamodel. Although this issue is investigated for visual languages (Krahn et al., 2008), research is needed to determine the accurate ways to describe such transformation.

Omg Modeling Infrastructure

Atkinson and Kuhne (2003) discussed problems with the OMG modeling infrastructure (4 metamodeling layers) depicted in Figure 1. One of them, they argued, that there is no explanation of how entities within the 4 layers infrastructure model relate to the real world. They questioned whether world elements are accommodated within the infrastructure, or do they lie outside? The other issue they raised is that the infrastructure model shows an implication that all instances of relationships between elements are fundamental of the same kind. The issue that needs more research to become, is this a valid approach? or should a model be more discriminating? Future research may provide explanations for these questions.

CONCLUSION

A system view occurs when it is represented by a model. Any model is built based on a specific meta-model. The meta-model consists of a set of (functional or structural) elements and of composition rules that allows building a model representing the system view. Computers use machine-readable languages for communication just like people use natural languages to communicate between them. Machine languages (e.g. programming languages) contain a large variety of meaningful elements. Therefore, a language consists of a syntactic notation (syntax), which is a set of legal elements, together with the meaning of those elements, which is expressed by relating the syntax to a semantic domain. A model of a language that takes the essential elements of the language that are used in system development is a meta-model. It includes the language elements, its textual and/or graphical syntax, and its semantics i.e. the meaning of the models and programs written in the language. This chapter aimed to provide an overview of the topic of meta-modeling, highlighting the important aspects of meta-models, their relationship to modeling languages, and recent OMG standards. This chapter discussed topics that are still unexplored in metamodeling and the need for more research to fill the gaps in this important area.

REFERENCES

Alfred, V., Sethi, R., & Ullman, J. D. (2007). *Compilers: PRINCIPLES, techniques, and tools* (2nd ed.). Addison-Wesley Longman Publishing.

Atkinson, C., & Kuhne, T. (2003). Model-driven development: A METAMODELING foundation. *IEEE Software*, *20*(5), 36–41. doi:10.1109/MS.2003.1231149

Baresi, L., & Miraz, M. (2011). A Component-oriented metamodel for the modernization of software applications. *IEEE International Conference on Engineering of Complex Computer Systems*, 179-187. 10.1109/ICECCS.2011.25

Basha, N., Abdul Moiz, S., & Rizwanullah, M. (2012). Model based software development issues & challenges. *Journal of Computer Science & Informatics*, *2*(1).

Chen, P. P. (1997). English, chinese and ER diagrams. *Data & Knowledge Engineering, 23*(1), 5–16. doi:10.1016/S0169-023X(97)00017-7

Czarnecki, K., & Hedin, G. (Eds.). (2012). Software language engineering. LNCS, 7745.

Dahanayake, A. (2000). *Computer aided method engineering: DESIGNING CASE repositories for the 21st century*. Idea Group Inc.

David, R., & Allah, H. (1994). Petri nets for modeling of dynamic system – A Survey. *Automatica, 30*(2), 15–202. doi:10.1016/0005-1098(94)90024-8

Domnguez, E., & Zapata, M. A. (2000). Mappings and interoperability: A META- modelling approach. In T. Yakhno (Ed.), *Advances in Information Systems, ADVIS'00* (pp. 352–362). Springer. doi:10.1007/3-540-40888-6_34

Drbohlav, M. (1999). Meta-modeling: Theory and practical implications. In System Development Methods for Databases, Enterprise Modeling, and Workflow Management. Kluwer Academic Publishing.

Fernandes, J. M., & Lilius, J. (2004). Functional and object-oriented views in embedded soft-ware modeling. *Proceedings of 11th International Conference on the Engineering of Computer Based Systems (ECBS 2004)*, 378-387.

Fowler, M. (2010). *Domain specific languages* (1st ed.). Addison-Wesley Professional.

Gajski, D., Fahid, F., & Narayan, S. (1994). *Specification and design of embedded systems*. Prentic- Hall.

Harel, D., & Rumpe, B. (2004). Meaningful modeling: What's the semantics of "semantics"? *IEEE Computer, 37*(10).

Hug, C., Front, A., Rieu, D., & Henderson-Sellers, B. (2009). A Method to build information systems engineering process metamodels. *Journal of Systems and Software, 82*(10), 1730–1742. doi:10.1016/j.jss.2009.05.020

ISO/IEC 24744 (2007). Software engineering - metamodel for development methodologies.

Jackson, E., & Sztipanovits, J. (2009). Formalizing the structural semantics of domain-speciðc modeling languages. *Software & Systems Modeling, 8*(4), 451–478. doi:10.100710270-008-0105-0

Jackson, M. (1992). The Jackson development methods. In J. Marciniak (Ed.), *Wiley Encyclopedia of Software Engineering*

Jensen, K. (1997), Colored petri nets: BASIC concepts, analysis methods and practical use: Vol. 1. Basic concepts. Springer

Jeusfeld, M. (2009). Metamodeling and method engineering with conceptbase. In M. A. Jeusfeld, M. Jarke, & J. Mylopoulos (Eds.), *Metamodeling for Method Engineering* (pp. 89–168). The MIT Press.

KerMeta. (n.d.). *Define the FSM metamodel*. http://www.kermeta.org/docs/fr.irisa.triskell.kermeta.samples.fsm.documentation/build/html.chunked/KerMeta-The-FSM-example/ch03.html

Kleppe, A. (2008). *Software language engineering: CREATING domain-specific languages using meta models*. Addison-Wesley Professional.

Krahn, H., Rumpe, B., & Völkel, S. (2007). Integrated definition of abstract and concrete syntax for textual languages. *Proceedings of the ACM/IEEE 10th International Conference on Model Driven Engineering Languages and Systems (MODELS 2007)*.

Krahn, H., Rumpe, B., & Völkel, S. (2008). MontiCore: MODULAR development of textual domain speciðc languages. *Proceedings of the 46th International Conference on Objects, Models, Components, Patterns (TOOLS-Europe)*, 297-315.

Kuhne, T. (2006). Matters of meta-modeling. *Journal of Software and Systems Modeling*, 5(4), 369–385. doi:10.100710270-006-0017-9

Lehmann, G., Blumendorf, M., Trollmann, F., & Albayrak, S. (2010). Meta-modeling runtime models. *Proceedings of the International Conference on Models in Software Engineering (MODELS'10)*, 209-223.

Mauw, S., Wiersma, W. T., & Willemse, T. (2004). Language-driven system design. *International Journal of Software Engineering and Knowledge Engineering*, 14(6), 625–663. doi:10.1142/S0218194004001828

Mernik, M., Heering, J., & Sloane, A. M. (2005). When and how to develop domain-speciðc languages. *ACM Computing Surveys*, 37(4), 316–344. doi:10.1145/1118890.1118892

Merriam-Webster's collegiate dictionary. (1993). 10th ed.). Merriam-Webster.

Mosānsa, G., & Kampars, J. (2020). *Development of light-weight web-based metamodeling tool*. 13th IFIP WG 8.1 Working Conference on the Practice of Enterprise Modelling, Riga, Poland.

OMF. (2002). *Specification version (1.4)*. https://www.omg.org/spec/MOF/1.4)

OMG. (2001). *MDA - The Architecture of choice for a changing world*. https://www.omg.org/mda/

OMG. (2003a). *Common warehouse metamodel (CWM) specification, Version 1.1, Volume1 formal/03-03-02*. OMG.

OMG. (2003b). *The Common Warehouse metamodel (specifications, papers, presentations)*. https://www.cwmforum.org/

OMG. (2005). *Software process engineering metamodel specification*. Version 1.1. OMG.

OMG. (2009). *Meta-object facility*. https://www.omg.org/mof/

Osis, J., & Donins, U. (2017). *Adjusting unified modeling language*. Elsevier Inc. doi:10.1016/B978-0-12-805476-5.00003-4

Pool, J. (2001). Model-driven architecture: VISION, standards and emerging technologies. *Annual European Conference on Object-Oriented Programming (ECOOP 2001)*.

Rumbaugh, J., Jacobson, I., & Booch, G. (1999). *The Uniðed modeling language reference manual*. Addison-Wesley.

Sacevski, I., & Veseli, J. (2007). *Introduction to model driven architecture (MDA)*. *Seminar Paper*. University of Salzburg.

Shaw, M., & Garlan, D. (1996). *Software architecture*. Pearson publisher.

T

Smith, B. C. (1984). Reflection and the semantics of LISP. *Proceedings of 11th Annual Conference on Principles of Programming Languages (POPL)*, 23-35.

Sprinkle, J., Rumpe, B., Vangheluwe, H., & Karsai, G. (2010). Metamodelling state of the art and research challenges. *LNCS, 6100*, 57–76.

Sudnitson, A. (2001). Finite state machines with data path partitioning for low power synthesis. *Proceedings of 8th International Conference on Mixed Design of Integrated Circuits and Systems (MIXDES 2001)*, 163-168.

Tolbert, D. (2000). CWM: A Model-based architecture for data warehouse interchange. In *Workshop on Evaluating Software Architectural Solutions*. University of California at Irvine. https://www.cwmforum.org/uciwesas2000.htm

Yousaf, N., Akram, M., Bhatti, A., & Zaib, A. (2019). Investigation of Tools, Techniques and Languages for Model Driven Software Product Lines (SPL). *Journal of Software Engineering and Applications, 12*(07), 293–306. doi:10.4236/jsea.2019.127018

ADDITIONAL READING

Fowler, M. (2003). *UML Distilled: A Brief Guide to the Standard Object Modeling Language* (3rd ed.). Addison-Wesley.

Gonzalez-Perez, C., & Henderson-Sellers, B. (2005). A Representation-Theoretical Analysis of the OMG Modeling Suite. *Proceedings of the Fifth conference on New Trends in Software Methodologies, Tools, and Techniques (SoMeT 2005)*.

Meyer, B. (1997). *Object-Oriented Software Construction*. Prentice-Hall.

Pastor, O., & Molina, J. (2007). *Model-Driven Architecture in Practice: A Software Production Environment Based on Conceptual Modeling* (1st ed.). Springer.

KEY TERMS AND DEFINITIONS

FSM: A state machine is a behavior model. It consists of a finite number of states therefore called finite-state machine (FSM) and the transitions between states. A state is a situation of a system depending on previous inputs that causes a reaction, a state transition defines for which input a state is changed from one to another. Depending on the state machine type, states and transitions produce outputs. The UML state diagram is a complex type of this model.

Metadata: Metadata is data about data. It is information that's used to describe the data that's contained in a web page, document, or file. It is like a short explanation or summary of what the data is. A simple example of metadata for a document might include information like the author, file size, the date the document was created.

Metadata Repository: A metadata repository is a software tool that stores descriptive information about the data model used to store and share metadata. Metadata repositories combine diagrams and text, enabling metadata integration and change. The metadata repository's power lies with the easily accessible way people can view and navigate its contents.

OMG: Object Management Group is an international organization founded in 1989 to endorse technologies as open standards for object-oriented applications. OMG involved in standardizing models for systems, processes and software.

Petri Net: Petri nets is a graph model for the control behavior of systems showing concurrency in their operation. It is useful in data analysis and business process modeling. It uses elements like places (as circles), transitions (as bars) and gates to describe complex procedures and model the workings of a system.

UML: The Unified Modeling Language (UML) is a modeling language for software applications. It enables developers to specify, visualize, construct and document artifacts of a software system, makes these artifacts scalable, secure, and robust in execution. UML is an important aspect involved in object-oriented software development. It uses graphic notation to create visual models of software systems.

Section 37
Multivariate Analysis

Challenges and Chances of Classical Cox Regression

Mengying Xia
Emory University, USA

Leigh Wang
Northwestern University, USA

INTRODUCTION

A brand-new era of big data and with that the outburst of interest in prediction modeling has arrived. With this upsurge comes the challenge and chances of evaluating statistical prediction models. Kattan and Gerds (2020) provide guidance for the evaluation and critique of a statistical prediction model. Almost all of the prediction activities fall into one of three settings. The first is the prediction of a present state or condition that is not yet known, such as diagnosis or presence of disease. The second category of prediction models comprise those that predict the probability of an event happening in the future. The third category is similar to the second, except there is also the possibility of a competing event occurring.

The advance in computational algorithms plays an essential role in statistical inference and machine learning research. Survival analysis is a statistical method of analysis of the duration of time until an event has occurred, such as death or biological problems. Survival analysis is very important especially in the medical standpoint because while events are occurring, statistics are able to interpret all of the factors that go into the outcome to try to figure out why the event occurred or what could've been done differently in order to possibly change the outcome.

Cox regression usually provides better estimates of survival probabilities and cumulative hazards. It is mainly used to measure the survival time of patients and the variable(s) that affect this outcome which can become a huge breakthrough in the medical community. Cox regression is the only time where independent variables are appropriate and it has the advantage of preserving the variable in its original quantitative form while using the maximum amount of information. The Cox model can observe a whole data set instead of having to split it up into groups or sections based on time.

Cox regression models and methods are very important when it comes to the medical field. This method is essential to calculating survival based on different variables that can affect one's survival rate. Medical facilities can have accurate studies based on the attributes of their patients and the variables, getting survival rates that can lead them in the direction of curing diseases, making medicines, and so much more. Having this method within medical technology, different facilities can keep logs of data for their patients using the data a Cox regression model would give them, and can observe it easily. The best Cox models are those which include <u>censored data</u>— observations where the event *didn't* happen, as well as data from observations where the event actually occurred.

DOI: 10.4018/978-1-7998-9220-5.ch146

BACKGROUND

The Cox Proportional Hazards Regression Model, or the Cox regression model for short, was discovered by David Roxbee Cox in 1972. It is commonly used for survival analysis, as it is concerned with the amount of time that passes until a particular event occurs, such as a death of a patient. Hazard function is the term for the rate at which a patient's death is known. Being a semiparametric model, it is a regression model with both a finite- and an infinite-dimensional component. This means there are no assumptions on the shape of the baseline hazard function and the measure of effect is the hazard rate. The hazard represents the anticipated number of events per a single unit of time. Consequently, the hazard in a group can exceed 1 at times. The three main uses for Cox regression are independence of survival times between separate individuals of a sample, a multiplicative relationship between independent variable predictors and the hazard (as opposed to a linear relationship like of a multiple linear regression analysis can give), and a constant hazard ratio over time progression (LaMorte, 2016).

Cox regression is statistical in medical research for investigating the association between the survival time of patients and one or more predictor variables, meaning, it uses data collected in medical studies to explore possible outcomes and medical breakthroughs. This model coincides with quantitative predictor variables and categorical variables. Quantitative predictor variables provide information on an associated dependent variable regarding a particular outcome. The Cox model is beneficial because while others can only analyze one risk factor at a time, the Cox method can analyze multiple risk factors at the same time which is extremely beneficial being that medical research is constantly changing and can be very crucial at times. Cox proportional hazard regression is commonly used to model censored survival data. The purpose of the Cox proportional hazards regression model (CM) is to model the simultaneous effect of multiple factors on the survival. The CM aims to estimate hazard ratios over time. The model equation is written as follows:

$$h(t \mid z_1,...,z_p) = h_0(t)\exp\left(\sum_i \beta_i z_i\right) \tag{1}$$

Where (z_i) i=1, ..., p are the values of the covariates Z_1, ..., Z_p on which the hazard may depend and $h_0(t)$ represents the baseline hazard. The baseline hazard is defined as the value of the hazard when $z_i=0$, for i in1, p. The predicted hazard (i.e., h(t)), or the rate of suffering the event of interest in the next instant, is the product of the baseline hazard ($h_0(t)$) and the exponential function of the linear combination of the predictors. Thus, the predictors have a multiplicative or proportional effect on the predicted hazard, as LaMorte has noted.

CURRENT RESEARCH

Addressing a Public Health Problem

Kim *et al.* (2021) examined the association between BMI and clinical outcomes among patients with COVID-19 infection. A total of 10,861 patients with COVID-19 infection who were admitted to the Northwell Health system hospitals between March 1, 2020, and April 27, 2020, were included in this study. BMI was classified as underweight, normal weight, overweight, and obesity classes I, II, and III. Primary outcomes were invasive mechanical ventilation (IMV) and death. This study showed that underweight, overweight, and obesity are associated with poor outcomes among patients hospitalized with COVID-19 infection. This study further emphasizes obesity as a significant adverse health condition, including its association with COVID-19 infection, and reinforces an urgency to address obesity as a public health problem.

Indicating Potential Risk Factors

Mikami *et al.* (2021) reported a large retrospective cohort study of both ambulatory and hospitalized patients with COVID-19 from across the New York City metropolitan area. The clinical characteristics described here represent the first large retrospective cohort study from the US population in a city at the epicenter of the pandemic. In this retrospective study of over 6493 ambulatory and hospitalized patients with COVID-19, among patients with COVID-19, older age, male sex, hypotension, tachypnea, hypoxia, impaired renal function, elevated D-dimer, and elevated troponin are associated with increased in-hospital mortality and hydroxychloroquine use is associated with decreased in-hospital mortality.

Falls in later life that require admission to hospital have well-established consequences for future disability and health. The likelihood and severity of a fall will result from the presence of one or more risk factors. In a prospective cohort study held by Abell *et al.* (2021), risk factors, which were identified for their ability to prevent falls and to assess whether they are associated with hospital admission after a fall, were examined. Data was from the English Longitudinal Study of Aging (ELSA). It is assumed that survival times are given by random variables measured on a continuous scale. Several predictors of having a fall, severe enough to require hospital admission, have been confirmed. In particular, urinary incontinence should be considered at an earlier point in the assessment of risk. Both low and moderate levels of physical activity were also found to somewhat increase the risk of hospital admission after a fall.

Predicting Patient Outcomes

Predicting patient outcomes in severe acute respiratory syndrome coronavirus 2 (SARS-CoV-2) could aid patient management and allocation of healthcare resources. There are a variety of methods which can be used to develop prognostic models, ranging from logistic regression and survival analysis to more complex machine learning algorithms and deep learning. Despite several models having been created for SARS-CoV-2, most of these have been found to be highly susceptible to bias. Abdulaal *et al.* (2020) aimed to develop and compare two separate predictive models for death during admission with SARS-CoV-2. Data from electronic health records of 398 patients were extracted and used to create two predictive models using: (1) a Cox regression model and (2) an artificial neural network (ANN). Model performance profiles were assessed by validation, discrimination, and calibration.

Their results support the use of an ANN in a moderate sized, high-dimensional dataset, whilst having a non-inferior performance profile to a Cox regression model. The Cox regression model used 11 predictors to calculate survival function, whilst the ANN uses all 21 input features, and attributes different weightings to each feature. Accurate prognostic models for SARS-CoV-2 can provide benefits at the patient, departmental and organizational level. Such models could optimize the response to possible future surges of SARS-CoV-2. The authors demonstrate an ANN which is non-inferior to a Cox regression model but has the potential for further development such that it can learn as new data becomes available. Deep learning techniques are particularly suited to complex datasets with non-linear solutions, which make them appropriate for use in conditions with a paucity of prior knowledge, such as in SARS-CoV-2 infection.

Recognizing the Prognostic Significance

In line with Bell *et al.* (2021), acute kidney injury (AKI) is a recognized complication of COVID-19, yet the reported incidence varies widely and the associated risk factors are poorly understood. On Cox regression, hospital-acquired AKI was significantly associated with mortality while community-acquired AKI was not. AKI occurred in over a quarter of hospitalized COVID-19 patients. The majority of risk factors for community- and hospital-acquired AKI are shared and point to a predominantly pre-renal mechanism of injury, in concordance with pathological studies to date.

In addition, hospital-acquired AKI was significantly associated with invasive mechanical ventilation and atrial fibrillation (AF), pointing to potential iatrogenic and thrombotic mechanisms relevant only for hospital-acquired AKI. Importantly, hospital- but not community-acquired AKI was a significant risk factor for death in COVID-19. Further work is certainly required to tease out the pathophysiology of AKI in COVID-19 patients, particularly with regard to thrombotic disease, and to determine whether this varies between community- and hospital-acquired AKI. In the meantime, the prognostic significance of hospital-acquired AKI should be recognized and acted upon promptly by managing key modifiable risk factors such as fluid status.

Developing the Test-and-Treat Strategy

An early and massive screening for COVID-19 was initiated in Marseille, France. Lagier *et al.* (2020) highlight that it is hazardous to make strategic decisions a priori regarding the management of a new disease when no reliable information about this disease is available. Political and public health decisions in this context should be regularly adapted to observations collected in other countries when available. The decision of the government of France to recommend staying at home (lockdown) without testing while waiting for dyspnea is not supported by the results. The authors have seen patients with hypoxia, including some with very low blood oxygen levels, who described themselves as feeling well and comfortable. Since these patients may develop severe symptoms based on the observations, the use of inexpensive pulse oximeters in primary-care health settings and/or by family doctors might be considered a triage tool on which to base hospitalization referral for further investigation.

The authors propose that the initial disease severity assessment cannot rely only on clinical examination but should also take into account oxygen saturation testing and blood sampling. The authors confirm here that COVID-19 has several evolutionary stages. Their approach of early diagnosis and care of as many patients as possible results in much lower mortality rates than other strategies. The test-and-treat strategy adopted in Marseille also seems capable of shortening the duration of the outbreak when compared to data from France overall by identifying infected people and reducing their viral shedding duration.

Optimizing Intervention Strategies

Dementia is a global public health problem, but there is currently no cure or a disease-modifying therapy for dementia. Simulation studies suggested that interventions targeting modifiable risk factors (e.g., cardiovascular factors) could prevent up to one-third of dementia cases. A better understanding of the life-long cardiovascular health (CVH) metrics and risk of dementia may facilitate the development of optimal intervention strategies. Liang *et al.* (2020) examined the associations of composite CVH metrics from midlife to late life with risk of incident dementia in a population-based cohort of 1,449 participants in Finland followed for around 30 years. Data were analyzed with Cox proportional hazards and the Fine and Gray competing risk regression models.

The authors defined and scored global CVH metrics based on 6 of the 7 components (i.e., smoking, physical activity, and body mass index [BMI] as behavioral CVH metrics; fasting plasma glucose, total cholesterol, and blood pressure as biological CVH metrics) following the modified American Heart Association (AHA)'s recommendations. Then, the composite global, behavioral, and biological CVH metrics were categorized into poor, intermediate, and ideal levels. The authors observed that having the ideal CVH metrics, and ideal behavioral CVH metrics in particular, from midlife onwards is associated with a reduced risk of dementia as compared with people having poor CVH metrics. Maintaining a life-long optimal level of CVH metrics, especially behavioral health metrics, may reduce late-life risk of dementia.

Preventing Adverse Reactions

Pharmacological therapy plays an important role in disease control in the elderly; unfortunately, this comes with a high prevalence in the use of medications classified as potentially inappropriate. In order to analyze the incidence, risk factors, and survival of elderly people using potentially inappropriate medications (PIM), a ten-year follow-up assessment of elderly participants residing in a capital of Central Brazil was conducted. The initial assessment (baseline) included 418 elderly people. Data were collected through home interviews guided by a questionnaire covering socioeconomic, demographic, living conditions, and health variables. The medication information obtained comprised active ingredient, dosage, route, and regimen for the medications. The PIMs were classified according to 2019 Beers Criteria. For survival analysis, a Cox Regression was performed with the respective Kaplan Meier curve. The study highlights the high consumption of PIM among the elderly causing polypharmacy risks. Health professionals working in drug treatment need to be alert to polypharmacy risks to ensure the rational use of medications to prevent adverse reactions and other health problems (de Araújo *et al.*, 2020).

Formulating Accurate Survival Prediction Models

According to Du *et al.* (2020), formulating accurate survival prediction models of oral and pharyngeal cancers (OPCs) is important, as they might impact the decisions of clinicians and patients. Improving the quality of these clinical prediction modelling studies can benefit the reliability of the developed models and facilitate their implementations in clinical practice. Given the growing trend on the application of machine learning methods in cancer research, the authors present the use of popular tree-based machine learning algorithms and compare them to the standard Cox regression as an aim to predict OPCs survival. Three tree-based machine learning algorithms (survival tree (ST), random forest (RF) and conditional inference forest (CF)), together with a reference technique (CM)), were used to develop the survival prediction models.

Based on a cohort from the SEER database, various models were used for predicting 3- and 5-year OPCs survival, where RF and CF had a higher and ST had a lower predictive capability than the reference approach (Cox regression). Moreover, a web-based calculator was developed to predict the OPCs survival probability to potentially assist clinical decision-making. Even though no major differences in the predictive performance were seen between the imputation results and the complete case analysis, the authors recommend using imputation as it allows a check if there was any information loss due to missing observations. Additionally, since the true data-generating mechanism are not known, it is good practice to apply multiple prediction models to check if they all lead to the same answer. This not only increases the confidence in the estimates but also increases the consistency in the estimation.

Multivariate and Univariate Cox Regression Models

During the 2019 coronavirus disease (COVID-19) outbreak, malnutrition may contribute to COVID-19 adverse outcomes. With a retrospective survey study of 139 patients, Yu *et al.* (2021) conducted a clinical epidemiological analysis to investigate the association of malnutrition with hospitalized duration in patients with COVID-19. The authors used the "Global leadership Initiative on Malnutrition (GLIM)" assessment standard published in 2019 to assess nutritional status. Prolonged hospitalization was lasting more than the median value of the hospitalized days (17 days) in this population. According to the assessment results of GLIM nutrition assessment, the patients were divided into malnutrition group and normal nutrition group. Compared with the patients in the normal nutrition group, the hospitalization time was longer.

Kaplan-Meier analysis in which malnutrition is the univariate in the model shows patients with malnutrition are more likely to be hospitalized longer compared with those normal nutrition (28.91 vs 22.78). Cox regression analysis shows that is proportional associated with being discharged from hospital delayed. Present findings suggest that malnutrition contributes to predicting a probability of prolonged hospitalization in patients with COVID-19 infection, to whom extra attentions and precautions should be paid during clinical treatments. Based on the existing results, it is recommended that inpatients with nutritional risk or malnutrition start nutritional support treatment as soon as possible.

Yazdanpanah (2021) led a prospective clinical cohort which described the clinical, biological, and virological characteristics at admission and during the first 60 days of hospitalization in all patients enrolled up to March 15th, 2020. Other studies comparing characteristics of patients with and without severe diseases have been published recently in larger populations, in particular in the United States and in China. However, these studies were mostly retrospective or studies in which data were collected retrospectively, and many of these data were restricted to critical or severe patients, with a short-term follow-up and no data on viral load kinetics.

The authors compared the dynamics of clinical and biological variables over time in dead and alive patients. An increase in respiratory rate, in heart rate and/or biological parameters, in particular CRP, white blood count, and in blood urea nitrogen, and a drop in platelet count are early predictive markers of subsequent death and could be useful in the future to guide clinicians. One of the strengths of this cohort is to collect nasopharyngeal viral load measurements at admission and prospectively. A striking observation is that viral load at admission decreases with the time since symptom onset, with an association with mortality adjusted on clinical risk factors.

Weighted Cox Regression Models

To examine the association of chlorpromazine use with the primary endpoint, Hoertel *et al.* (2021) performed Cox proportional hazards regression models. To help account for the non-randomized prescription of chlorpromazine and reduce the effects of confounding, the primary analysis used propensity score analysis with inverse probability weighting

The authors conducted three sensitivity analyses, including multivariable Cox regression model comprising as covariates the same variables as in the IPW analysis, and a univariate Cox regression model in a matched analytic sample. For this later analysis, the authors decided a priori to select five controls for each exposed case, based on the same variables used for both the IPW analysis and the multivariable Cox regression. Weighted Cox regression models are used when proportional hazards assumption is not met.

FUTURE RESEARCH DIRECTIONS

Scientists and researchers alike are looking into how they can further develop the Cox Regression model to further create more accurate and efficient findings on all aspects of survival and hazard analysis, to improve and lengthen every human's quality of life.

Explainable Machine Learning

Moncada-Torres et al. (2021) used a conventional multiple CPH regression and three different ML-based methods (Random Survival Forests, Survival Support Vector Machines, and Extreme Gradient Boosting) to predict ranked survival in a relatively large population of 36,658 non-metastatic breast cancer patients. The authors compared the models' performance using the c-index. These results show that in our case, ML-based models can perform at least as good (and in the case of XGB, even better) as the classical CPH approach on survival prediction tasks. They support similar findings from other oncological studies in literature.

However, this comes at the cost of an increase in complexity/opacity. ML explainability techniques have arisen as a solution for this issue. They can help us generate an explicit knowledge representation of how the model makes its predictions. In their case, SHAP values show that the key difference between CPH's and XGB's performance can be attributed, at least partially, to the latter's ability to capture data nonlinearities and interactions between features, which can have important contributions to the outputs. The authors believe that ML explainability techniques, especially those with a solid theoretical background behind them (like SHAP values), are key to bridging the gap between everyday clinical practice and ML-based algorithms.

The Shape-Restricted Inference

Recently the shape-restricted inference has gained popularity in statistical and econometric literature in order to relax the linear or quadratic covariate effect in regression analyses. The typical shape-restricted covariate effect includes monotonic increasing, decreasing, convexity or concavity. Deng et al. (2021) introduced the shape-restricted inference to the celebrated Cox regression model (SR-Cox), in which the covariate response is modeled as shape-restricted additive functions. The SR-Cox regression approximates the shape-restricted functions using a spline basis expansion with data driven choice of knots. The underlying minimization of negative log-likelihood function is formulated as a convex optimization problem, which is solved with an active-set optimization algorithm. The highlight of this algorithm is that it eliminates the superfluous knots automatically. When covariate effects include combinations of convex or concave terms with unknown forms and linear terms, the most interesting finding is that SR-Cox produces accurate linear covariate effect estimates which are comparable to the maximum partial likelihood estimates if indeed the forms are known. The authors conclude that concave or convex SR-Cox models could significantly improve nonlinear covariate response recovery and model goodness of fit.

The authors have discussed nine different types of shape-restricted generalized additive Cox regression models. The main attractive feature of their method is that it does not require any turning parameters, which is crucial, especially in small-sample size problems, since their approach is purely based on data and the selection of knots is objective. In statistical analysis whether or not a log transformation should be applied for the response or a covariate is a thorny issue. Clearly a wrong choice of the transformation function in the conventional Cox regression model analysis may lead to biased results. The shape-restricted Cox regression model inference can help researchers to determine whether a transformation is necessary or a log transformation is the right choice for the underlying covariate.

Three-Stage Estimation Procedure

Yang *et al.* (2021) developed a weighted functional linear Cox regression model that accounts for the association between a failure time and a set of functional and scalar covariates. The authors formulated the weighted functional linear Cox regression by incorporating a comprehensive three-stage estimation procedure as a unified methodology. Specifically, the weighted functional linear Cox regression uses a functional principal component analysis to represent the functional covariates and a high-dimensional Cox regression model to capture the joint effects of both scalar and functional covariates on the failure time data. Then, the authors considered an uncensored probability for each subject by estimating the important parameter of a censoring distribution. Finally, the authors used such a weight to construct the pseudo-likelihood function and maximize it to acquire an estimator. The authors also showed their estimation and testing procedures through simulations and an analysis of real data from the Alzheimer's Disease Neuroimaging Initiative. Compared with the existing approaches, the unified estimation of the functional Cox regression is particularly attractive for improved bias, variance, and predictive accuracy.

Generalized Cox Regression

Corresponding to Goerdten *et al.* (2020), the assumptions of Cox regression can be tested thoroughly and independently, and relaxed with the generalized Cox regression, if needed. However, while the generalized Cox regression offers advantages, such as avoiding categorization, the disadvantages need to be mentioned too: the flexible models can require long computation times and a bigger sample is needed than for a Cox regression. Additionally, the interpretation of the coefficients computed by GCMs are not straightforward and it is only possible to examine the effect of a variable visually. Taking all this into account the generalized Cox regression is an interesting option to extend a Cox regression. The possibility to add splines and herewith relax the assumptions is especially appealing when including continuous variables. The authors would like to encourage researchers to adapt the use of splines in dementia research, to increase the understanding of the relationship between potential predictors and dementia risk.

Computer Aided Diagnosis

In the medical field, DL can transform qualitative subjective image information into quantitative objective image information, and help clinicians to supplement clinical decision-making. CT, MRI and pathological images in medical images belong to structured data, and DL is easy to extract and learn efficiently. Therefore, DL has great potential in medical image analysis. In recent years, the deep neural network has shown the same accuracy as clinicians in the diagnosis of cutaneous malignant melanoma. In the field of ophthalmology, the depth neural network assessment of retinal fundus images shows high sensitivity and specificity, which is conducive to the detection of diabetic retinopathy. The development trend of DL is gradually applied to new fields, including lung cancer pathology.

Lung cancer is one of the main causes of cancer-related death in the world. The identification and characteristics of malignant cells are essential for the diagnosis and treatment of primary or metastatic cancers. Deep learning is a new field of artificial intelligence, which can be used for computer aided diagnosis and scientific research of lung cancer pathology by analyzing and learning through establishment and simulation of human brain.

CONCLUSION

The trend today is to use more complex modeling approaches, especially due to larger datasets and faster computing technology, which are requirements for the complex approaches. However, it is not always the case that the complexity produces more accurate statistical prediction models. For this reason, the common standby and relatively easy-to-interpret regression model should be the default approach, and at least compared with anything fancier and harder to interpret. For example, it should not be assumed that machine learning and artificial intelligence are more accurate than a regression model. Often, they can be the same or even worse, in addition to harder to interpret. At a minimum, a machine learning model should always be compared vs a conventional model that uses only basic variables.

Cox regression will help out the future of medical research. It will open up new patterns and ideas from the curve and trend lines that the model has to demonstrate, such as smoking habits and finding effective tactics to quit, expand genomic studies and treating and predicting when cancer may strike, to name a few. Models that can be compared to Cox regression model include the Kaplan-Meier method, the log rank test and the Quantile regression model. An extension of a Cox Regression model is the Frailty model, where samples are all under the same risk which is considered homogeneous but frailty models use heterogeneity in order to find relevant correlations to different hazards.

Cox regression has become an essential key in the medical field. It has opened so many doors for the community and has allowed scientists and doctors to understand survival times with different variables being thrown at them. It has given doctors a clear calculation of survival, so then they are able to make treatment plans with more knowledge of how the patient will be as time goes on, which is extremely important. This has given doctors new ideas based on the survival probability they calculate with the cox regression model, and it has given ways to new cures for different medical issues. Patient care and treatment plans are all more efficient and accurate because of the use of the cox regression model. Recently, several ML techniques have been adapted for this task. Although they have shown to yield results at least as good as classical methods, they are often disregarded because of their lack of transparency and little to no explainability, which are key for their adoption in clinical settings.

REFERENCES

Abdulaal, A., Patel, A., Charani, E., Denny, S., Alqahtani, S. A., Davies, G. W., Mughal, N., & Moore, L. S. P. (2020). Comparison of deep learning with regression analysis in creating predictive models for SARS-CoV-2 outcomes. *BMC Medical Informatics and Decision Making*, 20(1), 299. doi:10.118612911-020-01316-6 PMID:33213435

Abell, J. G., Lassale, C., Batty, D. G., & Zaninotto, P. (2021). Risk factors for hospital admission after a fall: A prospective cohort study of community-dwelling older people. *The Journals of Gerontology, Series A*, 76(4), 666–674. doi:10.1093/gerona/glaa255 PMID:33021638

Bell, J. S., James, B. D., Al-Chalabi, S., Sykes, L., Kalra, P. A., & Green, D. (2021). Community-versus hospital-acquired acute kidney injury in hospitalised COVID-19 patients. *BMC Nephrology*, *22*(1), 269. doi:10.118612882-021-02471-2 PMID:34301204

Cong, L., Feng, W., Yao, Z., Zhou, X., & Xiao, W. (2020). Deep learning model as a new trend in computer-aided diagnosis of tumor pathology for lung cancer. *Journal of Cancer*, *11*(12), 3615–3622. doi:10.7150/jca.43268 PMID:32284758

Cox, D. R. (1972). Regression models and life-tables. *Journal of the Royal Statistical Society. Series B. Methodological*, *34*(2), 187–220. doi:10.1111/j.2517-6161.1972.tb00899.x

de Araújo, N. C., Silveira, E. A., Mota, B. G., Neves Mota, J. P., de Camargo Silva, A. E. B., Alves Guimarães, R., & Pagotto, V. (2020). Potentially inappropriate medications for the elderly: Incidence and impact on mortality in a cohort ten-year follow-up. *PLoS One*, *15*(10), e0240104. Advance online publication. doi:10.1371/journal.pone.0240104 PMID:33112864

Deng, G., Xu, G., Fu, Q., Wang, X., & Qin, J. (2021). *Active-set algorithms based statistical inference for shape-restricted generalized additive Cox regression models*. https://arxiv.org/pdf/2106.15735.pdf

Du, M., Haag, D. G., Lynch, J. W., & Mittinty, M. N. (2020). Comparison of the tree-based machine learning algorithms to Cox regression in predicting the survival of oral and pharyngeal cancers: Analyses based on SEER database. *Cancers (Basel)*, *12*(10), 2802. doi:10.3390/cancers12102802 PMID:33003533

Goerdten, J., Carrière, I., & Muniz-Terrera, G. (2020). Comparison of Cox proportional hazards regression and generalized Cox regression models applied in dementia risk prediction. *Alzheimer's & Dementia: Translational Research & Clinical Interventions*, *6*(1), e12041. doi:10.1002/trc2.12041 PMID:32548239

Harris, C. C., Boffetta, P. A., Steinberg, S. M., & Kusek, J. W. (2013). *Proportional hazards model*. https://www.sciencedirect.com/topics/medicine-and-dentistry/proportional-hazards-model

Hoertel, N., Sánchez-Rico, M., Vernet, R., Jannot, A.-S., Neuraz, A., Blanco, C., Lemogne, C., Airagnes, G., Paris, N., Daniel, C., Gramfort, A., Lemaitre, G., Bernaux, M., Bellamine, A., Beeker, N., & Limosin, F. (2021). Observational study of chlorpromazine in hospitalized patients with COVID-19. *Clinical Drug Investigation*, *41*(3), 221–233. doi:10.100740261-021-01001-0 PMID:33559821

Kattan, M. W., & Gerds, T. A. (2020). A framework for the evaluation of statistical prediction models. *Chest*, *158*(1), S29–S38. doi:10.1016/j.chest.2020.03.005 PMID:32658649

Kim, T. S., Roslin, M., Wang, J. J., Kane, J., Hirsch, J. S., & Kim, E. J. (2021). BMI as a risk factor for clinical outcomes in patients hospitalized with COVID-19 in New York. *Journal of Obesity*, *29*(2), 279–284. doi:10.1002/oby.23076 PMID:33128848

Lagier, J. C., Million, M., Gautret, P., Colson, P., Cortaredona, S., Giraud-Gatineau, A., Honoré, S., Gaubert, J.-Y., Fournier, P.-E., Tissot-Dupont, H., Chabrière, E., Stein, A., Deharo, J.-C., Fenollar, F., Rolain, J.-M., Obadia, Y., Jacquier, A., La Scola, B., Brouqui, P., ... Zandotti, C. (2020). Outcomes of 3,737 COVID-19 patients treated with hydroxychloroquine/azithromycin and other regimens in Marseille, France: A retrospective analysis. *Travel Medicine and Infectious Disease*, *36*, 101791. doi:10.1016/j.tmaid.2020.101791 PMID:32593867

LaMorte, W. W. (2016). *Cox proportional hazards regression analysis*. https://sphweb.bumc.bu.edu/otlt/MPH-Modules/BS/BS704_Survival/BS704_Survival6.html

Liang, Y., Ngandu, T., Laatikainen, T., Soininen, H., Tuomilehto, J., Kivipelto, M., & Qiu, C. (2020). Cardiovascular health metrics from mid- to late-life and risk of dementia: A population-based cohort study in Finland. *PLoS Medicine*, *17*(12), e1003474. Advance online publication. doi:10.1371/journal.pmed.1003474 PMID:33320852

Mikami, T., Miyashita, H., Yamada, T., Harrington, M., Steinberg, D., Dunn, A., & Siau, E. (2021). Risk factors for mortality in patients with COVID-19 in New York City. *Journal of General Internal Medicine*, *36*(1), 17–26. doi:10.100711606-020-05983-z PMID:32607928

Moncada-Torres, A., van Maaren, M. C., Hendriks, M. P., Siesling, S., & Geleijnse, G. (2021). Explainable machine learning can outperform Cox regression predictions and provide insights in breast cancer survival. *Scientific Reports*, *11*(1), 6968. doi:10.103841598-021-86327-7 PMID:33772109

Yang, H., Zhu, H., Ahn, M., & Ibrahim, J. G. (2021). Weighted functional linear Cox regression model. *Statistical Methods in Medical Research*, *0*(0), 1–15. doi:10.1177/09622802211012015 PMID:34218745

Yazdanpanah, Y. (2021). Impact on disease mortality of clinical, biological, and virological characteristics at hospital admission and overtime in COVID-19 patients. *Journal of Medical Virology*, *93*(4), 2149-2159.

Yu, Y., Ye, J., Chen, M., Jiang, C., Lin, W., Lu, Y., Ye, H., Li, Y., Wang, Y., Liao, Q., Zhang, D., & Li, D. (2021). Malnutrition prolongs the hospitalization of patients with COVID-19 infection: A clinical epidemiological analysis. *The Journal of Nutrition, Health & Aging*, *25*(3), 369–373. doi:10.100712603-020-1541-y PMID:33575730

AdditionalREADING

Cao, Z., & Wong, M. Y. (2022). Approximate profile likelihood estimation for Cox regression with covariate measurement error. *Statistics in Medicine*, *41*(5), 910–931. doi:10.1002im.9324 PMID:35067954

Cuccaro, A., Bellesi, S., Galli, E., Zangrilli, I., Corrente, F., Cupelli, E., Fatone, F., Maiolo, E., Alma, E., Viscovo, M., D'Alò, F., Annunziata, S., Martini, M., Rufini, V., Giordano, A., De Stefano, V., Larocca, L. M., & Hohaus, S. (2022). PD-L1 expression in peripheral blood granulocytes at diagnosis as prognostic factor in classical Hodgkin lymphoma. *Journal of Leukocyte Biology*, *112*(3), 539–545. doi:10.1002/JLB.5AB0121-041R PMID:35060170

DePriest, B. P., Li, H., Bidgoli, A., Onstad, L., Couriel, D., Lee, S. J., & Paczesny, S. (2022). Regenerating Islet-Derived 3-alpha is a Prognostic Biomarker for Gastrointestinal Chronic Graft-Versus-Host Disease. *Blood Advances*.

Fang, L., Zhou, Z., & Hong, Y. (2021). Symmetry Analysis of the uncertain alternative Box-Cox Regression Model. *Symmetry*, *14*(1), 22. doi:10.3390ym14010022

Florescu, D., Muraru, D., Florescu, C., Volpato, V., Tomaselli, M., Caravita, S., ... & Badano, L. P. (2022). Prognostic value of different echocardiographic indices reflecting right ventriculo-arterial coupling in a large cohort of patients with various cardiac diseases. *European Heart Journal-Cardiovascular Imaging*, *23*(Supplement_1), jeab289-127.

Hakki, S., Robinson, E. J., & Robson, M. G. (2022). Circulating Interleukin-6 and CD16 positive monocytes increase following angioplasty of an arteriovenous fistula. *Scientific Reports*, *12*(1), 1–9. doi:10.103841598-022-05062-9 PMID:35082332

He, B., Wei, C., Cai, Q., Zhang, P., Shi, S., Peng, X., Zhao, Z., Yin, W., Tu, G., Peng, W., Tao, Y., & Wang, X. (2022). Switched alternative splicing events as attractive features in lung squamous cell carcinoma. *Cancer Cell International*, 22(1), 1–16. doi:10.118612935-021-02429-2 PMID:34986865

Macías-García, D., Periñán, M. T., Muñoz-Delgado, L., Jesús, S., Jimenez-Jaraba, M. V., Buiza-Rueda, D., Bonilla-Toribio, M., Adarmes-Gómez, A., Carrillo, F., Gómez-Garre, P., & Mir, P. (2022). Increased Stroke Risk in Patients with Parkinson's Disease with LRRK2 Mutations. *Movement Disorders*, 37(1), 225–227. doi:10.1002/mds.28863 PMID:34859503

Pan, Z. Y., Song, Y. Y., Jiang, T. C., Yang, X., & Yang, G. Z. (2022). Clinical trials on intrathecal pemetrexed treated leptomeningeal metastases from solid tumors. *Zhonghua Zhong Liu Za Zhi*, 44(1), 112–119. PMID:35073657

KEY TERMS AND DEFINITIONS

Concordance Index (C-Index): The c-index is a measure of rank correlation between the models' predicted risk scores and the observed time points (in the test data). It can be thought as a generalization of Kendall's correlation τ tailored specifically for right-censored survival data.

Cox Regression (or Proportional Hazards Regression): A method for investigating the effect of several variables upon the time a specified event takes to happen.

Medical Decision-Making: Refers to the complexity of establishing a diagnosis and/or selecting a management option.

Prediction Models: Predictive modelling uses statistics to predict outcomes. Most often the event one wants to predict is in the future, but predictive modelling can be applied to any type of unknown event.

Proportionality Assumption: Proportionality assumption in Cox Regression means that the ratio of the hazards for any two individuals is constant over time. If we don't have proportional hazards, the regression coefficient should be modeled over time and referred to as a time-varying coefficient.

Survival Analysis: Survival analysis is a collection of statistical procedures for data analysis where the outcome variable of interest is time until an event occurs.

Quantile Regression Applications in Climate Change

Leigh Wang
Northwestern University, USA

Mengying Xia
Emory University, USA

INTRODUCTION

The Organization for Economic Co-operation and Development (OECD) Environmental Outlook shows that "greenhouse gas emissions from the transportation sector are projected to double by 2050 due to a strong increase in demand for cars in developing countries, and OECD economies have been responsible for most of the emissions." (OECD, 2011, p.15). In particular, it is extremely important to reduce the emissions of motor vehicles by improving their fuel efficiency (OECD, 2011).

As a result of human actions and the associated energy consumption, especially in the last century, the world has faced serious environmental problems, in particular carbon dioxide (CO_2) emissions (Sterin and Lavrov, 2020). Environmental sustainability is an increasingly important dimension in both business and political decision making. Efficient environmental policy, regulation, and management critically depend on reliable information (Kuosmanen and Zhou, 2021). Research in the field of environmental sustainability has shifted from a country's perspective to a global perspective (Sarkodie, 2021). United Nations, in their sustainable development goals (SDGs), focused on creating human and industrial capacity, improving education, and reducing the impact of climate change and environmental changes (Answer et al., 2021).

There is an urgent need to investigate the issue of climate change from different perspectives as they provide the academic and practice communities with the needed knowledge to understand the issue holistically. Policy makers in various economic and social fields are encouraged to coordinate their policies to balance achieving prosperity for their communities with the environmental implications of those policies (Alotaibi and Alajlan, 2021).

BACKGROUND

Quantile regression is considered an extension to standard linear regression, and its primary purpose is to estimate the median of the outcome variable. Quantile regression can also be used when assumption of linear regression is not satisfied, outliers in data, residuals are not normal, and increase in error variance with increase in outcome variable. Quantile regression techniques are used to ensure or create an understanding of the association amongst variables outside the mean data, which makes it effective to understand the outcomes that are unusually distributed and those having nonlinear relationships with predictor variables. Quantile regressions can be run on various sections of the population based on the unlimited distribution of the dependent variables (Huang et al., 2017; Koenker, 2017).

DOI: 10.4018/978-1-7998-9220-5.ch147

Another rationale that justifies quantile regression's significance is that it enables scholars to abandon the presumption that variables have similar working means at the upper tails of the distribution as at the mean, and it also helps in identifying the factors that critically determine the variables. According to Wenz (2019), quantile regression is forecasting, introducing a purposed bias in the outcome. Rather than identifying the mean of the anticipated variable, this type of regression pursues the median and any other quantiles, which are often referred to as percentiles. The main benefit of quantile regression is that its measures are comprehensive against outliers in the outcome measurements. The central position about the quantile regression topic is that they surpass this and are beneficial when there are interests in conditional quantile functions.

Quantile regression is currently a famous approach to offer a broad description of the distribution of an outcome variable on a collection of inputs. A quantile regression number accounts for and measures the level of a particular quantile of the outcome distribution, which is shifted by a one-unit rise in the predictor variable (Huang et al., 2017). Although the goal and aim of regression analysis are to estimate the conditional means of a variable one is interested in, quantile regression is used in estimating any conditional quantile of any level. Many scholars have studied the subject of quantile regression both from frequentist and Bayesian perspectives. Quantile regression is generally essential and shows to be essential when an individual is interested in the relationship amongst sections of the distribution also on limits. Some researchers have also studied the relationship between quantile regression and risk assessment and modeling (Rahman & Vossmeyer, 2019).

Koenker (2017) reported that the quantile classification technique places similar observation numbers into every class. The technique is mainly used for data that is evenly distributed across the range. The primary issue related to this is that quantile regression methodology has features positioned within similar cases, which can have significantly different values, especially when there is no even distribution of data across the range. Wang et al. (2019) conducted a study to ascertain the different issues related to quantiles and quantile regression. When the values having small range differences are positioned into various sets, which suggests a significant difference in the dataset. Therefore, quantile regression can create classification gaps amongst the attribute values, whereby these gaps can cause an over-weighting to the outliers in such a class set. Chen et al. (2021) also provided another issue related to quantiles and quantile regression by saying that when there is incorrect creation of the number of classes having similar values, this can lead to two groups. The primary reason why most analysts and scholars rarely use quantile regression, especially in healthcare research, is that the interpretations appear to be unintuitive.

CURRENT RESEARCH

Socioeconomic Indicators

Alotaibi and Alajlan (2021) investigated the inclusive relationship between socioeconomic indicators and CO_2 emissions in G20 countries using two socioeconomic indicators: LPI for the period 2007 to 2019 and HDI for the period 2000 to 2019, which were chosen based upon the reliability and availability of data. Quantile regression was employed to simultaneously analyze the heterogeneous effects of the explanatory variables, which included four control variables beside the socioeconomic variables. The authors empirically selected the control variables based on their regression quality and introduced them in two empirical models for LPI and HDI. The selected control variables were fossil fuel consumption, gross domestic production, trade openness, and urbanization. The results of both models revealed that there was an association between increased socioeconomic development and reduced CO_2 emissions.

The socioeconomic relationship with CO_2 emissions described in this paper provides policy makers with a more inclusive overview about how to counter CO_2 emissions. Unlike the majority of previous works, there is no emphasis on a specific factor that drives CO_2 emissions. The authors approached the issue of CO_2 emissions and sustainable development from a relatively new perspective. Policy makers ought to understand that although socioeconomic development could lead to more CO_2 emission, the relationship is described in an inverted U-shaped manner, as described in the EKC hypothesis. This means that as a country becomes more developed, it should experience lower CO_2 emissions. This could be a result of a more advancement in technology, education, infrastructure, and other dimensions of socioeconomic development.

Technological Innovation

Cheng et al. (2021) focus on the impacts of technology innovation on CO_2 emissions by employing a balanced panel dataset for 35 OECD countries covering 1996–2015. Economic growth, fixed investment, and exports are chosen as control variables. To avoid possible biased results and obtain more information about the impacts, a newly developed panel quantile regression method with non-additive fixed effects is applied as the data are not normally distributed. The empirical results are heterogeneous across different quantiles. Moreover, the influencing mechanism of technological innovation is systematically analyzed. To be specific, the direct and moderating impacts of technological innovation on CO_2 emissions in OECD countries are discussed.

Technological innovation directly reduces CO_2 emissions through R&D investment and education expenditure. Technological innovation can offset the positive impacts of economic growth on CO_2 emissions by reducing energy intensity. Technological innovation can enhance the negative impacts of renewable energy on CO_2 emissions by facilitating the development of renewable energy industry in the low quantile countries. Based on the results and discussion, the following policy recommendations are proposed: 1). To effectively mitigate CO_2 emissions, the government should pay attention to R&D investment and education expenditure, as well as cooperate with the private sector. 2). The government should encourage the technologies related to the improvement of energy intensity. 3). The government should remove the barriers affecting the diffusion of technology and promulgate related environmental regulations.

Financial Policies

D'Orazio and Dirks (2021) study the effects of financial development, economic growth, and climate-related financial policies on carbon (CO2) emissions for G20 countries. The panel quantile regression approach has been applied throughout its conditional distribution. The total effect appears nevertheless negative, which indicates that these policies may improve environmental quality overall in G20 countries. This method takes the unobserved individual heterogeneity and distributional heterogeneity into consideration. This analysis is relevant because the devastating consequences of environmental degradation on humanity and economic systems represent a pressing issue for governments and societies. Indeed, according to the latest IPCC (2018) report, G20 countries need to cut their current emissions by at least 45% in 2030 (below 2010 levels) to be in line with global benchmarks set on 1.5°C. Against this backdrop, in the past two decades, G20 countries have implemented a wide range of policy instruments, including different climate-related financial policies, to affect climate change and achieve effective mitigation results.

The authors investigated the determinants of carbon emissions in G20 countries. Having compared with OLS mean regression, the authors used MMQR approach to obtain a complete understanding of the factors that affect their sample's carbon emissions distribution. Building on the evidence that climate-related financial policies can play a role in the mitigation strategy of G20 countries, they should be more actively promoted at the global level. Their study suggests that countries should not increase the number of measures implemented in this policy area but also aim for specific types of measures to witness improvements in environmental quality. Their investigation shows that the policies' impact on environmental quality has been larger for quantiles characterized by countries adopting mandatory prudential measures and credit allocation policies.

Anthropogenic Consequences

Gyamfi et al. (2021) examine the influence of economic growth, coal rent, nuclear energy, coal CO_2 damage and energy from oil gas energy on carbon emissions. It employs a panel dataset of E7 member states from 1990 to 2016. The study uses OLS and Quantile regression analyses to understand the dynamics of the hypothesized relationships. The quantile regression approach aids to get rid of the bias of the OLS estimator. The results from the estimation techniques reveal a positive effect of real GDP on carbon emission. Increasing economic activities recorded in the region as a result in industrialization and the adoption of more advanced production techniques have led to more environmental depletion. Thus, uncontrolled growth is seen as a driver of environmental degradation in E7 economies. Additionally, renewable energy is found to have a negative and significant impact on CO_2 emissions in E7 countries. This confirms the transition of countries from non-renewable energy (fossil fuels, coal) consumption to renewable energy consumption as a viable way to combat the rising CO_2 emissions and to meet the expectation of growing demand for energy resources.

Furthermore, nuclear energy sources exert a positive effect on carbon emission in E7 economies but only when energy consumption from nuclear sources is low whereas found to have insignificant negative coefficients when more energy is generated from nuclear sources. This implies that environmental degradation could be reduced if more energy can be generated from nuclear energy sources in E7 economies. The results for coal rent show a positive and statistically significant impact of coal rent on carbon emission in E7 economies. However, the influence is most prevalent where coal rent consumption is moderately charged. Also, the cost of carbon damage shows a positively significant effect on carbon emission. This implies that the rising carbon emissions in E7 economies are because of the increasing economic activities compounding pressure on the environment.

Technological Progress

Xie, Wu, & Wang (2021) applied *super*-efficiency slacks-based measure (*SBM*) *model* for estimating the carbon emission efficiency of 59 countries from 1998 to 2016. Consistent with the recommendations of existing literature, the authors constructed a system to measure technological progress based on the outputs and transformations of a country's technical progress level as it relates to carbon emission efficiency. Given that distinct disparities were shown to exist between countries in terms of their efficiency value, their study uses the panel quantile regression to distinguish the effects of technological progress on carbon emission efficiency in countries with low, medium, and high carbon efficiency. Since energy intensity is an important contributor to carbon emission efficiency, and is itself heavily affected by renewable energy technology, the authors further investigate the interaction effect between technological progress and energy intensity on carbon emission efficiency.

Obvious disparities were discerned in the characteristics of carbon emission efficiency and its change over time in the studied countries. The impact of technological progress on carbon emission efficiency was found to be statistically significant and positive, besides, the relationship between multiple technological progress and carbon emission efficiency varies in line with the efficiency level of the countries studied. The interaction effects of technological progress and energy intensity are shown here to exert complex impacts on carbon emission efficiency. Financial support plays an active role in the growth of R&D department of the industrial sector and enterprises. The carbon emission efficiency can be improved by transforming patent fruits into productivity and enhancing energy efficiency and carbon emissions reduction technology. The government should increase the capital and technology support for the R&D departments, and optimize the industrial structure by eliminating or upgrading the high energy consumption and pollutant enterprises.

ICT Infrastructure

Anser *et al.* (2021) examined the dynamic interlinkages between technological factors and CO_2 emissions in a panel of 26 selected European countries. The importance of information and communication technologies (ICT) infrastructure in economic development is widely visible in the academic and research arena. At the same time, this positivity is influenced by negative externality of the environment in the form of high mass CO_2 emissions that is emerged with massive, unsustainable production and consumption. The technological and material footprint hinders the global sustainable policy actions that need strong environmental regulations and cleaner production technologies to delimit the anthropogenic activities from the atmosphere.

The study verified the material footprint under the premises of the Environment Kuznets Curve (EKC). The trade liberalization policies and unsustainable industrial production vastly increase CO_2 emissions that influenced the United Nations SDA. The study concludes that green ICT infrastructure is imperative for long-term sustainable growth across Europe. The focal point of all this exercise is that we have to conserve our natural environment through socio-economic and environmental policies that should base upon cleaner technologies, tight environmental regulations, up-gradation of information and communication technologies, and ISO-sensitized certification that would deem desirable for making 'smart Europe' with IT-enabled development.

Clean Energy Investment

By employing instrumental variable quantile regression model, Chen, Fu, and Chang (2021) investigate the effects of climate change on clean energy investment according to global panel data of 44 countries during 1996 to 2018. This study focuses on whether countries with greater and lesser clean energy investment respond similarly to climate change. As the data of clean energy investment can be obtained mainly for solar, wind, and geothermal energy, the authors examine the effects of climate change on these three types, respectively. Based on the empirical results, the authors arrive at several main conclusions. The effects of climate change on clean energy investment vary significantly in countries with greater and lesser clean energy investment. Similarly, extreme temperature, drought, and flood produce significantly

Q

negative influences on solar and wind investments in countries with greater investment, but the impacts in countries with lesser investment are statistically insignificant.

In addition, the effects of greenhouse gases on solar and geothermal investments are significantly positive, while they are significantly negative on wind investment. One possible reason is that solar and geothermal energies are considered to be effective in reducing greenhouse gas emissions, while whether or not wind energy can reduce greenhouse gas emissions remains controversial. There exist significant differences in the impacts of socioeconomic factors on clean energy investment. Economic development, population, clean energy consumption, and clean energy policy are conductive to investments in solar, wind, and geothermal energies for all quantiles of the distribution. Natural resource rents produce significantly positive effects on investments in the three energies only at the upper quantiles. Trade can promote solar and wind energy investments significantly, but the effect on geothermal energy investment is insignificant.

Lagged and Asymmetric Effects

Unlike previous researchers who mostly apply mean-based models, Dawar et al. (2021) examine the dependence structure between WTI prices and renewable energy equity indexes using quantile regression to offer a more comprehensive dependence structure under diverse market conditions. Their empirical analyses provide solid evidence for the decreasing dependence of clean energy stocks on oil price movements. Additionally, the lagged effect of WTI prices on clean energy equity returns is generally significant, which indicates that clean energy stock returns react differently to new information on oil returns under different market conditions. Further analyses involving the presence of asymmetry in the relationship between crude oil returns on the returns of clean energy stock indices in various market conditions show strong effects of negative oil returns during bearish periods and an insignificant effect during bullish periods.

Understanding the connectedness between renewable energy stocks and traditional energy prices is of paramount importance to ethical investors, as this information is essential for gaining superior risk-adjusted returns through proper allocation of clean energy assets to a portfolio. Such knowledge further helps to identify whether and to what extent these stocks are sensitive to shocks emanating from other allied markets. It is worth mentioning that although ethical investors aim at decarbonizing their portfolios, they still attempt to receive healthy returns from their investments. Their findings will be of particular interest to those participants who want to invest in eco-friendly firms. Overall, these results could be useful in outlining sustainable business strategies and designing optimal portfolios.

Economic Growth and Health Expenditure

Bilgili et al. (2021) investigate the impact of health expenditures on CO_2 emissions in panel 36 Asian countries within the framework of the Environment Kuznets Curve (EKC) hypothesis. The panel sample period spans from 1991 to 2017. The paper, by employing fully modified OLS (FMOLS), generalized method of moments (GMM), and quantile regression methodologies, confirms the EKC in Asia. Empirical results show that as the income level of panel Asian countries grows, the environmental pollution (CO_2 emissions) gets lower. The parameters from FMOLS highlight that both public and private health care expenditures contribute to lower CO_2 emissions in panel Asian countries. On the other hand, the parameters from GMM highlight that only private health care expenditures contribute to lower carbon emissions. The difference in parameters obtained from two distinct methodologies was further investigated using the quantile regression method.

Results revealed that there is a significant effect of both public and private health expenditures in lowering CO_2 emissions for the 50th and 75th quantiles; however, the effect is insignificant for the 25th quantile. This shows that countries with a lower level of CO_2 emissions have a weak relation with health expenditures. This is worth considering finding as the effect of public and private health care expenditure on CO_2 emissions has not been studied for Asia by previous literature using the quantile regression method. Besides, this paper reached statistical evidence that both government sector and private health sector expenditures caused environmental pollution to decrease in Asia and that the negative impact of the private health sector on CO_2 emissions (in absolute value) is greater than that of the government health sector.

Heterogeneous Effects

BRICS economies significantly contribute to the world economic growth (EG) and CO_2 emissions. However, no study so far has been conducted on BRICS economies to estimate the growth effects of energy efficiency (EE). Likewise, from the methodological perspective, this research uses a Product, Quantity and Routing (PQR) analysis that is useful for outliers and provides more accurate estimates. Therefore, Akram et al. (2021) attempt to analyze the heterogeneous effects of EE, renewable energy (RE), and other factors on EG of BRICS countries for 1990–2014. This research used the normality test, along with cross-section dependency and slope heterogeneity test for empirical research. The findings provide ample evidence that the data is heterogeneous and non-normal so that quantiles regression analysis can be applied to the EE, renewable energy consumption (REC), and EG relationship. The findings reveal that EE is a significant factor of EG in BRICS countries. By using the fixed effect PQR approach, the findings clearly explain that the effect of all the specific factors on EG is heterogeneous along the quantiles.

The results disclose that PQR demonstrates the heterogeneous effects of EE, RE and other factors at different quantiles of EG. While CM regression (POLS) depicts the homogenous effects of EE, RE and other decisive factors along different quantiles of EG. The effect of EE is significantly positive across all the points, but the positive effect is more robust at 50th and 60th quantiles of EG. REC significantly decreases the EG in BRICS economies. The results obtained from the causality analysis explain the two-way causal relationship between EE and EG. This approves the feedback hypothesis between EE and EG in BRICS countries. The results also provide the two-way causal relationship between REC and EG of BRICS nations. Furthermore, a causal association is examined from EE to REC. It suggests that EE is also helpful in enhancing REC.

Income Inequality

This research investigates the impact of income inequality on household direct and indirect CO_2 emissions of 30 provinces in China from 2000 to 2015 by the panel quantile regression method. The Theil index is selected to measure income inequality. Population, household consumption level, energy intensity, urbanization and industrial structure are chosen as control variables. The results show that the level of regional inequality is gradually increasing from the east to the west. The household indirect CO_2 emissions in the east increased fastest, while household direct CO_2 emissions in the west increased fastest. Income inequality significantly promoted direct CO_2 emissions under all quantile levels, while it has no significant effect on indirect CO_2 emissions. Furthermore, the positive impact of income inequality on direct CO_2 emissions will decrease as the level of direct CO_2 emissions increases. Population and per capita consumption will promote direct and indirect CO_2 emissions.

The Chinese government should pay more attention to the rationality of income distribution while maintaining the steady growth of residents' income. Since the dual policy goals of reducing inequality and CO_2 emissions are compatible with each other, the environmental pressure can be alleviated to a certain extent when income distribution is more equitable. Furthermore, the government can guide the consumption of low-income households to shift to low-carbon products through subsidies. At the same time, targeted poverty alleviation should be further implemented in poverty-stricken areas. When formulating and implementing policies, the local governments should consider the differences of carbon emission levels in various regions, and implement targeted adjustment programs. The government should impose stricter standards on high-carbon emission regions, but never relax the supervision on carbon emission reduction in low-carbon emission regions.

FUTURE RESEARCH DIRECTIONS

Panel Semiparametric Quantile Regression Neural Network (PSQRNN)

Zhou and Wang (2021) propose a new model– PSQRNN. It combines panel data, semiparametric model and composite QR with QRNN, which keeps the flexibility of nonparametric models and maintains the interpretability of parametric models simultaneously. In order to train the PSQRNN, a penalized composite quantile regression with LASSO, ridge regression and backpropagation algorithm is considered. In addition, a differentiable approximation of the quantile loss function is adopted so that the quasi-Newton optimization can be conducted to estimate the model parameters. The prediction accuracy is evaluated by an empirical study of 30 provinces' dataset from 1999 to 2018 in China under three different scenarios, based on economic and climate factors. Compared to the QRNN model, the PSQRNN model is more robust and performs better for electricity consumption forecasting. Finally, the PSQRNN model is used to predict the electricity consumptions of provincial data over 2019-2023. The authors find that the trends of electricity consumption demand in the future varies from province to province, which is helpful for government decision-making.

There are some interesting future works: (1) For large dimensional panel data, some feature selection techniques, such as principal component analysis, factor analysis and Lasso, can be applied to our proposed PSQRNN. They can screen out more important factors from the social, economic and climatic factors associated with electricity consumption. Therefore, PSQRNN based on feature selection is worth studying for panel electricity consumption forecasting. (2) Build hybrid methods based on Machine Learning, for example, Boosting PSQRNN, PSQRNN with random forest, PSQRNN with GANs, etc. The above methods are supposed to improve the accuracy of prediction.

Expectile and Quantile Regression

The marginal abatement costs (MACs) of environmental bads such as carbon dioxide (CO_2) are a big concern. Several data-driven approaches to empirical estimation of MACs from observed input-output data are available, including econometric approaches, production economic approaches, and mathematical programming approaches. Kuosmanen and Zhou (2021) have developed a novel data-driven approach based on convex quantile regression and convex expectile regression to estimate shadow prices and marginal abatement costs for undesirable outputs such as carbon dioxide. The proposed approach effectively addresses three major shortcomings of the traditional approach to shadow pricing. The authors apply convex quantile regression or convex expectile regression to estimate shadow prices not only on the efficient frontier, but also in the interior of the production possibility set.

The proposed quantile approach ensures that shadow prices and marginal abatement costs for bad outputs are estimated at the actual level of performance by the evaluated units. The local estimation approach makes the proposed quantile approach less sensitive to the choice of the direction vector as there is no need to project inefficient firms to the efficient frontier. The proposed approach takes both noise and inefficiency explicitly into account in the estimation of quantiles or expectiles. New empirical evidence could convince policy makers around the world to pursue more stringent mitigation targets called for by the Intergovernmental Panel on Climate Change (IPCC). The method warrants further research, both in theory and in terms of systematic Monte-Carlo simulations. Developing operational methods for statistical inferences such as bootstrapping, and addressing econometric issues such as endogeneity in the present context, provide other important topics for future research.

Special Quantile Regression Forest (sQRF)

In line with Córdoba et al. (2021), rural land valuation plays an important role in the development of land use policies for agricultural purposes. The advance of computational software and machine learning methods has enhanced mass appraisal methodologies for modeling and predicting economic values. New machine learning methods, like tree-based regression models, have been proposed as an alternative to linear regression to predict economic values from ancillary variables, since these algorithms are able to handle non-normality and non-linearity in the data. However, regression trees are commonly estimated assuming independent rather than spatially correlated data. The authors model the relationship between a set of environmental variables and rural land values and develop a spatial version of a machine learning algorithm, as a new method for land unit values (LUVs) predictions. The main advantage of applying the sQRF methodology for mass appraisal is the possibility to handle big data and its high predictive accuracy.

The sQRF outperformed linear regression model (LR), regression kriging method (RK), and spatial Random Forest (sRF) in delivering LUV predictions, as shown by several validation measurements. The procedure was able to derive better predictions of LUVs at unsampled sites than the classical or even the spatial linear regression model. The algorithm sQRF uses site-specific explanatory variables and LUVs from neighboring sites to improve LUV predictions. Moreover, it has the ability to yield an uncertainty measure for the predicted LUVs. The findings showed that soil quality was the most important environmental variable in explaining farmland values in Córdoba. The methodology can be used for objective assessment of LUVs in other territories. The sQRF method can be implemented using free software and widely available territorial data; however, as other supervised machine learning methods, it lacks automation. Future research on automatic optimization of sQRF parameters will facilitate its use in digital economy.

CONCLUSION

Climate change, which resulting in a serious impact on environmental degradation, has become one of the biggest talks recently amongst the public but also become a major political standpoint. As Xie, Wu, & Wang (2021) indicate that, in the social context of enhancing environmental quality and mitigating climate change, the improvement of <u>carbon emission</u> efficiency has emerged as a hot topic recently due to its promise as an approach to reduce emissions and improve environmental quality. With the thrive of the informationization and knowledge economy, the resource conservation and environmental protection that is promoted by progress in <u>science and technology</u> is increasingly being relied upon for <u>achieving sustainable development</u> globally.

Quantile regression being used to help with climate change is exceptionally new. Quantile regression is a methodology that allows understanding relationships between multiple variables other than just the mean/average of a given set of data. What this allows for people to do is understand the exact or at least predict the outcome that is distributed across a nonlinear function. Recently quantile regression has been used to help learn about climate change and hopefully shed a little more light on the ever growing issue.

There are many important discoveries, such as more environmental degradation is attributed to the unequal distribution of power and wealth; increasing clean energy investment can dramatically decrease greenhouse gas; Energy conservation and emission reduction measures should be vigorously implemented to achieve resource-saving and environment-friendly development. Also, scientists believe that quantile regression can help predict how climate change will change in the future. This allows them to predict how temperatures will change and what could be causing it.

REFERENCES

Akram, R., Chen, F., Khalid, F., Huang, G., & Irfan, M. (2021). Heterogeneous effects of energy efficiency and renewable energy on economic growth of BRICS countries: A fixed effect panel quantile regression analysis. *Energy, 215*(Part B).

Alotaibi, A. A., & Alajlan, N. (2021). Using Quantile Regression to analyze the relationship between Socioeconomic Indicators and Carbon Dioxide Emissions in G20 Countries. *Sustainability, 2021*(13), 7011. doi:10.3390u13137011

Anser, M. K., Ahmad, M., Khan, M. A., Zaman, K., Nassani, A. A., Askar, S. E., Abro, M. M. Q., & Kabbani, A. (2021). The role of information and communication technologies in mitigating carbon emissions: Evidence from panel quantile regression. *Environmental Science and Pollution Research International, 28*(17), 21065–21084. doi:10.100711356-020-12114-y PMID:33405124

Bilgili, F., Kuşkaya, S., & Khan, M. (2021). The roles of economic growth and health expenditure on CO_2 emissions in selected Asian countries: A quantile regression model approach. *Environ Sci Pollut Res*. https://doi-org.ezproxy.montclair.edu/10.1007/s11356-021-13639-6

Chen, L., Galvao, A. F., & Song, S. (2021). Quantile regression with generated regressors. *Econometrics, 9*(2), 16. doi:10.3390/econometrics9020016

Chen, X., Fu, Q., & Chang, C. P. (2021). What are the shocks of climate change on clean energy investment: A diversified exploration. *Energy Economics, 95*, 105136.

Cheng, C., Ren, X., Dong, K., Dong, X., & Wang, Z. (2021). How does technological innovation mitigate CO2 emissions in OECD countries? Heterogeneous analysis using panel quantile regression. *Journal of Environmental Management, 280*.

Cheng, Y., Wang, Y., Chen, W., Wang, Q., & Zhao, G. (2021). Does income inequality affect direct and indirect household CO_2 emissions? A quantile regression approach. *Clean Technologies and Environmental Policy, 23*(4), 1199–1213. doi:10.100710098-020-01980-2

Córdoba, M., Carranza, J. P., Piumetto, M., Monzani, F., & Balzarini, M. (2021). A spatially based quantile regression forest model for mapping rural land values. *Journal of Environmental Management, 289.*

Dawar, I., Dutta, A., Bouri, E., & Saeed, T. (2021). Crude oil prices and clean energy stock indices: Lagged and asymmetric effects with quantile regression. *Renewable Energy, 163,* 288–299. doi:10.1016/j.renene.2020.08.162

D'Orazio, P., & Dirks, M. W. (2021). *Exploring the effects of climate-related financial policies on carbon emissions in G20 countries: A Panel Quantile Regression Approach.* https://www.researchsquare.com/article/rs-476273/v1.pdf

Gyamfi, B. A., Adedoyin, F. F., Bein, M. A., Bekun, F. V., & Agozie, D. Q. (2021). The anthropogenic consequences of energy consumption in E7 economies: Juxtaposing roles of renewable, coal, nuclear, oil and gas energy: Evidence from panel quantile method. *Journal of Cleaner Production, •••,* 295.

Huang, Q., Zhang, H., Chen, J., & He, M. (2017). Quantile regression models and their applications: A review. *Journal of Biometrics & Biostatistics, 8*(10).

Jiang, R., Hu, X., Yu, K., & Qian, W. (2018). Composite quantile regression for massive datasets. *Statistics, 52*(5), 980–1004. doi:10.1080/02331888.2018.1500579

Koenker, R. (2017). Quantile regression: 40 years on. *Annual Review of Economics, 9*(1), 155–176. doi:10.1146/annurev-economics-063016-103651

Kuosmanen, T., & Zhou, X. (2021). Shadow prices and marginal abatement costs: Convex quantile regression approach. *European Journal of Operational Research, 289*(2), 666–675. doi:10.1016/j.ejor.2020.07.036

Rahman, M. A., & Vossmeyer, A. (2019). Estimation and applications of quantile regression for binary longitudinal data. In Topics in Identification, Limited Dependent Variables, Partial Observability, Experimentation, and Flexible Modeling: Part B. Emerald Publishing Limited. doi:10.1108/S0731-90532019000040B009

Sarkodie, S. A., & Owusu, P. A. (2021). Impact of COVID-19 pandemic on waste management. *Environment, Development and Sustainability, 23*(5), 7951–7960. doi:10.100710668-020-00956-y PMID:32863738

Wang, H., Feng, X., & Dong, C. (2019). Copula-based quantile regression for longitudinal data. *Statistica Sinica, 29*(1), 245–264.

Wenz, S. E. (2019). What quantile regression does and doesn't do: A commentary on Petscher and Logan. *Child Development, 90*(4), 1442–1452. doi:10.1111/cdev.13141 PMID:30267567

Xie, Z., Wu, R., & Wang, S. (2021). How technological progress affects the carbon emission efficiency? Evidence from national panel quantile regression. *Journal of Cleaner Production, 307,* 127133.

Zhou, X., & Wang, J. (2021). *Panel semiparametric quantile regression neural network for electricity consumption forecasting.* arXiv:2103.00711 [stat.ML]

ADDITIONAL READING

Adebayo, T. S., Rjoub, H., Akinsola, G. D., & Oladipupo, S. D. (2022). The asymmetric effects of renewable energy consumption and trade openness on carbon emissions in Sweden: New evidence from quantile-on-quantile regression approach. *Environmental Science and Pollution Research International*, *29*(2), 1875–1886. doi:10.100711356-021-15706-4 PMID:34363156

Anwar, A., Malik, S., & Ahmad, P. (2022). Cogitating the role of Technological Innovation and Institutional Quality in Formulating the Sustainable Development Goal Policies for E7 Countries: Evidence from Quantile Regression. *Global Business Review*. doi:10.1177/09721509211072657

Awosusi, A. A., Adebayo, T. S., Altuntaş, M., Agyekum, E. B., Zawbaa, H. M., & Kamel, S. (2022). The dynamic impact of biomass and natural resources on ecological footprint in BRICS economies: A quantile regression evidence. *Energy Reports*, *8*, 1979–1994. doi:10.1016/j.egyr.2022.01.022

Bilgili, F., Ozturk, I., Kocak, E., Kuskaya, S., & Cingoz, A. (2022). The nexus between access to electricity and CO2 damage in Asian Countries: The evidence from quantile regression models. *Energy and Building*, *256*, 111761. doi:10.1016/j.enbuild.2021.111761

Gyamfi, B. A., Onifade, S. T., Nwani, C., & Bekun, F. V. (2022). Accounting for the combined impacts of natural resources rent, income level, and energy consumption on environmental quality of G7 economies: A panel quantile regression approach. *Environmental Science and Pollution Research International*, *29*(2), 2806–2818. doi:10.100711356-021-15756-8 PMID:34378136

Liu, C., Ou, G., Fu, Y., Zhang, C., & Yue, C. (2022). Application of a Panel Data Quantile-Regression Model to the Dynamics of Carbon Sequestration in Pinus kesiya var. langbianensis Natural Forests. *Forests*, *13*(1), 12. doi:10.3390/f13010012

Raza, M. Y., & Hasan, M. M. (2022). Estimating the multiple impacts of technical progress on Bangladesh's manufacturing and industrial sector's CO2 emissions: A quantile regression approach. *Energy Reports*, *8*, 2288–2301. doi:10.1016/j.egyr.2022.01.005

Sun, Y., Bao, Q., Siao-Yun, W., Islam, M., & Razzaq, A. (2022). Renewable energy transition and environmental sustainability through economic complexity in BRICS countries: Fresh insights from novel Method of Moments Quantile regression. *Renewable Energy*, *184*, 1165–1176. doi:10.1016/j.renene.2021.12.003

Syed, Q. R., Bhowmik, R., Adedoyin, F. F., Alola, A. A., & Khalid, N. (2022). Do economic policy uncertainty and geopolitical risk surge CO2 emissions? New insights from panel quantile regression approach. *Environmental Science and Pollution Research International*, *29*(19), 1–17. doi:10.100711356-021-17707-9 PMID:34981380

KEY TERMS AND DEFINITIONS

Climate Change: It is attributed to both natural variability and human activities. However, many of these changes are now considered attributable to human activities nowadays.

Environmental Protection: The practice of protecting the natural environment by individuals, organizations, and governments.

Greenhouse Gases: They are a natural part of the atmosphere that, through a natural process called the greenhouse effect, trap the sun's warmth and maintain the earth's surface temperature at the level necessary to support life.

Heterogeneous Effects: The nonrandom, explainable variability in the direction and magnitude of treatment effects for individuals within a population.

Quantile Regression: Quantile regression enables quantification of the relationship between dependent and independent variables across different quantiles of the conditional distribution of the dependent variable.

Renewable Energy (or Clean Energy): Collected from renewable resources, including carbon neutral sources like sunlight, wind, rain, tides, waves, and geothermal heat.

Socio-Economic Factors: Including occupation, education, income, wealth and where someone lives.

Section 38
Natural Language Processing (NLP)

Challenges and Opportunities in Knowledge Representation and Reasoning

Pankaj Dadure
National Institute of Technology, Silchar, India

Partha Pakray
National Institute of Technology, Silchar, India

Sivaji Bandyopadhyay
National Institute of Technology, Silchar, India

INTRODUCTION

Knowledge Representation and Reasoning (KRR) describes real-world information that can be used to explain and solve complicated real-life issues such as human-computer interaction through natural language. The knowledge representation is not only about the data representation but also enables a computer to learn from this representation and act intelligently as a human being. Modern computer applications have led to the generalized use of knowledge representations in various contexts, including information search, simulation, web semantic ontology description (Baral, 2015). Natural language and representation of knowledge are strongly aligned in nature. In any field of science, the intelligent systems highly depend on the representation and reasoning of knowledge. By applying the knowledge representation and reasoning techniques to the data that are already being available on the internet, initiate a revolution in representation, analysis, and use of a huge amount of available data. Moreover, there are numerous problems relating to the use of techniques to represent knowledge, such as important attributes, relations between attributes, the choice of granularity of representation, and the identification of the correct structure as required. The systems are quite passive in current approaches and researchers mainly manage the information and extensions to the knowledge base.

The key factor involved in building intelligent knowledge systems is the representation of knowledge. Knowledge representation and reasoning techniques mentioned in Figure 1 (Malhotra, 2015) deal with knowledge as connecting node at the time of input and processing. There is a need to design state-of-the-art knowledge representation techniques that can integrate innovative and intelligent knowledge representation and reasoning properties into the system.

BACKGROUND

The researchers of the AI community have believed that the knowledge in the human brain, and knowledge in intelligent information processing systems, is considered as a network of interconnected nodes. Moreover, the way nodes are organized, relations between the nodes and the effectiveness with which information is collected vary enormously in human brain networks and human knowledge systems. Network connections in the human brain provide different characteristics that lead to their rapid or slow

DOI: 10.4018/978-1-7998-9220-5.ch148

recovery of information (Sandberg, 2013). So, there is a demand to design an intelligent knowledge representation system which ensure that an autonomous node can determine the appropriate connectivity. Furthermore, communication among nodes is not only an appointed string relationship, but also the network intelligence.

Figure 1. Evolution of Knowledge Representation Techniques

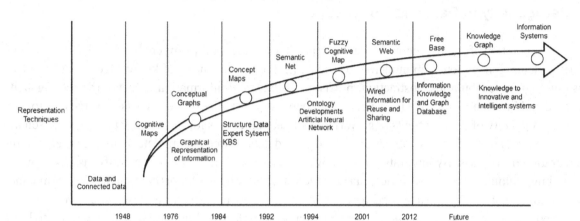

Relation Between Knowledge and Intelligence

In the modern era, knowledge plays a crucial role and leads to state-of-the-art decision-making techniques of artificial intelligence (Ackerman, 2005). It depicts the smart actions of AI agents or systems. Only with awareness or experience of the input is it possible for an individual or device to act correctly. The key issue of artificial intelligence lies in knowledge representation and reasoning: to recognize the essence of intelligence and cognition so well that computers can be programmed to show human skills.

Let's take an example to understand this relationship:

Figure 2. Decision-maker

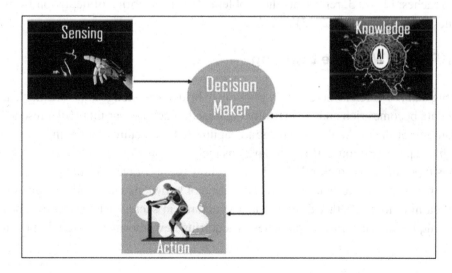

The example shown in Figure 2, there is one decision-maker whose actions are validated by understanding the environment using knowledge. But, if the knowledge part is discarded from here, it will not able to perform any intelligent action.

CHALLENGES IN KNOWLEDGE REPRESENTATION AND REASONING

Heterogeneity in Data and Knowledge

The incorporation of heterogeneous information and knowledge is the prime challenge in KRR (Machery, 2010). Heterogeneity exists in numerous variants: (a) the heterogeneity of knowledge structures (such as ontologies, vocabularies, abstraction, precision of data, and information objects), (b) heterogeneity of data and information objects (exls versus unicode), and structure (table versus csv versus vector) (c) the heterogeneity of data elements (e.g., variance of data object ids for the same data object), in semantics. The integration of diverse objects, knowledge, and data source in complete form is greater than the integration of its parts. By integrating the knowledge generated from various scientific assessments, or combining findings of various species, can gain the valuable insights. Robots contain multiple commands and controls that can view in a new behavior or advise the robot to learn more. Researchers work on various methods of heterogeneous knowledge and data, from tight coupling and incorporation to the loose coupling of the components which required for project completion. Whereas the issue of heterogeneity remains a sacred pillar of KRR research and poses many challenges, a series of innovations have opened up new chances to make a significant difference over the next few years such as: 1. academic credit from data citations is becoming more popular and this exchange of data, contribute to greater collaboration and inclusion, 2. crowd-based sourcing technology: Freebase, DBpedia and Wikidata systems enable the individuals to insert their own knowledge into a shared model, 3. the growing involvement of scientists and civilians in the global knowledge, 4. increased KRR backend capabilities: inexpensive storage, collateral hardware and software, finer logistical systems, allow us to scale to billions of triples. In the recent era, adequate storage, bandwidth and computing power allow efficient data sharing and enhance the ability to collaborate, 5. In big data cloud models, KRR is the fastest way to achieve the promise of identification and recording (for group exchange) of artifacts. Scientists are increasingly realizing the need for comprehensive semantic annotations to model results and allow resource interviews over the system. 6. Big data are helpful in many cases both in terms of high precision, poor recall and low-accuracy approaches. Figure 3, represents the problems at various forms of depiction from raw data to structured knowledge (Noy N. a., 2013).

Bridging KRR and Machine Learning

In the era of big data, research is increasingly growing to bridge knowledge and machine learning. Since the available data becomes rich and intrinsically organized, machine learning (ML) research requires a rich understanding of the available knowledge to capture data structure, source information and other essential quality aspects (Bottou, 2014). ML analysis includes complex models and hypotheses that can reflect various types of entity, their relationships and how these evolve over the period of time. At the same time, the research in representation and acquisition of knowledge takes advantage of newly evolving machine learning methods that discover data structures in secret or latent form. These structural discovery techniques can be helpful approaches to acquiring new information, ranging from the model-

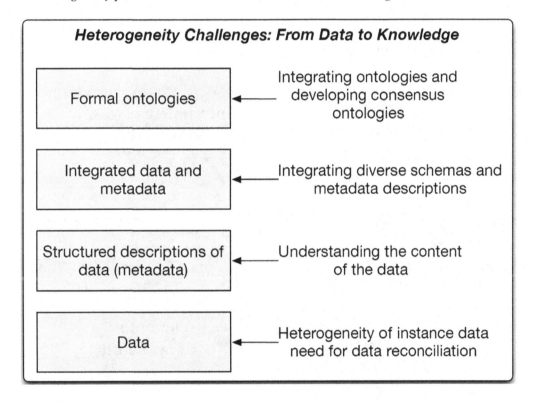

ing of a subject that discovers a single latent variable to rich statistical relation models that can uncover new relations and hierarchical models. More important, it provides the chance to close the gap between data-driven knowledge exploration and knowledge-based theory: by deploying the richer languages of knowledge representation, the features used in a machine learning algorithm can be searched for new structures which can be incorporated into the representation of knowledge and used in additional structures. Moreover, systems are needed to combine logic with probability and make a combination of deductive and statistical reasoning to close the loop. Adaptive areas of research such as applied statistical learning and probabilistic logic programming are promising avenues, aimed at using statistical and logical representations as well as rationalization methods.

Figure 3. Heterogeneity problems between data and structured knowledge

Data and Experiments Matching

The researchers are increasingly required to use and incorporate the data provided by the experiments of physical framework and data obtained from sensors and different methods of data gathering (Couper, 2017). Generally, the researcher designed the framework and gathered the data by executing various modelling assumptions at a different time, using different languages and at different timescales. Nevertheless, the ability to fuse the knowledge from the various designs and take wise decisions on the basis of these design, the data is essential. Modelling languages, which can handle data in a stable, extendable and understandable way, are very important. Applications to such languages include climatic, environmental, energy grids, ecological modelling, production, medical, and health framework.

Irrationality, Uncertainty and Inadequacy

The latest development has contributed to the increasing number of knowledge foundations, which contain inadequate or irrational knowledge (Johnny, 2020). These knowledge foundations are automatically obtained, partially created, or built up by a distributed user knowledge sharing platforms. These foundations contained linguistic knowledge bases like FrameNet, WordNet, and VerbNet, worldwide knowledge bases for instance ConceptNet, DBpedia, Freebase, and Google Knowledge Graph. This knowledge is inconsistent, uncoordinated, unavoidably incomplete. Users represent knowledge at various levels of abstraction and have different contexts and views. The knowledge derives from big data is often seem incoherent or incomplete, because the absence of origin metadata is unable to clarify variations in the measurements. This are the challenges for reasoning systems which perform and scale in full and uniform knowledge.

Figure 4. Imperfect state of knowledge

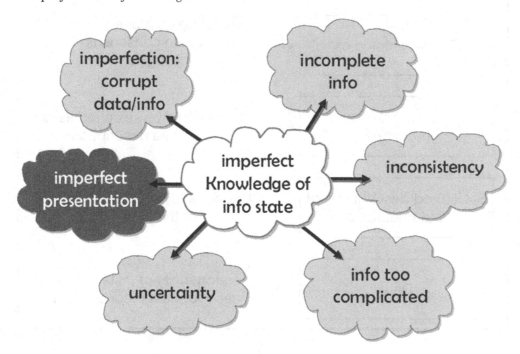

Robust Reasoning

In server-based applications, the current reasoner performance is always inadequate. The stable and extensible reasoning with very little utilization of resource is required for all type of inputs, also in the presence of many facts, consideration of broad ontologies and numbers of regulations (Haghighi, 2012). There are numerous reasoning frameworks for languages with minimal demonstrative ability which address the level of growth, for instance, a large number of RDF systems (Ozsu, 2016). One main objective is to boost the efficiency of these systems in order to compete with the quickest storage and query systems. Another important objective is to reach comparable performance levels in more expressive languages.

Parallel calculation and distributed storage may contribute to reasoning efficiency boosting but not a complete solution. The careful consideration of all aspects of efficiency, not simply the wall-and-clock time but also the impact of memory hierarchies, transmission expenditure as well. Moreover, the sophisticated centralized control is required for successful reasoning over the inexpressive parallel language.

Effective Human-Scale Reasoning

The biggest divergence between AI based reasoning systems and human reasoning is that human reasoning appears to be too accurate and successful as human understand more (Zhang, 2020). By comparison, AI systems generally need careful handmade optimisation in order to attain considerable efficiency. One important research question is to understand the space for reasoning tasks and architectures which handle them optimally. Another fascinating question in research is how human reasoning in software can achieve its desirable properties. Human reasoning is robust, scalable and works across large knowledge fields. It would be ground breaking to understand how to build equally operating software, in terms of our science and economic expertise.

Knowledge-Data Representation Gap

The KRR research community has established specialized languages and ontologies to reflect expertise in different fields, but as a total percentage of available data, the volume of data represented by a KRR models is continuing to compact. The increased number of data is available as part of Linked Open Data cloud (Bizer, 2011). Although, the most of this information is available in the RDF by utilizing the original data sources schema alone. While some Linked Data sources have rich ontologies, these are the exceptions rather than the rules. Then the rest of the data available on the web. On the internet, the data and services in any of the forms are accessible and no effort is made to explain the data semantic. Attempting to solve the gap in knowledge representation bring tremendous change in the ability to use diverse knowledge sources. Just consider the field of biology where major investments are being made in science, instruments and data collection. The capability to identifying and recycling of data is immensely narrow because the data produced by other investigators are primarily manual. However, if all data within this region are recorded in terms of common field ontologies, researchers would be able to easily discover and then use this knowledge to conduct their research in a more efficient way. To close this gap, a new approaches, tools and techniques are required to represent and reason over the large amount of currently available data.

Acquiring Knowledge from People

The smart systems are able to gain people's knowledge about new ways of executing tasks or simply people's expectations for their behaviour (Strohmaier, 2012). Knowledge acquired directly from people, even if they are affording to attain much more knowledge by using machine learning, is often an essential skill for smart systems. The prime questions in this field: How the information of a system can be extended? How do people understand and enable the system to broaden its awareness on its own? How can misunderstandings in an information system be corrected? How do smart systems learn from many other people who have knowledge overlapping?

Capturing Knowledge from Text

The extraction of relational information from the text has a rich history of utilizing methods that are focused upon manually encoded patterns, and machine learning techniques (Amini, 2014). Moreover, sometimes, the same text contains details of variety of relationships. For example, biological connections such as relationships between gene-disease, gene-drug, drug-mutation, and etc extracted from the biological texts. In addition to this, a new approach is needed, which can extract arbitrary relationships, if the relation is defined in user query. An even greater challenge in extracting the knowledge from texts is to get more precise details. To address this challenge, the translation of text into formal information representation is ultimately important. In many applications, such translation is required, such as (a) creating a device capable natural language commands and directives (e.g. human-robotics interaction), (b) correlates the correctness of students' answers to gold standards responses in an intelligent tutoring system, (c) which can interpret scenario statements and hypothesize of missing knowledge to make the observations by knowledge utilizing and inexplicable inspection, and (d) important developments in the capture of textual knowledge often involve the creation of KRR formalism that is especially suitable for extracting knowledge from text, like structure of dynamic and temporal connective logic or non-monotonic structure. The preference of a specific structure will rely on the type of text, and a specific methodology is required to identify the correct structure.

Constructing the Large Common-Sense Knowledge Bases

The human reasoning is one of the important part of artificial intelligence and cognitive science studies which depends on an immense build-up of knowledge (Davis, 2015). This knowledge expands from top abstractions (e.g., number concepts) to real-life data. Without such knowledge, any question-answering system can generate the answer in nonsensical manner. A well design software with these same logical capacities is necessary to make it more independent and trustworthy in order to resolve the impasse in their operations. Creating broad common sense knowledge bases offers a modern knowledge framework for cyber-physical systems as they are used across various systems. However, an understanding of what is required to develop, how to use and how to maintained common sense knowledge bases, become key challenges.

FUTURE RESEARCH DIRECTIONS

As numerous challenges in the data and information-driven domain, the representation of knowledge is crucially important. Data extraction, the development of new applications powered by knowledge, and creation of new demonstrative knowledge will possibly activate the success in numerous areas. Approximately any application that has information to process needs the advancement in KRR research. In practically, KRR already is used in biomedical, environmental science, oil, gas and renewable energy industries, engineering, earth sciences, bioscience, autonomous robotics, education, digital sciences, social sciences (census and decision making), culture studies, business, defence, geosciences and material sciences. In this fields, KRR methods play an crucial role to help in knowledge management and recovery, data collection and analysis, machine learning, sensor data processing, agent's association, engineering system representation, and comprehension of natural languages. To illustrate the use cases and the opportunities that KRR offers are gathered below.

Education

The rise of intelligent tutoring/smart teaching systems has one of the AI and Cognitive Science's biggest success stories (d Baker, 2006). Smart teaching systems and educational outcomes provide functionally described knowledge base and gaining experiences. In a number of fields like studying algebra, such programs have already been shown to be useful (Melis, 2004), and near about half million students in the India adopted this technology. The previous work has acknowledged the strength of such systems in the advanced academic sector by providing guidance anytime, anywhere (Almasri, 2019). These automated interactive guidance methods are advantageous in all forms of education, from conventional classrooms teaching to large free online lessons. The availability of structurally represented domain knowledge is a key challenge in the implementation of such systems. In addition to this, the new forms of smart tutoring system are required which facilitate STEM learning (Science, Technology, Engineering and Mathematics). For example, helping students to create facts in order to understand the mechanisms of scientific knowledge instead of just their outcomes, necessitate understanding of the everyday task. The overview and deliverable outcome of intelligent tutoring system are shown in Figure 5 and 6.

Figure 5. Overview of intelligent tutoring system

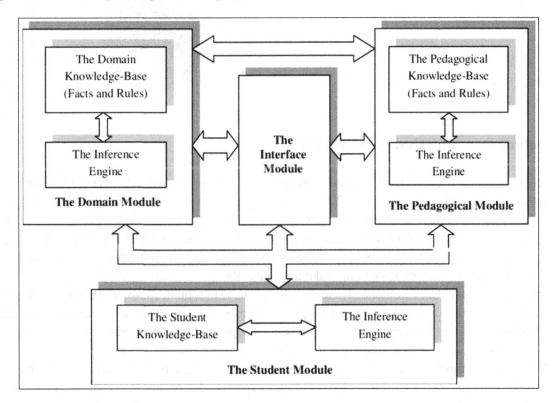

Figure 6. Deliverable outcome of intelligent tutoring system

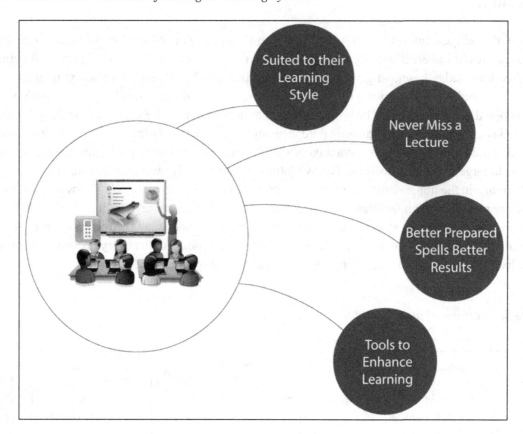

Robotics, Sensors, Computer Vision

The control of robotic agents has been an important motivating subject in artificial intelligence research since the early days of KRR (Sridharan, 2015). AI-based robot are sequences of control to accomplish a specific objective. A robust robot must have the ability to reasons about actions in which order to be done and how to execute them. In the recent years, a several research teams working on the design of robots which work on a regular basis for managing tasks such as the apartment cleaning, the preparation of salads, popcorn, pancakes, cloths folding and many more. Recently, the advancement in robots physical capabilities have taken huge progress. Therefore, there is need to rethink about the aspect of representation and reasoning of knowledge in the representing and reasoning of actions in the complex situation. It can also consider the learning problem which is often separated from the update of values, since the information is learned or modified may be more abstracted or dynamic over a longer period of time.

Actions reasoning: Robot agents are not able to carry out ambiguous tasks such as 'pick-up bottle' 'settle table' and 'arrange the meal' except a detailed expertise. Therefore, to investigate and establish methods of knowledge processing with a vague mission, there is need to supply the necessary information in a suitable manner with the appropriate resources (Tenorth, 2012). If robots are to be so professional, then their reasoning cannot stop to perform action like finding an item. For simple task like pick-up a glass, the robot must determine where to stand, which hands to use, how to reached their, which kind of grasping is needed, how many fingers is needed, how much force is needed to pick up. These choices are context-specific and task-conditional. How a bottle can be grasped depends on whether it is loaded or empty. If the processing of knowledge does not understand these aspects of robot operation, then there is a great effect on robot efficiency.

Uncertainty: The robot is facing three key issues to accomplish their task such as household operations: a mixed-constantly discrete state region of infinite aspects, significant uncertainty about current situation, and the consequences of intervention & long-range planning horizons (Amiri, 2020). For example, a robot must have to find some combination of possibilities to find jam bottle in the rear of a refrigerator. The robot requirements demonstrate its confidence based on the present state of the refrigerator, like what objects are supposed to take place and where they can arise. All these acts eventually occur in real continuous space and should be chosen depend on the present belief state of the robot.

Advancement in Healthcare Sector

In several fields, continuous and comprehensive data analyses can contribute to new insights. For instance, medical profile analysis illustrates the safety and effectiveness of medicinal products that are beyond the potential of costly clinical studies (De Brouwer, 2018). The site PatientsLikeMe (Frost, 2011) has been able to arrange a self-reported drug study for patients with amyotrophic lateral sclerosis (ALS). To add details and to match patients to clinical trials automatically, KRR is one of the prime needs. It is also able to tackle the complexities of individual medicine by deploying knowledge representation and reasoning by establish personal care strategies, classify people with related rare diseases, exploit test results, literature and common practice. The team at IBM Watson is already heading in this way.

Biomedical and Pharmaceutical Research

Progress in biomedical and pharmaceutical research is dependent on previous knowledge and requires simple and efficient access to information hidden in science journals and partially noted small and wide data sets (Woods, 2007). Currently, a considerable effort is required to curate articles in order to provide an idea of the component functionality. Modern scientific data management is focused on ontology to construct machine-understandable representations of information and is an important part of generating usable data for question answering and analysis. There are numerous opportunities and obstacles for biomedical and pharmaceutical research and exploration, with hundreds of ontologies currently available for semantic annotations and for formal representation. Enrichment analysis is the most well-known application of ontology in biomedical science (Hoehndorf, 2016). The purpose of enrichment analysis is to identify a collection of attributes that are substantially improved in a target set and also share that attribute over some backgrounds. While new research requires the plenty of ontologies to automatically add text-based explanations such as scientific papers, researchers reveal new connections between unlinked entities. But such studies are relatively easy to carry out. A major difficulty is that these comparisons must be balanced with previous information and a website of data includes large empirical statements, experimental data results from particular methodologies with experimental findings. Further analysis needs to be geared towards gathering of evidence to provide plausibility, trust and interpretation.

Question Answering

Question answering system is a system that answer questions about the collection of documents, mostly in natural languages and where text is included in the documents and other types of information such as videos and websites. Question answers are useful in a number of areas, including knowledge analyzes, answers in medical transcripts, answers to research literature queries, the discovery of answers in previous legislation cases and replies to patent databases (Khashabi, 2018). At the top, answering a question requires the interpretation and formulation of questions, text understanding and other details. In each of these steps, the representation and reasoning of knowledge plays an important role (Clark, 2018). In the construction of questioning schemes, there is also a substantial possibility for KRR. Questions and texts are primarily concerned with interpreting natural language. Constructing natural language systems include translating the text into KRR formalism, raising it through different types of knowledge including common sense, domain and linguistic knowledge and reasoning with them in order to create subsets of answers which used to generate answers. When answering questions, direct database operations, such as joins are appropriate for some types of questions. Researchers have made such formalizations such as forecast responses, definitions, diagnostics and counter factual questions with regard to the basic fields of operation in certain contexts. Far more must be achieved. In a biological area, knowledge includes compound of (a) ontological information of elements, characteristics, classes and sub-classes (b) when it may occur and their influence. "Why" "How" and "What- If " issues remain difficult in this domain.

Understanding Spatial and Spatio-Temporal Data

A huge amount of spatial knowledge comes from cameras and others devices, such as GPS transceivers in mobile users. Many applications demand or can be usefully extended from monitoring mobile assistance and environmental surveillance to a sophisticated understanding of such data. The use of qualitative spatial representations not only relieves the size and noise of such data, but also allows integration of various types of spatial information (Atluri, 2018). Computer vision's interpretation of visual data has been a challenge for many decades and, while a lot of progress has been made on approaches that seek to understand such data using ongoing/numeric methods, interest has only begun in trying to eliminate high-level symbolic depictions from video data. Due to the existence of noise in visual data (for example by adjusting lighting), symbolic observations are extremely difficult to extract (Faghmous, 2014). The difficulty is made even tough by the amount of data, whether "out of the web" or in-real life; but on the other way the huge volume of data often mitigates the problems because redundancy is also present. In addition to this, the method of mitigation can be created by understanding how the environment and how events evolve so that data can be interpreted, noise can be corrected, and contradictory data can be combined and fused. This brings a challenge to the source of such context information, especially whether it must be manually defined or it can be acquired by data mining or machine learning approaches.

CONCLUSION

Human beings are good at understanding, reasoning and interpreting of knowledge and based on that they performed different tasks in the real world. Representing and reasoning of real-world information for a machine to learn, and then use it to address complex real-life issues is a strenuous one. The prior study of knowledge representation demonstrates how an intelligent agent can communicate his views, intentions and conclusions for automated reasoning. This book chapter has discussed about the key factor of knowledge representation and reasoning, analyzed the major challenges, and new opportunities where novel knowledge representation and reasoning research has major impact. In future, there is a need to design novel knowledge representation technique that will incorporate innovative and intelligent knowledge retrieval properties into the knowledge reasoning system.

C

ACKNOWLEDGMENT

The authors would like to express gratitude to the Department of Computer Science and Engineering and Centre for Natural Language Processing, National Institute of Technology Silchar, India for providing infrastructural facilities and support.

REFERENCES

Ackerman, P. L. (2005). Knowledge and intelligence. In Handbook of understanding and measuring intelligence (pp. 125-139). Sage. doi:10.4135/9781452233529.n8

Almasri, A. N. (2019). *Intelligent tutoring systems survey for the period 2000-2018*. IJARW.

Amini, B., Ibrahim, R., Othman, M. S., & Selamat, A. (2014). Capturing scholar's knowledge from heterogeneous resources for profiling in recommender systems. *Expert Systems with Applications*, *41*(17), 7945–7957. doi:10.1016/j.eswa.2014.06.039

Amiri, S., Shokrolah Shirazi, M., & Zhang, S. (2020). Learning and reasoning for robot sequential decision making under uncertainty. *Proceedings of the AAAI Conference on Artificial Intelligence*, *34*(03), 2726–2733. doi:10.1609/aaai.v34i03.5659

Atluri, G., Karpatne, A., & Kumar, V. (2018). Spatio-temporal data mining: A survey of problems and methods. *ACM Computing Surveys*, *51*(4), 1–41. doi:10.1145/3161602

Baker, R. S. (2006). Adapting to when students game an intelligent tutoring system. In *International conference on intelligent tutoring systems* (pp. 392-401). Springer.

Baral, C. a. (2015). Knowledge representation and reasoning: What's hot. *Twenty-Ninth AAAI Conference on Artificial Intelligence*.

Bizer, C. L. (2011). Linked data: The story so far. In *Semantic services, interoperability and web applications: emerging concepts* (pp. 205–227). IGI Global. doi:10.4018/978-1-60960-593-3.ch008

Bottou, L. (2014). From machine learning to machine reasoning. *Machine Learning*, *94*(2), 133–149. doi:10.100710994-013-5335-x

Clark, P. a. (2018). *Think you have solved question answering? try arc, the ai2 reasoning challenge*. arXiv preprint arXiv:1803.05457.

Couper, M. P. (2017). New developments in survey data collection. *Annual Review of Sociology*, *43*, 121–145.

Davis, E., & Marcus, G. (2015). Commonsense reasoning and commonsense knowledge in artificial intelligence. *Communications of the ACM*, *58*(9), 92–103. doi:10.1145/2701413

De Brouwer, M., Ongenae, F., Bonte, P., & De Turck, F. (2018). Towards a cascading reasoning framework to support responsive ambient-intelligent healthcare interventions. *Sensors (Basel)*, *18*(10), 3514. doi:10.339018103514 PMID:30340363

Faghmous, J. H. (2014). Spatio-temporal data mining for climate data: Advances, challenges, and opportunities. *Data mining and knowledge discovery for big data*, 83-116.

Frost, J., Okun, S., Vaughan, T., Heywood, J., & Wicks, P. (2011). Patient-reported outcomes as a source of evidence in off-label prescribing: Analysis of data from PatientsLikeMe. *Journal of Medical Internet Research*, *13*(1), e6. doi:10.2196/jmir.1643 PMID:21252034

Haghighi, A. O. (2012). A robust shallow temporal reasoning system. In *Proceedings of the Demonstration Session at the Conference of the North American Chapter of the Association for Computational Linguistics: Human Language Technologies* (pp. 29-32). Academic Press.

Hoehndorf, R. a. (2016). Large-scale reasoning over functions in biomedical ontologies. *Formal Ontology in Information Systems*, 299-312.

Johnny, O., & Trovati, M. (2020). Big data inconsistencies and incompleteness: A literature review. *International Journal of Grid and Utility Computing*, *11*(5), 705–713. doi:10.1504/IJGUC.2020.110057

Khashabi, D. a. (2018). Question answering as global reasoning over semantic abstractions. *Proceedings of the AAAI Conference on Artificial Intelligence*, 32. 10.1609/aaai.v32i1.11574

Machery, E. (2010). The heterogeneity of knowledge representation and the elimination of concept. In *Behavioral and brain sciences* (Vol. 33). Cambridge University Press. doi:10.1017/S0140525X10000932

Malhotra, M., & Nair, T. R. G. (2015). Evolution of knowledge representation and retrieval techniques. *International Journal of Intelligent Systems and Applications*, *7*(7), 1–18. doi:10.5815/ijisa.2015.07.03

Melis, E. a. (2004). Activemath: An intelligent tutoring system for mathematics. In *International Conference on Artificial Intelligence and Soft Computing* (pp. 91-101). Springer. 10.1007/978-3-540-24844-6_12

Noy, N. a. (2013). *Research Challenges and Opportunities in Knowledge Representation*. Academic Press.

Ozsu, M. T. (2016). A survey of RDF data management systems. *Frontiers of Computer Science*, *10*(3), 418–432. doi:10.100711704-016-5554-y

Sandberg, A. (2013). Feasibility of whole brain emulation. In *Philosophy and theory of artificial intelligence* (pp. 251–264). Springer. doi:10.1007/978-3-642-31674-6_19

Sridharan, M. a. (2015). *A refinement-based architecture for knowledge representation and reasoning in robotics*. arXiv preprint arXiv:1508.03891.

Strohmaier, M., & Kröll, M. (2012). Acquiring knowledge about human goals from search query logs. *Information Processing & Management*, *48*(1), 63–82. doi:10.1016/j.ipm.2011.03.010

Tenorth, M. a. (2012). A unified representation for reasoning about robot actions, processes, and their effects on objects. In *IEEE/RSJ International Conference on Intelligent Robots and Systems* (pp. 1351-1358). IEEE. 10.1109/IROS.2012.6385529

Woods, N. N. (2007). Science is fundamental: The role of biomedical knowledge in clinical reasoning. *Medical Education*, *41*(7), 1173–1177. doi:10.1111/j.1365-2923.2007.02911.x PMID:18045369

Zhang, C. a. (2020). Read, Attend, and Exclude: Multi-Choice Reading Comprehension by Mimicking Human Reasoning Process. *Proceedings of the 43rd International ACM SIGIR Conference on Research and Development in Information Retrieval*, 1945-1948. 10.1145/3397271.3401326

ADDITIONAL READING

Bettini, C., Brdiczka, O., Henricksen, K., Indulska, J., Nicklas, D., Ranganathan, A., & Riboni, D. (2010). A survey of context modelling and reasoning techniques. *Pervasive and Mobile Computing*, *6*(2), 161–180. doi:10.1016/j.pmcj.2009.06.002

Blasch, E. a. (2006). Issues and challenges of knowledge representation and reasoning methods in situation assessment (Level 2 Fusion). In *Signal Processing, Sensor Fusion, and Target Recognition XV*. International Society for Optics and Photonics. doi:10.1117/12.669779

Bouquet, P., Ghidini, C., Giunchiglia, F., & Blanzieri, E. (2003). Theories and uses of context in knowledge representation and reasoning. *Journal of Pragmatics*, *35*(3), 455–484. doi:10.1016/S0378-2166(02)00145-5

Gottlob, G., Pichler, R., & Wei, F. (2010). Bounded treewidth as a key to tractability of knowledge representation and reasoning. *Artificial Intelligence*, *174*(1), 105–132. doi:10.1016/j.artint.2009.10.003

Haarslev, V., Hidde, K., Möller, R., & Wessel, M. (2012). The RacerPro knowledge representation and reasoning system. *Semantic Web*, *3*(3), 267–277. doi:10.3233/SW-2011-0032

Hotz, L. a. (2014). *Configuration knowledge representation and reasoning*. Morgan Kaufmann. doi:10.1016/B978-0-12-415817-7.00006-2

Lakemeyer, G. a. (1994). *Foundations of knowledge representation and reasoning*. Springer. doi:10.1007/3-540-58107-3

Liu, H.-C. H.-Y., Xu, D.-H., Duan, C.-Y., & Xiong, Y. (2019). Pythagorean fuzzy Petri nets for knowledge representation and reasoning in large group context. *IEEE Transactions on Systems, Man, and Cybernetics. Systems*, *51*(8), 5261–5271. doi:10.1109/TSMC.2019.2949342

Noy, N. a. (2013). *Research Challenges and Opportunities in Knowledge Representation*. Academic Press.

Ozsu, M. T. (2016). A survey of RDF data management systems. *Frontiers of Computer Science*, *10*(3), 418–432. doi:10.100711704-016-5554-y

Perttunen, M. a. (2009). Context representation and reasoning in pervasive computing: A review. *International Journal of Multimedia and Ubiquitous Engineering*, *4*(4), 1–28.

KEY TERMS AND DEFINITIONS

Knowledge: The fact or condition of knowing something with familiarity gained through experience or association.

Knowledge Representation and Reasoning: It's a process to encode human knowledge into a symbolic language so that it can be used by the information systems.

Heterogeneity: A sample or population where each members have different characteristics.

Inadequacy: A condition of being not enough or not good enough.

Irrationality: Irrationality is cognition, thinking, talking, or acting without inclusion of rationality.

Uncertainty: Uncertainty refers to epistemic situations involving imperfect or unknown information.

Section 39
Nature–Inspired Algorithms

Spatial Audio Coding and Machine Learning

S

Karim Dabbabi

Faculty of Sciences of Tunis, Research Unit of Analysis and Processing of Electrical and Energetic Systems, University of Tunis El Manar, Tunis, Tunisia

INTRODUCTION

The development and improvement of spatial sound rendering techniques is the result of the advent of consumer mixed reality products, which are becoming addressed to a large user base. In this regard, acoustics processing and modeling in the field of audio analysis has found rapid inception and adoption using many machine and deep learning methods to meet the domain-specific requirements of acoustic research. This requires new approaches and architectures to be adapted. Such methods were inspired from image processing and adapted to audio processing, such as adversarial approaches and 2D convolutional operators.

In fact, the challenges posed by the processing of acoustic signals are numerous which are linked on the one hand to their nature and their representations as well as to the nature of the anisotropy of their time-frequency representations with the short-term Fourier transform, and on the other hand to the multi-scale nature of musical events as well as to the effect of psychoacoustics. Spatial audio also has its specific complexity that influences detection performance for humans and machines (Zieliński, Lee, Antoniuk, & Dadan, 2020). It is mainly devoted to the localization of sound ensemble around, in front of or behind a listener. On the Internet, human objects took on the role of remote testing, but their accuracy was low (Gabrielli, Fazekas, & Nam, 2021). In contrast, very high classification results have been obtained in tests with deep learning methods under unknown conditions (Gabrielli, Fazekas, & Nam, 2021).

In this chapter, spatial audio coding standards will be discussed with the aim of presenting the importance of their applicability and showing their strengths and weaknesses Among these standards, a focus will be made on spatial audio coding techniques (SAC), followed by a brief passage on the psychoacoustic principle of spatial sound, then the historical reception of multichannel audio will be presented by listing the main approaches. After that, the suggested SAC techniques will exposed. The way to improve the quality accuracy for the reconstructed audio, and the evaluation of the quality of the reconstructed audio signal will be given successively at the end of this first section. MPEG standards for encoding multi-channel audio signal, such as MPEG Surround, MPEG Spatial Audio Object Encoding, and MPEG-H 3D Audio Encoding, will be introduced in the second section. The applications of machine learning (ML) in acoustics and their exploration for spatial sound scenes will then be successively integrated and analyzed. At the end, other research directions in spatial audio and machine learning (ML) are suggested and analyzed.

DOI: 10.4018/978-1-7998-9220-5.ch149

BACKGROUND

Nowadays, many technological inventions have been made and integrated into the market, such as three-dimensional (3D) audio technology, also called spatial audio (Rumsey, F., 2001). The latter has many application areas, such as digital audio entertainment media like ultrahigh definition television (UHDTV), many other generations of television broadcasting, etc. As for the UHDTV standard, up to 20 multiple speakers have been explored to provide realistic 3D audio perception to users. Thus, a single audio channel feeds each speaker; therefore, multi-channel audio signals will be requested. Some broadcasting companies which have continuously adopted these audio chain technologies in recording, transmission and production include the BBC, UK and NHK, Japan.

In audio spatial, the active component that plays a major role is perceptual audio coding (Pan, D., 1995; Painter, T., & Spanias, A., 2000; Bosi, M., & Goldberg, R. E., 2002; Brandenburg, Faller, Herre, Johnston, & Kleijn, 2014).

The latter has been developed in such a way that it can compress the size of audio data incredibly so that the properties of the audio signal that would not be detected by our hearing system simply have to be removed. This task is carried out on the basis of knowledge about psychoacoustics. Indeed, the emergence of perceptual audio coding refers to the 1990s, when the first and well-known MPEG-1 layer 3 digital audio compression standard, known as MP3, was explored. In fact, spatial audio coding (SAC) (Herre, Faller, Disch, Ertel, Hilpert, Hoelzer, Linzmeier, Spenger, & Kroon,2004; Herre, J., 2004). is one of many other audio coding techniques that have been invented and standardized to accurately model multi-channel audio signals. The goal behind the use of spatial audio coding is not only limited to increasing the compression rate over advanced multi-channel audio coding methods but is being extended to provide more opportunities to be applied in other systems, such as the legacy broadcasting system. Surround MPEG is considered a well-used SAC standard, which has aroused the interest of researchers due to its rich functionalities, such as artistic stereo mixing and binaural rendering. In addition, an option was provided for users to interact and update the audio scene composition and spatial characteristics of the rendered surround sound by integrating object-based audio.

This makes it more interesting audio rendering system. There are many applications that are keen to apply technology based on objects, such as musical reconstruction, games, teleconferencing, sports broadcasting, karaoke system and improving dialogue (Oldfield, Shirley, & Spille, 2014; Oldfield, Shirley & Satongar, 2015; Jot, Smith & Thompson, 2015; Bleidt, Borsum, Fuchs, & Weiss, 2015).

FOCUS OF THE ARTICLE

Standards of Spatial Audio Coding

Spatial Audio Coding (SAC) is more its primary consideration as not being a pure compression method, it is counted as an approach to represent multi-channel audio signals by a lower number of channels (i.e., a (mono) or two (stereo)) with preservation of the spatial properties of the audio signals. Typically, the process responsible for reducing the number of channels is called down-mixing, as shown in Figure 1. For transmission and storage tasks, the encoding of the down-mix signals should be done using compression techniques, such as Universal Speech and Audio Coding (USAC) (Quackenbush, S., & Lefebvre, R.,,2011; ISO/IEC,2012;Neuendorf, Multrus, Rettelbach, Fuchs, Robilliard, Lecomte, & Grill,2013;Oh, E., & Kim, M., 2011)., MPEG 1 layer 3, and Advanced Audio Coding (AAC) (Bosi, Brandenburg, Quackenbush,

Fielder, Akagiri, Fuchs, Dietz, Herre, Davidson, & Oikawa,1997; Brandenburg, K., & Bosi, M.,1997; Chon, Choi, Moon, & Seo, 2005;Herre, Faller, Ertel, Hilpert, Hoelzer, & Spenger, 2004). As for the spatial parameters, they are considered as secondary information. This helps to reconstruct multichannel audio signals when needed, by expanding the down-mix signal according to the orientation of the spatial parameters. However, there is regularly no need to reconstruct multichannel audio signals, especially if the user equipment can only consider down-mix audio rendering where spatial parameters can simply be eliminated. The possibility of reducing the number of audio channels is the main advantage of this technique, which allows the use of fewer audio signals for compression. This is especially important in relation to the conventional multichannel audio coding process where each channel had to be coded separately. Therefore, it allows the representation of the audio data to be carried out on a lower number of bits and the reproduction of the channel configuration to be performed differently from the original multi-channel format. Among the main advantages of spatial audio coding is its subnormal similarity which leads to a progressive update of the recent mono and stereo audio broadcasting systems by including a multichannel audio content.

In fact, there are many approaches that have been proposed for efficiently encoding multichannel audio signals on the basis of spatial audio encoding (SAC). All methods are generally relying on the extracted spatial parameters and they can be divided into two groups: channel-based relationship approaches and those based on virtual source position. For the first group, it is based on the relationship between audio channels to represent the spatial characteristics of the audio scene and relies on the coherences and differences in time and level between several channels or between two of them only for the extraction of the spatial parameters. Thus, the channel relationships remain the same as the original when multichannel audio signals are created. In addition, this group includes MP3 Surround (Grill, Hellmuth, Hilpert, Herre, & Plogsties, 2006; ISO/IEC,2006; ISO/IEC, 2009)., Parametric Stereo (PS) (Breebaart, van de Par, Kohlrausch, & Schuijers, 2005; Schuijers, Breebaart, Purnhagen, & Engdegard, 2004; Schuijers, Oomen, den Brinker, & Breebaart,2003). and Binaural Cue Coding (BCC) (Baumgarte, F., & Faller; 2002; Baumgarte, F., & Faller,2003; Faller, C., & Baumgarte, F.,2003). With regard to the second group; the audio scene is associated with a virtual audio source by the approaches it contains. As for the representation of the position of the virtual audio source, it is performed by a direction vector where its determination can be effectuated from any configuration of multichannel audio signals. Among the SAC approaches that are involved in the second group, the author can mention Directional Audio Coding (DAC) (Goodwin, M. M., & Jot, J.-M.,2008;31 Pulkki, V., & Faller, C., 2006; Pulkki, V.,2006;Pulkki,V., & Karjalainen, M., 2008;Vilkamo, Lokki, & Pulkki,2009) and Spatial Audio Scene Coding (SASC) (Goodwin, M. M., & Jot, J.-M., 2006; Goodwin, M. M., & Jot, J.-M., 2006; Jot, Merimaa, Goodwin, & Laroche, 2007; Goodwin, M. M., Jot, J.-M.,2007; Goodwin, M. M., Jot, J.-M.,2007; Goodwin, M. M., & Jot, J.-M.,2007). Moreover, Vector Based Amplitude Panning (VBAP) has been applied for the purpose of reproducing multichannel audio signals by replicating the sound field from virtual sources located in the coordinates provided by the direction vector.

Psycho-Acoustic of Spatial Sound

In early approaches to audio coding, the phenomenon on the human auditory system was widely explored, such as the silent and temporal / frequency masking threshold. However, SAC techniques in particular require more cues from human hearing ability to discern the spatial specification of the sound wave. In fact, the human brain has the ability to detect inter-auditory time and level differences of a sound wave delivered by a sound source position under its two ears, which then explored to form a perception on the location of the sound source. By exploring these major clues, human can locate the position of an incoming sound source even if he cannot see more clues like head movement which must be taken into account in a more complicated situation.

Figure 1.

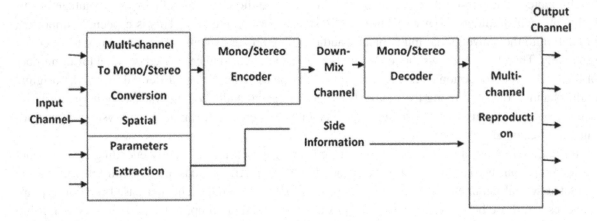

History of Perception

Based on the terminology that multichannel audio typically includes stereo (two channels), the SAC technique therefore begins to emerge with the integration of parametric based encoding of stereo audio signals, such as Mid-Side stereo encoding (MS) and Intensity Stereo (IS), offering a more precise Stereo Parametric (PS) approach that was subsequently approved as an MPEG standard.

For stereo audio signals, they can be analyzed using a parametric stereo approach to calculate the following stereo parameters: Inter-channel Coherence (ICC), Inter-channel Intensity Difference (IID) and Inter-channel Phase Difference (IPD), which are basically calculated on the basis of the inter-auditory time difference of the human hearing system (Pulkki, V., & Hirvonen, T., 2005). After that, the stereo audio signals were down-mixed and later encoded by AAC standard. To expand the approach to a larger number of audio channels, an attempt has been made by offering MP3 Surround and Binaural Cue Coding (BCC). Indeed, BCC seems to be more common where different audio encoders can be explored to compress down-mix audio signals, whereas MP3 Surround is precisely destined to extend the practice of the MP3 encoder; as an extensively used codec, to multi-channel audio configuration.

Suggested SAC Techniques

There are many encoding methods that have been suggested with different spatial parameters such as Spatial Audio Scene Coding (UPS) that performs the extraction of direction vector as spatial parameter for a three-dimensional representation of spatial sound. As for audio reproduction, in order to reproduce sound field from virtual sources situated in positions that provided by the direction vector, Vector Based Amplitude Panning (VBAP) is used. Directional Audio Coding (DAC) is further a suggested approach to explore the directional vector as spatial parameters although it contains the technology of a microphone array (Blauert, J, 2001; S-Amling, Kuech, Kallinger, Galdo, Ahonen, & Pulkki, 2008; Kuech, Kallinger, S-Amling, del Galdo, Ahonen, & Pulkki, 2008; Kallinger, M., Kuech, F.,S-Amling, del Galdo, Ahonen,

S

& Pulkki, 2008). to process audio recording and production. Diffuseness is additionally transmitted as a parameter representing the ambient sound specifications. Also, another approach has been proposed to compress multi-channel audio signals by taking advantage of the panning technique (Ahonen, Pulkki, Kuech, Kallinger & Schultz-Amling, 2008; Cheng, Ritz, & Burnett, 2006; Cheng, Ritz, & Burnett, 2007; Cheng, Ritz, & Burnett, 2008; Cheng, Cheng, Ritz, & Burnett, 2008). This approach makes it possible to reduce a sound field of 360 degrees to a smaller number (e.g., 60 degrees). Basically, it does not require spatial parameters, in particular for low bit rates operation. On the contrary, the location of audio sources can cause ambiguity when the reverse panning technique is explored to produce multi-channel audio signals.

Ameliorating Reconstructed Audio Accuracy

The introduction of the Closed-loop SAC method [(Elfitri, I., & Kurnia, 2014; Elfitri, I., Kurnia, R., & Harneldi, D., 2014; Elfitri, I., Muharam, M., & Shobirin, 2014; Elfitri, I., H. D., & Laksono, A., 2015; Elfitri, I., & Luthfi, A.,2015). was intended to improve the accuracy of the rendered audio signals and to further improve the performance of any SAC method by reducing the error and distortion generated by the procedures of encoding and quantization. It is mainly considered as a minimization method applied to the front of the SAC technique. Various approaches have been also suggested which comprise balanced-delay filter bank to support this closed-loop configuration.

In many applications, Analysis by Synthesis (Abs) concept (Elfitri, Shi, & Kondoz, 2014; Elfitri, Gunel, & Kondoz,2011; Günther, G., 2002; Yang, Jia, Bao, & Wang,2015). has been extensively applied and used in this technique to carry out a trial-and-error procedure to enhance the quality of the reconstructed audio signals. Despite the fact that Abs was carried out at the front of the perception-based system, however, improved perception quality has been reported, although waveform-based error criteria were explored to compare the original audio signals and those reproduced.

Quality Assessment of Reproduced Audio Signal

To assess the quality of the reconstructed audio signal, a subjective audio test is generally considered as the only valid approach (ITU-R, 1997; ITU-R,2014;ITU-R,2015;ITU-R,2001;ITU-R,2003;ITU-R,2014;ITU-R,2015;Cheng,Ritz,& Burnett, 2007). This refers to the fact that the objective test such as signal-to-noise ratio cannot detect artifacts (Liu, Hsu, & Lee, 2008). inserted into the perceptual audio coding. Nevertheless, objective perception-based testing such as Perceptual Evaluation of Audio Quality (PEAQ) is advisable as a secondary evaluation for perceptual audio coding. As the assessment in real time systems is not possible, objective perception-based testing has to be further developed, particularly for multi-channel audio reproduction.

MPEG Standard for Encoding Multi-Channel Audio Signals

Three international standards for encoding multi-channel audio signals will be presented in this section: MPEG Surround [(ITU-R, 2001;Breebaart, Herre, Faller, Roden, Myburg, Disch, Purnhagen, Neusinger, Kjorling, & Oomen, 2005; Breebaart, Hotho, Koppens, Schuijers, Oomen, & de Par, 2007;Herre, Purnhagen, Breebaart, Faller, Disch, Kjorling, Schuijers, Hilpert, & Myburg, 2005;Herre, Kjörling, Breebaart, Faller, Disch, Purnhagen, & Chong,2008;81 Hilpert, J., & Disch, S.,2009; ISO/IEC, 2007;Samsudin, Kurniawati, & George, 2014; Tournery, Faller, Kuech, & Herre, 2010)., MPEG-H 3D (Herre, Hilpert,

Kuntz, & Plogsties,2015). and MPEG SAOC (Breebaart, Engdegård, Falch, Hellmuth, Hilpert, Hoelzer, & Terentiev, 2008; Terentiev, Falch, Hellmuth, Hilpert, Oomen, Engdegard, & Mundt, 2009). Table 1 shows the key technologies explored in many MPEG standards, where generally MPEG Surround explores the channel-based system, MPEG SAOC uses an object-based system, and MPEG-H 3D Audio Coding exploits three-dimensional audio reproduction technology. Additionally, hybridization of the decorrelator and the filter bank (Engdegard, Purnhagen, Roden, & Liljeryd, 2004; Chen, Hsiao, Hsu, & Liu, 2010). has been explored in MPEG standards. Indeed, the bank-filter is practical for the decomposition of the audio signal and its processing in the critical band, like our hearing system. Using hybrid system, a sub-band signal can be provided with different frequency resolution. On the other hand, the correlator may lead to improve the spatial effects of the reproduced audio signals, especially for low bit rate implementation.

Table 1. Summary of key technologies explored in MPEG spatial audio standards

No	Standard	Reproduction Mode	Key Features	Main Applications
1	MPEG Surround	Channel-based audio	Binaural rendering Artistic stereo down-mix	Audio broadcasting Teleconference
2	MPEG SAOC	Object-based audio	MPEG Surround transcoder	Music recomposition Gaming, Karaoke
3	MPEG-H 3D Audio	3D audio	Higher order ambiosonic	Ultra HDTV

MPEG Surround

The MPEG Surround standard was introduced in 1990 and is considered the first international standard benefiting from the spatial audio coding concept. The representation of multi-channel audio signals has been constructed as mono, stereo or 5.1 down-mix signals despite the fact that the exploration of the stereo down-mix is mainly reported. For spatial parameters based on perception, it is composed of the Channel Prediction Coefficient (CPC), Channel Level Differences (CLD) and Inter-Channel Coherence (ICC), which are explored.

When high bit rate operation is allowed, the generation of the residual signal and its inclusion in the bit-steam spatial parameter to compensate for the error caused by the down-mix and up-mix processes allowing the waveform reconstruction of audio signals. Otherwise, a synthetic residual signal is produced by the decorrelator which is included in the MPEG Surround decoder, therefore more spatial parameters can be offered in the reproduced audio signals. In fact, MPEG Surround can be accordant to any legacy audio codec since it is an SAC-based standard. Moreover, it hybridizes very well with High Efficiency AAC (HE-AAC) (Wolters, Kjorling, Homm & Purnhagen, 2003; Herre, J., & Dietz, M., 2008). because the latter and MPEG Surround explore the same bank-filter to carry out the time-frequency decomposition of audio signals.

At very low bit rates such as 64 and 96 kb/s (Mason, Marston, Kozamernik, & Stoll, 2007; Marston, Kozamernik, Stoll, & Spikofski, 2009)., formal subjective tests have demonstrated that high quality audio reproduction was achieved, but performance was significantly improved when operating at higher bit rates up to 256 kb/s as concluded in (Roden, Breebart, Hilpert, & Purnhagen, 2007). In addition, binaural rendering can be supported by MPEG Surround in terms of functionality, where multi-channel audio reproduction can be enjoyed by users through their headphones. To preserve existing customers who only have a stereo decoder instead of the multi-channel one and capture the best stereo content, the MPEG Surround encoder can also produce artistic stereo down-mix signals.

MPEG Spatial Audio Object Encoding

With the concept of object-based audio (Herre, J., & Disch, S., 2008; Herre, J. & Terentiv, L., 2011; Gorlow, Habets, & Marchand, 2013; Fug, Holzer, Borb, Ertel, Kratschmer, & Plogsties, 2014)., a new method of multi-channel audio reproduction has been introduced. It was fundamentally not similar to conventional channel-based audio where customers were offered the option to interact with the multi-channel reproduction system in order to update the reconstructed audio composition (AS shown in Figure 2). For example, customers can adjust the anchor volume only in news broadcasting; however, other background sounds are kept as they are. This feature gives music composers the ability to vary the existing musical composition according to their preferences. Furthermore, it provides the facility to update the spatial effects of the reproduced sound relating to the video display for game players and movie viewers. To apply this method, the encoder side requires the capture of each audio object, which is hoped to be done to perform the adjustment on the decoder side. Moreover, metadata and object parameters are such object audio source positions, where their generation and transmission have to be done to the decoder. The metadata and these parameters should provide the opportunity to be used to reproduce multi-channel audio signals without requiring any assistance from the users on the decoder side.

The development of the MPEG SAOC standard is carried out using the foundation of object-based audio reproduction. To reproduce multi-channel audio reproduction, MPEG SAOC exploits MPEG Surround decoder by offering conversion from metadata and object parameters to channel-based spatial parameters. In fact, some methods have been suggested to ameliorate the performance and usability of MPEG SAOC.

The combination of MPEG SAOC with DirAC in (Herre, Falch, Mahne, Galdo, del Kallinger, & Thiergart, 2012). was done for the purpose of providing a spatial teleconferencing system; however the integration of its two-step encoding structure (Kim, Seo, Beack, Kang, & Hahn, 2011) was for improving the performance of each rendered audio object. As shown in (Park, Kim & Hahn, 2013; Park, Kim & Hahn, 2011), the transmission of harmonic information to the decoder side can be also performed in order to improve the vocal removal efficiency of MPEG SAOC on a music re-composition application.

Figure 2.

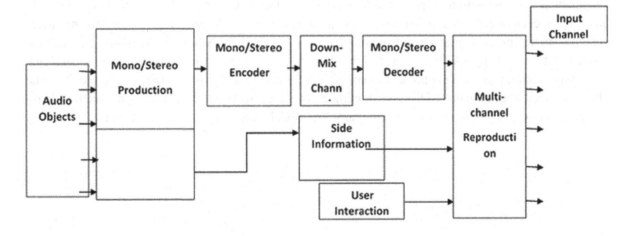

MPEG-H 3D Audio Encoding

To support more audio reproduction systems (such as 10.2 (Kim, Lee, & Pulkki, 2010). and 22.2 (Hamasaki, Nishiguchi, Okumura, & Nakayama,2007; Sugimoto, Nakayama, & Oode,2014; Ando, Hamasaki, Imai, Iwaki, Kitajima, Nakayama, & Sugimoto, 2007; Matsui, K., & Ando, A.,2013; Hamasaki, K.,2011). audio systems) in addition to a larger number of loudspeakers during the application of wav field synthesis (WFS) approach (Berkhout, Vries, & Vogel, 1993; Theile, G., 2004)., MPEG-H 3D audio encoding was introduced as a new MPEG standard. This therefore offered the opportunity to achieve true three-dimensional (3D) audio reproduction. On the one hand, the exploration of a greater number of loudspeaker setup is particular because it is destined to reproduce sound field that is higher than the position of the listener via the elevated loudspeakers. On the other hand, the WFS approach has attracted a lot of attention because it allows the reconstruction of a realistic audio wave-front by using a large number of loudspeakers. Moreover, the reproduction of any audio format can be sent from the encoder side to different loudspeaker configurations.

For encoding down-mix signals, the Unified Audio Speech Coding Standard (USAC) has been recommended to strengthen the coding of audio and speech signals. In fact, tests have shown satisfactory 3D audio perception when testing the MPEG 3D standard at very high bit rates such as 512 and 1200 kbps.

SOLUTIONS AND RECOMMENDATIONS

Application of Machine Learning (ML) in Acoustics

Biology, communications, marine and earth sciences represent the main range of applications from which acoustic data can be provided from scientific and engineering insights. There are many recent advances in machine learning (ML) and their transformative potential in the field of acoustics, including deep learning. Indeed, ML is a large family of techniques that are primarily rely on statistics, automatic detection, and the use of patterns in data. Also, it is considered data driven compared to signal processing and conventional acoustics.

Complex relationships can be offered by ML between labels and features, between features and actions, or between features themselves. In the big training data scenario, ML can find models modeling sophisticate acoustic phenomena such as reverberation and human speech. In acoustics, ML is experiencing rapid development with convincing results and great promise for the future.

Nevertheless, data analysis for all application domains is considered sophisticated due to many challenges such as reverberation, large data volume, data corruption, missing and sparse measurements. As instance, speech interference and source localization is considered to be a difficult task for machines due to a single utterance or an event from multiple acoustic arrivals. Although the significant progress made by ML-based approaches in acoustics in achieving superior performance over conventional signal processing techniques, these approaches have a clear limitation which is that they are data driven and therefore need huge amounts of data for training and testing. Additionally, conventional methods have the potential to be more interpretable than many ML models, especially in deep learning.

Machine Learning (ML) for Spatial Audio Scenes

Commonly used web browsers are now adopting binaural technology, which allows real-time application of spatial audio scenes (Zieliński, S. K., & Lee, H., 2019). As the number of applications exploring binaural technology continues to grow, binaural recordings constituting large repositories will still be created. Thus, many challenges related to the retrieval and semantic search of spatial audio content will be addressed. By this way, the search for binaural audio sources on the Internet for a hypothetical user of future multimedia systems can be done according to their spatial properties and not only according to their genre (sound effects, jazz, pop music, etc.).

The description of complex spatial audio scenes was performed according to Rumsey's spatial audio scene-based paradigm using perceptual attributes describing acoustic environments, sets of sources, and individual audio sources (Rumsey, F., 2002). In this look, the limitation of the majority of models is to localize individual audio sources (May, Ma, & Brown, 2015; Ma, N., & Brown, G.J., 2016; Ma, Gonzalez, & Brown,2018; Benaroya, Obin, Liuni, Roebel, Raumel, Argentieri, 2018; Lovedee-Turner, M., & Murphy, D., 2018). and ignore higher-level attributes characterizing complex spatial audio scenes.

The inspiration of early machine-listening algorithms from spatial hearing in human were described as single-source localization methods because of their abilities to locate only one source at a time (Jeffress, L.A., 1948). Multiple-source localization models have been developed more recently (May et al., 2015; Ma, N., & Brown, G.J., 2016; Ma et al., 2018; Benaroya et al., 2018)., which represented a major step towards the quantification of higher-level attributes, ultimately contributing to a holistic specification of complex spatial audio scenes. Despite the fact that these models have achieved good accuracy, their applicability is still limited due to their often reliance on prior knowledge regarding their signal characteristics and the number of sources of interest. Being developed and tested using predominately speech signals (May et al., 2015; Ma, N., & Brown, G.J., 2016; Ma et al.,2018; Benaroya, 2018)., is also itself a drawback for the multiple-source binaural localization models. Their applicability to musical recordings is therefore unknown.

In common practice, machine-listening systems are now used based on artificial intelligence-based algorithms, unlike the first models (Breebaart, van de Par, & Kohlrausch, 2001). Gaussian mixture models (GMM) (May et al., 2015). and neural networks (Ma, N., & Brown, G.J., 2016). are such approaches included in these algorithms. Additionally, deep neural networks and conventional networks represent the recent trends in machine learning and have been explored to develop binaural models (Ma, N., & Brown, G.J., 2016; Ma et al.,2018; Han, Y., Park, J., & Lee, K, 2017).

Spatial hearing in humans is governed by three types of binaural cues: Interaural coherence (IC), interaural level difference (ILD), and interaural time difference (ITD). For interaural coherence (IC), it has an impact on the apparent width of the source, whereas ILD and ITD are mainly intended to localize audio sources in the horizontal plane. Spectral cues have been explored in addition to binaural ones in an effort to assist humans locate sources in the sagittal plane and to offer aid in front-back disambiguation (Blauert, J., 1974).

The performance of binaural models can be potentially degraded due to two factors: acoustic reverberations combined with background noise and front-back confusion effect (Blauert, J., 1974). However, the localization error (May et al., 2015) can be reduced when artificially simulating head movements. A motorized dummy-head microphone, the integration of a spatial audio renderer, are necessary for such models and they are essential tools to dynamically synthesize binaural stimuli through simulated head rotation. To partially minimize the negative effect of reverberations on accuracy of binaural models, room reflections and direct sounds should be treated separately. However, breaking down audio recordings into their main and ambient components is still a difficult task (Ibrahim, K.M., & Allam, M., 2018). The remaining solutions include integrating a precedence effect model (Hummersone, C.H., Mason, R., & Brookes, T., 2010) or a multi-conditional training (May et al., 2015).

In summary, significant ameliorations have been performed over the past two decades, with respect to binaural modeling of human hearing, particularly with respect to multi-speaker localization in binaural speech signals (May et al., 2015; Ma, N., & Brown, G.J., 2016; Ma et al., 2018; Benaroya et al.,2018). However, there is no formal studies dealing with the automatic specification of complex audio scenes in binaural recordings of music according to the authors in (Zieliński, S. K., & Lee, H. 2019), apart from the work of (Zieliński, S.K., & Lee, H., 2018). summarizing the pilot experiment.

FUTURE RESEARCH DIRECTIONS

Spatial audio has the opportunity to transform the future by diving deeper into the potential of many active fields of which it proves its strong implications in the good design of products intended for example for the digital world, health and well-being, etc. In audio processing, high resolution is provided by offering enhanced personal listening experiences (i.e. phone calls, spoken words, music, video, wellness content, etc.) and hence specialists, sellers and marketers are encouraged to prioritize their spatial audio-based products in the markets.

Despite the fact that this kind of products are still far away in the design of the industry's perennial objects, however the initiative taken by well-industrial competitors to produce high-quality spatial sound-based products has a good impact.in the emergence of such new products, which open new doors and guidelines for businesses and consumers to market and own these innovative products. Beyond improving the bottom line for audio content producers and hardware manufacturers (headphones, speakers, hearing aids, etc.), the new constellation of spatial audio applications is similarly finding its own place in healthcare, which also has its share in providing products and healthier experiences. Realizing the bridge between digital health and music represents one of the main roles of spatial audio in this field of research by being a promising environment to provide a mountainous net positive effect on the lives of millions of people around the world. Additionally, streaming audio naturally through audio content is in itself a healthy way to reduce stress and improve well-being, making the listening experience immersive and more enjoyable.

When it comes to Space, there are few apps that have been made based on Spatial Audio, making it a current trend. On the contrary, many excellent platforms dedicated to gaming have been built by major software companies, which encourages them to launch new applications in this area in addition to other new areas.

While listing all the above application areas for spatial audio, one should not forget the dynamic function of machine learning approaches especially exploring the high performance offered by advanced deep learning algorithms. This in itself represents a trend that requires even more improvements and refinements to meet the demands of real-world applications.

CONCLUSION

In this chapter, an overview of the main spatial audio coding technology has been presented. Indeed, the main design, the suggested techniques, as well as various spatial parameters were studied. In addition, the fundamentals of object-based and channel-based audio were exposed. MPEG Surround, MPEG-H 3D Audio Coding, and MPEG SAOC, which together belong to the MPEG standards, were also presented. Additionally, the main applications of machine learning (ML) approaches in acoustics and spatial audio scenes were given.

As additional work, the author suggests to focus on the integration of spatial audio coding in recent technologies and to see its performance especially in real time using advanced machine learning algorithms (ML). Moreover, the author proposes to broaden the application of spatial audio coding to include other research areas such as the spatial domain.

CONFLICT OF INTEREST

The author declares no conflict of interest.

REFERENCES

Ahonen, J., Kallinger, M., Küch, F., Pulkki, V., & Schultz-Amling, R. (2008, May). Directional analysis of sound field with linear microphone array and applications in sound reproduction. In *Audio Engineering Society Convention 124*. Audio Engineering Society.

Ando, A., Hamasaki, K., Imai, A., Iwaki, M., Kitajima, S., Nakayama, Y., & Sugimoto, T. (2007, May). Production and live transmission of 22.2 multichannel sound with ultra-high definition TV. In *Audio Engineering Society Convention 122*. Audio Engineering Society.

Baumgarte, F., & Faller, C. (2002, April). *Why binaural cue coding is better than intensity stereo coding*. Presented at the *112th Convention of the Audio Engineering Society*.

Baumgarte, F., & Faller, C. (2003). Binaural cue coding-Part I: Psychoacoustic fundamentals and design principles. *IEEE Transactions on Speech and Audio Processing, 11*(6), 509–519. doi:10.1109/TSA.2003.818109

Benaroya, E. L., Obin, N., Liuni, M., Roebel, A., Raumel, W., & Argentieri, S. (2018). Binaural localization of multiple sound sources by non-negative tensor factorization. *IEEE/ACM Transactions on Audio, Speech, and Language Processing, 26*(6), 1072–1082. doi:10.1109/TASLP.2018.2806745

Berkhout, A. J., de Vries, D., & Vogel, P. (1993). Acoustic control by wave field synthesis. *The Journal of the Acoustical Society of America, 93*(5), 2764–2778. doi:10.1121/1.405852

Blauert, J. (1974). *Spatial hearing: The psychology of human sound localization*. The MIT Press.

Blauert, J. (2001). *Spatial Hearing: The psychophysics of human sound localization*. MIT Press.

Bleidt, R., Borsum, A., Fuchs, H., & Weiss, S. M. (2015). Object-based audio: Opportunities for improved listening experience and increased listener involvement. *SMPTE Motion Imaging Journal, 124*(5), 1–13. doi:10.5594/j18579

Bosi, M., Brandenburg, K., Quackenbush, S., Fielder, L., Akagiri, K., Fuchs, H., Dietz, M., Herre, J., Davidson, G., & Oikawa, Y. (1997). ISO/IEC MPEG-2 advanced audio coding. *Journal of the Audio Engineering Society, 45*(10), 789–814.

Bosi, M., & Goldberg, R. E. (2002). *Introduction to digital audio coding and standards*. Springer Science & Business Media.

Brandenburg, K., & Bosi, M. (1997, September). ISO/IEC MPEG-2 advanced audio coding: Overview and applications. In Audio Engineering Society Convention 103. Audio Engineering Society.

Brandenburg, K., Faller, C., Herre, J., Johnston, J. D., & Kleijn, W. B. (2013). Perceptual coding of high-quality digital audio. *Proceedings of the IEEE, 101*(9), 1905–1919. doi:10.1109/JPROC.2013.2263371

Breebaart, J., Engdegård, J., Falch, C., Hellmuth, O., Hilpert, J., Hoelzer, A., & Terentiev, L. (2008, May). Spatial audio object coding (SAOC)-The upcoming MPEG standard on parametric object based audio coding. In *Audio Engineering Society Convention 124*. Audio Engineering Society.

Breebaart, J., Herre, J., Faller, C., Roden, J., Myburg, F., Disch, S., Purnhagen, H. H. G., Neusinger, M., Kjorling, K., & Oomen, W. (2005, October). *MPEG spatial audio coding/ MPEG surround: Overview and current status*. Presented at the *11th Convention of the Audio Engineering Society*.

Breebaart, J., Hotho, G., Koppens, J., Schuijers, E., Oomen, W., & de Par, S. V. (2007). Background, concepts, and architecture for the recent MPEG Surround standard on multichannel audio compression. *Journal of the Audio Engineering Society, 55*(5), 331–351.

Breebaart, J., van de Par, S., & Kohlrausch, A. (2001). Binaural processing model based on contralateral inhibition. I. Model structure. *The Journal of the Acoustical Society of America, 110*(3), 1074–1088. doi:10.1121/1.1383297 PMID:11519576

Breebaart, J., van de Par, S., Kohlrausch, A., & Schuijers, E. (2005). Parametric coding of stereo audio. *EURASIP Journal on Advances in Signal Processing, 2005*(9), 1–18. doi:10.1155/ASP.2005.1305

Chen, D. P., Hsiao, H. F., Hsu, H. W., & Liu, C. M. (2010, May). Gram-schmidt-based downmixer and decorrelator in the MPEG surround coding. In *Audio Engineering Society Convention 128*. Audio Engineering Society.

Cheng, B., Ritz, C., & Burnett, I. (2006, November). Squeezing the auditory space: a new approach to multi-channel audio coding. In *Pacific-Rim Conference on Multimedia*. Springer.

Cheng, B., Ritz, C., & Burnett, I. (2007, April). Principles and analysis of the squeezing approach to low bit rate spatial audio coding. In *2007 IEEE International Conference on Acoustics, Speech and Signal Processing-ICASSP'07*. IEEE. 10.1109/ICASSP.2007.366604

Cheng, B., Ritz, C., & Burnett, I. (2007). *Advances in multimedia information processing-PCM 2007*. Springer.

Cheng, B., Ritz, C., & Burnett, I. (2008, March). A spatial squeezing approach to ambisonic audio compression. In *2008 IEEE International Conference on Acoustics, Speech and Signal Processing*. IEEE. 10.1109/ICASSP.2008.4517623

Cheng, E., Cheng, B., Ritz, C., & Burnett, I. (2008, December). Spatialized teleconferencing: Recording and squeezed rendering of multiple distributed Sites. In *2008 Australasian Telecommunication Networks and Applications Conference*. IEEE. 10.1109/ATNAC.2008.4783360

Chon, S. B., Choi, I. Y., Moon, H. G., Seo, J., & Sung, K.-M. (2005, October). Virtual source location information for binaural cue coding. In *Audio Engineering Society Convention 119*. Audio Engineering Society.

Elfitri, I. H. D., & Laksono, P. A. (2015, May). Balanced-delay filter bank for closed-loop spatial audio coding. In *2015 International Seminar on Intelligent Technology and Its Applications (ISITIA)*.IEEE.

Elfitri, I., Gunel, B., & Kondoz, A. M. (2011). Multichannel audio coding based on analysis by synthesis. *Proceedings of the IEEE*, *99*(4), 657–670. doi:10.1109/JPROC.2010.2102310

Elfitri, I., & Kurnia, R. (2014, October). Investigation on objective performance of closed-loop spatial audio coding. In *2014 6th International Conference on Information Technology and Electrical Engineering (ICITEE)*. IEEE. 10.1109/ICITEED.2014.7007926

Elfitri, I., Kurnia, R., & Harneldi, D. (2014, October). Experimental study on improved parametric stereo for bit rate scalable audio coding. In *2014 6th International Conference on Information Technology and Electrical Engineering (ICITEE)*. IEEE. 10.1109/ICITEED.2014.7007922

Elfitri, I., & Luthfi, A. (2015, October). R-TTT module with modified residual signal for improving multichannel audio signal accuracy. In *2015 International Conference on Automation, Cognitive Science, Optics, Micro Electro-Mechanical System, and Information Technology (ICACOMIT)*. IEEE. 10.1109/ICACOMIT.2015.7440207

Elfitri, I., & Luthfi, A. (2017). Reviews on technology and standard of spatial audio coding. *Journal Nasional Teknik Elektro*, *6*(1), 44–56. doi:10.25077/jnte.v6n1.372.2017

Elfitri, I., Muharam, M., & Shobirin, M. (2014, October). Distortion analysis of hierarchical mixing technique on MPEG surround standard. In *2014 International Conference on Advanced Computer Science and Information System*. IEEE. 10.1109/ICACSIS.2014.7065868

Elfitri, I., Shi, X., & Kondoz, A. M. (2014). Analysis by synthesis spatial audio coding. *IET Signal Processing*, *8*(1), 30–38. doi:10.1049/iet-spr.2013.0015

Engdegard, J., Purnhagen, H., Roden, J., & Liljeryd, L. (2004, May). Synthetic ambience in parametric stereo coding. In *Audio Engineering Society Convention 116*. Audio Engineering Society.

Faller, C., & Baumgarte, F. (2003). Binaural cue coding-Part II: Schemes and applications. *IEEE Transactions on Speech and Audio Processing*, *11*(6), 520–531. doi:10.1109/TSA.2003.818108

Fug, S., Holzer, A., Borb, C., Ertel, C., Kratschmer, M., & Plogsties, J. (2014, October). Design, coding and processing of metadata for object-based interactive audio. In *Audio Engineering Society Convention 137*. Audio Engineering Society.

Gabrielli, L., Fazekas, G., & Nam, J. (2021). Special issue on deep learning for applications in acoustics: Modeling, synthesis, and listening. *Applied Sciences (Basel, Switzerland)*, *11*(2), 473. doi:10.3390/app11020473

Goodwin, M. M., & Jot, J.-M. (2006, May). A frequency-domain framework for spatial audio coding based on universal spatial cues. In *Audio Engineering Society Convention 120*. Audio Engineering Society.

Goodwin, M. M., & Jot, J.-M. (2006, October). Analysis and synthesis for universal spatial audio coding. In *Audio Engineering Society Convention 121*. Audio Engineering Society.

Goodwin, M. M., & Jot, J.-M. (2007, March). Multichannel surround format conversion and generalized up mix. In *Audio Engineering Society Conference: 30th International Conference: Intelligent Audio Environments*. Audio Engineering Society.

Goodwin, M. M., & Jot, J.-M. (2007, April). Primary-ambient signal decomposition and vector-based localization for spatial audio coding and enhancement. In *2007 IEEE International Conference on Acoustics, Speech and Signal Processing-ICASSP'07*. IEEE. 10.1109/ICASSP.2007.366603

Goodwin, M. M., & Jot, J.-M. (2007, October). Binaural 3-D audio rendering based on spatial audio scene coding. In *Audio Engineering Society Convention 123*. Audio Engineering Society.

Goodwin, M. M., & Jot, J.-M. (2008, October). Spatial audio scene coding. In *Audio Engineering Society Convention 125*. Audio Engineering Society.

Gorlow, S., Habets, E. A. P., & Marchand, S. (2013, May). Multichannel object-based audio coding with controllable quality. In *2013 IEEE International Conference on Acoustics, Speech and Signal Processing*. IEEE. 10.1109/ICASSP.2013.6637710

Grill, B., Hellmuth, O., Hilpert, J., Herre, J., & Plogsties, J. (2006, May). Closing the gap between the multi-channel and the stereo audio world: Recent MP3 surround extensions. In *Audio Engineering Society Convention 120*. Audio Engineering Society.

Günther, G. (2002). *Vision, Modeling, and Visualization 2002*. IOS Press.

Hamasaki, K. (2011). *The multichannel sounds and its reproduction at home and personal environment.* In AES 43rd International Conference, Pohang, Korea.

Hamasaki, K., Nishiguchi, T., Okumura, R., & Nakayama, Y. (2007, May). Wide listening area with exceptional spatial sound quality of a 22.2 multichannel sound system. In *Audio Engineering Society Convention 122*. Audio Engineering Society.

Han, Y., Park, J., & Lee, K. (2017). Convolutional neural networks with binaural representations and background subtraction for acoustic scene classification. *The Detection and Classification of Acoustic Scenes and Events (DCASE)*, 1-5.

Herre, J. (2004, October). *From joint stereo to spatial audio coding-recent progress and standardization.* In *Sixth International Conference on Digital Audio Effects (DAFX04)*, Naples, Italy.

Herre, J., & Dietz, M. (2008). MPEG-4 high-efficiency AAC coding. *IEEE Signal Processing Magazine*, *25*(3), 137–142. doi:10.1109/MSP.2008.918684

Herre, J., & Disch, S. (2007, July). New concepts in parametric coding of spatial audio: From SAC to SAOC. In *2007 IEEE International Conference on Multimedia and Expo*. IEEE. 10.1109/ICME.2007.4285045

Herre, J., Falch, C., Mahne, D., Galdo, G., del Kallinger, M., & Thiergart, O. (2012). Interactive teleconferencing combining spatial audio object coding and dirac technology. *Journal of the Audio Engineering Society*, *59*(12), 924–935.

Herre, J., Faller, C., Disch, S., Ertel, C., Hilpert, J., Hoelzer, A., Linzmeier, K., Spenger, C., & Kroon, P. (2004, October). Spatial audio coding: Next-generation efficient and compatible coding of multi-channel audio. In *Audio Engineering Society Convention 117*. Audio Engineering Society.

Herre, J., Faller, C., Ertel, C., Hilpert, J., Hoelzer, A., & Spenger, C. (2004, May). MP3 surround: Efficient and compatible coding of multi-channel audio. In *Audio Engineering Society Convention 116*. Audio Engineering Society.

Herre, J., Hilpert, J., Kuntz, A., & Plogsties, J. (2015). MPEG-H audio—The new standard for universal spatial/3D audio coding. *Journal of the Audio Engineering Society*, *62*(12), 821–830. doi:10.17743/jaes.2014.0049

Herre, J., Kjörling, K., Breebaart, J., Faller, C., Disch, S., Purnhagen, H., ... Chong, K. S. (2008). MPEG surround-the ISO/MPEG standard for efficient and compatible multichannel audio coding. *Journal of the Audio Engineering Society*, *56*(11), 932–955.

Herre, J., Purnhagen, H., Breebaart, J., Faller, C., Disch, S., Kjorling, K., Schuijers, E., Hilpert, J., & Myburg, F. (2005). *The reference model architecture for MPEG spatial audio coding*. Academic Press.

Herre, J., & Terentiv, L. (2011). *Parametric coding of audio objects: Technology, performance, and opportunities*, Presented at the 42nd Int. Conference: Semantic Audio, Il menau, Germany.

Hilpert, J., & Disch, S. (2009). The MPEG surround audio coding standard. *IEEE Signal Processing Magazine*, *26*(1), 148–152. doi:10.1109/MSP.2008.930433

Hummersone, C. H., Mason, R., & Brookes, T. (2010). Dynamic precedence effect modeling for source separation in reverberant environments. *IEEE Transactions on Audio, Speech, and Language Processing*, *18*(7), 1867–1871. doi:10.1109/TASL.2010.2051354

Ibrahim, K. M., & Allam, M. (2018, April). Primary-ambient source separation for up mixing to surround sound systems. In *2018 IEEE International Conference on Acoustics, Speech and Signal Processing (ICASSP)*. IEEE. 10.1109/ICASSP.2018.8461459

ISO/IEC. (2006). Information technology - generic coding of moving pictures and associated audio information, Part 7: Advanced audio coding, ISO/IEC. Int. Standards Organization, Geneva, Switzerland.

ISO/IEC. (2007). *Information technology - MPEG audio technologies, Part 1: MPEG surround, ISO/IEC*. International Standards Organization.

ISO/IEC. (2009). *Information technology - coding of audio-visual objects, Part 3: Audio, ISO/IEC*. International Standards Organization.

ISO/IEC. (2012). Information technology - MPEG audio technologies, Part 3: Unified speech and audio coding, ISO/IEC. Int. Standards Organization, Geneva, Switzerland.

ITU-R. (1997). *Method for subjective assessment of small impairments in audio systems including multichannel sound systems*, Recommendation ITU-RBS.

ITU-R. (2001). *Method for subjective assessment of intermediate quality level of coding systems*, Recommendation ITU-RBS.

ITU-R. (2001). *Method for objective measurements of perceived audio quality*, Recommendation ITU-RBS.

ITU-R. (2003). *Method for Subjective Assessment of Intermediate Quality Level of Coding Systems*, Recommendation ITU-R BS.

ITU-R. (2014). *Method for subjective assessment of small impairments in audio systems*, Recommendation ITU-RBS.

ITU-R. (2014). *Method for subjective assessment of intermediate quality level of audio systems*, Recommendation ITU-RBS.

ITU-R. (2015). *Method for subjective assessment of small impairments in audio systems*, Recommendation ITU-RBS.

ITU-R. (2015). *Method for subjective assessment of intermediate quality level of audio systems*, Recommendation ITU-RBS.

Jeffress, L. A. (1948). A place theory of sound localization. *Journal of Comparative and Physiological Psychology*, *41*(1), 35–39. doi:10.1037/h0061495 PMID:18904764

Jot, J., Smith, B., & Thompson, J. (2015). *Dialog control and enhancement in object-based audio systems*. Presented at the *139th Convention of the Audio Engineering Society*.

Jot, J.-M., Merimaa, J., Goodwin, M. M., Krishnaswamy, A., & Laroche, J. (2007, October). Spatial audio scene coding in a universal two-channel 3-D stereo format. In *Audio Engineering Society Convention 123*. Audio Engineering Society.

Kallinger, M., Kuech, F., S-Amling, R., del Galdo, G., Ahonen, J., & Pulkki, V. (2008, May). Enhanced direction estimation using microphone arrays for directional audio coding. In *Hands-free speech communication and microphone arrays*. IEEE.

Kim, K., Seo, J., Beack, S., Kang, K., & Hahn, M. (2011). Spatial audio object coding with two-step coding structure for interactive audio service. *IEEE Transactions on Multimedia*, *13*(6), 1208–1216. doi:10.1109/TMM.2011.2168197

Kim, S., Lee, Y., & Pulkki, V. (2010, November). New 10.2-channel vertical surround system (10.2-vss); comparison study of perceived audio quality in various multichannel sound systems with height loudspeakers. In *Audio Engineering Society Convention 129*. Audio Engineering Society.

Kuech, F., Kallinger, M., S-Amling, R., del Galdo, G., Ahonen, J., & Pulkki, V. (2008, May). Directional audio coding using planar microphone arrays. In *2008 hands-free speech communication and Microphone Arrays*. IEEE.

Liu, C., Hsu, H., & Lee, W. (2008). Compression artifacts in perceptual audio coding. *IEEE Transactions on Audio, Speech, and Language Processing*, *16*(4), 681–695. doi:10.1109/TASL.2008.918979

Lovedee-Turner, M., & Murphy, D. (2018). Application of machine learning for the spatial analysis of binaural room impulse responses. *Applied Sciences (Basel, Switzerland)*, *8*(1), 105. doi:10.3390/app8010105

Ma, N., & Brown, G. J. (2016, September). Speech localisation in a multitalker mixture by humans and machines. In *Proceedings of INTERSPEECH 2016*. ISCA. 10.21437/Interspeech.2016-1149

Ma, N., Gonzalez, J. A., & Brown, G. J. (2018). Robust binaural localization of a target sound source by combining spectral source models and deep neural networks. *IEEE/ACM Transactions on Audio, Speech, and Language Processing*, *26*(11), 2122–2131. doi:10.1109/TASLP.2018.2855960

Marston, D., Kozamernik, F., Stoll, G., & Spikofski, G. (2009, May). Further EBU tests of multichannel audio codecs. In *Audio Engineering Society Convention 126*. Audio Engineering Society.

Mason, A., Marston, D., Kozamernik, F., & Stoll, G. (2007, May). EBU tests of multi-channel audio codecs. In *Audio Engineering Society Convention 122*. Audio Engineering Society.

Matsui, K., & Ando, A. (2013, October). Binaural reproduction of 22.2 multichannel sound with loudspeaker array frame. In *Audio Engineering Society Convention 135*. Audio Engineering Society.

May, T., Ma, N., & Brown, G. J. (2015, April). Robust localisation of multiple speakers exploiting head movements and multi-conditional training of binaural cues. In *2015 IEEE International Conference on Acoustics, Speech and Signal Processing (ICASSP)*. IEEE. 10.1109/ICASSP.2015.7178457

Neuendorf, M., Multrus, M., Rettelbach, N., Fuchs, G., Robilliard, J., Lecomte, J., ... Grill, B. (2013). The ISO/MPEG unified speech and audio coding standard—Consistent high quality for all content types and at all bit rates. *Journal of the Audio Engineering Society, 61*(12), 956–977.

Oh, E., & Kim, M. (2011, September). Enhanced stereo algorithms in the unified speech and audio coding. In *Audio Engineering Society Conference: 43rd International Conference: Audio for Wirelessly Networked Personal Devices*. Audio Engineering Society.

Oldfield, R., Shirley, B., & Satongar, D. (2015, October). Application of object-based audio for automated mixing of live football broadcast. In *Audio Engineering Society Convention 139*. Audio Engineering Society.

Oldfield, R., Shirley, B., & Spille, J. (2014, October). An object-based audio system for interactive broadcasting. In *Audio Engineering Society Convention 137*. Audio Engineering Society.

Painter, T., & Spanias, A. (2000). Perceptual coding of digital audio. *Proceedings of the IEEE, 88*(4), 451–515. doi:10.1109/5.842996

Pan, D. (1995). A tutorial on MPEG/audio compression. *IEEE MultiMedia, 2*(2), 60–74. doi:10.1109/93.388209

Park, J., Kim, K., & Hahn, M. (2011, January). Harmonic elimination structures for Karaoke mode in spatial audio object coding scheme. In *2011 IEEE International Conference on Consumer Electronics (ICCE)*. IEEE. 10.1109/ICCE.2011.5722879

Park, J., Kim, K., & Hahn, M. (2013). Vocal removal from multiobject audio using harmonic information for karaoke service. *IEEE Transactions on Audio, Speech, and Language Processing, 21*(4), 798–805. doi:10.1109/TASL.2012.2234116

Pulkki, V. (2006, June). Directional audio coding in spatial sound reproduction and stereo up mixing. In *Audio Engineering Society Conference: 28th International Conference: The Future of Audio Technology--Surround and Beyond*. Audio Engineering Society.

Pulkki, V., & Faller, C. (2006, May). Directional audio coding: filterbank and STFT-based design. In *Audio Engineering Society Convention 120*. Audio Engineering Society.

Pulkki, V., & Hirvonen, T. (2004). Localization of virtual sources in multichannel audio reproduction. *IEEE Transactions on Speech and Audio Processing, 13*(1), 105–119. doi:10.1109/TSA.2004.838533

Pulkki, V., & Karjalainen, M. (2008). Multichannel audio rendering using amplitude panning. *IEEE Signal Processing Magazine, 25*(3), 118–122. doi:10.1109/MSP.2008.918025

Quackenbush, S., & Lefebvre, R. (2011, October). Performance of MPEG unified speech and audio coding. In *Audio Engineering Society Convention 131*. Audio Engineering Society.

Roden, J., Breebart, J., Hilpert, J., Purnhagen, H., Schuijers, E., Koppens, J., Linzmeier, K., & Holzer, A. (2007, October). A study of the MPEG surround quality versus bit-rate curve. In *Audio Engineering Society Convention 123*. Audio Engineering Society.

Rumsey, F. (2002). Spatial quality evaluation for reproduced sound: Terminology, meaning, and a scene-based paradigm. *Journal of the Audio Engineering Society, 50*(9), 651–666.

Rumsey, F. (2011). *Spatial Audio*. Academic Press.

S-Amling, R., Kuech, F., Kallinger, M., Galdo, G. D., Ahonen, J., & Pulkki, V. (2008, May). *Planar microphone array processing for the analysis and reproduction of spatial audio using directional audio coding*. In 124th AES Convention, Amsterdam, The Netherlands.

Samsudin, S., Kurniawati, E., & George, S. (2014, August). A direct MPEG surround encoding scheme for surround sound recording with coincident microphone techniques. In *Audio Engineering Society Conference: 55th International Conference: Spatial Audio*. Audio Engineering Society.

Schuijers, E., Breebaart, J., Purnhagen, H., & Engdegard, J. (2004, May). Low complexity parametric stereo coding. In *Audio Engineering Society Convention 116*. Audio Engineering Society.

Schuijers, E., Oomen, W., den Brinker, B., & Breebaart, J. (2003, March). Advances in parametric coding for high-quality audio. In *Audio Engineering Society Convention 114*. Audio Engineering Society.

Sugimoto, T., Nakayama, Y., & Oode, S. (2014, October). Bit rate of 22.2 multichannel sound signal meeting broadcast quality. In *Audio Engineering Society Convention 137*. Audio Engineering Society.

Terentiev, L., Falch, C., Hellmuth, O., Hilpert, J., Oomen, W., Engdegard, J., & Mundt, H. (2009, February). SAOC for gaming–The upcoming MPEG standard on parametric object based audio coding. In *Audio Engineering Society Conference: 35th International Conference: Audio for Games*. Audio Engineering Society.

Theile, G., & Wittek, H. (2004). Wave field synthesis: *A promising spatial audio rendering concept. Acoustical Science and Technology, 25*(6), 393–399. doi:10.1250/ast.25.393

Tournery, C., Faller, C., Kuech, F., & Herre, J. (2010, May). Converting stereo microphone signals directly to MPEG-surround. In *Audio Engineering Society Convention 128*. Audio Engineering Society.

Vilkamo, J., Lokki, T., & Pulkki, V. (2009). Directional audio coding: Virtual microphone-based synthesis and subjective evaluation. *Journal of the Audio Engineering Society, 57*(9), 709–724.

Wolters, M., Kjorling, K., Homm, D., & Purnhagen, H. (2003, October). A closer look into MPEG-4 high efficiency AAC. In *Audio Engineering Society Convention 115*. Audio Engineering Society.

Yang, Z., Jia, M., Bao, C., & Wang, W. (2015, December). An analysis-by-synthesis encoding approach for multiple audio objects. In *2015 Asia-Pacific Signal and Information Processing Association Annual Summit and Conference (APSIPA)*. IEEE. 10.1109/APSIPA.2015.7415383

S

Zeng, X., Ritz, C., & Xi, J. (2012). Encoding navigable speech sources: A psychoacoustic-based analysis-by-synthesis approach. *IEEE Transactions on Audio, Speech, and Language Processing*, *21*(1), 29–38.

Zeng, X., Ritz, C., & Xi, J. (2012, March). Encoding navigable speech sources: An analysis by synthesis approach. In *2012 IEEE International Conference on Acoustics, Speech and Signal Processing (ICASSP)*. IEEE.

Zieliński, S. K., & Lee, H. (2019). Automatic spatial audio scene classification in binaural recordings of music. *Applied Sciences (Basel, Switzerland)*, *9*(9), 1724. doi:10.3390/app9091724

Zieliński, S. K., Lee, H., Antoniuk, P., & Dadan, O. (2020). A comparison of human against machine-classification of spatial audio scenes in binaural recordings of music. *Applied Sciences (Basel, Switzerland)*, *10*(17), 5956. doi:10.3390/app10175956

Zieliński, S. K., & Lee, H. F. (2018, September). Feature extraction of binaural recordings for acoustic scene classification. In *2018 Federated Conference on Computer Science and Information Systems (FedCSIS)*. IEEE. 10.15439/2018F182

ADDITIONAL READING

Han, Y., Park, J., & Lee, K. (2017). Convolutional neural networks with binaural representations and background subtraction for acoustic scene classification. *The Detection and Classification of Acoustic Scenes and Events (DCASE)*, 1-5.

Herre, J., Hilpert, J., Kuntz, A., & Plogsties, J. (2015). MPEG-H audio—The new standard for universal spatial/3D audio coding. *Journal of the Audio Engineering Society*, *62*(12), 821–830. doi:10.17743/jaes.2014.0049

Ibrahim, K. M., & Allam, M. (2018, April). Primary-ambient source separation for up mixing to surround sound systems. In *2018 IEEE International Conference on Acoustics, Speech and Signal Processing (ICASSP)*. IEEE. 10.1109/ICASSP.2018.8461459

Lovedee-Turner, M., & Murphy, D. (2018). Application of machine learning for the spatial analysis of binaural room impulse responses. *Applied Sciences (Basel, Switzerland)*, *8*(1), 105. doi:10.3390/app8010105

Ma, N., & Brown, G. J. (2016, September). Speech localisation in a multitalker mixture by humans and machines. In *Proceedings of INTERSPEECH 2016*. ISCA. 10.21437/Interspeech.2016-1149

Ma, N., Gonzalez, J. A., & Brown, G. J. (2018). Robust binaural localization of a target sound source by combining spectral source models and deep neural networks. *IEEE/ACM Transactions on Audio, Speech, and Language Processing*, *26*(11), 2122–2131. doi:10.1109/TASLP.2018.2855960

Zieliński, S. K., & Lee, H. (2019). Automatic spatial audio scene classification in binaural recordings of music. *Applied Sciences (Basel, Switzerland)*, *9*(9), 1724. doi:10.3390/app9091724

Zieliński, S. K., Lee, H., Antoniuk, P., & Dadan, O. (2020). A Comparison of Human against Machine-Classification of Spatial Audio Scenes in Binaural Recordings of Music. *Applied Sciences (Basel, Switzerland)*, *10*(17), 5956. doi:10.3390/app10175956

KEY TERMS AND DEFINITIONS

Binaural Recordings: Binaural recording is a method of recording sound that explores two microphones with the aim of creating a 3D stereo sound sensation for the listener to actually be in the room with the performers or instruments.

Machine Learning: Machine learning is a computer programming technique that uses statistical probabilities to give computers the ability to learn on their own without explicit programming.

Machine-Listening Systems: Machine-listening systems consist of recording, decoding and interpreting sounds (voice, music, noises, etc.).

MPEG Surround: MPEG Surround is based on breaking down the original signal into two signals: a stereo (or mono) signal on the one hand, and a channel of spatialization data on the other.

MPEG-H 3D Audio Coding: It is an audio coding standard developed by the ISO/IEC Moving Picture Experts Group (MPEG) to support audio coding as Audio Channels, Audio Objects, or Higher Order Ambisonics (HOA).

Spatial Audio Coding: The concept of spatial audio coding is to represent two or more audio channels by means of down mixing, along with parameters to design the spatial attributes of the original audio signals that are missed by the down mixing procedure.

Spatial Audio Object Coding: It is a proprietary spatialization system that makes it possible to render a mix on a variable configuration of loudspeakers from an object-oriented audio stream.

About the Contributors

John Wang is a professor in the Department of Information Management and Business Analytics at Montclair State University, USA. Having received a scholarship award, he came to the USA and completed his Ph.D. in operations research at Temple University. Due to his extraordinary contributions beyond a tenured full professor, Dr. Wang has been honored with two special range adjustments in 2006 and 2009, respectively. He has published over 100 refereed papers and seventeen books. He has also developed several computer software programs based on his research findings.

* * *

Nassir Abba-Aji, PhD, is a Senior Lecturer at the Department of Mass Communication, University of Maiduguri, Borno State, Nigeria, and the Sub-Dean, Faculty of Social Sciences of the university. He is a one-time Chairman, Jere Local Government Area, Borno State, as well as Commissioner for Religious Affairs during the Senator Ali Modu Sheriff Administration in Borno State. Dr Nassir has published several articles and book chapters, and has presented papers at several conferences.

Peter Abraldes completed his BA in political science at the University of Pittsburgh. He completed graduate work in statistics and earned his masters in data analytics at the Pennsylvania State University. Peter also spent time studying development economics in Argentina and Brazil, especially how international trade impacts developing countries. His studies include labor economics, trade export policies, and national industrial development policies. He is a maritime trade analyst for the Philadelphia Regional Port Authority, focused on optimizing the organization's cargo development strategy. The strategy includes understanding how the port can differentiate itself and make it more resilient to supply chain disruptions and international policy changes. He has been the scholarship chair for the World Trade Association of Philadelphia since 2018.

Anal Acharya is currently Assistant Professor in Computer Science department in St. Xavier's College, Kolkata. His current research interest is Educational Data Mining.

Prageet Aeron is presently an Assistant Professor at the department of Information Management at MDI Gurgaon. He is a Fellow (FPM) of Computers and Information Systems Group from the Indian Institute of Management Ahmedabad, and a B.Tech from the Indian Institute of Technology-BHU, Varanasi. He has over 10 years of teaching experience across various B-schools in NCR and is actively engaged in teaching and research in the areas of Entrepreneurship, Strategic Information Systems, e-Commerce and Big Data Applications in Management. His research work has been regularly accepted in reputed International Journals and Conferences.

Javier M. Aguiar Pérez is Associate Professor at University of Valladolid, and Head of the Data Engineering Research Unit. His research is focused on Big Data, Artificial Intelligence, and Internet of Things. He has managed international research projects and he has contributed in the standardisation field as expert at the European Telecommunications Standards Institute. He serves as editor, guest editor and reviewer, and author in several international journals, books and conferences. Furthermore, he has been involved as reviewer and rapporteur in several international research initiatives.

Gilbert Ahamer is inclined to analyse fundamentals of philosophy for the target of designing new paradigms driven by foresight when it comes to develop policies for mastering globalisation. As a physicist, environmentalist, economist, technologist, and geographer, he suggests that radically new concepts might beneficially contribute to solving the pressing problems of global change. He co-founded the 'Global Studies' curriculum at Graz University, Austria, studied and established global long-term scenarios when affiliated to the International Institute for Applied Systems Analysis IIASA, and is active in institutionalised dialogue-building for the Environment Agency Austria in Central Asia, Ukraine, and Georgia since his earlier affiliation to the Austrian Academy of Sciences.

Md. Omar Al-Zadid is currently working as a Senior Officer in Bank Asia Limited, Dhaka, Bangladesh. He began his career as a corporate professional in The Daily 'Prothom Alo', one of the top ranking newspapers in Bangladesh. His primary responsibilities in Prothom Alo included key account management and customer relationship management in advertisement department. He achieved 2nd Category Ptak Prize Award in recognition of global supply chain understanding and leadership in the young supply chain community organized by International Supply Chain Education Alliance (ISCEA) in 2013. He obtained Certificate of Achievement for completion of ITES Foundation Skills Training on Digital Marketing under NASSCOM IT-ITES sector Skill Council Certification in 2015. He holds an MBA in Marketing from the University of Dhaka, Bangladesh. His principal research interests include marketing analytics, innovation adoption, digital marketing, online banking, consumer behavior and psychology, Blue Ocean marketing strategy etc.

İnci Albayrak is an Professor in the Department of Mathematical Engineering at Yildiz Technical University (YTU),Turkey, where she has been a faculty member since 1992. She received her BS in 1990, MS in 1993 and PhD in 1997 in Mathematical Engineering from Yildiz Technical University. She had studied spectral theory and operator theory. She has lots of papers in these areas. In recent years, she has collaborated actively with researchers and focused on fuzzy mathematics. She has ongoing research projects about fuzzy linear equation systems and fuzzy linear programming problem.

Dima Alberg is a Researcher in SCE – Shamoon College of Engineering. His areas of specialty are financial data mining, scientific programming, and simulation methods. His current and future research plans focus on developing new models and tools that allow researchers and practitioners to analyze and solve practical problems in data science research areas.

Miguel Alonso Felipe received his M.S. degrees in telecommunication engineering from the University of Valladolid, Spain. In addition, he is PhD Candidate at University of Valladolid and Researcher of the Data Engineering Research Unit. His research is mainly focused on Big Data, Artificial Intelligence, and Internet of Things. Besides, he is co-author of some publications in journals, dealing with topics related to his lines of research.

Yas Alsultanny is the scientist of machine learning, data mining, and quantitative analysis, he is a computer engineering and data analysis PhD holder. He was spent his past 30 years of his life dedicated to the advancement of technological convergence and knowledge transfer to students. He was developed a high standard of research methods for graduate students and MBA through his supervising 100 MSc and PhD theses, and consulting 140 MBA projects, moreover he supervised 40 higher diploma projects and 100 BSc projects. Professor Alsultanny served for a reputed university in Bahrain: Arabian Gulf University (AGU), French Arabian Business School, and University of Bahrain. In Jordan: Applied Science University (ASU), Amman Arab University, Al-Balqa Applied University, and the Arab Academy for Banking and Financial Sciences. In Iraq: University of Baghdad, University of Technology, Al-Mustansiriya University, and Institute of Technology. In Germany: Arab German Academy for Science and Technology (online). Besides these, he was held position director of the AGU University Consultations, Community Services, Training, and Continuous Teaching Centre in Bahrain. And the position of head of the Computer Information Systems department and vice dean College of Information Technology in ASU University in Jordan. Alsultanny was worked a chair of statistical and KPIs committees in AGU University, chair of quality assurance and accreditation committee in Amman Arab University, member of quality assurance and accreditation committee in ASU and AGU Universities, member of establishing PhD Innovation Management programme in AGU University, member of establishing the college of Information Technology, ASU University, member of establishing Graduate College of Computing Studies, Amman Arab University, member of developing MSc Technology Management programme, member council of College of Graduate Studies, AGU University, and member council of College of Information Technology, ASU University. He is a trainer and a consultant for several public and private organizations, he led more than 100 workshops, and main speaker in many symposiums and conferences. He is a main writer of the UN Environment report, as well as member of writing AGU university strategic plans. In addition, he is reviewer and editor for various international journals.

Gerardo Amador Soto is a PhD student in Energy Systems from the National University of Colombia, Researcher in Energy Efficiency for Complex Systems.

Billie Anderson is an Assistant Professor of Applied Statistics at UMKC's Henry W. Bloch School of Management. Billie earned her Ph.D. in Applied Statistics from the University of Alabama, Masters of Mathematics and Statistics from the University of South Alabama, and her Bachelor of Mathematics from Spring Hill College. Before entering academia, Billie was a Research Statistician for SAS. SAS is a statistical software company headquartered in North Carolina. Billie wrote data mining algorithms for the banking and insurance industries. Billie maintained a consultancy relationship with SAS as an analytical trainer from 2012-2020. In this role, she taught analytical-based classes to professionals in organizations to help promote best statistical practices. And, she has consulted with different companies like Ann Taylor, Dunn & Bradstreet, Blue Cross Blue Shield of Michigan, Lowes Home Improvement Store, and Starbucks. She assisted these organizations in applying analytics to solve their business problems. Billie's research focus is in the statistical modeling of credit scoring with a particular interest in reject inference.

Issa Annamoradnejad is a Ph.D. candidate at the Sharif University of Technology, Tehran, Iran.

Rahimberdi Annamoradnejad wrote a chapter on the current and potential application of machine learning for predicting housing prices. He is an Iranian urban planner and an associate professor of geography and urban planning at the University of Mazandaran.

Joel Antúnez-García was born in Ensenada B. C., México, in 1975. He received the B. Sc. degree in Physics from Universidad Autónoma de Baja California (UABC), México, in 1999. The M. Sc. from Centro de Investigación Científica y de Educación Superior de Ensenada (CICESE), México, in 2004. The Ph. D. in Physical-Industrial Engineering from Universidad Autónoma de Nuevo Léon (UANL), Méxio, in 2010. From 2012 to 2013, he did a postdoctoral stay at Centro de Nanociencias y Nanotecnología at UNAM, working on DFT calculations to obtain different zeolites' electronic properties. From 2013-2015 he worked as a professor at Centro de Enseñanza Técnica y Superior (CETYS university). From 2016 to date, he has been involved in the theoretical study of bi-and tri-metallic catalysts based on MoS2 compounds and zeolites.

Dounia Arezki (), after obtaining an MSc in Artificial Intelligence, pursued her Ph.D. program in information technology at the Computer Science faculty of Science and Technology university of Oran (USTO) from 2017 to 2021. January 2022, she started an MSc program in international business. Presently her research interests are focused on spatial data processing, clustering algorithms, data analysis, risk, and project management.

Heba Atteya is the Senior Director of Business Intelligence and Data Analytics unit at The American University in Cairo (AUC). She led the founding team who built AUC's enterprise data-warehouse and business intelligence (BI) platform. In her current role, she manages the full-spectrum of the BI process including: setting AUC's BI roadmap, leading the data architecture and modeling functions, as well as the automated data extraction from the different source systems. Heba completed her MSc in Computer Science at AUC in Spring 2017 in the topic of visualizing large datasets. She earned her bachelor of science in Information Systems with honors in 2010 and joined AUC as a full-time staff member since 2011. She had a successful track record of achievements which qualified her for the position of BI and Data Analytics Director in 2017. Ever since then, she has successfully expanded the BI platform to extract data from the main ERP of the University, the main student information system, and the university CRM, as well as several other source systems providing a 360-degree view of student, faculty, staff and alumni of the University. Recently, she has led the efforts of the AUC's first big data project, analyzing Wi-Fi big data streams to support COVID-19 contact tracing process, as well as AUC's first AI-powered Chat-bot supporting the IT Help Desk function. She has always found inspiration in working with data and finding its underlying hidden patterns. She believes that informed decision-making is what every institution needs to compete in this highly competitive market.

Antonio Badia is an Associate Professor in the Computer Science and Engineering department at the Speed School of Engineering, University of Louisville. His research focuses on database systems and data science; his previous projects have been funded by the National Science Foundation and US Navy. He's the author of over 50 publications and 2 books.

Youakim Badr is an Associate Professor of Data Analytics in the Great Valley campus of the Pennsylvania State University, USA. He earned his Ph.D. in computer science from the National Institute of Applied Sciences (INSA-Lyon), where he worked as an associate professor in the computer science and engineering department. Over the course of his research, Dr. Badr has worked extensively in the area of service computing (distributed systems) and information security. His current research strategy aims at developing a new software engineering approach for designing and deploying "smart connected devices" and building "smart service systems" for the Internet of Things.

Surajit Bag is an Associate Professor at the Institute of Management and Technology, Ghaziabad, India (AACSB accredited). He is also working as a Visiting Associate Professor in the Department of Transport and Supply Chain Management, University of Johannesburg, South Africa. He has 11 years of industry experience. He has teaching experince from India, Morocco, South Africa and U.K. Educationally, Dr. Surajit earned his second Ph.D. in Information Management from the Postgraduate School of Engineering Management, University of Johannesburg, South Africa, and holds his first Ph.D. in Supply Chain Management from the School of Business, University of Petroleum and Energy Studies, India. Prior to getting a Ph.D., he obtained an MBA in Marketing Management (major) from MAKAUT (formerly the West Bengal University of Technology), India. His substantive areas of interest include Industry 4.0, big data, artificial intelligence applications in marketing and supply chain, sustainability. His expertise lies in the areas of Multivariate Data Analysis Techniques, Mediation Analysis, Moderation Analysis, and Structural Equation Modeling. He is familiar with data analysis software such as WarpPLS, PLS-SEM, SPSS, and Python. Surajit has published some of the most cited papers in the Industrial Marketing Management, International Journal of Production Economics, International Journal of Production Research, Technological Forecasting & Social Change, Production, Planning & Control, IEEE Transactions on Engineering Management, Journal of Cleaner Production, Annals of Operations Research, Information Systems Frontiers, Journal of Business Research, and Supply Chain Management: An International Journal. He is the proud recipient of the "AIMS-IRMA Young Management Researcher Award 2016" for his significant contribution to management research. He is the proud recipient of best "Doctoral Research Award 2020" from the Postgraduate School of Engineering Management, University of Johannesburg in recognition of the outstanding academic excellence. Dr. Surajit was listed in World's Top 2% Scientists which was released by Stanford University. He is a professional member of the Association of International Business, (AIB), Chartered Institute of Procurement and Supply (CIPS); Association for Supply Chain Management (ASCM); Institute of Electrical and Electronics Engineers (IEEE); Indian Rubber Institute; Association of Indian Management Scholars (AIMS International); and Operational Research Society of India (ORSI).

Sikha Bagui is Professor and Askew Fellow in the Department of Computer Science, at The University West Florida, Pensacola, Florida. Dr. Bagui is active in publishing peer reviewed journal articles in the areas of database design, data mining, Big Data analytics, machine learning and AI. Dr. Bagui has worked on funded as well unfunded research projects and has 85+ peer reviewed publications, some in highly selected journals and conferences. She has also co-authored several books on database and SQL. Bagui also serves as Associate Editor and is on the editorial board of several journals.

Samir Bandyopadhyay is presently a distinguished professor of The Bhawanipur Education Society College.

Soumya Banerjee is the Chief Technical Advisor & Board member of Must with specialised on ML & Security.

Sarang Bang is currently Studying at Vellore Institute of Technology, Vellore (India) pursuing Btech in Computer Science with Specialization in Data Science. He completed his schooling from Bhavan's Bhagwandas Purohit Vidya Mandir, Nagpur wherein he secured 10 cgpa in 10th grade and few other merit awards . He has been District Level Volleyball player during his schooling year. After choosing PCM and completing his 12th grade with 86.7 percentage he developed a lot of interest in coding and hence chose Computer Science as his career. In VIT, he is core committee member at VIT Mathematical Association Student chapter and also member at Lions Club International Leo Club Victory, Nagpur. He is passionate about Web Development and has worked on many projects as well as contributed to Hackathons as a front end developer. He also has interest in flutter development, machine learning. He wants to focus on a career in research and is currently exploring Machine learning and Artificial Intelligence.

Bazila Banu is a Professor and Head in the Department of Artificial Intelligence and Machine Learning at Bannari Amman Institute of Technology, India. She received her PhD degree in Information and Communication Engineering at Anna University, India in 2015 and guiding PhD Scholars. She holds 16 years of professional experience including academic and software Industry. She published 15 articles in National and International journals . She is an active reviewer and Guest Editor for International journals and technical committee member for International conferences. Her research interest includes Big Data and Data Analytics. She has filed three National level Patents and received grants from AICTE for Margdarshan scheme (19 Lakhs) and National Commission for women.

Isak Barbopoulos, PhD, has worked as a research psychologist studying the situational activation of consumer motives. He is currently working as a data scientist at Insert Coin, where he is developing and implementing a system for adaptive gamification.

Mikel Barrio Conde is a PhD candidate at University of Valladolid, who received his M.S. degrees in telecommunication engineering from the University of Valladolid, Spain. He is researcher of the Data Engineering Research Unit and his research is focused on Artificial Intelligence, and Internet of Things. Also, he is co-author of some publications in journals, dealing with topics related to his lines of his research.

Sotiris Batsakis is a Laboratory Teaching member of the Technical University of Crete, Greece and he has worked as Affiliated Senior Researcher and Senior Lecturer at the University of Huddersfield, UK. He received a diploma in Computer Engineering and Informatics from the University of Patras, Greece with highest distinction, and a Master's degree and a Ph.D. in Electronic and Computer Engineering from the Technical University of Crete Greece. He is an experienced researcher having participated on various research projects and with over 50 research publications in the areas of Knowledge Representation, Artificial Intelligence and Information Retrieval.

Andrew Behrens is an Instructor of business analytics courses at Dakota State University and is pursuing a Ph.D. in Information Systems at Dakota State University. He has worked with Cherie Noteboom for three years and has published in IS Conferences (MWAIS, IACIS, and AMCIS).

Santiago Belda https://orcid.org/0000-0003-3739-6056 (ORCID ID) From 2011 to 2015, he engaged in a PhD in Mathematical Methods and Modeling in Science and Engineering at Universidad de Alicante. He worked in various projects and is currently affiliated to Universidad de Alicante as a Distinguished postdoc researcher Presently his research interests are Astronomy, VLBI, Earth Orientation Parameters, Terrestrial and Celestial Reference Frames. Santiago Belda was partially supported by Generalitat Valenciana SEJIGENT program (SEJIGENT/2021/001), European Union – NextGenerationEU (ZAMBRANO 21-04) and European Research Council (ERC) under the ERC-2017-STG SENTIFLEX project grant number 755617.

Zakaria Bendaoud is an associate professor at the University of Saida. His research focuses on information retrieval, supply chain and transportation.

Mustapha Benramdane is a Ph.D. student in Computer Science at CNAM. His main research domains are matchmaking and Intent-based Contextual Orchestration inside Digital Business Ecosystems and Platforms.

Níssia Bergiante is a Doctor in Transportation Engineering (COPPE UFRJ– Federal University of Rio de Janeiro - Brazil). Production Engineer with a Master in Production Engineering (UFF-Brazil). Background in Production Engineering, focusing on Operational Management and Operational Research, acting on the following subjects: Decision Analysis and Soft Operation Research (Problem Structuring Methods); Operation Management and Process improvement.

Aditi A. Bhoir is a final year undergraduate student, currently pursuing Bachelor of Technology (B. Tech.) in Mechanical Engineering, at Sardar Patel College of Engineering, Mumbai, India. She will be doing Master of Science (MS) in abroad from fall 2022. Her focus research interest is design and robotics.

Trevor J. Bihl is a Senior Research Engineer with the Air Force Research Laboratory, Sensors Directorate where he leads a diverse portfolio in artificial intelligence (AI) and autonomy. Dr. Bihl earned his doctorate in Electrical Engineering from the Air Force Institute of Technology, Wright Patterson AFB, OH, and he also received a bachelor's and master's degree in Electrical Engineering at Ohio University, Athens, OH. Dr. Bihl is a Senior Member of IEEE and he has served as a board member as Vice President of Chapters/Fora for INFORMS (The Institute of Operations Research and the Management Sciences). His research interests include artificial intelligence, autonomous systems, machine learning, and operations research.

Sanjay Krishno Biswas is a faculty of Anthropology at Shahjalal University of Science and Technology, Bangladesh. He is currently pursuing his Ph.D. His academic interest includes Anthropological Theory, Mobility, and Migration, Diaspora and Transnationality, Ethnicity and Marginality, and Ecology and Climate Change. Mr. Biswas has a number of articles in reputed journals and book chapters from reputed publishers including Routledge.

Karim Bouamrane received the PhD Degree in computer science from the Oran University in 2006. He is full Professor of computer Science at the same university. He is member of computer science laboratory (LIO). He is the head of the team decision and piloting system. His current research interests deal with decision support system, transportation system, risk management, Health system, bio-inspired approach. He participates in several scientific committees' international/national conferences in Algeria and others countries in the same domain and collaborate in Algerian-French scientific projects. He is co-author of more than 60 scientific publications and communications.

Samia Bouzefrane is Professor at the Conservatoire National des Arts et Métiers (Cnam) of Paris. She received her PhD in Computer Science from the University of Poitiers (France) in 1998. After four years at the University of Le Havre (France), she joined in 2002 the CEDRIC Lab of Cnam. She is the co-author of many books (Operating Systems, Smart Cards, and Identity Management Systems). She is a lead expert in the French ministry. She is involved in many scientific workshops and conferences. Her current research areas cover Security and AI Internet of Thing.

Paul Bracewell is Co-Founder of New Zealand-based data science firm, DOT loves data and Adjunct Research Fellow at Victoria University of Wellington. He received his PhD in Statistics from Massey University and has contributed to more than 50 peer reviewed publications.

James Braman is an Associate Professor in the Computer Science/Information Technology Department at the Community College of Baltimore County for the School of Business, Technology and Law. He earned a B.S. and M.S. in Computer Science and D.Sc. in Information Technology from Towson University. He is currently pursuing a M.S. in Thanatology from Marian University. From 2009 to 2017 he was a joint editor-in-chief for the European Alliance for Innovation (EAI) endorsed Transactions on E-Learning with Dr. Giovanni Vincenti. Dr. Braman's research interests include thanatechnology, virtual and augmented reality, e-Learning, affective computing, agent-based technologies, and information retrieval.

Alexis D. Brown is an Assistant Professor in the Computer Science & Information Technology Department at the Community College of Baltimore County. They hold a master's degree in Management Information Systems from the University of Maryland Baltimore County. Their main research interests focus on education and instructional technology but includes varied technology-related topics.

Joseph Budu is an award-winning research scholar within the information systems discipline. He received the University of Ghana Vice Chancellor award for the outstanding doctoral dissertation for the humanities for the 2019/2020 academic year. Prior to this feat, he has undertaken several academic research and consultancies. Dr. Budu has written one mini-book, and one research workbook to guide students in conducting academic research. See https://bit.ly/BuduContentfolio for various contents Joseph has produced (e.g. manuals, blog posts, lead magnets, and presentations).

Rachel Cardarelli graduated from Bryant University with a degree in Actuarial Mathematics and concentration in Applied Statistics. Since graduating, she has been working as an Actuarial Analyst.

Ferhan Çebi is a Professor in Istanbul Technical University Faculty of Management, Management Engineering Department. She holds a B.S. in Chemical Engineering from ITU, a M.S. and a Ph.D. in Management Engineering from ITU. She gives the lectures on Operations Research and Operations Management at the undergraduate level and graduate level. Her main research areas are application of Operations Research techniques to the manufacturing and service problems, production planning and control, fuzziness and mathematical modelling, decision analysis, decision support systems, information technology for competitiveness. She is acting scientific committee member and organization committee member for a number of national & international conferences. Ferhan Cebi is member of editorial boards of International Journal of Information Systems in the Service Sector, International Journal of Information & Decision Sciences, and International Journal of Data Sciences. Her works have been published in several international and national conference proceedings and journals such as Computers and Industrial Engineering, Information Sciences, Information Systems Frontiers, Journal of Enterprise Information Management, Logistics Information Management, International Journal of Information and Decision Sciences.

Shuvro Chakrobartty has made significant contributions to identifying, conceptualizing, and formulating the research objective and methodology, the proposed framework, and the analysis of the findings. With a prior educational background in Computer Science and Business, currently, he is a Ph.D. student of Information Systems at Dakota State University. His research interests lie in responsible AI and data analytics. He has work experience in multiple industries within the software, cloud, and data engineering domain. He is a member of the Association for Information Systems (AIS) professional organizations and serves as a peer-reviewer for multiple conferences, books, and journal publications.

Hannah H. Chang is Associate Professor of Marketing at Lee Kong Chian School of Business, Singapore Management University. She received a PhD in Marketing from Graduate School of Business, Columbia University.

Hsin-Lu Chang is a professor in the Department of Management Information Systems, National Chengchi University. She received a Ph.D. in information systems at the School of Commerce, the University of Illinois at Urbana-Champaign. Her research areas are in E-Commerce, IT value, and technology adoption. She has published in Decision Support Systems, Information Systems Journal, International Journal of Electronic Commerce, Journal of Organizational Computing and Electronic Commerce, and Information Systems and e-Business Management.

D. K. Chaturvedi is Professor in Electrical Engineering at DEI, Agra, India.

Akhilesh Chauhan is a fourth-year Ph.D. (IS) student in the College of Business and Information Systems at the Dakota State University (Madison, S.D., USA). He is received a master's degree in Analytics from Dakota State University. He is currently working as a graduate research assistant at DSU. His current research interest includes association rule mining, machine learning, healthcare informatics, transfer learning, text mining, and data mining.

Tanvi Chawla completed her B.Tech in Information Technology (IT) from MDU, Rohtak in 2012 and received her M.Tech in Software Engineering (SE) from ITM University, Gurgaon in 2014. She has completed her Ph.D. in Computer Science and Engineering (CSE) from Malaviya National Institute of Technology (MNIT), Jaipur in 2022. During her Ph.D. she published articles in premier journals and conferences. Her research interests are Semantic Web, Big Data, Distributed Data Storage, and Processing.

Xi Chen is a lecturer in the College of Humanities at Beijing University of Civil Engineering and Architecture. She is also a research assistant in the Beijing Research Base for Architectural Culture. Her current research interests include English academic writing, settlement evolution, and urbanization in China and the U.S., etc.

Xiaoyan Cheng is a professor at University of Nebraska at Omaha. Dr. Cheng's research has been published in Auditing: A Journal of Practice & Theory, Advances in Accounting, Review of Quantitative Finance and Accounting, Research in Accounting Regulation, Global Finance Journal, Asian Review of Accounting, and Review of Pacific Basin Financial Markets and Policies.

Xusen Cheng is a Professor of Information Systems in the School of Information at Renmin University of China in Beijing. He obtained his PhD degree from the University of Manchester, UK. His research is in the areas of information systems and management particularly focusing on online collaboration, global teams, the sharing economy, e-commerce, and e-learning.

Paula Chimenti is an Associate Professor of Strategy and Innovation at COPPEAD graduate school of business, Federal University of Rio de Janeiro, Brazil. She holds a PhD in Administration from Coppead. She is the coordinator of the Center of Studies in Strategy and Innovation, where she develops research about the impact of disruptive innovations on business ecosystems. She has several works published in journals in Brazil and abroad, such as JGIM and JCR. Her article on Business Ecosystems received the first prize in one of the most important academic conferences in Brazil. She teaches Management Networked Businesses, Digital Marketing and Research Methodology in the Executive MBA, Master's and Doctorate programs at COPPEAD / UFRJ. She coordinated the Master program and Executive MBA programs at COPPEAD. Paula is the cases for teaching Editor for RAC - Revista de Administração Contemporânea, one of the top journals in Brasil.

Jahid Siraz Chowdhuy is a Fellow Ph.D. the program, Department of Social Administration and Justice, Faculty of Arts and Social Sciences, University of Malaya, 50603, Kuala Lumpur, Malaysia and Ex-faculty of Anthropology, Shahjalal University of Science and Technology, Bangladesh.

Parvathi Chundi is a professor of computer science at University of Nebraska at Omaha. Her primary research interests are in the fields of data mining, big data, and computer vision. She is currently focused on developing algorithms for automatic labeling of data for semantic and instance segmentation of biofilm images.

William Chung is an associate professor of Management Sciences at the City University of Hong Kong. He earned his Ph.D. in Management Sciences at the University of Waterloo, Canada. His personal research interests mainly focus on developing mathematical methodologies for energy-environmental policy problems, like large-scale equilibrium models, benchmarking methods for the energy consumption performance of buildings, and decomposition analysis of energy intensity. His papers can be found in the following journals: Operations Research, European Journal of Operational Research (EJOR), Computational Economics, Energy Economics, Energy Policy, Energy, Applied Energy, and Energy and Buildings. In addition, he is the director and founder of the Energy and Environmental Policy Research

Unit at the City University of Hong Kong. He was a visiting professor of the Center for International Energy and Environment Strategy Studies, Renmin University of China.

Mateus Coimbra holds a PhD in Administration from COPPEAD school of business in Federal University of Rio de Janeiro, Brazil.

Mirko Čubrilo is BSc in Mathematics, MSc in Mathematics, PhD in Computer Science (all from Zagreb University, Croatia). Full professor with tenure (Zagreb University, Croatia). Currently engaged at the University of the North (Varaždin, Croatia). Scientific interest includes mathematical logic, theory of algorithms, logic programming, artificial intelligence in a broad context, including neural nets and deep learning. Author of two books on the topics of mathematical logic and programming and more than fifty papers, published in journals and conference proceedings around the world (Germany, Japan, UK, USA, Egypt, Slovakia, Greece, Italy).

Marcin Czajkowski received his Master's degree (2007) and his PhD with honours (2015) in Computer Science from the Bialystok University of Technology, Poland. His research activity mainly concerns bioinformatics, machine learning and data mining, in particular, decision trees, evolutionary algorithms and relative expression analysis.

Jeya Mala D. has a Ph.D. in Software Engineering with Specialization on Software Testing and is currently working as 'Associate Professor Senior' in Vellore Institute of Technology, Chennai, India. She had been in the industry for about 4 years. She has a profound teaching and research experience of more than 24 years. She has published a book on "Object Oriented Analysis and Design using UML" for Tata McGraw Hill Publishers, also she has published 2 edited books for IGI Global, USA. She has published more than 70 papers about her research works at leading international journals and conferences such as IET, ACM, Springer, World Scientific, Computing and Informatics etc. As a researcher, Dr. Jeya Mala had investigated practical aspects of software engineering and object oriented paradigms for effective software development. Her work on Software Testing has fetched grants from UGC under Major Research Project scheme. Her dissertation has been listed as one of the best Ph.D. thesis in the CSIR – Indian Science Abstracts. She has successfully guided numerous Software Development based projects for the IBM- The Great Mind Challenge (TGMC) contest. The project she has mentored during 2007, has received national level Best Top 10 Project Award – 2007, from IBM. Currently she is guiding Ph.D. and M.Phil research scholars under the areas of Software Engineering and optimization techniques. She is a life member of Computer Society of India and an invited member of ACEEE. She forms the reviewer board in Journals like IEEE Transactions on Software Engineering, Elsevier – Information Sciences, Springer, World Scientific, International Journal of Metaheuristics etc. She has organized several sponsored national level conferences and workshops, notably she is one of the organizers of "Research Ideas in Software Engineering and Security (RISES'13) – A run-up event of ICSE 2014 sponsored by Computer Society of India". She has been listed in Marquis Who's Who list in 2011. She has completed certification on Software Testing Fundamentals, Brain bench certification on Java 1.1 programming, IBM certification as Associate Developer Websphere Application Studio. She is a proud recipient of several laurels from industries like Honeywell, IBM and Microsoft for her remarkable contributions in the field of Software Development and Object Orientation.

Karim Dabbabi is currently working as an assistant professor at the Faculty of Sciences of Tunis (FST). He held the postdoctoral position for a year and a half at the same faculty. He obtained his doctorate degree in electronics in July 2019 from the FST in addition to that of a research master's degree in automatic and signal processing from the National School of Engineers of Tunis in 2014. He has worked on various research projects in Automatic Speech Recognition (ASR), speaker diarization, automatic indexing of audio documents, audio segmentation and natural language processing (NLP) in general. In addition, he has worked on the identification of different neurological diseases, including Parkinson's and Alzheimer's using different voice features.

Indraneel Dabhade completed his M.S. in Engineering at Clemson University. He is a CISSP and has studied Cybersecurity from the Massachusetts Institute of Technology Center for Professional Education. He is currently pursuing an advanced certification in information security at the Stanford Center for Professional Development. Indraneel is a published author in Data Science, Human Factors, and Intellectual Property Rights. He has over 7 years of industry experience. Currently, Indraneel heads an automation firm (O Automation) in India.

Debabrata Datta is currently an Assistant Professor In Computer Science at St. Xavier's College (Autonomous), Kolkata. His research interest is Data Analytics and Natural Language Processing.

Magdalene Delighta Angeline D. is currently in the Department of Computer Science and Engineering as Assistant Professor, Joginpally B.R Engineering College, Hyderabad, India. Her research area includes data mining, computer networks. She has a good number of research publications.

Boryana Deliyska is professor retired in Department of Computer Systems and Informatics of University of Forestry, Sofia, Bulgaria. She obtained a PHD Degree in Computer Science from Technical University of Sofia, BG. She has long-standing research and practical experience in Semantic Web technologies, e-learning, computer lexicography, ontology engineering, web design and programming, geographical information systems (GIS), databases and information systems. She teaches information technologies, programming, CAD, computer graphics and computer networks. She is an author of 4 monographies, 7 Elsevier's dictionaries, 18 textbooks, more of 130 journal articles and conference papers.

Javier Del-Pozo-Velázquez received his M.S. degrees in telecommunication engineering from the University of Valladolid, Spain. In addition, he is PhD Candidate at University of Valladolid and Researcher of the Data Engineering Research Unit. His research is mainly focused on Big Data, Artificial Intelligence and Internet of Things. Besides, he is co-author of some publications in journals, dealing with topics related to his lines of research.

Chitra A. Dhawale (Ph.D in Computer Science) is currently working as a Professor Department of Computer Engineering P.R. Pote College of Engineering and Management, Amravati (MS), India. Earlier She worked as a Professor at Symbiosis International University, Pune (MS). To her credit, 06 research scholars have been awarded PhD. so far under her guidance, by S.G.B. Amravati and R.T.M. Nagpur University. Her research interests include Image and Video Processing, Machine Learning, Deep Learning, Multi-Biometric, Big Data Analytics. She has developed many projects for Machine Learning, Deep Learning, Natural Language Processing Algorithms using python. She also has hands on experience in

R-Programming, Hadoop-MapReduce, Apache Spark, Tableau. She has published 02 books, 08 Book Chapters, 26 Research papers in Journals (02- SCI-Indexed,15-Scopus Indexed, 06-UGC Journals and 03 in other research journals) and presented 35 papers in International Conferences (Abroad Conference-08, IEEE-18, ACM-02, Elsevier-01,Springer-04, Others-02) and 19 papers in National Conferences. She has reviewed 09 books for various publishers.

Kritika Dhawale is working as Deep Learning Engineer at SkyLark Drones, Bangalore. She has published 2 book chapters on Deep Learning. Her Research interest is Deep Learning and Cloud Computing.

Harini Dissanayake is a research student at Victoria University of Wellington, New Zealand working on her project 'Data informed decision bias.' The project focuses on identifying discriminatory bias in operational algorithms and remedying sample selection bias in datasets used for informing both commercial and government decisions.

Emmanuel Djaba is an early-stage academic with an avid interest in data science and machine learning. With extensive experience in industry, he is interested in doing innovative research that can be readily applied to interesting problems. He is currently a PhD student at the University of Ghana where he is pursuing a PhD in information systems.

Matt Drake has been a researcher in supply chain management for twenty years, focusing mainly on the areas of supply chain education and ethics. He has published over 30 articles and book chapters during this time. His chapter discusses the use of IoT technology to improve supply chain management. As firms look to improve their supply chain resilience in response to the COVID-19 pandemic and other disruptions, IoT data increases visibility, traceability, and can help firms to mitigate risks through added agility and responsiveness. The improved decision making made possible from IoT data creates a competitive advantage in the market.

Dorin Drignei received his PhD in Statistics from Iowa State University in 2004. Following his graduation, he was a postdoctoral researcher at the National Center for Atmospheric Research for two years. In 2006 he joined Oakland University where he is currently a Professor of Statistics. His current research interests include statistical modeling of big time series data.

Yuehua Duan is a PhD student in Computer Science Department at the University of North Carolina, Charlotte. Her research interests include recommender systems, business analytics, data mining, natural language processing, and machine learning.

Dishit Duggar is currently Studying at Vellore Institute of Technology, Vellore (India) pursuing Btech in Computer Science with Specialization in Information Security. He completed his schooling from Delhi Public School, Jaipur wherein he secured 10 cgpa in 10th grade and was a gold medal recipient for being a scholar for 6 consecutive years. After choosing PCM and completing his 12th grade with 93.8 percentage, He developed a lot of interest in coding and hence chose Computer Science as his career. In VIT, he is the App Lead of VinnovateIT which is a lab setup by Cognizant and also a member at Student Technical Community which is backed by Microsoft. He is passionate about Apps, Blockchain and Machine Learning and has worked on many projects as well as contributed and lead teams in multiple Hackathons. He wants to focus on a career in research and is currently exploring Cyber Security and Artificial Intelligence.

Ankur Dumka is working as Associate Professor and head of department in Women Institute of Technology, Dehradun. He is having more than 10 years of academic and industrial experience. He is having more than 60 research papers in reputed journals and conferences of repute. He contributed 4 books and 12 book chapters with reputed publisher. He is also associated with many reputed journals in the capacity of editorial board members and editor.

Abhishek Dutta has completed BS in Computer Science from Calcutta University and MS in Data Science and Analytics from Maulana Abul Kalam Azad University of Technology, Kolkata, India in 2020. He has authored seven conference papers which are published in IEEE Xplore and Springer Link. His research areas include Machine Learning, Deep Learning and AI applications in Finance.

Santosha Kumar Dwivedy received the Ph.D. in Mechanical Engineering from Indian Institute of Technology Kharagpur (IIT Kharagpur), India in 2000. He is currently Professor in Department of Mechanical Engineering at Indian Institute of Technology Guwahati (IIT Guwahati). He was also a Visiting Professor at Institute of Engineering and Computational Mechanics, University of Stuttgart, Germany under DAAD-IIT faculty exchange scheme. He has over 180 journal and conference publications with a focus on integrating robotics and dynamics in various fields. His research interests include both industrial and medical robotics, biomechanics, nonlinear vibration, and control along with the applications.

Brent M. Egan, MD, is Vice-President, Cardiovascular Disease Prevention in the Improving Health Outcomes group of the American Medical Association. He also serves as Professor of Medicine at the University of South Carolina School of Medicine, Greenville and as Past-President of the South Carolina Upstate affiliate of the American Heart Association. He received his medical degree and training in medicine and hypertension at the University of Michigan. He also served on the Board of Directors and President of the International Society of Hypertension in Blacks for many years. His professional interests center on hypertension, metabolic syndrome and vascular disease, which led to some 350 original papers and reviews. Dr. Egan remains committed to working with colleagues to translate the evidence-base into better cardiovascular health, especially for medically underserved populations.

Amal El Arid has earned a Masters' degree in Electrical and Computer Engineering from the American University of Beirut. She has been an instructor in the Department of Computer Science and Information Technology at the Lebanese International University since 2012. In addition, she specializes in programming and networking fields, earning a trainer certificate from the CISCO organization as a CCNA instructor since 2016. She is now working in the artificial intelligence and machine learning research field.

Houda El Bouhissi graduated with an engineering degree in computer science from Sidi-Bel-Abbes University - Algeria, in 1995. She received her M. Sc. and Ph. D. in computer science from the University of Sidi-Bel-Abbes, Algeria, in 2008 and 2015, respectively. Also, she received an M. Sc. in eLearning from the University of sciences and technologies, Lille1, France. Currently, she is an Assistant Professor at the University of Bejaia, Algeria. Her research interests include recommender systems, sentiments analysis, information systems interoperability, ontology engineering, and machine learning.

Mohamed El Touhamy is a Senior Data Engineer at The American University in Cairo (AUC). He completed his undergraduate studies at the Faculty of Computers and Information, Cairo University, earning a bachelor's degree in Computer Science. Mohamed started his journey in data science in 2017, participating in and leading many mega projects. He has excellent experience in big data engineering, data extraction using different technologies, data quality checks automation, and data warehouse enterprise solution management. He is also a graduate student at The American University in Cairo, seeking his master's degree in Computer Science.

Caner Erden, currently working as Assistant Professor in the Faculty of Applied Sciences, Sakarya University of Applied Sciences, Sakarya, Turkey. He worked as resarch assistant of Industrial Engineering at Sakarya University and researcher at Sakarya University Artificial Intelligence Systems Application and Research between 2012-2020. He holds a PhD degree in Industrial Engineering from Natural Science Institue Industrial Engineering Department, Sakarya University, Turkey with thesis titled "Dynamic Integrated Process Planning, Scheduling and Due Date Assignment". His research interests include scheduling, discrete event simulation, meta-heuristic algorithms, modelling and optimization, decision-making under uncertainty, machine learning and deep learning.

Omar El-Gayar has made a significant contribution to the conceptualization and formulation of the research objective and methodology, the proposed framework, and the interpretation of the findings. He is a Professor of Information Systems at Dakota State University. His research interests include analytics, business intelligence, and decision support. His numerous publications appear in various information technology-related venues. Dr. El-Gayar serves as a peer and program evaluator for accrediting agencies such as the Higher Learning Commission and ABET and as a peer reviewer for numerous journals and conferences. He is a member of the association for Information Systems (AIS).

Gozde Erturk Zararsiz is a faculty member in Biostatistics Department of Erciyes University. Her research mostly focuses on statistical modeling, method comparison, survival analysis and machine learning. Zararsiz completed her M.Sc. from Cukurova University, Institute of Health Sciences, Department of Biostatistics with the thesis entitled as "Evolution of Competing Risks Based on Both Dependent-Independent Real and Simulated Data by Using Self-Developed R Program". In 2015, Zararsiz has started her Ph.D. in Department of Biostatistics of Eskisehir Osmangazi University. During her Ph.D. in 2016, Zararsiz worked as a visiting researcher under the supervision of Prof. Dr. Christoph Klein at the laboratory of the Dr von Hauner Children's Hospital, LMU in Munich. During her research period, Zararsiz has published international papers and received awards. Zararsiz completed her PhD with the thesis entitled as "Bootstrap-Based Regression Approaches in Comparing Laboratory Methods".

Tasnia Fatin is a PhD Candidate in Management at Putra Business School, UPM, Malaysia. She has been a Lecturer of Marketing at Northern University Bangladesh (BBA, MBA) where she has taught Brand Management, Strategic Marketing, Principles of Marketing and Marketing Management. She had also been a Lecturer at Independent University Bangladesh. She takes keen interest in Entrepreneurship and has been running her own Business Solutions Agency and a Skill Training Institute. She holds an

MBA in Marketing from the University of Dhaka. She has also worked as a Strategic Marketing Manager for Prasaad Group of Companies to develop real estate projects home and abroad. She has also separately worked on projects in Urban Waste Management and Sustainable Agriculture that has been presented at George Washington University (USA), MIT (USA), Queens University (Canada) and at KLCC (Malaysia). Her research interests include digital marketing, disruptive innovations and the way they shape the world, IoT (Internet of Things), and sustainable business practices. She participated in several national level, Government level, and International level Youth Conferences and Forums home and abroad mentored by Industry leaders, experts, and professors from Harvard, Oxford, and many other prestigious institutions.

Arafat Febriandirza is a junior researcher at the Research Center for Informatics, The Indonesia Institute of Sciences (LIPI), Indonesia since 2020. He obtained his bachelor degree in Electrical Engineering from University of General Achmad Yani, Indonesia in 2008. He earned a Master's degree in Information Technology from the University of Indonesia in 2011 and a Doctorate in Communication and Transportation Engineering from Wuhan university of Technology in 2018. Arafat Febriandirza's research interests include issues in the field of Machine Learning, Modeling, Simulation, and Social Informatics.

Egi Arvian Firmansyah is a permanent lecturer at the Faculty of Economics and Business Universitas Padjadjaran, Indonesia. He has been published numerous journal articles and conferences proceedings. He is also a finance and managing editor at Jurnal Bisnis dan Manajemen, which is an accredited and reputable journal in Indonesia. Currently, he is a Ph.D student in finance at Universiti Brunei Darussalam.

Robert Leslie Fisher was educated in New York City. He attended Stuyvesant High School, a special science high school, has a bachelors degree (cum laude) in sociology from City College of New York, and a graduate degree in sociology from Columbia University. He is the author of several books including "Invisible Student Scientists (2013)" and the forthcoming Educating Public Interest Professionals and the Student Loan Debt Crisis." He has previously contributed chapters to encyclopedias and handbooks published by IGI Global including John Wang International Handbook of Business Analytics and Optimization as well as the International Encyclopedia of Information Sciences and Technology, and the International Encyclopedia of Modern Educational Technologies, Applications, and Management (both edited by Mehdi Khosrow-Pour). Mr. Fisher resides in the USA. He is an independent contractor.

Wendy Flores-Fuentes received the bachelor's degree in electronic engineering from the Autonomous University of Baja California in 2001, the master's degree in engineering from Technological Institute of Mexicali in 2006, and the Ph.D. degree in science, applied physics, with emphasis on Optoelectronic Scanning Systems for SHM, from Autonomous University of Baja California in June 2014. By now she is the author of 36 journal articles in Elsevier, IEEE, Emerald and Springer, 18 book chapters and 8 books in Springer, Intech, IGI global Lambert Academic and Springer, 46 proceedings articles in IEEE ISIE 2014-2021, IECON 2014, 2018, 2019, the World Congress on Engineering and Computer Science (IAENG 2013), IEEE Section Mexico IEEE ROCC2011, and the VII International Conference on Industrial Engineering ARGOS 2014. Recently, she has organized and participated as Chair of Special Session on ''Machine Vision, Control and Navigation'' at IEEE ISIE 2015-2021 and IECON 2018, 2019. She has participated has Guest Editor at Journal of Sensors with Hindawi, The International Journal of Advanced

Robotic Systems with SAGE, IEEE Sensors, and Elsevier Measurement. She holds 1 patent of Mexico and 1 patent of Ukraine. She has been a reviewer of several articles in Taylor and Francis, IEEE, Elsevier, and EEMJ. Currently, she is a full-time professor at Universidad Autónoma de Baja California, at the Faculty of Engineering. She has been incorporated into CONACYT National Research System in 2015. She did receive the award of "Best session presentation" in WSECS2013 in San-Francisco, USA. She did receive as coauthor the award of "Outstanding Paper in the 2017 Emerald Literati Network Awards for Excellence". Her's interests include optoelectronics, robotics, artificial intelligence, measurement systems, and machine vision systems.

Jeffrey Yi-Lin Forrest is a professor of mathematics and the research coach for the School of Business at Slippery Rock University of Pennsylvania. His research interest covers a wide range of topics, including, but not limited to, economics, finance, mathematics, management, marketing and systems science. As of the end of 2020, he has published over 600 research works, 24 monographs and 27 special topic edited volumes.

Raksh Gangwar is working as Professor and Director in Women Institute of Technology, Dehradun. He is having more than 35 years of experience. He has guided many Ph.D and M.Tech scholars. He is also member of many committee of national/international repute. He has contributed many research papers. He has also contributed many patents under his name.

Ge Gao is a Professor at Zhuhai College of Science and Technology and Management School at Jilin University. Her research focuses on Blockchain application, Supply Chain Management, Big Data application, user interface management in mobile commerce, and Social electronic commerce.

Araceli Gárate-García is a full-time professor at the Universidad Politécnica de Baja California (UPBC) since 2017. She received her PhD in electronics and telecommunications in conjoint between the CICESE research center, Mexico and the IRCCyN research center of the ECN university, France in 2011, the M.Sc. degree in electronics and telecommunications from CICESE research center in 2006 and her bachelor degree in Electronic Engineering in 2003 from the ITM university. Her main research interests are the analysis and control of nonlinear systems with and without time delays and the symbolic computation.

María J. García G. is Bachelor in Chemistry and has a master in Operations Research (OR). Together others authors had increase their investigations, already two hundred and forty, mainly in the areas of Evaluation and Management of Projects, Knowledge Management, Managerial and Social Decision making and OR, especially in multi-criteria decision. They have been presented or published in different countries, having publications and offering their reports, chats or conferences in: Azerbaijan, Finland, Poland, Croatia, Switzerland, Greece, Germany, Italy, Czech Republic, Iceland, Lithuania, Spain, France, Portugal, United States, Panama, Uruguay, Brazil, Mexico, Argentina and Chile besides attending as guest speaker, in lectures to relevant events in Colombia, Peru, Spain and Venezuela. Among other works she is coauthor of: "Inventories control, the Inventory manager and Matrixes Of Weighing with multiplicative factors (MOWwMf)"; "A Methodology of the Decision Support Systems Applied to Other Projects of Investigation"; "Matrixes Of Weighing and catastrophes"; "Multiattribute Model with Multiplicative Factors and Matrixes Of Weighing and the Problem of the Potable Water"

Nuno Geada has a Master's degree in Systems Information Management by Polytechnic Institute of Setúbal - School of Business Sciences and Management -Setúbal, Degree in Industrial Management and Technology by Polytechnic Institute of Setúbal - School of Technology of Setubal. He has written chapters, and papers to journals about topics regarding information technology management and strategic change management. He is from the Editorial Board - Associate Editor from International Journal of Business Strategy and Automation (IJBSA). He is the Editor of the book Reviving Businesses with New Organizational Change Management Strategies. His main research interests in information systems management, strategy, knowledge management, change management, and information technology management adoption in business contexts throw models and frameworks. He works as a Professor and a Researcher.

Natheer K. Gharaibeh is currently Associate Professor at College of Computer Science & Engineering at Yanbu - Taibah University from June 2016. He has more than 17 years of experience: He worked as Assistant Professor at College of Computer Science & Engineering at Yanbu – Taibah University from September. 2013 till June 2016. Before that he worked as an Assistant Professor at Balqa Applied University. He also worked as part-time Lecturer at Jordan University of Science and Technology (JUST) and other Jordanian universities. He published many papers in International Journals and participated in several International Conferences. His current research interests are: Business Intelligence, NLP, IR, Software Engineering, and Knowledge Societies. He got a grant for a joint project from the DFG with Rostock Technical University - Germany. He is editorial board Member, reviewer, and Keynote speaker in many International Journals and Conferences, he also has membership in many International and Technical Societies.

Abichal Ghosh is a final year B.E. student pursuing his degree in Computer Science from BITS Pilani K.K. Birla Goa campus. His field of interest lies in the research areas of Artificial Intelligence, Machine Learning, Deep Learning, Image Processing, Computer Vision and their application in various fields such as Desalination by Membrane technology, Ozonation, and more. Recently, he has been working for the prediction of the optimal conditions of Thin Film Nanocomposite Membranes for efficient desalination. For the topics related to Computer Vision, he has previously worked in the topic of Segmentation and is also currently working on the topic of Learned Image Compression.

Christoph Glauser was born in Berne in 1964. After studying History, Political Science and Media Science in Berne and Law in Geneva, he obtained a doctorate at the University of Berne in 1994. Christoph Glauser then participated in the national research programme, NFP27 at the University of Geneva. As a lecturer in Journalism and Online Research, he worked at various universities. He lectured in the subject, „Organisational Learning" in Social Psychology at the University of Zurich and for six years, he was the leading researcher and lecturer at ETH Zurich. In 1997-1998 he was a Visiting Lecturer at the University of Washington in Seattle, for which he continued to lecture their graduate students in Rome until 2006. During that time, he was Visiting Lecturer for online research at various universities both in Switzerland and abroad. Since 1998, Christoph Glauser has developed a successful career as online expert, CEO and delegate of governing boards, in particular (delete 'of') MMS – Media Monitoring Switzerland AG - and in diverse IT companies. Since 1994, he has been running the Institute for Fundamental Studies in Computer-assisted Content Analyses IFAA in Berne. In 2001, Glauser founded the URL study factory for competition analyses, ArgYou (Arguments for You), in order to study content of websites on the internet and compare these via search engines with the searched-for content (online effect research). In 2006, this company evolved into ArgYou AG in Baar (Switzerland), where he has remained as Chair of the governing board up to the present. For some years, Glauser has been serving on several European committees as an expert in e-governance. Subsequently, in 2007, he was one of the sixteen members of the jury for the European Union e-Government award, which honours the best European e-government projects on behalf of the European Commission. Since 2014 he has been operating the IFAAR find-engine set up directly for purposes of digital evaluation.

Rajesh Godasu is pursuing a Ph.D. in information systems at Dakota State University, his research interest is Deep learning in medical images. He has worked with Dr. Zeng for the past three years on different Machine Learning, Data Science, and Predictive Analytics topics. Conducted research on the Topic "Transfer Learning in Medical Image Classification" and published two papers in Information systems conferences, MWAIS and AMCIS.

Jorge Gomes is a researcher at ADVANCE, ISEG, School of Economics & Management of the Universidade de Lisboa. He holds a PhD in Management from ISEG and a Masters in Management Sciences from ISCTE-IUL, He also have a post-graduation in Project Management from INDEG/ISCTE, and a degree in Geographic Engineering from the Faculty of Sciences of the Universidade de Lisboa. During the past 30 years, he has worked as an engineer, project manager, quality auditor and consultant. Teaches Management at ULHT, Lisboa. His research interests include Benefits Management, Project Management, Project Success, Maturity Models, IS/IT Investments, IS/IT in Healthcare, and IS/IT Management.

Hale Gonce Kocken is an Associate Professor in the Department of Mathematical Engineering at the Yildiz Technical University (YTU), Istanbul, Turkey. She has been a faculty member of YTU since 2004. She completed her Ph.D. entitled "Fuzzy approaches to network analysis" in Applied Mathematics (2011) from the same department. Her current area of research is mathematical programming, supply chain management, and some related Operational Research subjects in multi-criteria and fuzzy environments.

Rick Gorvett is Professor and Chair of the Mathematics Department at Bryant University. He is a Fellow of the Casualty Actuarial Society.

M. Govindarajan is currently an Associate Professor in the Department of Computer Science and Engineering, Annamalai University, Tamil Nadu, India. He received the B.E, M.E and Ph.D Degree in Computer Science and Engineering from Annamalai University, Tamil Nadu, India in 2001, 2005 and 2010 respectively. He did his post-doctoral research in the Department of Computing, Faculty of Engineering and Physical Sciences, University of Surrey, Guildford, Surrey, United Kingdom in 2011 and at CSIR Centre for Mathematical Modelling and Computer Simulation, Bangalore in 2013. He has visited countries like Czech Republic, Austria, Thailand, United Kingdom (twice), Malaysia, U.S.A (twice), and Singapore. He has presented and published more than 140 papers at Conferences and Journals and also received best paper awards. He has delivered invited talks at various national and international conferences. His current research interests include Data Mining and its applications, Web Mining, Text Mining, and Sentiment Mining. He has completed two major projects as principal investigator and has produced four Ph.Ds. He was the recipient of the Achievement Award for the field in the Conference in Bio-Engineering, Computer Science, Knowledge Mining (2006), Prague, Czech Republic. He received

Career Award for Young Teachers (2006), All India Council for Technical Education, New Delhi, India and Young Scientist International Travel Award (2012), Department of Science and Technology, Government of India, New Delhi. He is a Young Scientists awardee under Fast Track Scheme (2013), Department of Science and Technology, Government of India, New Delhi and also granted Young Scientist Fellowship (2013), Tamil Nadu State Council for Science and Technology, Government of Tamil Nadu, Chennai. He also received the Senior Scientist International Travel Award (2016), Department of Science and Technology, Government of India. He has published ten book chapters and also applied patent in the area of data mining. He is an active Member of various professional bodies and Editorial Board Member of various conferences and journals.

Ashwin Gupta has currently completed his BSc with Major in Computer Science from St. Xavier's College, Kolkata. His current research interest is Data Analytics and Machine Learning.

Neha Gupta is currently working as an Professor, Faculty of Computer Applications at Manav Rachna International Institute of Research and Studies, Faridabad campus. She has completed her PhD from Manav Rachna International University and has done R&D Project in CDAC-Noida. She has total of 12+ year of experience in teaching and research. She is a Life Member of ACM CSTA, Tech Republic and Professional Member of IEEE. She has authored and coauthored 30 research papers in SCI/SCOPUS/Peer Reviewed Journals (Scopus indexed) and IEEE/IET Conference proceedings in areas of Web Content Mining, Mobile Computing, and Web Content Adaptation. She is a technical programme committee (TPC) member in various conferences across globe. She is an active reviewer for International Journal of Computer and Information Technology and in various IEEE Conferences around the world. She is one of the Editorial and review board members in International Journal of Research in Engineering and Technology.

Jafar Habibi is an associate professor at the Computer Engineering Department, Sharif University of Technology, Iran. He has been the head of the Computer Society of Iran and the Department of Computer Engineering. His main research interests are Internet of Things, Simulation, System Analysis and Design, and Social Network Analysis.

Christian Haertel studied business informatics at Otto von Guericke University Magdeburg. He joined the VLBA research team in 2021 and accompanies research projects with external partners (e.g., Google Cloud, Accenture Digital). The modelling and development of concepts in the areas of data science and cloud computing are his main areas of research.

J. Michael Hardin is the Provost and Vice President and Professor of Quantitative Analysis at Samford University. Dr. Hardin came to Samford University in July 2015 from the University of Alabama at Tuscaloosa, where he served as the Culverhouse College of Commerce and Business Administration dean. Dr. Hardin had previously served as Culverhouse's senior associate dean, associate dean for research, director of the University of Alabama's NIH Alabama EPSCoR Agency and director of Culverhouse's Institute of Business Intelligence. Dr. Hardin's service as a Culverhouse professor of quantitative analysis, business and statistics was widely credited for establishing the University of Alabama as an internationally-known resource in the field of data analytics. His Culverhouse career followed his numerous administrative and faculty appointments at the University of Alabama in Birmingham in biostatistics, biomathematics, health informatics and computer science. Dr. Hardin holds a Ph.D. in Applied Statistics from the University of Alabama, M.A. in Mathematics from the University of Alabama, M.S. in Research Design and Statistics from Florida State University's College of Education, B.A. in Mathematics from the University of West Florida, B.A. in Philosophy from the University of West Florida and M.Div. from New Orleans Baptist Theological Seminary. He is an ordained Southern Baptist minister. Dr. Hardin has authored or co-authored more than 150 papers in various journals, edited numerous professional journals, authored multiple book chapters, presented more than 250 abstracts at national meetings and given more than 150 invited lectures or talks. For 25 years he served as a National Institutes of Health (NIH) grant reviewer and participated as Investigator or co-Investigator on more than 100 U.S. Department of Health and Human Services/NIH-funded projects. He has served as a consultant for other national healthcare and financial organizations and was among the inventors receiving a U.S. patent licensed to MedMined, a Birmingham-based firm dedicated to controlling hospital infection rates and improving patient care.

Shanmugasundaram Hariharan received his B.E degree specialized in Computer Science and Engineering from Madurai Kammaraj University, Madurai, India in 2002, M.E degree specialized in the field of Computer Science and Engineering from Anna University, Chennai, India in 2004. He holds his Ph.D degree in the area of Information Retrieval from Anna University, Chennai, India. He is a member of IAENG, IACSIT, ISTE, CSTA and has 17 years of experience in teaching. Currently he is working as Professor in Department of Computer Science and Engineering, Vardhaman College of Engineering, India. His research interests include Information Retrieval, Data mining, Opinion Mining, Web mining. He has to his credit several papers in referred journals and conferences. He also serves as editorial board member and as program committee member for several international journals and conferences.

Budi Harsanto is a lecturer at Universitas Padjadjaran, Bandung, Indonesia. His research interests are in sustainability innovation, and operations and supply chain management.

Md Salleh Salleh Hassan, Prof., PhD, is a retired Professor at the Department of Communication, Faculty of Modern Languages and Communication, Universiti Putra Malaysia. He has graduated many PhD, master's and undergraduate students. He was once the Deputy Dean of the Faculty, and has published many research papers, attended many conferences both local and international.

Miralem Helmefalk, PhD, is an assistant senior lecturer at the Department of Marketing in School of Business and Economics at Linnaeus University in Sweden. Miralem's research interests lie in concepts within consumer psychology, digitalization, gamification as well as sensory marketing. He believes that machine learning represents the perfect storm for his research interests.

Gilberto J. Hernández is a Bachelor in Chemistry and have a master in Technology of foods. Together others authors had increase their investigations, mainly in the areas of Food technologies, Playful, in particular in the fantastic sports leagues, Knowledge Management, Managerial and Social Decision making, Logistics, Risk Management and Operations research, especially in multi-criteria decision and making decision under uncertainty and risk. They have been presented or published in different countries, having publications and offering their reports, chats or conferences in: Finland, Poland, Croatia, Switzerland, Greece, Czech Republic, Spain, Portugal and United States besides attending as guest speaker, in lectures to relevant events in Costa Rica and Venezuela. Among other works he is coauthor of: "Enterprise Logistics, Indicators and Physical Distribution Manager"; "Multiattribute Models with Multiplicative factors in the Fantasy Sports"; "The Industrial design manager of LoMoBaP and Knowledge Management"; "Dynamic knowledge: Diagnosis and Customer Service".

José Hernández Ramírez is a Chemical Engineer and have a master in Operations Research. Together others authors had increase their investigations, already above two hundred and forty, mainly in the areas of Knowledge Management, Managerial and Social Decision making, Logistics, Risk Management and Operations research, especially in multi-criteria decision. They have been presented or published in different countries, having publications and offering their reports, chats or conferences in: Azerbaijan, Finland, Croatia, Switzerland, Greece, Germany, Italy, Czech Republic, Iceland, Lithuania, Spain, France, Portugal, United States, Panama, Paraguay, Uruguay, Brazil, Cuba, Mexico, Argentina and Chile besides attending as guest speaker, in reiterated occasions, in lectures to relevant events in Colombia, Peru, Costa Rica, Brazil, Spain and Venezuela. Among other works he is coauthor of: "Teaching Enterprise Logistics through Indicators: Dispatch Manager"; "Enterprise diagnosis and the Environmental manager of LoMoBaP"; "Logistics, Marketing and Knowledge Management in the Community of Consumer".

Thanh Ho received M.S. degree in Computer Science from University of Information Technology, VNU-HCM, Vietnam in 2009 and PhD degree in Computer Science from University of Information Technology, VNU-HCM, Vietnam. He is currently lecturer in Faculty of Information Systems, University of Economics and Law, VNU-HCM, Vietnam in 2018. His research interests are Data mining, Data Analytics, Business Intelligence, Social Network Analysis, and Big Data.

Victoria Hodge is a Research Fellow and Software Developer in the Department of Computer Science at University of York. Her research interests include AI, outlier detection, and data mining. She is currently researching the safety assurance of machine learning for autonomous systems. A focus of this research is assuring robot navigation including localisation. She is on the editorial board of two journals and has authored over 60 refereed publications. She has worked in industry as a software architect for a medical diagnostics company; and as a software developer on condition monitoring in industrial environments, and deep learning for robot navigation.

Essam H. Houssein received his PhD degree in Computer Science in 2012. He is an associate professor at the Faculty of Computers and Information, Minia University, Egypt. He is the founder and chair of the Computing & Artificial Intelligence Research Group (CAIRG) in Egypt. He has more than 100 scientific research papers published in prestigious international journals in the topics for instance meta-heuristics optimization, artificial intelligence, image processing, IoT and its applications. Essam H. Houssein serves as a reviewer of more than 40 journals (Elsevier, Springer, IEEE, etc.). His research interests include WSNs, IoT, AI, Bioinformatics and Biomedical, Image processing, Data mining, and Meta-heuristics Optimization techniques.

Adamkolo Mohammed Ibrahim is a Lecturer at the Department of Mass Communication, University of Maiduguri, Nigeria and a PhD Research Scholar at Bayero University, Kano (BUK), Nigeria. He received his master's degree in Development Communication at Universiti Putra Malaysia (UPM) in 2017. In 2007, he had his first degree (BA Mass Communication) at the Department of Mass Communication, University of Maiduguri, Nigeria. Currently, he teaches mass communication at the University of Maiduguri. He conducts research and writes in ICT adoption for development, social media, cyberbullying, cyber terrorism/conflict, gender and ICT, gender and conflict and online shopping. He has published several journal articles, book chapters and a few books. His most recent work explores the impacts of fake news and hate speech in Nigerian democracy and proposes a theoretical model as a fact-checking tool. More details on his most recent works and all his other publications can be accessed on his website: https://unimaid.academia.edu/AdamkoloMohammedIbrahim. Malam Adamkolo is currently serving as an Editorial Board Member of Jurnal Komunikasi Ikatan Sarjana Komunikasi Indonesia (the Communication Journal of the Indonesian Association of Communication Scholars) and a co-researcher in a research project by The Kukah Centre, Abuja, Nigeria. The proposed title of the research is: "Engaging Local Communities for Peacebuilding, Social Cohesion, Preventing and Countering Violent Extremism in Nigeria's northeast". Adamkolo has received Publons Top Reviewer Award in 2018 (for being among the top 1% global peer reviewers in Psychiatry/Psychology). In 2017, Elsevier had awarded him a certificate of outstanding peer review with one of Elsevier's prestigious journals, Computers in Human Behaviour (CHB) which he reviews for; he also reviews for Emerald's Journal of Systems and Information Technology (JSIT) and several other journals. Much earlier, from 2000 to 2010, he worked as a broadcast journalist in Yobe Broadcasting Corporation (YBC) Damaturu, and from 2008 to 2010 was deployed to Sahel FM (formerly Pride FM, a subsidiary of YBC Damaturu as DJ-cum-producer/presenter/journalist). From 2008 to 2010, he worked as YBC's focal person on UNICEF and Partnership for the Revival of Routine Immunisation in Northern Nigeria-Maternal, newborn and Child Health (PRRINN-MNCH). From September to October 2018, he served as a consultant to ManienDanniels (West Africa Ltd.) and MNCH2 programme.

Funda Ipekten's research focused on a statistical analysis of high-throughput metabolomics data, multi-omics data integration, feature selection for multi-omics.

Adelina Ivanova is Assisted Professor Dr. in Department of Computer Systems and Informatics of University of Forestry, Sofia, Bulgaria. Her research interests are in the areas of ontology engineering, sustainable development, databases, and office information systems.

Sajan T. John is an Associate Professor of Industrial Engineering in the Department of Mechanical Engineering at Viswajyothi College of Engineering and Technology, Vazhakulam, Kerala. He received PhD from the National Institute of Technology Calicut in 2015. His research interests are in the areas of operations research, mathematical modelling, supply chain management and reverse logistics. He has published papers in international journals and proceedings of international and national conferences.

Rachid Kaleche is a PhD student of computer science since 2018. He is member of computer science laboratory (LIO) of Oran 1 university in Algeria. His current research interests deal with artificial intelligence, transportation system, logistic systems, machine learning, and bio-inspired approach. He is co-author of many publications and communications.

Reddi Kamesh received B.Tech in Chemical engineering from Acharya Nagarjuna University, Guntur, India, in 2011, and M.Tech and Ph.D. from Academy of and Innovative Research (AcSIR), CSIR-Indian Institute of Chemical Technology (IICT), Campus, Hyderabad, India, in 2014 and 2019 respectively. Dr. Kamesh has extensive experience in the field of Process Systems Engineering (PSE), Artificial Intelligence (AI) and Machine Learning methods, Integrated Multi-Scale Modelling methods, and Process Intensification. He is working as a scientist in CSIR-IICT since 2016. He has actively engaged in basic research as well as applied research. He has developed process model-based as well as AI-based methodologies to simulate, design, control, and optimize processes, for accelerated product and process design, and to achieve performance improvements to existing processes in terms of improving productivity and selectivity while maintaining their safety and environmental constraints. Dr. Kamesh was a recipient of the Ambuja Young Researchers Award in 2014 from Indian Institute of Chemical Engineers (IIChE).

Shri Kant has received his Ph. D. in applied mathematics from applied mathematics departments of institute of technology, Banaras Hindu University (BHU), Varanasi in 1981. He is working as a Professor and head of "Center of Cyber Security and cryptology", Department of Computer Science and Engineering of Sharda University, India and involved actively in teaching and research mainly in the area of cyber security and Machine learning. His areas of interest are Special Functions, Cryptology, Pattern Recognition, Cluster Analysis, Soft Computing Model, Machine Learning and Data Mining.

Nurdan Kara is an Assistant Prof. in the Department of Mathematics at National Defence University (MSU), Istanbul, Turkey. She has been a faculty member of Ankara University since 1998. She completed her Ph.D. entitled "Fuzzy approaches to multiobjective fractional transportation problem" in Applied Mathematics (2008) from Yildiz Technical University. Her current area of research is mathematical Programming, fractional programming, supply chain management and some related Operational Research subjects in multi criteria and fuzzy environments.

Prasanna Karhade is Associate Professor of IT Management, Shidler College Faculty Fellow and a Faculty Fellow at the Pacific Asian Center for Entrepreneurship [PACE] at the University of Hawai'i at Mānoa. His research interests include digital innovation and digital platforms in growing, rural, eastern, aspirational and transitional [GREAT] economies.

Bouamrane Karim received the PhD Degree in computer science from the Oran University in 2006. He is Professor of computer Science at Oran1 University. He is the head of "Decision and piloting system" team. His current research interests deal with decision support system and logistics in maritime transportation, urban transportation system, production system, health systems and application of bio-inspired based optimization metaheuristic. He participates in several scientific committees' international/national conferences in Algeria and others countries in the same domain and collaborated in Algerian-French scientific projects. He is co-author of more than 40 scientific publications.

Joseph Kasten is an Assistant Professor of Information Science and Technology at the Pennsylvania State University in York, PA. He earned a PhD in Information Science at Long Island University in Brookville, NY, an MBA at Dowling College in Oakdale, NY, and a BS in engineering at Florida Institute of Technology in Melbourne, FL. Before joining academia, Joe was a senior engineer with the Northrop-Grumman Corp. where he worked on various military and commercial projects such as the X-29 and the Boeing 777. His research interests center on the implementation of data analytics within the organization as well as the application of blockchain technology to emerging organizational requirements. Professor Kasten's recent research appears in the International Journal of Business Intelligence Research and International Journal of Healthcare Information Systems and Informatics.

Tolga Kaya is a full-time researcher and lecturer at the department of Management Engineering in Istanbul Technical University. His research areas are consumer modeling, statistical decision making, input-output modeling, multicriteria decision making, machine learning and fuzzy applications in business and management. He has published several papers and presented his research at a number of international conferences in these areas.

Wei Ke, Ph.D., is the Adjunct Associate Professor of Quantitative Revenue and Pricing Analytics at Columbia Business School. Previously, he was Managing Partner and the head of financial services practice in North America at Simon-Kucher & Partners. Wei received a Ph.D. in Decision, Risk, and Operations from Columbia Business School, and a BSc in Electrical Engineering & Applied Mathematics, summa cum laude, from Columbia University.

Vanessa Keppeler is a Senior Associate with PwC Germany's Financial Services Consulting practice. She specializes on the design and implementation of Data and AI Governance. Her research and studies focus on the practical enablement of Explainable AI in Financial Institutions. Vanessa holds a master's degree in Management (Finance).

Mehrnaz Khalaj Hedayati is an Assistant Professor of Management at Georgia College & State University, J. Whitney Bunting College of Business. Mehrnaz received her Ph.D. from the University of Rhode Island in 2020. Mehrnaz has published several academic journal articles. She is a Lean Six Sigma Certified from the URI College of Business. She has taught undergraduate and master's level courses in Business Quantitative Analysis, Business Statistics, and Operations Management. She has also served as ad-hoc reviewer for several academic journals.

Fahima Khanam is a Lecturer in the department of Aviation Operation Management at Bangabandhu Sheikh Mujibur Rahman Aviation and Aerospace University. Prior to joining the BSMRAAU, she served as Lecturer in the Department of Business Administration at Sheikh Burhanuddin Post Graduate College, European University, Victoria University and German University, Bangladesh where she taught Principles of Marketing, Marketing Management, Operations Management, International Business, and Business Communication. She also worked as a corporate professional in The Daily 'Prothom Alo', one of the top daily newspapers in Bangladesh. She holds an MBA in Marketing from University of Dhaka, Bangladesh. Her most recent publication appeared in the International Journal of Big Data and Analytics in Healthcare (IJBDAH). Her principal research interests include e-commerce, online shopping, social media marketing and branding strategy, marketing strategy and technology adoption.

Shardul Khandekar has his BE completed in E&TC and his research area includes machine learning and deep learning.

Mubina Khondkar serves as a Professor in the Department of Marketing at the University of Dhaka. She has interdisciplinary knowledge in the areas of marketing and development economics. She has both industry and research experiences with organizations including ANZ Grindlays Bank, Care Bangladesh, USAID, DFID, Concern, IFPRI, World Bank, SEDF, IFC, JICA, CIDA, UNICEF, BIDS, the University of Manchester, and the University of Cambridge. Her research interests include value chain analysis, marketing, poverty, microfinance, development economics, gender, and women's empowerment. Further details can be found here: https://www.researchgate.net/profile/Mubina-Khondkar.

Soumya Khurana has his BE completed in E&TC and his research area includes machine learning and deep learning.

Necla Koçhan is currently working as a postdoctoral researcher at Izmir Biomedicine and Genome Center, IBG. Her research interests are computational biology, statistical data analysis, fuzzy theory, classification, and biostatistics.

Koharudin is a master student in IPB University, Indonesia. In 2014 he joined the Bureau of Organization and Human Resource, Indonesian Institute of Sciences (LIPI), as IT Engineering. In 2020 He moved to Center for Scientific Data and Documentation, Indonesian Institute of Sciences (LIPI). His current roles include building and maintaining web applications, designing database architecture, integrating data and providing data through service point. He obtained his bachelor degree in Computer Science from the Sepuluh Nopember Institute of Technology in 2011. He has developed some applications such as Human Resources Information System, Mobile applications and API Gateway. His research interests include Bioinformatics, High Performance Computing and Machine Learning.

Tibor Koltay is Professor retired from the Institute of Learning Technologies at Eszterházy Károly Catholic University, in Hungary. He graduated from Eötvös Loránd University (Budapest, Hungary) in 1984 with an MA in Russian. He obtained there his PhD in 2002. In 1992 he was awarded the Certificate of Advanced Studies in Library and Information Science at Kent State University, Kent. OH.

Xiangfen Kong is an Associate Professor from the Civil Aviation University of China. Her research interests include smart airports, system reliability, operational research, and big data.

Elena Kornyshova is an Associate Professor at CNAM, Ph.D. in Economics and Management Sciences and Ph.D. in Computer Science. Her main research domains are method and process engineering, decision-making, enterprise architecture, and digitalization. She is/was involved in organization of multiple international conferences and workshops. She has significant experience in industry and consultancy sector mainly in the fields of IS engineering and enterprise architecture.

Maximiliano E. Korstanje is editor in chief of International Journal of Safety and Security in Tourism (UP Argentina) and Editor in Chief Emeritus of International Journal of Cyber Warfare and Terrorism (IGI-Global US). Korstanje is Senior Researchers in the Department of Economics at University of Palermo, Argentina. In 2015 he was awarded as Visiting Research Fellow at School of Sociology and Social Policy, University of Leeds, UK and the University of La Habana Cuba. In 2017 is elected as Foreign Faculty Member of AMIT, Mexican Academy in the study of Tourism, which is the most prominent institutions dedicated to tourism research in Mexico. He had a vast experience in editorial projects working as advisory member of Elsevier, Routledge, Springer, IGI global and Cambridge Scholar publishing. Korstanje had visited and given seminars in many important universities worldwide. He has also recently been selected to take part of the 2018 Albert Nelson Marquis Lifetime Achievement Award. a great distinction given by Marquis Who´s Who in the world.

Mika Kosonen is a graduate student in University of Lapland. He has bachelor's degree in social sciences and is currently finishing his master's degree. His bachelor's thesis was concerning artificial intelligence and ethics, and master's thesis contributes to morality in human-technology interaction, both with excellent grades. With strong interest in technology and human experience he is always wondering the world where technology mediates the reality, whether in suburbans or the wilderness found in northernmost parts of Europe.

Anjani Kumar is a Ph.D. student of computer science at the University of Nebraska at Omaha. He is working as a Data Scientist at Data Axle Inc. His primary research interests are in the fields of Big Data, Deep Learning, and Machine Learning.

Sameer Kumar is an Associate Professor at Universiti Malaya, Malaysia.

Madhusree Kundu is presently Professor, Department of Chemical Engineering, National Institute of Technology Rourkela, Orissa, India. Currently, HOD, Central Instrument Facility (CIF), NIT Rourkela. Experience: Worked as Process Engineer in Simon Carves India Limited (A Design Consultancy). First Academic Appointment: Assistant Professor, Birla Institute of Technology and Science (BITS) Pilani, Rajasthan, India. PhD: Indian Institute of Technology Kharagpur Research Interest: Fluid Phase equilibrium and its application, Modeling, & Simulation and Control, Chemommetrics/Machine Learning applications, Process Identification monitoring and Control, Biomimetic device development and Digitized Sustainable Agriculture.

Mascha Kurpicz-Briki obtained her PhD in the area of energy-efficient cloud computing at the University of Neuchâtel. After her PhD, she worked a few years in industry, in the area of open-source engineering, cloud computing and analytics. She is now professor for data engineering at the Bern University of Applied Sciences, investigating how to apply digital methods and in particular natural language processing to social and community challenges.

Kevin Kwak is an Information Systems and Accounting student at the University of Nebraska at Omaha. He received a Master's in Accounting and as of this writing is pursuing a Master's in Information Systems. His current interests of study are accounting, data security, and data mining. Currently, he has had five articles published in various journals.

Wikil Kwak is a Professor of Accounting at the University of Nebraska at Omaha. He received Ph.D. in Accounting from the University of Nebraska in Lincoln. Dr. Kwak's research interests include the areas of mathematical programming approaches in bankruptcy prediction, capital budgeting, transfer pricing, performance evaluation and Japanese capital market studies. He has published more than 57 articles in the Engineering Economist, Abacus, Contemporary Accounting Research, Review of Quantitative Finance and Accounting, Management Accountant, Journal of Petroleum Accounting and Financial Management, Business Intelligence and Data Mining, Review of Pacific Basin Financial Markets and Policies, and Multinational Business Review.

Georgios Lampropoulos received his BSc degree with the title of Information Technology Engineer specialized as a Software Engineer from the Department of Information Technology at Alexander

Technological Educational Institute of Thessaloniki (currently named International Hellenic University) in 2017 and he received his MSc in Web Intelligence from the same department in 2019. Currently, he is a PhD candidate and Visiting Lecturer in the Department of Information and Electronic Engineering at International Hellenic University and a MEd student in Education Sciences at Hellenic Open University. He has published his work in several peer reviewed journals and conferences, he has taken part in international research programs and he has also served as a reviewer and a member of the organizing and scientific committees of international conferences and international journals.

Torben Larsen is an MSc Econ from University of Aarhus and an international Degree in Strategic Management from University of Maryland-Tietgenskolen Dk. He has broad experience in regional planning of healthcare with Academic Awards from 1) Association of Hospital Managers in Norway, Lundbeck Fonden Dk and MIE96. He is a former Chief Research Consultant at University of Southern Denmark which included leadership of an EU-sponsored research project in Integrated Homecare. He has been involved with various courses and conferences and has written research papers in Health Economics, Neuroeconomics, Meditation and Biofeedback. 2017 he published "Homo Neuroeconomicus" (IJUDH(1)). 2020 he published "Neuroeconomic Pcyshology. 3 Modules for End-users . . . .", IJPCH Actually, he is giving guest lectures in cybernetic economics.

Matthias Lederer is Full Professor of Information Systems at the Technical University of Applied Sciences Amberg-Weiden. Prior to this, he was a professor at the ISM International School of Management Munich and at the same time Chief Process Officer at the IT Service Center of the Bavarian justice system. His previous positions include research assistant at the University of Erlangen-Nuremberg and strategy consultant at the German industrial company REHAU. His research and studies focus on business process management and IT management. Prof. Lederer holds a doctorate as well as a master's degree in international information systems and is the author of over 70 scientific publications in this field.

Eva Lee applies combinatorial optimization, math programming, game theory, and parallel computation to biological, medical, health systems, and logistics analyses. Her clinical decision-support systems (DSS) assist in disease diagnosis/prediction, treatment design, drug delivery, treatment and healthcare outcome analysis/prediction, and healthcare operations logistics. In logistics, she tackles operations planning and resource allocation, and her DSS addresses inventory control, vehicle dispatching, scheduling, transportation, telecom, portfolio investment, public health emergency treatment response, and facility location/planning. Dr. Lee is Director of the Center for Operations Research in Medicine and HealthCare, a center established through funds from the National Science Foundation and the Whitaker Foundation. The center focuses on biomedicine, public health and defense, translational medical research, medical delivery and preparedness, and the protection of critical infrastructures. She is a subject matter expert in medical systems and public health informatics, logistics and networks, and large-scale connected systems. She previously served as the Senior Health Systems Engineer and Professor for the U.S. Department of Veterans Affairs and was Co-Director for the Center for Health Organization Transformation. Dr. Lee has received numerous practice excellence awards, including the INFORMS Edelman Award on novel cancer therapeutics, the Wagner prize on vaccine immunity prediction, and the Pierskalla award on bioterrorism, emergency response, and mass casualty mitigation She is a fellow at INFORMS and AIMBE. Lee has served on NAE/NAS/IOM, NRC, NBSB, DTRA panel committees related to CBRN and WMD incidents, public health and medical preparedness, and healthcare systems innovation. She holds ten patents on medical systems and devices. Her work has been featured in the New York Times, London Times, disaster documentaries, and in other venues.

Jinha Lee is an Assistant Professor in the Department of Public and Allied Health at Bowling Green State University. His research interests include healthcare operations, data analytics, economic decision analysis, and system modeling in healthcare service. His work has examined practice variance and systems analysis for quality and process improvement and new clinical guidelines establishment. Also, his research has focused on economic analysis on industry networks, resource allocations, and the R&D process in healthcare services. His research primarily utilizes large datasets and clinical observations derived from various healthcare databases and field studies in clinical facilities. He has collaborated actively with hospitals, healthcare research institutes, and healthcare delivery organizations both in the U.S. and in foreign countries.

Ulli Leucht is a Manager in PwC Germany's Financial Services Technology Consulting team. He is an expert in AI and its use in Financial Institutions - which includes how AI use cases are identified, perceived, implemented, operated and surrounding governance, compliance, and legal requirements. Prior to joining PwC Germany, he worked with some of the most innovative FinTechs in the United Kingdom and the United States in the context of AI. Ulli's research and studies focus is the usage of AI in Financial Institutions. He holds a master's degree in Sensors and Cognitive Psychology.

Carson Leung is currently a Professor at the University of Manitoba, Canada. He has contributed more than 300 refereed publications on the topics of big data, computational intelligence, cognitive computing, data analytics, data mining, data science, fuzzy systems, machine learning, social network analysis, and visual analytics. These include eight chapters in IGI Global's books/encyclopedia (e.g., Encyclopedia of Organizational Knowledge, Administration, and Technology (2021)). He has also served on the Organizing Committee of the ACM CIKM, ACM SIGMOD, IEEE DSAA, IEEE ICDM, and other conferences.

Siyao Li is a student at the City University of Macau. She studies in the International Business program.

Gilson B. A. Lima is a Professor in the Industrial Engineering Department at Federal Fluminense University (UFF), Brazil. He received his PhD in the Rio de Janeiro Federal University, Brazil. His current research interests include industrial safety, risk management, industrial maintenance and industrial environmental management.

Yu-Wei Lin is an assistant professor in the Leavey School of Business, Santa Clara University. He received a Ph.D. in information systems at Gies College of Business, the University of Illinois at Urbana-Champaign. His research interests are in User-Generated Content, Healthcare Analytics, Online Review Analysis, Machine Learning, Decision Making, and Decision Support Systems.

Fangyao Liu is an assistant professor in the College of Electronic and Information at the Southwest Minzu University, China. He received Ph.D. in Information Technology from the University of Nebraska at Omaha, USA. Dr. Liu's research interests include the areas of data mining, artificial intelligence, and statistics. He has published more than 20 articles in the International journal of Computers Communications & Control, Journal of Urban Planning and Development, Journal of software, Journal of Asian Development, Journal of Contemporary Management, Procedia Computer Science, and several IEEE conferences.

Haoyu Liu is an assistant professor at the Faculty of Business, City University of Macau. He received an MPhil and a PhD in Operations Management from HKUST Business School in 2017 and 2020, respectively. He serves as a reviewer for Manufacturing & Service Operations Management (MSOM), Naval Research Logistics (NRL), International Journal of Applied Management Science (IJAMS), International Journal of Retail & Distribution Management (IJRDM), International Journal of E-Business Research (IJEBR), International Conference on Information Systems (ICIS), and INFORMS Conference on Service Science (ICSS). He has broad interests in issues related to healthcare, emerging technologies, charitable organizations, and marketing. In solving problems, he employs various techniques, ranging from game-theoretical and stochastic models to typical tools in empirical and experimental studies.

Ran Liu is an Assistant Professor in the Marketing department at Central Connecticut State University. His research focuses on online relationships, user-generated content (UGC), data modeling, and International businesses. He serves as Associate Editor (Asia) for Journal of Eastern European and Central Asian Research (JEECAR) and Faculty Advisor for American Marketing Association Collegiate Chapter.

Cèlia Llurba is currently a PhD student in Educational Technology in the Department of Pedagogy at the URV. Graduate in East Asian Studies from the UOC and a graduate in Mining Engineering from the UPC. She is currently a teacher of Technology in a high school in Cambrils (state employee) and also teaches in the subjects of Vocational Guidance and Citizenship, and Educational Processes and Contexts, within the Master's Degree in Teacher Training at the URV. Her main lines of research are: intellectual learning environments, data analytics and artificial intelligence in intellectual areas.

Manuel Lozano Rodriguez is American University of Sovereign Nations (AUSN) Visiting Prof. in his own discipline that takes bioethics off the medical hegemony to land it on social sciences, futurism, politics and pop culture through metaphysics of displacement. Born in Barcelona in 1978, Ph.D. in Bioethics, Sustainability and Global Public Health, AUSN; Master of Science in Sustainability, Peace and Development, AUSN; Graduate in Fundamentals of Sustainability Organizational, Harvard.

Lorenzo Magnani, philosopher, epistemologist, and cognitive scientist, is a professor of Philosophy of Science at the University of Pavia, Italy, and the director of its Computational Philosophy Laboratory. His previous positions have included: visiting researcher (Carnegie Mellon University, 1992; McGill University, 1992–93; University of Waterloo, 1993; and Georgia Institute of Technology, 1998–99) and visiting professor (visiting professor of Philosophy of Science and Theories of Ethics at Georgia Institute of Technology, 1999–2003; Weissman Distinguished Visiting Professor of Special Studies in Philosophy: Philosophy of Science at Baruch College, City University of New York, 2003). Visiting professor at the Sun Yat-sen University, Canton (Guangzhou), China from 2006 to 2012, in the event of the 50th anniversary of the re-building of the Philosophy Department of Sun Yat-sen University in 2010, an award was given to him to acknowledge his contributions to the areas of philosophy, philosophy of science, logic, and cognitive science. A Doctor Honoris Causa degree was awarded to Lorenzo Magnani by the Senate of the Ştefan cel Mare University, Suceava, Romania. In 2015 Lorenzo Magnani has been appointed member of the International Academy for the Philosophy of the Sciences (AIPS). He currently directs international research programs in the EU, USA, and China. His book Abduction, Reason, and Science (New York, 2001) has become a well-respected work in the field of human cognition. The book Morality in a Technological World (Cambridge, 2007) develops a philosophical and cognitive theory of the relationships between ethics and technology in a naturalistic perspective. The book Abductive Cognition. The Epistemological and Eco-Cognitive Dimensions of Hypothetical Reasoning and the last monograph Understanding Violence. The Intertwining of Morality, Religion, and Violence: A Philosophical Stance have been more recently published by Springer, in 2009 and 2011. A new monograph has been published by Springer in 2017, The Abductive Structure of Scientific Creativity. An Essay on the Ecology of Cognition, together with the Springer Handbook of Model-Based Science (edited with Tommaso Bertolotti). The last book Eco-Cognitive Computationalism. Cognitive Domestication of Ignorant Entities, published by Springer, offers an entirely new dynamic perspective on the nature of computation. He edited books in Chinese, 16 special issues of international academic journals, and 17 collective books, some of them deriving from international conferences. Since 1998, initially in collaboration with Nancy J. Nersessian and Paul Thagard, he created and promoted the MBR Conferences on Model-Based Reasoning. Since 2011 he is the editor of the Book Series Studies in Applied Philosophy, Epistemology and Rational Ethics (SAPERE), Springer, Heidelberg/Berlin.

Mazlina Abdul Majid is an Associate Professor in the Faculty of Computing at University Malaysia Pahang (UMP), Malaysia. She received her PHD in Computer Science from the University of Nottingham, UK. She held various managerial responsibilities as a Deputy Dean of Research and Graduate Studies and currently acts as the head of the Software Engineering Research Group in her Faculty. She also taught courses on the undergraduate and master's levels. She has published 130 research in local and international books, journals and conference proceedings. She is also a member of various committees of international conferences. Her research interests include simulation, software agent, software usability and testing.

Jasna D. Marković-Petrović received her B.Sc. (1992) and M.Sc. (2011) degrees in electrical engineering and her Ph.D. degree (2018) in technical sciences, all from the University of Belgrade, Serbia. She is with the Public Enterprise "Electric Power Industry of Serbia" for more than 25 years. Her activities involve implementation of the technical information system, participation in projects concerning upgrading the remote control system of the hydropower plant, and implementation of the SCADA security system. She is a member of the Serbian National CIGRÉ Study Committee D2. As author or coauthor, she published a number of book chapters, journal articles and conference papers in her field. Her main research interests involve smart grids, SCADA and industrial control systems security, and cyber risk management.

Roberto Marmo received the Laurea (cum laude) in Computer Science from Salerno University (Italy) and Ph.D. in Electronic and Computer Engineering obtained from the University of Pavia (Italy). He is presently contract teacher of computer science at Faculty of Engineering of Pavia University, Italy. His most recent work is concerned with mathematical models and software for social network analysis. He is author of "Social Media Mining", a textbook in Italian language on extraction of information from social media, website http://www.socialmediamining.it.

Nikolaos Matsatsinis is a full Professor of Information and Decision Support Systems in the School of Production Engineering and Management of the Technical University of Crete, Greece. He is President of the Hellenic Operational Research Society (HELORS). He is Director of DSS Lab and Postgraduate Programs. He has contributed as scientific or project coordinator on over of fifty national and international projects. He is chief editor of the Operational Research: An International Journal (Impact Factor 2020: 2.410) and International Journal of Decision Support Systems. He is the author or co-author/editor of 25 books and over of 120 articles in international scientific journals and books. He has organized and participated in the organization of over of ninety scientific conferences, including EURO 2021, and he has over of one hundred and ninety presentations in international and national scientific conferences. His research interests fall into the areas of Intelligent DSS, Multi-Agent Systems, Recommendation Systems, Multicriteria Decision Analysis, Group Decision Making, Operational Research, e-Marketing, Consumer Behaviour Analysis, Data Analysis, Business Intelligence & Business Analytics.

Hubert Maupas is graduated from Ecole Centrale de Lyon (France) and holds a PhD in Integrated Electronics, obtained with several patents and publications. He has spent most of his career in medical device industry and is currently working as COO of MUST, a all-in-one B2B Metaverse platform to manage DBE (Digital Business Ecosystem) embedding advanced matchmaking algorithms.

Iman Megahed is the AVP for Digital Transformation, Chief Strategy and Knowledge Officer at the American University in Cairo (AUC). She is currently responsible for all Information Technology, Information Security, Business Intelligence and institutional effectiveness functions. She co-founded the business intelligence and data governance functions to support informed based decision making. She also founded the office of Online Student Services which applied web services and portal technology to enhance student services. With a successful track record in technology and effectiveness administrative positions in Higher Education since 1992, Iman has accumulated extensive technical expertise, unique project management skills coupled with results-oriented leadership style and passion for informed based decision making. Iman earned her PhD in Organizational Behavior from Cairo University, MBA and BS in Computer Science from The American University in Cairo.

Natarajan Meghanathan is a tenured Full Professor of Computer Science at Jackson State University, Jackson, MS. He graduated with a Ph.D. in Computer Science from The University of Texas at Dallas in May 2005. Dr. Meghanathan has published more than 175 peer-reviewed articles (more than half of them being journal publications). He has also received federal education and research grants from the U. S. National Science Foundation, Army Research Lab and Air Force Research Lab. Dr. Meghanathan has been serving in the editorial board of several international journals and in the Technical Program Committees and Organization Committees of several international conferences. His research interests are Wireless Ad hoc Networks and Sensor Networks, Graph Theory and Network Science, Cyber Security, Machine Learning, Bioinformatics and Computational Biology. For more information, visit https://www.jsums.edu/nmeghanathan.

Abelardo Mercado Herrera has a PhD from the National Institute of Astrophysics, Optics and Electronics (INAOE), specializing in Astrophysics, Postdoctorate in Astrophysics from the Institute of Astronomy from the National Autonomous University of Mexico (UNAM), Electronics Engineer from the Autonomous University of Baja California (UABC). He is a specialist in the mathematical-statistical description of stochastic processes and/or deterministic systems, nonlinear systems, complex systems, chaos theory, among others, as well as its application to physical phenomena such as astronomy, medicine, economics, finance, telecommunications, social sciences etc., in order to determine the dynamics underlying in such processes, and given the case, its connection with real physical variables and possible prediction. He has worked on the development of interfaces and programs to carry out electrical tests in industry, as well as in scientific instrumentation, applied to telemetry, infrared polarimetry, optics and spectroscopy. He has also specialized in image analysis, measurement techniques and noise reduction.

Shivlal Mewada is presently working as an Assistant Professor (contact) in the Dept. of CS, Govt. Holkar (Autonomous, Model) Science College, Indore, India. He shared the responsibility of research activities and coordinator of M.Phil.(CS) at Govt. Holkar Sci. Collage, Indore. He has also received JRF in 2010-11 for M.Phil. Programme under UGC Fellow scheme, New Delhi. He is a member of IEEE since 2013 and editorial member of the ISROSET since 2013. He is a technical committee and editorial member of various reputed journals including Taylor & Francis, Inderscience. He chaired 5 national and international conferences and seminars. He organized 2 special for international conferences. He also contributed to the organization of 2 national and 4 virtual international conferences. Mr. Mewada has published 3 book chapters and over 18 research articles in reputed journals like SCI, Scopus including IEEE conferences. His areas of interest include; cryptography, information security and computational intelligence.

Tanish Ambrishkumar Mishra is an undergraduate student at Sardar Patel College of Engineering, Mumbai, India. Currently pursuing his Bachelor of Technology (B.Tech) in Department of Mechanical Engineering. His research areas of interest are mobile robotics, biomimetic robot design, robotic prosthetic limb design, control systems and AI/ML.

Mayank Modashiya is a Data Scientist 1 at Kenco Group, Chattanooga, TN, USA. He earned is Bachelor's in Engineering in Mechanical Engineering, India. He earned his Masters in Industrial Engineering from the University of Texas at Arlington. Mayank has passion for applying machine learning (ML) and artificial Intelligence (AI) to solve complex supply chain problems. Mayank has more than 2 years' experience in developing and implementing AI/ML for problem solving. His research interest includes supply chain networks, logistics and manufacturing. He is member of INFORMS and IISE.

Jordi Mogas holds a PhD in Educational Technology and a Bachelor's in Information and Documentation with mention in information systems management. Currently, he is a postdoc researcher at GEPS research center (Globalisation, Education and Social Policies), at the Universitat Autònoma de Barcelona, and belongs to ARGET (Applied Research Group in Education and Technology). Dr. Mogas teaches at both the Department of Pedagogy at the Universitat Rovira i Virgili (professor associate) and at the Department of Education at the Universitat Oberta de Catalunya (professor collaborador). His main research lines are: Smart Learning Environments, Virtual Learning Environments and Self-Regulated Learning.

Siddhartha Moulik is working as a Scientist in CSIR-IICT. His field of specialization deals with wastewater treatment, cavitation based advanced oxidation processes, sonochemistry as well as in membrane separation technology along with experiences in practical field applications.

Adam Moyer is an Assistant Professor in the Department of Analytics and Information Systems at Ohio University's College of Business. Moyer received a BBA from Ohio University and has had experience managing information systems for non-profit organizations, has worked as a systems engineer, and has consulted for various companies. While earning an MS in Industrial & Systems Engineering at Ohio University, Adam developed and taught courses related to information systems, programming, system design and deployment, business intelligence, analytics, and cybersecurity at Ohio University. After gaining additional professional experience in the counterintelligence community, Moyer returned to Ohio University and earned a Ph.D. in Mechanical and Systems Engineering.

Anirban Mukherjee is faculty in marketing. He received a PhD in Marketing from The Samuel Curtis Johnson Graduate School of Management, Cornell University.

Anweshan Mukherjee has completed his BSc with Major in Computer Science from St. Xavier's College, Kolkata and is currently pursuing MSc in Computer Science from the same college. His current research interest is Data Analytics and Machine Learning.

Partha Mukherjee, assistant professor of data analytics, received his bachelor's degree in mechanical engineering in 1995 from Jadavpur University in India. He received his Master of Technology in Computer Science from Indian Statistical Institute in 2001. He earned his second graduate degree in computer Science from the University of Tulsa in 2008. He completed his Ph.D. from Penn State in information and technology with a minor in applied statistics in 2016.

Fabian N. Murrieta-Rico received B.Eng. and M.Eng. degrees from Instituto Tecnológico de Mexicali (ITM) in 2004 and 2013 respectively. In 2017, he received his PhD in Materials Physics at Centro de Investigación Científica y Educación Superior de Ensenada (CICESE). He has worked as an automation engineer, systems designer, as a university professor, and as postdoctoral researcher at Facultad de Ingeniería, Arquitectura y Diseño from Universidad Autónoma de Baja California (UABC) and at the Centro de Nanociencias y Nanotecnología from Universidad Nacional Autónoma de México (CNyN-UNAM), currently he works as professor at the Universidad Politécnica de Baja California. His research has been published in different journals and presented at international conferences since 2009. He has served as reviewer for different journals, some of them include IEEE Transactions on Industrial Electronics, IEEE Transactions on Instrumentation, Measurement and Sensor Review. His research interests are focused on the field of time and frequency metrology, the design of wireless sensor networks, automated systems, and highly sensitive chemical detectors.

Balsam A. J. Mustafa holds an MS.c in Information Systems from the UK and earned her Ph.D. in Computer Science (Software Engineering) from Malaysia. Her research interests are in the areas of empirical software engineering, intelligent health care systems, and data mining & analytics. Dr. Balsam has served on more than 25 international conference program committees and journal editorial boards, and has been a keynote and invited speaker at several international conferences. She is a member of IEEE and a professional member of the Association of Computing Machinery (ACM). Dr. Balsam has published 30 technical papers in various refereed journals and conference proceedings.

Ambika N. is an MCA, MPhil, Ph.D. in computer science. She completed her Ph.D. from Bharathiar university in the year 2015. She has 16 years of teaching experience and presently working for St.Francis College, Bangalore. She has guided BCA, MCA and M.Tech students in their projects. Her expertise includes wireless sensor network, Internet of things, cybersecurity. She gives guest lectures in her expertise. She is a reviewer of books, conferences (national/international), encyclopaedia and journals. She is advisory committee member of some conferences. She has many publications in National & international conferences, international books, national and international journals and encyclopaedias. She has some patent publications (National) in computer science division.

Jyotindra Narayan is a regular doctoral fellow at the Department of Mechanical Engineering, Indian Institute of Technology Guwahati, currently practicing and working on "Design, Development and Control Architecture of a Low-cost Lower-Limb Exoskeleton for Mobility Assistance and Gait Rehabilitation". Moreover, he employs the intelligent and soft computing algorithms in his research. He has a substantial experience in kinematics, dynamics and control of robotic devices for medical applications. He has published several journals, book chapters and conference papers on the broad topic of medical and rehabilitation devices.

Ghalia Nasserddine is a Ph.D in information technology and systems. She has been an assistant professor at Lebanese International University since 2010. In addition, she is active research in machine learning, belief function theory, renewable energy and High voltage transmission.

Son Nguyen earned his master's degree in applied mathematics and doctoral degree in mathematics, statistics emphasis, both at Ohio University. He is currently an assistant professor at the department of mathematics at Bryant University. His primary research interests lie in dimensionality reduction, imbalanced learning, and machine learning classification. In addition to the theoretical aspects, he is also interested in applying statistics to other areas such as finance and healthcare.

Van-Ho Nguyen received B.A. degree in Management Information System from Faculty of Information Systems, University of Economics and Law (VNU–HCM), Vietnam in 2015, and Master degree in MIS from School of Business Information Technology from University of Economics Ho Chi Minh City, Vietnam in 2020, respectively. His current research interests include Business Intelligence, Data Analytics, and Machine Learning.

Shivinder Nijjer, currently serving as Assistant Professor in Chitkara University, Punjab, has a doctorate in Business Analytics and Human Resource Management. She has authored books and book chapters in the field of Business Analytics, Information Systems and Strategy for eminent publication groups like Taylor and Francis, Emerald, Pearson and IGI Global. She is currently guiding two PhD candidates and is on reviewer panel of three Scopus indexed journals.

Roberto Nogueira is Grupo Globo Full Professor of Strategy at COPPEAD Graduate School of Business, The Federal University of Rio de Janeiro, where he is also executive director of the Strategy and Innovation Research Center. He joined COPPEAD in 1984 and since that teaches at the MSc, PhD and Executive Education courses. He was visiting professor at the University of San Diego (USA), San Jose State University (USA), Alma Business School (Italy), Audencia (France) and Stellenbosch (South

Africa). He is co-founder and board member of the Executive MBA Consortium for Global Business Innovation, encompassing Business Schools from five continents - Alma Business School (Italy), Cranfield (UK), Coppead (Brazil), ESAN (Peru), FIU (USA), Keio Business School (Japan), Kozminski (Poland), MIR (Russia), Munich Business School (Germany), San Jose State (Silicon Valley - USA) and Stellenbosch (South Africa) promoting the exchange of Executive MBA students. Nogueira wrote two books and has published dozens of scholarly articles on such topics as Corporate Strategy, Business Ecosystems, Innovation and Emerging Technologies and Business Reconfiguration, analyzing sectors such as Health, Energy, Education, Media and Entertainment and Space.

Cherie Noteboom is a Professor of Information Systems in the College of Business and Information Systems, Coordinator of the PhD in Information Systems and Co-Director of the Center of Excellence in Information Systems at Dakota State University. She holds a Ph.D. in Information Technology from the University of Nebraska-Omaha. In addition, she has earned an Education Doctorate in Adult & Higher Education & Administration & MBA from the University of South Dakota. She has a BS degree in computer science from South Dakota State University. She researches in the areas of Information Systems, Healthcare, and Project Management. Her industry experience runs the continuum from technical computer science endeavors to project management and formal management & leadership positions. She has significant experience working with Management Information Systems, Staff Development, Project Management, Application Development, Education, Healthcare, Mentoring, and Leadership.

Zinga Novais is a project manager. She holds a Master's in Project Management from ISEG, School of Economics & Management of the University of Lisbon. She also holds a post-graduation in Project Management and a postgraduation in Management & Business Consulting, both from ISEG - University of Lisbon; and a degree in Public Administration from ISCSP, School of Social and Political Sciences of the University of Lisbon.

Poonam Oberoi is an Associate Professor of Marketing at Excelia Business School. She joined Excelia Group in 2014 after successfully defending her thesis at Grenoble Ecole de Management the same year. On the research front, Dr. Oberoi's primary focus is in the area of innovation and technology management. Her work examines the technology and innovation sourcing decisions that firms make, and the consequences of these decisions. Since her appointment at Excelia Business School, she has published research papers on these topics in well-regarded, peer reviewed, international journals such as M@n@gement and Journal of Business Research. Furthermore, she has published many book chapters and case studies on related topics. For more information, please visit: https://www.excelia-group.com/faculty-research/faculty/oberoi.

Ibrahim Oguntola is a Research Assistant, Industrial Engineering, Dalhousie University, Canada.

Kamalendu Pal is with the Department of Computer Science, School of Science and Technology, City, University of London. Kamalendu received his BSc (Hons) degree in Physics from Calcutta University, India, Postgraduate Diploma in Computer Science from Pune, India, MSc degree in Software Systems Technology from the University of Sheffield, Postgraduate Diploma in Artificial Intelligence from the Kingston University, MPhil degree in Computer Science from the University College London, and MBA degree from the University of Hull, United Kingdom. He has published over seventy-five international research articles (including book chapters) widely in the scientific community with research papers in the ACM SIGMIS Database, Expert Systems with Applications, Decision Support Systems, and conferences. His research interests include knowledge-based systems, decision support systems, blockchain technology, software engineering, service-oriented computing, and ubiquitous computing. He is on the editorial board of an international computer science journal and is a member of the British Computer Society, the Institution of Engineering and Technology, and the IEEE Computer Society.

Ramon Palau is a researcher and lecturer in the Pedagogy Department of the Rovira and Virgili University. As a researcher he did internships in UNESCO París and Leipzig University. His current work as a researcher is in ARGET (Applied Research Group of Education Technology) focused in e-learning, digital technologies, digital competences and educational application of digital technologies. In this group he has participated in several research projects. Currently his research is centered in smart learning environments publishing the first fundings. He has worked as a content developer for several institutions as Universitat Oberta de Catalunya, Fundació URV, Fundació Paco Puerto, Editorial Barcanova and Universitat de Lleida. Previously of the works in academia, he has worked as a primary and secondary teacher as a civil servant. From 2003 until 2007 he had been a principal in a public school. Concerning teaching, in higher education level, he has taught in Master of Educational Technology in Universitat Rovira i Virgili and Universitat Oberta de Catalunya and the Master of Teaching in Secondary School where is the director of the program.

Adam Palmquist is an industrial PhDc at the department of Applied IT at Gothenburg University and works as Chief Scientific Officer (CSO) at the Swedish Gamification company Insert Coin. Palmquist has a background in learning and game design. He is the author of several books addressing the intersection of design, technology, and learning. Adam has worked as a gamification and learning advisor for several international companies in the technology and production industries. His PhD-project is a collaboration between Gothenburg University and Insert Coin concerning Gamified the World Engine (GWEN), a unique system-agnostic API constructed to make gamification designs scalable. The interdisciplinary project transpires at the intersection of Human-Computer Interaction, Design Science in Information Systems and Learning Analytics.

Chung-Yeung Pang received his Ph.D. from Cambridge University, England. He has over 30 years of software development experience in a variety of areas from device drivers, web, and mobile apps to large enterprise IT systems. He has experience in many programming languages, including low-level languages like Assembler and C, high-level languages like COBOL, Java and Ada, AI languages like LISP and Prolog, and mobile app languages like Javascript and Dart. For the past 20 years he has worked as a consultant in various corporate software projects. He worked in the fields of architecture design, development, coaching and management of IT projects. At one time he was a lead architect on a project with a budget of over $ 1 billion. In recent years, despite limited resources and high pressure in some projects, he has led many projects to complete on time and on budget.

Severin Pang completed a combined degree in mathematics, statistics, and economics at the University of Bern. He also received the Swiss federal state diploma for computer engineers. He has more than 10 years of experience in computing engineering in companies such as Swiss Re, Zurich Insurance and IBM. At IBM he implemented AI functionalities for a hovering robot to support ISS astronauts. Severin Pang is currently working as a data scientist at Cognitive Solutions & Innovation AG in Switzerland, where he formulates mathematical models for predictive maintenance of machines, develops an intelligent sensor to detect anomalies in the frequency spectrum, and verifies the effectiveness of fuel-saving measures for Airbus aircraft and optimizes the energy consumption of more than 6000 hotels around the world. He has contributed to a number of publications in the fields of data science, AI, and software engineering.

Renan Payer holds a PhD and a Master's degree in Production Engineering from Fluminense Federal University (Brazil). Graduated in Chemical Engineering (University of the State of Rio de Janeiro UERJ) in Industrial Chemistry (Fluminense Federal University - UFF). He has an MBA in Production and Quality Management. It carries out academic research in the area of sustainability, circular economy and digital transformation.

Jean-Eric Pelet holds a PhD in Marketing, an MBA in Information Systems and a BA (Hns) in Advertising. As an assistant professor in management, he works on problems concerning consumer behaviour when using a website or other information system (e-learning, knowledge management, e-commerce platforms), and how the interface can change that behavior. His main interest lies in the variables that enhance navigation in order to help people to be more efficient with these systems. He works as a visiting professor both in France and abroad (England, Switzerland) teaching e-marketing, ergonomics, usability, and consumer behaviour at Design Schools (Nantes), Business Schools (Paris, Reims), and Universities (Paris Dauphine – Nantes). Dr. Pelet has also actively participated in a number of European Community and National research projects. His current research interests focus on, social networks, interface design, and usability.

María A. Pérez received her M.S. and Ph.D. degrees in telecommunication engineering from the University of Valladolid, Spain, in 1996 and 1999, respectively. She is presently Associate Professor at University of Valladolid, and member of the Data Engineering Research Unit. Her research is focused on Big Data, Artificial Intelligence, Internet of Things, and the application of technology to the learning process. She has managed or participated in numerous international research projects. She is author or co-author of many publications in journals, books, and conferences. In addition, she has been involved as reviewer in several international research initiatives.

Vitalii Petranovskii received the Ph.D. degree in physical chemistry from the Moscow Institute of Crystallography in 1988. From 1993 to 1994, he worked as a Visiting Fellow at the National Institute of Materials Science and Chemical Research, Japan. Since 1995, he has been working with the Center for Nanotechnology and Nanotechnology, National University of Mexico, as the Head of the Department of Nanocatalysis, from 2006 to 2014. He is a member of the Mexican Academy of Sciences, the International Association of Zeolites, and the Russian Chemical Society. He has published over 160 articles in peer-reviewed journals and five invited book chapters. He is also a coauthor of the monograph Clusters and Matrix Isolated Clustered Superstructures (St. Petersburg, 1995). His research interests include the synthesis and properties of nanoparticles deposited on zeolite matrices, and the modification of the zeolite matrices themselves for their high-tech use.

Frederick E. Petry received BS and MS degrees in physics and a PhD in computer and information science from The Ohio State University. He is currently a computer scientist in the Naval Research Laboratory at the Stennis Space Center Mississippi. He has been on the faculty of the University of Alabama in Huntsville, the Ohio State University and Tulane University where he is an Emeritus Professor. His recent research interests include representation of imprecision via soft computing in databases, spatial and environmental and information systems and machine learning. Dr. Petry has over 350 scientific publications including 150 journal articles/book chapters and 9 books written or edited. For his research on the use of fuzzy sets for modeling imprecision in databases and information systems he was elected an IEEE Life Fellow, AAAS Fellow, IFSA Fellow and an ACM Distinguished Scientist. In 2016 he received the IEEE Computational Intelligence Society Pioneer Award.

Birgit Pilch studied Biology and then Technical Protection of Environment at Graz University and Graz University of Technology.

Matthias Pohl is a research associate in the Very Large Business Application Lab at the Otto von Guericke University Magdeburg since 2016. His main research and work interests are data science, statistical modeling and the efficient design of innovative IT solutions. Matthias Pohl studied Mathematics and Informatics and holds a Diplom degree in Mathematics from Otto von Guericke University Magdeburg.

Peter Poschmann, M.Sc., works as a research associate at the Chair of Logistics, Institute of Technology and Management, at the Technical University of Berlin. Within the scope of several research projects, he focuses on the technical application of Machine Learning to logistic problems, in particular the prediction of transport processes. Previously, he worked as a research associate at a Fraunhofer Institute with a focus on Data Science. He graduated in industrial engineering with a specialization in mechanical engineering at the Technical University of Darmstadt.

Brajkishore Prajapati is an associate Data Scientist at Azilen Technologies Pvt. Ltd. He is living in Gwalior, Madhya Pradesh. He is very passionate and loyal to his work and finishes his work on time. His dream is to become one of the great researchers in the field of Artificial Intelligence. He is a very big fan of cricket and reading.

Sabyasachi Pramanik is a Professional IEEE member. He obtained a PhD in Computer Science and Engineering from the Sri Satya Sai University of Technology and Medical Sciences, Bhopal, India. Presently, he is an Assistant Professor, Department of Computer Science and Engineering, Haldia Institute of Technology, India. He has many publications in various reputed international conferences, journals, and online book chapter contributions (Indexed by SCIE, Scopus, ESCI, etc.). He is doing research in the field of Artificial Intelligence, Data Privacy, Cybersecurity, Network Security, and Machine Learning. He is also serving as the editorial board member of many international journals. He is a reviewer of journal articles from IEEE, Springer, Elsevier, Inderscience, IET, and IGI Global. He has reviewed many conference papers, has been a keynote speaker, session chair and has been a technical program committee member in many international conferences. He has authored a book on Wireless Sensor Network. Currently, he is editing 6 books from IGI Global, CRC Press EAI/Springer and Scrivener-Wiley Publications.

Abdurrakhman Prasetyadi is a junior researcher at the Research Center for Data and Information Science, The Indonesia Institute of Sciences (LIPI), Indonesia since 2019. He was a researcher at the Center for Information Technology (UPT BIT LIPI) for 6 years. He obtained his bachelor's degree in

Library and Information Sciences from the University of Padjadjaran, Indonesia in 2008. He earned a Master's degree in Information Technology for Libraries from the IPB University in 2017. Abdurrakhman Prasetyadi's research interests include issues in the field of Library and Information Science, Social Informatics, and Informetrics.

Bitan Pratihar obtained his Bachelor of Technology degree in Chemical Engineering from National Institute of Technology Durgapur, India, in 2017. He completed his Master of Technology degree in Chemical Engineering department of National Institute of Technology Rourkela, India, in 2019. His research interests were the application of Fuzzy Logic in data mining, controller design, and soft sensor design for several chemical engineering applications and others. Currently, he is a doctoral student in Membrane Separation Laboratory of Chemical Engineering Department, Indian Institute of Technology Kharagpur, India.

Alessandro Puzzanghera is a PhD student at the University for foreigners "Dante Alighieri" in Reggio Calabria. He worked many years as legal assistant at the FIDLAW LLP a law firm in London. He successfully completed her studies in the Master of Studies (MSt) postgraduate level degree program of the European Law and Governance School at the European Public Law Organization in Athens. His fields of research include: Artificial Intelligence, Administrative law, Personal Data in particular about GDPR. He published papers for Hart publishing (Oxford), EPLO publication (Athens) and various italian scientific journals.

John Quinn is a Professor of Mathematics at Bryant University and has been teaching there since 1991. Prior to teaching, he was an engineer at the Naval Underwater Systems Center (now the Naval Undersea Warfare Center). He received his Sc.B. degree from Brown University in 1978, and his M.S. and Ph.D. degrees from Harvard University in 1987 and 1991, respectively. Professor Quinn has published in multiple areas. He has done previous research in mathematical programming methods and computable general equilibrium models. He currently does research in probability models and in data mining applications, including the prediction of rare events. He is also doing research in pension modeling, including the effects of health status on retirement payouts.

Parvathi R. is a Professor of School of Computing Science and Engineering at VIT University, Chennai since 2011. She received the Doctoral degree in the field of spatial data mining in the same year. Her teaching experience in the area of computer science includes more than two decades and her research interests include data mining, big data and computational biology.

Sreemathy R. is working as Associate Professor in Pune Institute of Computer Technology, Savitribai Phule Pune University, India. She has her Master's degree in Electronics Engineering from college of Engineering, Pune. Savitribai Phule Pune University and Doctoral degree in Electronics Engineering from Shivaji University, India. Her research areas include signal processing, image processing, Artificial Intelligence, Machine Learning and Deep Learning.

Kornelije Rabuzin is currently a Full Professor at the Faculty of organization and informatics, University of Zagreb, Croatia. He holds Bachelor, Master, and PhD degrees - all in Information Science. He performs research in the area of databases, particularly graph databases, as well as in the field of data warehousing and business intelligence. He has published four books and more than eighty scientific and professional papers.

Kaleche Rachid is a PhD student of computer science since 2018. He is member of computer science laboratory (LIO) of Oran1 university in Algeria. His current research interests deal with artificial intelligence, transportation system, logistic systems, machine learning, bio-inspired approach. He is co-author of many publications and communications.

Rulina Rachmawati earned a bachelor degree in Chemistry from the Sepuluh Nopember Institute of Technology, Indonesia, in 2009. She started her career as a technical librarian at the Library and Archive Agency of the Regional Government of Surabaya city, Indonesia. Her passion for librarianship brought her to pursue a Master of Information Management from RMIT University, Australia, in 2019. Presently, she is a librarian at the Center for Scientific Data and Documentation, the Indonesian Institute of Sciences. Her current roles include providing library services, providing content for the Indonesian Scientific Journal Database (ISJD), and researching data, documentation and information. Her research interests include bibliometrics, library services, information retrieval, and research data management.

Nayem Rahman is an Information Technology (IT) Professional. He has implemented several large projects using data warehousing and big data technologies. He holds a Ph.D. from the Department of Engineering and Technology Management at Portland State University, USA, an M.S. in Systems Science (Modeling & Simulation) from Portland State University, Oregon, USA, and an MBA in Management Information Systems (MIS), Project Management, and Marketing from Wright State University, Ohio, USA. He has authored 40 articles published in various conference proceedings and scholarly journals. He serves on the Editorial Review Board of the International Journal of End-User Computing and Development (IJEUCD). His principal research interests include Big Data Analytics, Big Data Technology Acceptance, Data Mining for Business Intelligence, and Simulation-based Decision Support System (DSS).

Vishnu Rajan is an Assistant Professor in the Production & Operations Management Division at XIME Kochi, Kerala, India. His current research interests include supply chain risk management, operations research, reliability engineering, manufacturing systems management, quantitative techniques and statistics. He has published research articles in reputed peer-reviewed international journals of Taylor & Francis, Emerald, Inderscience, Elsevier, IEEE and IIIE publications. He also has a scientific book chapter to his credit. Besides this, Vishnu serves as an editorial board member of the International Journal of Risk and Contingency Management (IJRCM) of IGI Global.

T. Rajeshwari is freelancer and Yagyopathy researcher. She usually writes up article in science forums related to Hindu Mythology and their scientific proofs. She belongs to Kolkata and travels across globe for social work and spreading the science of Hindu rituals.

P. N. Ram Kumar is Professor in the QM & OM area at the Indian Institute of Management Kozhikode. Prior to this appointment, he had worked as a Post-Doctoral Research Fellow in the School of Mechanical and Aerospace Engineering at the Nanyang Technological University, Singapore. He obtained his Bachelor in Mechanical Engineering from the JNTU Hyderabad in 2003, Master in Industrial Engineering from the PSG College of Technology, Coimbatore in 2005 and PhD from the IIT Madras in 2009.

His primary areas of research include, but not limited to, transportation network optimisation, military logistics, reliability engineering and supply chain management. He has authored several international journal papers and his work has been published in reputed journals such as Journal of the Operational Research Society, Defense and Security Analysis, Strategic Analysis, and Journal of Defense Modeling & Simulation, to name a few.

Perumal Ramasubramanian holds BE, ME from Computer Science and Engineering from Madurai Kamaraj University and PH.D Computer Science from Madurai Kamaraj University in the year 1989, 1996 and 2012. He has 31 years teaching experience in academia. He was published 55 papers in various international journal and conferences. He has authored 14 books and has 135 citations with h-index 5 and i10 index 4. He is also actively involved in various professional societies like Institution of Engineers(I), Computer Science Teachers Association, ISTE, ISRD, etc.

Célia M. Q. Ramos graduated in Computer Engineering from the University of Coimbra, obtained her Master in Electrical and Computers Engineering from the Higher Technical Institute, Lisbon University, and the PhD in Econometrics in the University of the Algarve (UALG), Faculty of Economics, Portugal. She is Associate Professor at School for Management, Hospitality and Tourism, also in the UALG, where she lectures computer science. Areas of research and special interest include the conception and development of business intelligence, information systems, tourism information systems, big data, tourism, machine learning, social media marketing, econometric modelling and panel-data models. Célia Ramos has published in the fields of information systems and tourism, namely, she has authored a book, several book chapters, conference papers and journal articles. At the level of applied research, she has participated in several funded projects.

Anshu Rani has more than 12 years of experience in teaching and learning at various reputed institutes. She is a researcher associated with the online consumer behaviour area.

Bindu Rani is a Ph.D. scholar from Department of Computer Science and Engineering, Sharda University, Greater Noida, India and works as assistant professor in Information Technology Department, Inderprastha Engineering College, Ghaziabad, Dr. A.P.J Abdul Kalam Technical University, India. She received Master in Computer Science and Application degree from Aligarh Muslim University (AMU), India. Her research interests are Data Mining, Big Data and Machine learning techniques.

N. Raghavendra Rao is an Advisor to FINAIT Consultancy Services India. He has a doctorate in the area of Finance. He has a rare distinction of having experience in the combined areas of Information Technology and Finance.

Zbigniew W. Ras is a Professor of Computer Science Department and the Director of the KDD Laboratory at the University of North Carolina, Charlotte. He also holds professorship position in the Institute of Computer Science at the Polish-Japanese Academy of Information Technology in Warsaw, Poland. His areas of specialization include knowledge discovery and data mining, recommender systems, health informatics, business analytics, flexible query answering, music information retrieval, and art.

Rohit Rastogi received his B.E. degree in Computer Science and Engineering from C.C.S.Univ. Meerut in 2003, the M.E. degree in Computer Science from NITTTR-Chandigarh (National Institute of Technical Teachers Training and Research-affiliated to MHRD, Govt. of India), Punjab Univ. Chandigarh in 2010. Currently he is pursuing his Ph.D. In computer science from Dayalbagh Educational Institute, Agra under renowned professor of Electrical Engineering Dr. D.K. Chaturvedi in area of spiritual consciousness. Dr. Santosh Satya of IIT-Delhi and dr. Navneet Arora of IIT-Roorkee have happily consented him to co supervise. He is also working presently with Dr. Piyush Trivedi of DSVV Hardwar, India in center of Scientific spirituality. He is a Associate Professor of CSE Dept. in ABES Engineering. College, Ghaziabad (U.P.-India), affiliated to Dr. A.P. J. Abdul Kalam Technical Univ. Lucknow (earlier Uttar Pradesh Tech. University). Also, he is preparing some interesting algorithms on Swarm Intelligence approaches like PSO, ACO and BCO etc.Rohit Rastogi is involved actively with Vichaar Krnati Abhiyaan and strongly believe that transformation starts within self.

Mark Rauch is a database administrator and a graduate student in the program for Database Management at the University of West Florida. Mark Rauch is actively working in the healthcare industry and has experience working with several Oracle database platforms as well as SQL Server. His experience extends across Oracle 11g, 12c, and 19c. He has also supported several aspects of Oracle Middleware including Oracle Data Integrator, Oracle Enterprise Manager, Web Logic, and Business Publisher.

Yuan Ren is an instructor in Shanghai Dianji University. He was born in 1984. He got his bachelor's degree in mathematics from Jilin University in 2007, and doctor's degree in computer software from Fudan University in 2013. His multidisciplinary research interests include image understanding, artificial intelligence, and data science.

M. Yudhi Rezaldi is a researcher at the Research Center for Informatics, National Research and Innovation Agency (BRIN). His academic qualifications were obtained from Pasundan Universiti Bandung for his bachelor degree, and Mater degree in Magister of Design from Institut Teknologi Bandung (ITB). He completed his PhD in 2020 at Computer Science from Universiti Kebangsaan Malaysia (UKM). And he is also an active member of Himpunan Peneliti Indonesia (Himpenindo). His research interests include visualization, modeling, computer graphics animation, multimedia design, Information Science, particularly disaster. He received an award The best researcher in the 2011 researcher and engineer incentive program in Indonesian Institute of Science (LIPI). and once received the Karya Satya award 10 years in 2018 from the Indonesian government for his services to the country.

Moisés Rivas López was born in June 1, 1960. He received the B.S. and M.S. degrees in Autonomous University of Baja California, México, in 1985, 1991, respectively. He received PhD degree in the same University, on specialty "Optical Scanning for Structural Health Monitoring", in 2010. He has written 5 book chapters and 148 Journal and Proceedings Conference papers. Since 1992 till the present time he has presented different works in several International Congresses of IEEE, ICROS, SICE, AMMAC in USA, England, Japan, turkey and Mexico. Dr. Rivas was Dean of Engineering Institute of Autonomous University Baja California, Since1997 to 2005; also was Rector of Polytechnic University of Baja California, Since2006 to 2010. Since 2012 to 208 was the head of physic engineering department, of Engineering Institute, Autonomous University of Baja California, Mexico. Since 2013 till the present time member of National Researcher System and now is Professor in the Polytechnic University of Baja California.

Julio C. Rodríguez-Quiñonez received the B.S. degree in CETYS, Mexico in 2007. He received the Ph.D. degree from Baja California Autonomous University, México, in 2013. He is currently Full Time Researcher-Professor in the Engineering Faculty of the Autonomous University of Baja California, and member of the National Research System Level 1. Since 2016 is Senior Member of IEEE. He is involved in the development of optical scanning prototype in the Applied Physics Department and research leader in the development of a new stereo vision system prototype. He has been thesis director of 3 Doctor's Degree students and 4 Master's degree students. He holds two patents referred to dynamic triangulation method, has been editor of 4 books, Guest Editor of Measurement, IEEE Sensors Journal, International Journal of Advanced Robotic Systems and Journal of Sensors, written over 70 papers, 8 book chapters and has been a reviewer for IEEE Sensors Journal, Optics and Lasers in Engineering, IEEE Transaction on Mechatronics and Neural Computing and Applications of Springer; he participated as a reviewer and Session Chair of IEEE ISIE conferences in 2014 (Turkey), 2015 (Brazil), 2016 (USA), 2017 (UK), 2019 (Canada), IECON 2018 (USA), IECON 2019 (Portugal), ISIE 2020 (Netherlands), ISIE 2021 (Japan). His current research interests include automated metrology, stereo vision systems, control systems, robot navigation and 3D laser scanners.

Mário José Batista Romão is an Associate Professor of Information Systems, with Aggregation, at ISEG – University of Lisbon. He is Director of the Masters program in Computer Science and Management. He holds a PhD in Management Sciences by ISCTE-IUL and by Computer Integrated Manufacturing at Cranfiel University (UK). He also holds a MsC in Telecommunications and Computer Science, at IST - Instituto Superior Técnico, University of Lisbon. He is Pos-Graduated in Project Management and holds the international certification Project Management Professional (PMP), by PMI – Project Management International. He has a degree in Electrotecnic Engineer by IST.

James Rotella did his BS in physics at Pennsylvania State University and MS in physics at the University of Pittsburgh. While at the University of Pittsburgh he focused on doing epigenetic research in the biophysics department. He went on to work for 4 years as a failure analysis engineer at a Dynamics Inc. working on improving their lines of flexible microelectronics. He focused on improving yield internally in the factory, and designing and carrying out accelerated life and field tests to improve field performance. After working at Dynamics, he moved on to begin work programming at K&L Gates where he maintains analytics pipelines, models, and databases. While at K&L Gates, he completed an Masters in Data Analytics at Pennsylvania State University.

Anirban Roy is the founder of Water-Energy Nexus Laboratory in BITS Pilani Goa Campus Founder and Promoter and CEO of Epione Swajal Solutions India LLP, focussing on Membrane Manufacturing. Experience in membrane synthesis, manufacturing, handling, devices, and prototypes.

Parimal Roy studied in Anthropology. Later he obtained papers on MBA, Project management, and Criminology (paper is better than a certificate) to enhance his knowledge. He is currently working in a state own institution in the field of Training & Development. Decolonizing, Marginal community, subaltern voice, Project management - all are interest arena in academic world. His written book is

Extra-marital love in folk songs. Co-author of Captive minded intellectual; Quantitative Ethnography in Indigenous Research Methodology; and so many book chapters and journals.

Saúl Rozada Raneros is a PhD candidate at University of Valladolid, who received his M.S. degrees in telecommunication engineering from the University of Valladolid, Spain. He is researcher of the Data Engineering Research Unit and his research is focused on Internet of Things, and Virtual Reality. Also, he is co-author of some publications in journals, dealing with topics related to his lines of his research.

Rauno Rusko is University lecturer at the University of Lapland. His research activities focus on cooperation, coopetition, strategic management, supply chain management and entrepreneurship mainly in the branches of information communication technology, forest industry and tourism. His articles appeared in the European Management Journal, Forest Policy and Economics, International Journal of Business Environment, Industrial Marketing Management, International Journal of Innovation in the Digital Economy and International Journal of Tourism Research among others.

Rashid bin Mohd Saad is an educationist and serving as an Assistant professor at the Department of Education at Universiti Malaya. At present, he is working in the Drug Discoveries of Indigenous communities in Bangladesh.

Sheelu Sagar is a research scholar pursuing her PhD in Management from Amity University (AUUP). She graduated with a Bachelor Degree of Science from Delhi University. She received her Post Graduate Degree in Master of Business Administration with distinction from Amity University Uttar Pradesh India in 2019. She is working at a post of Asst. Controller of Examinations, Amity University, Uttar Pradesh. She is associated with various NGOs - in India. She is an Active Member of Gayatri Teerth, ShantiKunj, Haridwar, Trustee - ChaturdhamVed Bhawan Nyas (having various centers all over India), Member Executive Body -Shree JeeGauSadan, Noida. She is a social worker and has been performing Yagya since last 35 years and working for revival of Indian Cultural Heritage through yagna (Hawan), meditation through Gayatri Mantra and pranayama. She is doing her research on Gayatri Mantra.

Rajarshi Saha has currently completed his BSc with Major in Computer Science from St. Xavier's College, Kolkata. His current research interest is Data Analytics and Machine Learning.

Sudipta Sahana is an Associate Professor at a renowned University in West Bengal. For more than 11 years he has worked in this region. He has passed his M.tech degree in Software Engineering and B.Tech Degree in Information Technology from West Bengal University of Technology with a great CGPA/DGPA in 2010 and 2012 respectively. He completed his Ph.D. from the University of Kalyani in 2020. He has published more than 60 papers in referred journals and conferences indexed by Scopus, DBLP, and Google Scholar and working as an editorial team member of many reputed journals. He is a life member of the Computer Society of India (CSI), Computer Science Teachers Association (CSTA), and also a member of the International Association of Computer Science and Information Technology (IACSIT).

Pavithra Salanke has more than a decade of experience in Teaching and she is an active member in the research area of HR using social media.

Hajara U. Sanda, PhD, is an Associate Professor at the Department of Mass Communication, Bayero University, Kano, Kano State, Nigeria. She is also a former Dean, Student Affairs of the university, and has published many research articles, presented many conference papers, and published a couple of books.

Enes Şanlıtürk holds B.S. in Industrial Engineering in Istanbul Technical University and M.S. in Management Engineering in Istanbul Technical University. Also, his Ph.D. education continues in Industrial Engineering in Istanbul Technical University. He has study in Machine Learning. His main contributions is enhancing defect prediction performance in machine learning on production systems. In addition, he works in private sector as an Analyst.

Loris Schmid was born in 1992 in Visp, Switzerland. Studying at the University of Berne he attained a Master of Science in Economics. During the UMUSE2 (User Monitoring of the US Election) project, Loris Schmid was employed by the University of Neuchâtel from August 2020 until February 2021 performing data analysis and processing. He works as an Analyst and Research Assistant at IFAAR since 2019.

Dara Schniederjans is an Associate Professor of Supply Chain Management at the University of Rhode Island, College of Business Administration. Dara received her Ph.D. from Texas Tech University in 2012. Dara has co-authored five books and published over thirty academic journal articles as well as numerous book chapters. Dara has served as a guest co-editor for a special issue on "Business ethics in Social Sciences" in the International Journal of Society Systems Science. She has also served as a website coordinator and new faculty development consortium co-coordinator for Decisions Sciences Institute.

Jaydip Sen obtained his Bachelor of Engineering (B.E) in Electrical Engineering with honors from Jadavpur University, Kolkata, India in 1988, and Master of Technology (M.Tech) in Computer Science with honors from Indian Statistical Institute, Kolkata in 2001. Currently, he is pursuing his PhD on "Security and Privacy in Internet of Things" in Jadavpur University, which is expected to be completed by December 2018. His research areas include security in wired and wireless networks, intrusion detection systems, secure routing protocols in wireless ad hoc and sensor networks, secure multicast and broadcast communication in next generation broadband wireless networks, trust and reputation based systems, sensor networks, and privacy issues in ubiquitous and pervasive communication. He has more than 100 publications in reputed international journals and referred conference proceedings (IEEE Xplore, ACM Digital Library, Springer LNCS etc.), and 6 book chapters in books published by internationally renowned publishing houses e.g. Springer, CRC press, IGI-Global etc. He is a Senior Member of ACM, USA a Member IEEE, USA.

Kishore Kumar Senapati's experiences at BIT, Mesra complement both teaching and research, which brought innovation culture at academia and Industry. He has significant Industry driven research and teaching experience in the leading organizations of the country working nearly two decades, including ≈ 16 years at current place as an Assistant Professor in the Department of Computer Science and Engineering at Birla Institute of Technology, MESRA, Ranchi, INDIA. He has obtained PhD in Engineering from Birla Institute of Technology, MESRA. He has Master of Technology in Computer Science from UTKAL University, ODISHA. He has more than 18 years of teaching and research experience. He has guided more than 41 students of ME & M. Tech and four PhD scholars are currently working under his supervision in Computer Science field. He has capabilities in the area of algorithm design, Image processing, Cyber Security and Machine learning. He has published more than 40 peer reviewed papers on various national and international journals of repute including conference presentations. He has delivered invited talks at various national and international seminars including conferences, symposium, and workshop. He is also professional member of national and international societies. He was also active members in various program committees of international conference and chaired the sessions. He serves as editor of International and National Journal of high repute. He has successfully conducted several workshops in his organization on various topics. He is an honorary computer science expert and serves the nation in multiple areas.

Oleg Yu. Sergiyenko was born in February, 9, 1969. He received the B.S., and M.S., degrees in Kharkiv National University of Automobiles and Highways, Kharkiv, Ukraine, in 1991, 1993, respectively. He received the Ph.D. degree in Kharkiv National Polytechnic University on specialty "Tools and methods of non-destructive control" in 1997. He received the DSc degree in Kharkiv National University of Radio electronics in 2018. He has been an editor of 7 books, written 24 book chapters, 160 papers indexed in Scopus and holds 2 patents of Ukraine and 1 in Mexico. Since 1994 till the present time he was represented by his research works in several International Congresses of IEEE, ICROS, SICE, IMEKO in USA, England, Japan, Canada, Italy, Brazil, Austria, Ukraine, and Mexico. Dr.Sergiyenko in December 2004 was invited by Engineering Institute of Baja California Autonomous University for researcher position. He is currently Head of Applied Physics Department of Engineering Institute of Baja California Autonomous University, Mexico, director of several Masters and Doctorate thesis. He was a member of Program Committees of various international and local conferences. He is member of Academy (Academician) of Applied Radio electronics of Bielorussia, Ukraine and Russia.

Martina Šestak received her Master's degree in Information and Software Engineering from the Faculty of Organization and Informatics, University of Zagreb in 2016. She is currently a Ph.D. student in Computer Science at Faculty of Electrical Engineering and Computer Science in Maribor. She is currently a Teaching Assistant and a member of Laboratory for Information Systems at the Faculty of Electrical Engineering and Computer Science, University of Maribor. Her main research interests include graph databases, data analytics and knowledge graphs.

Rohan Shah is a Director in the Financial Services practice at Simon-Kucher & Partners. Rohan holds a Master's degree in Operations Research, specializing in Financial and Managerial Applications from Columbia University in the City of New York.

Aakanksha Sharaff has completed her graduation in Computer Science and Engineering in 2010 from Government Engineering College, Bilaspur (C.G.). She has completed her post graduation Master of Technology in 2012 in Computer Science & Engineering (Specialization- Software Engineering) from National Institute of Technology, Rourkela and completed Ph.D. degree in Computer Science & Engineering in 2017 from National Institute of Technology Raipur, India. Her area of interest is Software Engineering, Data Mining, Text Mining, and Information Retrieval. She is currently working as an Assistant Professor at NIT Raipur India.

Michael J. Shaw joined the faculty of University of Illinois at Urbana-Champaign in 1984. He has been affiliated with the Gies College of Business, National Center for Supercomputing Applications, and the Information Trust Institute. His research interests include machine learning, digital transformation, and healthcare applications.

Yong Shi is a Professor of University of Nebraska at Omaha. He also serves as the Director, Chinese Academy of Sciences Research Center on Fictitious Economy & Data Science and the Director of the Key Lab of Big Data Mining and Knowledge Management, Chinese Academy of Sciences. He is the counselor of the State Council of PRC (2016), the elected member of the International Eurasian Academy of Science (2017), and elected fellow of the World Academy of Sciences for Advancement of Science in Developing Countries (2015). His research interests include business intelligence, data mining, and multiple criteria decision making. He has published more than 32 books, over 350 papers in various journals and numerous conferences/proceedings papers. He is the Editor-in-Chief of International Journal of Information Technology and Decision Making (SCI), Editor-in-Chief of Annals of Data Science (Springer) and a member of Editorial Board for several academic journals.

Dharmpal Singh received his Bachelor of Computer Science and Engineering and Master of Computer Science and Engineering from West Bengal University of Technology. He has about eight years of experience in teaching and research. At present, he is with JIS College of Engineering, Kalyani, and West Bengal, India as an Associate Professor. Currently, he had done his Ph. D from University of Kalyani. He has about 26 publications in national and international journals and conference proceedings. He is also the editorial board members of many reputed/ referred journal.

Aarushi Siri Agarwal is pursuing an undergraduate degree in Computer Science Engineering at Vellore Institute of Technology Chennai. Her interest is in using Machine Learning algorithms for data analysis, mainly in areas such as Cyber Security and Social Network Analysis.

R. Sridharan is a Professor of Industrial Engineering in the Department of Mechanical Engineering at National Institute of Technology Calicut, India. He received his PhD in 1995 from the Department of Mechanical Engineering at Indian Institute of Technology, Bombay, India. His research interests include modelling and analysis of decision problems in supply chain management, job shop production systems and flexible manufacturing systems. He has published papers in reputed journals such as IJPE, IJPR, JMTM, IJLM, IJAMT, etc. For the outstanding contribution to the field of industrial engineering and the institution, he has been conferred with the Fellowship award by the National Council of the Indian Institution of Industrial Engineering in 2017.

Karthik Srinivasan is an assistant professor of business analytics in the School of Business at University of Kansas (KU). He completed his PhD in Management Information Systems from University of Arizona and his master's in management from Indian Institute of Science. He has also worked as a software developer and a data scientist prior to joining academia. His research focuses on addressing novel and important analytics challenges using statistical machine learning, network science, and natural language processing. His research has been presented in top tier business and healthcare analytics conferences and journals. Karthik teaches database management, data warehousing, big data courses for undergraduates and masters students at KU.

Gautam Srivastava is working as an Assistant Professor with GL Bajaj Institute of Management and Research. He has 15+ years of academic experience. He has completed his Ph.D. from the University of Petroleum and Energy Studies, India. His area of specialization is Marketing. He has published and presented many research papers in national and international journals.

Daniel Staegemann studied computer science at Technical University Berlin (TUB). He received the master's degree in 2017. He is currently pursuing the Ph.D. degree with the Otto von Guericke University Magdeburg. Since 2018, he has been employed as a research associate with OVGU where he has authored numerous papers that have been published in prestigious journals and conferences, for which he is also an active reviewer. His research interest is primarily focused on big data, especially the testing.

Mirjana D. Stojanović received her B.Sc. (1985) and M.Sc. (1993) degrees in electrical engineering and her Ph.D. degree (2005) in technical sciences, all from the University of Belgrade, Serbia. She is currently full professor in Information and Communication Technologies at the Faculty of Transport and Traffic Engineering, University of Belgrade. Previously, she held research position at the Mihailo Pupin Institute, University of Belgrade, and was involved in developing telecommunication equipment and systems for regional power utilities and major Serbian corporate systems. Prof. Stojanović participated in a number of national and international R&D projects, including technical projects of the International Council on Large Electric Systems, CIGRÉ. As author or co-author she published more than 170 book chapters, journal articles, and conference papers in her field. She was lead editor of the book on ICS cyber security in the Future Internet environment. Mirjana Stojanović also published a monograph on teletraffic engineering and two university textbooks (in Serbian). Her research interests include communication protocols, cyber security, service and network management, and Future Internet technologies.

Frank Straube studied Industrial Engineering, received his doctorate in 1987 from the Department of Logistics at the Technical University of Berlin under Prof. Dr.-Ing. H. Baumgarten and subsequently worked in a scientifically oriented practice, including more than 10 years as head of a company with more than 100 employees planning logistics systems. After his habilitation (2004) at the University of St. Gallen, Prof. Straube followed the call to the TU Berlin and since then has been head of the logistics department at the Institute for Technology and Management. He is a member of the editorial boards of international logistics journals. Prof. Straube founded the "International Transfer Center for Logistics (ITCL)" in 2005 to realize innovative planning and training activities for companies. He is a member of different boards at companies and associations to bridge between science and practice.

Hamed Taherdoost is an award-winning leader and R&D professional. He is the founder of Hamta Group and sessional faculty member of University Canada West. He has over 20 years of experience in both industry and academia sectors. Dr. Hamed was lecturer at IAU and PNU universities, a scientific researcher and R&D and Academic Manager at IAU, Research Club, MDTH, NAAS, Pinmo, Tablokar, Requiti, and Hamta Academy. Hamed has authored over 120 scientific articles in peer-reviewed international journals and conference proceedings (h-index = 24; i10-index = 50; February 2021), as well as eight book chapters and seven books in the field of technology and research methodology. He is the author of the Research Skills book and his current papers have been published in Behaviour & Information Technology, Information and Computer Security, Electronics, Annual Data Science, Cogent Business & Management, Procedia Manufacturing, and International Journal of Intelligent Engineering Informatics. He is a Senior Member of the IEEE, IAEEEE, IASED & IEDRC, Working group member of IFIP TC and Member of CSIAC, ACT-IAC, and many other professional bodies. Currently, he is involved in several multidisciplinary research projects among which includes studying innovation in information technology & web development, people's behavior, and technology acceptance.

Toshifumi Takada, Professor of National Chung Cheng University, Taiwan, 2018 to present, and Professor Emeritus of Tohoku University Accounting School, served as a CPA examination commissioner from 2001 to 2003. He has held many important posts, including the special commissioner of the Business Accounting Council of the Financial Service Agency, councilor of the Japan Accounting Association, President of the Japan Audit Association, and Director of the Japan Internal Control Association. Professional Career: 1979-1997 Lecturer, Associate Professor, Professor of Fukushima University, Japan 1997-2018 Professor of Tohoku University, Japan 2018-present Professor of National Chung Cheng University, Taiwan.

Neeti Tandon is Yagypathy researcher, scholar of fundamental physics in Vikram University Ujjain. She is active Volunteer of Gayatri Parivaar and highly involved in philanthropic activities.

Ahmet Tezcan Tekin holds B.S. in Computer Science in Istanbul Technical University and Binghamton University, a M.S. and Ph.D. in Management Engineering in Istanbul Technical University. He has studies in Machine Learning, Fuzzy Clustering etc. He gives lectures on Database Management and Big Data Management in different programs. His main contributions in this research area is improving prediction performance in machine learning with the merging Ensemble Learning approach and fuzzy clustering approach.

Gizem Temelcan obtained her Ph.D. entitled "Optimization of the System Optimum Fuzzy Traffic Assignment Problem" in Mathematical Engineering from Yildiz Technical University in 2020. She is an Assistant Professor in the Department of Computer Engineering at Beykoz University, Istanbul, Turkey. Her research interests are operational research, optimization of linear and nonlinear programming problems in the fuzzy environment.

Ronak Tiwari is a graduate student of Industrial Engineering and Management in the Department of Mechanical Engineering at National Institute of Technology Calicut, India. He worked in the industry for two years after receiving his bachelor's degree. He received his bachelor's degree in Industrial Engineering, in 2018, from Pandit Deendayal Petroleum University, Gujarat, India. He also received a silver medal for his academic performance during his undergraduate studies. He received a Government of India Scholarship under INSPIRE scheme to pursue basic sciences. He is an active researcher, and his research interests are mainly in supply chain risk, supply chain resilience, location theory problems, and humanitarian logistics. He has also acted as a reviewer of some internationally reputed journals.

Carlos Torres is CEO of Power-MI, a cloud platform to manage Predictive Maintenance. Born in San Salvador, 1975. Mechanical Engineer, Universidad Centroamericana "José Simeon Cañas", El Salvador. Master in Science Mechatronics, Universität Siegen, Germany. INSEAD Certificate in Global Management, France. Harvard Business School graduated in Global Management Program, USA.

Cahyo Trianggoro is Junior Researcher at Research Center for Informatics, Indonesia Institute of Science (LIPI). Cahyo is completed study from University of Padjadjaran, where he received a Bachelor degree in Information and Library Science and currently pursue for master degree in graduate school University of Padjadjaran. Cahyo having research interest study in data governance, digital preservation, and social informatics.

B. K. Tripathy is now working as a Professor in SITE, school, VIT, Vellore, India. He has received research/academic fellowships from UGC, DST, SERC and DOE of Govt. of India. Dr. Tripathy has published more than 700 technical papers in international journals, proceedings of international conferences and edited research volumes. He has produced 30 PhDs, 13 MPhils and 5 M.S (By research) under his supervision. Dr. Tripathy has 10 edited volumes, published two text books on Soft Computing and Computer Graphics. He has served as the member of Advisory board or Technical Programme Committee member of more than 125 international conferences inside India and abroad. Also, he has edited 6 research volumes for different publications including IGI and CRC. He is a Fellow of IETE and life/senior member of IEEE, ACM, IRSS, CSI, ACEEE, OMS and IMS. Dr. Tripathy is an editorial board member/reviewer of more than 100 international journals of repute.

Gyananjaya Tripathy has completed his graduation in Information Technology in 2012 from Biju Patnaik University of Technology, Odisha. He has completed his post graduation Master of Technology in 2016 in Computer Science & Engineering (Specialization- Wireless Sensor Network) from Veer Surendra Sai University of Technology, Burla (Odisha) and pursuing his Ph.D. degree in Computer Science & Engineering from National Institute of Technology Raipur, India. His area of interest is Wireless Sensor Network and Sentiment Analysis.

Klaus Turowski (born 1966) studied Business and Engineering at the University of Karlsruhe, achieved his doctorate at the Institute for Business Informatics at the University of Münster and habilitated in Business Informatics at the Faculty of Computer Science at the Otto von Guericke University Magdeburg. In 2000, he deputized the Chair of Business Informatics at the University of the Federal Armed Forces München and, from 2001, he headed the Chair of Business Informatics and Systems Engineering at the University of Augsburg. Since 2011, he is heading the Chair of Business Informatics (AG WI) at the Otto von Guericke University Magdeburg, the Very Large Business Applications Lab (VLBA Lab) and the world's largest SAP University Competence Center (SAP UCC Magdeburg). Additionally, Klaus Turowski worked as a guest lecturer at several universities around the world and was a lecturer at the Universities of Darmstadt and Konstanz. He was a (co-) organizer of a multiplicity of national and international scientific congresses and workshops and acted as a member of several programme commitees, and expert Groups. In the context of his university activities as well as an independent consultant he gained practical experience in industry.

Mousami Turuk is working as Assistant Professor in Pune Institute of Computer Technology, Savitribai Phule Pune University, India. She has her Master's degree in Electronics Engineering from Walchand College of Engineering, Sangli, Shivaji University Kolhapur. She has Doctoral degree in Electronics Engineering from Sant Gadge Baba, Amaravati University India. Her research areas include computer vision, Machine Learning and Deep Learning.

M. Ali Ülkü, Ph.D., M.Sc., is a Full Professor and the Director of the Centre for Research in Sustainable Supply Chain Analytics (CRSSCA), in the Rowe School of Business at Dalhousie University, Canada. Dr. Ülkü's research is on sustainable and circular supply chain and logistics management, and analytical decision models.

Mahmud Ullah is an Associate Professor of Marketing at the Faculty of Business Studies, University of Dhaka, Bangladesh. He teaches Behavioral and Quantitative courses in Business, e.g., Psychology, Organizational Behavior, Consumer Behavior, Business Mathematics, Business Statistics, Quantitative Analyses in Business etc., in addition to the Basic and Specialized Marketing courses like Marketing Management, Non-Profit Marketing, E-Marketing etc. He also taught Basic & Advanced English, and IELTS in a couple of English language Schools in New Zealand during his stay over there between 2002 and 2006. He has conducted a number of research projects sponsored by different international and national organizations like the World Bank (RMB), UNICEF, UNFPA, USAID, JAICA, AUSAID, IPPF, PPD, Die Licht Brucke, Andheri Hilfe, BNSB, FPAB etc. He did most of his research in the field of Health, Education, and Environment. His research interests include ethical aspects of human behavior in all these relevant fields, specifically in the continuously evolving and changing field of Digital Business and Marketing.

Nivedita V. S. is an Assistant Professor in the Department of Computer Science and Technology at Bannari Amman Institute of Technology, India. She is pursuing her doctoral degree in Information and Communication Engineering at Anna University, India. She holds 6 years of professional experience in academic institutions affiliated under Anna University. Her research interests include information filtering and retrieval, explainable intelligence, big data, etc.

Satish Vadlamani is a Director of Data Science and BI at Kenco Group, Chattanooga, TN, USA. He earned B.Tech. in Electronics and Communications Engineering, India. A Masters and Ph.D. in Industrial and Systems Engineering from Mississippi State University, USA. Before joining Kenco, Dr. Vadlamani worked at other global supply chain companies like APLL and XPO. Dr. Vadlamani has passion for applying operations research, machine learning (ML) and artificial (AI) intelligence to solve complex supply chain problems. Dr. Vadlamani has seven years of experience applying ML and AI for problem solving. Dr. Vadlamani has published at multiple journals and conferences and teaches data science and analytics to people around the globe. His research interests include networks, wireless sensor networks, wireless ad-hoc networks, supply chain networks, network interdiction, location problems, transportation, and meta-heuristics. Dr. Vadlamani has been an invited speaker at various colleges, universities, and other professional organizations across the globe. He is a member of IEOM, INFORMS and IISE.

Phuong Vi was born in Thai Nguyen, Vietnam. She is a lecturer at the Faculty of Journalism - Communications, Thai Nguyen University of Science, Vietnam. Her current research focuses on the following: Media culture; Social Media; Journalism History; Online newspaper; Journalism and public opinion; Public Relations. Her research is articles about journalism - modern media; books and book chapters have been published in prestigious international journals. "I am a journalist, researcher, author, writer, and university lecturer that never tires of learning and learning and teaches others for posterity, and for social development."

Takis Vidalis completed his basic legal studies at the University of Athens. In 1995, he received his Ph.D. in law. In 2001 he was elected a senior researcher and legal advisor of the Hellenic National Bioethics Commission (now, Commission for Bioethics and Technoethics). He is the author (or co-author) of 7 books and more than 50 academic papers in topics related to ethics and law of advanced technologies, constitutional law, philosophy of law, and sociology of law. Currently, he teaches "Artificial Intelligence: Ethics and Law", at the Law School of the Univ. of Athens, and "Biolaw and Bioethics," at the International Hellenic University. He is the president of the Research Ethics Committee of the National Centre for Scientific Research "Democritos" (the largest multidisciplinary research centre of Greece), and a member of the European Group on Ethics in Science and New Technologies (European Commission).

Fabio Vitor is an Assistant Professor of operations research in the Department of Mathematical and Statistical Sciences at the University of Nebraska at Omaha. He received a Ph.D. in Industrial Engineering and M.S. in Operations Research from Kansas State University, and a B.S. in Industrial Engineering from Maua Institute of Technology, Brazil. Dr. Vitor has nearly 10 years of industry experience, working for companies such as Monsanto, Kalmar, and Volkswagen. Dr. Vitor's research includes both theoretical and applied topics in operations research. His theoretical research creates algorithms to more quickly solve continuous and discrete optimization problems while some of his applied research has involved the application of optimization models and other operations research tools to reduce inventory costs, improve delivery routings, optimize nursery planting allocation, improve airport operations, and create strategies to overcome human trafficking.

Rogan Vleming is the Head of Data Science & Engineering at Simon-Kucher & Partners. Rogan received an M.B.A. in Finance specializing in financial engineering from McMaster University's De-Groote School of Business, and a B.Sc. in Mechanical Engineering from McMaster University.

Haris Abd Wahab, PhD, is an Associate Professor in the Department of Social Administration and Justice, Faculty of Arts and Social Sciences, University of Malaya, Malaysia. He graduated in the field of human development and community development. He has conducted studies on community work, community development, volunteerism, and disability. He has extensive experience working as a medical social worker at the Ministry of Health, Malaysia.

Chaojie Wang works for The MITRE Corporation, an international thinktank and operator of Federally Funded Research and Development Centers (FFRDC). In his capacity as a principal systems engineer, Dr. Wang advises the federal government on IT Acquisition & Modernization, Data Analytics & Knowledge Management, Health IT and Informatics, and Emerging Technology Evaluation & Adoption. Dr. Wang currently serves as the Editor-in-Chief for the International Journal of Patient-Centered Healthcare (IJPCH) by IGI Global and is on the Editorial Review Board of the Issues in Information System (IIS) by the International Association for Computer Information Systems (IACIS). Dr. Wang teaches Data Science graduate courses at University of Maryland Baltimore County (UMBC) and Healthcare Informatics graduate courses at Harrisburg University of Science and Technology. Dr. Wang holds a Bachelor of Engineering in MIS from Tsinghua University, a Master of Art in Economics and a Master of Science in Statistics both from the University of Toledo, an MBA in Finance from Loyola University Maryland, and a Doctor of Science in Information Systems and Communications from Robert Morris University.

Di Wang received his B.S. and M.S. degree in electrical engineering from Fuzhou University, China and Tianjin University, China. He is currently pursuing his Ph.D. degree in the Industrial Engineering Department, University of Illinois at Chicago, USA. His current research interests include multi-agent systems, distributed control, and energy schedule in the smart city.

Yue Wang is a doctoral candidate at the Computer Network Information Center, Chinese Academy of Sciences. Her research interests cover data mining, machine learning, user behavior analysis, etc. She has been working at the intersection of machine learning and information management for several years. Recently, she is working on NEW ARP technical research. In this paper, she handles the research on the technologies of the NEW ARP.

Manuel Weinke works as a research associate at the Chair of Logistics, Institute of Technology and Management, at the Technical University of Berlin. Within the scope of several research projects, he focuses on the utilization of Machine Learning in logistics management. Previously, he worked as a senior consultant in a management consultancy. He graduated in industrial engineering with a major in logistics, project, and quality management at the Technical University of Berlin.

Thomas A. Woolman is a doctoral student at Indiana State University's Technology Management program, with a concentration in digital communication systems. Mr. Woolman also holds an MBA with a concentration in data analytics from Saint Joseph's University, a Master's degree in Data Analytics from Saint Joseph's University and a Master's degree in Physical Science from Emporia State University. He is the president of On Target Technologies, Inc., a data science and research analytics consulting firm based in Virginia, USA.

Brian G. Wu received his Bachelor of Arts in Mathematics & Piano Music from Albion College in 2014. He pursued his graduate education at Oakland University, where he received his MS in Applied Statistics in 2016 and his PhD in Applied Mathematical Sciences, Applied Statistics Specialization, in 2020. His PhD thesis addressed computational and modeling aspects of big time series data. He will continue his career as a Visiting Assistant Professor at Southwestern University in the 2021-22 academic year.

Tao Wu is an assistant professor of Computer Science at SUNY Oneonta. He has extensive research experience in the fields of data science, information science, wireless communications, wireless networks, and statistical signal processing. He is also an expert in computer hardware and programming.

Mengying Xia's research interests focus on molecular epidemiology and women's health. Her current research involves molecular predictors of ovarian cancer severity, recurrence, and prognosis.

Hang Xiao is a project manager in SSGM at State Street Corporation. He earned a M.S. in Information System from Northeastern University in 2012. His research interests include IoT, AI, Big Data, and Operational Research.

Khadidja Yachba (born in Oran, Algeria) is a Teacher (Assistant Professor) in Computer sciences department of University Centre Relizane and a research assistant at LIO Laboratory, Oran, Algeria. She received her Ph. D. in transport maritime and optimization at University of Oran 1, Ahmed Benbella in 2017. Her research interests are in Decision Support Systems (urban, road, maritime transportation, and health), Optimization, Simulation, Cooperative and Distributed System, Knowledge bases and Multi Criteria Decision Making. Khadidja Yachba has published in journals such as transport and telecommunication, International Journal of Decision Sciences, Risk and Management.

Ronald R. Yager has worked in the area of machine intelligence for over twenty-five years. He has published over 500 papers and more then thirty books in areas related to artificial intelligence, fuzzy sets, decision-making under uncertainty and the fusion of information. He is among the world's top 1% most highly cited researchers with over 85,000 citations. He was the recipient of the IEEE Computational Intelligence Society's highly prestigious Frank Rosenblatt Award in 2016. He was the recipient of the IEEE Systems, Man and Cybernetics Society 2018 Lotfi Zadeh Pioneer Award. He was also the recipient of the IEEE Computational Intelligence Society Pioneer award in Fuzzy Systems. He received honorary doctorates from the Azerbaijan Technical University, the State University of Information Technologies, Sofia Bulgaria and the Rostov on the Don University, Russia. Dr. Yager is a fellow of the IEEE and the Fuzzy Systems Association. He was given a lifetime achievement award by the Polish Academy of Sciences for his contributions. He served at the National Science Foundation as program director in the Information Sciences program. He was a NASA/Stanford visiting fellow and a research associate at the University of California, Berkeley. He has been a lecturer at NATO Advanced Study Institutes. He is a Distinguished Adjunct Professor at King Abdulaziz University, Jeddah, Saudi Arabia. He was a distinguished honorary professor at the Aalborg University Denmark. He was distinguished visiting scientist at King Saud University, Riyadh, Saudi Arabia. He received his undergraduate degree from the City College of New York and his Ph. D. from the Polytechnic University of New York. He was editor and chief of the International Journal of Intelligent Systems. He serves on the editorial board of numerous technology journals. Currently he is an Emeritus Professor at Iona College and is director of the Machine Intelligence.

Jing Yang is an associate professor of management information systems at the State University of New York at Oneonta. She has authored multiple research papers on consumer reviews that have been published in a variety of high-quality peer-reviewed journals, including Decision Support Systems, Nakai Business Review International, Wireless Personal Communications, and the International Journal of Operations Research and Information Systems.

Lanting Yang is a student at the City University of Macau. She studies in the International Business program.

Pi-Ying Yen is an assistant professor at the School of Business, Macau University of Science and Technology. She received her PhD in Industrial Engineering and Decision Analytics from HKUST in 2020. She serves as a reviewer for Manufacturing & Service Operations Management (MSOM) and Naval Research Logistics (NRL). Her research interests include socially responsible operations, supply chain management, and consumer behavior.

Iris Yeung received her B.Soc.Sc. Degree from the University of Hong Kong, M.Sc. degree from Imperial College, University of London, and a Ph.D. degree from University of Kent at Canterbury, UK. Her major research and teaching areas are time series analysis and multivariate data analysis. She has published articles in the Journal of Statistical Computation and Simulations, Statistica Sinica, Journal of Royal Statistical Society: Series C, Journal of Applied Statistical Science, Environmental Monitoring and Assessment, Environmental Science and Pollution Research, Waste Management, Marine Pollution Bulletin, Energy Policy, Applied Energy, Energy and Buildings, and Energy for Sustainable Development. She has participated in a number of consulting projects, including the British Council, Mass Transit Railway Corporation, Hong Kong Ferry (Holdings) Co. Ltd., Greenpeace East Asia, and Environmental Protection Department, The Government of the Hong Kong Special Administrative Region.

Selen Yılmaz Işıkhan carried out an integrated master and doctorate education in biostatistics department of Hacettepe University Faculty of Medicine. She has been working as a lecturer at the same university since 2010. Some examples of her research interests are machine learning, data mining, multivariate statistical analyses, regression analysis, meta analysis, and gut microbiota analysis.

Ambar Yoganingrum is a senior researcher at the Research Center for Informatics, National Research and Innovation Agency (BRIN), Indonesia, since 2019. She was a researcher in Center for Scientific Documentation and Information, Indonesian Institute of Sciences (PDII LIPI) for 18 years. She obtained her bachelor degree in Pharmaceutical Sciences from University of Padjadjaran, Indonesia in 1990. She earned a Master's degree in Health Informatics from the University of Indonesia in 2003 and a Doctorate in Information Systems from the same university in 2015. Ambar Yoganingrum's research interests include issues in the field of Library and Information Sciences, Information processing, Applied Informatics for Social Sciences purposes, and Multimedia.

M. Yossi is an Associate Professor and the Head of the Department of Industrial Engineering and Management at SCE – Shamoon College of Engineering. His areas of specialty are work-study, DEA, and ranking methods. He has published several papers and six books in these areas. He received his BSc, MSc, and Ph.D. (Summa Cum Laude) in Industrial Engineering from the Ben-Gurion University of the Negev, Israel.

William A. Young II is the Director of the Online Masters of Business Administration (OMBA) program, the Director of the Online Masters of Business Analytics (OMBAn), and a Charles G. O'Bleness Associate Professor of Business Analytics in the Department of Analytics and Information Systems. As an Associate Professor, Young received Ohio University's University Professor Award in 2020. Young earned his doctorate in Mechanical and Systems Engineering from Ohio University's Russ College of Engineering and Technology in 2010. William also received a bachelor's and master's degree in Electrical Engineering at Ohio University in 2002 and 2005, respectively. William has collaborated with multidisciplinary teams of faculty, students, and professionals on projects and programs that have been funded by General Electric Aviation, the National Science Foundation, Sogeti Netherlands, and Ohio's Department of Labor. Young's primary research and teaching interests relate to business analytics and operations management.

Jianjun Yu is currently the researcher, doctoral supervisor at the Computer Network Information Center, Chinese Academy of Sciences. His research interests cover big data analysis, collaborative filtering recommendations, and cloud computing. Recently, he is working on New ARP technical research.

Gokmen Zararsiz is a PhD researcher working in Dept. of Biostatistics, Faculty of Medicine, Erciyes University, Turkey.

Alex Zarifis is passionate about researching, teaching and practicing management in its many facets. He has taught in higher education for over ten years at universities including the University of Cambridge, University of Manchester and the University of Mannheim. His research is in the areas of information systems and management. Dr Alex first degree is a BSc in Management with Information Systems from the University of Leeds. His second an MSc in Business Information Technology and a PhD in Business Administration are both from the University of Manchester. The University of Manchester PhD in Business Administration is ranked 1st in the world according to the Financial Times.

David Zeng is a faculty member in College of Business and Information Systems at Dakota State University. David received his PhD at University of California, Irvine specializing in Information Systems. David's Teaching Interests include Predictive Analytics for Decision-making, Programming for Data Analytics (Python), Business Intelligence & Visualization, Deep Learning, AI Applications, Applied AI & applications, and Strategy & Application of AI in Organizations. David's research has been published at top-tier, peer-reviewed journals including MIS Quarterly, and has been funded by both internal and external grants. David received the Merrill D. Hunter Award of Excellence in Research in 2020. David is the Director of Center for Business Analytics Research (CBAR) at DSU.

Jin Zhang is a full professor at the School of Information Studies, University of Wisconsin-Milwaukee, U.S.A. He has published papers in journals such as Journal of the American Society for Information Science and Technology, Information Processing & Management, Journal of Documentation, Journal of Intelligent Information Systems, Online Information Review, etc. His book "Visualization for Information Retrieval" was published in the Information Retrieval Series by Springer in 2008. His research interests include visualization for information retrieval, information retrieval algorithm, metadata, search engine evaluation, consumer health informatics, social media, transaction log analysis, digital libraries, data mining, knowledge system evaluation, and human computer interface design.

Peng Zhao is a data science professional with experience in industry, teaching, and research. He has a broad range of practical data science experience in different industries, including finance, mobile device, consumer intelligence, big data technology, insurance, and biomedical industries. He is a leading machine learning expertise in a Big Data & AI company in New Jersey. He also manages a data scientist team providing a variety of data consulting services to individuals, businesses, and non-profit organizations.

Yuehua Zhao is a research assistant professor at the School of Information Management, Nanjing University, China. Her research interests include consumer health informatics, social network analysis, and social media research.

Index

D

F

G

H

M

P

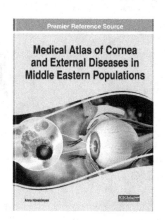
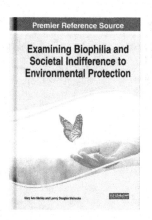

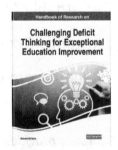